ENCYCLOPEDIA OF
U.S. Labor and Working-Class History

ENCYCLOPEDIA OF
U.S. Labor and Working-Class History

VOLUME 1
A–F
INDEX

Eric Arnesen

EDITOR

 Routledge
Taylor & Francis Group
New York   London

Routledge is an imprint of the
Taylor & Francis Group, an informa business

Routledge
Taylor & Francis Group
270 Madison Avenue
New York, NY 10016

Routledge
Taylor & Francis Group
2 Park Square
Milton Park, Abingdon
Oxon OX14 4RN

Printed in the United States of America on acid-free paper
10 9 8 7 6 5 4 3 2 1

International Standard Book Number-10: 0-415-96826-7 (Hardcover)
International Standard Book Number-13: 978-0-415-96826-3 (Hardcover)

Library of Congress Cataloging-in-Publication Data

Arnesen, Eric.
   Encyclopedia of U.S. labor and working-class history / Eric Arneson.
      p. cm.
   Includes bibliographical references and index.
   ISBN 0-415-96826-7
   1. Labor--United States--History--Encyclopedias. 2. Working class--United States--History--Encyclopedias. 3. Industrial relations--United States--History--Encyclopedias. I. Title. II. Title: Encyclopedia of United States labor and working-class history.

HD8066.A78 2006
331.0973'03--dc22
                                                   2006048640

Visit the Taylor & Francis Web site at
http://www.taylorandfrancis.com

and the Routledge Web site at
http://www.routledge-ny.com

CONTENTS

ASSOCIATE EDITORS

vii

CONTRIBUTORS

María Graciela Abarca
University of Buenos Aires, Argentina

Ellen S. Aiken
University of Colorado

Lindsey Allen
Independent Scholar

Edie Ambrose
Xavier University

David M. Anderson
Louisiana Tech University

Ronald Applegate
Cornell University

Eric Arnesen
University of Illinois at Chicago

Andrew Arnold
Kutztown University of Pennsylvania

Dexter Arnold
University of Cincinnati

Steve Ashby
University of Indiana

Carl L. Bankston, III
Tulane University

Lucy G. Barber
National Archives and Records Administration

James R. Barrett
University of Illinois at Urbana-Champaign

Kathleen M. Barry
University of Cambridge, UK

Rachel A. Batch
Widener University

Beth Thompkins Bates
Wayne State University

Joshua Beaty
College of William and Mary

Mildred Allen Beik
Independent Scholar

Evan P. Bennett
Independent Scholar

Michael J. Bennett
Independent Scholar

Julie Berebitsky
University of the South

Timothy A. Berg
McHenry County College, Illinois

Aaron Max Berkowitz
University of Illinois at Chicago

Matthew S. R. Bewig
University of Florida

Mary H. Blewett
University of Massachusetts at Lowell

Kevin Boyle
Ohio State University

Lauren H. Braun
University of Illinois at Chicago

Douglas Bristol
University of Southern Mississippi

David Brody
University of California at Davis (emeritus)

Jamie L. Bronstein
New Mexico State University

Edwin L. Brown
University of Alabama at Birmingham

CONTRIBUTORS

Victoria Bissell Brown
Grinnell College

David Brundage
University of California at Santa Cruz

Emily Brunner
University of Chicago

Robert Bruno
University of Illinois at Urbana-Champaign

Nicholas Buchanan
Massachusetts Institute of Technology

Peter H. Buckingham
Linfield College

Stephen Burwood
State University of New York at Geneseo

Robert Bussell
University of Oregon

Jenny Carson
University of Toronto

Theresa A. Case
University of Houston

Kenneth M. Casebeer
University of Miami Law School

James G. Cassedy
National Archives and Records Administration

Marisa Chappell
Oregon State University

Robert W. Cherney
San Francisco State University

Daniel Clark
Oakland University

Catherine Clinton
Independent Scholar

Andrew Wender Cohen
Syracuse University

Peter Cole
Western Illinois University

Stephen Cole
Notre Dame de Namur University

Timothy C. Coogan
LaGuardia Community College, New York

Axel B. Corlu
Binghamton University, State University of New York

Seth Cotlar
Willamette University

Evan Matthew Daniel
*Tamiment Library/Robert F. Wagner Labor Archives,
New York University*

Catharine Christie Dann
College of William and Mary

Colin Davis
University of Alabama at Birmingham

G. V. Davis
Marshall University

Greta de Jong
University of Nevada at Reno

John D'Emilio
University of Illinois at Chicago

Dennis A. Deslippe
Australian National University

Anthony DeStefanis
College of William and Mary

Ileen A. DeVault
Cornell University

Victor G. Devinatz
Illinois State University

Steven Deyle
University of California at Davis

Steven Dike-Wilhelm
University of Colorado

Brian Dolinar
Claremont Graduate University

Colleen Doody
DePaul University

Gregory Downey
University of Wisconsin at Madison

Michael V. Doyle
Skidmore College

Alan Draper
St. Lawrence University

Philip Jacques Dreyfus
San Francisco State University

Melvyn Dubofsky
Binghamton University, State University of New York

Douglas R. Egerton
Le Moyne College

Kathleen L. Endres
University of Akron

Beth English
Princeton University

John Enyeart
Bucknell University

Steve Estes
Sonoma State University

Candace Falk
University of California at Berkeley

Rosemary Feurer
Northern Illinois University

Lisa Michelle Fine
Michigan State University

Leon Fink
University of Illinois at Chicago

Michael W. Fitzgerald
St. Olaf College

John H. Flores
University of Illinois at Chicago

Mary E. Fredrickson
Miami University of Ohio

Joshua B. Freeman
Graduate Center, City University of New York

John D. French
Woodrow Wilson International Center for Scholars

Daniel Geary
University of California at Berkeley

Gregory Geddes
Binghamton University, State University of New York

Erik S. Gellman
Northwestern University

Gene C. Gerard
Tarrant County College, Texas

Kristin Geraty
Indiana University

Larry G. Gerber
Auburn University

Heidi Scott Giusto
Duke University

Lawrence B. Glickman
University of South Carolina

Susan M. Glisson
University of Mississippi

Chad Alan Goldberg
University of Wisconsin

Steve Golin
Bloomfield College

Risa L. Goluboff
University of Virginia

Elliott J. Gorn
Brown University

Thomas M. Grace
Cornell University

George N. Green
University of Texas at Arlington

Jean-Denis Grèze
Independent Scholar

James Green
University of Massachusetts at Boston

Brian Greenberg
Monmouth College

Richard A. Greenwald
Drew University

CONTRIBUTORS

John Grider
University of Colorado

Andrew Gyory
Independent Scholar

Pamela Hackbart-Dean
Georgia State University

Greg Hall
Western Illinois University

Daniel Harper
University of Illinois

Kenneth J. Heineman
Ohio University

John Heinz
Chicago Maritime Society

Jeffrey Helgeson
University of Illinois at Chicago

Danielle Hidalgo
Independent Scholar

Frank Tobias Higbie
University of Illinois at Urbana-Champaign

Matthew Hild
Georgia State University

Adam J. Hodges
University of Houston at Clear Lake

Sean Holmes
Brunel University, United Kingdom

Michael Honey
University of Washington-Tacoma

Adam Howard
University of Florida

Tera Hunter
Carnegie Mellon University

Maurice Isserman
Hamilton College

Maurice Jackson
Georgetown University

Catherine O. Jacquet
University of Illinois at Chicago

Elizabeth Jameson
University of Calgary

Robert F. Jefferson
Xavier University

Richard J. Jensen
University of Nevada at Las Vegas (emeritus)

John B. Jentz
Raynor Memorial Libraries, Marquette University

Edward P. Johanningsmeier
Independent Scholar

Robert D. Johnston
University of Illinois at Chicago

Gwen Hoerr Jordan
University of Wisconsin at Madison

Yevette Richards Jordan
George Mason University

Lisa Kannenberg
The College of Saint Rose

Anthony Kaye
Pennsylvania State University

Brian Kelly
Queens University Belfast, Northern Ireland

Kevin Kenny
Boston College

Andrew E. Kersten
University of Wisconsin at Green Bay

Lionel Kimble, Jr.
Chicago State University

Marta M. Knight
California State University at Sacramento

Steven D. Koczak
New York State Senate Research Service

David Koistinen
American University of Beirut, Lebanon

James C. Kollros
St. Xavier University

Robert Korstad
Duke University

Molly Ladd-Taylor
York University

Clarence Lang
University of Illinois at Urbana-Champaign

Jennifer Langdon-Teclaw
University of Illinois at Chicago

R. Todd Laugen
Metropolitan State College of Denver

Bruce Laurie
University of Massachusetts, Amherst

Mark Lause
University of Cincinnati

John Leggett
Rutgers University

Steven Leikin
San Francisco State University

Karen Leroux
Drake University

Steven C. Levi
Independent Scholar and Author

Alex Lichtenstein
Rice University

Robbie Lieberman
Southern Illinois University

Joseph Lipari
University of Illinois at Chicago

Rebecca S. Lowen
Independent Scholar

Stephanie Luce
University of Massachusetts at Amherst

Jennifer Luff
Service Employees International Union

John M. Lund
Keene State College, University of New Hampshire

Brigid Lusk
Northern Illinois University

John F. Lyons
Joliet College

Robert Macieski
University of New Hampshire

Nancy MacLean
Northwestern University

Anastasia Mann
Princeton University

Geoff Mann
Simon Fraser University

Wendi N. Manuel-Scott
George Mason University

Kathleen Mapes
State University of New York at Geneseo

Sharon Mastracci
University of Illinois at Chicago

Joseph A. McCartin
Georgetown University

John Thomas McGuire
State University of New York at Cortland

Elizabeth McKillen
University of Maine at Orono

Robert C. McMath, Jr.
University of Arkansas

Eden Medina
Indiana University

Ronald Mendel
University of Northampton, United Kingdom

Timothy Messer-Kruse
University of Toledo

Jack Metzgar
Roosevelt University

Steven Meyer
University of Wisconsin at Milwaukee

Gregory M. Miller
University of Toledo

Heather Lee Miller
Historical Research Associates, Inc.

James A. Miller
George Washington University

CONTRIBUTORS

Timothy Minchin
La Trobe University

Samuel Mitrani
University of Illinois at Chicago

Marian Mollin
Virginia Polytechnic Institute and State University

Scott Molloy
University of Rhode Island

Paul D. Moreno
Hillsdale College

Alexander Morrow
University of Oregon

Scott Nelson
College of William and Mary

Caryn E. Neumann
Ohio State University

Mitchell Newton-Matza
Lexington College

Bruce Nissen
Florida International University

Mark A. Noon
Bloomsburg University of Pennsylvania

Stephen H. Norwood
University of Oklahoma

Kathleen Banks Nutter
Smith College

Kathryn J. Oberdeck
University of Illinois at Urbana-Champaign

Edward T. O'Donnell
College of the Holy Cross

Richard Oestricher
University of Pittsburgh

Brigid O'Farrell
Stanford University

Amy C. Offner
Dollars and Sense *Magazine*

John S. Olszowka
Mercyhurst College

Colleen O'Neill
Utah State University

Liesl Miller Orenic
Dominican University

Annelise Orleck
Dartmouth College

Merideth Oyen
Georgetown University

David Palmer
Flinders University, Australia

Karen Pastorello
Tompkins Cortland Community College, New York

Barry Pateman
University of California-Berkeley

Brad Paul
National Policy and Advocacy Council on Homelessness (NPACH)

Ruth Percy
University of Toronto

Michael Perman
University of Illinois at Chicago

Jean Pfaelzer
University of Delaware

Lori Pierce
DePaul University

Michael Cain Pierce
University of Arkansas

Jerald Podair
Lawrence University

Kevin Noble Powers
Georgetown University

David Purcell
University of Cincinnati

Peter Rachleff
Macalester College

Bruno Ramirez
University of Montreal, Canada

Scott E. Randolph
Purdue University

Padma Rangaswamy
South Asian American Policy and Research Institute

David C. Ranney
University of Illinois at Chicago (emeritus)

Gerda W. Ray
University of Missouri at St. Louis

Jonathan Rees
Colorado State University at Pueblo

Steven A. Reich
James Madison University

David M. Reimers
New York University (emeritus)

Ester Reiter
Atkinson College, York University

Rachel R. Reynolds
Drexel University

Christopher Rhomberg
Yale University

Lawrence Richards
University of Richmond

Elizabeth Ricketts
Indiana University of Pennsylvania

Steven A. Riess
Northeastern Illinois University

Howard Rock
Florida International University

John C. Rodrigue
Louisiana State University

Marc S. Rodriguez
University of Notre Dame

Donald W. Rogers
Central Connecticut State University and Housatonic Community College

Gerald Ronning
Albright College

Margaret Rose
University of California at Santa Barbara

Sarah F. Rose
University of Illinois at Chicago

John J. Rosen
University of Illinois at Chicago

Doug Rossinow
Metropolitan State University

Kate Rousmaniere
Miami University

Margaret C. Rung
Roosevelt University

Jason Russell
York University

John Russell
Georgia State University

Francis Ryan
Moravian College

Joseph C. Santora
Essex County College

Ralph Scharnau
Northeast Iowa Community College, Peosta

Ronald W. Schatz
Wesleyan University

Michael Schiavone
Flinders University, Australia

Kevin E. Schmiesing
Acton Institute

Dorothee Schneider
University of Illinois at Urbana-Champaign

Katrin Schultheiss
University of Illinois at Chicago

Rima Lunin Schultz
University of Illinois at Chicago

Carlos A. Schwantes
University of Missouri at St. Louis

CONTRIBUTORS

James Searing
University of Illinois at Chicago

Karin A. Shapiro
Duke University

Paul Siegel
Independent Scholar

Michael W. Simpson
University of Wisconsin at Madison

Joseph E. Slater
University of Toledo

Eric Richard Smith
University of Illinois at Chicago

Michael Spear
City University of New York

Robyn Ceanne Spencer
Pennsylvania State University

Sarah Stage
Arizona State University, West Campus

Howard R. Stanger
Canisius College

Richard Stott
George Washington University

David O. Stowell
Keene State College, University of New Hampshire

Shelton Stromquist
University of Iowa

Thomas Summerhill
Michigan State University

Paul Michel Taillon
University of Auckland, New Zealand

Vanessa Tait
University of California at Berkeley

Clarence Taylor
Baruch College, City University of New York

Kieran W. Taylor
University of North Carolina at Chapel Hill

Michael M. Topp
University of Texas at El Paso

Frank Towers
University of Northern Colorado

Martin Tuohy
National Archives and Records Administration, Great Lakes Branch

Mary C. Tuominen
Denison University

Joseph M. Turrini
Auburn University

Emily E. LaBarbera Twarog
University of Illinois at Chicago

William E. Van Vugt
Calvin College

Susannah Walker
Virginia Wesleyan University

Wilson J. Warren
Western Michigan University

Peter Way
Bowling Green State University

John Weber
College of William and Mary

Edmund F. Wehrle
Eastern Illinois University

Carl R. Weinberg
Indiana University

Robert E. Weir
Mount Holyoke College

Virginia Wright Wexman
University of Illinois at Chicago

Carmen Teresa Whalen
Williams College

Jeannie M. Whayne
University of Arkansas

John White
Independent Scholar

Marcus Widenor
University of Oregon

John Fabian Witt
Columbia University

David Witwer
Lycoming College

Kenneth C. Wolensky
Pennsylvania Historical and Museum Commission

James Wolfinger
Northwestern University

Chris Wonderlich
University of Illinois at Chicago

John Chi-Kit Wong
Washington State University

Robert H. Woodrum
Clark Atlanta University

Gerald Zahavi
State University of New York at Albany

Minna P. Ziskind
University of Pennsylvania

David A. Zonderman
North Carolina State University

ALPHABETICAL LIST OF ENTRIES

THEMATIC LIST OF ENTRIES

Concepts and Developments

Abolitionism
Affirmative Action
American Exceptionalism
American Standard of Living
Anarchism
Anticommunism
Apprenticeship
Arbitration
Artisans
Arts and Crafts Movement
Assembly Line Production
Blacklists
Boycotts
Capital Flight
Catholic Church
Central Labor Unions
Child Care
Child Labor
Civil Rights
Cold War
Collective Bargaining
Company Towns
Convict Labor in the New South
Cooperation
Coxey's Army
Culture, Working-Class
De-Industrialization
Disfranchisement
"Don't Buy Where You Can't Work" Campaigns
Dorr War
Dual Unionism
Education, Labor
Emancipation and Reconstruction
Environmentalism
Family Wage
Film
Five Dollar Day
Foreign Policy
Fourierism

Free-Soilism
Gender
Globalization
Gold Rush
Great Migration
Great Society/War on Poverty (1960s)
Historiography of American Labor History
Hoboes
Housework
Immigration Restriction
Indentured Servitude
Industrial Democracy
Industrial Unionism
Injunctions
Labor Day
Labor Republicanism
Labor Theory of Value
Living Wage
Living Wage Campaigns
Maquiladoras
May Day
Migrant Farmworkers
Music
New Left
New South
New York City Fiscal Crisis (1970s)
No-Strike Pledge
Novels, Poetry, Drama
Operation Dixie
Organized Crime
Pattern Bargaining
Peonage
Philadelphia Plan
Plumb Plan
Politics and Labor, Nineteenth Century
Portal-to-Portal Pay
Protocol of Peace
Racketeering and RICO
Rosie the Riveter
Sacco and Vanzetti
Sexual Harassment
Sharecropping and Tenancy

Legal Cases, Acts, and Legislation

Management

Labor-Management Cooperation
National Civic Federation
National Right to Work Committee
Personnel Management
Pinkerton Detectives
Welfare Capitalism

Organizations

A. Philip Randolph Institute
Actors' Equity Association
African Blood Brotherhood
Alliance for Labor Action
American Alliance for Labor and Democracy
American Labor Party
Association of Catholic Trade Unionists
Black Lung Associations
Black Panther Party
Black Workers Congress
Brookwood Labor College
Bryn Mawr Summer School for Women Workers
    in Industry
Civil Rights Congress
Colored Farmers' Alliance
Communist Party
Conference for Progressive Political Action
Delmarva Poultry Justice Alliance
DRUM, FRUM, ELRUM
Farmer-Labor Party
Future Outlook League of Cleveland
Greenback-Labor Party
Highlander Folk School/Highlander Research and
    Education Center
Home Club
Hull-House Settlement (1889–1963)
Illinois Woman's Alliance
International Labor Defense
International Workers' Order
Jewish Labor Committee
Justice for Janitors
Know-Nothing Party
Ku Klux Klan (Reconstruction and WWI Era)
Labor Research Association
Labor's Non-Partisan League (1936–1944)
League for Industrial Democracy (LID)
League of Revolutionary Black Workers
Liberal Party
Locofoco Democrats
Lowell Female Labor Reform Association (LFLRA)
Loyal Legion of Loggers and Lumbermen
March on Washington Movement
Miners for Democracy
Molly Maguires

National Ad Hoc Committee of Black Steelworkers
National Association for the Advancement of
    Colored People (NAACP)
National Association of Colored Graduate Nurses
National Child Labor Committee
National Consumers League
National Labor Reform Party
National Negro Congress
National Negro Labor Council
National Urban League
New England Labor Reform League
New England Workingmen's Association
Poor People's Campaign
Popular Front
Populism/People's Party
Professional Air Traffic Controllers Organization
Socialist Labor Party
Socialist Party of America
Socialist Trade and Labor Alliance
Socialist Workers' Party
Sons of Liberty
Trade Union Unity League
Unemployed League (1930s)
Union League Movement
Union Summer
Wages for Housework
Women's Trade Union League
Workers Alliance of America
Workers' Defense League
Working Girls' Clubs
Zoot Suit Riots

Periods

Antebellum Era
Civil War and Reconstruction
Colonial Era
Dominance and Influence of Organized Labor: 1940s
Gilded Age
Great Depression: 1930s
Politics and Labor, Twentieth Century
Progressive Era
Revolution and Early National Period
Significant Gains and Missed Opportunities: 1950s
    and 1960s
Unemployment, Insecurity, and the Decline of Labor:
    1970s
Vietnam War
Wage Losses and Union Decline: 1980s through the
    Early 2000s
Worker Mobilization, Management Resistance: 1920s
World War I
World War II

Racial and Ethnic Categories of Workers

Regions

Strikes

Trade Unions

INTRODUCTION

At the dawn of the twenty-first century, the scholarly field of labor history is a large, sophisticated, and diverse one. Prior to the 1960s, economists, political scientists, and historians largely took individual trade unions and the labor movement as the subjects of their academic investigations. Since the 1960s, however, the emergence of the "new labor history" has broadened the investigative lens considerably, embracing countless topics that earlier scholars might not even recognize as belonging to their field. Trade unions and labor movements continue, of course, to be legitimate subjects of exploration, but labor history has come to embrace much more. Initially concerned with grassroots activism, the experiences of the rank and file, and working-class communities and their cultures, the "new labor history"—which by 2006 is no longer very new—is deeply concerned with politics, law, race, ethnicity, gender, law, and migration. The sheer heterogeneity of America's working classes now stands at the heart of much of the field. Historians clearly recognize that just as there was no single working class possessing shared interests, so too was there no single working-class identity, culture, or ideology.

Today, a large and growing number of labor historians and labor studies scholars have produced a large and rich body of literature on a vast array of subjects. The Labor and Working-Class History Association and the Labor Studies Association boast hundreds of members, the field publishes multiple journals, articles on labor's past regularly find their way into non-labor oriented journals, and the themes explored by labor historians are routinely covered in U.S. history textbooks. To a significant extent, labor history, long considered by its practitioners to be a vital component of the larger drama of American history, is recognized as such by the larger field of American historians as well.

The *Encyclopedia of U.S. Labor and Working-Class History* builds upon the past several generations of scholarship to explore numerous dimensions of the working-class past. Its conception of what constitutes labor history is expansive and capacious, its sense of the borders between different fields porous. While attentive to the field's traditional focus on skilled craft and semi-skilled manufacturing workers, it devotes considerable attention to occupations that have only more recently attracted scholarly attention, such as longshoring, domestic service, prostitution, nursing, teaching, hair styling, computer programming, sleeping car portering, housework, and agriculture. It erodes the artificial boundaries between labor history and African-American history, treating the subjects of slavery, the slave trade, slave rebellions, and abolitionism, for instance, as integral to the recounting of the history of American labor. The heterogeneity of the working class is a central theme, with the *Encyclopedia* providing extensive coverage of race and gender divisions and the experiences of a multitude of immigrant groups.

How to Use This Book

Organization

The *Encyclopedia of U.S. Labor and Working-Class History* is organized in a straightforward and easy to use **A to Z format**. Users will find a number of useful features accompanying the entries, including **References and Further Reading** and **See Also** suggestions for easy cross-referencing. The volumes each include a thematic list of entries, in addition to an alphabetical list of entries and a **thorough, analytical index**.

Illustrations

The *Encyclopedia* includes 78 illustrations. These photographs, culled from the archives of the Library of Congress, accompany specific entries, and depict strikes, union meetings, workers, and influential leaders.

Thematic Coverage

The *Encyclopedia of U.S. Labor and Working-Class History* features 662 independent entries ranging in length from 500 to 6,000 words. The topics covered fall into 11 broad categories:

Concepts and Developments: Entries included in this category look in depth at central concepts, ideas, and broad developments in the history of American workers. American exceptionalism, sexual harassment, music, affirmative action, syndicalism, strikebreaking, living wage campaigns, immigration restriction, indentured servitude, and the historiography of labor history are only a few of the subjects treated in this broad-ranging category.

Government Agencies and Committees: Entries falling into this category examine government agencies affecting labor. Among the many covered are the Fair Employment Practice Committee, the LaFollette Civil Liberties Committee, the U.S. Women's Bureau, and the Federal Bureau of Investigation.

Individuals: Entries in this category cover a diverse set of figures intimately involved in labor relations and working-class life over the past two and a half centuries. Familiar figures like Walter Reuther, Jimmy Hoffa, George Meany, and A. Philip Randolph will be found in this section. But the list of key figures includes a host of less familiar names, including labor poet George Lippard, community activist Saul Alinsky, settlement house leaders Florence Kelley and Jane Addams, the mythic figure John Henry, labor troubadour Joe Hill, African-American labor activists Richard L. Davis, Willard Townsend, and Maida Springer, anarchist Lucy Parsons, and labor journalist John Swinton.

Legal Cases, Acts, and Legislation: This category focuses on laws and court cases affecting labor relations and working-class life. Examples in this group include the Chinese Exclusion Acts, the Civil Rights Act of 1964, Aid to Families with Dependent Children (AFDC), the Immigration and Nationality Act of 1965, and the North American Free Trade Agreement.

Management: Business organizations and programs (such as labor-management cooperation, welfare capitalism, and the National Right to Work Committee) are examined in this category.

Organizations: Organizations that are not unions, but nonetheless were working-class associations or bodies that dealt with working-class issues, compose another category. The Socialist Party of America, the Colored Farmers' Alliance, the Populist Party, and the March on Washington Movement fall into this category.

Periods: Lengthy chronological entries provide broad coverage of the principal contours of the evolution of labor systems and labor relations from the colonial era to the present. The period covered in each essay (the colonial era, the antebellum era, the Gilded Age and Progressive Era, the 1940s, and 1980 to the present, for example) conforms to an established periodizaiton or logical block of time corresponding to key developments.

Racial and Ethnic Categories of Workers: Racial and ethnic/immigration groups constitute another category of entries, with coverage of a wide range of groups including the Irish, Mexican and Mexican Americans, French Canadians, and recent immigrants from Southeast and South Asia and Central America.

Regions: Key geographical regions with a defined historical scholarship (including the South, the Pacific Northwest, the Southwest, and California) are explored in this category of entries.

Strikes: Strikes and labor-related conflicts represent a significant group of entries. Well-known events such as the Pullman Strike of 1894, the 1912 Lawrence Textile Strike, the 1937 Memorial Day Massacre, and the J.P. Stevens campaign are examined, as are many lesser known conflicts including the 1881 Atlanta Washerwomen's Strike, the 1919 Bogalusa, Louisiana strike, and the 1891–1892 Tennessee Convict Uprising.

Trade Unions: Numerous entries explore the history of trade unions in the nineteenth and twentieth centuries. While commonly recognized and major unions and union federations such as the United Steelworkers of America, the Knights of Labor, the International Brotherhood of Teamsters, and the Industrial Workers of the World are covered, so too are unions that are not household names, such as the Stockyards Labor Council, the International Fur and Leather Workers Union, and the United Hatters', Cap and Millinery Workers' International Union. Particular attention is paid to unions and labor associations composed of non-white workers and women, including the Brotherhood of Sleeping Car Porters, the United Farm Workers of America, the Southern Tenant Farmers Union, the Women's Trade Union League, and the Coalition of Labor Union Women.

A total of 298 scholars in the United States and Europe have contributed to the *Encyclopedia*. These individuals are specialists in their fields and bring to the project a vast wealth of knowledge and expertise. They share no historiographical or political perspective, and each has approached their subjects as she or he saw fit. Indeed, the interpretations offered are those of the authors and, at times, similar topics are explored from different or even conflicting interpretive positions.

Acknowledgments

Since the actual labor that goes into creating an encyclopedia of this sort is vast and collective, numerous people necessarily contributed significant to bringing this project to fruition. The five associate editors—Leon Fink, Cindy Hahamovitch, Tera Hunter, Bruce Laurie, and Joseph McCartin—are all superb scholars of labor's past who devoted considerable time and energy to conceptualizing the volume, identifying potential authors, and reading, editing, and engaging the arguments of the hundreds of entries in this volume. Without their editorial care and expertise, this project would have been impossible to complete. At Routledge, Mark L. Georgiev helped shape the project in its early stages, while Kristen Holt oversaw the massive logistical operation of contacting authors, answering queries, and shepherding the project through the editorial process. Closer to home, fellow historian Katrin Schultheiss provided her usual and invaluable intellectual support and guidance throughout the project's life, while our children Rachel, Samuel, and William patiently, and sometimes not so patiently, endured my continual thinking-out-loud about the project and countless of its individual subjects. While their interests remained largely fixed on baseball, soccer, and children's fiction—they provided no editorial support but did occasionally ask good questions—I suspect that they learned something about the history of labor and the craft of history in the process. I look forward to the day when they too can use and learn from the *Encyclopedia*.

Eric Arnesen

A

A. E. STALEY STRIKE (1995)

From 1992–1995, the Staley workers were at the forefront of a labor upsurge in central Illinois. In 1988, Tate & Lyle, the largest sugar conglomerate in the world, bought the A. E. Staley Company and launched an assault on the union at Staley's largest corn-processing plant in Decatur, Illinois. The company demanded the union replace its 117-page contract, culminating 50 years of collective bargaining, with the company's 16-page contract. The local union, which began the conflict as Allied Industrial Workers Local 837 but in January 1994, merged with the paper workers to become United Paperworkers International Union Local 7837, responded by educating and mobilizing the 850 unionists in a 9-month work-to-rule campaign, then built a national solidarity movement when the company locked the unionists out of the plant.

When the Staley workers were joined on the picket lines in 1994–1995 by striking United Auto Workers Local 751 Caterpillar workers and United Rubber Workers Local 751 Bridgestone/Firestone workers, the *New York Times* labeled Decatur "Strike City, USA." Decatur unionists united forces in what they labeled the Illinois war zone. "Decatur was a turning point," says AFL-CIO staffer Joe Uehlein. "What happened in Decatur during that period, and the Staley workers right on point with it, was as big a moment as was the Homestead strike of 1892."

In October 1992, when A. E. Staley first imposed a contract with 12-hour rotating shifts, loss of seniority, and gutted grievance procedures, workers brought in St. Louis-based Jerry Tucker, founder and director of the New Directions caucus in the United Auto Workers union, to coordinate an in-plant strategy known as "work-to-rule." "The workers engaged in one of the most creative and ultimately empowering activities I've seen in years," declared Tucker, labor's foremost expert on the tactic. Rather than bring their wealth of experience and skill to the job, workers would strictly follow the contract and company work rules. In many ways, the Decatur Staley plant was ideal for a work-to-rule campaign. It was an old plant, run by an experienced workforce. Much of the machinery was decades old, and some machinery dated back to the origins of the plant in 1912. "You just did what you had to do to get by," explained Staley worker Mike Dulaney. "The little extras that you might have done on your own to make things run smoother, we didn't do that."

After Tate & Lyle took over A. E. Staley, the new management fired half of the white-collar workforce, including dozens of plant supervisors, most of whom had cordial, respectful relationships with the union workforce and decades on the job. Most Staley workers had more than two decades in the plant, often working at the same job. The newly hired supervisors were ignorant of the idiosyncrasies of the aging plant and thus contributed to the success of the workers' work-to-rule effort. "With work-to-rule, you leave your brain outside the plant," said Staley worker Dan Lane. "People were very aggressive with that.

Production started flying down, things were going the way we wanted to. It was getting to be like a real strike *in* the plant."

In addition to impacting production, the workers launched a series of actions that demonstrated the magnitude of their solidarity and their resolve for a just contract. Both types of actions were fundamental to the campaign and served to fuel one another. The Staley workers regularly wore red union T-shirts to work, along with union caps and an extensive array of union buttons. Workers honked their car horns as they drove out of the plant parking lot after their shift. At times the union leadership called for demonstrations where hundreds of workers gathered at the plant gate before they marched *en masse* into work.

Often when a worker was called into a supervisor's office to be reprimanded, large numbers of Staley workers stopped work and went to the meeting. When the company began mandatory in-plant meetings, workers responded with creative tactics. At one meeting, workers suddenly stood and sang "God Bless America" in the midst of management's presentation; and at another meeting, workers recited the Pledge of Allegiance. At other meetings, workers chanted loudly, "No contract, no peace!" and "Union, union, union!" In one department, Staley worker Nancy Hanna bought Groucho Marx masks at a novelty store; when management began its presentation, workers put on the masks, then got up and walked out.

"This is the most solid group of people I've ever seen in my life," noted worker Bob Willoughby in the union's *Deadly Corn* video. "It's almost like a school of fish. When one turns, they all turn." The company ended dues check-off, but 97% of the members turned their dues, which the membership had voted to increase fivefold to $100 a month, in to their stewards. The work-to-rule campaign reached a peak in June 1993, when production was cut by one-third and nearly the entire workforce staged a two-day walkout over dangerous conditions in the plant.

When the company locked out the workers one week later on June 27, 1993, and began to hire hundreds of scab replacement workers, the unionists launched a national solidarity campaign. Rank-and-file workers, calling themselves Road Warriors, hit the road to build support, organize dozens of Staley Worker Solidarity committees, and build activism around the local's corporate campaign coordinated by union adviser Ray Rogers and his Corporate Campaign, Inc., staff.

A corporate campaign is a mobilization of the labor movement and the community to tarnish a corporation's image and to inflict serious economic damage on the company to pressure management to negotiate a fair contract. A corporate campaign hits the company from every conceivable angle. As AFL-CIO Secretary-Treasurer Rich Trumka explains it, "You fire fifty arrows out of the quiver. Each one of them has some effect, but you don't know how much. But collectively they achieve the result you want to get to. And you keep firing arrows" until the employer breaks down and agrees to bargain a fair contract. If a corporation that is attacking its workers has received tax subsidies from local or state governments, then this may be a way to build an alliance with homeowners burdened with high property taxes. If a corporation has a record of damaging the environment through toxic emissions into the city's air, water, and ground, then neighborhood groups, civic leaders, and environmental organizations may be a natural ally of the embattled union.

A central aspect of the Staley workers' corporate campaign was targeting the company's largest purchasers of Staley high-fructose corn syrup, Miller Beer and Pepsi Cola. The Staley Workers Solidarity committees distributed flyers at supermarkets, then-Pepsi subsidiaries Taco Bell and Kentucky Fried Chicken, and at company-sponsored festivals and concerts to ask people to tell Staley's customers to end their financial relationship with Staley. The campaign had its first big success in early 1994, when Miller Beer announced it was switching to another corn syrup manufacturer.

Solidarity committees also mobilized hundreds of people to attend Decatur rallies, held local rallies, raised funds, and organized local unions to adopt a family with a $600 monthly pledge. Over the course of the lockout, $3.5 million was raised by the Road Warriors and Solidarity committees. The Staley local also welcomed unpaid, full-time organizers from Detroit, St. Louis, and Chicago into the union's Campaign for Justice office, further strengthening ties to the solidarity committees.

Before the lockout, the Staley workers had gone door-to-door four times in Decatur explaining the local's stance. Most Decatur residents were sympathetic, and when the lockout occurred, hundreds posted signs of support on their lawns. Community outreach continued during the lockout as workers built a labor-religious coalition that advocated for the unionists. Father Martin Mangan of Decatur's St. James Catholic Church soon became a spokesperson for the workers. African-American workers organized a caucus and two marches on the theme of labor rights equals civil rights.

After the local brought in activists for training on nonviolent civil disobedience, 50 supporters staged a sit-in at the main A. E. Staley gate on June 4, 1994, blocking trucks and virtually shutting down the plant for the day. Three weeks later, five thousand protesters marked the first anniversary of the lockout, and over four hundred people crossed the Staley property line in a nonviolent protest. Police sprayed the crowd with pepper gas, with the rank-and-file Staley workers in front suffering the worst of its effects. The union and its solidarity committees rapidly distributed hundreds of copies of *Struggle in the Heartland*, second video produced by the St. Louis–based Labor Vision independent film group, which depicted the two civil disobedience actions and the police assault.

Problems of racism and sexism troubled the local and initially hampered broader support. In the 50 years of its existence, only one woman and no African-American had ever been elected to the Executive Board. With only 7% and 10% of the membership, respectively, a woman or black candidate would need broad support from the white male majority. During the lockout, and as a result of marches initiated by the African-American caucus, Jeanette Hawkins, the first African-American woman to be hired at the plant, was elected to the bargaining committee. Three white male candidates who supported diversifying the leadership withdrew their own candidacies and campaigned for Hawkins' election. Prior to the marches, only one African-American had been traveling regularly with the Road Warriors, but soon a number of locked-out African-Americans became regulars on the road.

Early in the fight, the local ignored its by-laws and began holding weekly solidarity meetings that welcomed spouses, children, and supporters. The wives and women workers later formed a bimonthly support group where the women shared the hardships of the lockout on family life and organized support for the union.

In December 1995, under severe financial duress, under pressure from paper workers, and having failed to gain the promised escalation of labor solidarity from newly elected AFL-CIO President John Sweeney, the membership voted to accept the company's contract. Although the company, after downsizing the workforce and outsourcing jobs, offered work to just 350 union members, barely a hundred Local 7837 members returned to the plant.

STEVEN ASHBY

References and Further Reading

Ashby, Steven, and C. J. Hawking. *The Staley Workers and the Fight for a New American Labor Movement*. Champaign: University of Illinois Press, forthcoming.

Franklin, Stephen. *Three Strikes: Labor's Heartland Losses and What They Mean for Working Americans*. New York: Guilford Press, 2001.

A. PHILIP RANDOLPH INSTITUTE

In 1965, in the wake of the twentieth century's two greatest civil rights legislative victories, A. Philip Randolph, Bayard Rustin, and a group of labor and civil rights activists established the A. Philip Randolph Institute (APRI) to blaze a new path for progressive change. Supported by a $25,000 grant from the American Federation of Labor (AFL)–Congress of Industrial Organizations (CIO), Randolph and Rustin transformed their old Brotherhood of Sleeping Car Porters headquarters in Harlem into the first national headquarters for the APRI. The institute's leaders shared a belief that the future struggle would not be centered on gaining access to public accommodations. Rather they were convinced that the social movement created in part by Randolph and propelled by such people as Martin Luther King, Jr., must face the deep-seated political and economic injustices suffered by working-class Americans of all backgrounds. The institute's goal therefore has been, in the words of Rustin, to forge "a new and dynamic unity between black Americans and those other groups that advocate social progress— the trade union movement, religious organizations, liberals, and students." This unity was intended to lend support to trade unions; to work to increase progressive political participation; to expand governmental programs from education to health care; to advocate integration, nonviolence, democratic reform; to instigate and support job-training and job creation programs; and to voice sympathy for other people and movements in the world engaged in related struggles.

To fulfill its mission, the institute pursued a number of strategies. After the 1965 Voting Rights Act passed, the institute sponsored registration and voting drives. It also actively sought to bridge the gulf between white and black trade unionists through conferences and educational campaigns. Finally in 1970, the institute's associate director, Norman Hill, spearheaded an operation to open branch offices in cities that had large black populations. Since 1974, the A. Philip Randolph Institute has operated roughly 150 branch offices in 36 states.

In all its activities, the A. Philip Randolph has been an advocate for the working poor of all backgrounds and has sought to improve race relations by supporting unionization and economic reforms that ameliorate the conditions of poverty. Perhaps its most radical idea was the Freedom Budget. Randolph himself introduced the plan in 1966. In the midst of a national social crisis in which some advocated violence to change society, Randolph called on the federal government to invest nearly $20 billion over a decade to eradicate poverty in the United States. Randolph did not receive the support of any politicians, so he in turn questioned the commitment of President Johnson and his administration to the antipoverty and civil rights programs of the Great Society. Regardless the Freedom Budget did represent well the institute's philosophy and outlook.

Since the 1960s, the A. Philip Randolph Institute has continued to fight for economic, political, and social justice. Its support of César Chávez and the United Farm Workers, the 1968 Memphis Sanitation Strike, and the 1969 General Electric Strike were important but generated little public controversy. However the institute did take several controversial stands. For example, unlike Dr. Martin Luther King, Jr., and the Southern Christian Leadership Conference, Randolph and the APRI did not attack President Johnson on his cold war foreign policy or even the Vietnam War.

Furthermore the institute's involvement in the 1968 New York City public school teachers' strike generated much contention. In 1968, the city's board of education attempted to reassign white teachers in the Ocean Hill–Brownsville district in order to introduce more black and Hispanic teachers in that area. The move precipitated a United Federation of Teachers' strike and created one of the most divisive political and racial episodes in New York City's history. In a response that some young black radicals and nationalists saw as betrayal, the APRI stood behind the UFT. Randolph and the institute were seen as sell-outs and opponents to the black power movement. Both then and now, the institute has honored its namesake by taking controversial and even unpopular positions to advance the cause of unions and civil rights.

ANDREW E. KERSTEN

References and Further Reading

Anderson, Jervis B. *A Philip Randolph: A Biographical Portrait*. New York: Harcourt, Brace, Jovanovich, 1972.
Pfeffer, Paula F. *A Philip Randolph: Pioneer of the Civil Rights Movement*. Baton Rouge: Louisiana State University Press, 1990.
Podair, Jerald E. *The Strike That Changed New York: Blacks, Whites, and the Ocean Hill-Brownsville Crisis*. New Haven, CT: Yale University Press, 2002.
Rustin, Bayard. "The History of the A. Philip Randolph Institute." *Debate and Understanding* 1 (Winter 1976): 29–35.

See also **American Federation of Labor-Congress of Industrial Organizations; Brotherhood of Sleeping Car Porters; Ocean Hill-Brownsville Strikes (1968); Randolph, A. Philip; Rustin, Bayard**

ABOLITIONISM

Abolitionism, or the movement to end slavery in the decades before the Civil War, had two important predecessors—gradualism and African colonization—that differed from one another and from their successor. Gradual emancipation, which typically required the children of slaves to remain in service until their late twenties, was the preferred solution of the Revolutionary and Federalist eras. Following the precedent established in 1780 by the state of Pennsylvania, more and more states in the North passed gradualist laws, the last being New York (1799) and New Jersey (1804), which together had half the slaves in the region. Not long after gradualism ran its course, colonizationism rose to the fore. This movement, which formally began in 1816–1817 with the formation of the American Colonization Society (ACS), promoted emancipation of slaves followed by the emigration of free blacks and former slaves to Africa or the Caribbean. Though the ACS attracted leading jurists and politicians in the North and South, it failed in its own right and especially by comparison to gradualism. The ACS settled only a few thousand African-Americans in Africa (notably Liberia, which the ACS established in 1822), a puny figure compared to the 75,000 slaves freed by the actions of the Revolutionary generation. Both movements are important, not only for what they did or did not achieve; but because they served as negative reference points for the abolitionist movement that took shape in the early 1830s.

Most leading abolitionists in the 1830s started out as colonizationists. This included William Lloyd Garrison of Boston, the new movement's towering figure. The son of a struggling Newburyport, Massachusetts, ship captain who abandoned his family when Garrison was still a toddler, young Garrison was raised by his mother in want and poverty. As a teenager he became an apprentice to a local printer, completing his training in newspaper shops in Boston and Bennington, Vermont, before returning to Boston in 1828 to work for The *Genius of Universal Emancipation*. This abolitionist sheet was founded in 1821 by the Quaker activist Benjamin Lundy who lured Garrison to Baltimore in 1829 when he moved the paper there. Historians used to believe that Garrison found his lifetime calling as an antislavery agitator partly because of Lundy's influence and partly because of his firsthand experience with the horrors of slavery in Baltimore. It appears however that he was also influenced by black men who can justly be considered the founders of the abolitionist movement before the Civil War as we have come to know it. It was they who rejected the gradualism of the

Revolutionary Era and the colonizationism of the Era of Good Feelings.

African-American activists in the major northern port cities in the second half of the 1820 loudly denounced colonization. In Boston David Walker joined together with fellow blacks to form the Massachusetts General Colored Association (MGCA), one of the earliest anticolonizationist groups in the nation. At first blush Walker appears to be a very unlikely source of inspiration for the pacifistic, nonviolent Garrison. After all his 1829 blockbuster, *An Appeal to the Colored Citizens of the World*, calling for resistance to slavery by the slaves themselves, is laced with withering denunciations of white injustice and apocalyptic visions of black revolution. However the larger project of the *Appeal* and of the MGCA, for that matter, was immediate emancipation, or what became known simply as immediatism, along with equal rights for blacks following emancipation. The policies of immediate liberation and civil rights along with anticolonizationism made a huge impression on Garrison and his followers.

Having jettisoned colonizationism by the late 1820s, Garrison and his colleagues moved quickly to put together a movement premised on immediatism and equality. In January 1831, he published the first edition of the *Liberator*, the voice of the movement in New England and the larger movement's best-known sheet. A year later he called the meeting that launched the New England Anti-Slavery Society (renamed the Massachusetts Anti-Slavery Society in 1835). Similar groups in New York, Boston, and other cities gathered in Philadelphia in 1833 to begin the American Anti-Slavery Society, the national voice of the movement. This small group of some 62 white male delegates (four women and three blacks attended as observers) launched a crusade that would boast nearly 200,000 acolytes by the end of the decade. It was to exercise influence far in excess of it numbers.

Who were these people? Apart from Garrison and perhaps a few of his counterparts who were nationally known, the more prominent leaders, and not a few local ones, were rich and well-born. This exclusive circle included the New York merchants and financiers Arthur and Lewis Tappan, as well as the Boston Brahmin Wendell Phillips, to name just a few. The vast majority of the membership however consisted of neither the rich nor the poor of the city nor the farmer nor landless laborer of the country. Most were drawn from the ranks of the "middling sort"– petty professionals, small employers, and working people in the villages and small towns of the country disproportionately located in New England and western New York as well as in pockets of the Midwest settled by

Yankee migrants. About a third of them and possibly more were women.

This geographic pattern hints at the intellectual sources of abolitionism. New England and western New York were "burned over" by the revivals of the Second Great Awakening, which left in its wake thousands of converts and born-again Christians girded to prepare the world for the second coming of Christ by cleansing it of depravity. Most of them eagerly joined the crusade against liquor. A smaller but significant minority of the newly churched identified slavery as sin, and such evangelicals formed the vast majority of abolitionism's rank and file. Some quickened Christians found slavery to be a violation of the rights of man enshrined in the Declaration. It appears however that advocates of equal rights were a separate group and probably a much smaller one. The evangelicals gave the movement its moralistic ethos—and defining strategy as well. They would end slavery, neither through violence nor political action, but with the "bibles and tracts" policy of converting all Americans, including southern planters, to their version of Christianity—that is, through moral suasion.

The New York office, funded mainly by wealthy merchants, built support through a busy agenda of activities. Led by the transplanted Yankees Joshua Leavitt and Elizur Wright, the New Yorkers hired and coordinated a field staff to carry out national policy and promote debates and discussions on slavery as well as lectures featuring appearances by fugitive slaves testifying firsthand to the brutality that was slavery. One of their chief projects was the great propaganda drop in spring 1835, alternatively known as the pamphlet or postal campaign because it involved distributing unheard-of numbers of tracts and other pieces of antislavery propaganda. This massive effort was made possible by using the recently invented steam press, which elevated output to unimagined levels. In 1835 alone, the New York office sent out over a million items, nearly ten times the 1834 rate. The second project involved petitioning Congress in the name of emancipation, an effort that also began in 1835 with the national office and then devolved in 1836 to state and local organizations. The second project easily rivaled and perhaps surpassed the postal campaign in scope, barraging lawmakers with petitions demanding the abolition of slavery in Washington, D.C., and of the slave traffic in the South as well as banning the admission of more slave states to the union.

These initiatives at once strongly affected national politics and abolitionism itself. The postal campaign outraged politicians and officials in the South, who appealed to the national administration for relief. Postmaster Amos Kendall responded in late 1835 by banning abolitionist material from the mail service even though he knew it was illegal. The petitions continued to pour into Washington, some 30,000 in 1836, further angering southern Democrats and their allies in the North, popularly known as Doughface Democrats, who drew together to pass a resolution automatically tabling petitions on slavery and thereby choking off debate on the subject. These groups approved similar gag rules every year until 1840, when a four-year rule was imposed. Such audacious violations of free speech and expression probably turned some northern Democrats against slavery and may well have recruited abolitionists.

There is no question that the petition campaign deeply impressed a faction of abolitionists previously associated with moral suasion. Garrison was not among them. The premier moral suasionist of the age, "the great agitator" had come around to the position that political action of all sorts—up to and including voting—was morally repugnant and wholly unacceptable because politics required sacrificing principle to compromise and coalition building. Garrison and his friends took a harder and harder line against political engagement as the 1830s wore on, insisting that moral cleansing had to precede voting. The middle of the new decade found Garrison asking why people found it so hard to see that voting was "not moral action—any more than a box on the ear is an argument? (*Liberator*, Mar. 13, 1846). He simultaneously came out for women's rights in the second half of the decade, siding with a small faction of women in the movement chastised by men for having stepped out their sphere and determined to lay claim to equal rights.

A substantial faction of abolitionists, already impatient with Garrison's feminist sympathies, was even more discouraged by his tendentious opposition to politics. Men like Wright and Edwin B. Stanton, husband-to-be of Elizabeth Cady, had seen potential in the petition campaign in 1836 and in several abolitionist forays into electoral politics in 1838 and 1839 in New York and Massachusetts. The sides sparred with one another over political action at the state and national levels in 1837 and 1838 and then had a showdown at the 1839 national convention of the AASS. Garrison mustered enough votes to sink a resolution that would have committed the organization to political action. Defeated on the convention floor, Wright and the New Yorkers' faction in 1840 organized the Liberty Party, the nation's first political organization committed to the abolition of slavery. The split between old-org and new-org abolitionists transformed the movement forever.

Old-org and new-org abolitionism developed over the next two decades in the context of tightening sectional tensions over slavery in national politics. First came the Mexican War in 1846–1848, a war many northerners in both parties saw as a southern plot for appropriating additional slave land. The 1850 compromise that disposed of the land taken in the war only heated northern tempers. Northerners, and Yankees especially, felt that the South benefited disproportionately from the settlement, taking special umbrage at the Fugitive Slave Act for investing the federal government with more power to return runaway slaves and punishing those who obstructed government agents. Yankee outrage over that law was only beginning to abate in 1854 when Congress passed Stephen Douglas's Kansas-Nebraska Bill, which repealed the Missouri Compromise and theoretically at least opened new territory in the West to slavery. On top of all that came the hated Dred Scott decision in 1857 in which the Supreme Court ruled that Congress had no power to limit the property rights of slaveholders. The court said in effect that the Missouri Compromise was null and void, that the South had been right all along when it insisted that slaves were property protected by no less a force than the Constitution. Taken together such events lend credence to the northern idea that "slave power" ran the nation.

Through all of that, old and new org remained divided against one another despite shared goals and objectives. Garrison's old org proved far more hostile and uncooperative, routinely rejecting overtures from new-org men and openly condemning them as opportunists. Garrison clung fast to apolitical agitation into the early 1840s, then adopted the extreme position of letting the South secede if it chose to do so under the slogan "no union with slaveholders." His reasoning was that if the South left the Union, both regions would be better off because the North would become a haven for runaways, which would gradually erode the southern economy and eat away at what remained of slavery. He also continued to support civil rights for blacks, relentlessly assailing racism and organizing popular demonstrations against Jim Crow in private and public accommodations. Even historians who doubt the efficacy of Garrison's abolitionist strategy applaud his principled stand for racial equality, arguing that the old org had a moral edge over the new org.

This distinction between the factions is only partly correct on the question of abolitionism. The new org beat something of a retreat from the immediatism of the Garrisonians because its dominant voices took the position that the federal government could not interfere with slavery where it existed. It therefore supported policies that would weaken the South politically—such as ending the three-fifths clause and prohibiting the admission of more slave states to the union—or that would weaken slavery itself—such as cutting off the internal traffic. However others argued strongly that the federal government could act to end slavery itself, and not simply prohibit its expansion. Libertyites who adhered to this line of reasoning, such as Lysander Spooner, were full-blown abolitionists, not compromising antislavery advocates.

The new party was also divided over legal equality. In New York, and possibly in Ohio as well, Liberty men balked at extending the rights of citizenship to black men and showed very little interest in fighting Jim Crow; in New England, where African-American men enjoyed the vote (except in Connecticut), Libertyites were as liberal-minded on civil rights as the Garrisonians. Having gained the balance of power in the elections of 1842 in Massachusetts, Liberty politicians had the legislature repeal an ancient law barring intermarriage between the races and pass a personal liberty law that prohibited state officials from cooperating with federal authorities in the trail of runaway slaves. When the legislature came within a few votes of forcing railways to end separate accommodations for African-Americans, the carriers caved in and ended segregation on their own. Several cities and towns soon integrated their public schools.

The civil rights laws approved by the Bay State legislature in 1843 were not the work of white abolitionists alone. Prominent African-Americans who were personally loyal to Garrison and putative advocates of apolitical moral suasion came out strongly for the personal liberty law and for the effort to desegregate the railways; several years later, they started the drive for school desegregation that featured a massive boycott of Boston's Jim Crow classrooms. This group included William Cooper Nell, Garrison's former apprentice, and Charles Lenox Remond, a close friend of Garrison, who nonetheless testified before the Bay State legislature on the need for laws to end segregation on public carriers. They gained new colleagues in the second half of the 1840s when several runaway slaves—Lewis Hayden and Leonard Grimes, for instance—arrived in the city of Boston and quickly emerged as leaders. Though such men continued to admire Garrison, they thought less and less of his hostility to politics. Nearly all joined the Free Soil party, which subsumed the Libertyites in 1848. The new party proved hospitable despite the stigma later attached to it by historians as a white supremacist force. It nominated African-Americans for public office and supplied legal assistance for suits filed against racist school boards that refused to close black schools.

Nor did Free Soil support for blacks end there. Slaveholders and their agents in the early 1850s sought to take advantage of the Fugitive Slave Act. Nowhere did they face stiffer resistance than in Massachusetts. Free Soilers tried without success to strengthen the personal liberty law of 1843 (a feat achieved by the Know-Nothings in 1855). In Boston white party activists, working separately but in cooperation with blacks, held massive rallies against the hated law and hounded and harassed southerners on the prowl for fugitive slaves, on one occasion intimidating two of them into giving up and leaving town. Free Soilers proved no less compromising on the question of slavery. Instead of opposing expansionism, they denounced slavery itself, coming within several votes in 1851–1852 of putting the state house on record against slavery.

So it went into the 1850s when the Know-Nothings replaced the Free Soilers and the Republicans replaced the Know-Nothings. Black and white abolitionists in Massachusetts supported an end to Jim Crow as well as an end to slavery. That they did not always succeed in the legislature is unsurprising. They were after all participants in broad coalitions in the successive third-party organizations that cropped up in the 1850s, coalitions that grew broader and more popular with each insurgency. They were a plurality among the Free Soilers and probably smaller still among the Republicans. They were not egalitarians. They instead are best understood as paternalists with patronizing attitudes toward blacks who hoped that integrated public schools and other public accommodations would literally integrate blacks into the dominant culture. They were not much different from Garrison on the question of race.

The point is neither to lionize political abolitionists nor to make Massachusetts a stand-in for the North. The Bay State's liberal version of political abolitionism coexisted with a more narrow expression of antislavery, which one scholar aptly calls a "northern rights" outlook. This position, first articulated in the early 1840s by the Libertyite Joshua Leavitt, held that slavery was wrong, not because it was sinful, but because it was economically backward and burdensome. Slavery diverted investment that would have gone into more productive pursuits in the North, holding down growth in the region as a whole and penalizing workers in particular. Free labor and slave labor could not coexist without the latter constraining the former in the North. Such a northern rights outlook found its way into Free Soilism and Republicanism, intensifying the regional consciousness, which itself was an important byproduct of antislavery politics. It was the dominant outlook of Free Soilers and Republicans in the Middle West and quite common in

New England as well. In New England at least it was not inconsistent with political abolitionism, for the same people who saw slavery as contrary to Scripture also saw it as contrary to sound economics. It is still unclear if this intellectual pattern prevailed in antislavery parties elsewhere.

As with abolitionism, so with race. Garrisonianism was not the sole voice of racial toleration, limited though it was, in the North before the Civil War. Some political abolitionists fought to overcome their region's legacy of racism and Jim Crow. Their seeming failure does not mean that we can ignore them. It means instead that civil rights politics in the North was more complicated than we have been led to believe. It is a story that has not been properly told. It cannot be told without looking at what political actors—and workers especially—actually did, without delving more deeply into state and local politics, and without paying more serious attention to black activists.

BRUCE LAURIE

References and Further Reading

Barnes, Gilbert H. *The Anti-Slavery Impulse, 1830–1844.* New York: D. Appleton-Century, 1933.

Berlin, Ira. *Slaves without Masters: The Free Negro in the Antebellum South.* New York: Pantheon Books, 1974.

Dumond, Dwight L. *Antislavery: The Crusade for Freedom in America.* Ann Arbor: Univ. of Michigan Press, 1960.

Frey, Sylvia. *Water from the Rock: Black Resistance in a Revolutionary Age.* Princeton, NJ: Princeton Univ. Press, 1991.

Goodman, Paul. *Of One Blood: Abolitionism and the Origins of Racial Equality.* Berkeley: Univ. of California Press, 1998.

Kraut, Alan M., ed. *Crusaders and Compromisers: Essays on the Relationship of the Antislavery Struggle to the Second Party System.* Westport, CT: Greenwood Press, 1983.

Liberator [Boston], 1831–1865.

Laurie, Bruce. *Beyond Garrison: Antislavery and Social Reform.* New York: Cambridge Univ. Press, 2005.

Merrill, Walter H., and Louis Ruchames. *The Letters of William Lloyd Garrison.* 6 vols. Cambridge: Harvard Univ. Press, 1971–1981.

Quarles, Benjamin. *Black Abolitionists.* New York: Oxford Univ. Press, 1968.

Rael, Patrick. *Black Identity and Black Protest in the Antebellum North.* Chapel Hill: Univ. of North Carolina Press, 2002.

Sewell, Richard H. *Ballots for Freedom: Antislavery Politics in the United States, 1837–1860.* New York: Oxford Univ. Press, 1976.

Stewart, James Brewer. *Holy Warriors: The Abolitionists and American Slavery.* New York: Hill & Wang, 1976.

Thomas, John L. *The Liberator, William Lloyd Garrison.* Boston: Little, Brown, 1963.

Yellin, Jean F., and John C. Van Horne, eds. *The Abolitionist Sisterhood: Women's Political Culture in Antebellum America.* Ithaca, NY: Cornell Univ. Press, 1994.

ACTORS' EQUITY ASSOCIATION

In its origins, the Actors' Equity Association (AEA), a trade union founded in 1912 to represent performers working on the so-called legitimate stage, was an institutionalized response to a radical restructuring of the commercial theater business in the late nineteenth century that transformed the relationship between actors and their employers. In the wake of the depression of the early 1870s, combination companies, groups of actors touring the country in shows that were built around the talents of a single star performer, began to displace resident stock companies as the chief purveyors of theatrical entertainment in the United States. Stripped of their role as producers, theater managers were left with little alternative but to reinvent themselves as theatrical shopkeepers, traveling each summer to New York, the emergent capital of the entertainment industry, to book shows for the upcoming season.

In its early years, the combination system was characterized by intense and unrestricted competition. To combat the resulting problems, theater managers began to group their theaters into circuits, a strategy that strengthened their bargaining position by making it possible for them to offer touring companies several weeks of business in a single transaction. In the wake of this shift, enterprising businessmen in New York began to set themselves up as booking agents. Initially they were simply theatrical middlemen coordinating negotiations between New York-based producers and representatives of the theatrical circuits. As their businesses prospered however, they expanded their operations, investing in theaters and eventually setting themselves up as producers in their own right. During the 1890s, the most successful of these theatrical entrepreneurs began to pool their resources, creating chains of theaters that extended across the entire country. By 1910, two rival groups of producing managers—the Theatrical Syndicate and the Shubert Organization—had established an iron grip over the theater business in the United States.

What contemporary commentators were quick to label the theater trusts transformed U.S. show business, centralizing and rationalizing a wasteful and inefficient booking system and generating vast profits in the process. Among the thousands of men and women who earned a living treading the boards, however, they aroused considerable hostility. Though they injected an element of stability into a notoriously volatile industry, they did little to improve the working conditions of ordinary actors and actresses. In the absence of a standard theatrical contract, they were free to dictate the terms of an actor's employment.

Crowd of striking actors on 45th Street, New York City. Library of Congress, Prints & Photographs Division [LC-B2-4997-10].

If they reneged on their contractual responsibilities, the actor had little recourse beyond a long and costly legal battle. So dominant was their position that any performer who challenged them in the courts risked being permanently frozen out.

Of the 18 founder members of the AEA, all were male and most belonged to that large and amorphous group of performers who had successfully plied their trade on the metropolitan stage but whose careers had peaked some way short of stardom. They were bound together by their grievances against the new-style businessmen of the theater and a shared perception that actors, in their failure to organize, were out of step with other occupational groups. Successful professionals with a great deal invested in the prevailing theatrical order, they were not looking for a radical reconfiguration of labor-management relations in the theater industry. Framing their objectives in terms of the well being of the theatrical community as a whole, they put forward a proposal for the adoption of a standard theatrical contract that would, in their words, "protect the high-minded actor and high-minded manager in equal part." What they were offering to the producing managers was a mutually beneficial compact: In return for standardized conditions of employment they would serve up a compliant theatrical workforce. To a group of employers who, no less than their counterparts in other sectors of the economy, needed disciplined and reliable workers,

such an arrangement had much to recommend it. Even so the theater magnates quickly concluded that they did not wish to relinquish something that they saw as a key managerial prerogative—the right to determine the terms on which individual performers were employed—and they rejected the AEA's demands. In the face of managerial intransigence, actors' leaders soon concluded that "the only Trail out of the Wilderness" was affiliation with the organized labor movement. But for many actors, the idea of allying themselves with industrial workers was anathema, and for the next few years, a bitter debate about the wisdom of pursuing such a course raged within the acting community. With the managers refusing to give any ground however, frustration among the men and women of the legitimate stage began to mount, and in July 1919, Equity members voted overwhelmingly to cast their lot with organized labor. Eager to accommodate a group of workers who, in the eyes of most contemporary commentators, made rather incongruous trade unionists, the American Federation of Labor (AFL) issued an international charter covering the entire field of theatrical entertainment under a new umbrella organization, the Associated Actors and Artistes of America. Shortly thereafter Equity members passed a resolution to the effect that they would not work for any member of the Producing Managers' Association (PMA), an association that represented the collective interests of the managerial establishment until the entire PMA membership recognized the AEA and signed its standard minimum contract. The subsequent walkouts eventually brought production in the metropolitan theater to a standstill.

An unlikely victory in the month-long strike brought recognition to the AEA, but its position remained far from secure. Even in the wake of the settlement, irreconcilables within the managerial camp continued to evade their contractual responsibilities. Moreover with the benefits of the Equity contract available to all actors regardless of whether or not they were union members, most newcomers to the legitimate stage chose not to join the AEA, while many one-time loyalists simply stopped paying their dues. Faced with a precipitous decline in membership, AEA leaders put forward a scheme for the gradual implementation of an Equity shop, an arrangement whereby Equity members would be forbidden to play alongside non-Equity performers. It was a move that provoked outrage on the part of the major producers for whom anything even remotely akin to a closed shop was anathema. Their growing reliance on outside capital however meant that they could not risk another strike, and in 1924, they signed a compromise agreement that allowed them to employ non-Equity performers as long as they did not make up more than 20% of any given cast.

Having established itself as the legitimate bargaining agent for the U.S. stage actor, the AEA proceeded to transform labor-management relations in the theater industry in the United States. To the men and women of the stage, it brought vast improvements in working conditions, standardizing conditions of employment and eliminating the worst abuses to which they had been subjected. In an effort to eliminate the managerial practice of stranding unsuccessful touring companies wherever a show happened to close, for example, the AEA began checking the credentials of prospective producers and warning its members against accepting work with employers who did not appear to be financially secure. As a direct result, the number of companies left stranded in the theatrical hinterland fell from 56 during the 1921–1922 season to just four during the 1924–1925 season. The AEA also did much to redress the power imbalance between actors and their employers by vigorously enforcing the 2-week notice clause in the standard Equity contract and preventing producing managers from discharging performers without warning. The AEA worked hard moreover to protect members against loss of earnings resulting from canceled performances, insisting, for example, that if a star fell ill and could not complete the run of a show, the supporting cast should still get paid.

For all their concern for the welfare of their members however, Equity leaders were no less committed to upholding managerial authority in the workplace, insisting that actors no less than their employers had a responsibility to uphold the sanctity of the theatrical contract. Performers who reneged on that responsibility felt the full weight of their union's coercive powers. The AEA was particularly tough on contract jumpers, demanding that actors, like managers, abide by the terms of the 2-week notice clause and routinely requiring those who failed to do so to pay their former employers the equivalent of 2 weeks' salary. If Equity officials felt that a contract-jumping instance had damaged a show's chances of success, they imposed an even stiffer penalty, suspending offenders from the AEA, sometimes indefinitely, and thereby making it almost impossible for them to earn a living on the legitimate stage. By the late 1920s, most theatrical employers, large and small, had accepted that they had as much to gain from a strong actors' union as their employees. "If Equity were wiped out tomorrow," producer Brock Pemberton told an industrial relations analyst in 1926, "we'd revert to barbarism."

Just as significant as the AEA's efforts to monitor the contractual relationship between actors and their employers was the campaign it conducted in the 1920s to cleanse the acting community of the taint of immorality. Anxious to purge the U.S. stage of undesirables, its leaders undertook to extend their authority beyond the confines of the rehearsal room and the theater and into the private lives of their members. Against the backdrop of Prohibition, drunkenness emerged as a particularly significant issue. A performer who drank to excess was a threat not only to the livelihood of his or her fellow performers but also to the occupational aspirations of the acting elite, so Equity officials worked hand-in-hand with both actors and managers to rid the theater of inveterate drunkards. The AEA's incursions across the ill-defined boundary between the public and the private did not end with its often overzealous efforts to regulate the drinking habits of its members. Where possible it attempted to police their sexual lives as well, imposing harsh penalties on performers whose conduct brought them into conflict with prevailing notions of respectability, most obviously sexually promiscuous women and gay men. The campaign also had an important external dimension. Eager to reshape popular perceptions of the stage performer as a socially marginal figure, for example, Equity officials repeatedly petitioned the Methodist church to open its doors to actors and to lift its ban on theater attendance.

Even as the AEA sought to impose its authority on the U.S. stage-acting community, the cultural landscape of the United States was changing. By the early 1920s, the movie theater had displaced the playhouse as the principal arena for the consumption of popular entertainment, and screen acting had emerged as an important area of artistic endeavor in its own right. Seemingly blind to the implications of this upheaval, Equity leaders continued to claim the right, as practitioners of the highest expression of the actors' art, to speak for the entire acting community, and they resolved to extend their jurisdiction to the movie industry. A series of organizing drives in Hollywood in the mid-1920s yielded little in the way of permanent gains. The advent of sound and the subsequent migration of hundreds of stage performers to the West Coast however created a new window of opportunity for the AEA, and in June 1929, its leaders announced that their members would no longer accept non-Equity contracts or work alongside non-Equity performers. The quasi-strike split the Hollywood acting community in two. Thousands of lesser players flocked to the Equity banner. A majority of the stars in contrast reacted with hostility to what they saw as an attempt by the old theatrical aristocracy to "Broadwayize" the movie industry. Without the support of Hollywood's biggest names, the AEA had no chance of forcing the movie moguls to terms, and in August 1929, it called off its job action and withdrew from the motion picture studios in disarray.

The onset of the Depression entirely transformed both the economic and political contexts in which the AEA operated. In the wake of the Wall Street Crash, the theatrical economy, already seriously weakened by overexpansion on Broadway, rising production costs, and competition from the movies, collapsed. In the provinces, theatrical activity ground to a virtual halt. From 1927–1931, the number of resident stock companies operating outside New York City fell from 165 to just 30. By 1933, there were only 12 cities in the country capable of supporting first-class touring companies. In New York City, the collapse was almost as precipitous. The number of shows opening on Broadway slumped from an all-time peak of 264 in the 1927–1928 season to 187 in the 1930–1931 season. As production fell off, unemployment in the perennially overcrowded acting profession rose dramatically. Paid-up membership in the AEA, a reasonably accurate indicator of the number of performers finding steady work in the legitimate theater at any given historical moment, dropped from 9,857 in 1930 to 3,364 in 1933. Even for actors and actresses who did find work, times were hard. With salaries declining to less than 50% of their pre-Depression levels, a growing number of performers found it impossible to make ends meet.

Faced with a crisis of unprecedented proportions, the AEA began to reorient its activities, working with producers under the aegis of the National Industrial Recovery Administration for example to negotiate a minimum wage for its members. In the politically charged atmosphere of the 1930s however, traditional patterns of deference within the acting community were breaking down, and such measures notwithstanding, the power and authority of the Equity old guard was on the wane. In 1934, disgruntled rank-and-filers formed a pressure group, the so-called Actors' Forum, to agitate for a more effective response to the problems facing the men and women of the U.S. stage. Its leaders, self-confessed radicals who had cut their ideological teeth in New York City's left-wing theater groups, accused Equity officials of having lost touch with the average performer and called on them to adopt a program of reforms that would meet the basic economic needs of their constituents. At a highly charged emergency meeting in November 1934, attended by almost two thousand members, the AEA leadership fought off a challenge from the Actors' Forum, winning a vote of confidence by a margin of more than two to one. But the AEA emerged from the controversy not only more sensitive to the bread-and-butter concerns of ordinary stage actors but also more willing to enlist the assistance of the federal government in addressing them. In an effort to maximize job opportunities for its members, it entered into an interchangeability agreement with the Screen Actors Guild, the American Guild of Musical Artists, and the American Federation of Radio Artists that made it easier for performers to move between different branches of the commercial entertainment industry. More significantly it gave its full backing to the Federal Theatre Project (FTP), a branch of the Works Progress Administration (WPA) set up in 1935 both to provide jobs for unemployed theatrical workers and to bring theatrical entertainment to a wider audience than ever before. When the Dies Committee, a precursor of the House Committee on Un-American Activities, charged the FTP with engaging in subversive activities and called for its dismantling, the AEA campaigned vigorously, though ultimately unsuccessfully, to save a body that had become a major employer of theatrical talent.

The AEA emerged from the economic and political turbulence of the 1930s intact but deeply divided. Its growing politicization moreover meant that it was vulnerable to the attacks of conservative elements both inside and outside the theatrical community. In July 1940, for instance, Congressman William P. Lambertson accused seven members of the Equity Council of being Communists. Anxious to insulate themselves against charges of subversion, union leaders refused to put the seven members forward for re-election. When one of the seven ran successfully without the endorsement of the Equity leadership, 10 senior officials resigned in protest. Nor did the in-fighting end there. In 1945, Frank Fay, a one-time vaudevillian and star of the hit play *Harvey*, called for the expulsion of five Equity members who had appeared in a benefit show for the Spanish Republic in 1936 at which both the Catholic church and the pope had been heavily criticized. Though the AEA eventually cleared all five of anything that might have constituted a breach of union rules, the controversy demonstrated the vulnerability of performers who had associated themselves with progressive causes in the 1930s to the conservative backlash that followed in the wake of World War II. To its credit the AEA acted promptly to pre-empt an internal witch hunt, censuring Faye and passing a rule forbidding any Equity member from defaming another. Unlike the Screen Actors Guild moreover, the AEA spoke out forcibly against blacklisting, passing a resolution in September 1951, condemning the practice of denying performers employment on account of their political views and promising to help blacklisted members to continue to work in the theater. In a further demonstration of its liberal credentials, the AEA also placed itself in the vanguard of the struggle against racial segregation. In 1947, for example, it announced that unless the National Theatre in Washington, DC, abandoned its policy of audience segregation within a year, it would forbid its members to play there. Rather than submit to the AEA's demands, the National's management opted to turn it into a movie theater. When the National reopened its doors as a legitimate playhouse 5 years later however, it did so to an integrated audience.

Since the 1950s, the theatrical landscape of the United States has undergone profound transformations, most notably the advent of Off-Broadway and Off-Off-Broadway entertainment and the massive expansion of regional theater. Even so the AEA has remained relatively consistent in terms of how it has operated. The economic well being of the men and women of the U.S. stage has remained central to its mission. In May 1960, for example, it shut down Broadway for 2 weeks in response to the refusal of the League of New York Theatres and Producers to back its proposals for a pension plan for actors. Its members returned to work only after Mayor Robert

Wagner, Jr., agreed to scrap the city's amusement tax so that theatrical employers could afford to donate a portion of box office receipts to a pension fund. In February 1964, another strike ended after just 27 hours with a settlement, again brokered by Wagner, that brought an increase in the minimum salary for actors and the equalization of performance and rehearsal pay. In November 1970, the AEA extended its campaign for improved pay and working conditions to Off-Broadway, ordering its members to strike and eventually winning a salary increase and the extension of the Equity shop to Off-Broadway theaters. The AEA has not always relied on industry action to bring about improvements in the working conditions of U.S. stage actors, however. In 1980, for instance, it managed to negotiate the insertion of a just-cause clause into its standard contract to protect actors against arbitrary dismissal. Nor has the AEA confined its activities to regulating the contractual relationship between actors and their employers. During the mid-1980s, it emerged as a major player in the fight against AIDS, setting up the Equity Fights AIDS Committee to raise funds for victims of an epidemic that has disproportionately impacted the theatrical community. As an extension of its role as the guardian of the collective interests of U.S. stage actors, the AEA has also been a perennial advocate of federal funding for the theater. From 1959–1965, Equity officials appeared before nine congressional committees to speak in favor of the creation of a governmental agency to promote the arts, and over the last 40 years, the AEA has been an outspoken supporter of the National Endowment for the Arts. Though its members have always resisted proposals to merge with unions representing other sections of the acting community, the AEA has managed to cast off many of the antilabor prejudices that characterized it during its formative years. As recently as 2003, it gave its unqualified backing to the American Federation of Musicians in its battle with the League of New York Theatres and Producers over minimum orchestra size requirements. The AEA has remained firm in its commitment to the principle of equality, campaigning vigorously to increase employment opportunities for members of racial and ethnic minorities and embracing wholeheartedly the principle of nontraditional casting to break down barriers of race, gender, age, and disability. It has also been steadfast in its opposition to blacklisting, even backing the British actress Vanessa Redgrave in her 1984 lawsuit against the Boston Symphony Orchestra for allegedly terminating her contract on account of her political views.

SEAN P. HOLMES

References and Further Reading

Harding, Alfred. *The Revolt of the Actors*. New York: William Morrow and Company, 1929.

Holmes, Sean P. "All the World's A Stage: The Actors' Strike of 1919." *Journal of American History* 91, 4 (2005): 1291–1317.

———. "And the Villain Still Pursued Her: The Actors' Equity Association in Hollywood, 1919–1929." *Historical Journal of Film, Radio, and Television* 25, 1 (2005): 27–50.

———. "The Shuberts and the Actors' Equity Association, 1913–1924." *The Passing Show: Newsletter of the Shubert Archive* 23 (2003): 21–32.

ACTORS' STRIKE (1919)

In studies of the great wave of labor unrest that swept the United States in the wake of World War I, the actors' strike of 1919 rarely receives more than a cursory mention. It is significant however, and not simply for what it reveals about industrial relations in the commercial entertainment industry. It highlights many of the problems in organizing workers in the culture industries and draws our attention to the resources that such workers are able to deploy in their struggles with their employers.

The roots of the strike lay in the restructuring of the U.S. theater that took place in the late nineteenth century as pre-industrial modes of production gave way to something more closely akin to modern business practice. By 1910, two rival groups of producing managers—the Theatrical Syndicate and the Shuberts—had established an iron grip over the so-called legitimate theater in the United States, operating national entertainment networks that integrated the processes of production, distribution, and exhibition. Though the rise of the so-called "theater trusts" injected an element of stability into a notoriously volatile business, it also led to worsening working conditions across the industry. The Actors' Equity Association (AEA), a body founded in 1913 to protect the interests of stage performers and to raise the collective status of acting as an occupation, responded to growing resentment among ordinary actors and actresses by launching a campaign for the introduction of a standard contract. The theatrical magnates however were unwilling to relinquish the right to determine the terms on which individual performers were employed, and though they negotiated intermittently with the AEA through their employers' association, the Producing Managers' Association (PMA), they refused to give any ground. In July 1919, convinced that only militant action would force concessions, Equity members voted to affiliate with the American Federation of Labor (AFL). Less than a month later, on August 7 1919, they passed a resolution to the effect that they would not work for any manager who belonged to the PMA until the PMA had recognized the AEA as the legitimate bargaining agent of the U.S. actor.

The odds in the strike were heavily stacked against the AEA. With a large pool of nonunion talent at their disposal—chorus girls and vaudevillians, as well as the hundreds of legitimate performers who had never embraced the Equity cause—the managers began rebuilding their shows immediately. Union leaders moved quickly to win the allegiance of nonmembers, setting up a chorus auxiliary to address the needs of young women who earned their living in the chorus lines and welcoming performers from every branch of the acting profession into their ranks. Reinvented as a genuine mass movement of theatrical workers, the AEA was able to turn up the pressure on the managers. Strikers in New York City took their fight into the streets, where they used their celebrity status to transform the streets into an entertainment spectacle, charming theater goers with parades, playlets, and song-and-dance routines and shifting the balance of public opinion decisively in their favor. Consumers as well as objects of consumption, strikers also secured the support of the many small-business owners in the theater district—restaurant proprietors, shopkeepers, landladies of theatrical boarding houses, barbers, and so forth—who depended on their continued patronage and goodwill. To raise funds, they organized a series of benefit shows that proved spectacularly successful both critically and financially. The theater magnates hit back by filing lawsuits against the AEA collectively and several hundred of its members individually. However their legal counteroffensive had the unanticipated effect of persuading members of other theatrical unions, most notably the stagehands and musicians, to walk out in support of the striking actors. With theatrical production at a virtual standstill, the venture capitalists who had brokered the massive expansion of the entertainment industry in the early twentieth century began to grow restive, sensing that their investments might be at risk. Shorn of their support, the producing managers had no alternative but to give in to the AEA's demands, and on September 6, 1919, the strike ended.

Though the managerial moguls cautioned its leaders against crowing, the AEA had won a significant victory. Over the course of the month-long strike, its membership had risen from around 2,700 to over 14,000, and the amount of money in its coffers increased. By the time its members returned to work, the AEA had secured the right to bargain collectively on behalf of the men and women of the

U.S. stage and established itself as a permanent feature of the theatrical landscape.

SEAN P. HOLMES

References and Further Reading

Harding, Alfred. *The Revolt of the Actors.* New York: William Morrow and Company, 1929.
Holmes, Sean P. "All the World's a Stage: The Actors' Strike of 1919." *Journal of American History* 91, 4 (2005): 1291–1317.

ADAIR V. UNITED STATES (1908)

In *Adair v. United States*, the Supreme Court invalidated a federal law that had prohibited contracts that required employees to promise not to join a union while employed. This decision essentially legalized "yellow dog" contracts and undermined Congress' ambivalent efforts to assuage labor unrest in the railway industry.

After the Civil War, railroad companies aggressively expanded the railway system with little government regulation. Characterized as robber barons, owners demanded dangerous labor from their employees while paying low and unpredictable wages. In response railroad workers, similar to laborers in other fields, organized into trade unions and increasingly protested this treatment through strikes. In 1888, after more than a decade of railway strikes, including extensive and violent strikes in 1877 and 1885–1886, Congress attempted to intervene. It passed the Arbitration Act, which authorized establishing panels with investigative powers to identify the source of labor disputes and issue nonbinding opinions. Railroad companies refused to arbitrate, so the act proved ineffective.

A decade later in response to continued labor unrest, Congress passed the Erdman Act (1898). This act also authorized voluntary arbitration, but unlike its predecessor, it made panel decisions binding. Further Section 10 made it a misdemeanor to discriminate against employees of an interstate carrier for belonging to a union. While this provision provided some legislative support for labor unions, it was not decisive. In 1908, in a case involving the Louisville and Nashville Railroad Company (L&NRR), the United States Supreme Court found Section 10 to be unconstitutional.

The L&NRR, as a common carrier engaged in interstate commerce, was subject to Section 10. When L&NRR agent William Adair fired employee O. B. Coppage for being a member of the Brotherhood of Locomotive Firemen, federal prosecutors charged Adair with a misdemeanor. The district court found Section 10 constitutional and Adair guilty.

Adair appealed on the grounds that Section 10 violated the Fifth Amendment of the U.S. Constitution by depriving L&NRR of its liberty and property without due process.

The Supreme Court reversed its decision, finding that Section 10 did violate the Fifth Amendment. The Court reasoned that L&NRR and its agent Adair had a liberty and property right in its employment decisions and that these rights were protected so long as they did not injure a public interest. The Court acknowledged that Congress had the power to override those rights to regulate interstate commerce but found that in this case, there was no legal or logical connection between an employee's membership in a labor organization and carrying on interstate commerce. Therefore it deemed that Congress could not make it a crime for an employer to fire an employee because of union membership.

The two dissenting opinions, by Justices McKenna and Holmes, identified a larger public policy issue raised by the case: The negative effect on the public welfare of continued conflict between railroad companies and railroad employees' unions. Both suggested that employers' Fifth Amendment rights were not absolute and that the provisions of the Erdman Act were permissible restraints to further important public policy. Nonetheless yellow dog contracts remained legal until 1932 when Congress passed the Norris-LaGuardia Act, which the Supreme Court upheld in 1938.

GWEN HOERR JORDAN

References and Further Reading

Arnesen, Eric. *Brotherhoods of Color: Black Railroad Workers and the Struggle for Equality.* Cambridge, MA: Harvard University Press, 2001.
Forbath, William E. *Law and the Shaping of the American Labor Movement.* Cambridge, MA: Harvard University Press, 1991.
Lovell, George I. *Legislative Deferrals; Statutory Ambiguity, Judicial Power, and American Democracy.* Cambridge, MA: Cambridge University Press, 2003.

Cases and Statutes Cited

Adair v. United States 208 U.S. 161 (1908).
United States Supreme Court in Lauf v. Shinner. 303 U.S. 323 (1938).

ADAMSON ACT

The demand for an 8-hour workday has a long history in U.S. labor affairs. Despite nearly continuous efforts by various labor organizations dating back many decades into the nineteenth century, the 8-hour day did not become the norm for industrial workers until well into the twentieth century. The Adamson Act, drafted hurriedly in the midst of a strike crisis, was the genesis of that change. For all its wider significance, the bill itself applied only to a small subset of railway employees, the members of the four brotherhoods—conductors, engineers, trainmen, and firemen—in all less than 20% of the total railroad workforce. Castigated by railway executives as a craven capitulation to threatened economic violence, the Adamson Act was a momentous victory for the railway brotherhoods and a clear statement of the breadth of the power of Congress to regulate interstate commerce.

The narrative of the act begins in the fall of 1915. Executives of the railway brotherhoods, responding to a persistent clamor from within their ranks, announced their decision to present 52 major railroads with a demand for an 8-hour day and time-and-a-half pay after 8 hours. They stated further that they would not submit to the arbitration of the United States Mediation Board established under the provisions of the Newlands Act of 1913. The carriers received the formal proposal on March 30, 1916, and announced their rejection of its terms in mid-June. At that time they offered to submit the issue to arbitration. The brotherhoods responded by setting a strike deadline of September 4, 1916. Throughout that spring and summer, the brotherhoods prepared for a national strike, setting up committees and obtaining strike authorizations. Railroad managers, likewise determined to defeat the brotherhoods, set plans to operate the trunk lines with supervisory personnel and strikebreakers.

By early August President Woodrow Wilson concluded that a catastrophic national railway strike was imminent and the issue at hand so contentious as to preclude the parties negotiating any resolution without outside assistance. From August 13 to August 27, Wilson alternately lectured, cajoled, and threatened the disputants in an effort to arrange some reasonable compromise. Wilson personally sympathized with the brotherhood's demand for an 8-hour day, but he believed that the appeal for time-and-a-half was without merit. Equally convinced of the rectitude of their respective positions, the carriers and the brotherhoods adamantly refused to negotiate despite the efforts of the President. On August 28, concerned that a strike would hinder military preparedness, Wilson decided he had no other choice but to request the passage of legislation granting an 8-hour day to train service employees.

Wilson outlined his proposal in a joint address to Congress on August 29. He asked for a prohibition on strikes to give a proposed federal commission the opportunity to investigate railway labor issues; called

for an expansion of the size of the Interstate Commerce Commission, with a mandate to assess whether the increase in labor costs warranted a rate increase; and for the executive branch, sought the authority to compel the operation of the railways for military purposes. The bill drafted by William C. Adamson, chair of the House Interstate Commerce Committee, and Claude Kitchen, House Majority Leader, reflected political realities and the need for swift legislative action with the strike deadline looming. It stated that "eight hours shall, in contracts for labor and service, be deemed a day's work and the measure or standard of a day's work for the purpose of reckoning the compensation of all employees who are now or may hereafter be employed by any common carrier by railroad...." The law further stipulated that the wages previously paid for a full day, generally understood to be 10 hours, were now to be paid for 8 hours, and called for the creation of a temporary three-member federal commission to study railroad problems in general.

Railroad executives immediately challenged the constitutionality of the act. The carriers asserted that Congress did not possess the power to determine the length of a workday. Further if it did possess that authority, it was strictly limited and the act clearly exceeded those limitations. Because the carriers, the brotherhoods, and the Wilson administration all sought a swift resolution of the case, they agreed to a number of measures—including dismissal of union representatives from the suit—that hastened its movement through the court system. Consequently the Supreme Court heard arguments on January 8–10, 1917, as *Wilson v. New*. While the court considered the case, it enjoined the application of the wage provisions of the bill but required the railroads to maintain a record of the wages they would have to pay retroactively should it uphold the law. The brotherhoods, fearful of a reversal, responded with a general strike order on March 15, 1917. Finally on March 19, 1917, the court upheld the Adamson Act in its entirety on a 5 to 4 vote. Ironically under great pressure from President Wilson and the Council of National Defense, the carriers had capitulated the previous day, agreeing to abide by the provisions of the law in the interest of national unity. With the looming threat of war, both sides concentrated their efforts on the terrible gridlock and car shortages that plagued the industry throughout the remainder of the year.

The bill is significant for a number of reasons. First it set an 8-hour standard for industrial labor, a pattern that would later became ubiquitous. Second it seemed to confirm for many railway managers the onset of active antipathy toward the industry by the state. Third it firmly established the power of Congress in regulating interstate commerce. Fourth Wilson's support of the 8-hour day opened a new phase in the relationship between union labor and politics, moving such conservative labor unions as the brotherhoods into direct collaboration with the Democratic party. Finally the prominent role of the brotherhoods in the political debates before and after the passage of the 1920 Transportation Act is evidence of that shift.

SCOTT E. RANDOLPH

References and Further Reading

Dubofsky, Melvyn. *The State and Labor in Modern America.* Chapel Hill: University of North Carolina Press, 1994.
Kerr, K. Austin. *American Railroad Politics, 1914–1920.* Pittsburgh: University of Pittsburgh Press, 1968.
Lecht, Leonard A. *Experience under Railway Labor Legislation.* New York: Columbia University Press, 1955.
Link, Arthur. *Woodrow Wilson and the Progressive Era, 1910–1917.* New York: Harper and Row, 1954.
Montgomery, David. *The Fall of the House of Labor: The Workplace, the State, and American Labor Activism, 1865–1925.* Cambridge: Cambridge University Press, 1987.

Cases and Statutes Cited

Adamson Act, 39 Stat. 721, chap. 436 (1916).
Newlands Act, 38 Stat. 103 (1913).
Wilson v. New, 243 U.S. 332 (1917).

Jane Addams. Library of Congress, Prints & Photographs Division [LC-USZ61-144].

ADDAMS, JANE (1860–1935)
Chicago Settlement House Leader, Social Reformer, and Peace Activist

Jane Addams used her position as head resident of Chicago's Hull-House settlement to operate as a middle-class ally of the labor movement and an advocate for the interests of the working class from the 1890s until her death in 1935. Born in Cedarville, Illinois, at the start of the Civil War, Addams grew up in material comfort under the tutelage of her father, a successful grain miller, banker, and Republican state senator. A four-year education at Rockford Female Seminary, her father's death, and 6 subsequent years of illness, family duty, and European travel left Addams impatient for the authority of a steward in society but without an avenue for realizing her ambition. It was in an effort to find a demanding, independent, and socially useful role for herself that Addams, along with her friend, Ellen Gates Starr,

decided to import to Chicago the British concept of the settlement house, where they would settle among the working poor and offer their neighborly services.

Addams and Starr insisted from the start that Hull-House was not a charity, nor was it devoted to Protestant evangelizing. But when the settlement opened, its novice leaders knew little about the daily struggles of their working-class neighbors and less about labor organizing or labor legislation. In impressively short order however, Addams democratized her ambitions to be a steward, recognizing that her neighbors had as much to teach her as she had to teach them. By 1892 and for the subsequent 43 years, Addams was a persuasive advocate for the pragmatic view that a democratic state relies on the "character of its citizens, therefore if certain industrial conditions are forcing the workers below the standard of decency," it is appropriate for workers to organize to alter industrial conditions and equally appropriate for the state itself to regulate those conditions (Jane Addams,

Twenty Years at Hull-House with Autobiographical Notes, 1910). Her dual advocacy of labor unions and labor legislation often put her at odds with partisans of each approach, but it is consistent with her pragmatic view that any method that improves the living standards of the working class benefits the ultimate goal: An expanded and strengthened democracy.

The keystone in Addams' role as a middle-class advocate for working-class interests is her persistent focus on a harmonious, class-diverse, and culturally diverse democracy. That focus grew out of her daily experiences at Hull-House, her philosophical commitment to pacifist Christian humanism, and her aversion to conflict. The combination of ideology and personality, along with her considerable rhetorical skill, made Addams the most famous, most articulate, most stubborn, and most annoying advocate for peaceful, cross-class cooperation in U.S. history. She irritated labor unionists by chiding them for being so materialistic and combative that they strayed from the noble high road of democratic brotherhood; she infuriated socialists for offering a programmatic "speck in an ocean of misery," and she regularly enraged procapitalists for what they viewed as her prolabor and, therefore, her "socialistic" stance (Jane Addams, "An Oft-Told Tale," 1912). In the bitterly divided world of pre-World War I industrial relations, Addams persistently defined her role as that of mediator because she held the pacifist's conviction that only arbitration would achieve the desired democratic end. Among all the industrial foxes, Addams was the hedgehog; she knew one thing and she knew it well: Peaceful, cross-class cooperation produces political, economic, and social democracy. Her record of activism on behalf of the working class only makes sense within that firm philosophical context.

The Pullman Strike of 1894 is often cited as Addam's baptism in the labor struggle, but she had felt "almost forced into the trades unions" years before that dramatic strike because of the desperate conditions her neighbors faced. By the end of 1891, she had offered Hull-House as a meeting place for the Women's Bookbinding Union, led by Mary Kenney. In early 1892, Addams welcomed Florence Kelley, a forceful advocate for socialist ideals, as a new Hull-House resident, and she was deeply influenced by Kelley's own shift from revolutionary socialism to cross-class endeavors on behalf of prolabor legislation. Ultimately Kelley's path was more attractive to Addams than Starr's path, which led toward passionately partisan Christian socialism. Addams fully supported Kelley's sweatshop investigations in the summer of 1892 alongside immigrant labor leaders like Abraham Bisno, endorsed Kelley's Factory Inspection Bill in 1893, and delighted when the

bill's passage meant Kelley could serve from her Hull-House base as the nation's first female factory inspector. Addams drew on her disappointment when the Illinois State Supreme Court ruled the Inspection Act unconstitutional whenever she argued that workers' alienation was increased by the "growing distrust of the integrity of the courts" and their justifiable suspicion that judges' "whole view of life is on the corporation side" (Jane Addams, "Remarks on John R. Commons' Paper," 1907).

Addams's unsuccessful attempt to mediate the Pullman Strike in June of 1894 did not mark an end to her occasional role as a labor mediator; over the course of her career, she met both success and failure in her efforts to use arbitration to bring about peaceful compromise between striking workers and resistant employers. But hands-on labor arbitration was not Addams primary contribution to the history of the labor movement or working-class advocacy. It was as a writer and public speaker that Addams proved most useful to the cause of labor, affirming workers' rights to organize by rhetorically assuming such rights were obvious in a modern industrial democracy and then explaining to her middle-class audiences why "we must all acknowledge" that the obligation to satisfy the fundamental demands of the labor movement is a duty belonging "to all of us." Indeed, wrote Addams in 1895, those who did not recognize that "the injury to one" must be "the concern of all," had fallen "below the standard ethics of [the] day" (Jane Addams, "The Settlement as a Factor in the Labor Movement," 1895).

It was in the 1890s that Addams crafted her most significant statements on the rights of labor and on the most appropriate means within a democracy for ensuring those rights. Her analysis of the Pullman Strike in her 1894 essay, "A Modern Lear," reads today like an even-handed critique of both George Pullman's outdated paternalism and workers' impulsive indulgence in anger, but it was regarded at the time as so harsh toward Pullman that Addams could not get the essay published until 1912. In 1895 she included "The Settlement as a Factor in the Labor Movement" in the collection of essays, *Hull-House Maps and Papers,* which secured the Chicago settlement's status as a leader in social reform. And early in 1899, Addams published "Trades Unions and Public Duty" in the *American Journal of Sociology,* gathering together in that 15-page essay the arguments that she had been developing over the course of a decade of public speeches (Jane Addams, "A Modern Lear," 1912; "The Settlement as a Factor in the Labor Movement," 1895; "Trades Unions and Public Duty," 1899).

In "The Settlement as a Factor in the Labor Movement," Addams performed a signature maneuver: She asserted that "organization for working people was a necessity" in order to translate "democracy into social affairs," and then positioned the settlement between workers and employers as the agent capable of taking "a larger and steadier view than is always possible to the workingman, smarting under a sense of wrong; or to the capitalist . . . insisting upon the inalienable right of 'invested capital' to a return of at least four percent." The settlement, said Addams, could "recall them both to a sense of the larger development," which she defined as "the unity of life . . . the betterment not of one kind of people or class of people, but for the common good" (Jane Addams, "The Settlement as a Factor in the Labor Movement," 1895).

Four years later in "Trades Union and Public Duty," Addams made a surprisingly aggressive argument for the logic of labor union strategies, defending unionists' harsh treatment of scab labor and their use of the walking delegate, the boycott, sympathy strikes, and limited apprenticeships as utterly logical given the circumstances workers faced. At the same time, she told the readers of the *American Journal of Sociology* that if they did not like such divisive tactics, then it was their "public duty" to insist that the state achieve the "noble purpose of trades unions" and stop blaming labor unions for struggling to do "alone . . . what the community as a whole should undertake." While endorsing organized workers' goals and nonviolent means, Addams maintained that "if the objects of trades unions could find quiet and orderly expression in legislative enactment, and if their measures could be submitted to the examination and judgment of the whole without a sense of division or of warfare, we should have the ideal development of the democratic state" (Jane Addams, "Trades Unions and Public Duty," 1899).

Addams advanced the cause of labor by insisting that any harmonious ideal in a modern, industrial, democratic state had to take seriously workers' demands, their right to make demands, and their right to a place at any policy-making table. But her detached commitment to the higher ideal of unity and the common good often made Addams a frustrating ally for labor unionists. She aligned with the general cause of labor but refused to abandon her philosophical commitment to mediation in order to become a full-fledged partisan for organized labor. As Margaret Dreier Robins of the Women's Trade Union League put it, Addams was the only person in the United States who could "reach the honorable conservatives of this country and raise for them a rallying cry," yet Addams's insistence on criticizing both labor and capital for an insufficiently cooperative spirit did not feel like much of a rallying cry to organizers engaged in daily struggle on the ground ("Margaret Dreier

Robins to Jane Addams," 1907). From the perspective of some labor leaders at the time and labor historians since, Addams's reticence to take sides with labor against capital appeared inconsistent with her support of labor's goals. From Addams's pacifist perspective, her stance was most consistent with democracy; her support for labor strikes was a major concession on her part to industrial reality; and her mediationist approach to unions and legislation had the greatest chance of long-term success. Still she saw the problems with her approach and admitted in her autobiography that her "desire to bear independent witness to social righteousness often resulted in a sense of compromise difficult to endure, and at many times it seemed to me that were destined to alienate everybody" (Jane Addams, *Twenty Years at Hull-House*, 1910).

VICTORIA BISSELL BROWN

References and Further Reading

Addams, Jane. *Twenty Years at Hull-House with Autobiographical Notes*. New York: Macmillan Company, 1910.
———. "Remarks on John R. Commons' Paper, 'Is Class Conflict in America Growing and Inevitable.'" In American Sociological Society, *Papers and Proceedings* 2 (Dec. 28-31, 1907). P. 155.
———. "The Settlement as a Factor in the Labor Movement." *Hull-House Maps and Papers*. Boston: Thomas Y. Crowell & Co., 1895. Pp. 83–204.
———."A Modern Lear." *Survey* 29 (Nov. 2, 1912): 131–137.
———. "Trades Unions and Public Duty." *American Journal of Sociology* 4 (Jan. 1899): 448–462.
———. "An Oft-Told Tale." The *New York Call*. Apr. 25, 1912.
"Adolphus Bartlett to Jane Addams." Dec. 2, 1900; "Margaret Dreier Robins to Jane Addams." Feb. 18, 1907. Jane Addams Memorial Collection. Chicago: University of Illinois-Chicago.

See also **Hull-House Settlement (1889–1963)**

ADKINS V. CHILDREN'S HOSPITAL (1918)

In 1918, the United States Congress passed a minimum wage law for women and children workers in the District of Columbia. Children's Hospital, one of the national capital's largest employers, sued Jesse C. Adkins, the head of Washington, D.C.'s minimum wage board, claiming that the statute violated its due process rights under the U.S. Constitution's Fifth Amendment. The case eventually reached the nation's highest court in early 1923.

While the U.S. Supreme Court had upheld a minimum wage law for men in 1917, two factors presaged a possible defeat for the minimum wage law in *Adkins.* First the Supreme Court had ruled twice in 1918 and 1922 against federal child labor legislation. Second President Warren G. Harding had appointed conservative Republicans to the nation's highest court, including George Sutherland and William Howard Taft. These new appointments tipped the Supreme Court toward judicial support of the "freedom of contract" principle, which held that the state could not interfere with an employment contract.

Harvard Law School professor Felix Frankfurter and his assistant, Mary Williams (Molly) Dewson, argued in their brief supporting the minimum wage law that the statute proved constitutional for two reasons. First they asserted that a mandated floor wage preserved living standards for working women. Second they emphasized the contribution of a minimum wage to business efficiency.

In early April 1923, a six-to-three majority of the Court ruled that the District of Columbia's minimum wage law violated the freedom of contract principle. Thus legislatures could not pass laws regulating wages for women workers, regardless of economic realities. Surprisingly Chief Justice Taft dissented from the majority decision.

Adkins v. Children's Hospital became a turning point for reformers in the United States, particularly Florence Kelley, general secretary of the National Consumers' League (NCL). Ever since *Muller v. Oregon,* the 1908 Supreme Court case that upheld an Oregon hours law for working women, Kelley and her coworkers in the NCL's legal network, such as Frankfurter and Dewson, had hoped that working women's legislation could provide an entering wedge for the inclusion of all workers under state protection. *Adkins* now proved a difficult obstacle to that objective. Eventually Kelley broke with Frankfurter, the NCL's counsel, over what approach to take to the decision.

Throughout the 1920s and early 1930s, sharp divisions continued among progressive reformers about a response to *Adkins.* Some urged that minimum wage laws be promoted in state legislatures, but others argued that until the Supreme Court reversed itself, further action would prove futile. There was also a concern that minimum wage laws might lead to a double standard, with workers of color excluded from state protection. Not until the Great Depression of the early 1930s would reformers again aggressively promote minimum wage legislation. The Supreme Court would reverse *Adkins* in *West Coast Hotel Co. v. Parrish* (1937), thus establishing a judicial precedent for the introduction of the Fair Labor Standards Act of 1938.

JOHN THOMAS MCGUIRE

References and Further Reading

Hart, Vivien. *Bound by Our Constitution: Women Workers and the Minimum Wage.* Princeton, NJ.: Princeton University Press, 1994.
McGuire, John Thomas. "From the Courts to the State Legislatures: Social Justice Feminism, Labor Legislation, and the 1920s." *Labor History* 45, 2 (2004): 225–246.
Zimmerman, Joan. "The Jurisprudence of Equality: The Women's Minimum Wage, The First Equal Rights Amendment, and Adkins v. Children's Hospital, 1905–1923." *Journal of American History* 78, 1 (1991): 188–225.

Cases Cited

Adkins v. Children's Hospital, 261 U.S. 525 (1923).
West Coast Hotel Co. v. Parrish, 300 U.S. 379 (1937).

AFFIRMATIVE ACTION

Affirmative action was the policy answer activists and public officials developed in the 1960s to remedy the cumulative injustice inflicted on African-Americans in the United States. Because the country was founded on slavery, the U.S. working class was divided at its creation. For generations the racial division of labor, which originated in slavery and was later enforced by government-sponsored white supremacy, impoverished African-Americans, strained black families and communities, and limited chances of black children relative to their white counterparts in every class. Affirmative action began first in employment, and then it was adapted to educational institutions. A key demand of the civil rights movement since the 1960s, it was then embraced as a strategy for inclusion by other groups, most prominently women and Mexican-Americans.

The phrase affirmative action became popular in the mid-1960s as an umbrella term for a range of active strategies to break down segregation and ensure inclusion of those historically excluded from full citizenship. Plans may be voluntary, as they typically are in education, adopted through conciliation with such government agencies as the Equal Employment Opportunities Commission (EEOC), or imposed by the courts. Some programs have been promoted by labor unions in collective-bargaining agreements. The specific content varies. All include soft measures to expand applicant pools: More pro-active recruitment, for example, using black media, community organizations, and institutions. The plans often provide for training those who have the ability to perform the work, but not the specific skills needed. Some programs also include hard measures: Numerical goals and timetables for hiring or admitting the underrepresented. The toughest affirmative action, such as programs requiring that for every white person hired a black person must also be hired, is the rarest form and typically results from litigation. The precedent-setting cases involved the construction industry beginning in 1969, as courts found perpetrators guilty of chronic discrimination and saw demonstrated unwillingness to change course without supervision. In 1969, the Nixon administration also instituted the landmark Philadelphia Plan, which imposed hiring goals and timetables on Philadelphia construction employers and unions to overcome their continuing refusal to allow blacks into skilled work.

These policies answered decades of grassroots struggle against job discrimination on the part of African-American activists, who traced the problems of poor black communities to the lack of good jobs and saw the racial division of labor as the pivot of U.S. apartheid. The commission of inquiry into the causes of the Harlem riot in 1935, chaired by the eminent sociologist E. Franklin Frazier, came to this conclusion. Its report, suppressed by Mayor Fiorello La Guardia, recommended that the city deny contracts to firms that discriminated. During the Depression community activists in cities across the country also mounted "don't buy where you can't work" boycotts of stores that refused to hire black workers. In 1936, the Public Works Administration responded to the demand for jobs by requiring contractors to hire set numbers of blacks on public-housing construction projects. The pressure for fair employment grew with the mass March on Washington Movement, organized by A. Philip Randolph during World War II. It led to the wartime federal Fair Employment Practices Committee, a watershed in government recognition of discrimination as a serious problem demanding action. Gunnar Myrdal's massive 1944 study, *An American Dilemma,* confirmed that of all the forms of discrimination African-Americans faced, economic discrimination concerned them most.

The Communist left, which played an important role in organizing several unions in the Congress of Industrial Organizations (CIO), believed racism was the Achilles' heel of the U.S. labor movement and developed precursors of affirmative action to address it in the 1940s especially. In New York, the center of a vibrant black left, progressive labor and black organizations often worked together to end discrimination

in employment and to get blacks into better paying jobs. In the recession of 1949, Communists fought to preserve the foothold blacks had acquired in industry during the war years. Communists argued that seniority should be suspended to keep blacks, the last hired, from being first fired. In the two left-led unions that also had a say in hiring, they ensured that one in every four workers placed in jobs was black and pushed for work sharing instead of layoffs. But the Cold War then accelerating fueled domestic anticommunism that inflicted mortal blows on such civil rights unionism. It also weakened the National Association for the Advancement of Colored People (NAACP), since it emboldened the opponents of both labor and civil rights, notably southern white supremacists and northern business interests.

The mass civil rights movement that developed in the mid-1950s relied on the newly merged American Federation of Labor (AFL)-CIO as a lobbying partner but found it could not trust unions to practice solidarity on the shop floor. The building trades of the AFL proved the most recalcitrant. As craft unions, they had historically relied on restricting the workforce to elevate wages and conditions for their members, an economic strategy reinforced by racism. Through their control of training in apprenticeship programs and of hiring in the referral system, the skilled trades locked out blacks, sometimes even building racial exclusion and nepotism into their constitutions. Industrial unions in contrast enabled black workers to achieve considerable advances in wages, conditions, and job security, and occasionally, as the case of the United Packinghouse Workers of America best illustrates, in civil rights as well. Still even some of the most progressive industrial unions, such as the United Auto Workers, kept white workers in a privileged position and black workers in a subordinate position by maintaining separate departmental seniority lines that entrenched occupational segregation.

Aided in particular by the labor secretary of the NAACP, Herbert Hill, black workers waged mounting challenges to job segregation in the late 1950s and 1960s. On the one hand, especially in the South, they worked to outlaw discrimination. On the other hand, they also fought for race-conscious measures that would remedy long and continuing exclusion from better jobs. Contrary to popular belief today, no one made the case for such measures more eloquently than Martin Luther King, Jr. In his 1963 book, *Why We Can't Wait,* King urged "some compensatory consideration for the handicaps" blacks had "inherited from the past" and insisted that what is today called color blindness was not enough. "It is impossible to create a formula for the future which does not take into account that our society has been doing something special *against* the Negro for hundreds of years," reasoned King. "How then can he be absorbed into the mainstream of American life if we do not do something *for* him now, in order to balance the equation and equip him to compete on a just and equal basis?" (Martin Luther King, Jr., *Why We Can't Wait*, 1963). Fairness demanded more than formal equality. Such arguments persuaded President Lyndon Johnson; his famous Howard University speech in 1965, which announced that "freedom is not enough," borrowed its central metaphor from King.

An often-unrecognized factor that made such policies necessary was conservative opposition to other strategies of fighting discrimination, such as cease-and-desist orders and criminal penalties for perpetrators, both of which were proposed by civil rights advocates. In Congress, the anti-Deal alliance of southern Dixiecrats and northern business Republicans became the anti-civil rights alliance, backed by a growing popular right at the grassroots level and encouraged by such public intellectuals as William F. Buckley and other writers for the *National Review*. As blacks faced strong resistance to what seemed to so many as elementary fairness and few U.S. whites proved willing to work for universal policies to achieve more equity, such as mass job creation or classic redistributive policies, the demand for affirmative actionlike policies grew. Ironically the exceptionally sharp differentials in rewards to different kinds of labor in the United States, a system that AFL-CIO leaders had come to accept, also pushed workers toward targeted remedies that promised to break down the division of labor and open better jobs to all.

Not only abstract justice but also practical concerns made pro-active measures seem urgent. Thanks to the mechanization of southern cotton farming and the shift of much northern industry to the suburbs, poverty was growing worse among African-Americans in the midst of the nation's longest economic boom. The 1963 March on Washington for Jobs and Freedom and the National Urban League's campaign for a Domestic Marshall Plan that started in the same year contributed to passage of the 1964 Civil Rights Act but won few visible practical gains. Riots erupted in black ghettos across the country in the mid-1960s, most notably in Watts, California; blacks vented widespread rage over the failure of civil rights legislation to deliver improvement to the most strapped communities, especially to end chronic unemployment and underemployment. Affirmative action seemed to offer an economically cheap and politically feasible response to the mounting crisis. The policy appealed

to working-class blacks shut out of higher paying blue-collar and white-collar jobs, to middle-class African-Americans expecting the better jobs for which their training had prepared them, to government officials juggling many urgent problems tied to low incomes, and even to large employers seeking protection from costly lawsuits for discrimination.

As policymakers sought language to frame what they were doing, they borrowed the phrase affirmative action from the 1935 Wagner Act. President John F. Kennedy first used the phrase in association with racial justice in a 1961 executive order on federal contracts. But the policies took their current form as first Lyndon Johnson and then Richard Nixon issued executive orders broadening the mandate of the Office of Federal Contract Compliance (OFCC) to require employers who accepted government contractors to take active steps to include black workers in particular. Most important the employment section of the Civil Rights Act of 1964, Title VII, empowered courts to order such "affirmative action as may be appropriate" to remedy discrimination. In carrying out the mandate of Title VII, the courts have built up a large body of case law defining discrimination and delineating equal access.

Meanwhile other long-excluded groups covered by Title VII also began fighting discrimination more actively and seeking inclusion in affirmative action policies. The National Organization for Women (NOW), soon the nation's best-known feminist group, came into being out of anger over the Equal Employment Opportunity Commission's (EEOC's) early refusal to take sex discrimination seriously—even though two of every five complaints to the agency came from women. The new feminist movement fought hard for affirmative action programs thereafter, a commitment that has since united women's groups from the Girl Scouts to the Gray Panthers. Mexican-Americans also mobilized from the 1960s onward for affirmative action through such organizations as the American GI Forum and the League of United Latin American citizens.

The combination of conservative resistance, a weak left, and unreliable labor allies drove seekers of inclusion to look more and more to the courts and affirmative action for help. These policies worked where little else had to open jobs and opportunities. Nearly all civil rights experts and social scientists who have studied the impact agree that these policies worked far better than their predecessors and that they had a limited but significant impact on improving employment and reducing poverty in the heyday of their application in the 1970s. Yet job loss due to economic restructuring has undercut progress in the industries where working-class blacks scored the greatest gains, packinghouse, textiles, and steel among these. Efficacy then declined markedly in the Reagan era as federal commitment gave way to federal hostility and as the problems of the poor became more distinct from those of other African-Americans due to the altered labor market and the growing concentration of poverty. Antidiscrimination efforts have also been enervated over the years by chronic underfunding and government unwillingness to cancel large contracts even for egregious discrimination.

As the mass movement that had won reform receded in the mid-1970s, affirmative action also proved amenable to agitation by a growing conservative mobilization. The spread of such policies coincided with a major recession that turned much of corporate United States against the regulatory state and opened many white workers to zero-sum arguments about why they faced mounting layoffs. As economic restructuring devastated black and white employment in once better paying blue-collar jobs, tough questions arose about who should get the remaining jobs and on what basis: Long group exclusion or seniority. The AFL-CIO hostility to work-sharing compromises widened the gap, and right-wing politicians moved in to fill it. The classic example was North Carolina U.S. Senator Jesse Helms, who ran a campaign ad featuring a white worker crumpling a pink slip. "You needed that job," intoned the voice-over, "but it had to go to a minority because of a racial quota."

The outcome by the early years of the twenty-first century was a seeming stalemate on affirmative action: Unlikely to be rescinded entirely, it also seemed unlikely to advance or to achieve as much as it had in the 1970s. Meanwhile affirmative action had acquired backers from new sources, among them some corporations eager to avoid lawsuits for discrimination and to demonstrate their diversity to promising new consumer markets at home and abroad. The business edge they sought was far from the social justice that King and other movement supporters of race-conscious policies envisioned. That affirmative action advocates more and more made their case in the language of diversity rather than social justice seemed a measure of the toll decades of being on the defensive had taken. The policies were preserved but at a cost to the more robust egalitarian vision that originally inspired them.

NANCY MACLEAN

References and Further Reading

Arnesen, Eric. *Brotherhoods of Color: Black Railroad Workers and the Struggle for Equality*. Cambridge, MA: Harvard University Press, 2002.

Bergmann, Barbara R. *The Economic Emergence of Women*. New York: Basic Books, 1986.

Graham, Hugh Davis. *The Civil Rights Era: The Origins and Development of National Policy*. New York: Oxford University Press, 1990.

MacLean, Nancy. *Freedom Is Not Enough: The Opening of the American Workplace*. Cambridge, MA: Harvard University Press and the Russell Sage Foundation, 2006.

Minchin, Timothy J. *Hiring the Black Worker: The Racial Integration of the Southern Textile Industry, 1960–1980*. Chapel Hill: University of North Carolina Press, 1999.

————. *The Color of Work: The Struggle for Civil Rights in the Southern Paper Industry, 1945–1980*. Chapel Hill, University of North Carolina Press, 2001.

Needleman, Ruth. *Black Freedom Fighters in Steel: The Struggle for Democratic Unionism*. Ithaca, NY: Cornell University Press, 2003.

Nelson, Bruce. *Divided We Stand: American Workers and the Struggle for Black Equality* Princeton, NJ: Princeton University Press, 2001.

Robinson, Jo Ann Ooiman, ed. *Affirmative Action: A Documentary History*. Westport, CT.: Greenwood Press, 2001.

Skrentny, John D. *The Minority Rights Revolution*. Cambridge, MA: Harvard University Press, 2002.

AFRICAN-AMERICANS

The shortage of labor in the European colonies of the New World brought about a new kind of servitude: Large-scale, race-based, hereditary chattel slavery. In the English North American colonies that became the United States, this system had taken coherent shape by 1700. The approximately 600,000 Africans who were brought there endured a variety of experiences and changes over time, growing into four million free people after the Civil War.

Slaves were owned throughout the 13 colonies and engaged in almost every kind of labor. They composed very little of the northern colonial population but were perhaps 20% of New York City's population in the eighteenth century. They comprised nearly half of the Chesapeake colonies' population (Virginia and Maryland), where they worked mostly in tobacco cultivation. Slaves were a majority of the deep South's colonies (South Carolina and Georgia), working principally in rice and indigo, and later in sugar and cotton, which spread into the southwestern territories and became the mainstay of the southern economy. Generally labor was more arduous and lethal the further south one went. Slaves also mastered skilled trades and domestic work needed for largely self-sufficient plantations—nearly 30% of South Carolina male slaves, and 9% of females, were skilled workers in 1790. Perhaps a third of Virginia female slaves worked in domestic service in 1800.

The typical slave lived on a large plantation, though the typical slaveholder owned few slaves, and three-fourths of white southerners owned no

An African-American laborer at Wheeler Dam, Alabama, carrying a construction tool. Library of Congress, Prints & Photographs Division, FSA/OWI Collection [LC-USZ62-116592].

slaves. This produced a variety of labor systems. The largest plantations used overseers and gang labor; some farms worked on the "task" system; the smallest might see owner and slave toiling beside one another. The slave population was stratified. The vast bulk of field hands considered lower in status than skilled slaves and domestics, with illegitimate children of masters passing into the free black population or even passing for white.

The Constitution permitted Congress to prohibit the importation of African slaves in 1808, and this ensured that the southern United States would remain a white majority slave society—unusual among New World slave regimes. A significant free black population emerged in the nineteenth century. Almost all Delaware African-Americans were free by 1860, as were nearly half of Maryland's. A few free blacks owned slaves themselves. Free blacks faced a number of legal disabilities (including outright exclusion from several states), and white workingmen's organizations often lobbied for relief from competition from slave or free black labor. Though there were few large cities in the antebellum South, free blacks gravitated toward these cities, and even slaves enjoyed greater autonomy there, sometimes being hired out by their masters and allowed to keep some surplus earnings. Free blacks engaged in almost every kind of work in antebellum cities except those involving authority over whites, or those that might promote slave resistance. Frederick Douglass's oft-told autobiography highlighted the hazards of urban slavery. In northern cities blacks began to lose ground in trades that they had held under slavery, a pattern that would be repeated in the postemancipation South. Free blacks declined from nearly 40% to under 30% of New York City's artisanal force from 1790–1810. The influx of immigrants in the 1840s and 1850s intensified the crisis of northern black tradesmen.

During the Civil War the Union adopted a policy of emancipation and abolition gradually, and as it did, it provoked the question of the postwar position of African-American workers. northern workers were ambivalent about black freedom, many fearing the competition of emancipated slaves. Proposals for colonization addressed this concern. For their part, African-Americans sought economic opportunity and the legal equality needed to protect their right, as Lincoln put it, "to eat the bread, without the leave of anybody else, which his own hand earns."

Republicans believed that blacks could be integrated into their philosophy of free labor. In this theory, part of the Anglo-Scot Enlightenment liberal theory most often associated with Adam Smith, labor relations were ideally voluntary and contractual. Employer and employee were equally free to bargain; the relation was individual, "at will," and equally terminable. Employers could not compel employees to work (this was the essence of slavery); nor could employees compel employers to pay certain wages (as labor unions sought to do).

Many southern whites were determined to keep the freedmen in a situation as close to slavery as possible. Southern legislatures expressed this goal in the Black Codes of 1865, which limited black rights to own land, firearms, and engage in certain occupations and provided harsh punishments for breaches of labor contracts, disrespect to employers, and vagrancy. Laws also protected white artisans from competition from former slaves.

Republicans in Congress responded with the Civil Rights Act of 1866 and the Fourteenth Amendment. These acts emphasized the principal Republican goals of economic freedom and equality before the law. The rights in the Civil Rights Act were fundamentally economic: "The right to make and enforce contracts; to sue, be parties, and give evidence; to inherit, purchase, lease, sell, hold and convey real and personal property; and to full and equal benefit of all laws and proceedings for the security of person and property." When President Johnson vetoed the Civil Rights bill and the southern states refused to ratify the Fourteenth Amendment, Congress imposed black suffrage on the former Confederate states.

Republican concern for limited government, federalism, property rights, and a desire to restore the Union with as few recriminations as possible from the southern white majority, led them to eschew plans to confiscate antebellum plantations and redistribute the land to the freedmen—the promise of 40 acres and a mule. Nor did the most racial of southern Reconstruction governments, where blacks had the most influence, enact such laws. White landowners and black workers usually accepted a compromise system known as sharecropping. In exchange for a share (usually one-third) of the crop, owners provided land, tools, seed, and other capital, while the freedmen supplied the labor. While land ownership

would not have provided a panacea for the freed people's economic needs, it surely would have improved their fortunes. Up to World War I, African-American workers remained overwhelmingly southern and agricultural, in many ways trapped in an isolated, undesirable regional labor market.

The organized labor movement, which had been revived by the economic growth and strain of wartime industrialization, largely rejected the liberal or *laissez faire* philosophy of free labor and the wage system and sought collective action to empower workers. Like most contemporary historians, they concluded that industrialization had made the individualistic free labor philosophy obsolete. The overwhelming market power of corporate enterprises enabled them to impose wage slavery on their workers. However most unions continued to exclude and discriminate against black workers. Despite the appeals of its national leaders, the National Labor Union, the first U.S. national labor federation, did not act against the discriminatory policies of its member unions. This led Isaac Myers, a black shipwright, to form a parallel Colored National Labor Union that would organize black workers and also support the Republican party. Though some black and white workers cooperated against employers, for the most part they remained competitors who often broke one another's strikes. Both labor associations were largely eliminated by the depression of 1873. The relationship of blacks and white unions were not off to a good start, as reflected in the title of Frederick Douglass' 1874 essay, "The Folly, Tyranny, and Wickedness of Labor Unions."

Black workers made considerable economic progress in the late nineteenth century; in relative terms probably greater than any other period in history. Though they tried, planters were unable to conspire to depress agricultural wages, and African-Americans exercised their freedom to move in search of better working conditions. Perhaps 10% of black South Carolinians left the state during Reconstruction, and many blacks headed to the southwest frontier of Mississippi, Texas, or Kansas. When collective action such as labor organization was unsuccessful, this strategy of moving, or threatening to move (known as exit), often improved their circumstances.

In the period after white Democrats regained control of the former Confederate states (completed by 1877), and especially after the 1890s, southern states enacted a variety of laws to restrict black exit. Convict labor was the most direct and brutal means. The Thirteenth Amendment permitted involuntary servitude "as a punishment for crime whereof the party shall have been duly convicted." The state then leased these convicts to southern employers. Laws also punished enticement—offering higher wages to somebody working under an annual labor contract. Licensing laws restricted black employment in skilled construction trades and even in barbering. Heavy license fees also prevented emigrant agents from telling blacks about economic opportunities elsewhere. "White capping," lynching, and other terrorist devices also kept black workers in place. Before the Supreme Court declared them unconstitutional in 1910 (and sometimes after), debt peonage laws kept blacks tied to their plantations. Finally the formal segregation that began in the 1890s also limited black job opportunities, and disfranchisement prevented them from doing much about it.

The labor movement revival of the 1880s, led by the Noble and Holy Order of the Knights of Labor, did a better job than the National Labor Union at including black workers. Perhaps fifty to a hundred thousand blacks joined the Knights, whose total membership was estimated at 700,000, forming separate Colored assemblies. But the Knights of Labor was so disparate an organization, a combination of utopians, anarchists, trade unionists, and others, that it was unable to provide the spearhead of a national labor movement. It collapsed nearly as quickly as it rose after the Haymarket bombing of 1886, and by 1894 it called for the voluntary expatriation of blacks to Africa.

After emancipation, African-Americans lost ground in many skilled trades, particularly in construction, that they had occupied under slavery, and they were excluded from new, technologically advanced trades like electrical work. Blacks were almost entirely excluded from the cotton textile industry, whose sponsors engaged in a promotional campaign depicting it as a benefit for Confederate veterans, widows, and orphans and a refuge for white workers from black competition. Iron and steel promoters made a similar paternal appeal to racial solidarity, but workers in this industry relied instead on their union for job security and kept blacks limited to undesirable jobs. In coal mining blacks were well-represented in the South from the outset, and there was more cooperation between white and black workers in the United Mine Workers than in perhaps any other union. Outside of the South however, white coal unionists resisted black competition, often by violent means.

On the whole the relationship between blacks and organized labor was largely a negative one after the turn of the century. The great Pullman strike of 1894 was coordinated by the American Railway Union, which excluded lacks. Thus Chicago blacks formed an Antistrikers Railroad Union to help break the strike. The next year Booker T. Washington, the most prominent black leader after Frederick Douglass's death that year, emphasized *laissez faire* principles in his famous Atlanta Compromise

address. He called on blacks to "cast down your bucket" among southern whites, whom he also exhorted to "cast down your bucket among these people who have, without strikes or labor wars, tilled your fields, cleared your forests, built up your railroads and cities, and brought forth treasures from the bowels of the earth." Washington believed that blacks could benefit in a system of separate-but-equal if their right to work was respected. However black economic progress only augmented white hostility, and without the vote African-Americans had few remedies.

The mainstream U.S. labor movement that emerged in the 1890s, the American Federation of Labor (AFL), also established segregation as its system of race relations. The AFL was constitutionally committed to worker organization without regard to race, and during the early 1890, AFL president Samuel Gompers did act to force member unions to remove color bars from their constitutions. This did not however result in black admission to such unions, for informal means were available to keep them out. By the end of the decade, the AFL had abandoned even the pretense of racial equality. When black workers could not be excluded entirely, they were relegated to federal labor unions with few of the privileges of white national unions. While Gompers recognized that keeping blacks outside of organized labor allowed employers to use them to break strikes, he blamed black leaders like Washington, not discriminatory white unions, for the problem. The exclusion of blacks by these unions was part of their general strategy of controlling the labor supply, which led them to demand the end of Chinese immigration and the restriction of white immigration. Moreover the AFL was composed primarily of craft, or skilled, unions and exerted little effort in organizing unskilled workers, among whose ranks blacks were concentrated. While Gompers and the AFL became more exclusionist in the early twentieth century, black workers were able to gain footholds in some unions, such as construction, dock work, and coal mining, where they were too numerous to exclude. They also preserved their jobs in southern railroad occupations despite the hostility of the white brotherhoods.

Blacks did the best that they could in the system of segregation, which actually provided opportunities for black businessmen and union leaders in a captive market. Blacks were also able to control their own segregated local unions, a position that they usually lost in integrated ones. Booker T. Washington's emphasis on black entrepreneurship and control of black organizations recognized this—an idea shared by black separatists and nationalists throughout U.S. history. Though sociologists and historians usually denigrate the phenomenon of black capitalism, there was considerable black entrepreneurship in the early twentieth century, one that compared favorably to new immigrant groups. Though a black business and professional class did exist, the class structure among African-Americans was compressed toward the bottom: The best-off strata of blacks comparable to middle-class whites, middle-class blacks comparable to working-class whites, and a large poor segment at the bottom. In 1910, 90% of black women were engaged in agricultural or domestic service. In the late nineteenth century, about half of African-American women were in the labor force, compared to only 17% of white women, a gap that persisted until the later twentieth century.

An important organization to arise out of the black bourgeoisie, in response to the general progressive neglect of or disdain for blacks, was the National Association for the Advancement of Colored People (NAACP). While the association concerned itself primarily with issues of social and political equality, it also kept an eye on economic discrimination. The next year black leaders more sympathetic to Booker T. Washington launched the National Urban League, which worked more closely with employers—its detractors accusing it of serving as a strike-breaking agency.

And blacks did often break strikes as a way of entering border state and northern industries. But African-American strike breaking was often exaggerated—most strike breakers were white, and most blacks did not enter northern industries as strike breakers. White unionists often exaggerated the black role in strike breaking, accusing employers of playing a nefarious game of divide-and-conquer, while themselves trying to capitalize on white racial animosity. Upton Sinclair's lurid description of black strike breakers in the *Jungle* (1906) is a good example. For African-Americans excluded from unions strike breaking was a perfectly rational and just economic tactic. Moreover it often demonstrated that blacks were courageous and capable, and many race leaders believed that black competition was good for race relations and would ultimately convince white unions to cease exclusion and discrimination.

Racial job competition intensified in the World War I period. The return of the Democratic party to power in 1913 was good for the AFL and bad for black workers. At the same time, southern blacks began to move in great numbers to northern cities in the Great Migration. The outbreak of World War I in 1914 effectively curtailed European immigration, and black migrants began to take the place of white immigrants in northern industries. Black industrial employment doubled in the 1910s. The migration and integration into northern job lines accelerated when the United States entered the war in 1917. The Wilson administration augmented the power of the AFL as part of the national economic mobilization, and the AFL used that power to resist the efforts of employers to maintain an open (nonunion) shop. Rapid migration and job competition also produced two of the worst race riots in U.S. history, in East St. Louis in 1917, and Chicago in 1919.

When the war ended, the Republicans regained control of the government and ended most of the pro-union policies of the wartime years. While the war years appeared to have only intensified black union hostility, migration assured that blacks would be a major factor in the great mass production industries of the North—steel, meatpacking, and automobiles especially.

The power of organized labor did not abate entirely in the 1920s. The railroad unions in particular won extended powers under the Railway Labor Act of 1926 and used it and its later amendments to drive blacks out of the railroad workforce. The U.S. blacks also acquired more political power by the Great Migration, which continued, as Congress severely restricted European immigration in 1921 and 1924. In northern cities where they could vote, black organizations sought to use political power to soften the practices of the AFL. The most prominent figure in the cautious black union *rapprochement* of the 1920s was A. Philip Randolph. Randolph had been a socialist union organizer and editor before the war and had denounced the AFL as "the most wicked machine for the propagation of race prejudices in the country" in 1919. After his disillusionment with the Communists, Randolph then took the presidency of the Brotherhood of Sleeping Car Porters and attempted to gain affiliation in the AFL. By the end of the decade, the federation conceded only nine federal charters to the brotherhood. While the NAACP and AFL both opposed President Hoover's nomination of John J. Parker to the Supreme Court in 1930, they did not work together in their lobbying efforts.

The Great Depression and New Deal altered fundamentally the place of organized labor in the U.S. political economy and the relationship of blacks to organized labor. At first it appeared that the power of organized labor (which had supported the Democrats) would be used to increase discrimination against blacks (who had remained Republican). The first major pieces of Roosevelt's New Deal, the National Industrial Recovery Act (NRA) and Agricultural Adjustment Act, also had deleterious effects on black workers and farmers in their attempts to reduce production and raise prices and wages. The black press called the NRA the "Negro Run-Around," "Negro Removal Act," or "Negro Ruined

Again." Most blacks remained southern and agricultural in the 1930s, and New Deal agricultural policies affected them harshly. Acreage reduction incentives fell most heavily on black sharecroppers, and displaced black farmers—especially men—had trouble making a sudden adjustment to nonagricultural work in a period of high unemployment. Blacks also faced discrimination in New Deal public works and relief programs.

At the same time the New Dealers did begin to make some provision for U.S. blacks. The most important of these was in relief programs—these more than anything else won black voters to the Democratic party in the 1934 and 1936 elections. The Public Works Administration established racial quotas for black employment in federal construction contractors—much less than a racially proportionate share and less than African-Americans would have gotten in a free market but recognition nevertheless. Local black organizations also took advantage of pro-union legislation by engaging in their own direct-action job campaigns, known as the "Don't Buy Where You Can't Work" movement, forcing white employers in black neighborhoods to hire blacks.

Employers resisted early New Deal legislation, and the Supreme Court struck most of it down, which limited the damage that it did to black workers. When Congress enacted a more effective plan, the National Labor Relations (Wagner) Act of 1935, black organizations had reason to fear its effects. The act imposed compulsory, majority unionism on employers—they must bargain with the organization chosen by a majority of their employees. The act made no exception for unions that excluded or discriminated against minorities. Both the NAACP and Urban League warned of its potential to harm black workers, but the AFL refused to agree to an amendment to protect them. Urban League president Lester Granger later called the Wagner Act "the worst piece of legislation ever passed by Congress."

At the annual AFL convention later that year, the federation leadership effectively stifled a committee effort to reform union racial practices. At the same time, the convention also saw the rise to prominence of the Committee on (later Congress of) Industrial Organizations (CIO), unionists who sought to organize unskilled workers in the mass production industries. Since blacks were present in these industries in such large numbers, a new departure in black union relations was likely.

Black workers responded in a variety of ways to the great CIO-organizing campaigns that followed Roosevelt's 1936 re-election. Along with the change in national labor policy, state governments enacted "little New Deals," and state and local officials took the side of strikers against owners. Some remained suspicious of union appeals, others joined enthusiastically. By the end of the decade however, black organizations and workers could see that law and politics had shifted the balance of power to the union side, and they went along with the shift.

The CIO did a great deal to improve the relations of blacks and organized labor. Its inclusiveness forced the AFL to broaden its appeal to black workers. The living standards of blacks who joined unions certainly improved. And the period from 1940–1965 saw the most significant advances in relative black economic status since the late nineteenth century. On the other hand, industrial union organization often shifted the locus of discrimination from admission and hiring to job assignment, seniority, and promotion. More important the organization of the core, mass-production sector of the economy ultimately reduced employment in this area, though war deferred this decline until the 1950–1960s. Most blacks remained in the unorganized, peripheral sectors of the economy. Unemployment became a permanent feature of the U.S. economy, and the black unemployment rate was usually double the white rate. And this gap was even wider when it included those African-Americans who had dropped out of the labor force altogether.

The federal government took the first major steps to end employer and union discrimination on the eve of World War II. A. Philip Randolph organized a "March on Washington Movement" to protest discrimination in U.S. industry, and he threatened to bring thousands of marchers to the capital unless President Roosevelt prohibited job discrimination and segregation in the armed forces. President Roosevelt agreed to the former in a June 1941, executive order that created the Fair Employment Practice Committee (FEPC). The committee publicized extensive discrimination and was able to win some improvement in black employment, though some recalcitrant contractors and unions were able to ignore FEPC directives. It was effective enough that southern Democrats cut off its funding in 1946, and civil rights groups lobbied for Congress to create a new one for the next 20 years.

The federal courts and the states built on the FEPC effort. Courts sustained black workers' lawsuits against discriminatory unions. In suits against the railroad brotherhoods, the Supreme Court ruled that unions, since federal legislation had given them special privileges, they had a duty of "fair representation." They could not use government power to discriminate against black workers—though the Court did not require them to admit blacks as members.

World War II dealt a serious blow to the ideology of white supremacy, with the United States fighting

Hitler's race-based regime. The United States then needed to bolster its reputation for democracy and equality in its rivalry with the Soviet Union for influence in the postcolonial Third World. The challenge for the white United States to make its behavior conform to its egalitarian ideals was expressed in Gunnar Myrdal's *An American Dilemma* (1944).

The postwar industrialization of the South, and continued urbanization of blacks North and South, added to the movement for equality. The desire to attract investment often moderated southern resistance to desegregation. The AFL and CIO (the federations merged in 1955), supported desegregation but faced significant resistance from southern locals, especially after the 1954 *Brown* decision. At the same time, a host of postwar government policies at the national and state levels—the location of transportation and public housing, reinforcing private-sector housing discrimination—tended to augment residential segregation, which in turn restricted the job opportunities available to black workers.

While Congress did not enact a fair employment statute until 1964, many states in the Northeast, upper Midwest, and on the West Coast did. These agencies made some progress against discrimination in the first decade after the war but faced increasing problems thereafter. These agencies adopted an individual rights, equal treatment, color-blind approach to discrimination, which could have only limited effect given the profound historical and structural aspects of racial inequality in the United States. Quite simply equal treatment produced unequal outcomes. Moreover the supply of low-skilled, high-paying jobs began to decline after 1955 as the U.S. economy became more service-oriented and faced global competition. But black migration into northern cities continued long after jobs began leaving these cities as northern states adopted more generous welfare policies. By the 1960s, a permanently unemployed and socially devastated underclass existed.

The federal government added some impetus to the antidiscrimination campaign. Presidents Truman, Eisenhower, and Kennedy established executive orders against discrimination in government contracting, but they all suffered from the weaknesses of the original FEPC—lack of statutory authority and budget especially. By 1960, these committees began to pressure contractors to grant racial preferences to blacks and to take affirmative action to ensure equal employment opportunities, but civil rights organizations dismissed these as token efforts.

Both state and executive antidiscrimination organizations could do little against union exclusion. Partly this was because unions were not direct government contractors; partly it was because organized labor was a powerful constituency in the Democratic party. The National Labor Relations Board also handled unions with kid gloves, regarding itself as a labor–management rather than a civil rights agency.

Ten years after the *Brown* decision, in the midst of increasingly intense civil rights protest and segregationist reaction, Congress finally outlawed racial job discrimination throughout the nation in the Civil Rights Act of 1964. The act was written in color-blind language; it would be equally illegal to discriminate in favor of as against minorities. The act was also prospective, providing no remedies for discrimination that had taken place in the past and explicitly securing *bona fide* union seniority rights and prohibiting racial quotas. But the interpretation of the Civil Rights Act changed rapidly in the face of urban riots and increasing black militancy in the late 1960s.

Bureaucrats and judges turned the Civil Rights Act from a simple command of desegregation into a mandate for integration and affirmative action. President Johnson's commencement address at Howard University in 1965 set the tone. "You do not take a person who, for years, has been hobbled by chains and liberate him, bring him up to the starting line of a race and then say, 'you are free to compete with all the others,' and still justly believe that you have been completely fair . . . . We seek not just freedom but opportunity. We seek not just legal equity but human ability, not just equality as a right and a theory but equality as a fact and equality as a result." Perhaps the most important government policy affecting black employment in the 1960s was the expansion and improvement of government employment itself. As public sector employment grew and became proportionately more African-American, it raised the socioeconomic status of black women especially. Whereas black women were the least well-off group in the labor market in 1950, they had pulled ahead of black men and approximately equal to white women by the end of the century. For black men construction and transportation—industries heavily affected by government spending—were the principal areas of employment. But both African-American men and women participated in a much greater variety of occupations, and saw more intraracial social stratification, than at the beginning of the century.

The Civil Rights Act certainly helped to open job opportunities for African-Americans, particularly in southern manufacturing. Black female employment in clerical work increased from under 10% to over 30% in the decade after 1964. Overall black professional employment doubled from 1961–1977. Both the Equal Employment Opportunity Commission, established to enforce the Civil Rights Act, and the Labor Department, which took over the enforcement of executive orders against discrimination in government contracting, began to require preferential treatment for racial minorities and women. Employers were not permitted to use tests that had a "disparate impact" on minority applicants unless they were shown to be clearly necessary to the operation of the business. Similarly courts abrogated union seniority systems that made it riskier for blacks to move out of previously all-black job lines. The most visible and controversial of these programs was the Philadelphia Plan, in which the Labor Department required government contractors to establish hiring quotas for minorities. Initially adopted for the most exclusive skilled construction crafts in a few U.S. cities, the program soon covered all government contractors—nearly half of the U.S. labor market. The government also used the threat of loss of government contracts to pressure employers to adopt voluntary affirmative action plans. Colleges and universities also extended preferential treatment to black applicants, though not using overt quotas. In these ways the government could uproot the "present effects of past discrimination" despite the text of the Civil Rights Act.

The establishment of legal equality in the labor market did little more than counteract the ill effects that earlier government policies had on black workers but could not control the great changes in the U.S. economy in the last quarter of the century. The United States faced global competition as a free-trade nation for the first time since the Civil War. One out of every seven manufacturing jobs were lost in the 1979–1982 recession. The little-noted Immigration Reform Act of 1965 also increased competition in the labor market for low-skilled, native-born workers.

African-Americans were more heavily unionized than white Americans by the end of the century—a remarkable inversion of the long-term under-representation of blacks in unions. The South at last caught up to the national average in economic terms, and African-Americans began to migrate from the urban North to the South. At the same time, the unionized share of the U.S. workforce shrunk to pre–New Deal levels. Simultaneous with the erosion of the industrial core of the U.S. economy and its unions, there was an explosion of public-sector employment and unionization. Public employment grew from 7% to 16% of overall employment from 1940–1970. The African-American share of public employment rose from 6% to 14%. Government employees began to unionize in the 1950s, and the organized proportion of public employment rose while the proportion of private employees declined. While seniority and affirmative action caused dissension between civil rights organizations and blue-collar unionists in the private

sector, public employee unions were close to African-American organizations.

While there were some notable clashes between blacks and public unions—the 1968 New York City teachers' strike among the most prominent—for the most part a solid black union alliance prevailed. But the growth of public-sector employment reached a limit by the 1980s, as public reaction to statism set in. The problems of unemployment, welfare reform, and education had a disproportionate impact on African-Americans. The concentration of blacks in the low-wage, service sector of the economy, and the need for unions to organize them, led to a serious turnover of AFL-CIO leadership in 1995 and a schism in 2005.

Debate continues regarding the overall economic effects of affirmative action. The clearest benefits occurred in the decade immediately after the Civil Rights Act, and especially in the South. Similarly, widespread disagreement exists over the relative position of blacks and whites in the U.S. economy. On the whole there has not been much improvement in the relative position of African-Americans since the 1960s. Black per capita income remains around 60% of the white average, and nearly every statistic of socioeconomic well-being shows U.S. blacks to be less well-off than whites. Notable achievements at the top of the social scale have been seen alongside acute deprivation at the bottom. Even more intense debate surrounds the question of whether these disparities are due to discrimination or cultural differences. The anguish and tortured discussion of the concentration of black poverty and crime in the aftermath of Hurricane Katrina in New Orleans exposed the continuing problem.

PAUL D. MORENO

References and Further Reading

Arnesen, Eric. "Specter of the Black Strikebreaker: Race, Employment, and Labor Activism in the Industrial Era." *Labor History* 44 (2003).
Bates, Beth. *Pullman Porters and the Rise of Protest Politics in Black America, 1925–45*. Chapel Hill: University of North Carolina Press, 2001.
Foner, Philip S., and Ronald L. Lewis, eds. *The Black Worker: A Documentary History from Colonial Times to the Present*. 8 vols. Philadelphia: Temple University Press, 1978–1984.
Harris, William H. *The Harder We Run: Black Workers Since the Civil War*. New York: Oxford University Press, 1982.
Higgs, Robert. *Competition and Coercion: Blacks in the American Economy, 1865–1914*. Cambridge: Cambridge University Press, 1977.
Jones, Jacqueline. *American Work: Four Centuries of Black and White Labor*. New York: Norton, 1998.

Katz, Michael B., Mark J. Stern, and Jamie J. Fade. "The New African American Inequality." *Journal of American History* 98 (2005).

McCartin, Joseph A. "Abortive Reconstruction: Federal War Labor Policies, Union Organization, and the Politics of Race." *Journal of Policy History* 9 (1997).

Northrup, Herbert, et al. *Negro Employment in Basic Industry: A Study of Racial Policies in Six Industries (Automobile, Aerospace, Steel, Rubber Tires, Petroleum, and Chemicals)*. Philadelphia: Wharton, 1970.

Northrup, Herbert. *Organized Labor and the Negro*. New York: Harper, 1944.

Shulman, Steven, and William Darity, eds. *The Question of Discrimination: Racial Inequality in the U.S. Labor Market*. Middletown, CT: Wesleyan University Press, 1989.

Spero, Sterling D., and Abram L. Harris. *The Black Worker: The Negro and the Labor Movement*. New York: Columbia University Press, 1930.

See also **Agriculture Adjustment Administration; Civil Rights Act of 1964/Title VII; Fair Employment Practice Committee; Gompers, Samuel; March on Washington Movement; National Industrial Recovery Act; Randolph, A. Philip; Slave Trade**

AFRICAN BLOOD BROTHERHOOD

An organization of black militants based in Harlem, the African Blood Brotherhood (ABB) existed as an independent body from October of 1919 until 1922, when it was absorbed by the Communist party.

Historians dispute whether or not the African Blood Brotherhood was ever independent of the political control of the Communist party or if it was essentially the black branch of the party from its inception. In either case the African Blood Brotherhood offered a class-based critique of racism that competed with Marcus Garvey's ideas in the period after World War I. Before the ABB's founding, Cyril Briggs, its main leader, had published a newspaper called the *Crusader*, which became the organ of the ABB in 1919. Briggs was attracted to communism by the example of the Russian Revolution and the USSR's denunciation of colonialism and racism. He argued that Woodrow Wilson and the Allies offered no hope for colonized peoples, since they applied the idea of national self-determination only to Europe while extending the colonial empires of France and Britain after the war. The *Crusader* was clear however that black people needed to rely on their own forces both for their own defense and for their eventual liberation from racial oppression. It called for black people to defend themselves with arms during the race riots of 1919 in Chicago and East St. Louis and 1921 in Tulsa.

Membership figures for the ABB and the circulation of the *Crusader* are widely disputed. Briggs himself was unclear on the matter, claiming from 3,000–30,000 members for the organization at its peak and from 4,000–36,000 for the circulation of the paper. In any case the ABB was not a mass organization, and it was dwarfed in its time by Garvey's Universal Negro Improvement Association (UNIA). The one major fight that the ABB might have led took place in Tulsa. A group of black Tulsans who might have been organized as a branch of the ABB defended Dick Rowland from a lynching. This event touched off the Tulsa race riot in which whites burned down the Greenwood section of that city where most black Tulsans lived. The evidence is inconclusive as to whether or not the black Tulsans who defended Rowland were actually ABB members, but it seems clear that they were influenced by the ABB and the ideas of black self-defense promoted by the *Crusader*.

The main importance of the ABB lies in the intellectual connection that its members drew among communism, working class militancy, and black liberation, rather than its limited organizational successes. In an era when race starkly divided the U.S. working class and when the dominant black organizations looked to the black middle class, the ABB argued that black workers could be at the forefront of the fight against racism. The intellectual foundations laid by the ABB were later built on by black Communists in the 1930s.

SAMUEL MITRANI

References and Further Reading

Hill, Robert. "Racial and Radical: Cyril V. Briggs, The *Crusader* Magazine, and the African Blood Brotherhood, 1918–1922." In The *Crusader* (bound set), vol. 1. New York: Garland Publishing, 1987.

Solomon, Mark. *The Cry Was Unity, Communists and African Americans, 1917–1936*. Jackson, MS: University Press of Mississippi, 1998.

See also **African-Americans; Communist Party**

AFRICANS (TWENTIETH CENTURY)

People of African descent have lived on the North American continent for centuries, but it was not until the Immigration Act of 1965 eliminated country-by-country quotas to admit peoples by regions of the world that large new numbers of Africans began voluntarily coming from Africa to the United States. Initially the majority of post-1965 immigrants from sub-Saharan Africa came to the United States for educational opportunities, and large numbers returned to the African countries from which they came. Since the late 1980s however, permanent African immigration has increased greatly, as many sought opportunities for work overseas when conditions in their home countries declined. Structural adjustment policies administered by the International Monetary Fund and the World Bank accompanied the retreat of the state from the realms of health, education, and public security, incurring a decline in numbers of jobs, job security, and the availability of healthcare and education. In some cases immigrants also come abroad to evade political and ethnic persecution and civil war. Of all Western nations, the United States accepts the largest numbers of African immigrants, and today there are at least one million foreign-born Africans living in the United States, making up 3% of the total foreign-born population.

African immigrant experiences reflect how Africa is the most underdeveloped and most indebted region of the world. Relatively wealthy and well-educated Africans, or those with wealthy sponsors on the continent or within the United States, tend to be the only people who have the means to emigrate. Additionally African refugees originating from contexts of political persecution or wars in their home countries also receive international and nonprofit assistance in their journeys to the United States.

African immigrants are very diverse, coming from over 50 countries and countless African ethnic groups with separate traditions and languages. As of 2002, the largest African national groups within the United States. were Nigerians (139,000), Ethiopians (87,500), and South Africans (70,000). Of the 69,000 refugees arriving in the United States in 2001, 28% percent were from Africa, mostly from Sudan and Somalia. Even with such a diversity of cultural and economic backgrounds, within the United States, African immigrants can be roughly divided into three labor groups: Professionals, nonprofessionals (including most refugees), and international itinerant traders.

Professional immigrants from Africa come from the wealthiest and best-educated sectors of African countries, draining local economies and institutions of valuable human capital. Indeed African immigrants in the United States have the highest educational levels of all post-1965 immigrant groups; more than half have college degrees. Most professional immigrants leave Africa for the United States to ensure their access to dignified, stable and relatively high-paying professional employment, better education for their children, and for secondary issues like access to health care or to build up retirement assets. Additionally high numbers of U.S. professional African immigrants are native to countries where English is an official language or is at least widely taught in schools. Immigrants who speak no European languages or who come from countries in which French or Portuguese is the official language have greater difficulty finding professional employment. Once in the United States, a large number of these immigrants obtain H1B professional visas, or in the case of younger immigrants, they may have enrolled in additional higher education to obtain student visas, thereby continuing to attain education, greater earning potential, and better chances at becoming naturalized citizens. (Some well-educated immigrants do enter nonprofessional employment sectors, as later discussion shows.) These African physicians, teachers, accountants, engineers, and middle- and upper-level managers typically settle in the neighborhoods and suburbs where their professional peers live, and they often integrate relatively seamlessly into the U.S. mainstream. Their children have of late been the center of controversy at U.S. colleges and universities, where ethnically African (and Caribbean) students have qualified for minority scholarships that some African-American advocates claim were intended for the descendents of nineteenth-century U.S. slaves.

Since the early 1990s, recently arriving Africans have increasingly entered into nonprofessional labor markets in the United States, settling in major U.S. major cities and taking such wage jobs as valets, car parks, and child-care workers. These nonprofessionals are also joined by many highly educated Africans who may have difficulty finding professional work either because of visa problems or problems with validating their African educational credentials within U.S. institutions. Many nonprofessional immigrants were also raised outside of English-speaking regions on the continent, and although they may learn English quickly, they have less cultural experience and comfort level with U.S. professional and mainstream work and educational environments. Nonprofessional immigrants tend to settle in loosely knit African enclaves within working-class African-American neighborhoods in such cities as Houston, Philadelphia, New York, Chicago, and Washington, D.C. There is also a trend in which Africans arriving in large cities decide to explore semiskilled work and unskilled factory labor in smaller U.S. cities, notably Greensboro, North Carolina, which has a significant African labor force. Additionally nonprofessional Africans enter the U.S. labor force by taking paraprofessional training in fields that have chronic worker shortages, like allied health care. It is noteworthy that African women tend to work outside the home even when children are present, relying on friends and relatives for child care as is the custom in Africa. Besides taking wage labor, many Africans in the United States become entrepreneurs and are visible to the general public through their own small businesses like hair salons, travel agencies, shops, restaurants, and cabs. Like many other post-1965 immigrant groups in the

United States, Africans have higher rates of savings and home ownership than native-born U.S. citizens at the same income levels.

A unique group of African itinerant traders have built up a complex international business sector, traveling and selling goods across the United States as well as Europe, the Middle East, and even Japan. Traders in African cloth, statuettes, and other Afro-centric merchandise, these itinerant businessmen (and a few women) generally hail from Francophone West African countries and are Muslims; they often rely on personal contacts through Islamic organizations in the United States to conduct their business. Although many traders are based in the United States legally, running large, legitimate business operations, other traders are undocumented, plying their trade on the streets of U.S. cities in the informal sector, selling items like bootlegged video and audio recordings, and counterfeit trademarked goods.

Most African immigrants intend to resettle in their countries of origin, although there is wide variation in the numbers who can and do return. In general African small-business owners and unskilled workers from politically stable and relatively prosperous countries like Ghana, Senegal, and Kenya are more likely to return after sojourning in the United States, using savings to purchase homes and businesses in Africa. Especially pressing on all immigrants however is the burden of remittances. Remittances involve sending home monies regularly to support family, build family homes, and to contribute to important public works projects, for example, the mosque in the city of Tuba in Senegal, or to build local schools and operate Catholic missions in Nigeria. In Ghana in 2003, private remittances from immigrants abroad made up over 13% of the Ghanaian GDP, with approximately half of those monies coming from North America.

Most Africans who come abroad to the United States. rely on ethnic networks to find housing, employment, and advice or advocacy for obtaining visas. These ethnic networks are often formalized as mutual assistance organizations or home town associations. Mutual assistance organizations provide rotating credit and financial education for members, for example, by helping members to obtain licenses to operate taxi cabs, an expense which can run into the tens of thousands of dollars. Home town associations (made up of individuals from a single region) provide referrals, information and opportunities to socialize, and they also engage in development projects in the home country, projects that help members maintain transnational connections. Besides groups within African immigrant communities, long-established U.S. settlement agencies are adapting to the needs of these new immigrant populations. With recent conflicts in Eritrea, Sudan, and Liberia, U.S. nonprofit organizations like Catholic Charities and Lutheran Social Services have resettled refugees in smaller and midsized U.S. cities, where Africans work at low-wage service jobs, ideally while pursuing education in paraprofessional or professional fields.

RACHEL R. REYNOLDS

References and Further Reading

Arthur, John A. *Invisible Sojourners: African Immigrant Diaspora in the United States.* New York: Praeger, 2001.

Balch Institute. *Extended Lives: The African Immigrant Experience in Philadelphia.* www.hsp.org/default.aspx?id=85, (2001–)

Holtzman, Jon D. *Nuer Journeys, Nuer Lives; Sudanese Refugees in Minnesota.* Boston, MA: Allyn and Bacon, 2000.

Howes, Arthur. *Benjamin and His Brother.* Documentary video, 2002.

Stoller, Paul. *Money Has No Smell: The Africanization of New York City.* Chicago: University of Chicago Press, 2002.

AGRICULTURAL LABOR RELATIONS ACT (1975)

California's Agricultural Labor Relations Act (ALRA) of 1975 was the first exception to the total exclusion of farm workers from labor relations law in the United States. It also signaled a transformation in the conflict between the United Farm Workers of America (UFW) and corporate agriculture in California. Beginning with the Delano Grape Strike in 1965, which marked the emergence of the National Farm Workers Association (NFWA), the precursor to the UFW, there had been continuous labor unrest in the fields. During the 10-year period, the UFW, led by César Chávez, launched strikes, engaged in protracted contract negotiations, built an impressive international boycott network, and developed a strong political power base. In response growers directed their vast economic and political resources to resist unionization, but in contrast to past disputes, they were unable to suppress labor organization of the largely Mexican-heritage and Filipino workforce. The early 1970s had witnessed the most violent relations as the UFW, growers, and Teamsters clashed in the lettuce fields and battled over the renewal of the expiring contracts with Gallo Winery and table-grape growers. In the face of this bitter confrontation, government mediation provided a possible alternative to unresolved labor strife. Politicians, agribusiness, and union officials gave serious consideration to historical precedents in formulating a legislative compromise they hoped would end the continuous turmoil in the fields.

In the 1930s, the National Labor Relations Act (NLRA) had authorized the federal government to mediate conflicts between industries and their workers. The NLRA affirmed workers' right to organize freely and required employers to sign collective-bargaining agreements with duly elected union leaders. The NLRA had given organized labor legal protection against employers' power to fire labor organizers, suppress strikes, and stifle unions, but the law specifically excluded unskilled workers, domestic laborers, and agricultural workers from its coverage. Thus agricultural workers could be intimidated and fired for labor activism, which dampened enthusiasm for organizing. The only benefit of exclusion from coverage was that farm workers had license to use strategies that were proscribed by U.S. labor law after the Taft-Hartley Act in 1947. Nevertheless the NLRA offered a precedent, and politicians in California saw it as a model on which to craft new legislation.

The limits imposed by Taft-Hartley left agricultural union leaders with mixed feelings about the prospect of including farm workers in federal labor relations law. As a result the UFW's position on legislation shifted over the years. Initially Chávez supported the inclusion of agricultural labor under the NLRA. But after grower resistance, acrimonious strikes, and extended boycotts, Chávez came to reject the tactic of simply including farm workers under the act's provisions. His objections concerned the restrictive Taft-Hartley Amendment of 1947. In addition to prohibiting mass picketing and sympathy strikes, it had also authorized the U.S. president to order strikers to return to work, and it held unions legally responsible for damages if their members struck in violation of union contracts. Most significantly it banned the use of the secondary boycott, which had become the UFW's most effective tool in its struggle with corporate agriculture.

Growers and their allies, confident of support from Republican Governor Ronald Reagan and President Richard Nixon, saw an opportunity in the early 1970s to push for a legislative resolution to the disorder in the fields. Progrower politicians drafted a bill that specified a craft rather than the industrywide approach to organization used by the UFW. This meant that workers would be divided into various groups (machine operators, truck drivers, irrigators, pruners, harvesters) rather than by farm or ranch. The measure provided for grievance hearings prior to an election, which could suspend or delay the voting process until after the harvest when most workers had left the area. The proposed law also prohibited the use of the secondary boycott.

Other unions were also interested in pursuing a legislative solution. Engaged in a jurisdictional contest with the UFW, the Teamsters had raided UFW contracts up for renewal in 1973. Growers preferred negotiating "sweetheart" contracts with the Teamsters, who wanted legislation that would protect the existing contracts they currently held. Packinghouse workers and the building trades wanted language inserted that exempted their members from the proposed law. Finally the Butchers' and Retail Clerks' unions, who felt the secondary boycott jeopardized their jobs, increasingly pressured the American Federation of Labor (AFL)-Congress of Industrial Organizations (CIO), under George Meany, to reign in the UFW. Meany grew increasingly frustrated by the independent UFW that proudly proclaimed its social movement origins and pursued unorthodox approaches in recruiting young, idealistic volunteers instead of paid professionals. The AFL-CIO president believed the UFW would become a more conventional union under government regulation.

The momentum for legislation continued even when Governor Reagan declined to run for re-election, opening the way for Democrat Jerry Brown's successful campaign for the statehouse. The Brown administration actively stepped into the fray to fashion an acceptable bill from all the competing proposals submitted by the UFW and growers. After considerable wrangling, negotiators reached a compromise. The ALRA established a five-person Agricultural Labor Relations Board (ALRB) charged with supervising secret-ballot elections. It stipulated that in order to petition for an election, 50% of the workforce had to sign authorization cards for union representation. Strikebreakers hired after the outbreak of a strike would not be able to vote. Elections would be held quickly, during peak harvest time, reflecting the unique conditions of agricultural labor. Challenges and grievances would be postponed until after an election in order to forestall procedural delays from impeding the election process. Workers were organized on a basis similar to the industrial form of organization by farm or employer as opposed to the craft approach by individual job classification. The already existing Teamster contracts were validated. Most importantly to the UFW, no limitations were placed on primary boycotts or harvest-season strikes. However restrictions were imposed on a secondary boycott (the union's most effective strategy); it could not be used to gain union recognition as a bargaining agent. It could be used only after an election and only to pressure unwilling growers to negotiate a union contract.

After the bill won the endorsement of the UFW, other unions, and representatives of agribusiness, its final passage was expedited through a special legislative session called by Brown. The governor appointed the five members of the ALRB. Growers and Teamsters attacked the board for its alleged pro-UFW bias. Some UFW members opposed the law because of its limitations on the secondary boycott. Nevertheless passage of the ALRA unleashed a torrent of organizing. And with this scramble, additional problems arose. Primary among them was the issue of access to laborers at the work site. While the ALRB granted access to workers in the fields 1 hour before and after work and during the lunch break, growers argued that this policy infringed on their property rights—even as they blocked entry to UFW organizers while granting it to Teamster organizers. The board was also overwhelmed by unfair labor practice charges, such as threats of worker dismissals, firing of UFW supporters, company hiring of workers who agreed to vote either for the Teamsters or no union. Despite the heated competition, the UFW won over 50% of the elections; the Teamsters prevailed at around 40%; and votes of no-union accounted for the remainder. After 5 months of operation, the ALRB had conducted 423 elections involving over 50,000 workers. It had received 988 unfair labor charges, dispatching 254 of them. Inundated with election petitions and irregularities, the board exhausted its operating budget. Unable to force modifications to the law, a progrower coalition consisting of Republicans and conservative, rural Democrats defeated an effort to appropriate supplemental funding. To counter this effort, the UFW mobilized to place an initiative on the ballot, making it difficult to amend the law. Although endorsed by Governor Brown and presidential candidate Jimmy Carter, Proposition 14 was defeated in 1976. But the ALRA received increased funding in the next budget.

Although agribusiness has tried to amend ALRA provisions, such as the access rule, the make-whole remedy (which required grower payment of lost wages for bad-faith bargaining), and the secondary boycott, the law has remained intact and developed a body of case law. With the ALRA the UFW entered a new phase as the law introduced stability into agricultural labor relations. As a consequence of the law, the UFW moved away from its original identity as a social movement to the model of a more conventional union. After the first year of intensive organizing, the act slowed unionization campaigns and ultimately curbed the power of the UFW; but it also provided the union with a legislative foundation to secure its existence. Unwarranted delays and the tendency of the ALRB to become politicized depending on the ideology of officials making appointments continually frustrate workers and union officials. Although the ALRB provided a model for similar legislation in other states, it has been extremely difficult for farm workers to achieve similar legislation elsewhere. With the exception of California, the majority of states, including Florida and North Carolina, two of the largest users of agricultural labor, have failed to provide farm workers with basic protections denied to them under U.S. federal law. In fact the minimum levels of protection established by state laws are often lower than those recognized under federal law, and state funds allotted for enforcement are generally inadequate. Even with this landmark legislation, the UFW has continued an uphill struggle for the rights of farm workers 30 years after the passage of the ALRA.

MARGARET ROSE

References and Further Reading

Jenkins, J. Craig. *The Politics of Insurgency: The Farm Workers Movement in the 1960s.* New York: Columbia University Press, 1985.

Levy, Jacques. *Cesar Chavez: Autobiography of la Causa.* New York: W.W. Norton & Company, Inc, 1975.

Majka, Linda C., and Theo J. Majka. *Farm Workers, Agribusiness, and the State.* Philadelphia: Temple University Press, 1982.

Martin, Philip, "Labor Relations in California Agriculture: 1975–2000," http://migration.ucdavis.edu/cf/comments

Rose, Margaret. "Dolores Huerta: The United Farm Workers' Union." In *The Human Tradition in American Labor History*, edited by Eric Arnesen. Wilmington, Delaware: Scholarly Resources, Inc, 2004. Pp. 211–229.

See also **Chávez, César Estrada; Delano Grape Strike (1965–1970); Huerta, Dolores C.; United Farm Workers of America**

AGRICULTURAL WORKERS ORGANIZATION

Members of the Industrial Workers of the World (IWW), also known as Wobblies, began organizing agricultural workers soon after they had formed their union in 1905. In Washington, California, and North Dakota, Wobblies established a presence first in cities where they hoped to reach migrant farmworkers. Spokane, Fresno, and Minot were cities frequented by itinerant workers who would arrive in search of employment, a place to spend their wages, or a place to hole up for the winter. Much of the Wobbly presence was built out of free speech fights. Although advancing the First Amendment rights of free speech, the Wobblies did little to help organize migrant farmworkers. It was on-the-job organizing that positioned the IWW as a pragmatic labor union.

The Wheatland Strike in California, along with other organizing efforts in eastern Washington and

North Dakota in the early 1910s, motivated Wobblies at the September 1914 IWW convention to call for a conference of agricultural Wobblies. In April 1915, IWW delegates from various agricultural regions of the country, but primarily from western states, met at an agricultural workers conference in Kansas City, Missouri. Here they established initiation fees, monthly dues, and elected Walter T. Nef as secretary-treasurer and a five-member supervisory committee to head the new Agricultural Workers Organization (AWO). One of the most innovative features of the AWO was the field delegate system. The field delegates lived and worked among agricultural laborers whom they were trying to organize. Field delegates carried union application materials, union membership dues books, dues stamps, Wobbly literature, and other items essential for organizing and informing workers of the AWO's mission. Over the course of 1915 and 1916, the AWO (or harvest Wobblies) organized thousands of agricultural workers in California, the Pacific Northwest, and in the Great Plains.

In late 1916, the AWO claimed a membership of eighteen thousand laborers. Among those members were workers in various agricultural jobs but also workers in logging and construction. Bill Haywood and other members of the IWW leadership grew concerned that the AWO exercised too much influence on the IWW as a whole. At the November 1916 IWW general convention in Chicago, AWO delegates made up 75% of the delegates on the convention floor. Haywood and others were also concerned that the AWO would break free of the IWW to become an independent national union. Therefore Haywood and the executive board worked to persuade the convention delegates to support a restructuring of the member unions of the IWW into industrial unions under the supervision of the leadership in Chicago. They were successful. The Agricultural Workers' Industrial Union (AWIU) was created and charged with organizing only agricultural laborers.

By summer 1917, harvest Wobblies had established an effective, pragmatic, industrial union that could organize thousands of migrant and seasonal farmworkers in the western countryside. The reason that the AWIU proved more successful in the West than in any other region had to do with the sociocultural nature of the workforce. The Wheat Belt of the Great Plains, the agricultural zones of the Pacific Northwest, and the industrial-agricultural valleys of central California together required hundreds of thousands of migrant and seasonal farmworkers. The majority of these workers were itinerant, white, native-born, young men, which was the predominant membership of the AWIU. Harvest workers had to steal rides on freight trains to get to job sites, and

many stayed in makeshift "jungle" camps between jobs. They confronted hostile townsfolk and a criminal element that preyed on migrant harvest workers. The AWIU members shared this work life culture, which helped in recruiting new members.

With passage of the Espionage and Sedition Acts during World War I, Wobblies and thousands of other U.S. citizens and resident aliens experienced intense repression at the hands of the federal government and frequent violations of their civil rights. Before the AWIU, and the IWW as a whole, could rebound from federal wartime persecution, Wobblies had to endure a second wave of law enforcement attacks in the form of state criminal syndicalism statutes. California would be the most aggressive state in repressing harvest Wobblies with its criminal syndicalism laws, though other states in the Far West and in the Great Plains would use the same tactic for similar effect. Despite this legal offensive against the IWW in the West that included criminal syndicalism and vagrancy arrests, harvest Wobblies continued to work in the fields and orchards, institute organizing campaigns, and attend to AWIU affairs.

Harvest Wobblies persevered through the immediate postwar years. In the short term, the AWIU emerged in 1921 with renewed strength, assisting the IWW to achieve several years of noteworthy resurgence as a militant labor organization. By the mid-1920s, however, the AWIU went into steep decline. West Coast farm workers became increasingly more socially and culturally diverse as families of harvest workers, Latinos, and Asians made up a great share of the workforce. They along with the still-predominant white, native-born harvest workers in the Wheat Belt drove their own vehicles to work sites and avoided the jungle camps. The AWIU never found a way to accommodate these changes within its organizing strategy. Moreover mechanization of wheat harvesting eliminated thousands of agricultural jobs in the Wheat Belt after 1930.

Harvest Wobblies are historically significant for several reasons. They established one of the first unions to organize U.S. farmworkers. The AWO and the AWIU were the largest and most dynamic constituencies of the IWW. From 1915–1925, over half of the IWW's finances originated from the AWO or the AWIU. The agricultural branch of the IWW became a proving ground for many of the best organizers and leaders of the union, such as Walter Nef, Edwin Doree, George Speed, Mat Fox, and E. W. Latchem. Harvest Wobblies personified some of the most indelible features of the union membership. They were the militant casual laborers of the U.S. West, riding the rails, living in jungles, and preaching industrial unionism and revolution in the workplace. They, along with other Wobblies of the West, helped to create the footloose, masculine, rebel worker culture of the IWW.

GREG HALL

References and Further Reading

Dubofsky, Melvyn. *We Shall Be All: A History of the Industrial Workers of the World.* Chicago: Quadrangle Books, 1969.

Foner, Philip S. *History of the Labor Movement in the United States*, vol. 4. *The Industrial Workers of the World, 1905–1917.* New York: International Publishers, 1965.

Hall, Greg. *Harvest Wobblies: The Industrial Workers of the World and Agricultural Laborers in the American West, 1905–1930.* Corvalis: Oregon State University Press, 2001.

Higbie, Frank Tobias. *Indispensable Outcasts: Hobo Workers and Community in the American Midwest, 1880–1930.* Urbana: University of Illinois Press, 2003.

Kronbluh, Joyce L., ed. *Rebel Voices: An IWW Anthology.* Chicago: Charles H. Kerr Publishing Company, 1988.

Sellars, Nigel. *Oil, Wheat, and Wobblies: The Industrial Workers of the World in Oklahoma, 1905–1930.* Norman: University of Oklahoma Press, 1998.

Taft, Philip. "The I.W.W. in the Grain Belt." *Labor History* 1 (Winter 1960): 53–67.

See also **Industrial Workers of the World**

AGRICULTURE ADJUSTMENT ADMINISTRATION

On May 12, 1933, President Franklin D. Roosevelt signed the Agriculture Adjustment Act, creating the Agriculture Adjustment Administration (AAA) within the U.S. Department of Agriculture. Farm commodity prices, which had been falling through the 1920s, accelerated downward with the advent of the Great Depression in 1929. Under this New Deal legislation, Congress and the President sought to increase the price of such key agricultural commodities as cotton, tobacco, wheat, corn, and dairy products in an effort to give farmers the same purchasing power they had during the prosperous years of 1909–1914. Unlike legislative efforts of the 1920s, this measure downplayed market expansion as a means to increase demand and instead encouraged farmers to limit production, or supply, in exchange for benefit payments from the AAA. A tax levied on processors of agricultural commodities paid for the program.

Charged with overseeing the implementation of this system, the AAA created a vast network of local, county, state and federal officials who coordinated administration. Like many New Deal programs, AAA officials built their network around existing structures and organizations, most notably the agriculture extension services, which operated on a state and local level. Extension services helped promote the program and worked with federal officials to establish state and county committees, which were responsible for setting production quotas, publicizing the program, as well as overseeing the signing and enforcement of contracts.

Although it had a reputation as a well-managed agency, the AAA faced significant criticism. First of all the public found it disturbing that the government would cut agricultural production when many people did not have enough to eat or wear. Second contracts mandated that landowners share benefit payments with their tenants and sharecroppers, but this rarely happened, and enforcement remained lax because planters dominated committees charged with overseeing the contracts. Third landowners were now using smaller portions of their holdings and consequently began to evict tenants and sharecroppers. Finally many farmers began to invest in mechanization, sometimes using their benefit payments to purchase machines, which further lessened their need for workers. Estimates suggest that mechanization displaced one- to two-fifths of farmers in the 1930s. The situation was particularly dire on cotton plantations. Many tenants and sharecroppers became homeless and were forced to become farm wage laborers. Frustrated, one group of Arkansas tenants and sharecroppers decided to fight back by organizing the interracial Southern Tenant and Farmers' Union (STFU) in July 1934. They used collective action in an attempt to win enforcement of Section 7 of the AAA contracts, which outlined tenant rights.

Confronted with large numbers of written complaints from tenants and sharecroppers, a small faction of AAA officials began to verbalize their discontent with AAA's inaction on this issue. Within the agency a growing rift appeared between those, such as Assistant Secretary of Agriculture Rexford Tugwell, who perceived the program as an opportunity to enact needed social reforms, and those who perceived the AAA as an administrative agency that should stay focused on commodity prices, not labor relations. Many of the latter believed that landlords had certain rights, including the right to lay off workers, whereas many of the former thought the AAA had an obligation to support tenants in their fight against the landlords. To this end reformers led by AAA legal counsel Jerome Frank formed a Committee on Landlord Tenant Relationships. The AAA's first administrator, George N. Peek, however felt that the agency should focus on monitoring contract negotiations and facilitating benefit payments. Peek's successor, Chester Davis, also clashed with agency reformers. Eventually this division led Davis to fire some reformers and move others into different posts. Tenants in general, and the STFU specifically, received very little support from the AAA or the federal government. Overall the farm program, especially for cotton, tended to benefit larger landowners over small ones, and certainly over sharecroppers and tenants.

Conservatives too complained about the AAA's activities, and in 1936, the Supreme Court declared the Agriculture Adjustment Act unconstitutional in *U.S v. Butler*, stipulating that Congress had overstepped its regulatory functions and that because of this, the processing tax was invalid. Rather than eliminate a program popular with landowners and that seemed to have some success in raising farm prices, Congress reconstituted the AAA under the Soil Conservation and Domestic Allotment Act of 1936. It abolished the processing tax and paid for the program through general revenues. With a new stress on soil conservation as a means of keeping production levels low, the AAA began to use farms rather than commodities as the basic contract unit. A reorganization of AAA from divisions based on crops to geographic regions reflected this shift in focus. Two years later Congress once again revised the law. This time it sought to control oversupply through a storage system and by monitoring interstate marketing and to provide loans to farmers. It also enacted the first federal crop insurance program.

Some commodity prices rose from 1933–1939, but they did not necessarily improve because of AAA programs. A good portion of the rise seemed to be due to a cut in supply caused by such natural disasters as the severe droughts of the early-to-mid-1930s rather than AAA's efforts to decrease farm output. As late as 1939, farm prices on most commodities had still not recovered to pre-1914 levels or even to pre-1929 prices.

During World War II, the AAA reversed course, working with farmers to increase production to meet new demand. In 1942, it changed its name to the Agricultural Adjustment Agency, and 3 years later, it ceased to exist as an entity, although its work lived on in other divisions. The AAA set a precedent for federal agriculture subsidies. Its mission of applying business models to the agricultural sector also oriented the subsidy program toward economic concerns rather than such social reform as improved labor and living standards for farm tenants, sharecroppers, and wage workers.

MARGARET C. RUNG

References and Further Reading

Agricultural Adjustment Act, Act of May 12, 1933, c. 25, 48 Stat 31.
Daniel, Pete. "The New Deal, Southern Agriculture, and Economic Change." In *The New Deal and the South*, edited by James C. Cobb and Michael V. Namorato. Jackson, MS: University Press of Mississippi, 1984. Pp. 37–61.
Finegold, Kenneth, and Theda Skocpol. *State and Party in America's New Deal*. Madison, WI: University of Wisconsin Press, 1995.
Kester, Howard. *Revolt among the Sharecroppers*. New York: Covici Friede Publishers, 1936.
Perkins, Van L. *Crisis in Agriculture: The Agriculture Adjustment Administration and the New Deal, 1933*. Berkeley, CA: University of California Press, 1969.
Saloutos, Theodore. *The American Farmer and the New Deal*. Ames, IA: Iowa State University Press, 1982.
United States v. Butler 297 U.S. 1 (1936).

See also **Agricultural Labor Relations Act; Agriculture Adjustment Administration; Agricultural Workers Organization; Great Depression; Sharecropping and Tenancy; Southern Tenant Farmers' Union**

AID TO FAMILIES WITH DEPENDENT CHILDREN

Aid to Families with Dependent Children (AFDC), commonly referred to as welfare, was a joint federal-state grant-in-aid program for children of poor single parents, predominantly mothers. From its inception in the Social Security Act of 1935 to its demise in the Personal Responsibility and Work Opportunity Reconciliation Act (PRWORA) of 1996, AFDC provided minimal financial support for some single-mother families, consistently one of the largest groups of impoverished Americans.

The Origins and Structure of AFDC, 1900–1935

Most scholars locate AFDC's origins in Progressive Era mothers' pension programs, a response to the specific problem of poor fatherless families and the more general disruptions wrought by industrialization, immigration, and urbanization. By the late nineteenth century, middle-class and elite reformers, along with working-class advocates, demanded a multitude of laws and programs aimed at improving the social and economic conditions of the laboring classes. While some efforts to regulate hours, wages, and working conditions overcame political elites' commitment to *laissez faire* economic policy, state governments and Congress scuttled proposals for social welfare provisions like old-age, health, and unemployment insurance programs. At the same time, women reformers began to define single motherhood as a particular social problem as fatherless families became more visible with the breakdown of traditional patriarchal families and communities, increased geographic mobility, and the shift away from family-based economies toward wage labor. Their campaign to establish public responsibility for needy single mothers and their children proved more successful than other welfare proposals: State-level mothers' pensions legislation spread rapidly after Illinois enacted the first program in 1911 to affect 39 states by 1920 and all but two states (Georgia and South Carolina) by 1935.

The success of mothers' pension legislation reflected both ideological changes and political developments. By the early twentieth century, social reformers rejected institutionalization of poor children and emphasized the importance of a mother's care. Their celebration of home life and consequent commitment to keeping poor single mothers and their children together found sympathy among the editors of mass-circulation women's magazines reaching millions of middle-class readers across the country. At the same time, U.S. political circumstances—early achievement of universal white manhood suffrage, weakness of labor unions, and lack of a labor party, failure of civil service reform, and consequent weak bureaucracies, the intensity of *laissez faire* attitudes among elites, and the expansion of higher education for women—opened political space for a unique force: middle-class women. Prominent female social reformers in the nation's settlement houses demanded mothers' pensions as part of a larger campaign for social justice and as a recognition of both poor women's vulnerability in the labor market and their service to the state as mothers. Meanwhile the nearly two million members of federated women's clubs lobbied state legislators with more traditionalist arguments about the sacredness of motherhood.

Administration of mothers' pensions foreshadowed some of AFDC's later weaknesses. State laws authorized, but did not require, counties to provide aid, and a majority did not. Concerns about undermining fathers' breadwinning responsibilities along with chronic underfunding and reliance on private charity workers (who opposed outdoor relief) for administration combined to encourage stringent eligibility requirements. Many states limited the program to widows, long-time residents, and citizens, while social workers conducted home visits to evaluate recipients' fitness as mothers. Not surprisingly then, pensioners were overwhelmingly native-born whites or, in major cities, European immigrants, while black and Mexican women were virtually excluded. Immigrant recipients had to participate in Americanization campaigns, which included classes in English, citizenship, infant care, and nutrition. And despite reformers' rhetoric, pensions did not enable most recipients to devote themselves full-time to childrearing. Instead administrators—either social workers or juvenile court judges—channeled poor single mothers into low-wage labor both by denying aid to women considered able to work (particularly African-American women) and by requiring that recipients and their older children supplement pensions with part-time, low-wage labor (such as taking in laundry, outwork, or part-time domestic service). A 1923 study found that more than half of all mothers aid recipients performed some kind of wage labor.

When the Great Depression pushed federal lawmakers to establish a broader welfare state, mothers' pensions became a federal program, Aid to Dependent Children (ADC). Title IV of the Social Security Act authorized federal funds for the support of families "deprived of parental support" because of death, absence, or incapacity. One of the act's least controversial features, ADC proved weak from its inception. Officials of the Children's Bureau, female social reformers who wrote the ADC title, were more concerned with maternal and infant health provisions. Convinced also that social insurance programs for male breadwinners would ultimately solve the problem of women's and children's poverty, they proposed a small ADC program. The bureau's commitment to state and local administration—reinforced by powerful southern legislators' defense of their region's low-wage agricultural labor force and racial order—precluded national benefit standards or federal administration. Congress refused to assure that grants offered "reasonable subsistence compatible with decency and health," lowered federal funding for ADC, and tightened the definition of eligible children. As important, Congress gave administration of ADC not to its only institutional supporter, the Children's Bureau, but to the newly created Social Security Board, which launched a campaign to promote its social insurance programs by stigmatizing both public assistance programs (ADC, Old Age Assistance, and Aid to the Blind) and their clientele. Even among the public assistance programs, ADC was disadvantaged: It received lower funding levels (Congress raised the federal share in 1939, 1946, and 1948), but until the 1960s, the average monthly benefit was less than a quarter of the average monthly earnings of a manufacturing worker.

Reforming ADC for a New Clientele, 1940–1962

During the late 1940s and 1950s, changing and rising ADC rolls ignited backlash in many states and prompted reformers to rethink the program. The 1939 Social Security Amendments folded the widows and children of insured workers into the system's primary tier, turning Old Age Insurance into Old

Age and Survivors' Insurance. This change removed "deserving widows" from ADC and changed the program's clientele. The percentage of ADC children with widowed mothers declined to 20% by 1942 and 8% by 1961. The rest were children of divorced, deserted, or never-married mothers. In addition the percentage of nonwhite recipients rose to 30% by 1948 and 40% by 1960. This changing clientele rendered the ADC population increasingly vulnerable to racism as well as anxieties about female sexual immorality and male irresponsibility. After World War II, the rolls also began to rise, tripling from 1945–1960 to become the country's largest public assistance category, while postwar inflation and tax increases fueled resentment against welfare spending.

In response almost half of all states, mostly in the South and Southwest, sought to restrict AFDC rolls. During the 1950s, at least 18 states followed Georgia's lead by specifically denying aid to mothers who bore out-of-wedlock children. Many states also instituted residency and "substitute parent" or "man-in-the-house" regulations, by which welfare administrators deemed any man in the mother's life as responsible for child support and invaded recipients' privacy with surprise home inspections, dubbed midnight raids. Employable mother rules cut off welfare when agricultural labor was needed. Opinion polls revealed significant support for this kind of welfare reform, and Social Security Board statements opposing restrictions had little effect. Congress joined in the backlash in 1950 and 1951 with the Notice to Law Enforcement Officials (NOLEO), which required welfare workers to interrogate applicants about deserting fathers, and the Jenner Amendment, which allowed states to publicize welfare rolls.

A coalition of welfare and social work professionals centered in the American Public Welfare Association (APWA), along with allies in foundations and the academy, responded to the postwar welfare backlash by emphasizing its character as a family program (ADC became AFDC in 1960) and by changing the program's emphasis from an income support program to rehabilitation. While they pushed for higher federal funding levels, national standards (which consistently failed passage), and expanded coverage, their most innovative reform was to include in 1956 and 1961 federal funding for services aimed at improving family life and increasing recipients' employability. The 1961 reform also gave states the option to extend aid to two-parent families with an unemployed breadwinner (the AFDC-Unemployed Parent program), which never reached a majority of states and remained a tiny portion of AFDC rolls. Emphasis on employability and the inclusion of fathers muddied the program's stated purpose of

supporting full-time motherhood and justified the first AFDC-related work relief program, the Community Work and Training Program, explicitly opened to (volunteer) mothers in 1962.

Welfare Crisis and Backlash, 1967–1969

Welfare became the topic of sustained national debate in the late 1960s when rolls increased from 3.1 million in 1960 to 4.3 million in 1965 to 6.1 million in 1969 to 10.8 million by 1974. Most sources at the time blamed this welfare explosion on increasing illegitimacy, part of a broader "culture of poverty" that researchers and pundits associated especially with African-Americans. Most famously, the Labor Department's Daniel Patrick Moynihan implicated AFDC for reinforcing black matriarchy as part of a "tangle of pathology" rooted in black male disadvantage. Scholars have since demonstrated that rising AFDC rolls were the result not of increasing numbers of single-mother families but rather of more eligible families applying and getting aid. African-American migration outside the South enabled more black women to qualify, civil rights activism and urban rioting loosened welfare administration, and AFDC mothers began to join together to protest restrictions, publicize regulations, and pressure administrators. Funded by religious organizations and foundations, many groups in 1966 formed a National Welfare Rights Organization (NWRO), an unprecedented organization of poor, mostly black women who demanded "jobs or income now." In addition, federal Legal Aid attorneys successfully challenged welfare restrictions and established recipients' right to due process. As a result of these changes, the proportion of eligible families who received grants rose from one-third in 1960 to over 90% by the 1970s.

While many liberals hoped to solve the welfare crisis with full employment and a guaranteed income, most Americans supported conservative efforts to restrict welfare. Congress considered several punitive reforms but focused on moving AFDC mothers into jobs. In 1967, lawmakers allowed recipients to keep a portion of their wages without losing benefits and required some recipients to seek employment through the Work Incentive Program (WIN). Limited funding for job training and child care, administrators' emphasis on *male* employment, recipients' low educational levels, and women's (particularly minority women's) relegation to the low-wage labor market limited the ability of most recipients to climb out of poverty, whether through welfare or wage labor.

The conservative case against AFDC gained ground by the 1980s as part of a larger assault on federal social spending. Increasing numbers of mothers in the labor market undermined support for a program that theoretically paid mothers to stay home with their children, while pundits and journalists emphasized the link between AFDC and a so-called underclass of poor, inner-city African-Americans. Perhaps most important in provoking opposition to AFDC was a sustained corporate funded attack. Conservative think-tanks funded a host of books and articles like Martin Anderson's *Welfare* (1978) and Charles Murray's *Losing Ground* (1984), which blasted AFDC for breaking up families, discouraging wage labor, and deepening social dysfunction, while politicians promoted the welfare queen stereotype to gain support for restrictive reforms ranging from mandatory paternity identification to stricter work requirements. In the Omnibus Budget Reconciliation Act of 1982, the Reagan administration targeted wage-earning recipients by cutting funding for child care and job training as well as reducing AFDC grants. As a result, the proportion of poor families with children under 18 receiving AFDC declined from an estimated 83% in the 1970s to 63% in 1983.

The Family Support Act of 1988 (FSA) sought once again to replace AFDC with wage labor, reflecting a shift toward employment-based welfare reform that reached back to the post-World War II period. It required AFDC mothers with children over age three to participate in Job Opportunities and Basic Skills (JOBS), a mandatory education, training, job-search program. The FSA also stepped up child support enforcement efforts and mandated that all states establish an AFDC-UP program. At the same time, the federal government permitted states to impose a series of conditions on welfare, from family caps to children's school attendance to vaccinations. Despite the fanfare surrounding the FSA, recession pushed the number of welfare recipients up from 10–11 million throughout the 1970s and early 1980s to a high of 14 million by the early 1990s, providing further pressure for reform.

The End of AFDC

By the 1990s, welfare reform had come to mean reducing rolls and cutting spending, even though AFDC represented a mere 1% of federal spending in the mid-1990s. Republican lawmakers included welfare reform in their 1994 "Contract with America," and Democratic President Bill Clinton, long an advocate of welfare reform as part of the New Democrat strategy, vetoed two bills as too punitive. But in 1996, he signed the Personal Responsibility and Work Opportunity Reconciliation Act (PRWORA), fulfilling his promise to "end welfare as we know it." The bill replaced AFDC with Temporary Aid to Needy Families (TANF), a capped block grant to states, which were given almost complete control over eligibility and benefits. In addition to tightening child support enforcement, denying aid to legal immigrants, and requiring teenaged recipients to live with parents or other adults, the PRWORA limited welfare receipt to 2 years at a time and 5 years over a lifetime, effectively eliminating the federal government's 61-year guarantee to ensuring aid to poor female-headed families.

Most public discussion has declared the termination of AFDC a success. By June 1999, welfare rolls had fallen 49% from their historic high of five million families in 1994, likely as much a result of a booming economy accompanied by rising real earnings, expanded government aid to the working poor (through the Earned Income Tax Credit and expanded child care and Medicaid eligibility), and vigorous deterrence on the part of local welfare administrators. Yet while welfare rolls have declined, studies show that poor single mothers and their children are no better off financially, and often worse off, whatever combination of wage labor, government benefits, and other sources of support they draw on.

MARISA CHAPPELL

References and Further Reading

Abramovitz, Mimi. *Under Attack, Fighting Back: Women and Welfare in the United States.* New York: Monthly Review Press, 1996.

Edin, Kathryn, and Laura Lein. *Making Ends Meet: How Single Mothers Survive on Welfare and Low-Wage Work.* New York: Russell Sage Foundation, 1997.

Goodwin, Joanne L. *Gender and the Politics of Welfare Reform: Mothers Pensions in Chicago, 1911–1929.* Chicago, Illinois: The University of Chicago Press, 1997.

Gordon, Linda. *Pitied But Not Entitled: Single Mothers and the History of Welfare, 1890–1935.* New York: The Free Press, 1994.

Gordon, Linda, ed. *Women, the State, and Welfare.* Madison, Wisconsin: The University of Wisconsin Press, 1990.

Ladd-Taylor, Molly. *Mother-Work: Child Welfare and the State, 1890–1930.* Urbana, Illinois: The University of Illinois Press, 1994.

Law, Sylvia A. "Women, Work, Welfare, and the Preservation of Patriarchy." *University of Pennsylvania Law Review* 131, 6 (1983): 1249–1339.

Mink, Gwendolyn. *The Wages of Motherhood: Inequality in the Welfare State, 1917–1942.* Ithaca, New York: Cornell University Press, 1995.

Mittelstadt, Jennifer. *From Welfare to Workfare: The Unintended Consequences of Liberal Reform, 1945–1965.* Chapel Hill, North Carolina: The University of North Carolina Press, 2005.

Murray, Charles. *Losing Ground: American Social Policy, 1950–1980.* New York: Basic Books, 1984.

Nadasen, Premilla. *Welfare Warriors: The Welfare Rights Movement in the United States.* New York: Routledge, 2004.

Patterson, James T. *America's Struggle Against Poverty, 1900–1994.* Cambridge, MA: Harvard University Press, 1994.

Quadagno, Jill. *The Color of Welfare: How Racism Undermined the War on Poverty.* New York: Oxford University Press, 1994.

Reese, Ellen. *Backlash against Welfare Mothers: Past and Present.* Berkeley, CA: University of California Press, 2005.

Skocpol, Theda. *Protecting Soldiers and Mothers: The Political Origins of Social Policy in the United States.* Cambridge, MA: Harvard University Press, 1992.

Stoesz, David. *A Poverty of Imagination: Bootstrap Capitalism, Sequel to Welfare Reform.* Madison: The University of Wisconsin Press, 2000.

Cases and Statutes Cited

Family Support Act of 1988, Public Law 100-485

Omnibus Budget Reconciliation Act of 1981, Public Law 97-35

Personal Responsibility and Work Opportunity Reconciliation Act of 1996, Public Law 104-193

Social Security Act of 1935, Public Law 76-379

Social Security Amendments of 1956, Public Law 84-880

Social Security Amendments of 1961, Public Law 87-64

Social Security Amendments of 1967, Public Law 90-248

See also **Workfare**

AIR LINE PILOTS' ASSOCIATION

In 1930, David L. Behncke, a United Airlines pilot, held secret meetings with a group of key men from several airlines including United, American, Eastern, and Northwest, to organize pilots employed by commercial airlines. Pilots interested signed undated letters of resignation and put down 50 dollars in escrow money. In 1931, the pilots officially formed the Air Line Pilots' Association (ALPA) and made their first successful stand at United Airlines when they confronted the company over hourly wages and their method of computation. Soon after Behncke convinced the pilots to affiliate with the American Federation of Labor (AFL), which chartered ALPA to represent the "craft of airline pilot." This distinction separated ALPA from earlier pilots' associations, including those open to all employed pilots and an earlier association of pilots working under contract with the U.S. Postal Service. The ALPA differed because membership was open only to pilots employed by commercial airlines and because of the formal tie to the labor movement.

While wages and working conditions on most airlines were comparable to those offered by the U.S. Postal Service (post office airmail service ended in 1928), low wages and longer flying times resulted in the first labor showdown in the industry in 1932, when Century Air Lines slashed wages for pilots employed in the Midwest after hiring pilots on the West Coast at much lower rates. The ALPA members were locked out although the incident is known as the Century Air Line Strike. The ALPA turned to Democratic New Deal allies who helped crush Century's hopes for airmail contracts, which had to be approved by a congressional appropriations committee. This first critical strike exposed the insecurity caused by substantial numbers of unemployed pilots eager to fly and the importance of regulation for pilots. During the 1930s, ALPA's support of Franklin Roosevelt's cancellation of airmail contracts granted during Hoover's administration and its lobbying efforts resulted in federal protections through Decision 83 of the National Labor Board and later the Civil Aeronautics Board, which set pilot wages and working conditions. The ALPA also successfully lobbied for inclusion of the airline industry under the Railway Labor Act (RLA) in 1936, arguing that the RLA's mediation board system would promote labor peace in the industry and serve the public better.

The ALPA signed its first contract with American Airlines in 1939. Under Behncke's leadership the union bargained contracts at all the principal air carriers by 1947 with a total membership of over 5,000 pilots. During the 1940s, ALPA created such affiliates as the Airline Stewards and Stewardesses Association and the Airline Agents Association to organize workers in other craft categories with some success. In 1946, ALPA pilots at Transcontinental and Western Airlines walked out in the first nationwide strike in the industry. With a war-weary public (including blue-collar union members) skeptical of a strike by "Golden Boys," some earning $10,000 a year, an enormous sum, ALPA (and especially Behncke) successfully opposed industrywide bargaining and held out for a federal resolution for computing wages on newer and much faster aircraft. In 1948, pilots and other workers struck National Airlines for over 6 months. While the airline employed replacement pilots, ALPA carried on a successful public relations campaign questioning the safety of National's operations, which resulted in a significant slump in passenger loads for National. In both strikes airlines and ALPA battled publicly over safety and the exclusive and glamorous image of airline pilots.

Behncke's health trouble, growing disconnectedness with a rapidly changing industry, and erratic behavior forced internal troubles at ALPA to a head. Frustrated by his autocratic style and grandstanding tactics during negotiations, a new era of college-educated pilots and the ALPA staff (who formed its own union) both pushed for his ouster. In 1951, by special committee, Clarence N. Sayen, then executive vice-president, replaced the self-educated, working-class Behncke as president, although he battled his removal for another year. Behncke died a year later.

Sayen, a copilot for Braniff Airways with a master's degree in geography, worked to democratize ALPA's constitution and by-laws to avoid the complicated struggles at the end of the Behncke era. During Sayen's tenure, ALPA made substantial gains in wages and work rules for pilots as the industry introduced jet aircraft. The ALPA also battled with the Flight Engineers International Association (FEIA)–American Federation of Labor-Congress of Industrial Organizations (AFL-CIO) with membership extended to all cockpit crew and then fought for all-pilot crews on new jet aircraft. Pushing to maintain full control of the cockpit, ALPA argued that all cockpit employees must be pilots, including those serving as flight engineers, and that FEIA was an illegal union challenging ALPA's jurisdiction. While the AFL-CIO Executive Council unsuccessfully urged the unions to merge, ALPA filed a petition with the National Mediation Board over representation of flight crews at United Airlines. By 1964, through cockpit crew complement, pilot training, Federal Aviation Administration (FAA) regulation, new technology, and ALPA crossing FEIA picket lines, the ALPA-FEIA struggle was over. Sayen, criticized for never having been a captain, resigned from his post in 1962, during a bitter strike at Southern Airways.

According to ALPA historian George E. Hopkins, ALPA's next president, Charles H. Ruby, faced the retirement of the first generation of ALPA pilots and a rank and file disinterested in union politics. Ruby was politically conservative like much of ALPA's membership, and under his tenure, the union distanced itself from the rest of organized labor. In 1963, American Airlines pilots left ALPA and formed the Allied Pilots Association in a long-running dispute over national involvement in local union affairs, the FEIA struggle, and strike benefits.

Under the leadership of John J. O'Donnell, ALPA repaired its relationship with the rest of the labor movement and weathered two major crises: Skyjacking and deregulation. With 160 skyjackings of U.S. aircraft from 1968–1972, skyjacking was a job safety issue for flight crews, and ALPA pushed for increased security measures on the ground and the Antihijacking Act of 1974. The Deregulation Act of 1978 transformed the industry, and thousands of pilots lost their jobs through mergers, bankruptcies, and concession

bargaining through the 1980s. Since the 1990s, the attractive wages and working conditions bargained by ALPA also faced tremendous pressure from the success of low-cost and commuter airlines since deregulation where nonunion often fly for one-third the pay. The hijackings of September 11, 2001, pushed air safety again to center stage, and the bankruptcies and concession bargaining that followed have increased downward pressure on wages and working conditions. In 2004, ALPA represented 64,000 pilots, up from 24,000 in 1968, at 44 U.S. and Canadian airlines.

Flying overwhelmingly remains the domain of white males. In 1990, of the nearly 110,000 airplane pilots and navigators in the United States, over 102,000 were white males.

LIESL MILLER ORENIC

References and Further Reading

Davies, R.E.G. *Airlines of the United States since 1914.* Washington, D.C.: Smithsonian Institution Press, 1971.
Hopkins, George E. *The Airline Pilots: A Study in Elite Unionization.* Cambridge, MA: Harvard University Press, 1971.
———. *Flying the Line: The First Half-Century of the Airline Pilots Association.* Washington, D.C.: The Air Line Pilots Association, 1982.
———. "Air Line Pilots Association." In *The Airline Industry*, edited by William M. Leary. New York: Facts on File: 1992. Pp. 17–20.
———. "David L. Behncke." Ibid. Pp. 52–55.
———. "Clarence N. Sayen." Ibid. Pp. 420–422.
Kahn, Mark L. "The National Air Lines Strike: A Case Study." *Journal of Air Law and Commerce* 19, 1 (1952): 11–24.
Kaps, Robert W. *Air Transport Labor Relations.* Carbondale: Southern Illinois University Press, 1997.
Kommons, Nick. *The THIRD Man, a History of the Airline Crew Complement Controversy, 1947–1981.* Washington, D.C.: Department of Transportation, Federal Aviation Administration, 1987.
Northrup, Herbert, Armand Thiebolt, Jr., and William N. Chernish. *The Negro in the Air Transportation Industry.* Philadelphia: Wharton School of Finance and Commerce, University of Pennsylvania, 1971.
Smith, Henry Ladd. *Airways: The History of Commercial Aviation in the United States.* New York: A. A. Knopf, 1942.
Solberg, Carl. *Conquest of the Skies: A History of Commercial Aviation in America.* Boston: Little, Brown, and Co., 1979.
Walsh, David J. *On Different Planes: An Organizational Analysis of Cooperation and Conflict among Airline Unions.* Ithaca, NY: ILR Press, 1994.
Whitnah, Donald R. "Airline Deregulation Act of 1978." In *The Airline Industry*, edited by William M. Leary. New York: Facts on File: 1992. Pp. 15–17.

See also **Airlines (Operation and Service), Railway Labor Acts**

AIRCRAFT CONSTRUCTION

The Wright brothers' epic flight in 1903 stood as truly one of the monumental technological achievements of the twentieth century. With the advent of the airplane, peoples, societies, and cultures became drawn together more closely geographically than ever before. Still in the decade following the Wrights' momentous flight at Kitty Hawk, the full technological potential of manned flight remained untapped, as aviation's innovators struggled to define a market for their novelty. Given the lack of economic development, aircraft construction in the period from 1903 until the onset of World War I remained centered in small workshops, highly dependent on the skills, abilities, and knowledge of its craft workers.

During this early era of aviation, small gangs of skilled craftsmen labored together building the entire wooden structure. Wheels were laid on the ground, with the group then setting to work on building the machine from the ground up, overseeing every aspect of the production process from construction to first flight. In terms of planning and engineering, the process had minimal preparation or overall organization beyond rudimentary drawings and calculations usually scrawled on the shop walls. Instead the process remained heavily dependent on the knowledge accumulated by a myriad of such skilled craftsmen as cabinetmakers, woodworkers, machinists, and

mechanic. These workers served as the pioneers in the earliest days of aviation.

The pre-industrial methods of aircraft manufacturing underwent a dramatic shift with the advent of the Great War in 1914. Warring nations suddenly looked to use this new aeronautical technology, adapting it to their war machines. Thus an industry that prior to 1914 typically produced no more than 40 airplanes in total during any given year suddenly became overwhelmed by requests for thousands of flying machines. The change brought an economic boom to an industry whose financial fate had always been tenuous. Still by far the most significant change occurred on the shop floor, since military demands for airplanes required an alteration in the manufacturing process, moving construction away from small craft shops to large-scale industrial enterprises.

To meet the war demands, companies began to break down the construction process. Manufacturing became divided into distinct phases or tasks. For example at the Curtiss Aeroplane & Motor Company, considered to be the largest aircraft manufacturer in the United States, production was centered in five separate departments: Motors, woodworking, metal or machine parts, hulls for seaplanes, and special government orders. Afterward the various manufactured components came together in an assembly department where the final airplane was pieced

Three men in shop polishing airplane propellers. Library of Congress, Prints & Photographs Division [LC-USZ62-93432].

together by semiskilled and unskilled laborers. This process at Curtiss was replicated throughout the industry during the war era as companies looked to meet military demands.

During the wartime reorganization, skilled work continued to remain a vital component of the production process. Trades ranging from woodworkers to mechanics continued to be used. Similarly countless new trades were also introduced into the process, bringing onto the shop floor electricians, painters, machinists, pipe fitters and toolmakers. However the autonomy and independence that once accompanied early manufacturing no longer existed. Planning became more orderly, with engineers and draftsmen designing the airplanes with an eye toward greater standardization. Likewise a system of managers and foremen emerged to oversee the production process, further removing the independence of manufacturing from the craftsmen. The days of aircraft workers building an entire airplane, and experimenting freely in the process, ended with World War I. Instead workers now toiled in an environment where they built distinct components of the machine under the direct supervision of trained professionals.

The 1920s and 1930s brought continued changes in the pattern of aircraft construction. First the industry's wartime trend of rationalizing the work environment continued in the postwar period. Employers continued to reorganize the construction process, seeking to limit production costs and control manufacturing schedules. This trend brought a growing reliance on laborsaving machinery on the shop floor and further broke down shop-floor production patterns. The second significant shift came with the industry's move toward metal aircraft. During the 1920s, metal increasingly became the material of choice in constructing aircraft. The process began gradually, starting with the introduction of metal fuselages. By the 1930s, the move to metal would become complete, resulting in aircraft entirely constructed of metal.

The net effect of these manufacturing changes fundamentally altered the composition of the industry's workforce. New trades and occupations entered the industry. Carpenters, cabinetmakers, and other highly skilled wood trades, once the dominant crafts in the prewar era, were replaced by machine operators and metal workers. Still by far the biggest change occurred in terms of the skilled composition of aircraft workers. Throughout the interwar period, changes in aircraft manufacturing ushered in a steady decline in the use of craft workers. According to a study by the Aeronautical Chamber of Commerce, in 1922 nearly 75% of the industry's labor force held the designation of skilled labor. Conversely by 1938 only 10%–15% continued to be classified as skilled workers. Instead

the industry became the domain of semiskilled and unskilled laborers.

Further impacting the industry's manufacturing patterns, and by extension its labor force, were the external economic constraints placed on the industry in the 1920s and 1930s. Manufacturers, reliant almost entirely on the sparse military contracts for their livelihood, struggled in the postwar era. Often times a company's financial fate hinged on winning a single military contract, and more often than not, manufacturers lived from contract to contract. This atmosphere produced a boom or bust environment that not only impacted the economic well-being of the manufacturers but also shaped the experiences of workers on the shop floor. Companies financially struggling in the postwar period often sustained the barest labor force, selectively maintaining a skeletal force of workers who mastered the major skills required of aircraft manufacturing. Only on securing a military contract did companies begin expanding their labor force, looking to meet the new production demands. In the months that followed, the size of the labor force grew, with companies often hiring hundreds of new employees. Then as the contract neared completion, companies soon began scaling back their labor force until the contract was finally completed; at that point the company laid off the remaining new employees hired in the previous months and returned to the employment level of its core group of workers at the start of the process.

The cyclical manufacturing patterns that defined aircraft in the 1920s and 1930s exerted an enormous impact on workers. Stable and steady employment remained a benefit limited to a small segment of workers. These workers were highly skilled, representing a cross-section of trades employed in the industry. For the company these workers served as the foundation on which to expand production facilities as contracts dictated, maintaining continuity in production and serving as a liaison who could teach the new workers entering the factory gates at times of expansion. In return these workers or aircraftsmen, as they came to be termed, gained employment stability, remaining insulated from the employment fluctuations plaguing the industry. Aircraftsmen also enjoyed a degree of economic stability that few on the shop floor shared, since they received wages that typically exceeded local market standards. Additionally being among the ranks of aircraftsmen also brought the possibility of mobility, since companies periodically promoted these workers to positions of midlevel management, opening the doors to positions as foremen, group leaders, or inspectors.

In contrast the new hires or temporary workers were often most noticeable by their youth. Often times they were just removed from vocational school, possessing no real industrial work experience beyond the classroom. Laboring in aircraft allowed them the opportunity to hone their skills and gain useful experience for future employment outside aviation. Likewise this arrangement proved appealing to manufacturers who, because of limited market demand, were unable to maintain the large labor force needed to operate their facilities. Under this cyclical production setting, the firm gained valuable workers who made it possible to meet the immediate contractual demands over short periods of time. Yet most importantly it did so at a relatively low cost, since these inexperienced workers typically labored at extremely low wages.

Worker-based efforts to try to counter the economic divisions proved difficult to maintain as employers skillfully balanced the dichotomy existing between aircraftsmen and temporary workers throughout the 1920s and early 1930s. As a result an open-shop environment dominated labor relations in the interwar era. Only with the onset of the Great Depression, as the economic conditions of both aircraftsmen and temporary workers were threatened, did organized labor begin to play a role in the industry.

The first true move toward unionization started with the emergence in 1933 of an independent union known as the Aeronautical Workers' Union (AWU), which operated from aircraft plants in Buffalo, New York. Early AWU success at Curtiss Aeroplane and Consolidated Aircraft drew the attention of the American Federation of Labor (AFL), which granted the aircraft union a charter as Federal Labor Union No. 18286. Soon AWU organizers successfully brought into its ranks workers at Glenn Martin (Baltimore), Boeing (Seattle), Pratt-Whitney (Hartford), Sikorsky (Bridgeport), and 12 other facilities. Yet despite the optimistic start, the AWU's success proved short-lived, disbanding in 1934 due to employer repression, jurisdictional infighting within the AFL, and continued economic divisions between temporary workers and aircraftsmen.

The defeat of the AWU ushered a rise in independent organizations that varied from limited worker-based unions, such as the Aircraft at Curtiss Aeroplan, to company unions, such as the Douglas Employees Association, which operated out of Douglas Aircraft in Santa Monica. National organization did not emerge in aircraft until after 1940 when both the AFL and the Congress of Industrial Organizations openly committed their unions to organizing the industry and its growing labor force. By 1945, all the major aircraft manufacturing companies became organized whether under the auspices of the International Association of Machinists (AFL) or United Automobile Workers (CIO).

JOHN S. OLSZOWKA

AIRLINES (OPERATION AND SERVICE)

In the first three decades of the twentieth century, the U.S. airline industry grew through government support and regulation, the infusion of capital led by high-profile businessmen, the skill and popularity of former World War I pilots, and the U.S. public's frenzied obsession with flight. Flying the U.S mail, not passengers, provided the profit for, and regulation of, early commercial air transportation. The United States Post Office opened its first regular airmail route between New York and Washington, D.C. in 1918. In 1925, the Kelly Act permitted postal contracts with private companies for mail transport at specified rates over designated routes. Among the first 12 contracts, 10 went to airlines that later became United, American, TWA, and Northwest. In response to growing concerns about air safety for those in the air and on the ground, Congress passed the Air Commerce Act of 1926, which created the Bureau of Aeronautics to regulate airways, airports, and navigation systems, license pilots and aircraft, and oversee the safe operation of a national air transportation system. In 1930, the Watres Act allowed for long-term airmail contracts with established airlines and encouraged experimentation with passenger service. That year the industry employed fewer than 3,500 people as pilots, mechanics, stewards and stewardesses, traffic agents, and office personnel nationwide, and fewer than a hundred of them were women. Scandal over the Watres Act soon erupted over unpublicized meetings between the Post Office and select airlines, and in 1934, the Black-McKellar Act restructured jurisdiction over aviation, including the regulation of hours and benefits of airline pilots and aircraft mechanics and airline executive salaries. In 1936, the Douglas DC-3 made passenger transport profitable, thus challenging the dependence airlines had on airmail. In 1938, President Franklin Roosevelt signed the Civil Aeronautics Act, which regulated safety, defined personnel qualifications, required adherence to labor regulation, and allowed commercial competition under the authority of the Civil Aeronautics Authority and the Civil Aeronautics Board (CAB). This system basically remained in effect until deregulation in 1978.

Early Organizing

In 1931, pilots at United Airlines formed the Air Line Pilots' Association (ALPA) and made their first successful stand when they confronted the airline over possible changes in hourly wages and their method of

Library of Congress, Prints & Photographs Division, FSA/OWI Collection [reproduction number, LC-USF34-081926-E].

computation. Low wages and longer flying times resulted in the first labor showdown in the industry in 1932, when Century Air Lines slashed wages for pilots employed in the Midwest after hiring pilots on the West Coast at much lower rates. ALPA members were locked out although the incident is known as the Century Air Line Strike. The ALPA turned to Democratic New Deal allies and crushed Century's hopes for airmail contracts. In 1933, the International Association of Machinists (IAM) made initial inroads into the airline industry by organizing aircraft mechanics at Eastern Air Transport. In 1936, lobbied by both unions, President Roosevelt amended the Railway Labor Act (RLA) to include the airline industry. The ALPA and the IAM signed their first contracts with the airlines in 1939.

The World War II Era

The airline industry experienced tremendous growth during World War II as a supplier of aircraft, modification services, manpower, and training under lucrative federal contracts. In 1940, the industry employed over 22,000 people, 86% of them white males, almost all (92%) of them native-born. By 1945, 68,281 people worked in air transportation, with white women and African-American men and women employed at least for the duration in aircraft modification centers and at airport operations. While white women found work as mechanics helpers and office staff (and stewardesses), most African-Americans worked as laborers, cleaners, or porters. Turnover among workers on the ground was high, reaching 50% in some regions, since wages were lower than in other industries. By the war's end the industry secured its position as essential for domestic transportation and national security. As a workplace the airlines changed from a rather informal and somewhat rustic place to work to a modern bustling terminal.

Wartime Organizing

During the war and immediately after, both American Federation of Labor (AFL) and Congress of Industrial Organizations (CIO) unions organized airline employees. Frustrated by layoffs, long hours, and low wages, wartime workers seemed less convinced to make sacrifices for the glamorous image of the industry or its prominent and sometimes revered leaders. Workers responded by organizing and going on strike. From 1937–1947, airlines and unions entered into 168 agreements, with the majority bargained from 1944–1947, and from 1946–1953, went on strike 32 times. The IAM, the Transport Workers' Union of America (TWU), the United Auto Workers, and the Brotherhood of Railway and Steamship Clerks all organized skilled and unskilled ground employees, especially aircraft mechanics, fleet service clerks, store and stock employees, and porters, sometimes competing with smaller independent or company unions. Competition among the unions was fierce, and a sort of fragmented craft unionism developed. The ALPA created such affiliates as the Air Line Stewardesses Association and the Air Line Agents Association to organize workers in other craft categories, and the IAM and the TWU created separate airline divisions within their unions to appeal to these workers, many of whom viewed themselves as different from production workers in other industries. Personnel or job definitions, particularly among skilled employees, such as navigators, radio operators, and dispatchers, launched new unions, including the Flight Engineers International Association and the Air Line Dispatchers Association. Jurisdictional conflicts under the "craft or class" structure of the RLA and the CAB created conflicts among unions as they organized difficult-to-define work groups. For example ongoing disputes between the ALPA and FEIA and the BRC and IAM were heard before the National Mediation Board over flight engineers and equipment servicemen, respectively.

1950s Expansion and Conflict

In 1948, pilots, office workers, and mechanics at National Air Lines went on strike for 6 months. The length of the disputes, the unprecedented use of replacement workers by the airline, and public relations tactics by labor ushered in a new era of labor relations in the industry. National lost passengers during the strike and market share after; its image suffered; and it faced the possible loss of routes under CAB regulations. Air service as a perishable and regulated commodity could be profitable only through improved productivity, better service, and newer equipment. The airlines expanded welfare capital programs and training procedures to encourage loyalty and efficiency; invested in new equipment, such as the DC-6; and bargained hard on wages and work rules, particularly for flight crews and mechanics.

By 1955, air transportation carried 38 million passengers and employed over 122,000 people, over 95% of them white and 80% male. By the mid-1950s, most of the industry's crafts were organized, and by the end of the decade, union density at the top 10 airlines ranged from 50%–85%. Airlines responded to labor conflict and high union density by creating the Mutual Aid Pact (MAP) to protect profits and market share during strikes and in bargaining with such unions as ALPA and the IAM, which used "whip-saw" or pattern bargaining where individual contracts could push up wages and conditions across the industry. Through the MAP airlines paid struck airlines based on the increased revenue earned through shifted passenger traffic. Airline unions opposed the pact and formed the short-lived Association of Air Transport Unions to enforce common contract expiration dates and strategize across the industry.

The Jet Age

The airlines used MAP in 1966 during the industry's biggest strike when 35,400 IAM members went on strike at five major airlines after a year of joint negotiations and emergency board hearings over proposed 3.2% wage caps (the Johnson Administration's policy to curb wartime inflation), and health and welfare benefits. The strike halted 61% of the nation's certified air traffic. President Lyndon Johnson brought both sides to the table, but the IAM membership shocked the nation by rejecting the agreement. Faced with legislation that would result in longer back-to-work periods and compulsory arbitration, both sides went back to the table and settled the

43-day strike with a 3-year contract that favored the union's demands.

Technological advances transformed the airline industry. From 1958–1959, the airlines introduced turbojet aircraft, and over the next decade, jet aircraft cut flight time, fuel, and airframe maintenance costs and increased carrying capacity through seat space and containerized loading. Safety, training, and the staffing demands of the new aircraft were concerns for airline workers. The industry also faced the cultural and political climate of the Civil Rights Era but not without resistance. In 1961, the industry came under Executive Order 10925, which called for the equal employment of African-Americans at businesses engaged in interstate commerce. Cases before the Supreme Court and the Equal Employment Opportunity Commission and state fair employment practice committees ended racial discrimination in the hiring of African-American pilots and flight attendants and ended the marital restrictions for all female flight attendants. From 1960–1970, the air transportation labor force rose from nearly 200,000 to 388,000, and it diversified slightly in both racial and gender terms. Women went from 22% to 27% of the total workforce while African-Americans increased from only 5% to 6% of the workforce. Although the gross employment figures for African-American men and women rose significantly, they mostly found positions in such lower skilled ground jobs as fleet services.

Deregulation and Beyond

While the average airline worker experienced a 51% increase in wages (national average: 28%) from 1968–1972, the industry was on the verge of crisis. As the airlines introduced new wide-body jets, a recession curbed the demand for air travel, and rising oil prices dramatically increased operating costs. The airlines asked the CAB for higher fares to offset rising costs, thereby sparking consumer protest and calls for deregulation, particularly from free-market advocates associated with the Gerald Ford Administration. In April 1978, Congress passed the Airline Deregulation Act, which deregulated the industry and abolished the Civil Aeronautics Board (air traffic safety, including personnel certification, came under the jurisdiction of the Federal Aviation Administration in 1958). Intense competition among airlines ensued, with daily fare discounting and new airlines entering the market. A second recession in the early 1980s proved deadly to many smaller airlines, and larger airlines responded with new route systems, such as the "hub and spoke," and more efficient aircraft. Hostile takeovers and explosive labor relations also marked the 1980s, first with the air traffic controllers union (PATCO) strike and then airline layoffs, the use of replacement workers and concession bargaining resulting in two-tier wage scales and outsourcing. Financiers like Frank Lorenzo and Carl Icahn purchased and merged various airlines, including TWA, Continental, and Eastern, resulting in extended and bitter battles with labor, particularly in the case of Eastern, where a standoff between Lorenzo and the IAM resulted in Eastern's demise. This new generation of airline executives reflected a management style that did not include a romantic attachment to flight.

By the early 1990s, with one exception, all the airlines started after deregulation had folded. The legacy carriers, such as United, American, TWA, Delta, and Northwest, controlled most of the domestic air market. By the late 1990s, low-cost start-up carriers with newer equipment and lower labor costs challenged the legacy carriers. With the hijacking of four U.S. airplanes by terrorists on September 11, 2001, the airline industry entered another crisis phase. The following severe drop in air travel, high debt levels and labor costs, poor management strategies, and high fuel costs served to push several major carriers to the brink of or into bankruptcy. Since 2001, airline unions and management have struggled over concessions and restructuring plans under the scrutiny of the federal government. Old-guard airline unions, such as the TWU and the IAM, have faced raiding by independent craft unions, such as the Allied Ground Workers, which hopes to represent fleet service clerks and the Airline Mechanics Fraternal Association, which represents mechanics at United and Northwest airlines. In 2003 air transportation employed 634,000 people, women were 40% of the workforce and minorities, 30% .

LIESL MILLER ORENIC

References and Further Reading

Bernstein, Aaron. *Grounded: Frank Lorenzo and the Destruction of Eastern Airlines.* Washington, DC: Beard Books, 1999.
Cimini, Michael, H. *Airline Experience under the Railway Labor Act.* U.S. Department of Labor, Bureau of Labor Statistics. Washington, DC: U.S. Government Printing Office, 1971.
Cohen, Isaac. "David L. Behncke, the Airline Pilots, and the New Deal: The Struggle for Federal Labor Legislation." *Labor History* 41, 1 (2000): 47–62.
Davies, R. E. G.. *Airlines of the United States since 1914.* Washington, D.C.: Smithsonian Institution Press, 1971.
Hopkins, George E. "Air Line Pilots Association." In *The Airline Industry*, edited by William M. Leary. New York: Facts on File: 1992. Pp. 17–20.
Kahn, Mark L. "The National Air Lines Strike: A Case Study." *Journal of Air Law and Commerce* 19, 1 (1952): 11–24.
Kaps, Robert W. *Air Transport Labor Relations.* Carbondale: Southern Illinois University Press, 1997.
Northrup, Herbert, Armand Thiebolt, Jr., and William N. Chernish. *The Negro in the Air Transportation Industry.* Philadelphia: Wharton School of Finance and Commerce, University of Pennsylvania, 1971.
Orenic, Liesl Miller. "Rethinking Workplace Culture: Fleet Service Clerks in the American Airline Industry, 1945–1970." *Journal of Urban History* 30, 3 (2004): 452–464.
Smith, Henry Ladd. *Airways: The History of Commercial Aviation in the United States.* New York: A. A. Knopf, 1942.
Solberg, Carl. *Conquest of the Skies: A History of Commercial Aviation in America.* Boston: Little, Brown, and Co., 1979.
Van der Linden, F. Robert. *Airlines and Air Mail: The Post Office and the Birth of the Commercial Aviation Industry.* Lexington: University Press of Kentucky, 2002.
Walsh, David J. *On Different Planes: An Organizational Analysis of Cooperation and Conflict among Airline Unions.* Ithaca, NY: ILR Press, 1994.
Whitnah, Donald R. "Airline Deregulation Act of 1978." In *The Airline Industry*, edited by William M. Leary. New York: Facts on File: 1992. Pp. 15–17.

See also **Air Line Pilots' Association; Association of Professional Flight Attendants; International Association of Machinists and Aerospace Workers; Railway Labor Acts; Transport Workers Union**

ALIEN CONTRACT LABOR LAW

The Alien Contract Labor Law, also known as the Foran Act, was enacted by Congress on February 26, 1885. The bill was sponsored by Rep. Martin A. Foran, a Democrat from Ohio and former president of the Coopers International Union. The Alien Contract Labor Law prohibited the practice of contracting with laborers overseas and importing them into the United States; it was subsequently amended in 1887 and 1888 in order to create specific mechanisms for enforcement. The Alien Contract Labor Law was formally repealed with the Immigration and Nationality Act of 1952.

The United States in the mid-nineteenth century experienced a labor shortage, so business and factory owners looked to immigrant labor to meet their needs. Workers were often imported in large groups under a system of contract labor that was quite similar to the indentured servitude of the Colonial Era. These contracts usually required the immigrant to repay the costs of importation by working wage-free for a period of time. The system of contract labor was supported by Congress with the Contract Labor Law of 1864, a law that provided federal enforcement for overseas labor contracts. The system of immigrant contract labor was opposed most notably by the

National Labor Union, which lobbied actively to repeal the Contract Labor Law. The opposition of organized labor stemmed from a fear of being undercut by contract laborers, both in terms of competition for work and the use of immigrant laborers as strikebreakers; racism played a role as well.

The Contract Labor Law was repealed in 1868, thanks in large part to the lobbying efforts of the National Labor Union, but this merely ended government support for the contracts; the practice could continue as before. Opposition to immigrant labor escalated, and in the years leading up to 1885, Congress received numerous petitions calling for restrictions on immigration. Congress responded with three bills designed to curtail contract labor, but it was the anticontract labor bill sponsored by Foran that made it through committee and after a few revisions, was voted into law on February 26, 1885. This first law lacked any enforcement mechanisms, and consequently the Knights of Labor lobbied for revisions: The amendment of 1887 empowered the Secretary of the Treasury to enforce the law and required that all immigrants be interrogated at point of entry, while the 1888 amendment provided for the expulsion of illegal immigrants and added incentives for individuals who turned in offenders. The Alien Contract Labor Law and its amendments were part of a larger constellation of late nineteenth- and early twentieth-century legislation aimed at securing the United States from undesirable immigration. Many state and federal cases have cited the act or its amendments to support immigration restrictions, forming part of an edifice of precedence that has sought to protect U.S. workers from competition and has also sought to keep away populations deemed racially undesirable by U.S. citizens or their representatives in government.

JOHN RUSSELL

References and Further Reading

Briggs, Vernon M., Jr. "Immigration Policy and American Unionism: A Reality Check," http://digitalcommons.ilr.cornell.edu/briggsIV/13, (2004–).

Daniels, Roger. *Guarding the Golden Door: American Immigration Policy and Immigrants since 1882.* New York: Hill and Wang, 2004.

Hutchinson, Edward P. *Legislative History of American Immigration Policy, 1798–1965.* Philadelphia: University of Pennsylvania Press, 1981.

Statutes Cited

Act of October 19, 1888, c. 1210, 25 Stat. 566.

Alien Contract Labor Law, Act of February 26, 1885, c. 164, 23 Stat. 332.

Contract Labor Law, Act of July 4, 1864, c. 246, 13 Stat. 385.

Contract Labor Law, Act of February 23, 1887, c. 220, 24 Stat. 414.

Immigration and Nationality Act, Act of June 27, 1952, c. 477, 66 Stat. 163 at 279.

See also **Indentured Servitude; Knights of Labor; National Labor Union**

ALINSKY, SAUL DAVID, AND THE INDUSTRIAL AREAS FOUNDATION

Often referred to as an agitator, troublemaker, and Communist, Saul Alinsky (1909–1972) began his community organizing work in Chicago's Back of the Yards neighborhood in the late 1930s. He believed that social justice could be achieved by ordinary people through democratic means and argued that controversy was necessary in affecting social change. Alinsky's legacy can be found in modern organizing efforts by broad-based community organizations across the United States, including the organization he founded, the Industrial Areas Foundation (IAF). Additionally Alinsky's vision and organizing tactics, as well as his trainees, can be seen in other democratic movements, including the Civil Rights Movement and the Farmworkers Movement.

Born in 1909 to Russian immigrants, Alinsky grew up in a Jewish ghetto in Chicago. After obtaining a graduate degree in criminology from the University of Chicago, he worked briefly as a criminologist at a state prison in Joliet, Illinois. Before he emerged as a community organizer, Alinsky spent time during the 1930s working with the Congress of Industrial Organizations (CIO). Specifically he helped organize the CIO Newspaper Guild and supported dissident members of the United Mine Workers. Strongly influenced by labor leader John L. Lewis (whose biography he wrote in 1949), he shifted his energy to community organizing and sought to empower politically and socially marginalized groups in society by teaching them how to use self-interest in order to bring disparate groups together toward a common goal. In Chicago's Back of the Yards neighborhood, home to the city's meat-packing industry and the setting for Upton Sinclair's *The Jungle*, Alinsky worked closely with community leader Joe Meegan and Chicago Bishop Bernard Sheil to form his first broad-based community organization called the Back of the Yards Council in 1939. Drawing support from the Catholic Church, the CIO, business leaders, and community members, and using a variety of militant tactics, Alinsky's group won major concessions from the city.

In his work with the Back of the Yards Council and with subsequent organizations, Alinsky relied on and further developed the tactics and strategies he learned from the CIO. Alinsky's philosophy of community organizing used controlled conflict as its most important tool in extracting power from elites and redistributing that power among community members. Much like the CIO, Alinsky and his fellow organizers needed to be invited to a community, and that community needed to raise money on its own to support the organizing effort. Alinsky borrowed other strategies from the CIO, including his emphasis on organizing around multiple salient issues and his tactic of polarizing and personalizing the enemy in campaigns. Structurally Alinsky's organizations also resembled CIO unions. A typical Alinsky organization was governed by an annual convention, with monthly meetings of board members and representatives of member organizations.

In August of 1940, with financial assistance from Marshall Field III, Alinsky founded the IAF, which he intended to serve as an umbrella organization for the community groups he was developing across the United States. Unlike the modern IAF, Alinsky's initial organization included just a handful of professional organizers whose only training consisted of following Alinsky from city to city. In 1945, while spending time in jail for supporting union efforts in Chicago, the IAF leader documented his organizing vision and his experience with the Back of the Yards Council in *Reveille for Radicals,* in which he argued that the poor must salvage democracy through the creation of broad-based citizen's organizations. While these organizations would not be formed to fight for a specific issue or cause, the organizations would engage in issue-specific campaigns, with the broader goal of empowering local leaders.

Following his work in the Back of the Yards neighborhood, Alinsky and his small staff of two or three organizers continued to form organizations across the United States. Among these organizations were the Citizens Foundation of Lackawanna in Lackawanna, New York; the Organization for the Southwest Community in Chicago; The Woodlawn Organization (TWO) in Chicago; the BUILD Organization in Buffalo, New York; and Freedom, Integration, God, Honor, Today (FIGHT) in Rochester, New York.

Following the Montgomery bus boycott against racial segregation in public transportation in 1955, Alinsky began to think about ways to challenge residential segregation in Chicago. He created the first large-scale civil rights effort in the North with the Woodlawn Organization (TWO), born in January 1961. The organization was funded primarily by the Catholic church, the Presbyterian church, and the Schwarzhaupt Foundation and was led by IAF organizers Nick Von Hoffman and Bob Squires. After an inspiring community reaction to a visit from a group of Freedom Riders working to integrate southern cities, Von Hoffman organized a massive African-American voter registration drive in the Woodlawn community. A caravan of 46 buses, with over 2,500 black passengers traveled to city hall to register voters and made TWO a serious player in city politics for several decades to follow.

The FIGHT's civil rights battle in Rochester, New York, is one of Alinsky's most well-documented campaigns. After a summer of race riots in 1964, the Rochester Council of Churches raised enough money to bring Alinsky to Rochester. Before he even arrived, Alinsky's critics denounced him as an outside agitator and argued against bringing the IAF to New York. This reaction was pleasing to Alinsky, since it created controversy for his new organization in Rochester without having to do any work. Alinsky named Edward Chambers lead organizer of the new broad-based community group whose main concern was the lack of jobs available to the African-American population in Rochester. Alinsky, Chambers, and the new organization, which called itself FIGHT, set their sights on Eastman Kodak, the largest employer in Rochester at the time. The FIGHT demanded that Kodak meet its social and community responsibilities by sponsoring a job-training program for unemployed community residents. After applying pressure in the form of mass community rallies, a Kodak negotiator initially signed an agreement with FIGHT to help develop job opportunities. However Kodak executives soon backed out of the agreement, and Alinsky and Chambers developed an innovative approach to get Kodak's attention. Using stock proxies and purchasing Kodak stock, FIGHT leaders were able to attend a Kodak shareholders' meeting to demand that the company honor the agreement it signed. While this tactic was not immediately successful, it put a significant amount pressure on the corporation, and it eventually gave into FIGHT's demands.

Leadership Transition

Alinsky died suddenly at the age of 63 in June of 1972. After working with Alinsky for 16 years, Edward Chambers took the helm of the IAF. A few years prior to Alinsky's death, Alinsky, Chambers, and fellow organizer Dick Harmon had created a training institute to teach future organizers the skills Alinsky had been developing in communities around the country and to institutionalize the organizing profession. While Alinsky traveled from one college campus to another speaking to young activists in the late 1960s, Harmon and Chambers focused on developing the institute, designed to train both poor and working-class organizers from across the country with the goal that they would return to their communities armed with the skills necessary to revitalize democracy.

With the shift in leadership from Alinsky to Chambers came an institutionalization of many of the things Alinsky had done more casually. While Alinsky had trained organizers on the ground during campaigns, Chambers and other IAF leaders developed the training institute to teach potential organizers in larger numbers about the skills Alinsky had taught on the street. While Alinsky had required an invitation to a community from local leaders, Chambers developed a system in which a local organization interested in organizing its community and the IAF would sign a letter of agreement, stating the terms of the relationship. Beginning with the Back of the Yards Council, the IAF always desired to form strong organizations that could eventually function effectively without the IAF's assistance. Alinsky often admitted that his passion was in the birth of an organization and the controversy surrounding it. Chambers' IAF differs from Alinsky's in that it maintains a closer relationship with its local affiliates over time. Finally the process by which the IAF joins forces with local community groups has become more deliberate than it was under Alinsky. After determining that a significant amount of racial, ethnic, and religious diversity exists in a community and that community members are not focused on just one issue, the IAF begins to guide local leaders through the process of building an organization. Sponsoring committees form in the community to assess the level of interest and financial support available, and key leaders begin to attend IAF training sessions.

Modern IAF

Under the direction of Chambers, the modern IAF, a nonpartisan and not-for-profit organization, has refined Alinsky's vision and created a complex network of broad-based organizations across the United States. These organizations, located in New York, Maryland, Texas, California, and Illinois, among other places, bring institutions that are central to public life, such as churches, synagogues, unions, and neighborhood associations, together in local communities. The IAF organizers seek to revive democracy in these communities, so that the act of voting is not the only aspect of public life for community members. Institutional members, including religious institutions, as well as other community groups and associations, contribute annual dues to the local IAF affiliate to finance the

operation. The organizations' specific goals reflect the community's agenda and priorities and are developed through a series of individual and group meetings IAF organizers have with community leaders. Although each affiliate is led by a professional organizer employed by the IAF, developing local leaders is a central element in the IAF philosophy. Alinsky's creation of the broad-based citizens' organization that used leaders in pre-existing institutions demonstrated the importance of fostering grassroots leadership to create an organization that can survive long-term.

While each IAF organization develops its own agenda dependent on community members' priorities, the process by which that agenda is brought to life is consistent across IAF organizations. Each organization holds actions in which local political leaders and other targets are held publicly accountable for their actions. Following each action, professional organizers and local leaders gather together to evaluate their work. This required evaluation process allows the organization to reflect on the extent to which it has reached its goals, to assess its targets' reactions, and to plan subsequent action.

One example of a successful modern IAF organization is the Community Organized in Public Service (COPS), founded in 1973 in San Antonio, Texas. In 1990, there were 26 member churches in COPS, representing 50,000 families. Led by IAF regional supervisor, Ernesto Cortes, Jr., COPS has been victorious on issues ranging from education to city infrastructure. Departing from Alinsky's philosophy of leaving an organization to survive on its own, the modern IAF has maintained close relationships with its affiliates, evidenced by COPS's fifteenth anniversary in 1988. Another major victory for the modern IAF began in East Brooklyn, New York, with the Nehemiah Homes movement. In this devastated part of the city, IAF affiliate East Brooklyn Congregations (EBC) built 2,100 single-family houses that low-income families could afford. This program was replicated in other parts of New York, Baltimore, and California, and it was the model program for the National Housing Opportunity Act of 1988.

Since Alinsky founded the IAF in 1940, the organization has created over 60 independent organizations across the United States and has assisted in creating similar organizations in the United Kingdom, Germany, and South Africa. Although the daily activities of IAF affiliates are coordinated by local leaders and regional organizers, 10-day national training sessions and regular network meetings ensure philosophical continuity across the various IAF organizations. Unlike the days of Alinsky's IAF, the modern IAF now maintains close, continued relationships with the organizations it helps create. While the pedagogical and philosophical foundation of the modern IAF is very much rooted in Alinsky's vision of broad-based organizing, the organization's relationship with its affiliates, professional organizers, and local leaders has become more institutionalized, allowing it to grow into a sophisticated network of organizations.

KRISTIN GERATY

References and Further Reading

Betten, Neil, and Michael J. Austin. *The Roots of Community Organizing: 1917–1939.* Philadelphia: Temple University Press, 1990.

Chambers, Edward T. *Roots for Radicals: Organizing for Power, Action, and Justice.* New York: Continuum International Publishing Group, 2004.

Horwitt, Sanford D. *Let Them Call Me Rebel: Saul Alinsky– His Life and Legacy.* New York: Alfred A Knopf, 1989.

Industrial Areas Foundation. "IAF 50 Years: Organizing for Change." San Francisco: Sapir Press, 1990.

Sanders, Marion K. *The Professional Radical: Conversations with Saul Alinsky.* New York: Harper and Row Publisher, 1970.

ALLIANCE FOR LABOR ACTION

The Alliance for Labor Action (ALA) was founded in June of 1969, by the United Auto Workers (UAW) and the Teamsters at the prompting of Walter Reuther, then head of the UAW. By the late 1960s, the union leadership was in crisis about how to address the political situation of the day. Four main issues divided the traditional leadership, epitomized by George Meaney, head of the American Federation of Labor (AFL)-Congress of Industrial Organizations (CIO), and a dissident minority that wanted to revitalize the unions by seeking new allies within the social movements of the day at the expense of the old allies within the Democratic party. These issues were the war in Vietnam, the nature of the relationship between labor and the Democratic party, the problem of organizing the unorganized, and the internal structure of governance within the AFL-CIO.

In the late 1960s, the AFL-CIO was seen by many of those involved in the antiwar movement and the black movement as a part of the establishment that maintained the status quo. The AFL-CIO had defended the war and spent millions of dollars promoting anti-Communist unions in Vietnam. The AFL-CIO opposed reform in the Democratic party during and after the 1968 convention, and while many union leaders had supported civil rights, they were slow to promote many black workers into the union leadership and demanded moderation from black leaders. Many within the labor movement also accused Meaney and those around him of running the AFL-CIO in a dictatorial fashion. Reuther, who had traditionally represented labor liberalism, wanted to change this image by reinvigorating the unions.

In 1968, Reuther demanded that Meaney call a special convention where the UAW could present its plan for revitalizing the labor movement. When Meaney refused, Reuther pulled the UAW out of the AFL-CIO and brought the Teamsters with him. Reuther wanted to organize the unorganized, who were being ignored by the old union federation, especially in the South and in the communications industries. The ALA was formed as an alternative to the AFL-CIO that would devote more energy and resources to recruiting new members and that would take more progressive stances on the issues of the day. To this end the ALA focused on Atlanta and sent many experienced organizers into that city. It spent millions of dollars on an advertising campaign in the local Atlanta media praising the benefits of union membership. These advertisements successfully branded the ALA. According to one poll, 43% of Atlanta residents knew the name. After 2 years however, the ALA had convinced only 4,590 people to vote to join the ALA unions. The ALA had spent $1,200 per potential recruit.

The ALA failed to tap into the political energy of young people, African-Americans, or the women's movement. It used corporate methods of advertising and organizing that reinforced popular perceptions of the unions as part of the establishment. Also the northern organizers sent to Atlanta had few ties with the local community and were unable to build them. While it spent more money on organizing than the AFL-CIO, it used the same methods then current within the labor movement.

The ALA also took a stronger stand against the Vietnam War than the AFL-CIO. While Meaney and the AFL-CIO publicly stood for a negotiated peace, the ALA called for the immediate withdrawal of U.S. troops. However it devoted few resources to the anti-Vietnam movement.

In 1970, Reuther died in a plane crash. Without this motivating force and with few results to show for its efforts, the ALA was dissolved in 1972.

SAMUEL MITRANI

References and Further Reading

Foner, Phillip. *U.S. Labor and the Vietnam War.* New York: International Publishers, 1986.

Lichtenstein, Nelson. *Walter Reuther, the Most Dangerous Man in Detroit.* Champaign: University of Illinois Press, 1997.

Tait, Vanessa. *Poor Workers' Unions, Rebuilding Labor from Below*. Boston: South End Press, 2005.

See also **American Federation of Labor-Congress of Industrial Organizations; Reuther, Walter; United Automobile Workers**

AMALGAMATED ASSOCIATION OF IRON AND STEEL WORKERS

The Amalgamated Association of Iron and Steel Workers was the only important trade union in the U.S. iron and steel industries between its founding in 1876 and 1937. As the word amalgamated implies, the union was formed by the merger of four separate craft unions: the United Sons of Vulcan; the Associated Brotherhood of Iron and Steel Heaters, Rollers, and Roughers; the Iron and Steel Roll Hands' Union; and the United Nailers. While the iron puddlers from the Sons of Vulcan who made up most of its membership had been able to exercise extraordinary control over the production process during previous decades, an 1874–1875 Pittsburgh lockout, as well as the gradual changeover from iron to Bessemer steel production, signaled to workers that they had reason to fear for the future. Therefore despite the reputed power of the Amalgamated, the creation of the union was really a defensive measure.

The Amalgamated Association was always concerned with preserving the wage scale of its highly skilled core constituency. Therefore it negotiated uniform wage scales with employers each year. As wages in iron mills were generally paid as piece rates, the union had ultimate control over output. For the same reason, the union generally opposed the 8-hour day for iron workers, since this stood to decrease their compensation. This is a reflection of how skilled workers totally dominated the organization.

Two iron workers straddle steel girders on top of the Empire State Building as it nears completion. Library of Congress, Prints & Photographs Division, NYWT &S Collection [LC-USZ62-120926].

In order to judge the Amalgamated Association's strength, it is important to differentiate between two sectors of the industry. The power of the Amalgamated Association was overwhelmingly concentrated in the iron-producing sector of the industry, which became increasingly irrelevant as the size of the steel sector grew ever larger starting in the 1870s. The reason the Amalgamated Association was stronger in the older sector had to do with the difference between iron- and steel-producing technology. Bessemer steel production did not require puddling, a difficult process essential to iron making that took years of training to master. Yet an immigrant, nonunion, common laborer could become a skilled steelworker in as little as a few weeks. Despite this situation the union did not object to employers introducing new technology into their mills. In fact the Amalgamated had so little power over steel making that one might argue that it had no choice.

Because the Amalgamated Association had always concentrated its organizing efforts on highly skilled workers, less-skilled workers tended to view the union with contempt. Indeed the group's constitution did not even make common laborers eligible for membership. Therefore, the industry's increased need for less-skilled labor damaged the long-term viability of the organization. The Amalgamated Association was never able to organize even half the steel workers in the Pittsburgh district.

Because of the changing situation in the industry, the Amalgamated Association suffered a long series of setbacks at mills across the country beginning in the late-1880s. However unlike most of the strikes the union had lost in the past, the Amalgamated lost these mills permanently. In 1891, the Amalgamated Association lost strikes at iron and steel mills across Pennsylvania and neighboring states. In 1892, the conflict spread further. Virtually every firm in both the iron and steel sectors of the industry found the Amalgamated Association scale unacceptable that year. Most companies that had previously signed the scale refused that year. In fact manufacturers from every sector of the industry and every region of the country began proposing deep wage cuts even before the union first proposed its wage scale. In the struggle that followed, steel makers across the country managed to banish the Amalgamated permanently from their facilities.

But most of the attention of the public focused on the fight at Andrew Carnegie's mill in Homestead, Pennsylvania. Carnegie Steel had fought the union there in 1889 and eventually agreed to a 3-year contract instead of the 1-year scale that most firms signed. This is a sign of Carnegie's preference to work with the union at that time. But by 1892, the market for the steel that Carnegie made had turned sour, and therefore Carnegie's attitude toward the Amalgamated changed drastically. While many observers have blamed Carnegie for destroying the Amalgamated Association, in truth it had terrible difficulties long before the infamous Homestead lockout occurred. In fact very few workers at the Homestead Works were Amalgamated members when the lockout began. It is better to think of Carnegie Steel as drastically accelerating the union's decline rather than initiating the process.

The damage that the Amalgamated suffered before Homestead is largely hidden by the growth of another steel-making sector. The McKinley Tariff of 1892 jumpstarted the U.S. tin plate industry, which was used primarily for roof shingles and cans. Starting in 1892, a flood of pro-union Welsh workers into the new industry masked the failure of the union to ever capture a significant portion of the steel industry's workforce. This is reflected in the union's decision to change its name to the Amalgamated Association of Iron, Steel, and Tin Workers in 1897.

After Homestead the Amalgamated Association retained a presence in those sectors of the industry that still required skilled workers. When United States Steel formed in 1901, the union hoped to take advantage of what it perceived to be a vulnerable position by striking. It lost, and since they struck in mills that had already signed contracts, the walkout also damaged the union's public reputation. In 1909, a lockout removed the Amalgamated Association from the last of U.S. Steel's plants. For the next few decades, the union existed only in a few specialty steel plants in the Midwest. When unorganized steel workers instigated the largest strike in the industry's history at that time in 1919, Amalgamated Association President Michael Tighe (nicknamed "grandmother" because of his conservatism) pulled his skilled constituents off the picket line just a month-and-a-half into the conflict in order to preserve the remaining power base of his now-inconsequential organization. By doing so he doomed the Great Steel Strike to failure.

In 1933, the largest union in the industry was still the Amalgamated Association. By this point this long-dormant organization was hardly even a shadow of its former self. Amalgamated membership dropped from 31,500 in 1920 to approximately 4,700 in mid-1933. Nearly all of these union members were highly skilled employees working in sheet mills or at wrought iron furnaces. Even though congressional debates over Section 7(a) of the National Industrial Recovery Act (NIRA) and the Iron and Steel Code set up under the same legislation had received an enormous amount of media attention, the Amalgamated Association had not planned to conduct an organizing campaign.

For this reason the initiative for an organizing campaign after the passage of the NIRA came from American Federation of Labor President William Green. Eventually the Amalgamated leadership relented to Green's cajoling. The union sent 106 organizers into the field during that summer of 1933. Most of them had few qualifications for the job. Many were retired Amalgamated members who used outdated organizing techniques from decades past or friends of the central union office who went into the field without training. From September 1933 to May 1934, the union reduced its organizing staff from 106 to 15. Potential recruits were essentially left to organize themselves.

And they did by the thousands. These new union members gave the old Amalgamated leadership lots of trouble. In February 1935, President Tighe felt compelled to revoke the charters of 13 lodges that supported the use of more militant organizing tactics. Together all the expelled lodges represented approximately 75% of the union's membership. Although the leadership re-admitted some locals in an October 1935 settlement, by then the Amalgamated Association's earlier membership gains had almost completely disappeared. Only 5,300 of the 100,000–150,000 recruits who had signed cards during the previous 2 years remained union members. Furthermore new organizing had completely ceased. The Amalgamated gained only four new lodges during the entire 1935 calendar year. When the Amalgamated ceded control of its own organizing to the Committee of Industrial Organizations' Steel Workers Organizing Committee, a new, more-successful union would be born.

JONATHAN REES

References and Further Reading

Brody, David. *Steelworkers in America: The Nonunion Era.* Urbana: University of Illinois Press, 1998. [Originally published in 1960]

Fitch, John A. *The Steel Workers.* Pittsburgh: Pittsburgh University Press, 1989. [Originally published in 1911.]

Rees, Jonathan. *Managing the Mills: Labor Policy in the American Steel Industry during the Nonunion Era.* Lanham, MD: University Press of America, 2004.

AMALGAMATED ASSOCIATION OF STREET RAILWAY EMPLOYEES/ AMERICAN ASSOCIATION OF STREET AND ELECTRICAL RAILWAY EMPLOYEES

Urban mass transportation seemed like the poor stepchild to the nation's burgeoning railroad system when in the 1830s lumbering omnibuses and primitive railed horse cars appeared on the streets of New York City together. These slow, fledgling carriers patiently awaited the arrival of electric technology almost 50 years later that ignited the speed of a trolley system that crisscrossed the nation's cities and outstripped train service in frequency and capacity.

Despite the romance of horse cars as both machine and garden in a congested urban setting, transit workers—drivers and conductors—experienced a host of problems that would bedevil them even more with the widespread introduction of electric propulsion in the last decade of the nineteenth century. Shifts that stretched from sun-up to sun-down, overcrowded vehicles, truncated schedules, and a host of other irritants precipitated strikes as early as the 1860s and led to organizing drives in the 1880s by the Knights of Labor, especially in large, impersonal urban settings.

When the Knights' empire faltered in the late 1880s, Samuel Gompers, the first president of the American Federation of Labor (AFL), issued a call for the formation of a national union of horse car and trolley workers. Fifty representatives of varied transit employees' interests answered the proclamation in 1892 in Indianapolis and formed the Amalgamated just as horse cars gave way to electrification and rationalization of service. Within a year the incipient organization faced the financial problems of the depression of 1893 but secured the services of William D. Mahon, who started his career with the reins of a horse car in Columbus, Ohio, before taking the reins of the new labor group. He led the union for 52 years until 1946 and like Gompers and the AFL, imprinted his personality on the infant organization.

Under Mahon, who was a close friend of Gompers as well as socialist Eugene V. Debs, the Amalgamated paralleled the practices of the Federation by stressing centralized organizing, health and safety, vocational skills, high wages, and a concomitant dues structure. On the other hand, the Amalgamated often skirted AFL guidelines by placing all members—skilled and unskilled—into the same union rather than fragmenting them into individual craft unions, especially in smaller operations. Mahon was a practical socialist like his colleague Debs.

However the Amalgamated instituted a scorched earth policy against hostile employers. The union harnessed the seething anger of ordinary citizens against the trolley enterprises, central targets of society's wrath as the excesses of the Gilded Age provoked the activism of the Progressive Era. Trolley workers, the public face of transit operations, centered around the conductor, who continued to collect fares as in horse car days. Horse drivers morphed into motormen in the technological shakeup. These employees, who

Baltimore, Maryland. Trolley car conductor. Library of Congress, Prints & Photographs Division, FSA/OWI Collection [LC-USW3-022047-E].

long haul, mechanization proved cheaper than expensive and vulnerable horses.

In this framework the Amalgamated organized disgruntled employees at a rapid pace, often in a violent manner. The union participated in 200 strikes during its first quarter of a century. Mahon cagily massaged the Progressive Era mentality by always offering to arbitrate any questions about collective bargaining, knowing full well any such tender would be refused outside of a few enlightened transit managers. The Amalgamated initiated walkouts that paralyzed mass transportation and hindered the employment of strikebreakers with inspired riots by irate passengers, who now stood on the street with the motormen and conductors, united against out-of-state corporations. Deaths and injuries in these battles, which eventually seemed to grip most cities in the United States sooner or later, totaled almost as many casualties as strikes in the country's coal-mining regions. Well-heeled companies at least initially combated the union in close cooperation with local militia, police, and judges—all of them usually under Republican control. Win or lose, the Amalgamated always seemed to return for another confrontation, since conditions seldom improved for employees without union recognition.

By 1919, the Amalgamated represented 300 properties. It unionized so thoroughly that it issued only 40 charters for the whole decade of the 1920s due to a lack of unorganized transit establishments. Mahon, re-elected president until his retirement in 1946, remained a progressive if crusty commander.

The Amalgamated endured as a major union on the U.S. scene until the demise of the streetcar and the trackless trolley after World War II. However as early as the 1920s and the proliferation of automobile ownership, many transit properties sought savings by replacing two-man crews with a single employee who collected fares and operated the vehicle at the same time. The widespread introduction of buses in the same period only facilitated the one-man operation. World War II, replete with automobile gas rationing on the home front, rejuvenated mass transportation at least for the duration of the conflict.

By the 1950s, many transit systems failed economically. Some state and local governments underwrote operations until the passage of the federal Urban Mass Transportation Act in 1964 that provided financial assistance for the transit infrastructure. The Amalgamated became adept at lobbying Congress and helped secure funding for bus, subway, and a few remaining railed operations.

Demographic changes in the United States favored automobile travel in the second half of the twentieth century, and mass transit lost most of its working and

toiled together as a team, often lived on the same line they operated for decades, building a social network of daily solidarity with passengers almost unique in the world of work at the time. Courtesies between car men and riders cemented lifetime friendships that provided a phalanx of active supporters during trolley strikes, colloquially known as car wars, that punctuated the period from the union's formation in 1892 through World War I.

The widespread electrification of mass transportation in the 1890s set the stage for militant unionization. The alacrity of the new motor power that flowed from ubiquitous, overhead power lines through trolley poles that charged streetcar motors provided the fastest local service ever seen in urban corridors and eventually in rural areas as well. Horse car operations merged into single electric operations whose speed and convenience drew the public in unprecedented numbers with expanding schedules and longer destinations.

Vehicles soon rivaled steam cars in size, capacity, and in some suburban areas, speed as well. Ironically for the motormen at least operating an electric trolley took less dexterity than managing a team of horses; on the other hand, the conductors had to collect fares from more passengers than ever. Accidents increased dramatically as did the injured and dead, both among passengers and crews. Management also cut wages in order to pay for the capitalization of the expensive new system that required steel rails, miles of electric wire, and sophisticated trolleys. However over the middle-class riders. The Amalgamated still retained its representation on most properties, while the membership of the union included significantly more minorities and women.

SCOTT MOLLOY

References and Further Reading

Harring, Sidney L. "Car Wars: Strikes, Arbitration, and Class Struggle in the Making of Labor Law." *Review of Law and Social Changes* 14 (1986): 849–872.
Molloy, Scott. *Trolley Wars: Streetcar Workers on the Line*. Washington, DC: Smithsonian Press, 1996.
N.A. A History of the Amalgamated Transit Union. Washington, DC: Amalgamated Transit Union, 1992.

See also **American Federation of Labor; Debs, Eugene V.; Gompers, Samuel**

AMALGAMATED CLOTHING WORKERS OF AMERICA

Officially founded in 1914, the origins of the Amalgamated Clothing Workers of America (ACWA) date back to the 1910 Chicago Men's Garment Workers Strike when on September 22, 1910, a small group of female workers led by Bessie Abramowitz walked off their hand-sewing jobs at Hart, Schaffner, and Marx (HSM) Shop Number 5 to protest the last in a series of arbitrary wage cuts. Chicago manufacturers produced more men's garments than any other city in the country and HSM was the largest firm in the city. Although known for its modernized management techniques, the factory's employees were not immune from the exploitive practices of meager wages and lengthy hours that plagued the industry. Workers in other shops where conditions were even worse soon joined these young, mostly immigrant women.

Within 3 weeks the more skilled male workers, including apprentice cutter and future union president, Sidney Hillman, packed their tools and left their jobs to join the strikers. By the beginning of October, strike ranks swelled to almost 40,000, virtually shutting down the production of men's clothes. Jane Addams, Hull-House founder, and Margaret Dreier Robins, Women's Trade Union League (WTUL) president, were among the first community members to come to the aid of the strikers. They offered organizing assistance and financial aid as well as meeting space for the strike leaders. The only union in the industry, the United Garment Workers (UGW), had no interest in organizing the mostly unskilled immigrant workers. Despite the fact that the unionized male cutters were involved in the strike, union leaders initially refused to help the strikers.

Sidney Hillman, former President [of] Amalgamated Clothing Workers of America, C.I.O. Library of Congress, Prints & Photographs Division [LC-USZ62-127378].

Dragging on over 5 months, the strike turned violent as Chicago police on horseback smashed picket lines. Hundreds of strikers were injured, and two were killed. The strikers' plight provoked public sympathy and enlisted the support of a number of prominent Chicago citizens, including John Fitzpatrick, Chicago Federation of Labor president. A Citizen's Committee comprised of civic and business leaders made a number of unsuccessful attempts to settle the strike. In early November Thomas Rickert, UGW president, betrayed the strikers by secretly negotiating an agreement that provided for arbitration of grievances without union recognition.

Finally in January 1911, HSM employees represented by labor lawyer Clarence Darrow and the company owners agreed to settle the conflict. The agreement permitted unionization and guaranteed that an arbitration board would be established to mediate worker grievances at HSM. The tens of thousands of workers in the other shops went back to work the following month with no concessions or lost their jobs altogether. Yet despite the partial victory for the workers, the strike had several important consequences that laid the groundwork for future unionization. In addition to the establishment of an arbitration system that soon became the national model for collective bargaining in the men's garment industry, the cross-class alliances generated by the cooperation of progressive Chicago marked the beginning of influential relationships that endured for at least half a century. More importantly the core group of strikers that emerged as leaders, such as Abramowitz, Hillman, Frank Rosenblum, A. D. Marimpietri, and Sam Levin, proved that they could unite multiple ethnic groups in the fight for industrial democracy. Hillman served as a worker representative on the arbitration board and along with Abramowitz and WTUL member Mary Anderson, he helped to organize workers into the reconfigured Chicago Local 39.

In October 1914, at the UGW convention in Nashville, Tennessee, the clothing worker delegations with the exception of those from Chicago were denied seats. Angered by this treatment, the clothing worker delegates began to leave the convention hall to reconvene a few blocks away to decide their course of action. The Chicago delegation stayed behind to make a case for the clothing workers, but when convention leaders declined to address their pleas, they too left for the Duncan Hotel. They wired Hillman, who at the time was working as an arbitration representative for the International Ladies' Garment Workers' Union, to inform him of their actions and to encourage him to step in to lead them. When this group of so-called militants met in late December in New York, they renounced all connections to the UGW and adopted an entirely new name for their organization—the Amalgamated Clothing Workers of America (ACWA). They united with the Tailors' Industrial Union, adopting a constitution calling for an industrial union that entitled all workers in the men's garment industry to membership regardless of their trade. The 134 delegates representing more than 40,000 clothing workers in 68 local unions decided to start an organizational campaign among female workers, who comprised roughly 60% of the workers in the men's garment industry. The convention also adopted resolutions for the 8-hour workday and division of work in slack seasons. The new union reinstated many of the insurgent leaders from the Nashville convention as its officers, and Hillman was elected as the first president.

During the 32 years Hillman spent at the ACWA's helm, the union surpassed all competition to become the largest organization of men's clothing workers in the country, and Hillman would become one of the most powerful labor leaders of the twentieth century. His vision for industrial democracy for the rank and file included "new unionism," where workers and management would work together to achieve greater efficiency and autonomy in the workplace. Collective bargaining practices became a vital part of the new

unionism in the men's garment industry. Hillman was not averse to politicizing the labor movement. He advocated for full citizenship rights for workers so that they could become active in their communities and enjoy a satisfying standard of living. Education and the right to vote were primary concerns for the rank and file, which in the beginning consisted of a large number of immigrant workers. Amalgamated leaders realized that worker education was crucial to establishing a broad base of loyal and community-minded unionists. The ACWA promoted education by offering classes in English, labor history, and trade union organizing by 1916. It established its own education department in 1921 and funded a national director. Union leaders encouraged workers to attend labor schools like the Brookwood Labor Institute and the Bryn Mawr Summer School for Women Workers. Yet in spite of its initial popularity, by the mid-1920s labor education lost some of its appeal for the increasingly native-born rank and file. The national director of education, J. B. S. Hardman, believed that workers learned from experience, and not from books. A hard-line socialist, he supported education that could be used for political purposes.

A series of intense campaigns to organize the nation's leading clothing centers punctuated the early years of the union's existence. The largest organizational drive took place in Chicago where unorganized shops remained notorious for sweatshop conditions and employer resistance. After several unsuccessful attempts to meet with employers, Hillman called a strike in September 1915. After 25,000 employees held out against police brutality, the UGW, the city administration, and individual employers began to capitulate. Even without a general agreement or modifications in the number of hours employees were allowed to work, Hillman considered the open-shop practices in the over 90 firms now operating under union contracts a victory. The Amalgamated gained the support of the workers and solidified the commitment of many involved in the city's reform circle, including lawyer Harold Ickes and his wife; George Mead, University of Chicago professor; Carl Sandburg, then a young reporter covering the strike; and Ellen Gates Starr from Hull-House. On May 3, 1916, Hillman married Abramowitz, by then a business agent for Local 152 and a member of the ACWA's General Executive Board. After their marriage the Hillmans relocated to New York to be closer to union headquarters. Bessie Hillman remained active in the union throughout her life.

By 1917, the union reached across the Canadian border, organizing workers in Montreal. Rochester, New York, one of the leading centers for the production of high-quality men's garments was organized in 1919. Rapid progress eluded the union in Baltimore, but by 1920 the majority of the city's major firms fell under the union banner. New York presented another challenging situation: From 1920–1921, the New York City Manufacturers' Association tried to break the union by locking workers out of plants. Hillman relied on the skills of his centralized organization to deliver relief supplies and inform the locals on strike by calling mass meetings of workers. After 6 months Amalgamated leaders won a settlement. World War I provided a short-lived boost for union workers in military union factories awarded government contracts. By 1920, Amalgamated membership was at an all time high. The union claimed 177,000 members who enjoyed higher wages, a shorter workweek, and the benefits of the arbitration system. With a stable foundation the union began to implement such social benefits for its members as unemployment insurance for Chicago members and a cooperative bank and housing in New York.

Yet when the economy began to spiral downward in the late 1920s, membership also began to plummet. Racketeers demanding protection money from ACWA affiliates like the Cutters' Union and leftists vying for power in other locals exacerbated an already dire situation. Hillman acted quickly to expel both the criminal elements and the Communists from the union. For the most part, Hillman's efforts to oust undesirables from the union were successful. Acting on a policy of constructive cooperation, the ACWA lent money to financially strapped factories in an effort to keep jobs available to workers. The union created employment exchanges to match unemployed workers to jobs. Union leaders reorganized the union's structure so that one regional joint board dealt with all locals in that region. The joint boards reported directly to national ACWA headquarters. Despite the measures taken to solidify its foundation, by 1929 the ACWA had lost over 65,000 members. An anxious Hillman realized that the situation was beyond his control. To counter the divisive effects of the Depression, Hillman brought his union into the American Federation of Labor.

Like countless other Depression Era Americans, by 1933 Hillman turned to the government and to Franklin Delano Roosevelt, in particular, to remedy the economic catastrophe. Immediately after the passage of the National Industrial Recovery Act on June 15, 1933, Hillman committed the ACWA to organizing. The Amalgamated concentrated most of its resources in the drive to organize the shirt workers. In the 1920s and early 1930s, many of the manufacturers attempted to avoid union jurisdiction by closing their shops and leaving New York and other organized metropolitan areas. These "runaway shops" were re-established in small towns throughout Connecticut, New Jersey, Upstate New York, and Pennsylvania. Rather than put workers out of work by forcing these shops to close, from 1933–1934, the ACWA exerted a massive effort to organize these workers. The majority of factory owners refused to allow their employees voluntarily to join the union, and as a result strikes erupted across the runaway regions. Many individuals came to the aid of the striking workers to lend support, including Cornelia Bryce Pinchot, wife of the governor of Pennsylvania, who garnered much publicity for her efforts in Northhampton, Pennsylvania's Baby Strike, where so many of the strikers appeared to be child workers. In the mining towns where many of the owners relocated purposely so that they could offer jobs to the wives and children of miners, the United Mine Workers aided the strike leaders by helping to man the picket lines. Where the runaway outposts offered the most resistance, the shirt worker campaign continued until the end of the decade.

Both the newly organized shirt workers and the New York laundry workers campaign from 1937–1939 added thousands of new members to the ACWA's roster. In 1939 the union boasted almost 260,000 members. Old world ties were still visible as the depression began to lift. Southern and Eastern Europeans predominated in the organization. By the late 1930s Jewish unionists, who along with the Italian membership filled the majority of leadership positions, taken together accounted for approximately 75% of the union's membership (Italians 40% and Jews 35%). Fifteen percent of the members were Poles, 5% Lithuanians, and 10% fell into the other category, which included native-born workers.

The Laundry Workers campaign also marked the first time that union leaders actively recruited black workers into the ACWA. Largely as a result of their work bringing black workers into the laundry workers ranks, the ACWA began to advocate for civil rights. Education programs were revived in an effort to educate these new members—shirt workers and laundry workers–about the benefits of union membership. A national education department was re-established with a special branch dedicated to laundry worker education. Classes on current events, economics, and labor issues became part of the standard curriculum, and teachers who volunteered their services taught classes or were employees of the Works Progress Administration. Amalgamated members also attended Hudson Shore Labor School, one of the first of its kind to admit black students.

Hillman became a major figure in New Deal politics and a key advisor to Roosevelt. Hillman became a member of FDR's Labor Advisory Board of the National Recovery Administration in 1933 and a member of the Industrial Advisory Board in 1934. He helped influence the passage of the National Labor Relations Act that guaranteed workers' right to organize and established collective bargaining as the mechanism for industrial disputes. He championed labor's cause by establishing codes in the clothing industry guaranteeing minimum wages and lobbying for the Fair Labor Standards Act penned by Frances Perkins, Secretary of Labor, which granted minimum wages, maximum hour regulations, and limited child labor on its passage in 1938. Through his involvement in government agencies, he brought the ACWA into political affairs first by helping to establish Labor's Non-Partisan League in the mid-1930s to join labor's diverse interests under one banner with the potential of creating an independent party geared toward labor interests in the future. By the mid-1940s, Hillman created a Political Action Committee so that labor could raise funds and votes to secure Roosevelt's election to a fourth term.

In 1935, Hillman along with John L. Lewis of the United Mine Workers founded the Congress of Industrial Organizations (CIO)—a national umbrella for all industrial unions. Two years later, the CIO headed by Lewis established the Textile Workers' Organizing Committee, which by 1939 evolved into the Textile Workers' Union of America (TWUA). With the U.S. participation in World War II imminent, Hillman reached the apex of his personal power. In December of 1940, Roosevelt appointed him associate director of the Office of Production Management. Hillman moved his staff to Washington and traveled home on the weekends. In the meantime the ACWA converted its Department of Cultural Activities into the Office of War Activities. Bessie Hillman stayed behind at New York headquarters to serve as the director of the new department. She helped to coordinate volunteer efforts designed to aid U.S. forces. She also coordinated a massive Russian food drive. When the War Manpower Commission replaced the Office of Production Management in 1942, Hillman did not receive an appointment. Physically exhausted and emotionally overwhelmed, he suffered his third heart attack shortly afterward.

Roosevelt may have failed to offer Hillman an official position in his last administration, but Hillman remained a trusted confidant and advisor for the remainder of FDR's tenure. By mid-1943, in an effort to maintain labor's voice in politics and to ensure the election of Roosevelt to an unprecedented fourth term, Hillman, under the auspices of the CIO created a Political Action Committee (PAC). Hillman's political activism came under scrutiny when the Republicans attempted to discredit FDR's candidacy by fostering a *New York Times* article that reported when Democratic party leaders asked for an endorsement of the 1944 vice-presidential candidate, FDR supposedly replied, "Clear it with Sidney."

Nevertheless as the war continued, the union gained strength and benefited from government contracts in military uniform and parachute production. A year after the war ended, 59-year-old Hillman suffered a fatal heart attack at his Point Lookout residence on Long Island. Survivors included his wife, who was elected to the General Executive Board in 1946, and his two daughters, Philoine and Selma. At the conclusion of his impressive career, the Amalgamated numbered 350,000 workers—all of whom benefited from the passage of legislation that protected their rights as workers and improved their overall standard of living. During the war years an increasing number of African-Americans, Mexicans, Puerto Ricans, and southern white women became ACWA members. Female workers continued to outnumber men in the Amalgamated. Hillman's legacy lived on with the establishment of the Sidney Hillman Foundation, which provides grants for excellence in media and publishing. In 1951, the first of many union health centers named for him was opened in New York City.

In the wake of Hillman's death, Jacob Potofsky became president of the ACWA. Potofsky had been a loyal follower of Hillman and an intimate family friend. A young boy at the time of the Chicago strikes, Potofsky had served as an organizer and vice president of the union for decades. In the aftermath of the war, Potofsky along with the leaders of the nation's other labor organizations grappled with anti-union sentiment. The Taft-Hartley Act passed in 1947 negated many of the Depression Era gains, making organization of workers more difficult. Uncomfortable with assuming a defensive posture, the CIO launched Operation Dixie, an extensive drive to organize southern workers. The CIO leaders believed that organizing the South's largest industrial sector, cotton textile production, was the key to organizing the entire region. Both the ACWA and TWUA participated, lending funds and organizers to the effort. The ACWA and the TWUA were the only CIO unions to send female organizers into the field. Although over two million dollars was spent and over two hundred organizers participated, the labor movement failed to organize more than 15% of southern textile workers. Racist attitudes on the part of both owners and workers and accusations of Communist sympathy that lay submerged in the labor movement extinguished the fires of unionization by 1953.

In 1952, the ACWA signed the first master contract in the industry. The contract covered all the workers in the manufacture of men's clothing. The union continued its emphasis on economic and social benefits for its members. Health centers and union banks sprang up across the country. Lobbying endeavors paid off in 1956 when an amendment to the Fair Labor Standards Act pushed the federal minimum wage to $1.00. Yet the union was not free from internal dissention.

In the postwar years female members in the Amalgamated began to protest their secondary status in the union. In the mid-1920s, they enjoyed the benefits of a separate Women's Department, but when its director, Dorothy Jacobs Bellanca, stepped down, the department was dissolved. Union women had always comprised more than half of the membership of the Amalgamated. They served as organizers, education directors, and even presidents of locals, but with the exception of Bessie Hillman, women did not have representation at the national level. At a 1961 Industrial Union Conference for female trade union leaders, 72-year-old Amalgamated Vice-President Bessie Hillman departed from her usual collegial demeanor to give a keynote address that took many in attendance by surprise. Speaking from her own experience, she articulated her labor feminist principles. Hillman accused male union leaders of offering women only token positions in their respective organizations or limiting their opportunities for leadership altogether. She encouraged female members to take the initiative to become leaders in their unions and to fight for their rights as workers. Acting on Hillman's cue in 1974 female labor activists established the Coalition of Labor Union Women to continue to seek civil and social rights for women in unions and broader U.S. society. In 1968, the union opened the first labor-sponsored day care center in the United States. Other centers, including one named for Bessie Hillman in the state office complex in Harrisburg, Pennsylvania, followed.

Organizational drives entered unchartered territory during the 1970s. The ACWA organizers traveled to Puerto Rico to organize garment workers there, and when no other union would, the Amalgamated stepped in to organize the production workers at Xerox in Rochester, New York. By 1973, the ACWA claimed a membership of 365,000 in almost 797 local unions. The number of Latino workers continued to increase, as did the number of Asian workers joining the union. In 1974, a 22-month strike at the Farah Manufacturing Company, a renowned El Paso, Texas, manufacturer of men's and boys' pants, culminated with organization. In 1979, the union won a victory at the J. P. Stevens plant in Drakes Branch, Virginia, followed the next year with other Stevens contracts, ending a 17-year struggle depicted in the movie *Norma Rae,* whose leading actress, Sally Field, won an Oscar Award. The J. P. Stevens workers reaped the benefits of victory in more stringent health and safety measures, contract enforcement, and educational programs. Other textile plants, like Fieldcrest Cannon Mills in the old company town of Kannapolis, North Carolina, proved more difficult to organize, with especially resistant employers who avoided unionization until 1999.

In 1976, the union initiated the first in a series of mergers, joining with the TWUA to form the Amalgamated Clothing and Textile Workers' Union (ACTWU). The United Shoe Workers' Union and the Hatters, Cap, and Millinery Workers' International Union affiliated with the ACTWU within a decade after its establishment. By 1993, the union joined forces with the International Ladies' Garment Workers' Union, workers, environmentalists, and consumers in the United States, Canada, and Mexico to achieve international workers' rights and environmental and social standards in all trade agreements. Together the two unions collaborated effort resulted in the first union contracts for workers in the Free Trade Zones of the Dominican Republic. These contracts were aimed at protecting the jobs of North American workers through fair trade policies and improvement of conditions for workers in the Third World. Closer to home the ACTWU initiated sit-ins at National Labor Relations Board offices around the country, demanding fair and democratic labor laws for U.S. workers. In 1994, the union and Levi-Strauss and Company announced a groundbreaking partnership agreement to reorganize the workplace in Levi's North American factories and distribution centers. In 1995, in the largest victory in a National Labor Relations Board election since 1979, 2,300 Tultex workers in Martinsville, Virginia, voted overwhelmingly for the ACTWU.

In 1995, the ACTWU merged with the International Ladies' Garment Workers' Union to establish the Union of Needle Trades, Industrial, and Textile Employees (UNITE). On July 12, 2004, UNITE joined forces with the Hotel Employees and Restaurant Employees (HERE) to form UNITE/HERE. On September 14, 2005, UNITE/HERE Executive Board members voted to disaffiliate from the American Federation of Labor (AFL)-Congress of Industrial Organizations (CIO) over strategic differences. Today UNITE/HERE represents 450,000 workers in the hotel, gaming, laundry, apparel and textile manufacturing, retail and food service sectors. It is part of a larger coalition—Change to Win—committed "to organizing new members and a proworker bipartisan political agenda."

KAREN PASTORELLO

References and Further Reading

Amalgamated Clothing Workers of America. *ACWA Biennial Convention Proceedings* and *Reports of the General Executive Board* (1914–1975).

———. *The Advance* (1917–1975).

———. *Bread and Roses: The Story of the Rise of the Shirtworkers, 1933–1934*. New York: Amalgamated Clothing Workers of America, 1935.

———. "Needle and Thread, 1915–1960: Forty-Five Years of the Amalgamated Clothing Workers of America." New York: New York Joint Board, 1960.

Argersinger, Jo Ann E. *Making the Amalgamated: Gender, Ethnicity, and Class in the Baltimore Clothing Industry*. Baltimore, MD: Johns Hopkins University Press, 1999.

Bae, Youngsoo. *Labor in Retreat: Class and Community among Men's Clothing Workers of Chicago, 1871–1929*. Albany: State University of New York, 2001.

Bookbinder, Hyman. *To Promote the General Welfare: The Story of the Amalgamated Clothing Workers of America*. New York: The Amalgamated Clothing Workers of America, 1950.

Fraser, Steven. *Labor Will Rule: Sidney Hillman and the Rise of American Labor*. New York: The Free Press, 1991.

Hardman, J. B. S., et al. *Fiftieth-Anniversary Souvenir History of the New York Joint Board, ACWA*. New York: Amalgamated Clothing Workers of America, 1964.

Josephson, Matthew. *Sidney Hillman: Statesman of American Labor*. New York: Doubleday, 1956.

Lamar, Elden. *The Clothing Workers in Philadelphia: History of Their Struggles for Union and Security*. Philadelphia: Philadelphia Joint Board, 1940.

Marimpietri, A. D. "From These Beginnings: The Making of the Amalgamated Clothing Workers of America." Chicago: Amalgamated Clothing Workers of America, Chicago Joint Board, 1928.

Mayer, Harold. *The Inheritance*. A film commemorating the fiftieth anniversary of the Amalgamated Clothing Workers of America (1964).

Records of the Amalgamated Clothing Workers of America, Kheel Center for Labor-Management Documentation, Martin P. Catherwood Library, Cornell University, Ithaca, New York.

Women's Trade Union League of Chicago. *Official Report of the Strike Committee, Chicago Garment Workers' Strike October 29, 1910–February 18, 1911*. Chicago: Women's Trade Union League, 1911.

Zaretz, Charles E. *The ACWA: A Study in Progressive Trades Unionism*. New York: Ancon Publishing Company, 1934.

See also **Hillman, Sidney**

AMALGAMATED MEAT CUTTERS AND BUTCHERS WORKMEN

The Amalgamated Meat Cutters and Butchers Workmen (AMC) was founded in Cincinnati, Ohio, by Homer D. Call, a meat cutter from Syracuse, New York; George Byer, a butcher from Kansas City: John F. Hart, a butcher from Utica, New York; and John F. O'Sullivan, a union organizer of the American Federation of Labor (AFL) from Boston in 1897, as the first national organization of packinghouse workers granted a charter under the AFL. In its early years Michael Donnelly, a sheep butcher from Omaha, Nebraska, was elected the first president of the growing union and oversaw the union's organizing activities in smaller packinghouse communities before leading an operation to organize Chicago's stockyards in 1900. In Chicago the AMC fell into the traditional patterns of organizing skilled labor and focused the bulk of its energies on organizing skilled butchers. However unlike other AFL unions, which maintained a policy of organizing only skilled laborers, by 1901 Amalgamated removed such restrictions; recruited a number of interpreters from ethnic groups within the stockyards; and began to organize the growing numbers of unskilled ethnic Poles, Bohemians, and Lithuanians, who moved into the meatpacking industry following strikes in 1886 and 1894, into department-based unions.

From 1901–1904, the AMC reached it epoch in popularity and boasted a membership exceeding 56,000 members. However despite these numbers, serious division, along both ethnic and skill lines, permeated throughout the organization as union leadership struggled with strategies designed to encourage a broader vision of class solidarity, where workers would see themselves as part of a broader movement rather than merely identify with a specific occupation. As the AMC grew, conflicts between union leadership and the rank-and-file became more apparent as conservative-minded AMC officials tried to contain more militant shop-floor activism over issues of better hours, wages, and working conditions.

In 1902, such job campaigns forced the packers to institute 10-hour days along with overtime provisions. These gains far exceeded the gains secured by the AMC national contract of the same year. By the summer of 1904, the general membership of the union called for an industrywide wage increase and rejected calls for moderation from Donnelly. When the packers refused their demands, a strike ensued. However this action undertaken by the AMC failed largely because many African-American, Greek, Slavic, and Lithuanian unskilled workers, who refused to organize with the AMC, remained in the plant. As a result of this failure, the union lost much of its prestige and membership: Membership dropped from 34,400 in 1904 to 6,200 in 1910.

With the beginning of U.S. involvement in World War I, the AMC, aided by the creation of the Stockyards Labor Councils (SLC) in July 1917, again began to organize the packinghouse industry. The SLC, which grew out of a conference of all local unions

Butchers idle at meat counter during meat boycott. Library of Congress, Prints & Photographs Division [LC-DIG-ggbain-04488].

that held jurisdiction over packinghouse workers, in its early stages worked to bring a growing number of African-American workers into the AMC. Although the AMC and the SLC officially remained a separate entity, the SLC's recruitment of black workers forced the AMC to reconsider its own treatment of African-Americans within its locals, since previous efforts led to *de facto* segregation in the stockyards. This move would prove vital to the long-term success of the AMC as the 1904 strike failed, in part because many African-Americans, who comprised 20% of the stockyard workforce by 1918, were not affiliated with the union, and a number of crafts and unions within the yards did not admit African-Americans or organized them into segregated locals. Amalgamated achieved some success in organizing black workers alongside white workers inside the stockyards. However the unions still faced obstacles as only one-third of black workers joined. In addition the packers continued their efforts to hold the allegiances of African-American workers by increasing the number of black workers in the plants, using demagogues who encouraged black workers to join pseudo-unions, and increasing racial tension by replacing laid-off white union members with unorganized African-Americans.

Despite the effort by the packers to curtail black membership into the Meat Cutters' union, by late 1917 Amalgamated and the other stockyard unions presented a list of demands to the packers. The packers refused to meet with union officials. However before any strike vote could be taken, the President's Mediation Commission interceded because a strike would negatively impact wartime meat production. Instead employers and union officials agreed to allow a federal arbitrator, Judge Samuel S. Alschuler, to settle any dispute between the two sides for the duration of the war.

With the conclusion of the war, the drives by Amalgamated in the yards to attract new members continued. Amalgamated pushed for, and was successful in attaining, far higher membership numbers by building on a promise of higher postwar wages. This success was short-lived however, because in July 1919, Chicago experienced a race riot. The intense conflict between union workers and packinghouse employers appears to have been among the causes for this riot. African-Americans, who were unable to reach the stockyards during the weeklong violence, returned to work under the protection of federal troops, and when the troops were withdrawn, a number of black workers found it difficult to remain loyal to the union. In addition to these racial tensions, by 1920 delegates at an annual convention approved a "100 percent American" resolution that stipulated that all officers had to be U.S. citizens. This resolution came only 3 years after delegates who apparently saw the demographic shifts within the organization resolved to print some union reports and articles in Polish, Lithuanian, Bohemian, German, English, and Spanish. Moreover racial tension within the membership increased, and by 1921, new fears regarding unemployment surfaced.

Amalgamated suffered another setback as it faced competition from a newly formed company-backed union and an expiration deadline of the collective-bargaining agreement in 1921. Later that year the AMC called a strike to protest wage cuts, but unable to call on a firm base of support in the plants, the union faced severe challenges. Among these challenges were the facts that the Teamsters and Elevated Engineers chose to cross picket lines rather than remain on strike and that the AMC lost substantial black membership as many chose to remain loyal to the packers instead of aligning with the union. By January 1922, Amalgamated was driven out of the yards.

Although Amalgamated continued to exist during the Depression Era, it did not become an organizing force in the stockyards until the New Deal. During this period Amalgamated competed with various company unions and the Communist-led Packinghouse Workers' Industrial Union for members. Because of this new competition, the AMC faced difficulties in regaining its hold on the industry, especially because many white laborers still resented African-American workers for crossing the strike lines during the 1921–1922 strike. Moreover during the New Deal, the AMC fell under the control of more conservative-minded leadership of the AFL, whose industry made little effort to organize unskilled workers aggressively in the yards. By the time the United States entered World War II, the AMC faced another challenge from the Congress of Industrial Organizations (CIO)-led Packinghouse Workers Organizing Committee (PWOC), which later became the UPWA in 1943, whose direct-action campaigns and liberal racial positions seemed more attractive to many workers.

The UPWA and the AMC co-existed in the stockyards during the wartime and postwar period; however at times the groups presented less than a united front. For example in 1946, the AMC reluctantly worked with the UPWA as plans were developed to impose a strike deadline. Initially AMC leadership announced that its membership would remain at work in the event of a strike. However when it was seen that the packers were no more willing to negotiate with the AMC than they were with the UPWA, the AMC agreed to a work stoppage alongside the UPWA.

In another example the AMC sided with the packers in 1948 when the UPWA launched a strike. Following the 1948 strike, the AMC attempted to re-establish itself in the industry by claiming to be an alternative to the UPWA. However with the passage of the Taft-Hartley Act, it appeared as if the influence union organizing held in the packing industry was fading.

By 1963, it was becoming more obvious that much of the organizing activities in the stockyards of the previous 63 years were waning. In was during this period when, facing a decline in prestige and in an attempt to sustain a semblance of industrial unionism in the meatpacking industry, the AMC and Butcher Workmen absorbed what was left of its rivals the UPWA. With the increase in nonunion shops in the meat industry during the 1970s and 1980s, the remnants of the Amalgamated union were forced to merge with the Retail Clerks to form the United Food and Commercial Workers (UFCW). By the 1980s, the AMC found it impossible to launch any job campaigns with anemic membership and the closing of much of the meatpacking industry across the United States.

LIONEL KIMBLE, JR.

References and Further Reading

Brody, David. *Butcher Workmen: A Study of Unionization.* Cambridge, MA: Harvard University Press, 1964.

Cayton, Horace R., and George S. Mitchell. *Black Workers and the New Unions.* Chapel Hill: University of North Carolina Press, 1939.

Halpern, Rick. *Down on the Killing Floor: Black and White Workers in Chicago's Packinghouses, 1904–54.* Urbana: University of Illinois Press, 1997.

Herbst, Alma. *The Negro in the Slaughtering and Meatpacking Industry in Chicago.* New York: Arno Publishing, 1971.

Horowitz, Roger. *"Negro and White Unite and Fight!" A Social History of Industrial Unionism in Meatpacking, 1930–1990.* Urbana: University of Illinois Press, 1997.

AMERICAN ALLIANCE FOR LABOR AND DEMOCRACY

The American Alliance for Labor and Democracy (AALD) was created in the summer of 1917 by American Federation of Labor (AFL) leaders, prowar socialists, and officials from the Central Federated Union of New York to encourage worker loyalty to the U.S. government during World War I and to prevent disruptive strikes that might hinder wartime production. Concerned that pacifist organizations like the Peoples' Council were encouraging worker unrest in such important New York industries as the Jewish-dominated garment trades, AFL President Samuel Gompers first worked with labor union leaders from the Central Federated Union of New York to develop plans for an American Alliance for Labor and Democracy designed to counteract pacifist propaganda. Since Gompers, like President Woodrow Wilson, believed that immigrant workers were particularly prone to pacifist appeals, he also sought to use the proposed alliance to Americanize the working class in New York City. Such prowar socialists as Robert Maisel, J. G. Phelps Stokes, and John Spargo soon expressed interest in the AALD and at a meeting at the Continental hotel in New York on July 28, 1917, agreed to cooperate in launching the new organization. Gompers was appointed the president of the AALD and Maisel its director. Significantly Gompers was not authorized either by the AFL Executive Council or constituent AFL unions to create the AALD. Most prominent socialists who participated in founding the AALD had already left the Socialist party due to its antiwar positions.

Bankrolled by the government-sponsored Committee on Public Information, the AALD produced a steady stream of prowar propaganda, held labor loyalty and liberty loan rallies, and organized local chapters throughout the country to coordinate their activities. To promote the organization further, Gompers finally sought to gain the official endorsement of the AFL for the AALD and its activities at the federation's convention in November of 1917. The proposed endorsement provoked a bitter debate at the convention that raised fundamental questions about what role organized labor should play in supporting or opposing government foreign policy during a time of national crisis. Some questioned whether it was necessary or appropriate for the AFL to support an organization promoting labor loyalty to the government. They believed that the AFL ought to maintain its independent position as a representative of the working class. Others expressed concern that the AALD did not more systematically oppose the Wilson administration's suppression of civil liberties, for this had long been a critical function of labor organizations. Still others wondered why Gompers wanted to Americanize the labor movement. Yet the convention ultimately endorsed the AALD by a vote of 21,602 to 402.

Opposition to the Alliance however remained strong within some urban union movements, especially those with significant socialist or large Irish, German, and Jewish constituencies who were opposed to the Wilson administration's war policies. In New York City the AALD became involved in a bitter feud with the United Hebrew Trades and Amalgamated Clothing Workers of America. In Chicago, home to one of the most militant labor movements in the country, leaders of the municipal federation of labor expressed concern about some of the tactics of the AALD when solicited to create a local chapter and chose to ignore frequent angry pleas from Maisel to form an organization there. Poor attendance at AALD meetings by AFL delegates in 1917 may also have indicated a lack of enthusiasm for the organization among important segments of the labor movement.

During 1918, the AALD focused on promoting Wilson's 14 points, but its efforts were undercut by financial problems. Maisel continuously lobbied the Committee on Public Information to support new labor programs but was instead asked to restrict spending. The financial situation became particularly dire when Congress cut appropriations for the Committee on Public Information, and the AALD was placed under the financial direction of the Industrial Relations Division of the Committee on Public Information. The AALD however received a significant infusion of cash from the AFL when it was entrusted with creating a labor loyalty press to thwart alleged German activity in Mexico and South America in the summer of 1918.

Gompers and others expressed hope that the AALD would continue in peacetime as an AFL propaganda agency that would work to promote the AFL's public image, gain continued representation for labor on government councils, and oppose labor radicalism. But the AALD was depleted of funds by November of 1919 and disbanded.

ELIZABETH McKILLEN

References and Further Reading

Gompers, Samuel. *Seventy Years of Life and Labor: An Autobiography*. New York: E. P. Dutton, 1925.
Grubbs, Frank L. *The Struggle for Labor Loyalty: Gompers, the A.F. of L., and the Pacifists, 1917–1920*. Durham, NC: Duke University Press, 1968.
Larson, Simeon. *Labor and Foreign Policy: Gompers, the AFL, and the First World War, 1914–1918*. London: Associated University Presses, 1975.
McCartin, Joseph. *Labor's Great War: The Struggle for Industrial Democracy and the Origins of Modern American Labor Relations, 1912–1921*. North Carolina: University of North Carolina Press, 1997.
McKillen, Elizabeth. *Chicago Labor and the Quest for a Democratic Diplomacy, 1914–1924*. Ithaca, NY: Cornell University Press, 1995.
Radosh, Ronald. *American Labor and United States Foreign Policy*. New York: Vintage Books, 1969.

See also **Central Labor Unions; Chicago Federation of Labor; World War I**

AMERICAN ANTI-BOYCOTT ASSOCIATION

The American Anti-Boycott Association (AABA) represented the interests of business owners in court from 1902–1919. The AABA furnished employers with legal counsel in a number of precedent-setting cases that challenged various union tactics, including picketing, sympathetic strikes (refusals to deal with businesses that sell the products of a struck firm), and boycotts. It quickly earned a reputation as one of the most vocal and successful advocates of the management prerogatives over employees.

Two hat makers from Danbury, Connecticut, Dietrich Eduard Loewe and Charles Hart Merritt, created the AABA to protect themselves and other entrepreneurs from what they saw as the unfair efforts by unions to impose closed-shop agreements, which required employers to hire only members of a given union. Closed-shop movements, the organization's founders argued, denied employers the fundamental right to hire whomever they chose and infringed on workers' constitutional right not to join a union. Adopting the motto "a just man armed is potent for peace," Loewe and Merritt envisioned an association whose members would pool their financial resources to defend these rights in the courtroom through a series of carefully selected cases.

The character of the businesses that the AABA actually represented is open to debate. Its leaders claimed to speak for small business owners in competition with rich and powerful corporate competitors. These corporations supposedly had the luxury of cooperating with some unions' demands in order to maintain peaceful relations with their workers, leaving the smaller firms at the mercy of organized labor. Yet as historian Andrew Wender Cohen has pointed out, many of the AABA's allies, such as the Employers' Association of Chicago, the Citizens' Industrial Alliance of America, and especially the National Association of Manufacturers, included owners of large firms and corporations.

In any case Daniel Davenport, the AABA's chief counsel, pursued the organization's pro-employer agenda aggressively. Under his direction the association's lawyers argued test cases before courts throughout the nation in the hope of establishing binding legal precedents. In 1903, they represented the Kellogg Switchboard Company during a strike in Chicago. They successfully convinced the state courts to issue an injunction, or court order, that forbade union members to use threats, pickets, or even persuasion in their efforts to convince strikebreakers to leave the company's employ.

Perhaps the most important cases argued during Davenport's tenure as legal director were *Loewe v.*

Lawlor and *Gompers v. Bucks Stove & Range Company*. *Loewe v. Lawlor* came to be known as the "Danbury Hatter's Case." The dispute had actually provided the initial motivation for Loewe and Merritt's decision to organize the AABA in the first place. In 1902, the United Hatters of North America union had imposed a national boycott against hats made by Loewe's and Merritt's businesses because the two manufacturers had refused to sign closed-shop agreements. The litigation in this case lasted over 10 years and made its way twice to the United States Supreme Court. The Court's first decision, handed down in 1908, declared that the boycott in this instance violated the Sherman Antitrust Act of 1890. The ruling signified the first definitive declaration that the Sherman law applied to labor unions as well as businesses. In the Supreme Court's second decision, submitted in 1915, the justices ruled that every single member of the Hatters' union was personally responsible for paying the large damage award granted to the hat manufacturers. In other words the court had set a precedent for holding all union members liable for the actions of union officers. In *Gompers v. Buck's Stove & Range Company*, the U.S. Supreme Court in 1911 upheld a court order that forbade the American Federation of Labor (AFL) from urging its members to boycott the products of a business that the American Federation of Labor deemed unfair to workers.

The holdings in these two cases strengthened the claims of AABA's leaders that they worked to secure individual rights and to protect business owners' property from harmful labor actions. For these leaders the Danbury Hatters' Case ensured that unscrupulous unionists could no longer hide behind the actions of their leaders, while the *Buck's Stove* case defended businesses from concerted, nationally organized attacks. Union supporters on the other hand argued that these cases unfairly exposed financially constrained workers to endless liability and impinged on union members' freedom of speech by forbidding them to urge consumers to refuse to patronize certain products.

By 1919, Walter Gordon Merritt had become head of the organization and renamed it the League for Industrial Rights. Merritt, the son of one of the original founders, Charles Hart Merritt, saw the League as more representative of corporations than the older AABA had been. But he continued the policy of defending management prerogatives in court. In the 1921 case *Duplex Printing Press Company v. Deering*, for example, his lawyers attacked the Clayton Antitrust Act of 1914. The Supreme Court's *Duplex* decision eviscerated the act's exemption of labor unions from antistrike injunction. In other words the case reaffirmed organized labor's subjection to hostile court orders.

In its short career the AABA had successes and setbacks. The organization succeeded remarkably at bringing its conception of individual rights to national attention. *Loewe v. Lawlor* and *Gompers v. Buck's Stove & Company* weakened workers' efforts to (in its view) coerce businesses to recognize unions because the decisions upheld sweeping court orders that forbade one of organized labor's most effective tools, the boycott. But some of these victories were Pyrrhic ones. Loewe was unable to collect all his damages from the Danbury case because the workers held liable did not own enough property to compensate him fully. More important the AABA never achieved one of its most cherished goals, a declaration that any strike for the purpose of establishing a closed shop be in and of itself illegal. The courts refused to accede completely to the organization's claim that all individuals had a constitutional right not to face compulsory union membership. One thing is clear however: The American Anti-Boycott Association serves as a reminder of the importance of the law in the evolution of labor relations in the United States.

DANIEL HARPER

References and Further Reading

Cohen, Andrew Wender. "Business Myths, Lawyerly Strategies, and Social Context: Ernst on Labor Law History." *Law & Social Inquiry* 23, 1 (1998): 165–183.
Ernst, Daniel R. *Lawyers against Labor: From Individual Rights to Corporate Liberalism.* Urbana and Chicago: University of Illinois Press, 1995.

Cases Cited

Christensen v. Kellogg Switchboard & Supply Company, 110 ILL. App. 61 (1903).
Gompers v. Buck's Stove & Range Company, 221 U.S. 418 (1911).
Lawlor v. Loewe, 235 U.S. 522 (1915).
Loewe v. Lawlor, 208 U.S. 274 (1908).

See also **Clayton Antitrust Act; Danbury Hatters Case: Loewe v. Lawlor (1908, 1915); Gompers v. Buck's Stove and Range Co.; Law and Labor; Sherman Antitrust Act**

AMERICAN EXCEPTIONALISM

In 1906, the German sociologist Werner Sombart posed a question that has continued to influence discussions about U.S. labor ever since. In his book, *Why Is There No Socialism in the United States,* Sombart advanced the notion that U.S. workers were exceptional in comparison to workers in other industrial nations by virtue of their lack of support for socialism and their failure to develop a sense of class consciousness. Although at the time Sombart wrote, socialism was hardly a less potent political force in the United States than it was in Britain, his question would prove prescient about the future of socialism in the United States. Over the course of the twentieth century, the United States would in fact be the only industrial democracy in the world in which a socialist party did not permanently establish itself as a major factor in national politics.

Sombart and another early exponent of the theory of U.S. labor exceptionalism, labor economist Selig Perlman, saw the lack of support for socialism directly linked to the lack of class consciousness among U.S. workers. Workers throughout the rest of the industrialized world came to see themselves as a class apart and therefore to support the development of labor-based parties whose goal was to bring about socialism. Most U.S. workers on the other hand developed what Perlman, in his highly influential *A Theory of the Labor Movement* (1928), described as a form of "job consciousness" that caused them to focus on quite limited bread-and-butter issues relating to wages and working conditions and to eschew radical politics. The U.S. workers and their unions worked within the existing economic and political system instead of trying to replace it.

Sombart, Perlman, and other later proponents of the idea of U.S. exceptionalism offered a variety of explanations for what they saw as the U.S. labor movement's distinctive pattern of development. They argued that a higher standard of living and greater opportunities for upward social mobility produced by the rapidly expanding U.S. economy made U.S. workers more likely than their counterparts in Europe to see themselves as beneficiaries rather than victims of capitalism. The U.S. workers generally did not view themselves as part of a permanent working class, believing that if they did not themselves achieve prosperity, at least their children would have the opportunity to improve their social status. The pervasive individualism and emphasis on economic opportunity in U.S. society, including the historic opportunity provided by the safety valve of the frontier, thus undercut the development of class consciousness and worker support for efforts to put an end to a system based on the pursuit of individual profit.

The U.S. political system is also often cited as a factor in U.S. labor exceptionalism. Workers in Europe were largely excluded from the franchise until the twentieth century and saw support for socialist labor parties as an important means of gaining access to political power. In contrast universal white male suffrage became the norm in the United States well before the full-scale industrialization that followed the Civil War. As a result U.S. wage earners had a history of regarding themselves as citizens who enjoyed equal rights in the body politic. Rather than acquiring an identity as members of an excluded and oppressed class in need of their own political party, U.S. workers had developed well-established partisan loyalties to the Republican or Democratic parties dating back to the nineteenth century—loyalties that were passed on from generation to generation. Workers in the United States therefore proved difficult recruits for the American Socialist party. The U.S. two-party system, with its winner-take-all form of presidential elections, also militated against the emergence of a socialist third party, because small minority parties had far less chance to influence public policy than did minority parties in a parliamentary system. In addition Sombart and Perlman pointed to the U.S. system of federalism as another barrier to the development of socialism. Because of the wide dispersal of power over many different political jurisdictions in the United States, workers had less incentive to seek political solutions to their problems than in more centralized European polities in which the effort either to capture or at least influence centralized authority offered a greater prospect of reward.

Although Sombart was silent on the issue, Perlman and many later commentators have argued that the development of a cohesive sense of class consciousness among U.S. workers was also significantly impeded by the much greater ethnic and racial diversity of the working population in the United States as compared to other industrial nations. Ethnic groups that had been traditional enemies in Europe had trouble working together on behalf of a common working-class agenda, and new immigrants were continually entering the U.S. labor market, making the development of a common working-class identity particularly difficult. White-black racial divisions were if anything even more of an obstacle to the formation of a single working-class identity, especially because employers often used African-Americans as strikebreakers when union-organized work stoppages occurred.

Post-World War II Expressions of U.S. Exceptionalism

The idea of U.S. exceptionalism was first fully developed early in the twentieth century, but this interpretation may have achieved its widest acceptance in the Cold War environment that emerged after the World War II. In the postwar period, labor exceptionalism was reinforced by the pluralist approach that came to dominate U.S. political science. Pluralists, such as David Truman and Robert Dahl, argued that U.S. society was largely free of the sharp class divisions of European nations because people in the United States tended to identify with many different and cross-cutting groups based on religion, region, ethnicity, and other factors, and thereby failed to develop an overarching identity as members of a single class. Politics became an intricate game of building ever shifting coalitions composed of many different interest groups, so that there was little opportunity for a class-based party with a sweeping ideological agenda to gain any traction in the United States.

The consensus interpretation of U.S. history put forward by such scholars such as Louis Hartz also complemented the theory of U.S. labor exceptionalism. Consensus historians emphasized the lack of fundamental ideological conflict in a nation in which most people shared a belief in private property, the profit motive, individualism, and limited government. Hartz was especially influential in claiming in his widely read *Liberal Tradition in America* (1955) that the lack of a feudal past explained the overwhelming dominance of liberalism in the United States. Having been born equal, without the deeply entrenched social distinctions that characterized European societies, the United States failed to develop either a true conservative tradition that sought to defend the philosophical and social legacy of feudalism or a powerful socialist movement that sought to root out the remaining hierarchical vestiges of a feudal past.

Industrial relations experts in the postwar era, such as John Dunlop and Clark Kerr, helped to articulate a conception of industrial pluralism that was in many ways an extension of the theory of U.S. labor exceptionalism and had much in common with the dominant pluralist framework of political science and the consensus view of U.S. history. When Sombart first posed his famous question, few U.S. workers belonged to unions. The theory of U.S. labor exceptionalism however was not predicated on the assumption that U.S. workers were unlikely to join unions, only that they lacked a sense of class consciousness that would cause them to see themselves as having fundamentally different interests from their employers and that would propel them to support socialist politics. Perlman and his mentor, John Commons, one of the founders of the fields of labor economics and industrial relations, contended that the bread-and-butter unionism represented by Samuel Gompers's American Federation of Labor was entirely consistent with the narrowly focused job consciousness that they believed distinguished U.S. from European workers.

When U.S. workers finally began to join unions in large numbers in the two decades after the passage of the National Labor Relations Act (NLRA) in 1935, industrial pluralists saw the conservative collective-bargaining system that emerged in the postwar United States as in essence a confirmation of the exceptional character of the U.S. labor movement. The U.S. unions gained greater power, but they did not seek to create a truly independent political voice, nor did they challenge the premises of U.S. capitalism. Instead they focused on winning legally enforceable collective bargaining agreements, which included narrowly defined work rules, improved wages, and fringe benefits, and on providing political support for the Democratic party.

Challenges and New Directions

Beginning in the 1960s many historians began to challenge certain aspects of the theory of U.S. labor exceptionalism, including the notion that U.S. workers had never developed a sense of class consciousness. They brought new attention to the long history of labor violence in the United States and to the fact that in the late nineteenth century, many contemporary observers saw the U.S. labor movement as among the most militant in the world. The failure of socialism in their view was not necessarily a product of workers' contentment or their unquestioning acceptance of U.S. capitalism. Some radical historians pointed to state repression, especially that associated with World War I and its aftermath, as a critical factor in the collapse of what had been a growing socialist movement.

In the 1980s, Eric Foner, Aristide Zolberg, and others questioned the entire exceptionalist analytical framework. They argued that it was premised on the assumption that there was a single model of working-class development leading to the rise of labor-backed socialist parties that applied to all other industrial nations except the United States. Yet they contended that national variations among the labor movements of Europe have been so great as to invalidate the assumption that a single norm of historical development could be said to exist. Moreover the divergence in labor politics and labor relations between the United States and other Western industrial democracies that may have emerged in the first half of the twentieth century seemed to be disappearing in the last decades of the century as European Social Democratic parties appeared to back away from their historic commitment to socialism and unions began to lose power.

While some social scientists and historians have begun to question the validity of the exceptionalist framework, many more have continued to accept its basic assumption of the distinctive character of the U.S. labor movement but have sought to refine or amend Sombart and Perlman's original explanations for the failure of socialism to take hold in the United States. Political sociologists Seymour Martin Lipset and Gary Marks have provided a significant updating of Sombart in *It Didn't Happen Here* (2000). Lipset and Marks discount the importance of many of the factors cited by both Sombart and Perlman, including the constitutional structure of U.S. politics and the early granting of the franchise to U.S. workers. They still emphasize what they see as the pervasive and deeply rooted antistatism of U.S. society and the widely held belief in the possibility of social mobility as inhibiting factors in the development of socialism. They also acknowledge the significance of the ethnic and racial diversity of the U.S. working population.

Lipset and Marks however move beyond most earlier explanations of U.S. exceptionalism in arguing that the dominance of craft unions in the U.S. labor movement has distinguished organized labor in the United States from union movements in other Western industrial nations and was a crucial factor in the failure of U.S. workers to support the creation of a labor party. They contend that what they label exclusive craft unions are less likely than more inclusive general or industrial unions to turn to politics or to support a class-based political party to advance the interests of their members. Inclusive unions seek to organize large numbers of workers but have a very difficult time controlling their labor market through traditional union tactics because it includes unskilled as well as skilled workers. Consequently such unions typically view political involvement and legislative action as a key to accomplishing their objectives. Exclusive craft unions on the other hand seek to control a much smaller labor market and are much less likely to see concerted political action as a key to their success. Lipset and Marks argue that only in the United States did craft unions remain the dominant force in the organized labor movement into the twentieth century. Whereas in Western Europe inclusive unions played leading roles in every nation's labor movement and in supporting the development of labor parties, in the United States the dominance of craft unions caused organized labor movement to adopt an approach that relied on business unionism rather than on a more class-based strategy of labor politics. Not only did the U.S. union movement fail to coordinate its activities with the American Socialist party that emerged in the early twentieth century;

it often came to see itself as a rival to the more ideologically oriented socialist organization. Lipset and Marks argue that the split proved crucial because it denied U.S. socialism a critical mass base on which to build, while socialist parties in other industrial nations benefited from the support of union movements characterized by more inclusive forms of organization.

William Forbath and Victoria Hattam offer a different revision of the traditional theory of exceptionalism. Writing in the 1990s, both scholars revisited the issue of how the structure of U.S. government may have worked to prevent the growth of a viable socialist movement. Each has separately argued that U.S. unions did in fact initially pursue political solutions to many of their problems, but the U.S. labor movement continually was thwarted by the judiciary's independent power to rule against union interests. British workers, they note, also encountered hostile judicial rulings, but because judges in Britain were subject to parliamentary supremacy, union involvement in politics was successful in reversing such judicial rulings. In the United States on the other hand, according to Forbath and Hattam, organized labor was continually frustrated at its inability to use its influence on the legislative process to overcome the antilabor decisions of judges. This experience, not some deeply ingrained ideological predisposition, led U.S. unions finally to adopt an antistatist position and to conclude that investing time and resources in electoral politics or the creation of a labor party was impractical.

While Sombart's initial framing of the problem of exceptionalism still helps to shape much of the ongoing discussion about the U.S. labor movement, a number of scholars have attempted to reformulate the issue by turning away from the issue of socialism and instead focusing on what they see as the distinctive nature of labor-management relations in the United States. Sanford Jacoby sums up the view of many other historians when he claims that one of the most distinctive features of U.S. industrial relations has long been the strength of employer opposition to unions and the ability of employers throughout most of U.S. history to prevent their employees from organizing. Although the NLRA seemed to have marked an historic change in the ability of employers to interfere with efforts at unionizing, the law's effects proved rather transitory, and the last decades of the twentieth century would see a resurgence of successful efforts by employers to reduce the role of unions in the U.S. economy. Thus both before the passage of the NLRA, and once again in the last quarter of the twentieth century, the United States had a lower level of union membership among its workers than most other industrial democracies.

Even when collective bargaining has occurred, it has taken a form that many observers see as peculiarly U.S. Whereas multi-employer and industrywide bargaining has been common in other nations, in the United States bargaining has typically taken place in a decentralized manner involving unions negotiating with individual employers. In fact the NLRA legally prohibited industrywide bargaining. Moreover collective bargaining in the United States has been distinctive because it became a means of developing highly detailed agreements about working conditions that were legally enforceable, a pattern that was generally not found in other industrial democracies. Labor historian David Brody has called this system workplace contractualism.

Brody and other economic and business historians, such as William Lazonick, offer one theory that may explain not only the exceptionally strong resistance of U.S. employers to unions, but also the form of collective bargaining that became fairly widespread for a relatively short period following the passage of the NLRA. They argue that in contrast to Britain and most other industrial nations, the United States witnessed the development of mass production carried out by huge, bureaucratically organized firms before unions had achieved a solid foothold in U.S. industry. In Britain until well into the twentieth century, manufacturing typically took place in relatively small-scale firms that did not have sufficient resources to build up large managerial hierarchies. These firms came to rely on already established unions to exercise a certain degree of control and supervision over the shop floor. Employers in Britain and elsewhere were also more willing to recognize unions than were employers in the United States because they sought to avoid competition over wages with other small-scale producers in the same industry. Industrywide collective bargaining agreements were one means of limiting cutthroat or unpredictable wage competition. In the United States on the other hand, the most influential employers sought to maintain total control over the production process and resisted unionization as an impediment to achieving that goal. Moreover the large scale of many U.S. firms meant that they were less concerned about chaotic competition with other firms in the same industry and hence saw little need for multi-employer collective bargaining. Once it became impossible to avoid unions altogether, U.S. employers favored a bureaucratic approach to collective bargaining that would limit their workers' ability to challenge managerial prerogatives.

Although a number of prominent labor historians in the 1980s and 1990s seemed ready to proclaim the demise of the theory of U.S. labor exceptionalism, Sombart's question seems likely to generate debate and discussion for many years to come. Even if other Western industrial democracies continue to become in certain respects more like the United States, the failure of U.S. workers in the twentieth century to sustain a viable socialist party and the reasons for the historic weakness of unions in the U.S. political economy will remain fascinating questions subject to a variety of interpretations.

LARRY G. GERBER

References and Further Reading

Brody, David. "Workplace Contractualism in Comparative Perspective." In *Industrial Democracy in America: The Ambiguous Promise*, edited by Nelson Lichtenstein and Howell John Harris. Cambridge, UK: Cambridge University Press, 1993.

Forbath, William E. *Law and the Shaping of the American Labor Movement*. Cambridge, MA: Harvard University Press, 1991.

Gerber, Larry G. "Shifting Perspectives on American Exceptionalism: Recent Literature on American Labor Relations and Labor Politics." *Journal of American Studies* 31, 2 (1997): 253–274.

Hartz, Louis. *The Liberal Tradition in America: An Interpretation of American Political Thought since the Revolution*. New York: Harcourt, Brace, 1955.

Hattam, Victoria Charlotte. *Labor Visions and State Power: The Origins of Business Unionism in the United States*. Princeton, NJ: Princeton University Press, 1993.

Heffer, Jean, and Jeanine Rovet, eds. *Why Is There No Socialism in the United States?* Paris: Editions de L'école des Hautes Etudes en Sciences Sociales, 1988.

Jacoby, Sanford M. "American Exceptionalism Revisited: The Importance of Management." In *Masters to Managers: Historical and Comparative Perspectives on American Employers*, edited by Sanford M. Jacoby. New York: Columbia University Press, 1991.

Lazonick, William. *Competitive Advantage on the Shop Floor*. Cambridge, MA: Harvard University Press, 1990.

Lipset, Seymour Martin, and Gary Marks. *It Didn't Happen Here: Why Socialism Failed in the United States*. New York: W. W. Norton, 2000.

Perlman, Selig. *A Theory of the Labor Movement*. New York: Macmillan, 1928.

Shafer, Byron E., ed. *Is America Different? A New Look at American Exceptionalism*. Oxford, UK: Clarendon Press, 1991.

Sombart, Werner. *Why Is There No Socialism in the United States?* Trans. Patricia M. Hocking and C. T. Husbands. White Plains, NY: M. E. Sharpe, 1976. Reprint, Tubingen, DR: Verlag von J. C. B. Mohr, 1906.

Voss, Kim. *The Making of American Exceptionalism: The Knights of Labor and Class Formation in the Nineteenth Century*. Ithaca, NY: Cornell University Press, 1993.

Zolberg, Aristide. "How Many Exceptionalisms?" In *Working-Class Formation: Nineteenth-Century Patterns in Western Europe and the United States*, edited by Ira Katznelson and Aristide R. Zolberg. Princeton, NJ: Princeton University Press, 1986.

See also **Commons, John Rogers; Perlman, Selig**

AMERICAN FEDERATION OF GOVERNMENT EMPLOYEES

A disagreement between the leadership of the National Federation of Federal Employees (NFFE), representing government workers, and the American Federation of Labor (AFL) led to the establishment of a new civil service union, the American Federation of Government Employees (AFGE). When members of NFFE voted to leave the AFL in 1931, a group of disaffected NFFE members worked with AFL leaders to form a rival union, AFGE. Chartered in August 1932, the core of the union consisted of former NFFE members and Washington, D.C., lodges that had not favored the break with the AFL. A third general federal union, the United Federal Workers of America (UFWA), formed in 1937 from a group of suspended AFGE lodges and affiliated with the Congress of Industrial Organizations (CIO).

The AFGE's first convention, held at the Hamilton Hotel in Washington, D.C., attracted 42 delegates, 14 of whom were women. They elected David R. Glass, an employee of the Veteran's Administration, as their first national president. Reflecting the significant presence of women in civil service unions, they chose convention chair Helen McCarty (later Voss) of the Navy Department as their chief organizer. McCarty Voss would serve the union for 38 years. In 1935, Berniece Heffner became secretary treasurer, a post she held for 18 years. During numerous transition periods, Heffner served as interim president.

In its early years AFGE had a reputation for attracting managers and supervisors into its ranks. It had a strong presence for instance in the Civil Service Commission, and many of its presidents had ties to managerial or upper-level positions. Charles Stengle, AFGE president from 1936–1939, was a former congressman and secretary for the New York City Civil Service Commission. James Yaden, a longtime national vice-president who served as president from 1948–1950, was the chief of the Civil Service Commission's Examining Division, and James Campbell, president from 1951–1962, had been director of the Civil Service Commission's St. Louis office. In the union's first few years, some of its more progressive members sought to bar Civil Service Commission officials from holding office, but they were defeated. In the late 1960s and early 1970s, at least one national vice-president echoed this sentiment, suggesting that supervisors should not be able to join the union, but as with the earlier effort, it did not succeed.

Although AFGE had only 562 members in early 1932, it recorded rapid growth through the mid-1930s. By 1936, it boasted 37,199 members in 328 lodges. In the late 1940s and early 1950s, membership rolls once again burgeoned, and the union counted 61,315 members in 1952, the same year that UFWA folded. The AFGE's most rapid growth occurred in the 1960s, due to a major organizing campaign initiated by President John Griner (1962–1972), the civil rights movement, and a presidential executive order, which recognized the right of federal employees to join unions and negotiate on a limited number of issues. By December 1970, the union had over 300,000 members. This number declined starting in the mid-1970s, leveling off in the next decade to 180,000. It rose again through the 1990s, reaching 200,000 members in 1100 locals in 2002, representing occupations ranging from food inspector to plumber to lawyer.

Strategies

In the mid-1930s, young, idealistic workers who had joined AFGE because of its strong ties to the AFL and labor movement felt increasingly alienated by AFGE's conservative leadership. Agitating for the union to use more militant tactics, these members and their lodges soon found themselves at odds with AFGE leaders. In 1934, AFGE Lodge 91 and others picketed National Recovery Administration (NRA) headquarters after NRA head Hugh Johnson fired their lodge president during negotiations over an employee grievance. The AFGE leaders responded by adopting a no-picketing rule at the 1936 convention. Other lodges also earned the ire of leaders when they formed a Committee against False Economy in 1937 to protest President Franklin D. Roosevelt's budget cuts. The union's 1937 constitution stated that the union was "unequivocally opposed to and will not tolerate strikes, picketing [,] or other public acts against government authority which have the effect of embarrassing the Government." From 1936–1937, AFGE leaders suspended a number of lodges for insubordination, alleged ties to the Communist party, and engaging in acts deemed embarrassing to the union. These lodges eventually formed the nucleus of UFWA-CIO.

Like most civil service unions, AFGE focused on improving work conditions and pay for workers, while conceding that it could not engage in collective bargaining. Because taxpayers paid the salaries of federal workers, AFGE agreed with politicians that workers could not bargain with an employer but instead could improve pay and benefits only by lobbying Congress, the representative of taxpayers. The AFGE's ties to management and emphasis on political pressure led it to work as much as possible within the system to publicize the interests of federal employees.

The AFGE's tone and tactics shifted in the 1960s with the advent of limited bargaining rights. By the late 1970s and 1980s and into the twenty-first century, when government budget cuts threatened federal jobs, the AFGE began to undertake more public demonstrations to promote its agenda. For instance it clashed publicly with the administration of George W. Bush, which it felt was seeking to undermine public-sector jobs and union rights. In 2002, for instance, the administration announced its desire to open large segments of government work to competition from private companies. Under this plan up to one-half of all federal jobs could become private-sector positions. In the late twentieth century and into the twenty-first century, the union emphasized legislative and political action along with collective bargaining. This shift in the union's identity was mirrored by its decision in 1968 to change the name of units from lodges, which connoted membership in a fraternal association, to locals, a name more in line with labor organizations.

This later stress on agency negotiations emerged after President John F. Kennedy issued Executive Order 10988 on January 17, 1962. This order not only explicitly recognized the right of federal workers to join a union, but also offered these workers limited bargaining rights. It established three levels of recognition—informal, formal, and exclusive—based on the percentage of employees belonging to a union in any given unit. If a majority of employees in an agency or unit of an agency belonged to the same union, the union earned exclusive recognition and the right to bargain with agency heads over general work conditions, personnel policies and practices, and grievances. The range of issues up for negotiation turned out to be narrow, because the order explicitly excluded negotiations over any personnel matter governed by congressional statute, which included pay and position classification. The order also recognized broad management rights, such as the right to hire, promote, transfer, demote, discharge, and discipline employees, as well as the ability to implement any personnel action deemed essential to accomplish agency objectives. In 1978, the Civil Service Reform Act (CSRA) institutionalized collective bargaining, expanding slightly the types of work conditions and personnel practices open to negotiation while maintaining the exclusion of such personnel policies as wages set by Congress. It also preserved extensive management rights. The law established boards to oversee agreements and protect whistleblowers. By the early 1990s, AFGE had achieved exclusive recognition for 26 of its units. Over a thousand locals had attained some form of recognition with agreements covering some 700,000 workers.

Yet AFGE felt far from secure as a public-sector union. In 2002, AFGE along with other unions became locked in a bitter battle with President George W. Bush over the union status of employees in the proposed Department of Homeland Security (DHS). Bush asked for the power to hire, fire, and establish pay for DHS employees, which the union considered an assault on the merit system. In addition Bush requested that all DHS employees be exempt from collective bargaining rights as established under CSRA. The AFGE officials accused President Bush of anti-union bias; Bush had previously denied collective bargaining rights to employees of the Transportation Security Administration and to some employees in the Justice Department on the grounds of protecting national security. Eventually Congress compromised with the president, facilitating his ability to dismiss DHS employees to protect national security but also maintaining the right of these workers to join unions and bargain collectively.

Agenda

The AFGE women had a long tradition of setting union objectives. In the mid-1930s for instance, the union came out in opposition to Section 213 of the Economy Act, which sought to limit the number of married couples working for the federal government. The law disproportionately affected women. Publicly McCarty Voss argued that the law applied equally to the wives of legislators, and Heffner simply stated that job selection should be made solely on merit. In the 1950s, the union supported maternity leave policies, and in the early 1960s, Esther Johnson, secretary treasurer of the union from 1956–1970, served on President Kennedy's National Conference on the Status of Women. In 1974, the union established a Department of Women's Affairs to address discrimination.

Not until the 1960s would the AFGE begin to address noticeably the problem of racial discrimination. While its constitution did not explicitly bar African-Americans, it did not commit initially to fighting discrimination, and union officials did not actively recruit African-Americans during its first decades. After the merger of the AFL and CIO in 1955, and the emergence of the civil rights movement, greater numbers of African-Americans joined, and several national vice-presidents and district leaders brought attention to the issue of discrimination. By 1968, the union had established a Fair Practices Department, and more African-Americans took leadership roles, culminating in the election in 1988 of John N. Sturdivant, who had previously served as executive vice-president. Sturdivant held the presidency until his death in 1997.

In its early years the AFGE's agenda resembled its rival NFFE. The AFGE supported extension of the merit and classification system, lobbied Congress for better pay, including overtime pay for holiday work as well as night differentials, and in 1936 began a drive to set a minimum wage of $1,500 a year for all federal workers. It advocated for retirement benefits, in-service training and promotion from within, improvements to sick leave, greater transparency in the efficiency-rating process, and employee representation on personnel bodies. Although it suspended conventions during World War II, the union continued its activism, spearheading opposition to the government's decision to move a number of agencies out of Washington, D.C., because of overcrowding. During the 1950s, AFGE focused much of its attention on improved benefits, such as health, accident, death, hospitalization insurance, and travel per diems. In 1969, it helped win amendments to the Federal Retirement System. Starting in the 1950s and continuing into the 1990s, the union undertook a campaign against the growing practice of contracting out government work. Faced with significant reductions-in-force during the 1980s and 1990s, members and leaders also strove for greater control and oversight of layoff procedures. Calls for smaller government starting in the 1970s prompted AFGE to fund programs to fight negative images of federal employees. From the 1970s until the early 1990s, the union challenged the 1939 Hatch Act, which had severely limited the political activities of civil servants. Revisions to the act in 1993 enabled federal employees to run for local political offices without having to take a leave of absence and to engage in partisan activities on their own time and outside the office. The AFGE took particular note of the latter provision, because in 1985 the Merit Systems Protection Board successfully charged AFGE President Kenneth T. Blaylock with violating the Hatch Act for supporting Walter Mondale's run for the presidency.

From its inception AFGE used its AFL affiliation to build its membership and strengthen its legislative efforts. Its changing membership and agenda mirrored its evolving identity as a labor organization. This shift was evident in its growing desire to use the tactics and pursue an agenda traditionally associated with the private-sector labor movement.

MARGARET C. RUNG

References and Further Reading

"AFGE History," www.afge.org/Index.cfm?Page=History (2005).

Johnson, Eldon. "General Unions in the Federal Civil Service." *Journal of Politics* 1 (February 1940): 23–56.

Kearney, Richard C., and David G. Carnevale. *Labor Relations in the Public Sector*. 3rd ed. New York: Marcel Dekker, 2001.

Levine, Marvin, and Eugene G. Hagburg. *Public Sector Labor Relations*. St. Paul, MN: West Publishing Co., 1979.

Nevin, Jack, and Lorna Nevin. *AFGE—Federal Union: The Story of the American Federation of Government Employees*. American Federation of Government Employees, 1976.

Rung, Margaret. *Servants of the State: Managing Diversity and Democracy in the Federal Workforce, 1933–1953*. Athens, GA: University of Georgia Press, 2002.

Spero, Sterling D. *Government as Employer*. New York: Remsen Press, 1948.

See also **American Federation of Labor; National Federation of Federal Employees; United Government Employees; United Public Workers of America/United Federal Workers of America**

AMERICAN FEDERATION OF LABOR

The American Federation of Labor (AFL) was the most successful of a series of attempts to create cross-union labor organizations in the nineteenth century. While groups like the General Trades' Union of New York or the National Labor Union failed largely because they could not withstand the worst dips of the business cycle, the AFL's emphasis on organizing skilled, high-paying workers into craft unions provided the financial cushion needed for it to remain (albeit now as the AFL-CIO) to this day. Its politics were generally conservative and often aligned with employers on issues like tariffs and wars. This contributed to the group's longevity by preventing it from being the target of antiradical crackdowns like those waged against the Knights of Labor or Industrial Workers of the World.

The origins of the AFL can be found in disgruntled workers in the Knights of Labor. In 1881, a group of trade unionist Knights, unhappy with the policies of Knights leader Terence Powderly, wanted to set up a national organization under which the officers of the union could be held more accountable, just as was the case with union locals. The new organization founded that year was called the Federation of Organized Trades' and Labor Union of the United States and Canada (FOTLU), and one of its founding officers was a cigar maker named Samuel Gompers. His union had gained great stability through concentration during the 1870s, and Gompers's presence on the board of the FOTLU reflected his belief that the same thing done on a national scale could improve the lot of organized labor in general.

Unfortunately the FOTLU had no program besides a series of legislative demands, and even then it did not have enough power to get them enacted. While 108 delegates from member unions attended the group's first convention in Pittsburgh, only 18 delegates attended the convention in Cleveland next year. While many believed an organization like the FOTLU would be helpful, few national unions were willing to sacrifice their autonomy to create a lasting national federation at this time. According to Philip Taft, this organization "made only a slight contribution to the subsequent policies and practices of the A. F. of L."

The Early Years

Continued competition with the Knights was the chief reason that the FOTLU disappeared and the AFL formed in its place with many of the same member unions. The AFL originated at a December 1886, meeting in Columbus, Ohio. Its first president, Gompers, would serve as president with the exception of 1 year until his death in 1924. The founding national unions in the AFL were the iron molders, the typographers, the granite cutters, the stereotypers, the miners and mine laborers, the journeyman tailors, the journeymen bakers, the furniture workers, the metal workers, the carpenters and joiners, and the cigar makers. There were also local unions of barbers, waiters, bricklayers, and city trades councils from Baltimore, Chicago, St. Louis, Philadelphia, and New York. Ten more international unions joined the AFL during its first year of existence.

The unions that took part in the Federation were of unequal strength. The largest and most successful of these unions, like the International Molders' Union, could wield disproportionate power over the weaker organizations. The vast majority of them (the mine workers being the notable exception) were craft unions, meaning they concentrated on organizing skilled workers. This differentiated the AFL from the Knights of Labor, their chief rival. The railway brotherhoods, whose membership contained workers who were perhaps the most skilled workers in the United States, did not affiliate because they had little need for the AFL's aid. While the AFL was an umbrella organization for national unions, throughout its history there were also many locals that were directly affiliated with the AFL because no national union existed in that industry. Part of the mission of the AFL was to organize the unorganized, and it employed organizers to achieve that goal. While the initial result of these efforts would be directly affiliated locals, the eventual result in ideal circumstances was supposed to be the creation of new national AFL affiliates.

Gompers's chief objective as president was to improve the economic position of the membership of the AFL's member unions. In his report to the 1890 AFL convention, Gompers wrote:

> I am willing to subordinate my opinions to the well being, harmony and success of the labor movement; I am willing to sacrifice myself upon the alter of any phase or action it may take for its advancement; I am willing to step aside if it will promote our cause; but I cannot and will not prove false to my convictions that trade unions pure and simple are the natural organizations of wage workers to secure their present and practical improvement and to achieve their final emancipation. (Samuel Gompers, "Report to the 1890 AFL Convention")

While the phrase pure and simple unionism is often used to describe the AFL's program, it is quite vague. What pure and simple trade unionism definitely did not include at this juncture was entanglement with party politics. Gompers's chief opponents within the AFL during the early years of his presidency were socialists who had a different view than he on the question of politic involvement by the organization. But the AFL recognized that even though newly established unions often wanted to strike, such times were not conducive to victory, since new labor organizations were often unstable. Socialists instigated Gompers's defeat for the presidency by United Mine Workers' President John McBride at the 1894 Denver convention for this reason. Since Gompers was returned to the presidency the next year, he liked to refer to 1895 as his sabbatical year.

Besides its emphasis on craft unionism, another reflection of the AFL's conservatism was its hostility toward organizing workers of other races. While the AFL claimed to be race-blind, it did not really practice what it preached. It did not allow unions to bar African-Americans workers, but its emphasis on organizing skilled workers meant that most black workers were tacitly excluded. Those black workers in AFL member unions were usually relegated to segregated locals and were admitted only in order to prevent black workers from sabotaging future strikes. Similar prejudice can be seen in the AFL's attitude toward Chinese workers. Gompers's cigar makers union had been at the forefront of lobbying for the Chinese Exclusion Act in 1882. In 1903, when sugar beet workers struck in Oxnard, California, Gompers offered to let the victorious workers directly affiliate with the AFL as long as they denied membership to Chinese workers.

The Progressive Era, World War I, and the 1920s

While many Progressive Era reform groups worked to improve the lot of U.S. workers, the AFL was suspicious of state involvement in industrial relations. Certainly some of this attitude is a reflection of the AFL's constituency of skilled workers, who were more likely to survive on their own than their less-skilled counterparts. However it also reflects a suspicion of government brought on by its hostility toward organized labor. A Bill of Grievances, drawn up by the AFL and submitted to Congress in 1906, included such complaints as the failure to enact an 8-hour law. The AFL also urged its members to be more politically active for the first time.

Faced with this kind of hostility from the public and private sector, it is no wonder that AFL leaders turned to more moderate employers to find some kind of common ground. Gompers and other AFL union presidents, such as John Mitchell of the United Mine Workers, were members of the National Civic Federation (NCF), a group of businessmen and labor leaders organized in 1899. In fact Gompers served as the group's vice-president. The NCF wanted to lower the rancor associated with industrial controversy by opening up lines of communication across the class divide. It intervened in many of the strikes of the era in the hopes of mediating a solution. While it had no luck with large disputes like the steel strike of 1901, it did help settle over one hundred industrial disputes. Another important part of the NCF's mission was to promote welfare work (historians now call it welfare capitalism), amenities provided by management to labor that went beyond ordinary monetary compensation.

Critics from the left condemned the organization as aiding in management attempts to steer workers away from class conflict. In 1905, a socialist resolution condemning Gompers's membership in the organization was voted down at the AFL convention. In 1911, three resolutions not directly tied to socialists (including one from the United Mine Workers, which had changed its position since Mitchell had been that group's president) were voted down. In truth Gompers's membership in the NCF was a perfect reflection of the AFL's willingness to compromise with the political and economic establishment. The

AFL officers remained part of the NCF's board until 1935.

When prolabor Democrat Woodrow Wilson became president in 1913, the AFL welcomed its new-found influence. While the Republicans had rebuffed the AFL repeatedly, Wilson gladly wrote Gompers long letters. The most important fruit of this relationship was the AFL's support for the successful passage of the Clayton Act in 1914. Designed in part to end the prosecution of unions under the Sherman Antitrust Act, it included language that stated that "the labor of a human being is not a commodity or article of commerce." The act was widely hailed as "labor's Magna Carta," but the Supreme Court's narrow reading of the act left workers everywhere terribly disappointed.

When World War I began, the United States was not part of it, and the AFL wanted to keep it that way. But as time passed and the nation inched closer to war, the AFL grew increasingly supportive of the United States getting more involved. Once World War I began, the AFL signed an agreement with the government in which some union workers in defense industries forswore the right to strike in exchange for certain rights being protected. This was later extended to other industries through the rulings of the National War Labor Board (NWLB), which the government formed to regulate industrial relations during the conflict. Whether labor's rights under this agreement included the right to strike was always a matter of controversy; however there is no doubt that AFL unions grew significantly in membership during the war because of the NWLB's labor-friendly rulings.

Perhaps the best sign that the labor movement increased in stature during the war was the new-found respect that the government showed the AFL. In 1917, President Wilson visited its convention in Buffalo, the first time it had ever had such an important guest. Not only did the administration ask Gompers for advice on whom to appoint to certain government boards that dealt with labor matters, Gompers himself received an appointment to a government board that planned how labor would be allocated during the war. As wartime assaults on labor by employers increased, Gompers had the ear of President Wilson. An organization that had once eschewed politics had now found a way to make it work to its advantage.

The 1924 U.S. presidential election marked a significant turning point in the history of the AFL's political activity. Unhappy with both parties for their failure to provide any positive policies to aid labor, the AFL endorsed independent candidate Robert La Follette. Perhaps even more significant than this was the enthusiasm with which the AFL endorsed him. Gompers, while ill, came to the AFL convention.

Perhaps Gompers's efforts were the last bit of energy he had, since the longtime AFL president died shortly after the election. The leadership replaced Gompers with William Green, the secretary-treasurer of the United Mine Workers.

The Depression, the New Deal, and the Split

When the Depression struck, the AFL began by debating proposals to help unemployed union members. It backed shorter hours to promote work sharing in 1930, and eventually unemployment insurance. The AFL also strongly supported unemployment relief long before Roosevelt became president. The first great victory for the AFL during the Roosevelt administration was the inclusion of Section 7(a) in the National Industrial Recovery Act (NIRA). Although who suggested the exact language by which the government recognized the right of employees to organize for the first time has been lost to history, there were many drafts circulating in AFL headquarters beforehand. Some unions (such as the Mine Workers) made more of this vague legislation than others (such as the Amalgamated Association of Iron, Steel and Tin Workers, which essentially left its potential constituents to organize themselves). To Green's credit however, he did his best to prompt such slower unions to take action.

When the Supreme Court invalidated the NIRA, the AFL threw itself behind a replacement sponsored by Senator Robert Wagner of New York. Indeed AFL leaders met with Wagner to help design a bill that would protect their interests and be easier for the government to enforce. Once it passed, President Green even submitted names to the president for consideration as members of the National Labor Relations Board (NLRB), and one of their suggestions was accepted. The AFL's opinion of the NLRB would soon change, since its leaders came to believe that it favored a rival federation during disputes.

That rival federation was of course the Congress of Industrial Organizations (CIO, first called the Committee of Industrial Organizations until its member unions were suspended in 1937). From the AFL's perspective, the primary sin of John L. Lewis' new industrial union movement was the fact that it was a dual union even though the CIO's member unions intended to concentrate on organizing workers in largely unorganized industries. Nevertheless the existence of tiny craft unions in industries like steel and in shipyards were enough to make the CIO look like traitors in the eyes of the AFL's leadership. The issue of whether to start organizing along industrial lines had been debated for years by the time of the break-up, and the CIO unions had always lost. While the AFL technically suspended the CIO only after a 1937 trial, the severe charges that the AFL brought against the CIO strongly suggested that a break was coming and that the AFL was playing for the sympathy of workers who had yet to choose sides.

Peace talks between the two organizations in late-1937 failed, in large part because the AFL leadership was divided on whether to let the CIO back and the CIO itself was too committed to its efforts to want to return. In fact you can make a good case that rivalry with the CIO was good for the labor movement in the late-1930s, since it stimulated both organizations to make successful organizing efforts. The membership that the AFL lost when the CIO union left was more than made up for by 1938. While this did not compare to the unprecedented growth rate that the CIO experienced over the same time period, it certainly improved morale at AFL headquarters.

From World War II to the Merger

In late 1941, the AFL and CIO came together to support another no-strike pledge during the coming conflict. Over the course of World War II, representatives from the AFL and CIO met regularly in an effort to stop labor infighting from harming needed production. The no-strike pledge included the promise that the government would enforce maintenance of membership and dues check-off on employers with war contracts. This meant that the membership of both federations grew sharply over the course of the conflict. The chief problem that AFL leadership faced during the war was to get the administration to drop wage controls, embodied under the NWLB's "Little Steel" decision. This was the cause of many wildcat strikes by member union locals during the war, but in the end the government did not budge on this issue.

After the war the government offered the AFL the chance to participate in the postwar-planning process. The AFL also developed a foreign policy, reaching out to mainstream European labor through its newly formed International Affairs Department. The ex-Communist Jay Lovestone and the AFL's representative in Europe, Irving Brown, also tried to influence developing countries away from Soviet influence. Although many contend that the AFL took money from the Central Intelligence Agency once the Cold War began, the AFL (and later the AFL-CIO) has always denied this charge. Despite its efforts to be good citizens, the AFL suffered a series of legislative setbacks in the late-1940s, most notably the Taft-Hartley ACT of 1947. The clause in the act that required union leaders to take loyalty oaths in order to benefit from the National Labor Relations Act led to the redisaffiliation of the United Mine Workers (which had rejoined the federation after a fallout between John L. Lewis and CIO President Philip Murray).

While there had been unity talks going on for years, the deaths of Green and CIO leader Murray in the early 1950s meant that there were new people at the top of each organization, leaders who did not participate in all the rancor of the late-1930s. George Meany, Green's secretary-treasurer, assumed the AFL presidency in 1952. Merger talks began with the signing of a mutual no-raiding agreement in 1954. The merger plan, ratified in 1955, solidified jurisdictional lines between member unions, recognized the independence of each member union, and recognized the legitimacy of industrial organization (the issue that had caused the split in the first place).

JONATHAN REES

References and Further Reading

Kaufman, Stuart. *Samuel Gompers and the Origins of the American Federation of Labor, 1848–1896*. Westport, CT: Greenwood Press, 1973.

Lorwin, Lewis. *The American Federation of Labor: History, Politics, and Prospects*. New York: Sentry Press, 1971. [Originally printed in 1933.]

Taft, Philip. *The A. F. of L. from the Death of Gompers to the Merger*. New York: Harper and Brothers, 1959.

———. *The A. F. of L. in the Time of Gompers*. New York: Harper & Brothers, 1957.

See also **Gompers, Samuel; Knights of Labor, National Civic Federation; National Industrial Recovery Act**

AMERICAN FEDERATION OF LABOR-CONGRESS OF INDUSTRIAL ORGANIZATIONS

The American Federation of Labor and Congress of Industrial Organizations (AFL-CIO) is a federation of autonomous labor unions in the United States, Canada, Mexico, Panama, and U.S. dependencies. The merger of the American Federation of Labor (AFL) and the Congress of Industrial Organizations (CIO) created the organization in 1955. Headquartered in Washington, D.C., officially the federation is governed by a quadrennial convention (originally biannual) and an executive council. Day-to-day power is vested in a president, an executive vice-president, and a secretary-treasurer. Key federation departments include International Affairs, Legislation, Civil Rights,

Organization, Research, and Industrial Unions. The Committee on Political Education (COPE) focuses on political mobilization for the federation.

From its start, the AFL-CIO's primary function has been to provide support and organizational services for affiliates, especially political lobbying on the national level. Although critics have maligned the AFL-CIO as more of an interest group than the spearhead of a movement, from its founding, the federation has been a conspicuous national force pressing for liberal reform and the interests of U.S. workers.

In December 1955, delegates from both the AFL and the CIO gathered in New York City with the goal of putting a permanent end to divisions that had wracked the labor movement since the 1930s. The deaths in close succession of AFL President William Green and CIO President Philip Murray in 1952 placed in power a new generation of leaders less tied to the conflicts of the past. Likewise by midcentury, a consensus based on Keynesian economics, anti-communism, and liberal reform at home emerged within the labor movement. Since the AFL was the larger, more prosperous of the two organizations, the merger tended to be on its terms. AFL President George Meany and AFL Secretary-Treasurer William F. Schnitzler thus, respectively, became president and secretary-treasurer of the new federation. The CIO President Walter Reuther took one of many vice-presidential slots and was placed at the head of the new Industrial Union Department.

While the quest for unity inspired the merger, fostering harmony between key AFL-CIO leaders still proved challenging. The ambitious Reuther pressed Meany and the AFL-CIO to take a more activist posture, particularly on the key issue of organizing. Likewise A. Philip Randolph, the legendary president of the Brotherhood of Sleeping Car Porters and an AFL-CIO vice-president, led a sometimes frustrating crusade against discriminatory practices in some federation trade unions. When Randolph rose at the 1959 AFL-CIO convention to press his cause, Meany snapped back: "Who the hell appointed you as the guardian of all the Negroes in America?"

Although a general anti-Communist consensus united federation leaders, differences regarding foreign policy also caused divisions. Jay Lovestone, the former head of the American Communist party turned sharply anti-Communist, had become a key advisor to Meany and the AFL leadership. Although Lovestone did not originally head the new AFL-CIO International Affairs Department (a position he took in 1963), he remained a forceful, controversial influence on Meany and others. Under Lovestone's sway, the AFL-CIO maintained a principled no-contact policy with trade unions in Communist countries.

Meanwhile Reuther and others in the AFL-CIO resented Lovestone's heavy-handed influence and pressed for dialogue with Communists and neutralists.

The early years of the AFL-CIO also saw continuing struggles over the corruption/racketeering endemic in some unions. In the late 1950s, congressional investigations into the Teamsters brought the issue again to the forefront. As evidence mounted, Meany moved against the Teamsters. In 1957, the AFL-CIO Executive Council suspended Teamsters President Dave Beck for violating the federation's ethical practices code. When the equally controversial Jimmy Hoffa replaced Beck, Meany expelled the Teamsters from the federation despite the union's yearly contribution of over $800,000 to the AFL-CIO. Although Meany hoped to forestall federal action by handling corruption in-house, in 1959 Congress passed the Landrum-Griffin Act, expanding federal regulation of internal union affairs. Meany openly lamented that Congress "was stampeded" by public pressure into passing the new regulations.

Frequent recessions, growing concerns over automation, and conservative fiscal policies rendered the Eisenhower years frustrating for AFL-CIO leaders. The federation therefore eagerly embraced Senator John F. Kennedy's 1960 campaign for president and its mantra of "we can do better." Only a month after JFK's inauguration, the AFL-CIO Executive Council marveled: "The new administration has given the nation a new sense of purpose, urgency and hope."

In retrospect the early and mid-1960s were the federation's golden years. The rapid growth of public employee unions augmented union membership even as traditional unions began to lose numbers with the first signs of de-industrialization. Meanwhile the liberalism laced with strong anticommunism of JFK and his successor Lyndon Johnson, who quickly forged unprecedented bonds with federation leaders, echoed labor's long-held political agenda. The AFL-CIO applauded Johnson's War on Poverty and advances in the civil rights arena, although the AFL-CIO resisted openly endorsing the 1963 March on Washington, fearing the influence of a radical element. Meany celebrated the harmonious labor/liberal alliance times as he opened the 1965 AFL-CIO convention: "To a greater degree than ever before in the history of this country, the stated goals of the administration and of Congress, on the one hand, and of the labor movement on the other are practically identical."

During this era, the federation also expanded its foreign operations, working ever closer with the U.S. government, especially Kennedy's Agency for International Development (AID). Since World War II in fact, both the AFL and CIO had established an increasingly strong international presence as part of their campaign against the perceived threat of communism. Beginning first in Western Europe then expanding to the Third World, labor operatives worked around the globe, sometimes closely with the CIA. Lovestone and other federation officials maintained close ties to the CIA well into the 1980s. Encouraged by Lovestone the federation founded in 1962 the American Institute for Free Labor Development (AIFLD) to support anti-Communist trade unionism in Latin America. Two years later the federation christened the African Labor College, and in 1968, it organized the Asian American Free Labor Institute. In each case AID provided the majority of funding, while the AFL-CIO administered the semi-private organizations.

But the federation's stalwart anticommunism and extensive foreign operations quickly proved the source of controversy—especially with the beginning of the Vietnam War. Given its virulent anticommunism and its close ties to a trade union movement in Saigon, the AFL-CIO jumped to support intervention in Vietnam, offering its unstinting support for the war. In response an antiwar movement sprang up at the rank-and-file grassroots level. Among the rank-and-file, polls showed trade unionists as even more likely than the average citizen to oppose escalation and favor withdrawal—understandable given the working-class roots of many of those sent to Southeast Asia. As liberal doves ramped up attacks on the Johnson administration, the federation found itself alienated from many of its liberal allies. The controversial war also worsened relations between Meany and Reuther. In 1966, Victor Reuther, the activist brother of Walter, gave an extended interview to the *Los Angeles Times* in which he revealed the federation's joint work with the CIA. Other revelations quickly followed. The *Washington Post* soon was complaining that "a union which does secret government work is not the kind of 'free trade union,' responsive to its members' will, which American ideals enshrine."

The ordeal of the 1968 presidential campaign only added to a sense of crisis. Federation leaders were particularly shocked at President Johnson's withdrawal from the race in March 1968. "I don't know how long it will take me to recover from the atomic bomb which President Johnson hurled," wrote Lovestone to Meany. The federation then pumped unprecedented resources into the campaign of Vice-President Hubert Humphrey, but to no avail.

Meanwhile discouraged by the war and frustrated by what he saw as the stagnant, unimaginative leadership of the AFL-CIO, Walter Reuther moved to pursue an independent destiny. In March 1968, he demanded a special AFL-CIO convention to modernize and revitalize the labor movement. When it

became clear that Meany would control such a convention, Reuther pulled his UAW out of the AFL-CIO. Initially Reuther hoped to weld together an alliance of former CIO unions to challenge Meany's leadership. But even among his allies, he found little support. Instead Reuther turned to the two million-member Teamsters, ousted by Meany in the late 1950s. In 1968, with the renegade Teamsters, Reuther launched the Alliance for Labor Action (ALA). With a membership of roughly 3.5 million, the new organization aimed to re-energize the labor movement, focusing on organization and forging alliances with liberal and radical groups. But with strong opposition from Meany and deep cultural and philosophical divides between the UAW and Teamsters, the organization struggled. Walter Reuther's death in a plane crash in 1970 effectively ended the experiment.

During the Nixon years, the federation strove to maintain its support for the war in Vietnam and to repair ties with its former liberal allies—both with limited success. Having won with a meager 43% of the popular vote, President Richard Nixon hoped to expand his political base. While Nixon relied largely on patriotic symbolism and his quest for "peace with honor" in Vietnam to attract blue-collar voters, his actions often undercut his cultivation plan. Nixon's successive nominations in 1969 of Clement F. Haynsworth and G. Harrold Carswell met with fierce opposition from the AFL-CIO, which could take pride in contributing to their defeat. Likewise the administration's introduction of the so-called Philadelphia Plan, a model requiring contractors on federal projects to make good faith efforts to integrate their workforce in accordance with the local black-white population ratio, also met with resistance from the federation.

As the first signs of inflation overtook the economy, many in Nixon's administration openly blamed labor, specifically construction workers, for rising prices. Nixon's suspension of the Davis-Bacon Act in 1971 and his introduction of price and wage controls that same year further angered AFL-CIO leaders. Meany, despite his reputation as a hawkish anachronism, emerged a leading critic of the president's economic plan. When Nixon appeared before the AFL-CIO biannual convention in November 1971, Meany and assembled delegates greeted the president with a notable lack of enthusiasm (some claimed a notable rudeness).

Yet despite tensions with Nixon, no fundamental reconciliation with liberals occurred. While the AFL-CIO hoped that a hawkish moderate, such as Senator Henry Jackson, might successfully challenge Nixon, federation leaders watched with anxiety the accession of liberal dove Senator George McGovern to the

Democratic nomination. Dismayed at McGovern's foreign policy stance and his dismissive treatment of labor, the AFL-CIO Executive Council voted 27-3 in favor of neutrality in the 1972 election. Nixon's overwhelming reelection however hardly mended fences between the federation and the president. By the fall of 1973, in the midst of the Watergate scandal, the AFL-CIO Executive Council called for Nixon's resignation or impeachment "in the interest of preserving our democratic system of government."

Grave concerns about a weakening economy—with unemployment running at 8.5% in 1975—also preoccupied the federation by the mid-1970s. Facing a deep recession, the AFL-CIO maintained its calls for full-employment policies, including lower interest rates, public works projects for the unemployed, and increased federal spending. Meany particularly assailed Nixon's successor, Gerald Ford, as heading a "government of negativism." Ford's veto of situs picketing legislation in early 1976 particularly infuriated Meany, who blasted the president's "nihilistic use of veto power."

But the federation proved unable to recover the political power it lost in the late 1960s. During the 1976 campaign, the AFL-CIO found itself a potential liability for the Democratic candidate Jimmy Carter. Republican Vice-Presidential candidate Robert Dole brazenly suggested, "[I]f Jimmy Carter is elected . . . Meany would have the key to the front door and the back door of the White House." Relief at Carter's election, on which the federation had spent considerable funds and energies, quickly turned to frustration when the new president showed little interest in reversing controversial elements of the Taft-Hartley and Landrum-Griffin Acts. Nor could the AFL-CIO take much solace in the passage of the Humphrey-Hawkins Full Employment Act, which was so watered down by Congress it made little impact. Soon Meany was maligning Carter as a conservative. Meany's death in 1979 and his replacement by the staid Lane Kirkland served as only further confirmation that the era of labor power had passed.

Still the election of ultraconservative Ronald Reagan, with considerable support from blue-collar workers fed up with inflation and joblessness, came as a jolt to the federation. To rally opposition to Reagan's economic plans, the AFL-CIO organized a massive Solidarity Day march on Washington, which drew some 500,000 protesters. The 1980s also saw something of a spirit of reconciliation within the labor movement as both the Teamsters and United Auto Workers re-affiliated with the federation. Seeking to improve organized labor's public relations, Kirkland also created the Labor Institute for Public Affairs. A graduate of Georgetown University's Foreign Service School, Kirkland, like Meany, was deeply drawn to foreign affairs and spent significant federation resources supporting the Solidarity movement in Poland.

While Kirkland could take credit for success in Poland, the AFL-CIO's fortunes at home continued to falter. While unionized workers made up 33% of the workforce in 1960, the figure fell precipitously to 14% by the early 1990s. Even the election of Democratic William J. Clinton in 1992 appeared a mixed blessing, since the new president proved a vigorous supporter of the North American Free Trade Agreement and other free trade initiatives. Meanwhile a generation of activists, centered in the Service Workers' International Union (SWIU), rallied against the lethargy of Kirkland and the AFL-CIO. When Republicans took control of both the House and the Senate in the 1994 off-year elections, the activists felt it was time to move. The next year SWIU President John Sweeny announced he would challenge Kirkland for the AFL-CIO presidency. Foreseeing his own defeat, Kirkland retired in favor of AFL-CIO Secretary-Treasurer Thomas R. Donahue. The reform, New Voice ticket headed by Sweeney however soundly defeated Donahue at the federation's 1995 convention.

Sweeney aimed to bring a new relevance to the AFL-CIO in part by pouring federation funds and energies into organizing and political campaigns. The new leadership introduced such ambitious programs as Union Summer, a 5-week internship program for young activists. The success of the 1997 AFL-CIO-sponsored strike against United Parcel Services seemed to herald a new day for the federation and organized labor. But continuing Republican control of Congress and the defeat of AFL-CIO supported candidates in the presidential elections of 2000 and 2004 dealt severe blows to Sweeney's political strategy. Likewise union membership continued to drop, and expensive organizing and political campaigns depleted federation coffers. In the summer of 2005, both the Teamsters and SWIU (Sweeney's own union) defected from the federation and formed the rival Work to Change alliance. Federation membership, which peaked in 1974 at 14 million, fell to a meager 9 million (representing 54 unions) by 2005. Still Sweeney managed re-election in the fall of 2005 and vows that the AFL-CIO will remain an active force fighting in the interest of workers.

EDMUND F. WEHRLE

References and Further Reading

Goldberg, Arthur. *AFL-CIO: Labor United*. New York, 1956.

Lichtenstein, Nelson. *Most Dangerous Man in Detroit: Walter Reuther and the Fate of American Labor.* New York, 1995.

Moody, Kim. *An Injury to All: The Decline of the American Labor Movement.* London, 1986.

Morgan, Ted. *A Covert Life, Jay Lovestone, Communist, Anti-Communist, and Spymaster.* New York, 1999.

Robinson, Archie. *George Meany and His Times.* New York, 1981.

Wehrle, Edmund. *"Between a River and a Mountain": The AFL-CIO and the Vietnam War, 1947–1975.* Ann Arbor: University of Michigan Press, 2005.

Zieger, Robert H. *American Workers, American Unions, 1920–1985.* New York, 1986.

AMERICAN FEDERATION OF MUSICIANS

The American Federation of Musicians (AFM) was established in Indianapolis on October 19, 1896. The formation of the AFM effectively ended a period of intense competition between the Knights of Labor and the American Federation of Labor (AFL) to organize musicians, since the majority of musician's guilds previously in the National League of Musicians joined the AFM. The AFM determined that any musician paid for his or her services could be considered a professional musician and was therefore eligible for membership. This new system of inclusion expanded the AFM's membership immediately; from 3,000 original members to 45,000 by 1906, and by World War II, the AFM had become the largest entertainers' union in the world. After peaking with a membership of over 200,000 during the 1950s, the AFM's membership has declined but remains strong at approximately 100,000 today. While the AFM has faced problems common to many unions, for much of its history the organization's principle concern has been the battle against technological displacement. The union has fought primarily to retain steady employment for its members, to preserve live musical performances, and to help musicians reap appropriate portions of the benefits derived from their recorded music.

In its early years, the AFM's primary threat was competition from European and military bands. European bands toured extensively in the United States from the middle of the nineteenth century, and were favored by U.S. booking agents because of their relatively low cost and high public appeal. The AFM, led by Joseph Weber (president, 1900–1914, 1915–1940), repeatedly fought to exclude European bands under the Alien Contract Labor Law of 1885, but the United States Congress continually rejected their case because they considered musicians artists, a category of worker exempted under that law. Only in 1932 did Congress narrow the definition of artist to restrict competition from European musicians. The AFM had earlier but less-definitive success staving off competition from military bands. Military bands, effectively subsidized by the U.S. government, undercut union musicians with cheaper rates. Consistent lobbying efforts by the AFM eventually convinced Congress to restrict military bands from competing with civilian musicians in 1916, but after World War II the order was rescinded, and military band competition remained a problem until 1978, when the AFM voted to allow U.S. military personnel to join the union.

Through the years the naturally mobile nature of musicians and their work, the frequently blurred line between professional and amateur, and the ephemeral nature of the musician's product has made enforcing union lines difficult. Tensions between traveling and local musicians have risen within the AFM since its inception. In 1902, the AFM addressed jurisdictional problems through the transfer system, whereby a musician working in a new city could get a transfer card, pay limited dues, and play limited engagements. The AFM has tweaked the transfer system over the years, and since 1934, it has included a surcharge on traveling musicians' contracts. The transfer system has been an organizational and financial success. The surcharge has accounted for up to two-thirds of yearly union revenues collected nationally, and musician and historian George Seltzer credited it with the union's early growth in membership.

The maturation of recording technology and the increased use of canned, or recorded, music by the entertainment industry during the 1920s marked a turning point for musicians and the AFM. The development of recording and listening devices, the birth of talking movies, and the expansion of commercial radio changed the means and opportunities for musicians to earn a living. Theater musicians, who formed an important component of the AFM due to their steady employment and good wages, were particularly hard hit. Prior to the 1927 release of the *Jazz Singer*, the first talking picture, movie theaters employed tens of thousands of musicians nationally to provide musical accompaniment to silent films. By the Great Depression, the new movie technology resulted in 22,000 national theater musicians being replaced by just a few hundred studio musicians in Hollywood. The concurrent rise in commercial radio created new employment opportunities, but not nearly fast enough or in large enough numbers. Initially stations relied on musicians playing for publicity. Some used network and recorded programming. Even after major radio networks determined talent was worth paying for, however, employment was concentrated in a few major cities and fell far short of replacing jobs lost in the theater business.

The AFM leadership and rank-and-file fought technological displacement and Depression-related unemployment with limited results from 1927–1936. Although the AFM leadership, led still by President Weber, initially believed that the public would reject canned music in favor of live performances, this proved false. The AFM launched an unsuccessful publicity campaign aimed at convincing the public that recorded music debased the artform. In fact the popularity of movies with sound undermined the position of theater musicians over the course of the decade. While Chicago musicians successfully struck theaters in 1927, New York's theater musicians were unable to generate a popular boycott of theaters during the 1930s. Although WPA programs relieved some of the pressure caused by unemployment, by the late 1930s, the AFM rank and file were unsatisfied and turned to new leadership.

In 1940, the AFM chose James Caesar Petrillo to be its new president, largely on the basis of Petrillo's aggressive tactics to ensure employment for musicians. As president of the Chicago Federation of Musicians (CFM), Petrillo had effectively used strikes, and the threat of recording bans, to preserve jobs, force radio stations to bargain collectively and to hire standby musicians, and to organize hotel musicians. An outspoken critic of the AFM's failed publicity campaign tactics, Petrillo argued that musicians who made recordings were unique in actually creating the product that replaced them and argued that the music industry should share profits to ensure live musical performance. In 1942, Petrillo organized the first of two major labor actions under his reign, declaring that AFM musicians would no longer make recordings. The AFM sought to force music companies to pay a surcharge on recorded music, a fee that the AFM would use to hire unemployed musicians to play free, public concerts. Despite public pressure to end the wartime ban, the AFM eventually forced recording companies to concede. The result was the Recording and Transcription Fund (RFT), which required record labels to pay to the AFM a few cents per record, money that was then used to pay for live performances. The RTF was made illegal by the 1946 Lea Act (also known as the Anti-Petrillo Act), which also banned musicians from bargaining collectively with radio stations. In response Petrillo called for yet another recording ban in 1948, one that circumvented the legal logistics of the first. The resulting Musicians Performance Trust Fund (MPTF) eventually collected and paid millions of dollars for concerts.

While the AFM reached its peak membership during the 1950s, the diversity within its membership created new problems. The MPTF exposed one fault line between full-time, well-compensated musicians and their part-time, or moonlighting, counterparts. Some of the elite musicians and the companies who employed them for instance balked at their recordings being used to subsidize the MPTF. The Los Angeles local was a particularly active opponent of the MPTF, since some of its members believed the surtax encouraged the entertainment industry to hire foreign competition. The disagreement hit a critical point in 1958, when the disgruntled musicians, many employed by national radio and television networks, formed a dual union, the Musicians Guild of America (MGA). The impasse was settled only when Petrillo stepped down as AFM president in 1958, and his handpicked successor, Herman Kenin, reduced the required contributions to the MPTF.

Black union members also challenged AFM practices during the 1950s. Since 1902, with the notable exception of New York Local 802, the AFM had segregated black musicians into separate or subsidiary locals. Again the initial challenge came from California. In 1953 Los Angeles's black and white locals decided to merge, and in 1956 they used the national AFM convention to propose an end to segregated locals nationwide. Petrillo actively resisted integration, and change occurred only slowly under Kenin. The issue of integrating locals was a divisive one, and one that did not break down simply or strictly along racial lines. Many white locals resisted integration, but many black locals resisted similarly, not wanting to give up their assets and fearing that their autonomy and representation would be curtailed in majority white locals. Throughout the 1960s, local activists, and Kenin at the national level, slowly worked out merger agreements in the majority of cities, and by the early 1970s, only two segregated locals remained. In many instances however, locals' mergers did not result in equitable unions, and initially few blacks achieved leadership positions.

The AFM's simple mandates remain the same today as they did at its inception: Securing good, full-time jobs for musicians and controlling their recorded product. For example it remains difficult for many musicians to earn a living playing live music. A 2003 National Endowment for the Arts report found that two-thirds of jazz musicians make less than $7,000 a year. In addition the AFM has remained active in promoting legislation to secure musicians' rights to their recorded product. Since 1980, the AFM has supported several pieces of federal legislation designed to curb piracy. Considering recent technological advances, such as the growth of the internet, it appears likely that the AFM will find technological changes a major issue well into its second century of existence.

CHRIS WONDERLICH

References and Further Reading

Seltzer, George. *Music Matters: The Performers and the American Federation of Musicians*. Metuchen, NJ: The Scarecrow Press, Inc., 1989.

Spivey, Donald. *Union and the Black Musician: The Narrative of William Everett Samuels and Chicago Local 208*. New York: University Press of America, 1984.

Zinn, Howard, Dana Frank, and Robin D. G. Kelley. *Three Strikes: Miners, Musicians, Salegirls, and the Fighting Spirit of Labor's Last Century*. Boston: Beacon Press, 2001.

See also **Petrillo, James Caesar**

AMERICAN FEDERATION OF STATE, COUNTY, AND MUNICIPAL EMPLOYEES (AFSCME)

Despite its start as an organization representing less than a hundred Wisconsin civil service employees in 1932, the American Federation of State, County, and Municipal Employees (AFSCME, pronounced afs-mee), grew to become the largest and one of the most powerful unions in the United States by the end of the twentieth century. The AFSCME's dynamic growth in the post-1945 period sets it apart from the downward trends experienced by organized labor through this era. The union's success comes from a variety of factors, largely the corresponding expansion in government employment in the twentieth century, and that fact that unlike the industrial sector, government service employment cannot be outsourced beyond U.S. boundaries. The AFSCME's unique position within the U.S. labor movement has drawn on its ability to pioneer in organizing sectors of the economy traditionally overlooked by craft and industrial unions, including health care services, higher education, clerical, technical, and professional employees in both the government and nonprofit sectors. Its power within the U.S. labor movement has also been characterized by highly visible national leadership committed to political activism and a kind of social movement unionism that seeks to connect workplace issues with the concerns of the broader community. This tradition of social unionism within AFSCME is usually associated with the major social changes of the 1960s, although the union's origins date back to the early New Deal period.

Local Origins of a National Union

The origins of the AFSCME trace back to 1932, when a small group of Wisconsin state employees organized to protect their jobs against a wave of politically based firings. Before the 1932 gubernatorial election in Wisconsin, Col. A. E. Garey, Wisconsin's director of civil service, met with Republican Governor Philip LaFollette to discuss the possibility of establishing a state employee's organization. LaFollette accepted the idea just as Democratic victories in November ushered in the beginning of political dismissals, with jobs given to the victorious party's loyalists in disregard of existing civil service law. With LaFollette's favorable nod, Garey and a small group of organizers put together the Wisconsin State Employees' Association (WSEA), consisting of about 50 state administrators as well as clerical and technical employees. The small organization developed a campaign that called on local labor, farmer, women's, and veteran's groups to support them in their struggle. The WSEA, with help from this coalition of citizens, succeeded in both saving the jobs of its members and in strengthening the existing state civil service code. This early success gained the WSEA notoriety across the state, and the organization gradually grew.

Arnold Zander, Wisconsin's state personnel administrator, emerged as the early leader of the association. Active in the original organizing campaign and the chief architect of the publicity drive to save state jobs, Zander believed that the politicized climate of government employment demanded a permanent organization to represent state workers against the possibility of future attacks against the civil service system. Zander envisioned a union of professionals, men and women in all areas of government service who sought to make their government jobs respectable careers, rather than the spoils rewarded them for loyalty to specific political sponsors. Under his leadership the state organization grew, forming new units and incorporating existing civil service associations and mutual aid groups. Soon after forming, in an attempt to legitimatize the association with labor councils, WSEA was granted an American Federation of Labor (AFL) charter as Federal Labor Union 18213. With continued success in membership drives through 1934, Zander was convinced that a larger, more powerful national organization of state and local government workers could be formed. Meetings with AFL President William Green provided Zander with the mandate to form a national union to organize local and state government workers not represented by existing federal organizations. Established in 1935 as a chapter within the American Federation of Government Employees (AFGE), the organization soon emerged as its own chartered union the following year, with Zander elected its first president, a position he would hold for almost 30 years.

In August 1936, AFSCME had 119 locals with just under 4,000 members, expanding to 9,737 by the end of the year. The union continued to expand in these early years, although its membership rates never equaled the successes of industrial unions of this period. The limited ability of public-sector unions to expand, despite the millions of potential members, reflected the realities of the legal environment faced by organized public employees of this era. Following the passing of the Wagner Act in 1937, new federal labor legislation guaranteed U.S. workers the right to join unions for the first time in U.S. history, leading to an unprecedented upward spike in membership and political influence. Government employees however at both federal and local levels were not covered by these laws. Their exemption reflects a long tradition of hostility to public employee organizations, both by public administrators and most of the tax-paying public. Even in the mid-1930s, the legacy of the failed 1918 Boston Police Strike, where civil chaos erupted after the city's police officers walked off the job, still shaped negative opinions about the unionization of government employees. Although federal organizations, such as the American Federation of Government Employees (AFGE) existed, along with the AFL's International Association of Firefighters (IAFF) and scores of local police associations and mutual aid societies, these organizations lacked the legal rights to challenge power on the job formally and remained a weak presence, both in the government workplace and within the ranks of organized labor.

By 1940, AFSCME's numbers had grown to 29,087, claiming members in 33 states, including chapters in the South and Far West. The largest sections of the union in these early years were in Cincinnati, Milwaukee, and Wayne County, Michigan, all with membership from 1,000–2,000. Philadelphia emerged as an early innovator within the federation, with 2,500 members in the city's Public Works Department, and succeeded in pressuring the city's Republican administrations for wage increases, civil service reforms, and a say in workplace regulations and hiring practices. The typical local however was quite small and midwestern, such as the Davenport, Iowa, local of 48 members. Considering its national membership, AFSCME had a truly polyglot union, with locals representing white-collar employees and such professionals as librarians and social workers, clerical staff of all ranks, as well as blue-collar divisions made up primarily of public works employees. The AFSCME also innovated in the revival of police unionism in the late 1930s, representing 36 locals of police officers in 1946 in addition to units representing employees at county and state correctional facilities. The AFSCME was also known for organizing a wide range of workers traditionally overlooked by industrial and craft unions, including accountants, supervisors and inspectors, playground workers, tree surgeons and grounds crew workers, life guards, and zookeepers. This broad jurisdictional scope marks AFSCME's membership to this day and largely accounts for its steady growth in the postwar period. The AFSCME experienced modest membership increases during World War II, raising its base to 61,082 by 1945.

The Rise of Civil Service Unionism

For most of the locals that AFSCME represented, the terms of union membership rarely included actual collective bargaining agreements, which were the norm in private industry. In 1946, AFSCME claimed 94 agreements with county administrators, city managers, and councils, 42 of which were legally binding contracts. In most of its dealings with government managers, AFSCME secured advancements in the workplace through memoranda, resolutions, statements of policy and ordinances. The early years of AFSCME are characterized mostly by a union philosophy that stressed the advancement of civil service regulations as the key to better government labor relations, a program that clearly set it apart from the rest of the labor movement. The union's agenda was advanced by Zander, who stood out as unique among the new cadre of U.S. labor leaders of the New Deal period. An intellectual with a Ph.D. from the University of Wisconsin, Zander was heavily influenced by the urban reform and management programs that dated back to the progressive period. Believing that the government workplace could be perfected through application of scientific management procedures administered by experts, Zander stressed the introduction of the merit system as key to the improved workplace.

The merit system would allow for uniformity in government employment, providing specific rules for wages and pensions, vacation time, promotion through testing, and immunity from political contributions and service that marked government workplaces across the country. As an advocate of these measures, Zander was active in national civil service reform movements, a member of the National Civil Service Reform League, and served on the executive board of the Civil Service Assembly of the United States and Canada. Although largely a technical revisionist of the workplace, Zander was a visionary who sought to revolutionize the entire system and culture of U.S. government workplace relations that had dominated since the Jacksonian era.

The goals of civil service unionism were expressed in the union's official journal, the *Public Employee*, which highlighted union achievements across the country, articulated union priorities, often with editorials stressing the need for civil service reform. With headquarters in Madison, Wisconsin, until the late 1940s, the national office acted as a major clearing house for civil service reform literature used in education and lobbying campaigns with elected officials, public workers, and the broader taxpaying public.

Strikes by AFSCME locals were rare, though not unheard of. In 1946, municipal workers joined industrial workers across the country in the nation's greatest strike wave, with 43 public employee strikes in cities with populations over 10,000. Certain AFSCME locals had reputations for militancy. Philadelphia's branch was fiery, with sections going out on strike five times from 1937–1944—with even more threats along the way. Locals in Buffalo and Cleveland also went out on strike, putting pressure on city officials by curtailing basic city services. One of the most famous strikes of the immediate postwar period that showed the potential militancy of local government employees occurred in May 1946, when a newly chartered AFSCME local in Rochester, New York, walked off the job for union recognition and wage increases. Following the firing of almost 500 union members, AFSCME reached out for public support and received official support from the city's AFL and CIO councils, which organized a general strike that brought Rochester to a halt. Within a day of this labor holiday, city workers succeeded in winning back their jobs, although falling short of achieving official union recognition.

The union's reluctance to use the strike weapon also reflected the spirit of public employee unionism as envisioned by its founder, Zander. The AFSCME was different from other unions because its interests ultimately extended beyond bread-and-butter issues of union membership to the protection of the wider public they served. Public employee organizations had a responsibility to citizens, not just because they ultimately paid their wages, but because they deserved the highest standards of professional service. This emphasis on public concern would mark the union's culture into the twenty-first century. The AFSCME also stressed citizenship issues in its recruitment rhetoric with potential members, claiming that the control exercised over public servants by political bosses negated the rights of government workers to function as independent citizens who could vote according to their own conscience rather than in accordance with the logic of the spoils system.

Not all embraced AFSCME's philosophy of civil service unionism. The first decade of the organization's existence was characterized by major jurisdictional factions with competing organizations vying for allegiance of local government workers. The AFSCME's main rival was the similarly sounding State, County, and Municipal Workers of America (SCMWA), which was chartered by the CIO in the summer of 1937. Headed by Abram Flaxer, a social worker from New York City's Department of Welfare who had previously served as a vice-president of AFSCME, SCMWA embraced the CIO's industrial-unionizing tactics, organizing across government classifications, and generally engaging in more militant membership drives that sought not only to strengthen civil service laws, but to gain actual collective-bargaining contracts. Despite this rhetoric of militancy however, SCMWA recognized the legal limits of its programs and instituted no-strike clauses in its original constitution. Strongest in New York City, where it reached just over 10,000 members in sanitation, welfare, and clerical bureaus, SCMWA also had a presence in such cities as Milwaukee, Chicago, and Pittsburgh. A significant split between the rival organizations centered on politics, with Flaxer's organization considered more left leaning. This political agenda was apparent in the formation of the United Public Workers of America (UPWA), which incorporated the SCMWA and the United Federal Workers in 1946. In 1950, following the CIO crackdown on suspected Communist-influenced unions, the UPWA was disbanded. Although the CIO chartered a new union in its place, the Government and Civic Employees' Organizing Committee, the breaking of the UPWA gave AFSCME almost unrivaled jurisdiction in representing local government workers within the U.S. labor movement.

The jurisdictional advantages for AFSCME following the collapse of its CIO rival in the McCarthy era were most apparent in New York City. There a small and neglected AFSCME council was revived by the leadership of Jerry Wurf, a socialist who assumed control of the city's AFSCME District Council 37 in 1952. Wurf conducted tireless campaigns to organize New York's municipal workers, even taking on a city job himself to facilitate contact with potential workers. His bold campaigns and his mastery of the city's media gained him a reputation that helped to secure more members and gain important concessions from New York City government. Starting with a council of about 400 workers in 1952, Wurf transformed the union to become one of the most respected in the city, with 20,000 members in 1960. Wurf's successes would gain him an independent support base within AFSCME, projecting him into a national leadership position that would eventually shift the union's historical course.

The New Militancy of the 1960s

The year 1964 is usually seen as the dividing point in AFSCME's history, when the organization broke from earlier patterns of civil service reform toward a more militant form of unionization that sought to achieve parity with private sector workers. In that year Wurf defeated Zander as AFSCME international president after 6 years of internal disputes that divided AFSCME into two camps. Wurf brought a fundamentally different vision of AFSCME's role and transformed the union into a fighting organization committed to social-based unionism that fused workplace issues with such broader community campaigns as the African-American freedom movement. Initial reforms included an overhaul of the union's constitution, implementing more democratic procedures, tighter financial regulations, and the redrawing of the union's jurisdictional map to facilitate broader organizing campaigns. Wurf also changed the public image of the union by establishing green as the official color of the union. Used on posters, literature, and official letter head, green had long been used by Wurf in organizing campaigns in New York City, symbolizing the spirit of renewal, the symbol for go, and the color of money.

Wurf instituted the most aggressive unionizing campaign in the history of the organization, encouraged by a new legal environment that asserted a new day for government workers. Following President Kennedy's signing of Executive Order 10988 in 1962, the earlier achievement of collective bargaining rights in Wisconsin in 1959, and legal support from such groups as the American Civil Liberties Union and the American Bar Association's Section on Labor Relations Law, government workers of all levels organized in unprecedented numbers. The AFSCME led the way, achieving a remarkable organizing rate of 1,000 new members daily by 1969. The most famous and fateful organizing campaign of the late 1960s was the 1968 Memphis Sanitation strike, where over 2,000 predominantly African-American sanitation workers protested for higher pay, better work conditions, and union representation. The striking men forged ties within the African-American community with church groups and political organizations to place pressure on Memphis city council. Seeing their struggle as a basic attempt at human dignity, Martin Luther King came to Memphis to support the strikers and their families, where he was assassinated on April 4, 1968. Overwhelming national public pressure caused Memphis officials to grant the demands to the workers in the wake of King's death and linked AFSCME with the broader cause of the African-American freedom movement.

The 1970s saw the period of greatest growth for AFSCME. In 1973, Gerald McEntee concluded a 3-year organizing campaign of Pennsylvania's Commonwealth employees, bringing 75,000 workers into a single statewide council that signed a binding contract covering wages and health benefits. This campaign—the largest in U.S. labor history—became the blueprint for similar ones across the country and launched McEntee into national leadership—he was elected as AFSCME international president following Wurf's death in 1981. By that time AFSCME had grown to become one of the largest unions in the country, eclipsing the one million mark in 1978, with the incorporation of the Civil Service Employees' Association of New York. Under McEntee's leadership, the union continued to grow through the 1980s and 1990s, both through new organizing campaigns of such diverse working groups as university employees and nursing home staff and through major mergers with existing organizations, such as the United Nurses of America and Hospital Workers' Union 1199c.

Since the late 1960s, AFSCME has become one of the most politicized unions in the AFL-CIO, forging a political power base through such organizations as its political arm, the Public Employees Organized to Promote Legislative Equality (PEOPLE), one of the largest political action committees in the United States. Since 1972, the union has consistently been one of the primary forces within the progressive wing of the Democratic party, playing a major role in setting the legislative agenda and in choosing Democratic presidential candidates. The AFSCME's increased political role, its influence within the AFL-CIO, and its ongoing commitment to a social unionism that addresses community as well as workplace themes continue to make the union a model of twenty-first century unionism.

FRANCIS RYAN

References and Further Reading

Bellush, Bernard, and Jewel Bellush. *Union Power and New York: Victor Gotbaum and District Council 37.* New York: Praeger, 1984.
Billings, Richard N., and John Greenya. *Power to the Public Worker.* Washington, D.C.: R. B. Luce, 1974.
Goulden, Joseph C. *Jerry Wurf: Labor's Last Angry Man.* New York: Atheneum, 1982.
Kramer, Leo. *Labor's Paradox: The American Federation of State County and Municipal Employees, AFL-CIO.* New York and London: Wiley, 1962.
Slater, Joseph. *Public Workers: Government Employee Unions, the Law, and the State, 1900–1962.* Ithaca, NY: ILR Press, 2004.
Spero, Sterling *Government as Employer.* New York: Remsen Press, 1948.

See also McEntee, Gerald; McEntee, William J.; Nursing and Health Care; Wurf, Jerry

AMERICAN FEDERATION OF TEACHERS

The American Federation of Teachers (AFT) is a major national union of white-collar workers that is affiliated with the American Federation of Labor and Congress of Industrial Organizations (AFL-CIO). Historically the AFT has been concerned with the problems of elementary, high school, and college teachers, but in the past 30 years the organization has embraced workers in health care and public service.

The AFT has its origins among public school teachers who organized to improve their working lives and the schools. In Chicago elementary public schoolteachers led by Margaret Haley and Catharine Goggin formed the Chicago Teachers' Federation (CTF) in 1897, seeking higher salaries, pensions, job security, and a greater say in classroom management. In November 1902, the 4,000-member CTF affiliated with the Chicago Federation of Labor (CFL), the municipal arm of the American Federation of Labor (AFL), becoming the first group of teachers to affiliate with a local labor federation. Teachers in San Antonio, Texas, became the first group of schoolteachers to join organized labor when it directly affiliated with the AFL a few months earlier. Other groups of teachers followed their lead. Men and women and high school and elementary teachers formed separate unions that reflected gender differences in pay, promotion prospects, and working conditions among teachers. In the segregated southern school districts, black and white teachers organized separate locals, but in the North racially integrated locals emerged.

As teacher unions began to appear in other towns and cities across the country, Chicago public schoolteachers played a major role in organizing a nationwide teachers' association. In April 1916, after the Chicago teachers' organizations issued a call for a national organization of teachers, eight locals formed the AFT. Chicago became the first headquarters of the AFT, and Charles Stillman of the Chicago Federation of Men Teachers became the first AFT president. Subsequently the AFT was governed by an annual convention and an executive council comprised of regional vice-presidents, but the AFT remained a loose federation of a few strong urban locals. The federation adopted a no-strike policy and pursued their demands by appealing to public opinion, lobbying local politicians, and depending on the strength of organized labor. The AFT distinguished itself from its main rival, the National Education Association (NEA), by its affiliation with organized labor and its insistence on excluding school administrators from membership. With wartime conditions favoring labor organization, membership of the AFT reached 11,000 in approximately 100 locals in 1919, 1.5% of the teaching force.

The AFT faced persistent opposition to its attempts to organize public schoolteachers. Teachers, it was commonly believed, should be selfless and not pursue their own demands at the expense of the school system and the students. The public expected female teachers in particular to eschew unions and maintain proper decorum and not participate in demonstrations or strikes. Presidents, governors, mayors, and judges argued that the public schools belonged to all the people who controlled the schools through their elected representatives and their appointees. For school administrators to share their decision-making authority with unelected union leaders would violate the sovereignty of the government and the democratic will of the people. As the popular term public servant signified, teachers were seen as servants of the whole public who should not show allegiance to any particular segment of society, such as organized labor. Superintendents suggested that to help public education, teachers should join the NEA, which represented the whole education profession and sought to improve the professional development of teachers rather than a special interest groups like labor.

The World War I years saw a concerted nationwide attempt to destroy the fledgling teacher unions by politicians and boards of education. The onslaught started in Cleveland in 1914, when the board of education announced that it would not rehire teachers who were members of a labor union. Inspired by the events in Cleveland, unionized teachers were fired in St. Louis, New York, and Washington, D.C. In June 1916, the Chicago Board of Education refused to re-employ 68 teachers, the majority of whom were members of Margaret Haley's CTF. In return for the re-instatement of the teachers, in May 1917, the CTF, one of the most influential affiliates of the AFT, disaffiliated from the CFL and the AFT, thus breaking all formal links with organized labor. Facing enormous hostility from local school administrators, politicians, and the rival NEA, which dubbed teacher unions unprofessional, the AFT struggled to sustain itself as an organization over the next decade. During the presidencies of grade schoolteachers Florence Rood from St. Paul, Minnesota, and Mary C. Barker from Atlanta, Georgia, many locals collapsed, and membership declined to 7,000 in 1930. As a result the organization had little impact on local or national education policy.

During the Depression of the 1930s, when public education was curtailed as cities and states cut public expenditures, AFT membership steadily climbed again until it reached 33,000 in 1939. Many public schools closed, and schoolteachers who faced wage cuts, months without pay, and deteriorating working conditions turned toward unions to pursue their demands. The National Labor Relations Act of 1935, which helped private-sector unions to organize and bargain with employees, however did not apply to public-sector workers. In the larger cities, where there was a strong labor federation and politicians and administrators who tolerated teacher unionism, teachers were able to organize unions if not bargain with school boards. The Chicago Teachers' Union formed by an amalgamation of elementary and high school locals in 1937, and with over 8,000 members by the end of the decade, two-thirds of the workforce, became the largest teachers' local in the country. In smaller communities the AFT found it much harder to prosper. While a third of industrial workers had joined unions by the end of the decade, only 3.4% of the teacher workforce joined the AFT.

While the majority of AFT members were found in the nation's public schools, the organization also included college instructors. In the 1930s, teachers in higher education, such as the progressive educator John Dewey, became influential in the union. The first presidents of the AFT were high school and elementary schoolteachers, but in the 1930s, college teachers came to the fore. In 193, Jerome Davis, a Yale University professor of theology, became the sixth AFT president, and in 1939, George Counts, a professor at the Teachers' College in New York, became the seventh president.

If the AFT gained new members in the 1930s, it also faced major ideological conflicts between Communists and their opponents. With the apparent failings of capitalism in the depression, and the Communist party willing to forge alliances with liberals during its Popular Front period, Communist influence increased in some locals and in the national organization. Whereas the CTU included few Communist members and remained the center of anti-Communist activity in the AFT, the 4,000-strong New York teachers' union probably had close to 1,000 Communist party activists in its ranks. One of the major conflicts centered on the Communist attempt to affiliate the AFT with the newly formed Committee (later Congress) of Industrial Organizations (CIO). The CIO, formed in November 1935 by John L. Lewis, president of the United Mine Workers of America, and other AFL union leaders, sought to organize across industrial lines all the unorganized, including those the AFL had been reluctant to organize:

The unskilled, blacks, and women. Because the AFL remained politically powerful in most cities, the AFT voted against affiliation with the CIO. Finally three Communist-controlled locals, one in Philadelphia and two in New York, with a combined membership of over 8,000, were ejected from the federation in 1941.

The post-World War II years saw the largest teachers' strike wave yet seen in U.S. history and another surge in AFT membership. As price controls were lifted in 1946, and inflation cut into teachers' already low salaries, teachers turned to the AFT and to militant action to gain improved pay. The AFT leadership reasserted the no-strike policy in 1947, but many AFT locals ignored the pledge. The first official strike by an AFT local occurred in St. Paul, Minnesota, in November 1946, when public schoolteachers demanded higher salaries. Altogether some 57 teacher strikes took place from 1946–1949, while only 12 had occurred from 1940–1945. The AFT membership rose from 22,000 in 1941 to 42,000 in 1947, or 4.5% of the workforce. The militancy of the AFT declined as states outlawed teacher strikes and the Red Scare of the 1950s penetrated deep into the classroom and frightened teachers away from political and union action. The AFT continued to campaign for more spending on public education and teachers' salaries by demanding federal aid for education, but a conservative-dominated Congress refused all appeals.

The AFT achieved little at the national level in the 1950s, but at the local level female elementary teachers in the AFT and the NEA successfully campaigned for the introduction of single, or equal, salary schedules for both elementary and high school teachers. The first single salary schedule for teachers was developed in the Denver, Colorado, school system in 1920. By 1931, 22% of school systems used the single-salary schedule, and in 1941, it was 31%. In larger cities where separate salary schedules had long been in operation, there was resistance from administers to any change that would increase costs and from male high school teachers who saw their higher status threatened. Only in 1943 did the first city out of the 14 with a population over 500,000—Detroit—adopt the single-salary scale. The living costs of elementary schoolteachers rose during the war as greater opportunities opened up for women outside the teaching profession, which dramatically altered the expectations of female teachers and the concerns of administrators. By 1947, 64% of school districts used the single-salary schedule, and in 1951 it was 97%. By 1952, Chicago and Boston remained the only two cities out of 17 with a population over 500,000 that had not adopted a full single-salary schedule in terms of equal pay and equal hours of work.

During the presidency of Chicago high school teacher Carl Megel (1952–1964), the issue of civil rights for African-Americans became a dominant one for the organization. In the early 1950s, the AFT made a concerted effort to integrate its racially segregated southern locals. After its southern affiliates showed little progress in integration, in 1957, the AFT expelled the segregated locals and lost 7,000 members in the process. Although the support for civil rights varied from local to local, the national organization continued to back the rights of African-Americans. The AFT filed an amicus brief in support of the plaintiffs in the *Brown v. Board of Education* Supreme Court decision of 1954, which desegregated the public schools and appeared on civil rights platforms throughout the country.

The attainment of collective-bargaining rights for teachers also became a major AFT aim during the presidency of Megel. Although some AFT locals bargained with their boards of education, the overwhelming majority of public schoolteachers had not established bargaining rights. As teachers saw the salaries and working conditions of unionized workers in private industry improve dramatically in the 1950s, AFT teachers turned to collective bargaining to improve their own position. Many AFT locals lobbied state legislators to pass legislation to allow collective bargaining between public-sector workers and local authorities. By 1959, however, Wisconsin was the only state with collective-bargaining legislation. Consequently teachers began to campaign for local boards of education unilaterally to grant collective bargaining without state legislation to sanction it.

The most dramatic breakthrough in collective bargaining came in New York in 1960. Under the leadership of David Selden and Albert Shanker, a number of AFT locals merged to from the United Federation of Teachers (UFT) and campaigned for collective-bargaining rights. In November 1960, 5,000 of New York City's 50,000 teachers staged a 1-day strike, and in June 1961, New York teachers overwhelmingly voted for collective bargaining in a ballot. In December 1961, in another ballot, the teachers voted for the UFT as their sole bargaining agent, and in June the following year, the UFT negotiated the first comprehensive collective-bargaining agreement in a major city. In 1963, the AFT repealed its no-strike pledge. In the following years teachers all across the country, encouraged by the New York teachers, turned to collective bargaining and strikes to win their demands. Between July 1960 and June 1974, the country experienced over 1,000 teacher strikes involving more than 823,000 teachers. By the end of the 1970s, collective-bargaining agreements covered 72% of public schoolteachers. The AFT membership grew from 59,000 in

1960 to over 200,000 in 1970 and 550,000 in 1980. After the dramatic success of the UFT, the numerical and ideological strength of the AFT shifted decisively from Chicago to New York City. From the mid-1960s to the end of the century, every AFT president came from the New York local.

In the late 1960s, when AFT locals attained collective-bargaining rights and became a junior partner in determining school policy and the civil rights movement became more militant, some union locals clashed with the black community. While the newly empowered teachers wanted to prioritize pay in negotiations with school boards, black parents and students in the inner cities wanted them to join in their campaigns for educational improvements. They wanted increased funding for the schools, more say in school policy, more black teachers, and a black studies curriculum. The attainment of collective-bargaining rights also brought increased demands on the union from the black teachers, who faced discriminatory teacher certification exams, were excluded from leadership positions in the union and the schools, and often taught in the most overcrowded and underfunded schools. Because of the inability of the union to address issues connected with the black community, many black teachers chose to support the parents and students rather than the union during disputes.

This conflict between unionized teachers and the black community gained national headlines in the fall of 1968, when Shanker and the UFT called a citywide strike in a conflict with the African-American and Puerto Rican community-controlled schools in Ocean Hill-Brownsville, New York City. The predominantly white schoolteachers wanted to protect teachers' seniority rights and job security, whereas the community of Ocean Hill-Brownsville sought to replace white teachers with black ones. In other districts, AFT locals faced less conflict as they incorporated the black community's demands into their negotiations with school boards and helped to produce major changes in the union and the public school system. The growth in the number of black school administrators, the establishment of a multicultural curriculum, and the introduction of more African-Americans into leadership positions in teacher unions remains a legacy of this turbulent era.

After the dramatic upsurge of the 1960s and early 1970s, the AFT grew in national significance. In 1968, the AFT moved its headquarters from Chicago to its present location in Washington, D.C., to be nearer the seat of political power. The AFT was now one of the largest affiliates of the AFL and a major influence in national politics. Shanker, elected AFT president in 1974, became one of the most recognizable union leaders in the country. With national newspaper columns and the respect of politicians, Shanker used his position to oppose merit pay for teachers, campaign for more federal funding for education, and promote educational innovations. After his death in 1997, another New York teacher, Sandra Feldman, was elected AFT president.

In the last three decades, the AFT has grown into a trade union representing workers in public schools, higher education, health care, and public service. Approximately 60% of its membership works directly in education. Since the late 1960s, the NEA, who shifted its position on collective bargaining and strikes, and the AFT have been involved in merger talks. In 1998, the membership of the NEA rejected a proposed unification with the AFT. With over 900,000 members organized in 2,500 locals, predominantly in the urban school districts, the AFT's membership is half that of the NEA's. The AFT offers its members such benefits as liability insurance and group, health, life, and accident insurance. Its legal defense fund upholds academic freedom and protects teachers from arbitrary dismissal. The AFT publishes a number of important research reports and periodicals, including *American Educator* and *American Teacher,* and takes an active interest in legislative matters.

Along with the labor movement as a whole, the AFT declined in influence, if not in numbers, since the 1980s. Republican Presidents Ronald Reagan and George H. Bush sought cuts in public expenditure and attacked the liberal and labor influence in public education. Criticized by commentators for their self-interest and opposition to charter schools and unable to convince politicians to reform the unequal distribution of school funding, the AFT remains on the defensive. Nevertheless since it grew in influence in the 1960s, public schoolteachers' working conditions, salaries, and benefits have improved enormously, and the AFT has established itself as a major influence in both the labor movement and the public education system.

JOHN F. LYONS

References and Further Reading

Braun, Robert J. *Teachers and Power: The Story of the American Federation of Teachers.* New York: Simon and Schuster, 1972.

Eaton, William Edward. *The American Federation of Teachers, 1916–1961: A History of the Movement.* Carbondale, IL, Southern Illinois University Press, 1975.

Lyons, John F. "The Chicago Teachers' Union, Politics and the City's Schools, 1937–1970." PhD thesis, University of Illinois at Chicago, 2001.

Murphy, Marjorie. *Blackboard Unions: The AFT and the NEA, 1900–1980.* Ithaca and London: Cornell University Press, 1990.

O'Connor, Paula. "Grade-School Teachers Become Labor Leaders: Margaret Haley, Florence Rood, and Mary Barker of the AFT." *Labor's Heritage* 7 (Fall 1995): 4–17.

Taft, Philip. *United They Teach: The Story of the United Federation of Teachers.* Los Angeles: Nash Publishing, 1974.

Urban, Wayne J. *Why Teachers Organized.* Detroit, MI: Wayne State University Press, 1982.

See also **Ocean Hill-Brownsville Strikes (1968)**

AMERICAN LABOR PARTY

New York labor leaders formed the American Labor Party (ALP) in 1936 as part of a national plan to create labor parties in states across the country. Although labor parties in other states failed to take hold, the ALP became a crucial third party in New York State politics for the next decade. The party was initially intended only to help re-elect President Franklin Roosevelt and congressional supporters of his New Deal program in 1936 and then disband. Many ALP leaders however wanted a permanent option for New York voters who desired to elect New Deal Democrats without having to support the whole Democratic line of candidates. Several successes followed over the next decade, but by 1944, a split occurred within the party over Communist influence among the leadership, and many of the conservative socialists within the ALP broke ranks to form the Liberal Party of New York. This left the ALP, under significant Communist control, leading the party to support the Progressive party's candidate, Henry Wallace, in the 1948 presidential campaign instead of President Truman. By the early 1950s, the ALP weakened in the anti-Communist climate of the era and ended its own existence by 1956.

The Congress of Industrial Organizations (CIO) leaders Sidney Hillman and John L. Lewis joined forces to form the Labor Non-Partisan League (LNPL) to play a role in the 1936 presidential election. President Roosevelt's campaign appointed the AFL's Dan Tobin to lead the Democratic party's labor committee, and this left the newly formed CIO without a role in the campaign. The CIO leadership believed it crucial that Roosevelt be reelected, especially after the Supreme Court had ruled in 1935 that many key components of the New Deal were unconstitutional. Individual chapters of the LNPL formed in various states, and in New York, such notable labor leaders as Hillman, David Dubinsky, and Max Zaritsky established a LNPL chapter that became known as the ALP. In New York, this party would prove crucial in offering thousands of trade unionists and liberals a voice in New York politics.

Hillman and other CIO officials viewed the LNPL and ALP as one-time affairs meant solely to secure labor votes for Roosevelt in the 1936 presidential election. They wanted to ensure the continuation of New Deal policies, which benefited U.S. labor unions greatly during the decade. To Hillman's surprise, many ALP leaders dismissed the disbanding of the party after the 1936 presidential election and enthusiastically called for the permanent status of the party. They designed the ALP to provide an alternative for New York liberals who could vote for President Roosevelt without supporting the entire Democratic ticket, which typically included Democrats perceived by labor officials as corrupt Tammany Hall politicians. Since Tammany Hall dominated New York State's Democratic party, labor leaders sought this alternative so they could vote for Roosevelt while also endorsing candidates for lower offices who voted for New Deal legislation. These could be Democrats, Republicans, or ALP candidates.

With the major garment unions behind the ALP, the party developed into an important player in presidential elections as well as New York mayoralty, senatorial, and gubernatorial races. From 1936–1946, the ALP provided crucial support in the elections of Mayors Fiorella LaGuardia and William O'Dwyer, Senators Robert Wagner and James Meade, Governor Herbert Lehman, and District Attorney Thomas Dewey. In 1938, the ALP elected its own candidate, former Republican Vito Marcantonio, to the House of Representatives.

In 1939, with the signing of the Molotov-Ribbentrop Pact between Germany and the Soviet Union, Communists within the ALP turned against Roosevelt. This infuriated most of the non-Communists within the party, who feared the Communists would try to prevent the ALP endorsement of Roosevelt's 1940 election campaign. After a bitter battle, the non-Communists put Roosevelt on its ballot, but the friction caused by the episode led to a final break 4 years later. In 1944, most non-Communists bolted from the ALP after Communists gained control of the party apparatus, leading such ALP anti-Communists as Dubinsky and Rose to view the party as a Communist front. Of the founding ALP leadership, only Hillman believed he could work with (and control) the Communists, and he opted to stay in the party. Despite Hillman's pleading with Dubinsky and Rose to remain, the two influential union leaders formed the rival Liberal party of New York, which would eventually succeed the ALP as the leading third party of New York State.

With Hillman's sudden death in 1946, there were no more barriers to complete Communist control of the ALP. Accordingly in 1948, the ALP rejected Harry Truman's presidential candidacy in favor of former vice-president and commerce secretary, Henry Wallace. In February, the ALP demonstrated to New York Democrats its strength with a special election victory of its candidate Leo Issacson over the Democratic candidate Karl Propper as well as the Liberal party candidate Dean Alfange. This special election victory galvanized the party and deeply concerned the Truman administration. The ALP victory also led New York Democrats to distance themselves from Truman's campaign and focus their resources on local candidates.

Ultimately Truman's victory in November precipitated the demise of the ALP. The party's support of Wallace, who had been associated with Communists and criticized for his conciliatory attitude towards the Soviet Union, alienated many in the Democratic and Republican parties, which had been willing to work with the ALP previously. The intense anti-Communist environment of the 1950s made matters worse for the ALP. In 1952, the ALP attempted to rally support for Vincent Hallinan, the Progressive party's candidate for president, but Hallinan failed to make any headway in the election. With the ALP's 1954 failure to garner 50,000 votes for the New York governor's race, the ALP lost its place on the state ballot. By 1956, this led to the party's committee to vote itself out of existence.

ADAM HOWARD

References and Further Reading

Davin, Eric Leif. "Defeat of the Labor Party Idea." In *We Are All Leaders: The Alternative Unionism of the Early 1930s*, edited by Staughton Lynd. Chicago: University of Illinois Press, 1996.

Dubinsky, David, and A. H. Raskin. *David Dubinsky: A Life with Labor*. New York: Simon and Schuster, 1977.

Epstein, Melech. *Jewish Labor Movement in the USA*, vol. 1-2. New York: Ktav Publishing House, Inc., 1969.

Fraser, Steven. *Labor Will Rule: Sidney Hillman and the Rise of American Labor*. New York: The Free Press, 1991.

Parmet, Robert D. *The Master of Seventh Avenue: David Dubinsky and the American Labor Movement*. New York: New York University Press, 2005.

AMERICAN LABOR UNION

The American Labor Union (1898–1905), originally called the Western Labor Union, was a short-lived but significant effort of mainly western workers to build an alternative to the American Federation of Labor (AFL). The organization grew out of the rapid industrialization and growing social inequality that transformed the American West in the late nineteenth century. These changes led to a great deal of labor conflict, especially in the hard-rock mining industry, which was rocked by a series of strikes in such states as Idaho and Colorado that led to the 1893 birth and subsequent growth of the Western Federation of Miners (WFM). Though the WFM affiliated with the AFL in 1896, the metal miners' organization increasingly embraced industrial unionism and independent political action, opposing the craft and pure-and-simple union models favored by the AFL. Many western workers also felt that the AFL's domination by eastern trade unionists made it unresponsive to their needs, especially after the WFM's bitter defeat in the Leadville, Colorado, strike of 1896–1897, which its leaders partly blamed on lack of financial support from the AFL. At its May 1997 convention, the WFM decided to withdraw from the AFL.

In November 1897, the Montana State Trade and Labor Council adopted a resolution calling for the establishment of a western federation of labor. The WFM's executive board expressed support for this in December and shortly afterward issued an invitation to all western unions to send representatives to a meeting at Salt Lake City, May 10–12, 1998. With 119 delegates from a number of western states and British Columbia in attendance (77 of them WFM members), the meeting founded the Western Labor Union (WLU) and elected Daniel McDonald, leader of the Butte, Montana, Iron Molders Union, as its president. Though never an actual officer, WFM President Edward Boyce exerted great influence at this meeting and on the organization as a whole until his retirement in 1902. The new organization endorsed industrial unionism, independent political action and the goal of uniting all labor unions west of the Mississippi.

The WLU grew steadily over the next few years. In October 1999, it claimed 65 affiliated unions in Montana, Colorado, and Idaho, along with one in Rossland, British Columbia. Local unions of clerks, laundry workers, cooks and waiters, butchers, lumber workers, bricklayers and stonemasons, and musicians affiliated with the WLU, though its core constituency remained hard-rock miners. Unlike the AFL, the WLU advocated fundamental social and economic change. In 1899, it called for government ownership of all "natural monopolies," and in 1901, it endorsed the Socialist party. Most importantly it stood for organizing the unorganized—especially unskilled workers—in industrial unions. But it was less the WLU's positions than the fact that it threatened to become a rival labor center in the West that led to tension with the AFL. Fearing that large industrial unions like the United Mine Workers and the Brewery Workers might leave the federation, AFL leaders decided to try to destroy the WLU.

After 1900, AFL organizers began to appear in the western states they had previously neglected, engaging in controversial practices like creating competing unions in trades organized by the WLU and encouraging strike breaking during WLU strikes. In Denver, which became a major center of the WLU, conflict between the two federations was extremely bitter, and in March 1902, the Denver Trades Assembly returned its charter to the AFL and affiliated with the WLU. At the WLU's third convention, held in Denver in June 1902, the conflict came to a head. Frank Morrison, secretary-treasurer of the AFL, addressed the delegates, calling on the WLU to disband or face opposition from AFL unions all over the West.

Rejecting these threats and responding positively to a powerful speech by the socialist leader Eugene V. Debs, who was present, the delegates voted to change their name to the American Labor Union (ALU) and to challenge the AFL throughout the nation. They re-elected McDonald as president of the renamed organization, along with D. F. O'Shea of Cripple Creek, Colorado, as vice-president and Clarence Smith of Butte as secretary-treasurer. McDonald would serve as president of the ALU until replaced by the Colorado labor leader, David C. Coates, in 1905. Despite this continuity of leadership however, the ALU differed from the WLU by claiming a national rather than regional jurisdiction and by encouraging unions already affiliated with the AFL to affiliate instead with the ALU. The ALU also endorsed the platform of the American Socialist party in its entirety.

The AFL now began a major organizing drive in the West, but since its goal seemed simply to destroy the ALU, it ended up hurting the AFL's cause. The ALU grew rapidly for a time, claiming 276 local unions in 24 different states, territories, or Canadian provinces and a membership of 100,000 by its 1903 convention, though these figures were surely exaggerated. Two international unions, the United Brotherhood of Railway Employees and the United Association of Hotel and Restaurant Employees, affiliated with the ALU, and it grew especially rapidly in Colorado, Montana, Idaho, Washington, California, and British Columbia. Western locals of the Brewery Workers (dominated by German Americans) affiliated with the ALU, and the Brewery Workers' Union as a whole for a time considered affiliation. In early 1903, McDonald established six ALU locals of shoe workers in St. Louis, and ALU locals of shoe workers appeared in Chicago and Lynn, Massachusetts, as well.

Nonetheless western metal miners remained the most important group within the ALU, and as a result, males dominated its ranks as they had that of the WLU. In Cripple Creek, Colorado, for example, just 65 out of more than four thousand WLU members were women in 1901. And although the ALU formally called for the organization of female workers on an equal basis, not all of its leaders agreed. R. E. Croskey, the national president of the ALU's Hotel and Restaurant Employees' Union, for example, strongly opposed the employment of women as cooks in restaurants or hotels.

Although it reached out to unskilled European immigrants, the organization's stance towards Asian immigrants, who faced intense white working-class opposition throughout the West, was mixed. At the 1900 WLU convention, McDonald expressed alarm at the growing numbers of Japanese laborers in the United States and recommended that the 1882 Chinese Exclusion Act be extended to all Asians. But by January 1903, ALU members were debating the issue, with one British Columbia activist criticizing the focus on Asian exclusion as antithetical to the ALU's belief that "all men and women are sisters and brothers." In May 1903, the WFM announced that it would begin organizing Chinese and Japanese laborers, and the ALU, though divided, followed suit in June, amending its constitution to read "no working man or woman shall be excluded from membership in local unions because of creed or color." Although such formal positions did not overcome the racism of large numbers of white rank-and-file ALU members, they represented a new development in the western labor movement and pointed toward the more sweeping racial inclusiveness of the Industrial Workers of the World (IWW, 1905–).

The ALU hit its peak membership in fall 1903 and for a number of reasons, began to decline thereafter. Despite the ALU's commitment to socialism and the support from left-wing socialists like Debs, the main body of the American Socialist party, seeking to work for socialism within the AFL, opposed the ALU as an unacceptable example of dual unionism. The ALU was also hurt by its low-dues structure, which limited it financially. Most harmful of all was the national open-shop drive, which hit the ALU in the so-called Colorado labor wars of 1903–1904. Backed by local employer groups and Colorado's anti-union governor, mine owners engaged in a concerted effort to destroy the WFM and the ALU. Bloody battles, mass arrests, and deportations of miners in communities like Cripple Creek and Telluride brought the ALU to near extinction. Moving its headquarters from Butte to Chicago and turning its weekly publication, the *American Labor Union Journal*, into a monthly in 1904 did nothing to stop the decline. In June 1905, after its representatives played a central role in founding the IWW, the ALU disbanded.

Though short-lived, the ALU occupies an important place in U.S. labor history. It drew attention to the AFL's neglect of western workers and forced it to pay more attention to their needs. Its call for organizing the unskilled in industrial unions was later taken up by the IWW and the Congress of Industrial Organizations in the 1930s. And its racial inclusiveness, while limited, pointed toward the more sweeping egalitarianism of later radical labor organizations.

DAVID BRUNDAGE

References and Further Reading

Brundage, David. *The Making of Western Labor Radicalism: Denver's Organized Workers, 1878–1905*. Urbana, IL: University of Illinois Press, 1994.

Dubofsky, Melvyn. *We Shall Be All: A History of the Industrial Workers of the World*. New York: Quadrangle, 1969.

Emmons, David M. *The Butte Irish: Class and Ethnicity in an American Mining Town, 1875–1925*. Urbana, IL: University of Illinois Press, 1989.

Jameson, Elizabeth. *All the Glitters Class, Conflict, and Community in Cripple Creek*. Urbana, IL: University of Illinois Press, 1998.

Laslett, John. *Labor and the Left: A Study of Socialist and Radical Influences in the American Labor Movement, 1881–1924*. New York: Basic Books, 1970.

McCormack, A. Ross. *Reformers, Rebels, and Revolutionaries: The Western Canadian Radical Movement, 1899–1919*. Toronto: University of Toronto Press, 1977.

See also **American Federation of Labor; Debs, Eugene V.; Dual Unionism; Hardrock Mining; Morrison, Frank**

AMERICAN NEGRO LABOR CONGRESS

During the spring of 1925, the American Communist party, under the guidance of the Communist International, prepared the way for the formation of the American Negro Labor Congress (ANLC), which was conceived as a forum for addressing racism in labor unions and the workplace.

The first meeting of the ANLC, held on October 25 in Chicago and headed by Lovett Fort-Whiteman, received much attention from both national and international sources. The ANLC was inspired, in part, by the frustration the black and white left felt toward the American Federation of Labor, whose official bureaucracy failed to address the needs of black workers and in part by the desire to use the ANLC to organize the black working class outside the influence of mainstream black institutions. Great hopes were placed on the ability of the ANLC to alter the racial landscape in the United States. Although few of those hopes were realized, the organization raised issues of race and class within the trade union movement even as it highlighted the politics of white chauvinism within the Communist party.

In May the Communist party held mass meetings in black communities on Chicago's South Side to broadcast its message of support for the forthcoming labor congress devoted to issues of importance to African-Americans. The Communists, promoting themselves as the champions of the oppressed of the world, had a lot to say about the class struggle but were brief on the topic of race and self-determination for African-Americans. The ANLC organizers had hoped that union and nonunion black workers, farmers, intellectuals, and radicals from all backgrounds would attend the founding convention. Despite much advance work preparing the way, only 33 accredited delegates were seated at the October convention, hardly an auspicious beginning for an organization some hoped would usher in a new day in race relations. Black Communists Otto Huiswoud and Richard B. Moore, who had warned the party of the danger of placing issues germane to white Communists in the forefront of advanced publicity about the ANLC, were not surprised. Huiswoud and Moore suggested that all publicity should resonate with working-class blacks, and a black presence should be evident at all levels.

The opening convention foreshadowed challenges the ANLC was never able to resolve, challenges that ultimately contributed to its short duration. On opening night Lovett Fort-Whiteman, a graduate of Tuskegee Institute, drama critic for the *Messenger* and the *Crusader*, and member of the American Communist party, addressed a relatively large group of black and white workers from the Chicago area. Moore, a gifted speaker, also delivered an impassioned plea for all enlightened and radical African-Americans to unite under the ANLC banner to abolish all manner of social and political discrimination, which ended with his reading from Claude McKay's "If We Must Die."

However after the invocations from Fort-Whiteman and Moore, the following days of the convention were poorly attended. Only official delegates, already members of the American Communist party, remained for the business meetings. They had scant success recruiting outside the ranks of the party's membership, and there were very few new black recruits. While the convention did not represent a broad cross-section of the black community, its working-class presence was unmistakable in the credentials of cooks, plumbers, laborers, janitors, and hod carriers. Finally there were no black artists on the convention's program, which featured performances by Russian ballet and theater groups.

Black leaders and the black press gave the gathering mixed reviews. The *Baltimore Afro-American* welcomed the congress; *Opportunity*, the voice of the National Urban League, rejected the Communist agenda but agreed with the list of grievances outlined by the ANLC. W. E. B. Du Bois and Abram L. Harris, a professor of economics at Howard University, thought it was important to explore the Communist-led challenge to racism on the industrial front. A. Philip Randolph and Chandler Owen, editors of the *Messenger,* were the most vocal critics of the ANLC, using the pages of the magazine to argue for organizing black workers by cooperating with the existing labor movement. Randolph was also in Chicago during October 1925, testing his approach. As the president of the recently formed Brotherhood of Sleeping Car Porters (BSCP), Randolph hoped to organize Pullman sleeping car porters and maids in the BSCP and gain a place as a full member for the BSCP in the American Federation of Labor.

The *Negro Champion,* a product of the advanced publicity, became the voice of the ANLC when it could find the means to publish. Immediately following the founding convention, Fort-Whiteman went on a cross-country speaking tour to garner support for the congress. He was not entirely successful. The organization was forever underfunded, and memberships remained low, but the congress created more than 45 local chapters by 1927. The Chicago local remained the largest, with approximately 70 members; the rest were half that size.

With the organization in trouble, the Communist party called for a reorganization of ANLC. Fort-Whiteman was replaced by Richard Moore, assuming leadership in 1927 soon after he drafted the "Common Resolution on the Negro Question," as the ANLC's representative, in February at the Brussels International Congress against Colonial Oppression and Imperialism. His colleague, Huiswoud, expanded ANLC activities in the Caribbean by using it as a means to help form the Jamaican Trades' and Labor Union. Moore focused on turning the ANLC around. He moved the headquarters to New York City in 1928, hoping to organize the community by building networks around issues that appealed to black workers. He started the Harlem Tenants League that year and found that interest was higher for housing issues than equality in the trade union movement. Hermina Huiswoud and Grace Campbell, two important female voices from the black left, rose to prominence as leaders in the tenants' rights network.

The ANLC never did gain its footing within the black community and was, throughout its short duration, considered suspect in the eyes of many African-Americans. Above all, while white Communists had hoped the organization would serve to pull the black working class into the party, black Communists and other black activists hoped the ANLC would pay close attention to the interests and issues that resonated in the work and lives of African-Americans. One emphasized class, the other race. The ANLC held its last convention in the summer of 1930, after which it ceased to exist.

BETH TOMPKINS BATES

References and Further Reading

Foner, Philip S. *Organized Labor and the Black Worker, 1619–1981.* New York: International Publishers, 1981.
Foner, Philip S., and James S. Allen, eds. *African Communism and Black Americans: A Documentary History, 1919–1929.* Philadelphia: Temple University Press, 1987.
Harris, William H. *The Harder We Run: Black Workers since the Civil War.* New York: Oxford University Press, 1982.
Solomon, Mark. *The Cry Was Unity: Communists and African-Americans, 1917–1936.* Jackson, MI: University Press of Mississippi, 1998.

See also **American Federation of Labor; Brotherhood of Sleeping Car Porters**

AMERICAN POSTAL WORKERS' UNION

The postal service is among the longest running enterprises in the history of the United States, originated by the Second Continental Congress in July 1775, a year before the Declaration of Independence. For more than two centuries, postal workers have been a microcosm of the U.S. working class. They have been the country's most widespread group of workers—town and city, rural and urban, North and South, East and West—sharing a single employer. They have also been among the most diverse workforces, including African-Americans, Asian Americans, Chicanos, European immigrants and their descendants, and women as well as men. Their jobs have ranged from manufacturing (bags, locks, shipping equipment, and so forth) and trucking to sorting and delivery to window clerks serving the public to accountants and bookkeepers handling payroll and finances.

Despite their remarkable everyman status, many postal workers toiled under onerous conditions for meager compensation. Conditions in sorting facilities were unhealthy, dangerous, and dismal. Buildings were dank, poorly lit, crowded, and unventilated. Wages were low. Postal employees were required to work long hours of overtime without additional pay. Until 1883, when Congress passed a civil service law, many postal jobs were handed out as political patronage or as rewards for bribes and favoritism.

In the late nineteenth century, in the era of the Knights of Labor and the emergence of the American Federation of Labor, postal workers began to organize. Local unions appeared in different cities, offering their members mutual benefit and insurance features and sought to lobby the government for improvements. There were also a variety of national efforts. As early as 1874, railroad mail clerks joined together to create the Railway Mail Mutual Benefit Association, and in 1891, they expanded into the National Association of Railway Postal Clerks. In the 1880s and 1890s, meetings of delegates from a number of local unions created the United National Association of Post Office Clerks, and in 1906, delegates from seven cities, reaching from Nashville to San Francisco, received an American Federation of Labor (AFL) charter for the National Federation of Post Office Clerks. All of these efforts faced determined resistance. President Theodore Roosevelt issued an executive order denying all federal employees their right to participate collectively in political action or to solicit members of Congress, which President Taft later extended. Still postal workers of all sorts continued to organize local unions, building a base of mutual benefits and seeking the help of the AFL in improving their conditions.

The employment conditions of postal workers remained in the hands of Congress and the executive branch of the federal government. Their situation improved somewhat in the Progressive Era. The 1912 Lloyd-LaFollette Act rescinded the previous gag rules and established the right of federal and postal employees to organize unions. Congress adopted a Federal Employees' Compensation Act for workers injured on the job, voted for the first Civil Service Retirement Act, and provided a 10% nighttime differential. But the Great Depression saw such gains rolled back, as wages were cut 15% and workers faced temporary furloughs. And then Congress specifically excluded them (and all federal employees) from the collective-bargaining rights established by the National Labor Relations Act of 1935. They remained caught between the powers of different branches of government as wage increases voted for by Congress were vetoed by the president, which happened several times during the Eisenhower administration.

Still postal workers sought to organize to gain some power over their situation. Motor vehicle employees, maintenance workers, and special delivery messengers organized in the 1920s and 1930s, joining the letter carriers and the clerks as unionized workers. All formed separate craft organizations however, with little collaborative action. Those who wanted to build a unitary national organization faced not only craft divisions but also racial divides (frustrated by the particular problems they experienced, African-American postal workers had organized themselves into the National Alliance of Postal and Federal Employees), tensions between large urban and small town locals as to the voice they might have in a national organization, and disagreements about union strategy. Meanwhile the federal government withheld formal recognition from all the organizations while postal workers' wages fell behind those of other workers and their working conditions deteriorated.

In the 1960s, as public-sector workers at the federal, state, and local levels began to organize themselves and demand legislation that would provide recognition and sanction collective bargaining over wages as well as the conditions of employment, postal worker union activists increased their discussions of mergers and organizational development. In 1966, Roy Hallbeck, president of the United Federation of Postal Clerks (UFPC) and an advocate of United Federation of Postal Clerks—National Postal Union (UFPC-NPU) merger, note, "We have paid a frightful price for disunity." But efforts to bring postal worker unions together failed several times.

The national postal wildcat strike of March 1970 brought the organizations together. More than 200,000 postal workers in more than 30 cities struck out of frustration with the government's inaction on wages and working conditions. Not only did this strike bring the rank-and-file workers and their local union leaders together in joint action (militant, illegal action, at that), but it also prompted the passage of the Postal Reorganization Act, which granted unions recognition and the right to negotiate with management over wages, benefits, and working conditions. Five unions—the two largest unions, the UFPC and the NPU, which represented the men and women who worked the windows and sorted and processed the mail behind the scenes; the National Association of Post Office and General Service Maintenance Employees, which represented those who serviced and repaired the motor vehicles used by the postal service and cleaned and serviced the facilities; the National Federation of Motor Vehicle Employees, whose members drove, repaired, and serviced motor vehicles; and the National Association of Special Delivery Messengers—merged on July 1, 1971, to become the American Postal Workers' Union (APWU). Members of the National Alliance of Postal Employees, the African-American organization, joined the APWU as individuals over the next months and years, but many also maintained locals of their own organization, albeit without recognition or bargaining rights. The National Association of Letter Carriers refused to join in the merger process, and the National Postal Mailhandlers' Union, which was long part of the Laborers' International Union, chose to remain in its own organization.

For the next decade, the major postal worker unions bargained jointly with the U.S. Postal Service,

and wages, benefits, economic security, and working conditions of postal workers improved significantly. The APWU distinguished itself for its racial diversity, its national presence, its existence in smaller towns as well as larger cities, its progressive political stances, and its support of local union newsletters and internal education. By the mid-1980s and on, the APWU, the other postal unions, and postal workers suffered a fate similar to that of other unions in the era of economic neoliberalism. Technological change, the reorganization of mail processing, privatization, deregulation, globalization, and hostility to unions have undermined the accomplishments of the 1970s. Sadly interunion solidarity and collaboration have also suffered despite energetic internal rank-and-file movements for "One Postal Union" and "Organizing the Private Sector," leaving postal workers less able to defend their achievements. As we enter the twenty-first century, postal workers are no longer confident of their job security or that their compensation and working conditions will continue to improve.

PETER RACHLEFF

References and Further Reading

Freeman, Richard, and Casey Ichniowski, eds. *When Public Sector Workers Organize*. Chicago, IL: University of Chicago Press, 1988.

Rachleff, Peter. "Machine Technology and Workplace Control: The U.S. Post Office." In *Critical Studies in Organization and Bureaucracy*, Frank Fischer and Carmen Sirianni, eds. Philadelphia: Temple University Press, 1984.

Walsh, John, and Garth Mangum. *Labor Struggle in the Post Office: From Selective Lobbying to Collective Bargaining*. Armonk, NY: M.E. Sharpe, 1992.

See also **Postal Strike (1970)**

AMERICAN RAILWAY UNION

During the nineteenth century, the American Railway Union (ARU) was the largest and for a brief time most influential union in the United States organized along industrial lines. Although most commonly identified with the Pullman strike and boycott of 1894, the ARU grew out of railroad workers' organizational experimentation under the Knights of Labor (KOL) and a number of efforts to federate railroad brotherhoods. Despite a massive effort by employers after the Pullman strike to blacklist railroad workers associated with the ARU, remnants of the union survived in western states and in the early twentieth century, formed the United Brotherhood of Railway Employees (UBRE).

The railway strikes of 1877 ignited renewed organization among railroad workers. The brotherhoods of the operating trades were among the initial beneficiaries of this new organizational enthusiasm. With the vast majority of railroad workers outside the existing craft jurisdictions, the rapidly growing KOL moved into the breach in many localities by organizing mixed assemblies of railroad workers, trade assemblies of various shop crafts, and in some cases District Assemblies (DA) of all railroad trades on whole rail systems. The most notable of these were DA 101, which led the Great Southwest Strike of 1886 on the Gould lines, and DA 82, covering the Union Pacific Railroad.

As railway strikes grew in number and scale during the 1880s, many members of the brotherhoods associated themselves with local or district assemblies of the KOL. Such dual unionism was evident on many divisions of the Chicago, Burlington, and Quincy railroads, whose enginemen struck in 1888, supported by sympathetic shop men, trackmen, and switchmen associated with the KOL.

The Burlington strike defeat led midwestern and western railroad workers more actively to search for a new type of organization that would unite their efforts to resist the corporate rationalization and cost-cutting on highly competitive transcontinental railroads. During the later stages of the strike, an alternative grievance committee formed to widen the boycott of CB&Q cars and form a more durable federation of railroad organizations. Three of the four major brotherhoods formed the Supreme Council of the United Orders of Railway Employees, a federation of national officers "from the top" that gave them control over calling strikes by their respective unions. The KOL on the Union Pacific and the Burlington workers' grievance committee promoted a very different model of federation "from below." Formed in late 1889, the Supreme Council lasted into 1892 when it collapsed after brakemen scabbed against switchmen on the Chicago & Northwestern and switchmen in Buffalo lost a bitter strike. By this time, J. N. Corbin and the KOL on the Union Pacific had been joined by railroad workers across the West in a renewed effort to unite from below. In July 1890, dissatisfied delegates from brotherhood locals and KOL men had held an exploratory conference in Denver signaling their intention to organize a general union of railroad workers. Brotherhood officials Eugene V. Debs and G. W. Howard attended the meeting. Within the year Debs resigned his position as secretary-treasurer of the BLF, and Howard begun actively to organize a new general union of railway men.

Specific steps toward the organization of a general union of railroad workers began in the early spring of 1893 when Debs, Howard, Rogers, and other former brotherhood men drafted a "Declaration of Principles." They criticized the brotherhoods for failing to protect their members and called not for federation but a unified organization embracing "all classes, one roof to shelter all." Warning that the current methods of organization had "filled the land with scabs," they promised to reach out to the unemployed and former railway men. The American Railway Union was officially launched in Chicago at a June 1893 meeting of 50 men from diverse trades and locales. The initial constitution declared "all classes of railway employees...of good character" eligible for membership, but at the first convention the following year, delegates voted by a close margin to admit only members "born of white parents."

Organizers fanned out across the country and met an immediate and enthusiastic response on western roads. By November, 96 lodges had organized, and before the year's end, the organization was virtually complete on a number of key systems, among them the Union Pacific, the Denver & Rio Grande, the Northern Pacific, and the Southern Pacific. Members flocked from the brotherhoods, leaving their ranks depleted in many localities. But on railroads in the East and South, the ARU had a negligible presence.

Even as the ARU grew in the early months of 1894, two strikes foreshadowed troubles on the horizon. The first in early April involved James J. Hill's Great Northern, running west from St. Paul. Hill's men, newly organized in the ARU, demanded a rescission of wage cuts imposed earlier in the year. Hill's refusal precipitated a strike of virtually all employees on the road, and within a few weeks, through the mediation of Twin Cities businessmen, the strike was settled in the union's favor. The victory ignited a renewed wave of organizing in the West. By June 1894, 456 lodges and some 150,000 men had joined the ARU.

A second strike of recently organized ARU members at the Pullman Palace Car Works in Pullman, Illinois, stemmed from depression-induced wage cuts, lay offs, and high rents for company housing. Although discouraged from striking by ARU vice-president, George Howard, the Pullman workers walked out on May 11 after the company discharged three members of the grievance committee. Despite moral support from ARU leaders and lodges and mediation by Chicago's Civic Federation, the Pullman Company refused to negotiate.

On June 12, 1894, more than four hundred ARU delegates gathered in Chicago for the organization's first national convention. Testimony from a committee of Pullman strikers deeply stirred the sympathy of the delegates. Despite cautioning words from Debs and Howard, the delegates, following constitutionally prescribed procedures, solicited guidance from local lodges for a referendum calling for a national boycott of all Pullman sleeping cars. The locals wired back overwhelming support, and a boycott commenced on June 26.

The ARU entered the strike buoyed by its dramatic growth, reminiscent of the KOL in 1885–1886, and by the victory over James J. Hill. But it faced a determined foe well-prepared for a showdown with this upstart union. The General Managers' Association (GMA) had collaborated to meet previous strike threats, most notably the general strike for the 8-hour day on May 1, 1886. Its subcommittees went into action recruiting scab workers, facilitating the movement of freight, seeking court injunctions, and mobilizing private guards and local and state law enforcement personnel to prevent strikers' interference with railroad operations. Most importantly, it actively campaigned for federal government intervention, which materialized after Attorney General Richard Olney appointed former railroad attorney Edwin Walker as special prosecutor.

The first few days of the strike appeared to confirm the power of the ARU. Rail traffic in and out of Chicago came to a virtual standstill as strikers refused to handle trains with Pullman cars and then struck railroads that dismissed employees for such refusals. The strike spread rapidly in the West. On the Northern Pacific for instance, traffic west of the Twin Cities ceased on June 28 and did not resume until July 13. General management lost all contact for more than a week with a number of western divisions. Similar patterns played out on many but not all western roads. The CB&Q had seen only limited recovery of union activity since the bitter 1888 enginemen's strike. Most of the members of the largely secret ARU locals on that road were discharged with the onset of strike activity.

Beginning on July 2, the special prosecutor issued a series of blanket injunctions that prohibited strikers from interfering with the movement of trains. Following the deployment of federal troops on July 4 to enforce the injunctions, the ARU faced a formidable challenge. Violence erupted on a scale not seen during the early days of the strike. In Chicago alone, 13 people were killed and 53 seriously wounded before the strike was declared over. Strike leaders, including Debs, Howard, Keliher, and Rogers, were indicted by a grand jury on July 10 for conspiracy to interfere with interstate commerce and the mails and promptly arrested. At meetings in Briggs House, ARU leaders had tried unsuccessfully to enlist leaders of the American Federation of Labor (AFL) and their members in a general strike to pressure Pullman and the GMA to settle.

Although ARU members had disrupted rail traffic throughout the West and enjoyed broad-based community support in localities as far flung as Raton, New Mexico, Sacramento, California, Ogden, Utah, and Glendive, Montana, the combination of federal injunctions and aggressive actions by federal troops gradually restored rail service to even the most remote divisions. The arrest of strike leaders interrupted ARU communications and left many locals isolated. By the last week in July, strike activity had largely ceased and on August 2, ARU delegates hastily gathered in Chicago to call off the strike.

In September, Debs and his fellow ARU directors were tried on contempt of court charges for violating injunctions based on the Sherman Anti-trust Act's prohibition of "combinations or conspiracies in restraint of trade." On December 14, Judge William A. Woods announced their conviction. The defendants would serve terms ranging from 3–6 months in the Woodstock, Illinois, jail, commencing January 8, 1895.

The *Railway Times* reported some renewal of ARU organizing activity in the West during 1895. But the incarceration of the union's leaders and the impact of the blacklist on ARU activists took a serious toll. On July 15, 189,7 two-dozen ARU delegates gathered in Chicago and at Debs' urging, voted to dissolve the union and create a new political organization—the Social Democracy of America. The controversial decision left some western railroad men frustrated and others divided over whether to pursue the new organization's goals through founding western cooperative colonies for blacklisted workers or more conventional political action.

Some former ARU members formed the United Brotherhood of Railway Employees in 1901. By 1903, its official organ, the *Railway Employees' Journal* listed 56 lodges active in the Far West and Texas. Denied affiliation with the AFL, the UBRE eventually joined the American Labor Union and in 1905, the Industrial Workers of the World.

SHELTON STROMQUIST

References and Further Reading

Carwardine, William. *The Pullman Strike*. Chicago: Charles Kerr, 1894.

Foner, Philip S. *History of the Labor Movement in the United States*, vol. 2. New York: International Publishers, 1955.

Lindsey, Almont. *The Pullman Strike: the Story of a Unique Experiment and of a Great Labor Upheaval*. Chicago, IL: University of Chicago Press, 1942.

Salvatore, Nick. *Eugene V. Debs: Citizen and Socialist*. Urbana: University of Illinois Press, 1982.

Schneirov, Richard, Shelton Stromquist, Nick Salvatore, eds. *The Pullman Strike and the Crisis of the 1890s: Essays on Labor and Politics*. Urbana: University of Illinois Press, 1999.

Stromquist, Shelton. *A Generation of Boomers: The Pattern of Railroad Labor Conflict in Nineteenth-Century America*. Urbana: University of Illinois Press, 1987.

See also **Knights of Labor; Pullman Strike and Boycott (1894)**

AMERICAN STANDARD OF LIVING

The "American standard of living" has been a keyword of the labor movement in the United States since shortly after the Civil War. Although they rarely defined the American standard of living, workers and their allies generally invoked the term to refer to the dignity of the U.S. laborer in a time of transition. As the reality for U.S. workers shifted from independent proprietorship to wage-labor employment, the American standard, like the parallel concept of the living wage, provided a means for workers to link economic demands to political rights. Proponents of the American standard did this by claiming that a high level of consumption was necessary for working-class Americans to experience full citizenship in the republic.

A parallel discourse about the American standard of living was carried out in the late nineteenth century by the first generation of labor statisticians, notably Carroll Wright, the longtime head of the Massachusetts Bureau of Statistics of Labor (1873–1888) and the United States Bureau and Department of Labor (1885–1905). For these statisticians, the American standard of living was something quantifiable; a scientific measure of how U.S. workers lived, based on survey, wage, budget, and interview data. These statistical measures contributed to the Progressive Era attempt in many states to set a minimum wage for workers.

According to its advocates in the labor movement, the American standard should have been a reflection of the dignity of U.S. laborers, who in the "producerist" thinking shared by most Americans in the nineteenth century, lay at the heart of the republic. Workers understood the American standard as the just reward of their labor. They did not shy away from specifying what this meant in material terms, holding up contemporary standards of luxury as properly within the purview of U.S. producers. The American mechanic, according to George McNeill, the New England trade union leader and writer, should have "a parlor with a carpet on it, a mantelpiece with ornaments on it, pictures on the wall, books on the tables, kitchens with facilities" (Lawrence

Glickman, *Living Wage*, 1997). Similarly the mine workers' leader John Mitchell wrote in 1898 that American workers should be able to purchase "a comfortable house of at least six rooms," which contained a bathroom, good sanitary plumbing, parlor, dining room, kitchen, sleeping rooms, carpets, pictures, books and furniture (quoted in Alice Kessler-Harris, *A Woman's Wage: Historical Meanings and Social Consequences*, 1990). Other labor leaders incorporated symbols of modern consumerism—recreational opportunities, home ownership—into their definitions of the American standard.

Proponents of the American standard posited a correlation between character and desires. They defined the American standard as the quality of having many wants as well as the means to fulfill them. The worker who possessed the American standard could actually help to set the wage rate by consenting only to high-paying jobs. The activist and one-time Massachusetts gubernatorial candidate Edwin Chamberlin, like many other labor reformers, concluded that "the greater the wants, the higher the wages" (quoted in Lawrence Glickman, *Living Wage*, 1997). In making this claim, They reversed the view that income determined one's proper level of consumption. Instead they posited that wants were a good in and of themselves; a reflection of a proud workforce and a spur to demands for higher wages.

According to its champions, U.S. workers were characterized by a high level of consumption and an ever-increasing desire for, in the famous words of Samuel Gompers, the American Federation of Labor leader, more. "The American Standard of Living in the year 1903 is a different, a better and higher standard than the American Standard of Living in the year 1803," claimed John Mitchell (Lawrence Glickman, *Living Wage*, 1997). Just as living wage advocates were leery of setting an absolute measurement of what this entailed for fear that "the minimum would become the maximum," proponents of the American standard of living understood it as a level of consumption that would continually increase.

High standards redounded to the benefit of the entire working class and the nation as a whole. This meant, according to proponents, that old ideas that equated thrift with virtue would need to be updated. In the new era of wage labor, high standards of living and high levels of consumption were better indicators of virtue and solidarity than excessive economy. The American standard of living would ensure that the nation's workers were comfortable, politically active, and through their power as consumers, willing and able to assist their fellow workers. Rather than peons to thrift, promoters of the American standard saw it as their duty to highlight the social benefits of consumption. As the worker A. S. Leitch wrote in 1887, "The wage workers' extravagance is the wage-workers' salvation....Suppose all workingmen of the United States...at a certain time conclude to squander no more of their earnings in the purchase of tobacco— thousands of tobacco workers would soon go hungry. Or beer: the brewers would be ruined. To shut down on 'superfluous luxuries' of books and papers, the printers would get a tough deal." Leitch concluded with a defense of working-class extravagance, which gives employment to thousands of our brother wage slaves by means of which they gain a livelihood and provide the comfort that workers needed to exercise virtue and citizenship (Lawrence Glickman, *Living Wage*, 1997).

From the beginning, national identity was critical to the meaning of the American standard. Proponents of the American standard held that as the labor intellectual Ira Steward said in the 1870s, low wages were "eminently un-American" and conversely, good wages were as integral to the success of American democracy as the "frequency and freedom of elections." (Lawrence Glickman, *Living Wage*, 1997). Connecting consumption to patriotism, American workers argued that a high standard of living was necessary in a country newly dominated by wage earners rather than farmers and small producers. "In a political sense, the high standard of living is a chief requirement for the preservation of republican institutions," as one working-class group claimed in 1888. "And it is a public duty of the most sacred kind to protect the workingmen of the country . . . to secure a high standard of living." "The safeguarding of liberty and virtue" was not merely a political matter; workers could not ensure these without an expansive level of consumption (Lawrence Glickman, *Living Wage*, 1997). In order to maintain a "self-governing Republic," the Anthracite Coal Commission declared several decades later, "all American wage earners have a fundamental economic right to at least a living wage, or an American standard of living" (Lawrence Glickman, *Living Wage*, 1997). Typically this justification for a high standard of living was political as much as economic: Without it "there could not be an intelligent and sound citizenship."

The language of the American standard served a function analogous to the earlier republican language of virtue. Possessing the American standard would allow wage workers to fight injustice in the form of low wages and long hours, just as virtue enabled antebellum artisans to fight it in other forms, such as the concentration of political power. An unjust economy however would ensure that the American standard could not be perpetuated. Like virtue, it was a quality reciprocally linked to economic and political life. Its presence was a symbol of a healthy republic, its absence a telltale sign of danger. As the labor leaders who contributed to the *Voice of Labor* noted, "The wage earners' standard of living, which rests so largely upon the wages received and upon the hours of labor, determines the physical, mental and moral foundations of the masses upon which the structure of American institutions must rest" (Lawrence Glickman, *Living Wage*, 1997).

Another political aspect of the American standard was the connection it drew between high wages and national identity. Whereas previously labor had argued that the United States was distinct from other countries because of the sovereignty of its large class of small producers, in the late nineteenth century, it began to argue that America's high standards set it apart. This led to a new category of American exceptionalism: The need for high wages and the ability to consume properly distinguished Americans from others. The patriotism of the American standard discourse sometimes shaded into jingoism and even beyond that into xenophobia and racism. While some proponents of the American standard understood it as a quality that all workers could aspire to, others understood it as being possessed exclusively by white, male American-born workers. The claims of the Texas labor reformer and minister B. W. Williams in 1887 were typical: "The American laborer should not be expected to live like the Irish tenant farmer or the Russian serf. His earning ought to be sufficient to enable him to live as a respectable American citizen" (Lawrence Glickman, *Living Wage*, 1997). In this view, American workers had more wants and desires than other workers and therefore were willing to insist on higher wages. The labor intellectual and pamphleteer George Gunton contrasted "stupefied peasants who have no new wants" with "the multiplication of wants and tastes" in the American worker (Lawrence Glickman, *Living Wage*, 1997). Gunton and others described the American standard as a quality rather than a quantity, one seemingly possessed more naturally by native-born, white, American workers than by suspect immigrants.

The flipside of this nationalist interpretation of the American standard was a fear of those perceived as having lower standards of living. This fear often took on a hateful tone, revealing deeply ingrained racist and sexist assumptions imbedded in labor's political economy. Proponents declared that an American standard stood for national health; a low standard represented a grave danger to the country. If the "standard of living is the measure of civilization," as Boston labor leader Frank Foster wrote in 1900, low standards threatened civilization. "The low standard of living has produced the degradation of labor witnessed among the Orientals," noted the *Voice of*

Labor, selecting the group most frequently denounced for threatening the American standard and replacing the American worker with brutes. By equating brutishness and despotism with the low standard of living, American standard proponents highlighted the danger to the republic. "If this standard is lowered," they concluded, "American citizenship would be debased" (quotations from Lawrence Glickman, *Living Wage*, 1997).

By defining the American standard as a quality ingrained in white male wage earners, through years of cultural habit, it became easy for these workers to declare that others lacked the acculturation and genetic make-up necessary to maintain such standards. Not only was the American standard used to separate the United States from other countries, it also promoted a hierarchy within the country. Organized workers wielded the American standard against immigrants, blacks, and women as often as they deployed it against stingy employers.

Being an American wage earner in this view implied a particular standard of living *vis-a-vis* other less civilized groups: "An American will starve or strike rather than accept Chinese wages," wrote Gunton, "because the American standard of living demands higher wages." According to the same logic, those with few wants (paradigmatically, the Chinese) would necessarily receive low wages (Lawrence Glickman, *Living Wage*, 1997). In keeping with their new political economy, workers ground their critique of groups that threatened American standards in the realm of leisure rather than productive labor. White workers routinely conceded that the Chinese worked hard and competently; it was in the area of leisure that they found the Chinese to be deficient. "While the Chinaman works industriously enough, he consumes very little, either of his own production or of ours," declared Samuel Gompers and a union colleague in a 1906 anti-Chinese pamphlet tellingly titled, *Meat vs. Rice: American Manhood against Asiatic Coolieism. Which Shall Survive?* As a result, they noted, "The white laboring man . . . is injured in his comfort, reduced in his scale of life and standard of living, necessarily carrying down with it his moral and physical stamina." The title of one section of the pamphlet, "Asiatic Labor Degrades as Slave Labor Did," suggests that trade unionists treated the subversion of American standards as the moral equivalent of slavery. While granting that the Chinese were tireless workers, a San Francisco newspaper criticized them in 1901 for their "mean-living": They present the American workingman with the alternative of committing suicide or coming down to John Chinaman's standard of wages and living" (quotations from Lawrence Glickman, *Living Wage*, 1997). In this scenario,

maintaining the American standard was literally a matter of life or death for white workers.

American standard proponents argued that they could not compete with groups that possessed lower standards without threatening the foundation of the republic. They often framed this argument in racial terms. "It is an insult to the respectability and manhood of an American to expect him to compete in the labor market with the heathen of Asia," declared two members of the Knights of Labor. "Such competition is an utter impossibility," since no "American can offer to work for wages so low that the Chinese will not bid lower." Caucasians, Samuel Gompers bluntly wrote in 1905, "are not going to let their standard of living be destroyed by negroes, Chinaman, Japs, or any others." In 1885, an article in *John Swinton's Paper* declared that Chinese standards imposed impossible burdens on American workers struggling to maintain their standards: "Does any one class imagine it can compete with men who live like vermin, whose families cost nothing, and whose food and clothing are but nominal in cost?" In contrast, American workers defined themselves by their elegant lifestyle and expansive purchasing habits (Lawrence Glickman, *Living Wage*, 1997).

In the twentieth century, American workers continued to promote the idea of the American standard, but they sought to make it more inclusive. Rather than using the term as a club against immigrants, by the 1930s, the American standard came to be a battle cry of an increasingly multi-ethnic and racially diverse working class, one aspect of the great upsurge in union participation during the middle decades of the century. As the idea became less associated with labor's particularism and racism, other groups began to invoke the term as a symbol of American exceptionalism. As the historian Marina Moscowitz has noted, the idea became central to middle-class Americans, who sought to define (and partake in) common standards of etiquette, design, home furnishings, and other aspects of daily life. Politicians with no loyalties to the labor movement, picked up the idea, and especially during the Cold War, when the concept metamorphosed into the American way of life, the high standard of living of American workers was taken as proof of the superiority of capitalist democracy. In the early twenty-first century concerns about outsourcing and global competition have led many pundits to voice concern that the era of the American standard of living may be coming to an end. But the idea that American workers deserve a decent and ever-growing standard of living continues to motivate many members of the American working class.

LAWRENCE B. GLICKMAN

101

References and Further Reading

Anderson, Margo. "Standards, Statuses, and Statistics: Carroll Wright and the American Standard of Living." *Advancing the Consumer Interest* 9 (Spring 1997): 4–12.

Brown, Claire. *American Standards of Living 1918–1988.* Oxford, UK and Cambridge, MA: Blackwell, 1994.

Glickman, Lawrence. *A Living Wage: American Workers and the Making of Consumer Society.* Ithaca, NY: Cornell University Press, 1997.

Kessler-Harris, Alice. *A Woman's Wage: Historical Meanings and Social Consequences.* Lexington: University Press of Kentucky, 1990.

Moscowitz, Marina. *Standard of Living: The Measure of the Middle Class in Modern America.* Baltimore and London: Johns Hopkins University Press, 2004.

Shergold, Peter R. *Working-Class Life: The "American Standard" in Comparative Perspective, 1899–1913.* Pittsburgh: University of Pittsburgh Press, 1982.

ANARCHISM

Since its emergence in the nineteenth century, anarchism in the United States has been characterized by the coexistence of two distinct strands of thought—a native tradition that was largely individualist and an immigrant tradition heavily based on collectivism. Deriving inspiration from the writings of Thomas Paine, Ralph Waldo Emerson, and Henry David Thoreau, individual anarchism supported the existence of a stateless social order characterized by voluntary social interactions among the citizenry, the maintenance of private property, and a market economy with wages paid in accordance with the labor theory of value. Based on these principles, Josiah Warren, a gifted musician and inventor who had left Robert Owen's colony of New Harmony in 1827, established the Village of Equity with six families in Ohio in 1834. Considered the first individual anarchist settlement in the United States, the community's collapse resulted not from economic breakdown but from the spread of malaria and influenza. In 1846, Warren founded Utopia, which survived as an individual anarchist community for nearly two decades with approximately 100 residents before evolving into a more traditional village with cooperative leanings.

The primary advocate of this philosophy in the latter half of the nineteenth century was Benjamin R. Tucker, a publisher by trade and the translator who first brought the writings of two prominent anarchists, Pierre-Joseph Proudhon and Mikhail Bakunin, to the American public's attention. An effective polemicist who maintained an extreme individualist anarchism throughout his life, he vehemently opposed collectivist anarchism, arguing that freedom was irreconcilable with any form of communism and believed that collectivist anarchism's support of the "propaganda of the deed" (see the following section) was basically morally wrong. From 1881–1908, Tucker published the foremost individual anarchist newspaper, *Liberty: Not the Daughter but the Mother of Order*, which drew acclaim from H. L. Mencken, George Bernard Shaw, and Walt Whitman. When the publication of *Liberty* ceased, not only did a primary forum of indigenous American radicalism disappear but so, for the most part, did the individualist anarchist tradition in the United States.

Collectivist Anarchism in the United States

The collectivist form of anarchism, also known as anarchocommunism, inspired the majority of anarchists in the United States. Promoted primarily by immigrants who advocated the overthrow of capitalism, these anarcho-Communists favored an egalitarian society that contained neither markets nor wages but was guided by the Marxist principle of "from each according to their ability, to each according to their need." Without the existence of the state to administer economic and political affairs, self-managing worker councils and assemblies would be established, with direct worker control of the means of production. All production decisions would be made by these worker organs; community institutions would also be self-managed by its members. Substituting for the role of the state, federations and networks established by free association would link workplaces and communities together.

The roots of this immigrant anarchism in the United States can be traced to the 1880 split in the German immigrant-dominated Socialist Labor party. Although still viewing themselves as Marxists, the dissidents established Socialist Revolutionary Clubs in New York, Chicago, and other large cities as a precursor to the development of anarchism. With the formation of the International Working People's Association, also known as the Black International, in London in 1881, in order to revitalize the previous left-wing internationalism of the First International, the Socialist Revolutionary Clubs, with its strongest base in Chicago, formally supported and affiliated with this new International. At the same time, a grouping of native-born Americans from San Francisco, led by Burnette G. Haskell, an affluent lawyer, formed the International Workingmen's Association, or Red International, and joined the Black International. Finally a third group of anarchists derived their inspiration from Johann Most, a charismatic lecturer and journalist, who re-established *Die Freiheit* on his arrival in New York in 1882. Most of these anarchists advocated the "propaganda of the deed," or the use of violence in promoting social change, and refused to work within labor unions.

By the time of the International's second Congress in Pittsburgh in 1883, Chicago had become the national center of anarchist activity. The conference resulted in a dramatic increase in both membership and activity in the city. Of the International's 6,000 members in the United States, half were in Chicago groups, with the majority being either German or Czechs. However the Chicago anarchists' influence was certainly broader and deeper than its membership figures indicated. A Central Labor Union, guided by the International, was established in 1883, and by the start of 1886, the bulk of the city's unions supported the anarchists. Finally from 1883–1886, the International published five newspapers in the city with a circulation exceeding 30,000.

The events of 4 May 1886, often referred to as the Haymarket incident or affair, where a bomb exploded killing police after they attacked the anarchist-led Haymarket Square demonstration, eventually led to the decimation of the anarchist movement. The aftermath of the demonstration, which was held as a memorial to the two McCormick Works employees killed by police on 3 May when striking for the 8-hour work day, resulted in severe repression against 8-hour strikers, anarchists, and labor leaders not only in Chicago but to some degree throughout the nation. Culminating in the trial of eight anarchists who were found guilty in August 1886 of conspiracy to murder a policeman killed at Haymarket, four were hanged in November 1887, one took his own life in prison while three remained in jail until 1893 when Illinois' Governor Altgeld pardoned them, conceding the inherent unfairness of the trial.

The Birth of U.S. Jewish Anarchism

Shortly after Haymarket, anarchism's limited mass following in the United States melted away. The Chicago events also led to the Black International's collapse and with it, the cessation of most of its publications. Thus by 1887, anarchism in this country had become largely a movement only among Jewish, German, Italian, and Spanish immigrants and their children. The largest and most active of these immigrant groups were the Yiddish-speaking Jewish anarchists, who did not begin to register a major impact on anarchism in this country until after the first massive wave of immigration from Tsarist Russia in the 1880s.

The Haymarket trial led a handful of young rank-and-file workers from New York's Lower East Side to form the first U.S. Jewish anarchist group, the Pioneers of Liberty (Pionire der Frayhayt), on 9 October 1886, the day that the eight Chicago anarchists were sentenced for their alleged crime. Immediately affiliating with the Black International, this tiny group threw themselves into the campaign to save the Chicago anarchists from execution by conducting meetings, holding rallies, and raising funds for their legal appeals. In addition, from their Orchard Street headquarters in the center of the Lower East Side, the Pioneers churned out Yiddish language literature, including a pamphlet discussing the Haymarket affair, and organized weekly lectures that drew an enthusiastic throng of participants.

Knowledge of the Pioneers' activities spread to other eastern cities with large concentrations of Yiddish-speaking immigrants. Under the group's sponsorship, workers' educational clubs sprouted in Baltimore, Boston, and Providence, while groupings containing both socialists and anarchists began to emerge, the most significant being the Knights of Liberty (Riter der Frayhayt) founded in Philadelphia in 1889. Composed of anarchists who had resided in London prior to arriving in the United States, the Knights organized anarchist lectures that attracted workers by the hundreds each Sunday afternoon.

With the continued growth of the Jewish anarchist movement in the United States, the Pioneers of Liberty proclaimed in January 1889 that it would begin to publish a weekly paper in New York, to be named the *Varhayt* (Truth). The inaugural issue, which rolled off the presses on 15 February 1889, was the first Yiddish (purely) anarchist journal not only to appear in the United States but throughout the world. Lasting only 5 months due to a lack of funds, during its short existence, the paper published articles authored by Johann Most and Peter Kropotkin, a summary of Marxist economics, and essays on political and labor events. A whole issue was even devoted to memorializing the Paris Commune's eighteenth anniversary. However a little over a year later, the Pioneers of Liberty, the Knights of Liberty, and other groups launched the anarchist *Fraye Arbeter Shtime* (Free Voice of Labor) on 4 July 1890, which became the longest running Yiddish newspaper in the world when it ended publication in December 1977. Throughout the paper's nearly 90 years of existence, it exerted a major influence on the Jewish labor movement in the United States while publishing some of the most trenchant analysis of distinguished writers and poets in the Yiddish language.

After the promising 1880s and 1890s, the Jewish anarchists realized by the turn of the twentieth century that social revolution was no longer on the horizon. Moving to a more pragmatic perspective in fighting for social reform, the Jewish anarchists threw themselves into establishing libertarian schools and cooperative organizations while becoming increasingly active in the labor movement. By the early twentieth century, they were organizing unions in all trades and industries in which Jewish workers were found, including bookbinding, cigar making, and house painting, becoming particularly active in the International Ladies' Garment Workers' Union (ILGWU) and the Amalgamated Clothing Workers of America (ACWA). In these two heavily Jewish garment unions, the anarchists took part in strikes, fighting both corruption and bureaucracy.

Consistent with the anarchists' new practical positions, they helped to organize the Workmen's Circle, the socialist-leaning Jewish fraternal order, which provided an array of benefits, including life insurance, in addition to offering various educational and cultural programs throughout the United States and Canada. They also participated in the ILGWU's and the ACWA's housing cooperatives in New York City.

When the Communists appeared on the verge of obtaining control of the ILGWU and the ACWA, the anarchists successfully united with their former socialist adversaries from 1923–1927 in beating back this challenge. However during this faction fight, the anarchists became entangled in the union officialdom, with Morris Sigman elected to the ILGWU presidency and Rose Pesotta and Anna Sosnovsky obtaining union vice-presidencies.

Well-known figures in the history of U.S. anarchism that emerged from the Jewish anarchist movement were Alexander Berkman and Emma Goldman. Berkman is best known for his failed assassination attempt of Henry Clay Frick, the plant manager of the Homestead (Pennsylvania) steel mill, in 1892 after Frick's hiring of Pinkerton guards led to the shooting of strikers. Goldman, a lifelong friend of Berkman, sought to Americanize anarchism through her writing and by conducting lectures directed to English-speaking readers and audiences. To this end, and in an attempt to revitalize an anarchist movement flagging since the early twentieth century, she published an anarchist monthly journal, *Mother Earth*, from 1906–1917, when the federal government quashed it. Although the journal's circulation was only 3,000–5,000 copies an issue, it achieved prominence for connecting European anarchist philosophy with indigenous traditions of American radicalism.

Anarchism's Decline in the United States

A deathblow to anarchism in the United States came with government repression during World War I, which led to the deportation of foreign-born activists, the closing of newspapers, and the targeting of specific anarchist groups. In addition although many anarchists enthusiastically supported the Russian Revolution and the Bolshevik government, only later to turn against it, the formation and growth of the U.S. Communist party usurped the terrain to the left of the Socialist party of America, a space that the anarchist movement had claimed as its own since the turn of the twentieth century. Even the publicity surrounding the Sacco and Vanzetti trial and the subsequent execution of these two anarchists during the 1920s failed to revive a fading movement. The annihilation of a once vibrant anarchism in Spain in the aftermath of the country's civil war reduced the U.S. anarchists' role on the eve of World War II to publishing literature and to providing relief for their surviving Spanish comrades.

Postwar Developments in U.S. Anarchism

In the post-World War II period, the ideology of anarchism continued to have a marginal influence on American society. The intermingling of anarchist ideas with pacifism resulted in the creation of Pacifica Radio in the San Francisco Bay area and later influenced Beat Generation writers. In the next decade, *Liberation*, a more or less anarchopacifist magazine, prepared the way for the New Left's arrival in the 1960s. With the growth of the largest of the New Left organizations, the Students for a Democratic Society, its major principle of "participatory democracy," the idea that people should run the institutions that affect their everyday lives, was inspired by anarchism. With the New Left's disintegration, anarchist ideas became associated with the ecology movement; particularly its confrontational direct-action branch represented by such groups as Friends of the Earth. The emergence of punk rock in the 1970s exposed a younger generation to anarchist ideas, although they were often expressed in an openly nihilistic manner. A generation later, beginning in the late 1990s, various anarchist groups became major participants in the antiglobalization movement, helping to mobilize the successful protest against the World Trade Organization (WTO) meeting in Seattle in 1999. In the first decade of the twenty-first century, these anarchists continue to organize demonstrations against state cartels, including the WTO, the World Bank, the Group of Eight, and the World Economic Forum.

VICTOR G. DEVINATZ

References and Further Reading

Anderson, Carlotta R. *All-American Anarchist: Joseph A. Labadie and the Labor Movement.* Detroit, Wayne State University Press, 1998.

Avrich, Paul. *Anarchist Voices: An Oral History of Anarchism in America.* Princeton, NJ: Princeton University Press, 1994.

———. *Anarchist Portraits.* Princeton, NJ: Princeton University Press, 1988.

Buhle, Paul. "Anarchism and American Labor." *International Labor and Working Class History* 23: (Spring 1983): 21–34.

DeLeon, David. *The American as Anarchist: Reflections on Indigenous Radicalism.* Baltimore, MD: Johns Hopkins University Press, 1978.

Falk, Candace. *Love, Anarchy, and Emma Goldman.* New York: Holt, Rinehart, and Winston, 1984.

Jacker, Corinne. *The Black Flag of Anarchy: Anti-Statism in the United States.* New York: Scribner, 1968.

Martin, James J. *Men against the State: The Expositors of Individualist Anarchism in America, 1827–1908.* Colorado Springs, CO: Myles Publishers, 1970.

Nelson, Bruce C. *Beyond the Martyrs: A Social History of Chicago Anarchism, 1870–1900.* New Brunswick, NJ: Rutgers University Press, 1988.

Reichert, William O. *Partisans of Freedom: A Study in American Anarchism.* Bowling Green, OH: Bowling Green University Popular Press, 1976.

Woodcock, George. *Anarchism.* New York: Penguin, 1986.

See also **Berkman, Alexander; Goldman, Emma; Haymarket Affair (1886)**

ANDERSON, MARY (AUGUST 27, 1872–JANUARY 29, 1964)
Women's Bureau, Department of Labor

Mary Anderson ascended from her immigrant roots through the ranks of trade unionism to become a union president and eventually head of the Women's Bureau of the United States Department of Labor. Devoted to achieving improved conditions for female workers, Anderson was the first working-class woman to achieve such a prominent position in a federal agency.

Mary Anderson was the youngest of seven children born to Mangus and Matilda (Johnson) Anderson near Lidkoping, Sweden, on August 27, 1872. Anderson attended a Lutheran elementary school before her family fell on hard economic times and lost their farm. In 1889, at the age of 16 Mary and her sister, Hilda, immigrated to the United States to work with their older sister Anna in a rural Michigan lumber camp. Within three years, Mary Anderson tired of her dishwashing job and relocated to Chicago where,

due to the economic decline of 1893, she weathered a number of slack periods to become a skilled boot and shoe worker. Within a year after she secured a job at Schwab's shoe factory, her coworkers elected the 22-year-old Anderson to the presidency of the all-women Boot Stitchers' Local 94.

Comfortable in the working-class environs, Anderson expanded her connections in the labor arena, serving as the union representative at the citywide Chicago Federation of Labor meetings. Her work also exposed her to the vibrant women's political culture centered around Chicago's Hull-House settlement. Anderson credited Hull-House founder Jane Addams with "open[ing] a door to a larger life." Addams introduced Anderson to others working to alleviate the plight of workers, including National Women's Trade Union League (WTUL) President Margaret Dreier Robins, who became a lifelong mentor to the young Anderson. Mary McDowell, the "angel of the stockyards," along with Hull-House resident, Chief Factory Inspector of Illinois, and founder of the National Consumers' League Florence Kelley would also become good friends of Anderson. The ties between Anderson and the middle-class social reformers and their affiliated organizations encouraged Anderson's advocacy on behalf of protective legislation for female workers throughout her life.

Through her membership in the WTUL, Anderson participated in the 1910 Chicago Men's Garment Workers' Strike. During the strike she befriended strike leaders Bessie Abramowitz and her future husband, Sidney Hillman. Anderson helped them to organize and sustain the strikers over the brutal winter of 1910–1911. Although the strike ended with mixed results, Anderson helped to negotiate the collective-bargaining agreement between the city's largest garment firm, Hart, Schaffner, and Marx (HSM), and its more than 8,000 employees. Following the strike, Anderson worked full-time for the WTUL helping to ensure that the workers' grievances were properly channeled through the arbitration system established after the strike.

With suffrage for women on the horizon, Anderson became an American citizen in 1915. She continued to advance the WTUL's goal of bringing women into trade unions by expanding her organizational activities to workers in department stores, stockyards, and candy factories. Anderson and her middle-class allies, including Robins and the director of industrial studies for the Russell Sage Foundation, Mary Van Kleeck, viewed the U.S. entry into World War I as an opportunity to advance the cause of better wages and working conditions for female workers in the defense industries. Van Kleeck became the director of

Woodrow Wilson's new Women in Industry Service, and Anderson served as her assistant.

In 1920, when Congress transformed the Women in Industry Service into a permanent Women's Bureau within the United States Department of Labor, Anderson became its first director. During her almost 25-year tenure, she berated all forms of discrimination against women. As a single, self-supporting woman, Anderson fought to counter the widespread belief that women worked for pin money rather than out of economic necessity. She criticized Depression Era discrimination against married women, calling it "unjust and unsound." A close friend of the Roosevelts during the New Deal years, Anderson found fault with the National Recovery Administration's wage and hour industrial codes, many of which discriminated against workers on the basis of race and gender. Relying on one of the many Women's Bureau investigations she initiated, she found the problems facing black female industrial workers, particularly their working conditions and wages appalling. Due to the prevailing public sentiments, which endorsed racism and sexism, these prejudices were virtually impossible to overcome. She established a special committee to abolish industrial homework that proved much more successful. A longtime advocate of minimum wages, maximum hours, and regulation of child labor at the federal level, Anderson considered the passage of the Fair Labor Standards Act in 1938 a victory for workers.

In 1940, even before the United States became officially involved in World War II, the Women's Bureau issued guidelines for employing women in defense industries. With the outbreak of the war, Anderson directed the effort to employ women in nontraditional jobs and to monitor their standards of employment, including safety provisions for hazardous occupations. She fought a futile battle to have a woman appointed to the War Manpower Commission. Instead a separate Women's Advisory Committee was established. However women on the committee acted in a solely advisory capacity rather than influencing policy formulation. The Women's Bureau revealed union contracts allowed discrimination against women in the areas of wage and seniority rights. Women's wartime gains were inadequate—they were paid less than men for performing the same jobs, and they were continually denied equal employment opportunities.

Anderson felt that the Women's Bureau's most important accomplishment under her administration were the reports published regarding the conditions of women's employment, including wages and hours in 32 states. Anderson proved adept at circumventing the government bureaucracy to, in Assistant Secretary of Labor Esther Peterson's words, "give working women a voice in government." Anderson's greatest desire was to achieve equal pay for equal work for women. Anderson retired from her official position "tired and discouraged," when Roosevelt's Secretary of Labor, Frances Perkins, failed to support the Bureau's programs financially and refused to cooperate with Anderson. After her retirement in 1944, she devoted much of her time to writing her memoirs and occasionally guest speaking at various labor-related functions. Anderson died in 1964 at the age of 92, one year after the Equal Pay Act passed into law.

KAREN PASTORELLO

References and Further Reading

Anderson, Mary, and Winslow, Mary N. *Woman at Work: The Autobiography of Mary Anderson*. Minneapolis: The University of Minnesota Press, 1951.

Mary Anderson's Papers. In the Papers of the Women's Trade Union League and Its Principal Leaders. Schlesinger Library, Radcliff College, Cambridge, MA.

Women's Bureau, United States Department of Labor, Record Group 86. National Archives and Record Center, Washington, DC.

See also **Department of Labor; Women's Bureau**

ANTEBELLUM ERA

The labor movement in the antebellum United States unfolded in a broader economic, political, and demographic context that at once encouraged and discouraged trade unionism. Such contradictory tendencies gave the early labor movement its peculiar shape. This essay will sketch out that context before moving on to the labor movement itself.

Industrial transformation, bolstered by the Embargo of European imports in the War of 1828, developed its own momentum in the 1820s. It gave rise to two distinctive workplaces, the factory and the outworking system. The modernized factory had a limited compass that embraced a few pursuits, namely the production of cotton and woolen cloth and the making of iron and iron implements. Iron mills scattered in the Northeast through the countryside in small, remote towns near iron deposits; textile factories in New England bunched on inland streams, notably in Pawtucket, Rhode Island, as well as Waltham and Lowell, Massachusetts. Textiles proved to be the most advanced industry in the nation, marked as it was by relatively large factories with up to 50 workers, powered by water wheels, and equipped with the latest machines. The firms tended to be incorporated businesses with managerial hierarchies that included foremen and supervisors who directed a unique work force consisting of families, as in Rhode

Island, or single women in their late teens to early twenties, as in Massachusetts, recruited from hardscrabble farms nestled in the New England countryside. The women were subjected to a paternalistic order, living two or three to a room in dormitories managed by matronly women who encouraged church attendance and enforced nightly curfews. Such control was supposed to shield the women in Lowell and other such places from gritty industrialism, popularly associated with the degraded labor in the "dark and satanic mills" in England. Lowell's workforce would be different. The women were not only protected; they were also expected to be temporary workers who would leave the mills after earning enough money to help parents pay off mortgages, send brothers to college, or accumulate dowries in order to improve their own marriage prospects. And for a time it worked. The women earned relatively high wages and benefited from the relatively light hand of paternalistic management, which not only saw to it that they were housed and fed but also allowed episodic trips home to care for ailing parents or do their part for the spring planting or fall harvest. It also helped that most had abbreviated careers in the mills, working two or three years before trading wage labor for marriage and child rearing.

Many more women and most men did not work in factories before the 1850s. They either toiled at home as outworkers in various trades under the putting-out system; men worked in smallish shops. Historians used to believe that the transformation of craftwork into specialized tasks coincided with the advent of Jacksonian Democracy. More recent work indicates specialization, the solvent of craft work before the application of machine technology, began around the time of the Revolution; it accelerated substantially however in the 1820s with the onset of the Transportation revolution, which pried open new markets throughout the North and West. Employers out to tap such markets increased production by reorganizing labor and introducing hand tools, not by using machines or herding workers into factories. Shoemaking for instance was transformed from three basic tasks—cutting leather into tops and bottoms, sewing the tops, and affixing the tops to bottoms—into 40 or so different steps before the sewing machine was adapted to leather in the mid-1840s. It was only in the early 1850s that factories appeared in shoemaking and other trades. For the greater part of the antebellum period, shoemakers and other tradesmen worked in shops with under a dozen workers in which labor relations were intensely personal and equally supple.

Small shops cleaved neatly into two groups depending largely on the trade. In the luxury trades of jewelry making or the higher end of crafts otherwise in decline, workers carried on pretty much as they had in the past, learning their trades through apprentice training, or on-the-job instruction, and deliberately making custom goods on relatively casual work schedules. Relations between employer and employee at this level of production remained comparatively harmonious. Other workplaces degenerated into early-day sweatshops in which workers churned out standard items, doing specialized tasks under the strict supervision of foremen or employers. Some historians characterize this as "the drive system," a regime featuring strict control from above.

The harsh social relations of the sweatshop made fertile ground for unionization. Such workplaces after all prevailed in trades with long conventions of labor relations in which journeymen, as early employers were called, plied craft skills and had enjoyed some autonomy. At the same time however, deteriorating conditions were mitigated some by the fluidity of the social order of the handicrafts. Journeymen still aspired to setting up on their own across a wide spectrum of crafts, and relatively low start-up costs made for easy entry to ownership. The line between master and journeyman, employer and employee, remained porous through this period. The old adage of "today's journeyman, tomorrow's master," still applied, softening labor relations in the crafts.

A form of ambiguity also characterized the early workforce itself. What the historian Herbert Gutman once called "the first American working class" was ethnically and racially homogenous. The vast majority were native-born Americans of American or English stock before the great influx of Irish and German immigrants after the turn of the 1840s. Thus in the 1820s, under 10,000 immigrants arrived from Europe, and only 143,000 came a decade later when the labor movement thrived; the total soared to 600,000 in the 1840s and leapt upward again to 1.7 million in the 1850s due to the Irish famine and political turmoil in Germany. Though we are accustomed to associating the great influx from 1845–1855 with the famine generation, the fact is that nearly as many Germans arrived as Irish. Irish immigrants, impoverished former peasants and land laborers, entered the workforce at the bottom, forming the vast army of unskilled labor on construction sites, canal diggings, and wharves and docks. Some would find work at semiskilled tasks in the lower end of tailoring and shoemaking. The Germans by contrast carried craft skills with them and were found in a broad array of trades in their new home. For their part African-Americans were few in number—Philadelphia's black population of 20,000 in 1850 being the largest in the North—and most of them concentrated in unskilled labor in and around waterfronts in eastern port cities. As a result the ethnic tensions that would divide group against group were largely absent before the 1850s when Irish and German immigrants all but took over the bastardized crafts in New York and Philadelphia and to a lesser extent in Boston. If ethnic uniformity eased the task of labor organization, geographic mobility complicated it. Study after study of cities and towns in this period demonstrates that working people were footloose, moving from place to place at a dizzying pace. The majority of workers at the start of a decade in one place simply up and left by the start of the next one. No one believes that such sojourners sought fortunes or the fabled opportunities on the frontier; instead most left one city or town for another. Such geographic volatility thwarted labor organization, making it extremely difficult for workers to maintain their organizations over time. Very few nations, the evidence suggests, had such a mobile working class.

Nor did many industrializing nations develop along the same political lines as the United States. In Europe, and more particularly in England, the working class developed in a context of political repression in which workers were barred from voting. English workers who unionized could be prosecuted under the Combination Acts in the 1820s, and the suffrage reform of a decade later offered no relief, enfranchising the middle class and not the working class. Such conditions necessarily intensified class consciousness in England and on the Continent. Not so in the United States. Though American unionists were sometimes subjected to hostile court decisions, they were not barred from collective action by statute law. Indeed in the United States, the national government was weak to begin with and weaker still as industrialism spread and deepened; state government, though stronger and growing more active, did not inhibit labor organization. As if that were not enough of a complication, nearly every state in the North extended the franchise to ordinary white men coincident with the rise of mills and factories. American workers were not alienated from their government as individuals or as a class. They instead thought of government as *their* government. This posed an opportunity and a challenge—an opportunity because it opened up politics as an avenue of organization and amelioration, and a challenge because workers had the chance to organize as a class when they were still a minority and in a political system whose parties cut across class lines and did not easily admit to the politics of class.

It was out of these contradictory forces that the first American labor movement was born in the late 1820s. Craftsmen in eastern cities had organized trade societies as early as the 1780s, usually to fight for wage increases. Their organizations were fleeting and confined to single trades, with printers, carpenters, and shoemakers in the vanguard of self-organization. The intensification of craft transformation in the 1820s however set off an upsurge in protest as groups of construction workers in 1827 in Boston and Philadelphia went on strike for a 10-hour day, signaling broader and deeper disquiet. The unrest spread outward and quickly spilled into the political arena across the North and into the Middle West. Political insurgencies under the banners of Working Men's parties, Working Men's Republican parties, People's parties, and so on, shot up in 15 states and scores of cities and towns from New York to Carlisle, Pennsylvania and beyond. Some were factions of dissidents with no political affiliations, others were "outs" disaffected with the newly formed Democrats or National Republicans and unaffiliated with unions or working-class organizations of any sort. Weaker and ephemeral parties in the towns of the countryside campaigned on populist platforms. Working men's organizations in the major cities honed a sharper class edge.

The Working Men's parties in New York and Philadelphia were founded by labor radicals determined to find an alternative to market capitalism that would restore personal independence. The leaders were heavily influenced by the work of the classical economists and primitive socialists in England informed by the value of labor, the simple but powerful axiom that identified manual labor, not capital investment, as the mainstay of wealth. Workers created wealth by fashioning products from raw materials. In New York the key figures were the English immigrant Robert Dale Owen, who championed a radical system of boarding schools for all children, along with Thomas Skidmore, the one-time teacher cum machinist, who proposed an ambitious plan to confiscate all personal and private property for redistribution in equal parts to all male family heads. Their counterpart in Philadelphia was William Heighton, an English immigrant who arrived with his family around the War of 1812 and in the mid-1820s studied the work of John Gray, the English radical who had assailed competition and argued for cooperative production in his *Lecture on Human Happiness* (1825). In two addresses delivered in April and November 1827, Heighton gave formal expression to the labor theory of value and laid out a plan for an umbrella union, which became the Mechanics' Union of Trade Associations (MUTA), the nation's first organization of craft unions. He also encouraged what a modern historian of the Populist party in the 1890s called a "movement culture," that is, a complex of didactic and self-help organizations designed to nurture class consciousness, a task he thought to be well beyond the scope of trade unions. He thus organized the *Mechanics' Free Press*, the nation's first trade union paper, as well as a library that doubled as a reading room and debating club for discussion of such issues as the evils of banks and corporations as well as the desirability of cooperative production. He also encouraged several consumer cooperatives plus a barter store styled "labour for labour," which reckoned labor time as the medium of exchange. His counterparts in New York and Boston followed suit, organizing their own presses, libraries, and debating societies.

Heighton endorsed trade unionism for its capacity to raise wages and improve conditions. He argued however that workers needed stronger medicine if they were to raise their horizons and transform the economy. He envisioned the unions in his adoptive city not as instruments of struggle but as the base of an independent political organization that would give expression to the peculiar class interests of labor. Several months after the formation of the MUTA, he and his fellows in early 1828 persuaded the union to form an independent party. The Working Men's party, the first labor party in the land, became his consuming passion, so much so that the MUTA went into eclipse and soon passed from the scene. The new party itself adopted a platform that closely followed the reforms of its counterparts elsewhere, stressing the importance of free public education in place of humiliating pauper schools for children of the poor and working poor; endorsing tax reform; and railing against banks, corporations, and other institutions of emergent capitalism. After a rough inaugural in 1828, the Philadelphia Working Men polled nearly a third of the vote in 1829, the same proportion as their New York comrades, only to fall victim to factionalism and apathy. In addition, in New York and Philadelphia, if not in Boston, a wing of the Democratic party adopted the more moderate plans in the Working Men's platform and opened space for Working Men's politicians. Other labor parties cropped up in the early 1830s here and there, but the Working Men' insurgency was a spent force. The disappointing foray into the political arena poisoned the well of third partyism for labor activists, who well into the antebellum bent energies toward unionism. Very few of them however thought of unionism or indeed the larger project of self-organization as ends in themselves. They would routinely be drawn to labor reform—notably programs for access to land and cooperative production—that promised to reduce competition and restore personal independence.

Starting in the early 1830s with the New England Association of Farmers, Mechanics, and Other Working Men (1831) and New York and Baltimore (1833), the labor movement re-emerged in the form of revitalized trade unions, which came together in bodies called general trades' unions. With the notable exception of the New England Association, which included factory hands and mill workers, city central unions represented craftsmen and skilled workmen, overlooking the great numbers of unskilled workers on docks and at construction sites. This unionist phase of the labor movement had a more limited geographic orbit than the political phase, embracing about 15 cities, and initially focused on more immediate demands. The 10-hour day galvanized the New England Association as well as scores of unions in several larger cities. Boston workers struck unsuccessfully for 10 hours in 1832 and 1835 but helped arouse the movement in Philadelphia in June 1835 by distributing the so-called "Ten-Hour Circular," a manifesto for a shorter workday penned by Seth Luther and his associates. Its effect, said the Philadelphia handloom weaver John Ferral was electric, sparking the first general strike in the nation and one of the more successful work stoppages of the decade. Quaker City unionists and others also struggled to improve their wages and strengthen apprentice training in order to freeze out cheaper labor, but unionists in this period scarcely lost sight of the reform spirit. They continued to experiment with cooperative production and discuss schemes for land reform short of Sidmore's radical scheme. Indeed their National Trades' Union (NTU), a national body of delegates representing urban unions that met from 1834–1836, recommended cooperation again and again in several committee reports. An 1836 report on education concluded that by organizing into cooperatives, workers would be able to sell directly to consumers, eliminating speculative middle men and thereby realizing "a full reward for their labor." Another committee the same year issued a preliminary report that concluded if tradesmen invested their funds in cooperatives instead of unions, "a much more permanent benefit would be rendered" (Commons et al., *Documentary History*, 1957).

The labor movement was already in trouble when the NTU met for the last time in 1836. Employers had launched robust counteroffensives to defeat strikes and collapse unions, and city centrals slipped into division and acrimony over jurisdiction and access to strike funds. Already weakened, the labor movement suffered a deathblow from the panic of 1837 and devastating 7-year depression, which effectively wiped the field of unions.

The ensuing two decades saw both continuities and discontinuities with the past. The trickle of foreign immigration swelled into a torrent by the end of the 1840s, flooding the sweated trades with new arrivals from Ireland and Germany, disrupting old solidarities within trades, and frustrating efforts to rebuild labor organization. Some unionists and labor radicals in New York and those who had pioneered the movement a decade earlier continued the struggle. Many more dropped from view. The most troublesome continuity was the volatile economy, the boom-and-bust cycle that encouraged unions in good times and killed them in bad times.

Several general patterns of labor agitation gradually took shape. Urban workingmen tried to regroup, typically in spurts in 1843–1844, and at the turn of the 1840s, at first as single unions unaffiliated with larger bodies but then increasingly as components of city central-styled industrial congresses that mimicked the general trades' unions of a decade before. The unionist upsurge of the late 1840s showed a new militancy, nowhere more obvious than in New York where a general strike of American and German tailors, along with some Irish, brought in the police. Two strikers were shot dead, many more were injured, and at least 40 arrested, marking the first time urban workers ran afoul of official violence.

On the other hand, some veterans of the 1830s, along with such new figures as Albert Brisbane, developed utopian schemes premised on cooperative labor and retreated to the countryside. Brisbane's phalanxes or rural utopias had some appeal to wage earners, as if the advance of industrialism evoked renewed interest in alternatives to it. George Henry Evans, the former leader of the New York Working Men, who had retreated to the New Jersey countryside for a decade, reappeared in the mid-1840s in New York to champion a program he called National Reform, which envisioned dividing the national domain into communities with 360-acre homesteads, a watered down and appealing alternative to Skidmorean radicalism. Armed with his *Young America* and a small but enthusiastic band of followers who added cooperative production to his program, Evans worked tirelessly to enlist unionists in his crusade for land reform, showing up at labor conclaves throughout the Northeast.

Modern historians no longer argue, as their forebears once did, that labor reform reflected a class chasm that cast reformers as middle-class utopians meddling in the labor movement and leading hard-headed working people astray. Brisbane's phalanxes, recent evidence shows, were heavily populated by workers, not middle-class dreamers. Workers who rejected utopianism moreover proved receptive to both land reform and cooperation. Perhaps the best such example was the New England Workingmen's Association (NEWA), a regionwide organization that brought together unions and labor reform groups organized in cities and towns. The NEWA, inspired mainly by renewed 10-hour sentiment in the region, not only endorsed land reform and cooperation; it also came out against slavery from an abolitionist perspective.

The most intriguing affiliate of the NEWA was the Lowell Female Labor Reform Association (LFLRA). Organized by women led by Sarah G. Bagley and Huldah Stone in the nation's showcase industrial city, the LFLRA reflected the withering of Lowell's signature paternalism. Lenient foremen from the old regime were replaced with tougher managers who extracted more work for less pay and extended the workday into early evening. The women responded with petition drives in 1845 and 1846 aimed at convincing lawmakers to make 10 hours a legal day's work. Bagley and her friends however were as enthusiastic about labor reform as their male colleagues, supporting antislavery as well as temperance and other features of moral reform. When their 10-hour campaign faltered after 1846, the Lowell women embraced Protective Unionism, a movement of consumer cooperatives popular in their region after 1845. The "Spindle City" boasted no fewer than eight such stores by midcentury.

Labor's durable fascination with land reform could not help but have larger political ramifications in an era of growing concern in the North over the issue of slavery. In 1848, the Second Party System reeled from disaffection by abolitionists and antislavery activists who launched the Free Soil party, the most successful third-party insurgency of its time. The new party ran particularly well in New York and Massachusetts, polling no less than a third of the vote in the Bay State in the 1848 election. Free Soilism appealed to workers in part by campaigning against the expansion of slavery and by endorsing the 10-hour day, the issue of the hour for workers in the region. In Massachusetts, where Free Soilism had more staying power, Free Soilers formed a coalition with antislavery Democrats to put a 10-hour statute on the books. Though they failed by a few votes, they proved threatening enough to convince mill owners to cut the workday by an hour. Their colleagues in Pennsylvania and New Hampshire did push through such laws but defeated their purpose by attaching provisions allowing workers to contract for as many hours as they saw fit.

The question is whether Free Soilism also reflected working-class racism, or what some modern historians call "whiteness." There is no doubt that a good segment of the working class in the North was racist and that such workers saw Free Soilism as an instrument that would not only open a portal from the factory to farm; it would also keep Western lands lily white, a refuge from blacks. Not a few Free Soil politicians after all campaigned on a platform of excluding blacks from the territories. And they were not alone. Populist Democrats in eastern cities also raged against African-Americans, none more flamboyantly than

ANTEBELLUM ERA

Mike Walsh, the Irish immigrant who arrived in New York in 1839 brimming with political ambition. Sporting a diamond ring and silver-tipped cane, the Irish demagogue drew together a boisterous band of loyalists organized into a political club cum gang styled the Spartan Band as well as his own newspaper, the *Subterranean*, which played to the masses with a blend of cooperation, land reform, and white supremacy. Walsh was of a kind in a stylistic sense but had plenty of political sympathizers in other cities, notably Philadelphia, where Irish and probably some American workers staged bloody race riots through the 1840s under the approving eye of Democratic politicians. It is pointless to deny the racism of white workers.

It is misleading however to tar all workers with the racist brush or to assume that northern workers were preoccupied with their racial identity. In Massachusetts and elsewhere, good numbers of workers who supported Free Soilism and later Republicanism were abolitionists not unsympathetic to blacks. If not egalitarians, they were not fire-breathing racists and were tolerant of blacks as long as they stayed in their place. More to the point, such workers were less concerned with race than with religious and regional identities. They were Yankees and nativists first and foremost by this time, less concerned about blacks and race than about the "Slave Power" and about the Irish who were flooding into Boston and the major industrial centers. The Free Soil party was arguably more nativistic than racist in state politics, supporting anti-Catholic policies that included deporting the most impoverished of the Irish to their homeland.

The nativism that commingled with antislavery in Free Soilism received fuller expression in the American party, more popularly called Know-Nothings, which burst on the northern scene in the elections of 1854. The Know-Nothings swept the Massachusetts elections and rose to power in other industrial states in the East (they were somewhat weaker in the West) in alliance with blocs of political regulars. In the Bay State and presumably in neighboring states as well, a faction of Know Nothings supported laborist issues, including a mechanics' lien law, broader and better public schools, and legal limitations on the length of the workday. The new party was an effervescent force, giving way nearly everywhere with a year or so to the surging Republicans. Nonetheless, nativism lingered longest in Lowell and strongly influenced Republican organizations throughout the industrial Northeast, testifying to the durability of working-class xenophobia.

Nativism affected working-class organizations, as well. Petty bourgeois politicians and civic leaders tried to steer American workmen away from labor organizations by integrating then into nativistic lodges and fraternities. Anti-Catholics spawned in the initial nativist outburst in the 1840s grew and proliferated in the early 1850s. The Order of United American Mechanics offered social benefits together with rites and rituals that smacked of patriotism and religious parochialism. The closest it came to addressing the labor question boiled down to boycotting Irish businesses and blacklisting Irish workers.

Such measures did not suit more militant workmen in the major cities, who in 1853 and 1854 formed a spate of trade unions that launched a rash of strikes, chiefly in trades heavy with American and German workers. An early labor historian counted some 400 strikes in 1853–1854, a presumed high for the era, adding that union sentiment eventually reached an unprecedented numbers of trades, far more than in the 1830s when labor organization reached its peak. Some workers tried to emulate the spirit of the printers who formed the National Typographical Union. Efforts to form city centrals however generally failed, and most unions collapsed in the abrupt downturn in winter 1854. Some revived over the next few years only to fall apart in the economic slide of 1857. Despite this pattern of volatile organization with trades and the fitful outbursts of multi-union groups, the decade of the 1850s stands out for recrudescent union organization and robust class strife. It deserves more attention from students of labor.

Irish workers, who had born the brunt of nativist animus through the politically raucous 1850s, also began to stir. Though some of them may well have taken part in the labor unrest of the 1850s, they sometimes found themselves on the wrong side of labor militancy. That was surely the case in 1852 when mill hands in Amesbury and Salisbury, Massachusetts, went on strike for a 10-hour day, encouraged, interestingly enough, by Free Soil politicians working for a legislative solution. Angered by the intransigence of their employers, the Yankee workers vented frustrations on Irish immigrants brought in to break the strike. Such scabbing was the act of desperate people eager to curry favor with employers offering work at any price and willing to bear the censure of fellow workers who had no use for them in any circumstances. The tables were turned by the end of the decade however when the Irish learned the new rules of the industrial game. Irish women were in the forefront of an obscure but clearly important strike in Lowell in February 1859, a strike that appears to have been thwarted by Yankee strikebreakers. The episode nonetheless marked an important step for the Irish, and Irish women especially, who would feature prominently in labor leadership by the Gilded Age.

111

The shoemakers of Lynn also anticipated the future, if in a different way. Few workers exemplified more emphatically the confluence of trade unionism and labor radicalism. Their town was a center of early unionism, Free Soilism, and antislavery, with more than a hint of support for cooperative production. Free Soilers garnered nearly half the vote in 1848, far surpassing the statewide average of 30%. Several unions and labor organs had come and gone since the early 1830s when the town labor movement was born. By the early 1850s, Lynn workingmen and women were at it again, this time in response to being forced into factories with tighter and more demanding work regimes. They were thrown back on their heels by layoffs and wage cuts in the panic of 1857, which stifled organizing but produced widespread need and want. Protest meetings in winter 1857–1858 laid the groundwork in spring 1859 for the Lynn Mechanics' Association and a new organ, the *New England Mechanic*; a year later the association announced a strike to reverse the recent rate reductions.

The strike brought the busy shoe town to a halt. Some 20,000 workers came out in support, about half the employees in the region, and stayed out for 6 long weeks. Some owners, by no means all, conceded, but most did not, and the strike was counted as a failure. It was also a taste of what lay ahead in the Gilded Age. Like most strikes in single-industry towns, this one threw local organizations and businesses to the side of labor. Town fire companies and militia units marched in the parades and processions that clogged Lynn streets in the first weeks of the strike. Grocers and other suppliers of necessities offered credit and support for the beleaguered strikers. Large rallies—including a separate one organized by women—heard labor militants denounce the regime of the factory as slavery and vow never to be slaves, the metaphors of the age for degraded labor as well as the language of men and women who moved effortlessly from labor rallies to antislavery meetings.

Impressive though it was, the ardor was not enough. Jostling between police and workers as the strike began turned more ominous when the authorities arrested five men for trying to intercept shipments of leather destined for strikebreakers out of own. A day of so later, just as the strike began, a contingent of police arrived from Boston bolstered by a company of militia. The police and soldiers provoked scuffles and harsh words, if not injuries or fatalities, and withdrew after a few days. The show of force, coupled with the ability of the employers to wait out the workers, was quite enough.

Lynn's workers trekked back to work as the Republican party geared up for the nation's most momentous election. They would support the party of Lincoln and antislavery in overwhelming numbers. But neither their prosaic Republicanism nor the sectional strife could mask the fact that labor organization, however fragile and feeble, reflected the aspirations of workers for a more equitable share of the products of their labor. One of their number put it in verse: "You will live by your honest toil/ But never consent to be slaves." Thus did the working people in Lynn carry on the struggle inaugurated by the workers in Philadelphia 30 years earlier, a struggle that would be pursued with more vigor by the Knights of Labor when they returned from the battlefields of civil war.

BRUCE LAURIE

References and Further Reading

Blewett, Mary. *Men, Women, and Work: Class, Gender, and Protest in the New England Shoe Industry, 1780–1910.* Urbana: Univ. of Illinois Press.

Bridges, Amy. *A City in the Republic: Antebellum New York and the Origins of Machine Politics.* Ithaca, NY: Cornell Univ. Press, 1984.

Commons, John R, et al. *Documentary History of American Industrial Society. 1910–1911.* Vols. 4-8. New York: Russell & Russell, 1958.

——— *The History of Labour in the United States.* Vol. 1. New York: The Macmillan Company, 1918.

Dawley, Alan. *Class and Community: The Industrial Revolution in Lynn.* Cambridge, MA: Harvard Univ. Press, 1976.

Dublin, Thomas. *Women at Work: The Transformation of Work and Community in Lowell, Massachusetts, 1826–1860.* New York: Columbia Univ. Press, 1979.

Guarani, Carl J. *The Utopian Alternative: Fourierism in Nineteenth-Century America.* Ithaca, NY: Cornell Univ. Press, 1991.

Hirsch, Susan E. *The Roots of the American Working Class: The Industrialization of Crafts in Newark, 1800–1860.* Philadelphia: Univ. of Pennsylvania Press, 1978.

Kamphoefner, Walter D., Wolfgang Helbich, and Ulrike Sommer. *News from the Land of Freedom: German Immigrants Write Home,* Ithaca, NY: Cornell Univ. Press, 1991.

Laurie, Bruce. *Working People of Philadelphia, 1800–1850.* Philadelphia: Temple Univ. Press,

———. *Beyond Garrison: Antislavery and Social Reform.* New York: Cambridge Univ. Press, 2005.

Miller, Kerby A. *Emigrants and Exiles: Ireland and the Irish Exodus to North America* New York: Oxford Univ. Press, 1985.

Montgomery, David. *Citizen Worker: The Experience of Workers in the United States with Democracy and the Free Market during the Nineteenth Century.* New York: Cambridge Univ. Press, 1993.

Pessen, Edward. *Most Uncommon Jacksonians: The Radical Leaders of the Early Labor Movement.* Albany, NY: State University of New York Press, 1967.

Roediger, David. *The Wages of Whiteness: Race and the Making of the American Working Class.* New York: Verso, 1991.

Ross, Steven J. *Workers on the Edge: Work, Leisure, and Politics in Industrializing Cincinnati, 1788–1890.* New York: Columbia Univ. Press, 1985.

Steffen, Charles G. *The Mechanics of Baltimore: Workers and Politics in the Age of Revolution, 1763–1812.* Urbana: Univ. of Illinois Press, 1984.

Stansell, Christine. *City of Women: Sex and Class in New York, 1789–1860.* New York: Knopf, 1986.

Sutton, William R. *Journeymen for Jesus: Evangelical Artisans Confront Capitalism in Jacksonian Baltimore.* University Park: The Pennsylvania State Univ. Press, 1998.

Ware, Norman. *The Industrial Worker, 1840–1860: The Reaction of American Industrial Society to the Industrial Revolution. 1924.* New York: Quadrangle, 1964.

Wilentz, Sean. *Chants Democratic: New York City and the Rise of the Working Class.* New York: Oxford Univ. Press, 1984.

ANTHRACITE COAL STRIKE (1902)

From May 12 to October 23, 1902, 150,000 coal miners in the anthracite coal region of Eastern Pennsylvania struck for higher wages, better working conditions, and the right to negotiate such issues through the United Mine Workers of America (UMW). By the strike's end, they had gained national attention, intervention from the White House, and a role in jump starting the Progressive movement, as well as a 10% raise in wages and a shorter workday. They failed to gain formal recognition of their union. In his memoirs, labor leader Samuel Gompers named this strike the single most important incident in the history of the American labor movement: "from then on the miners were not merely human machines to produce coal," he wrote, "but men and citizens."

As the summer months of 1902 dragged on, the coal needed to heat urban households throughout the nation grew scarce and expensive. (Eastern cities required that residents use anthracite, available only from this small region, for heating purposes. Other types of coal, while far cheaper, were also far sootier.) Republican leaders, such as Senator Marcus Hanna

Strike Arbitration Commission appointed by President Roosevelt. Library of Congress, Prints & Photographs Division [LC-USZ62-95897].

of Ohio and President Theodore Roosevelt, became increasingly concerned that the crisis would be laid at their door. Roosevelt wrote friends and colleagues that he feared riots in the streets if there were no coal. Newspapers predicted a coal famine.

While the UMW offered to accept arbitration, the coal railroad executives who controlled this little corner of American industry refused to negotiate as a matter of right. Wrote George Baer, one of their leaders to Father John J. Curran of the anthracite region, let the strike "cripple industry, stagnate business or tie up the commerce of the world, and we will not surrender." The UMW, coal operators insisted, represented only competing coal regions and terrorism. This strike and unionism itself attacked their most sacred, constitutionally guaranteed property rights, as well as the right of individuals to work as individuals for any wages they desired. But more, it attacked their god-given American way of life. Baer's letter to Father Curran continued, "The rights and interests of the laboring man will be protected and cared for, not by the labor agitators, but by the Christian men to whom God in his infinite wisdom has given control of the property interests of the country."

Nevertheless in early October, the coal operators agreed to participate in the deliberations of a federal commission named by Roosevelt and to accept its recommendations. It had been a long road to the table. In June Roosevelt's Commissioner of Labor Carroll D. Wright investigated the situation and issued a report. Building on Wright's efforts, the Chicago-based National Civic Federation (NCF) of business and labor leaders pressed operators to negotiate. In August the NCF suggested that a presidential commission be named, with the miners to go back to work during deliberations. The UMW President John Mitchell refused to send the men back without a guarantee that the coal operators would accept the commission's final award. Pressing the coal operators through the offices of banker J. P. Morgan, Theodore Roosevelt invited both sides to the White House to discuss the matter in early October. Mitchell again offered to accept arbitration from a presidential tribunal if the coal operators would agree to it. The coal operators refused the notion, denounced the coal miners as criminals, and demanded that the president order in federal troops. After the meeting Mitchell again refused to ask the coal miners to return to work, pending a presidential investigation, pointing out that the coal operators had shown no willingness to accept any such arrangements. On October 6, the Pennsylvania Militia deployed nearly 9,000 men to the region to protect any coal miners who wished to go to work. Nevertheless two days later, mass meetings of coal miners throughout the region renewed their commitment to the strike.

After heavy pressure from Roosevelt and J. P. Morgan, the operators agreed to accept the decision of a presidential commission. The miners went back to work on October 23. The operators had one main condition: The commission was not to acknowledge the union. Their second condition focused on the composition of the commission. It was to include an officer from the engineering corps of the military, a mining engineer, a federal judge from eastern Pennsylvania, a man who had been active in mining and selling anthracite coal, and "a man of prominence, eminent as a sociologist." Roosevelt also added a Catholic priest. When Mitchell asked that a union man be added as such, the coal operators refused. Roosevelt reported that their reaction verged on the hysterical. But when the president offered instead to appoint a labor leader as the eminent sociologist, the operators accepted him with relief. Roosevelt mocked them for accepting a labor leader as long as he was called something else. Yet for the railroad men, negotiations had always turned on such nice ideological considerations. The commission saw hundreds of witnesses and investigated every aspect of life in the coalfields. Lead attorney for the UMW was Clarence Darrow, assisted from Boston by future Supreme Court justice Louis D. Brandeis, and in person by activist author Henry Demarest Lloyd. In addition to John Mitchell, the commission's star witnesses were breaker boys, men, and women from the mines who spoke of the realities of living in the coal regions. The commission eventually granted the coal miners a 10% raise and a shorter workday.

The anthracite strike of 1902 marked the first time that the United States government put its full weight behind labor negotiations. It is in part this intervention that gives the 1902 anthracite strike its importance in U.S. history. It served as an early victory for Progressives and a triumph for Roosevelt's vision of an active presidency. The miners won a small but significant improvement in wages and conditions. They failed to gain recognition of their right to be represented collectively through their union. Nevertheless their victory came in an era still dominated by *laissez faire* economic assumptions that left no room whatsoever for governmental intervention on behalf of labor. If the anthracite strike helped to define such a role for the national government, it also suggested the limitations of this approach. Nevertheless a six-man arbitration commission split between union and management representatives continued to meet over the next several years, granting additional raises and changes in work conditions from time to time. The union gained de facto union recognition and a steady membership in the anthracite region only after 1912, when the arbitration commission established formal pit committees in each mine to negotiate local conditions.

ANDREW B. ARNOLD

References and Further Reading

Blatz, Perry K. *Democratic Miners: Work and Labor Relations in the Anthracite Coal Industry, 1875–1925.* Albany, NY: State University of New York Press, 1994.

Cornell, Robert J. *The Anthracite Coal Strike of 1902.* Washington, DC: The Catholic University of America Press, 1957.

Gowaskie, Joseph M. "John Mitchell and the Anthracite Mine Workers: Leadership, Conservatism, and Rank-and-File Militancy." *Labor History* 27, 1 (Winter 1985–1986): 54–84.

Phelan, Craig. *Divided Loyalties: The Public and Private Life of Labor Leader John Mitchell.* Albany: State University of New York Press, 1994.

Wiebe, Robert H. "The Anthracite Strike of 1902: A Record of Confusion." Mississippi *Valley Historical Review* 48, 2 (September, 1961): 229–251.

ANTICOMMUNISM

Anticommunism is the opposition to radical leftist political ideologies that emphasize equal wealth, worker control of industry, and atheism. While American anticommunism is often associated with the Cold War, it in fact has a much longer history. Anticommunism, or more correctly, antiradicalism developed in the United States during the late nineteenth century as the nation industrialized. While manufacturing boomed during this period, immigrants flooded into American cities to fill industry's need for cheap labor. This unprecedented immigration and urbanization led many Americans to worry that alien radicals threatened the nation. Recurring economic depressions and often-violent strikes confirmed this fear for many native-born citizens. Some workers, in response to low wages, long hours, and poor working conditions, did embrace radical doctrines, such as anarchism, socialism, and communism. Opponents of radicalism argued that these ideologies violated American ideals of private property rights.

As Americans struggled to maintain control over burgeoning industries and cities, many feared that radicals would spread their dangerous ideas to other workers and spark a radical uprising similar to those that were occurring in Europe. When Parisian workers established their own government in March 1871, some American newspapers speculated that the United States might not be resistant to such a revolution. European immigrants were instrumental in bringing radical beliefs to the United States, although not all radicals were immigrants. Many refugees fled from the failed European uprisings of the midnineteenth century and came to the United States to work. As a result native-born Americans often viewed communism, socialism, and anarchism as alien ideologies. This equation held particularly true during the 1886 Haymarket affair, the first major red scare in the United States. Haymarket occurred in Chicago, a booming industrial metropolis where labor activists found a sympathetic audience for their ideas. On May 1, 1886, Chicago was roiled by a general strike in support of an 8-hour workday. Three days later, Chicago police shot picketing workers who were fighting with strike breakers. In response anarchists organized a protest meeting for the following night at Haymarket Square. Although the demonstration was small and nonviolent, Chicago police broke up the crowd. In response someone threw a bomb at the charging policemen, who then began firing on the crowd. By the end of the evening, one policeman was dead, six were injured, and dozens of protesters were wounded. Panicked city business and political leaders immediately demanded justice. Although no one knew who actually threw the bomb, the city's anarchist leaders were targeted for creating an environment conducive to violence. Chicago's anarchists had a reputation for belligerence, largely because they often lauded dynamite as a great social leveler in their writings. Eight local anarchists, six of whom were German immigrants, were tried for murder. The subsequent trial was a travesty of justice. Some of the accused had not even been at Haymarket the night of the bombing. Nevertheless all eight defendants were found guilty, and four were subsequently hanged.

The crushing of Chicago's anarchists not only weakened the city's radical movement but also undermined moderate labor's demands for the 8-hour day. The city's business leaders and newspapers equated the labor movement with anarchism. Chicago's elites ensured that the local government and court system were fully mobilized against the city's labor activists. Not surprisingly when the American Federation of Labor (AFL) was formed later in 1886, its leaders emphasized "pure and simple" unionism and rejected radical doctrines in an attempt to distance themselves from Haymarket and anarchism.

At the start of the twentieth century, antiradicalism shifted from cities to rural areas, especially western lumber and mining regions. In response to the poor working conditions in these industries, the Industrial Workers of the World (IWW) developed. The Wobblies, as the IWW was popularly called, sought worker control, rejected capitalism, and organized workers by industry rather than craft until workers were joined in "one big union." However the aspect of the IWW ideology that most scared management was their embrace of general strikes and often-violent industrial sabotage. In response managers often used vigilante action against the Wobblies. The most famous of these occurred in the copper-mining town of Bisbee, Arizona, in July 1917. Local businessmen and mine officials seized over one thousand Wobblies, forced them into boxcars, shipped them to the desert, and abandoned them.

World War I and the Great Red Scare

Antiradicalism increased once the United States entered World War I, largely because socialists and anarchists opposed the war. Eugene Debs, leader of the Socialist party, argued that the conflict was between capitalist nations who employed workers to do the actual fighting. Since the war did not serve workers' interests, Debs urged the working class to sit out the fight. The IWW argued a similar position and thus refused to stop striking throughout the conflict. This opposition to the war convinced many antiradicals that the left was not only a danger to private property and American businesses but also to the nation. The Russian Revolution of November 1917 further confirmed this view. When Lenin and the Bolsheviks seized control of Russia in the midst of World War I, they declared that the war was a conspiracy by the international ruling class against the workers of the world. The Bolsheviks called for an end to the fighting and urged soldiers on both sides to revolt. As a result, the Bolsheviks negotiated a separate peace treaty with the Germans and pulled Russian troops off the front. Pro-war Americans felt betrayed and worried that the Bolsheviks had handed the Germans a potentially crucial victory. They responded angrily when American radicals, like Eugene Debs, Big Bill Haywood of the IWW, and anarchist Emma Goldman, celebrated the Bolsheviks' victory. Radicals thus solidified their reputation for disloyalty to American interests and became firmly associated with the Soviet Union in the minds of many Americans.

World War I marked the first time that the federal government used its powers against radicals. In response to antiwar opposition, Congress passed laws to silence opponents. The Espionage Act made obstructing military enlistment or interfering with either military operations or industrial production illegal. Debs was arrested and imprisoned under this legislation after he gave a speech in which he encouraged soldiers to refuse to join the military. The IWW

leaders, such as Big Bill Haywood, were punished, since their wartime strikes interfered with industrial production. In 1918, Congress passed the Sedition Act, which made it a crime to speak language disloyal to the American government or Constitution. Ultimately over 1,500 people were arrested for violating these two laws. The federal government also targeted Wobblies by passing the Literacy Test Act of 1917, which allowed the government to deport any aliens who advocated anarchism, the unlawful destruction of property, or the violent overthrow of the government. Since much of this legislation was designed to expire at the end of the war, Congress also passed laws that targeted radicals after the war. The Immigration Act of 1918 allowed the United States to deport any alien who supported the violent overthrow of the government. The federal government used this law extensively against pro-Communist immigrants.

Once the war ended, the United States experienced a strike wave that led to what became known as the Great Red Scare. This anti-Communist campaign grew out of World War I and the Bolshevik revolution. In 1918, Soviet Communists sought to extend their revolution by urging workers throughout the world to revolt. This call appeared successful—Bolshevik uprisings occurred in Germany, Hungary, Austria, and Bulgaria. In the United States, a series of strikes broke out once the wartime prohibition against labor stoppages ended. Although most of these developed in reaction to postwar pay cuts and rising inflation, the strikers appeared to many Americans to be responding to the clarion call of Bolshevik revolution. Management in response to some of these work stoppages used anticommunism to break the strikes. In the steel industry, for instance, corporate executives successfully split striking workers along nativist lines by portraying nonnative strikers as Communists and urging skilled American workers to cross the picket lines. In the midst of this labor unrest, the leftwing of the Socialist party broke away and two competing American Communist parties were formed—one constituted of foreign language groups and one of English speakers—that advocated the violent overthrow of the American government in their party platforms. When a series of mail bombs were sent to the attorney general, the mayor of Seattle, and prominent businessmen, like John D. Rockefeller and J. P. Morgan, it appeared to many Americans that the revolution had begun.

In response the federal government began a major crackdown. Attorney General J. Mitchell Palmer, only recently spared from the bomb sent to his home, created the General Intelligence Division of the Bureau of Investigation and placed young J. Edgar Hoover in charge. The division investigated radical organizations, raided their headquarters, arrested their leaders, and then deported any aliens. These so-called Palmer raids led to over six thousand arrests and hundreds of deportations. The division, which later became the Federal Bureau of Investigation (FBI), played a central role in the campaign against Communists for the next 50 years.

The Great Red Scare of 1918–1919 ended rather quickly as some Americans criticized the gross violations of civil liberties that occurred in the Justice Department's round-ups. Nevertheless the scare had tremendous implications for both American Communists and organized labor. The raids weakened the American Communist party and confirmed it as an alien organization in many Americans' minds. Organized labor also found its power attenuated, even though mainstream labor leaders like the AFL's Samuel Gompers argued that the federation, not the radicals, authentically represented the interests of American workers. Nevertheless management easily linked labor and communism during the great strike wave, and the failure of key strikes in the postwar period proved devastating for the AFL. While the federal government backed away from the worst abuses of the Palmer era, it continued to fight against radicalism by restricting immigration. The Immigration Acts of both 1921 and 1924 limited the number of immigrants from southern and eastern Europe, two areas that were perceived as radical hotbeds. By the mid-1920s, the federal government, in conjunction with the nation's major industrialists, appeared to have finally defeated communism and ended any threat subversives posed to the nation's economic order.

The New Deal and World War II

The Great Depression of the 1930s resurrected labor's vitality and led ultimately to a resurgence in both communism and anticommunism. Unemployment rates for male industrial workers as high as 50% led some Americans to turn to communism to explain capitalism's collapse and to ameliorate the terrible poverty they saw. The Soviets helped the Communist Party of the United States (CPUSA) and Communist parties around the world when it changed the party line in 1935. Communists were to stop working for revolution and were instead supposed to join with liberal democrats in a popular front against fascism, which was on the rise in Europe. American Communists as a result emphasized such issues as helping the unemployed, organizing workers, ending legalized segregation, supporting the New Deal, and fighting

against fascism at home and abroad. Party members thus worked closely with labor organizers in the newly formed Congress of Industrial Organizations (CIO) and with liberal Democrats who worked for the New Deal. Because of this alliance, AFL leaders bitterly attacked the CIO for being Communist-led and argued that Communists would betray American workers if labor's interest conflicted with that of the Soviet Union. In response to this Communist resurgence, the Catholic church became more vocal in its opposition. The Vatican had long criticized communism for denying the spiritual nature of man. However the Spanish Civil War of the late 1930s convinced the Vatican that increased Communist power would lead to the church's destruction. In the United States, Catholic anticommunism appeared among both leftist Catholics, as labor priests and the Association of Catholic Trade Unionists (ACTU) appealed to workers to organize and rid their unions of Communist influence, and among more conservative Catholics, who rallied behind Father Charles Coughlin.

The Popular Front came to a sudden halt in September 1939 when the Soviet Union and Nazi Germany signed a peace pact. This shocking agreement alienated American liberals and marginalized the CPUSA. Party members, who had been prominent opponents of fascism, now found themselves defending Stalin's alliance with the Nazis and criticizing American war efforts as imperialistic. Anticommunism in the United States reached a new peak, as non-Communists on the left joined with traditional anti-Communists and lashed out angrily against the party for privileging Soviet needs over those of Americans.

This brief red scare ended when the Nazis invaded the Soviet Union in June 1941. Communist parties around the world revived the Popular Front for the duration of the war. Communists now threw their whole-hearted support behind Roosevelt's efforts to help the British defeat the Nazis and after Pearl Harbor, behind the American war effort. As a result of the American alliance with the Soviet Union, domestic anticommunism waned during the war.

The Cold War

American anticommunism reached perhaps its greatest strength during the Cold War. A number of factors led to this increase. On the one hand, big business was emboldened by its success during World War II and sought to roll back the gains made by both labor and the New Deal state. In addition Soviet actions in

Eastern Europe at the end of the war infuriated Catholics, who complained bitterly that the Red Army was destroying churches and arresting prominent Catholics in Poland, Hungary, and Czechoslovakia. Most importantly tensions between the United States and the Soviet Union increased as these new superpowers recognized that their strategic interests now conflicted. As a result, containing the spread of communism abroad became a major American foreign policy concern for the first time. Thus at home Communists were viewed as *saboteurs* working in the interests of a foreign enemy. This view of Communists as saboteurs was a real if exaggerated, fear. During World War II, the Soviets, in response to the secret Manhattan project, developed an espionage program to gain information about this atomic research. The American government knew about the Soviet spy network because it had broken the Soviet code. During the late 1940s and early 1950s, the United States prosecuted atomic spies like Julius Rosenberg, although it did not make public the classified information that incriminated these secret agents. Republicans, who had been out of power for most of the previous two decades, exploited public fears of espionage and argued that the Roosevelt and Truman administrations were filled with Communists. This charge had tremendous resonance after both the Communist victory in the Chinese Revolution and the successful Soviet atomic bomb test in 1949. Senator Joseph McCarthy in particular greatly exaggerated the existence of internal subversion and used this charge to return a Republican to the White House in 1952.

American Communists were also attacked by their former popular-front allies, who again accused the CPUSA of privileging Soviet needs over those of American workers. Labor liberals turned against them and expelled Communist-led unions from the CIO in 1949 and 1950. Civil rights organizations like the NAACP purged Communists, including founding member W. E. B. DuBois, from their ranks. The Truman administration systematically investigated all federal employees and fired hundreds who had ties to Communist or popular-front groups, even though there was no evidence of subversion. Harassed from all sides, the CPUSA virtually disappeared.

While domestic anticommunism dissipated after the 1950s with the near destruction of the CPUSA, anticommunism continued to guide American labor leaders' policies overseas until the fall of the Berlin Wall in 1989. The AFL-CIO aided the CIA's attempts to thwart Communist labor movements in Europe and Latin America during the 1950s, and the federation supported the Vietnam War. In addition Lane Kirkland, the head of the AFL-CIO, actively backed the anti-Communist Solidarity movement in Poland during the 1980s.

COLLEEN DOODY

References and Further Reading

Heale, M. J. *American Anticommunism: Combating the Enemy Within, 1830–1970*. Baltimore, MD: Johns Hopkins Press, 1990.

Levenstein, Harvey. *Communism, Anticommunism, and the CIO*. Westport, CT: Greenwood Press, 1981.

Powers, Richard Gid. *Not without Honor: The History of American Anticommunism*. New York: The Free Press, 1995.

Zieger, Robert H. *The CIO: 1933–1955*. Chapel Hill: University of North Carolina Press, 1995.

ANTI-RENT WARS (NEW YORK)

The anti-rent wars took place on the great estates (or manors) of eastern New York from 1839 to approximately 1850 and were the most dramatic of a series of tenant insurgencies in the state from 1750–1880. The anti-rent movement began in 1839, when Steven Van Rensselaer III passed away, leaving his heirs to collect thousands of dollars of back rents that he had allowed to accumulate on Rensselaerwyck—a massive estate encompassing much of Albany and Rensselaer counties. His heirs demanded immediate repayment of all arrears and threatened to evict delinquents. Tenants in Albany County immediately organized a committee to request leniency. Many owed years of back rent and had no hope of repaying the landlord, especially those living on hill farms.

The new landlords refused to negotiate, prompting farmers to issue a "Declaration of Independence" that stated that tenant labor, in the form of improvements, had given the manor lands value; therefore tenants had earned title to the land. In addition they charged that manor leases were feudal. Manor leases transferred title in fee to tenants in perpetuity, yet any failure to pay rent, or the violation of attendant clauses, empowered the landlord to evict the tenant. As well, the landlord retained all mineral, water, and timber rights. Also deemed degrading were clauses requiring labor service to the landlord. Last, the landlord levied a fee, or "quarter sale," on every transfer of the lease (usually one-quarter of the sale price). Such terms, tenants charged, placed them in a dependent relationship on the landlord that was out of step with republican values. Tenants resolved to pay no more rents until the landlords agreed to sell the land to them at a fair price.

Rioting broke out when Albany County lawmen attempted to evict delinquents, serve process, or conduct sheriff's sales to liquidate tenant debts. They were greeted by "calico Indians"—disguised, armed insurgents—who prevented the enforcement of the law and tarred and feathered their more persistent adversaries. Anti-rent associations soon formed throughout the region. Associations performed a number of functions: They negotiated with landlords; petitioned the legislature; mounted title suits; corresponded with other committees; taxed members to fund activities; conducted rent strikes and boycotts; and secretly organized calico Indian tribes to intimidate enemies and battle state and local authorities. Extralegal activity—riots, anonymous threats, arson, tarring and feathering—also erupted, creating deep community rifts between "down" and "up-renters." By 1844, the insurgency spread to Rensselaer, Schoharie, Columbia, Greene, Ulster, Delaware, Dutchess, Montgomery, Sullivan, and Otsego counties—virtually the entire Catskill-Hudson region. Many estates in these areas were let on life leases. When the lives named in the contract (usually three) expired or a farmer was evicted for not paying rent, the landlord re-entered the property. The value of improvements made to the plot was thus lost. Anti-rent demands for title based on a labor theory of value appealed to these tenants.

The primary focus of anti-rent associations was to pressure the state legislature to promote land reform. They first attempted to find a legal means to challenge landlords' titles, which tenant rioters as early as the 1750s had charged were faulty or fraudulent. However both political parties—Democrats and Whigs—had factions favorable to the landlords, and tenant petitions requesting legislative action repeatedly failed. The movement radicalized quickly in the face of this inaction. In 1843, Dr. Smith A. Boughton of Rensselaer County (the calico Indian orator Big Thunder) rose to leadership and helped bring anti-rent into alliance with national reformers, radical free-soil advocates, and labor reformers. Thomas A. Devyr, Alvan Bovay, and George Henry Evans stumped eastern New York calling for a rural-urban workingmen's alliance to end the manor system as the first in a series of democratic reforms to benefit labor. The two groups united to form the Anti-Rent Equal Rights party in 1844, a nonpartisan political organization that would throw its votes behind candidates from either party who supported an anti-rent agenda. The party proved very successful at electing sympathetic candidates to the state legislature in 1844, and anti-rent appeared destined to achieve its goals.

However the new Democratic governor, Silas Wright, did not support anti-rent and especially deplored the disorderly activities of the calico Indians. Wright took office at the height of Indian violence in January 1845 and demanded and received a law making it a felony to appear in disguise. Law-and-order posses stepped up efforts to root out Indian cells, and anti-rent strongholds descended into civil war as posses and Indians engaged in pitched battles; Indians tarred and feathered deputies; and shootings, arson, and other lawless acts increased.

New Yorkers responded with mixed feelings. Most believed the manor leases oppressive, yet they deplored Indian vigilantism. Many therefore supported calls for a plebiscite on the ballot in 1845 to hold a constitutional convention in 1846 that promised to address land and other reforms. That effort nearly was shattered by the murder of Delaware County Deputy Osman Steele in August by Indians gathered to prevent a sale at the farm of Moses Earle in Andes. Governor Wright and Delaware County officials declared a state of insurrection in the county and sent the militia to help the sheriff crush the rebellion. Law-and-order tactics proved so brutal and the trial of the insurgents so staged however that voters statewide rallied to the anti-rent cause, overwhelmingly approving the measure for a constitutional convention.

The 1846 constitution effectively ended the anti-rent movement. Tenants won a number of important concessions. The document outlawed perpetual leases, though old leases remained in force. As well, democratic reforms promised to undercut the power of the well to do. More county and state offices were made elective, especially in the judiciary. Tenants believed that they had substantially eroded landlord power even though systematic land reform eluded them. Thereafter the movement rapidly dissolved.

With land reform only partially achieved, the most enduring legacy of the movement was in politics, where anti-rent splintered the Democratic and Whig parties. Many tenants gravitated toward Free Soil in 1848; others subsequently joined nativist, temperance, or abolitionist parties. By and large antirent counties moved toward the newly formed Republican party and its free-soil message in 1856. In the end anti-renters succeeded in partly dismantling the manor system and helped transform the political system of the state.

THOMAS SUMMERHILL

References and Further Reading

Bruegel, Martin. *Farm, Shop, Landing: The Rise of Market Society in the Hudson Valley 1790–1860*. Durham, NC: Duke University Press, 2002.

Christman, Henry. *Tin Horns and Calico: An Episode in the Emergence of American Democracy*. New York: Henry Holt & Co., 1945.

Ellis, David M. *Landlords and Farmers in the Hudson-Mohawk Region, 1790–1850*. Ithaca, NY: Cornell University Press, 1946.

Huston, Reeve. *Land and Freedom: Rural Society, Popular Protest, and Party Politics in Antebellum New York.* New York: Oxford University Press, 2000.

McCurdy, Charles W. *The Anti-Rent Era in New York Law and Politics, 1839–1865.* Chapel Hill: University of North Carolina Press, 2001.

Summerhill, Thomas. *Harvest of Dissent: Agrarianism in Nineteenth-Century New York.* Urbana: University of Illinois Press, 2005.

APPRENTICESHIP

The origins of American apprenticeship can be found in medieval England, notably the Statute of Artificers (1563), under which parents, unless they possessed the means to educate their sons privately, had to apprentice them in either a craft or in farm labor. Within a craft, the terms were longer, until either age 21 or 24. Children without means were bound to the local parish. Entry into the crafts (and thus apprenticeship) in England was controlled by guilds to ensure that there was not an oversupply in their crafts, thus lowering the prices of their goods.

In the United States guilds never took hold, and there was no control on the number of apprentices given indentures in any single trade. This meant that while masters might employ a larger number of apprentices, thus avoiding the need of hiring journeymen (wage laborers), the apprentices would eventually become journeymen and often masters, particularly in trades involving little capital, such as tailoring and shoemaking. This oversupply would inevitably lower the living standards of artisans in these trades. To enter such a low-paying, low-prestige, and numerous trade, no premium was required. To enter a more lucrative trade, such as goldsmithing, silversmithing, and watch making, the father of the apprentice often had to pay a fee.

Apprenticeships were drawn up between the parents and the master craftsman. These were legal documents, enforceable in court. In return for room, board, clothing, and a minimal education, the apprentice was placed under the master *in loco parentis.* "The apprentice was to faithfully serve [his master], his secrets keep, his lawful commands readily obey." The apprentice was subject to the master's discipline, including corporal punishment, but was to be taught the "trade or mystery" of the craft and to receive a basic education as well as clothing on his completion of indenture. If he ran away, the master could legally advertise for his capture and return, and many colonial and early national newspapers contained ads with descriptions of the runaway and rewards for his safe return.

Young men training in blacksmithing at Hampton Institute, Hampton, Virginia. Library of Congress, Prints & Photographs Division [LC-USZ62-119867].

Within a craft there were traditional duties performed by the apprentice. In the printing business, made famous by the Boston apprenticeship of Benjamin Franklin to his demanding brother James, an apprentice was in charge of inking the press, feeding and removing the sheets of paper in the press, cleaning the type, preparing the balls of ink, and overseeing the ink vat after the master had prepared it. Occasionally as his indenture matured, the apprentice might be allowed to set type or operate the press, provided he was physically able to do so.

The advent of American independence brought significant changes to the status of apprenticeship. The American economy grew at a rapid pace in the 1790s and into the early nineteenth century, but it was also subject to serious downturns during the Embargo, 1807–1808, and the War of 1812. Masters saw new economic horizons after the Revolution, but the new economy also demanded higher capital investments to begin a business, especially in printing and other elite crafts. Too, the pressures on the crafts for mass production (orders of chairs or shoes numbering in the thousands for shipment to the West Indies) often called more for speed than skill. In jobs often simplified by a marked division of labor, the master often needed less a highly trained apprentice than a moderately skilled journeyman who might work for lower wages than a highly skilled craftsman who required years of training. Many apprentices were lured away at an early age by the prospect of earning cash wages and of being liberated from the control of a paternalistic master. Moreover the publication of trade secrets in the form of new guidebooks to the crafts also eroded the power of the masters, since apprentices could learn the mystery for themselves with the use of these publications.

There were also noneconomic reasons for the decline of apprenticeships. The evangelical Christianity of the 1790s that emphasized family love rather than hierarchy often created resentment among apprentices against the master's authority. Most significantly the Jeffersonian movement, emphasizing egalitarianism and the concept of personal liberty and opposed to traditional modes of deference, led many apprentices to resent the authority of their masters and to leave their indentures early. Masters complained constantly of saucy apprentices who talked back to them, who left work without permission, who frequented grog shops or horse races, and who refused to learn the required skills. However courts after 1790 began siding with apprentices, finding the masters guilty of assault, for example, for corporal punishment. At times municipalities showed concern over delinquent apprentices in the streets, but the trend was clearly to undermine the master's authority, so much so that often no indentures were even signed after 1800; in its place informal agreements were arranged between a youth and a master.

By the 1830s, a number of large local firms emerged, most notably the textile mills of New England and government armories that demanded a large number of highly trained machinists who learned these skills from traveling from machine shop to machine shop throughout the country. However they also needed a continuous supply of relatively unskilled labor and paid an immediate cash wage to those who applied (when business was brisk). Apprenticeship was not an option at these operations. There was no place and no need to train workers over a long period of years. The cash wage was replacing apprenticeship in more and more situations. Even in the small craft enterprises, it would not be unlikely to see the apprentice receive a wage and be living outside the home of the owner of the shop. This made the apprentices even more independent, aware of their hours and conditions. After the Panic of 1837 and into the 1840s, economic conditions were difficult and advancement slow. This only exacerbated the plight of apprenticeship.

Mechanization before the Civil War spelled the death knell for traditional apprenticeship. To take printing as an example, the development of the steam press revolutionized the industry in the 1830s. It allowed the production of large, inexpensive newspapers, leading to a much wider reading public and the penny press, as well as greater production of inexpensive books and magazines. However traditional presswork disappeared, replaced by pressmen and roller boys seeking work as typesetters. The master printers hired many more apprentices to do simplified and narrow jobs than they did skilled journeymen. The same thing happened in other crafts, particularly those dealing with expensive machinery. Masters became more and more distant from their employees, and the working classes needed less and less technical knowledge. Given this depersonalization, the personal relationship between master and apprentice, already severely strained, disappeared. By the 1850s, in many crafts apprentices were low-paid industrial workers.

There were efforts at reform. Many of the traditional masters formed institutes in an attempt to maintain the original system. These often had extensive libraries and lecture programs that lasted beyond the Civil War, especially in the trades that were less likely to be affected by industrialization and high capital costs. The New York Mechanics Society is an excellent example. It had long had a school for its members' children and others who paid tuition, but with the advent of the public school movement, it closed down in 1858 in favor of an evening school for apprentices. The school, which is still in operation, only enrolled a few hundred apprentices in traditional crafts. The society also opened a library for apprentices, with the majority of its books on science and geography. By the 1840s, there were over 9,000 books and 2,000 readers, but this still represented a small number of apprentices. In reality the various mechanic societies were able to assist masters in traditional trades but were unable to halt the decline of the apprenticeship.

The decline of apprenticeship can be in part seen as a cause of the rise of gangs and urban crime and violence in the antebellum period as well as of nativist parties, which owed their strength to adolescents who were unable to find an easy entry into the marketplace and who deeply resented the large numbers of immigrants challenging them for the semiskilled jobs that were replacing the highly skilled crafts of the late eighteenth and early nineteenth centuries. While the apprenticeship has never completely disappeared, and a number of crafts still maintain limited entry systems within a unionized framework, and while mechanics societies still offer courses, for most adolescents the entry to the workplace is through a vocational school or community college into a wage earning position. The paternalism of the traditional apprenticeship system, one that lasted over four hundred years, was a victim of modern capitalism.

HOWARD ROCK

References and Further Reading

Rorabaugh, W. J. *The Craft Apprentice: From Franklin to the Machine Age in America*. New York: Oxford University Press, 1986.
Wilentz, Sean. *Chants Democratic: New York City and the Rise of the American Working Class, 1788–1850*. New York: Oxford University Press, 1984.

See also **Antebellum Era; Artisans; Civil War and Reconstruction; Revolution and Early National Period**

ARBITRATION

Arbitration of industrial relations disputes in the United States gained wide acceptance and legitimacy only in the last half of the twentieth century. Labor-management arbitration, a quasi-judicial process, is of two types, interest, and rights. Interest arbitration defines a compulsory obligation of the parties to submit to an umpire when they reach an impasse in contract negotiations. It is more common in the public sector, where employees do not have the right to strike. In the private sector, interest arbitration remains relatively rare. Rights, or grievance arbitration, on the other hand, exists in an estimated 98% of collective-bargaining agreements in both the public and private sector. Here disputes over interpretation or application of the parties existing collective-bargaining agreement is voluntarily resolved when an arbitrator, chosen by the parties, makes a final and binding enforcement decision based on the merit of evidence and arguments submitted by both parties during a formal hearing.

Interest arbitration has a longer history in the United States, first recorded in the 1829 Constitution of the Journeyman Cabinetmakers of Philadelphia. The Knights of Labor in 1869 recommended interest and rights arbitration to prevent strikes, an economic and political weapon they opposed. During the 1870s and 1880s, a period of extraordinary labor strife, the Knights chief rival, the American Federation of Labor (AFL), opposed compulsory arbitration. The United Mine Workers (UMW) in 1890 included an arbitration provision in their constitution. The U.S. government in the nineteenth and early twentieth centuries tentatively encouraged voluntary interest-arbitration clauses in the railroad industry, first with the passage of the Interstate Commerce Act in 1887. After 1910, the piece-rate clothing shops in New York City endorsed a proposal by future Supreme Court Justice Louis Brandeis of permanent arbitration to prevent strikes. In 1913, the Department of Labor established the U.S. Conciliation Service primarily to mediate labor disputes, but the service also had the authority to recommend arbitration. Little evidence exists however of employer willingness to accede to arbitration during this era. Further expansion of arbitration would require intervention by the federal government.

The Federal Transportation Act of 1920 defined for the first time in the railroad industry a distinction between interest and rights disputes, recognizing separate resolution procedures. Six years later, the Railway Labor Act (and as amended in 1934) went one step further when it created the National Railroad Adjustment Board (NRAB). Grievances between employees and a carrier over application and interpretation of agreements when handled in the "usual manner up to and including the chief operating officer," yet not resolved, became the jurisdiction of the NRAB. If the parties were unable to resolve, or refused to participate in a NRAB conference, a separate agency, the National Mediation Board (NMB) intervened, first to help mediate or failing that to encourage the parties to submit their dispute to arbitration. Outside of the railroad industry, The U.S. Arbitration Act (1925) created a legal basis for employment arbitration by individuals, stating that arbitration agreements "shall be valid, irrevocable and enforceable." Following this emerging trend the American Arbitration Association formed the next year and within two decades became the chief nonpublic organization providing arbitrators to settle labor-management disputes. Significant expansion of arbitration however came with the advance of collective-bargaining rights with the passage of the National Labor Relations Act of 1935 (NLRA) and the National Labor Relations Board (NLRB), which interpreted and enforced the act.

A labor union, once certified by the NLRB, became under the act the sole representative of all employees within a bargaining unit "for the purposes of collective bargaining in respect to rates of pay, wages, hours of employment, or other conditions of employment." Labor-management disputes under the NLRA, while not specifically mentioning or endorsing arbitration, gave "any individual employee or group of employees . . . the right at any time to present grievances to their employers." The NLRA, through a series of contradictory decisions by the federal courts and NLRB, left a legal construction that on the one hand gave employees the right to present grievances but the certified union the exclusive right to settle grievances.

While confusion remained on the role arbitration would play in American industry, the organizing successes by the Congress of Industrial Organizations (CIO) in primary industries, for example, steel, rubber, and autos during the 1930s, increasingly saw the inclusion of negotiated provisions to arbitrate rights cases. The 1937 collective-bargaining agreement between General Motors (GM) and the United Auto Workers (UAW) included an arbitration clause where both parties had to agree to submit a dispute. The 1940 agreement amended this earlier clause providing for voluntary arbitration where either party could request arbitration. Every agreement since has contained this clause. Nonetheless prior to World War II, grievance arbitration clauses existed in less than 10% of contracts. World War II changed that.

Several events during the war made grievance arbitration a permanent feature of U.S. industrial relations. During the war labor organizations voluntarily forfeited the right to strike in order to sustain American production. The loss of labor's principal economic weapon required the development of some mechanism to resolve inevitable disputes. Prior to 1940, arbitration, although not prevalent, had proven successful in preventing strikes over grievances. President Franklin D. Roosevelt in 1942, in an effort to further stabilize industrial relations, established the War Labor Board (WLB) with jurisdiction over labor disputes. The tripartite board (with four labor representatives, four management and four public representatives) in a series of decisions settled on arbitration as the preferred means to resolve grievances once negotiations reached

an impasse. The WLB was not neutral and actively promoted the inclusion of arbitration clauses, supporting the enforcement of an arbitrator's decision as final and binding on both parties. By the end of the war, 73% of collective-bargaining agreements had voluntary arbitration clauses, similar in content to what GM and the UAW negotiated in 1940.

After the war a conservative U.S. Congress through the Labor Management Relations Act of 1947 (LMRA), focused in Sections 201 and 203(d) on workplace disputes and explicitly favored that the final resolution of grievances be done through procedures agreed on by the parties. In Section 30, Congress created a substantive means to enforce collective-bargaining agreements through suits brought in federal district court. This section, in the view of the U.S. Congress, would give rise to labor-management stability in industrial relations. The LMRA expanded significantly the scope and jurisdiction of the federal judiciary in labor-management relations.

A series of four decisions by the U.S. Supreme Court interpreting Section 301 upheld not just the federal courts right to enforce contracts but the legitimacy of arbitration and the role of the arbitrator in resolving disputes. In *Textile Workers v. Lincoln Mills* (1957), the union appealed to the court to enforce the parties' agreement to arbitrate. Justice William O. Douglas, writing for the majority, ruled for enforcement, noting that an agreement to arbitrate was the *quid pro quo* for a union no-strike pledge. Section 301 expressed a government policy, Douglas wrote, "[that] courts should enforce these agreements . . . and that industrial peace can best be obtained only in this way."

Three cases decided in 1960, *American Manufacturing, Warrior & Gulf*, and *Enterprise Wheel* (popularly termed the *Steelworkers Trilogy*) put, as Charles J. Morris wrote in the *Developing Labor Law*, grievance or rights arbitration in the center of the common law of the collective bargaining agreement. Two of the three cases dealt specifically with arbitrability. Employers after the passage of the LMRA increasingly refused union demands to arbitrate, arguing in federal courts that the issue in dispute was not arbitrable. The *Warrior & Gulf* decision agreed that the federal courts alone determined whether an issue were arbitrable, adding with emphasis, however, that doubts to coverage should favor the use of arbitration, not the federal courts. In *American Manufacturing*, the employer challenged the arbitrator's prerogative to decide a case by claiming the case itself lacked merit. The U.S. Supreme Court disagreed and ruled that decisions on merit were at the discretion of the arbitrator. The final piece was *Enterprise Wheel*, which protected the integrity of the arbitration process through limiting the ability of either party to appeal an arbitrator's opinion to the federal courts. The *Trilogy* effectively deferred to the arbitrator's judgment, with the judiciary giving the process of arbitration a legitimacy it had lacked. Arbitration had value, according to the *Trilogy*, over court intervention in that it voluntarily bound the parties, it was cheaper, faster and less formal, and created a stabilizing extension of collective bargaining.

Grievance arbitration, whether it takes place in the public or private sector, is for all practical purposes the same. Generally after the parties in a systematic process are unable to resolve a grievance through negotiation, either party can then demand arbitration, and the other must comply. There are industry and union differences in the arbitration process. Most common is the selection of one *ad hoc* arbitrator that the parties agree on, or if they are unable to agree, select through the agency of the American Arbitration Association or the Federal Mediation and Conciliation Service. Less frequently the parties use a three-person panel with management and labor each appointing a member, with the third appointment an impartial arbitrator. In a large majority of arbitration agreements, the cost of the arbitration hearing is divided evenly between the parties. In a minority the losing party pays all costs.

Disputes in grievance arbitration are of two types: contract interpretation or discipline and discharge. Contract interpretation grievances usually are over issues of job assignments, overtime distribution, layoff procedures, subcontracting, and the like. Procedurally the moving party in interpretation cases is the union, and the presumption favors the status quo or management. In discipline cases, the moving party is management, where it has the burden to prove its action was for a "just cause." The arbitration hearing, while less formal, resembles a court proceeding. Each party submits evidence through witnesses and exhibits subject to rules of discovery, objection, and cross-examination. In a majority of cases, a court stenographer prepares a record of the hearing. Both parties generally prepare written posthearing briefs, restating their evidence and arguments and rebutting the arguments of the other side. The arbitrator then issues a written decision that is final and binding.

Grievance arbitration is the norm in labor-management relations in unionized workplaces in the United States and increasingly is found in nonunion settings when enforced by state statute. Union employees, when surveyed, generally support grievance procedures that include arbitration as the final step. Its advantage is the stability and predictability it brings to industrial relations while at the same time giving employees an instrumental voice in their working conditions.

EDWIN L. BROWN

References and Further Reading

Elkouri, Frank, and Edna Asper Elkouri. *How Arbitration Works*. 6th ed. Washington, DC: Bureau of National Affairs, 2003.

Morris, Charles J. "Historical Background of Labor Arbitration: Lessons from the Past" In *Labor Arbitration: A Practical Guide for Advocates*, edited by Max Zinny, William F. Dolson, and Christopher A. Barreca. Washington, DC: Bureau of National Affairs, 1990.

Morris, Charles J., ed. *The Developing Labor Law*. Washington, DC: Bureau of National Affairs, 1987.

Repas, Bob. *Contract Administration*. Washington, DC: Bureau of National Affairs, 1984.

Taylor, Benjamin J., and Fred Witney. *Labor Relations Law*. Englewood Cliffs, NJ: Prentice Hall, Inc., 1987.

Cases and Statutes Cited

Interstate Commerce Act of 1887.

Labor Management Relations Act of 1947.

National Labor Relations Act of 1935.

Railway Labor Act of 1926, amended 1934.

Textile Workers' Union v. Lincoln Mills of Alabama, 353 U.S. 448 (1957).

Transportation Act of 1920.

Steelworkers v. American Manufacturing Co., 363 U.S. 564 (1960).

Steelworkers v. Enterprise Wheel & Car Corp., 363 U.S. 593 (1960).

Steelworkers v. Warrior & Gulf Navigation Co., 363.U.S. 574 (1960).

ARTISANS

Skilled craftsmen played a critical role in the early United States. Though found throughout the colonies, they were most heavily concentrated in towns and cities, especially the major seaports, where they were constituted the largest sector of the population. They worked in a panoply of trades ranging from goldsmithing, silversmithing, and cabinetmaking at the top to baking, butchering, and carpentry in the middle to tailoring and shoemaking at the bottom. The most populous trades were the building crafts, particularly carpentry and masonry, which might employ 40% of craftsmen during construction season. Tailoring and shoemaking followed in size.

Mid–eighteenth-century artisans could be classified as either wage earners (the beginning of a working class) or master craftsmen (incipient bourgeois entrepreneurs) because in the course of a colonial career, they were often both. Normally a lad of 13 or 14 would contract with a master craftsman to learn a trade. He boarded with his master, who was responsible for his rudimentary education and clothing as well as teaching the art of the trade. Learning the mysteries of the most demanding trades, such as

Cabinet work. Pauls Valley Training School. Library of Congress, Prints & Photographs Division, National Child Labor Committee Collection [LC-DIG-nclc-05249].

cabinetmaking or watch making, took many hours at the hands of the ablest craftsmen, who passed down knowledge gained from centuries of craftsmanship. The more rudimentary trades, such as shoemaking, with awl and hammer skills, took less time to master.

Following release from indentures at 21, the apprenticed boy would be a wage earner or journeyman, often working in various cities for master craftsmen. If competent and savvy, he would then open his own business. A master's dwelling commonly included a lower story shop, with his family living above. Mobility to master craftsman standing was common except for the poorest trades. Artisans in those trades, even those owning small shoemaker or tailoring shops, often earned only a subsistence living, with little sense of social security in event of personal crisis or economic recession. Shoemaker George Robert Twelves Hewes, the last survivor of the Boston Tea party, was imprisoned early in his career for small debts; such were the perils of his trade. Too, artisans were prey to the scourge of epidemics, especially smallpox and yellow fever that ravaged the nation's seaports. Still artisans were clearly a rank above unskilled laborers and indentured servants and immeasurably distant from slaves, who made up close to 10% or more of New York's and Philadelphia's population and close to half of Charleston's.

Upward mobility beyond craftsman standing was possible among the colonial craftsmen, particularly among the more elite artisans who managed at times to nearly co-equal status with merchants. Some artisans, such as cabinetmakers, participated directly in colonial trade, shipping thousands of Windsor chairs, while others worked closely with merchants in a nascent capitalist economy operating under the rules of British mercantilism. The vast majority of artisans in colonial United States remained at that level throughout their lives, and most could be said to be in the middling or lower middling ranks of society. This was the case in the major seaports with the exception of Boston, a city ravaged by wars and the need for poor relief, where some craftsmen sank below subsistence levels.

Skilled craftsmen possessed a venerable heritage. They were products in part of English guild traditions that supervised their trades, limiting admission, controlling prices, and setting rules of their trade. The privileged members of these guilds built elegant headquarters and occupied a notable place in their city's life. While a few trades established benevolent societies and tradition of apprenticeship indentures and workshop practices crossed the Atlantic, colonial United States had no guild tradition, nor did it develop one. On the one hand this meant that it was a more open society, and many craftsmen in major seaports often gained freemanship. Also artisans were generally literate and politically aware and proud of their craft skills even if they lacked the legal imprimatur of a guild. On the other hand, they were unable to gain guild privileges with regard to price control, limitation of craft membership, or status. Moreover while men who possessed demanding skills and well-fashioned tools were clearly above the level of laborers who worked on the docks, they were subject to a tradition that classified anyone who performed manual labor, however refined, as well beneath the rank of gentlemen. Lacking breeding, wealth, and education, they were expected to defer willingly to their mercantile and professional betters, who regarded mechanics (as they were commonly known) with a measure of condescension. There was no guild membership to mediate that standing.

Skilled craftsmen had a strong social identity. With their noted leather aprons, they dressed similarly, kept common hours, and shared social traditions that separated them from the elite as well as unskilled laborers. As independent entrepreneurs who owned their own shops, they were freemen entitled to vote, part of the political mix in the eighteenth-century urban politics. If they seldom attained significant political positions, their voices were considered by elite factions seeking office. They could easily make the difference in such factional struggles as that between the Delanceys and Livingstons in New York. They developed, if not a class consciousness, a sense of their own interests and a willingness to ensure that their concerns were addressed. Their outlooks were also influenced by their ethnic and religious backgrounds.

There were skilled craftsmen in the rural communities as well. They were most likely to be more of the jack-of-all-trades variety, in which a joiner could fix a wheel, mend a coach, or build a chair. There were only a few craftsmen for each farming community, though occasional such villages as that of other Moravians in Rowan County, North Carolina, were known for their craftsmanship, male and female, in leather and textile.

During the Revolutionary Era, skilled craftsmen became central players in the movement toward independence. Not that there were no loyalist artisans; those with strong Anglican roots or allegiance as well as Scottish or recent immigrants (except for Irish) often inclined to the British position. However compared to the other sectors of the population, artisans tended to be more radical in opposition to British measures. In Boston, New York, and especially in Philadelphia, artisans formed their own committees and took on part of the *ad hoc* governing committees that emerged in New York and Philadelphia. While New York soon fell under British occupation, in Philadelphia artisans and radical small merchants came into control of the political process for much of the revolution, producing the era's most radical state constitution, a unicameral body calling for free public education and eliminating the property requirement for voting. In the battle over ratification of the Constitution, most urban artisans supported the new federal charter in hopes of gaining protective tariffs for their crafts and due to their patriotic allegiance to the new nation.

The period from 1790–1830 was the golden age of the U.S. craftsman. The era left a great legacy in craftsmanship, as federal furniture remains the greatest craft work produced in the American tradition; artisan crafts gave birth to the American labor movement and to manufacturing and entrepreneurship innovation; and artisans emerged as a major player in American politics.

The craftwork produced by such cabinetmakers as Duncan Phyfe and Charles-Lonore Lannuier, to name but a few, is almost priceless in the antique market today. Replacing the Chippendale style that dominated the eighteenth century, a style that combined Chinese, rococo, and pseudo-Gothic styles in heavily and ornately carved furniture, was a new style emphasizing grace, linearity, proportion, artful display of color, including inlays and painted designs. Based on neoclassical design, it became popular in England beginning in the 1770s. American furniture and craftsmanship drew on the English, Greek, and Roman models but with subtle differences in proportions. Given the spirit of republicanism that pervaded the era, it is not surprising that much of the furniture and silver and grandfather clocks and other fine works displayed the American eagles and other symbols of the new American nation blended with the classical republican symbols.

The business of a craft in the early national period was far more extensive than in the Colonial Era. First the economic ambitions and horizons of craftsmen were enhanced by the revolution. Independence meant more than political rights; it meant the opportunity to enter the marketplace and prosper to the limitations only of one's abilities in craft and business skills. Craftsmen were deft users of advertisement, credit, and banking. In 1810, New York incorporated the Mechanics Bank, the highest capitalized bank ($1.5 million) that specified that $600,000 be devoted to the state's mechanics. Successful artisan entrepreneurs used division of labor and hired many employees; Duncan Phyfe employed over one hundred journeymen, with sections of turners, upholsterers and carvers, and gilders. His quarters included a workshop, a warehouse, and display rooms. Large numbers of furniture were built and stocked in the city, ranging in quality, for sale to the mercantile elite in the city and to brokers in the West Indies and other American cities.

Many crafts prospered with the strong economic growth of the Napoleonic Wars. Shipbuilding contractors employed large numbers of craftsmen in production of clipper and naval vessels. In construction master builders would contract to construct a home and then hire carpenters, masons, and stonecutters. A number of crafts remained small businesses, but many bakers, butchers, and watchmakers still had their own shops. The city's largest crafts, notably printing, cabinetmaking, construction, shoemaking, and tailoring, became large-scale enterprises requiring considerable capital investment; type and printing presses were for example well beyond the means of an aspiring journeyman. In these trades masters tended to become cost-conscious employers rather than the paternal master craftsman who nurtured journeymen and apprentices on their way to master standing. Journeymen as well had to accept that fact that they were unlikely to become master craftsmen. In so doing journeymen printers, shoemakers, cabinetmakers, carpenters, and masons in American seaports formed their own benevolent associations. These provided benefits in case of illness or death, but also negotiated conditions of employment with employers. More and more journeymen lived in boardinghouses rather than with masters, and more and more apprentices left their indentures early for wages in crafts that demanded less skill.

As masters sought to maintain lower prices for labor, journeymen responded by demanding negotiated wages either by the hour (construction) or by piecework (tailoring and shoemaking). When the two sides could not agree, the journeymen were not unwilling to walk out of either a single master, stage a citywide walk out, or even to open their own store. They demanded that masters hire only those who belonged to their journeymen societies. It was this demand and the walkouts that ensued when violations occurred that led to major labor conspiracy trials against shoemakers in both New York and Philadelphia. Journeymen were charged with conspiring under English Common Law against the rights of other journeymen who wanted to work. The trials ended in convictions, and though the fines assessed were not severe, they limited the ability of journeymen to establish a powerful countervailing force in the marketplace.

Politically artisans became the pivotal voting bloc in the nation's seaports. Supporters of the Constitution, they saw the new charter as offering trade protection and a more advantageous market position and so were originally strong followers of the Federalist party. However the Jeffersonian appeal of egalitarianism made headway, especially against the expected deference and arrogance of Federalist leaders. The Jeffersonian appeal to the artisans was not that of the agrarianism espoused by John Taylor of Caroline. Rather in such pivotal states as Pennsylvania and

New York, it was a sense of equality in the marketplace and of attack against enhanced economic privilege. Artisan masters ought to be allowed to exploit the new economy. Artisan journeymen had the right to fight for their rights and not to be intimidated by Federalist employers who expected them to vote as instructed. Republicans exploited incidents of such coercion through an active press. Too, many artisans joined the Democratic-Republican Societies in support of the French Revolution, in stark opposition to the Federalists. A number of artisans followed Painite deism, and these were welcome into Republican ranks (though others formed the backbone of new Baptist and Methodist congregations). Enough artisans shifted their votes in Philadelphia and New York City by 1800 to give Jefferson the presidency and maintain Jeffersonian political dominance even into the hard years of the War of 1812; at such a moment many craftsmen were willing to sacrifice their economic welfare temporarily for the greater good espoused by Madison. Federalism retreated to a New England fortress.

In the age of Jackson, the artisan experience was marked by what one historian has termed metropolitan industrialization and the bastardization of craft. Once again the division between the more- and less-respectable crafts came to the front, as the more populous but less-refined crafts, such as tailoring and shoemaking, were most deeply affected. However this tension also affected a number of respectable trades, including some of the furniture-making crafts as well as building and printing. In these trades the labor supply was greatly increased by the influx of millions of Irish and German immigrants into the major American cities. In addition workers now focused on the ready-made rather than on custom orders. Masters became foremen who were pressured by intense competition to lower wages in order to manufacture large and inexpensive supplies of shoes and garments. A few highly skilled cutters might do well, as would a number of industrialists, but the average wage for an artisan slipped well below the subsistence level, and all family members had to work to stay afloat. Not surprisingly artisans resented the loss of their income and standing and in 1829 organized a Workingman's party influenced by such radical thinkers as Thomas Skidmore, who called for the equalization of property; and George Henry Evans, who demanded free land distribution. This party lasted only a couple of years and was beset by divisions, but the new economy pushed artisans to form stronger unions, such as, in New York, the General Trades' Union that called 40 strikes and included 50 separate unions in the early 1930s. The union movement was hurt by the Panic of 1837 but reemerged in the 1850s.

Artisans became the core of the emerging U.S. working class, forming organizations that would lead to the modern labor unions and third parties that would offer ideas that would influence major party politics in years to come.

HOWARD ROCK

References and Further Reading

Foner, Eric. *Tom Paine and Revolutionary America*. New York: Oxford University Press, 1976.

Lewis, Johanna Miller. *Artisans in the North Carolina Backcountry*. Lexington: University of Kentucky Press, 1995.

Montgomery, Charles F. *American Furniture: The Federal Period, 1788–1825*. New York: The Viking Press, 1966.

Pessen, Edwin. *Most Uncommon Jacksonians: The Radical Leaders of the Early Labor Movement*. Albany, NY: SUNY Press, 1967.

Rilling, Donna J. *Making Houses. Crafting Capitalism: Builders in Philadelphia, 1790–1850*. Philadelphia: University of Pennsylvania Press, 2001.

Rock, Howard B. *Artisans of the New Republic, the Tradesmen of New York City in the Early Republic*. New York: New York University Press, 1979.

———. *The New York City Artisan, 1789–1825: A Documentary History*. Albany, NY: SUNY Press, 1989.

Schultz, Ronald. *The Republic of Labor: Philadelphia Artisans and the Politics of Class, 1720–1830*. New York: Oxford University Press, 1997.

Smith, Billie G. *The "Lower Sort": Philadelphia's Laboring People, 1750–1800*. Ithaca, NY: Cornell University Press, 1990.

Stott, Richard. *Workers in the Metropolis, Class, Ethnicity, and Youth in Antebellum New York*. Ithaca, NY: Cornell University Press, 1990.

Wilentz, Sean. *Chants Democratic: New York City and the Rise of the American Working Class, 1788–1850*. New York: Oxford University Press, 1984.

See also **Apprenticeship; Revolution, and Early National Period**

ARTS AND CRAFTS MOVEMENT

The Arts and Crafts movement emerged in the 1870s in response to the dramatic social and economic changes that transformed Europe and the United States over the course of the nineteenth century. Arts and Crafts reformers lamented the degradation of labor, despoliation of nature, and decline in aesthetic sensibilities that they believed were brought about by industrialization. They believed that the employment of large numbers of once-independent craftspeople in large factories and the growing emphasis on the mass production of machine-made goods had radically altered both the character of work itself and the aesthetic quality of the products that work yielded. Labor that had once been creative and meaningful had become repetitive, dull, and meaningless. Objects that had once expressed the artistic imagination and skills of their human creators now reflected only the productive capacities of disembodied machines and corporations.

Arts and Crafts reformers, who never formed a cohesive group in Europe or the United States, sought in various ways to combat these nefarious developments. While some sought to reorganize production around a mythologized version of the medieval craft guild, others advocated the establishment of self-sufficient utopian handicraft communities apart from modern society. Still others were more modest in their ambitions, aiming to reform existing industrial practices; establish new design schools; or organize craft unions, shows, and philanthropies. Some reformers, especially the British Arts and Crafts leaders of the 1870s and 1880s, imbued their aesthetic and labor initiatives with a radical, sometimes socialist, political agenda, but many in Europe and the United States either confined their radicalism to the realm of aesthetics or embraced a conservative nationalism that celebrated the authenticity of folk culture and art. Whatever their political inclinations, all Arts and Crafts reformers believed in the need to reform industrial society through the reunification of art and labor.

The Arts and Crafts movement had its roots in England, where it also took its most radical political form. As the world's first and—still by the mid-nineteenth century—most highly industrialized urbanized nation, England also produced the century's first critics of the aesthetic and social effects of the development of factories and mass production. The renowned art historian John Ruskin (1819–1900) voiced already at midcentury his conviction that factory work degraded labor, drained the creativity out of workers, and turned them into mere appendages of machines. Only the elimination of machine production and a return to handicraft could restore dignity and meaning to labor and thereby restore joy and meaning to workers' lives. Ruskin abhorred uniformity, symmetry, and regularity, whether in machine-produced objects or in classical art and architecture. Instead he championed a more natural aesthetic of irregularity and asymmetry that he maintained was a truer embodiment of human creativity.

The most influential and well-known leader of the English Arts and Crafts movement was William Morris (1834–1896). Although Morris did not follow Ruskin in the latter's wholesale rejection of machinery, like Ruskin he believed above all in the socially and morally regenerative capacity of craft. In 1861, Morris, along with a group of prominent artists and artisans, established the firm of Morris, Marshall, Faulkner, and Company (later Morris and Co.) with the aim of producing high-quality handmade home furnishings and decorative arts for the general populace. Morris himself designed wallpaper patterns, tapestries, and carpets, while his colleagues produced furniture, tiles, embroidery, and stained glass, among other things. Morris soon found that the company could not realize in practice the ideals of its founders: In order to sustain themselves, the producers had to price their handcrafted items beyond the means of all but the wealthy. To cut costs, Morris was compelled to break down the production process into simpler tasks that could be performed quickly and repetitively, thereby replicating the very pattern of labor organization that he found so troubling in industrialized England. Frustrated by these economic constraints, Morris turned in the 1880s to socialism as a political solution to the problem of reforming work. Morris had numerous admirers and followers in England and elsewhere, including C. R. Ashbee (1863–1942), who made numerous trips to the United States and whose Guild of Handicraft served as a model for handicraft societies in America. Although nearly all of Morris's followers shared his passion for craft, design, and their capacity to re-invest labor with meaning, few shared his radical political vision.

The American Arts and Crafts movement peaked during the two decades surrounding the turn of the twentieth century. As in England, the broadly defined movement in the United States was the product of growing middle-class anxiety about the effects of a rapidly changing society and culture. While some focused primarily on the loss of beauty and taste brought on by industrial manufacturing, others worried more about the growing immiseration and unhappiness of the working class and its implications for social and political stability. All agreed however that these two alarming trends were fundamentally linked. By reforming design principles along simpler, more utilitarian, and more naturalistic lines and by reorganizing labor to make it more co-operative, creative, enriching, and more spiritually (as well as economically) rewarding, Arts and Crafts leaders saw themselves as responding to a looming social crisis.

Although a common social vision of the unity of art and labor underlay the many initiatives that fell under the broad umbrella of the Arts and Crafts movement, those efforts took a wide variety of forms, including the establishment of small utopian craft-agricultural communities, the foundation of co-operative design and production workshops, the organization of craft exhibition societies, and the publication of journals promoting the ideals and practices of craftsmanship.

Arts and Crafts reformers also represented a range of political perspectives. Mary Ware Dennett (1872–1947), a leader of the Boston Society of Arts and Crafts, stressed the need for industrial democracy as a prerequisite for achieving the independence of craft workers and criticized the society for privileging the production of objects over the amelioration of working conditions. By contrast the architect Ralph Adams Cram (1863–1942) extolled the Middle Ages as the embodiment of the spirit of social fellowship and co-operation. That spirit, he argued, was later destroyed by the Renaissance, with its emphasis on individualism, materialism, and democracy from which modern society still suffered. Cram became a leader of a Gothic Revival movement steeped not only in medieval architectural style but in an enthusiasm for monarchy, premodern Christianity, and precapitalist economic forms. At the same time, Cram's contemporary, the architect and designer Frank Lloyd Wright (1867–1959), celebrated the liberating potential of the machine, as long as machines remained under the control of the artist. Wright's commitment to the unity of structure and aesthetics and his belief that style must reflect the materials and uses of a building or object were as much an expression of Arts and Crafts ideals as were Cram's nostalgia for a premodern era and Dennett's vision of industrial reform.

Among the most prominent proponents of the American Arts and Crafts movement were the furniture-maker and publisher Gustav Stickley (1858–1942) and the businessman and printer Elbert Hubbard (1856–1915). Both Stickley and Hubbard built successful commercial enterprises by promoting the craftsmanship ideal to the burgeoning middle-class market. Stickley opened a furniture-making workshop in Syracuse, New York, which produced clean, simple, designs—later called mission style—the majority by machine. His journal, the Craftsman, promoted Stickley's products and aesthetic by printing ruggedly simple designs for houses, furniture, and various crafts. Though a consistent critic of commercialism and factory production, Stickley was no political radical. He revered the simplicity and naturalness that he ascribed to premodern and native Indian cultures and remained committed above all to the independence of the individual craft worker.

Unlike Stickley, Elbert Hubbard saw no contradiction between his craftsman ideals and commercialism. He established the Roycroft workshops in 1896 as a commercial enterprise that would produce and market a wide variety of handcrafted goods. The elaborate Roycroft catalog, first issued in 1901, marketed home furnishings and other items to middle-class consumers. Ostensibly predicated on Arts and Crafts labor reform principles, Roycroft evolved into an efficient manufacturing enterprise that embraced more conventional ideas of paternalism and welfare capitalism. Hubbard's emphasis on good working conditions, training opportunities, and leisure time and space for workers was balanced by his practice of maintaining low wages and retaining complete control of the enterprise.

Although inspired and influenced by the idealism of Ruskin and the radicalism of Morris, the American Arts and Crafts movement was more heterogeneous and less clearly tied to a particular political agenda than its English counterpart. At its core the movement was an expression of middle-class unease about modern society fueled by worries about the effects of commercialization, competition, mass production, and greed on American society. In the end the Arts and Crafts movement had little lasting impact on the organization of labor or industrial production, since one after another, the various short-lived experiments in alternative, craft-based production failed. But the influence of the Arts and Crafts movement on American style was profound throughout the twentieth century and remains evident into the twenty-first in the perennial popularity of rustic, mission-style furniture; in the middle-class fascination with home decorating and interior design; and in the proliferation of pottery and woodworking classes for hobbyists. The Arts and Crafts movement failed to bring about the social revolution that Morris dreamed of. It did however foster a revolution in style, albeit a style that is now fully compatible with commercialization and mass production.

KATRIN SCHULTHEISS

References and Further Reading

Anscombe, Isabelle. *Arts and Crafts Style*. London: Phaidon Press, 1991.

Boris, Eileen. *Art and Labor: Ruskin, Morris, and the Craftsman Ideal in America*. Philadelphia, PA: Temple University Press, 1986.

———. "'Dreams of Brotherhood and Beauty': The Social Ideas of the Arts and Crafts Movement." In Kaplan, *"The Art That Is Life": The Arts and Craft Movement in America (1875–1920)*. Boston: Little, Brown, and Company, 1987.

Kaplan, Wendy. "'The Lamp of British Precedent': An Introduction to the Arts and Crafts Movement." Ibid.

Stansky, Peter. *Redesigning the World: William Morris, the 1880s and the Arts and Crafts*. Princeton, NJ: Princeton University Press, 1985.

ASSEMBLY LINE PRODUCTION

Henry Ford, one of the numerous fathers of American history, bears the title of father of the assembly line. On one hand, father is a misattribution, since the creation of modern mass production was the evolution of trends in American industry since the mid-nineteenth century and the collective effort of many people in the Ford Highland Park plant—Ford, his plant superintendents and managers, industrial engineers, foremen, and ordinary workmen. On the other hand, the term assembly line is a misnomer for what this collective effort tried to accomplish in the Ford Highland Park factory from 1910–1914, since it hoped to create what it labeled a system of "progressive production" to manufacture and to assemble the enormously popular "motorcar for the great multitude"—the Model-T Ford.

Once Ford and others decided to manufacture this inexpensive and well-built automobile for the ordinary person, they inaugurated a technical and industrial process that gradually but thoroughly transformed industrial production in the United States and in the world. The huge and increasing popular demand for the Model-T Ford lead to a continuous effort to refashion and to reshape the means and methods for the efficient production of the automobile. At the time Ford managers, engineers, technicians, and skilled workers were quite aware of the recent ideas and innovations in scientific management and the latest developments in machine tool technology that were in the collective industrial consciousness.

The crucial decision was the one to manufacture a standardized and uniform product—the Model-T Ford. As Ford later noted, he wanted to manufacture an automobile that was as standardized and as unvarying as a match or pin, a product so standardized that the customer could have any color so long as it was black. Once a standardized product was decided, the next phase was to use Frederick W. Taylor's principles of the division and subdivision of labor to standardize and to simplify all work tasks and work routines throughout the Highland Park factory. Combined with the high-volume production that the immense popular demand generated, the standardized work allowed for the investment in single-purpose machine tools to produce the same part over and over again in the Ford machine shops. Instead of resting on the multiple skills of an all-round machinist, the Ford machine operator became an unskilled worker whose major attributes were the speed to load and unload the machine and the ability to endure repetitive and monotonous work.

The next phase involved the conception of all machine and assembly operations as a completely integrated and interconnected system. The notion and method of progressive or line production began in the Highland Park machine shops. At the time machines were traditionally organized according to the class or type of machine tool. Under the traditional arrangement, Ford managers and engineers noticed the huge number of workers required to move or to truck parts back and forth from one type of machine operation to another. They determined that the arrangement of machines in the sequence of machining operation on a casting would result in a large labor savings through the elimination of truckers needed to move the parts back and forth from shop to shop. They also recognized production efficiencies in the sequential arrangement of machine operations. The use of a fast and adept worker, or a pace setter, at the beginning of a series of machine operations established the pace of the rest of the workers down the line of machines. Additionally shop supervisors and foremen could readily detect the underperforming workers by the piles of unprocessed materials next to them.

The final stage in the development of progressive production was the actual development of what we now know as the assembly line. Technical folklore holds that Ford conceived of the assembly line as an inversion of ideas used in midwestern meat-packing plants, which meant in effect disassembled animals. After the realization of the efficiencies of progressive production with machine tools, Ford managers, engineers, and skilled workers next moved on to apply similar progressive or line principles to the assembly of automobile parts and components and ultimately to the assembly of the entire automobile. They began with the hand assembly of small components, such as magnetos and pistons, which were passed by hand from worker to worker. Then gravity slides, overhead chains, and conveyor belts moved the work from assembly station to assembly station. As in the classic Charlie Chaplin film, *Modern Times*, the mechanical movement of conveyor belts had the added advantage of pacing Ford automobile workers. After the successful development of line assembly of smaller parts and components, Ford officials moved to larger and more complex automobile components, such as the transmissions and engines.

By the end of 1913, the creation of the final assembly line represented a culmination of four years of technical innovation in the Ford shops and ultimately of the evolution of the modern manufacture at home and abroad. Ford officials, engineers, and workers initially attempted to use a windlass to pull a wheeled chassis down a long shop room. Groups of workers followed the chassis and attached parts and components stationed along the way for the final assembly of the Model-T Ford. Eventually Ford workers positioned themselves with the stacked parts and components and attached them as the chassis moved down the line on a conveyor belt. The modern assembly line was born.

All in all progressive production envisioned the Ford Highland Park factory as a systematically integrated system of automobile production. Work-in-progress flowed through the factory from raw materials into the plant to the foundry to the machine production lines to the subassembly lines and to the final assembly line. The principles of line production and line assembly established new forms of control, organizational and technical, over automobile workers. The organizational control of work tasks was a consequence of arranging work in a line so that each worker paced the other. The technical control involved how the cycle of the single-purpose machine and how the conveyor belt paced automobile workers.

The application of specialized machine tools and of line production and assembly methods greatly enhanced the worker effort and factory output in the Ford Highland Park plant. In the late 1910s and early 1920s, other automobile firms and other industries adopted and adapted Ford mass-production principles and methods. Through the 1920s, Fordism, called Fordismus in Germany and Fordizatsiia in the Soviet Union, quickly and globally became synonymous with modern industrial practices and set the pattern for twentieth-century industrialization. As the film *Modern Times* suggested, the assembly line was a central metaphor for the "machine civilization" debate of the 1920s.

STEVEN MEYER

References and Further Reading

Biggs, Lindy. *The Rational Factory: Architecture, Technology, and Work in America's Age of Mass Production.* Baltimore, MD: Johns Hopkins University Press, 1996.

Gartman, David. *Auto Slavery: The Labor Process in the American Automobile Industry, 1897–1950.* New Brunswick, NJ: Rutgers University Press, 1986.

Hounshell, David A. *From the American System to Mass Production: The Development of Manufacturing Technology in the United States.* Baltimore, MD: Johns Hopkins University Press, 1984.

Meyer, Stephen. *The Five-Dollar Day: Labor Management and Social Control in the Ford Motor Company, 1908–1921.* Albany, NY: SUNY Press, 1981.

ASSOCIATION OF CATHOLIC TRADE UNIONISTS

The Association of Catholic Trade Unionists (ACTU) was in existence from 1937 to the early 1970s. Comprising of Catholic union members, its dual aim was to promote the goals of organized labor and to push labor in directions consistent with Catholicism, in particular by stemming Communist influences.

The ACTU's original organizers were a group of Catholic Workers and union members, including John Cort, Edward Squitieri, Edward Scully, George Donahue, William Callahan, Michael Gunn, Joseph Hughes, and Martin Wersing. Labor priest John Monaghan joined the group as chaplain. Cort was a leader in Dorothy Day's New York Catholic Worker chapter and became the organization's president. Wersing was the president of the Edison Electric Workers' Union.

The first meeting of the ACTU occurred at the headquarters of the Catholic Worker in New York in February of 1937. Cort and the other Workers present believed that the Worker movement was too far removed from labor struggles. They were displeased as well that Day and her followers seemed insufficiently concerned about the influence of Communists in organized labor.

In March 1938, the ACTU acquired its own office in New York, located above a local Communist party headquarters. The organization's management had established two requirements for membership: Membership in a labor union and good standing in the Catholic church. Concerning its relationship to the church, the ACTU would be lay and autonomous; that is, its leadership and direction would come from Catholics who were not priests or bishops. In Cort's words, "The intention was not to create Catholic unions, but to provide a religious and educational organization for the Catholic members of existing organizations" (John C. Cort, *Making of a Catholic Socialist*, 2003). Catholic clergy nonetheless exerted significant influence through their positions as chaplains.

The ACTU organized a legal team, the Catholic Labor Defense league, and established labor schools for the training of workers and union leaders. The league's activities included representing workers who were prevented by management from organizing; representing workers who were fired for organizing; assisting new or unaffiliated unions in contract negotiations; and representing individual workers in disputes with their own unions. The labor schools, which spread rapidly and engaged thousands of students, were often affiliated with a Catholic educational institution—the first was attached to Fordham University.

Initially dominated by American Federation of Labor (AFL) members, the ACTU quickly attracted participation from Congress of Industrial Organizations (CIO) unionists as well. By 1940, there were seven chapters besides New York, including Chicago, Boston, Detroit, and San Francisco. Though there was a national council, the ACTU remained largely a local affair, with individual chapters displaying various ideological emphases. The relatively powerful Detroit local promoted the re-organization of economic life along the lines suggested by papal social encyclicals, such as Pope Pius XI's *Quadragesimo Anno* (1931). It pushed for the creation of joint boards made up equally of representatives from worker associations and employer associations. These boards would control every aspect of their respective industries, including wages, prices, and production.

Notwithstanding such sweeping goals, most ACTU activity focused on the immediate needs of its members. In its support of union activity, the ACTU lent organizational aid to strikes and demonstrations. In the late 1930s, local chapters supported in their respective skirmishes with management the Amalgamated Utility Workers in New York; the Newspaper Guild in Chicago; and the United Auto Workers (UAW) in Detroit. In the 1939 UAW Chrysler strike, the ACTU was credited with bringing Detroit Archbishop Edward Mooney and the diocesan newspaper into alliance with the union, thereby turning the tide of the conflict in the UAW's favor.

In many chapters, anti-Communist programs soon became the chief activity. The ACTU undermined Communist influence through its labor schools and attacked it directly through its organizational apparatus and legal arm. Actists (as members called themselves) led and cooperated in campaigns to defeat Communists in union elections and supported dismemberment, through the tactics of raids and splits, of unions that did not reject Communist leadership. One long-term struggle occurred between the ACTU and the Transport Workers' Union (TWU). Beginning in 1939, when the ACTU urged transportation workers to join the United Mine Workers instead of the TWU, the ACTU's fight against Communist leadership within the TWU continued through the 1940s.

Within the context of the Catholic church nonetheless, the ACTU occupied a position on the political left. It countered claims from conservatives that for example the CIO was dominated by Communists.

Except for a slower period caused by the war from 1942–1945, the ACTU was active and influential from its founding to the end of the 1940s. At its height, the ACTU's membership numbered approximately 10,000 workers in 24 local chapters. Many Actists gained lofty union posts. Detroit ACTU vice-president Paul Saint-Marie was in 1941 elected the top official in UAW Local 600, the largest local in the world.

Given the ACTU's shift to focus on anticommunism in the 1940s, the comprehensive expulsion of radicals from American unions accomplished by the end of the decade removed much of the organization's purpose. In the 1950s, its clout and activity declined rapidly. The last surviving chapter, in New York, ceased publication of its newsletter, the *Labor Leader*, in 1959, though the group existed into the 1970s.

That the ACTU exerted a conservative influence on American labor is not in dispute, though scholars disagree as to the extent of that influence. Some believe the ACTU was the decisive force in preventing more radical union action, while others argue that organized labor in the United States would have rejected Communist tendencies in any case; in the latter view, the ACTU was simply one factor among many. From another perspective, the ACTU smoothed relations between the Catholic church and organized labor. By providing institutional support for Catholic union members and by defending unions in general against the charge of communism, it was instrumental in building a mostly positive relationship between unions and American Catholics.

KEVIN E. SCHMIESING

References and Further Reading

Betten, Neil. *Catholic Activism and the Industrial Worker.* Gainesville: University Presses of Florida, 1976.

Cort, John C. *Dreadful Conversions: The Making of a Catholic Socialist.* New York: Fordham University Press, 2003.

Seaton, Douglas P. *Catholics and Radicals: The Association of Catholic Trade Unionists and the American Labor Movement from the Depression to the Cold War.* East Brunswick, NJ: Bucknell University Press, 1981.

See also **Catholic Church; Day, Dorothy**

ASSOCIATION OF PROFESSIONAL FLIGHT ATTENDANTS

As larger aircraft and regulation encouraged the expansion of passenger business in the fledgling airline industry, airline companies modeled customer service after the purser or Pullman porter models and hired young white or African-American males to help with passenger boarding and in-flight services. In 1930, Ellen Church, a registered nurse who had learned to fly an airplane, approached Boeing Air Transport seeking employment as a pilot. Management instead hired her and seven other nurses to work in the aircraft cabin on a trial basis. Ellen Church and her colleagues became the first female crew members in U.S. commercial aviation. The presence of young women trained to aid and comfort the queasy or nervous passengers was immediately popular with the flying public, and the career of "stewardess" was born.

Despite the attention and the glamour, the cold unpressurized aircraft cabin, grueling schedules, and low pay made stewardessing (and stewarding) a difficult job. In 1936, the DC-3 aircraft made flying passengers profitable for the airlines. With up to 21 passengers onboard, and a coast-to-coast range including five stops, flight attendants faced dramatically increased workloads. World War II both heightened the glamorous image of flight work and exacerbated already difficult working conditions. Because of wartime military contracts, the airline industry operated only half its aircraft for commercial service, although passenger demand actually increased. Because of wartime nursing shortages, stewardesses were no longer required to have medical training, although weight, height, pregnancy, and marital status restrictions remained.

While airline pilots organized in the 1930s, flight attendants and airline workers on the ground participated in organizing drives during and immediately after World War II. Considered the low-paid temporary work for middle-class young women, much of organized labor doubted stewardesses' interest in organizing. In 1944, Ada J. Brown, Sally Thometz, and Frances Hall, stewardesses at United Air Lines, founded the Air Line Stewardesses Association (ALSA). With some guidance from the Air Line Pilots' Association (ALPA), Brown and the others filed for certification under the Railway Labor Act and began negotiations with United in December 1945. The ALSA's first contract included an 85-hour limit on monthly flight hours, the first increase in the base wage since 1930, and a grievance process. In 1949, ALSA merged with the Air Line Steward and Stewardesses' Association (ALSSA), an affiliate of ALPA formed in 1946.

In the 1950s, changes to the Railway Labor Act allowing the union shop and changes to civil aeronautics law requiring in-flight personnel for safety strengthened the position of flight attendant unions. By their first convention in 1951, ALSSA held contracts with 18 airlines. In 1953, ALSSA members elected Rowland K. Quinn, Jr., a steward from Eastern Airlines, as president. While ALSSA continued to call on ALPA for guidance and legal resources, conflict between ALSSA and ALPA developed over ALSSA's repeated applications for a separate charter from the American Federation of Labor (AFL) (and AFL-CIO [Congress of Industrial Organizations]).

The introduction of jet aircraft, the Landrum-Griffin Act, and pressure from competing unions further complicated relations between ALSSA and ALPA. Conflicts over flight hour limits and pay differentials on the new larger and faster aircraft and honoring picket lines tested the affiliation. In 1960, ALSSA's leadership removed its records and furniture from the ALPA building and set up new offices in downtown Chicago. In response ALPA crafted a new Stewards and Stewardesses Division and worked with AFL-CIO leadership to bring the ALSSA dissidents back into ALPA. At the same time, the Transport Workers' Union (TWU), which represented flight attendants at Pan American Airways, offered affiliation to ALSSA. Elections for ALSSA members resulted in an even split between ALPA and TWU affiliation. Raiding between TWU and ALPA-affiliated locals and the International Brotherhood of Teamsters followed.

By the late 1960s, the women's liberation movement and jumbo jet aircraft spurred on important changes in flight attendant unionism. Because jumbo jet aircraft required increased cabin staffing, flight attendant membership in ALPA began to outpace that of pilots. Fearing a "stewardess problem," pilot leadership in ALPA agreed to a gradual transition of the Stewards and Stewardesses Division of the Air Line Pilots' Association (S & S Division) to independence as the Association of Flight Attendants (AFA) in 1973.

The glamorous image, airline regulations regarding age, appearance, and marital status worked against building solidarity among flight attendants. According to AFA historian Georgia Panter Nielsen, the marriage rule and low pay ensured that the average flight attendant career lasted less than two years. Prior to the Civil Rights Act of 1964, ALSSA and the TWU attempted to end marital restrictions through negotiations. The TWU grievances at Pan American Airways on this matter were denied at arbitration through the Railway Labor Act's (RLA's) System Board of Adjustment. The ALSSA brought similar cases to arbitration on behalf of flight attendants at Trans World Airlines (TWA) and Braniff Airlines.

Using Title VII of the Civil Rights Act of 1964, flight attendants began to challenge the physical and marital status regulations for female flight attendants. Within a decade, over a dozen cases had been filed with the Equal Employment Opportunity Commission (EEOC) on the issue of weight standards alone, S & S Division vice-president Kelly Rueck (later AFA president) spearheaded these efforts. A class action lawsuit over marriage restrictions at United Airlines resulted in 10 years of litigation over seniority, reinstatement, and remedies (*United Airlines, Inc. v. Mcdonald*, 432 U.S. 385 [1977]). During the 1970s, flight attendants also challenged the airlines' increasingly provocative advertising campaigns. The AFA leadership joined members of the activist group Stewardesses for Women's Rights in protesting "Fly Me" campaigns and threatened slowdowns marked by a "spontaneous loss of enthusiasm" and filed lawsuits alleging hostile working conditions. Rank-and-file flight attendants invigorated by feminism and collective activism also expressed their frustration with union leadership and disaffiliated from the AFA and the TWU, forming independent unions at Continental, American, TWA, and Pan Am.

In 1984, the AFA received its charter from the AFL-CIO, making it the first union to be chartered with all women leaders. The AFA activism in the 1980s served to counter some of the downsizing and streamlining challenges presented in the postderegulation era.

The AFA safety campaigns countered efforts to reduce FAA standards for cabin crew size and pushed for improved exit lighting, carry-on limits, smoking regulations, and material flammability standards.

In 1994, AFA members at Alaska Airways instituted CHAOS (Create Havoc Around Our System), a successful strategy of surprise intermittent local strike actions that disrupted flights and made it nearly impossible to replace strikers. Flight attendant activism has increased in the post-9/11 era with lobbying for airline and airport security regulations. The AFA continued to use CHAOS through the 1990s, and in the post-9/11 airline industry, the AFA has used this strategy at the threat of contract nullification at airlines under bankruptcy protection. In 2002, AFA membership reached 50,000 members. In 2004, AFA members voted to merge with the Communication Workers of America.

LIESL MILLER ORENIC

References and Further Reading

Albrecht, Sandra L. "'We Are on Strike!' The Development of Labor Militancy in the Airline Industry." *Labor History* 45, 1 (200): 101–117.
Cobble, Dorothy Sue. "'A Spontaneous Loss of Enthusiasm': Workplace Feminism and the Transformation of Women's Service Jobs in the 1970s." International Labor and Working-Class History 56 (1999): 23.
Kaps, Robert W. *Air Transport Labor Relations*. Carbondale, IL: Southern Illinois University Press, 1997.
Nielsen, Georgia Panter. *From Sky Girl to Flight Attendant: Women and the Making of a Union*. Ithaca, NY: ILR Press, 1982.
———. "Flight Attendant Labor Organizations." In *The Airline Industry*, edited by William M. Leary. New York: Facts of File, 1992.
Walsh, David J. *On Different Planes: An Organizational Analysis of Cooperation and Conflict among Airline Unions*. Ithaca, NY: ILR Press, 1994.
Whitnah, Donald R. "Airline Deregulation Act of 1978." In *The Airline Industry*, edited by William M. Leary. New York: Facts on File, 1992.

ATLANTA WASHERWOMEN'S STRIKE (1881)

In the summer of 1881, African-American washerwomen defied all expectations by organizing the largest strike at that point in the city's history. Given the broad support and participation within the black community and the wide range of white households that relied on their labor, the entire city was impacted. Organized protests by domestic workers were not new in this era: There were strikes in Jackson, Mississippi, in 1866, and Galveston, Texas, in 1877, but neither of them surpassed the Atlantans' scale and scope.

The washerwomen drew on the leadership and political skills developed during Reconstruction in Republican party activities, labor associations, churches, secret societies, and informal neighborhood networks. In 1877, they first mobilized to address pay issues. In 1879 and 1880, they coalesced into a protective association. And in July 1881, they created the Washing Society.

At the inaugural meeting held at a local black church, the members elected officers, appointed committees, designated subsidiary societies in each of the city's five wards, and established a uniform rate for their labor. Within a few weeks, the "washing Amazons," as they were christened by opponents, called a citywide strike. Unlike other domestic workers who toiled away in the homes of employers, laundresses brought bundles of dirty clothing home and often cleaned them at communal wash sites, which enabled their mobilization. "Visiting committees" built from this existing base by canvassing from door-to-door throughout black neighborhoods to urge nonaffiliated women to join the organization and honor the strike. The effectiveness of this strategy, along with regular decentralized ward meetings, was visibly demonstrated in the swelling of their ranks from 20 to 3,000 strikers and sympathizers within 3 weeks.

At least a minority of washerwomen resisted joining the strike, which prompted confrontations. The police also accused the visiting committee of threatening to use violence against resisters. Several strikers and at least one of their husbands was arrested for disorderly conduct and quarreling, fined, and in some cases, jailed. Relatively little information is known about the leaders other than what is available on those who were arrested. They were mostly older, married women with children, and some had unemployed husbands. Their willingness to jeopardize even the sole family income shows their determination despite their precarious circumstances.

Whites in Atlanta, as represented in the *Atlanta Constitution*, the leading voice of the opposition, begrudgingly acknowledged the magnitude of the strike and were forced to take it more seriously than anticipated. But they also had difficulty imagining that the women were capable of independent thought and action. One source claimed that an unnamed white man headed the organization, without producing evidence to substantiate it. While some employers waited for an impending doom, others searched for methods to bring the strike to a halt. Consistent with the ambitions of the city's elite, leading capitalists raised funds for an industrial steam laundry and offered to employ "smart Yankee girls" who would presumably make manual workers obsolete. Municipal authorities undertook the most direct action not only by arrests and fines, but also by proposing that each member of any washerwomen's organization pay a business tax of $25. Not coincidentally the City Council introduced this resolution on the same day the backers of the industrial laundry sought a tax exemption status. Another group of businessmen invoked welfare payments as a form of social control by threatening to deny winter aid to strikers, and the *Constitution* warned of the corresponding dangers of provoking landlords to raise the costs of rent if the strikers persisted with "exorbitant demands."

The washerwomen responded to these measures in early August by calling a meeting attended by five hundred women and men at the Wheat Street Baptist Church. They wrote a letter to Mayor Jim English that denounced the council's actions and defiantly suggested that they would pay the taxes and turn them into protective fees. In reality the women could not afford the equivalent of several months in wages, but they articulated an important principle of self-regulation. This letter is a rare extant document of ordinary black women of this era speaking in their own voices to protest their work conditions. It shows that although the stakes weighed heavily against them, they refused to be disarmed.

The laundry workers' actions also inspired other black workers: Cooks, maids, and children's nurses demanded higher wages, too. Black waiters at the National Hotel refused to work until their employers agreed to increase their monthly wages. The atmosphere of black labor unrest gave them new leverage and their employers conceded.

The conclusion of the strike is left open to interpretation. The newspaper's reports petered out without a clear explanation of how it was resolved. In at least some cases, employers relented to paying the women more money, but most did not, as indicated by the continuation of low wages as a central point of contention long after the strike ended. More important, the strike succeeded on the political level, as suggested by a tidbit of information that appeared in the newspaper in September. The washerwomen threatened to organize a general strike of all domestic workers at the October opening of the International Cotton Exposition, the first world's fair to be held in the South. The newspaper told white housewives to prepare for a massive walkout at a time of unparalleled need; a warning that would have been unnecessary had the first strike completely failed. There is no evidence that the second strike came to fruition, but the shrewd strategy that undergirded the mere threat of a general strike was symbolic. Atlanta was preparing to showcase its pre-eminence as a model city of the new South. Such dissension would have severely tarnished its image and reneged on the fulfillment of southern hospitality promised to the multitude of expected guests. Though strikes, whether real or threatened, were rare, black working-class women would continue to channel their discontent in a variety of creative and often more surreptitious forms as the era of *de jure* segregation approached and hardened.

TERA W. HUNTER

References and Further Reading

Hunter, Tera W. *"To 'Joy My Freedom": Southern Black Women's Lives and Labors after the Civil War*. Cambridge, MA: Harvard University Press, 1997.

Jones, Jacqueline. *Labor of Love, Labor of Sorrow: Black Women, Work, and the Family from Slavery to the Present*. New York: Basic Books, 1985.

Rabinowitz, Howard N. *Race Relations in the Urban South, 1865–1890*. New York: Oxford University Press, 1978.

Sterling, Dorothy, ed. *We Are Your Sisters: Black Women in the Nineteenth Century*. New York: W. W. Norton, 1984.

AT-WILL EMPLOYMENT

The United States is the only industrialized country that has continuously adhered to a rule that indefinite-term employment contracts should be construed as at-will. All others require either a notice before discharge, severance pay, just cause, or some combination.

The origin of the rule appears sometime in the 1870s. The usual rule looked to pay periods to resolve indefiniteness, but sometimes indefiniteness voided the contract. An Albany practitioner, H. G. Wood, first clearly stated the rule in a *Treatise on Master and Servant* in 1877. Although he acknowledged that employment contracts were capable of implied terms, he stated, "The one must be bound to employ, and the other to serve, for a certain definite time, or either is at liberty to put an end to the relation at any time, and there is no contract of hiring and service obligatory beyond the will of either party." The first case to adopt Wood's construction was actually a tortuous interference-with-business case arising when a railroad prohibited its employees from trading with a general store. Because the employees were at-will, they could be fired for good reason, bad reason, or no reason at all. *Payne v. The Western & Atlantic Railroad Co.*, 81 Tenn. Rpts. 507 (1984).

Several causes of the rule have been suggested: The rise of liberty-of-contract legal theory, industrialization, a class-based attempt to limit the power of middle-class managers. None are completely satisfying. Neither a pure legal theory nor rapid economic change could be considered without the other, and in any event, the contract theory focused on a meeting of the minds that allowed implied terms. While the early adoptions of the rule all involved middle-class employees, the rule was soon applied to all workers. However with reconstruction and the Thirteenth Amendment, it is true that all workers must be free to bind themselves only by voluntary contract. A principle of mutuality suggested that employers should have the same power to condition employment only by contract as free labor. Furthermore such employer power promoted mobility of capital, promoting *laissez faire* capitalism.

In fact in 1915, *Coppage v. Kansas*, 236 U.S. 1 (1915), codified the at-will rule against government in Constitutional law. The Supreme Court reasoned based on four mutually reinforcing premises, two pairs of economic and legal assumptions. At the micro-social level, it assumed first the economic principle of mobility: Every individual should be free to move themselves or their capital to its contractually valued highest use. Second this right should be legally mutual for the employer and employee. At the macrosocial level, the Court assumed first that society's wealth would be maximized by the aggregate of such free contracts. Second such rules as reinforce such a market are legally neutral between employer and employee.

After the recognition that unequal bargaining power justifies governmental regulation in virtually all other types of contracts, and the rejection of the *Coppage* theory in Constitutional law by 1937, what now explains the persistence of the at-will rule to the present? Some states, for example, Florida, cite certainty of business expectations or business promotion. What is clear is that maintaining the rule makes employers "the sovereign of the job." Coupled with the reserve of labor maintained by unemployment insurance, employers need not tie their hands against business cycles by definite-term employment for most employees and can always hold the disciplinary threat of discharge over at-will employees. The result is that over 60% of the U.S. labor force is employed at-will.

The first exception to the at-will rule occurred in 1959, in the California case, *Peterman v. International Brotherhood of Teamsters*, 174 Cal. App. 2d 184 (1959). An at-will employee refused to perjure himself for the benefit of the company and was discharged. The court held the discharge to be against public policy and void because suborning perjury undermined the integrity of the justice system. In another early development, an implied covenant of good faith and fair dealing prevented discharge of an employee who refused a supervisor's sexual advances, *Monge v. Beebe Rubber Co.*, 316 A. 2d 549 (N.H. 1974). Third employer assurances of just cause before discharge written into an employee handbook were held binding on an employer, *Toussaint v. Blue Cross and Blue Shield of Michigan*, 292 N.W. 2d 880 (Mich. 1980). At present, only seven states have refused to modify their at-will rule by such judicially created exceptions.

The impact of these exceptions can be overstated. The most frequent exception holds a discharge void as against public policy only if the policy can be found in legislation or state constitution, with a handful of states allowing policy to be found in judicial pronouncements. Second public policy exceptions are usually restricted to attempted interference with judicial or administrative legal procedures. Only California has recognized an exception based on the economic waste of firing a worker with employment longevity, *Pugh v. See's Candies, Inc.*, 116 Cal. App. 3d 311 (1981). A minority of states, including California and other western states, sound the doctrine in tort rather than contract, providing for greater damages and thus realistic access to attorneys. Only a handful of states recognize an implied covenant of good faith. Finally the handbook exception really does not bind an unwilling employer, who never has to issue such a guarantee and can always retract any such promise prospectively.

The continued persistence of the at-will employment rule thus continues to mirror the weak status of labor regulation in the United States generally.

KENNETH M. CASEBEER

References and Further Reading

Casebeer, Kenneth M. "Teaching an Old Dog Old Tricks: *Coppage v. Kansas* and At-Will Employment Revisited." *Cardozo Law Review* 6 (Summer 1985): 765–797.

Feinman, Jay M. "The Development of the At-Will Rule." *The American Journal of Legal History* XX (1976): 118–135.

Jacoby, Sanford M. "The Duration of Indefinite Employment Contracts in the United States and England: A Historical Analysis." *Comparative Labor Law Journal* 5 (1982): 85–128.

Morriss, Andrew P. "Exploding Myths: An Empirical and Economic Reassessment of the Rise of Employment At-Will." *Missouri Law Review* 59 (1994): 679–773.

Summers, Clyde W. "Employment At-Will in the United States: The Divine Right of Employers." *U. Pa Journal of Labor and Employment Law* 3, 1 (2000): 65–86.

Wood, Horace G. *A Treatise on Master and Servant*, S 134. Albany, 1877.

Cases Cited

Coppage v. Kansas, 236 U.S. 1 (1915).

Monge v. Beebe Rubber Co., 316 A. 2d 549 (N.H. 1974).

Payne v. The Western & Atlantic Railroad Co., 81 Tenn. Rpts. 507 (1984).

Peterman v. International Brotherhood of Teamsters, 174 Cal. App. 2d 184 (1959).

Pugh v. See's Candies, Inc., 116 Cal. App. 3d 311 (1981).

Toussaint v. Blue Cross & Blue Shield of Michigan, 292 N.W. 2d 880 (Mich. 1980).

See also **American Exceptionalism**

B

BACON'S REBELLION

Bacon's Rebellion, or the Virginia Rebellion of 1676, was a popular revolt in colonial Virginia named for its leader, Nathaniel Bacon. The Rebellion was both a struggle over Virginia's Indian policy and a revolt by disenfranchised colonists and their sympathizers against ruling government officials, such as Governor William Berkeley.

In the late 1600s high taxes, declining tobacco prices, commercial competition from Maryland and the Carolinas, frequent Indian attacks, lack of voting privileges for nonlandowners, and poor weather and crop yields all frustrated colonists, especially small planters in the backcountry. Many of the planters who pushed into western Indian lands were former indentured servants and dependents of the landholding gentry in Virginia. Since taking the office of Governor in 1641, Berkeley discouraged widespread education, stifled elections, granted the bulk of frontier lands and political offices to his supporters, and levied high taxes to support his regime. His policies, in addition to creating tensions with Indians, garnered resentment on the part of backcountry settlers and those opposed to Berkeley's faction.

In 1676, conflict between colonists and indigenous tribes escalated. Settlers in the Northern Neck of Virginia experienced an attack by the Doeg Indians. In retaliation, frontier militiamen wrongly killed members of the Susquhannock tribe and fanned the flames for additional native response. Backcountry settlers petitioned Governor William Berkeley to take action against the tribes, but he refused. While Berkeley was not particularly sympathetic to Indians, he had lucrative trade interests with the natives to protect. The Governor did begin an investigation into the attacks and requested that settlers refrain from contact or further retaliation. Angered by this position, Nathaniel Bacon ignored the request and seized a number of Appomattox Indians on the charge of stealing corn. Berkeley reprimanded Bacon and called the "Long Assembly." At this meeting government officials declared war on enemy Indians and called for higher taxes to support an increased defensive guard around the colony.

Many small farmers and settlers resented additional tax increases and limited access to backcountry trade resulting from the government actions. Colonists desired protection from Indian attacks but also wanted to maintain access to valuable land and resources. In turn they rallied around Bacon as a representative of their rights. Bacon agreed to lead attacks against Indians and to cover the cost of the raids. Although Bacon and his followers were often successful at overcoming Indian tribes, Berkeley declared them rebels and traitors to the crown because of their extralegal actions.

Local landowners sympathetic to Bacon and his cause voted him into the Virginia House of Burgesses. Upon his arrival at the Legislative Assembly of June 1676, Bacon immediately apologized to Berkeley and the council. The Governor then issued a pardon, allowing Bacon to take his seat and argue for continued protection of the frontier. The meeting broke into arguments, however, and Bacon and his men surrounded the statehouse at Jamestown and forced Berkeley to allow campaigns against the Indians without government interference. Berkeley broke this agreement and Bacon's men took over Jamestown from July to September of 1676. Bacon issued his "Declaration of the People," which stated that Berkeley was corrupt, played favorites, and protected the Indians for his own interests. During this time Berkeley fled first to his home at Green Spring and then to a plantation on the Eastern Shore of Virginia.

Eventually Berkeley returned to recapture Jamestown with the aid of the English militia. Bacon made last-ditch efforts to maintain control but eventually burned the capitol and fled. When Bacon abruptly died of the "Bloody Flux" and "Lousey Disease" on October 26, 1676, the Rebellion quickly ended. After regaining control of the government, Berkeley subdued the rebels, confiscated a number of estates, and hanged 23 men. This severe response caused the English crown to remove Berkeley from office and recall him to England. A royal commission was also sent to create treaties of pacification with the Indians and guaranteed them small land reserves.

Other than these land grants, Bacon's Rebellion did not create immediate changes in Indian policy or drastically upset the ruling gentry. At no point did white settlers stop the process of expansion into western lands or their attempts to control the backcountry. There was no real shift in power that occurred as a result of the Rebellion, since many of the same landholders continued to dominate the economics and politics of colonial Virginia. While Berkeley was ousted, the crown and English rule remained strong. The events did raise questions among leaders as to the threat to social order imposed by freed slaves, servants, and small planters and landowners. During the events of 1676 both Bacon and Berkeley offered freedom to servants and slaves, white and black, who joined their cause. But Bacon was clearly more successful in attracting support from these largely disenfranchised people. While there were many additional factors in the increased entrenchment of slave labor in the Chesapeake, the struggle heightened awareness of the gentry's vulnerability to usurpation by united forces of former indentured servants and poorer sorts. Some historians have argued that in order for the gentry to create an alliance between all whites, race-based slavery became more attractive as a method of control.

For many years, historians viewed the Rebellion as early stirrings of sentiment leading toward the American Revolution. Creating such a trajectory between the events of 1676 and 1776 is often downplayed by current scholars. While there are similarities in the events, Bacon's force of "common men" reacting against abuses by an unjust government should not be equated with the revolutionary efforts of a century later.

Modern historians have used the Rebellion to examine ties between gender, race, and dominance that permeated society in seventeenth-century Virginia. Another current interpretation views the Rebellion as an expression of an ideological unity between colonists interested in seeking local autonomy over the interests of the state. Others view the Rebellion as merely a personal competition between the strong personalities of Bacon and Berkeley. The Rebellion is best remembered as an occasion where, if ever so briefly, former servants and other disenfranchised people were able to articulate their grievances against the established government and members of the ruling gentry.

CATHARINE CHRISTIE DANN

References and Further Reading

Breen, T. H., and Stephen Innes. *Myne Own Ground: Race and Freedom on Virginia's Eastern Shore, 1640–1676.* New York: Oxford University Press, 1980.

Brown, Kathleen M. *Good Wives, Nasty Wenches, and Anxious Patriarchs: Gender, Race, and Power in Colonial Virginia.* Chapel Hill: University of North Carolina Press, 1996.

Carson, Jane. *Bacon's Rebellion, 1676–1976.* Jamestown, VA: Jamestown Foundation, 1976.

McCulley, Susan. "Bacon's Rebellion," www.nps.gov/colo/Jthanout/BacRebel.html, June 1987.

Morgan, Edmund Sears. *American Slavery, American Freedom: The Ordeal of Colonial Virginia.* New York: W. W. Norton and Co., 1975.

Washburn, Wilcomb E. *The Governor and the Rebel.* Chapel Hill: University of North Carolina Press, 1957.

Webb, Stephen Saunders. *1676: The End of American Independence.* New York: Alfred A. Knopf, 1984.

Wertenbaker, Thomas Jefferson. *Torchbearer of the Revolution: The Story of Bacon's Rebellion and Its Leader.* Princeton, NJ: Princeton University Press, 1940.

BAGLEY, SARAH GEORGE (APRIL 29, 1806–?)
Women's Rights Labor Activist

Sarah Bagley was a pioneering female labor leader in the 1840s, one of the first to speak publicly for women's rights at work and the 10-hour day. Drawing on nearly a decade of labor in the textile mills of Lowell, Massachusetts, Bagley broke down barriers based on stereotypes of female modesty and testified to the people, the press, and the politicians about harsh conditions of factory labor and the need to regulate hours of work. After her days as a crusading "Lowell Mill Girl" were over, she eventually became a homeopathic physician in New York.

Bagley was born in Candia, New Hampshire, where her parents—Nathan and Rhoda—farmed land inherited from Nathan's father. The Bagley family's hold on their farm, however, became increasingly tenuous in the early nineteenth century. As a child, the third of five, Bagley saw her family move to a new farmstead in Gilford, New Hampshire. When her father lost a lawsuit in 1822, the household moved again to what is now Laconia, New Hampshire. But Nathan Bagley never owned another home in his own name.

Like other young women from northern New England farming families facing hard times, Bagley looked to employment in the Lowell textile mills as a means for earning her own money, and thereby easing the economic burden on her parents. Yet Bagley's story was also atypical in several ways. She was older than most of her coworkers and may have come to Lowell with previous mill experience. Bagley started work as a weaver for the Hamilton Company in 1837 at the age of 31, when most operatives would have been in their late teens or early 20s. Given her relatively advanced age, and the especially precarious economic status of her family, she also probably approached work not as a brief sojourn to earn a dowry for an expected marriage, but as a possible long-term employment option for a single woman seeking an independent living. Moreover, Bagley likely used some of her earnings to make a down payment in 1840 on a house her family had been renting back in New Hampshire. Thus she embodied, more than many of her fellow employees, the ideal of the selfless operative toiling to support her poverty-stricken family that factory defenders invoked to praise the Lowell mills; even as she also emerged as one of the corporation's leading critics! Over time, Bagley proved to always be a hard worker—whatever the cause—but never a deferential one.

Though her first writings, in the procorporation *Lowell Offering*, praised the factory system, by the mid-1840s Bagley was a frequent contributor to the prolabor *Voice of Industry*. Being older and more attuned to the possibility that mill work might be her job for a long time, Bagley probably drew on her particular perspective to develop her arguments against long hours, declining wages, and increasing workloads. Having now worked in Lowell for nearly a decade, in both the weaving and dressing rooms of several companies, she scathingly dissected the system

she believed compromised her health and made women increasingly dependent on autocratic overseers and distant owners.

When the Lowell Female Labor Reform Association (LFLRA) was founded in the winter of 1845, Bagley became president and presided over its rapid growth during the following year. She encouraged the association to purchase the *Voice of Industry* and used that organ to promote not only the rights of Lowell mill girls but also women's suffrage and legal equality, abolition of chattel slavery, pacifism, and even utopian socialism (Fourierism). Bagley also emerged as a champion of the 10-hour crusade: circulating political petitions, speaking at rallies and even workingmen's conventions, not to mention testifying before the Massachusetts state legislature. She stressed that a shorter workday would protect women's (indeed, all workers') physical, mental, and spiritual health. Thus, she combined a bold sense of women's political rights and public presence to defend female operatives not only as workers but as citizens and future mothers.

Bagley's role as a public spokeswoman for labor rights and other social reforms came to an abrupt end in late 1846 under pressure, not from corporate officials, but from other editors at the *Voice of Industry*. Throughout her years of battle with the mill owners and managers, Bagley was never blacklisted and continued to live in corporate housing with her brother Henry, a skilled engraver at the printworks, and his family. Perhaps the companies did not want to make her a martyr for the cause of labor reform, or face even more of her tongue-lashings from outside the city. It is also possible that by mid-1845 Bagley had left mill work to try her hand at dressmaking—she may have been "encouraged" to leave the weave room, or she may have wanted more control over her time to continue working for the 10-hour day. Meanwhile, fellow labor journalists found Bagley's political and social critiques too radical and undignified for a woman in their ranks. Seemingly fed up with both mill work and male labor activists who would no longer publish what she wrote, Bagley took a job at the telegraph office in Springfield, Massachusetts. She angrily quit one year later, when she discovered that the man who had previously held her position earned higher wages for the same job. Still feeling responsible for supporting her aging parents back in New Hampshire, she returned to Lowell for a final six-month stint of factory work in 1848; but now she was wary of expending precious time or money on more reform crusades.

By 1849, Bagley's father had died, and the mortgage on the family farm was paid off. Bagley was now living in Philadelphia and working as the secretary for the Rosine Association—a Quaker organization dedicated to reforming prostitutes. Shortly thereafter, she married a physician—James Durno—and moved to Albany, New York. Durno was a widower, 10 years older than Bagley, with at least one young child. Bagley, marrying for the first time at nearly 45 years of age, had no children of her own. For the next decade, the Durnos ran a patent medicine business. As James became increasingly involved in the finances, Sarah became the medical practitioner—still disregarding traditional expectations for a middle-aged married woman such as herself. She advertised in the city directory as a specialist in the diseases of women and children. By the early 1860s, the couple had moved to Brooklyn and their medical practice flourished. James died about a decade later, and Sarah stopped practicing medicine by 1875. She was last listed in the city directory of 1883 and may have died at that time—being close to 80 years old. But no death certificate or probate inventory has been found.

Yet, for that brief moment in the mid-1840s, Sarah Bagley emerged as one of the earliest public advocates for working women's rights in the emerging industrial economy of antebellum New England. She combined years of personal experience in the textile mills of Lowell with a deep sense of justice and equality to articulate a probing critique of the factory system and a vision of social reform to ensure the rights and freedom of all men and women.

DAVID A. ZONDERMAN

References and Further Reading

Most of Bagley's published work appears in the *Voice of Industry*, 1844–1847.

Dublin, Thomas. *Women at Work: The Transformation of Work and Community in Lowell, Massachusetts, 1826–1860*. New York: Columbia University Press, 1979.

Early, Frances H. "A Reappraisal of the New England Labor Reform Movement of the 1840s: The Lowell Female Labor Reform Association and the New England Workingmen's Association." *Social History [Histoire Sociale]* 13 (1980): 33–54.

Foner, Philip S., ed. *The Factory Girls*. Urbana: University of Illinois Press, 1977.

Murphy, Teresa. "Sarah Bagley: Laboring for Life," in Arnesen, Eric, ed., *The Human Tradition in American Labor History*. Wilmington, DE: Scholarly Resources, 2004.

Murphy, Teresa. *Ten Hours' Labor: Religion, Reform, and Gender in Early New England*. Ithaca, NY: Cornell University Press, 1992.

Wright, Helena. "Sarah G. Bagley: A Biographical Note." *Labor History* 20 (1979): 398–413.

Zonderman, David A. *Aspirations and Anxieties: New England Workers and the Mechanized Factory System, 1815–1850*. New York: Oxford University Press, 1992.

See also **Fourierism; Lowell Female Labor Reform Association (LFLRA); Textiles**

BAKERY AND CONFECTIONERY WORKERS UNION

The Journeymen Bakers Union, founded in 1880 by Bohemian journalist George Block, would eventually evolve into the Bakery and Confectionery Workers International Union (B&C), the largest bakers' union in the United States. Block's first attempt at organizing a bakers' union was short lived. In May of 1881, only a year after the union had been formed, the organized bakers of New York City led a premature strike, leading to the organization's collapse. The working conditions of nineteenth-century bakers, however, who frequently labored for 16 hours on weekdays and 23 hours on Saturdays, quickly led to further attempts at organization. Block himself went on to form the first journal devoted to union bakers in the United States, the *Deutsche-Amerikanische Baeckerzeitung*, in 1885 and to the creation of the first national bakers' union, the Journeymen Bakers National Union, in 1886.

These early organizations were composed almost entirely of Germans. The official journal of the bakers' union did not begin to publish articles in English until 1895. The German character of the union was reflected in the politics of its members, many of whom embraced the equally German Socialist Labor Party (SLP) of Daniel De Leon. The second secretary of the union, August Delabar (1888–1892), was also an active member of the SLP, running for the mayoralty of New York City on the party's ticket. Moreover, the union went so far as to endorse the SLP's platform in 1891. This close connection between the union and the SLP eventually led to Block's resignation as editor of the union's journal.

While the union maintained its socialist leadership well into the Great Depression of the 1930s, after 1892 the B&C leadership began a move away from political action and toward the model of business unionism. This move was strengthened early in the twentieth century when maximum hours legislation, which the union had helped pass, was struck down by the U.S. Supreme Court as unconstitutional in its *Lochner v. New York* decision. The creation of a "business union" entailed both a centralization of authority in the union's national officers and the creation of a national strike fund, which the national officers could use to exert control over the decisions of locals. These moves created considerable resistance among some union locals, many of which were fiercely autonomous and jealous of their right to "home rule." This tension over centralization would generate conflict up through the postwar period. Some of the conflict's major results were repeated failure to create a compulsory sick and death benefit for union members, significant resistance to regional and companywide negotiation strategies, and, in 1913, the expulsion of a number of New York locals, which would eventually become the Amalgamated Food Workers Union.

The B&C's organizing strategy in the nineteenth century had necessarily focused on small bakeries, as the majority of shops then had fewer than four workers. The second decade of the twentieth century, however, saw the rise of large bread trusts. These trusts quickly forced many small competitors out of business and hence put many union bakers out of work. The rise of the trusts led the B&C to move from its older strategy of boycotts to one of citywide union label campaigns. These campaigns, along with the relatively union-friendly environment of the war years, allowed the B&C to gain some ground even within the trusts. However, the open-shop drives in the immediate post-WWI period and the onset of the Depression prevented the B&C from fully capitalizing on its gains during the war. However, the union's out-of-work benefits system helped mitigate some of the effects of the Depression, and by lowering dues and encouraging the organization of new locals, the B&C managed to gain over 20,000 members between 1933 and 1936.

The B&C continued to grow in the 1940s and 1950s. The union further centralized its negotiations, focusing on regional and companywide contracts whenever possible. Under Curtis Sims, the leader of Local 25 in Chattanooga, the union began a concerted and successful effort to organize in the South. Helped by a companywide contract with the A&P, which gave the union a membership base across the region, the B&C went on to charter interracial locals throughout the South, bringing a large number of African-American members into the union. These successes, however, would be tempered by the selection of Jim Cross to succeed William Schnitzler as president of the union after Schnitzler ascended to become secretary-treasurer of the American Federation of Labor (AFL) under George Meany in 1952.

In 1956, Cross was accused by Curtis Sims of embezzling union funds. Although Cross denied the charges and managed to have Sims expelled from the union, an independent AFL investigation led to the B&C's expulsion from the labor federation in 1957. When the B&C was expelled, 95 locals broke with the union and affiliated with the newly created, AFL-chartered American Bakery and Confectionery Workers International Union (ABC). Meanwhile, B&C officials considered merging with the Teamsters, though the membership rejected attempts to unite with Jimmy Hoffa's union. Attempts to reunite the two unions were stymied by the personal animosities of Jim Cross and Curtis Sims, who became an officer

of the ABC. Convicted of another act of embezzlement in 1960, Cross was forced to resign as B&C president. When Curtis Sims resigned from the ABC in 1969, the two unions were able to reunite after 12 years of separation.

Later, the B&C merged with two other unions, leading to both an increase in size and a diversification of its membership. In 1978, the union merged with the Tobacco Workers International Union, and in 1999 with the American Federation of Grain Millers. These mergers led to an increase in membership in both Canada and the U.S. South, and it also dramatically increased the number of women in the union. Moreover, shifts in the baking industry over the latter half of the twentieth century have led to a dramatic increase in Latino and African-American members in the Bakery, Confectionery, Tobacco Workers and Grain Millers International Union.

AARON MAX BERKOWITZ

References and Further Reading

Kaufman, Stuart. *A Vision of Unity: The History of the Bakery and Confectionery Workers International Union.* Champaign-Urbana: University of Illinois Press, 1987.

BARBERS

The history of barbers illustrates how skilled workers experienced dramatic changes in the American service sector over more than two centuries. During the colonial period, the prevalence of slaves and indentured servants in the trade led to a popular association of barbering with servitude. White men shunned barbering following the American Revolution, creating a lucrative economic niche for African-American men. By transforming the mundane act of personal grooming into a luxurious ritual that conferred status, black barbers firmly established the barbershop as a central place in the lives of nineteenth-century American men. White, immigrant barbers further upgraded the trade in the Gilded Age by forming a national union that successfully lobbied for state regulation. During the early twentieth century, corporate marketing campaigns for personal care products, most notably razors, frustrated this drive for professionalization and eroded the strong ties between white men and their barbers. Barbers responded by catering to increasingly segmented markets that emerged from the identity politics of the 1960s and 1970s. The fact that a highly skilled trade drew practitioners overwhelmingly from marginalized groups and failed to gain recognition for its expertise highlights the disadvantages workers have encountered in the service sector, especially when they perform personal services. At the same time, the ability of barbers to persist as independent businessmen in the face of corporate attempts to dominate the trade furnishes an insightful counterpoint to skilled workers in manufacturing.

Origins in Servitude

When the trade crossed the Atlantic with European colonists, barbers had a tradition of being liminal figures. Beaumarchis' satirical play, *The Marriage of Figaro*, illustrated this role. Although Figaro served as a custodian of gentility, helping aristocrats maintain the appearance expected of their rank, he was also the servant in the household of the Count, bound to serve his master even when he tried to woo Figaro's beloved. The appeal of colonial Americans' barbers had much to do with their origins in slavery and servitude, for customers could imagine they received the same services that gentlemen received from their valets on southern plantations and in imposing townhomes. Yet, as Americans became familiar with republican ideology during their struggle for independence, the cachet of being associated with genteel servants made barbers appear unfit for citizenship. Making a living in personal service fit the contemporary image of the dependent lackey. Consequently, native-born white men left the trade to a small number of French refugees and African-American slaves, who often used their skills as barbers to earn the goodwill or funds necessary to secure their freedom.

Nineteenth-Century Heyday

Black barbers went on to successfully compete for white customers throughout the nineteenth century. To secure the loyalty of white customers, black barbers adopted two strategies. A perceptive understanding of their customers allowed black barbers to capitalize on racial stereotypes. Because they understood how whites saw them, they were able to create rituals of deference that appealed to their customers. Black barbers reinforced the association of their services with distinction by locating their shops in shopping districts for the well-to-do and outfitting them with the trappings of a parlor in an aristocratic home. These innovations followed trends in hotels and other service establishments. However, black barbers maintained solidarity within their ranks by holding onto tradition. They maintained high levels of skill and reduced competition by preserving the artisan system.

While masters in other trades were becoming bosses, black barbers continued to take apprentices into their homes and helped promising journeymen open their own barbershops. The combination of entrepreneurial innovation and mutual aid formed the basis of an African-American tradition of enterprise that proved capable of being reworked to serve black customers in the twentieth century.

European immigrants worked for half a century in barbering to secure widespread public acceptance and decent working conditions. Between 1850 and 1860, immigrant barbers, mainly from Germany, surpassed their black counterparts in overall numbers, but they failed to win over affluent white customers. They worked, standing, 10- to 12-hour days, seven days a week, in so-called cheap shops that served working-class customers for as little as a nickel a shave and 15 cents for a haircut. By the 1880s, these barbers faced a crisis. Italian immigrants, more likely to know barbering when they arrived than any other trade, dramatically increased competition. In the next decade, the Panic of 1893 coincided with A. B. Moler establishing the first of a national chain of barber schools that undercut prices and produced minimally trained barbers who could compete only by offering lower prices. Barbers had organized local unions during the 1870s, but no national union existed until 1887, when barbers formed the Journeymen Barbers International Union of America (JBIUA). The JBIUA affiliated with the American Federation of Labor (AFL) the next year and expanded its membership from 50 in 1888 to 1,300 in 1891 and 11,600 in 1901. The JBIUA managed to limit competition and raise prices through a variety of measures, some undertaken within the trade union movement while others worked through state legislatures. By issuing union cards to barber shops with organized journeymen, the JBIUA found a way to pressure fellow trade unionists to pay higher prices and support union barbers. The JBIUA also developed the retiring card for paid-up members who decided to go into business for themselves. Since more than one half of those who retired later reverted to journeymen status, these aspiring businessmen had an incentive to keep a union shop and avoid price cutting. The blurred line between worker and employer, as well as the short life of most barbershops, made traditional collective bargaining agreements less relevant to the JBIUA. To deal with the problem of owner-operators vulnerable to competitive pressures, the JBIUA sought to create a legal framework that regulated hours and days of operation, minimum prices, and admission to the trade. The last issue, license laws, proved most controversial, prompting charges of discrimination from black barbers and lawsuits from barbershop owners.

Under license laws, a state board typically composed of JBIUA members decided who could enter and practice the trade. Union spokesmen argued that licensing would safeguard public health by ensuring hygienic barbershops. According to the JBIUA, union barbers possessed expertise in sanitation, which also validated a drive to have barbering recognized as a profession equivalent to dentistry. Licensing laws proliferated, with 20 states enacting licensing laws by 1914. By succeeding at convincing white Americans that hygiene, instead of the genteel deference for which black barbers were known, represented the most important qualification of a barber, union barbers finally won affluent white customers away from black barbers.

Challenges and Opportunities in the Twentieth Century

At the start of the twentieth century, barbers were at the apex of their trade. The majority of men relied on their barbers to treat their dandruff and baldness as well as trim their beards and cut their hair. King C. Gillette irrevocably altered the relationship between American men and their barbers with his successful campaign to sell disposable razors. Undercutting the barbers' claims to expertise in sanitation, company advertising emphasized its high-grade materials and sophisticated manufacturing process to imbue the Gillette razor with the mystique of high technology. The scientific design, Gillette claimed, made the product inherently sanitary and eliminated the need for skill in shaving. In addition, Gillette subtly appealed to class prejudice, reminding middle-class customers of how unpleasant it was to wait long hours while subjected to loquacious barbers. The U.S. military helped the Gillette Company during the First World War by purchasing 3.5 million razors for servicemen. When the Gillette company lowered the price of its original razor to one dollar in 1921, its product became affordable to working-class men, and the overwhelming majority broke their habit of visiting their barber two or three times a week for a shave.

From the 1920s onward, new sources of competition shrank the domain of barbers while expanding the market for personal grooming services and products. The JBIUA was ill-prepared for the 1960s revolution in hairstyles. Although the union offered training in styling longer hair and sponsored national competitions for barber stylists, rank-and-file barbers failed to keep up with the times. The union declined along with traditional barbers, finally merging with the United Food and Commercial Workers Union.

Within the African-American community, the popularity of new hairstyles demonstrated how identity politics splintered the traditional market of barbers. The Afro put many black barbers out of work until some developed methods of styling it, often in unisex shops. Hair-care manufacturers subsequently introduced products such as Afro Sheen. When braiding became popular in the 1970s, immigrants from Africa and the Caribbean offered the service in Afro-centric shops and fought attempts to make them get licensed as barbers or beauticians. Barbers also faced competition from national chains such as Fantastic Sams. As lifestyle became an increasingly key factor that determined where people sought hair care, the traditions of barbering had less and less relevance to the marketplace.

Douglas Bristol

References and Further Reading

Bristol, Douglas. "From Outposts to Enclaves: A Social History of Black Barbers from 1750 to 1915." *Enterprise and Society: The International Journal of Business History* 5 (Dec. 2004): 594–606.

———. "The Victory of Black Barbers over Reform in Ohio, 1902–1913." *Essays in Economic and Business History* 16 (1998): 1–10.

Hall, W. Scott. *The Journeymen Barbers' International Union of America.* Baltimore: Johns Hopkins Press, 1936.

Walker, Susannah. "Black Is Profitable: The Commodification of the Afro." In *Beauty and Business: Commerce, Gender, and Culture in Modern America*, edited by Philip Scranton, New York: Routledge, 2001.

BARRY-LAKE, LEONORA MARIE (KEARNEY) (AUGUST 13, 1849– JULY 15, 1930)

Leonora M. Barry was a pioneer organizer of women's assemblies for the Knights of Labor and a tireless advocate for women's suffrage and temperance. She was born in County Cork, Ireland, the daughter of John and Honor (Brown) Kearney. The Kearneys, like nearly two million others, left Ireland at the height of the Irish potato famine. They arrived in the United States in 1852 and settled on a small farm near the upstate New York village of Pierrepont. Leonora and a younger brother, Henry, grew up isolated from their native-born Protestant neighbors, and Leonora assumed many of the roles of a farm wife when her mother died in 1864. When John Kearney remarried a woman just five years older than Leonora with whom she clashed, Leonora left the farm, studied for six weeks, and secured a state teaching certificate.

At the age of 16, Leonora embarked on a teaching career, the aftermath of the Civil War occasioning a teacher shortage of which she took advantage. In 1871, she married William E. Barry, a Potsdam, New York, musician and painter. In accordance with state law, the now-married Leonora Kearney-Barry quit her teaching post. The Barrys had a daughter and two sons over the next nine years and moved their family several times among New York and western Massachusetts textile towns until settling in Amsterdam, New York, around 1880. More than 30 mills lined the Mohawk River, providing jobs in carpet weaving, knit goods, and other enterprises for the many Irish, Italians, and eastern Europeans who made their way there. Millwork was soon to be Leonora's fate; in 1881, her husband and her daughter, Marion, died of lung disease, leaving her the sole provider for sons William and Charles, aged eight and one. Barry secured a seamstress's position with the Pioneer Knitting Mill, where she toiled up to 70 hours per week in an industry ruled by a self-imposed speed-up, since most of the line workers were paid piece-rate.

Barry's entry into the mills coincided with the rise of the Knights of Labor (KOL), which had formed a local assembly in Amsterdam in 1882. In 1884, Barry joined newly formed Victory Assembly, which contained around 1,500 female mill operatives, dressmakers, and musicians. Barry became the Master Workman (president) of Victory Assembly in just one year. Long hours, low pay, and oppressive working conditions made Amsterdam's mills prime targets for KOL organization, and Barry immersed herself in said activity. By 1886, the year that Barry headed a successful Victory Assembly strike, 19 other KOL locals operated in and around Amsterdam.

Barry's zeal soon attracted the attention of KOL superiors. She was a delegate to New York's state KOL convention, and Terence V. Powderly, the KOL's national leader, asked her to mediate a dispute involving Philadelphia retail magnate John Wanamaker. The Knights saw strikes as a losing proposition for both labor and management; whenever possible, the KOL advocated arbitration, and it preferred to launch boycotts rather than sanction strikes if arbitration failed. Barry attracted more notice as one of only 16 women among the 658 delegates at the KOL's 1886 General Assembly. At that convention, Powderly personally endorsed Barry to fill the newly created post of General Investigator for Women's Work.

Barry's elevation to this post reflected the KOL's explosive growth after 1885 and its ongoing foray into the organization of women. The KOL, founded in 1869, experienced only modest growth into the 1880s, but its membership skyrocketed from 111,395 members in June 1885 to an official total of 729,677 one year later, a tally that was understated because members poured into the KOL faster than it could process applications. Many joined after an unexpected 1885 strike victory over railroad and telegraph baron Jay Gould, a hated figure among late nineteenth-century workers. However, growth also occurred because of the KOL's ongoing commitment to organizing immigrants, African-Americans, and women. Women were first admitted into the KOL in 1880, and by the early 1890s, more than 70,000 passed through the organization's ranks. Barry's position was created to investigate women's employment conditions, build new assemblies, agitate for the KOL's principle of equal pay for equal work, and integrate women into the Knights.

Barry soon found her role amorphous, hardly surprising given that the 1886 spike in membership proved an anomaly. During the heady days of 1886, the KOL created a bureaucratic infrastructure designed for a larger organization than it was destined to become. Barry served simultaneously as an organizer, researcher, lobbyist, executive board member, and lecturer, but greatly preferred the speaker's podium to her other duties. She won fame as a fiery and engaging lecturer, but earned the ire of General Secretary Treasurer John Hayes, who openly questioned why Barry assumed that role when the KOL already employed paid lecturers. This became problematic after 1887, when employer crackdowns in the wake of the Great Upheaval saw the KOL hemorrhage members and money.

Barry was ordered to redirect her energy to investigating women's work conditions and organizing women's assemblies. In 1886 and 1887, Barry traveled along the Eastern seaboard and filed detailed reports on the shocking abuses she witnessed. But those same reports often berated the sexism of male Knights, a complaint that did not sit well with Hayes. She was among the first labor leaders to insist that women's organizing models ought to be different from those of men, another idea to which Hayes took umbrage. It did not help Barry that Hayes originally came to power at the behest of the anti-Powderly Home Club; Powderly often enlisted Barry as a spy to feed him information on his enemies, further alienating Hayes.

In 1888, Barry visited a hundred cities, distributed nearly two thousand leaflets, organized scores of local assemblies, and delivered over a hundred lectures, only to see her Women's Department placed under Hayes's supervision. Hayes belittled and slandered Barry in a systematic manner that would today be labeled sexual harassment. In 1889, he dispatched her to the South, where she witnessed Dickensian conditions that shocked even a hardened veteran like herself. To make matters worse, she contracted malaria. Her pessimistic 1889 General Assembly report declared the Women's Department a failure, recommended its dissolution, and proffered her resignation. Delegates compelled her to stay on, but Barry's effectiveness within the KOL was over.

In April 1890, Barry delivered a bombshell by marrying St. Louis printer Obadiah Reed Lake, resigning her KOL post, and declaring that a woman's proper place was in the home. Barry-Lake maintained her KOL membership, did some work for the Knights, and continued to write positively of it. Her resignation and defense of domesticity were assuredly gestures designed to save face and avoid embarrassing the Knights, as Barry-Lake did not pursue a life of domestic bliss. She was an in-demand lecturer on both the lyceum and Chautauqua circuits, joined a successful 1893 Colorado women's suffrage campaign, and was active in both the Women's Christian Temperance Union and the Catholic Total Abstinence Society. She eventually retired to Minooka, Illinois, where she died of throat cancer in 1930.

ROBERT E. WEIR

References and Further Reading

Kepes, Betsy. "Leonora Barry: First Voice for Working Women." *Labor's Heritage* 12:1 (Winter/Spring 2003): 38–50.

Levine, Susan B. *Labor's True Woman: Carpet Weavers, Industrialization, and Labor Reform in the Gilded Age.* Philadelphia: Temple, 1984.

Weir, Robert E. *Knights Unhorsed: Internal Conflict in a Gilded Age Social Movement.* Detroit: Wayne State, 2000.

BEAUTICIANS

Beauty work emerged as a significant skilled occupation for American women at the beginning of the twentieth century. It was part of the development of a commercialized beauty industry that accompanied the growth of mass consumer culture in the United States. Throughout most of the nineteenth century, the majority of women took care of their own hair. If she was wealthy or worked in the theater, a woman might have had a personal servant to do the job or she might have hired a professional hairdresser to wash, brush, and arrange her hair, but hairdressing was a rare occupation for women. Kathy Peiss notes that, as increasing numbers of women entered the work force toward the end of the nineteenth century, beauty culture emerged as one of a few occupations (along with millinery and dressmaking) that offered women the chance to become entrepreneurs and get paid for doing creative work. As it grew, the beauty industry

was shaped by racial and class divisions, changing ideas about women's work, and tensions over professionalization and regulation of the industry.

Race and Beauty Work

African-American and white beauty culture developed more or less separately in the twentieth century. Some of the most prominent early professional hairdressers of the late nineteenth century were, in fact, black women, but they served wealthy white clients. Marjorie Joyner, a prominent twentieth-century beautician, was one of a few black women who went to a white beauty school and served both white and black women in her Chicago shop for a short time. Nevertheless, by 1916, Joyner, who became the leading hairstyling educator for the Madame C. J. Walker Manufacturing Company for over 50 years, primarily trained black women, a shift that reflected hardening lines of segregation in the beauty industry. This separation reflected segregation in American life, as well as differing beauty practices. White women began to patronize beauticians in significant numbers around World War I. In her history of beauty shops, Julie Willett attributes this to the emergence of bobbed hair and the development of the permanent wave machine. When long, more or less unprocessed hair was the fashion, the average white woman could care for her hair without professional help. Cutting hair, however, did require some expertise. Initially, the young women who bobbed their hair went to male barbers, but as the style became more fashionable, men began to resent female intrusion of their spaces and many women shied away from the less-than-genteel atmosphere they often found at barbershops. Beauty shops offered women an enjoyable experience as well as a commercial service by creating more feminine spaces for their clients and featuring a range of beauty services from hair coloring and permanent waving to facials, manicures, and make-up consultations.

Professional hairdressing had an earlier start for African-American women. By the turn of the century, certainly well before 1910, black women could choose from a number of commercial methods of hair care. Many needed to straighten their hair to achieve the long, flowing look still fashionable then. While home methods to do this had existed since before the Civil War, the recently invented technique that used oils and a heated steel comb to straighten hair was best performed by a professional hand. The wavy, bobbed styles popular by the 1920s continued to begin, for a lot of black women, with straightening.

Racial prejudice further widened the gap between white and black beauty culture. Segregation in white beauty schools and beauticians' organizations prompted African-American women to build their own professional associations, start their own beauty colleges, and hold their own trade conferences. Early on at least, African-American women (most notably Madam C. J. Walker, Annie Turnbo Malone, and Sara Washington) dominated the black beauty industry leadership. While many prominent white entrepreneurs also emerged during the early years of the beauty shop (Elizabeth Arden and Helena Rubinstein, for example), men, who had for decades run beauty product companies catering to white women, continued to wield considerable power in the established beauty trade organizations.

Beauty Culture as an Occupational Choice for Working Women

The appeal of beauty work for women in the first half of the twentieth century crossed racial and class lines even as class and race shaped the occupational identities of beauticians. Gender discrimination in employment left women who needed or wanted to work with limited options. Women who had higher education, both black and white, sometimes found in beauty culture opportunities to use their skills to run their own businesses, which was often a desirable alternative to the handful of "female" professions college-educated women could choose from. Working-class women who faced waged labor in low-paying services and industries could also find beauty work an attractive choice, even if their wages and hours did not improve. Willett observes that, in fact, the average beauty shop worker faced long hours standing on her feet and made little more money than she would in other semi-skilled jobs. A significant portion of beauticians did not work for wages at all, but rather rented booths from salon owners or worked out of their homes, essentially becoming independent businesswomen in their own right. While this did not often improve beauticians' incomes, it did allow them a great deal of flexibility in their work schedules, and allowed many working-class women to feel that they were independent businesswomen rather than waged employees. For working-class African-American women, who faced even fewer occupational choices and frequently ended up working for white employers in domestic service jobs, this independence, and the chance to earn a living working for other black women, held tremendous appeal, even though African-American beauticians faced even lower wages and longer, more erratic hours than whites did.

Professionalization, Regulation, and the Occupational Identities of Beauticians

Beauticians saw themselves as professionals, and this had a significant effect on the work culture and organization of beauty shops. Most beauty culturists resented any suggestion that theirs was a service occupation. Paradoxically, this too had racial implications. White beauticians were fiercely protective of their perceived professional status and resisted being put in the same occupational category (as they were by the National Recovery Administration during the Depression, for example) with the domestic service jobs they associated with racial minorities. At the same time, African-American beauticians also claimed professional status, often promoting their occupation as a route to escaping the drudgery and exploitation of domestic service.

Beauticians expressed their professional identities through education, trade associations, and work practices. Beauty schools often required academic courses in chemistry and anatomy, and frequently offered such collegiate amenities as dorms, extracurricular activities, and formal commencement exercises for graduates. Trade journals and conferences encouraged beauticians to equate themselves with other creative and scientific professionals and to keep up with current styles and new technologically sophisticated methods. In many salons beauticians dressed like nurses and maintained strict standards of cleanliness and decorum. These practices were widespread, but nevertheless, professionalization efforts could reflect class divisions within the industry, particularly when it came to the issue of regulation. Starting in the 1930s and well established by the 1960s, state cosmetology boards emerged to make rules for training and certifying beauticians and to set standards for wages, hours, and working conditions in shops. Owners of the more affluent shops as well as their employees (many of whom identified as middle class) often welcomed more stringent licensing policies as a way of raising the status of beauty culture. Laws increased the number of hours beauty school students had to spend in training and limited the number of on-the-job training hours one could count toward certification. But poorer women often found it difficult to fulfill these more expensive training requirements, and owners of less lucrative shops, who depended on booth renters and apprenticeships to keep their shops in business, chafed under cosmetology boards' attempts to curtail both practices. It was equally difficult to regulate wages and hours for waged beauty workers. Shop owners complained that booth renting and unregulated home salons led to price gouging, which made it impossible for them to pay a fair wage, whereas the booth renters and home operators countered that there was no other way for them to make a decent living. It was in the beauty shops that catered to the poorest populations (particularly the African-American shops) and during the most economically stressful times (such as the Great Depression) that these sorts of economic divisions in the industry emerged most starkly.

According to Willett, the American beauty shop went through a "golden age" from the 1940s through most of the 1960s. It was a period marked by continuing racial and gender segregation in employment paired with increased spending power for American women, black and white. This combination allowed for significant growth and economic success for beauty shops and helped beauty work reach the apex of its prestige and compensatory appeal as a female occupation. By the 1970s and 1980s, the civil rights and women's liberation movements opened up new educational and professional opportunities for women, and beauty salon chains emerged to challenge independently owned shops and further standardize beauty work. Today beauty culture remains a popular semi-skilled occupation for women interested in creative service-based work, but the overall appeal and significance of beauty work for women has nevertheless receded over the past several decades.

SUSANNAH WALKER

References and Further Reading

Blackwelder, Julia Kirk. *Styling Jim Crow: African American Beauty Training during Segregation.* College Station: Texas A&M University Press, 2003.

Peiss, Kathy. *Hope in a Jar: The Making of America's Beauty Culture.* New York: Henry Holt & Company, 1998.

Willett, Julie. *Permanent Waves: The Making of America's Beauty Shop.* New York: New York University Press, 2000.

BECK, DAVID (1894–1993)
President, International Brotherhood of Teamsters

President of the International Brotherhood of Teamsters (IBT) from 1952 to 1957, David Beck helped transform that union by broadening its jurisdiction and centralizing its organization. He also drew controversy when he became the subject of a congressional committee investigation in 1956–1957. Faced with charges of misusing union funds, Beck chose not to run for reelection and later served jail time for charges that stemmed from his handling of union funds.

Beck was born in Stockton, California, in 1894, and grew up in Seattle, where as a young man he began driving a laundry delivery truck. He joined the Teamsters and by the age of 29 became the secretary-treasurer of his local union. Ambitious and smart, Beck soon led the Seattle Teamsters Joint Council. Under his leadership the Teamsters organized the local truck drivers by arranging a network of collusive agreements with local employers. Laundry owners, for instance, would agree to hire only Teamsters Union drivers, and in turn the union would help the owners enforce a cartel arrangement to control prices and competition. In this way employers accrued financial benefits from signing their employees up with the Teamsters Union.

While such collusive agreements were not new within the Teamsters, Beck did pioneer new regional strategies of organization that drew on the growth of inter-city trucking in the 1930s. He organized inter-city trucking firms by refusing to have Teamsters unload or exchange freight loads with nonunion firms. Then trucking terminals in other cities could be organized by refusing to have Teamsters deliver freight to nonunion destinations. To coordinate these efforts, he brought all of the locals in Washington State into the Seattle Teamsters Joint Council, thus breaking with a long tradition within the Teamsters that had limited Joint Councils to only a citywide jurisdiction. He used this same pattern of organization in Oregon and later throughout the western states, creating the first regionwide-level organization within the Teamsters, the Western Conference of Teamsters, in 1937.

Even as he built these new regional organizing strategies, Beck also worked to increase the size of the union by expanding its jurisdiction. Using a variety of pretexts, including a need to forestall organizing efforts by the Congress of Industrial Organizations (CIO), Beck pushed the Teamsters to lay claim to a wider range of occupations, including warehouse employees and cannery workers, among others.

In 1952, Beck won election to the union's presidency and worked to spread the innovations he had developed in the Teamsters Western Conference to the rest of the union. Four years later, a Senate investigating committee called him in to testify at hearings on union corruption. Asked about evidence that he had used Teamsters Union funds for his own benefit, Beck invoked his constitutional privilege against self-incrimination. The revelations of the committee and his reaction to them undercut his position within the union, and he chose not to run for reelection. James R. Hoffa, who may have provided congressional investigators with their initial leads on Beck, won the election to replace him.

DAVID WITWER

References and Further Reading

Garnel, Donald. *The Rise of Teamster Power in the West.* Berkeley: University of California Press, 1972.
McCallum, John D. *Dave Beck*. Mercer Island, WA: The Writing Works, 1978.

See also **International Brotherhood of Teamsters; McClellan Committee Hearings**

BELLAMY, EDWARD (MARCH 26, 1850– MAY 22, 1898)
Journalist

Edward Bellamy was a journalist whose 1888 utopian novel *Looking Backward* focused attention on social inequities in the late nineteenth century and inspired political reformers and visionaries.

Bellamy was born and lived most of his life in Chicopee Falls, a western Massachusetts town located along a cascade on the Connecticut River that provided power for local textile and paper mills. Both his father and grandfather were Baptist ministers and instilled in him a strong moral sense, though Bellamy did not fully grasp the magnitude of poverty's effects until he witnessed it firsthand as an 18-year-old studying in Germany. Bellamy graduated from Union College in 1867 and passed his bar exams in 1871, but never practiced law. Instead, he pursued a career in journalism, first with the *New York Evening Post*. In 1872, he returned to Chicopee Falls to become associate editor of the nearby *Springfield Union* newspaper. He also published short stories in *Scribner's* and other magazines, and his first novel, *Six to One: A Nantucket Idyl* [sic], appeared in 1878. He married Emma Sanderson in 1883, a union that produced two children, Paul and Marion.

Bellamy wrote several more novels, scores of short stories, and lectured on social topics on the lyceum circuit, but enjoyed only minor success until the publication of *Looking Backward*, which was an instant success and sold more than a million copies in his lifetime. Bellamy struck resonant chords with the book. First, he employed a time travel plot device, which was popular in Victorian fiction. Second, the novel featured a romance between two of its major characters, which pleased members of the middle class, who made up the bulk of its readership. Its main appeal, however, lay in its optimistic prediction for a prosperous and peaceful future. Although *Looking Backward* was set in the year 2000, it also excoriated the violent, strike-prone, poverty-ridden world of the late–nineteenth-century United States.

Bellamy's novel opens amidst social turmoil and tension so severe as to lead the book's protagonist, the well-heeled but insomniac Julian West, to employ a mesmerist to induce sleep. West left instructions with his servant to wake him the next morning, but an evening fire destroyed his Boston home and, presumably, West himself. West remained in his trance until builders unearthed his subterranean lair and he was revived by Dr. Leete. West awakens in the year 2000 to find that all traces of his troubled world have disappeared. In its place stands a modern socialist utopia in which the State is the sole employer, producer, retailer, and arbiter of disputes. Poverty and inequality have been vanquished by a system that requires all citizens to work in the Industrial Army until the mandatory retirement age of 45, yet allows one to pursue whatever occupation one wishes, and remunerates each equally irrespective of position. Gone were corruption, money, lawyers, taxes, banks, middlemen, war, servants, social class, and customary gender relations.

The book's structure is essentially a series of questions posed by West followed by lectures delivered by Leete, punctuated only by occasional remarks from Leete's daughter, Edith, with whom West eventually falls in love. By modern standards, *Looking Backward* is problematic. Although Bellamy anticipated innovations like radio and credit cards, his views of gender, though advanced on some levels, remain mired in Victorian sentimentality, and many aspects of his utopia betray middle-class naiveté. But despite the book's clunky narrative and didactic tone, the nineteenth-century public was fascinated by both the futuristic world Bellamy constructed and the rational and peaceful path by which it occurred. His evolutionary socialism seemed a perfect antidote to Victorians conditioned by the depression of the early 1880s and such violent upheavals as railroad strikes and the 1886 Haymarket riot.

Although the middle class devoured Bellamy's book more than any other group of readers, the book proved an inspiration for progressive reformers around the world. A term coined in the novel, "Nationalism," sparked an eponymous movement of reform-minded citizens devoted to making Bellamy's utopia a reality. Bellamy's fame spread overseas, where he was hailed as a modern prophet. His ideas were especially popular in Australia, Canada, The Netherlands, and New Zealand, and each had strong Bellamyite movements. Bellamy edited *The Nationalist*, the movement's official journal, from 1889 until 1891, as well as its successor,

New Nation, which was published from 1891 to 1894. In all, about 165 Nationalist and Bellamy clubs formed within 10 years of the novel's publication.

Although Bellamy's utopia remained elusive, his writings were widely discussed by People's Party (Populists) supporters, who in 1892 consolidated local efforts to form a national third party. Several of Bellamy's ideas made their way into the Populists' platform. Bellamy's ideas were embraced by such influential progressives as Oscar Ameringer, Clarence Darrow, Eugene Debs, Daniel De Leon, Elizabeth Gurley Flynn, Charlotte Perkins-Gilman, Henry Demarest Lloyd, Scott Nearing, and Upton Sinclair. They were also endorsed by both the Knights of Labor (KOL) and the American Federation of Labor (AFL) in Bellamy's lifetime, and posthumously by some members of the Industrial Workers of the World (IWW). *Looking Backward* was also widely read among socialists in the United States and abroad, and Russian translations were popular with revolution-minded Petrograd workers during their abortive 1905 upheaval.

The mass appeal across ideological lines points to a problem inherent with Bellamyite Nationalism: ambiguity. Critics charged that Bellamy's utopia was imprecise, impractical, and impossible to achieve. Bellamy tried to address many of their charges in Nationalist journals and in his 1897 sequel novel, *Equality*. The latter, stripped of its Victorian romance, was a commercial and critical flop. By the time of his death in 1898, whatever overarching vision Bellamy may have possessed disappeared amidst what his many admirers wanted it to mean.

Of Bellamy's six novels, only *Looking Backward* enjoyed success, though Charles Kerr spun off a chapter of *Equality*, "The Parable of the Water-Tank," as a moderately successful pamphlet. The Nationalist movement was in deep decline by Bellamy's passing, one of many Great Upheaval movements whose early promise ended in disappointment. As a thinker, Bellamy was more of a visionary than an ideologue, his version of socialism being too malleable to sustain an organized movement. However, aspects of his utopianism made their way into movements as diverse as Populism, the Socialist Party, Progressivism, and the New Deal. Bellamy deserves credit for the inspiration he induced.

ROBERT E. WEIR

References and Further Reading

Bellamy, Edward. *Looking Backward*, 1888.
Bowman, Sylvia et al. *Edward Bellamy Abroad: An American Prophet's Influence*. New York: Twayne, 1962.
Coleman, Peter J. *Progressivism and the World of Reform*. Lawrence: University of Kansas, 1987.

BENNETT, HARRY (1893–1979)
Ford Motor Company's Service Department

Harry Bennett, ex-navy boxer and head of the Ford Motor Company's Service Department, assembled what became during the 1930s the world's largest private army, whose purpose was to disrupt union organizing efforts using espionage, physical intimidation, and violence. Bennett's spies maintained tight surveillance over workers in plants and neighborhoods. From 1932 until 1941, the Ford Service Department, with Henry Ford's strong encouragement, considered itself at war against unionism and frequently initiated bloody assaults on union organizers. Although all the auto companies and their parts suppliers vigorously opposed unionism, none fought it as long and as tenaciously as Ford. Bennett was centrally involved in two of the most dramatic episodes of anti-union violence in American labor history, the Ford Hunger March of 1932, when his Servicemen participated in the killings of men demonstrating against unemployment, and the Battle of the Overpass in 1937, in which they seriously injured union leafleters. Bennett, although he knew little about business or production, wielded more power in the company than anyone besides Henry Ford during the last years of the "Old Man."

Ford was impressed by Bennett's swagger and fighting prowess, and in the early 1920s made him head of plant police at the company's River Rouge plant, soon to be the flagship, in Dearborn, Michigan. To Ford, Bennett became not only a trusted advisor, but a surrogate son, whom he favored over his own son, Edsel. Bennett's rise to the pinnacle of power at Ford owed much to his influence with organized crime. Henry Ford feared that his grandchildren would be kidnapped and believed that Bennett's friendships with gangsters offered them protection. Alarmed by the threat of unionization during the 1930s, Ford encouraged Bennett to build the Service Department into a large-scale mercenary army to keep the company nonunion.

Many members of Detroit's criminal gangs joined Bennett's Service Department. Appointed to Michigan's Parole Board, he had men who had been convicted of violent crimes released so they could enter his service. To strengthen the Service Department, Bennett gave mobsters Ford dealerships and concessions at company plants.

In May 1937, Bennett unleashed massive violence to derail the United Auto Workers (UAW) union's first major drive to organize Ford. In the Battle of the Overpass outside the River Rouge plant, his Servicemen badly mauled unionists attempting to distribute handbills, including the leaders of the UAW Ford campaign, Walter Reuther and Richard Frankensteen. Servicemen inflicted savage beatings and whippings on unionists in Dallas and Memphis. The UAW compared Ford's repressive methods to those of European fascism, and branded the Service Department "Ford's Gestapo."

When the UAW launched a strike at the River Rouge plant in 1941, Bennett's use of violence, which Henry Ford backed, provoked a split in company management. Bennett sought to undermine the union by inciting racial violence, which he hoped would precipitate state intervention against the strike. Bennett armed black strikebreakers, some of them recently recruited Southern migrants, with knives and crowbars, and ordered them to assault white pickets. Public support for the strike and a divided management allowed the UAW to win a favorable settlement, and Ford became the first of the Big Three auto manufacturers to grant a union shop.

In 1945, Edsel Ford's widow and son, Henry Ford II, took control of the company away from the aged Henry Ford. Henry Ford II, who favored collective bargaining, assumed the Ford presidency and immediately discharged Bennett, sweeping his supporters out of the company. Although he lived over three more decades, Bennett never returned to company management. He devoted some of his time to organized crime activity, and died in obscurity.

STEPHEN H. NORWOOD

References and Further Reading

Norwood, Stephen. *Strikebreaking and Intimidation: Mercenaries and Masculinity in Twentieth-Century America.* Chapel Hill: University of North Carolina Press, 2002.

BERGER, VICTOR (FEBRUARY 28, 1860–AUGUST 7, 1929)
Socialist Party of America

An activist and a newspaper editor, Victor Berger was one of the founders of the Socialist Party of America in 1901, a tireless advocate for the workingperson and the first Socialist Party (SP) member elected to the United States Congress, in 1910. Berger was considered one of the leaders of the SP's "right wing." As a congressman he championed the cause of organized labor, although he believed that union organization was ultimately secondary to the triumph of democratic socialism.

Berger was born in Austria-Hungary on 28 February 1860 and came to the United States in 1878. He settled in Milwaukee, which was the home to a large number of German-Americans and was the center of an active trade union movement. Berger joined Daniel De Leon's Socialist Labor Party (SLP), married Meta Schlichting, and became the editor of two influential Milwaukee newspapers, the *Social Democratic Herald* and the *Milwaukee Leader.* Berger disagreed with De Leon's insistence on setting up an alternative trade federation to the American Federation of Labor (AFL) and was an active participant at many AFL conventions. He later became disillusioned with the AFL, although he always remained hostile to more militant forms of unionism, such as the syndicalist Industrial Workers of the World (IWW).

As an SP leader and a congressman, Berger supported nearly all the goals of AFL-style trade unionism, including the desire for better pay and a higher standard of living and the need for better working conditions. He introduced legislation advocating pensions for senior citizens, and won a major congressional victory in 1912—and was lauded by the IWW—when he sponsored hearings to investigate the great Lawrence (Massachusetts) strike of mill workers. Berger, Eugene Debs, and Adolph Germer also led an SP investigation into the conditions of miners in West Virginia in 1913.

Berger cautioned that the constant fight between labor and capital was an inevitable one, and that the structures of a capitalist political system—government, the military, and the courts—would necessarily favor the side of capital. Unions had some temporary importance, in Berger's view, in waging the daily battles against entrenched capital. It was inevitable, Berger believed, that members of trade unions, once aware of their options, would choose the socialist alternative. Berger did not believe that a true labor party was possible and essentially wanted labor and the SP to work along parallel lines. In addition, although he was a socialist, Berger had reactionary racial attitudes.

Berger was a gradualist. He was secure in his assumption that socialism would triumph in the United States, but he decried organizations like the IWW and events like the French Revolution of the 1780s. Although Berger thought that the Second Amendment protected the workingperson, he believed that ultimate change had to come through electoral politics and the ballot box. Berger did not believe in Communism. Berger's democratic socialism did

Victor Louis Berger, socialist, representative of Wisconsin, head-and-shoulders portrait, facing front. Library of Congress, Prints & Photographs Division [LC-USZ62-100903].

References and Further Reading

Berger, Meta. *A Milwaukee Woman's Life on the Left: The Autobiography of Meta Berger*. Madison: State Historical Society of Wisconsin, 2001.

Buhle, Mari Jo, Paul Buhle, and Dan Georgakas, eds. *Encyclopedia of the American Left*. Urbana: University of Illinois Press, 1992. Originally published by Garland Press, 1990.

Hyfler, Robert. *Prophets of the Left: American Socialist Thought in the Twentieth Century*. Westport, CT: Greenwood Press, 1984.

Miller, Sally. *Victor Berger and the Promise of Constructive Socialism, 1910–1920*. Westport, CT: Greenwood Press, 1973.

BERKMAN, ALEXANDER (1870–1936)
Anarchist

Alexander Berkman was a Russian-American anarchist, whose influence in the history of anarchism and labor transcends the United States. He was a lifelong friend of and companion to Emma Goldman, author and editor of numerous publications, including *Mother Earth*. Berkman is also known for the unsuccessful assassination attempt on the chairman of the Carnegie Steel Company in 1892.

Alexander Berkman was born in 1870 to Jewish parents in Vilna, Russia. During his childhood and adolescence, Russia went through one of the most turbulent and violent periods of its history, with news of violence from radical movements circulating daily, culminating in the assassination of Tsar Alexander II in 1881. When Berkman migrated to the United States in 1888 as an orphan, he already had a past accentuated with confrontations against authority, including the school he attended, where he experienced trouble because of an essay denouncing the existence of God.

Once in the United States, Berkman was surrounded by the rich cultural and political environment of immigrant life in New York, with Russian, Jewish, and German anarchist circles, among others, providing the background for his dedication to anarchism. The political atmosphere of the 1880s in the United States was hardly less turbulent than Berkman's native Russia, as the recent Haymarket bombing and the execution of anarchists allegedly involved in the bombing still stirred debate and anger among the politically active immigrant communities. His association with Emma Goldman as well as Johann Most, one of the most significant figures of the time among anarchist groups in the United States, began during this period.

mean collective ownership of capital, but it allowed for private savings and did not advocate expropriation of all private property.

When war broke out in Europe, Berger eventually endorsed the SP's antiwar position. Berger's *Milwaukee Leader*'s second-class postage status was revoked during the war, and Berger was indicted for conspiracy in 1918 under the Espionage Act and convicted—later overturned—in 1919. Nevertheless, Berger was elected to Congress in November 1918, only to be denied his seat.

Berger's political party and his newspaper survived the "red scare," but both suffered greatly. He was returned to Congress three more times in the 1920s, however, and remained involved with the *Leader* until his death in 1929.

GREGORY GEDDES

Selected Works

Berger, Victor. *Broadsides*. Milwaukee: Social-Democratic Publishing Company, 1913.

Anarchist Alexander Berkman speaking in Union Square, NYC, May 1, 1914. Library of Congress, Prints & Photographs Division [LC-USZ62-33541].

In 1892, when the news of the violence at Homestead reached Berkman and Goldman, Berkman decided to act on his beliefs. In what was clearly an act of "propaganda by the deed," Berkman obtained a pistol and a dagger and targeted Henry Clay Frick, the chairman of the Carnegie Steel Company who had hired the Pinkerton detective agency in order to crush the strike at the steel mills, with disastrous results. Berkman had hoped that the killing of Frick, more than an act of simple revenge, would serve as a catalyst to incite the people against the oppressive elite. The assassination attempt, despite the use of both the pistol and the dagger, proved unsuccessful, as Frick recovered from his wounds. The act cost Berkman 14 years of his life, spent in the Western Penitentiary of Pennsylvania.

By the time Berkman was released in 1906, Johann Most was dead, which left Berkman and Goldman among the foremost anarchists in the United States. He edited Goldman's highly influential and relatively long-lived *Mother Earth* magazine, as well as writing his experiences and thoughts during his imprisonment (*Prison Memoirs of an Anarchist*). Amidst all the activity, Berkman worked on promoting the Ferrer School in New York, a testing ground for new and anarchism-inspired ideas for education, while trying to raise support for events such as the Lawrence strike of 1912. The duration of World War I, especially after the entry of the United States to the war in 1917,

witnessed Berkman's agitation against the war and conscription. During the years of the "Red Scare" at the end of the war, Berkman was targeted along with Goldman and many other prominent anarchists, which resulted in another term in prison followed by his deportation to Russia in 1919.

Berkman and Goldman both toured Russia, participating in several cultural activities for a short period of time, before their observation of the Bolshevik Revolution and its brutal suppression of anarchists in the Ukraine and during the Kronstadt uprising of 1921 led them, disillusioned, to a life of exile in various European countries. Berkman's communist anarchism, wary of a "new tyranny," emphasized the elements of popular initiative, spontaneous self-organization, and cooperation against the rational planning and centralized organization he witnessed in the new Soviet republic. In 1936, Berkman, suffering from several operations, chronic health problems, and continuous poverty, committed suicide in his Nice (France) apartment, three weeks before the start of the Spanish Civil War.

AXEL B. CORLU

References and Further Reading

The Alexander Berkman Archive, http://dwardmac.pitzer. edu/anarchist_archives/bright/berkman/berkman.html.

Avrich, Paul. *Anarchist Portraits*. Princeton, NJ: Princeton University Press, 1988.
Berkman, Alexander. *Prison Memoirs of an Anarchist*. New York: Mother Earth Publishing Association, 1912.

See also **Anarchism; Goldman, Emma; Haymarket Affair (1886); Homestead Strike (1892); Lawrence Strike (1912); Ludlow Massacre (1914)**

BISBEE DEPORTATION/COPPER STRIKE (1917)

On July 12, 1917, Sheriff Harry Wheeler, aided by deputies and vigilantes, rounded up 1,185 union members and sympathizers and marched them two miles from Bisbee to a baseball park in Warren, Arizona. After passing through a gauntlet of armed men, the strikers and their supporters boarded box cars on a train that would carry them out into the New Mexican desert and abandon them there. Known as the "Bisbee Deportation," this event proved to be devastating for the future of organized labor in Arizona.

This incident brought an end to a 15-day-old strike organized by members of the Metal Mine Workers Industrial Union (MMWIU), an affiliate of the Industrial Workers of the World (IWW). The strike itself was not particularly violent, well organized, or militant. In fact, workers in the mining district were deeply divided over the role of the IWW in the struggle. A rival union, the International Union of Mine, Mill, and Smelter Workers (Mine-Mill), condemned the IWW's efforts and encouraged its members to cross the picket line. It had been trying to organize the miners since 1906, but had been unsuccessful in securing a union contract. To make matters worse, the International had revoked Mine-Mill's local charter due to growing support for the IWW within its ranks. But the Wobblies (as IWW activists were called) were running out of strike funds, and American Federation of Labor (AFL) unions had barred them from participating in the district trades council.

In light of these conditions, the response from the company-backed deputies and vigilantes might seem like a profound overreaction. But from the mining company's perspective, the IWW was a serious threat and was gaining increasing support from workers in Arizona's mining districts. The Phelps Dodge Corporation was beginning to develop its open-pit operation in Bisbee, a move that would employ a majority of surface workers rather than the more highly skilled underground miners, a category it defined in racialized terms.

Part of the IWW's strike demands included a significant dismantling of the wage differentials between surface workers and underground miners. It called for a raise in pay from $4.00 to $6.00 a day for underground work and $2.50 to $5.50 a day for surface labor. In addition to wage increases, IWW appealed for improved working conditions, reducing the work day to six hours, requiring two men to a drilling machine and eliminating blasting underground during shifts. Since the majority of surface workers were Mexican, the IWW's efforts to narrow the wage gap threatened to blur the color line that had been so characteristic of Bisbee's labor market.

Bisbee's history of racial segregation included an unwritten law that prohibited Chinese people from staying in town overnight. Chinese truck farmers could come to Bisbee to sell their produce, but they would have to leave before the sun went down. Town promoters and AFL leaders made great efforts to distinguish the district from Clifton and Morenci and other mining areas, boasting that Bisbee was a "white man's camp." Miners there earned a white man's wage, a distinction that excluded Mexicans, who were not allowed to work in the better-paying underground jobs. By 1917, thousands of Italians and Slavs made up a kind of "in-between" race, neither clearly white nor Mexican. While the rhetoric surrounding the deportation was filled with anti-Mexican references, most of the deportees were Euro-American and European immigrants.

Immediately after the deportation, federal troops rescued the men stranded in the desert and housed them in a makeshift camp near Columbus, New Mexico. Rifle-wielding guards posted at the town's entrance prohibited the miners from going back to Bisbee. Husbands, sons, and brothers were cut off from their wives, sisters, and mothers. The women of Bisbee organized relief committees, gave depositions, and attempted to attract public attention to the injustices they faced on a day-to-day basis. Rosa McKay, who had been elected to the state legislature before women had the vote nationwide, led the women's efforts, gathering food and clothing and coordinating covert trips to Columbus to deliver supplies to the men. The wife of an AFL member and mother of three, McKay wired President Wilson, asking him for protection, "before we are burned up like the women and children were in Ludlow." William B. Cleary, a famous civil rights lawyer, pressed the deportees' legal claims. Despite a presidential investigation and criminal and civil trials, the vigilante action remained unchecked.

One historian has characterized the deportation as an outgrowth of World War I nativism, a community's act of self-defense against "foreign" influences. Indeed, many IWW leaders were outspoken critics of the war, characterizing it as a capitalist conflict they could best oppose by organizing workers worldwide. Detractors accused union members of disloyalty and circulated rumors that the IWW harbored German spies. George Hunt, a populist Democrat who had served as Arizona's first governor from 1912 to 1917, came to the aid of the deported men and disputed such claims in communication with President Woodrow Wilson. His census of the deportees showed that most were not even IWW members. Many of the men were registered for the draft and had even purchased war bonds.

Another historian has interpreted the event more broadly and argues that the Bisbee deportation was just one of the many draconian labor practices, including similar incidents in other mining districts, that helped to undermine the influence of organized labor in Arizona politics in the early twentieth century. Others have framed the incident in racial and gendered terms, connecting the struggle to white racial fears of Mexican labor militancy and Bisbee's proximity to the revolutionary violence that raged in nearby border towns.

The long-term effects are difficult to gauge. While the deportation undermined the influence of the IWW in the region, Mine-Mill eventually established a foothold in the district. However, it would not be until after World War II that Bisbee's dual wage system would begin to fade as Mexican-Americans gained access to higher skilled jobs.

COLLEEN O'NEILL

References and Further Reading

Benton-Cohen, Katherine. "Docile Children and Dangerous Revolutionaries: The Racial Hierarchy of Manliness and the Bisbee Deportation of 1917." *Frontiers: A Journal of Women's Studies* 24 (2003): 30–50.

Byrkit, James W. *Forging the Copper Collar: Arizona's Labor-Management Wars of 1901–1921.* Tucson: University of Arizona Press, 1982.

Dubofsky, Melvyn. *We Shall Be All: A History of the Industrial Workers of the World.* Urbana: University of Illinois Press, 1988.

Jensen, Vernon H. *Heritage of Conflict: Labor Relations in the Nonferrous Metals Industry up to 1930.* Ithaca, NY: Cornell University Press, 1950.

Lindquist, John H. and James Fraser. "A Sociological Interpretation of the Bisbee Deportation." *Pacific Historical Review* 37:4 (1968): 401–422.

Mellinger, Philip. *Race and Labor in Western Copper: The Fight for Equality, 1896–1918.* Tucson: University of Arizona Press, 1995.

O'Neill, Colleen. "Domesticity Deployed: Gender, Race and the Construction of Class Struggle in the Bisbee Deportation." *Labor History* 34 (Spring/Summer 1993): 256–273.

Taft, Philip. "The Bisbee Deportation." *Labor History* 13:1 (1972), 3–40.

See also **Industrial Workers of the World; Mexican and Mexican-American Workers; World War I**

BISNO, ABRAHAM (1866–1929)
International Ladies' Garment Workers' Union

Abraham Bisno, an early leader of the International Ladies' Garment Workers' Union (ILGWU), was the best-known trade unionist among the Jewish garment workers in Chicago and New York in the late nineteenth and early twentieth century.

Bisno was born in Russia in 1866 as the son and grandson of tailors. According to family custom, he became a tailor's apprentice. When his poverty-stricken family migrated to the United States in 1881 to escape a Russian pogrom, he went to work at once. Though not equipped by nature to become a skilled hand tailor, Bisno proved to be a skilled sewing-machine operator. He worked as a tailor in Atlanta, where the family first lived, and served as the family spokesman because of his quickness at picking up both English and American business customs. He then worked in Chattanooga and Chicago, where the Bisno family finally settled. By the age of 16, Bisno had become a successful contractor who obtained work for his family, consulted with designers, bought sewing machines, hired additional workers, and organized the work process.

In Chicago, Bisno became interested in improving conditions for workers. The women's garment industry in the last third of the nineteenth century and first decades of the twentieth century was notorious for cutthroat competition that drove down both prices and wages. The workers, chiefly Jewish immigrants from Eastern Europe, labored for excessively long hours, in unsanitary and dangerous conditions, for relatively little money. In 1888, Bisno helped organize the Workingman's Educational Society, which sponsored lectures by trade unionists, socialists, and anarchists. Shortly afterward, in 1890, the society formed the Chicago Cloak Makers' Union, with Bisno as president. The union was one of the forerunners of the ILGWU. Bisno served as chief clerk of the Joint Board of the ILGWU in New York City for a year in 1911. Upon leaving as chief clerk, he continued briefly as general manager of the Joint Board.

One of the early participants in the activities at Jane Addams' Hull-House, he joined these progressive reformers in campaigning for legislation to abolish sweatshops in Illinois. The agitation led the state legislature to appoint an investigating commission, for which Bisno and Florence Kelley collected information. When Kelley received an appointment as chief factory inspector, Bisno became one of her deputy inspectors for four years.

Bisno focused on providing security for union workers. He was a socialist, though political concerns were always secondary in importance in his mind to trade unionism. Like other unionists, Bisno suffered periods of unemployment and blacklisting when strikes were lost and the union was too weak to support its leader. At these times, he worked at heavy, unskilled factory labor or collected tickets on the elevated railroad lines.

Not known for his tact or patience, Bisno struggled to keep the loyalty of radical workers, win the support of more conservative national union officers, and obtain cooperation from the manufacturers. Once the garment trade was organized, it did not need a man as combative as Bisno. He left the union in 1917. Bisno devoted most of the remainder of his life to his real estate business. He died in Chicago in 1929.

CARYN E. NEUMANN

References and Further Reading

Seidman, Joel, ed. *Abraham Bisno: Union Pioneer*. Madison: The University of Wisconsin Press, 1967.

See also **Addams, Jane; International Ladies' Garment Workers' Union (ILGWU) (1900–1995)**

BLACK LUNG ASSOCIATIONS

The Black Lung Associations were first organized in the Appalachian coal fields at the end of the 1960s. The associations have been the main organizational vehicles for a rank-and-file movement demanding compensation, prevention, and treatment of black lung disease (coal workers' pneumoconiosis).

Historical Roots: Neglect and Denial; Ferment and Insurgency

In both the nineteenth and twentieth centuries, autopsy evidence, as well as disease and disability rates among coal miners, led a number of observers to identify long-term coal dust exposure as a source of chronic shortness of breath and coughing that was progressive, debilitating, and in many cases, ultimately fatal. Given the massive numbers of U.S. coal miners, especially throughout the first half of the twentieth century, the human toll was considerable. New technologies, such as cutting machines, loading machines, and "continuous miners," were progressively introduced

over many decades, and each innovation multiplied the number of tiny airborne dust particles that became lodged in coal miners' lungs. Yet, the coal industry and its allies within the medical profession, the insurance industry, and government agencies promoted the notion that only silicosis, caused by sand and certain rock dusts, could cause disabling occupational lung disease. Coal dust was even said to be beneficial to miners' health. The result was a failure to carry out dust control, and an ineffectual state workers' compensation system excluded most disabled miners through "Catch-22"-type time limits on the filing of claims and through the refusal to recognize specifically coal dust-caused disease as compensable.

The 1960s rank-and-file rebellion among coal miners, from which the Black Lung Associations emerged, was not only directed at coal mine operators. It also sought, successfully, to reclaim the United Mine Workers of America (UMWA) from the criminal and corrupt post-John L. Lewis leadership of Tony Boyle. During that era, two physicians in West Virginia, Drs. I. E. Buff and Donald Rasmussen, grew frustrated with the longstanding black lung cover-up. They began bringing the medical facts about coal dust disease directly to the miners and their families in the hollows where they lived. In doing so, they validated what the miners had long believed about the effects of coal dust. Their actions catalyzed a movement.

The "Heroic Period" (1968–1970)

The history and character of the Black Lung Associations can be understood in the context of three periods. The first began in late 1968, with the death of 78 miners in the Farmington mine explosion that focused national attention on the tragic neglect of mine safety. In its wake, a few local UMWA presidents and disabled miners in the Kanawha Valley area formed the West Virginia Black Lung Association. The initial core included African-American miner Charles Brooks and Arnold Miller. Pooling their own resources, they developed a model state black lung compensation bill. The association spread to other southern West Virginia counties and mobilized 3,000 miners to rally in Charleston. The Boyle UMWA leadership responded with a combination of hostility and co-optation, charging the association with "dual unionism," while putting forth its own weaker bill. The black lung movement then became increasingly bound up with the growing insurgency against Boyle. In February 1969, a wildcat strike started over a local dispute near Beckley, West Virginia. In the context of the evolving black lung movement, the walkout became infused with the demand for a black lung bill and soon spread, closing down virtually all the coal mines in West Virginia.

This rarity in the United States, a strike making political demands upon the state, produced historic results when West Virginia passed a strong black lung law. The reverberations extended further, however, and by the end of 1969, under the threat of another walkout, President Nixon reluctantly signed the Federal Coal Mine Health and Safety Act. The groundbreaking legislation took federal responsibility for workplace health and safety beyond anything that would have been dreamed possible a decade before. Among its provisions were a federal black lung compensation program (initially seen as temporary) for miners disabled by black lung and for widows, and a federally mandated limit on respirable dust in the mines, with mechanisms for enforcement.

The Fight for Implementation; Failed Bid for a Broad Coalition (1971–1988)

The ferment of the late 1960s produced both the federal black lung program and the end of the Boyle era. Arnold Miller, an association founder, won the presidency of the UMWA in 1972. Concomitantly, Black Lung Associations formed in several Appalachian states, and in 1976, displaced disabled miners organized a chapter in the Chicago area. A loose coordinating structure, soon known as the National Black Lung Association (NBLA), emerged under Bill Worthington, an African-American disabled miner from Harlan County.

The emergence of new associations was, in considerable part, a response to widespread grassroots disappointment with the fledgling federal compensation program, and the associations became largely defined by that response. Restrictive rules and bureaucratic abuse led to numerous denials and endless delay of claims. Association leaders organized militant confrontations and meetings with federal officials and lobbying trips to Washington, and also functioned as "lay" (nonattorney) representatives in individual claims. They played important roles in winning favorable congressional amendments in 1972 and 1978 which, among other things, made the federal compensation program permanent and created clinics for diagnosis and treatment. The associations were able also to impose particularly effective "interim regulations" for the backlogs of cases reopened and reviewed under both sets of amendments, resulting in the payment of several hundred thousand claims.

However, by 1978, the UMWA's legislative staff was in control of the lobbying effort, and most coalfield associations were not growing in strength. Then, the juggernaut of "Reaganomics" in 1981 brought about amendments that made the compensation program more restrictive. Although a UMWA-sponsored one-day "moratorium" on work, early in 1981, brought thousands of working miners to Washington in a rally to defend the compensation program (and possibly rescued it from abolition), tensions between the UMWA and the associations, which had existed beneath the surface, were evident. The associations were further harmed by indictments that charged a few lay representatives with taking illegal fees from miners for assistance on claims.

NBLA President Worthington placed his hopes in a nationwide organization that would unite all people exposed to workplace hazards. The black lung movement had indeed inspired Brown and White Lung Associations among textile and asbestos workers, respectively. The three associations' efforts sparked the Breath of Life Organizing Campaign, which led actions against President Reagan's attacks on Social Security Disability and developed a proposal for a comprehensive federal compensation program. However, by 1988, the coalition had withered in the face of growing conservatism, perhaps falling victim to its very reliance upon demands for comprehensive federal action.

Partial Revival; Limited Victories (1989–2001)

The UMWA's militant Pittston strike to rescue endangered pensions, a scandal around widespread coal industry fraud in the federal coal dust sampling program, and then the emergence of Cecil Roberts as UMWA president and Mike South as NBLA president revitalized the historic ties of working miners with disabled miners and widows. As associations revived in several states, the two organizations put aside old tensions and moved to an unprecedented degree of working unity. Facing an uncertain future with a dramatic decline in the number of union miners, they accepted the political impossibility of winning new federal legislation on black lung. They instead waged a victorious campaign around the more limited, but still substantial, goal of revising the Department of Labor's regulations for the federal black lung benefits program. As in times past, the associations and the UMWA enlisted the support of doctors (including the venerable Rasmussen) and health workers, as well as lawyers and legal workers. The death of South, who had worked tirelessly in the face of severe lung disease, was a setback. But the Black Lung Associations' demise has been prematurely announced in the past, and they have proved too feisty to oblige. That may yet be the case.

The associations have always been characterized by a periodically declining and reviving leadership core of militant disabled miners. African-Americans have notably served as key leaders, especially in the earlier period, despite their steep decline relative to the work force. The core has organized ad hoc support from health and legal workers, usually with no paid staff. Perhaps reflecting an ambiguous relationship with the UMWA, the associations have been loosely structured and only a few chapters, at various times, have had substantial numbers of formally enrolled rank-and-file members and a well-defined organizational life. It also is likely that the magnitude of the 1969 victory focused the movement's attention so heavily upon implementing and protecting the federal law that it limited the associations' organizational development.

Yet, the associations have succeeded in tapping the deepest emotional wellsprings in the coalfields, sustaining a kind of social contract between generations—the working miners and those who have been "used up" into disability. The creative energies that the Black Lung Associations unleashed, and the movement they represent, have helped to shape the late–twentieth-century history of American coal miners and their relationship to the American political economy.

PAUL SIEGEL

References and Further Reading

Barth, Peter S. *The Tragedy of Black Lung: Federal Compensation for Occupational Disease.* Kalamazoo, MI: W. E. Upjohn Institute for Employment Research, 1987.
Derickson, Alan. *Black Lung: Anatomy of a Public Health Disaster.* Ithaca, NY: Cornell University Press, 1998.
———. "The Role of the United Mine Workers in the Prevention of Work-Related Respiratory Disease, 1890–1968." In *The United Mine Workers of America: A Model of Industrial Solidarity?* edited by John H. M. Laslett, 224–238, University Park: University of Pennsylvania Press, 1996.
Green, James R. "'Tying the Knot of Solidarity': The Pittston Strike of 1989–1990." In *The United Mine Workers of America: A Model of Industrial Solidarity?* edited by John H. M. Laslett, 513–544, University Park: University of Pennsylvania Press, 1996.
Harris, Gardner, and Ralph Dunlop. "Dust, Deception and Death." Series in *The Courier Journal.* April 19–April 26, 1998. Louisville, KY.
Hume, Brit. *Death and the Mines: Rebellion and Murder in the United Mine Workers.* New York: Grossman Publishers, 1971.
Judkins, Bennett M. *We Offer Ourselves as Evidence: Toward Workers' Control of Occupational Health.* New York: Greenwood Press, 1986.
Lewis, Ronald L. *Black Coal Miners in America: Race, Class and Community Conflict, 1780–1980.* Lexington: University Press of Kentucky, 1987.
Nyden, Paul. *Miners for Democracy: Struggle in the Coal Fields* (Ph.D. Dissertation). Ann Arbor, MI: University Microfilms International, 1974.
Smith, Barbara Ellen. *Digging Our Own Graves: Coal Mines and the Struggle over Black Lung Disease.* Philadelphia: Temple University Press, 1987.

Statutes Cited

Black Lung Benefits Act of 1972, PL 92-303
Black Lung Benefits Amendments of 1981, PL 97-119
Black Lung Benefits Reform Act of 1977, PL 95-239
Federal Coal Mine Health and Safety Act of 1969, PL 91-173

See also **Federal Coal Mine Health and Safety Act; Miller, Arnold; Miners for Democracy; United Mine Workers of America**

BLACK PANTHER PARTY

The Black Panther Party (BPP), founded by Huey P. Newton and Bobby Seale in Oakland, California, in 1966, was one of the leading organizations of the modern black freedom movement. Newton and Seale met as students at Oakland's Merritt College in September 1962. Their friendship was cemented by their desire to address the racism, police brutality, housing discrimination, and inferior education they'd experienced growing up in working-class Oakland. Critical of their experiences as activists in local black nationalist organizations, Newton and Seale turned to Malcolm X, a vocal critic of nonviolent resistance and one of the most forceful advocates for black self-determination and self-defense, and international revolutionary theorists such as Amilcar Cabral, Kwame Nkrumah, Fidel Castro, Franz Fanon, and Mao Tse-tung for ideological inspiration. On October 15, 1966, they founded the BPP and drafted a mission statement, called the "10-Point Program and Platform," demanding freedom, self-determination, full employment, reparations from the federal government, decent housing, education representative of the black experience, freedom for black prisoners, an end to police brutality, exemption of all black men from military service, and land, bread, housing, education, clothing, justice, and peace. The BPP defined itself as a vanguard organization critical of both class and racial inequities and espoused a revolutionary nationalist ideology that advocated the socialist transformation of the United States.

The BPP's initial activities—patrolling the Oakland police armed with law books, tape recorders, and legally carried weapons, and marching on the

Black Panther Convention, Lincoln Memorial. Library of Congress, Prints & Photographs Division [LC-U9-22860-27].

state legislature to protest the passage of a law banning openly carried weapons—earned it national and international publicity. Within one year of its creation, the BPP had approximately 75 members, an office, a newspaper, and a growing core of supporters. Newton's arrest in October 1967 for killing a police officer further thrust the BPP into the spotlight; "Free Huey" became a rallying cry for supporters who believed that Newton was a political prisoner being persecuted for his beliefs. Although the Free Huey movement broadened the Panthers' base of support to several hundred members, it was the murder of Martin Luther King in 1968 and the murder of the Panthers' first recruit, Bobby Hutton, by local police a few days later that fueled the Panthers' nationwide expansion. By 1969, Panther chapters had formed in dozens of cities around the country, including Los Angeles, Seattle, and Chicago. The Panthers launched

community programs such as free food distribution, sickle-cell anemia testing, free health clinics, and free breakfast for school children to highlight the government's failure to address poverty. By providing free social services for thousands of poor people all around the country, the Panthers hoped to demonstrate the viability of socialist principles.

As the BPP grew in numbers and influence, it became the major target of COINTELPRO, an FBI program to "expose, disrupt, misdirect, discredit, or otherwise neutralize the activities of black nationalist, hate-type organizations and groupings, their leadership, spokesmen, membership, and supporters and to contain their propensity for violence and civil disorder," launched in 1967. The FBI, in concert with local police departments and the CIA, used tactics ranging from wiretaps and false letters to spies and agents provocateurs in an attempt to destroy the BPP.

COINTELPRO created a climate of suspicion and paranoia among BPP members, undermined personal relationships and political alliances, isolated the organization from sources of support, shaped the public perception of the Panthers, and resulted in violence. In one of the most well-known incidents, the FBI and Chicago police killed Panther leaders Fred Hampton and Mark Clark during a raid of Hampton's apartment in 1969. COINTELPRO helped fuel internal debates about the role of armed struggle in the BPP's political program, the centralization of power in the Oakland national headquarters, and the lack of internal democracy. After a public dispute between Newton and Panther leader Eldridge Cleaver in 1971, the BPP splintered under the weight of mass resignations, expulsions, and violent fratricide. The largest group of dissenters formed the Black Liberation Army, an armed underground organization, to carry on their vision of social change.

Although many observers believed that the BPP had died, Oakland leaders sought to restructure the organization by dismantling many remaining chapters around the country and centralizing the BPP's membership base, skills, and resources in Oakland. Under Newton's leadership, they shifted from fighting for the systemic transformation of the U.S. socioeconomic system to seeking reform within that system. The Panthers expanded the range of their community programs and founded the Oakland Community School (OCS), which grew to serve approximately 150 students and earned a nationwide reputation for excellence in community-based education. Tactically, they turned to electoral politics to mobilize and organize the black community and gain a legitimate voice in the local political scene. They marshaled the votes of a multiracial coalition of supporters to become a formidable local political machine that was able to place Panther candidates on school boards, neighborhood councils, and antipoverty boards. In 1972, Elaine Brown ran for a city council seat and Seale ran for mayor on a progressive political platform that emphasized social programs such as housing, preventative medical health care, childcare, educational improvement, and environmental protection. Although both Brown and Seale's candidacies were unsuccessful, Seale garnered over 40% of the vote, forcing a runoff election with the incumbent mayor, and the Panthers successfully registered close to 15,000 new voters. This newly revitalized electorate would be pivotal in the election of Oakland's first black mayor and Panther ally, Lionel Wilson, in 1977. Despite local political visibility, the organization was weakened by its increasingly corrupt leadership strata—Newton, in particular, faced criminal charges ranging from murder to embezzlement in the 1970s—declining membership, and

financial problems. By 1982, the OCS closed its doors and the organization officially came to an end.

In the early 1990s, popular and scholarly interest in the BPP reemerged. Newton's murder by an Oakland drug dealer in 1989 thrust the Panthers into the national spotlight and launched a public dialogue about the legacy of the organization and its relevance to contemporary urban socioeconomic conditions. Former Panthers joined younger activists to create Panther-influenced organizations in communities of color around the nation, such as the Commemoration Committee for the Black Panther Party in Oakland, the New African Vanguard Movement in Los Angeles, and the Black Panther Collective in New York. The Panthers' legacy of working-class progressive political action continues to inform the black freedom movement.

ROBYN CEANNE SPENCER

References and Further Reading

Churchill, Ward, and Jim Vander Wall. *The COINTELPRO Papers: Documents from the FBI's Secret Wars against Domestic Dissent*. Boston: South End Press, 1990.
Cleaver, Kathleen, and George Katsiaficas, eds. *Liberation, Imagination and the Black Panther Party: A New Look at the Panthers and Their Legacy*. New York: Routledge, 2001.
Foner, Philip S., ed. *The Black Panthers Speak: The Manifesto of the Party, the First Complete Documentary Record of the Panthers' Program*. Philadelphia: J. B. Lippincott Company, 1970.
Jeffries, Judson L. *Huey P. Newton: The Radical Theorist*. Jackson: University Press of Mississippi, 2002.
Jones, Charles E., ed. *The Black Panther Party [Reconsidered]*. Baltimore: Black Classic Press, 1998.
Seale, Bobby. *Seize the Time: The Story of the Black Panther Party and Huey Newton*. New York: Random House, 1968

BLACK WORKERS CONGRESS

Formed in 1971, the Black Workers Congress (BWC) was the product of the heightened racial consciousness of black working-class youth who came of age after World War II in northern and western cities and the by-product of the success of the League of Revolutionary Black Workers, which was formed in Detroit in 1969. The new outlook among black youth, in conjunction with the experience of urban uprisings of the late 1960s, the rise of black power, and the increasingly black work force in the automobile industry, raised the question of what role black workers could play at the national level in a revolutionary union movement. When the League of Revolutionary Black Workers (LRBW) addressed that question through its multipronged challenges to racism within the automobile companies and the United Auto Workers (UAW) union, black auto workers responded enthusiastically. The LRBW was credited with significant improvements in the quality of life on the line for black workers. Since the long-term objective of the League was to develop the radical potential of black workers in order to bring about a socialist America, the question of nationalizing the LRBW model rose to the fore, which, in turn, led to a manifesto calling for the formation of a Black Workers Congress.

The BWC's manifesto cited over 30 objectives for the organization, which included gaining more control over production, ending racism, leading the way toward women's liberation, and educating workers about foreign policy issues. Actual construction of BWC units would grow out of alliances already in place around the country. Since the BWC was to be the vehicle for "franchising" the LRBW model, the original plan was that the League would be one of the principal building blocks of the nationwide congress. Instead, the process of trying to create the BWC contributed to the decline of the League.

Although the manifesto was well received at first, tensions within the leadership of the League soon erupted, creating a split in June 1971. General G. Baker Jr. and Chuck Wooten believed more time needed to be spent on the ground in Detroit to nurture continued success within the automobile plants. They were concerned that concentrating the League's efforts on the creation of organizational ties with revolutionaries throughout the country would dilute its resources and threaten its success on the shop floor. A key issue was whether the BWC would be serving black workers or black intellectuals, what became known within the BWC as the struggle between the masses and the cadre.

Internal dissension continued over the issue of the BWC for over a year, ending when Ken Cockrel, Mike Hamlin, and John Watson formally resigned from the LRBW on June 12, 1971. Cockrel, Hamlin, and Watson vowed to build a BWC that was totally independent of the League. Moreover, they hoped the BWC, which had been actively forming units across the nation during this time, would emerge as a mass revolutionary movement in the cities by the end of 1971. Instead, the BWC fell victim to the internal ideological dispute that continued in various forms for the next several years, and the League morphed into the Communist League.

Nevertheless, hopes were high when the first national convention was held in Gary, Indiana, in September 1971 and attended by more than 400 delegates from all regions of the country. The BWC connected the interests of African-Americans to the larger world shaped by the toil of third-world workers and overlapping interests of American capitalism. In a conscious attempt to build a revolutionary movement on a wider base than the League, the BWC tailored its opening address to the concerns of third-world people and the interests of working women. John Watson's keynote address stressed the need to view all workers as brothers and sisters, reminding his audience that the industrial giants—such as General Motors, IBM, and U.S. Steel—gained their power and prominence by exploiting black as well as brown workers. The BWC took great care to appeal to women, committing the congress to the establishment of day care centers and equal pay for equal work; approximately one third of the delegates were women. Although the BWC's goals were lofty, most of its ideas were never put into practice as the organization got bogged down in bureaucratic and strategic questions related to how to proceed.

Under the tutelage of James Forman, an SNCC (Student Nonviolent Coordinating Committee) leader in the early 1960s who by the late 1960s had gained national prestige as a leading black revolutionary theorist and organizer, the BWC was dominated by theory and ideological pronouncements, with little attention given to practice. As a result it never developed a broad mass base, substituted mountains of paper—proposals and manuals—for organization, and even, according to its own accounts, never had more than approximately 500 members. Eventually, Forman's leadership was questioned, and he was attacked from within. Forman was officially expelled from the BWC in April 1973, accused of destroying the League and contributing to weakening the BWC. Mike Hamlin was chairman of the BWC until another split divided the organization in 1975.

BETH TOMPKINS BATES

References and Further Reading

Foner, Philip S., and Ronald L. Lewis, eds. *Black Workers: A Documentary History from Colonial Times to the Present.* Philadelphia: Temple University Press, 1989.

Georgakas, Dan, and Marvin Surkin. *Detroit: I Do Mind Dying.* 2nd ed. Cambridge, MA: South End Press, 1998.

Geschwender, James A. *Class, Race, and Worker Insurgency: The League of Revolutionary Black Workers.* Cambridge: Cambridge University Press, 1977.

See also **League of Revolutionary Black Workers**

BLACKLISTS

Blacklists usually refer to efforts by business owners to prevent the employment of those they deem undesirable, although in some cases the word "blacklist" has been used to refer to unions' refusal to allow their members to work for "unfair" employers. Since at least the late 1800s, blacklisting has served as a tool of management to discipline the work force and to combat union organizing. In consequence, workers and supporters of organized labor have sought laws to forbid the practice.

Origins and Attempts at Anti-Blacklisting Legislation through the Early 1900s

In order to be effective, blacklists require an efficient mechanism for sharing information about the labor force. It comes as no surprise, then, that the Burlington Railroad Company made one of the first systematic efforts in the United States to blacklist employees. With over 20,000 laborers, the company felt the need to make sure that a worker fired for incompetence at one of its divisions could not gain employment at another. From 1877 until 1892, the Burlington maintained a centralized clearinghouse of records that stated the cause for the discharge of each employee. The discharge records made special note of workers whom the business fired for offenses that it considered particularly egregious, such as alcohol abuse or stealing, and placed these employees on a blacklist to militate against their rehiring. Almost 5% of names on the blacklist had been discharged for pro-union activity or strike agitation.

Punishing pro-union workers was, in fact, the best-known, if not most common, use of blacklists, and employers used a variety of means to guard themselves against new hires with ties to organized labor. The most brazen was firing outright workers known to be union members or refusing to rehire union leaders after failed strike attempts. Other approaches were subtler. Some managers required all new employees to sign "iron-clad agreements" or "yellow dog contracts." Under these agreements, which courts usually enforced before 1935, new workers promised not to join unions. Other bosses might devise a system of work tickets, or employment certificates. Under such a system, employers would agree to hire workers only if they possessed a card issued by an employers association, and workers could obtain such cards only by renouncing any plans to join a labor organization.

Union supporters saw blacklists as threats to their right to work and endeavored to pass laws banning the practice. Several states passed laws prohibiting blacklisting. The Illinois legislature, for example, passed the Cole Anti-Boycott Law in 1887 that banned both union boycotts and employer blacklisting, and in 1893 it enacted a statute that outlawed iron-clad agreements. At the national level, opponents of blacklisting tried unsuccessfully in 1897 to secure passage of House Bill 9490, which would have made the practice a violation of the Sherman Anti-Trust Act. A year later, however, they succeeded in passing the Erdman Act, which forbade yellow dog contracts.

Employers defended themselves against such laws by arguing that blacklists were both a necessity and a constitutional right. Many business owners, with the support of such organizations as the National Association of Manufacturers and the various Citizens Alliances across the country, claimed that they were simply protecting their enterprises from radical, potentially violent agitators intent on destroying their property. Management also believed that blacklists were simply a counterpoint to boycotts, or efforts by unionists to dissuade consumers from patronizing businesses deemed unfair to its workers. The Constitution, employers contended, guaranteed their right to hire whomever they pleased.

The courts usually sided with employers' cases designed to test the constitutionality of these laws. In the 1900 case *Gillespie v. People*, the Illinois Supreme Court voided the state's law against iron-clad agreements. Four years later, an Indiana court struck down an anti-blacklisting law. In the 1908 case of *Adair v. United States*, the federal Supreme Court nullified the Erdman Act. In declaring such laws unconstitutional, the courts accepted the argument of managers and business owners that these measures impaired their constitutional right to negotiate the best possible terms when hiring employees.

Anti-Blacklisting Components of the Wagner Act and Landrum-Griffin Act

In the 1930s, opponents of blacklisting had more success in passing legislation to ban the practice under President Franklin D. Roosevelt's New Deal reforms that were enacted to pull the country out of the Great Depression. In 1935, Congress passed the National Labor Relations Act, also known as the Wagner Act. As part of its aim to provide government protection of unions, section 8 of the new law forbade what it called "unfair labor practices" by employers. One of these practices referred to blacklisting, making illegal "discrimination in regard to hire or tenure of employment or any term or condition of employment to encourage or discourage membership in any labor organization." In the landmark 1937 case *National Labor Relations Board v. Jones & Laughlin Steel*

Corp., the United States Supreme Court affirmed the constitutionality of the prohibition against these employer practices.

As the historian Robert Michael Smith has pointed out, some employers tried to get around the Wagner Act's proscriptions by contracting anti-union consulting firms that engaged in tactics reminiscent of blacklisting. One of the largest of such firms was the Labor Relations Associates, founded by Nathan W. Shefferman. The Associates administered employment tests that nominally examined applicants' psychological stability but in practice were designed to screen against union sympathizers. The agency also set up sham grievance committees and employee front groups for the purpose of identifying pro-union workers and exposing them to summary discharge. Section 203 of the Labor Management Reporting and Disclosure Act of 1959, also known as the Landrum-Griffin Act, sought to limit management's ability to use third-party agencies. The law required employers to disclose to the Secretary of Labor any use of funds to engage a consulting firm for the purpose of reporting on employees' union proclivities.

The Wagner Act and Landrum-Griffin Act fared better in the courts than the anti-blacklist legislation earlier in the century. However, their enforcement was often weak or sporadic. The Department of Labor, for example, seldom pressed businesses to observe the reporting requirement concerning labor consulting firms, and employers continued to use them with little fear of punishment.

Political Blacklisting in the Age of McCarthyism

What is known as the age of McCarthyism produced one of the most famous eras of blacklisting. In the late 1940s and 1950s, the commencement of the Cold War, which pitted the United States and the Soviet Union in a struggle for world domination, fueled an anticommunist "red scare" at all levels of government and in the private sector. Wishing to protect the country against what they believed to be the communist threat to national security, Congress, the Federal Bureau of Investigation, various cabinet-level agencies, and various other public and private entities conducted investigations into the loyalty of employees. Investigations often resulted in the summary dismissal of employees deemed a threat to national security because of their alleged political sympathies. Particularly suspect were those individuals who refused to participate in the investigations by asserting their Fifth Amendment right against self-incrimination.

According to the historian Ellen Schrecker, more than 10,000 people lost their jobs as a result of the hysteria, including civil servants, members of left-wing unions, and high school and university teachers.

Some of the most visible victims of McCarthyism were the actors, directors, and screenwriters whom the movie, television, and radio industries blacklisted for their left-wing political views or for declining to name colleagues alleged to have communist sympathies. In 1947, the House Un-American Activities Committee cited 10 members of the movie industry for contempt because they refused to cooperate with a congressional investigation of communists in the movie industry. The Association of Motion Picture Producers fired the "Hollywood 10" promptly, and its members declared that they would refuse to employ any suspected communists. In 1950, a publication entitled *Red Channels* listed actors and screenwriters who had pursued allegedly procommunist activities. For the next decade, those tainted with the blacklist found it difficult or impossible to find work. Many who did find work, like writer Dalton Trumbo, had to use pseudonyms to keep their jobs.

Blacklists during the McCarthy Era differed from anti-union blacklists because the former relied on ascertaining a person's alleged political affiliation. Employers refused to hire suspected communists as much out of fear of public censure as out of concern about labor militancy. Nevertheless, management used the anticommunist hysteria to serve anti-union ends as well. A provision of the Labor Management Relations Act of 1947, also known as the Taft-Hartley Act, removed unions from government protection if their officers refused to take noncommunist oaths. Business owners in some cases could use the refusal of a union's officers to sign such an oath as a reason to decertify it, that is, remove its status as the recognized representative of the workers.

By the 1990s, the anticommunist hysteria had subsided and laws against blacklisting against union supporters had survived. But enforcement of these laws remained difficult because employers continued to rely on labor consultants and in most states were not legally obligated to show cause when they discharged employees. At the same time, these laws did compel management to be at least circumspect if it decided to take a job applicant's views on labor organizations into consideration.

DANIEL HARPER

References and Further Reading

Beckner, Earl R. *A History of Labor Legislation in Illinois.* Chicago: University of Chicago Press, 1929.
Black, Paul V. "Experiment in Bureaucratic Centralization: Employee Blacklisting on the Burlington Railroad,

1877–1892." *The Business History Review* 51, no. 4 (Winter 1977): 444–459.

Forbath, William E. *Law and the Shaping of the American Labor Movement.* Cambridge, MA: Harvard University Press, 1991.

Schrecker, Ellen. *The Age of McCarthyism: A Brief History with Documents.* 2nd edition. New York: Bedford/St. Martins, 2002.

Smith, Robert Michael. *From Blackjacks to Briefcases: A History of Commercialized Strikebreaking and Union-busting in the United States.* Athens: Ohio University Press, 2003.

Cases and Statutes Cited

Adair v. United States, 208 U.S. 161 (1908)
Gillespie v. People, 188 Ill. 176 (1900)
National Labor Relations Board v. Jones & Laughlin Steel Co., 301 U. S. 1 (1937)
Wabash Railroad Co. v. Young, 162 Ind. 102 (1904)
Erdman Act, Act of June 1, 1898, 30 Stat. 424
Labor Management Relations Act (also known as the Taft-Hartley Act), Act of June 23, 1947, 61 Stat. 136
Labor Management Reporting and Disclosure Act (also known as the Landrum-Griffin Act), Act of September 14, 1959, 73 Stat. 519
National Labor Relations Act (also known as the Wagner Act), Act of July 5, 1935, 49 Stat. 449

*See also **Adair v. United States** (1908); At-Will Employment; Boycotts; Erdman Act; Landrum-Griffin Act (1959); Law and Labor; **National Labor Relations Board v. Jones-Laughlin Steel Corporation** (1937); Taft-Hartley Act*

BLOOR, ELLA REEVE (JULY 8, 1862–AUGUST 10, 1951)
American Communist Party

Ella Reeve Bloor, lifelong labor leader, organizer, and agitator, is typically remembered as the most prominent woman leader of the American Communist Party during the 1930s and 1940s. Bloor's political career, however, traversed a broad spectrum of the American Left; beginning in the 1890s, Bloor spent over 50 years participating in the temperance, women's suffrage, socialist, antiwar, and communist movements.

Bloor was born in 1862 to a middle-class family in Staten Island, New York. Her parents, Charles Reeve and Harriet Amanda Disbrow, raised her along with 11 siblings in a relatively affluent neighborhood in New Jersey. Charles Reeve ran his own drugstore in Bridgeton, New Jersey, and when Harriet died in 1879, the children and household were put under Ella's charge. After marrying and having children of her own, Bloor found her domestic life lackluster and she began actively campaigning for both the temperance and suffrage movements.

A combination of influences initiated Bloor's urge to become politically active. Her great uncle Dan Ware, a freethinker and abolitionist, introduced her to the works of philosophers and scientists early on. This led her to pursue a degree from the University of Pennsylvania, where Bloor was introduced to the works of Marx and Engels. During this time period she learned firsthand of the struggles of women weavers in Philadelphia and joined the Workers Textile Union in their support. From this time forward, Bloor maintained active involvement in reform movements.

Bloor belonged to Eugene Debs's Social Democracy of America and Daniel De Leon's Socialist Labor Party, before finding political accord with the Socialist Party in 1902. During her 16-year tenure with the Socialist Party, Bloor served as a party state organizer in Delaware, Connecticut, Ohio, and New York. Over time she worked on strike support, child labor investigations, raising money for worker relief, recruitment efforts, lecturing, and writing for the Socialist press. In 1906, Bloor and fellow Socialist party member Richard Bloor traveled to Chicago to investigate labor conditions in the meatpacking industry for Upton Sinclair. Although she never married Bloor, Ella took his name as her own and was known as Ella Reeve Bloor from that time forward.

From the earliest days of her reform efforts, Bloor showed a commitment to women, both those in the paid and unpaid labor forces. This commitment informed her organizing strategies and approach throughout her political career. As an advocate for women's suffrage, Bloor sought to integrate her advocacy of women with her Socialist Party work. In 1910, Bloor introduced an amendment to the Socialist Party Congress that would commit the party to continued cooperation with the woman's suffrage movement. Bloor also worked for both the National American Woman Suffrage Association and the National Woman's Party in Connecticut.

During the 1910s, Bloor expanded her agenda. She came to be known as "Mother Bloor," a name she retained for the remainder of her political career. Bloor constantly traveled the country to support and organize striking workers. She struggled alongside textile workers, steel workers, and miners. In 1911, she joined striking miners in West Virginia. Two years later, Bloor visited Calumet, Michigan, to aid the area's striking copper miners. She worked closely with the women's auxiliaries while in Calumet. In 1914, she aligned with the United Mine Workers of America in Ludlow, Colorado, who were striking against Rockefeller's Colorado Fuel and Iron Company mines. This was one of many occasions where Bloor confronted the darker sides of the labor struggle. The Colorado state militia made a surprise attack on the strikers the night of April 20, 1914, murdering miners and their families. This incident spoke to Bloor's conviction that labor and family issues should not be separated. Over the next 40 years, she fought to reconcile unionism with the family and community.

With the onset of World War I, Bloor began agitating against the war. She was actively involved in antiwar groups, including the People's Council of America for Democracy and Peace and the Liberty Defense Union. She also helped to organize the Workers' Defense Union, precursor to the International Labor Defense. As the war continued, Bloor became increasingly disappointed with the Socialist Party's lack of a firm antiwar stance. In 1919, she separated from the party and, enthralled with the Bolshevik message, Bloor became a founding member of the American Communist Party.

Bloor spent the next 23 years of her life as a national organizer and agitator for the Communist Party. By the 1930s, she was a national spokeswoman for the party and a contributor to the Communist journal *Working Woman*. She advocated for the organization and political education of women as well as the full integration of women into all aspects of party life. Regarding the centrality of women as a necessity for a strong labor movement, Bloor rejected the masculinization of the Communist Party and promoted women workers as symbols for the movement. She stood as a key figure in the transformation of Communist Party politics during the 1930s to a grassroots community-based approach.

During the early 1930s, Bloor began actively organizing for the United Farmers' League. She helped to organize the First Farmers' National Conference in Washington, D.C., in 1932. Throughout the 1930s she continued to travel nationally, organizing farmers in Iowa, Montana, Nebraska, and the Dakotas.

Bloor maintained her militant antiwar stance during the interwar period. She traveled to Paris in 1934 as a delegate to the Women's International Congress Against War and Fascism. Here she was elected to serve on the World Committee Against War and Fascism. During the late 1930s, as a member of the National Executive Committee of the American League Against War and Fascism, she worked to fuse the labor and peace movements.

By the late 1930s, Bloor was recognized as the most prominent woman leader and public symbol of the American Communist Party. Her presence shaped grassroots campaigns as she organized from state to state and agitated with miners, farmers, steel workers, machinists, and needle trade workers. In Ann Barton's 1937 tribute to Mother Bloor, fellow Communist Party member Elizabeth Gurley Flynn wrote of her, "We love and honor this extraordinary American woman as a symbol of the militant American farmer and working class, of the forward sweep of women in the class struggle and in our Party, as an example to young and old of what an American Bolshevik should be." Jailed over 30 times as a result of her various reform movement activities and with a lifetime of commitment to reform movements, Ella Reeve Bloor made significant contributions to the strategies and successes of the American Left.

CATHERINE O. JACQUET

References and Further Reading

Barton, Ann. *Mother Bloor: The Spirit of 76.* New York: Workers Library Publishers, 1937.

Bloor, Ella Reeve. "The Higher Ideals of Trade Unionism." *Cloth, Hat, Cap, and Millinery Workers Journal* 1 (Oct.–Nov. 1916): 15–16.

———. "Michigan Strike Letter." *Miners Magazine* 15 (March 1914): 10.

———. *We Are Many.* New York: International Publishers Co., 1940.

———. "The Woman Question in the Hat Trade." *Cloth, Hat, Cap, and Millinery Workers Journal* 1 (September 1916): 8–9.

Brown, Kathleen A. "The 'Savagely Fathered and Un-Mothered World' of the Communist Party, U.S.A.: Feminism, Maternalism, and 'Mother Bloor.'" *Feminist Studies* 25, no. 3 (Fall 1999): 537–571.

Flynn, Elizabeth Gurley. *Daughters of America: Ella Reeve Bloor and Anita Whitney.* New York: Worker's Library, 1942.

Sternsher, Bernard, and Judith Sealander, eds. *Women of Valor: The Struggle against the Great Depression as Told in Their Own Life Stories.* Chicago: Ivan R. Dee, Inc., 1990.

Tode, Charlotte. "Mother Bloor: A Fighter of the Working Class for Many Years." *Working Woman* (July 1931).

See also **International Labor Defense**

BOGALUSA LABOR CONFLICT OF 1919

The Bogalusa, Louisiana, labor conflict of 1919 produced the most dramatic display of interracial labor solidarity in the Deep South in the first half of the twentieth century. The Great Southern Lumber (GSL) Company's systematic use of violence to disrupt the organizing of loggers and sawmill workers caused the Louisiana State Federation of Labor at the time to denounce its anti-union campaign as among the most brutal in American history. The United Brotherhood of Carpenters and Joiners (UBCJ) and the International Brotherhood of Timber Workers (IBTW), both American Federation of Labor (AFL) affiliates, welcomed Bogalusa's blacks into their ranks early in the organizing drive because they feared the company could mobilize them as strikebreakers. Blacks made up a significant proportion of the lumber industry's labor force.

Bogalusa's white and black workers drew much closer together as the organizing campaign proceeded, in part because company gunmen and pro-employer vigilantes violently assaulted unionists of both races. In addition, several factors peculiar to the lumber industry made white loggers and sawmill workers more receptive to including blacks in their unions. The dangerous and physically demanding nature of work in the forests and sawmills caused whites and blacks to respect each other's courage, strength, and endurance, qualities they considered central in defining masculinity. In the lumber industry, where tasks were relatively homogeneous, blacks and whites often worked closely together. Blacks were therefore less likely to be stigmatized in the least desirable jobs.

GSL's violent campaign of intimidation against the union effort revealed the limits of company paternalism. Entrepreneurs from Buffalo, New York, had established Bogalusa as a model town in 1906, intended as an alternative to the dilapidated shack settlements surrounding most southern lumber mills. GSL touted Bogalusa as a "New South City of Destiny" centered around the world's largest lumber mill. The company deliberately dispersed housing to avoid congestion and boasted that it provided modern recreational facilities and schools for each race. But it also tightly controlled town government and maintained its own heavily armed police force. While fiercely anti-union, GSL denounced the organizing of blacks in particularly venomous terms, charging that the unions threatened the racial hierarchy on which social order depended.

The unions never explicitly challenged Louisiana's Jim Crow system, organizing racially separate locals. Yet in the process of organizing, black and white lumber workers mixed together at meetings, causing the company to accuse the unions of showing contempt for southern custom by failing to properly segregate the races.

The enthusiasm for the union campaign in Bogalusa's black community reflected an increasing African-American determination to confront discrimination in the immediate postwar period. This was illustrated by the assertiveness of returning black World War veterans and the appearance of militant publications challenging Jim Crow, like A. Philip Randolph's *The Messenger*, developments that alarmed white supremacists.

Aware of the threat company gunmen posed to pro-union African-Americans, in June 1919 white lumber workers, in an action probably unprecedented in the Deep South, marched into Bogalusa's black section openly displaying guns, to protect the black workers' union meeting. The company waged a persistent terror campaign against the unions through the fall, as its gunmen beat and arrested many of their white and black supporters.

GSL sought to delegitimate the UBCJ-IBTW campaign by comparing its organizers to Reconstruction "carpetbaggers," suggesting that unionism was alien to the South and that violence was justified in combating it. Ironically, GSL was owned and largely managed by northern transplants, while southerners directed the union drive. With GSL's assistance, merchants and professional men in Bogalusa established the Self-Preservation and Loyalty League (SPLL), modeled on the Reconstruction Ku Klux Klan. Its purpose was to intimidate unionists, whom it accused of championing "social equality." By including the word "Loyalty" in its name, the SPLL also exploited the postwar fear of Bolshevism to portray the union as subversive.

In October–November 1919, GSL prepared to totally eliminate unionism in Bogalusa by discharging union activists of both races and evicting them from company housing, and escalated its violence. A mob of company gunmen and SPLL members fired into the home of Sol Dacus, leader of Bogalusa's African-American union of sawmill workers and loggers, nearly hitting his wife and two children. Fearing lynching, Dacus fled into a swamp as the mob ransacked his house.

The next day Dacus met two white unionists, J. P. Bouchillon and Stanley O'Rourke, who volunteered to escort him to union headquarters in Bogalusa. The white men carried shotguns, and proceeding down Bogalusa's main avenue, they announced that they would protect Dacus. Several white Bogalusans summoned city authorities, who had arrest warrants issued, charging the three union men with disturbing the peace. To carry out the arrests, the authorities assembled a posse of company gunmen and SPLL members, which surrounded union headquarters, heavily outnumbering the men inside.

Accounts of who fired first conflict, but within minutes the posse had shot dead Lem Williams, president of Bogalusa's Central Trades and Labor Council; Bouchillon; and another white union carpenter, Thomas Gaines; and mortally wounded O'Rourke. However, Dacus, the posse's main target, escaped once again. One SPLL member was wounded.

The killings of the four white union men and the near-lynching of Dacus put a permanent end to the union campaign in Bogalusa. Workers were so inti-midated they would not talk to newspaper reporters.

Backed by the Louisiana State Federation of Labor, Dacus sued GSL for damages stemming from loss of all his property in the mob attack on his home. Lena Williams, Lem Williams's widow, in a striking display of interracial solidarity, testified for Dacus, claiming that the mob had intended to murder him. But a New Orleans jury ruled in the company's favor.

A suit that Lena Williams filed against GSL, charg-ing it had had her husband murdered, reached the U.S. Supreme Court, which unanimously ruled against her in 1928. It declared that Bouchillon and O'Rourke had committed a "breach of the peace" because they intended to prevent Dacus's arrest by force. At its 2005 national convention, the UBCJ rejected a motion to build a memorial to the slain UBCJ members Williams, Bouchillon, O'Rourke, and Gaines.

STEPHEN H. NORWOOD

References and Further Reading

Norwood, Stephen H. "Bogalusa Burning: The War against Biracial Unionism in the Deep South, 1919." *Journal of Southern History* 63, no. 3(1997): 591–628.

BORDERS: MEXICO/U.S.

The U.S.-Mexico border runs for more than two thousand miles from the twin cities of Brownsville, Texas, and Matamoros, Tamaulipas, to the twin cities of San Diego, California, and Tijuana, Baja Califor-nia Norte. The international boundary runs through four states of the United States (Texas, New Mexico, Arizona, and California) and six Mexican states (Tamaulipas, Nuevo Leon, Coahuila, Chihuahua, Sonora, and Baja California Norte). While the loca-tion of the border dividing these two nations has not changed location since 1853, this region has under-gone severe upheaval and change from its earliest European settlement to the present day.

The border region has been sparsely populated for most of its history, and has in fact only been a border region since the wars of 1836 and 1846–1848 sepa-rated the present-day U.S. Southwest from Mexico. Prior to Spanish colonization of Mexico and the Southwest, this region was populated by Native Americans, who were then displaced by small groups of settlers sent to the frontier region by the Spanish. By the time of Mexico's independence from Spain in 1821, the only large settlement concentration in the present-day border region was in the mountains of northern New Mexico. Northern Mexico, Texas, and California remained largely empty.

This began to change shortly after Mexico's inde-pendence, when settlers from the United States began to flow into Texas. By the 1830s the Anglo settlers greatly outnumbered Mexicans in Texas, alarming the far-away government in Mexico City, which hoped to use Texas as a buffer zone against encroachments from the United States, not as its leading edge. The independence of Texas was achieved in 1836 through a combination of a liberal revolt against the conser-vative government of Santa Anna, a slaveholders' uprising against abolition, and a conspiracy by Anglo landowners to bring Texas into the United States. Texas independence was followed 10 years later by the U.S. Army's invasion of Mexico and eventual defeat of the Mexican military in 1848. The resultant Treaty of Guadalupe-Hidalgo gave the present-day Southwest to the United States and created the U.S.-Mexico border. The Gadsden Pur-chase of 1853, acquired in order to build a rail link to the West Coast, produced the present shape of the border.

The Early Development of the Border: 1848–1910

From its first days as an international boundary, the border region behaved more as a unified whole than a divided frontier. Mexicans and Americans crossed the boundary line freely, as commerce and culture ig-nored the solely legalistic distinction of an interna-tional boundary. In fact, for much of the nineteenth century neither Mexico nor the United States was able to integrate the U.S.-Mexico border region into the larger national polity in any but the most cursory ways because it was so far distant from the seats of national power. Lacking the consolidation of central-ized power from Mexico City and Washington, D.C., the border region evolved differently from the rest of each respective nation, remaining economically, cul-turally, and politically peripheral.

Despite this cross-border cultural unity, the border region was not peaceful or particularly stable during the second half of the nineteenth century. The most important conflicts that took place in the border re-gion in the years after the U.S.-Mexico War involved landholding. According to the Treaty of Guadalupe-Hidalgo, all Mexican land titles would be honored by the United States, but such was not the case. Many factors combined to create this situation, from unclear Mexican titles and land grants to con-flicting national and state regulations regarding land ownership, but in the end the Mexican landholders, both individual landowners and communal village holdings, lost most of their property to a combination of long-lasting litigation, rising property values, and outright thievery by Anglo newcomers. The federal government did little to stop the dispossession of Mexican landholders, especially after the California Gold Rush and the development of railroad networks into the West sent real estate values skyrocketing.

Still, the border region continued to languish under the benign neglect of each country into the 1870s. This disregard was especially apparent during the 1860s, when the U.S. Civil War and the French Intervention in Mexico kept each nation from integrating the border region more fully into its centralized state. Things began to change in the following decade when Reconstruction in the United States and the rise of Porfirio Diaz in Mexico brought strong centralist tendencies to both national governments. Massive changes in the border region followed over the next few decades as technological and economic advancement began to push these areas out of their peripheral status. Most important was the entry of railroads into both the U.S. Southwest and Northern Mexico by the 1880s. This allowed the traditional basic extractive economy of the border region to diversify and expand, as transportation costs fell and new markets opened up. On both sides of the boundary, mining, commercial agriculture (especially cotton), and livestock increased in importance. This economic growth helped bring both investment money and workers into the area, creating all at once a more dynamic but also more dependent border region, which was now reliant on centralized governmental structures.

Economic growth was far from painless, however. Political consolidation and economic centralization created a new elite at the top of border society (such as the Terrazas-Creel family in Chihuahua and the King-Kleberg clan in Texas), but it also bred anger among many borderlanders. While many gained from the changes occurring in the Southwest and northern Mexico, there were many others who fought to keep these changes from destroying their way of life. In several instances this led to outright rebellion. The *Gorras Blancas* in New Mexico; the Juan Cortina, Catarino Garza, and Plan de San Diego rebellions in Texas; the Tomochic rebellion in Chihuahua; and the Cananea labor rebellion in Sonora are just a few of the bloody rebellions that convulsed the border region in the last decades of the nineteenth century and early years of the twentieth century. Indeed, the border region would play a primary role in the next major turning point in Mexican and U.S. history: the Mexican Revolution.

The Mexican Revolution and the Further Evolution of the Border: 1910–1940

The border region had long served as a refuge for political dissidents from both nations. In the early years of the twentieth century, Mexican dissidents, forced to leave the increasingly repressive Mexico of Porfirio Diaz, settled in the U.S. Southwest in large numbers while working to undermine the decades-long dictatorship in their homeland. San Antonio, Texas, and Los Angeles, California, became the headquarters for dissidents such as Francisco Madero and Ricardo Flores Magon, who would play major roles in the coming revolution. In addition, many workers in the North traveled to the United States regularly to work, giving them firsthand knowledge of the nature of change occurring on both sides of the border. These transnational workers were also the ones with the greatest consciousness of the continued dispossession that accompanied capital expansion and political centralization. In fact, much of the early fighting that drove Diaz from power in 1911 began in the northern Mexican border region. Thus, while much of the North had benefited from the economic modernization and forced centralization of the Diaz years, it was northerners who began the fight against the Diaz dictatorship.

The years 1910–1930 witnessed a fierce civil war within Mexico, which quieted down after 1920 but continued to simmer for another decade as a series of regional rebellions threatened the fragile postrevolutionary peace. Large portions of northern Mexico were destroyed during the intense fighting, forcing hundreds of thousands to cross the border into the southwestern United States in the first two decades of military chaos. Thus, a huge population of largely working-class Mexicans entered the U.S. border region in the decades after 1910. This demographic change caused by the Mexican Revolution would have consequences for the United States that were every bit as important as for Mexico. The border states, especially Texas and California, now had the labor supply necessary to cut costs and compete for ever larger markets for their products. Irrigation increased as capitalist agriculture spread into regions where ranching and other activities had previously been dominant. Thus, the U.S. Southwest capitalized on the devastation of Mexico's North by developing on the backs of these new Mexican emigrants. Combined with the economic boom of the World War I years in the United States, the Southwest grew rapidly while northern Mexico continued to languish through war and uneasy peace.

The period from the outbreak of the Mexican Revolution to the outbreak of World War II also saw the first systematic codification of U.S. immigration laws. The first U.S. border posts were created in 1891, but only six officials staffed these outposts by the turn of the century. Beginning in 1917 and continuing in 1921 and 1924, the federal government put restrictions on who could enter the United States, though each time legislation was passed, Mexicans were exempted from the new quota systems under pressure from agricultural interests which opposed any legislation that reduced the flow of Mexicans into the United States. Mexicans were now expected to pass through an inspection station on the border, but otherwise they were able to pass freely across the border. A Border Patrol was formed in 1924, but it aimed primarily to make sure that Chinese and European immigrants, excluded by restrictive immigration legislation, did not use Mexico as a "back door" into the United States. It was not until 1965 that immigration quotas were applied to Mexicans. Still, the pressures exerted by the economic collapse and social dislocation of the Great Depression led to the massive forced repatriation of over a million Mexicans during the 1930s. As with any boom economy, the economic collapse of the 1930s hit the U.S. Southwest especially hard. The disintegration of migrant labor streams that employed hundreds of thousands of Mexicans and Mexican-Americans, combined with the fears of repatriation, made the Depression years extremely difficult for Latinos in the Southwest.

World War II and State-Sponsored Immigration

The outbreak of World War II began a new era in the history of the U.S.-Mexico border. With the economic collapse of the 1930s gone and the end of the forced repatriation of Mexicans, a new wave of immigrants crossed the border into the United States seeking employment in the rapidly growing war economy. Additionally, with large numbers of American laborers entering the armed forces, many employers complained that they faced a labor shortage. Responding to the anguished cries of agricultural interests, the U.S. government set out to make an agreement with the Mexican government to import workers through the official sponsorship of the two nations. Under this plan, known as the Bracero Program, hundreds of thousands of Mexican workers came to the United States under the nominal protection of the federal government during the war. Hoping to protect its citizens, the Mexican government was able to extract guarantees of safe passage and good treatment for the braceros. While the official prohibition of Texas was maintained

throughout the war, illegal immigration flourished along the Texas-Mexico border.

The Bracero Program did not end in 1945, however. Instead, agricultural interests in the Southwest and Midwest were able to pressure the government to continue extending the program until it was finally killed in 1964. The continued extension of the program required consent from Mexico, but in many instances the Mexican government was coerced into continuing the Bracero Program. The primary example of this was the massive forced repatriation drive launched in 1953 and 1954 under the name "Operation Wetback." While negotiators from the United States and Mexico stalemated in their attempts to extend the program, the U.S. government used the Immigration and Naturalization Service (INS) to force Mexico's hand. With millions of Mexicans repatriated to Mexico, remittance payments to Mexico would cease and social problems were sure to result from the reintroduction of such a large population. The only way to keep this from happening was to extend the Bracero Program according to the terms dictated by the United States.

World War II and the Cold War years also witnessed a dramatic increase in federal spending along the border. Texas and California were flooded with billions of dollars in defense spending. This increased expenditure allowed the U.S. border states to move beyond their reliance on primary-sector economic activity and into more diversified industrial and commercial ventures. The same occurred in northern Mexico, as the Mexican government began to promote manufacturing in the border region, primarily in the maquilas, which were supposed to substitute Mexican manufactured goods for imports as well as boost export revenues. One example of this development was the industrial and commercial complex that grew between San Antonio, Texas, and Monterrey, Nuevo Leon. Monterrey developed into a manufacturing center, while San Antonio became the distribution center for Mexican products entering the United States. Thus, the changes of World War II and the Cold War extended to both sides of the border.

The Modern Border: 1965 to Today

The exclusion of Mexico from immigration quota systems ended in 1965 with the passage of the Immigration and Nationality Act. This law limited the number of legal immigrants from all Western Hemisphere nations to 170,000 a year. Yet large numbers of immigrants continued to flow across the border in spite of the new regulations. It is impossible to say how many illegal immigrants crossed the border in the year after 1965, but the number of apprehensions of illegal immigrants in the United States, the vast majority of whom came across the U.S.-Mexico border, was continually higher than the number of legally admitted immigrants. At the very least there were hundreds of thousands of illegal crossings each year, with many repeat crossings. Additionally, as the nations of Central America were caught up in a series of bloody civil wars from the late 1950s until the late 1980s, many began to escape through Mexico and across the border into the United States. This additional immigrant source served to heighten tensions along the U.S.-Mexico border as the INS and the U.S. military scrambled to slow down illegal immigration at the same time that public fears of a drug epidemic in the United States enflamed the border region. These same concerns and fears would continue to plague the border region into the 21st century.

The years after the 1960s also saw the explosive growth of Mexican maquila production along the border, especially after the passage of the North American Free Trade Agreement in 1994. In the late twentieth century and early 21st century, these factories were primarily foreign-owned and received massive tax breaks from the Mexican government. When they first appeared, it was hoped that they would create related economic linkages, meaning that they would spawn new Mexican-owned companies that would provide supplies and services for the maquilas. For the most part, however, these linkages and new companies were not created. Instead, the maquilas remained largely detached from the larger Mexican economy, sending their products to foreign markets and their profits to foreign owners.

At the beginning of the 21st century, as it always has, the U.S.-Mexico border served to both unite and divide the two countries. While it divided the border region into two different legal states, the international boundary also united the border region into one cultural space united by migration and commerce. Further, with advances in transportation and communication, the border continued to expand further into both the United States and Mexico as people and products circulated between the two nations.

JOHN WEBER

References and Further Reading

Acuna, Rodolfo. *Occupied America: A History of Chicanos.* 3rd ed. New York: Harper Collins, 1988.

Hart, John Mason, ed. *Border Crossings: Mexican and Mexican-American Workers.* Wilmington, DE: Scholarly Resources, 1998.

Lorey, David E. *The U.S.-Mexican Border in the Twentieth Century.* Wilmington, DE: Scholarly Resources, 1999.

Martinez, Oscar J. *Troublesome Border.* Tucson: University of Arizona Press, 1988.

McWilliams, Carey. *North from Mexico: The Spanish-Speaking People of the United States.* New York: Praeger, 1990 [1948].

Miller, Tom. *On the Border: Portraits of America's Southwestern Frontier.* Tucson: University of Arizona Press, 1981.

Mora-Torres, Juan. *The Making of the Mexican Border: The State, Capitalism, and Society in Nuevo Leon, 1848–1910.* Austin: University of Texas Press, 2001.

Rouse, Roger. "Mexican Migration and the Social Space of Postmodernism." *Diaspora* 1:1 (1991): 8–23.

Ruiz, Ramon Eduardo. *On the Rim of Mexico: Encounters of the Rich and Poor.* Boulder, CO: Westview, 2000.

Vanderwood, Paul. *The Power of God against the Guns of Government: Religious Upheaval in Mexico at the Turn of the Nineteenth Century.* Stanford, CA: Stanford University Press, 1998.

Weber, Devra. *Dark Sweat, White Gold: California Farm Workers, Cotton, and the New Deal.* Berkeley: University of California Press, 1994.

Young, Elliot. *Catarino Garza's Revolution on the Texas-Mexico Border.* Durham, NC: Duke University Press, 2004.

See also **Alien Contract Labor Law; Bisbee Deportation/Copper Strike (1917); California; Cannery and Agricultural Workers Industrial Union; Capital Flight; Central Americans; Chavez, César Estrada; Corona, Burt; Delano Grape Strike (1965–1970); Globalization; Gold Rush; Great Depression: 1930s; Guatemalans; H-2 Program; Huerta, Dolores C.; Immigration and Nationality Act of 1965; Immigration Restriction; McCarran-Walter Act (1952); Mexican and Mexican-American Workers; Migrant Farmworkers; North American Free Trade Agreement; Pueblo Revolt (1680); San Joaquin Valley Cotton Strike (1933); Southwest; United Cannery, Agricultural, Packing, and Allied Workers of America; United Farm Workers of America; World War I; Zoot Suit Riots**

BOYCOTTS

A boycott is a refusal to conduct business—whether buy, sell, or trade—with a particular person or company believed to be engaged in unfair practices. Sometimes a boycott is not necessarily meant to cause economic damage. Boycotts could also involve the refusal to promote a business, such as not watching a particular news program because the television station advocated a controversial view or did not hire enough reporters of a certain gender or racial/ethnic group. Therefore, a boycott may be conducted as a way to cause embarrassment to a person or company by drawing attention to alleged bad practices.

For organized labor, a boycott is a powerful weapon against an employer thought to be unfair toward its workers. There are both *primary* and *secondary* boycotts. In primary boycotts, the actions are those described above; that is, refusing to conduct business with a specific person or company. In secondary boycotts, the economic pressure is put upon those who conduct business with the individual or company being complained about.

The word "boycott" comes from Ireland. Captain Charles Cunningham Boycott was an agent of Lord Erne, managing the lands for the absentee British landlord. Boycott refused a request by the tenants for a rent reduction. In their protest, the tenants refused to perform any work, especially harvesting, and also used the power of word of mouth to berate and tarnish Boycott's image throughout the community. Faced with no workers, and in need of some protection, Boycott received help when volunteers from Irish Unionists and the British army stepped in. Later on, the Irish Land League, among others, then used the term around the year 1880 to signify a refusal to patronize an enemy.

In the United States, boycotting itself was not an established word at first, but the practice was well known. One of the first known boycotts in the United States came in 1830. The National Negro Convention, a group dedicated to improving the condition of blacks, including a mass migration to Canada, advocated a boycott of slave-made products as a way to protest the abomination of slavery by cutting into any potential profits made by such labor. But as a viable economic weapon, the use of the boycott would need a few more years to develop.

For the U.S. labor movement, the use of the boycott became a major form of protest in the post-Civil War era as the movement gained momentum. Many believed that boycotting was a more sensible alternative to striking. One reasoning for this belief is that in a strike the workers suffered a usually temporary loss of wages (although in some instances the striking workers were never rehired, forcing them to try to find new employment). Through a boycott, only the employer would suffer monetary loss, although, as sometimes happens with a strike, a big enough loss of income could prompt an employer to close its doors, thus throwing all of its employees out of work.

With the formation of the Knights of Labor (KOL), the use of boycotts was considered to be a much more powerful tool than that of a strike. As a way to settle grievances, or gain bargaining power, the KOL believed the boycott to be a much more efficient, and peaceful, form of protest. Not only did the KOL call for numerous boycotts, but the actions were publicized. However, while there were a few successes in using this method, by and large the potential of using a boycott was never realized by the KOL.

The boycott became quite well known during the infamous Pullman Strike of 1894. In protesting wage cuts instituted by the Pullman Company against its workers, the American Railway Union (ARU), which was under the direction of Eugene V. Debs, called for a boycott of Pullman railroad cars to accompany the strike. Railroad workers across the country heeded the call for this secondary boycott, and within two weeks the Middle Western railroad system was shut down as workers refused to handle any Pullman cars.

The Pullman Company turned to President Grover Cleveland for assistance. Under the guise of protecting the mails, Cleveland sent in federal troops to both maintain order and protect the mails and interstate commerce. This action was taken over the protest of Illinois Governor John Peter Altgeld, and also since the Chicago police, who sympathized with the strikers, would not take action. Upon the arrival of troops, violence broke out, complete with gunfire and the burning of railroad cars. A federal court issued an injunction forbidding any interference with the mails or commerce, an action that Debs and the ARU ignored. Debs was jailed for contempt of court, and the strike eventually failed.

As a means of protest, the boycott is a powerful, yet nonviolent, means of protest. Yet, many states cracked down on its use. Organized labor conducted numerous boycotts during the last two decades of the nineteenth century. Many of these were protests against the use of products made by prison labor. As with curbing strikes, employers looked for ways to battle the use of the boycott. In Illinois, for example, the passage of the Cole Anti-Boycott law in 1887 sought to curb its use. According to this law, "if two or more persons conspired together or the officers or executive committee of any society or organization uttered or issued any circular or edict instructing its members to institute a boycott or blacklist, they shall be deemed guilty of a conspiracy." A fine of up to two thousand dollars and a possible prison sentence of up to five years were the penalties assigned. The one interesting aspect of this law was that employers were banned from creating a blacklist, a practice against which labor frequently fought. The Cole Anti-Boycott law survived well into the twentieth century, although subsequent amendments and court decisions altered its impact.

The idea of conducting boycotts, whether direct or secondary, became a legal question for a number of years. In a statement to Congress in 1908, Henry Kraus wrote, "Now, what do workmen do when they boycott? They tell their friends, they tell their neighbors, they tell their fellow citizens of the hard or degrading terms imposed by the boycotted person or firm; and they ask these friends, neighbors, and fellow citizens, to assist in ameliorating these hard or degrading terms of employment imposed by the boycotted persons."

The federal government would become involved in the boycott issue, especially during the twentieth century. In 1890, Congress passed the Sherman Antitrust Act, a law designed to curb corrupt business practices, especially those involved in the restraint of trade. While meant to restrict the owners of industry, the law was soon turned around and used against organized labor. One of the first instances of the Sherman Act being used as such was in the 1909 U.S. Supreme Court decision in *Loewe v. Lawlor*, also known as the *Danbury Hatters* case. This case involved the actions of the United Hatters of North America, which was failing in its attempt to organize the workers of D. E. Loewe in Danbury, Connecticut. The union called for a nationwide boycott of the company's products. In response, the company brought suit against the union under the Sherman Act, arguing that the boycott was in restraint of trade. The Supreme Court agreed with the company, ruled that the union was subject to an injunction, and assessed it treble damages.

The Sherman Act was not intended to be used against organized labor. Keeping this in mind, Congress passed the 1914 Clayton Antitrust Act, called the "Magna Carta of Labor." This act sought to protect many of the rights to which labor felt it was due and that were supposedly protected under the Sherman Act. Among these rights were the strike, boycott, and peaceful picketing. Injunctions were not to be issued against labor for participating in these activities, unless there would be irreparable harm to property.

The U.S. Supreme Court weighed in on the boycott issue with the 1921 decision *Duplex Printing Press v. Deering*. The case involved a secondary boycott, which was being defined as "economic pressure by a union upon an employer with whom the union has no dispute." In order to achieve this, the union would apply the boycott against one company as a way to dissuade it from doing business with the company with whom it had the dispute.

The *Duplex* case involved the International Association of Machinists, an affiliate of the American Federation of Labor (AFL). The union was trying to organize workers at the Duplex Printing Press Company, located in Battle Creek, Michigan. The company had no intentions of allowing the unions in. Furthermore, the standards used by the company were considerably lower than those the union negotiated with other businesses. To the union, this gave Duplex an unfair economic advantage and could also affect the contracts signed with the unionized companies. With New York being Duplex's best market, the union sought to stop the sales in that region. In addition to the boycott, the union also employed strikes, and even threats, toward those transporting Duplex machines.

When the Supreme Court heard the case, it ruled on behalf of the company. The Court held that the secondary boycott was enjoinable under the Clayton Act, citing the union was acting within the term "restraint of trade." To the Court, the union was not acting within its lawful and legitimate purpose. Labor organizations across the country protested the Court's decision and then turned to their own state legislatures to pass acts that would hopefully further protect labor's right to use activities such as boycotts.

The New Deal years were certainly kinder to labor than any previous time. In his efforts to revive the slumping economy, President Franklin D. Roosevelt thought that granting some concessions to labor would prevent conflicts and thus bring stability to industry. In the post-World War II years, though, any gains labor made were slowly stripped away or watered down. In 1947, over the veto of President Harry S. Truman, Congress passed the Taft-Hartley Labor Act, officially known as the Labor-Management Relations Act. Truman referred to the law as a "slave labor bill." Taft-Hartley amended the 1935 Wagner Act, also known as the National Labor Relations Act, which permitted labor several long-sought-after benefits, such as the right to collective bargaining. Among the list of prohibited actions and practices included jurisdictional strikes, secondary boycotts, and "common-situs picketing," which is similar to a secondary boycott whereby unions picket, strike, or refuse to do business with a company with whom they have no grievance but that conducts business with one they do. In 1959, the restrictions against secondary boycotts were strengthened with the Labor Management Reporting and Disclosure Act.

Probably one of the most famous boycotts in U.S. history was the one led by the United Farm Workers (UFW) from 1965 to 1970. Farmers suffered a loss of workers during World War II due to the flocks of workers taking on positions in the factories. As a result, farmers were allowed to hire Mexican workers on a temporary basis, who were called braceros. The stipulation was that no bracero could replace an American worker, if one was to be found. Well after the war, wage disputes concerning the braceros and domestic workers came to the forefront. Many Filipino workers, who were organized under the AFL's Agricultural Workers' Organizing Committee, objected to a lower pay rate than the braceros, although federal rules prohibited domestics receiving a lower rate. Other grievances addressed were the deplorable living conditions, along with the lack of water and bathroom services. The Filipinos, joined by Mexican-Americans, walked off the job.

The key figure in the boycott was César Chávez. Although an agreement was struck not to pay Mexican immigrant workers more, compliance was ignored by many. Furthermore, the workers wanted unionization. Thousands of workers went on strike. Chávez pleaded with the American people not to buy grapes without the union label. Some wine growers signed agreements with the striking workers. The strike was successful, and as a result the farm workers received higher wages and better benefits.

Later, the boycott took on different proportions. Not just a tool of the labor movement to strike at allegedly unfair businesses, the boycott was adopted by many to achieve a specific goal. The term "girlcott" was used by the African-American track star Lacey O'Neal during the 1968 Olympics, urging others not to avoid the games and instead gain recognition. The tennis star Billy Jean King used the same word to protest against the unequal pay for women in the Wimbledon tournament. Probably the most famous noneconomic boycott was when President Jimmy Carter refused to allow the country to participate in the 1980 Olympic Games in Moscow in protest of the Soviet Union's activities in Afghanistan, a move that drew much criticism.

MITCHELL NEWTON-MATZA

References and Further Reading

Friedman, Lawrence. *A History of American Law*. New York: Simon and Schuster, 1985.
Hall, Kermit. *The Magic Mirror*. New York: Oxford University Press, 1991.
Jones, Lynn, and Isaac Mankita. "The 1965 Grape Boycott: A Case Study in Strategy." *United Farm Workers' Union* (4 June 2003).
Kraus, Henry. *Judicial Usurpation: An Open Letter to Congress Showing This in the Injunctions in Labor Disputes*, 1908.
Taylor, Benjamin, and Fred Witney. *U.S. Labor Relations Law*. Englewood Cliffs, NJ: Prentice Hall, 1992.

Cases and Statutes Cited

Duplex Printing Press Co. v. Deering, 254 U.S. 443 (1921)

See also **Knights of Labor; Pullman Strike and Boycott (1894)**

BOYLE, W. A. (TONY) (1904–1985)
President, United Mine Workers of America

William Anthony "Tony" Boyle became president of the United Mine Workers of America (UMWA) in 1963, three years after the retirement of John L. Lewis, who led America's unionized coal miners for 40 years. Lewis had handpicked the aging, ill Thomas Kennedy as president, while designating Boyle as vice president and heir apparent. Boyle's decade-long tenure and fall from power over America's oldest industrial union was dominated by the challenge of an insurgent movement against entrenched corruption, violence, and ultimately murder within the UMWA.

Boyle, from a family of Scottish immigrant miners, became Lewis's administrative assistant in 1947, after seven years as a UMWA district president in Montana. His move into Lewis's inner circle coincided with a gradually growing corruption within the UMWA national leadership. Lewis's vision of a dynamic industrial union increasingly hardened into the protection of his own power in the context of the coal industry's post-World War II retrenchment and economic crisis. Boyle fit in well. He engaged in nepotism that extended to opposing proposed state safety laws in Montana on behalf of one sibling, a coal mine owner, and to conferring the District 27 UMWA presidency on another sibling, who had never worked in a mine.

During that era, Boyle was a key player in Lewis's largely unsuccessful attempts to "bring around" the UMWA's nemesis—the recalcitrant, difficult-to-organize small mines, especially in parts of Virginia, Tennessee, and Kentucky. On the one hand, violence and intimidation were employed on both sides, with little involvement of rank-and-file miners in organizing. On the other hand, there were sweetheart deals with nominally union operators. From that milieu, specifically District 19 in Tennessee, Boyle would eventually select a pliant union official to recruit hired assassins.

As UMWA president, Boyle consolidated power, in part from a base of locals made up entirely of retired miners susceptible to influence and control. The Boyle machine manipulated the *United Mine Workers' Journal* to endlessly promote Boyle's name and to denigrate any opposition. Boyle also continued Lewis's destruction of district autonomy. Despite his self-promotion, Boyle enjoyed little or none of Lewis's immense personal prestige among miners. The growing problems of job loss, lagging wages, black lung disease, and unsafe mines produced a rank-and-file coal miners' movement. Boyle responded with inconsistent endorsements of change, alongside increasing hostility to the dissenters, employing violence to enforce uniformity at the 1964 UMWA convention.

Boyle's isolation from the growing rank-and-file anger was illustrated and exacerbated when the Mannington mine exploded in 1968, killing 78 miners. Despite a history of safety violations at the mine, he declared fatalistically that such disasters were inherent in the industry, and he vouched for the good intentions of Consolidation Coal, owners of the mine. This stood in stark contrast to collective memories of John L. Lewis visiting the sites of disasters and eloquently denouncing the operators. Added to Boyle's isolation from the lives of the members was the increasingly evident corruption, over which he presided.

When veteran Pennsylvania district leader Joseph "Jock" Yablonski broke with Boyle and ran for UMWA president in 1969, massive fraud tainted the election, which Boyle won. As the movement looked forward to Yablonski's continuing challenge, Boyle engineered the reform leader's assassination on December 31, 1969. Yablonski's wife and daughter were also killed. The shocking carnage and the militant miners' movement woke up the previously complacent U.S. Justice Department, leading to a 1972 court order that overturned the election and to a criminal indictment of Boyle for illegal use of union funds. Campaigning while free on bail, and still operating from a formidable political and financial base, Boyle lost the federally supervised new election to Miners for Democracy candidate Arnold Miller. By 1974, the trail of evidence had worked its way up, and Boyle was indicted for the murder of Yablonski. Sentenced to life, he later died in prison.

Perhaps the most remarkable thing about Boyle's career was the veneer of legitimacy he achieved, including a 1968 tribute from Hubert Humphrey, and even a folk song about him by Joe Glazer. It stemmed from past UMWA successes and from Boyle's control of institutionalized bureaucratic structures, such as collective bargaining and administration of the Health and Retirement Funds. While his methods were venal and undemocratic, those structures functioned in ways that maintained a degree of stability between the UMWA leadership and the industry. The veneer and the stability were ended by the combination of Boyle's overreaching into cold-blooded murder and the persistence of the rank-and-file movement, which included growing wildcat strikes. The insurgent UMWA miners won an end to federal complacency and rescued their union.

PAUL SIEGEL

References and Further Reading

Brody, David. *In Labor's Cause: Main Themes in the History of the American Worker*. New York: Oxford University Press, 1993.
Clark, Paul F. *The Miners' Fight for Democracy: Arnold Miller and the Reform of the United Mine Workers*. Ithaca: New York State School of Industrial and Labor Relations, Cornell University, 1981.
Dubofsky, Melvyn, and Warren Van Tine. *John L. Lewis: A Biography*. New York: Quadrangle, 1977.
Finley, Joseph, E. *The Corrupt Kingdom: The Rise and Fall of the United Mine Workers*. New York: Simon and Schuster, 1972.
Hume, Brit. *Death and the Mines: Rebellion and Murder in the United Mine Workers*. New York: Grossman Publishers, 1971.
Nyden, Paul. *Miners for Democracy: Struggle in the Coal Fields* (Ph.D. Dissertation). Ann Arbor, MI: University Microfilms International, 1974.

See also **Black Lung Associations; Federal Coal Mine Health and Safety Act; Miller, Arnold; United Mine Workers of America; Yablonski, Joseph A. "Jock"**

BRANDEIS BRIEF

The Brandeis Brief is today widely known as the first influential legal brief to rely on social scientific data to prove its case before the Supreme Court. Yet the Brandeis Brief grew out of a crucial episode in American labor history, *Muller v. Oregon* (1908), and the brief's successful argument portended much of the justification for government regulation on behalf of twentieth-century workers.

In 1905, the U.S. Supreme Court decided the case of *Lochner v. New York*, striking down a New York law limiting baker hours to 10 per day and 60 per week as a violation of workers' rights to liberty of contract. The case seemed to prohibit all government regulation of workers' wages, hours, and employment conditions. Soon after the *Lochner* decision, however, Oregon courts began passing judgment on a 1903 statute preventing women from working more than 10-hour days. Portland laundry owner Curt Muller gave his name to the case when he required his foreman to force ardent unionist Emma Gotcher to work more than 10 hours on Labor Day, 1905.

Advocates of government protection of workers and regulation of the economy looked to this new case as a possible crack in the seemingly all-encompassing capitalist conservatism of *Lochner*. While certain groups such as the American Association of Labor Legislation still hoped to press the case of laws that would protect all workers, the female-dominated National Consumers' League (NCL) realized that such an approach was doomed to fail. In the social Darwinist legal and intellectual environment of the early twentieth century, the only likely hope for protection of any workers was to begin by supporting the protection of women alone. General laws might then proceed from this "entering wedge."

In 1907, the Oregon Consumers' League notified national headquarters that it should begin to defend the Oregon 10-hour law. Florence Kelley, the dynamic and socialist general secretary of the NCL, and Josephine Goldmark, the head of the League's committee on labor law, first solicited the prominent but conservative New York lawyer Joseph Choate. When he turned down the case, Kelley and Goldmark gladly turned to Louis Brandeis—conveniently the latter's brother-in-law. Brandeis agreed to serve as long as the Oregon attorney general made him the state's official attorney in the case.

Brandeis was one of the shining stars of the Progressive legal firmament. A wealthy attorney from Louisville and an active Zionist, Brandeis, despite his privilege, turned against the era's dominant laissez-faire philosophy. He crusaded in the political arena against monopolies, earning the undying hatred of many corporate elites. Yet Brandeis's defense of the rights of small business earned him the respect of Woodrow Wilson, who would go on to appoint him to the Supreme Court in 1916—making him the first Jew to hold that post.

In the legal arena, Brandeis was convinced that courts had not only the ability but the obligation to aid those who were too weak to help themselves. Yet given the hostile judicial environment, and the decision not to launch a full-scale assault on *Lochner*, Brandeis had to resort not to moral suasion but to one of the favorite entities of Progressive Era reformers: "the facts." Brandeis believed that the collection and deployment of supposedly neutral data, uncovered by experts, would allow for the proper sorting out of good and evil. And in this case, the evil was long hours for women.

Brandeis set Goldmark to work on researching the voluminous facts that would become the heart, and indeed almost the entire body, of the Brandeis Brief. Goldmark in turn worked with 10 other researchers (including her sister Pauline and Florence Kelley) to uncover data on the physical, moral, and social impact of women's hours of wage labor. Based in the New York Public Library and the Columbia University libraries, Goldmark and her comrades dug through reports of medical and labor commissions, finding particularly invaluable information in British government publications. The result was a 113-page report—only the first two pages of which laid out a traditional legal argument based on previous cases. The rest, titled, "The World's Experience," was largely a series of quotations and often-undigested information from decidedly nonjudicial authorities, ranging from physicians to factory inspectors.

The brief used such social science to argue, above all, that long work hours were "disastrous" to the well-being of women and their offspring. Nature had made women weaker than men, the brief contended, and overwork led to fatigue, headaches, anemia, and a variety of other ailments. Perhaps most critical, long hours interfered in women's most important purpose: the bearing and raising of children. Exploitative labor caused miscarriages, premature births, and infant mortality, and children who did survive were enfeebled and often immoral. It was this appeal on behalf of the health and well-being of the entire human race that the justices most likely found to be the brief's most compelling argument; they ended up upholding the Oregon statute unanimously.

Americans initially greeted the decision in *Muller v. Oregon* with great enthusiasm. The claims of humanity finally seemed to have trumped the greed of rapacious employers. Yet even at the time, feminists were concerned about the gendered arguments on behalf of the Oregon statute, and on behalf of protective labor legislation for women more broadly, that portrayed women as victims. Feminist scholars have continued to hone this critique over the last century. By turning women into passive subjects who needed to be protected, Brandeis and Goldmark effectively disempowered them both at the workplace and before the judicial bench. This indefatigable duo did not even seek to interview contemporary female laundry (or other) workers; their mission was simply to protect, not to understand or interact with them—much less nurture their political activism.

Louis Brandeis later told his law clerk Dean Acheson that the proper title for the brief should have been "What Every Fool Knows." Yet while we should honor the genuine generosity and the humanitarianism of the Brandeis Brief, we today generally think quite differently from Brandeis and his allies. Their brief has now become just as much a symbol of the inegalitarian politics of much twentieth-century welfare-state liberalism as a victory of pure enlightenment.

ROBERT D. JOHNSTON

References and Further Reading

Baer, Judith A. *The Chains of Protection: The Judicial Response to Protective Labor Legislation.* Westport, CT: Greenwood, 1978.

Brandeis, Louis D., and Josephine Goldmark. *Women in Industry.* New York: Arno, 1969 [reprint of 1908 edition]. Contains the Brandeis Brief and the *Muller* decision.

Erickson, Nancy S. "*Muller v. Oregon* Reconsidered: The Origins of a Sex-Based Doctrine of Liberty of Contract." *Labor History* 30 (Spring 1989): 228–250.

Strum, Philippa. *Louis D. Brandeis: Justice for the People.* Cambridge, MA: Harvard University Press, 1984.

Woloch, Nancy. *Muller v. Oregon: A Brief History with Documents.* Boston: Bedford, 1996.

Cases Cited

Lochner v. New York 198 U.S. 45 (1905)
Muller v. Oregon 208 U.S. 412 (1908)

BRIDGES, HARRY RENTON (JULY 28, 1901–MARCH 30, 1990)
President, International Longshoremen's and Warehousemen's Union

For a generation of Americans, Harry Bridges personified militant, left-wing unionism. Born in a working-class suburb of Melbourne, Australia, Bridges derived his early political views from a favorite uncle who advocated trade unionism and served as an organizer for the Australian Labor Party. Later, working as a merchant seaman in the United States, he briefly joined the Industrial Workers of the World (IWW) and adopted many of their views on race and class, organizing, and union democracy. In 1922, he began working on the San Francisco docks. Longshore work was demanding and often dangerous. Hiring came through a daily shape-up when gang bosses (who acted as foremen for the longshoremen who worked a single hold of a ship) selected their work gang; there was no security of employment. In 1933, when the International Longshoremen's Association (ILA) chartered Local 38-79 in San Francisco, Bridges quickly emerged to leadership. He served as chairman of the strike committee during the 1934 coastwise longshore strike and came out with a reputation as a forceful and radical leader. Afterward, he became president of his local, then of the Pacific Coast District of the ILA, and then of the International Longshoremen's and Warehousemen's Union (ILWU, now the International Longshore and Warehouse Union), which was chartered by the Congress of Industrial Organizations (CIO) in 1937.

Bridges and the ILWU

One of the most important objectives in the 1934 strike was a union-controlled hiring hall in each port, replacing the shape-up in some ports and employer-controlled hiring halls elsewhere. The strike settlement specified that the hiring halls were to be financed jointly by the union and the employers but that each dispatcher was to be elected by union members. Thereafter, for Bridges and the members of his union, the slogan became "the hiring hall is the union." In 1935, while Bridges was president of Local 38-79, the local used the hiring hall to equalize earnings among longshoremen, to gain greater control over working conditions, and to ban racially segregated work gangs.

In the 1930s and 1940s, in California, Oregon, Washington, British Columbia, Alaska, and Hawaii, the ILWU forged a strong union among longshoremen and some warehouse workers. Expulsion from the CIO ended ILWU efforts—never very successful—to organize longshoremen and warehouse workers in eastern states. In Hawaii, after World War II, the ILWU became the largest union and a powerful political force, representing a highly racially diverse work force in the longshore, warehouse, sugar, pineapple, transportation, and hotel industries. By organizing sugar and pineapple field workers, the ILWU became the first union to achieve lasting success in bringing collective bargaining to agricultural workers.

Bridges consistently advocated "a lot of rank-and-file democracy and control." Under his leadership, the ILWU institutionalized extensive member participation in union decision making, including a requirement in the San Francisco local that officers could not serve consecutive terms. Within the ILWU, major decisions have usually been made through a membership referendum, and officers have been elected by all union members. Bridges often reminded his members, especially his critics, that a petition by 15% of the membership could suspend him—or any international officer—and force a recall election. In the longshore caucus, delegates from all the waterfront locals meet regularly to decide contract issues. "On the Beam," Bridges's column in *The Dispatcher*, the ILWU newspaper launched in 1942, regularly presented his views on union and public issues.

Bridges understood the power of symbols for minimizing the distance between leaders and members. He argued that a union officer should not earn more than the highest paid member of that union, and he stuck to that commitment throughout his career. Of 36 union presidents listed in a news magazine salary survey in 1964, none received less than Bridges. Bridges's personal lifestyle reflected the same values. When he and his wife bought a home, it was a modest row house in a middle-class neighborhood. Away from home, he often stayed in cheap hotels. Nothing earned his contempt faster than making a personal profit from the trust of union members.

Bridges consistently advocated the unity of labor. He helped to create and lead the Maritime Federation of the Pacific Coast, an ambitious effort to unite all West Coast maritime unions. Initially successful, the federation conducted a three-month strike in 1936–1937 that contributed to conflict between its two largest organizations, the ILA Pacific Coast District and the Sailors' Union of the Pacific (SUP). In 1937, Bridges led the Pacific Coast District into the CIO as the ILWU and became its first president, but the SUP opted for the American Federation of Labor (AFL) and left the Maritime Federation in 1938. Later, in 1946, Bridges took the lead in organizing the short-lived Committee for Maritime Unity, hoping to develop common bargaining among the six CIO maritime unions. By the late 1950s, the ILWU and Teamsters were working together to resolve jurisdictional disputes and eventually undertook some joint bargaining. As ILWU president, Bridges eventually sought a reconciliation with the ILA. One of his last public statements was to endorse affiliation with the AFL-CIO when ILWU members voted on that measure in 1988.

Bridges and the Communist Party

Bridges frequently described himself as a Marxist. His Marxism was never rigid, but he claimed that his class analysis kept him grounded in negotiations. No matter how well he got along with the men on the other side of the bargaining table, he claimed, he always knew that they represented the "class enemy." He approached race relations from a class analysis, arguing consistently for full racial integration of the work force and the union, and he argued for class solidarity across the lines of race, ethnicity, gender, and craft. Similarly, he worked from his ideological perspective to define the role of union president, to foster rank-and-file democracy, to advocate for civil rights and civil liberties, and to take positions on foreign policy issues.

Bridges consistently supported and defended the Communist Party (CP) and the Soviet Union. For Bridges, the enemies of the CP and the Soviet Union were his enemies—including both red-baiters and Trotskyists. Though Bridges acknowledged that "all the evidence introduced against me in that fight with the government was 95% true," he always denied that he had ever become a member of the CP.

The papers of the Communist Party of the United States at the Russian State Archive of Social and Political History, Moscow, were opened to researchers after the collapse of the Soviet Union. Though fragmentary and largely limited to the period before 1937–1938, those files suggest that Bridges took part in CP discussions of strategy and tactics beginning in 1934 and was elected to the Central Committee of the CPUSA in 1936. Historians are likely never to know the precise relationship between Bridges and the CP, but the records in Moscow suggest that he sometimes took positions contrary to the party line and did not always carry out decisions made in party caucuses.

After Bridges emerged as a strike leader in 1934, some business leaders, public officials, and American Legion officers claimed, on dubious evidence, that he was a Communist and should be deported to his native Australia. In 1939, bowing to political pressure, Secretary of Labor Frances Perkins ordered the Immigration and Naturalization Service (INS) to determine whether Bridges should be deported. When the hearing officer ruled in Bridges's favor, the House of Representatives passed a bill to deport Bridges. Undoubtedly unconstitutional, the measure died in the Senate. However, partially in response to the uproar over the hearing decision, Congress moved INS from Labor to Justice and established new criteria for deportation. Attorney General Robert Jackson then ordered the FBI to investigate Bridges; by 1956, Bridges's FBI file had grown to nearly 38,000 pages. In a second INS hearing, in 1941, the hearing officer found against Bridges. Upon appeal, the Supreme Court reversed that decision (*Bridges v. Wixon*, 1945), and Bridges completed his naturalization.

With the onset of the Cold War, left-wing unions came under pressure from CIO leadership to espouse anti-Communist views. In 1948, however, Bridges and the ILWU opposed CIO leaders by criticizing the Marshall Plan and supporting the presidential candidacy of Henry Wallace. The CIO subsequently expelled the ILWU on the grounds that it was communist-led. In 1949, with Bridges and the ILWU under attack within the CIO, federal authorities brought Bridges to trial, charging him and his two witnesses with lying at his naturalization when he swore he had never belonged to the Communist Party. In 1950, they were convicted of criminal conspiracy. In *Bridges v. U.S.* (1953), the Supreme Court overturned the conspiracy conviction on procedural grounds. In 1955, federal attorneys initiated yet a fourth trial, but the trial judge dismissed the charges.

Throughout his hearings and trials, Bridges's defense committees attracted widespread support from labor, the left, liberals, and eventually even business leaders. Most ILWU members considered him a martyr, suffering repeated trials solely because he was a successful union leader, and many others saw him as the victim of federal harassment. At the same time, however, the attacks on Bridges and his union drained enormous amounts of time, energy, and resources just for defense. Bridges's support for the CP—and similar support by other ILWU activists—led the CIO to expel the union, and led to the loss of the ILWU's few eastern locals. The ILWU tried to take in the Marine Cooks and Stewards Union—also expelled from the CIO—but lost that jurisdiction, too. The ILWU did take in the West Coast locals of the Fishermen's Union, another expelled union, and added a few other locals from other unions that had been expelled and were being raided. Thus, despite Bridges's commitment to labor unity, for 38 years—27 of them under Bridges's leadership—the ILWU stood outside the mainstream of organized labor.

Bridges and Longshore Labor Relations

Bridges always led the ILWU negotiating committee during bargaining for the coastwise longshore contract. In 1948, representatives of waterfront employers refused to negotiate with him because of his political views. After a bitter three-month strike, several key companies bolted from the previous employers' association, formed the Pacific Maritime Association (PMA), and hired new negotiators. This initiated a "New Look" in Pacific Coast longshore labor relations. Thereafter, Bridges and the ILWU built a stable—sometimes even comfortable—relationship with the PMA.

In the late 1950s, recognizing that technology could transform longshoring, Bridges argued that the ILWU should not fight change but instead try to benefit from it. After extensive discussion in the union newspaper and union meetings, and with endorsement by the membership, Bridges led negotiations through which the ILWU accepted full mechanization in return for generous retirement arrangements and a guarantee of full pay for those who did not retire. The ILWU-PMA Modernization and Mechanization Agreement (M&M) of 1960 led Secretary of Labor James P. Mitchell to judge that "next only to John L. Lewis, Bridges has done the best job in American labor of coming to grips with the problems of automation." Shipping companies rapidly converted to containers, greatly reducing the cost of shipping, but arguments that Bridges settled too cheaply were largely from hindsight. Some ILWU members, however, criticized the M&M for undermining the hiring hall by permitting employers to choose "steady men" for certain jobs. The steady-man issue, especially, fueled a four-month strike in 1971–1972.

Conclusion

Despite his lifelong, outspoken admiration for the Soviet Union, Bridges after 1960 was often praised for his contributions to the maritime industry and even lauded as a "labor statesman." He disavowed such honorifics, claiming that he had not changed his views. As early as the 1950s, Bridges had become a living legend—the militant, democratic leftist who repeatedly triumphed over federal persecution. Many ILWU members did not share Bridges's left-wing politics nor his admiration for the Soviet Union, but most nonetheless pledged him their respect, loyalty, and affection. In 1992, a group of ILWU pensioners in the Pacific Northwest demonstrated this by collecting a million dollars—mostly in small amounts from pensioners—to endow a Harry Bridges Chair in Labor Studies at the University of Washington.

ROBERT W. CHERNY

References and Further Reading

Cherny, Robert W. "Constructing a Radical Identity: History, Memory, and the Seafaring Stories of Harry Bridges." *Pacific Historical Review* 70, no. 4 (Nov. 2001): 571–600.

———"The Making of a Labor Radical: Harry Bridges, 1901–1934." *Pacific Historical Review* 64, no. 3 (Aug. 1995): 363–388.

———"Prelude to the Popular Front: The Communist Party in California, 1931–1935." *American Communist History* 1, no. 1(June 2002): 5–37.

Harry and Nikki Bridges Papers, Labor Archives and Research Center, San Francisco State University.

Harry Bridges Legal Collection, Southern California Library for Social Studies and Research, Los Angeles.

Kutler, Stanley I. "'If at first . . . ': The Trials of Harry Bridges." In *The American Inquisition: Justice and Injustice in the Cold War*, New York: Hill and Wang, 1982.

Larrowe, Charles P. *Harry Bridges: The Rise and Fall of Radical Labor in the United States.* New York: Lawrence Hill and Co., 1972.

Mills, Herb, and David Wellman. "Contractually Sanctioned Job Action and Workers' Control: The Case of the San Francisco Longshoremen." *Labor History* 28 (1987): 167–195.

Nelson, Bruce. *Workers on the Waterfront: Seamen, Longshoremen, and Unionism in the 1930s.* Urbana and Chicago: University of Illinois Press, 1988.

Norman Leonard Collection, Labor Archives and Research Center, San Francisco State University.

Schwartz, Harvey. "Harry Bridges and the Scholars: Looking at History's Verdict." *California History* 59, no. 1 (Spring 1980): 66–79.

Selvin, David. *A Terrible Anger: The 1934 Waterfront and General Strikes in San Francisco.* Detroit: Wayne State University Press, 1996.

Ward, Estolv E. *Harry Bridges on Trial.* New York: Modern Age Books, Inc., 1940.

Wellman, David. *The Union Makes Us Strong: Radical Unionism on the San Francisco Waterfront.* New York: Cambridge University Press, 1995.

Zalburg, Sanford. *A Spark Is Struck! Jack Hall and the ILWU in Hawaii.* Honolulu: University Press of Hawaii, 1979.

See also **International Longshoremen's Association; Maritime Labor**

BRISBANE, ALBERT (1809–1890)
Social Theorist

The nineteenth-century social thinker Albert Brisbane almost single-handedly transformed the way that Americans thought about the prospects for communal living, by importing, popularizing, and adapting to the American environment the ideas of the French communitarian Charles Fourier. Brisbane's efforts, which illustrate the importance of the transatlantic transmission of radical ideas in the antebellum period, resulted in a wave of Fourierite experiments throughout the northern United States between 1845 and 1855.

Born in Batavia, New York, into a middle-class family, Brisbane claimed to have discovered and rebelled against social inequality in the United States from the time that he was 15 years old. However, it was not until he had the opportunity to study at the Sorbonne, and then embark on a tour of Europe, that he discovered, and became completely obsessed by, the philosophy of Charles Fourier. Brisbane presented himself at Fourier's office and offered him 5 francs an hour to tutor Brisbane in his theory.

An eccentric French philosopher, Fourier had proposed that industry could be made more attractive to people if their natural inclinations were followed in the choice of, and practice of, an occupation. In Fourier's view, with plenty of variety, compatible workmates, friendly competition, and the right modifications made to the workplace for fun and comfort, work could excite the mind and delight the soul. At the very moment that mechanization was beginning to alienate the European worker, and by extension to menace the American worker, these ideas were powerful.

With the fervor of the newly converted, Brisbane sought to convert Fourier's system into reality. He toned down elements of Fourier's program that would have alienated American audiences, including Fourier's notion that the planets of the solar system copulated and that monogamy was unnatural. The result was a template for communitarianism that preserved individual family units and cohered with reigning American moral codes.

Brisbane's skill lay in exploitation of modern technology to popularize Fourier's ideas. He gave lectures, organized societies, and wrote several books, including *Social Destiny of Man* (1840) and *A Concise Exposition of the Doctrine of Association* (1843), which became patterns for the 25 Associationist "phalanxes" or communities that were erected during the 1840s—including Brook Farm, in Massachusetts, and the North American Phalanx, in Red Bank, New Jersey. Brisbane also edited two Fourierite newspapers, *The Future* and *The Phalanx*. By bringing the editor Horace Greeley into the Associationist fold early in the 1840s, Brisbane was able to use Greeley's *Tribune* to outline the ills of civilization and the Fourierite solution.

By the late 1840s, almost all of the Fourierite phalanxes had folded, falling prey to financial bad management and to individual disasters like the fire that consumed the major buildings at the North American Phalanx. Even successful communities, like the phalanx at Ceresco, Wisconsin, found it hard to repel the attractions of development and were folded into nearby towns. Nonetheless, Brisbane continued to try to keep Fourierism alive. In the 1850s, he worked with the French communitarian Victor Considerant to bankroll and plan a French colony based on Fourierite principles in La Réunion, Texas.

Brisbane continued to adapt Fourier's writings to changing times, proposing that phrenology be used to assign Fourierists to suitable work and suggesting that phalanxes could prosper if they adopted modern technology and used very large tracts of land. When not focusing on the social regeneration of mankind, he turned his mind to other, rather eccentric improvements, including a vacuum oven and a giant mausoleum that would be a monument to all of the nation's dead. Brisbane died in 1890, and was outlived by two years by the last Fourierite colony, the Kansas Cooperative Farm, which folded in 1892.

JAMIE L. BRONSTEIN

References and Further Reading

Bestor, Arthur. "Albert Brisbane: Propagandist for Socialism in the 1840's." *New York History* 28 (1947): 128–158.
Guarneri, Carl. *The Utopian Alternative: Fourierism in Nineteenth-Century America.* Ithaca, NY: Cornell University Press, 1991.
Mattek, Michael Charles. *Brisbane and Beyond: Revising Social Capitalism in Mid-Nineteenth-Century America.* Ph.D. thesis, Marquette University, 2002.
Pettit, Norman. *Albert Brisbane: Apostle of Fourierism in the United States, 1834–1890*, Ph.D. thesis, University of Miami, 1982.
Rohler, Lloyd Earl Jr. *The Utopian Persuasion of Albert Brisbane, First Apostle of Fourierism.* Ph.D. thesis, Indiana University, 1977.

See also **Fourierism**

BROOKWOOD LABOR COLLEGE

Established in 1921, Brookwood Labor College was the most influential worker education school of its generation, shaping the programs of hundreds of similar institutions across the United States, and serving as an important training base for many of the labor activists of the 1930s. Situated on a 53-acre estate in Katonah, New York, about 40 miles from New York City, the school's central purpose was to provide a practical education for labor leaders, and it held the distinction of being the first full-time residential institution in the United States dedicated exclusively to workers' education.

Brookwood's early supporters were predominantly socialist, and the school maintained a reputation as being an institution of the labor movement's left wing. Despite this, no single political orthodoxy marked the college's faculty or student body throughout its 16 years of existence. As an institution that had many ties to organized labor, and which saw its central purpose as advancing its development, Brookwood managed to remained independent, supported through direct student contributions, which were often paid through union scholarship funds. While not the first labor college in the United States, Brookwood was unique as a model of progressive education methods, implemented by the school's earliest educational director, A. J. Muste, a former executive secretary of the Amalgamated Textile Workers Union and a personal friend of progressive educator John Dewey, who was also an early booster of the Brookwood experiment.

The standard program offered at Brookwood consisted of a two-year course load focused entirely in the humanities, including classes in labor history, contemporary politics, sociology, economics, world civilization, English literature, and language studies taught by activists and college teachers allied with the cause of labor. Seeking to merge intellectual development with practical leadership skills, Brookwood's curriculum developed strong public speaking skills among its students, with standard rhetoric courses, organizing debate panels, and inviting such influential figures such as Norman Thomas and Robert Lynd to campus. Brookwood was also known for the strength of its labor journalism courses, which oversaw the publication of an in-house journal, *The Brookwood Review*, training many who later became journalists and newspaper editors for local unions. Another innovative program initiated at Brookwood College was a student theater organization, the Brookwood Labor Players, which toured the United States in the mid 1930s to much critical acclaim. The educational program at Brookwood extended beyond the classroom into a communal setting where both faculty, students, and guests participated in daily housekeeping chores, as well as extracurricular activities such as hikes, dances, and athletic competitions.

Students, consisting of both men and women—most of whom did not complete high school—represented a wide array of occupations, with most students coming from the New York City area. Some of the more famous Brookwood students included Walter and Roy Ruether, who both later taught extension courses for the college, and Nat Weinberg and Brendan Sexton, the postwar directors of the United Auto Workers research and education departments. Brookwood also pioneered such adult education pedagogies as correspondence courses and extension classes for workers who could not attend classes on campus and in organizing special summer programs. By 1937, Brookwood's unique program was modeled by dozens of new labor schools across the United States, which ironically resulted in its demise. Still, Brookwood remains as one of the most successful experiments in worker education in U.S. labor history.

FRANCIS RYAN

References and Further Reading

Altenbaugh, Richard J. *Education for Struggle: The American Labor Colleges of the 1920s and 1930s.* Philadelphia: Temple University, 1990.
Bloom, Jonathan D. "Brookwood Labor College: The Final Years, 1933–1937." *Labor's Heritage* 2, no. 2 (1990): 23–43.
Levine, Arthur. "An Unheralded Educational Experience: Brookwood Remembered." *Change* 13, no. 8 (1981): 38–42.

See also **Muste, A. J.; Reuther, Walter**

BROPHY, JOHN (1883–1963)
Congress of Industrial Organizations

Born in England and raised in the western Pennsylvania coalfields, John Brophy challenged President John L. Lewis for leadership of the United Mine Workers of America (UMWA) in the 1920s and went on to play a key role in the Congress of Industrial Organizations (CIO) in the 1930s and 1940s.

Patrick and Mary Brophy moved their family from St. Helens, Lancashire, to Philipsburg, Pennsylvania, in 1892, when John was nine. The family moved frequently to find work, and young Brophy had only a few years of schooling. He joined his father in the coal mines in Urey, Pennsylvania, in Indiana County, at the age of 11. At 15, he joined the South Fork UMWA local, in neighboring Cambria County. In 1906, Brophy participated in his first strike, as miners sought to restore wage cuts the UMWA had agreed to in 1904. Due to blacklisting, Brophy and his father were forced to head west for work. After a brief stint in Illinois, they returned to Pennsylvania and found work in the Cambria County town of Nanty Glo, where John Brophy joined Local 1386 and soon was elected local president.

Over these years, Brophy established himself as an articulate, disciplined, and militant union leader. He supplemented his meager schooling with correspondence courses and read widely. Rejecting the idea that miners' and operators' interests could be harmonized, he was strongly influenced by the Socialist faction of the UMWA led by Frank Hayes and Adolph Germer of Illinois. Later, Brophy would also be influenced by the social teachings of the Catholic Church, exemplified by *Rerum Novarum* issued by Pope Leo XIII in 1891 and *Quadragesimo Anno* proclaimed by Pope Pius XI in 1931. In 1916, Brophy was elected president of District 2 of the UMWA, which included Indiana, Cambria, and 15 other counties east of Pittsburgh.

Brophy is best known for the challenge he mounted to the UMWA leadership of John L. Lewis in 1926, which originated with Brophy's call for nationalization of the mines. The UMWA had endorsed this idea in principle in 1919, influenced by the popular Plumb Plan, which proposed to nationalize the railroads. Brophy made a formal proposal at a regional UMWA convention in 1921 in Du Bois, Pennsylvania, and published it as *The Miners' Program*. To shore up his progressive credentials for his challenge to Samuel Gompers for the presidency of the American Federation of Labor (AFL) that year, Lewis appointed Brophy to the UMWA's Nationalization Research Committee. In District 2, Brophy led an effort to broaden the education of coal miners on this topic through scholarships to Brookwood Labor College in Katonah, New York. When it became clear that Brophy was taking the nationalization program too seriously, Lewis blocked promotion of it in the *United Mine Workers Journal* and red-baited Brophy. Lewis's conduct during the 1922 coal strike further convinced Brophy that the union leadership had to be changed. Nonunion miners in Somerset quickly joined the national strike, facing down evictions from company housing and private police violence. But as the strike dragged on, Lewis and the national UMWA leadership agreed to a settlement that did not include the previously nonunion Somerset fields.

Brophy's program to challenge Lewis for the presidency of the UMWA, called "Save the Union," had three primary planks: nationalization of the mines, organizing the nonunion fields, and a labor party. Brophy's strongest support came from the Socialist-influenced Illinois miners, as well as Alexander Howat of Kansas. He also worked closely with activist Powers Hapgood and leaders of the Communist Party, such as William Z. Foster, whose Trade Union Educational League had been active in the UMWA. Lewis campaigned against Brophy by accusing him of organizing a "Bolshevik plot." In the 1926 UMWA election, marked by vote fraud, Lewis officially defeated Brophy 170,000 to 60,000. In the 1927 UMWA convention, Lewis loyalists physically attacked Brophy supporters, and in 1928, the Nanty Glo local complied with Lewis's orders to expel Brophy from the UMWA on the charge of dual-unionism. In light of his later anticommunism, Brophy's activity following the failed 1926 election attempt is notable: he traveled to the Soviet Union in 1927 as part of a labor delegation to gain U.S. diplomatic recognition of the new Soviet regime.

Expelled from the union, Brophy and his wife Anita (Anstead) Brophy, whom he married in 1918, had two small children, Philip and Jacqueline, to support. To make ends meet, Brophy took a job as a salesman at the Columbia Conserve Company, an experiment in cooperative capitalism run by Powers Hapgood's father, William, that began to dissolve as the Depression hit. In 1933, as prospects for rebuilding the UMWA brightened, Lewis asked Brophy back into the UMWA. Brophy served him as an ombudsman, keeping tabs on the Progressive Miners in Illinois and serving on an AFL committee to investigate A. Philip Randolph's charges of racism in the unions.

Their collaboration deepened in 1935 when Lewis formed the CIO and appointed Brophy as its executive director. Brophy assembled a team of talented staffers, including Len DeCaux and Katherine Ellickson, both of whom he knew from Brookwood. Brophy helped negotiate the agreement that ended the Flint sit-down strike and organized support for striking Akron rubber workers. After political differences led Lewis to leave the CIO in 1940, President Philip Murray appointed Brophy as national director of Industrial Union Councils. By fall 1944, Brophy oversaw 36 state and 232 local and area councils. During World War II, Brophy served as a member of the Fair Employment Practice Committee and allied with the two black members of the board to pressure Roosevelt to take racism more seriously. Brophy also served on the War Labor Board, resenting the Little Steel Decision but vigorously supporting the CIO's no-strike pledge.

Brophy completed his union career enforcing anti-Communist CIO discipline. He authored a CIO 1945 report that recommended against any third-party political efforts, and weighed in against local industrial councils, such as in Los Angeles, where Communist Party members had substantial influence, to ensure support for the Marshall Plan and opposition to the 1948 presidential candidacy of Henry Wallace. Brophy was instrumental in forming the anticommunist International Confederation of Free Trade Unions and traveled to southeast Asia in 1950 to promote anticommunist labor. Brophy also wrote in support of Catholic corporativist industrial council schemes. Until his retirement in 1961, Brophy served in the Community Relations department of the AFL-CIO.

CARL R. WEINBERG

References and Further Reading

Brophy, John (edited and supplemented by John O. P. Hall). *A Miner's Life*. Madison: University of Wisconsin Press, 1964.

————."The Industry Council Plan." *Commonweal* XLIX, no. 5 (November 2, 1948): 110–112.

————. "The Miner's Program." *Survey Graphic* 1, no. 6 (April 1922): 1026–1029.

————."Nationalization: The Miner's Plan." *Locomotive Engineer Journal* (March 1924): 178–179.

Bussel, Robert. "'Business without a Boss': The Columbia Conserve Company and Workers' Control, 1917–1943." *The Business History Review* 71, No. 3 (Autumn 1997): 417–443.

Cooper, Eileen Mountjoy. "That Magnificent Fight of Unionism: The Somerset County Strike of 1922." *Pennsylvania Heritage* 17, no. 4 (1991).

Dubofsky, Melvyn, and Warren Van Tine. *John L. Lewis: A Biography*. New York: Quadrangle/The New York Times Book Co., 1977.

Ricketts, Elizabeth "The Struggle for Civil Liberties and Unionization in the Coal Fields: The Free Speech Case of Vintondale, Pennsylvania, 1922." *Pennsylvania Magazine of History and Biography* 122 (October 1998): 319–352.

Singer, Alan. "Class-Conscious Coal Miners, Nanty-Glo Versus the Open Shop in the Post World War I Era." *Labor History* 29, no. 1 (Winter 1998): 56–65.

————. "Communists and Coal Miners: Rank-and-File Organizing in the United Mine Workers of America during the 1920s." *Science and Society* 55, no. 2 (1991): 132–157.

————. "John Brophy's 'Miner's Program': Workers' Education in UMWA District 2 during the 1920s." *Labor Studies Journal* 13 no. 4 (1988): 50–64.

Zieger, Robert H. *The CIO, 1935–1955*. Chapel Hill: The North Carolina University Press, 1995.

See also **Congress of Industrial Organizations; United Mine Workers of America**

BROTHERHOOD OF LOCOMOTIVE ENGINEERS

See **Railroad Brotherhoods**

BROTHERHOOD OF LOCOMOTIVE FIREMEN AND ENGINEMEN

See **Railroad Brotherhoods**

BROTHERHOOD OF MAINTENANCE OF WAY EMPLOYEES

See **Railroad Brotherhoods**

BROTHERHOOD OF RAILWAY CLERKS

See **Railroad Brotherhoods**

BROTHERHOOD OF SLEEPING CAR PORTERS

The Brotherhood of Sleeping Car Porters (BSCP) was the first national labor union of African-American workers awarded an international charter by the American Federation of Labor (AFL) and recognized by the leaders of a major American corporation. Formation of the union, a 12-year-long struggle that began on August 25, 1925, and ended on that same date in 1937, helped transform the perspective held in the black community toward labor unions. Although success of the BSCP meant shorter working hours and increased wages for Pullman porters and maids, the larger legacy of the union lay with the preconditions it provided for widespread unionization of black workers throughout the United States and its example as a social movement.

To understand the significance of the BSCP, it is necessary to put Pullman porters in historical context. Pullman porters were men who worked exclusively on railroad cars called Pullman sleeping cars, the brainchild of George Mortimer Pullman and the major means used by the wealthy to travel long distance before the era of air travel. The Pullman Palace Sleeping Car Company, organized in 1867 under the direction of George Pullman, revolutionized long-distance rail travel when it manufactured its palace on wheels, train cars that featured brocaded fabrics, plush red carpets, gilt-edged mirrors, silver-trimmed coal-oil lamps, and door frames and window sashes constructed from the finest polished woods. To win acceptance of his sleeping car by the traveling elite, Pullman added distinctive service when he explicitly chose recently freed black men to be porters on his sleeping

Ashley Totten, union official for the Brotherhood of Sleeping Car Porters, an unidentified man, Asa Philip Randolph, and Maida Springer-Kemp, union official for International Packing House workers. / A. Hansen Studio, New York, N.Y. Library of Congress, Prints & Photographs Division [LC-USZ62-104209].

cars. The idea was to evoke the comfort and style slaves provided for the gentry in the antebellum South when he created the position of the Pullman sleeping car porter to serve his patrons in a princely manner. The job description for the position included preparing berths, cleaning the cars, and rendering whatever small services customers desired to make them comfortable while traveling. Pullman sleeping cars were also serviced by conductors, who sold and collected tickets. Only porters waited upon the clients. Conductors handled money and had supervisory authority over the behavior, actions, and work requirements of the porters. Until the 1960s, all conductors were white; porters were exclusively black except for a brief period in the late 1920s when the Pullman Company, in an effort to break the back of the fledgling BSCP, hired Filipino porters.

When discussing their work, Pullman porters often observed that "Lincoln freed the slaves, and the Pullman Company hired 'em." If there is a measure of truth in this statement, it lies with the cloak of invisibility porters were advised to sustain while serving the white elite and the fact that porters were black. The cloak of invisibility, which included presenting the public with a smile and maintaining a fawning, submissive-looking stance, offered dual protection: it shielded porters from the charge of stepping out of place—the place assigned by the white world—or "being uppity"; at the same time it protected the sleeping car clients from the discomfort of having a white worker wait on them in the intimate and limited space of a sleeping car. The social distance that societal caste distinctions had created made the servile Pullman porter seem less intrusive than a white worker.

The invisibility was reinforced by the fact that in order to make enough in tips to supplement meager wages, porters assumed degrading postures and contributed to the stereotype of the porter as a clown, scuffling for a handout. But to earn decent tips, porters also had to take mental notes of the likes and dislikes, interests, and habits of patrons as a way to anticipate their clients' every need. All the while, they kept the mask glued to their faces, pretending not to understand or be privy to conversations they overheard. Such behavior led the patrons to regard porters as not fully formed, three-dimensional characters; to customers they were just "George"—property of the founder of the Pullman Company. Thus, the work culture of the job of Pullman porter, as much as issues of low wages and long hours, inspired the organization of the union.

Within the black community, the porter enjoyed prestige. Including in its ranks many of the best-educated black men in the country who could not get jobs in their areas of expertise because of discrimination, Pullman porters, especially before World War I, were considered members of the black middle class and thought of as among a community's "leading men." They clearly were the aristocrats among black workers because they did not have to get their hands dirty, were always on the move, and looked up to because they were able to let the community know what was happening in other areas of the country.

By the 1920s, the Pullman porter was perhaps the most recognized African-American in the white United States, and the Pullman Company employed approximately 12,000 African-Americans to serve over 35 million passengers who slept on Pullman sleeping cars, making it the largest private employer of black men in the United States. However, the status of the Pullman porter declined as World War I and the Great Migration led to rising expectations among African-Americans. The mostly younger black southerners who migrated north to Chicago in the aftermath of the war to make the world safe for democracy carried aspirations for economic and political integration into American society that rose above the status of working as a servant for the Pullman Company. African-Americans talked about the post-World War I era as an era when the "yesterdays are gone forever." The call went out for New Negroes, those willing to make demands and fight for rights of American citizenship. The Old Negro or Old Guard was characterized as "bent and twisted" from too much "bowing and kowtowing" to the wishes of white Americans. In contrast, the New Crowd or New Negroes stood tall, looked white Americans in the eye, and assumed their rightful place as full citizens in the United States.

In August 1925, a group of five porters—steeped in the thinking of the New Crowd and fed up with long hours, low pay, and the servile demeanor demanded by the Pullman Company—formed the Brotherhood of Sleeping Car Porters in New York City. The founders wanted shorter work hours and higher pay. In the 1920s, porters worked 400 hours a month for a monthly wage of $67.50. But they also wanted to rewrite the master-servant narrative that the Pullman Company's work culture had nurtured for so long. The organizers believed that until the myth connecting black people with the status of servants was destroyed, black Americans would never enjoy economic rights of citizenship. Ashley L. Totten, one of the five porters, asked A. Philip Randolph, editor of the *Messenger*, a progressive monthly magazine published in Harlem, to be head of the BSCP. Randolph was selected because he was an excellent public speaker, his magazine could serve as the voice of the new union, and he was beyond the reach of Pullman Company reprisals since he did not work in the industry. The initial organizing campaign in New York was fairly successful.

But the BSCP's campaign came to a halt when it reached Chicago, headquarters of the powerful, anti-union Pullman Company and home to more than a third of Pullman porters. To gain success, the Brotherhood had to win recognition from the Pullman Company and the black community. Chicago highlighted the difficulty of the task that lay ahead. For the next decade the Pullman Company flatly refused to recognize the existence or legitimacy of the BSCP. The organizers gained recognition and support from substantial portions of the black community before the Stock Market Crash in 1929, but even in that arena the union faced an uphill battle.

Through the years Pullman executives had cultivated close relationships with black leaders by pouring money into institutions in black Chicago and promoting the image of Pullman as a friend not just of workers, but the entire community. As a result, the majority of black leaders opposed the BSCP. Randolph chose Milton Price Webster, an ex-porter who worked as a bailiff and had close connections with the black Republican machine in Chicago, to be his second-in-command and head the Chicago district of the BSCP. Webster approached 45 or 50 prominent citizens before the first organizing meeting in Chicago, soliciting support and speakers. Only five agreed to speak at the first meeting, and only one showed up. The one was Dr. William D. Cook, minister of the Metropolitan Community Church. Dr. Cook not only agreed to speak but donated his church for the October 17, 1925, meeting. But because porters in Chicago, unlike those in New York City, lived in the shadow of the giant Pullman Company, very few porters signed up. Pullman's benevolent treatment of the black community paid off initially in terms of keeping black leaders from upsetting the racial status quo. Among the significant organs disseminating anti-Brotherhood propaganda were the *Chicago Defender*, *Chicago Whip*, and the Associated Negro Press.

The BSCP cadre launched a two-front war. On the national front, they turned the *Messenger* into the union's trade journal, publishing articles designed to educate readers about the goals of the union. A major objective was to publicize the concept of manhood rights and the BSCP's hope to restore the porter's manhood rights. From the first, Randolph harbored a vision of the BSCP as a vehicle for social and economic change for all African-Americans. In the pages of the *Messenger* Randolph wrote that the Brotherhood's mission was to pursue economic freedom. To reach that goal, Randolph believed industrial slavery had to be destroyed. The Brotherhood's manhood rights campaign was the link connecting the struggle for a union and resistance to the Pullman Company's company union with the struggle for recognition of black humanity within larger society. The BSCP used the idiom of manhood rights to describe the servile relations that prevailed. Porters had no manhood in the eyes of the company, which was why they were dismissed like children instead of treated like adults, according to the publicity circulated by BSCP organizers. A porter could be addressed as "George" by a 16-year-old messenger boy even though the porter might be four times the boy's age. Finally, organizers linked manhood rights to the concept as it had developed in nineteenth-century conflicts over the meaning of suffrage and citizenship in African-American history.

On the local front, the BSCP, using a community-based strategy, set out to win the hearts and minds of ministers, the press, and politicians who did not appreciate the role labor unions could play in the larger black freedom struggle. Here again the issue of manhood rights, which appealed to a broad audience, helped galvanize the larger community. One of the BSCP's first successful alliances in Chicago was with clubwomen who were drawn to the Brotherhood because they, too, identified with the concept of manhood rights, which they defined in universal, humanistic terms. Ida B. Wells-Barnett, internationally renowned antilynching activist, was among them. Clubwomen who educated the community about the Brotherhood appreciated the fact that the BSCP aspired to be not just a labor organization but a social movement. The alliance with a group of clubwomen and Dr. Cook was the foundation for the BSCP's Citizens Committee, formed in 1927, and was instrumental in helping the BSCP project its voice throughout black Chicago.

Beginning in January 1928, the BSCP's Citizens Committee in Chicago gave the agenda of the Brotherhood greater exposure through a Negro Labor Conference, the first of several it sponsored over the next five years. The conference, challenging patronage politics and asserting the right of black people to choose their own leaders, broke down resistance within the community even as it expanded the civil rights component of the Brotherhood's agenda. In the process, labor conferences made a pioneering effort to connect issues of labor with those for basic citizenship rights, bringing together citizens from all walks of life around the basic right of all Americans to pick their leaders. The BSCP's effort to focus on standing tall as a group and claiming a first-class place in society through collective organization, beyond the pay of a white politician, turned the labor conferences into a protest network, challenging the political status quo and, by extension, any black leadership dependent on white patronage.

The union also struggled to establish itself as a labor union in the eyes of both the Pullman Company and the AFL. The BSCP's application for an international charter in 1928 from the AFL was rejected; the intransigence of Pullman officials made it hard to negotiate with the company. During the spring of 1928, the BSCP threatened to strike the Pullman Company as a way to force the company to recognize the union. But within hours of the scheduled strike, after the Mediation Board refused to certify that an emergency existed in the railroad industry, Randolph called off the strike following the advice of William Green, president of the AFL. Many porters were confused and disappointed with the cancellation of the strike.

By 1929, the BSCP was having success within the community as black leaders began supporting the BSCP and its organizing networks and a prolabor perspective was taking shape. Shortly thereafter, fallout from the Depression, which included a severe decline in travelers, fewer jobs for porters, fewer tips for working porters, and fear associated with joining a union during hard times, contributed to a decline in BSCP membership (from a high of 7,300 in 1927, the BSCP dipped to 658 in 1933). While some observers decreed the BSCP had died, union porters simply refer to the period (1929–1933) as the "Dark Days."

The Brotherhood's fate changed through its relationship with the AFL, the coming of New Deal labor laws, and its relationship with black America. The AFL, which granted federal charters to 13 BSCP locals in 1929, provided very little financial assistance but gave the BSCP a platform from which to advance its call for greater economic opportunity for all black workers. In addition, favorable legislation promoted by the federal government also altered the union's destiny. The Amended Railway Labor Act of 1934 guaranteed railroad workers the legal right of collective bargaining, placing the National Mediation Board (NMB) at the service of the Brotherhood's union during elections. Finally, though the BSCP was reduced to a skeleton crew, the Brotherhood carried the gospel of unionism deep into the black community during the Dark Days by forging cross-class alliances with other groups challenging the racial status quo. Between 1930 and 1935, the Brotherhood helped forge alliances around issues related to the nomination of Judge Parker to the U.S. Supreme Court, the organization of black, female domestic and industrial workers, and the plight of Angelo Herndon. As activities of protest networks overlapped, a new crowd of leaders emerged, challenging the politics of civility that permeated old-guard relations in black Chicago. Protest networks active during the early Depression years included the labor conferences of the BSCP, the Brotherhood's Citizens Committee, and the industrial committee of the YWCA, which worked closely with the BSCP. By the time A. Philip Randolph became head of the National Negro Congress (NNC) in 1936, the Brotherhood was the nationally acknowledged voice of black workers.

Simultaneously, the AFL continued to support racist unions while hundreds of thousands of black workers in steel, meatpacking, and autos were poised for organization. Questions related to organizing black industrial workers erupted at the 1935 AFL convention when its leadership, refusing to endorse industrial unionism, set the stage for the emergence of the Congress of Industrial Organizations (CIO). Although the Brotherhood never did leave the AFL, the strength it had gained within the black community by 1935 pushed the AFL to grant the BSCP an international charter even as it voted to sustain union color bars against thousands of other black workers.

In 1937, the BSCP signed a historic labor contract with the giant Pullman Company, marking the first time representatives from a major American corporation negotiated a labor contract with a union of black workers. But the larger significance of the BSCP's community organizing during the Dark Days lay in popularizing unions and the labor movement, which played a significant role in the widespread unionization of black workers. The Brotherhood's manhood rights campaign, disseminated through its network of activists in labor conferences, the Citizens' Committee, clubwomen's networks, the YWCA, and other groups, prepared the way for the rise of trade unionism and a prolabor point of view within the black community. When the CIO began organizing black workers in mass-production industries in 1936, organizers relied on new-crowd networks formed during the previous decade to open doors in the black community. The new-crowd networks that overlapped with efforts of the BSCP's cadre of activists were not the only groups contributing to a new outlook toward labor, but the Brotherhood's struggle for manhood rights, aimed at gaining the confidence of middle-class leaders as well as workers, planted its labor rhetoric firmly in the soil of rights denied African-Americans as citizens. The collective organization of black workers was a means for African-Americans to gain greater control over the direction of their lives, for the process of labor organizing would be a tutorial for acquiring skills necessary to attain self-reliance and independence even as participants became more integrated within American society. Traditional labor unions, which in 1925 were judged on an individual basis—sometimes favorably, often not favorably—were not generally thought of as institutions for breaking down barriers to black inclusion into American society. Yet, by the mid-1930s, unions were increasingly perceived as vehicles for the advancement of African-Americans.

In 1941, A. Philip Randolph utilized BSCP networks, shaped during the organizing days of the union, to launch a march on Washington, scheduled for July 1941, to demand an end to segregation in the armed forces and discrimination in the job market. When President Roosevelt agreed to issue Executive Order #8802, prohibiting discrimination in defense industries and agencies of the federal government, and formed the Fair Employment Practice Committee (FEPC) to carry out the order, the march was called off. Because the FEPC lacked enforcement power, Milton Webster got himself appointed to the FEPC, and the BSCP formed the March on Washington Movement (MOWM) to act as a watchdog over enactment of 8802. For the next couple of years, the MOWM, led by a cadre connected with units of the BSCP network and using the power of collective action, mobilized large numbers of African-Americans around the advancement of the economic and social rights of black Americans.

By the 1950s, it was increasingly clear that Pullman porters would soon be an anachronism. As the cost of air travel decreased and the construction of highways increased, railroad travel fell into hard times and with it the fate of the porter's job. The Pullman Company was abolished in 1968, the same year Randolph stepped down as president of the union. C. L. Dellums, who had been with the BSCP since its earliest days as leader of the Oakland, California, porters, took over the presidency of the BSCP as the union struggled to remain financially viable. In 1971, most of BSCP's members were employed by Amtrak, and in 1978, it joined forces with the Brotherhood of Railway and Airline Clerks (BRAC).

But if the 1970s were truly the Dark Days for the Brotherhood, as the lights were turned out in BSCP headquarters across the country, its legacy shines bright in the example provided by such union stalwarts as A. Philip Randolph, C. L. Dellums, E. D. Nixon, and thousands more who were pioneers in mobilizing around a labor-oriented civil rights agenda.

BETH TOMPKINS BATES

References and Further Reading

Arnesen, Eric. *Brotherhoods of Color: Black Railroad Workers and the Struggle for Equality*. Cambridge, MA: Harvard University Press, 2001.

Bates, Beth Tompkins. *Pullman Porters and the Rise of Protest Politics in Black America, 1925–1945*. Chapel Hill: University of North Carolina Press, 2001.

Harris, William H. *Keeping the Faith: A. Philip Randolph, Milton P. Webster, and the Brotherhood of Sleeping Car Porters, 1925–1937*. Urbana: University of Illinois Press, 1977.

The Messenger, especially 7:8 (August 1925), 7:9 (September 1925), and 8:9 (September 1926).

See also **Dellums, C. L.; Fair Employment Practice Committee; National Negro Congress; Randolph, A. Philip**

BROTHERHOOD OF TIMBER WORKERS

First organized in Carson, Louisiana, in December 1910, the Brotherhood of Timber Workers (BTW) recruited within six months some 25,000 black and white lumber workers and forest farmers of the pine forests of southeast Texas and western Louisiana. The BTW's meteoric rise surprised even the most committed labor activists in this region of large-scale lumbering where unionism had shallow roots. Over-expansion of this extractive industry in the first decade of the twentieth century weakened workers' leverage with lumber operators by creating an industrial environment of labor surpluses, repeated production curtailments, an 11-hour work day, wage reductions, and sporadic payment in scrip. The BTW tapped growing resentment at the power of lumber operators among the people of the piney woods to build an organization dedicated to securing relief from the worst abuses of the lumber industry. The union demanded land reform, the abolition of commissary checks, the implementation of biweekly pay days, a union-sanctioned wage scale, a reduction in the hours of the working day, and a revision of doctor and hospital fees. In the summer of 1912, the BTW voted to affiliate with the Industrial Workers of the World (IWW) in a bid to strengthen its struggle against the lumber operators.

Despite its rapid rise, the union could not sustain its initial momentum. A vigorous employer counteroffensive of lockouts, blacklisting, espionage, violence, and the use of strikebreakers exposed the fragile foundations of the union's interracial alliance of farmers and industrial wage earners. Although organizational remnants of the BTW persisted until 1916, employers had broken the union by 1913. The union's failure to win recognition and concessions from the region's lumber operators notwithstanding, the BTW remains a significant episode in the history of interracial labor struggles in the Jim Crow South.

Origins and Membership

BTW activists envisioned a social transformation rooted nineteenth-century labor republicanism. In rhetoric reminiscent of the Knights of Labor (KOL), the BTW declared in its constitution that it aimed above all "to elevate those who labor—morally, socially, intellectually, and financially." Like the labor reformers who preceded them, BTW organizers did not imagine—at least in their constitution—an overthrow of capitalism but dreamed of a cooperative industrial future that honored and protected the toiler over the hoarder of wealth. The state, they argued, had the power and the moral responsibility to restore fairness and equality in economic relationships. To that end, the BTW worked to elect legislative candidates who pledged to protect the welfare of lumber workers and promised to break up the land trusts controlled by large-scale lumber operators.

Seeing the crucial division in society as one between those who worked and those who profited through idleness, the BTW built what it regarded as an alliance of the people against the Lumber Trust. Its expansive coalition of the working people of the piney woods included sawyers and other skilled lumber workers who were convinced that the gulf between skilled and common laborers paled in comparison with the social divide between all workers and lumber operators. Petty merchants, who resented company stores that controlled the region's retail trade, joined the ranks of the BTW. Even independent loggers and small sawmill operators, who had trouble competing for timber and securing fair shipping rates on piney-woods railroads owned and operated by subsidiaries of lumber companies, signed union cards and pledged to employ only union men.

The BTW also succeeded in uniting farmers and wage earners, something previous radical movements had accomplished with only limited success. A protracted struggle for control of the timberlands against outside lumber operators radicalized native farmers in the forest, making them ripe recruits for the BTW. Before lumber operators could expand their enterprises, they needed to clear title to the vast timberlands> they claimed. When they did so, farmers of the woods cried foul, asserting that their squatter claims gave them superior legal title to the forest land. Litigating these claims in the district courts, forest farmers, black and white, fared well in defending their right to the land. Numerous examples of white juries finding for black claimants over lumber operators demonstrated how a growing anticorporate sentiment spawned racial cooperation in the piney woods. Many of these initial legal victories, however, were reversed on appeal, empowering lumber operators to take possession of property long claimed by natives of the forest. Some of the BTW's most active recruits and locals, including a number of African-Americans, had direct experience in land litigation with lumber operators. Transformation of the countryside, as much as exploitation at the workplace, explains the widespread appeal of the BTW in this region.

The experience of biracial cooperation in land disputes provided one of the foundations for the BTW's interracialism. Although these workplaces were far from being free of racial conflict, black and white workers nevertheless shared common experiences that encouraged them to breach the color line. First, the labor force in these forest industries was biracial, so whites seldom viewed blacks as outsiders who threatened their job status. Second, because most work in these industries was unskilled, racial wage disparities were lower than in other southern industries. Because of the predominance of unskilled jobs, whites did not have a privileged job status to protect nor were blacks stigmatized for performing "nigger work," conditions that freed these work places of the racial distrust and conflict common to southern railroads, textiles, and building trades. Finally, a shared resentment of the company-town complex facilitated racial cooperation.

Like other biracial unions in the Jim Crow South, the BTW built its coalition on pragmatism. Activists tried to persuade white workers that it was in their own self-interest to join common cause with blacks, assuring them that joining a fight to achieve what they called "stomach equality" would not create social equality among the races. Unionists urged white workers to recognize the false promise of segregation, insisting that the color line, by artificially dividing workers, served only the interests of lumber operators. Although this raceless language of class avoided any recognition of the distinctive historical experiences of black workers, it is important to remember that thousands of African-Americans embraced stomach equality with their white counterparts. Although certainly well aware of the limitations of the union's ideas on race, African-Americans still endorsed the BTW's demands, both at the workplace and for land reform, which promised them tangible benefits. The BTW recognized the dignity of black workers, and the union claimed itself an active defender of their interests. Blacks assumed leadership positions, served as organizers, and challenged racial customs by speaking before mixed-race audiences with speeches that connected the black struggle for emancipation to the BTW's battle against the lumber trust.

Employer Counteroffensive

By the summer of 1911, the BTW had built an impressive, if fragile, interracial alliance of skilled and unskilled industrial workers, farmers, merchants, and independent loggers and mill operators. Large-scale lumbermen launched their own counteroffensive, seeking to exploit divisions within the tenuous alliances that sustained the union. First, they deployed a campaign to undermine public support for the BTW by portraying the union as a subversive organization led by a few dangerous outsiders who promoted their own self-interests by misappropriating union dues collected from poor mill workers. Lumber operators stoked the racist fears of whites in the region's newspapers, charging in a series of letters to the editor that the union's real objective was to impose social equality. To undermine black support for the BTW, employers hired black ministers and teachers who visited mill towns and preached the gospel of anti-unionism and schooled black workers in the merits of company loyalty. Employers also cast themselves as defenders of the family and of the general welfare of the region, who by providing steady industrial employment, elevated the standard of living in the piney woods and created vibrant, thriving communities in the woods. Joining the union, they warned, put those achievements, and family stability, at unnecessary risk.

Lumber operators also took more direct action to defeat the BTW. In July 1911, the Southern Lumber Operators' Association (SLOA), an organization of lumbermen dedicated to preventing the unionization of the industry, agreed to a plan to lock out the union. SLOA believed that member mills could afford to shut down plant operations indefinitely because most mills had substantial overstocks of lumber stored in their yards. Sawmill operators then agreed to determine the union status of their employees and reopen only after they could establish that they could do so with a nonunion labor force. But internal conflicts undermined SLOA's initial resolve. As one lumber operator remarked, he would rather donate his mills to charity than recognize the union. SLOA hired scores of labor spies to verify the union sympathies of the work force, allowing SLOA to compile an extensive blacklist that it shared with member mill operators. By the end of the summer, SLOA authorized the closing of 36 mills in what it called the "infected" areas of Louisiana and Texas, throwing some 10,000 men out of work.

Unionists adopted creative strategies to blunt this employer counteroffensive. In replying to employer accusations in the local press, activists did not take the race bait that employers dangled across the editorial page. Rather than deny that the union promoted social equality, activists simply kept silent on race. Instead, they refuted employer claims that mill hands prospered from large-scale lumbering and focused on wages, workplace safety, living conditions in mill towns, and land distribution. The BTW thus shifted public debate away from the explosive issue of social equality toward a conversation over the just distribution of the fruits of industrial expansion. The BTW was also well-positioned to weather the lockout as it came in the early autumn, just in time for that year's cotton harvest. Organizers secured cotton-picking contracts for sawmill hands displaced by the lockout and offered discharged unionists, especially African-Americans, cash assistance in relocating to the farms and cotton fields of the Southwest. Because of the extensive kinship links among sawmill workers and local farmers, many unionists relied on the mutual aid of family support networks that sustained them through the duration of the lockout.

Despite the BTW's ability to withstand the lockout, the operators' offensive sapped the BTW's strength by the end of 1911. Although unionists secured alternative employment and resources during the lockout, they had become so dispersed across the Southwest that the union lost its ability to collect dues with any consistency. By late autumn, the BTW's coffers were depleted. SLOA spies reported significant declines in membership and found that a number of locals had gone defunct. With its cadre of spies and a black list of 25,000 union members and sympathizers, SLOA established what it regarded as a centralized clearinghouse for labor that it urged member mills to use in reopening their plants. By late fall, operators pledged to restart their mills without union labor and began to recruit new workers from as far away as Georgia.

BTW unionists adopted new tactics to meet this next phase of the struggle against the lumber trust. First, they conducted a new but clandestine membership drive. As the cotton-picking season came to an end, BTW organizers urged returning members to return to work in the sawmills resuming production. To secure employment, the BTW advised unionists to change their names, take the employers' anti-union pledge, but continue paying dues to the BTW. Membership numbers rebounded throughout the spring of 1912, and at its second annual convention, held in Alexandria, Louisiana, the BTW voted to affiliate with the IWW, renaming itself the National Industrial Union of Forest and Lumber Workers, Southern District. The IWW provided critical resources that rejuvenated the BTW. The colorful Wobbly radical and Louisiana native Covington Hall started a union

newspaper, *The Lumberjack*, which provided the BTW with regional and national publicity and served as an important counterweight to the region's employer-dominated press. The IWW lent its experience in organizing, sustaining direct-action tactics, and maintaining the union's interracial membership. Backed by the IWW, the BTW mobilized this resurgent enthusiasm into a renewed campaign to organize the timberlands.

The lumber operators prepared to defeat the unionist challenge by whatever means necessary. Employers harassed stump speakers, deputized loyal workers, and infiltrated BTW locals with spies. They posted armed sentries outside their mills and company towns to prevent organizers from gaining access to non-union workers. In response, BTW activists held rallies outside the mills, making them family events that encouraged the participation of women and children as a strategy to protect themselves from violent attack. But mounting tensions eventually erupted into a massacre when company gunmen fired on some one hundred strikers and their families who had marched upon Grabow, Louisiana, home of the Galloway Lumber Company.

Armed unionists retaliated. Within 10 minutes, four men lay dead and 40 other people, including women and children, were wounded. Local authorities arrested more than 60 union activists and indicted them for the murder of an employed guard of the Galloway Lumber Company.

The riot at Grabow and the subsequent trial derailed the BTW's summer organizing campaign. The BTW redirected its energies into raising a legal defense fund and material support for the families of imprisoned unionists. Although the prisoners were eventually acquitted, the expense of the three-week trial exhausted union resources. The acquittal proved to be a Pyrrhic victory in other ways. The operators of the American Lumber Company in Merryville, Louisiana, the remaining stronghold of BTW activism, fired 15 of its employees who testified for the defense at the trial, goading the BTW's Local 218 to call a strike. Refusing to recognize the union, American Lumber closed the mill until it could reopen with nonunion labor. To defend the mill against unionists, American Lumber constructed a stockade around its property, intimidated strikers, and began to bring in replacement workers, principally African-Americans from other parts of Texas and Louisiana who were unfamiliar with the labor struggles of the preceding 16 months. Despite unionists' attempts to warn away strikebreakers, a sufficient number of them arrived under the protection of armed guards, allowing American Lumber to resume full operation. Most unionists saw defeat and left, but some three hundred black and white stalwarts kept the cause alive. Company deputies became ever more violent, the harassment culminating in a three-day campaign in February 1913, in which they and supporters of the company stormed and burned the union's soup kitchen and ransacked its headquarters. Although the strike officially lasted until June, the violence of mid-February brought an end to the struggle to unionize Merryville and the final collapse of the Brotherhood of Timber Workers' challenge to both the color line and the land and lumber trusts of Texas and Louisiana.

STEVEN A. REICH

References and Further Reading

Fannin, Mark. *Labor's Promised Land: Radical Visions of Gender, Race, and Religion in the South.* Knoxville: University of Tennessee Press, 2003.

Ferrell, Jeff. "'The Song the Capitalist Never Sings': The Brotherhood of Timber Workers and the Culture of Conflict." *Labor History* 32, no. 2 (1991): 422–431.

Ferrell, Jeff, and Kevin Ryan. "The Brotherhood of Timber Workers and the Southern Lumber Trust: Legal Repression and Worker Response." *Radical America* 19 (July–August 1985): 55–74.

Green, James R. "The Brotherhood of Timber Workers, 1910–1913: A Radical Response to Industrial Capitalism in the Southern USA." *Past and Present* 60 (1973): 161–200.

Hall, Covington. *Labor Struggles in the Deep South and Other Writings.* Edited and introduced by David R. Roediger. Chicago: Charles H. Kerr, 1999.

Morgan, George T. Jr. "No Compromise—No Recognition: John Henry Kirby, the Southern Lumber Operators' Association, and Unionism in the Piney Woods, 1906–1916." *Labor History* 10 (Spring 1969): 193–204.

Reed, Merl. "Lumberjacks and Longshoremen: The I.W.W. in Louisiana." *Labor History* 13 (Winter 1972): 41–59.

Roediger, David R. "Gaining a Hearing for Black-White Unity: Covington Hall and the Complexities of Race, Gender and Class." Chap. 10 in *Towards the Abolition of Whiteness: Essays on Race, Politics, and Working Class History.* London: Verso, 1994.

See also **Industrial Workers of the World**

BROWDER, EARL (MAY 20, 1891– JUNE 27, 1973)
American Communist Party

Earl Browder led the American Communist Party through the 1930s until his expulsion in 1946.

While loyal to the Soviet Union, Browder always remained very proud of being an American. Browder was born in Wichita, Kansas, to a family that could trace its roots in the New World back to the years before the American Revolution. His Kansas birth forever blessed him with a distinctive flat accent that emphasized his all-American background. By the time of Browder's birth, his farmer parents had suffered through a drought that took their crops, the deaths of two children to disease, and the loss of their farm to foreclosure. They lived in grinding poverty in a rented home and had lost all faith in the American system. The Browders raised their son Earl to rebel against a system that they viewed as unjust. In 1900, William Browder became an invalid, possibly because of a nervous breakdown. The tragedy forced the Browder boys to leave school to support the family. Earl became a department store errand boy before he could complete third grade. Later, he delivered messages for Western Union. Losing the opportunity of an education greatly affected Browder. Along with an unquenchable thirst for knowledge, he displayed a lifelong hostility toward the economic injustice that had cut short his childhood. To work for the overthrow of capitalism, Browder joined the Socialist Party at the age of 15 in 1906.

As a Socialist, Browder rubbed shoulders with radical unionists such as those who belonged to the Industrial Workers of the World (IWW). In 1912, Browder left the party in protest after the IWW leader Bill Haywood was removed from its executive committee because he advocated sabotage to weaken capitalism and benefit workers. Browder joined William Z. Foster's Syndicalist League of North America. Browder, now working as a bookkeeper for John D. Rockefeller's Standard Oil in Kansas City, served as the local head of the Bookkeepers, Stenographers, and Accountants, an American Federation of Labor (AFL)-affiliated organization. He resigned from Standard Oil in 1916 to manage a nearby farmer's co-op, sat on the Cooperative League of North America's national council, and wrote occasionally for the league's journal. In his spare time, he completed a college degree by taking correspondence courses.

American entry into World War I proved pivotal in Browder's life. In 1914, he had helped organize the League for Democratic Control, which sought to submit U.S. entry into the war to a popular vote. After the United States declared war, Browder was arrested for organizing protest meetings and evading the draft. He went to jail for three years, with two years of the sentence spent in Leavenworth Penitentiary with many of the IWW members including Haywood. While still jailed, Browder joined the newly formed American Communist Party. It had been formed by socialists who wanted a movement more to the political left. Browder left prison on November 5, 1920, as a dedicated communist, intent on devoting all of his time to promoting Leninism.

Browder's new life did not include his family. After Browder's release from jail, he resumed his interest in political activism but without his wife and infant son. He went to Chicago and left his family in Kansas. Browder abandoned both wife and son. However, he never obtained a divorce and continued to pay alimony. (Browder was finally divorced in 1959 when his first wife filed for an annulment.)

A seemingly faceless organization man, Browder became ever more deeply involved with Communism. As a trade union Communist, Browder joined others of his ilk in attempting to liquidate the party's underground, a relic of the First Red Scare and the Palmer Raids. Rising steadily in the ranks of American Communism, he attended the Communist International and the Red International of Labor Unions Congresses in Moscow in 1921. Back in the United States, he worked to get Communists accepted into a broad-based, reform-oriented Farmer-Labor Party for the national elections of 1924. The Communists enjoyed greatest success in the AFL's Chicago Federation of Labor, where they gained one fifth of the seats. Unfortunately, an attempt by the Communists to take control of the Farmer-Labor Party's 1923 convention with disguised delegates from paper organizations backfired. Angered by the actions of the Communists, the AFL subsequently banned the Communist-led Trade Union Educational League (TUEL), Browder's group. TUEL's attempt to work within AFL unions to develop a class-struggle unionism approach came to an end.

In the heart of Communism in Moscow, Browder was highly regarded as a party worker throughout the 1920s and 1930s. A good listener and keen observer, he had excellent political skills and could anticipate changes in Soviet politics. From 1927 to 1929, Browder worked in China for the Soviet Union-supported Pan Pacific Trade Union Secretariat. Upon his return to the United States in 1930, Browder's Moscow connections helped him become administrative secretary of the American Communist Party. He advanced to general secretary in 1934. In that same year, Browder devised the slogan, "Communism is Twentieth-Century Americanism," in an effort to identify the party with American traditions and institutions.

A sharp-dressed man with remarked-upon good manners, he made the Communist Party look good in the eyes of many Americans. Unlike other Communist leaders, notably Foster, Browder never participated in street battles. He produced necessary calls for revolt in future or conditional tenses. Publicly, he urged protestors not to demand seizures of city halls.

Under Browder's leadership, American Communists paid more attention to the concerns of women workers. When Congress passed the Economy Act of 1932, which permitted the dismissal of one spouse if a couple worked for the federal government, nearly 1,500 women lost their jobs. Private industry followed the government's lead and refused to hire married women. Browder spoke out against this discriminatory policy, denouncing it as a fascist effort to drive women from the labor market. The American Communists throughout the 1930s continued to advocate child care, birth control, and shared responsibility for housework. However, the party still saw women chiefly as wives and mothers instead of as workers. Women's issues played a subordinate role to industrial unionism, African-American rights, and the class struggle.

The Great Depression added to the appeal of Communism, since it appeared that capitalism had broken beyond repair. In May 1935, the Communists claimed about 35,000 members. Browder became the Communist Party presidential candidate in 1936. Running against Franklin D. Roosevelt, he polled 80,181 votes. No other Communist candidate has ever surpassed Browder's vote total. When Browder ran for a second time in 1940, while appealing a prison sentence, he garnered only 46,251 votes. Browder had been convicted and sentenced to four years' imprisonment for traveling on a false passport to Spain in support of anti-Franco Republicans. The jail sentence undoubtedly antagonized some voters, but disillusionment with the Communist support of the Hitler-Stalin nonaggression pact of 1939 cost Browder much support among an American public that did not turn out in large numbers for the election.

After Hitler invaded the Soviet Union in 1941, Browder's energetic support of the Allied war effort helped the Communist Party regain much of the support that it had lost. In *Victory—and After* (1942) and *Teheran: Our Path in Peace and War* (1944), Browder called for the postwar cooperation of labor and capital and the peaceful coexistence of Communism and capitalism.

However, after Cold War changes in Soviet policy, Browder lost the support of Moscow and was purged from the Communist ranks. He was criticized by the Communists for being right-wing, partly because he believed that his sons could achieve the American Dream through education. (Three of his four sons became college professors.) In 1945, Browder was replaced as the head of the American Communist Party by his hated rival, Foster. In 1946, Browder was expelled from the party. He subsequently made a living by serving as the U.S. representative for Soviet publishing houses.

The Cold War brought other difficulties for Browder. He was indicted in 1950 for refusing to answer questions at a Senate investigation but was acquitted in 1951. In 1952, Browder and his Russian-born wife, Raissa Luganovskaya, were indicted for false statements in her 1949 application for U.S. citizenship. The indictment was dropped in 1959. Browder spent the last years of his life as a lecturer and historical researcher.

CARYN E. NEUMANN

Selected Works

Marx and America: A Study of the Doctrine of Impoverishment. New York: Duell, Sloan, and Pearce, 1958.
The People's Front. New York: International Publishing, 1938.
Victory—and After. New York: International Publishing, 1942.
The Way Out. New York: International Publishing, 1941.

References and Further Reading

Isserman, Maurice. *Which Side Were You On? The American Communist Party during the Second World War.* Middletown, CT: Wesleyan University Press, 1982.
Klehr, Harvey. *The Heyday of American Communism.* New York: Basic Books, 1984.
Ryan, James G. *Earl Browder: The Failure of American Communism.* Tuscaloosa: The University of Alabama Press, 1997.

See also **American Federation of Labor; Anticommunism; Foster, William Z.; Haywood, William D. "Big Bill"; Industrial Workers of the World**

BRYN MAWR SUMMER SCHOOL FOR WOMEN WORKERS IN INDUSTRY

The Bryn Mawr Summer School for Women Workers in Industry opened its doors in 1921, the first workers education program designed for women in the United States. This experimental school was the idea of M. Carey Thomas, educator, suffragist, and president of Bryn Mawr College, and the project of Hilda Worthington Smith, whose dedication and patience made the Summer School a reality. They envisioned nurturing a new generation of women who would "work together for common ends," humanizing industry, improving working conditions, and raising wages. Each summer for 17 years the Bryn Mawr Summer School brought together one hundred women industrial workers from across the United States for a two-month term of study.

Summer School students came to Bryn Mawr from a variety of backgrounds, but all shared the effects of having entered factories between the ages of 10 and 14, working 12-hour shifts, and taking home wages to help support their families. A women's community that reached across class lines, racial barriers, and ethnic separations, the School admitted immigrant students, black women from the rural South, trade union activists, and workers from nonunion shops, who thrived in the school's nonhierarchical atmosphere. The decision was made in 1926 to racially integrate the Summer School, although Bryn Mawr College had yet to admit an African-American student. A total of 1,700 women came to Bryn Mawr between 1921 and 1938, from over 50 industrial communities; two thirds were from the Northeast, the remainder from across the country. The majority of these women workers were employed in the needle trades or in skilled craft industries. The School recruited organized workers from a range of unions, among them the International Ladies' Garment Workers' Union (ILGWU), the United Garment Workers, and the Amalgamated Clothing Workers. Most nontrade unions came to the School through the YWCA Industrial Department. Each year half the student body belonged to trade unions. Many students gained leadership positions in their unions after attending Bryn Mawr, and a number held national office, including Elizabeth Nord, of the Textile Workers of America, and Carmen Lucia, of the United Hatters, Cap and Millinery Workers. Worker-students at Bryn Mawr put into immediate practice the organizing strategies they were taught at the school, demanding, for example, that workers represent 50% of the Summer School Board and insisting on better working conditions for the housekeeping staff at the College.

Faculty invited to teach at the Bryn Mawr Summer School included women and men, prominent academics and trade union leaders. Among the 90 faculty hired between 1921 and 1938 were Alice Hanson Cook, Paul Douglas, Lillian Herstein, Amy Hewes, Leo Huberman, Broadus Mitchell, Gladys Palmer, Esther Peterson, Mark Starr, Caroline Ware, Colston Warne, and Theresa Wolfson. Most felt strongly that, as Caroline Ware put it, "Everybody had the sense that we had as much to learn from the students as the students had to learn from us." Teachers at the School combined a commitment to the political left with labor movement activism. They endorsed the principles of workers' education, always beginning with what their students knew and understood. Faculty encouraged students to write about themselves, and the stories that came pouring out became the basis for classes in economics and labor history. Students wrote plays and poetry, devised their own schema for economic recovery during the Depression, and shared stories and data about their jobs, wages, and communities. John Dewey visited the School and viewed it as a model of progressive education and experiential learning. Some described the School as a "salon" for the labor movement and the left, bringing together avant-garde women and men, including W. E. B. Du Bois, Norman Thomas, Margaret Sanger, Frances Perkins, and Eleanor Roosevelt, among others, who spoke to the students and joined in informal discussions with groups of faculty.

As the industrial reform movements of the 1920s gave way to heightened political and labor activism in the 1930s, conflicts between Bryn Mawr College and the Summer School flared almost annually. One College trustee asked the revealing question, "Why should we support your organizing workers to strike our husbands' plants?" The vision of cross-class feminism cherished by M. Carey Thomas and Hilda Smith shattered completely when the Board of Trustees disapproved of the involvement of faculty and students from the Summer School in a strike of agricultural workers at nearby Seabrook Farms, and the College Board of Trustees forced the Summer School to leave Bryn Mawr College in 1938. The remarkable thing about this history is that such an institutional alliance worked at all.

The Bryn Mawr Summer School served as a model for four other workers' education programs for women workers, including the Southern Summer School, the Summer School for Office Workers, the Vineyard Shore Labor School, and the Hudson Shore Labor School, a coeducational resident school established after the Bryn Mawr Summer School closed, at Hilda Smith's family home in New York State.

MARY E. FREDERICKSON

References and Further Reading

Bauman, Susan, and Rita Heller. "Women of Summer." Produced by Bauman and Heller. New York: Filmakers Library, Inc., 1985.
Heller, Rita. "Blue Collars and Bluestockings: The Bryn Mawr Summer School for Women Workers, 1921–1938," in Joyce Kornbluh and Mary Frederickson, eds., Sisterhood and Solidarity: Workers Education for Women, 1914–1984. Philadelphia: Temple University Press, 1984, pp. 107–145.
Hollis, Karyn L. Liberating Voices: Writing at the Bryn Mawr Summer School for Women Workers. Carbondale: Southern Illinois University Press, 2004.
Smith, Hilda W. Women Workers at the Bryn Mawr Summer School. New York: Affiliated Summer Schools for Women Workers in Industry, 1929.

BUNTING v. OREGON (1917)

Bunting v. Oregon is a relatively minor case—not because it did not establish an important principle, but because it came at a time when the United States Supreme Court proved itself quite inconsistent in sanctioning protective labor legislation. In many ways, Bunting serves as a kind of ideological (although not chronological) way station between the negation of such legislation represented by Lochner v. New York (1905) and Adkins v. Children's Hospital (1923) and the formal approval of such laws by the end of the New Deal.

The Bunting case grew out of a 1913 Oregon law that sought to regulate the wages and hours for all workers, not just the female laborers covered by Muller v. Oregon (1908). The statute made it a misdemeanor not to pay time-and-a-half for any work above 10 hours per day in the state's mills, factories, and manufacturing establishments (with the exception of security, repair, or emergency work). The law also prohibited any work at all over 13 hours a day.

Franklin Bunting, owner of the Lake View Flouring Mills, disregarded the law, was found guilty, and received a fine of $50. The Oregon Supreme Court upheld the conviction, and Bunting appealed to the nation's highest court. Represented by two of the state's most prominent corporate attorneys, Bunting argued that the law represented a violation of his rights to equal protection of the laws under the 14th Amendment.

The U.S. Supreme Court decided the case in favor of Oregon's 10-hour law 5-3, with Chief Justice Edward White and associate justices Willis Van Devanter and James McReynolds dissenting. (Louis Brandeis recused himself because he had, before his appointment to the bench, helped prepare—with the help of Josephine Goldmark—the nearly 1,000-page brief for the state of Oregon.) The court majority, however, carefully limited its support of the Oregon statute, endorsing its regulation of hours, but not (through the overtime provision) of wages. Despite the state of Oregon's explicit embrace of wage regulation in its brief, the court refused to touch that issue. In approving the regulation of hours, the Court generally followed the sociological perspective of Muller, recognizing the health benefits of limiting work to 10 hours and the broad prevalence of such limitations in Europe.

So, despite the Court's striking down of maximum hours legislation for New York bakers in the critically important Lochner case, the Supreme Court continued to support this extension of protective labor legislation, which involved not only men and women but, at least indirectly, wages as well. Yet the Court steadfastly refused to overturn Lochner. And when the issue of federal wage provisions for women workers came before the Court in *Adkins* in 1923, six of the justices resolutely struck down government power in that area. *Bunting* mattered much in the *Adkins* decision. Recalling the case as a crucial precedent, the majority of justices sharply demarcated the issue of wages from that of hours. In separate dissents, Chief Justice William Howard Taft and Associate Justice Oliver Wendell Holmes excoriated such a distinction. They also declared that, as far as they were concerned, *Bunting* had effectively served to overturn *Lochner.*

The New Deal judicial revolution that finally upheld government regulation of wages and hours would legally ratify—and indeed go well beyond—the principles of *Bunting*, although in the ensuing decades the case seemed to slip the memory of legal historians. Yet *Bunting v. Oregon* does show, at the least, that the Progressive Era Supreme Court never spoke with one voice when it came to the rights and protections of American workers.

ROBERT D. JOHNSTON

References and Further Reading

Frankfurter, Felix, with the assistance of Josephine Goldmark. *The Case for the Shorter Work Day.* New York: National Consumers' League, 1916.
Hall, Kermit L. *The Magic Mirror: Law in American History.* New York: Oxford University Press, 1989.

Cases and Statutes Cited

Adkins v. Children's Hospital 261 U.S. 525 (1923)
Bunting v. Oregon 243 U.S. 426 (1917)
Lochner v. New York 198 U.S. 45 (1905)
Muller v. Oregon 208 U.S. 412 (1908)

BUREAU OF LABOR STATISTICS

The Bureau of Labor Statistics (BLS) is the principal fact-finding agency for the federal government in the broad field of labor economics and statistics. Following the example of 13 states that created labor statistics bureaus on their own, particularly Massachusetts, Congress passed, and on June 27, 1884, President Chester A. Arthur signed, a bill establishing a labor statistics agency. The new agency was named the Bureau of Labor and placed in the Department of the Interior. Congress placed the Bureau under the direction of a Commissioner of Labor Statistics, to be appointed by the president with the consent of the U.S. Senate, for renewable terms of four years.

Spurning Terence Powderly, then head of the Knights of Labor (KOL), President Arthur selected Carroll D. Wright, who had been the head of the Massachusetts Bureau of Labor Statistics since 1873. Under Wright's leadership, the Bureau established a reputation for objectivity and for the production of high-quality reports. The various Bulletins, as well as Annual and Special Reports, covered subjects such as industrial depressions, strike investigations and industrial relations, working women and children, urban and ethnic matters, tariffs, wages and prices, and international labor matters.

President Cleveland recommended that the Bureau be enlarged to so that it could investigate the causes of labor disputes and perhaps serve as an arbitrator of labor disputes. At its convention in 1887, the KOL again recommended the establishment of a Department of Labor, and at the request of President Grover Cleveland, made recommendations as to the scope of the proposed department. Congress eventually passed a bill establishing a Department of Labor, but which did not give the department cabinet-level status. President Cleveland signed the bill on March 21, 1888.

The new department gained personnel and prestige, as Commissioner Wright reported directly to the president. The Department continued to be known for the quality and objectivity of its reports, and was recognized as the most important statistical agency of this period, exemplified as Wright supervised the completion of the 1890 census. Wright was also appointed by President Cleveland as chairman of a commission on the Pullman strike in 1894, and also played a role advising President Theodore Roosevelt during the 1902 Anthracite Coal Mine Strike, eventually serving as part of an arbitration commission that helped settle the strike.

In 1905, Dr. Charles P. Neill was appointed second commissioner of the Bureau of Labor, now part of the Department of Commerce and Labor, established in 1903. Neill strengthened the Bureau's headquarters-field fact gathering and statistical analysis work. His emphasis on studies for economic and social reform was in step with the ideas of the early Progressive movement.

Public Law 426-62, which created the Department of Labor on March 4, 1913, established the BLS within the new department. Section 4 of the Act mandated "that the Bureau of Labor Statistics, under the direction of the Secretary of Labor, shall collect, collate, and report at least once each year, or oftener if necessary, full and complete statistics of the conditions of labor, and the products and distribution of the products of the same, and to this end said Secretary shall have power to employ any or either of the bureaus provided for his department and to rearrange such statistical work and to distribute or consolidate the same as may be deemed desirable in the public interests." Dr. Royal Meeker was appointed the third commissioner of the BLS in August 1913 by President Woodrow Wilson.

Under Meeker, the Bureau faced a prewar recession and a wartime economy. The BLS began to produce regular reports on unemployment and employment, as well as a regular report on inflation, the Cost of Living Index, now known as the Consumer Price Index (CPI). The *Monthly Labor Review* was established in July 1915 to disseminate information from Bureau studies and remains the principal journal of fact, analysis, and research from the BLS.

In 1920, Dr. Meeker resigned his position to work for the International Labor Office of the League of Nations. Commissioner Ethelbert Stewart, a 33-year employee of the BLS and its predecessor agencies, succeeded Meeker. Under Stewart's tenure, the BLS initiated a series of comprehensive studies of specific industries and developed productivity indexes, the forerunners of many current economywide and sector indexes produced by the BLS.

Unfortunately for Stewart, who spent much of his 12-year tenure attempting to mitigate the impact of post-World War I budget cuts, conflicting employment statistics rankled the Department of Labor at the onset of the Great Depression of 1929. The U.S. Employment Service (USES), drastically cut back during the 1920s and staffed with partisan appointees, reported far more optimistic employment figures to Secretaries of Labor James J. Davis and William N. Doak than those reported by the BLS, which were usually six weeks after the USES reports.

In July 1932, the 74-year-old Stewart was forced to retire, replaced by Dr. Isador Lubin, an economist with the Brookings Institution, in July 1933. Closely associated with Secretary of Labor Frances Perkins, Lubin worked with the secretary, and outside consultants—including the American Statistical Association—to improve the Bureau's ability to provide reliable economic data essential to the new federal agencies established under Franklin Delano Roosevelt to foster recovery from the Depression.

Although Dr. Lubin formally remained Commissioner of Labor Statistics until 1946, he was assigned to the Labor Division of the National Defense Advisory Commission in June 1940, and was appointed special statistical assistant to President Roosevelt in May 1941. Mr. Ford Hinrichs, the BLS chief economist, acted as commissioner in Lubins's stead. Under Lubins and Hinrichs, additional regional offices were established to enhance the collection of wage, price, and employment information.

In addition to collection of information, the BLS actively sought new ways to analyze economic information. In the 1940s, the Bureau was one of the first organizations to use input-output analysis, invented by Dr. Wassily Leontief. An important concept in economics, input-output analysis shows the extensive process by which inputs in one industry produce outputs for consumption or for input into another industry. The Bureau's input-output work with Leontief had a direct effect on how the Agency measured the economy, leading to the development of producer price indexes. In addition, the Bureau's work with Leontief also had other effects on the Agency. When a still-being-assembled UNIVAC computer inverted a 1947 input/output matrix, the Bureau found itself at the vanguard of computing technology.

In August 1946, Ewan Clague was appointed commissioner, and was immediately faced with a draconian 1948 federal fiscal budget eliminating 700 of the Bureau's 1,700 positions. Increasing use of the statistics produced by the BLS, however, by the newly created Council of Economic Advisors (1946) and the Congressional Joint Economic Committee, and the 1948 agreement between the General Motors Company (GMC) and the United Auto Workers (UAW) calling for use of the Consumer Price Index for adjusting wages increased the public profile of the BLS.

Labor historians often refer to gradual establishment of postwar "corporate consensus" or "corporate liberalism" in the late 1940s and early 1950s. Corporate liberalism as a system can be characterized as one in which employers and labor leaders, with the encouragement of government, share a goal of day-to-day cooperation, guaranteed economic stability, and the protection of the rights of workers through nondisruptive collective action. Wages and benefits, rather than social reform, became the chief concern of unions. Perhaps the agreement between the GMC and the UAW to use the Consumer Price Index to adjust wages is emblematic of this corporate liberalism.

Clague continued to place emphasis on the BLS as a purveyor of reliable statistical indexes, revising the Consumer Price Index's market basket data in 1961–1962 and undertaking economic growth studies for the analysis and projection of economic growth trends. By the time of Clagues's replacement by Dr. Arthur M. Ross in 1965, the BLS had obtained a conventionally accepted public image as a nonpartisan professional organization issuing reliable statistics.

Under Dr. Arthur M. Ross, the BLS continued to modernize operations, particularly by increasing the use of automated data processing operations begun in the early 1960s. Under Ross, the BLS began to centralize its business operations. Dr. Geoffrey

H. Moore, formerly the president of the American Statistical Association, succeeded Ross as commissioner in 1970 and continued to centralize the operations of the BLS.

In July 1973, Julius Shiskin, formerly the head of the Office of Statistical Policy of the Office of Management and Budget (OMB), succeeded Geoffrey Moore as commissioner. Shiskin served as the chief economic statistician and assistant director of the Bureau of the Census, and the head economist of the Planning Division of the War Production Board from 1942 to 1945. At the Bureau of the Census he was instrumental in developing an electronic computer method for seasonally adjusting economic time series and for developing the *Business Conditions Digest*. At the OMB, he originated the *Social Indicators* report.

As commissioner during the Nixon, Ford, and Carter administrations, Shiskin was instrumental in preserving the political neutrality of the government's unemployment and work force statistics. By then, most federal wages, retirement, and entitlement programs, as well as most union collective bargaining contracts, had been linked with the Bureau's price indexes. Such indexation required complete confidence in the nonpolitical nature of the Bureau's operations. Shiskin also oversaw the complete overhaul of the preparation of the Consumer Price Index, as well as the Wholesale Price Indexes, which resulted in 1983 in the issuance of the present Producer Price Index.

Shiskin died while in office in October 1978 and was replaced by Dr. Janet L. Norwood, who was named acting commissioner. In March 1979, President Carter nominated her as the first woman to serve as commissioner. Except for a single acting commissioner, BLS commissioners serving since October 1978 have been women.

Early in her tenure, Norwood navigated a 12% budget cut in fiscal 1982, protecting the Bureau's core programs, and completed additional revisions of the CPI and Producer Price Index. Under her tenure, the BLS assumed responsibility for administering the Federal/State Cooperative national labor information programs.

Commissioner Norwood served until January 1, 1992, the effective date of her resignation. After an interim period of 23 months, during which William Barron served as acting commissioner, President Bill Clinton appointed Dr. Katharine G. Abraham as commissioner in 1993. During Commissioner Abraham's tenure, extensive research concerning the accuracy of the Consumer Price Index was done, laying the groundwork for several changes in the way the CPI was calculated. Much of the impetus for the revision of the CPI was the result of the work of a commission created by the Senate Finance Committee and chaired by the economist Michael J. Boskin of the Hoover Institute. In 1996, the Commission issued a report sharply criticizing the BLS for statistical deficiencies in the price index overestimating inflation rates.

Although Abraham served two terms as commissioner, and expressed an interest in serving a third, she was not reappointed in 2001, the first time in the history of the BLS that a commissioner who wished to stay on was not reappointed. Dr. Abraham was replaced by Dr. Lois Orr, who served as the acting commissioner from October 2001 to July 2002. In July 2002, President Bush appointed Dr. Kathleen P. Utgoff as the BLS commissioner. Utgoff was widely recognized for her work as the executive director of the Pension Benefit Guaranty Corporation, another agency within the Department of Labor.

During Utgoff's first term, the Bureau announced on August 5, 2005, that it would no longer collect the data on women workers in the Current Employment Survey (CES). The BLS defended its decisions against critics by noting first that the series imposed a significant reporting burden on survey respondents because payroll records do not typically include gender identification; second, the CES women workers series were little used; and finally the BLS would continue to provide extensive labor market information on women in other publications and reports.

As the BLS approached its 125th anniversary, the agency's veneer of nonpartisan objectivity appeared to shine less brightly, perhaps in partial result of the decline of the corporate liberal consensus of the 1950s and 1960s. In addition, as noted by former Commissioner Abraham, the BLS faced fundamental changes in the American economy, changes from a manufacturing to a service basis. Looking ahead, more comprehensive measurement of productive activities, however they may be organized, must be a priority within the Bureau of Labor Standards.

JAMES G. CASSEDY

References and Further Reading

Abraham, Katherine G. "What We Don't Know Could Hurt Us: Some Reflections on the Measurement of Economic Activity." *Journal of Economic Perspectives*, Volume 19, Number 3 (Summer 2005): 3–18(16).

Archival Records of the Bureau of Labor Statistics (Record Group 257) are available at the National Archives and Records Administration in College Park, Maryland (www.archives.gov). In addition, the Department of Labor has an extensive history section on its Web site at www.dol.gov.

Clague, Ewan. *The Bureau of Labor Statistics*. New York: Frederick A. Praeger, 1968.

Holdcamper, Forrest R., comp. *Preliminary Inventory of the Records of the Bureau of Statistics*. Washington, DC: National Archives and Records Service, 1964.

Kohli, Martin C. "The Leontief-BLS Partnership: A New Framework for Measurement." *The Monthly Labor Review* 124, No. 6 (June 2001): 29–37.

The United States Government Manual. Washington, DC: Federal Register, National Archives and Records Administration.

Unknown author. *Overall Administrative History of the Bureau of Labor Statistics*. Located in Finding Aids for the Records of the Bureau of Labor Statistics (Record Group 257). Washington, DC: National Archives and Records Administration, 1987.

C

C&O CANAL WORKERS STRIKE (1834)

In late January 1834, canal construction workers on the Chesapeake and Ohio (C&O) Canal violently attacked each other near Williamsport, Maryland, leading to the intervention of federal troops in a labor dispute for the first time. The violence pitted workers from the north of Ireland called Fardowns or Longfords against those from the south, denominated Corkonians. The trouble began when Corkonian workers attacked Longford canallers, leaving one dead. Several days later, 200 Longfordmen descended upon their enemies from Cork working below Williamsport. Four days thereafter, a full-scale battle raged between upward of 700 men of the Longford faction and 300 Corkonians, the latter being routed and chased from the field. Five to 10 men died. The canal company called in the state militia, which arrested 35 canallers and wounded many more. To ensure the continued stability of the line, the governor, at the behest of the C&O, requested that federal troops be stationed on the line. Two companies were dispatched from Baltimore and remained into the spring. Under their scrutiny, the two factions parleyed and signed a treaty.

Characterized by the C&O and the local authorities as merely an unusually violent Irish brouhaha, the 1834 disturbances resulted from workplace issues and were not an isolated incident. At least 10 riots or strikes erupted on the canal between 1834 and 1840, leading five times to the dispatching of the state militia and once to the intervention of federal troops. The 1834 C&O Canal Workers strike and its suppression illustrate much about the experience of unskilled labor, the intersection of class and ethnicity, and the unwillingness of the state to condone violent labor action, especially in the public works industry often backed by government funds.

The success of the Erie Canal (constructed 1817–1825) initiated a wave of speculative canal construction involving private companies and state agencies all purporting to perform the public work of facilitating trade and spreading progress. The C&O Canal Company, among the early imitators, planned to build an artificial waterway paralleling the Potomac River, and then crossing the Appalachian Mountains into the Ohio Valley. Construction began on July 4, 1827, with President John Quincy Adams turning the first spade of earth. From such auspicious beginnings soon flowed myriad problems. Canal construction suffered from chronic shortages of capital and labor. Private risk capital proved scarce, and the industry came to rely on state funds. Canal construction also required workers in unprecedented numbers for the era. The C&O, needing up to five thousand men in the mid-1830s, used different forms of labor, including slave and indentured, but relied primarily on wage laborers. The company passed the troublesome responsibility for the management of work and laborers onto contractors, who bid for the right to build sections of the canal. The company accepted the lowest bid, which forced contractors to cut their estimates as low as possible. Contractors, who were expected to employ, feed, and house an adequate work force, often confronted financial difficulties and found it difficult to pay the men on schedule or complete their sections. Insolvent builders commonly abandoned the canal, leaving their workers unpaid and unemployed, a cause of much labor unrest.

Canal work was dangerous and living conditions primitive. Canallers toiled from sunup to sundown, exposed to injuries common to physical labor and the epidemics that regularly swept public works construction—malaria, yellow fever, and cholera, which struck the C&O in 1832. At night, they retreated to shanties at the worksite, makeshift huts or bunkhouses. Theirs was a difficult existence marked by hard toil, rude conditions, a bare subsistence, and a high degree of transience.

Most canal laborers were Irish immigrants, though some native-born and German workers could be found on the line. In need of work, already on the move, and having a reputation as unskilled laborers, the Irish funneled into what was one of the most difficult types of labor at the time. On canals, their ethnicity acted as a social bond, but also as a source of friction. To protect themselves from conniving contractors or unduly harsh conditions, canallers banded together. The Irish secret society constituted their model for organization. Forged in the Irish peasantry's struggle with English domination, Irish laborers imported the tactic of clandestine violence to New World workplaces, where it proved equally adept in the struggle with employers. Instead of the Irish Whiteboys or Steelboys societies, the canallers formed factions based upon county of nativity in Ireland.

As the company's finances soured, canallers feared that failure threatened and contractors would not be able to pay them. In fact, one contractor owed money by the company discharged his men without fully paying them. These laborers formed the core of rioters. Such economic fears fractured the work force into traditional factions, as Corkonians and Longford men banded together in an attempt to control the remaining jobs for their own members. Class experience fused with ethnic cultural forms to produce violent labor action.

Collective labor violence pervaded the canal construction industry—160 incidents of riots and strikes took place on canals in the United States and Canada from 1780 to 1860. The authorities responded by calling in the militia or troops 32 times from 1829 to 1849. The secret societies or factions that fomented the labor unrest amounted to nascent labor organizations. The conflict took the form of Irish factional fighting but was an ethnic acting out of class conflict. Factions used violence to establish some control over the labor force, maintain employment, and drive up wages. At times, they fought directly with the canal

companies by staging strikes against nonpayment of wages or unacceptable workplace conditions. Though of an internecine variety, such violence, as the 1834 C&O Canal Workers strike demonstrates, constituted as valid an expression of class action, as did the strikes and parades of skilled artisans.

PETER WAY

References and Further Reading

Baird, W. David. "Violence along the Chesapeake and Ohio Canal: 1839." *Maryland Historical Magazine* 66 (Summer 1971): 121–134.

Beames, Michael. *Peasants and Power: The Whiteboy Movements and Their Control in Pre-Famine Ireland.* New York: St. Martin's, 1983.

Grimsted, David. "Ante-bellum Labor: Violence, Strike, and Communal Arbitration." *Journal of Social History* 19, no. 1 (1985): 5–28.

Morris, Richard B. "Andrew Jackson, Strikebreaker." *American Historical Review* 55 (October 1949): 54–68.

Way, Peter. *Common Labour: Workers and the Digging of North American Canals, 1780–1860.* New York: Cambridge University Press, 1993.

———. "Shovel and Shamrock: Irish Workers and Labor Violence in the Digging of the Chesapeake and Ohio Canal." *Labor History* 30, no. 4 (1989): 489–517.

See also **Irish**

CALIFORNIA

Native Americans were the first Californians whose work secured the wealth of others. In 1769, at San Diego, Father Junípero Serra and the Franciscans initiated a mission system designed to Christianize and Hispanicize the native peoples. Though the missionaries wished to save souls, their religious goals were inseparable from the Spanish state's aim of producing a class of Spanish-speaking Christian farmers and laborers who would defend Spain's imperial interests. The Law of the Indies anticipated 10 years of tutelage, but the priests repeatedly concluded that the full conversion of their charges was a remote prospect. Consequently, from the 1760s until the Mexican era of the 1830s, native Californians were encouraged and coerced into laboring in mission fields and pastures. After 1775, flight was subject to military capture and corporal punishment. As a captive, though technically not enslaved, labor force, mission Indians cultivated wheat, barley, and corn; tended olive orchards and vineyards; and raised cattle, sheep, and horses. Some became weavers, tanners, blacksmiths, masons, and carpenters. As mission growth caused the depopulation of native villages and the alteration of ecosystems, the missions' surpluses appealed to hungry Indians, thereby ensuring a supply of labor. By 1820, the

20 missions of Spanish California housed 20,000 neophytes, who raised thousands of livestock and produced 100,000 bushels of crops annually. Productivity was hampered, however, by measles and typhus epidemics, which especially ravaged reproductive-age women and the very young. Disease, overwork, and the humiliation of physical punishment also led to fugitivism and rebellion. In 1824, the Chumash of southern California reacted to their strict work regime and abuse by soldiers with a major uprising. The Chumash captured and occupied Mission La Purísima and Mission Santa Ynez for a month and Mission Santa Bárbara more briefly before fleeing to the interior. In 1828, similar circumstances prompted Estanislao's rebellion at Mission San José. Finally, in 1833, under the guidance of Mexico's liberal Vice President Valentín Gómez-Farías, the Mexican Congress secularized the California missions. Though secularization was supposed to provide the Indians with a share of former mission lands and herds, it actually left them as a pauperized and dependent labor force. Most found employment as agricultural laborers and cowboys on the ranchos of the 1830s and 1840s. As during the mission years, they were not paid in cash, but in food, clothing, and shelter. In the absence of urban growth and economic diversification, unpaid Indian workers in agricultural occupations remained the norm in California until U.S. annexation in 1848.

Gold Rush to 1900

The Gold Rush of 1849 stimulated migration into California from around the United States and from Western Europe, China, Canada, and Mexico. Early migrants were independent prospectors, but by 1850, the placer gold that could be collected by shovel and pan was gone. Mining companies employing capital-intensive extraction methods, such as hydraulic mining, ushered in a wage-earning economy for California's 150,000 people. Miners continued to be important, but their daily wages fell from $20 in 1848 to $3 by 1856. Other occupations emerged that were ancillary to the gold economy, in lumbering, transportation, metallurgy, and construction. San Francisco was the state's principal city, port, and manufacturing center. In June 1850, the San Francisco Typographical Society was born as the West Coast's first union, followed by a union of the city's teamsters in July. Economic instability in the form of a rapid sequence of booms and busts, coupled with high labor turnover, hampered organizing in the 1850s. Strikes were frequently unsuccessful, such as those by San Francisco sailors in August 1850 and

printers in October 1853. After 1859, silver from Nevada's Comstock Lode fueled San Francisco's continued growth, and conditions improved for organized labor. In 1863, the San Francisco Trades Union became the first citywide federation of unions on the West Coast. Unions agitated for the eight-hour day, and in June 1867, San Francisco was the first city in the nation to grant this to its government workers. In February 1868, a state law provided the same for most workers, but was not enforced. By 1870, San Francisco firms produced 60% of the West Coast's manufactured goods and employed one half of California's industrial workers.

A legacy of the Gold Rush migrations, thousands of Chinese workers in the state engaged in boot and shoe manufacturing, cigar making, and railroad construction. Race played a major role in the development of the California working class, as white workers invoked racial prerogatives to defend themselves against a perceived Chinese threat. In 1859, several San Francisco cigar makers faced boycotts for employing Chinese, while in February 1867, white boot and shoe makers struck against wage reductions that they blamed on Chinese competition. While whites declared the Chinese to be inassimilable into white society and union culture, over 3,500 Chinese construction workers struck against the Central Pacific Railroad in June 1867 for a 12-hour day and a raise in pay. Nevertheless, Chinese resistance to exploitation failed to ingratiate them with their white counterparts. When California faced the national depression of 1873, anti-Chinese sentiment took institutional form in the Workingmen's Party of California (WPC) in 1877. The WPC dominated San Francisco's working-class wards and elected one third of the delegates to the 1878–1879 state constitutional convention, whose product included a clause banning the employment of Chinese on public works and by corporations licensed in the state. Even after the new party's demise, white workers' attitudes were reflected in the anti-Chinese stance of the otherwise progressive Knights of Labor, which had over one hundred assemblies in California between 1878 and 1895, and in organized labor's agitation for the federal Chinese Exclusion Act of 1882. In fact, anti-Asian sentiment was a powerful unifying force for California's white labor movement.

In the aftermath of the depression of the 1870s, California workers enjoyed a decade of prosperity that produced some organizational gains. In March 1883, the San Francisco Trades Assembly succeeded in its campaign for a California Bureau of Labor Statistics, while Los Angeles plasterers won the first recorded strike in the city's history. In February, San Francisco carpenters had won a nine-hour day and elimination of piecework. The following year,

Los Angeles carpenters founded Local 56 of the United Brotherhood of Carpenters and Joiners, whose eight hundred members made it the largest union in southern California. In the spring of 1885, San Francisco sailors formed the Coast Seamen's Union—later a principal component of the Sailors' Union of the Pacific—while the city's ironworkers established the Federated Iron Trades Council, the first of its type in the country. In January 1886, San Francisco labor leaders created the Federated Trades and Labor Organization, dedicated to uniting all western workers and their organizations; and in September 1890, their counterparts in the south formed the Los Angeles Council of Federated Trades. Threatened by the rising tide of unionism, San Francisco employers banded together in the Manufacturers and Employers Association in August 1891, planning to drive unions from the city. The depression of 1893 made their efforts unnecessary, as union membership fell 75%. One important exception was the San Francisco Building Trades Council (BTC), founded in 1896, which soon became a potent political force. In 1900, with the depression over, the BTC won a major strike that enabled it to impose union-only hiring and the eight-hour day. The BTC may have enjoyed more power over its members' working conditions than any other union in the nation at that time.

1901 to the Great Depression

In the early decades of the twentieth century, the California labor movement grew rapidly and scored important economic, electoral, and legislative victories. However, new challenges emerged as the growth of large-scale agricultural enterprises affected the conditions and distribution of labor and as a southward shift in population caused Los Angeles to displace San Francisco by 1920 as the largest metropolis of the West. In 1901, the San Francisco Labor Council pressed successfully for a state law tightening child labor regulations. In June of that year, a two-month strike by the city's waterfront workers and teamsters culminated in the formation of the Union Labor Party, which governed San Francisco from 1901 to 1906 and 1909 to 1911, refusing to intervene on employers' behalf in labor disputes. The city's female garment workers, laundry workers, and waitresses all built unions during this period as well.

Los Angeles, by comparison, offered a less hospitable environment for labor organizations. An industrial late bloomer, nineteenth-century L.A. had been an agricultural town with few skilled workers and a shortage of capital. As late as 1890, L.A.'s population was only 50,000, one sixth of San Francisco's. Los Angeles had only one fifth as many industrial establishments as San Francisco, with 10% of the capitalization, and employing one tenth as many workers. When twentieth-century urban growth began in earnest, the *Los Angeles Times* publisher Harrison Gray Otis led that city's Merchants and Manufacturers Association in an effort to keep unions at bay and attract companies seeking a cheap labor force. In 1903, the Los Angeles Building Trades Council gave up its fight for the closed shop in the construction industry; a strike by iron molders ended with the imposition of open shop conditions by the Founders' and Employers' Association; and a strike of 1,400 Mexican laborers on the Los Angeles Railway Company was defeated as well. These latter workers belonged to one of the first Mexican-American unions, the Union Federal Mexicanos. Los Angeles employers were as effective at organizing themselves as were San Francisco workers. The Los Angeles labor movement suffered an additional blow when a huge explosion destroyed the Los Angeles Times building on October 1, 1910. Twenty people were killed, and two officials of the National Union of Iron Workers, John and James McNamara, were arrested and confessed to the crime.

Despite the unfavorable conditions that unions faced in L.A., in 1913 the administration of Republican Governor Hiram Johnson delivered new benefits to workers statewide, including workmen's compensation, an Industrial Welfare Commission that set minimum wages for women, an Industrial Accident Commission that enforced factory safety standards, and a California Commission of Immigration and Housing that regulated the living conditions of the migrant workers whose numbers grew as food cultivation and processing operations expanded.

By 1920, food processing was California's largest industry in terms of labor-force size and product value, followed by oil refining and shipbuilding. The state produced virtually all of the nation's lemons, olives, and apricots and 60% to 75% of its oranges, grapes, plums, and nuts. From 1900 to 1920, California's canned fruit and vegetable output grew from one quarter to one half of the national total. The seasonal workers in the fields and canneries were poorly paid and were often immigrants drawn from the mere 6% of Californians who were viewed as nonwhite. Shunned by the trade union movement, they occasionally organized themselves. In February 1903, California's first farm workers' union, the Japanese-Mexican Labor Organization, was formed in Oxnard. The new union's admission of Asians barred it from membership in the American Federation of Labor (AFL). In June 1908, the Industrial Workers of the

World (IWW) set up their first farm worker local in Holtville. In 1910, the IWW overcame Fresno's efforts to prevent their street speeches, but in 1912, vigilantes drove them out of San Diego. In August 1913, at the Durst hop ranch near Wheatland, IWW members led a protest over poor conditions after 2,800 men, women, and children arrived to fill half as many jobs. The event ignited into a shooting match, resulting in the death of two workers, the district attorney, and a sheriff's deputy, and the arrest and murder convictions of two IWW organizers, Blackie Ford and Herman Suhr. In 1919, largely in response to the IWW's militancy and opposition to the First World War, the state legislature enacted the Criminal Syndicalism Act, which criminalized the advocacy of violent change in industrial ownership and political power. With the IWW's postwar collapse, the AFL tried to organize agricultural workers into the Fruit and Vegetable Workers Association in 1920, but this lasted only until 1923. Early in the depression of the 1930s, the Communist-led Cannery and Agricultural Workers Industrial Union (CAWIU) rose to prominence in the industry. The CAWIU provided organizational support for strikes of Mexican and Filipino lettuce pickers in the Imperial Valley in 1930; of Santa Clara Valley cannery workers in 1931; and of Mexican, Filipino, Puerto Rican, and Italian pea pickers in Half Moon Bay in 1932. It was involved in the largest agricultural labor strike in U.S. history, involving 15,000 San Joaquin Valley cotton pickers in 1933. In response, growers formed the Associated Farmers organization, which fought unionism with violent vigilantism and contributed to the successful prosecution of CAWIU leaders under criminal syndicalism laws. The CAWIU dissolved in 1936.

New Deal Era and World War II

During the Great Depression, California workers joined in the national strike wave of 1933 to 1937. A longshoremen's strike in San Francisco in 1934 became a general strike authorized by the San Francisco Labor Council, and subsequent arbitration secured nearly all of the workers' demands. The pro-labor political environment characterized by congressional passage of the Wagner Act, which gave workers a federally protected right to organize, produced a doubling of union membership in San Francisco and significant gains even in L.A., where the Merchants and Manufacturers Association lost a battle with the Teamsters Union in 1937. The Pacific Coast District of the International Longshoremen's Association left the AFL and became the International

Longshoremen's and Warehousemen's Union of the new Congress of Industrial Organizations (CIO), which in turn chartered the United Cannery, Agricultural, Packing and Allied Workers of America (UCAPAWA), as well as leading drives among southern California's steel, automobile, rubber, and clothing workers. By 1940, the state had about 650,000 union members.

American participation in the Second World War tripled the state's manufacturing output and doubled its production labor force by 1947. The war stimulated shipbuilding in the San Francisco Bay Area, as characterized by the production of "Liberty Ships" at the Kaiser shipyards in Richmond. It also promoted the southern California aircraft industry, whose founders had been attracted to the area in the 1910s by its mild climate, cheap land, and nonunionized labor force. By 1945, almost 300,000 workers, 40% of whom were women, had built well over 100,000 aircraft for Lockheed, Douglas, Northrup, and other companies that drew 60% of all military contract funds in the state. Aside from bringing women into the industrial labor force, the war industries drew 340,000 African-Americans into California, where their numbers had always been negligible. Unions such as the International Brotherhood of Boilermakers, Iron Shipbuilders and Helpers of America forced the new workers into segregated auxiliaries. In 1943, at the Marinship yard in Sausalito, African-American workers withheld their union dues in protest against segregation and were barred from their jobs. In 1945, after an ineffectual investigation by the federal Fair Employment Practices Commission, the California Supreme Court ruled in *James v. Marinship* that segregated unions in a closed shop were unconstitutional. Nonetheless, shifting labor markets after the war left a growing number of African-Americans underemployed. Although the state of California had experienced economic inequities along racial lines since the Gold Rush, the declining fortunes of African-American workers added a new variant of inequality, once more familiar in the cities of the East.

Cold War to 2005

The Cold War drove new economic growth, as electronics and aerospace filled the void left by the decline of shipbuilding. By 1960, California firms received 25% of national defense spending. Population growth spurred the expansion of public infrastructure and public services, and thereby government employment. By 1951, over 40% of nonagricultural workers were unionized, but union membership declined over the next 20 years while public sector employment grew. African-American and Mexican-American workers benefited from government hiring, which was less discriminatory than in private enterprise. One of the principal challenges of the period was the anti-Communist climate. In 1947, the House Un-American Activities Committee launched an investigation into Communist influence in the Hollywood film industry among mostly unionized workers, 250 of whom were then blacklisted. Faced with the anti-Communist provisions of the Taft-Hartley Act, the CIO purged its Communist-led unions in 1949. While the labor movement thereafter shied away from social activism, it continued its battle for material benefits and contributed to the expansion of the state's middle class. In 1958, California's unions helped to defeat a "Right to Work" initiative at the polls that would have outlawed the union shop. A milestone of the era was the founding convention of the National Farm Workers Association (NFWA) in Delano on September 30, 1962. Led by César Chávez, the NFWA blended the strategies of the civil rights movement with Mexican-American identity politics and Catholic religious iconography to carry forward the mission of the old CAWIU and UCAPAWA. In September 1965, the NFWA joined with Filipino members of the Agricultural Workers Organizing Committee in launching the Delano grape strike. The two organizations eventually merged into the United Farm Workers union, which secured a favorable contract with the growers in July 1970 after a protracted struggle and consumer boycott. On September 22, 1975, Governor Jerry Brown signed the Agricultural Labor Relations Act, guaranteeing the collective bargaining rights of farm workers.

In 1968, reflecting the increasing importance and influence of public employees, the legislature granted these workers, except for teachers, full collective bargaining rights with the Meyers-Milias-Brown Act. Governor Brown ended the teachers' exclusion by signing the Rodda Act on the same day as the farm labor law. In September 1978, the Higher Education Employer-Employee Relations Act brought the last major group of public employees in the state under collective bargaining law. As public sector union membership expanded during the 1980s and 1990s, so did the organization of service workers. In 1987, Service Employees International Union (SEIU) Local 399 began its "Justice for Janitors" campaign in Los Angeles, seeking a pay raise, health insurance, and a single contract with all employers. On November 12, 1991, SEIU Local 660 led Los Angeles County workers in a successful one-day strike for a new contract. In November 1994, almost four thousand home health care aides in Alameda County, most of them

women, voted to join SEIU Local 616, the first time such workers had unionized in California. In 1999, in one of the biggest organizing achievements in U.S. history, 74,000 home care workers in Los Angeles joined SEIU Local 434B. In the early 2000s, California municipalities, including San Francisco, Oakland, San José, and Los Angeles, passed living wage ordinances for their employees and workers of companies on county and municipal contract. The decline of unionism in industrial employment since the 1960s, which California shared with the nation at large, was met with a rising tide of organization among public and service employees. This was opposed by economic conservatives, who played a partial role in the election of Governor Arnold Schwarzenegger in 2003.

PHILIP JACQUES DREYFUS

References and Further Reading

Cornford, Daniel, ed. *Working People of California.* Berkeley: University of California Press, 1995.
Cross, Ira B. *A History of the Labor Movement in California.* Berkeley: University of California Press, 1935.
Daniel, Cletus. *Bitter Harvest: A History of California Farmworkers, 1870–1941.* Berkeley: University of California Press, 1982.
Griswold Del Castillo, Richard, and Richard A. Garcia. *Cesar Chavez, a Triumph of the Spirit.* Norman: University of Oklahoma Press, 1995.
Hurtado, Albert. *Indian Survival on the California Frontier.* New Haven, CT: Yale, 1988.
Johnson, Marilyn. *The Second Gold Rush: Oakland and the East Bay in World War II.* Berkeley: University of California Press, 1993.
Kazin, Michael. *Barons of Labor: The San Francisco Building Trades and Union Power in the Progressive Era.* Urbana: University of Illinois Press, 1987.
McNichol, Liz. "Fighting of Many Fronts: SEIU in Los Angeles." *Labor Research Review* 9, no. 1 (1990): 37–43.
McWilliams, Carey. *Factories in the Field: The Story of Migratory Farm Labor in California.* Boston: Little, Brown, and Co., 1939.
Nelson, Bruce. *Workers on the Waterfront: Seamen, Longshoremen, and Unionism in the 1930s.* Urbana: University of Illinois Press, 1988.
Perry, Louis B., and Richard S. Perry. *A History of the Los Angeles Labor Movement, 1911–1941.* Berkeley: University of California Press, 1963.
Ruiz, Vicki. *Cannery Women, Cannery Lives: Mexican Women, Unionization, and the California Food Processing Industry, 1930–1950.* Albuquerque: University of New Mexico Press, 1987.
Saxton, Alexander. *The Indispensable Enemy: Labor and the Anti-Chinese Movement in California.* Berkeley: University of California Press, 1971.
Selvin, David F. *A Terrible Anger: The 1934 Waterfront and General Strikes in San Francisco.* Detroit: Wayne State University Press, 1996.
Stimson, Grace Heilman. *Rise of the Labor Movement in Los Angeles.* Berkeley: University of California Press, 1955.

CAMERON, ANDREW (1834–1890)
Civil War-Era Labor Activist

Andrew Cameron was an important leader of the American workers' movement in the period during and after the Civil War. Born in Berwick on Tweed, England, he worked as a printer in Chicago. He was one of the founders of the National Labor Union, along with William Sylvis. He attended the September 1869 Congress of the International Workingmen's Association, or First International, in Basle, as a delegate from the National Labor Union. He was a founder and president of the Chicago Trades Assembly in 1864, the same year that he began publishing the *Workingman's Advocate*, which lasted until 1877. In 1866, Cameron helped found the Eight Hour League and became its president. Throughout his life, he worked to both build the labor movement in Chicago and organize workers as a political force. Cameron was a skilled worker, however, who advocated uplift and temperance and was distrustful of foreign-born, Catholic workers. Especially after the late 1860s, Cameron advocated moderation within the labor movement. For example, in 1886, during the organizing drive that led to the eight-hour-day strikes of May Day, he spoke out against allowing socialists in the movement of the time. However, Cameron consistently pushed for reforms that would improve the lot of workers in Chicago and around the country.

The 1867 Midwest strike for the eight-hour day was an important turning point in Cameron's political evolution. Cameron and his compatriots had gotten the Republican-controlled state legislature in Illinois to pass a law stating that eight hours was a legal workday as long as no other contract was in place between workers and employers. Workers organized a large parade on May 1, 1867, and launched a citywide strike to enforce the eight-hour day. This strike was especially effective in the skilled trades that were already organized in unions and had been brought together in the Chicago Trades Assembly. It also included many construction workers in the Bridgeport neighborhood of Chicago. The strike also spread to other cities in Illinois, including Aurora and Springfield. Except for a few skilled workers, however, the strike failed to win its demands.

After the strike was repressed by the police, Cameron decided that counting on the two parties was not in labor's interest since many aldermen voiced support for the eight-hour law but winked at its violation. In 1868, the *Workingman's Advocate* promoted an independent labor slate. By 1869, however, Cameron and the *Workingman's Advocate* went back to traditional politics and endorsed "respectable" candidates. Cameron was to retain this distrust of independent working-class political organization. In 1873, when a People's Party slate backed by immigrant workers won control of the city council, Cameron called the party a "canker worm...gnawing at the city's vitals." Cameron was opposed to the People's Party's Catholic, anti-temperance flavor, and he allied with Chicago's traditional business elites rather than the Catholic, immigrant workers.

Despite his often conservative political ideas, throughout his life, Cameron was in favor of amalgamation of the various trade unions in a given industry under one organization. He was also in favor of cooperation between unions in different industries. Thus, while his political ideas after 1868 point toward those eventually advocated by Gompers and the American Federation of Labor (AFL), he was against the division of the various craft unions that eventually emerged.

Cameron consistently advocated a form of free-labor republicanism which held that dependence on either an employer or the state would rob a worker of his democratic citizenship. It was from this position that Cameron attacked both the then-current distribution of wealth and power and the socialists who aimed to change it by state control over industry. Cameron consistently opposed the socialists then active in Chicago, though he often defended socialism in Europe and came out in favor of the Paris Commune in 1871. This free-labor republican ideology also motivated Cameron's distrust of unskilled, intemperate immigrant workers, who struck him as incapable of maintaining the kind of independence that he and his followers valued so highly.

According to some historians such as Richard Schneirov, Cameron's type of labor reform activism helped lay the groundwork for the reforms of the Progressive Era by pushing upper-class, protestant reformers to abandon their militantly antilabor, laissez-faire ideology.

SAMUEL MITRANI

References and Further Reading

Schneirov, Richard. *Labor and Urban Politics: Class Conflict and the Origins of Modern Liberalism in Chicago, 1864–1897*. Champaign: University of Illinois Press, 1998.

See also **Haymarket Affair (1886); May Day; National Labor Union; Sylvis, William**

CANNERY AND AGRICULTURAL WORKERS INDUSTRIAL UNION

The roots of the Cannery and Agricultural Workers Industrial Union (CAWIU) date back to the summer of 1929 with the founding of the Trade Union Unity League (TUUL), the red industrial trade union federation established by the Communist Party USA (CPUSA). Created as dual unions during "Third Period Communism" as a rival to the craft-oriented American Federation of Labor (AFL) unions, the TUUL unions advanced the goal of organizing semi-skilled and unskilled workers who were traditionally ignored by the AFL. Delegates representing Mexican sugar beet workers from Colorado were present at the TUUL's founding conference, setting up the Agricultural Workers Industrial League (AWIL) as the precursor to the CAWIU because the AWIL was not yet large or powerful enough to operate as a union.

The AWIL's first real test was a baptism by fire when it took over the leadership of a strike that occurred in Imperial Valley, California. On January 1, 1930, a few hundred Mexican and Filipino lettuce workers in Brawley engaged in a spontaneous work stoppage, prompted by slashed wages and horrendous working conditions. Within days, 5,000 farm workers joined the walkout, making Imperial Valley the scene of a significant struggle. Early on, the Mexican Mutual Aid Society, the conservative and nationalistic organization directing the strike, was incapable of effectively combating employer assaults on meetings. Combined with the arrest of strikers, the work stoppage was threatened to be broken. Nevertheless, the walkout gained new life after the TUUL dispatched three young organizers, Frank Waldron (later known as Eugene Dennis), Harry Harvey, and Tsuji Horiuchi, from its affiliated AWIL to take over the strike leadership after learning about the walkout from the *Los Angeles Times*.

Once in Imperial Valley, the three activists, who had no prior organizing experience with agricultural laborers, worked behind the scenes to build up the strike's rank-and-file leadership. Upon emerging from the underground, the organizers immediately set up an AWIL chapter that included Filipino workers in all aspects of the work stoppage. Through promoting rank-and-file activism and stressing trade union issues, as opposed to advancing revolutionary ideology, the AWIL rejuvenated a deteriorating strike. However, with the three organizers' arrest, the authorities successfully prevented the distribution of strike relief. Faced with the risk of the arrest and deportation of the Mexican strikers, the union leaders ended the walkout on January 23 without achieving any demands.

The Imperial Valley strike served as a prototype for the organizing activity and other major work stoppages that the AWIL and its successor organizations—the Agricultural Workers' Industrial Union (AWIU) in early 1931 and the CAWIU in July 1931 after it took over the leadership of a cannery workers' walkout—conducted in 1931 and 1932. During much of these two years, the AWIU adopted a passive strategy of attempting to build the union through assuming the leadership of spontaneous work stoppages caused by wage cuts and intolerable working conditions, which were often brutally suppressed by the growers and authorities. In addition, at this time no serious effort was made at recruiting a stable, permanent base of members. Thus, by the end of 1932, the three CPUSA-led agricultural labor organizations had lost the four major strikes that they had directed since 1930 without obtaining any gains for the participating farm workers or for California agricultural unionism as a whole.

The CAWIU's fortunes changed dramatically in 1933. Of the 24 walkouts led by the union that year in California, involving nearly 37,500 workers, the CAWIU obtained partial wage increases in 20 work stoppages, while only four resulted in a total loss for the union. Apparently, the three years of defeated strikes had provided a training ground and important lessons for the CAWIU. Beginning the year with a group of well-trained and dedicated organizers respected by the state's farm workers, the union was more deliberate in its organization of walkouts. Preparing meticulous strike plans and formulating its demands through the diligent researching of wages, working conditions, and each crop's harvest schedule, the CAWIU also organized democratically elected farm committees, representing each ethnicity, at mass meetings in each growing district. After achieving a wage increase, although not union recognition, in its first solid strike victory among 1,000 cherry pickers in Santa Clara County in June, the union engaged in a series of largely successful work stoppages, obtaining wage increases during August among sugar beet workers in Ventura County, tomato pickers outside San Diego, pear pickers near San Jose, and peach pickers around Tulare. However, the most important strike was yet to come in October among the more than 15,000 cotton pickers in the San Joaquin Valley.

With wages in the industry having declined 75% in the last three years, cotton pickers were ready for unionization. After organizers built union locals, developed leaders, and constructed alliances with liberal groups for attaining public support for the ensuing work stoppage, the CAWIU called a general strike for October 4. The walkout was characterized by grower

Lennord Cannery worker feeding tomatoes onto conveyor belt. Library of Congress, Prints & Photographs Division, FSA/OWI Collection [LC-USF34-080632-C].

violence. Workers who would not go back to work or leave the region were attacked, and authorities arrested workers they believed to be strike leaders. Within one week, 12,000 pickers had struck the region, with no cotton being harvested.

Public pressure over the continuing violence prompted federal intervention. Relief was provided for the first time in U.S. labor history to strikers; and George Creel, a New Deal administrator, established fact-finding hearings, which recommended a 75-cent increase per hundred pounds to resolve the strike. On October 27, the union's central strike committee persuaded the strikers to accept the proposal, arguing that the walkout had already gone on too long. Thus, this major struggle ended with no clear winner.

Returning to Imperial Valley after four years, the CAWIU launched another lettuce worker strike in January 1934, which was easily defeated due to terror carried out by growers and law enforcement officials,

who were often one and the same. With the Communist International's shift in its line in early 1934 from organizing revolutionary industrial unions during the "Third Period" to a return to "boring from within" the reformist unions during the start of the Popular Front period, the TUUL officially folded its operation in March 1935.

The TUUL's abandonment meant the dissolution of the CAWIU, whose mantle was picked up by the CPUSA-led United Cannery, Agricultural, Packing and Allied Workers of America (UCAPAWA). Organized as a Congress of Industrial Organizations (CIO) affiliate in July 1937, UCAPAWA focused its organizing largely among the cannery and packing-shed workers as opposed to farm workers, deserting them in 1940. It would not be until the formation of the United Farm Workers (UFW) in the 1960s that California farm workers would obtain a voice and representation once more for their legitimate grievances.

VICTOR G. DEVINATZ

References and Further Reading

Bronfenbrenner, Kate. "California Farmworkers' Strikes of 1933." In *Labor Conflict in the United States*, edited by Ronald L. Filippelli. New York: Garland Publishing, 1990, pp. 79–83.

———. "California Pea Pickers' Strike of 1932." In *Labor Conflict in the United States*, edited by Ronald L. Filippelli. New York: Garland Publishing, 1990, pp. 86–87.

———. "Imperial Valley, California, Farmworkers' Strike of 1930." In *Labor Conflict in the United States*, edited by Ronald L. Filippelli. New York: Garland Publishing, 1990, pp. 255–256.

———. "Imperial Valley, California, Farmworkers' Strike of 1934." In *Labor Conflict in the United States*, edited by Ronald L. Filippelli. New York: Garland Publishing, 1990, pp. 257–258.

Daniels, Cletus E. *Bitter Harvest: A History of California Farmworkers, 1870–1941*. Ithaca, NY: Cornell University Press, 1981.

Jamieson, Stuart. *Labor Unionism in American Agriculture*. U.S. Bureau of Labor Statistics Bulletin No. 836. Washington, DC: Government Printing Office, 1945.

McWilliam, Carey. *Factories in the Fields: The Story of Migratory Farm Labor in California*. Boston: Little, Brown, 1939.

CAPITAL FLIGHT

Capital flight is the shift of production from existing facilities to new ones in locations where costs are lower and operating conditions are more favorable. Corporate managers engage in capital flight to escape the high wages and taxes, strict regulations, and especially the established unions typically found in areas where industries have long been in operation. "Disinvestment" is another term commonly used to describe the capital flight process. Since capital flight generally results in the downsizing or termination of production in the original location, it is a significant cause of de-industrialization. Although the terms "capital flight," "disinvestment," and "de-industrialization" are often used synonymously, the phenomena are not always equivalent.

Certain industries are more susceptible to capital flight than others. Relocation is virtually impossible for companies heavily dependent on inputs or skilled labor available only in the present location. Moving would be unattractive for a firm with very significant fixed investment at an existing facility or a union contract guaranteeing current workers the right to a job at a new location. Capital flight is much likelier to occur where none of these realities prevails. Business groups and government officials in less-developed regions frequently seek to build up the area economy by urging companies based elsewhere to set up local facilities. Incentives such as tax waivers are typically offered to encourage such investment. This kind of activity makes capital flight more probable.

The capital flight phenomenon burst into prominence in the 1970s. In the context of dramatic downsizing and restructuring of long-established industries, numerous firms shifted production to cheaper locales, often in less-developed countries. During this period, for example, American electronics producers and other large manufacturers moved work to new factories called *maquiladoras* just south of the Mexican border, where much lower wages could be paid. In the early years of the twenty-first century, numerous organizations transferred call centers and other white-collar functions to developing-world locations such as India. The latter moves were an important new manifestation of capital flight, as they demonstrated that what had been thought of as a phenomenon restricted to manufacturing could also take place in the service sector.

While capital flight began to attract significant attention in the late twentieth century, the phenomenon actually has a long history. European merchants of the sixteenth century, eager to avoid the expense of production by urban artisans in highly organized guilds, arranged for production to be carried out in a cheaper, more flexible manner by rural households. This process, known as "protoindustrialization," might be considered the first example of capital flight.

Early Examples of Capital Flight in the United States

Capital flight appeared in the United States relatively early in the industrial era. In the late nineteenth century, Massachusetts shoe manufacturers attempting to escape high wages and unionized labor set up plants in the towns of northern New England for the fabrication of their lower-quality goods. The garment industry of New York City saw significant capital flight during the early twentieth century as managers moved production out of a high-cost urban area with strong unions to locations in the surrounding states. After a successful mid-1930s union drive at its principal New Jersey factory, the Radio Corporation of America (RCA) shifted output of radios to a new plant in Bloomington, Indiana.

Companies that engaged in capital flight to escape unionized labor often found that this goal was only temporarily achieved. Northern New England's new shoe workers of the late nineteenth century joined the industry's Massachusetts-based labor organizations, sometimes participating with them in joint strikes. RCA's Bloomington operation was unionized in the mid-1940s. The inexperienced unionists at the newer factories were initially less militant, and even union pay rates in these locations were likely at first to be lower than elsewhere. Nevertheless, for the companies involved, it is unclear whether these (likely temporary) gains outweighed the expense and disruption of relocation. The labor movement as a whole may have actually benefited from these instances of capital flight, since the net effect was to spread unionism to areas of the country where it had previously been weak.

Difficulties in the Application of the Capital Flight Concept

The capital flight concept is often used in the general and academic literature in an overly broad, unnuanced manner. Labor scholars are particularly prone to making this mistake.

To begin with, the importance of capital flight can be exaggerated. Many writers tacitly assume that reducing production costs is the only factor motivating companies to relocate. In reality, however, firms move facilities for numerous reasons unrelated to the expense of production. Companies may do so to be closer to customers or needed inputs, or to consolidate production as part of a corporate reorganization. In each of the latter instances, capital is being *moved* (constituting local *disinvestment*, which may contribute to the original locale's *de-industrialization*). None of these are a case of capital *flight*, however.

There is also insufficient appreciation of the competitive context in which capital flight frequently takes place. Numerous industries saw the entry of new competitors at home and abroad over the course of the twentieth century, which led established producers to shift investment.

Events of the early twentieth century in the American cotton textile industry demonstrate the point. New England firms had long dominated the production of staple cotton goods but faced a new competitive threat after Reconstruction from swiftly expanding southern producers that benefited from the lower labor costs available in that region. By the 1920s, southern manufacturers had built up capacity and skill that enabled them to take over much of the national market for cotton goods. In response, some New England firms shifted production from their home region to the South, although most of the higher-cost producers in the northern region simply ceased operations. The action of the Yankee manufacturers that moved to the South was an example of capital flight, since these capitalists were indeed "fleeing" the high wages and unions of their home region. The circumstances,

however, hardly gave them a choice: if they had not relocated, most would surely have been forced out of business.

The example of New England cotton textiles had numerous parallels in the late twentieth century. Many American manufacturers that moved production to the developing world in the 1970s and after had come under fierce competitive pressure from producers based in Western Europe and East Asia.

DAVID KOISTINEN

References and Further Reading

Bluestone, Barry, and Bennett Harrison. *The Deindustrialization of America: Plant Closings, Community Abandonment, and the Dismantling of Basic Industry*. New York: Basic Books, 1982.

Cowie, Jefferson. *Capital Moves: RCA's Seventy-Year Quest for Cheap Labor*. Ithaca, NY: Cornell University Press, 1999.

Cowie, Jefferson, and Joseph Heathcott, eds. *Beyond the Ruins: The Meanings of Deindustrialization*. Ithaca and London: ILR Press, 2003.

Dublin, Thomas, and Walter Licht. *The Face of Decline: The Pennsylvania Anthracite Region in the Twentieth Century*. Ithaca, NY: Cornell University Press, 2005.

Koistinen, David. "The Causes of Deindustrialization: The Migration of the Cotton Textile Industry from New England to the South." *Enterprise & Society* 3, No. 3 (2002): 482–520.

See also **De-industrialization; Maquiladoras**

CAREY, JAMES (1911–1973)
Secretary, Congress of Industrial Organizations

James B. Carey was known as the "boy wonder" of the CIO workers movement, becoming president of a CIO union by age 25 and secretary of the CIO before he turned 30. His most important historical legacy was the dismemberment of the union that he had helped to found.

There was little in Carey's youth that suggested he might become involved in the labor movement. He was the fourth of 11 children, born in 1911 to a south Philadelphia Irish Catholic family. His father was a clerk at the U.S. Mint in Philadelphia and a staunch Democrat. James's goal was to become part of the middle class as an electrical engineer. He got a job at Philco but attended night school in engineering at Drexel and business management at the University of Pennsylvania's Wharton School of Finance. Carey's hopes were crushed by lack of opportunity, and he remained on the production line at Philco radio factory.

In the early years of the Great Depression, Carey was the leader of a group of young male inspectors interested in forming a union to combat harsh conditions and low pay. This group sought union recognition and went on strike, affiliating directly with the AFL as a federal labor union. Carey became an AFL staff representative for the large Philco local in 1934, and from this position he traveled across the Northeast, assisting other workers at radio and home appliance plants. Soon Carey sought an industrial union charter. The AFL continued to stall, but finally, in January 1936, they rejected his pleas, ordering him to take the locals he represented into the International Brotherhood of Electrical Workers, under Class B, or subordinate, membership status. In rebellion, Carey helped to organize the United Electrical Radio and Machine Workers of America (UE) in 1936, became its youthful president, and led it into the newly organized CIO six months later. By 1938, John L. Lewis, head of the CIO, had appointed him as secretary-treasurer for the CIO, the second most powerful position in the organization, though most scholars agree that this was done because Lewis thought he could control Carey.

Carey sought to represent the more conservative direction of the CIO movement, and several factors influenced his rebellion against the leadership of his own union, whom he accused of being influenced by Communist Party (CP) doctrines. The first was Roman Catholic social thought, which advocated support for trade unions but instructed Catholics to make them an alternative to radicalism rather than the base for a socialist agenda. In the 1930s, many Catholics were repulsed by the active role of the Communist Party in the organization of the CIO and, like Carey, felt that they should help to weed out all who were influenced or were members. Carey's anti-Communism had also been influenced by leaders of the Philadelphia hosiery workers, socialists who had won their positions through bitter factional struggles with Communists in the 1920s. From the early point of bargaining, Carey sought to assure managers that they harbored no design on managerial control.

By 1940, Carey had begun a rancorous critique of the union, even from his position as president. Carey wrote columns suggesting that the position of the other leaders on foreign policy issues was formulated by the CP and not for workers' interests. But in the end, Carey's own blunders in negotiations with management (more than one group of workers demanded he stay away) reduced his clout; he was defeated for president of the union, with even many right-wingers voting for his replacement, who was an ally of the left. Ironically, the CP wanted Carey to be re-elected

to stave off attacks on the union, but the left-wing leadership refused its suggestions. Carey continued his criticisms from his position in the CIO, but they were tempered during the wartime. Nevertheless, Carey began to cooperate with and enlist the aid of the FBI in 1943, asking them for background checks of unionists. By 1946, Carey was meeting with J. Edgar Hoover regularly to discuss Communists in the CIO and sought advice from him on how to target the left. Carey also reached out to labor priests, who helped him to organize an internal dissident group, the UE Members for Democratic Action (UEMDA), which labeled the UE as authoritarian and subordinate to Moscow. This continued relentlessly as the Cold War escalated. Finally, when the UEMDA proved unsuccessful in union elections, the CIO in 1949 expelled the UE along with 10 other unions and established another union, the International Union of Electrical Radio and Machine Workers (IUE), and appointed Carey as its head. Funded by over $1 million dollars in assistance by the CIO, the IUE won a majority of the members it contested, mainly on the argument that unions would be ineffective in bargaining if not associated with the CIO.

During the postwar period, Carey held key positions in the CIO. He helped to formulate the CIO's positions in respect to the global labor movement. Despite his fight with the Communists in the union movement in the United States in the immediate postwar, he sought to build bridges with workers across the globe, even those in the Soviet Union. As a delegate to the World Federation of Trade Unions (WFTU), created after WWII to be an international consortium for workers across the globe, Carey argued that Soviet Union workers should be included. But eventually he acquiesced to the State Department's anti-Soviet position and helped to bring the U.S. labor movement's foreign policy state in line with that of the U.S. government. Carey was appointed to the Marshall Plan's advisory committee, inaugurating his official status as labor statesman for the U.S. government, ended the affiliation with the WFTU, and endorsed the NATO alliance. He also worked to strengthen ties between the Democratic Party and the CIO. In order to reduce the possibility that the CIO's Political Action Committee might develop into a third-party challenge, he helped change rules that ensured its subordination to top CIO policy. He also advocated for a progressive position on civil rights within the CIO.

Carey's performance in the IUE increasingly came under attack after the UE was decimated. His critics, including those who had become his allies in the formation of the IUE, accused him of appointing cronies as organizers and of being personally responsible for failing to organize much of the decentralizing industry. Others suggested he was insane or at least delusional. Still others complained of corruption in the union. In 1965, he was defeated for union election and became a labor liaison for the United Nations Association. He died in 1973.

ROSEMARY FEURER

See also **Congress of Industrial Organizations**

CAREY, RONALD (1935–)
International Brotherhood of Teamsters

Ronald Carey, more commonly known as Ron Carey, is remembered in the chronicles of labor history for three acts. First, he was elected as a reform candidate to the presidency of the International Brotherhood of Teamsters (IBT) in 1991 in the first rank-and-file ballot in the union's history. Second, Carey led the successful strike against United Parcel Service (UPS) in 1997, which was one of labor's great victories since the 1960s. Finally, he is remembered for having been forced to step down as the Teamsters' president because of an illegal fund-raising scheme (although he was cleared of all charges); this led to the election of James Hoffa, Jr.

The son of a UPS delivery man, Carey also joined the company as a driver in 1955. Within two years, he was a shop steward, and in 1967, he became president of Teamsters Local 804 in Queens, New York. Carey was an exception to the vast majority of Teamster officials: he was not corrupt, had a modest salary (less than the chef at the Teamsters' headquarters), and was "militant." In the 1960s and 1970s, Carey was not afraid to lead his local out on strike to support his members. Likewise, in the 1980s, Carey opposed national contract settlements repeatedly. However, his greatest claim to fame occurred in the 1990s when under his presidency the Teamsters moved to the left and began to once again resemble a militant union.

In 1986, the U.S. government had begun investigations into the Teamsters through the Racketeer Influenced and Corrupt Organizations Act (RICO), believing that the Teamsters union was corrupt and had ties with the Mafia. Indeed, from 1957 to 1990, every president of the Teamsters, save Billy McCarthy, has been convicted and sentenced for a federal crime. In March 1989, the U.S. government and the Teamsters reached an agreement. The government dropped the RICO charges in return for the democratization of the Teamsters, including allowing the rank-and-file to elect national leaders.

Teamsters for a Democratic Union (TDU)—a reform caucus within the Teamsters committed to democracy and union militancy—decided not to field a candidate for the 1991 IBT presidential election but instead to endorse Carey because he supported its goals of union democracy and militancy in collective bargaining. TDU organized meetings in support of Carey; its members provided places for Carey to stay as he toured the country, and passed out literature, made phone calls, organized rallies, and got out the vote. This effort paid dividends. In December 1991, Carey and his entire slate won a three-way race, receiving 48% of the vote and giving Carey and his supporters control of the executive board. However, voter turnout was only 28%. In addition, through TDU efforts, the 1991 Teamsters convention saw 275 reform delegates elected (15% of the total delegates). However, this demonstrates the extent that the old hierarchy remained in office at different levels, as there were 1,900 delegates elected in total.

Nevertheless, under Carey's leadership, the Teamsters moved to the left. Carey was the leading voice against the North American Free Trade Agreement (NAFTA), and he increased the organizing budget, while reducing union officials' salaries. Likewise, he increased education for stewards and rank-and-file members; slashed the president's salary by $50,000; sold the union's jets, limousines, and condos; and put an emphasis on contract campaigns, local unions, and shop floor organizing. In addition, the Teamsters endorsed the 1992 Democratic presidential candidate Bill Clinton. However, the Teamsters did not endorse Clinton in the 1996 presidential election because of his support of NAFTA.

Carey's second great achievement is his leading of the Teamsters to victory over UPS in 1997. As the 1993 UPS contract failed to meet member expectations, the Teamsters implemented many new campaign tactics. The Teamsters prepared well in advance for the 1997 negotiations. The Teamsters conducted a survey of its UPS members in the lead-up to the contract negotiations. It asked for a list of contract priorities and activities workers were willing to undertake. It attempted to get all rank-and-file UPS Teamster members involved, even if Carey opponents headed their locals. This was crucial, considering the long-standing Teamsters tradition of decentralized power bases; that is, Teamster locals had a great deal of power and were often opposed to the national body. The Teamsters held rallies, built unity between full-time and part-time employees, and sought alliances with community groups and unions internationally in overseas UPS plants. Following the rejection of a "last, best, and final" contract offer from UPS, the Teamsters went on strike. Following a 15-day strike, UPS caved in to a majority of the union's demands. Carey claimed that the Teamsters' victory marked a new era where unions could once again stand up to big business. Indeed, it was thought that the Teamsters' victory would be the relaunching pad for the revival of the U.S. union movement.

However, the 1997 UPS negotiations were Carey's last major triumph. Instead of relying on the rank-and-file during his successful 1996 re-election campaign, as he did in 1991, Carey hired political consultants. Whether Carey needed the consultants to be re-elected is open to debate (Carey may have been concerned that only 28% of Teamsters voted in 1991, not to mention that the old hierarchy still had considerable resources and were in positions of power within the union). However, the consultants—the November group—implemented an illegal fund-raising scheme on Carey's behalf. The scheme saw the Teamsters "donate" $885,000 to political organizations and in return channel $221,000 into Carey's re-election campaign. Federal prosecutors, however, could not find enough evidence to lay charges relating to the fund-raising scheme. Instead, they accused Carey of perjury as he repeatedly denied involvement in the scheme to federal grand juries and the court-appointed monitors of the Teamsters. While Carey was eventually cleared of all charges by a Federal court jury, during the investigation the Justice Department forced Carey to step down as president and the Teamsters to conduct a new presidential election. In the election, James Hoffa, Jr.—Jimmy Hoffa's son—defeated the TDU-backed candidate Tom Leedham to become president of the International Brotherhood of Teamsters. Moreover, a federal oversight panel expelled Carey from the union, from holding any union office, and even from associating with friends and supporters within the Teamsters. Despite Carey's being acquitted of perjury and no charges ever being laid against him for involvement in the fund-raising scheme, these rulings remained in force.

Carey is remembered as a leader who reformed the Teamsters away from decades of corrupt business unionism toward becoming a progressive union and offered hope for those seeking the revival of the U.S. union movement.

MICHAEL SCHIAVONE

References and Further Reading

Brill, Steven. *The Teamsters*. New York: Simon and Schuster, 1978.
Corn, David. "The Prosecution and Persecution of Ron Carey." *The Nation*, April 6, 1998. www.thenation.com/doc/19980406/corn.
Crowe, Ken. "The Vindication of Ron Carey." *Union Democracy Review*, December/January 2001. www.uniondemocracy.org/UDR/22-vindication%20of%20Ron%20Carey.htm.
Plotz, David. "Ron Carey: A More Perfect Unionist." *Slate*, August 17, 1997. http://slate.msn.com/id/1829.

CATHOLIC CHURCH

The Catholic Church, with a worldwide membership of a billion believers and a long and sophisticated theological tradition, cannot be easily placed with respect to the labor movement. Its teachings promote justice in wages and worker solidarity while defending private property and the rule of law. The popes in their social encyclicals have envisioned the widespread distribution of property and harmonious relations between workers and owners of all classes. Catholic priests and laity have filtered Church teaching into their particular social, economic, and political situations in various and sometimes conflicting ways. In the United States, Catholics have been prominent in union membership and leadership; they have also been well represented among business managers, executives, and conservative political figures.

Historical and Theological Background

Arising out of Judaism, Christianity from the beginning has contained in tension two views of manual labor, both rooted in the Genesis account of creation. One view sees work as dignified and as participating with God in creation; the other sees toil as cursed, a result of the fall (original sin). The spread of Christianity, therefore, did not immediately and dramatically change the dominant views of the ancient Greek and Roman societies in which the new religion flourished, views which were themselves varied and often ambivalent.

The concept of the incarnation, of God being enfleshed as a man (and as a carpenter's son), did furnish additional theological support for the idea of labor as intrinsic to human dignity. In general, the early Church Fathers (ca. 100–500 AD) viewed labor positively. In addition, instead of idealizing the attainment of riches as had many of the ancients, they emphasized detachment from material goods and the obligation to share them freely. They generally recognized the validity of private property, but harshly criticized the wealthy and powerful who exploited the weakness of workers.

A significant development occurred with the promulgation of the monastic ideal promoted by St. Benedict of Nursia in the sixth century. Benedict's motto, *ora et labora*, expressed the view that work was exalted even to the level of prayer. Contemplation and toil became co-equal methods of serving God, and idleness was to be avoided. Such theological developments notwithstanding, medieval Europe remained for centuries stratified according to the tripartite arrangement of consecrated religious, warriors/political rulers, and serf or peasant laborers.

The rise of industrial organization that swept Europe beginning in the eighteenth century resulted in a shift in the relationships among workers, owners, and the Church. In terms of the new understanding of worker–owner relations that was regnant by the middle of the nineteenth century, Catholicism could not be simply identified with either labor or capital. Bishop Wilhelm von Ketteler of Mainz (1811–1877) led a Catholic movement for social reform and labor organization, while in many quarters Catholicism remained closely tied to the old regimes of Europe and to the principle of aristocratic privilege.

This was the context in which Pope Leo XIII wrote an encyclical letter that articulated the teaching of the Church with a view to the "new things" of the modern world. *Rerum Novarum* (1891) changed the perception of the Church among many contemporaries who had considered it a reactionary force. Leo wrote, for example, of the right of workers to a just wage, one that would maintain a breadwinner and his family in "frugal comfort." He criticized the concentration of wealth and power in the hands of the few and upheld the right of voluntary association, specifically commending labor unions. At the same time, he reiterated the Church's defense of private property, condemned socialism, and emphasized the need for Catholics to form and join unions that were not compromised by secular and revolutionary ideologies.

Pope John Paul II's encyclical *Laborem Exercens* (1981) elaborated on the themes of *Rerum Novarum*. John Paul stressed the dignity of work as a means to transform nature and achieve personal fulfillment. He extended the concept of worker to include those who manage business and those who perform intellectual work. He reiterated the "principle of the priority of labor over capital" but also denounced the Marxist view that the tension between laborers and owners could be overcome only by class struggle. Instead, he proposed a spiritual understanding of work and recognition of moral responsibilities on the part of owners, workers, and governments, which would alleviate the conflict generated by the materialist assumptions at the heart of both communism and liberal capitalism.

Catholic Church and Labor in the United States

In the United States, Catholics had been a miniscule percentage of the population until the arrival of large numbers of Irish and Germans after 1815. Immigration of Catholic Irish increased exponentially after the potato famine of 1845, and from that time on the Church was heavily urban and immigrant, with both its leaders and congregants usually of the laboring classes. Over the course of the second half of the nineteenth century, nativism, anti-Catholicism, and anti-unionism coalesced in Republican politics, and Catholics gravitated toward unions and the Democratic Party.

Leo's encyclical addressed several controversies that had been roiling the American church. Its defense of private property was seen as a rebuke to Henry George and his followers (among whom, prominently, was a New York priest, Edward McGlynn). Its endorsement of organized labor settled still simmering disputes over the role of Catholics in unions. It is estimated that at least half the membership of the Knights of Labor was Catholic (including its president from 1881 forward, Terence Powderly), but the organization came under scrutiny from some bishops because of its similarity to other "secret societies" (for example, the Masons) that the Church forbade its followers to join. The matter had been partially resolved in 1887, when Cardinal James Gibbons of Baltimore interceded in Rome and headed off a proposed condemnation of the Knights.

By 1891, the Knights were in decline, but *Rerum Novarum* provided new impetus for Catholics to become active in the labor movement, even if its exhortation to form specifically Catholic labor unions was widely interpreted as irrelevant to the pluralist context of the United States. While atheism underpinned many European unions and stimulated Catholic unionists to form separate labor federations, American unions' religious neutrality provided no such impetus. The cautious endorsement of organized labor by Church leaders is reflected in the assessment made by an author in the influential *Catholic Encyclopedia* (1907–1914): "Although the evil effects of the union are frequent, and sometimes very serious, they seem to be, on the whole, morally outweighed by its good effects."

Although Catholics often had direct control of religious unions in continental Europe, broad swaths of the labor movement were off limits. American Catholics, in contrast, seldom dominated unions, but they exerted influence across organized labor. The extent to which American unions were influenced by socialism is a matter of debate among historians, but it is certain that Catholic union members and leaders played important roles in steering American unions in nonradical directions.

Catholics, by 1910 numbering 16 million in a population of 92 million, were represented among all social classes and political persuasions, but they remained disproportionately Democrat and working class. They shared in the general ebb and flow of American labor organization. The effects of the postwar Red Scare and the prosperity and anti-union business activity of the 1920s led to declining union participation. Social Catholicism was not in hibernation, however. The new national organization of American bishops, the National Catholic Welfare Conference, commissioned a statement on social issues to be written by Catholic University of America professor Father John A. Ryan. The bishops' Program of Social Reconstruction (1919), which endorsed minimum wage laws and social insurance, was widely viewed as indicative of the official Church's coming into line with a progressive political agenda.

The early twentieth century witnessed the first appearance of "labor priests," who would become familiar characters to employers and workers across the country. Labor priests supported organized labor by providing spiritual and material support for strikers, preaching the benefits of organizing, and mediating between workers and owners. Among the best known were Peter Dietz in Milwaukee; Peter Yorke in San Francisco; Charles Owen Rice in Pittsburgh; John P. Boland in Buffalo; and George G. Higgins, who held John Ryan's old position as head of the bishops' Social Action Department. Jesuit John Corridan of New York became perhaps the most famous when his role among the longshoremen was depicted in the Oscar Award-winning film, *On the Waterfront* (1953).

Beginning in the 1930s, many Catholic institutions, in particular Jesuit colleges and universities, opened labor schools for the training of laity. At their peak in the 1940s, there were more than one hundred.

With the onset of the Great Depression, the identification of Catholics with the Democratic Party and with organized labor solidified. John Ryan was appointed to several positions in Franklin Roosevelt's administration, and Milwaukee diocesan priest Francis Haas became one of the Department of Labor's most active strike mediators. Bernard Sheil, an auxiliary bishop in Chicago, was a well-known champion of organized labor. In 1937, a group involved in Dorothy Day's Catholic Worker movement organized the Association of Catholic Trade Unionists. Catholic consensus in favor of the New Deal began to break down in the mid-1930s and

suffered a major blow when Roosevelt's court-packing plan disturbed Constitution-devoted Catholic intellectuals and writers. Radio priest Charles Coughlin had already turned against Roosevelt. Al Smith, a Catholic and erstwhile Democratic presidential candidate around whom Catholics had rallied in 1928, joined the Liberty League in denouncing Roosevelt in the 1936 election.

Catholics remained disproportionately Democratic-leaning for several decades, but they also shared in the revival of conservatism that began in the 1940s. Discontent with organized labor was one manifestation of this development. Father Edward Keller, an economist at the University of Notre Dame, advocated right-to-work legislation in the pages of Catholic scholarly and popular periodicals.

The conservative counter continued in 1955, when Catholic William F. Buckley Jr. founded *National Review* to promote, among other causes, limited government intervention in the economy. Conservatives were given a boost by geopolitical developments. The long-standing reputation of the Church as an anticommunist force benefited it when anticommunism became perhaps the dominant strand in post-World War II American politics and culture.

The Church's anticommunism did not by force of logic turn Catholics against organized labor—Catholic priests and labor leaders had long been fighting communist elements within unions. But the Soviet threat and attendant developments such as the rise of Senator Joseph McCarthy (a Catholic) brought into disrepute any person or organization deemed to be tainted by association, and distinctions between American trade and industrial unions and the international communist movement were easily lost.

By the 1960s, the labor priest was a less common figure, though he had not disappeared entirely. Bishop Hugh Donohoe in California continued the tradition of episcopal support for labor activity. But many Catholic priests—and increasingly sisters— joined civil rights and antiwar activists in a radicalism that departed from traditional Catholic social action and separated them from many union leaders and members who opposed those movements.

Catholic radicalism lacked the official backing of the Vatican and the hierarchy, as well as the support of a broad swath of laity, and would never come to dominate the American Catholic Church as organized labor and Democratic politics had. Instead, Catholics, far removed from the heyday of immigration and increasingly assimilated, became as a group undifferentiated from non-Catholic Americans. By the election of 1972, the choices of Catholic voters approximated those of the American electorate as a whole.

Yet even as the large-scale immigration of western and southern Europe faded into the past, a new, heavily Catholic wave of immigration swept into the nation's cities and southern countryside. Mexican-Americans in California, led by Catholic César Chávez's United Farm Workers (UFW), provided new strength to organized labor. The connection between old and new Catholic labor activism was evident in the bishops' selection of Monsignor George Higgins as liaison to the UFW.

In the closing decades of the twentieth century, as union membership in general declined, the prominence of organized labor as an issue on the Catholic agenda waned. Moral and cultural issues such as abortion and family breakdown overtook workers' rights—and eventually communism—as the chief concern of many Catholics. The shift was much remarked during the elections of the 1980s, when Catholic union members figured significantly among the so-called Reagan Democrats. Catholics nonetheless remain an important labor constituency, and the bishops' 1986 pastoral letter on the economy restated official support for many of the goals of organized labor.

KEVIN E. SCHMIESING

References and Further Reading

Betten, Neil. *Catholic Activism and the Industrial Worker*. Gainesville: University Presses of Florida, 1976.

Browne, Henry J. *The Catholic Church and the Knights of Labor*. Washington, DC: Catholic University of America Press, 1949.

Misner, Paul. *Social Catholicism in Europe: From the Onset of Industrialization to the First World War*. London: Darton, Longman, and Todd, 1991.

O' Brien, David J. *American Catholics and Social Reform: The New Deal Years*. New York: Oxford University Press, 1968.

Olsen, Glenn W. "*Ora et Labora*: Work in Medieval Europe," *Fides Quaerens Intellectum* 3 (2003): 31–61.

Pope John Paul II. *Laborem Exercens* (1981).

Pope Leo XIII. *Rerum Novarum* (1891).

Schmiesing, Kevin E. *Within the Market Strife: American Catholic Economic Thought from Rerum Novarum to Vatican II*. Lanham, MD: Lexington Books, 2003.

Wallace, Lillian Parker. *Leo XIII and the Rise of Socialism*. Durham, NC: Duke University Press, 1966.

See also **Association of Catholic Trade Unionists; Chávez, César Estrada; Knights of Labor**

CENTRAL AMERICANS

Central Americans have been coming to the United States since the nineteenth century, but the numbers were not large until after 1970. The immigrants who arrived during the 1930s formed communities in major American cities such as San Francisco and New York. These newcomers were generally middle class, educated, and often political refugees or labor leaders. A few were exiled military officers and politicians who had lost faith in the ability of their governments to promote what they believed needed to be done to develop their countries. Some others, not necessarily refugees, came in search of a better economic life.

A few more came during World War II when job opportunities opened in the United States. Another wave arrived during the 1940s and 1950s. The census reported that approximately 60,000 Central Americans entered prior to 1965. During the 1960s, another 100,000 arrived, marking the beginning of a steady movement of people from Nicaragua, El Salvador, Guatemala, Costa Rica, Panama, and Honduras. But it was the outbreak of civil war and violence, as well as failing economies, that propelled a substantial wave of these immigrants after 1970.

It is important to realize that people from these countries have different cultures, experiences, and motivations for emigration. In Nicaragua, a left-wing group, the Sandinista National Liberation Front, threatened the livelihood of many elite members of the old regime. Members of the dictatorship of the Anastasio Somoza Garcia family began to leave even before the Sandinistas seized power in 1979. Fifteen thousand members of the Somoza family and their followers headed for Miami, with many of them able to bring their money with them.

After the fall of Somoza, the U.S. government backed a revolutionary group based in Costa Rica and Honduras, the Contras, with the goal of replacing the left-wing Sandinistas with a government more acceptable to the United States. Because of the resultant violence, accompanied by economic difficulties, and the draft, working-class Nicaraguans also fled to the United States.

A problem the Nicaraguans shared with other Central Americans was becoming legal immigrants in the United States. Many lacked the necessary skills or family connections for visas. They came anyway, coming through Mexico and illegally crossing the southern border of the United States.

Because of the violence in their land, Nicaraguans sought refugee status. However, few were admitted as refugees. Once in the United States, many then applied for asylum, despite the availability of only a few thousand places annually. In addition, to win asylum, individuals had to prove that they had a "well-founded fear" that they would be persecuted if they returned to their native countries. Such individual claims were difficult to demonstrate, and the vast majority of Nicaraguans were denied asylum. Immigration officials said that they were economic, not political, refugees and claimed that being subject to a civil war and violence did not demonstrate that the asylum petitioners had a threat aimed directly at them.

Yet the Nicaraguans had supporters in the United States, mainly immigrant rights groups or religious leaders who believed that Central Americans deserved to remain in the United States. An immigrant judge in Florida said that he found the American government's position inconsistent. The judge noted that the United States was trying to overthrow a radical government in Nicaragua, but persons fleeing from that left-wing state were being denied asylum. Others rushed to their aid the approval rate increased briefly, but most Nicaraguans were still not granted asylum. Their case became weaker when the civil war ended and the Sandinistas were voted out of office in 1990. However, many Nicaraguans wanted to remain in the United States because they had established families and found employment during the 1980s. Finally, after prolonged debate, Congress passed the Nicaragua Adjustment and Central American Relief Act of 1997 (NACARA), which gave many of these refugees the opportunity to become legal immigrants. In the four-year period before NACARA was passed, only 21,000 Nicaraguans legalized their status; in the four-year period after NACARA, 66,000 Nicaraguans did so.

For Salvadorans and Guatemalans, the situation was somewhat different, but they too fled violence due to a civil war. The United States supported right-wing governments there. Indeed, the Central Intelligence Agency engineered a coup that installed a reactionary government in Guatemala in 1954, replacing an elected reformist regime, and Guatemala, too, was ruled by a right-wing government. Opponents of the governments in both nations resorted to guerilla tactics in an effort to replace those holding power. The United States supported the attempts to defeat the guerrilla movements, which resulted in civil wars that left tens of thousands of persons homeless, exposed to massive destruction and violence. Government military units were especially violent and feared by both Guatemalans and Salvadorans. Central America earned a reputation for being the most violent region of the world in the 1980s. An estimated 200,000 Guatemalans alone perished in conflict in the 1980s; most did not take sides in the war but were caught between the two sides. The response of many Guatemalans and Salvadorans was to flee their nations and cross into Mexico, where they found only a temporary haven. Many decided to head farther north and enter the United States legally or without proper immigrant papers if they could not qualify as resident aliens under the immigration laws.

Once in the United States, many of these nationals claimed asylum like the Nicaraguans had. However, the granting of asylum by the United States would be an admission that the U.S. government supported violent governments in power and the brutal tactics carried out by government troops. For those who had entered the United States illegally before 1982, an amnesty was possible as provided by the Immigrant Reform and Control Act of 1986, and 65,000 Guatemalans and a similar number of Salvadorans qualified. But most Central Americans entered after 1982, and over 90% of their claims for asylum were rejected. The federal government made it clear that it did not welcome a large-scale migration of "feet people," even those fleeing from a radical leftist government.

Another problem with obtaining asylum was the backlog, the majority of whom were Central Americans. This backlog reached 300,000 claims at its peak in the early 1990s—a figure that made it impossible for immigration authorities to consider their applications quickly and carefully. Before that time, groups sympathetic toward Central Americans provided help in the courts and forced the immigration authorities to follow proper procedures in handling asylum cases. As a result, a number of Central Americans received the right to remain in the United States by becoming resident aliens. NACARA was aimed mainly at Nicaraguans, but it also allowed some persons from the other two nations to become legal immigrants.

The end of civil conflicts created further difficulties for Central Americans seeking asylum. In Nicaragua, Sandinistas were defeated in an election, and peace returned after 1990. How could one claim political persecution under the newly elected regime? The ending of the civil wars in the early 1990s in El Salvador and Guatemala also made asylum nearly impossible to win for these nationals.

During the hostilities and even after, there was a way these Central Americans could remain in the United States, at least temporarily: the federal government could grant them extended voluntary departure, a temporary period to remain in the United States until peaceful conditions returned in their native lands. Before 1990, such a status was granted on an ad hoc basis but was made part of the Immigration Act of 1990 and called Temporary Protected Status (TPS). Several hundred thousand Central Americans received TPS, but it did not give them permanent residence. However, it provided them with a period of time in which they would not be deported. Receiving TPS was an admission that the United States recognized that conditions were not ideal in either El Salvador or Guatemala. While TPS allowed many to remain in the United States temporarily, it was possible to become an authorized immigrant by marrying an American citizen or finding employment that would qualify under the Immigration Act of 1965. It should be noted that a majority of persons in the 1990s who became immigrants were already in the United States; they adjusted their temporary status to legal immigrants, and these included a number of Central Americans.

A growing number of the claims of Central Americans for immigrant status in the United States were successful. In 2002, over 31,000 Salvadorans became immigrants. The figure for 2003 was 28,296, and for 2004 it was 29,795. El Salvador, which generated the largest flow, was becoming one of the main sources for immigration to the United States—seventh on the list of sending nations. In addition, immigration authorities recorded roughly 18,888 Guatemalan newcomers in 2004, the second largest source for Central American immigrants.

After the peace accords became effective in the 1990s, Central Americans continued to come and work and live in the United States as undocumented immigrants. Although estimates varied in the early twenty-first century, Central Americans made up nearly one fourth of all undocumented persons and possibly numbered one million persons.

Other Central American nations did not experience civil wars and extensive violence, though economic conditions in these countries were hardly ideal. The most stable Central American nation was Costa Rica, which also had the highest standard of living; as a result, few Costa Ricans headed north. Without a civil war to make them flee to the United States, immigration from Honduras, Panama, and Belize lagged behind their neighbors; and Costa Rica and Honduras housed many of the refugees from war, at least temporarily. Of these nations, Honduras sent the largest number north. The number from Honduras was half that from Guatemala and only one quarter of El Salvador's share. For Honduras, an additional problem occurred in 1998 when Hurricane Mitch ripped through Central America, which was centered on Honduras. Thousands fled to neighboring countries, and thousands of others went to the United States. In addition to those Hondurans already in the United States illegally, these undocumented immigrants were granted TPS, allowing them to remain legally, at least temporarily. TPS was extended until early 2005. Belize sent fewer than 1,000 persons to the United States as resident aliens annually. Panamanian entries averaged roughly 1,500 in the 1990s.

Overall, the Central American population grew substantially between the 1970s and the early twenty-first century. The 2000 census indicated that El Salvador was the largest Central American group with 665,000 recorded, followed by 372,000 Guatemalans and 217,000 Hondurans. Nicaragua totaled 177,000. It is not known how many others, mostly unauthorized, were left uncounted by the census or missed by the border patrols.

Searching for a New Life

One hundred thousand Nicaraguans followed the elite settlement of their countrymen to the Miami, Florida, region. While the elite often found better jobs because they were educated, many of those arriving as the civil war spread struggled. In Miami, Cubans sometimes aided these newcomers, because the first wave was fleeing a socialist regime in Nicaragua, just like the Cubans fleeing Fidel Castro's communist state in Cuba.

From elsewhere in Central America, many middle-class immigrants also fled. However, the vast majority of those coming from Central America were poor farmers or urban workers without money, hi-tech skills, and knowledge of English. For them, a new life in America meant starting at the bottom. Central Americans resemble Mexicans in their social and economic background. Whereas one quarter of white native-born Americans held college degrees, fewer than 10% of Salvadorans did. Fewer than 40% of Salvadorans had graduated from high school, compared with nearly 90% of white native-born Americans. Their incomes were low, and the proportion living in poverty was greater than that of the general American population. And it was common for both men and women to work. Guatemalans were similar to Salvadorans, and Hondurans and Nicaraguans were only slightly better off.

Central Americans settled in cities and communities where many of their countrymen had established themselves and where low-paying jobs beckoned to them. In Washington, DC, they were noticeable in restaurants—washing dishes and clearing tables—and if they were lucky and knew English, waiting tables. In other cities, a few found employment in garment factories or in hotels cleaning rooms. For women, domestic housework was available.

Los Angeles claimed the largest settlement of Central Americans, laboring in the lowest-paid jobs, such as the garment industry or as household workers. Because of their low incomes, Central American families often doubled up in their living arrangements. In some cases, three families shared a single apartment.

While most Central Americans settled in cities such as Los Angeles, one of the main themes in post-1990 immigration to the United States was the dispersal of resident aliens outside of the six major states for immigrants (California, Texas, New York, New Jersey, Florida, and Illinois). To be sure, roughly two thirds of the newcomers settled in these states in the first years of the twenty-first century, but those states' share of the foreign-born population had declined, as many immigrants headed for states such as North Carolina, Missouri, Minnesota, Arkansas, and Iowa, where few immigrants had been seen before.

Just as urban Central Americans used networks, so did those settling in smaller cities, towns, and suburbs. In 1987, a Guatemalan immigrant was hired by Perdue Farms, located in Georgetown, Delaware. Soon others followed, some of whom were relatives or from the same village as the first migrant. Soon whole communities of Central American immigrants appeared in towns where no immigrant communities had existed before 1990. Employment was a key to these networks, but so were churches and other familiar organizations.

While government officials labeled all Salvadorans and Guatemalans as Hispanics, many could scarcely speak Spanish. Rather, they were Maya but had many of the same reasons to leave their violent and poor land. They, too, built networks for the path to America. A Maya community developed in Indiantown, Florida, built around seasonal agriculture. In Morgantown, North Carolina, working-class jobs in the chicken-processing industry provided the lure, but these were undesirable positions. A large Maya community also developed in Los Angeles, and another was found in Houston. The first Maya to arrive in Houston was Juan Xuc, who came in 1979. He sent for relatives in his home village, and soon a steady stream of these Maya from Guatemala had built a Houston community.

For many young men without immigrant papers, the most difficult way to make a living was casual labor. In cities, and especially in suburbs, young men stood on selected street corners waiting for a day's work. If they were lucky, they would be hired in construction, which was booming in the early days of the twenty-first century. But many had to work in landscaping on a daily basis whenever such outdoor work could be performed. If unlucky, they received no employment at all and had to try again the next day. Some communities did not like young Central Americans (and Mexicans) standing on street corners, and several towns attempted, with little success, to halt these suburban informal hiring halls.

An important reason why these young men were willing to take such jobs was to earn money and send it home. Remittances were a vital part of these immigrant streams. Salvadorans sent $2.5 billion home

in 2004, the largest figure of the Central American nations. The men hoped, too, that their children back home, or those with them, would find a better future. Certainly second-generation Central Americans were better educated than their parents and were learning English. Their incomes exceeded their parents' but still lagged behind native-born white Americans. Central Americans were largely an immigrant community, and the future of the second generation was not clear.

DAVID M. REIMERS

References and Further Reading

Burns, Allan. *Maya in Exile: Guatemalans in Florida*. Philadelphia: Temple University Press, 1993.

Cordova, Carlos B., and Raquel Pinderhughes. "Central and South Americans." In *A Nation of Peoples: A Sourcebook on America's Multicultural Heritage*, edited by Elliott Robert Barkan. Westport, CT: Greenwood Press, 1999, pp. 96–118.

Coutin, Susan Bibler. *Legalizing Moves: Salvadoran Immigrants' Struggle for U.S. Residency*. Ann Arbor: University of Michigan Press, 2000.

Fink, Leon. *The Maya of Morgantown: Work and Community in the Nuevo New South*. Chapel Hill: The University Press of North Carolina, 2003.

Gordon, Jennifer. *Suburban Sweatshops: The Fight for Immigrant Rights*. Cambridge, MA: Harvard University Press, 2005.

Lopez, David E., Eric Popkin, and Edward Telles. "Central Americans: At the Bottom, Struggling to Get Ahead." In *Ethnic Los Angeles*, edited by Roger Waldinger and Mendi Bozorgmehr. New York: Russell Sage Foundation, 1996.

Louchy, James, and Marilyn M. Moors, eds. *The Maya Diaspora: Guatemalan Roots, New American Lives*. Philadelphia: Temple University Press, 2000.

Mahler, Sarah. *American Dreaming: Immigrant Life on the Margins*. Princeton, NJ: Princeton University Press, 1995.

Menjivar, Cecelia. *Fragmented Ties: Salvadoran Immigrant Networks in America*. Berkeley: University of California Press, 2000.

Portes, Alejandro, and Alex Stepick. *City on the Edge: The Transformation of Miami*. Berkeley: University of California Press, 1993.

Reimers, David M. *Other Immigrants: The Global Origins of the American People*. New York: New York University Press, 2005.

Repak, Terry A. *Waiting on Washington: Central American Workers in the Nation's Capital*. Philadelphia: Temple University Press, 1995.

CENTRAL LABOR UNIONS

Central labor unions (CLU) are localized groups that serve as an umbrella organization for unions, generally as a type of go-between between the local unions and the national association. While some of the purposes might have changed over the years, the basic concepts have remained in place.

CLUs serve several purposes. Quite often there are labor issues that cross the lines between skilled and unskilled labor, between jurisdictions, and between different locals and councils. CLUs help to formulate policies that will enable the different bodies to approach a situation in a unified manner. Such tactics may involve the calling of a strike or boycott, whether primary or secondary, sympathy strikes, or even activities where a protest is not an issue, such as a parade or picnic.

CLUs often walk a fine line between keeping the international organization satisfied, recognizing the differences between their affiliated locals, deflecting public opinion branding them as puppets for the main organization, and debunking rumors about not caring enough for local concerns. To those in the national organizations, there is sometimes concern that these CLUs may try to take control from them. The late AFL-CIO president George Meany saw the CLUs as appendages to the AFL-CIO.

Prior to the rise of the modern union, skilled craftsmen organized themselves into guilds. Each particular craft had its own guild—shoemakers, printers, carpenters, and so on. Many of the concerns that face the labor movement in modern times were also important to these guilds. These included the apprentice system, wage scales, the number of work hours, working conditions, and the drive for the closed shop, meaning that only members of the guild were permitted to work in a particular place. Strikes were not unheard of. In the early years of the New Republic, many guilds went on strike in order to protect their interests. These guilds also served social purposes. Many provided small libraries for the use of their members, and some established insurance programs to provide for the families of members who were injured or killed on the job. Until fraternal benefit organizations such as the Knights of Columbus were created, these guilds were instrumental in taking care of their members.

Some of the earliest forms of CLUs began during the 1820s. The Mechanic's Union of Trade Associations was formed in Philadelphia in 1827. In places such as Philadelphia and New York, the number of trade associations grew by at least 50% over the next decade or two. Throughout the nineteenth century, these early CLUs were far more independent than modern ones, which are now affiliated with a national organization.

What is known as the modern union began to rise during the post-Civil War era. Formed in 1866, the National Labor Union (NLU) welcomed unions and city trade assemblies within its fold. The NLU especially pushed for an eight-hour day for federal employees and created the National Labor Reform Party, a political entity to promote labor's agenda.

The Knights of Labor (KOL) was the next large national union, founded in 1869. This was an industrial, rather than a craft, union federation, open to those with and without particular skills. At first it was limited to the Philadelphia area, but then it expanded beyond those boundaries in 1874, thereby becoming a more national union. Like the NLU, however, the KOL would ultimately decline.

In New York, the CLU there was instrumental in organizing what many believe to be the first Labor Day in 1882. The New York CLU worked to both unionize and exert political power. Chicago would later in 1886 pick up on the idea of a recognized May Day.

The nation's largest labor organization, the AFL-CIO, first began in 1886, shortly after the deadly Haymarket Riot in Chicago, as the American Federation of Labor (AFL). The AFL was a craft union federation and persuaded many members of the KOL to join its ranks. Samuel Gompers, who held the presidency of the AFL (with a brief one-year exception) until his death in 1924, was opposed to industrial unionism. His "pure and simple" unionism focused on organization and economic power rather than political entanglements.

CLUs sprung up in all areas of the country. In Los Angeles, during 1884–1885, the printers, along with several other unions, established a Trades Council in order to support both a strike and a boycott. In order to support these actions, a daily labor paper was created in July 1885, but although it was on a firm financial footing, the paper wound up serving the cause of the printers exclusively. This new Trades Council also helped to mediate a labor dispute, a move that proved to be quite fruitful.

Other trades in Los Angeles followed this suit by establishing their own CLUs; the building trades, plasterers, painters, and carpenters all hoped to capitalize on this idea. These CLUs also went beyond trade organization by taking on political issues as well. A new Los Angeles Trade Council was formed in 1885, but this new organization failed to integrate many unions under its fold, as many of these locals were afraid to lose any form of autonomy. Another aspect of the problem was the intense anti-Chinese sentiment among the West Coast workers. Many of these workers feared that the new Trades Council would recognize, and incorporate, the Chinese workers. This fear was actually unfounded, as this new Trade Council even took part in an anti-Chinese convention in November 1885. Also, during that same year in March, a convention in San Francisco tried to unite the Pacific coast craft workers, but most unions showed little, if any, interest in the idea.

One very important CLU was formed in Chicago in 1896. Here, the AFL placed all the AFL-recognized unions under a central body, the Chicago Federation of Labor (CFL). There were some central bodies already in existence in the city, one of which was the Chicago Trades and Labor Assembly, formed in 1877. One of the main purposes behind creating the CFL was to curb corruption, especially amongst the leaders. Some leaders, such as Martin "Skinny" Madden and William Pomeroy, took corruption to heights none ever thought possible. Still, even after its formation, the CFL was still rife with graft. Madden continued to control the CFL, using strong-arm tactics to ensure his command.

Many of the city's other unions, as well as the Illinois State Federation of Labor (which was in itself a type of CLU, although on a state, rather than a city, level), worked to remove Madden from power. In 1905, this took place. Under the watchful eyes of the Chicago police, an election was held, and the Irish-born John Fitzpatrick was given the presidency. Fitzpatrick was known for his honesty, and he and Gompers had a long working relationship, although at times the CFL strayed from official AFL policy.

During the New Deal, the labor movement, especially the AFL, took advantage of the gains provided by the federal government. Union rolls swelled. In 1935, led by John L. Lewis of the United Mine Workers of America (UMW), a new federation was formed, the Committee of Industrial Organization (CIO—which changed its name in 1938 to the Congress of Industrial Organizations). As opposed to the AFL, the CIO was an industrial union, organizing workers regardless of their skill level. The two organizations were at odds for a number of years, eventually forming themselves into a single body, the AFL-CIO. But prior to that time, there was considerable bad blood. Some CLUs, such as the Central Labor Union of Great Falls, and the Rochester Central Trade and Labor Council, donated small amounts of money to the CIO in 1937. The result was that many AFL-affiliated unions would not recognize these organizations.

The AFL-CIO saw its share of troubles concerning CLUs and keeping them within the fold. During the first years of the 1930s, prior to the formation of the CIO, the auto workers in Ohio were making independent strides. Some CLUs were told to disband if they went against AFL policies. In 1934, the Cleveland Auto Council was determined to form its own international union. In 1935, the AFL Executive Council sent calls to all federal unions in the auto industry to send delegates to a convention in Detroit. Despite the

250 delegates in attendance, very little was accomplished, as there were persistent squabbles over issues such as the election and/or appointment of officers.

During 1995, the Teamsters and the Service Employees International Union (SEIU) withdrew from the AFL-CIO, causing a number of problems for central labor unions. Some of these problems were financial difficulties, loss of grassroots organizational activities, the feeling of disaffiliation, and loss of potential protection that might have been provided by the CLU and the AFL-CIO. In addressing these concerns, the AFL-CIO took several steps concerning the existing CLUs. These stipulations included the submission of financial statements, with financial assistance to those in arrears due to the disaffiliation, and meetings to establish plans of action. In addition, CLUs were not permitted to accept any unions or dues, or to allow access to records, participate in political or solidarity activities, or issue mobilization campaigns with disaffiliated unions. The AFL-CIO also began to make plans for establishing advisory bodies and strategy campaigns, and for strengthening working relationships with the still-affiliated CLUs.

MITCHELL NEWTON-MATZA

References and Further Reading

Burke, William. *History and Functions of Central Labor Unions.* New York: Macmillan, 1899.
Karson, Marc. *American Labor Unions and Politics, 1900–1918.* Carbondale: Southern Illinois University Press, 1958.
Roth, Herrich. S. *Labor: America's Two-Faced Movement.* New York: Petrocelli/Charter, 1975.
Stimson, Grace Heilman. *The Rise of the Labor Movement in Los Angeles.* Berkeley: University of California Press, 1955.
Taft, Philip. *The AFL from the Death of Gompers to the Merger.* New York: Harper and Brothers, 1959.

CHÁVEZ, CÉSAR ESTRADA (MARCH 31, 1927–APRIL 23, 1993)
President, United Farm Workers of America

César Chávez was the charismatic president of the United Farm Workers of America, AFL-CIO, who led the union for over 30 years. During his career, he dedicated himself to fighting for a decent standard of living as well as justice for agricultural laborers. Through his efforts, he obtained union representation and contracts for one of the poorest and most exploited groups in the United States. As a labor leader,

César Chávez, half-length portrait, facing left. Library of Congress, Prints & Photographs Division, NYWT & S Collection [LC-USZ62-111017].

he became a national symbol of the Mexican-American civil rights movement that emerged in the 1960s. In recognition of his achievements, schools, parks, and streets have been named after him. California declared his birthday, March 31, a holiday in his honor. It is the first American holiday honoring a Latino leader.

Born in 1927 near Yuma, Arizona, Chávez was named after his grandfather, who in the 1880s had fled the hardships of peonage under the dictatorship of Mexican President Porfirio Diaz. Chávez's father, Librado, married Juana Estrada, an immigrant from Chihuahua, in 1924. After the couple married, they left the family ranch and operated a general store, while Librado served as the local postmaster. The couple had six children. César was their second child and oldest son. The Great Depression caused severe hardship; the family lost their business and moved back to Librado's parents' farm. Drought coupled with depression economics and fraud forced the family off the ranch and into the migrant stream.

Desperate to survive, the family responded to notices of steady agricultural work in California. The relatively stable existence in Arizona presented a stark contrast with the migrant worker experience in California. Customary attendance at Laguna School outside Yuma, combined with farm chores, was replaced by frequent absences at some 30 schools in California's fertile valleys. Unpredictable harvests and the demands of the poverty-stricken migrant life dictated the family's precarious existence and limited access to education and adequate housing. The experience left an indelible impression on the 10-year-old Chávez.

Seasonal agriculture drove the family's routine. In a yearlong cycle, the Chávezes began their journey in the Imperial Valley, just over the California-Arizona border, picking peas and mustard greens and bunching carrots. In mid-spring, the family traveled to Oxnard for beans and then north to San Jose for the fruit harvest. Then it was on to the Sacramento Valley for the early summer harvest. In late summer, grapes, prunes, and tomatoes needed cultivating in the Fresno area. In the fall, the cotton crop in the San Joaquin Valley required laborers. The arduous sequence repeated itself when the Chávezes returned to their winter base in the Imperial Valley. The work was exhausting, the wages poor, the hours long, the conditions substandard, the housing inferior, and the labor contractors unscrupulous. After his father sustained an injury, Chávez left school to work full-time in the fields. With his graduation from the eighth grade in 1942 at age 15, he ended his formal schooling. Chávez credited his mother's strength and Mexican Catholicism for sustaining the family during these difficult years.

Enlistment in the U.S. Navy in 1944 interrupted the migrant cycle for Chávez. He served in the western Pacific as a deckhand. At the end of the war, he returned to California to work in the fields and in 1948 married Helen Fabela, a young farm worker he had previously courted during the many times his family had labored in the grape harvest in Delano. Characteristic of the high postwar birthrate, the couple had eight children between 1949 and 1959. With a growing family to provide for, Chávez returned to the migrant life, traveling up and down the state with his relatives, his young wife, and their small children. Like many young men of his generation, his military service had changed him. He grew dissatisfied with this dismal employment with no prospects. In the increasingly politicized racial and ethnic communities during the 1950s, this discontent propelled the establishment of groups committed to challenging injustice and prejudice intensified by wartime social tensions. Organizations spread quickly in cities and towns with large Mexican-heritage populations.

The CSO Years

In California, the Community Service Organization (CSO) was one of the associations that reflected the renewed interest in civic, social, and political activism. Started in Los Angeles in 1947 with joint financial support from the Chicago-based Industrial Areas Foundation (an initiative of social activist Saul Alinsky) and the Civic Unity League (established by Ignacio López), the CSO successfully backed the candidacy of Edward Roybal for the Los Angeles City Council. With this base, he was elected in 1962 to the U.S. House of Representatives, the first Hispanic from California to serve in Congress since 1879.

Capitalizing on its achievements in Los Angeles, the CSO launched an operation to organize chapters throughout California and the Southwest. In northern California, cities such as San Jose and Stockton were targeted. In San Jose, CSO organizer Fred Ross enlisted an initially skeptical Chávez, who was residing in the Mexican-American barrio Sal Si Puedes (which translated means "Get out if you can"). A reticent volunteer before becoming a paid organizer, Chávez quickly became the national director of the group in 1958. Assisting her husband's effort, Helen Chávez frequently relocated her family to central valley towns slated for membership drives and prepared mailings. Tirelessly conducting house meetings, recruiting organizers, and establishing new chapters, Chávez built a loyal membership, honed his leadership skills, and initiated contacts with other Mexican-American community activists, such as Dolores Huerta and Gilbert Padilla. In addition to conducting citizenship drives and voter registration campaigns, the group protested discrimination in housing, employment, and education; advocated for neighborhood improvements; and worked to curb police brutality. In the early 1960s, Chávez pressed the CSO to undertake a more difficult challenge. When the CSO board declined to endorse his plan to organize agricultural laborers, Chávez abruptly resigned from this organization in 1962.

The Founding of the Union

With Dolores Huerta and other sympathetic CSO colleagues, Chávez started the National Farm Workers Association (NFWA) in 1962. For a number of years, Chávez and Huerta concentrated on building membership. Chávez centered his efforts in Delano, supported by his wife, Helen, who worked in the fields and raised their family. Huerta, a single mother of seven children estranged from her second husband, based her operation in Stockton, where she received financial help from her relatives. After repeated requests, she finally consented to join Chávez in Delano.

Chávez and Huerta agreed to spend several years solidifying their support before directly confronting agribusiness. This plan abruptly ended in 1965. In that year, the Agricultural Workers Organizing Committee (AWOC), a predominately Filipino union under the leadership of Larry Itliong and financed by the AFL-CIO, asked Chávez and Huerta to respect their strike against Delano grape growers. The membership voted overwhelmingly to honor the walkout, thus launching the celebrated Delano grape strike.

For five difficult years, the United Farm Workers Organizing Committee, or UFWOC (after the AWOC and NFWA merged in 1966), fought the powerful California wine grape and, later, table grape growers. The union received a big boost with a visit and pledge of financial help from UAW President Walter Reuther and important support from Senator Robert F. Kennedy, when the U.S. Senate Subcommittee on Migratory Labor conducted hearings in Delano in March 1966. The struggle between the fledgling union and agricultural giants attracted significant coverage from the national media. Although the union achieved success with an agreement with Schenley Industries, Chávez soon realized that strikes in the fields were unlikely to yield lasting results, given the overwhelming resources and political power of agribusiness. Frustrated with the need to picket extensive areas and facing intimidation, anti-union tactics, and the entrenched influence of corporate agriculture, the UFWOC turned to civil rights-era strategies of massive demonstrations, civil disobedience, and fasts by Chávez. Energized by the philosophy of nonviolence successfully pursued by Mahatma Gandhi and Martin Luther King Jr., Chávez and his supporters mobilized support for a national boycott on behalf of farm workers. Linking civil rights activism with appeals to solidarity based on Mexican Catholicism, liberation theology, and a sense of ethnic pride, Chávez won contracts with well-known wine grape growers, vulnerable because of their highly visible brands. The UFWOC then focused its resources on the more intransigent table grape producers.

Building on the successful boycott that targeted wineries, Chávez called on farm worker families to fan out across the country to entreat urban unions, religious supporters, students, antiwar protestors, environmentalists, consumer groups, sympathetic politicians, Mexican-American organizations, African-American allies, and average housewives to create an international boycott to exact concessions from agribusiness. The boycott eventually forced table grape growers, first in Coachella and later in Delano, to negotiate. The breakthrough came in the 1970s when growers signed the historic contracts covering 85% of the industry.

Twenty Years of Struggle

Instead of ending the bitter struggle, the years from 1970 to 1975 marked a more unified stance by agribusiness against the United Farm Workers (UFW), which became a chartered affiliate of the AFL-CIO in this period. A more coordinated effort between California growers, their political allies, and the International Brotherhood of Teamsters materialized. Even before the union could fully savor its victory in the grape vineyards, it confronted a lettuce strike in the Salinas area and rival Teamster contracts with vegetable producers. This jurisdictional dispute spilled over into the contract renewal talks with grape growers. In 1973, the Teamsters decimated UFW membership by signing contracts with former UFW grape producers. Workers voted to strike, and Chávez reinforced the boycott, embarked on a national speaking tour, and organized protests across the country. Back in California, violence broke out. Kern County jails overflowed as a result of massive arrests of farm workers and their supporters. In addition to labor disputes with Gallo wines, the union entered into another protracted boycott of lettuce, grapes, wines, and other products.

After years of hostile relations with the Reagan administration, the union welcomed the election in 1974 of Governor Jerry Brown. Chávez and his political allies in the Democratic Party lobbied the governor to support legislation that would end the continual turbulence in the fields and provide a legal foundation for the union's existence. A legislative compromise between the Brown administration, corporate agriculture, the Teamsters, and the UFW resulted in the passage of the Agricultural Labor Relations Act (ALRA) in 1975. Although the union accepted restrictions on the secondary boycott, for the first time in California's history, farm workers had the right to engage in government-regulated collective bargaining.

With the appointment of members to the Agricultural Labor Relations Board (ALRB), Chávez's farm workers appeared on the threshold of a new epoch of labor relations. In a flurry of field organizing, the UFW did, in fact, win the majority of elections. But discord in the fields was not over, as the Teamsters mounted an aggressive organizing campaign and corporate agriculture marshaled its political power to terminate funding for the ALRB. Chávez fought back with the ultimately unsuccessful Proposition 14 ballot, aimed at making the ALRB a permanent part of the California constitution.

The 1980 presidential victory of pro-agribusiness Ronald Reagan signaled a national tilt toward conservatism and an antilabor climate. The election of Republican Governor George Deukmejian, a friend of corporate agriculture, exposed a similar shift in California. Additionally, the UFW experienced internal dissent regarding strategy and mounting criticism toward Chávez's centralized leadership. Strong differences of opinion and exhaustion from the intense battles led to the departure of longtime members of Chávez's inner circle. Union membership, which had peaked in the 1970s, drifted downward.

Unwavering in his commitment to farm workers, Chávez experimented with new tactics in the 1980s. Incorporating new technology, the UFW invested in direct mail and computer-generated mailing lists. Charges that Chávez had abandoned his original vision and de-emphasized field organizing grew. The decrease in activity, a characteristic that the UFW shared with the labor movement in general during the hostile Reagan era, prompted some observers to claim that Chávez had discarded his convictions and that his cause had lost its direction.

An Untimely Death

Ignoring the criticism, Chávez pressed ahead. In 1993, his sudden death in his sleep in San Luis, Arizona, not far from his birthplace, stunned his followers and admirers. He had gone there to testify in a legal suit against growers. Poor nutrition as a youngster, debilitating fasts, and the weight of leadership had extracted a heavy price. After years of declining membership and increasing indifference to farm worker concerns, Chávez's dream seemed to revive as a massive expression of grief over his unexpected passing overwhelmed farm workers and the many middle-class supporters whose lives he had touched. An estimated 40,000 mourners traveled to Delano to mourn and honor him. Millions more viewed the funeral on major national and international broadcasting outlets. His death promised to breathe new energy into "La Causa" (the farm workers' cause).

Despite his untimely death at age 66, Chávez remained an enduring symbol of change in many respects. His greatest aspiration was improving the lives of the men, women, and children who toiled in the fields. His dedication and drive awakened the conscience of a nation to the abject poverty and wretched circumstances of field workers, particularly those of Mexican heritage, in one of the wealthiest countries in the world. As a result of his charismatic leadership, workers and their middle-class supporters demanded dignity and respect; in addition, contracts negotiated wage increases and better work conditions, including the provision of water and sanitary facilities, pesticide protections, and grievance procedures through the collective bargaining process. Under union contracts, workers also received health and pension benefits and their own credit union. Chávez's vision served as a catalyst for the emergence of the Chicano rights movement, "*El Movimiento*," in the 1960s. *La Causa* mobilized farm workers, middle-class Latino organizations, Mexican-American students, and Chicanas (women) to espouse a new sense of cultural pride and to fight for their civic, political, social, and economic rights. With his appeal for justice, dignity, and nonviolence, Chávez's message connected with middle-class Anglos and other racial and ethnic groups in a cross-class and cross-race coalition for social change. The recipient of many awards, including the Medal of Freedom, the United States' highest civilian honor, bestowed posthumously by President Bill Clinton in 1994, the modest and soft-spoken Chávez eschewed the trappings of a major national figure and remained committed to his farm worker roots.

MARGARET ROSE

References and Further Reading

Dunne, John Gregory. *Delano: The Story of the California Grape Strike.* New York: Farrar, Straus & Giroux, 1967.

Etulain, Richard W. *Cesar Chavez: A Brief Biography with Documents.* Boston: Bedford/St. Martin's, 2002.

Griswold del Castillo, Richard, and Richard Garcia. *Cesar Chavez: A Triumph of Spirit.* Norman: University of Oklahoma Press, 1995.

Jenkins, J. Craig. *The Politics of Insurgency: The Farm Workers Movement in the 1960s.* New York: Columbia University Press, 1985.

Levy, Jacques. *Cesar Chavez: Autobiography of La Causa.* New York: W.W. Norton & Company, Inc., 1975.

London, Joan, and Henry Anderson. *So Shall Ye Reap: The Story of Cesar Chavez & the Farm Workers' Movement.* New York: Thomas Y. Crowell Company, 1970.

Majka, Linda C., and Theo J. Majka. *Farm Workers, Agribusiness, and the State.* Philadelphia: Temple University Press, 1982.

Matthiessen, Peter. *Sal Si Puedes: Cesar Chavez and the New American Revolution.* New York: Random House, 1969.

Meister, Dick, and Anne Loftis. *A Long Time Coming: The Struggle to Unionize America's Farm Workers.* New York: MacMillan Publishing Co., Inc., 1977.

Rose, Margaret. "Dolores Huerta: The United Farm Workers Union." In *The Human Tradition in American Labor History*, edited by Eric Arnesen. Wilmington, DE: Scholarly Resources Inc., 2004, pp. 211–229.

———. "Gender and Civic Activism in Mexican American Barrios: The Community Service Organization, 1947–1962." In *Not June Cleaver: Women and Gender in Postwar America, 1945–1962*, edited by Joanne Meyerowitz. Philadelphia: Temple University Press, 1994, pp. 177–200.

———. "Traditional and Non-traditional Patterns of Female Activism in the United Farm Workers of America, 1962–1980." *Frontiers* 11, no. 1 (March 1990): 26–32.

Taylor, Ronald B. *Chavez and the Farm Workers: A Study in the Acquisition & Use of Power.* Boston: Beacon Press, 1975.

See also **Agricultural Labor Relations Act (1975); Delano Grape Strike (1965–1970); Huerta, Dolores C.; United Farm Workers of America**

CHAVEZ-THOMPSON, LINDA (AUGUST 1, 1944–)
American Federation of Labor-Congress of Industrial Organizations

Linda Chavez-Thompson is a second-generation Mexican-American who was born in Lubbock, Texas. Chavez-Thompson learned about hard work early in life: as a 10-year-old child who weeded cotton in west Texas full-time during the summer, and as a 15-year-old who quit school to help support her family by "hoeing and picking cotton on a full-time basis." Over the next 35 years, as an adult, she held several staff and high-profile leadership positions in local, state, and national labor organizations. Elected executive vice president of the American Federation of Labor-Congress of Industrial Organizations (AFL-CIO) in 1995, she is the highest-ranking minority representative in the U.S. labor movement in the early twenty-first century.

Chavez-Thompson has been connected in some capacity to organized labor for more than 40 years. In 1971, as the international union representative for the American Federation of State, County, and Municipal Employees (AFSCME) in San Antonio, Texas, she was assigned to work in six "antilabor" states—Arizona, Colorado, New Mexico, Oklahoma, Texas, and Utah—in an attempt to increase union membership, particularly among the Spanish-speaking.

In the early 1970s, she gained considerable experience in union activities as the assistant business manager and then the business manager of AFSCME Local 2399. Chavez-Thompson undertook a major leadership role in labor through her position as the executive director of Local 2399 a few years later. In that capacity, she was responsible for creating policy, engaging in political action, and educating legislators about labor issues. As a result of several other labor appointments, for example, national vice president of the Labor Council for Latin American Advancement and the international vice president of AFSCME, she

CHICAGO FEDERATION OF LABOR

carved out an important place for herself in the labor movement.

From 1993 until the latter part of 1995, she served as the vice president of the AFL-CIO. In early 1995, many top-ranking AFL-CIO members had begun to recognize the spiraling decline of the organization. In order to stem the tide of this decline, several union leaders asked then president Lane Kirkland to step aside in favor of Tom Donahue, his vice president. Kirkland adamantly refused to step down, and Donahue declined to campaign for the AFL-CIO presidency. Chavez-Thompson became part of a triumvirate of union insurgents that included John Sweeney, head of the Service Employees International Union (SEIU), and Richard Trumka, head of the United Mine Workers of America (UMWA) that formed a slate to run for the AFL-CIO leadership offices to replace longtime AFL-CIO president Lane Kirkland and other incumbent union officials. Sweeney, Trumka, and Chavez-Thompson campaigned for substantive change in the AFL-CIO's operating philosophy and ran under the banner of "A New Voice for American Workers."

Their vision was to dramatically transform and reshape the 13 million member organization by making it more relevant for its membership, starting with their election in the late twentieth century. On October 25, 1997, Sweeney and the other members of the New Voice slate were swept into office after a hotly contested election between their camp and the camp of the interim AFL-CIO president, Tom Donahue, who had replaced Kirkland, who resigned as president prior to the 1995 convention.

As executive vice president, one of Chavez-Thompson's primary roles was "to reinvigorate the American labor movement." Toward that end, she advocated some innovative approaches to increasing the membership and the political activism of the AFL-CIO. She and the other labor leaders organized Union Summer, a project that sought to bring young people into the movement as union organizers and political activists. Chavez-Thompson was re-elected to a four-year term as executive vice president on September 30, 1997, and then re-elected for a second four-year term in 2001 and a third four-year term in 2005.

Chavez-Thompson has continued to play a significant role as one of the AFL-CIO's most prominent figures. She has focused her attention on the recruitment of Hispanic immigrants to increase the ranks of the AFL-CIO's dwindling membership, and she has sponsored several initiatives to develop coalitions with local, community, and women's rights groups and with nationally known civil rights organizations, such as the League of United Latin American Citizens and the National Council of La Raza and the National Association for the Advancement of Colored People.

Chavez-Thompson has also become a major spokesperson for the AFL-CIO through her key appointments to various labor and political boards of trustees. She is a member of the AFL-CIO's Housing Investment Trust (HIT) board of trustees, which is responsible for investing the pensions of union workers in various real estate projects (housing) and which oversees almost $4 billion in assets. Chavez-Thompson was appointed to President Bill Clinton's Initiative on Race and his Committee on Employment of People with Disabilities. In 2005, Chavez-Thompson was appointed as a vice chairperson of the Democratic National Committee (DNC) under the leadership of its chairperson, Howard Dean, the former governor of Vermont (1991–2003) and a Democratic candidate for president of the United States in 2004.

Chavez-Thompson continues to play a major role in the American labor movement.

JOSEPH C. SANTORA

Selected Works

Chavez-Thompson, Linda. "Communities at Work: How New Alliances Are Restoring Our Right to Organize." *New Labor Forum: A Journal of Ideas, Analysis and Debate* Fall/Winter (1998): 112–119.
———. "The Future of Populist Politics." Colorado College's 125th Anniversary Symposium: "Cultures in the 21st Century: Conflicts and Convergences," delivered at Colorado College on February 6, 1999.
———. "Repealing Safety." *The American Prospect Online.* March 6, 2001. www.prospect.org/web/page.ww?section=root&name=ViewWeb&articleId=321.
Figueroa, Maria. "An Interview with Linda Chavez-Thompson." http://members.aol.com/pobct/chavez.html.

See also **American Federation of Labor-Congress of Industrial Organizations**

CHICAGO FEDERATION OF LABOR

The Chicago Federation of Labor (CFL) was formed when two older labor organizations in Chicago, the Trades and Labor Assembly and the Labor Congress, merged in 1896 and applied for an American Federation of Labor (AFL) charter. From the Trades and Labor Assembly, the CFL inherited the membership and militant traditions of a group of local unions that included bricklayers, sailors, and carpenters, among many others. The Labor Congress, a group dominated by German-speaking socialists, bequeathed to the CFL its interest in the reform politics of the populist People's Party and the fledgling Progressive movement in Illinois. Although the Chicago Federation of Labor officially pledged to avoid political endorsements upon becoming an AFL affiliate and to follow the AFL's national policies, the Chicago labor organization remained, in historian Richard Schnierov's words, "politicized to its core" and often served as an independent and powerful voice within the AFL. The first program of the CFL endorsed federal ownership of the railroads and telegraphs and municipal ownership of all utilities.

During the early years of the twentieth century, the CFL's reputation was marred by the corruption and racketeering of its president, John "Skinny" Madden. But in 1905, reformer John Fitzpatrick was elected to the CFL presidency, a position he held from 1905 to 1907 and from 1909 to 1946. Fitzpatrick enjoyed a reputation for absolute integrity and was strongly committed to union democracy. At a time when many labor leaders advocated centralizing contract powers within national and international union bureaucracies, Fitzpatrick sought to restore these powers to local unions. He also made CFL meetings a forum for democratic debate, advocated referendums on major union issues, and sought to reform parliamentary procedures within the AFL convention.

The CFL president's advocacy of democratic reforms won him the support of a talented group of labor activists. Among these, some, like Fitzpatrick himself, clearly fell within a "progressive union" tradition and advocated moderate evolutionary change within the labor movement and American society. Foremost among this group were Ed Nockels, CFL secretary; Margaret Haley and Lillian Herstein of the Chicago Teachers Federation; and Robert Buck, editor of the CFL's insightful newspaper, the *New Majority* (1919–1924). Until a fateful split in 1923, Fitzpatrick also welcomed socialists and syndicalists, who sought to bore from within the AFL to promote class revolution. Among these was William Z. Foster, a future leader of the Communist Party who played a critical role in organizing Chicago's packinghouse and steel workers. An Irish immigrant and ardent Irish nationalist, Fitzpatrick also strengthened the CFL by forming close alliances with area immigrant leaders, hiring immigrant labor organizers, and making the local labor movement a center for immigrant nationalist activities. The combined efforts of progressives, radicals, and immigrant labor activists helped to transform the Chicago Federation of Labor into one of the largest and most militant city labor councils in the country.

World War I ushered in a particularly important era in the CFL's history as the organization became a center for pacifist politics as well as for major industrial organizing drives. CFL leaders like Fitzpatrick opposed American entrance into World War I, partly because of their ethnic ties to former homelands.

Equally important, however, was that many CFL activists were imbued with an ethos of international labor solidarity and believed that the business class was trying to drive the country into war for the sake of its own profits. They argued, however, that it would be workers who paid the price on the battlefields. In an effort to undermine the rush toward war, the CFL fought efforts to introduce military training in the schools, staged parades opposing military preparedness, and rallied on behalf of a movement demanding a democratic national referendum on the question of war or peace. The CFL also lobbied the AFL to demand that American citizens be prevented from entering war zones so as to prevent the escalating pattern of attacks that would inevitably lead to war.

At a carefully planned meeting of AFL representatives from which municipal labor leaders were excluded in March 1917, however, the AFL pledged its loyalty to the government in the event of war. Its efforts to mount a national antiwar campaign thwarted by the AFL, the CFL devoted 1917–1918 to using the wartime situation to labor's advantage. In particular, the CFL became, in the words of historian James Barrett, the "heart and brain of the two great World War I drives to organize mass-production workers in the steel and meat-packing industries." The campaigns scored some significant successes during the war but were undercut by fierce business counterattacks and by ethnic and racial divisiveness in the postwar era. The CFL's innovative campaigns nonetheless marked an important step forward in the march toward industrial unionism.

Disillusioned by the AFL's close relationship with the Wilson administration during the war, the CFL also launched independent city and county labor parties in 1919 and played a leadership role in creating the Illinois Labor party and the national Farmer-Labor party. The parties were particularly notable for their imaginative reinterpretation of American democratic ideals to justify democratic control of industry, majoritarian rule by a labor party, a democratic alternative to the League of Nations, and support for nationalist rebellions throughout the world.

Although Fitzpatrick lost decisively in his bid for mayor of Chicago in 1919, he fared surprisingly well for a third-party candidate. National Farmer-Labor Party presidential candidate Parley Christiansen, however, performed abysmally in 1920, undercut by AFL opposition, lack of funding, and a lack of press coverage. Subsequent efforts to build a more broadly based labor party movement faltered when communists packed one of the movement's conventions with their own delegates and wrested control of it from Fitzpatrick and his colleagues. Fitzpatrick subsequently disavowed the party that emerged from the convention, and a bitter animosity developed between the CFL and Chicago-area communists that would have divisive consequences for the future of the city's labor movement.

Censured by the AFL for its independent labor party politics and disillusioned by the fruits of its political labors, the CFL renewed its commitment to the officially nonpartisan policies of the AFL in 1924. Yet in many ways the CFL remained an independent and visionary force in the labor movement. The CFL secretary Edward Nockels, for example, continued to pursue his dream of an independent labor radio station, despite the early indifference of the AFL. Nockels, in contrast to many of his superiors in the AFL, was convinced of the revolutionary potential of the new technology and, according to historian Nathan Godfried, hoped to use a labor-owned radio station "both negatively, as a way to counter the propaganda of the capitalist media and positively, as a way to shape working-class culture and consciousness." The CFL secured a license to operate radio station WCFL, the "Voice of Labor," in 1926 and soon began broadcasting a creative mix of labor news shows, music, sports, and entertainment. WCFL fought many valiant battles with the Federal Radio Commission over the allocation of clear radio frequencies and changed greatly over time, but nonetheless continued to broadcast until 1978, when the CFL sold the station.

During the early years of the Great Depression, the CFL also continued to play a leadership role in the movement for industrial unions. Historian Barbara Newell has noted that after the Roosevelt administration successfully secured passage of the National Industrial Recovery Act, small locals sprang up in the meatpacking and steel industries that "formed around a nucleus of employees . . . who had been introduced to trade unionism in the earlier organizing attempts of Fitzpatrick and Foster." The CFL vigorously supported Chicago's meatpacking and steel locals, and they in turn played an important role in transforming the union movement in the two industries. Following the lead of the AFL, however, the CFL refused to aid the industrial union campaigns of the Congress of Industrial Organizations after it emerged in 1935. In part, CFL leaders feared a divided labor movement. Fitzpatrick, still bitter over the demise of the Labor Party, also distrusted the area communists who led many CIO organizing drives. The split in the ranks of labor isolated the CFL from key segments of the industrial union movement that it had previously nurtured.

The election of William Lee to the presidency of the CFL after Fitzpatrick's death in 1946 brought a significant shift in focus to the organization. Lee, who reigned as president until 1984, oversaw the merger between local AFL and CIO unions and became notable for cultivating close ties with the Cook County Democratic Party and the Democratic Mayor Richard J. Daley. Supporters argued that Lee's close relationship with Daley helped the CFL to expand its community influence: CFL representatives were awarded seats on the board of nearly every major public body in Chicago, including the Board of Education, Housing Authority, and Public Building Commission. Opponents charged that Lee undermined the independence and militance of the Chicago labor movement and aligned it on the wrong side of many civil rights struggles.

Since 1984, a succession of CFL presidents has revitalized campaigns to organize nonunionized workers and has mobilized to try to stem the national tide of deteriorating conditions for many union workers. The CFL has also demonstrated a renewed interest in global economic and foreign policy issues, as was evidenced in a vigorous discussion on the planned U.S. invasion of Iraq in February 2003. Campaigns and debates in the early twenty-first century suggested that many of the issues raised by twentieth-century labor activists would remain relevant into the twenty-first century.

ELIZABETH MCKILLEN

References and Further Reading

Barrett, James. *Work and Community in the Jungle: Chicago's Packinghouse Workers, 1894–1922*. Urbana: University of Illinois Press, 1987.
Chicago Federation of Labor. "Chicago Federation of Labor Historical Perspective." www.cflonline.org/links.php?id=1.
Chicago Federation of Labor. "Report on February 4 Chicago Federation of Labor Discussions of the War." www.Chicagocoal.org/antiwar/CFL-discussion-2003-0204.htm.
Cohen, Elizabeth. *Making a New Deal for Labor: Industrial Workers in Chicago, 1909–1939*. Cambridge: Cambridge University Press, 1990.
Godfried, Nathan. *WCFL: Chicago's Voice of Labor, 1926–1978*. Urbana: University of Illinois Press, 1997.
Keiser, John. "John Fitzpatrick and Progressive Unionism, 1915–1925." Ph.D. dissertation, Northwestern University, 1965.
McKillen, Elizabeth. *Chicago Labor and the Quest for a Democratic Diplomacy: 1914–1924*. Ithaca, NY: Cornell University Press, 1995.
Newell, Barbara. *Chicago and the Labor Movement*. Urbana: University of Illinois Press, 1961.
Schnierov, Richard. *Labor and Urban Politics: Class Conflict and the Origins of Modern Liberalism in Chicago, 1864–97*. Urbana: University of Illinois Press, 1998.
Strouthous, Andrew. *U.S. Labor and Political Action, 1918–24: A Comparison of Independent Political Action in New York, Chicago and Seattle*. New York: St. Martin's Press, 2000.

See also **Central Labor Unions; Farmer-Labor Party; Fitzpatrick, John; Foreign Policy**

CHICAGO TEACHERS' FEDERATION

The Chicago Teachers' Federation, founded in 1897 and powerful through the 1920s, was the largest teachers' association of its time and the first to affiliate with organized labor. Organized by and for elementary school teachers, its membership and staff consisted almost entirely of women, who dominated the teaching staff. At its height in the early 1900s, over half of six thousand Chicago elementary school teachers were members of the Federation. Its success was due primarily to its two officers, former teachers Catherine Goggin, who acted as secretary until her death in 1916, and Margaret Haley, who acted as business representative until her death in 1939. Haley, in particular, had a defining impact on the Federation during her 40 years of leadership, and she directed the organization's political agenda.

With a membership of disenfranchised women, the Federation held little power in the city and state offices with which it had to promote its cause. In order to bolster its authority, the Federation made an unprecedented alliance with organized labor, affiliating with the Chicago Federation of Labor in 1902. The membership led to a barrage of public criticism, yet it also led to salary increases and political power. In 1916, the Federation became Local 1 of the newly formed American Federation of Teachers. In 1917, however, the Federation was forced to withdraw from both organizations under a series of Board of Education regulations that effectively prohibited its teachers from memberships in labor unions.

The Federation was founded to defend a recently won pension law for elementary teachers and to protest a freeze on teacher salary increases, but its scope soon expanded into broader economic and political reform. In one of its earliest public actions, the Federation challenged corporate taxation exemptions that minimized the Board of Education budget, and it opposed the movement to reorganize city school administration away from community governance into a powerful, centralized superintendent's office. The Federation also joined with other Chicago organizations in campaigns for electoral and municipal reform, and with labor in opposing vocational education and school budget cuts.

The Federation functioned in part as an intellectual and political organization for women teachers, providing educational course work and promoting teacher participation in school management through democratic school and district councils. A regular Federation newsletter and monthly membership meetings kept the membership engaged in ongoing political work, and its tiny office in downtown Chicago was often jammed with teachers busily writing broadsides to promote current campaigns. Its female leadership advocated women's suffrage and equal pay for men and women teachers.

The Federation gained national recognition by challenging the policies of the administrator-dominated National Education Association (NEA) and demanding the participation of women teachers in that organization. Between 1897 and the 1920s, the Federation sent hundreds of teachers to the annual NEA meeting, forcing the organization to address the needs of classroom teachers and leading to the 1920 election of Chicago Superintendent Ella Flagg Young as the first woman NEA president. In these years, the Federation was known to teachers throughout the nation as a powerful advocate for women elementary teachers' rights, and it developed great political clout in Chicago and in the larger educational community.

Federation membership was overwhelmingly female and predominantly Irish-American. Concerned about the marginalization of their own group, Federation leaders were not willing to include men teachers or high school teachers in their organization. Long-standing ethnic bigotry also led them to ignore African-American teachers. As the Chicago teaching staff diversified in gender, race, and ethnicity with the expansion of secondary schooling after World War I, the Federation became increasingly isolated from the growing, and more inclusive, AFT locals, and it refused to join in the 1937 amalgamation that became the Chicago Teachers' Union. After Haley's death, the Federation limped along with its aging female membership, monitoring the pension and taking conservative stands on the persecution of communist teachers in the 1950s and on racial integration of schools in the 1960s. The Federation formally disbanded in 1968.

KATE ROUSMANIERE

References and Further Reading

Murphy, Marjorie. *Blackboard Unions: The AFT and the NEA 1900–1980*. Ithaca, NY: Cornell University Press, 1990.
Rousmaniere, Kate. *Citizen Teacher: The Life and Leadership of Margaret Haley*. Albany, NY: SUNY Press, 2005.
Urban, Wayne J. *Why Teachers Organized*. Detroit: Wayne State University Press, 1982.

See also **Haley, Margaret**

CHICAGO TEAMSTERS STRIKE (1905)

A bitter labor dispute, the Chicago Teamsters strike of 1905 lasted 105 days, from April to August 1905, and violence stemming from the strike left 416 people injured and 21 dead. The strike resulted from efforts by Chicago employers to reduce the power of the Teamsters Union, efforts that were only partially successful. In seeking to achieve their goal, employers promoted public concerns about union corruption and sought to fan racial tensions in the city.

In 1905, Chicago was a stronghold for the recently formed International Brotherhood of Teamsters (IBT). Nationwide, the union claimed a membership of 45,000 with about 30,000 of those members located in Chicago. Organizing efforts in Chicago had begun in 1899 and enjoyed great success by 1902. The union's rapid growth benefited from a network of collusive arrangements with team owners associations. In return for agreeing to a closed-shop contract, the union promised employers it would help enforce cartel arrangements controlling competition and price. These agreements led most team owners to support union organization of their employees, the drivers. As the union grew, it assumed an increasingly active role in the city's labor affairs. By choosing whether or not they would honor another union's picket line, team drivers often could determine the fate of a strike or organizing campaign. If the drivers refused to cross the picket line, they denied the employers needed supplies. In so doing, Teamsters were in fact engaged in a kind of sympathy strike. The union used this power to pressure employers in a range of industries to agree to accept the organization of their employees. In so doing, the Teamsters earned the ire of Chicago's business interests.

As union gains mounted across the country in the early years of the 1900s, an employer counteroffensive resulted, and Chicago employers took a leading role in this counteroffensive. Associations of employers, in Chicago and other cities, sought to engage in concerted efforts to break organized labor's power by attacking key union strategies, such as the union shop contract and the sympathetic strike. The Chicago Employers' Association (CEA) specifically hoped to confront the Teamsters Union, because of the latter group's strategic role in promoting organized labor in that city.

The CEA's opportunity came in early April 1905, when the Chicago Teamsters declared their intention to support a strike by the United Garment Workers Union (UGW), whose members had been fired several months earlier by Montgomery Ward & Company. When the Teamsters announced that their members would make no more deliveries to Montgomery Ward & Company until it came to terms with the UGW, the CEA responded by having all of the other city's department stores order their drivers to make the forbidden deliveries, forcing those Teamsters to join the walkout as well. In this way, the CEA spread the dispute beyond the initial company. When the UGW pulled out of the dispute in late April and the Teamsters tried to end it, the CEA kept the strike alive by refusing to allow the striking Teamsters to be rehired.

By early summer, about five thousand Teamsters were on strike, and on Chicago's streets, daily street battles took place between strike supporters and convoys of nonunion wagons with armed guards on board trying to negotiate the unfriendly city avenues. The city assigned the bulk of its police department to strike duty, but Mayor Edward F. Dunne, who had been elected with the support of organized labor, refused to have the crowds driven from the streets. Nor would he call for state or federal forces to enter the city and restore order. Without such a request from the mayor, neither Illinois's governor nor President Theodore Roosevelt was willing to intervene. As a result, the employers' wagons remained vulnerable and unable to make all of the needed deliveries.

The employers turned for help to the courts, where they received more sympathetic treatment. Court injunctions forbade further union picket activity. But more significantly, the employers convinced the state prosecutor's office to launch a union corruption investigation that could bring the Teamsters Union's leadership into disrepute. Meeting on a daily basis with the CEA, state prosecutors directed a grand jury probe that eschewed any investigation into employer activities and which came to focus on the private life of the Teamsters president, Cornelius P. Shea. Details about Shea's alleged visits to a brothel and an extramarital relationship became front-page news, supplemented by unsubstantiated charges of bribe taking. In July, the grand jury indicted Shea and other union leaders, not for corruption, but on conspiracy charges that stemmed from leading a sympathetic strike. Despite the bias of the investigation, the mud stuck; and the union's leaders, as well as the strike, were discredited in the eyes of many Chicagoans.

Just as corruption charges swirled around the strike, so too did racial tensions. African-Americans from southern cities made up a portion of the replacement drivers recruited by the CEA. Chicago newspapers highlighted the role of these black drivers, and in news stories and cartoons, the papers played on white racial antipathies. Similarly, the Chicago police encouraged violence against black replacement drivers, and at one point during the strike, police rioted through a district of town where some of the replacement drivers were staying. Some observers charged that the CEA sought to play on racial tensions in order to create a violent incident that would justify intervention by the state militia. But the Teamsters, which had from the beginning been a biracial union, urged its membership to avoid seeing the strike in racial terms.

By August 1905, the strike petered out to its end. The Teamsters accepted the fact that their striking members would not be rehired, and the CEA gave up its efforts to destroy the union. Although department store drivers remained nonunion for decades, most of the rest of the city's teamsters remained well organized. But a chastened Teamsters Union avoided further involvement in sympathy strikes. More significantly, the corruption charges had undercut the legitimacy of the union's power, which was now seen as abusive and irresponsible.

DAVID WITWER

References and Further Reading

Cohen, Andrew Wender. *The Racketeer's Progress: Chicago and the Struggle for the Modern American Economy, 1900–1940.* New York: Cambridge University Press, 2004.
Witwer, David. *Corruption and Reform in the Teamsters Union.* Urbana: University of Illinois Press, 2003.

See also **International Brotherhood of Teamsters**

CHILD CARE

As slave and unpaid labor in households, and as paid work in the market economy, the organization of child-care work by both gender and race plays a central role in the labor history of the United States. An analysis of the work of child care (both historical and contemporary) reveals continuity, as well as changes, in the ways in which gendered and racialized ideologies of motherhood and care organize social and economic life.

The Agricultural Economy, Slave Labor, and Child Care

Women's slave labor as field workers, care workers, and child bearers demonstrates the ways in which the gendered and racialized organization of labor benefited white land owners. Given the legal status of slave children as property constituting both future workers and "commodities" that could be sold, slave women's bearing of and caring for children enhanced the productivity and economic status of the master. If slave women were fortunate enough to keep their children, they were most often denied the opportunity to care for them. On larger plantations, slaves not capable of field work (older women and children) often assumed the work of providing collective care for slave children while their parents worked in field and house labor.

A small number of slave women worked as house servants and, while prohibited from caring for their own children, were deemed suitable to care for the children of their white masters. Slave women provided child care and served as wet nurses for the children of their masters while the white mistress managed the household (performing some direct household labor depending on the size of the plantation). This gendered and racialized organization of labor presages the status hierarchies further developed in the industrial economy—in the provision of paid and unpaid child care, as well as in other forms of labor.

The Industrial Economy: Gendered and Racialized Ideologies and Practices

In the mid-nineteenth century, the growth of industrialization in the United States fostered an increasingly dualistic, gendered, and racialized view of social and economic life: a division of labor into "separate spheres" of family and market. As production moved from plantations and farms to factories, households took on a new identity. Perceived to exist in the "private sphere," households were increasingly viewed as serving the social and economic roles of consuming rather than producing. In contrast, the market became identified as the sphere of production: the "public sphere." These transitions in the location and perception of work resulted in an ideology that not only distinguished the family from the market, but also identified these two spheres as explicitly gendered. The workplace, a place of paid labor, rationality, and competition, became identified with an ideology of masculinity. In contrast, women's behaviors and values were construed to be the result of their relational family experiences, and home and family became increasingly idealized as a place of feminine nurturance, affection, and care. This idealized notion of womanhood (often called the cult of domesticity or the cult of true womanhood) clearly conflicted with the reality of the lives of immigrant women, women of color, and poor white women whose paid labor was essential to the survival of their families. Nonetheless, the racialized, gendered, and class-based ideal took root, and the ideology of white womanhood and the full-time, at-home mother intensified in the American consciousness.

The competing need for women of color and poor women to provide unpaid domestic work (including child care) in their own homes, and the need for them as paid workers in the market economy, led to the first formally recognized day nurseries. With the growth of urban industrial production, poor women increasingly sought income through factory work and were unavailable to care for children within their own families. In response, philanthropists and wealthy women joined forces in the late nineteenth and early twentieth centuries to organize charitable "day nurseries." Often viewed as a "necessary evil" by whites (and some blacks), day nurseries were seen to provide a service for those families unable to transition smoothly to the ideal of the emerging industrial economy—a family in which wives engaged in unpaid domestic (household) labor while husbands engaged in paid industrial production. In contrast, the black clubwomen's movement, acknowledging both black mothers' employment and the racial segregation of most white-run nurseries, established day nurseries for black children. Under the leadership of the National Association of Colored Women (NACW), local affiliates organized urban day nurseries to care for African-American children in both the North and the South.

As a result of the reduction in both immigration and social reform activism, day nurseries declined following the Progressive Era and WWI. With the decline of charitable day nurseries, the subsequent major development in child care involved the emergence of private nursery schools and kindergartens serving middle- and upper-class families. While private nursery schools emerged as an institution of the middle and upper classes to promote early childhood education and development, day nurseries and child-care facilities were increasingly stigmatized as serving the working poor—families unable to achieve the ideal of a male breadwinner and female homemaker.

The Great Depression and World War II: Change and Continuity in Child Care

The Great Depression and WWII are often heralded as an era of dramatic change in both the public attitude toward and pubic provision of child care. While direct federal involvement in the provision of child care during the 1930s and 1940s represented a change from previous practice, a closer look at federal policy reflects historical continuity in its endorsement of gendered and racialized ideologies regarding women's labor—including the paid and unpaid care of children.

During the Great Depression, female-headed households increased through divorce and desertion, thereby challenging the ideology of the "separate spheres" with its male breadwinner and female homemaker. Without a male breadwinner, how could mothers provide full-time care for their children? Congress partially addressed this conflict with enactment of the Aid to Dependent Children (ADC) program in 1935. While publicly funded grants aided poor mothers in providing the basic necessities for their children, ADC continued to endorse the gendered division of labor and the ideology of the full-time, at-home mother. "Deserving" white mothers who were unable to sustain a male/female family structure through no fault of their own (for example, white widows) were viewed as most suitable for ADC. Limited support was available for divorced, separated, or deserted mothers; benefits were systematically denied to African-American mothers; and able-bodied women with school-aged children were disqualified from the program. In addition, while providing limited funds for the support of children, ADC provided no economic benefits to mothers themselves, further endorsing the need for the income of a male breadwinner in a family.

Given the growth of female-headed households and limited government support, women increasingly sought paid employment. In labor markets organized by race and gender, domestic service, including child care, served as one of the primary sources of employment available to immigrant women, women of color, and poor white women. Yet, Congress denied home-based workers rights under the labor legislation enacted during the New Deal—including the Fair Labor Standards Act, the National Industrial Recovery Act, the Social Security Act, and the National Labor Relations Act. This exclusion of women's home-based paid labor further reflects the historical privileging of white male industrial workers by policy makers and the unwillingness to recognize women's paid household and care work as legitimate labor.

In 1933, the Works Progress Administration (WPA) instituted Emergency Nursery Schools, primarily to provide jobs for unemployed teachers and, only secondarily, as a source of child care for working mothers. Many of the Emergency Nursery Schools were segregated, and qualified white teachers often refused to work in schools serving black children. In addition, employment turnover in nursery schools remained high, especially so with the growth of the war industry and the availability of more lucrative jobs for women in industrial production.

With the rearmament and mobilization programs of 1940–1941, the Federal Works Agency, with funding through the Lanham Act, took over the provision of child-care programs previously sponsored by the WPA. The war industry and federal government combined to train white women for industrial positions as welders, shipfitters, riveters, and machinists. Women of color, trained and hired to a much lesser degree in skilled industrial positions, found employment in clerical and janitorial jobs. Despite its recruitment of women workers, the War Manpower Commission appealed to mothers of young children to stay at home, and only when the majority of single women were employed in the war effort did the Commission seek to draw married women into production. Further, Congress clearly stated that the provision of publicly funded child care under the Lanham Act constituted a "war emergency measure" and that government funds were both limited and temporary. Reflecting Congress's position, at their peak in 1944, federally funded child-care centers cared for only a small portion of children in need—an estimated 120,000 children out of an estimated one million needing care. Unwilling to provide full public funding of group child care, the Federal Security Administration explicitly encouraged mothers to find individual care for their children.

The federal endorsement of child care as the private responsibility of families was further demonstrated at war's end when the government quickly dismantled federally funded child-care programs. By October 31, 1945, all federally subsidized child-care centers received notice of funding termination. In addition, government-funded publicity campaigns explicitly encouraged mothers to leave paid labor and return to the prewar ideal of the full-time, at-home mother.

The Postwar Period: Child Care Becomes an Enduring Public Issue

As policy makers terminated war-related child-care programs, the race- and class-based ideal of the full-time, at-home mother again grew and held sway well into the 1960s. Nonetheless, mothers continued to engage in paid labor in record numbers. While only 11% of mothers of young children reported engaging in paid labor in the immediate postwar period, that number grew dramatically, reaching 47% by 1980 and 62% by 2004. During these same years, black mothers of young children participated in paid labor at a rate 10% to 15% higher than their white counterparts. As mothers entered the labor force in record numbers, their previous availability as full-time, at-home mothers declined—yet the need for child care remained. Who would care for this growing number of children? Ironically, but not surprisingly, it is women (disproportionately women of color and often mothers themselves) who provide the child care that enables other women to work outside the home.

A Contemporary Perspective

The increased employment of white and middle-class mothers in the postwar period reflects the changing ideology of motherhood. Values central to the cult of true womanhood and the ideology of the full-time, at-home mother included motherhood as incompatible with labor force participation, the need for a clear gendered division of labor in families (male breadwinner and female homemaker), and child care as the private responsibility of families. In contrast, the reality of the lives of postwar white and middle-class mothers increasingly reflected the historical ideology of motherhood long applicable to poor women and women of color—motherhood is compatible with labor force participation; the paid labor of mothers is often needed to support families, and the government may provide limited child-care benefits in selected circumstances. With this change in both the practice and ideology of motherhood, the conflict between women's responsibilities as mothers and as paid employees became increasingly visible—as did the increased demand for child care as a service provided in the market economy.

Employed mothers use a variety of forms of institutional and noninstitutional care to meet the needs of their children. The most prominent form of care for young children of employed mothers remains informal care provided in families and households. In 2002, 52% of child care (both paid and unpaid care) used by employed mothers was provided in the informal economy by relatives, friends, and family members. The more visible form of child care is paid child care provided in both formal settings (for example, child-care centers, preschools) and home-based settings by family child-care providers (offering paid group care in the home of the provider), and by nannies and au pairs (see Chart 1). Despite the visibility of formal child-care centers as a source of paid care, in 2002, the majority of paid child care for young children (53%) was provided in home-based settings by family child-care providers and by nannies.

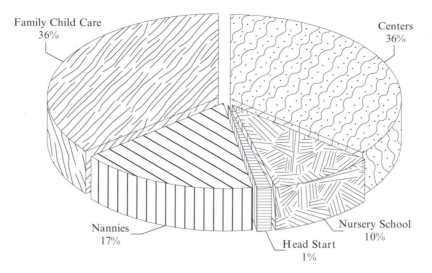

Child-Care Arrangements of Preschoolers of Employed Mothers: 2002
Source: Tabulations derived from "Who's Minding the Kids?" Child Care Arrangements Winter 2002, PPL Table 2a, U.S. Census Bureau, www.census.gov/population/www/socdemo/child.ppl-177.html, November 2005.

Paid Child-Care Work: Subsistence-Level Employment

In the first decade of the twenty-first century, child care stood as one of the 10 most rapidly growing industries in the United States. Despite this growth, the historical organization of paid child-care work by gender, race, and ethnicity remains constant. In 2003, women made up over 95% of paid child-care workers, and women of color made up one third of the child-care work force. Women of color disproportionately occupy the most poorly paid and lowest-status child-care jobs (as entry-level aides in centers and in homes as nannies and au pairs). In addition, the continued globalization of labor is reflected in child-care employment. As "transnational mothers," women from developing countries increasingly seek domestic employment in the United States, sending remittances from their domestic and home-based child-care work to others who care for their own children in their country of origin.

Child care remains a poverty-wage industry. Child-care workers earn one half as much as comparably educated women. In 2004, a quarter of child-care teachers and administrators reported incomes below 200% of the poverty line (roughly the minimum necessary to pay for basic necessities without public assistance). In the same period, nannies and family child-care providers reported earnings well below the minimum wage. In addition, domestic employees who worked as personal attendants (for example, nannies)

were explicitly excluded from federal legislation guaranteeing the right to a minimum wage.

In 2004, only one third of center-based teachers and administrators reported receiving health care as an employment benefit, and only one fifth reported participating in a pension plan. In the same period, home-based family child-care providers and nannies reported that they were not covered under even the most basic of medical insurance and had insufficient wages to invest in pension or retirement plans. Lack of benefits and low wages took their toll, as one third of center-based and home-based providers left child-care employment each year in the early twenty-first century—most often to seek higher-wage employment.

Turnover, wages, and quality of care are interrelated in child-care employment. As early as 1988, research identified the most important predictor of quality child care as the wages of teachers and providers. Multiple studies have documented the presence of well-compensated, well-educated, and consistent child-care providers as significant predictors of quality care for children. Short-term benefits of quality child care include children's ability to socialize and learn, while long-term social benefits include lower crime, higher employment, lower poverty rates, and greater economic productivity. Thus, the needs of children and families for quality care, as well as the long-term interests of society for productive citizens, are directly linked to higher-quality jobs for child-care workers. Meeting the needs of children, child-care providers, and the community proves to be mutually enhancing.

Addressing the Needs of Children, Child-Care Workers, and the Community

How might the need for high-quality care and high-quality jobs for child-care workers be addressed? Child-care workers and their advocates have used a variety of means to increase the quality of care, as well as the quality of child-care jobs. These include unionization, grassroots organizing, and campaigns for public funding of child care. While less than 5% of the child-care work force was unionized in 2003, in the same year five international unions reported active campaigns to organize child-care workers. Nonetheless, a union contract in and of itself is insufficient to change the wages of child-care teachers and providers. Given parents' limited ability to pay the full cost of quality care, as well as the public benefits that accrue from quality care, advocates, Unions, and policy makers have argued that public funding is essential to increase the stability, training, and compensation of the child-care work force. In 2001, 37 states reported funding indirect child-care compensation initiatives (for example, training and professional development programs). In the same year, 23 states reported programs to directly increase wages and benefits for child-care teachers and providers. The enactment of such programs implied public recognition that, as in K-12 education, long-term social benefits accrue through a public investment in the development and education of young children.

MARY C. TUOMINEN

References and Further Reading

Folbre, Nancy. *The Invisible Heart: Economics and Family Values*. New York: The New Press, 2001.

Glenn, Evelyn Nakano. *Unequal Freedom: How Race and Gender Shaped American Citizenship and Labor*. Cambridge, MA: Harvard University Press, 2002.

Helburn, Suzanne, and Barbara Bergmann. *America's Child Care Problem: The Way Out*. New York: Palgrave Macmillan, 2003.

Hondagneu-Sotelo, Pierrette. *Doméstica: Immigrant Workers Cleaning and Caring in the Shadows of Affluence*. Berkeley: University of California Press, 2001.

Michel, Sonya. *Children's Interests/Mothers' Rights: The Shaping of America's Child Care Policy*. New Haven, CT: Yale University Press, 1999.

Parreñas, Rhacel Salazar. *Servants of Globalization: Women, Migration and Domestic Work*. Stanford, CA: Stanford University Press, 2001.

Tuominen, Mary C. *We Are Not Babysitters: Family Childcare Providers Redefine Work and Care*. New Brunswick, NJ: Rutgers, 2003.

Whitebook, Marcy. *Working for Worthy Wages: The Child Care Compensation Movement: 1970–2001*. New York: The Foundation for Child Development, 2001.

CHILD LABOR

The commonly accepted twenty-first-century definition of child labor is the employment of children below a certain age as determined by custom or law. In most developed nations throughout the world, children working under the age of late adolescence— with exceptions made for schoolwork, household chores, and some paid work such as babysitting—is viewed as exploitative and unjust. The United States, as with other nations with advanced economies, passed through stages in its history wherein child labor was essential and normative, and only later came to be considered a social and economic problem. In developing nations functioning in the global economy of the twenty-first century, issues and challenges relating to child labor, to varying degrees, reflect many of those found in the United States at earlier stages of its economic growth.

Child labor in the United States has historically been integral to the family, or household, economy. Within the family economy, all members of the household contribute to the economic well-being of the familial unit. Middle- and upper-class families, especially those living in cities, often did not rely on the labor done or wages earned by their children for the economic survival of the household unit. But for poor and working-class families, as well as the majority of farming households, children and their labor power were vital and valuable resources. As the nation's economic development passed through various phases, the labor of children and their roles within both family and national economies have changed.

Child Labor in Colonial America

Child labor in the North American colonies was an expected and accepted aspect of everyday life. The colonies were land-rich but labor-poor, and as they matured, they faced chronic shortages of labor. The work of children was valued, not only as it was immediately used, but also as a preparation for a future, productive adulthood. As such, work itself and skills obtained in its execution were an integral part, or even the whole, of a child's formal education.

For children, their labor fell along a spectrum of "freeness" among the varying degrees of bound and free labor existing within the colonial economy. The spectrum ranged from work done within a free household headed by a child's own father to indentured servitude and to chattel slavery. Slaves labored as house servants in cities from Boston to Charlestown, on small farms in the North and the southern

Indiana Mfg. Co., Boy taking boards away from "double cut-off" machine. Library of Congress, Prints & Photographs Division, National Child Labor Committee Collection [LC-DIG-nclc-04487].

backcountry as labor supplementary to that of free-holder families, and constituted the largest component of the agricultural work force of the staple-crop plantation system that had firm roots in the southern colonies by the eighteenth century. Enslaved children worked where adult slaves worked, whether that were in the fields or the kitchens of their owners, or within the slaves' quarters as part of a family unit, as soon as they were able to learn how to perform even the most rudimentary tasks.

Indentured servitude was a system by which individuals, both male and female, were bound to a master for a term typically ranging from four to seven years, or until the child reached adulthood. These indentured servants worked in a variety of capacities, but especially in agriculture. In return for the rights to the servant's labor, the master was to provide food, shelter, clothing, and when the contract came to an end, "freedom's dues," which included rewards ranging from clothes and a small sum of money to livestock, tools, and sometimes land. In the cases of apprenticeship to skilled tradesmen, the bound child was typically male and living in an urban area, and the master provided education and training in a craft. Children bound to indentured servitude were often orphans or the children of poor, widowed, criminal, or dependent parents. Large numbers of apprentices came as well from families of middling economic means, while some slave owners apprenticed young,

male slaves so that they could learn trades that would make a household, farm, or plantation self-sufficient.

On small and large freeholder farms in New England, the Mid-Atlantic, and the southern backcountry, the household economy was largely self-sufficient. Here, immediate family members and possibly one or two hired hands, indentured servants, or slaves constituted the labor force. The household was the primary unit of production and consumption, and within this context the labor of children was vital. The very youngest children were responsible for tasks like feeding chickens or spooling thread. Older children, usually by the age of 10, if not earlier, mimicked the work done by their same-sex parent. For girls, they began learning the arts of "housewifery" from their mothers and did work which comprised in large part food preservation, cooking, sewing, cleaning, and medical and child care. Boys worked with their fathers doing numerous tasks that included plowing, sowing, and harvesting the fields, tending livestock, clearing land, and chopping wood.

Child Labor and Early Industrialization

After the American Revolution, the northern United States became increasingly market-oriented, industrial, and dependent on wage labor at the same time that slavery came to an end in the region. As the "market revolution" took place in the North, growing numbers of households changed from productive to consumptive units. With few exceptions, the South continued to base its social and economic foundation on agricultural pursuits and was a region where the economy was inexorably linked to slave labor and staple-crop production. Through the Civil War, work done by children in the South, whether the children of white yeoman farmers in the upcountry regions or enslaved children working on southern farms or plantations, remained much the same as it had been during the colonial era. The same may be said of those living of farmsteads in newly settled western territories.

But new and different demands for child labor emerged in the northern states through the antebellum period. Ever larger numbers of households devoted their time and labor power to specialized production for the marketplace. With immigration and in-migrations into cities as well as towns along transportation and travel routes to and from the West, markets for both foodstuffs and consumer goods grew exponentially. Farming families began growing crops or produce not for a household's sole use but for sale. Women and children began using their labor not to make clothes and foodstuffs for household consumption but to take in piecework, like sewing shoe uppers or ready-made garments, for cash payment that could purchase a range of household goods. Child labor, therefore, became an integral aspect of industrial homework in the rural countryside.

The putting-out system in which the "surplus labor" on family farms participated was part and parcel to the declining system of production of whole goods and apprenticeships within skilled trades. Master craftsmen, who became de facto bosses of semiskilled and unskilled workers, found that they could increase production and make the highest profits by breaking the manufacture of goods into smaller and more unskilled tasks that were "put out" into the countryside and done by rural women and children. Or the production of goods was carried out in industrial workshops by boys and men who would have formerly filled the ranks of apprentices and journeymen. Women and children in cities also took in piecework to support themselves or to supplement declining wages earned by husbands and sons now working in semiskilled or unskilled labor.

Industrial production also began drawing significant numbers of children into factories, especially into New England's cotton textile mills. Through the 1830s, these textile manufacturers tapped into local pools of surplus agricultural labor and recruited a work force of young, mostly single women. These women lived in boardinghouses owned by the mills, and many intended to work only a short time to supplement the earnings of a family farm or to earn a dowry. By the 1840s, however, an increased pace of production, declining workplace conditions, and lower wages paid for textile work drove many of these young women out of the mills at the same time that the first large numbers of Irish immigrants, pushed to the United States by poverty and famine, began taking jobs there. As this transition took place, mill owners abandoned the boardinghouse system and embraced instead a family labor system wherein the company hired multiple family members and set wage scales according to what a family rather than an individual might earn.

Textile manufacturing was just one of a growing number of manufacturing enterprises in the industrializing North that employed children. The workday in the mills averaged up to 12 hours a day during a six-day workweek, in poorly ventilated and often unsanitary conditions that left children with little time to attend school and that had likely adverse effects on their health and well-being. In addition, the low wages paid to children, especially within the context of the family labor and wage systems, had the effect of lowering wages paid to workers throughout individual industries. It was for these reasons that debates began over whether child labor was a positive good or a social and economic problem.

Child Labor and Reform

With the end of the Civil War came a reorganization of labor in the United States. Most significantly, slavery was abolished, and the entire nation, for the first time in its history, operated on a free-labor system. The war begat increased industrialization and consolidations of capital in the Northeast and Midwest. Rapid expansion and settlement in the territories of the far West began. And in the South the foundation was set on which railroad building and industrial development would be built in the 1870s and 1880s and continue apace on a scale not before seen in the region. Immigration from abroad and in-migrations to cities from the countryside accelerated as well and supplied the labor needed to fuel this industrial growth. While these changes created opportunity and great wealth for some, it created discontent and hardship for others.

As economic expansion in the United States continued at a brisk pace through the late nineteenth and early twentieth centuries, children were a continued presence in the agricultural and nonagricultural work forces, laboring on farms, in industrial homework, in the street trades, and in mills, mines, and factories. By 1890, the U.S. Census Bureau reported that over 1.5 million children ages 10 to 14 were gainfully employed, 6.5% of the nation's total farm and nonfarm work force. The number of these children employed in industrial jobs increased more than threefold between 1870 and 1900, from just over 350,000 to nearly 1.1 million. It was when this crush of youngsters began working on the streets as peddlers, newspaper boys, and messengers, at home manufacturing piece goods, and in various capacities in mills, mines, food canneries, and factories for 10, 11, and 12 hours a day that child labor came to be widely recognized as an alarming fact of modern American life that needed to be changed. Although children, native and immigrant and black and white alike, continued to work, and worked hard, on farms—whether as members of families working a plot of owned or rented land or employed on commercial farms as itinerant pickers—groups calling for child labor reform perceived this work as fundamentally different from and even healthful in a way that industrial employment in factories and homes was not. Many turn-of-the-century child labor reformers saw agricultural work in this way, because it usually occurred under the supervision of parents and out of doors. It therefore remained largely absent from the wider child labor dialogue and the legislation passed in the first three decades of the twentieth century to regulate it.

Organized labor had been a vocal opponent of child labor since early in the nineteenth century. During the 1880s, 1890s, and through the turn of the century, national unions like the Knights of Labor and the American Federation of Labor placed banning child labor high on their lists of objectives. These unions stressed the negative impact that long hours of work in unhealthy and unsafe surroundings had on children. But they also explicitly linked their attack on child labor to a broader assault on the family wage system, and to bolster calls for a living wage that would enable wage-earning men to support their families without wives, sons, and daughters working as well. Nonetheless, the reality of the situation remained that employers in general were recalcitrant about raising wages to a prescribed minimum, let alone a living wage standard, and the immediate, wholesale removal of children from the labor force would undoubtedly leave vast numbers of working families economically worse off than they currently were.

The issue of child labor, especially the humanitarian abuses seen inherent in it, also drew the attention of middle-class reformers by the turn of the century. What would be the future of the nation, these reformers asked, in a republic dependent on a strong,

educated, and engaged citizenry for its stability? The predominately white constituency of the child labor reform associations that had organized at the local, state, and national levels by the first decade of the twentieth century often articulated their arguments against child labor in nativist and racist terms. Reformers in northern and urban areas, in particular, questioned the ability of the nation to assimilate the large numbers of immigrants flooding into the United States if foreign-born children or children of foreign-born parents worked from childhood rather than attending school. Child labor reformers in the South, for their part, predicted a demise of the system of white supremacy that undergirded southern society should white children continue to labor sunup to sundown in mills and mines while their black counterparts went to school or worked in more healthful conditions on farms.

These arguments resonated with both the public and politicians during the Progressive Era, when both organized labor and middle-class reformers looked to the state to bring about effective child labor reform. Massachusetts passed the first child labor law in the United States in 1836. Through the turn of the century, state legislatures passed laws setting minimum ages and maximum hours of work for children, as well as compulsory education statutes in the industrialized North and Midwest, often at the behest of concerted lobbies representing organized labor and social reformers. By 1900, organized labor and child labor reform organizations concentrated their efforts on securing the passage of regulatory child labor laws in the South, and in 1903, Alabama passed the first twentieth-century child labor law in the region. In spite of such progress made at the state level, gaps remained from state to state in child labor regulations, school attendance laws, and their enforcement. While some child labor reformers continued their efforts at the state level, others began to work for a federal child labor law. Initial efforts did not result in the passage of a national law but facilitated the establishment of the U.S. Children's Bureau in 1912. Congress passed the first federal child labor regulation, the Keating-Owen Act, in 1916, but the U.S. Supreme Court declared it unconstitutional two years later. This was an important factor leading to a push, albeit unsuccessful, for a constitutional amendment granting Congress the authority to regulate child labor.

By the early 1920s, however, state child labor and compulsory education laws began having a measurable impact on the numbers of children working in industries throughout the United States, and the implementation of new technologies in numerous industries made work previously done by children obsolete. Yet, it was the onset of the Great Depression and federal legislation passed as part of the New Deal that facilitated the most precipitous decline of child labor nationwide. During the catastrophic economic crisis, public perceptions radically changed about the role and powers of the federal government, and during the prolonged period of high unemployment, public sentiment turned solidly against giving jobs to children and adolescents rather than to adults. The child labor provisions outlawing the employment of anyone under 16 years old that were part of the codes of competition developed under the 1933 National Industrial Recovery Act (NIRA) in many cases only reflected changes that had already occurred. Although the NIRA was declared unconstitutional in 1935, the Fair Labor Standards Act (FLSA) in 1938 banned the employment of children under 16 years of age in all mining and manufacturing industries engaged in interstate commerce. It was not until 1949, however, that Congress amended the FLSA to include the first provisions relating to commercial agriculture.

Child Labor in the Age of Globalization

Child labor in the United States was largely eradicated during the second half of the twentieth century. Nevertheless, in the early twenty-first century, it remained a persistent problem, especially among migrant agricultural workers and in the garment industry, where large numbers of immigrants worked, many of whom were in the United States illegally. Child workers were also found in industries worldwide—not uncommonly under dangerous, illegal, or exploitative conditions—in agriculture, manufacturing and mining, domestic and service industries, and numerous illicit trades ranging from drug trafficking to prostitution. Children were frequently employed directly or indirectly through subcontracted orders for companies headquartered in the United States or Western Europe, nations with stringent domestic child labor regulations. In fact, in the global economy, national child labor laws were not applicable beyond a single country's borders, and child labor reformers in the new millennium faced similar challenges that reformers in the United States faced at the turn of the last century, when vast disparities existed in child labor laws from state to state. Indeed, globalization had only hastened the "race to the bottom" in numerous industries, as capital was invested and reinvested in those places where operating costs were the lowest, which often came at the expense of the poorest in the global labor force. Globally, but most visibly in developing nations where opportunities for gainful employment were few, access to schools was limited, industrial regulations were nonexistent or routinely violated, and labor was cheap, unorganized, and often repressed, child labor continued to be a pressing social and economic issue in the twenty-first century.

BETH ENGLISH

References and Further Reading

Clement, Priscilla Ferguson. *Growing Pains: Children in the Industrial Age, 1850–1890*. London: Prentice Hall International, 1997.

Davidson, Elizabeth. *Child Labor Legislation in the Southern Textile States*. Chapel Hill: University of North Carolina Press, 1939.

Fauss, Paula, and Mary Ann Mason, eds. *Childhood in America*. New York: New York University Press, 2000.

Hindman, Hugh. *Child Labor: An American History*. Armonk, NY: M. E. Sharpe, 2002.

Human Rights Watch. "Children's Rights, Child Labor." www.hrw.org/children/labor.htm.

Illilck, Joseph. *American Childhoods*. Philadelphia: University of Pennsylvania Press, 2002.

Levine, Marvin. *Children for Hire: The Perils of Child Labor in the United States*. Westport, CT: Praeger, 2003.

Rorabaugh, W. J. *The Craft Apprentice: From Franklin to the Machine Age in America*. New York: Oxford University Press, 1986.

Sallee, Shelley. *The Whiteness of Child Labor Reform in the New South*. Athens: University of Georgia Press, 2004.

Trattner, Walter. *Crusade for the Children: The History of the National Child Labor Committee and Child Labor Reform in America*. Chicago: Quadrangle Books, 1970.

Zelizer, Viviana. *Pricing the Priceless Child: The Changing Social Value of Children*. New York: Basic Books, 1985.

See also **American Federation of Labor; American Standard of Living; Antebellum Era; Apprenticeship; Artisans; Children's Bureau; Civil War and Reconstruction; Colonial Era; Fair Labor Standards Act; Family Wage; Garment Industry; Globalization; Great Depression: 1930s; Indentured Servitude; Keating-Owen Child Labor Act (1916); Knights of Labor; Living Wage; Midwest; Migrant Farmworkers; National Child Labor Committee; National Industrial Recovery Act; New South; Prostitution; Revolution and Early National Period; Slavery; Textiles; World War II**

CHILDREN'S BUREAU

Established in 1912 within the Department of Commerce and Labor, the Children's Bureau was the first federal agency headed and staffed by women. Although it started off with a tiny budget and a mandate limited to research, the bureau played a major role in the development of U.S. children's policies. During the height of its influence, it published hundreds of studies on laws and social conditions affecting children, distributed child-rearing advice to millions of mothers, and spearheaded a mass women's movement that pressed the federal government to take greater responsibility for child welfare. Bureau officials shaped federal prohibitions on child labor and drafted the 1935 Social Security Act provisions for maternal and child health services and Aid to Dependent Children (welfare). The bureau is housed in the Department of Health and Human Services, where it provides grants to the states for foster care, adoption, and the prevention of child abuse.

The first two Children's Bureau chiefs, Julia Lathrop and Grace Abbott, were longtime residents of Jane Addams's Hull-House, and they shaped the bureau—and U.S. child welfare policy—according to their maternalist political beliefs. They saw childhood as a distinct stage of life requiring nurture and protection, believed that women had a special ability—and responsibility—for child welfare, and urged policy makers to make children their top political priority. Drawing on their extensive women's reform network, Lathrop and Abbott fashioned the Children's Bureau into a sort of national social settlement, the center of women's welfare activism. But their child welfare vision was distinctly middle-class: they believed all children needed education, a middle-class standard of living, and a "proper" home with a stay-at-home mother and a father who earned a decent wage.

The campaign against infant mortality was the bureau's first and most successful initiative. In 1915, 10% of all infants and almost 20% of infants of color died before their first birthday. To reduce infant and maternal deaths, the bureau improved the collection of vital statistics by expanding the birth registration area, distributed educational pamphlets, such as the bestselling *Infant Care* and *Prenatal Care*, and investigated the causes of infant and maternal mortality. Its infant mortality studies, based on interviews with mothers, were particularly innovative, for they mobilized community support while hammering home a key finding: the sharp correlation between poverty and infant death. By 1918, an estimated 11 million women had joined the bureau's baby-saving campaign.

The passage and implementation of the Sheppard-Towner Act between 1921 and 1929 marked the high point of the Children's Bureau's popular influence. The first federal social welfare measure in the United States and the first "women's" bill enacted after women won the vote, Sheppard-Towner provided matching grants to the states for prenatal and child health clinics, midwife training programs, visiting nurses, and other educational programs to reduce infant and maternal mortality. Despite providing no medical or nursing care, Sheppard-Towner was very popular with working-class mothers and contributed

to a modest reduction in infant mortality. Yet right-wing groups and the American Medical Association waged a bitter campaign against the bill, which they called a Bolshevik threat to the home, and eventually secured its defeat. The shutdown of Sheppard-Towner programs in 1929 brought the end of the maternalist movement. Although public health services for mothers and children were restored in the 1935 Social Security Act and expanded in the Emergency Maternity and Infant Care (EMIC) program of World War II, these strictly medical programs were targeted to specified populations and did not inspire broad popular support.

Child labor reformers had been the most vocal early advocates of a federal children's agency, and bureau officials made the abolition of child labor a top priority. The bureau administered the 1916 Keating-Owen Act, the nation's first child labor law, until it was overturned by the Supreme Court in 1918. Yet, unlike the baby-saving campaign, which received enthusiastic support from a broad cross-section of mothers, working-class parents who depended on their children's earnings did not necessarily share the bureau's middle-class ideas about the evils of child labor. Mothers could accept or refuse Sheppard-Towner health services, but restrictions on child labor were compulsory, and the bureau offered few alternatives to families' lost income. In any event, the U.S. Supreme Court struck down Keating-Owen, and a second child labor law passed in 1919. Bureau supporters responded with a vigorous campaign for a child labor amendment to the constitution, but it was not until 1938 that the Fair Labor Standards Act wrote prohibitions on child labor into federal law.

Historians have debated the Children's Bureau's impact on U.S. welfare policy. Some praise the agency for its expansive vision of a welfare state that served children from every region, race, and class. Bureau officials were unusually responsive to its constituents, they argue, and the agency functioned as a "women's branch" of the federal government for a short time. In contrast, other scholars emphasize the bureau's middle-class bias and moralistic views of family life. Bureau efforts to promote "scientific" child rearing and a bland diet undermined ethnic cultures and healing practices, including midwifery, while the strategy of "putting children first" reinforced conventional gender norms. Bureau officials promoted policies, such as Aid to Dependent Children, that punished women who were sexually active outside marriage and stigmatized single mothers. Well into the 1930s, the bureau opposed maternal employment and birth control.

For good or ill, the Children's Bureau helped to produce a major transformation in the lives of working-class mothers and children. By 1929, one half of U.S. babies were born to mothers touched by the agency's modern child-rearing advice. By the end of World War II, infants of every race, class, and region were born in hospitals, and infant and maternal mortality rates had declined. Nearly one hundred years after the bureau was founded, child labor remains largely illegal, childhood is recognized as a distinct life stage, and federal responsibility for child welfare is an established American value.

MOLLY LADD-TAYLOR

References and Further Reading

Gordon, Linda. *Pitied but Not Entitled: Single Mothers and the History of Welfare*. New York: Free Press, 1994.

Ladd-Taylor, Molly. *Mother-Work: Women, Child Welfare and the State, 1890–1930*. Urbana: University of Illinois, Press, 1994.

———. *Raising a Baby the Government Way: Mothers' Letters to the Children's Bureau, 1915–1932*. New Brunswick, NJ: Rutgers University Press, 1986.

Lindenmeyer, Kriste. *"A Right to Childhood": The U.S. Children's Bureau and Child Welfare, 1912–46*. Urbana: University of Illinois Press, 1997.

Muncy, Robyn. *Creating a Female Dominion in American Reform, 1890–1935*. New York: Oxford University Press, 1991.

Skocpol, Theda. *Protecting Mothers and Soldiers: The Political Origins of Social Policy in the United States*. Cambridge: Belknap Press, 1992.

See also **Addams, Jane; Child Labor; Hull-House Settlement (1889–1963); Keating-Owen Child Labor Act (1916)**

CHINESE EXCLUSION ACTS

The Chinese Exclusion Act, adopted in 1882, barred practically all Chinese immigrants from entering the United States for 10 years. It was the first federal law ever passed banning a group of immigrants based solely on race or nationality. The law also prevented Chinese immigrants from becoming American citizens. The Chinese Exclusion Act was renewed in 1892 and 1902, and made permanent in 1904. It was repealed in 1943.

Chinese immigrants began coming to America in large numbers in 1849, drawn by the gold rush to California. Many worked as miners, cooks, launderers, and agricultural and manufacturing laborers. Racial hostilities erupted in the mining camps when whites tried to drive all "foreigners"—Mexican, South American, and Chinese—from the region. Some Chinese immigrants had signed contracts in their native land to work for a set period of time at low wages, and miners and others singled them out for attack. Exploiting this sentiment, California politicians passed numerous discriminatory laws against the Chinese in the 1850s that restricted their settlement and forced them to pay special taxes. Despite these measures and the bigotry and violence, Chinese immigrants kept coming to California and the western United States. In the 1860s, the Central Pacific Railroad Company brought thousands of workers from China to build the western portion of the transcontinental railroad. By 1870, 63,254 Chinese were living in the United States: 49,310 (78.0%) of them in California and 62,864 (99.4%) in the West. Because few Chinese had settled east of the Rocky Mountains, Chinese immigration remained a regional rather than a national issue.

This changed in 1870 when a manufacturer in North Adams, Massachusetts, transported 75 Chinese immigrants from California to break a shoemakers' strike. Workers throughout the East and Midwest protested vigorously, denouncing this "importation" of Chinese laborers. Although lacing their comments with racism—a racism voiced in Congress and newspapers everywhere—workers did not oppose Chinese immigration, distinguishing carefully between "imported laborers" and "free immigrants."

The North Adams incident and ensuing uproar drew national attention to the Chinese issue, but California remained the hotbed of anti-Chinese activity. Chinese composed 8.5% of the state's population in 1870 and one fourth of San Francisco, the state's largest city. Because most Chinese immigrants were single men, they composed one third of the city's work force. When the Panic of 1873 ushered in a major nationwide depression and sent unemployment soaring, Chinese immigrants became a scapegoat throughout California. Politicians of both parties urged Chinese exclusion, and a candidate could not be elected governor or senator without advocating immigration restriction. With the aim of winning California in the presidential election of 1876, both the Republican and Democratic parties wrote anti-Chinese planks into their national platforms.

The national railroad strike of July 1877 sparked anti-Chinese riots in San Francisco. These riots gave birth to a new political organization, the Workingmen's Party of California (WPC), which sought to rein in corporate power and end Chinese immigration. WPC president Denis Kearney emerged as the leading anti-Chinese crusader, and the party quickly threatened Republican and Democratic dominance in the state.

In 1878, President Rutherford B. Hayes urged restriction of Chinese immigration and suggested renegotiating the Burlingame Treaty, an 1868 pact between the United States and China that permitted free immigration. Congress then passed a resolution endorsing this policy. In January 1879, the House of

Representatives passed the Fifteen Passenger Bill, a measure aimed at limiting to 15 the number of Chinese passengers on each incoming ship to the United States. When the bill reached the Senate in February, James G. Blaine became its most prominent sponsor. Senator Blaine was the leading contender for the Republican nomination for president in 1880. In championing the bill, Blaine argued that Chinese exclusion would defuse class and racial tensions and protect American workers. The Senate passed the bill, but President Hayes vetoed it on the grounds that it violated the Burlingame Treaty. He instructed the secretary of state to open formal negotiations with China to modify the treaty.

In 1880, both the Republican and Democratic platforms strongly endorsed Chinese immigration restriction. In accepting his party's nomination for president, Republican James Garfield, who prevailed over Blaine at the deadlocked convention, highlighted his opposition to Chinese immigration. Garfield won the election, and two weeks later, American and Chinese diplomats signed a new treaty giving the United States the power to restrict Chinese immigration, so long as "[t]he limitation or suspension shall be reasonable." The Senate ratified the treaty in May 1881 by a vote of 48 to 4, and in October, Chester Arthur, who had just become president following Garfield's assassination, proclaimed the treaty in effect.

As Congress began drafting an anti-Chinese measure, the Federation of Organized Trades and Labor Unions (FOTLU) held its first meeting in November 1881. The delegates, after vigorous debate, endorsed a resolution favoring Chinese exclusion. Samuel Gompers, one of the meeting's organizers, wrote that the FOTLU, which in 1886 would rename itself the American Federation of Labor, "was the first national organization which demanded exclusion of coolies from the United States." Ever since 1870, politically active union leaders and workers in the East had sought a ban on imported contract labor rather than on Chinese immigration. When the Fifteen Passenger Bill sailed through Congress in 1879, the labor movement expended scant effort on its behalf. In late 1881, however, with Congress poised to enact Chinese exclusion and a ban on imported labor nowhere in sight, some labor leaders in the East began moving toward an anti-immigration stance. The FOTLU's move signaled this new direction.

In March 1882, Congress passed a measure that would have banned Chinese immigration for 20 years. President Arthur vetoed this bill, arguing that the long suspension was not "reasonable," and thus a violation of the new treaty. Congress revised the bill, reducing the length of exclusion from 20 years to 10. Officially titled "An act to execute certain treaty stipulations relating to Chinese," the new bill passed overwhelmingly with bipartisan support in the House of Representatives, 201 to 37 (with 53 not voting), and in the Senate, 32 to 15 (with 29 not voting). Arthur signed the bill on May 6, 1882. The Chinese Exclusion Act banned all Chinese laborers from entering the United States, excepting only diplomats and their servants. The law set a precedent for all future anti-immigration laws and remained in effect for 61 years.

ANDREW GYORY

References and Further Reading

Chan, Sucheng, ed. *Entry Denied: Exclusion and the Chinese Community in America, 1882–1943*. Philadelphia: Temple University Press, 1991.

Coolidge, Mary Roberts. *Chinese Immigration*. New York: Holt, 1909.

Gyory, Andrew. *Closing the Gate: Race, Politics, and the Chinese Exclusion Act*. Chapel Hill: University of North Carolina Press, 1998.

Lee, Erika. *At America's Gates: Chinese Immigration during the Exclusion Era, 1882–1943*. Chapel Hill: University of North Carolina Press, 2003.

McClain, Charles J. *In Search of Equality: The Chinese Struggle against Discrimination in Nineteenth-Century America*. Berkeley: University of California Press, 1994.

Miller, Stuart Creighton. *The Unwelcome Immigrant: The American Image of the Chinese, 1785–1882*. Berkeley: University of California Press, 1969.

Peffer, George A. *If They Don't Bring Their Women Here: Chinese Female Immigration before Exclusion*. Urbana: University of Illinois Press, 1999.

Salyer, Lucy. *"Laws Harsh as Tigers": Chinese Immigrants and the Shaping of Modern Immigration Law*. Chapel Hill: University of North Carolina Press, 1995.

Sandmeyer, Elmer Clarence. *The Anti-Chinese Movement in California*. Urbana: University of Illinois Press, 1939.

Saxton, Alexander. *The Indispensable Enemy: Labor and the Anti-Chinese Movement in California*. Berkeley: University of California Press, 1971.

See also **Kearney, Denis**

CHINESE LABORERS' STRIKE ON THE TRANSCONTINENTAL RAILROAD (1867)

When it comes to labor unrest, one of the most unusual confrontations in American history was the Chinese strike against the Central Pacific Railway in June 1867. It was probably the first nonviolent strike of its size in American history.

The saga of the Central Pacific began with the creation of a loan by the U.S. Congress for the construction of a Transcontinental Railway. The concept was to link St. Louis, the most western depot in the East, with Sacramento, California, the closest reasonable depot to San Francisco. In those days, passage from Sacramento to San Francisco was by water. Four men in California, dubbed the "Big Four,"—Charles Crocker, Leland Stanford, Collis P. Huntington, and Mark Hopkins—created the Central Pacific Railway. The Central Pacific would require a substantial amount of manpower, which, in those days, California had in scant supply.

Traditionally viewed as amiable and passive, the Chinese were considered strike-proof. With this incentive, Charles Crocker imported 50 Chinese laborers from China in 1865. The Chinese proved to be so dependable and hardworking that more were imported. Called "Crocker's pets," they eventually numbered more than seven thousand. Not only were the Chinese hard workers, they were also fearless. At Cape Horn in the Sierra Nevada, for instance, the railway was stopped by an impassable rock wall that rose a sheer 4,000 feet. A tunnel could not be built through the wall, so a roadway had to be constructed up the sheer face of the precipice. To hew the roadway out of solid rock, the Chinese constructed two-man baskets of wooden strips. These were lowered into position from the top of the cliff, and dynamite charges were strategically placed. Then the men in the baskets were hauled out of danger as fast as the ropes could carry them. At least 37 men did not make it back up safely.

Chinese laborers became so efficient that they became a prime commodity on the labor market. In 1867, when Crocker tried to get more Chinese workers, he found them in short supply. To attract more workers, he was forced to raise wages, to $35 a month up from $31. Rather than being pleased with the wage increase, the Chinese already working on the railroad went on strike. On June 25, 1867, a large number of Chinese left their grading job and went back to their camp. There they demanded $40 a month, with the workday reduced to eight hours. (The workday was actually eight hours, but the foremen were lax in enforcing that rule.) They also wanted shorter shifts in the tunnels where the labor was cramped and dangerous, and, according to the *Sacramento Union* (July 12, 1867), they wanted to eliminate "the right of the overseers of the company to either whip them or restrain them from leaving the road when they desire to seek other employment."

When Central Pacific officials refused to negotiate, the Chinese raised their wage demands to $45 a month. The strike spread until workers all along the line quit their jobs. Construction came to a standstill.

For a week, the railway work was stalled. Crocker refused to raise wages and tried to find other workers to replace the Chinese. His plan was to use recently freed slaves because "a Negro labor force would tend to keep the Chinese quiet as the Chinese had kept the Irishmen quiet." But the labor market was too tight; Crocker could find no reliable and available alternative to the Chinese.

Crocker decided it was time to get tough. He cut off the food supply to the strikers. A week later, he visited the Chinese encampment and told the workers in no uncertain terms that he made the rules, and they did not. If they agreed to pay a fine and went back to work, all would be forgiven. If they did not, they would not be paid for any of the work done in June.

Four days later, the Chinese were back at work with no increase in wages or decrease in working hours. The few holdouts were harassed by a posse of Central Pacific employees. "If there had been that number of whites in a strike," Crocker remarked later, "there would have been murder, drunkenness and disorder." But with the Chinese, "it was just like Sunday. The men stayed in their camps. They would come out and walk around, but not a word was said; nothing was done. No violence was perpetrated along the whole line."

The legacy of the Chinese on the American West has largely been underemphasized. Without them, there would not have been a Transcontinental Railroad. They worked under the most dangerous of conditions, sometimes spending months underground. The Central Pacific had to build 15 tunnels through solid granite, a task most engineers thought was impossible. One of the most impressive was the Summit Tunnel, which was 1,659 feet in length. It was started from both ends and then, to speed up the work, a shaft was dropped from the top of the rock wall. Men were lowered into the shaft and worked from the inside out as other teams of men were working from the outside in. Even with 400-men shifts working around the clock, the tunnel progressed at less than a foot a day. And when winter came, the men burrowed tunnels in the snow to the work site. Windows and chimneys were cut into the snow tunnels, and for many months that was the only daylight the workers would see.

The labor was not without human cost. By the time the railway was completed, about 1,200 Chinese laborers had died. The bones of the dead were sent back to China, totaling approximately 10 tons.

STEVEN C. LEVI

References and Further Reading

Ambrose, Stephen E. *Nothing like It in the World: The Men Who Built the Transcontinental Railroad, 1863–1869.* New York: Simon & Schuster, 2000.

Dolan, Edward F. *The Transcontinental Railroad.* New York: Benchmark Books, 2003.

Saxton, Alexander. *The Indispensable Enemy: Labor and the Anti-Chinese Movement in California.* Berkeley: University of California Press, 1975.

Williams, John Hoyt. *A Great and Shining Road: The Epic Story of the Transcontinental Railroad*. Lincoln: University of Nebraska Press, 1996.

CIGAR MAKERS INTERNATIONAL UNION

The Cigar Makers International Union (CMIU), one of the founding unions of the American Federation of Labor, was one of the most important organizations of skilled workers in the late nineteenth-century United States. Often described as the prototype of the politically cautious craft union, it embodied many of the contradictions and problems of the American labor movement in its institutionally formative phase. Its members were ethnically diverse and for the most part highly skilled. The CMIU organized workers, from small town and urban environments; its members were often socialists, but political conservatives could also be found in the union.

Fraternal organizations, separated from each other by ethnicity and language, took the place of unions in the early years of the trade before the Civil War. These groups had almost no political profile. This changed with the founding of the Cigar Makers National Union in 1864 in New York City. The new organization comprised locals from New York, Pennsylvania, New Jersey, New England, and Ohio. This group was joined by locals from Chicago and Canada, changing the name to Cigar Makers International Union in 1867. By the late 1860s, the union had 5,900 members. In New York, Local 15 was the "English" (that is, English-speaking) local, while Local 10 organized a group of German-speaking cigar makers.

The decades from the 1870s to the early twentieth century were a period of transformation for the cigar industry. The introduction of the cigar mold, with its accompanying subdivision of labor and the decline of skilled cigar makers' status, brought new semiskilled workers from Eastern and East Central Europe into the trade in great numbers. In some areas, female, semiskilled workers soon began to dominate a growing industry. On the urban West Coast, Chinese immigrants entered the cigar trade as well. The Cigar Makers International Union struggled with these changes. It accepted only skilled craftsmen, and therefore excluded semiskilled workers such as stemmers as well as female workers in general. The union fought vigorously against Chinese cigar makers and became one of the core supporters of the anti-Chinese movement in the West.

But the industrial and economic crisis of the 1870s also propelled the union toward a more activist political stance. As part of a group of like-minded socialist immigrants, Samuel Gompers and his colleague Adolph Strasser started a local organization of politically active cigar makers in New York City in 1874 that they called the United Cigar Makers of North America. Its mostly German-speaking members were also active in the socialist labor movement of the city, and in 1875, they joined the CMIU as a third New York City local (Local 144). This self-consciously "American" union was open to workers of all backgrounds, at least in its early years. It soon gained members and influence. Samuel Gompers was its first president. In 1877, Adolph Strasser became the president of the CMIU and the editor of its monthly newspaper, the *Cigar Makers Official Journal*.

A disastrous 1877 strike of tenement workers in New York City, the union's stronghold, propelled the leaders of the CMIU into the national limelight as they tried to organize and direct the formerly non-union tenement workers. But when the strike was lost after a few months, it almost sank Local 144 and propelled its leaders into a much more conservative position in the years to come. With the economic depression of the mid-1870s hitting the cigar industry everywhere, the CMIU suffered a great decline nationwide in 1877 and 1878. By late 1877, the International Union numbered only 1,016 members nationwide. Only 17 locals remained in 1878.

By the early 1880s, the CMIU solidified its position as a union of skilled workers with a system of high dues (at first 10 cents, and by the 1880s 25 cents a week) and good benefits for its members in case of illness, unemployment, or death. A system of financial equalization allowed union members who traveled in search of work to join any local without initiation fees and to claim benefits nationwide, should the need arise. A restrictive system of strike approvals allowed union members to strike selectively (and claim benefits) but prevented the kind of mass walkouts that had crippled the union in 1877. While women and semiskilled workers were not explicitly excluded at first, these lower-paid workers were unable to afford the dues. Tenement workers were not admitted. With the worst of the economic hard times behind it, the CMIU once again began to grow in the early 1880s.

But the focus on benefits and financial stability and away from larger political questions also sowed discord. In 1882, a group of German socialists fielded an alternative slate of candidates for office in Local 144 and won. CMIU President Strasser declared the election invalid, and as a result, the largest and most influential local of the CMIU split. Soon the New York rebels were joined by dissident cigar makers elsewhere. Together they formed the Cigar Makers Progressive Union, a nationwide organization of socialist cigar makers.

1882–1886 were years of dual unionism for the cigar makers. This heightened the political profile of the trade nationwide. The Progressives proceeded to promote a program of politicized union activism and a more inclusive (and lower dues) membership policy. The CMIU stuck to its high dues program with extensive benefits, but also tried to organize Bohemian and German-speaking members in new locals. The CMIU was also one of the most important unions behind the founding of the Federation of Trades and Labor Unions of the United States (FOTLU) in 1882. CMIU Local 144 member Samuel Gompers became the president of this organization.

The labor upheavals of the mid-1880s strengthened the momentum for reunification of the union, and by the end of 1886, the Progressive Union and the CMIU merged. The Progressives were chartered as separate locals within the CMIU. Politically, the former Progressive union locals remained visible for decades as supporters of socialist ideas, platforms, and candidates in national debates and local elections and campaigns. In conventions in 1891 and 1893, members of the former Progressives demanded a political action clause in the union's platform, and in 1891, socialist members of the CMIU contributed to the majority that voted to elect the union president directly by membership vote rather than by a convention. As a result, President Strasser resigned. George Perkins became president of the CMIU, an office which he held until 1927. The union's headquarters, which had been in Buffalo since 1886, were moved to Chicago. The union had no conventions between 1896 and 1912.

By 1890, the CMIU counted 24,000 members nationwide in 276 locals in North America. The Clear Havana industry of Tampa, Florida, representing the high end of the industry, was the most significant segment of the cigar industry that remained largely outside the union's orbit. As the cigar industry expanded, the union grew with it in most parts of the country. Small and medium-sized shops were the core of the union membership, which numbered almost 34,000 in 414 locals by 1900. In 1909, the union had reached its zenith with about 44,000 members, between 40% to 48% of the nation's cigar makers. The CMIU's stronghold was in New England, though the largest locals continued to be in New York and Chicago.

The union's structure, administration, and benefit system reflected a community of men engaged in skilled craft manufacture, highly protective of their status. The union's organizing activity centered on promoting the union label among consumers and retailers, and its organizational strength rested on the fact that manufacturers felt compelled to produce their more expensive grades of cigars with a union label.

The CMIU's weak point lay in its inability to incorporate new forms of work and new classes of workers. Cigarettes were becoming the best-selling tobacco product by the early twentieth century. The cigar industry employed an increasing number of women so that by 1910, Edith Abbott began to call it a "woman's industry." Few of the female cigar makers were members of the CMIU. As mechanization crept into the cigar industry at the same time, skilled male workers became even more expendable. Despite a 1915 change in the union's constitution that allowed (women) team workers to become members, membership recovered only temporarily.

A series of strikes shook the industry and the union during and after World War I, with both women and men participating in the struggle for higher wages nationwide. But this two-year period of labor militancy (which the leadership tried to deflect, to no effect) did not change the position of the union's members in a changing and declining industry. By the early 1930s, the union's membership had declined to 19,000, fewer than half from a dozen years earlier. The average age of its members had already reached 64 by the late 1920s. When the Depression stuck, the cigar trade and its union were in a vulnerable position.

The CMIU never recovered from its decline in the 1920s, losing out to the American Tobacco Workers Union in the organization of tobacco and cigarette workers. About 2,000 members were all that remained of the CMIU in 1974, when this formerly mighty organization voted to merge with the Retail, Wholesale, and Department Store Union.

DOROTHEE SCHNEIDER

References and Further Reading

Cooper, Patricia. *Once a Cigar Maker: Men, Women, and Work Culture in American Cigar Factories, 1900–1919.* Urbana: University of Illinois Press, 1987.

Schneider, Dorothee. Trade Unions and Community: The German Working Class in New York City, 1870–1900. Urbana: University of Illinois Press, 1994.

CIVIL RIGHTS

Civil rights are rights, such as liberty, equality, and access to the political system, that come with citizenship. The fight to establish civil rights for all Americans regardless of race, creed, color, or gender has been the principal and most singular American struggle for almost four hundred years. This battle over what one commentator once labeled the "American dilemma"—a nation born in liberty but which denies it to many citizens—has touched every facet of American life and history. And it has involved Americans of every social station: average unionists and elite politicians, women and men, African-Americans and immigrants, and children and adults. A complete accounting is impossible here. Rather, this entry focuses on one aspect of civil rights history: the long and ongoing travail of workers to achieve fairness and equality.

Since the British first colonized the North American coastline, there have been differences between those engaged in labor and those for whom they worked over the right to freely enter into a contract, the right to freely leave that contract, and the right to negotiate the conditions of work. The British and other European colonists who eventually established the United States built their labor systems to some significant extent upon the backs of workers who were not free and had no civil rights. Enslaved American Indians, indentured colonists, and enslaved Africans and African-Americans labored in the British North American colonies in oppressive conditions where the rights and liberties enjoyed by first-class citizens of the empire were not bestowed upon them. Moreover, attempts to redress their grievances or to improve their lot were often met with violent repression.

In the American setting, this relationship between worker and employer became increasingly untenable. By the end of the eighteenth century, a group of British colonists rebelled against their imperial leaders, metaphorically arguing that these colonial rulers were attempting to enslave all English colonists. Although the British had no intention of putting all white Americans to work on plantations, images of slavery and antislavery were important to political rhetoric of the 1770s. The new nation that the American Revolution brought forth was predicated upon the idea that all citizens were entitled to the rights of life, liberty, and happiness. In practice, there were limits to the Declaration of Independence and later the Constitution. Women and minorities, particularly African-Americans, were denied their civil rights. Establishing first-class citizenship rights to property, profit, and politics has been the work of civil rights and labor activists for four centuries.

Although in the United States the phrase "civil rights" became popularized in the later nineteenth century and not the eighteenth century, there were nonetheless several important historical developments in the colonial era that had a great impact on later movements to create equality and equity in the United States. Among these developments was the creation of a segmented and segregated labor force in terms of race, gender, and ethnicity. During the colonial period, a central problem of the British North American colonies was the desperate labor shortage in the New World. As attempts to subjugate local Native Americans failed to fill English labor needs, colonial leaders turned to European, mostly British, indentured servants to work the fields and perform various tasks essential to sustaining the New World experiments. These workers did not have the same rights and liberties as planters and artisans. Some historians have argued further that the latter's rights were in fact based upon the former's subjugation.

From Virginia to Massachusetts, colonial promoters recruited young adults to work in the New World in less-than-free conditions. The deal seemed quite reasonable. Prospective recruits signed an indenture (that is, a contract), which bound them to work for a term of four to seven years on a plantation or with an artisan in exchange for passage to the British colonies. At the end of the term, each servant would be set free with "freedom's dues": a new set of clothes, a few tools, and 50 acres of land. Thousands jumped at the chance to build a new life in the colonies. From the early 1600s through the 1760s, eight out of every 10 migrants to the British North American colonies came as indentured servants. Most were single men between 15 and 24 years of age. They tended to work on tobacco plantations, laboring in the fields planting sprouts, transplanting seedlings, and grooming the plants. They also worked in barns curing tobacco and making it ready for transport.

At best, indentured servitude was a kind of apprenticeship. At worst, the system mirrored slavery in that servants worked at the master's irrational will and whim. Unfortunately, most servants experienced harsh, painful working lives in the colonies. Before 1650, two out of every three servants died before the end of their term of indenture as a direct result of disease, poor diet, and maltreatment. Physical abuse was not uncommon and rarely punished. Running away from one's indenture was not unheard of either. Punishments for that could be severe and included extensions of years of service. Moreover, if one was a black or a white female servant, other sets of rules applied. White male indentured servants were treated better than any of their counterparts. And yet, this was not saying much. Consequently, servant revolts in the colonial period were rare but not exceptional. The largest and most famous was Bacon's Rebellion in 1676. Instead of improving the working lives of British colonists following Bacon's revolt, Virginia planters and colonial leaders opted to invest in a more repressive labor system: slavery.

African slavery in the New World was already several hundred years old before the British fully adopted it. Moreover, even though it is clear that African slaves lived in the North American colonies in the early 1600s, the institution was not inescapable. Perhaps the best example remains the story of Anthony Johnson, an African slave who was sold to a white Jamestown planter in 1621. "Antonio the Negro" worked for his master for a little over a decade, when he was able to purchase his freedom. Declaring his freedom by choosing a new name, Anthony Johnson, he eventually became an influential planter in his own right. Johnson died in 1670 at the moment when the status of blacks in the colonies was changing. Because of revolts of white servants and freedmen as well as the continued severe labor shortage, more and more white planters began to import African slaves. From 1619 to 1810, over half a million Africans were forcibly brought to work in the British North American colonies and later the United States. For our purposes, what is significant about the slave experience was that (1) Africans and African-Americans were forced to work without contracts and without any rights to profit or property. In other words, they had no civil rights. (2) The status of slavery became a badge that all black Americans had to bear even after the Civil War. Their skin color became the mark of servitude and of a life of permanent discrimination against them and their progeny.

African-Americans were not the only group to be denied civil rights in the colonial period and after. Regardless of race and ethnicity, women did not share the same rights as white male workers. In the nineteenth century, some white women came to see their situation as akin to racial slavery. In fact, there were similarities. By accident of birth, society denied women political, economic, and social rights. They existed in a kind of permanent dependent status, legally covered first by their fathers, then by their husbands, and finally by their male children. As a general rule, they did not vote or hold office. They did run intricate and essential aspects of local economies, but even when those resulted in monetary profits, women did not always have full claim to them. Moreover, women workers often competed with men, and rarely did they win those contests. Take, for example, the life of Martha Ballard. Born in 1735, in Oxford, Massachusetts, Ballard became a midwife as well as an exceptional housewife. As a medical practitioner, she often battled local doctors over her patients and her treatments. Although she won many of the skirmishes, other midwives were not so successful. Eventually, midwives lost their battle with doctors, who frowned upon and delegitimized their craft. Similarly, in the early nineteenth century, men wrestled the dairy industry away from women, who had built it up, especially in New England, as part of their informal economy.

By the middle of the nineteenth century, as the antislavery movement gained momentum, the women's rights movement began to flourish. At the core of this women's movement was the demand for rights to control their working lives. In July 1848,

two hundred women activists and abolitionists (including 40 men, such as the pre-eminent civil rights leader Frederick Douglass) met in Seneca Falls, New York, to debate women's rights. The convention's public statement, titled the "Declaration of Sentiments," declared boldly that "we hold these truths to be self-evident; that all men and women are created equal; that they are endowed by their Creator with certain inalienable rights; that among these are life, liberty, and the pursuit of happiness." Mirroring its predecessor from the Revolutionary era, the Declaration of Sentiments then listed grievances: disenfranchisement, lack of all property rights including the right to wages, denial of education, and marriage, which made women "in the eye of the law, civilly dead." Thus, the women's rights movement was as much about women workers' civil rights as it was about political rights such as suffrage.

In the years before the Civil War, both the women's rights and abolitionist movements seemed to be moving toward a similar goal, the establishment of civil rights to Americans without respect to race or gender. In the antebellum period, there were few means to improve the working lives of women and minorities. One path was the law, but as abolitionists and women's rights advocates discovered, legal solutions to their problems were hard to find. There were some successes. In the antebellum period, several states, including New York, passed laws establishing property rights for married women. Similarly, by the early twentieth century, several states—all of them in the West—had granted women suffrage rights. But the gains were halting and not enough to improve the lives of women generally.

For African-Americans, the law offered little hope. Although northern states passed gradual emancipation laws after the American Revolution, the lives of free blacks remained precarious. On the one hand, they faced discrimination on the job, in politics, and in society. On the other hand, because of the various fugitive slave laws, many found themselves torn from their families and forced into slavery. In 1857, the U.S. Supreme Court dealt a serious blow to the efforts to widen the legal path toward freedom. Dred Scott had been a slave of an army surgeon, John Emerson. Emerson's tour of duty took him and Scott into the Wisconsin Territory, above the 36°30′ line demarking slave below and free above. After Emerson's death, Scott sued for his freedom on the grounds that he had lived in free territory. Speaking for the Court, Chief Justice Roger B. Taney ruled that Scott was not free because African-Americans were not citizens. The Dred Scott case propelled the abolitionist cause as well as fueled the political discontent that eventually would result in a Civil War.

The War of the Rebellion transformed America in a fundamental way. No longer were African-Americans excluded from first-class citizenship, at least constitutionally. During the Reconstruction that followed the war, the U.S. Congress passed three constitutional amendments that theoretically placed African-Americans on equal footing with other citizens. The Thirteenth Amendment (1865) abolished slavery and indentured servitude. Among other things, the Fourteenth Amendment (1868) established the principle that states cannot pass laws that deny citizens "life, liberty, or property" without due process. Finally, the Fifteenth Amendment (1870) provided all African-American men the right to vote. Additionally, during Reconstruction, the federal government created an agency to help ex-slaves move from slavery to freedom. The Freedmen's Bureau engaged in a variety of activities. It helped resettle displaced persons who had been uprooted as a result of the war. It gave out rations to those who could not feed themselves. From 1865 to 1869, the Bureau supplied 21 million meals to hungry black and white southerners. The Freedman's Bureau also fostered a new educational system in the former Confederacy in order to instruct the next generation of workers and leaders. Finally, Bureau agents aided freedmen and women in finding jobs and negotiated fair terms for employment. They helped draw up tens of thousands of contracts between these new wage employees and their employers. Ironically, many of these jobs were back on the plantations. As one historian has written, the old dependencies of white planters and black farmhands did not end once slavery died.

Regardless, from the Emancipation Proclamation in 1863 to the Compromise of 1877 when Reconstruction ended, African-Americans experienced tremendous advancement as workers and as members of the new southern polity. African-Americans were integral in the formation of the new southern state governments. They not only participated in the constitutional conventions but also after the new states were formed voted in large numbers and held office. Their political contributions extended to all facets of the government, from jury boxes to state houses. Ex-slaves fought hard for these gains, and they met stiff resistance at every turn. In general, whites resented the elevation of blacks to a status of equality. All across the South, white vigilante groups such as the Ku Klux Klan (KKK) threatened, attacked, and even murdered black politicians and activists. These groups also set their crosshairs on black workers. Although they were new to wage labor, African-American workers understood that to improve their working conditions, they had to organize and pressure employers. Labor unrest on plantations frightened not only white planters but Freedman's Bureau officials as well. Some southern whites responded with violence. Nevertheless, these nascent unionists pushed ahead.

The results of the 1876 presidential election, however, spelled doom for the generation of freedmen and women who emerged with new working lives after the Civil War. The movement to deny African-Americans their civil rights in the South predated the electoral fiasco. Before they were reconstructed, several states passed so-called Black Codes, which severely limited African-Americans' ability to rent or purchase property. Additionally, they could not freely enter or leave employment contracts, take time off work, testify in court, possess firearms, or speak freely. Momentarily suspended during Reconstruction, these laws came back in the late 1870s and through the 1890s. They were known as Jim Crow laws, and the U.S. Supreme Court eventually ruled them constitutional in 1896 in the infamous *Plessy* v. *Ferguson* decision.

In addition to legal measures enacted to keep blacks in a second-class position, some white southerners adopted violent methods. The KKK gained power and influence as the nineteenth century came to a close. As Ida B. Wells reported at the turn of the century, lynchings in the South were frequent occurrences. According to statistics compiled by the NAACP, from 1882 to 1931, 3,318 black men, women, and children were lynched. That is a rate of over 60 killings per year. As Wells so aptly demonstrated, many of these murders related to the economic successes of black workers and businessmen. Whites resented deeply the advances of former slaves. Lynching was but one way to abrogate civil rights; race riots were another. As blacks began to assert their civil rights, some whites tried to force them back into a slavelike condition. Such pressures sparked white-on-black riots in New Orleans (1865), Memphis (1866), and Hamburg, South Carolina (1876). The racial violence of the late nineteenth century demonstrates that free African-Americans still wore an indelible badge of inferiority. The Civil War had emancipated them, but they were not able to live and work as whites did.

At this critical juncture for African-Americans living in the Gilded Age, the central question was: how do we secure civil rights? One answer might have resided in the new labor movement. The National Labor Union (NLU), which arose during the years immediately preceding the Civil War, stood for interracial unionism. But rhetoric about equal did not translate into interracial organizing. Unlike the NLU, the Knights of Labor stated publicly both that black workers should be equal to white workers and that they all should belong to unions together. None other than Frederick Douglass and the pre-eminent black journalist T. Thomas Fortune supported the Knights. Unfortunately for black workers, the Knights did not last. After the 1886 Haymarket Square Massacre, the Knights suffered a decline and eventually gave way to the rival American Federation of Labor (AFL—established in 1881). The AFL was an umbrella group of craft unions. At its founding convention, many members of the Knights of Labor attended, including Jeremiah Grandison, an African-American worker and a member of the Knight's Local Assembly 1665 (Pittsburgh). It became clear to Grandison that the AFL was going to be much more conservative on racial issues. He spoke up during the conference, telling his colleagues that it would be absurd to ignore black wage earners who potentially could become strikebreakers. In fact, this had already occurred in the mining areas of Pennsylvania's Tuscarawas Valley. Grandison maintained that the only way to stop scabbing was to open the unions as widely as possible.

Initially, Grandison and those in the AFL who supported interracial unionism were able to sway official AFL policy. From 1886 to 1895, the AFL pushed craft unions toward racial inclusivity. For example, in 1890, the AFL refused to admit the International Association of Machinists until it dropped its constitutional clause denying African-American membership. But five years later, the AFL had abandoned its position. Although it still gave lip service to equality in employment, the AFL accepted the Machinists in 1895 when it transferred its ban on blacks from its constitution to its ritual. In 1896, the Boilermakers were accepted into the AFL without having removed its constitutional ban on black workers. Moreover, locals had considerable power to exclude workers not specified by union constitutions. In the absence of an international's mandate to a local about black workers, locals often established their own. Four major AFL affiliates (the Flint Glass Workers, the Brotherhood of Electrical Workers, the Plumbers and Steamfitters, and the Asbestos Workers) denied admittance to black workers by tacit consent of the locals.

By the twentieth century, the AFL had earned a well-deserved reputation for abiding, if not supporting, racial exclusion. Many of the AFL's international unions such as the Airline Dispatchers, Railroad Telegraphers, Railway and Steamship Clerks, Railway Mail Association, and Switchmen denied the right to join on racial grounds, limiting those eligible for membership to "white" workers. A few AFL unions such as the Railway Mail Association were more specific, stating that only those of the "Caucasian race or native American Indians" could join, while the Firemen's constitution defined "white" as excluding "Mexicans, Indians, or those of Spanish-Mexican extraction." Still other AFL unions (such as the Boilermakers, the Blacksmiths, the Maintenance of Way Employees, the Railway Carmen, and the Sheet Metal Workers) openly excluded African-American workers by admitting them into segregated, auxiliary unions. In some cases, notably among longshoremen, separate locals allowed some opportunities for black workers. However, in most cases, segregated locals created distinct disadvantages for African-Americans. Those auxiliaries had no voice in local or national union affairs, were completely represented by the white officers of the main local, had no grievance procedure, and frequently had fewer benefits than those afforded white members. As the black economist Robert C. Weaver once put it, black workers in these setups had second-class union status but paid first-class dues.

If most unions then protected the interests of their white members, they also guarded against any erosion in the status of male workers. Unions frequently functioned as a way for white male workers to privilege themselves over African-Americans and women as well as various ethnic group workers such as Chinese, French-Canadians, and Mexicans. Such was definitively the case with the American Federation of Labor. Since its inception, the AFL had refused to embrace women workers, preferring to keep them at arm's length. In 1881, when the AFL met for the first time, no women were present. This was at odds with the previous experiences of the labor movement. Women were the vanguard in industrial unions in the 1820s in New England textile mills. They were the bedrock of the shoemakers unions in the 1850s and 1860s. And, of course, they were instrumental to the success of the Knights of Labor, which had nearly 50,000 female members by the 1880s. In contrast to these organizations, the AFL developed a reputation for favoring the organization of women workers while not actually doing it. At its second convention in 1882, the AFL formally "extended to all unions of women equal opportunity to participate in future conventions with unions of men." This call netted one female delegate the following year, Charlotte Smith, the president of the Women's National Industrial League. Two years later, the AFL refreshed its call for women to join. Unsurprisingly, few did. In 1891, the AFL seemed to change course and hired a female organizer, Mary E. Kenney. After a year of unproductive work in New York City, AFL President Gompers fired her. During the 1892 and subsequent conventions, members highlighted the problems facing women workers and called for reform. Sometimes there were positive developments. In 1900, the AFL gave a charter to the new International Ladies' Garment Workers' Union, which had both male and female members. But generally, despite its public pronouncements, the AFL failed to take concrete steps to widely organize women workers.

In the absence of AFL organizing, working women and their allies pursued another strategy to establish civil rights, especially the right to determine the conditions of their labor. Beginning in the late nineteenth century, reformers sought protective legislation as a means to establish equality for women workers. The key moment came in 1908 when the United States Supreme Court ruled in *Muller v. Oregon* that a state law setting a maximum of 10 hours of work per day for factory women and laundresses was constitutional. This ruling overturned an earlier decision, *Lochner v. New York* (1905), in which the justices had struck down a 10-hour limit for bakery workers. Apparently, in the Muller case, the Supreme Court was swayed by future justice Louis D. Brandeis, who with the assistance of Florence Kelley and Josephine Goldmark of the National Consumers' League, had demonstrated the ill effects of long hours. Not only did excessive work outside the home damage women's health, but it hurt the family as well.

The *Oregon* decision and the state 10-hour workday law were demonstrable advances for female workers. Yet, in terms of civil rights, these victories and others like them had an ironic result. By upholding the Oregon law, the Supreme Court was in essence stating that unlike men, women did not have liberty of contract in all cases. Unlike first-class citizens, solely because they were women, they could not enter into contracts without any restrictions. This made women akin to child wards of the state. Thus, protective laws like the Oregon 10-hour statute rested upon the reality that women workers did not enjoy civil rights akin to their male counterparts. This legal trend reached a peak in the 1940s. By World War II, virtually all states, the District of Columbia, and every major territory including Puerto Rico had laws that limited women's wage workday to eight to 10 hours (per employer), established weekly limits of no more than 60 hours, and frequently prohibited or limited night work and the establishment of a minimum wage. The AFL, the nation's largest labor organization, wholeheartedly supported these statutes as long as they dealt with women. Unlike social reformers and feminists, who spearheaded reform campaigns for protective legislation, AFL leaders saw the laws as a means of shoring up the family and protecting their privileged status by discouraging employers from hiring women in the first place while ensuring reasonable conditions for those who did enter the labor force.

During the era of Franklin D. Roosevelt, new social and political movements were born that built upon the gains of the Progressive Era and dramatically reshaped the United States, making civil rights possible for women and minority workers. This historic change hinged on the advent of the New Deal. In 1933, President Roosevelt signed the National Industrial Recovery Act, which, among other things, established in its famous Section 7(a) the right for workers to organize unions and bargain collectively. Initially, most of the new unions and new unionists belonged to the American Federation of Labor. The AFL, however, was unable to handle the rising tide of unionization. In 1935, a group of labor leaders broke away from the AFL to form the Congress of Industrial Organizations (CIO). Among its founding principles, the CIO was dedicated to ending racial and sex discrimination in employment. For example, the United Packinghouse Workers of America (UPWA), which was affiliated with the CIO, was a progressive, interracial union. It worked to eliminate segregation on the job as well as wage differentials between northern and southern meatpacking factories. African-Americans also became leaders in the UPWA. Such high levels of interracial solidarity had a very tangible result. In 1954, the union began a 14-month strike against a Boston packing plant. Despite employer and some community pressure, the interracial union held together and saw the strike to a successful completion. The CIO was similarly dedicated to advancing the civil rights of women workers and ending discrimination. The CIO's unions, such as the United Electrical Workers, made equal pay for equal work a hallmark of their organizational campaigns.

In general, the revived labor movement—both the AFL and CIO—in the 1930s and 1940s transformed American politics. Black and white workers, men and women, now demanded equality in unions and in the labor market. They were unwilling to accept empty platitudes or one-sided compromises. The stellar example comes from the years leading up to American involvement in the Second World War. President Roosevelt's defense mobilization from 1939 to 1941 did release the American economy from the Great Depression's horrific grip. Yet, for the most part, the economic opportunities that preparedness created were for whites only. Discrimination was common in the South. In Texas, for instance, one out of every two new defense jobs was only for whites. However, this was no regional phenomenon. In Ohio, African-American workers were barred from eight out of every 10 jobs. To fight the discrimination in the "arsenal of democracy," in 1941, A. Philip Randolph, the leader of the all-black Brotherhood of Sleeping Car Porters, announced that unless President Roosevelt took decisive action to open the factory gates for all Americans, he would march 100,000 black workers down Pennsylvania Avenue in protest. Rather than bear the international embarrassment of such a march, FDR met with Randolph. In return for calling off the march, Roosevelt issued Executive Order 8802, which ordered defense contractors to end job discrimination on account of race, creed, color, or national origin. To enforce his edict, President Roosevelt established the Fair Employment Practice Committee (FEPC). Although the FEPC did not eliminate discrimination on the home front, it did advance civil rights by providing a model for future reform.

From the late 1940s through the mid-1960s, both the postwar African-American civil rights movement as well as the postwar feminist movement saw the re-creation of the FEPC as a key means to create first-class citizenship. Congressional conservatives had dismantled the wartime FEPC in 1946. In 1964, after an 18-year campaign, Congress bowed to public pressure from activists and from many labor unions and passed the Omnibus Civil Rights Bill, which outlawed employment discrimination on account of race, creed, color, national origin, *and* sex and which created the Equal Employment Opportunity Commission (EEOC) to enforce the law. Along with the other legislative milestone, the 1963 Equal Pay Act, the Civil Rights Act went far to remove the badges of inferiority that white women, all African-American workers, and many immigrants had been forced to wear for centuries.

Since the 1960s, the history of civil rights and workers has not been one of unalloyed success. In the late 1990s and through the new millennium, workers had to fight to maintain or to create civil rights in the workplace. One constant was the advocacy of the labor movement. Unions played critical roles in forcing companies as diverse as Wal-Mart and Mitsubishi Motors to become equal employment opportunity employers. And it was not always a successful struggle. Nonetheless, the parameters of the fight have been quite clear. At the start of the twenty-first century, American society remained a place where the blessings of liberty were bestowed on some more than on others. Since the 1930s and 1940s, the others in American history have increasingly demanded full citizenship rights. The story of this movement among African-American and women workers has been quite well documented. However, in the early twenty-first century, other disenfranchised Americans sought civil rights. In the future, historians will write about gay, lesbian, and "disabled" workers and the concept of first-class citizenship. In the United States, civil rights have been natural rights; workers have had to capture them and wrestle to keep them. It has been a centuries-long process and not a starting or ending point in history.

ANDREW E. KERSTEN

References and Further Reading

Arensen, Eric. *Brotherhoods of Color: Black Railroad Workers and the Struggle for Equality*. Cambridge, MA: Harvard University Press, 2001.

Bailyn, Bernard. *Voyagers to the West: A Passage in the Peopling of America on the Eve of the Revolution*. New York: Knopf, 1986.

Berlin, Ira. *Generations of Captivity: A History of African-American Slaves*. Cambridge, MA: Belknap Press of Harvard University Press, 2003.

Evans, Sara M. *Born for Liberty: A History of Women in America*. New York: Free Press, 1989.

Foner, Eric. *Reconstruction: America's Unfinished Revolution*. New York: Harper and Row, 1988.

Graham, Hugh Davis. *The Civil Rights Era: Origins and Development of National Policy, 1960–1972*. New York: Oxford University Press, 1989.

Halpern, Rick. *Down on the Killing Floor: Black and White Workers in Chicago's Packinghouses, 1904–1954*. Urbana: University of Illinois Press, 1997.

Harris, William H. *The Harder We Run: Black Workers since the Civil War*. New York: Oxford University Press, 1982.

Milkman, Ruth. *Gender at Work: The Dynamics of Job Segregation by Sex during World War II*. Urbana: University of Illinois Press, 1987.

Kersten, Andrew E. *Labor's Home Front: The AFL and the Second World War*. New York: New York University Press, forthcoming.

———. *Race, Jobs, and the War: The FEPC in the Midwest, 1941–1946*. Urbana: University of Illinois Press, 2000.

Kessler-Harris, Alice. *In Pursuit of Equity: Women, Men, and the Quest for Economic Citizenship in 20th Century America*. New York: Oxford University Press, 2001.

Morgan, Edmund S. *American Slavery, American Freedom: The Ordeal of Colonial Virginia*. New York: Norton, 1975.

Roediger, David R. *The Wages of Whiteness: Race and the Making of the American Working Class*. New York: Verso, 1991.

Shortall, Sally. *Women and Farming: Property and Power*. New York: St. Martin's Press, 1999.

Stampp, Kenneth M. *America in 1857: A Nation on the Brink*. New York: Oxford University Press, 1990.

Sugrue, Thomas J. *The Origins of the Urban Crisis: Race and Inequality in Postwar Detroit*. Princeton, NJ: Princeton University Press, 1996.

Ulrich, Laurel T. *A Midwife's Tale: The Life of Martha Ballard Based on Her Diary*. New York: Knopf, 1990.

Zieger, Robert H. *The CIO, 1935–1955*. Chapel Hill: University of North Carolina Press, 1995.

See also **American Federation of Labor-Congress of Industrial Organizations; Brotherhood of Sleeping Car Porters; Randolph, A. Philip**

CIVIL RIGHTS ACT OF 1964/TITLE VII

Congress ended a southern filibuster against federal civil rights legislation for the first time ever in June 1964, and on July 2, President Johnson signed the Civil Rights Act of 1964 into law. Title VII, Equal Employment Opportunity, is arguably the most important section of the entire act in that there was a quick and visible increase in women and minority group employment. In general, the act made it unlawful for an employer, employment agency, or labor organization to discriminate in employment against persons because of their race, color, religion, sex, or national origin.

Historical Precedents

The American at-will employment doctrine adopted by states has generally denied any remedy to employees treated arbitrarily by an employer, absent union representation or contract. An employer could hire and fire freely. For a short time, the federal courts even protected this doctrine as a Fifth Amendment right against a federal statute that prohibited firing employees for union membership. Congress relied on the commerce clause of the U.S. Constitution as a basis for Title VII. The commerce clause gives Congress the power to regulate commerce between the states and with foreign nations. In *Heart of Atlanta Motel*, the Supreme Court upheld Title II of the Civil Rights Act of 1964 with a broad interpretation of Congress's right to regulate interstate commerce that extends to local activity that has a substantial impact on commerce. Interestingly, the Court rejected the Fifth Amendment claim. This case made clear that the Supreme Court would defer to the power of Congress to prevent discrimination under the commerce clause and that claims of liberty and property deprivation by business would not prevail.

Federal law had addressed discrimination in federal civil service employment prior to the New Deal era of the 1930s and 1940s. Facing a mass march of African-Americans on Washington in 1941 organized by A. Philip Randolph, President Franklin Roosevelt signed Executive Order 8802, which extended protection from race, creed, color, and national origin employment discrimination to all defense contracts, federal employment, and federal vocational and training programs. The Fair Employment Practice Committee (FEPC) was established to investigate complaints, attempt resolution, and make recommendations. The FEPC expired in 1946. However, these efforts laid the foundation for Title VII and the Equal Employment Opportunity Commission of the 1960s.

During the late 1940s and 1950s, Presidents Truman and Eisenhower addressed discrimination in government contracting. Some members of Congress introduced legislation during this period to end various employment discrimination practices. However, rarely was such legislation considered by the full body, and no legislation was passed.

The Road to Passage

On June11, 1963, President John F. Kennedy addressed the nation on television and asked, "Who among us would be content to have the color of his skin changed?" Earlier that day, Alabama Governor George Wallace had stood in the doorway at the University of Alabama as a symbolic gesture opposing the admission of two black students. President Kennedy promised to strengthen his civil rights proposal. In the preceding months, Martin Luther King Jr. had been jailed in Birmingham for protesting segregation and issued his "A Letter from the Birmingham Jail." Robert Loevy, in his book *The Civil Right Act of 1964*, described King's letter as the "Declaration of Independence of the civil rights movement."

After the assassination of President Kennedy in November 1963, President Johnson placed the civil rights legislation as a high priority and a fitting tribute to the dead president. The conservative chairman of the House Rules Committee, Howard W. Smith, agreed to let the committee vote out the civil rights legislation in January 1964. As the House debated the bill, he moved to add an amendment prohibiting sex discrimination in employment in addition to race, color, religion, and national origin. Such action was intended to defeat the bill by dividing supporters. However, the strong support of liberals such as Martha Griffiths led to approval of the amendment in about two hours. The House of Representatives passed the bill on February 10, 1964.

Senate passage was required before the bill could be sent to the president for signature into law. Senate leaders attempted to bypass the Senate Judiciary Committee by placing the House bill directly on the Senate calendar. Opponents began a filibuster, an extended speech, to prevent voting or action by the Senate on the committee referral issue. They ended this after 16 days in order to avoid an early cloture (limit debate) vote.

The Senate debate on the House bill began soon after. Hubert Humphrey, the bill's Democratic floor leader, needed 67 votes out of the 100 senators to end the opposition filibuster to the main bill. The Democrats needed the support of some Republicans in order to close debate. Illinois Senator Dirksen formed a group of Republican senators to support cloture. However, some members of that group proposed three amendments. Any amendments would mean the bill would be sent back to the House if the bill passed the Senate. Needing the votes, the Democrats agreed to a consideration of the amendments. One amendment related to jury trials passed. The jury trial issue was important to opponents because of the historical use of white male juries to protect conservative values.

The Dirksen group of Republicans supported the cloture vote, and for the first time, the opposition filibuster to civil rights legislation had been stopped. The Senate approved the civil rights bill as amended, and the amended bill went to the House of Representatives. The bill did not have to return to the Senate when the House voted 289 to 126 to approve the Senate-amended legislation. President Lyndon Johnson signed the bill, which had become the Civil Rights Act of 1964, on July 2, 1964. This new act included Title VII on equal employment opportunity.

The Act

Title VII generally applies to employers of 15 or more, employment agencies, unions that operate hiring halls or have at least 15 members, and government. Both "disparate treatment" and "disparate impact" on protected groups and individuals are banned. Protected groups and persons are those subject to discrimination or harassment based on religion, national origin, race, color, or sex. Protected employees may include former workers for the employer as in *Robinson v. Shell Oil*, where a retaliation claim was made based upon a recommendation by Shell to a potential new employer. Claims must be filed rather quickly, generally within 180 days. Claims are made with the Equal Employment Opportunity Commission unless there is a state agency that enforces antidiscrimination laws.

The Cases

The U.S. Supreme Court's first major Title VII case, *Griggs v. Duke Power*, made clear that congressional intent was to remove barriers used in the past to favor whites. The Court struck down the requirements of a high school diploma and an intelligence test because neither was shown to be significantly related to requirements of the job, they worked to the substantial disadvantage of blacks vis-à-vis whites, and the jobs

had formerly been filled only by whites. These disparate impact cases often rely on statistical evidence.

Disparate treatment cases are often made on facial evidence or circumstantial evidence. Facial evidence is where the employers essentially advertises their bias. An example of such evidence might be an ad seeking "men only" for certain positions. Most cases involve circumstantial evidence. This evidence proves facts that allow people to infer the discriminatory intent. In *McDonnell Douglas Corp. v. Green* and *Texas Community Affairs v. Burdine*, the Court held that persons making disparate treatment claims must first show that they are a member of the protected groups, that they were qualified for the job or benefit, and that the job or benefit stayed open or was filled by a person not in the protected groups. If the employer fails to explain a clearly legitimate, nondiscriminatory reason for its action, the employee wins. If the employer makes such an explanation, the burden shifts to the employee to show that the reason given was a pretext or a cloak for the real discriminatory reason. The employer does not have to show that the person selected was better qualified.

Disparate treatment cases often involve a variety of motives, some of which may be legal and others not. Employee claimants then need to show that the wrongful motivation was a significant factor in the decision. The employer may claim that it would have taken the action even without the wrongful factor. Even if this is true, the 1991 Civil Rights Act allows the employee to certain relief and attorney fees.

Sexual harassment cases are of two types: quid pro quo or hostile environment. Quid pro quo means a deal, something given for something else. Here the employer or its agents condition employment or benefits on receipt of sexual favors. The Court held in *Meritor Savings Bank v. Vinson* that harassment creating a hostile or abusive work environment violates Title VII, even without economic loss to the employee. In *Harris v. Forklift Systems*, the Court held that actionable harassment is that which is sufficiently severe or pervasive to change the conditions of the environment and create an abusive work environment. More than mere offensiveness is needed, but less that tangible psychological injury.

Employers may in narrow circumstances have the Bona Fide Occupational Qualification (BFOQ) defense. This defense is not applicable to race. In *International Union, U.A.W. v. Johnson Controls*, the Court held that the trait the employer seeks must be essentially central to the business and pertain to the particular position. Substantially, all of the excluded group must be shown to lack necessary traits.

Title VII of the Civil Rights Act of 1964 has helped make women's work patterns more like those of men, according to the Bureau of Labor Statistics, although the impact may be less positive for poor women. Employment opportunities for minorities have increased greatly. Yet, gaps remain in education, employment, and income. Unions see diversity as strength, with 27% of union members being persons of color. In 2002, the Equal Employment Opportunity Commission received 84,000 complaints.

MICHAEL W. SIMPSON

References and Further Reading

Anderson, Terry H. *The Pursuit of Fairness: A History of Affirmative Action.* Oxford: Oxford University Press, 2004.
———. *The Sixties.* New York: Pearson Longman, 2004.
Bureau of National Affairs. *The Civil Rights Act of 1964.* Washington, DC, 1964.
Lewis, Harold S., and Elizabeth J. Norman. *Employment Discrimination Law and Practice.* St. Paul, MN: West Group, 2001.
Loevy, Robert D. *The Civil Rights Act of 1964: The Passage of the Law That Ended Racial Segregation.* Albany, NY: State University of New York Press.
U.S. Department of Labor. Bureau of Labor Statistics. "Women at Work: A Visual Essay." October 2003. www.bls.gov/opub/mlr/2003/10/ressum3.pdf.
———. Women's Bureau. "Quick Stats 2004." 2004. www.dol.gov/wb/stats/main.htm.

Cases and Statutes Cited

Griggs v. Duke Power, 401 U.S. 424 (1971)
Harris v. Forklift Systems, 510 U.S. 17 (1993)
Heart of Atlanta Motel v. United States, 379 U.S. 241 (1964)
International Union v. Johnson Controls, 499 U.S. 187 (1991)
McDonnell Douglas v. Green, 411 U.S. 792 (1973)
Meritor Savings Bank v. Vinson, 477 U.S. 57 (1986)
Robinson v. Shell Oil, 519 U.S. 337 (1997)
Texas Department of Community Affairs v. Burdine, 450 U.S. 248 (1981)
Civil Rights Act of 1964, Title VII, codified at United States Code Service 42 (2005), §§2000e et seq.

See also **Affirmative Action; At-Will Employment; Equal Pay Act of 1963; Fair Employment Practice Committee; Randolph, A. Philip**

CIVIL RIGHTS CONGRESS

The Civil Rights Congress (CRC) parried the mounting storm of Cold War hostility to defend the rights of African-Americans and leftist political activists from 1947 to 1956. In 1946, members of the National Negro Congress, a network of militant civil rights and union activists, the International Labor Defense, a legal defense group, and the National Federation for Constitutional Liberties formed the CRC. At its peak in the late 1940s, the New York City-based CRC boasted 10,000 members and 70 locals, with especially vibrant chapters in Detroit, New Orleans, Los Angeles, the Bay Area, and Seattle. Originally conceived as a mass-based organization, the CRC increasingly acted against particularly egregious cases of legal injustice. Its members fought against racial violence and incursions of civil liberties for specific defendants as well as created pamphlets and organized rallies to advocate justice through the court of public opinion. While the CRC lost most of its battles, its courageous members exposed McCarthyism and racial repression as twin impediments to democracy, piercing the aura of the "silent 50s" and serving as a precursor to the larger mass movement for racial equality during the next decade.

Civil Rights Congress leaders initially had ambitious plans for a mass movement. The CRC fought alongside labor unions and other progressive organizations in calling for the prosecution of the Klan, pressuring President Truman to support civil rights measures, and investigating racial violence against black veterans. One successful 1947 national campaign was its call to "Oust Bilbo." CRC chapters distributed 185,000 petitions that demanded Mississippi Senator Theodore Bilbo relinquish his seat due to his sponsorship of black and working-class disenfranchisement that continued to get him undemocratically elected. While Bilbo's death soon thereafter ended the campaign, it brought international publicity to widespread southern repression of voting rights. In addition to national campaigns, CRC chapters desegregated stores in places like Des Moines and Boulder, fought for jobs in Philadelphia, and registered voters in New Orleans.

The CRC never sustained a mass movement. Its leaders, including Aubrey Grossman and William Patterson, were self-critical of the CRC's strategy for not having a "union backbone." Aside from coordination with waterfront workers in New Orleans and the West Coast, the fur and leather workers in several cities, and autoworkers in Detroit, the CRC did not have a strong union membership. In addition, when in 1947 the attorney general labeled the CRC a "subversive organization," liberals and conservatives alike began to dismiss it and disassociate from it, calling it a "Communist front." With several Communists as prominent members, the CRC now had serious problems convincing liberals that they prioritized racial justice above loyalty to the Communist Party (CP). Soon thereafter, the CRC became a circumscribed network of leftist activists who focused on specific legal cases.

The CRC made international causes out of cases of racial injustice, like that of the Trenton Six. This case involved six young black men arrested for the murder of a white shopkeeper in New Jersey. Despite witnesses who reported having seen only one light-skinned black man at the scene, a 55-day trial resulted in convictions of all six defendants. The CRC entered the case in 1948 and dubbed it the "Northern Scottsboro." Their agitation led to the release of four of the original defendants, but the courts still convicted three black men of the crime. Meanwhile, local CRC chapters fought similar "legal lynchings." In its prolific Los Angeles chapter, for example, 30 CRC-affiliated attorneys fought 89 cases in 1949, most involving police brutality and racial discrimination.

In the South, CRC cases like that of Willie McGee and Rosa Lee Ingram confronted racial and sexual stereotypes. McGee, a black Mississippi truck driver, had an ongoing affair with a white woman, Willett Hawkins, for whom he did yard work. In 1946, Mississippi police arrested McGee after Hawkins's husband accused him of rape. The CRC fought the case for five years through the courts, held mass meetings, and exposed the frame-up in the press, but lost the battle for his reprieve when the state executed him in 1951. While this case relied upon Jim Crow notions that sex between black men and white women could only stem from rape, the case of Rosa Ingram in rural Georgia exposed another stereotype: that white men would never violate black women. John Stratford, a tenant farmer, hit Ingram with the butt of a rifle, and, by many accounts, tried to sexually assault her. Responding to her mother's screams, one of Ingram's sons hit Stratford over the head and killed him. Ignoring this self-defense, police arrested Ingram and two of her sons, and a jury sentenced all three to death in 1947. Less-militant organizations like the National Association for the Advancement of Colored People (NAACP), but especially a group of dedicated leftist black women who formed the Sojourners for Truth and Justice, agitated for a reversal of the verdict. The collaborative effort led to the Ingrams' release from prison in the early 1950s.

While fighting for domestic civil rights, the CRC also put racial injustice on the international stage to expose "the Achilles' heel" of U.S. foreign policy. The CRC linked its belief in freedom for racial minorities to anticolonial movements and opposed the Korean War as imperialist. By 1951, CRC leader William Patterson drafted, and then presented, a 240-page document called "We Charge Genocide" to the United Nations. The State Department and moderate civil rights groups like the NAACP scrambled to mute Patterson's indictment by releasing its own milder propaganda, sponsoring international tours of moderate African-Americans, and repressing CRC members back home (including the U.S. government's confiscation of Patterson's passport upon his return

from Europe). Nevertheless, progressive unions like the leather workers and longshoremen supported and sold copies of the petition, and people in places as far away as India challenged U.S. diplomats about racial oppression by posing specific questions about cases like Willie McGee and the Trenton Six.

As the Cold War became more repressive with the McCarran Act of 1950 and FBI infiltration of the CRC's chapters (with cooperation from NAACP leaders), the defense of its right to exist sapped its energy. Subversive Control Board prosecutions based on the McCarran Act cost the CRC hundreds of dollars weekly; a mob attacked Paul Robeson and other CRC supporters in Peekskill, New York, in 1949; police put members of the CRC bail fund in jail; and judges flouted the Sixth Amendment by prosecuting and refusing to allow CRC attorneys to defend clients like the Trenton Six. In addition, Communist leaders criticized the CRC for not doing enough to defend top Party members from prosecution for sedition under the 1940 Smith Act. The CRC came to the defense of the indicted CP leaders because its members saw this attack by the U.S. government as a threat against the first line of defense for civil liberties for all Americans. However, by defending top leaders like the "CP 11," the CRC gave credence to its critics, who labeled it the legal wing of the Communist Party. As the Cold War became more repressive, the CRC lost members and financial resources. This repression caused its demise in 1956, though the militant tactics and legal strategies it employed would arise again in the mass movements for civil rights during the next decade (its last case was the lynching of Emmett Till), but especially in campaigns against police brutality and government repression that re-emerged in the late 1960s.

ERIK S. GELLMAN

References and Further Reading

Anderson, Nancy. *Eyes off the Prize: The United Nations and the African American Freedom Struggle for Human Rights, 1944–1955*. New York: Cambridge University Press, 2003.

Horne, Gerald. *Communist Front? The Civil Rights Congress, 1946–1956*. Madison, NJ: Farleigh Dickinson University Press, 1988.

Papers of the Civil Rights Congress. Schomburg Center for Research in Black Culture. The New York Public Library, Harlem, New York.

CIVIL WAR AND RECONSTRUCTION

The Civil War and Reconstruction witnessed an upsurge in labor organizing that brought into being the first national trade federation, the end of slavery, and the first national strikes. By the end of Reconstruction, chances for a national labor movement that included the South and that was committed to equality without regard to race or gender had been weakened.

On the eve of the Civil War, America's 11.1 million workers fit into two broad legal categories, free and slave. The single most common occupation remained farming, which employed roughly 3.35 million whites and 2.52 million slaves, for a total of 53% of all workers. The growing manufacturing sector employed 1.5 million Americans (14% of the work force), of which one fifth were women. Approximately the same number found employment in construction and commerce, categories that encompassed everything from starched-collar merchants in their counting houses to shirtless stevedores unloading cargo on the docks. Women predominated among the 665,000 service workers, which included the single largest female occupation, domestic servant. Smaller cohorts labored in transportation, mining, and a variety of other pursuits.

Within each section, types of work varied by region. Most industrial workers (86%) lived in the free states of the North, but they were outnumbered by the North's farmers. Massachusetts, New York, and Pennsylvania contained just over half of the industrial work force, and another quarter lived in neighboring northeastern states. Farming mixed with a much smaller manufacturing sector in the old Northwest. The North housed 87% of the nation's 4.1 million foreign-born. Most immigrants had arrived from Ireland and Germany since the mid-1840s. The poorest immigrants gathered in the North's cities and took up low-paying jobs in commerce and industry.

In the South, slave-based agriculture was strongest in the seven states of the lower South, where enormous profits from the staples of cotton, sugar, and rice crowded out other activities. Slaves made up almost half of the lower South's population. In the eight states of the upper South, the slave population ranged from a high of 33% in North Carolina to a low of 2% in Delaware. Industrializing cities like Baltimore, Richmond, and St. Louis mixed with plantation districts and broad belts of small farms devoted to grain and livestock.

In the far West, the Gold Rush of 1849 spawned a mining and manufacturing boom in California, while Oregon attracted farmers. In California, 35,000 Chinese workingmen (9% of the state's population) toiled in mines, railroads, and urban sweatshops.

Although few northern white workers and farmers (or factory owners, professionals, or any other segment of the white population) endorsed immediate abolition and racial equality, many more supported free soil, the cheap distribution of federal land from

which slavery would be excluded. The opening of the West to settlement in the 1840s increased sectional conflict by raising the question of slavery's legality in this newly acquired federal territory. In the mid-1850s, a new party, the Republicans, emerged in the North as the free-soil rival to the Democrats, who were allied to southern slaveholders. In the South, small farmers occasionally clashed with wealthy slaveholders, but most supported slavery's expansion because of its perceived economic benefits and their commitment to white supremacy.

The erosion of traditional craft work arrangements and living standards provided an additional spur for workers to back free soil as an alternative to factories and sweatshops. The reality of permanent wage work for even the most highly skilled changed organizing strategies. In place of Jacksonian-era boycotts to enforce mechanics' price lists and Associationist calls for utopian industrial communities, workers turned to craft unions, which addressed issues related to their status as wage earners. During the 1850s, at least 26 national unions were formed. The Panic of 1857, followed by the secession-related business slump of 1860–1861, hampered these efforts. In February 1860, 20,000 shoemakers in Lynn, Massachusetts, staged the largest strike in pre-Civil War history to protest falling wages and the introduction of labor-saving machines. Many employers raised pay, but strikers failed to win collective bargaining rights. During the strike, some workers connected their demand for equal rights to emancipation. In 1860, only five national trade unions survived, and the combined membership of all unions, local and national, accounted for 10% of industrial workers.

Law and brute force prevented slaves from organizing unions, much less voting for antislavery politicians. Nevertheless, African-American slaves developed strategies for resisting their masters. They cooperated to control the pace of work, accumulated cash through garden plots and slave hiring, and organized a political community around church services and family networks. Slaves also defied the risks of recapture by running away and, much more rarely, by engaging in suicidal rebellions. Aided by free blacks in the cities, and by conductors on the Underground Railroad like Harriet Tubman, slaves were poised to strike for freedom when the opportunity arose.

The presidential election of 1860 provided that opportunity. The Republican Party drafted a free-soil platform and nominated Abraham Lincoln, an Illinois lawyer who emphasized his youthful career as a rail splitter. The Democratic Party split into northern and southern wings. Campaigning on the slogan "free soil, free labor, free men," Republicans appealed to workers and small farmers by promising to protect the right of ordinary Americans to gain access to productive property and claim a fair reward for their toil. Carrying only 40% of the popular vote, Lincoln won the election by garnering a majority in the electoral college that came exclusively from the free states.

Notwithstanding Lincoln's assurances that he would leave slavery alone where it already existed, southerners regarded his election as the first step toward general abolition. In December 1860, South Carolina, a leader of proslavery southern nationalism, quit the Union. During the next six months, 10 more slave states joined South Carolina to create the breakaway Confederacy. In line with public opinion in the North and four loyal border slave states, Lincoln vowed to preserve the Union with slavery intact in the South.

During the secession crisis, northern organized labor was divided. Few wanted war, but fewer still favored capitulation to the slaveholders. On February 22, 1861, trade union leaders from 12 states met in Philadelphia to advocate "concession not secession." Known as the Committee of Thirty-Four, the leaders supported the Crittenden Compromise, a peace plan that allowed slavery to expand south of the Missouri Compromise line. Despite the conciliatory efforts of some labor leaders, most farmers and workers agreed with Lincoln that slavery's expansion could not be permitted. After Confederate forces fired on Fort Sumter on April 12, 1861, even those in favor of compromise rallied behind Lincoln.

Northern workers backed the Union because the stakes were high. Defeat would weaken democracy, cut off the South's markets, and expand slavery westward, possibly even into the North. Several labor leaders organized their unions into military companies, causing their organizations to disband for lack of members. Radical fraternal societies, like the German *Turnverein*, volunteered *en masse*. In all, mechanics and laborers made up 42% of the Union military.

The response of southern labor was more complicated. In the 11 seceding states, poor whites solidly backed the Confederacy amidst the fervor created by secession and Lincoln's promised invasion. In 1861, the South's few cities harbored pockets of Unionism. In New Orleans, the largest Confederate city, the extreme Southern Rights candidate finished third in the 1860 presidential election. Some anti-secessionist workers, including the caulkers' union leader Richard Trevellick, left for the North, while others lay low until federal occupation in April 1862 allowed them to make a stand. In the border slave states, urban white workers fought secession. In Baltimore, gangs of pro-Union workers joined Union soldiers in combating a secessionist mob on April 19, 1861.

In St. Louis, German militia volunteers routed a Confederate force seeking to capture a federal armory.

Slaves welcomed the chance for freedom. News of Lincoln's election and secession prompted talk of escape, revolt, and cooperation with federal troops. Slaveholders near Natchez, Mississippi, put down one such slave conspiracy early in 1861.

Although southerners on both sides thought that Lincoln intended to abolish slavery, his administration began the war committed to maintaining the institution where it already existed. The pressure of war and the actions of slaves brought about a change of course. Despite the federal government's initial promise to return runaways to the masters, slaves understood that an enemy of their oppressor was by definition their friend. Slaves' awareness of this fact manifested itself prior to Fort Sumter. In March 1861, eight slaves arrived at federally held Fort Pickens, Florida, in search of freedom. The trickle that began at Fort Pickens turned into a flood of refugees by the end of 1861 as slaves fled to Union lines whenever federal troops approached. Fugitives made themselves valuable to their hosts by offering their services as cooks, laundresses, teamsters, blacksmiths, and common laborers and thereby freeing up soldiers for the front lines. Conditions were especially acute in federal outposts in the lower South, like Fortress Monroe near Norfolk, Virginia, and the Sea Islands off South Carolina. These acts of self-emancipation forced Union commanders to decide between ignoring Lincoln's orders and sheltering the fugitives, who by the summer of 1862 numbered in the tens of thousands, or returning them to Confederate slaveholders against whom their troops were fighting. In May 1861, Fortress Monroe's commander, Benjamin Butler, a Massachusetts Free-Soil politician and 10-hour-day advocate, banned the return of so-called contraband, or runaway slaves, to their secessionist masters. Other Union commanders from Missouri to South Carolina made similar judgment calls.

These acts of slave self-emancipation and the success of Confederate arms at Bull Run, the Peninsula, and many other battles in 1861 and 1862 persuaded Lincoln that a limited war would not work. In the summer of 1862, the Republican Congress enacted laws aimed at punishing the Confederacy and promoting free labor. These included nullification of the Fugitive Slave Acts, orders to seize slaves from rebels, government employment of African-Americans as laborers and soldiers, and the abolition of slavery in Washington, DC. The most significant of these laws was the Second Confiscation Act, passed on July 17, 1862, which set free any slave who entered Union lines and stated that his or her owner was disloyal. (The First Confiscation Act, passed on August 6,

1861, freed only those slaves directly employed in the Confederate war effort and was harder to enforce.) Passage of the Second Confiscation Act showed that despite Lincoln's wish to appease moderate slaveholders, slaves themselves had forced the Union to fight for universal liberty.

For farmers and workers, Congress banned slavery in federal territory; increased access to higher education; established a progressive income tax; and passed the Homestead Act, which gave 160 acres of public land to any settler who stayed on it for five years. On January 1, 1863, the Emancipation Proclamation freed all slaves in rebel-held territory. Although two and a half years of war remained, Lincoln's Republican Party had replaced a war for reunion with a war for freedom.

Because of its smaller population and lack of industry, the Confederacy confronted shortages of troops and supplies sooner than did the Union. On April 16, 1862, the Confederate government enacted conscription for all fighting-age white men. The draft law gave slaveholders one exemption from conscription for every 20 slaves they owned. Rich men could also pay a bounty or hire a substitute to take their place. The law outraged yeomen farmers torn between the demands of the army and pressing affairs at home. Like the draft, the collapse of the southern economy hurt poor southerners the most. Prices rose six times faster than wages, and some basic commodities like salt were completely unavailable. A tax in kind and impressments of supplies exacerbated complaints that the Confederate cause was a "rich man's war and a poor man's fight."

Dissent took many forms. In Appalachia, Unionists and deserters fought as guerrillas. On April 2, 1863, in the Confederate capital of Richmond, a mob of hungry women, many of whom were married to men working in local iron foundries, rioted to protest high prices and scarcities and then looted local shops. Despite these protests and a steady loss of territory and lives to the Union war machine, the Confederacy remained a popular cause with most whites living inside its borders. That loyalty enabled Confederates to fight until April 1865, long after major battlefield defeats made Union victory inevitable.

Despite having more people and resources, shortages became acute in the North by 1863. Although not as severe as in the South, workers' wages rose by half while the cost of living doubled. The withdrawal of millions of men to the military failed to raise wages above prices because employers replaced human labor with machinery and hired women in place of men.

More problematic for northern labor was the federal Conscription Act of March 3, 1863. Like Confederate officials, federal authorities allowed conscripts to pay a $300 commutation fee or furnish a substitute. Protests took place across the North. The most severe disorder occurred in New York City from July 13 to 16. Mob attacks on draft officers addressed grievances about conscription, but destruction of an African-American orphanage and lynching of black men spoke to racial hatreds stoked by exaggerated reports of black strikebreaking and resentment against Union efforts in behalf of slaves.

In New York City and in draft violence in central Pennsylvania, Irish immigrants stood out as rioters. Despite the sensational tales of rioting dockworkers and Molly Maguires, a far larger number of Irish-Americans fought for the Union army (144,221) than took part in antiwar violence.

Economic hardship generated a surge in trade union organizing between 1863 and 1865. Fifteen new national unions were organized, although several disappeared before the war ended. More successful were citywide trade assemblies and local unions. The movement for shorter hours took off in 1863 when Ira Steward, a leader of the Machinists' and Blacksmiths' International Union, organized the Boston Eight Hour League.

The upsurge in union activity extended to women workers whose numbers increased during wartime. In 1863, New York's female garment cutters created the Working Women's Protective Union to fight abuses and lobby for shorter hours and better wages. Branches of the union formed in Boston, St. Louis, Indianapolis, Chicago, and Philadelphia.

Strikes over pay and hours brought retaliation from employers, who were forming their own associations and who relied on federal troops to suppress strikes. The longest and most repressive federal intervention in a labor dispute occurred in Pennsylvania's anthracite region. Troops also broke strikes at munitions factories, docks, and railroads.

As northern workers struggled to advance the condition of free labor, southern slaves fought to make freedom universal and to win full equality with other citizens. Black military service spurred this effort. Black abolitionists like Frederick Douglass recognized that the public equated military service with citizenship, and they pressed Congress to enroll African-Americans. The enlistment of 186,000 African-Americans (90% of whom had been slaves before the war) undermined northern resistance to emancipation. Black military service helped turn the tide on the battlefield, and African-American veterans became leaders in the postwar struggle for equality.

In 1865, the Thirteenth Amendment to the Constitution abolished slavery throughout the United States and focused national attention on wartime experiments over what free labor would mean for ex-slaves. Those wartime experiments followed three paths. The first was the military itself, which employed one fifth to one third of the black men in several Confederate states. In a second model of free labor, ex-slaves settled on land confiscated from their masters. Limited to a few such as coastal South Carolina and the Mississippi plantation of Confederate President Jefferson Davis, land titles proved hard to maintain but freedmen in these locales did manage to establish control over their own labor and households. The closest resemblance to slavery existed in the federally controlled lower Mississippi Valley, where commanders used a contract labor system that paid the minimum for subsistence and perpetuated features of the old regime, such as work gangs.

At war's end, northern workers and southern freedpeople had fought together for freedom and shared common goals. Both groups wanted to expand their rights as workers in the American economy, both looked to the state as an agent of progressive social change, and both supported equal rights in the abstract. However, the commitment of white farmers and workers to racial equality was limited, and on that rock would founder efforts to create a more inclusive labor movement.

The North's limited commitment to ex-slaves enabled former Confederates to regain power in southern states under the lenient policies of President Andrew Johnson, who succeeded Lincoln after he was assassinated on April 14, 1865. In the South, former Confederates tried to re-establish slavery through discriminatory laws known as the Black Codes, which prevented African-Americans from quitting work, pursuing nonfarm occupations, or otherwise exiting the world of staple-crop agriculture. The injustice of wartime foes subjugating allies and vicious race riots in New Orleans and Memphis outraged northern public opinion sufficiently to bring the so-called radical wing of the Republican Party to power in 1867.

At their most ambitious, Radical Republicans sought to instill free labor values into southern society. More modest plans included guaranteeing blacks equality before the law, reinvigorating the southern economy, keeping ex-Confederates from power, and building the Republican Party in the South. Workers joined in the radical coalition with northern industrialists, middle-class reformers, women's rights activists, and southern freedmen, who won the right to vote in 1870.

For a brief time, Radical Reconstruction transformed racial and economic relations in the South. African-Americans not only voted but elected themselves to high office. The Fourteenth Amendment, passed in 1868, protected their civil rights. Civil Rights Acts passed in 1870 and 1871 (also known as the Enforcement Acts) provided recourse to federal courts for civil rights violations. State governments built schools, outlawed segregation, eliminated vestiges of slavery like the whipping post, banished debtor's prison, and democratized government by ending property qualifications for voting and instituting the secret ballot.

This transformation of southern society was short-lived. By 1877, former Confederates acting through the Democratic Party and the paramilitary Ku Klux Klan had retaken, or "redeemed," all of the South's state governments. Radical Reconstruction collapsed for many reasons, chief among which was the failure of northern whites to sustain their commitment to former slaves. Conflict between workers and employers and quarrels internal to the working class undermined northern resolve.

Already evident in wartime strikes, conflict between labor and capital intensified as workers pressed for changes that had been postponed during the war. Hope that labor would reap the rewards of military victory informed the eight-hour-day leagues that spread across the North in 1865. Simultaneously, state and national labor federations grew. In 1866, the National Labor Union (NLU) held its first meeting and called for laws mandating an eight-hour workday. Shorter hours angered businessmen, who otherwise supported Radical Reconstruction. Employers and many Radical Republican politicians understood free labor to mean freedom from interference in the marketplace, be it the coercion of slave owner or the meddling of government. To legislate the hours of work struck them as the entering wedge for wholesale tampering with property rights. Wealthy northerners viewed efforts by southern Republicans to redistribute land through tax seizures as part of the same dangerous movement.

In 1872, these disaffected Republicans abandoned the radicals for the Liberal Republican movement. Liberals nominated onetime Free-Soiler Horace Greeley on a platform of fiscal retrenchment and clean government. Greeley lost to incumbent Ulysses S. Grant, but his bolt from the party hurt the Radicals.

Labor activists had also grown restive with Republicans. Despite his lenient treatment of the South, President Andrew Johnson signed an eight-hour-day law for some federal employees, and the Democratic Party railed against bankers and Wall Street financiers. Unable to win significant legislation from the Republican Congress, workers turned toward the Democrats and third parties.

Conflict among workers further eroded support for equal rights under Radical Reconstruction. Seeking labor's support, women's suffrage advocates attended the NLU convention of 1869. The convention refused a seat to women's rights leader Susan B. Anthony both because delegates, almost all of whom were men, opposed woman's suffrage and because the Working Women's Protective Association, which Anthony represented, had engaged in strikebreaking.

The NLU and other trade unions had similar conflicts with black labor. In 1869, the NLU seated its first African-American delegates but otherwise refused to cooperate with black workers who were excluded from most unions. In 1869, Isaac Myers, a Baltimore ship caulker, founded the Colored National Labor Union (CNLU) to coordinate labor reform on behalf of African-American workers in 18 states. Although NLU president Richard Trevellick attended the initial meeting of the CNLU, the existence of a separate African-American national federation signified the failure of postwar labor leaders to overcome prejudice within their ranks. Unlike numerous white trades unionists, Meyers and his colleagues backed the Republican Party, which had fought for freedom during the war and resisted the Democratic attack on Reconstruction.

Racial identity also prevented labor solidarity in California. By 1870, Chinese workers made up one quarter of the state's work force. White unions excluded Chinese workers and boycotted Chinese-made products. Shunned by their coworkers, in 1867, Chinese railroad workers struck for higher pay on the Transcontinental Railroad. Railroad executives contemplated importing African-American strikebreakers from the South, but after a week, work had resumed at the old rate.

Some white workers fought against racism. Alonzo Draper, leader of the Lynn shoe strike, headed a regiment of the United States Colored Troops. Abolitionist Wendell Phillips participated in the eight-hour movement. NLU president William Sylvis toured the South to recruit blacks. Despite these efforts, conflicts over race, class, and gender weakened the labor movement.

The Panic of 1873, the longest economic contraction prior to the 1930s, dealt another blow to organized labor and Reconstruction. With unemployment at 25% in New York City and riots by the jobless occurring there and elsewhere in the industrial heartland, northern interest in helping the South's poor dried up.

In 1873 and 1874, strikes occurred on railroads and in northeastern textile mills. In 1875, Pennsylvania miners waged a long, unsuccessful strike that ended with the trial of the Molly Maguires. In July 1877, the Great Strike on the railroads—the first national strike in U.S. history—shut down several major cities and

once again brought labor into armed conflict with government troops. Already opposed to strikes, the NLU was led by these events further away from workplace activism. While middle-class reformers tried to make the NLU into a political party, some labor reformers gravitated toward socialism and currency reform, a remedy that also appealed to farmers hit hard by the Panic.

Other labor activists gravitated toward tightly organized semisecret unions like the Knights of St. Crispin, a shoemakers' organization, and the Noble and Holy Order of the Knights of Labor, which originated among Philadelphia garment makers in 1868. In 1870, the Knights of St. Crispin boasted 50,000 members, the largest of any contemporary union, and they won a strike in the old battleground of Lynn. An employer counterattack and the Panic of 1873 did away with the Crispins. The Knights of Labor, on the other hand, survived to carry forward the traditions of labor reform.

Cut off from the labor movement, former slaves in the South adjusted to Reconstruction's decline. Immediately after the war, the Freedmen's Bureau, an offshoot of the federal military, negotiated labor contracts between ex-slaves and their old masters. Over time, the contract system broke down because of cash shortages and resistance by freedpeople to white employer supervision. In its place, black families agreed to pay the landlord with a share of the crop in exchange for use of the land. From the perspective of former slaves, sharecropping, as this system was known, limited contact with white employers and gave blacks day-to-day control of their labor. Landlords opted for sharecropping because it solved the problem of cash scarcity and because tenant debt could be manipulated to keep black labor bound to the land. Redeemer governments passed crop lien laws to ensure that indebted tenants would remain in place.

Instead of sharecropping, some African-Americans, usually younger men, continued to contract for wages and migrated between plantations. Others moved to the cities of the South in search of jobs and relief from rural hardships. Southern manufacturers, however, routinely refused to hire blacks, and many found the cities no better than the countryside. Reluctantly, some African-Americans abandoned the South. In 1879, the Exodusters, a movement of 15,000 former slaves, migrated from the Mississippi Valley to Kansas.

By 1876, only three southern state governments remained in Republican hands. These were also the only states still to have federal troops defending African-American access to the courts and ballot box. Republican nominee Rutherford B. Hayes eked out an electoral college win over Democrat Samuel

Tilden, who won the popular vote. A stalemate lasted into 1877. Republicans who had already abandoned most of the South gave up their final outposts. They did so as much out of exhaustion with Reconstruction as from any deal cut with Democrats. Reconstruction's defeat also spelled defeat for the egalitarian promise of free soil, free labor, and free men, for which northern labor had gone to war in 1861.

FRANK TOWERS

References and Further Reading

Berlin, Ira, et al. *Free at Last: A Documentary History of Slavery, Freedom, and the Civil War.* New York: The New Press, 1992.

Bernstein, Iver. *The New York City Draft Riots: Their Significance for American Society and Politics in the Age of the Civil War.* New York: Oxford University Press 1990.

Foner, Eric. *Reconstruction: America's Unfinished Revolution, 1863–1877.* New York: Harper and Row, 1988.

Freehling, William W. *The South vs. the South: How Anti-Confederate Southerners Shaped the Course of the Civil War.* New York: Oxford University Press 2002.

Hahn, Steven. *A Nation under Our Feet: Black Political Struggles in the Rural South from Slavery to the Great Migration.* Cambridge, MA: Harvard University Press, 2003.

Huston, James L. *Calculating the Value of the Union: Slavery, Property Rights, and the Economic Origins of the Civil War.* Chapel Hill: The University of North Carolina Press, 2003.

Johnson, Russell L. *Warriors into Workers: The Civil War and the Formation of Urban-Industrial Society in a Northern City.* New York: Fordham University Press, 2003.

Kenney, Kevin. *Making Sense of the Molly Maguires.* New York: Oxford University Press, 1998.

Laurie, Bruce. *Artisans into Workers: Labor in Nineteenth-Century America.* New York: Hill and Wang, 1989.

Levine, Bruce. *The Spirit of 1848: German Immigrants, Labor Conflict, and the Coming of the Civil War.* Urbana: University of Illinois Press, 1992.

Montgomery, David. *Beyond Equality: Labor and the Radical Republicans, 1862–1872.* New York: Alfred A. Knopf, 1967.

———. *Citizen Worker: The Experience of Workers in the United States with Democracy and the Free Market in the Nineteenth Century.* Cambridge: Cambridge University Press, 1993.

Palladino, Grace. *Another Civil War: Labor, Capital, and the State in the Anthracite Regions of Pennsylvania, 1840–1868.* 1990. Reprint. New York: Fordham University Press, 2006.

Paludan, Phillip Shaw. *"A People's Contest": The Union and the Civil War, 1861–1865.* New York: Harper and Row, 1988.

Saville, Julie. *The Work of Reconstruction: From Slave Labor to Wage Labor in South Carolina, 1860–1870.* Cambridge: Cambridge University Press, 1996.

Saxton, Alexander. *The Indispensable Enemy: Labor and the Anti-Chinese Movement in California.* 1971. Reprint. Berkeley: University of California Press, 1995.

Stanley, Amy Dru. *From Bondage to Contract: Wage Labor, Marriage, and the Market in the Age of Slave Emancipation.* Cambridge: Cambridge University Press, 1998.

See also **Abolitionism; African-Americans; Chinese Laborers' Strike on the Transcontinental Railroad (1867); Free-Soilism; Fugitive Slave Acts; Germans; Greenback-Labor Party; Irish; Knights of Labor; Knights of St. Crispin and the Daughters of St. Crispin; Know-Nothing Party; Lynn Shoe Strike (1860); National Labor Union; Railroads; Railroad Strikes (1877); Sharecropping and Tenancy; Steward, Ira; Strikebreaking; Sylvis, William; Thirteenth Amendment; Trevellick, Richard; Tubman, Harriet**

CLAYTON ANTITRUST ACT (1914)

In 1914, in response to President Woodrow Wilson's support of the antitrust movement, Congress passed the Clayton Antitrust Act. The Act was a weak attempt to regulate the growing monopolies that gave a small number of businessmen immense power over the marketplace. Labor leaders' initial celebrations over the legislation were quickly replaced with disappointment as the Act and its implementation failed to provide meaningful reforms.

In the last decades of the nineteenth century, industrial workers, tradesmen, and reformers protested an economy that privileged the wealthy and disadvantaged the laboring classes. In the 1880s, they fostered a movement in opposition to trust building, the practice that allowed a small number of companies to gain disproportionate control over the economy. These trusts, broadly defined, included those business owners who forged agreements with owners of similar businesses in order to eliminate other competitors and monopolize the market. A few powerful companies, like Standard Oil, took control of businesses that supplied all the services involved in their industry, providing them with an advantage over less-integrated competitors. The antitrust movement campaigned for legislative reforms that would outlaw such activities.

In 1890, Congress passed the Sherman Antitrust Act as an initial measure to regulate certain business activities. The Sherman Act attempted to make it illegal to conspire or make contracts to form trusts that restrained free trade and commerce between states or with foreign nations. The Act, however, was vague, failing even to define its terms, and the probusiness-leaning Supreme Court rendered the Act ineffective. Congress failed to respond, but workers, who suffered from low wages, long hours, and dangerous working conditions that were the effects of these trusts, organized and went on strike.

Employers used the courts and physical violence to quash workers' protests. Business owners increasingly secured injunctions from the courts to prohibit unions from engaging in strikes and called on the police and militia to force protesters to disperse. The labor leaders who challenged these injunctions, including Eugene Debs in the 1894 Pullman strike, were found in contempt of court and jailed. Labor leaders responded by intensifying their campaign for additional legislation that would regulate against trusts and grant laborers the right to organize and act to protect their interests.

With slow, but growing, administrative support, under Presidents Theodore Roosevelt, William Howard Taft, and Woodrow Wilson, the antitrust movement made some tentative gains in the first decades of the twentieth century. AFL President Samuel Gompers and others lobbied the Congress, asking for antitrust laws that would outlaw trusts but exempt labor unions. In 1914, Congress finally acted. It passed the Clayton Antitrust Act ostensibly to outlaw trusts, which Gompers optimistically and incorrectly dubbed the working people's Magna Carta. Congress also passed the Federal Trade Commission Act, which created a commission authorized to regulate competition, charge violations, and gather trade information.

The Clayton Act tentatively attempted to fix loopholes in the Sherman Act. It prohibited pricing agreements that created monopolies and restrained trade, interlocking directorates in large corporations, firm acquisitions of stock in a competitor, and contracts that required purchasers to refrain from dealing with the sellers' competitors. The Act authorized holding officials of the corporation individually responsible for antitrust violations. Further, it exempted labor organizations from the antitrust restraints, explicitly providing that labor unions did not constitute unlawful combinations in restraint of trade. The Act, however, left ambiguous what union activities were permissible, allowing for the possibility of judicial regulation of labor organizations.

The federal courts used the ambiguities of the Act to strike down many of the regulations on business and to impose regulations on labor unions. Supporting these lower court decisions, in 1921, the U.S. Supreme Court ruled that the provisions of the Clayton Act did not impede the court's power to grant an injunction against labor unions. While the Court did acknowledge that laborers had the right to unionize, it ruled that any strikes or boycotts they conducted that impeded the flow of interstate commerce were illegal. As a result, employers continued to seek injunctions against labor unions to prevent strikes and boycotts, and courts continued to uphold them into the 1930s. Not until the New Deal and the passage of the Norris-LaGuardia Act in 1932 did the government provide meaningful antitrust policies and laws.

GWEN HOERR JORDAN

References and Further Reading

Ernst, Daniel R. *Lawyers against Labor: From Individual Rights to Corporate Liberalism*. Urbana: University of Illinois Press, 1995.

Forbath, William E. *Law and the Shaping of the American Labor Movement*. Cambridge, MA: Harvard University Press, 1991.

Franfurter, Felix, and Nathan Greene. *The Labor Injunction*. Glouster, MA: P. Smith, 1963, 1930.

Hattam, Victoria C. *Labor Visions and State Power: The Origins of Business Unionism in the United States*. Princeton, NJ: Princeton University Press, 1993.

CLERICAL WORK AND OFFICE WORK

Clerical work and office work are categories of white-collar work found in business offices and the administrative divisions of manufacturing establishments. Attached to the bureaucratic and record-keeping functions of capitalism, clerical and office work expanded with the growth of manufacturing, financial, commercial, and other economic activities over the last two hundred years. Specific jobs within the category of clerical and office work have changed considerably during U.S. history. In the earliest years of the United States, educated, well-connected young men with aspirations for advancements in the world worked as clerks in business, law, and commercial establishments and could have realistic expectations of rising through the ranks. Throughout the dynamic and volatile economy of the late nineteenth century, office and clerical work were a part of a growing service sector. Women took newly created positions such as typewriting. Even though women considered office work better than factory labor, they could not expect that their positions would provide advancement within the firm. Throughout the twentieth century, the clerical and office work sector grew as firms increasingly applied technology to office practice and employed women to do the work.

Most scholarship on clerical work and office work appeared after World War II. C. Wright Mills and Harry Braverman first alerted academics and the public to the situation, experience, and plight of the white-collar worker doing clerical and office work. Those interested in the world of work realized that this sector of the labor force could not be ignored. In addition to the growth in the size of the service sector generally, and the clerical sector specifically, scholars such as Mills and Braverman focused on the changing nature of twentieth-century capitalism and the alienating nature of some work in the clerical sector. Writing in 1951, Mills described a "new," albeit diverse, white-collar middle class emerging in the post-World War II period. Almost a quarter of a century later, Braverman described the ways in which this new clerical sector had become like factory work. Building upon Braverman's work, labor historians and women's and gender studies scholars from the 1970s on turned their attention to office and clerical work because it was recognized as the quintessential female job of the twentieth century. So powerfully had this job become gender typed, that when a man took the position, describing the gender was necessary; he was not a secretary, but a *male* secretary. Scholarship has focused on (1) the effects of technology and scientific management on office and clerical work and those who perform it; (2) the relationship between women and office work; (3) unionization; and (4) economic transformations of late twentieth-century capitalism.

Office and Clerical Work in the Nineteenth Century

The earliest clerical and office work fell into four categories: bookkeepers, office boys, copyists, and clerks. Basic literacy and mathematical skills, and a good hand, were the only skills required; however, since these were considered entry-level positions, employers hired only young men from good families. During the early nineteenth century, when firms and their bureaucratic requirements were small, record-keeping work was modest. Each business required unique skills from its male office staff. Office boys were younger, newer entrants into the firm with no expectation to move up through the ranks. Bookkeepers were in charge of important financial information and transactions and might use this job to improve their position in the firm. The category of clerk might contain a great variety of positions such as postal clerk, billing clerk, shopping clerk, railroad clerk, or hotel clerk, obviously contingent upon the enterprise. Men with skills in shorthand took stenographic transcriptions for trials and legal documents, depositions, and verbatim accounts of speeches. Men took clerk jobs in the growing bureaucracies in Washington DC as a way to enter a lifetime career of public service.

Throughout the nineteenth century, men not only filled a growing number of jobs in this category of employment but also availed themselves of opportunities to train for a variety of office jobs. To meet the demand for office workers, private business colleges appeared in many large cities during the middle of the nineteenth century. Before this sort of training and education was available in the public schools, these institutions provided basic business training to young, ambitious men who did not have family or business connections. These employment and educational opportunities were attractive to young men. According to Helen Lefkowitz Horowitz, in *Rereading Sex*, the young male clerk living and working alone in the city was "surrounded by a new 'sporting culture' with its many attractions." The city's amusements, which included taverns, theaters, and houses of prostitution, were nonworking equivalents to a masculine work space in the office. Some male office workers, like their brothers in the skilled trades, punctuated their workdays with trips to the office building's saloon for a quick shot. More respectable members of the clerking class could partake of leisure activities and housing provided by the Young Men's Christian Association and similar services provided to launch middle-class lives in the city.

Women and Clerical Work

The Civil War started the women's story in clerical and office work. When young men employed in government bureaucratic offices left their jobs to fight during the Civil War, women were called upon to fill the positions previously taken only by men in federal agencies and bureaucracies. Once women had broken through this important barrier and demonstrated that they had the skills and ability to do the work, there was no turning back. Starting in the 1870s, women enrolled in private business colleges, demanded clerical training courses in the public schools, took a large percentage of new positions available, and participated in conversations in trade journals and associations, asserting their right to take this new occupational opportunity for women. Between 1870 and 1930, women's share of the clerical labor force increased from less than 3% to over 50%. In Chicago in 1890, for example, roughly the same percentage of the male and female labor force, roughly 9%, worked at the 41,000 office positions. By 1930, when there were 238,000 office jobs, women dominated the jobs numerically, and over a third of all women in the labor force (and only 11% of the men) were doing office work.

The appearance of women in the office coincided with major changes in office work. The number of jobs in clerical and office work increased dramatically. Many new jobs were in existing categories, such as bookkeeping and clerkships, but some of the increase was from the creation of new jobs in the business office. The most important new position was the stenographer-typist, an office worker who took stenographic transcription of a text and typed it. This position resulted from the invention and widespread use of the typewriter and the pairing of this technology with stenography. This increased the educational and technological requirements of the copyist position. This office job also occupied a different position in the hierarchy of the firm. Stenographer-typists, later called secretaries, could be found working for one boss as a personal assistant, or in some of the larger firms, could be found working in a large, factorylike office with others doing similar work, later called a typing pool. Even though this was a new position that required new skills, because it was filled by young, white, native-born women, it was no longer a stepping-stone to advancement in the firm.

The growing importance of bureaucratic tasks and the growing numbers of individuals doing office work prompted many firms to develop a more efficient system of work. Magazines like *System* (1902–1930) shared scientific and practical information on how to improve office practice. Mechanical engineer William Henry Leffingwell applied the scientific management techniques of Frederick Winslow Taylor to clerical work. Certain office jobs resembled factory work, with the application of a variety of office machines. The adaptation of new technologies to the business world created new positions such as the switchboard operator and telephone receptionist. Women found jobs ranging from the exclusive private secretary to the lowly file clerk. Men were still found in certain types of office jobs, such as postal clerk and bookkeepers. Although they might still aspire to work their way up from the mailroom, women's career aspirations were limited to the clerical occupations themselves.

This limitation on women's advancement through the ranks of a firm, now known as the glass ceiling, was as much a result of the separation of many office jobs from male seniority lines as it was from occupational barriers attached to many office jobs. These occupational barriers resulted from assumptions about the sex, race, age, and class position of those taking office jobs at this time. Many companies would only hire young, native-born, white, and in most cases, Protestant women. Even though many young, second-generation working-class women saw a job in an office as a step up from factory work, clerical jobs were not open to all women. Individual firms might not hire African-Americans (the small number of African-American businesses certainly did), Catholics, Jews, certain ethnic groups, older women, married women, or women with children. The "marriage bar" for women was particularly powerful in office work before World War II. According to Sharon Hartmann

Strom, in *Beyond the Typewriter*, "the marriage bar was both a cultural convention and an arbitrary workplace requirement. The cultural norm before World War II was to expect that when women married, they would retire to home, especially if they had children." The marriage bar kept women's work separated from men's; it justified paying women less and kept women's wages low; and it supported the family wage ideal—the goal that men should earn enough to support a family.

It would be a mistake, however, to minimize the importance of the appearance of this occupational option to women at this time. Rationalized and restricted, office work still held promise to a group of women with limited occupational opportunities. Office work was clean, light, relatively well-paid employment for women. During the first decades of the twentieth century, women who took office jobs in the city, called businesswomen, participated in redefining the gendered nature of work and public space. Office work, previously a male job, took place in what had been considered male space, the business office. The prospect of women entering this work space, as well as a variety of spaces in the city, enlivened a conversation about women in the city. In an era when commentators were already concerned about "women adrift" and the "white slave trade," single women taking public transportation, striding unchaperoned on the streets, taking elevators in the new skyscrapers, and working side by side with unrelated men were not always considered acceptable. The reformer Jane Addams, in *A New Conscience and an Ancient Evil*, believed that female office workers, who were often the only women in their offices, were particularly susceptible to the temptation of becoming fallen women. If some women felt constrained by imagined restrictions or fear, many hundreds of thousands more demonstrated women's ability to move about the city and do this type of work by simply doing it. Progressive reformers of all types responded by providing a variety of services to girls training to become or working as office workers in the city by providing city lunch rooms, boarding houses, vocational educational and placement services, organized leisure activities, and professional organizations. Female office workers and their allies made the city and its skyscrapers their own.

Representations of the Office Worker

After Herman Melville immortalized the purgatory of the middle-aged man left behind at the clerk's desk in his short story "Bartleby the Scrivener" (1853), most representations of clerical and office workers were female. Female office workers were always interesting characters in U.S. popular culture. As Sinclair Lewis told the story of the life of a female office worker in *The Job: An American Novel (1917)*, he pondered the dilemmas of the modern, twentieth-century woman. The very earliest films, shorts shown in nickelodeons, featured female clerical workers in a variety of sensationalized and comprising positions. The plots of these films tapped into the audience's uncertainty about girls taking these positions. The female office worker could just as often appear as a young girl in an unwholesome environment, the victim of a predatory male boss, or a young, beautiful vamp seducing her boss away from his usually old-fashioned, battle-ax wife. During the 1920s, as the young, single, white, Protestant girl became a more regular feature in the downtown business office, her screen persona changed. During the flapper era, the office worker on film became the good girl next door trying to make her way in the world. She was thoroughly modern in her appearance and behavior but used new feminine wiles to get the rich, handsome husband at the end. Any controversy associated with women doing office work was resolved by the 1930s, when films such as *The Office Wife* (1930) promoted the message that good office workers make good wives.

In the postwar period, representations of female office workers reflected ongoing renegotiations of women's positions in the world of work. In *Desk Set* (1957), office worker Katherine Hepburn sparred with the man hoping to computerize the office, Spencer Tracy, about the indispensability of women over machines in every aspect of life. Influenced by the feminist movement of the 1960s and 1970s, the film *Nine to Five* (1980), with Lilly Tomlin, Jane Fonda, and Dolly Parton as office workers in the same office, humorously raised the issues of the glass ceiling and sexual harassment. This film also explored the importance of collective support and sisterhood among office workers to bring about change. *Working Girl* (1988) presented an ambitious female office worker, who not only bests her female Ivy League boss in business, but also steals her boyfriend. Once again, office work (and some very well-chosen outfits) was the recipe for female success and happiness.

Recent representations of office workers, male and female, take up the alienating and absurd nature of modern bureaucratic life. The popular comic strip *Dilbert* and the BBC situation comedy *The Office* (recently remade by a U.S. network) both present the office as the perfect setting for the theater of the absurd. Sitting in a cubicle, talking to disembodied voices at the other end of a wireless phone, e-mailing countless, faceless individuals throughout the globe, and engaging in meaningless rounds of work with no clear authority or purpose have become a symbol of alienation in the modern world.

Unionization

The mainstream labor movement has always considered office workers, particularly female office workers, difficult to unionize. The leaders of the dominant craft-oriented American Federation of Labor supported the family wage ideal and considered office workers, and other female workers, as only temporarily in the labor force. Nevertheless, there have been periods in U.S. history when office and clerical workers in many different industries have been successfully organized into unions. The changes in office practice at the start of the century and technological changes after World War II provided ripe conditions for workplace organizing, while feminism provided the ideology to justify it.

During the first decades of the twentieth century, the Women's Trade Union League (WTUL)—an AFL-affiliated organization dedicated to organizing and supporting women workers in a number of the largest U.S. cities—was only moderately successful in organizing office workers into unions. For example, the Chicago WTUL-affiliated Stenographers' and Typists' Association had a small membership of less than 200 in 1911. Chicago's civil service employees belonged to the more successful Office Employee Association that had a membership approaching one thousand by 1920. Female progressives and labor advocates undoubtedly perceived exploited female factory and sweatshop workers as more deserving of their attention than white-collar workers; and female office workers may have been less interested in participating in what they considered working-class activities.

The creation of the Congress of Industrial Organizations (CIO) and an upsurge in labor activism, often undertaken by communists and socialists in the labor movement during the late 1930s, brought about new efforts on behalf of office workers. According to Sharon Hartman Strom, the CIO chartered three office worker unions in 1937—the United Federal Workers, the State, County, and Municipal Workers of America, and the United Office and Professional Workers of America. They did well in the 1930s and 1940s but suffered during the communist purges in the 1950s. The AFL chartered its own union, the Office and Professional Employees Union, in 1944. Bringing together a number of locals in the private and public sector, it began with 22,000 members and today boasts 145,000 members. This union, however, often had male leaders, and this may have made it less appealing to the millions of female office workers in the United States in the era after World War II. Large industrial unions like the Steel Workers and particularly the United Automobile Workers (UAW) sought to organize white-collar workers in their industries. The United Automobile Workers, for example, began to pay attention to the white-collar employees as early as 1941, although certain large employers such as General Motors (GM) and Ford resisted any attempt to organize office staffs. With the creation in 1962 of the TOP (Technical, Office, and Professional) Department, the UAW began to make some progress toward organizing office staff. By the end of the 1960s, TOP had more than 80,000 members. The UAW also led efforts to organize office workers on college and university campuses.

The feminist movement of the late 1960s and 1970s inspired many female office workers to create new organizations to improve their work lives. Fed up with dress codes, sexual harassment, and a lack of respect and professional behavior at work, female office workers chanted slogans such as "Respect, Raises, and Roses" and formed new organizations like 9to5. While this brought a greater measure of fairness and equity to many work settings, the benefits of this activity were uneven and spotty. Office workers in public-sector workplaces (and at many colleges and universities) joined or created good unions. Gains in the private sector were spottier.

Recent Trends in Office Work: Technology and the Contingent Worker

Technology has altered office work throughout history. The invention of the typewriter during the 1870s provided the impetus for the creation of the job women took as they entered the office—the stenographer-typist. The term "typewriter" was used to refer to both the machine and the young female who operated it. Scholars often claimed that women could take this job because the new invention was gender neutral. This explanation, however, ignored the very powerful associations that already existed between young, white, middle-class familiarity with the piano keyboard and typewriting as a transferable skill. Young women with musical skills were, in fact, recruited for early typewriter work. A variety of office machines appeared in the business office after the typewriter, but the most important technological change in office practice occurred after World War II

with the application of computer technologies to a variety of clerical jobs. Keypunch operation was an early data processing function that required mind-numbing repetition and attention to detail. The electric typewriter contributed to the creation of the typing pool. Word processing systems appeared in the 1970s, and personal computers and terminals replaced many typewriters at workspaces. As more sophisticated machines came into the office, office workers needed greater technological skills. Scholars have noted that this has not always translated into any increase in pay or general recognition of these new skills. Office workers with extensive knowledge of new technologies are often classified as office managers and executive assistants. Those with limited or no technological skills are found in routinized and less-well-paid clerical duties. Contrary to dire predictions of the end of office work in the paperless office, office work has continued to change with new technologies and bureaucratic organization.

The woman behind the typewriter changed along with the machinery. During the 1950s, the age and race of female office workers began to change. Older and married women entered the clerical labor force after World War II, many returning to the labor force once their children were in school or out of the house. These middle-aged workers often claimed that the extra income allowed their families to send children to college or to buy a second car or vacation home. Marriage and pregnancy bars persisted until the 1970s, but many employers dropped these employment restrictions earlier. Many employers also began to hire African-American women. Discriminatory practices certainly persisted, but in many large companies, the first inroads of women of color in office work began in the post-World War II period.

Late twentieth-century changes in capitalism had a profound effect on office work. Shifts to the service and information technology sectors profoundly altered fundamental ideas about work. In an attempt to become lean and flexible, many firms increased the amount of temporary workers in their labor force. By using a greater percentage of temporary workers, companies could reduce benefit and health-care costs. Advances in technology have allowed some firms to rediscover homework. Outfitted with a PC at home, a worker, who was usually a woman with young children, could perform many paper-processing functions in her own home and at times that accommodated her schedule. This "electronic cottage" simultaneously evoked the sweatshop revisited and the solution to the post-feminist middle-class woman who wanted to have it all. That clerical homework has not completely replaced office employment is a testament to the isolation and exploitation of homework. Some firms have even found it profitable to contract out or "outsource" whole sectors of office practice, such as accounting, bookkeeping, or billing departments. All of these so-called contingent workers (temporary, homeworkers, outsourced) are a growing part of the clerical and office labor force.

Recent Trends in Office Work: Globalization

These technological and organizational changes in the nature of office and clerical work have created conditions allowing for the outsourcing of contingent workers overseas. In English-speaking nations in the Caribbean, India, and elsewhere, firms can employ cheaper workers for a whole series of front-office tasks (such as telemarketing) and back-office tasks (such as data entry and processing). The globalization of white-collar jobs has even provoked a recent congressional hearing, as many fear that white-collar work will suffer the same fate as manufacturing jobs. This will surely bring great change and, in some cases, hardship to workers in the United States. The effects on workers overseas, however, are still unfolding. The sociologist Jasmin Mirza studied the implications on gender roles as lower-middle-class Muslim women in Lahore, Pakistan, took jobs as receptionists, secretaries, telephone operators, draftswomen, computer operators, and designers during the last decade. Even though the number taking these jobs was small and the impact was still limited, this scholar concludes that women's appearance in the office and other public spaces challenged existing gender roles and expanded possibilities for women. Despite the real exploitation that office and clerical workers suffer as a result of new technologies and work arrangements, the transformative potential of women seeking white-collar jobs in offices in the city should never be underestimated.

LISA MICHELLE FINE

References and Further Reading

Addams, Jane. *A New Conscience and an Ancient Evil.* New York: The MacMillian Company, 1912.
Aron, Cindy Sondik. *Ladies and Gentlemen of the Civil Service: Middle-Class Workers in Victorian America.* New York: Oxford University Press, 1987.
Barnard, John. *American Vanguard: The United Auto Workers during the Reuther Years, 1935–1970.* Detroit: Wayne State University Press, 2004.
Boris, Eileen. *Home to Work: Motherhood and the Politics of Industrial Homework in the United States.* New York: Cambridge University Press, 1994.
Braverman, Harry. *Labor and Monopoly Capital: The Degradation of Work in the Twentieth Century.* New York: Monthly Review Press, 1974.
Cobble, Dorothy Sue. *The Other Women's Movement: Workplace Justice and Social Rights in Modern America.* Princeton, NJ: Princeton University Press, 2004.
Costello, Cynthia B. *We're Worth It!: Women and Collective Action in the Insurance Workplace.* Urbana: University of Illinois Press, 1991.
Davies, Margery W. *Woman's Place Is at the Typewriter: Office Work and Office Workers, 1870–1939.* Philadelphia: Temple University Press, 1982.
DeVault, Ileen A. *Sons and Daughters of Labor: Class and Clerical Workers in Turn-of-the-Century Pittsburgh.* Ithaca, NY: Cornell University Press, 1990.
Fine, Lisa M. *The Souls of the Skyscraper: Female Clerical Workers in Chicago, 1870–1930.* Philadelphia: Temple University Press, 1990.
Finley, Joseph E. *White Collar Union: The Story of the OPEIU and Its People.* New York: Octagon Books, 1975.
"The Globalization of White-Collar Jobs: Can America Lose These Jobs and Still Prosper?" Hearing before the Committee on Small Business, House of Representatives, One Hundred and Eighth Congress, First Session, Washington DC, June 18, 2003. Serial No.108-20. Washington, DC: U.S. Government Printing Office, 2003.
Horowitz, Helen Lefkowitz. *Rereading Sex: Battles over Sexual Knowledge and Suppression in Nineteenth-Century America.* New York: Vintage Books, 2002.
Kwolek-Folland, Angel. *Engendering Business: Men and Women in the Corporate Office, 1870–1930.* Baltimore: Johns Hopkins University Press, 1994.
Mills, C. Wright. *White Collar: The American Middle Classes.* New York: Oxford University Press, 1951.
Mizra, Jasmin. *Between Chaddor and the Market: Female Office Workers in Lahore.* Oxford, England: Oxford University Press, 2002.
Rotella, Elyce J. *From Home to Office: U.S. Women at Work, 1870–1930.* Ann Arbor, MI: UMI Research Press, 1981.
Snyder, Carl Dean. *White-Collar Workers and the UAW.* Urbana: University of Illinois Press, 1973.
Strom, Sharon Hartman. *Beyond the Typewriter: Gender, Class, and the Origins of Modern American Office Work, 1900–1930.* Urbana: University of Illinois Press, 1992.
———. "Challenging 'Woman's Place': Feminism, the Left, and Industrial Unionism in the 1930s." *Feminist Studies* 9, no. 2 (Summer 1983): 359–386.

COAL MINING
See **Mining, Coal**

COALITION OF BLACK TRADE UNIONISTS

The Coalition of Black Trade Unionists (CBTU) was formed in 1972 when more than 1,200 African-American union officials and rank-and-file members gathered in Chicago, Illinois, for two days to discuss the direction of the American Federation of

Labor-Congress of Industrial Organizations (AFL-CIO) and the role black workers could play in the larger labor movement. The initial meeting, which took place on September 23–24 at the LaSalle Hotel, was attended by representatives from 37 unions, making it the single largest gathering of black unionists in the history of the American labor movement.

Although the formation of the CBTU was the product of the frustration black trade unionists had felt within the labor movement, especially since the merger of the AFL-CIO in 1955, the catalyst was the neutral position the AFL-CIO Executive Council took in the 1972 presidential election between incumbent Richard Nixon and George McGovern. The five prominent black labor leaders issued the call for the first conference immediately after George Meany, president of the AFL-CIO, and the Executive Council ignored the voice of black American workers by endorsing neutrality at their meeting held in August. Those who objected to the Executive Council pronouncement thought it was tantamount to contributing to the re-election of Nixon. In the call that went out for the CBTU conference, the five leaders noted their concern over the upcoming presidential election, making clear their wish that George McGovern, the candidate of the Democratic Party, win the presidency. In the minds of CBTU leaders, the re-election of Richard Nixon would continue economic circumstances that did not favor the interests of labor. In particular, CBTU leaders cited continued unemployment, inflated prices, frozen wages, and the appointment of judges on the U.S. Supreme Court who would be insensitive to the rights of workers, minorities, and the poor. Finally, they were convinced that the election of Nixon over McGovern would result in the reversal or neglect of civil rights. The five who called the initial meeting were William Lucy, secretary-treasurer of the American Federation of State, County, and Municipal Employees; Charles Hayes, vice president of the Amalgamated Meatcutters and Butcher Workmen of North America; Nelson Jack Edwards, vice president of the United Auto Workers; Cleveland Robinson, president of the Distributive Workers of America, District 65; and William Simons, president of the American Federation of Teachers in Washington, DC, Local 6.

Charles Hayes, the first black trade unionist ever elected to Congress, chaired the meeting and mobilized those gathered by noting the need to create a structure for black and minority unionists that reached beyond the November elections. Hayes suggested an organization of the trade union movement that would give guidance and direction as well as assist minorities in overcoming some of the obstacles that black workers faced within the ranks of organized labor. Hayes, in an interview with this author, discussed hurdles placed before black labor by both employers and union officials. Thus, while the presidential election provided the moment for forming a new organization, the momentum was generated by the frustration many African-American trade unionists felt as minority players within the labor movement.

During the 1960s, black trade union officials had worked to end institutionalized racism on the job and in the unions through the Negro American Labor Council (NALC). But that organization, headed initially by A. Philip Randolph, was considered by many to be too inflexible and entrenched in the larger union bureaucracy by the early 1970s. Many of the leaders who called for the formation of the CBTU were activists in the NALC who thought that organization was shackled by the aura of Randolph. The CBTU activists, many of whom were once loyal followers of Randolph, felt Randolph was too comfortable with the status quo. One of these activists and Randolph's successor as head of the NALC, Cleveland Robinson, pledged NALC's resources to the fledgling organization of CBTU. Another, Charles Hayes, said he thought Randolph's moment as the voice for black labor had passed by the late 1960s. While acknowledging the incredible debt African-American labor owed to Randolph, Hayes was anxious to form an organization that would try to utilize the power of the nearly three million black workers in organized labor.

The vision the five organizers carried to Chicago was to make the labor movement more relevant to the needs and aspirations of black and poor workers. The emergence of the League of Revolutionary Black Workers in Detroit in the late 1960s highlighted the question of discrimination and lack of black representation within the labor movement. The CBTU liked to characterize its formation as the "awakening" of "the sleeping giant." The CBTU held its first convention five months later in May 1973 in Washington, DC.

There was opposition to the new organization. Bayard Rustin, an African-American colleague of Randolph from the 1940s, thought the CBTU was unnecessary. Rustin claimed that the new organization was redundant because, as he told *The New York Times*, black trade unionists had already assumed leadership roles in their unions and in their communities.

Accomplishments

The CBTU declared that its goal as a progressive forum for black workers was to help connect issues within unions to those within the black community. Through the years, the CBTU has been active in promoting black leadership within the union, advocating concerns of women workers, and mobilizing labor around human rights issues. The CBTU has led efforts to open more union leadership positions to African-American trade unionists, enhancing the viability of the labor movement through inclusion and diversity.

Since its first gathering, the CBTU has been influenced by the inclusion of African-American women. Between 35% and 40% of the 1,200 delegates who attended the initial 1972 meeting were black women. The CBTU's first executive committee was made up of five women. In 1982, the CBTU Executive Council organized the National Women's Committee as a way to form educational workshops focusing on teaching women how to play a leadership role within the union and address issues important to the larger community.

Political action has been high on the CBTU's agenda since its inception. Charles Hayes, as both a representative in Congress and founding member of the steering committee, was prominent in organizing the Congressional Black Caucus. Hayes was also a leader in the successful effort to elect Harold Washington as mayor of Chicago in 1983. Hayes and thousands of volunteers from the labor movement raised money and got out the vote in what was a very close election. The CBTU's efforts helped with the appointment of U.S. Labor Secretary Alexis Herman, the first African-American to hold that cabinet position.

The CBTU also added its weight to human rights causes, both in the United States and around the world, especially in Africa, Latin America, and the Caribbean. Domestically, it has been a voice for equal representation for residents of the District of Columbia. While taking a stand against Pinochet's military junta in Chile and the Abacha junta in Nigeria, it supported Caribbean workers exploited by American firms opposed to unions. The CBTU was in the vanguard with its positions against the apartheid state in South Africa. In 1974, it was the first American labor organization to pass strong resolutions calling for an economic boycott of South Africa, and CBTU President William Lucy was a founder of the Free South Africa Movement in 1984, which mobilized black workers into a grassroots anti-apartheid campaign. After Nelson Mandela was released from prison in 1990, Lucy raised over $250,000 from American unions, which helped finance Mandela's tour of the United States and ease the transition of the African National Congress in the new South Africa. The CBTU also passed resolutions highlighting political

and human rights issues involving workers in Namibia and Zimbabwe.

The CBTU has continued to grow since its formation in 1972. At the beginning of the twenty-first century, there were 57 chapters in the United States and one in Ontario, Canada, representing the interests of over 50 different international and national unions.

BETH TOMPKINS BATES

References and Further Reading

Foner, Philip S. *Organized Labor and the Black Worker, 1619–1981.* New York: International Publishers, 1981.
Foner, Philip S., and Ronald L. Lewis, eds. *Black Workers: A Documentary History from Colonial Times to the Present.* Philadelphia: Temple University Press, 1989.

COALITION OF LABOR UNION WOMEN

Since its founding convention in 1974 in Chicago, Illinois, the Coalition of Labor Union Women (CLUW) has sought to increase the empowerment of women in the labor movement. In 1974, more than 1,200 union women from across the United States met to create an organization that addressed the needs of millions of unorganized working women and make unions more responsive to the needs of all working women. CLUW is not a labor union. It is a coalition that provides its members with information and the tools necessary to bring about change in their local unions. CLUW provides a forum and structure where working women share common problems and concerns and develop action plans within the framework of their individual unions.

CLUW is the only organization that represents the interests of working women in the mainstream of the labor movement. It seeks affirmative action in the workplace to obtain equal hiring, promotion, classification, and pay for female union members. CLUW strives to strengthen the influence and participation of women within their unions, encourage political and legislative activity, and increase the number of union members in the female work force.

CLUW headquarters are in Washington, DC, under the direction of the national president and national staff, which comprises the organization's executive director, the director of the CLUW Center for Education and Research, the national organizer, and two additional staff positions. The organization has always maintained very close ties with organized labor not only to remain true to its founding mission, its international and national unions, and most of the unions from which CLUW members come are AFL-CIO member organizations.

The national executive council meets at least six times each year to act on organization business and to guide and plan biennial national conventions. National conventions have been held every other year since 1974 in cities across the United States. National- and local-level officers are elected each biennium, totaling more than 350 officers across the country. Convention workshops have covered such issues as sexual harassment; domestic violence; living with breast cancer; HIV/AIDS; juggling the demands of work, union, and family responsibilities; the mobilization for the inclusion of contraceptive coverage in health-care plans; organizing for immigrant rights; Social Security; meeting the needs of mature workers; and recruiting new generations of women workers. CLUW's initiative to recruit young working women includes demonstrating the union wage advantage, solidarity among fellow workers, and unity on issues affecting their lives.

Although domestic violence has been addressed by many organizations over several years, CLUW has focused its efforts on making domestic violence a union issue. With four million women experiencing domestic violence every year, the abuse directly affects union members, who can be both the victims of domestic violence, as well as the abusers themselves. CLUW has received federal grant money to create a video and training curriculum to inform its members on how to address this and several other issues. CLUW's program of internal union education seeks to provide its members and nonmembers alike with the resources to combat social and economic injustice.

National conventions have also coincided with the publication of newsletters and handbooks, and CLUW seeks to leverage its influence by participating with other working women's initiatives and organizations. Information gathering and distribution have always been at the core of CLUW's work. In 1975, CLUW published *Women and Health Security*, which was the first of several information resources released over the years. CLUW has sought to conduct research and distribute information on timely topics of interest to its membership and working women in general. Its publications have included: *Commitment to Child Care* (1977); *Effective Contract Language for Union Women* (1979); *Lead: A New Perspective on an Old Problem* (1981); *A Handbook for Empowerment of Union Women* (1982); *Bargaining for Child Care: A Union Parent's Guide* (1985); *Women and Children First: An Analysis of Trends in Federal Tax Policy* (1990); *Is Your Job Making You Sick? A CLUW*

Mrs. Elibia Siematter, working as a sweeper at the roundhouse, Clinton, Iowa. Library of Congress, Prints & Photographs Division, FSA-OWI Collection [LC-DIG-fsac-1a34803].

but also to preserve its interests on the agendas of its labor union partners.

National officers hold positions for four-year terms and include the offices of president, executive vice president, treasurer, recording secretary, and corresponding secretary. Several vice president and immediate past president positions, as well as an executive director and counsel, make up the remainder of the National Officers Council, which is the organization's governing body. The National Officers Council comprises 19 female union leaders. Members of the National Officers Council represent national labor unions from a wide range of occupations and trades, including the United Auto Workers (UAW), public-sector unions—the American Federation of Government Employees (AFGE) and the American Federation of State, County and Municipal Employees (AFSCME), the Office and Professional Employees' International Union (OPEIU), the United Association of Nurses (UAN), the International Federation of Professional and Technical Engineers (IFPTE), and the Utility Workers Union of America (UWUA). Indeed, CLUW members come from 60 international and national unions across the United States and Canada. CLUW is endorsed by the AFL-CIO and

Handbook on Health and Safety (1991); the *Family Medical Leave Act Resource Guide* (1993); and *Sharing Our Stories: Voices at Work* (1999). CLUW members participate in, and the organization cosponsors, many initiatives and efforts that are relevant to working women, including several United Nations Decade of Women conferences, as well as voter registration campaigns, the Women's Bureau of the U.S. Department of Labor's "Working Women Count" survey, Equal Pay Day, the Wal-Mart Day of Action, and the Seneca Falls, New York, anniversary celebration.

With the growth of the electronic medium, CLUW has been able to distribute information more broadly and with less expense than in the past. Since information gathering, outreach, and education remain at the core of the organization, more effective and efficient distribution of information has expanded its influence. From the organization's Web site, union leaders and women workers who are interested in organizing can find information on ways to develop a local chapter, contact persons for existing local chapters, sample recruitment materials to attract new members, tips for new chapters, and forms and policies. In addition, all publications, a calendar of events, and promotional items are found on the CLUW.org homepage, "The new online frontline for working women" (www.cluw.org).

The organization's standing committees cover administrative tasks like elections, archives, recruitment, and finance, and they also feature topical issues that CLUW intends to continually devote resources toward. Topical issues that maintain standing committees or task forces include affirmative action, family issues, nontraditional jobs, union organizing, women's health, young women workers, violence against women, and minority issues. Separately, the CLUW Education and Research Center was created in 1979 to address all of these issues and more, providing education and training to its chapters in order to fulfill the organization's mission. In addition, the Education and Research Center has awarded educational scholarships to young women in labor studies programs.

Although CLUW policy is determined at the national level, the local CLUW chapters are responsible for putting the strategies into action. Local chapters function to empower women to bring about changes in their local unions. Since the focus of activity for local CLUW members is within their own unions, the local CLUW chapter provides its members with resources and tools in order to effect change within their locals. CLUW local chapters educate members, keep them up-to-date on a variety of issues of concern to working families, and provide a support network for women in unions. Over 75 local chapters are in 29 states, from New York City and Washington, DC to Kenai, Alaska; Toledo, Ohio; and Frankston, Texas.

The four primary objectives of the organization have not changed over the past 30 years: CLUW seeks to promote affirmative action in the workplace; strengthen the role of women in unions; organize the unorganized women; and increase the involvement of women in the political and legislative process. These goals continue to provide the foundation for the organization's activities and have manifested in many diverse initiatives: equal pay, child and elder care benefits, job security, safe workplaces, affordable health care, HIV/AIDS awareness, contraceptive equity, and protection from sexual harassment and violence at work. CLUW received a multiyear $250,000 grant from the Centers for Disease Control and Prevention to increase awareness of HIV/AIDS in workplaces. CLUW has been very active in the class action discrimination lawsuit against Wal-Mart, charging that company with systematic discrimination against women in hiring and promotions. The suit charges that Wal-Mart fails to provide equal assignments, promotions, training, and pay and retaliates against women and men who complain about these practices. Women make up nearly two thirds of the firm's hourly sales employees but hold only one third of management positions, and are disproportionately concentrated in lower-paying, lower-mobility departments such as customer service, cosmetics, housewares, toys, fabrics, and clothes. In addition to class-action advocacy, CLUW has worked on Capitol Hill to lobby on behalf of other issues important to working women, including Social Security reform, the antisweatshop "Behind the Label" campaign, and the raising of awareness of women workers' plight at multinational manufacturing plants in and around Juarez, Mexico.

In addition to national conventions, workshops, and advocacy, CLUW has endeavored to achieve its four primary objectives through education and outreach to its membership. This outreach has taken many forms over the past 30 years and has included the aforementioned publications, bimonthly newsletters, and the production and sale of consciousness-raising job-site tools, including "The 9 to 5 Guide to Combating Sexual Harassment" and "It's Not Funny, It's Not Flattering...It's Sexual Harassment" note cards. For more than 30 years, CLUW has worked closely with other working women's organizations as well as its own membership and union organizations to address the full range of issues faced by working women and union parents.

SHARON MASTRACCI

COHN, FANNIA (1885–1962)
International Ladies' Garment Workers' Union

Thorny, thin-skinned, and highly emotional, Fannia M. Cohn was a member of the pioneer generation of Jewish immigrant women who built the International Ladies' Garment Workers' Union (ILGWU). A gifted organizer, Cohn came to the attention of American labor leaders when she led a largely teenage group of female underwear makers from 35 different countries in a massive and successful general strike in 1913. Three years later, at the age of 31, she became the first woman elected vice president of a major American labor union. Cohn remained a central figure in the ILGWU for half a century, promoting her vision of a labor movement that fed not only the body but the heart and mind as well. Of all the aspirations she had heard working women voice on picket lines, at meetings, and in late-night study groups, she believed one to be at the heart of their interest in trade unionism: the desire for personal development and education. She devoted her life to fulfilling that goal.

Skeptical about the efficacy of legislating change, Cohn believed that only through education could workers become truly liberated. Education, she thought, would give women the confidence to challenge gender as well as class inequalities. And only through education, Cohn felt, would men abandon their prejudices toward women. That worker education grew and flourished in the United States during the first half of the twentieth century was in large part due to Cohn's tireless, almost fanatical labors on behalf of that cause. Drawing the support of some of the nation's leading scholars and academics, Cohn became the driving force behind the creation of a vast network of worker education programs between 1915 and 1962: worker universities, night schools, residential colleges, lecture series, and union hall discussion groups. By the time of her death in 1962, worker education programs had taught hundreds of thousands of men and women across the United States who might otherwise never have had the chance to experience advanced schooling. And the name of Fannia Cohn was known to all throughout the world who were interested in bringing higher learning to the working classes. Her name, wrote ILGWU colleague Leon Stein at the time of her retirement, had come to "stand for pioneering efforts to increase the educational opportunities for men and women in the shops" (Orleck 1995:295).

Many young middle-class revolutionaries through history have talked of abandoning their comforts and privileges to join the working-class struggle. Cohn was one of the few who did. Born in Kletsk, Poland, to cosmopolitan parents who, according to Cohn, "distinguished themselves with culture, wealth, and humor," she was unusually well educated for an East European Jewish girl of her generation. Her parents prided themselves on holding progressive views both in terms of politics and the education of their daughters, all of whom were sent to an elite private school, where they were taught to read and write Russian as well as Yiddish. Cohn attributed her passion for learning to her mother. Cohn was, she said, "raised by mother on books...My mother wanted her children to be no less than professors" (Orleck 1995:22).

Cohn did make education her life's work. But her mother never imagined that study would lead her intense and emotional daughter where it did. Much to her family's dismay, 16-year-old Fannia Cohn joined the Minsk branch of the Socialist Revolutionary Party, an underground organization that hoped to spark peasant uprisings by assassinating hated government officials. Three years later, after her brother was almost killed in a pogrom, Cohn swallowed her revolutionary pride and accepted steamship tickets from her cousins in New York.

Her family was relieved to have fiery Fannia at a safe remove from revolutionary activity, but the young hothead soon angered them by refusing to accept a wealthy cousin's offer to put her through college and graduate school. "Coming as I did from a revolutionary background," she explained, "I was eager to be with the people...I was convinced that to voice the grievances, the hopes and aspirations of the workers, one must share in their experiences" (Orleck 1995:23). Like hundreds of thousands of Jewish immigrants of her generation, Cohn went to work in a garment shop. There she immediately began agitating for higher wages, improved working conditions, and shorter hours. For the next four years, she moved restlessly from shop to shop throughout Brooklyn's garment districts, carefully laying the ground for an uprising.

In 1913, Cohn led a strike of 35,000 "white goods" (underwear) makers, forging a new local union and earning her a seat on that union's first executive board. In 1915, she was hired by the ILGWU to organize Chicago dressmakers. Cohn achieved what other organizers before her, including Rose Schneiderman, had been unable to do. She founded the city's first dressmakers union. A Chicago newspaper, lauding her skill, style, and erudition, called her "one of labor's shrewdest diplomats" (Orleck 1995:79). She demonstrated that diplomacy at the 1916 ILGWU convention, where she was elected vice president. Cohn, perhaps to deflect resentment that a daughter of the middle class was the first woman to win a seat on the executive board of a major U.S. union, insisted that she had been drafted to run as part of a shop-floor movement to place a woman in union leadership. But colleagues recalled that Cohn wanted the position badly and had campaigned fiercely, and strategically, for the nomination.

Shortly after her victory, Cohn convinced the union's executive board to create an Education Department—modeled on the one she and Pauline Newman had helped found in Local 25, the shirtwaist makers' union. As secretary of the ILGWU Education Department, Cohn helped develop courses in history, economics, literature, and current events that opened up the possibility of higher education to thousands of garment workers. In a union whose membership was heavily female, women vastly outnumbered men in these early worker education courses. In classrooms, on field trips, and on retreats, Cohn urged women workers not to settle for small changes, but to seek empowerment in the broadest sense—an improved quality of life, economic advancement, and intellectual stimulation. They did. Newly emboldened by classes in history, politics, and literature, militant women garment workers began to call for greater representation in the leadership of their union. And they articulated an alternative vision of what the ILGWU could be—an egalitarian and socially transformative community of workers.

These women's shop-floor rebellion soon turned into open warfare with an immigrant male union leadership that was just beginning to gain political power through the conservative inner circles of the American Federation of Labor. The internecine struggles that followed nearly destroyed the garment unions. The Right-Left labor battles of the 1920s have usually been attributed to a split between members of the Socialist and Communist Parties. But the first shots were fired in the years after World War I, by women schooled to rebel in Cohn's early worker education classes.

Cohn chose to stay with the ILGWU when thousands of militant women and men left, but it was a choice that isolated and wounded her. The union's leadership never forgave her for refusing to condemn the rebellion she'd helped to spark. And many of the militants whom she had inspired now condemned her for appearing to capitulate to what they saw as a grasping and corrupt ILGWU leadership. By 1924, as a high-ranking official rooted in union headquarters, Cohn was cut off from the radical labor Democrats who would have been her most natural allies. In a poisonous atmosphere of mutual dislike and distrust, Cohn would struggle with the

ILGWU's male leaders ceaselessly for nearly four decades.

Fannia Cohn offset her strained relations with union leaders by cultivating some of the nation's leading intellectuals as allies and even instructors in her worker education courses. Economist John Kenneth Galbraith, literary critic Van Wyck Brooks, and historian Merle Curti taught during the 1930s in Cohn's worker education courses. Cohn would order pastrami sandwiches from Manhattan's famous Stage Delicatessen for her favorite scholars and cluck over them as they ate: "Es Nokh a sandwich, Kenneth," one colleague recalls her saying as she patted the back of the world-famous Galbraith after he finished a lecture for her garment workers.

The progressive historian Charles Beard became a lifelong friend and supporter, lauding Cohn for "splendid efforts in the field of labor education. No one in America is doing more than you are...You hearten workers throughout the country" (Orleck 1995:173). The labor economist Theresa Wolfson worked closely with Cohn for many years, as a friend, instructor in various programs for women workers, and one of the first academics to document the role of women in the labor movement. Wolfson also became Cohn's sounding board during a lifetime of doing battle with unappreciative union leaders. Cohn described herself as having "the sensitive heart and tender emotions of the artist and the poet." Wolfson understood how difficult it was for a woman with such a temperament to survive in the rough-hewn world of organized labor, telling Cohn that she "realized with such poignancy of feeling what it means to be a woman among men in a fighting organization" (Orleck 1995:190).

Cohn found supporters in the union among the younger generation of women and men whom she mentored and nurtured with great affection. "She loved the young people," recalled colleague Leon Stein, and the young people loved her." Cohn called the women activists who came of age in the 1930s "NRA babies," and she schooled them in the history of the union's early years. Among the most successful of Cohn's protégées from that era was black Panamanian garment organizer Maida Springer Kemp, who went on to become African affairs representative for the AFL-CIO. "Fannia Cohn, that name in ILG history," Springer said. "I respected and revered her" as one of the pioneers who built the labor movement. "When the men in the unions wanted to settle for less, these women were prepared to go on and be hungry and march into the winter" (Orleck 1995:202).

Cohn was widely respected by African-American trade unionists for being among a small handful of white labor activists who regularly reached out to black workers. A. Philip Randolph, founder of the Brotherhood of Sleeping Car Porters and the best-known black labor leader of the mid-twentieth century, wrote to thank Cohn for her unwavering support. "You have given encouragement, support and cooperation during the years and dark days of my struggle to organize the Negro workers...There is no comment on my humble efforts that I prize more highly than yours" (Orleck 1995:198).

Despite her international reputation and the high esteem in which Cohn was held among many academics and trade unionists, by the end of World War II, the male leadership of the ILGWU viewed Cohn as a burden to bear, a relic of the union's radical past. ILGWU President David Dubinsky likened her to U.S. Secretary of Labor Frances Perkins. "FDR has got Fannia Perkins," he was fond of saying. "And I've got Fannia Cohn. We've both got our cross to bear" (Orleck 1995:197). Dubinsky felt that Cohn did not understand the new realities of a union that was based as much in Pennsylvania and California as it was in New York, that was made up of native-born white Christians, Afro-Caribbeans, and Mexicans, not only immigrant Jews and Italians. Dubinsky and the ILGWU Executive Board wanted the aging woman warrior to step aside gracefully. Then the union could trot her out for ceremonial occasions, strike anniversaries, and Education Department dinners. Cohn was having none of it.

Finally, in September 1962, when Cohn was 77 years old, the union forcibly retired her. They held a testimonial luncheon at which her old detractors lauded her. The union newspaper *Justice* ran a two-part profile of the pioneering activist, giving her full credit for the role she had played both in the early strikes that had galvanized the ILGWU and in spreading worker education throughout the labor movement. Cohn accepted the tribute with her characteristic close-lipped smile, shook hands with her colleagues, and came back to work the next day—and every day after that. An exasperated David Dubinsky ordered her personal effects packed and her office cleared out to make room for Cohn's replacement. He changed the locks on her office door. Resolutely, Cohn continued to come in. She would sit for hours, with her coat and hat on, upright and silent in the hallway outside of her old office at union headquarters. The standoff lasted for a full four months, until on December 23, 1962, she failed to appear. Friends searched her apartment and found her body. The tiny, unswerving activist had died of a stroke. Nothing short of death could have kept her from her post at ILGWU headquarters.

ANNELISE ORLECK

References and Further Reading

Kessler-Harris, Alice. "Organizing the Unorganizable: Three Jewish Women and Their Union." *Labor History* 17, No. 1 (Winter 1976): 5–23.
———. "Problems of Coalition Building: Women and Trade Unions in the 1920s." In *Women, Work and Protest: A Century of U.S. Women's Labor History*, edited by Ruth Milkman. London: Routledge, 1985.
Orleck, Annelise. *Common Sense and a Little Fire: Women and Working-Class Politics in the United States*. Chapel Hill: University of North Carolina Press, 1995.
Wong, Susan Stone. "From Soul to Strawberries: The International Ladies Garment Workers Union and Workers Education, 1914–1950." In *Sisterhood and Solidarity: Workers' Education for Women*, edited by Joyce Kornbluh and Mary Frederickson. Philadelphia: Temple University Press, 1984.

See also **Dubinsky, David; International Ladies' Garment Workers' Union (ILGWU) (1900–1995); Schneiderman, Rose; Springer, Maida**

COLD WAR

The Cold War was the defining conflict of the second half of the twentieth century. Throughout the 50-year struggle between the United States and the Soviet Union, the American labor movement became one of the staunchest supporters of Cold War foreign policy. Even after the Democratic Party largely abandoned liberal anticommunism in the wake of the Vietnam War and Watergate, AFL-CIO leaders such as Lane Kirkland remained powerful voices opposed to Soviet imperialism, particularly in Poland.

Labor Anticommunism

Unlike in many Western European countries, the American labor movement had a long history of opposing communism and other leftist ideologies. While exceptions to this certainly existed, and while leftists and communists played important roles in the creation and maintenance of many unions, the leadership of the AFL-CIO and the vast majority of its constituent unions endorsed an anticommunist position and did their best to reduce or eliminate the presence of communists within unions.

While many scholars see labor's anticommunism as being a reflection of the anticommunism that pervaded much of Cold War American culture, the hostility of the mainstream of the labor movement toward the left goes back considerably farther. Instead, labor's hostility toward communism was rooted in two major factors: first, a belief that communists and other sectarian leftists placed the interests of their parties over the best interests of labor; and second, the fact that independent trade unions were usually one of the first casualties when a communist or leftist regime came to power. Both of these long predated the beginnings of the Cold War and largely motivated the AFL's anticommunist policy beginning with the late nineteenth-century attempts of the Socialist Labor Party to undermine and infiltrate the federation and its affiliates.

Things are more complicated when it comes to the CIO, however. It is certainly true that communists and other leftists played important roles in founding and organizing CIO unions. But the majority of CIO unions were neither left-led nor terribly friendly to communists and communism. And major CIO leaders, like John L. Lewis and Philip Murray, were hostile to the communists, even if they were willing to use them as organizers. When the CIO purged its communist-led unions in 1950, it was only partially a result of Cold War tensions and rising anticommunism. More important was the general hostility toward communism among Catholic workers and the fact that the CIO's left-led unions had backed Henry Wallace's third-party presidential campaign in 1948.

Cold War Liberalism and Labor

The American labor movement, particularly the AFL-CIO after the 1955 merger between the two labor federations, was one of the leading institutions of Cold War liberalism, an ideology which opposed both foreign communism and domestic conservatism. As part of the Cold War liberal consensus, the AFL-CIO supported a vigorous American foreign policy, with an emphasis on containing the expansion of the Soviet Union, along with an expansion of New Deal programs domestically. The AFL worked closely with a number of Cold War liberal institutions, particularly the Americans for Democratic Action (ADA), which formed one of the bases for the labor-liberal alliance that stretched from the 1940s through the end of the 1960s.

In many ways, the AFL-CIO became the last bastion of Cold War liberalism after its repudiation by most members of the Democratic Party in the late 1960s and early 1970s. A combination of the Vietnam War, Watergate, and the rise of the New Left led many Democrats to reject the staunch anticommunism that was at the heart of Cold War liberalism. This can perhaps best be seen in the endorsement of Eugene McCarthy over Hubert Humphrey by the ADA, up until then the premiere Cold War liberal

institution. As a result of the endorsement, a number of leading labor figures resigned from the organization, and the AFL-CIO became increasingly separated from its former allies in the labor-liberal alliance.

This split within American liberalism was reproduced, to a more limited extent, within the ranks of labor. A handful of unions, particularly those that had once been in the CIO, such as Walter Reuther's United Auto Workers (UAW), did not embrace the staunch anticommunism that had become AFL-CIO policy under George Meany and that continued under Lane Kirkland. In 1968, Reuther led the UAW out of the AFL-CIO, at least in part over the same ideological divisions that had split the labor-liberal coalition in the ADA. Moreover, this divide between the anticommunist liberals and the "anti-anticommunists" on their left within the AFL-CIO would only deepen during the 1970s and, particularly, the 1980s. Those AFL-CIO members and unions that opposed the executive board's position on international affairs would become stronger and more vocal as the Cold War drew to a close, and this division played a major part in the eventual ouster of Lane Kirkland as the head of the labor federation.

AFL-CIO and Latin America

After the breakup of the labor-liberal alliance, the AFL-CIO largely continued to support an anticommunist foreign policy abroad. However, this support became increasingly controversial within the labor federation. The foreign policy initiatives of the AFL-CIO under Lane Kirkland, in particular, provoked a strong reaction from the federation's more left-wing and progressive unions, which eventually resulted in his ouster. This was especially true with regard to the AFL-CIO's interventions in Latin America.

In both instances, the labor federation was committed to the support of free, independent labor unions abroad and opposed the control of both the authoritarian right and the communist left. This led the AFL-CIO to make enemies on both sides of the domestic political spectrum. Kirkland was forced to advocate a policy that alienated many in the labor movement, opposing the Republican Party's domestic agenda while at the same time generally opposing the foreign policy agenda of the Democrats. Despite these difficulties, however, Kirkland and the AFL-CIO remained committed to a vigorously liberal anticommunism throughout the Cold War.

The situation in Nicaragua during the 1980s illustrates nicely the difficulties faced by the AFL-CIO during that time. Before the Sandinistas came to power in 1979, the AFL-CIO had a pre-existing relationship with the Unified Workers Federation (CUS), a local Nicaraguan labor federation that had opposed the dictatorship of Anastasio Somoza. The Sandinistas, however, following a pattern set in many previous Marxist revolutions, aimed at exerting more centralized state control over labor unions and set up their own labor federation in competition with the CUS. The Sandinistas also placed serious restrictions on union activities, including attempts to ban strikes. As a result of these actions, the AFL-CIO took a strongly anti-Sandinista stance, largely on the grounds that the Nicaraguan regime undermined the rights of a free, independent labor movement.

Most of the American left, however, was highly sympathetic to the Sandinista regime and became increasingly hostile to the AFL-CIO and Lane Kirkland because of their anticommunist stance. In addition, the labor federation alienated many on the American right by refusing to support the Reagan administration's guerrilla Contra war against the Sandinistas. Kirkland and other members of the executive board were skeptical of the ability of CIA-backed insurgencies to install democratic regimes abroad, and thus opposed the Republican Party's major foreign-policy program in Nicaragua. In an attempt to support American-style trade unionism in Nicaragua, the AFL-CIO managed to isolate themselves from their natural allies on both the right and the left.

Solidarity and Poland

The AFL-CIO's stance in favor of the Solidarity movement in Poland resulted in many of the same ambiguities that arose from its Latin American policies. The labor federation quickly rallied to Solidarity's defense after its founding in 1980. Once again, however, their defense of independent trade unionism abroad failed to win them much support from the domestic right or the domestic left. While only a small percentage of the domestic left supported Poland's communist regime, large segments of the right and the left greatly feared anything that might lead to instability in the Eastern bloc. While remaining anticommunist, these domestic political forces, which largely included both the Reagan administration and the mainstream of the Democratic Party, feared that Solidarity's destabilizing of Poland might lead the USSR to intervene militarily in Eastern Europe or elsewhere.

Nevertheless, Kirkland and the AFL-CIO remained staunch supporters of Solidarity and have

been considered by some scholars to be the Polish union's strongest advocates in the United States. While most Western European nations refused to pressure Poland to lift the ban on Solidarity that had been imposed soon after its founding, the AFL-CIO loudly and consistently announced its support for the union and worked closely with its leaders to coordinate their strategies. Throughout Solidarity's years underground, the AFL-CIO became its principal supplier of material aid, including over $4 million in financial aid and considerable printing supplies. And when Solidarity was legalized in 1989 and won a successful election removing the communist regime from power, Kirkland and the AFL-CIO were widely hailed as one of the parties principally responsible for the movement's success.

Solidarity's victory in Poland is often considered the beginning of the end of the Cold War. In the end, Kirkland's policy of supporting free and independent trade unionism abroad was generally successful. The hostilities it generated, however, particularly among the left wing of the AFL-CIO, led to deep-seated resentment against the federation president. In 1995, a coalition of the largest trade unions in the AFL-CIO successfully pushed for Kirkland's resignation, arguing, among other things, that his foreign-policy initiatives had taken resources away from much-needed union organizing activities.

AARON MAX BERKOWITZ

References and Further Reading

Cherny, Robert, William Issel, and Kieran Walsh Taylor, eds. *American Labor and the Cold War: Grassroots Politics and Postwar Political Culture.* New Brunswick, NJ: Rutgers University Press, 2004.

Puddington, Arch. *Lane Kirkland: Champion of American Labor.* Hoboken, NJ: John Wiley & Sons, 2005.

Rosswurm, Steve, ed. *The CIO's Left-Led Unions.* New Brunswick, NJ: Rutgers University Press, 1992.

COLLECTIVE BARGAINING

Collective bargaining refers to the method of determining the standards of employment through negotiation by employers and union representatives. The term first came into use during the 1890s, coined, according to the English Fabians Sidney and Beatrice Webb, by her in 1891, and propagated in the United States by their landmark book, *Industrial Democracy* (1897). To some degree, nomenclature was only catching up with practice; American unions engaged in collective bargaining before it had a name. But naming it also underscored the temporal fact that collective bargaining was not coterminous with trade unionism. The constant was the collective effort to improve labor's condition—"job-consciousness," Selig Perlman called it, in *A Theory of the Labor Movement* (1928). Bargaining came later.

The presumption in collective bargaining is that employers are a party to the terms of employment. That was not the presumption of nineteenth-century artisans and craft workers. The standards for wages, hours, and work norms to which they adhered—expressive not of what the market would bear but of what they considered honorable and appropriate for their craft—were "legislated" by the union. Enforcing these terms on employers depended on the refusal of members to work with anyone not holding a union card or adhering to union standards. In industrial conflict, therefore, the pivotal issue was the closed shop. This regime was long-lived, enforced by union control over labor markets and by the autonomous nature of craft production. Over time, however, as the sustaining industrial conditions eroded, the unilateral exercise of craft power gave way to the trade agreement, although as late as the early 1920s the San Francisco building trades still set the terms of work and, while sometimes consenting to arbitration of disputed issues, balked at signing "time" agreements.

We define collective bargaining as a "method" of representing workers, but it was also an expression of job-consciousness, and in this guise part of a larger discussion about ultimate ends. Job-consciousness, although historically always robust, co-existed with alternate tendencies toward independent labor politics and, more grandly, toward labor-reform schemes like those advanced by the Knights of Labor. With the launching of the AFL, visions of an expansive, multifaceted labor movement faded. The argument of the pure-and-simple unionists who founded the federation was that an American movement could not afford anything but an exclusively job-conscious focus, and for them that meant, in instrumental terms, collective bargaining.

Pure-and-simple unionism never entirely carried the day. It was contested by the politically engaged left, sometimes operating inside the AFL, and, after 1905, explicitly rejected by the syndicalist International Workers of the World (IWW), which demonstrated that, in certain circumstances, workers were better off using pressure tactics than signing a labor agreement. Even so, collective bargaining was the dominant mode, sustained ideologically by the voluntarism espoused by Samuel Gompers and institutionally by the principle of trade autonomy, which acknowledged the supremacy within the AFL of the national unions responsible for collective bargaining.

The Webbs treated the advent of collective bargaining as an aspect of institutional maturation: the "primitive democracy" of unilateral action gave way to "representative government," and responsible leadership took command. But in the American context, market and technological forces were at least equally as important, instructing union leaders in the necessity of making employers parties to the terms of employment.

Consider the case of coal mining, where the most compelling fact was that cutthroat price competition translated directly into depressed wages and into petty forms of cheating—over coal weighing, unpaid dead work, and so on—by hard-pressed operators. Understanding this, miners focused from the earliest days on coal prices, even resorting after the Civil War to unilateral suspensions of work in hopes of reducing supplies and raising coal prices and then, in an attempt at regularizing price and wage movements, by negotiating sliding scales. By the 1880s, union leaders began to think more strategically. They concluded that the only way to defend their miners was by reducing the competitive pressures on the industry's labor relations through joint action with the industry.

Once operators accepted this proposition in 1897, a complex bargaining structure took shape, with a joint interstate conference that negotiated uniform standards for the "basing points"—equivalent districts in the participating states—that in turn became the basis for negotiating local tonnage rates and work rules at state and district conferences. The objective of all this machinery was the reverse of what industry-wide bargaining normally aims for—not to take wages out of competition, but to make wages the variable cost, enabling all operators in the Central Competitive Field, no matter how disadvantaged by location or by thin coal seams, to survive within a stabilized price structure. There was a name for this: competitive equality.

At the time, at the turn of the century, the joint interstate system in coal seemed emblematic of the coming of age of collective bargaining in America. It was a sign of the chastening effects of the labor strife of the 1890s that Attorney General Richard Olney, after brutally suppressing the great railway strike of 1894, thereafter advocated federal mediation of railway labor disputes and, to that end, became the principal architect of the Erdman Act (1898). A more comprehensive sign of public approval came from President McKinley's U.S. Industrial Commission, which in 1900 hailed collective bargaining as an expression of industrial democracy. In the private sector, prominent figures formed the National Civic Federation, with the specific mandate of encouraging collective bargaining. And in key industries, employers seemed disposed to give collective bargaining a try, famously including national agreements by metal-trades associations with the Machinists and Molders.

The expectation that collective bargaining would become the norm in American industry, however, proved illusory. The most ambitious of the experiments—in the metal trades, in meatpacking, at International Harvester—quickly foundered over disputed issues and strike actions. In other countries, such setbacks might have been accepted as part of the learning curve—as it was, for example, by the British metal trades at this time—but not by American employers. The National Metal Trades Association and the National Founders Association transformed themselves almost overnight from agencies for collective bargaining into the aggressive vanguard of a national campaign for the open shop. What this reflected, of course, was an abiding animus by American employers against dealing with workers collectively, an animus rooted in cherished principles of property rights and liberty of contract and nourished after 1900 by the new vogue for managerial control inspired by Frederick W. Taylor.

In the face of this resistance, union growth stalled around 1904 at two million, a tenth of the nonagricultural labor force. A third belonged to local trades, most notably, building and construction, but also printing, retail, food services, transportation, and a miscellany of crafts. What stymied collective bargaining in these local markets was an inability to leverage strength from one locality to another, so that the characteristic pattern was of a patchwork of union representation. In industries operating nationally or regionally, collective bargaining was best established in glass, certain branches of the metal trades (stove manufacture, shipyards, and machine fabrication), and mining. On the railroads, the operating brotherhoods were strongly organized and so, increasingly, were the nonoperating crafts, which, to surmount their fragmentation, began to advocate "system federation," that is, joint bargaining over entire railroad systems. Railroads resisted the shifts in power that this entailed—resulting in an epic four-year strike at the Illinois Central and Harriman lines—but in the end, largely gave way. System federation became the accepted way of conducting negotiations with the shop crafts.

The halting progress of collective bargaining manifestly was governed by some intricate, but favorable, calculus of union power and employer benefit. In the Central Competitive Field, the soft-coal operators had been forced to the bargaining table by an expectedly potent strike in 1897 and then won over by the promise of market stability. Anthracite, by contrast, had no such need; a cartel already controlled that sector. So the anthracite barons put up a stiffer

fight, succumbing finally in the great strike of 1902 to President Roosevelt's extra-ordinary intervention, but even then not conceding union recognition. Nor, despite the triumph of collective bargaining, was the Central Competitive Field itself sheltered from antiunionism. The challenge came from the open-shop West Virginia and Kentucky coalfields, whose cheaper product undercut the northern union operators and increasingly imperiled the joint interstate agreement.

In the clothing industry, the balance of forces shifted differently. As in soft coal, garment manufacturing in its various branches was furiously competitive, with very much the same exploitative effect: hard-pressed employers sweated and cheated workers for that extra penny. Clothing unions had no way of relieving the pricing pressures on employers, but they did have leverage on the production side. The crucial transaction there was the negotiation of endlessly varying piece rates. What the unions offered was a process for rationalizing this negotiation and, because they applied standards (not only for piece rates but over labor conditions) across shops, to some degree taking wages out of competition. It also became possible, once rate-setting gave the unions entry into the workplace, to take on the industry's chaotic methods of production and, by raising efficiency, carve out further space for higher wages. The celebrated innovation, originating in Louis D. Brandeis's Protocol for Peace that settled the great cloak-and-suit strike of 1910, was a joint system for adjudicating disputed rates and contract infractions, with an impartial umpire as the final arbiter. But no less important were the industrial-engineering departments set up by the unions to help bring the industry's shop practice into the twentieth century. Altogether, it was, say the historians Philip Taft and Selig Perlman, "a spectacular conquest of a new province for industrial government based on union recognition."

Arriving at "industrial government," however, had taken a wave of savage strikes and was no harbinger of industrial peace more generally. The country stood aghast at the murderous bombing of the *Los Angeles Times* building in 1910 by respected officials of the structural iron workers' union; at the successes of the IWW in leading mass strikes by textile workers in Lawrence, Massachusetts, in 1912, and Paterson, New Jersey, in 1913; and at a ghastly climactic episode in 1914, the torching by state militia of a tent city at Ludlow during a bitter Colorado coal miners' strike for collective bargaining that asphyxiated many strikers' wives and children and plunged Colorado into a virtual civil war.

With the "labor question" finally on the Progressive agenda, the newly installed Wilson administration appointed a blue-ribbon U.S. Commission on

Industrial Relations, whose job it would be, as the youthful journalist Walter Lippmann wrote, to explain the "deep-seated discontent" afflicting American workers. In its Final Report, the commission took note of "an almost universal conviction that . . . they, both as individuals and as a class, are denied justice." The core reason for industrial violence, including the McNamara bombing, was the fierce anti-unionism of American employers. In its most important recommendation, the Report called on the federal government to protect the right of workers to organize and engage in collective bargaining.

On its heels came World War I, and what had seemed, in 1915, an exercise in national education was suddenly translated into wartime policy (much of it by veterans of the commission). With war production its top priority, the Wilson administration imposed collective bargaining where unions already had a foothold (as in the railway shops and shipyards) and, where they did not, asserted the right of workers to organize and to representation by shop committees (a half-step, in the wartime context, to collective bargaining). Although the Wilson administration hastily reversed course after the Armistice, its wartime record left an indelible imprint, in at least four ways.

First, Wilson's penchant for elevating necessity into principle—the world safe for democracy, industrial democracy at home—invested the right to organize with an enduring legitimacy. Employers still fired union workers, only they could no longer justify doing so. That part of the debate was over. Second, the wartime resort to shop committees prompted employers, as a defensive measure, to set up their own employee representation plans (ERPs), which after the Armistice they deployed in their battles against trade unions. The ERPs, they argued, offered a legitimate alternative to collective bargaining. In so doing, they recast the terms of debate. The question became systemic: not either/or but "what kind?" Third, the labor crisis provoked by the war enflamed this debate and crystallized a next question: how should it be resolved? It should be resolved by putting it to the workers, "by representatives of their own choosing," concluded the president's Industrial Conference, as it sought, unsuccessfully, to mediate the great steel strike of 1919. In that phrase ("by representatives of their own choosing") is the kernel of a state-mandated regime of collective bargaining. Finally, "representatives of their own choosing" survived and became lodged in public policy because wartime control of the railroads led, when it came to labor, not to the restoration of past practice but to the Railway Labor Act (1926), which prohibited "interference, influence or coercion" by employers in the designation of representatives by employees. In this guise, under the rubric of company domination of a labor organization, "representatives of their own choosing" was definitively approved by the Supreme Court in 1930. And in the landmark Norris-LaGuardia Anti-Injunction Act (1932), the phrase was there, in the law's declaration of public policy embracing labor's right to organize and engage in collective bargaining.

All that was left for the New Deal was the discovery that "representatives of their own choosing" demanded more than barring company domination of labor organizations. In the case of the railroads, this had not been apparent because the 1926 law (which the unions had helped write) assumed the presence of the existing unions. But in the core mass-production industries, unions enjoyed no such standing. The furious battles over representation that broke out there during the early New Deal forced the NRA labor boards, in deference to the free-choice language of Section 7a, to fashion rules for determining whether workers preferred the company-created employee representation plans or outside unions. This was the genesis of Section 9 of the Wagner Act (1935): on a showing of majority support in an appropriate bargaining unit, a labor organization would be certified by the National Labor Relations Board (NLRB) as the exclusive bargaining agent with whom the employer had a "duty to bargain." To that extent, the employer's liberty of contract—sacrosanct in this realm for a hundred years—had been breached.

But in principle, no further. The Wagner Act mandated collective bargaining, but (as the Supreme Court stressed in upholding the law) "it does not compel any agreement whatever." Nor, in that spirit of free collective bargaining, did it undertake to meddle with the right to strike or the scope of bargaining, a point the law underlined by affirming the freedom of the parties to negotiate union-shop agreements. It was here, on the fraught issue of union security, that the fragility of the line drawn by the law's architects soon stood revealed, first by the imposition during World War II of maintenance of membership on open-shop employers, and then, as the pendulum swung, by the Taft-Hartley Act (1947), which authorized states to prohibit union-shop agreements. Right-to-work laws were touted as a victory for individual liberty, but they also infringed on a long-settled aspect of liberty of contract in labor agreements. The Taft-Hartley assault was, in fact, wide-ranging—on the right to strike (authorizing 80-day cooling-off periods), on economic weapons (declaring secondary boycotts unlawful), on eligibility (denied to foremen), and on the status of labor agreements (made, for the first time, legally enforceable). As for the NLRB, it became the policeman of good-faith bargaining, most intrusively by enforcing the distinction drawn after

Taft-Hartley between mandatory and permissive bargaining issues.

It turned out that by mandating that collective bargaining begin, the state also assumed a responsibility for how it proceeded. That truth, although resisted by the Wagner Act's authors, was almost at once evident in the case law interpreting the law; Taft-Hartley only drove it home.

Although collective bargaining began as soon as the Wagner Act passed constitutional muster in 1937—sooner, in fact, at the bellwether firms U.S. Steel and General Motors—a decade went by before its features fully emerged. Initially, while the Great Depression was still in effect, wages and benefits took a back seat to the workplace grievances that had fueled the unionizing drive and the wildcat aftermath. And then World War II intervened, bringing a halt to free collective bargaining. Far more than in World War I, the economy converted to war. Control on labor relations was virtually by fiat, with far-reaching, sometimes unforeseen consequences. Much that became distinctive—expansive fringe benefits, arbitration in the grievance system, formal job-classification systems—can be traced to World War II. The war, moreover, consolidated the grip of the industrial unions and stirred unparalleled militancy. After VJ Day, a great strike wave swept the country, causing 4,630 work stoppages and bringing out 4.9 million workers. In steel, automobiles, meatpacking, rubber, and other basic industries, union coverage was close to complete; overall, two thirds of all manufacturing workers were organized. Finally, the reconversion debate over economic policy amplified the context for collective bargaining. It became labor's responsibility, pronounced the CIO's Philip Murray, "to lay the groundwork for an era of full employment." That meant a high-wage, low-price program for spurring consumption and industrial production.

In the first round of postwar negotiations in 1945, Walter Reuther tested that proposition at General Motors. He demanded a 30% wage increase with no rise in GM prices, and when the company demurred, challenged it to "open the books." General Motors implacably resisted this "opening wedge" for prying "into the whole field of management." The company took a 113-day strike, rebuffed the government's intervention, conceded its market lead to competitors, and soundly defeated the United Auto Workers (UAW). Having made its point, GM laid out the terms for a durable relationship. It would accept the UAW as its bargaining partner. It would make the contract the engine for an ever-higher living standard of its worker—signaled by its offer in 1948 to peg wages to the cost of living (adjusted every three months) and to an annual productivity factor (3 cents

an hour). The price was that the UAW abandon its assault on the company's "right to manage." When it signed the five-year GM contract of 1950—the Treaty of Detroit, so-called—the UAW definitively accepted the company's terms.

The battle at General Motors was, of course, an exemplary case. But if events elsewhere were less sharply drawn, and outcomes more shaded and varied, the central tendency was everywhere the same. Surveying the scene in 1960, the great industrial-relations scholar Sumner H. Slichter was satisfied that labor and management had arrived at "a balanced relationship."

When leading academics and practitioners met that year at the University of Chicago to assess the "structure" of collective bargaining that had emerged, they took note of the bewildering array of bargaining arrangements. With about 150,000 contracts in effect, what else could have been expected? Within this diversity, however, seminar participants identified a clear tendency toward "centralization," in two main forms. Multi-employer negotiation was the norm in local (retail, construction) and regional (trucking, longshoring) markets. In basic industries like auto and steel, industrial unions generally engaged in "pattern" bargaining, negotiating companywide agreements with a lead firm that then diffused across the industry—a variant, in effect, of industrywide bargaining. In either case, the aim was the inclusion of all the enterprises that could be said to be in direct competition with each other. On that basis—by the ability to pass on collective-bargaining costs—enabling them to fulfill GM's pledge of a rising standard of living for American workers.

Weekly earnings for industrial workers went from $54.92 in 1949 to $71.81 (in 1947–49 dollars) in 1959. Over the decade, spendable real income for the average worker with three dependents increased by 18%. Collective bargaining delivered greater leisure (paid holidays and lengthier vacations) and, in a startling departure, a social safety net. The labor movement far preferred an expanded welfare state, as in Europe, but having lost that battle after World War II, it turned to the bargaining table. By the end of the 1950s, union contracts commonly provided defined-benefit pension plans (supplementing Social Security payments), company-paid health insurance, and for two million workers, mainly in auto and steel, supplementary unemployment benefits (SUB). The sum of these advances was that new sociological phenomenon, the "affluent" worker—as evidenced by relocation to the suburbs (half of all workers by 1965), home ownership, cars and other durable goods, and (the infallible signs of rising expectations) installment buying and a doubling in the number of working wives between 1945 and 1960. For industrial workers, the union contract was becoming the passport, as Reuther boasted, into the middle class.

The durability of the bargaining system that had produced this remarkable result seemed beyond question at the time, even among the seasoned experts attending the University of Chicago conference mentioned above. Yet one can already spot (with the benefit of hindsight) warning signs in its discussion of meatpacking. This was an emblematic CIO industry, highly concentrated, with master contracts generating wages and benefits just short of auto and steel. But in 1960, the dominant Big Four packers were losing market share. A host of competitors had sprung up, profiting from a transportation revolution that shifted livestock traffic from railroads to highway trucking and swept away the geographic advantage that old-line packers like Swift and Armour had enjoyed at the great Midwestern stockyards. By operating close to rural feedlots and cost-cutting producers—most notoriously, Iowa Beef Packers (IBP)—these competitors ultimately shattered the collective-bargaining system and restored meatpacking's grim reputation as a sweated, low-wage industry. Between 1982 and 1996, real hourly wages fell by 31.4% and by 2002 stood 24% below the national average for manufacturing.

Brutal as it was, meatpacking's devolution was historically unremarkable, only reaffirming the contingency that has always characterized American collective bargaining. When the sustaining economic environment shifts, the bargaining system either responds—as, for example, John L. Lewis did by abandoning Competitive Equality for an industrywide, high-wage strategy when coal lost ground to oil in the 1920s—or goes under—as Lewis's painstakingly built structure finally did when coal after the 1960s became an open-pit, western industry. What was historically remarkable, however, was the economic hurricane that meatpacking's devolution heralded. The environment on which the postwar bargaining system had been premised was largely swept away after the onset of "stagflation" in the early 1970s. In relative terms, manufacturing rapidly faded (accounting for scarcely 14% of GDP by 2002); the postwar era of sheltered markets ended, signaled by deregulation of the airlines, trucking, and communications; and as a register of its waning powers, labor virtually abandoned the right to strike. By 2005, collective bargaining covered fewer than 8% of all private-sector employees, a world away from the 35% of 1955.

Among the questions for historians to ponder is why, in light of the country's history of labor violence, this catastrophic contraction proceeded with so little social friction. Relatively few employers, in fact, actually broke unions. It could be done under the labor law, by decertification, but not easily, and generally not without first provoking a strike and bringing in permanent replacements. Employers preferred a less strife-ridden choice. If their operations were movable, they moved. Plant closing was, as a study of RCA revealed, a long-favored method of union-busting, even among high-end manufacturers. But globalization vastly increased the incentives, to the point, indeed, where union/nonunion no longer was determining. In industry after industry, no American operation could compete against Mexican or Chinese workers. Labor's decline might be described as deunionization by stealth: no jobs, no collective bargaining.

As for its actual practice, that was, predictably, mostly a function of the collapsing economic environment. Industrywide patterns that had taken labor costs out of competition fragmented and, in some firms, so did companywide agreements that had prevented "whipsawing" of plants. At both levels, negotiations pitted job security—the union priority—against reduced wages and benefits—the management priority—with outcomes conditioned by the company's financial distress. An ironic subtext of concession bargaining was its subversion of GM's precious right to manage. Asking for big concessions meant opening the books. And depending on how big, unions might take a seat on the board (Chrysler) or a stake in the company (United Airlines) or even, in the direst cases, total ownership (Weirton Steel). Unfortunately, what had seemed revolutionary in 1946 was, in failing companies 40 years later, a mostly empty victory. A variant of this development was an abortive effort at transforming "adversarial" collective bargaining into labor-management cooperation, driven especially by claims that rigid work rules damaged American "competitiveness," which was then abandoned in the mid-1990s as employers opted for a business model that embraced downsizing and outsourcing. Judged by its own standard, as a vehicle for maximizing the terms of employment, collective bargaining in fact did its job. If anything, the differential value for union workers increased at a time when employers were hell-bent on cutting costs and shedding benefits.

As for the 120 million others, inhabitants of a burgeoning service economy, a question arises about the relevance of a collective-bargaining system shaped by the nation's industrial past. Among labor's challenges—one sure to increase over time—is what kind of representation to offer to workers whose needs are not met by seniority, or work rules, or defined-benefit pensions, and perhaps cannot even be reduced to the terms of a union contract. The term "collective bargaining" was coined in the 1890s. It might be that a new term will have to be coined, corresponding to an economic transformation just as sweeping as the industrial revolution that gave rise to collective bargaining over a century ago.

DAVID BRODY

References and Further Reading

Brody, David. *Workers in Industrial America: Essays on the Twentieth Century Struggle*, 2nd ed. New York: Oxford University Press, 1993.

Commons, John R., ed. *Trade Unionism and Labor Problems: Second Series*. Boston: Ginn & Co., 1921.

Gompers, Samuel. *Labor and the Employer*. New York: E. P. Dutton & Co., 1920.

Laurie, Bruce. *Artisans into Workers: Labor in Nineteenth-Century America*. New York: Hill & Wang, 1989.

Lichtenstein, Nelson. *State of the Union: A Century of American Labor*. Princeton, NJ: Princeton University Press, 2002.

Millis, Harry A. *How Collective Bargaining Works*. New York: Twentieth Century Fund, 1942.

Montgomery, David. *The Fall of the House of Labor*. New York: Cambridge University Press, 1987.

Perlman, Selig. *A Theory of the Labor Movement*. New York: Kelley, 1928.

Slichter, Sumner H. *Union Policies and Industrial Management*. Washington: The Brookings Institution, 1941.

Slichter, Sumner H., James J. Healy, and E. Robert Livernash. *The Impact of Collective Bargaining on Management*. Washington, DC: The Brookings Institution, 1960.

Webb, Sidney and Beatrice. *Industrial Democracy*. 2 vols. London: Longman, Green & Co., 1897.

Weber, Arnold R., ed. *The Structure of Collective Bargaining: Problems and Perspectives*. New York: The Free Press of Glencoe, 1961.

COLONIAL ERA

A crushing demand for labor existed throughout all the colonies and provinces in seventeenth- and eighteenth-century British Colonial America. To meet the demand, various labor systems developed. The range of climates and the varieties of cash crops, as well as differences among the settlers themselves, determined the different types of labor regimes. In the early seventeenth century, three distinctive labor regimes took shape. The first came into being in the Chesapeake colonies (Virginia and Maryland), the second in the English West Indies (Barbados, Nevis, St. Christopher, Antigua, Montserrat, and Jamaica), and the third in the New England colonies (Plymouth, Massachusetts Bay, Rhode Island, Connecticut, and New Haven). With the growth of English settlement, especially after the restoration of Charles II in 1660 and the establishment of Great Britain in 1707 (created from the union of England and Scotland), the established labor systems of the earlier colonies expanded into new regions. Various forms of free and unfree labor existed throughout British Colonial America. The self-sufficient artisans and tradesmen who made up the ranks of free laborers promoted the idea of upward social mobility, laying the foundation in the process for what has since been celebrated as the American Dream. At the same time, British Colonial Americans relied on various forms of unfree labor, such as indentured servitude and slavery. The use of unfree labor repeatedly led to resistance. Indeed, the history of the colonial era is replete with narratives of runaway servants as well as insurrections and rebellions by both servants and slaves. By any measure, the adoption of racially based chattel slavery as a solution to chronic labor shortages constitutes the most disturbing aspect of the entire era. While slavery was centered in the British West Indies and the British southern mainland colonies, it existed in every colony. Slavery, originating during the colonial era, bequeathed to American civilization the festering problem of racism, a problem that continues to haunt the United States in the twenty-first century.

Chesapeake Colonies: Virginia and Maryland

Tobacco production in the Chesapeake colonies of Virginia (England's first permanent colony in North America founded in 1607) and Maryland (founded in 1634) spurred the migration of thousands of young, white indentured servants. These young laborers, often from impoverished backgrounds, flocked to Virginia and Maryland in the 1700s seeking a better life. Young, unmarried men composed the majority of these English laborers. They voluntarily signed a labor contract, called an indenture, in which they pledged to work for a number of years. Usually an indentured servant served a term of between four to seven years. In exchange for their labor, they were promised passage to America, food, board, clothing, and in some cases, a plot of land at the expiration of their contract. During most of the 1600s, a brisk trade in white indentured servants existed in the Chesapeake colonies as white servants composed the dominant labor regime that produced, harvested, and loaded the Chesapeake tobacco for export to Europe. Africans, who were first brought to Virginia in 1619, labored raising tobacco along with white servants. Because laws creating chattel slavery, by which blacks were reduced to the status of property, did not exist in the early decades of English colonization in the Chesapeake, these Africans labored as servants. Indeed, chattel slavery was unknown in England. Thus, the English colonists had no example of slavery to draw on.

During the early and mid-1600s, some Africans in the Chesapeake, especially those who converted to Christianity, became landowners and had servants of their own. For reasons that are still debated by historians, Africans increasingly found themselves reduced to the status of chattel slaves. Some scholars argue that this transition is best understood as the result of a maturing colonial society in which some planters had grown wealthy enough to afford slaves, a more expensive form of labor than indentured servants. Other scholars point to the social unrest in the 1670s—especially a Virginian uprising in 1675–1676 known as Bacon's Rebellion—as an important step on the road to the adoption of slavery in the Chesapeake. This uprising, which briefly toppled Virginia's royal government in 1676, originated from discontent among whites, including a large number of enraged former white indentured servants, whose prospects of owning land had dimmed. According to some scholars, this uprising led planters to increasingly turn to slavery, a type of labor they hoped would be more manageable than unruly white servants.

By the beginning of the 1700s, chattel slavery had been encoded into law in Virginia and Maryland. Defined as property, Africans, who were brought in increasing numbers to the Chesapeake in the 1700s, were bought and sold by Anglo planters. The traffic in slaves increased dramatically in the eighteenth century, resulting in a sizable African Creole population in the Chesapeake. While a handful of Africans in the eighteenth century gained freedom, the majority were relegated to the dehumanizing status of chattel, subject to the will and caprice of whites. During the 1700s, convict labor formed another type of unfree labor in the Chesapeake. Transported to the Chesapeake for crimes committed in Britain, these laborers worked for longer terms, depending on their crime. For the most serious offenses, convict laborers served for life. Yet, the adoption of slavery in the Chesapeake has arguably had the most lasting and troubling consequences. Historians, most notably Edmund Morgan, have argued convincingly that African slaves not only did the backbreaking labor but also provided whites with a sense of racial privilege. Among whites, racial solidarity trumped differences in economic status. Race therefore served to unite poor whites and wealthy white planters. By the time of the American Revolution (1775–1783), African slavery provided American revolutionaries with a way to understand their struggle against perceived British tyranny. White solidarity set alongside black slavery provided meaning to the founding fathers' sense of liberty.

English West Indies

In the English West Indies, including Barbados, Nevis, St. Christopher, Antigua, and Montserrat, planters turned to African slavery much sooner than the English colonists in the Chesapeake colonies. First settled by the English in the 1620s and 1630s, these islands initially followed in the example of the Chesapeake colonies by producing tobacco. Just as in the Chesapeake, young, white, male indentured servants rushed to the English Islands to grow tobacco. By the 1640s and 1650s, however, the planters focused on the production of sugar, a crop that thrived in the tropic climate of the islands and was far more lucrative than tobacco. With the transition from tobacco to sugar, planters in the English West Indies invested heavily in African slaves. The flow of white indentured servants slowed so that by the late seventeenth century few made the journey to the islands. By then, planters in the West Indies, including the island of Jamaica, which had been taken from the Spanish in 1655, imported thousands of Africans to toil on sugar plantations.

In the eighteenth century, the British islands stepped up their forced migration of Africans. Olaudah Equiano, one of the thousands sold into slavery, arrived in Barbados in 1756. He described the West Indies as a death trap, a place of widespread and unimaginable brutality, where Anglo planters raped, mutilated, and murdered Africans with impunity. Acts of resistance by slaves led to especially gruesome reprisals by white authorities. The horrendous treatment in the English West Indies of African slaves resulted in a staggering loss of life. According to Equiano, planters had to import thousands of new Africans each year in order to maintain a steady population of slaves.

New England

The labor system in the New England colonies differed significantly from the labor systems in the English West Indies and the Chesapeake colonies. The New England colonies were established by zealous Protestants, known as Puritans, during a burst of emigration in the 1630s and early 1640s known among some scholars as the "Great Migration." Unlike the Chesapeake and the West Indies, the cold climate and rocky soil of New England did not sustain cash crops during the colonial period. Instead, New Englanders turned to traditional agriculture, fishing, and the maritime trade to make their living.

In comparison with the other regions of English settlement, New England was relatively poor.

While indentured servitude and slavery existed in New England, it was the reliance on child labor that set the New England colonies apart from the other early zones of English colonization. Because colonial New England families tended to be very large, with six or more children being the norm, the region essentially produced its own labor force. New England's child labor regime served several purposes beyond simply meeting the demand for labor. First, in colonial New England, where the Puritan faith predominated, children received religious instruction in the households where they worked. In this way, the New England child labor system created communities bound together by shared religious belief. Second, this system of child labor allowed for extensive supervision over the large number of young people in New England. The placement of children in the households of relatives increased the degree of oversight and control. (The Puritan emphasis on the doctrine of original sin, which in practice meant children were viewed as natural-born sinners, helped to maintain New England's labor regime.) Some of the strains experienced by New England's child laborers found expression in cases of witchcraft. The historical record illustrates that on several occasions young servants believed the Devil was tempting them with promises of easing the burden of work if they would serve him. Slavery was practiced throughout New England, though the number of slaves in comparison to the Chesapeake colonies and West Indies was relatively small. Thus, the New England colonies are best described as societies with slaves as opposed to slave societies. Only wealthy New Englanders could afford slaves, and these slaves usually served to further advertise elite status. The majority of New England slaves were concentrated in the maritime communities, especially in port towns like Newport, Rhode Island, and Boston, Massachusetts.

Restoration Colonies

After the restoration of Charles II in 1660, England significantly expanded its mainland American holdings. Indeed, by the mid-1700s, a continuous line of British colonies, stretching from Maine to Georgia, had replaced what had been the scattered seventeenth-century English outposts. The new English possessions, known collectively as the Restoration colonies, included the middle colonies of New York (1664), New Jersey (1664), and Pennsylvania (1681).

The Restoration colonies also included North and South Carolina. New Hampshire, established by royal decree in 1679, formed another Restoration colony. In all these possessions, the older systems of unfree labor expanded.

Middle Colonies

Various unfree labor systems thrived in the Middle Colonies. New York City, which had been founded by the Dutch as New Amsterdam in 1624 and conquered by the English in 1664, had a mixed unfree labor force of white indentured servants and slaves. As in other areas of British Colonial America, the racial divide separating white servants and black slaves solidified during the 1700s. After a number of fires broke out in 1741 in New York City, for example, white authorities suspected a conspiracy by black slaves to take over the colony. They arrested and tried scores of slaves. Many slaves were brutally executed. The 1741 fear of a conspiracy provided the pretext for white New Yorkers to clamor for strict laws restricting the activities and movements of the city's enslaved population. As in other areas of British Colonial America, New York City's reliance on slavery and resulting fears of slavery rebellion among whites provided the foundation for a racially divided society.

New Jersey, taken from the Dutch in the 1660s, and Pennsylvania absorbed large numbers of indentured servants. The experience of William Moraley, an indentured servant, provides one example of what life was like for servants in the Middle Colonies. Falling on hard times in England as young man, Moraley set sail to America after signing an indenture in London. He arrived in Philadelphia in 1729, where he was sold to a New Jersey Quaker. Unhappy with working in New Jersey and hoping to be sold to someone in Philadelphia, Moraley followed the path of many indentured servants by running away. He was caught, however, and returned to his master. When he fulfilled the term of his indenture, Moraley failed to find his place in colonial society. He traveled throughout Pennsylvania, New Jersey, and New York before returning to England in 1734. He published his memoirs in 1743, in which he described the differences between servants and slaves in the Middle Colonies. Slaves suffered greatly. Those who endeavored to escape were flogged unmercifully. At the same time, masters who murdered their slaves escaped any punishment at all. Servants, too, suffered at the hands of their masters, who legally controlled their actions. Unlike slaves, servants could not marry.

Lower South

The labor system in the lower South that took root in the late seventeenth and eighteenth centuries largely derived from the model established in Barbados. Indeed, the majority of the English colonists who settled in what is now Charleston, South Carolina, in 1670 had left Barbados. In the decades following the first settlement, the English replicated the slave labor they knew from the West Indies. South Carolina's culture and dependence on slavery spread northward into North Carolina. It also spread southward into Georgia, a colony founded in the early 1730s as a buffer between South Carolina and Spanish Florida. Though the founders of Georgia banned slavery, the prohibition was repealed in the late 1740s, and slavery soon flourished. Unlike the West Indies, rice proved to be the most lucrative crop for Carolinians. Rice production, beginning in the 1690s, further propelled the expansion of chattel slavery in the lower South. By the 1710s, black slaves formed a majority in South Carolina. In 1739, slaves in South Carolina began the largest slave rebellion in British Colonial America. The Stono Rebellion began when slaves learned that Spanish Florida would provide asylum to escapees from the British colonies. The promise of freedom motivated nearly two dozen slaves in South Carolina to begin the trek south to Spanish Florida. As they moved south, they killed whites and recruited other slaves. The rebellion faltered as whites tracked down and killed the slaves. None of the slaves who took part in the Stono Rebellion ever reached freedom in Spanish Florida.

Free Labor in British Colonial America

In the pre-industrial world of British Colonial America, the majority of inhabitants worked the land. In these agricultural colonies, the ultimate goal for the majority of the migrants was to own land. Indeed, it was the prospect of becoming a landowner that spurred the migration of thousands of English colonists. Promoters of colonization carefully created an image of British America as a land of small, independent farmers. Throughout all the colonies, attaining the status of yeoman farmer—a colonist who controlled at least a small estate—served as the standard of respectability. In particular, land ownership conferred on colonial Americans the coveted status of independence, free from being dependent on others. The much-prized sense of personal independence derived from holding land fee simple (in absolute possession) also had political ramifications. In most colonies, only those who achieved the status of yeoman farmer could take part in local political decisions by exercising the right to vote. Many writers, including the Frenchman J. Hector St. John de Crevecouer, celebrated the opportunities in British Colonial America to own land. Arguably, Thomas Jefferson provided the most famous statement of the exalted place of the independent farmer. "Those who labour in the earth," Jefferson wrote, "are the chosen people of God, if ever he had a chosen people." This version of the colonies and the early republic as a world of small, prosperous farms assumed that the yeoman farmer was a white male. Indeed, the independent yeomanry by definition excluded women and non-whites.

Eighteenth-century British Colonial America was also a world of free working people. The counterparts to the independent yeoman in the countryside were the artisans and tradesmen in colonial towns and seaports. The path to the status of artisan and tradesman began with an apprenticeship. Unlike an indentured servant, who had to perform any labor his/her master commanded him/her to do, an apprentice was tasked with learning a specific trade or profession by working for a master artisan or tradesman, who agreed to teach the apprentice the mysteries of a given trade. After completing an apprenticeship, the laborer took on the status of journeyman. A journeyman had mastered a given trade but had not reached the full status of master artisan. Journeymen instead labored for wages under the direction of a master artisan. Only when a journeyman had accumulated enough capital to set up his own shop did he attain the rank of artisan or tradesman. Benjamin Franklin's almanac (published from 1733 to 1758 under the pseudonym "Poor Richard" Saunders) and his *Autobiography* presented advice for how to become a successful and self-made tradesman. According to Franklin, the artisan and tradesman who gained material wealth and the respect of his peers had to be hard-working, sober, and in general, adhere to an ethic of constant self-improvement. Indeed, artisans and tradesmen created a culture that promoted a spirit of both individual independence and mutual support. In a larger context, Franklin's depiction of America as a place of potentially unlimited social mobility for the diligent and careful young tradesman provided the basic formula for the American rags-to-riches narrative. Yet the success of artisans and tradesmen in British Colonial America was abetted by the existence of vast numbers of slaves and other unfree workers who never had the chance to succeed.

New France

Far fewer French settlers came to North America than English colonists. Nonetheless, the French created a large, if sparsely populated, New World empire that stretched from the St. Lawrence River, through the area of the Great Lakes, through the Mississippi Valley south to New Orleans.

In the seventeenth century, the majority of French immigrants came as indentured servants ("engages"), who served terms of three years. They performed the brunt of the heavy labor in New France. At the expiration of their three-year term, many engages returned to France. The French colony of Louisiana, claimed by the French explorer René-Robert Cavelier, sieur de La Salle in 1682 and named in deference to Louis XVI, enslaved Native Americans and imported black slaves to grow a variety of crops, the most profitable of which was indigo. Sugar was introduced in the 1750s and gradually supplanted indigo as the major cash crop.

Spanish Colonial Florida and New Mexico

Florida and New Mexico composed the two major Spanish Colonial holdings in what is now the United States. Founded in 1565, St. Augustine, Florida, served as the Spanish military outpost responsible for protecting the annual treasure fleets that sailed from Havana to Spain from pirates and, in the seventeenth and eighteenth centuries, from encroachments by the British in the North. While the Spanish in Florida relied on black slave labor, a 1693 Spanish royal decree also provided official sanctuary for slaves from British South Carolina if the escapees converted to Catholicism. In 1738, the town of Gracia Real de Santa Teresa de Mose was founded as a free black town. The Spanish hoped the town of Mose would destabilize the British colonies of Georgia and South Carolina. The Spanish plan partially succeeded: the existence of Mose spurred the 1739 Stono Rebellion in South Carolina. During the colonial era, the town of Mose attracted hundreds of slaves seeking to escape slavery in British Colonial America.

When the Spanish began to subjugate the Pueblo Indians of New Mexico in 1598, soldiers were rewarded with *encomiendas*, which required the Pueblo to make tribute payments of cloth, skins, and corn. The Spanish used Native Americans as servants and, even though slavery was banned in New Mexico, Native Americans were also held in bondage. The *genizaros*, or Indian slaves, were usually Apache or Navajo who had been captured in war. Spanish labor practices and the efforts to convert the Pueblo to Catholicism in colonial New Mexico had disastrous consequences for the colonists in 1680. Organized by the medicine man Popé, the Pueblo Revolt of 1680 toppled Spanish New Mexico. Sante Fe and other Spanish outposts fell to the Pueblo. It took 12 years before the Spanish reconquered New Mexico.

From Mercantilism to Free Trade

Colonial-era labor history is also the history of economic systems in transition and economic thinking in fluctuation. Indeed, the various labor practices in colonial America played an important role in stimulating change. Throughout much of the colonial era, mercantilism composed the dominant economic theory. Mercantilists believed a fixed amount of wealth, measured in bullion, existed in the world and that the state's ability to amass wealth depended on creating a favorable balance of trade. To that end, mercantilists argued that government must control trade to increase the power and financial standing of the state. Thus, Spain attempted to control the flow of silver and gold, mined by unfree labor in its American possessions, by employing heavily guarded treasure fleets. England followed the logic of mercantilism by passing a series of acts in the seventeenth century known collectively as the Navigation Acts. The English Navigation Acts prohibited foreign ships from trading in the colonies and required that the most important colonial crops, such as sugar from Barbados, Chesapeake tobacco, and Carolina's rice, be shipped directly to England. The Navigation Acts also required that colonial commodities be transported on vessels where the majority of the crew, as well as the captain, were English. The logic of mercantilism also found expression in the slave trade with the formation of the Royal African Company in 1672. The company exercised a monopoly over the English slave trade until the 1690s.

Various forces worked against mercantilism during the colonial era, however. Perhaps the greatest force for change was a powerful strain of individualism and individual liberty that motivated British colonists to chafe at what they viewed as the limitations imposed by mercantilism. In British America, colonists frequently disregarded the provisions of the Navigation Acts, preferring instead to insist on their right to freedom of trade. Benjamin Franklin, who advised colonists that "God helps those who help themselves" and emphasized freedom of private enterprise and individual initiative, contributed to the new economic outlook. Tragically, Franklin's viewpoint originated in an age when the existence of unfree labor, especially slavery, profoundly shaped the vision of potentially unlimited upward social mobility and individual wealth for laboring whites.

JOHN M. LUND

References and Further Reading

Allison, Robert J., ed. *The Interesting Narrative of the Life of Olaudah Equiano: Written by Himself.* Boston: Bedford/St. Martin's, 2006.

Beckles, Hilary McD. *White Servitude and Black Slavery in Barbados, 1627–1715.* Knoxville: University of Tennessee Press, 1989.

Berlin, Ira. *Many Thousands Gone: The First Two Centuries of Slavery in North America.* Cambridge, MA: Belknap Press of Harvard University Press, 1998.

Dunn, Richard. *Sugar & Slaves: The Rise of the Planter Class in the English West Indies, 1624–1713.* Chapel Hill: Published for the Omohundro Institute of Early American History and Culture by the University of North Carolina Press, 1972.

Franklin, Benjamin. *The Autobiography and Other Writings.* Edited by L. Jesse Lemisch. New York: New American Library, 1961.

Greer, Allan. *The People of New France.* Toronto: University of Toronto Press, 1999.

Gutierrez, Ramon A. *When Jesus Came, the Corn Mothers Went Away: Marriage, Sexuality, and Power in New Mexico, 1500–1846.* Stanford, CA: Stanford University Press, 1991.

Hotten, John Camden. *The Original Lists of Persons of Quality, Emigrants, Religious Exiles, Political Rebels, Serving Men Sold for a Term of Years, Apprentices, Children Stolen, Maidens Pressed, and Others Who Went from Great Britain to the American Plantations, 1600–1700.* New York: J. W. Bouton, 1874.

Kolchin, Peter. *American Slavery 1619–1877.* New York: Hill and Wang, 1993, 2003.

Landers, Jane. "Gracia Real de Santa Teresa de Mose: A Free Black Town in Spanish Colonial Florida." *American Historical Review* 95 (1990): 9–30.

Lepore, Jill. *New York Burning: Liberty, Slavery, and Conspiracy in Eighteenth-Century Manhattan.* New York: Alfred A. Knopf, 2005.

Morgan, Edmund S. *American Slavery, American Freedom: The Ordeal of Colonial Virginia.* New York: Norton, 1975.

Wood, Peter H. *Black Majority: Negroes in Colonial South Carolina from 1670 through the Stono Rebellion.* New York: W.W. Norton, 1974.

Waldstreicher, Franklin. *Runaway America: Benjamin Franklin, Slavery, and the American Revolution.* New York: Hill and Wang, 2004.

COLORED FARMERS' ALLIANCE

Between its formation in late 1886 and its demise by the end of 1892, the Colored Farmers' Alliance organized at least one million African-American farmers and farm laborers into an organization that promoted unity and self-help among its members. When the organization became involved in economic, labor, and political activism, however, it encountered harsh and sometimes violent white opposition. This white backlash against the Colored Alliance, along with the organization's failure to significantly improve its members' financial condition, led to its downfall, but even as it disintegrated, it still mobilized many African-Americans in support of the People's (or Populist) Party, which was a force in southern and western politics from 1892 until at least 1896.

Like the all-white Southern Farmers' Alliance (formally known as the National Farmers' Alliance and Industrial Union), the Colored Farmers' Alliance began in Texas. White farmers in central Texas formed the Southern Alliance during the mid-to-late 1870s, and that organization was just beginning to enter its period of major growth when African-American farmers, with a modicum of assistance from whites, formed the Colored Alliance in east Texas in 1886. As many as five different Colored Alliance organizations were formed during 1886–1887, but the two primary groups were one formed in 1886 in Lee County, led by the white "general organizer" Andrew J. Carothers, and another formed in December of that year in Houston County, led by the white "general superintendent" R. M. Humphrey, a Baptist minister, and black president J. J. Shuffer. The latter group eventually absorbed the others and named itself the Colored Farmers' National Alliance and Cooperative Union, more generally known as the Colored Farmers' Alliance. The organization established chapters in all 11 states of the former Confederacy as well as Delaware, Ohio, Illinois, Indiana, Missouri, and Nebraska.

According to its declaration of principles, the Colored Farmers' Alliance aimed "to promote agriculture and horticulture," "to educate the agricultural classes in the science of economic government, in a strictly nonpartisan spirit," "to develop a better state mentally, morally, socially, and financially," "to aid its members to become more skillful and efficient workers," to "protect their individual rights," to raise funds "for the benefit of sick or disabled members, or their distressed families," and to facilitate "the forming [of] a closer union among all colored people who may be eligible to membership in this association," among other goals. Like the Southern Farmers' Alliance, the Colored Alliance established cooperative stores for its members as well as large cooperative exchanges in Houston, New Orleans, Mobile, Charleston, and Norfolk, Virginia. But also like the Southern Alliance, the Colored Alliance lacked the capital and business acumen needed to

Sam Crawford oiling (i.e., greasing) tractor on his Maryland farm / Cooper. Library of Congress, Prints & Photographs Division, Visual Materials from the NAACP Records [LC-USZ62-130378].

succeed in many of these enterprises. The Colored Alliance succeeded in other tangible ways, though, such as raising money for the construction of schools and churches for African-Americans and for the aid of sick members and the families of deceased members.

Nevertheless, the Colored Alliance, which relied upon dues from its generally cash-strapped membership, failed to improve the material conditions of most of its members through these endeavors. When Colored Alliance leaders tried to take more direct measures for the financial assistance of the rank and file, however, disastrous, even tragic results often followed. In 1889, in Leflore County, Mississippi, for example, a Colored Alliance leader named Oliver Cromwell encouraged members to do business with a Southern Farmers' Alliance cooperative store in a neighboring county rather than with local white merchants, who held many black farmers in a state of debt peonage through the crop-lien or credit system. Leflore County whites soon ordered Cromwell to leave the county, but Colored Alliancemen boldly rose to his defense. Subsequently, armed whites—led by the Mississippi National Guard—attacked and killed not only Cromwell but about 25 other African-Americans as well. Similarly, when R. M. Humphrey called for a regional strike of southern black cotton pickers in September 1891 for the purpose of procuring higher wages (which were as low as 50 cents per hundred pounds), white planters, including Southern Alliancemen, denounced the plan as unwise and dangerous. Most black cotton pickers agreed and ignored the strike call, but in Lee County, Arkansas, some pickers walked off the job and tried to coax or intimidate others into doing the same. A biracial posse led by the white county sheriff put a decisive end to the strike, killing at least 15 African-Americans in the process.

Such attempts at economic or labor activism by the Colored Alliance underscored the tensions between the organization and its southern white counterpart. While the two organizations sometimes collaborated in cooperative ventures and made some identical demands for reform, such as currency and land reform and government ownership of railroads, they differed on some fundamental issues of economics and politics. The Southern Alliance vehemently opposed Congress's proposed Lodge Election Bill, which would have provided for federal supervision of federal elections, while the Colored Alliance, whose members were most likely to be victimized by violence or intimidation during elections, supported the bill. Furthermore, the Southern Alliance represented many middle-class farmers or farm operators, many of whom employed Colored Alliance members, male and female, and thus were threatened by Colored Alliance efforts at economic improvement.

After the failure of the cotton pickers' strike, the Colored Farmers' Alliance rapidly deteriorated; by the end of 1892, the organization had virtually disappeared. Nevertheless, the Colored Alliance's presence continued to be felt in politics through its influence on the Populist movement. The Colored Alliance had preceded the Southern Alliance in calling for the formation of a third political party, despite its self-avowed "nonpartisan spirit," and a number of Colored Alliance leaders and organizers worked actively for the Populist Party even as (and after) the Colored Alliance disintegrated. Of course, the Populist Party itself collapsed by the end of the nineteenth century, but in retrospect, the failure of most of the Colored Farmers' Alliance's efforts at economic, labor, and political activism should not diminish its significant place in history as the largest organization of African-American farmers and farm laborers during an era in which most African-Americans were tillers of the soil.

MATTHEW HILD

References and Further Reading

Ali, Omar H. *Black Populism in the New South: Between Reconstruction and Jim Crow, 1886–1898.* Jackson: University Press of Mississippi, forthcoming.
Gaither, Gerald H. *Blacks and the Populist Movement: Ballots and Bigotry in the New South.* Rev. ed. Tuscaloosa: University of Alabama Press, 2005.

COMMISSION ON INDUSTRIAL RELATIONS (1910s)

Battered by the open-shop movement and shamed by the McNamara brothers' surprise confession to bombing the *Los Angeles Times* building in 1912, the American labor movement caught a break from the U.S. Commission on Industrial Relations (CIR) in 1913. Chair Frank P. Walsh turned a government investigation into a partisan tribunal that blamed employers for violence on picket lines. While labor organizations like the AFL and the Industrial Workers of the World (IWW) rejected state solutions to the labor problem, the CIR called for federally protected labor rights and ultimately helped shape World War I labor policy.

In 1912, in the wake of the McNamara confessions, Progressive intellectuals and reformers petitioned Republican President William Taft to convene a special commission to investigate industrial violence. Once Taft announced the creation of the Commission, AFL President Samuel Gompers demanded that AFL union leaders should be allotted Commission seats and recommended AFL Treasurer John Lennon, James O'Connell from the AFL Metal Trades Department, and Austin Garretson of the Order of Railway Conductors. Progressives denounced Gompers's choices as reactionary bureaucrats. After Congress funded the Commission, the AFL, National Civic Federation, and National Association of Manufacturers lobbied for their appointees (and found common ground in opposing the appointment of an IWW representative). When Democrat Woodrow Wilson won the 1912 presidential election, none of the commissioners had yet been approved by the Senate.

Wilson took up the matter in early 1913, agreeing to retain Gompers's nominees. To represent business, Wilson proposed California government official Harry Weinstock, flour mill owner Thruston Ballard, and railroad executive Frederick Delano. Democratic fund-raiser Florence Jaffray Harriman and Wisconsin labor economist John R. Commons were put forward to represent the public. Louis Brandeis turned down a seat, so President Wilson turned to Kansas City labor lawyer Frank P. Walsh to chair the committee. Walsh had started out as a corporate lawyer, but in a road-to-Damascus transformation, on January 1, 1900, he abandoned his old practice and flung himself into Progressive reform and radical agitation. Largely unknown on the national scene, his nomination aroused little opposition. Walsh eagerly accepted the appointment and won Senate confirmation in September 1913.

Walsh convened the Commission and launched a series of dramatic public hearings on the strikes and industrial conflicts of the day. The Commission visited textile strikers in Paterson and Atlanta, garment workers in New York, and tenant farmers in the South. After mineworkers' tents caught fire in Ludlow, Colorado, the CIR sent investigators to the coalfields and interrogated mine owner John D. Rockefeller in a Manhattan auditorium before large crowds. Walsh won the enduring admiration of American workers for his pointed questioning of employers and his sympathetic ear for laborers. However, some of his fellow commissioners grew uncomfortable with Walsh's open partisanship. Commissioner Commons had expected research by the CIR's industrial economists, which included W. Jett Lauck, Sumner Slichter, William Leiserson, and Selig Perlman, to inform a deliberate inquiry and propose legislation. Walsh preferred spectacle to staff analysis.

This conflict intensified by early 1915, as Commons pushed for more impartial study and evenhanded treatment of employers. Walsh deflected the challenge, but tension remained. As the CIR's funding ran out, the Commission turned to drafting a final report. Walsh and the three labor representatives produced a radical manifesto calling for constitutional amendments to protect workers' rights to organize, investigation of employer misconduct by the Federal Trade Commission, restrictions on private detectives, and taxes on inheritances and land. This was too much for Commons. He wrote his own report calling instead for national mediation boards run by nonpartisan staffers. Harriman signed Commons's report, while the employer representatives produced a third report that condemned employer brutality as well as the closed shop, sympathy strikes, and the boycott. The failure of commissioners to agree on a single report struck observers as a failure.

As the CIR closed down, Walsh convened a private version of it called the Committee on Industrial Relations. Progressives organized mini-Committees in cities to lobby for the legislation proposed in Walsh's CIR report, while Walsh organized progressives to support strikers and called for both Democratic and Republican platforms to include federal labor reforms. Needing the votes, Wilson embraced the CIR, granting rail workers the eight-hour day with the 1916 Adamson Act and delivered progressives and unionists to the Democrats in the 1916 election. The CIR foreshadowed both the New Deal coalition and the AFL-CIO split over the proper role of the state in labor relations and shifted public attention from union thuggery to bosses' depredations.

JENNIFER LUFF

References and Further Reading

Adams, Graham Jr. *Age of Industrial Violence, 1910–15: The Activities and Findings of the United States Commission on Industrial Relations.* New York: Columbia University Press, 1966.

Greene, Julie. *Pure and Simple Politics: The American Federation of Labor and Political Activism, 1881–1917.* Cambridge and New York: Cambridge University Press, 1998.

McCartin, Joseph A. *Labor's Great War: The Struggle for Industrial Democracy and the Origins of Modern American Labor Relations, 1912–1921.* Chapel Hill: University of North Carolina Press, 1997.

See also **Adamson Act; Commons, John Rogers; Ludlow Massacre (1914); McNamara Brothers**

COMMONS, JOHN ROGERS (1862–1945)
Labor Historian

Commons was the scholar most responsible for institutionalizing the university study of labor history and contemporary labor issues. The basis for Commons's academic innovations was his distinctive challenge to academic orthodoxy and his career-long incorporation of labor studies into economics. When his mature program generated specialized fields in labor economics, industrial relations, and labor history, he gained renown for founding the "Wisconsin School" of scholarship in each specialty. Wisconsin School scholarship was closely identified with "institutionalism," the cross-disciplinary movement that Commons helped launch. Institutionalists sought to supplant the prevailing version of social science, focused on the hypothetical behavior of individuals, with analysis emphasizing the actual role of collective actors in organizing and governing modern capitalist societies. The connection between the theoretical restructuring advanced by institutionalists and the practical restructuring of American capitalism by Progressive reformers was manifested across Commons's career. A builder of institutions as well as a scholar of institution-building, Commons shaped his research program to support his evolving reform agenda for altering the labor-capital power imbalance. Due to his success in combining social reform and social science, Commons influenced labor history as well as labor historiography.

Commons's introduction to labor scholarship began in 1888 at Johns Hopkins University, where he studied "labor problems" with the subject's academic pioneer, Richard Ely. With Ely as his sponsor, Commons developed his own approach during his tenure at the University of Wisconsin's Economics department (1904–1932). Ely initially hired Commons to increase the department's coverage of labor topics and to enlarge the empirical base for labor scholarship by directing the department's American Bureau of Industrial Research. The curriculum featured labor history after Commons taught the initial course in 1905. Within a decade, he achieved a series of firsts for labor studies: an undergraduate minor, a graduate field, and a faculty team of specialists. As Bureau director, Commons led his students (several became his colleagues during the process) in producing the 10-volume *A Documentary History of American Industrial Society* (1910–1911), followed by the two-volume *History of Labour in the United States* (1918), which analyzed "labor organization" across the nineteenth century.

Commons provided the interpretive framework for the Bureau's analytical history. His focus centered on wage workers' collective actions to contest their employers' control over their industrialized labor. But his account emphasized how workers repeatedly shaped their organizations to respond to nonindustrialized features of American political economy. Commons drew particular attention to the extension and structuring of markets during the prolonged stage of merchant capitalism, since workplace power depended on workers' organizational capacity to curb market competition. He also stressed workers' unprecedented access to partisan politics, where their issues were routinely sacrificed and individualistic ideologies impeded their elaboration of collectivist alternatives. Based on his reading of the documentary record, Commons presented America's political-economic institutions as effectively constraining workers' efforts to build the labor institutions necessary to advance their class interests. His perception of workers successfully using, and changing, the institutional environment was confined to the century's end, when they responded to newly ascendant employer capitalism by mobilizing to establish "constitutional government in industry."

While completing novel labor history projects, Commons was active in the university-government collaboration called the Wisconsin Idea, framing reforms that established the state of Wisconsin as a national leader in the public regulation of business. His labor legislation included factory safety standards, workers' compensation for workplace accidents, and centralized regulation under a tripartite authority: the Wisconsin Industrial Commission. Commons had previously participated in groundbreaking initiatives to investigate labor-capital relations (U.S. Industrial Commission, 1900–1902) and to promote labor-capital bargaining for trade agreements (National Civic Federation, 1902–1903). Through his leadership in the Wisconsin Idea, he tied his program's research agenda to the cutting edge of labor reform. "Commons and associates" served as investigators for the Russell Sage Foundation's Pittsburgh Survey (1906–1907) and the U.S. Commission on Industrial Relations (1913–1916). For the American Association for Labor Legislation and the Wisconsin Industrial Commission, organizations whose creation they facilitated, their roles included administration as well as research.

The experience of combining labor research with labor reform shaped the remainder of Commons's career. As a practitioner, he focused his later activities on expanding the organized constituency for federal-level worker insurance programs and labor market regulation. The reach of his network-building was manifested in his honorific leadership positions: codirector, National Bureau of Economic Research (1920–1928); president, Stable Money Association (1922–1924); and president, National Consumers' League (1923–1935). Many of his students followed his lead, with the majority devoting their careers to labor-related policy making and public administration. They came to national prominence through their involvement in a wide range of New Deal initiatives, including drafting Social Security legislation and directing the National Labor Relations Board. Their visible impact reinforced the acclaim Commons received for pioneering significant elements of the vision and practice that came to fruition in New Deal labor reform.

After presiding over the American Economic Association (1917) during a period of heralded political-economic reconstruction, Commons focused his scholarship on reconstructing economics. In two major studies, *Legal Foundations of Capitalism* (1924) and *Institutional Economics* (1934), he located the changing institutional governance of capitalist economies at the center of economic analysis. By redefining the subject matter of economics, Commons revised its scope to include "nonmarket" modes of control—particularly, the control exercised by labor unions, business corporations, and public regulatory bodies. During this period, his Wisconsin associates extended their historical survey to 1932 with the publication of two final volumes of *History of Labor in the United States* (1935). Selig Perlman led the later effort,

while publishing the theoretical study that influentially defined American unionism as "job-conscious unionism." Perlman's interpretation, which blended Commons's analysis of unionism under merchant capitalism with Samuel Gompers's practice of trade unionism, became synonymous with the Wisconsin School approach to labor history.

Through mid-century, the historical studies produced by Commons and his students provided the dominant framework for studying labor. However, by the 1960s, the Wisconsin School approach lost its appeal, considered overly historical and institutionalist by most labor economists and insufficiently historical and institutionalist by a new generation of historians interested in labor. Champions of the "new labor history" challenged the interpretive hold of the "old labor history," criticizing the shortcomings of Commons and his associates. Because of their exclusive focus on organized labor, their histories omitted the majority of workers. Due to their narrow conception of labor organization, their institutional focus slighted the social and cultural institutions workers used to challenge the control capitalists wielded over workplaces and America's free-market economy. New labor historians initially emphasized the limitations of old labor history in order to transcend them. With subsequent syntheses of how structures of social power and structures of social meaning have intersected in workers' lives, continuities as well as departures define the relation between old and new labor histories.

Commons's legacy ultimately rests on the realism that informed his labor scholarship. The importance he placed on studying workers' interactions with changing institutional realities still resonates in debates over how to historicize workers' experience with American capitalism. Likewise, his realist stance still applies to the positions scholars take in the wider contest over whether the study of capitalism will be grounded in capitalism's actual history. Commons's historical investigation of the nonmarket institutions governing economic development was designed to promote a double transformation First, to overturn the social science that represents economic interactions and outcomes as solely governed by market institutions in accordance with natural laws. Second, to overcome the attendant social philosophy that denies the persistence of power struggles among collective actors to configure America's economic governance structure. Of the continuities between Commons and his successors, the most consequential is the shared commitment to providing the realism missing in conventional wisdom.

RONALD APPLEGATE

Selected Works

A Documentary History of American Industrial Society, ed. with others. Cleveland, OH: Arthur H. Clark, 10 vols., 1910–1911.
History of Labour in the United States, with others. New York: Macmillan, vols. I & II, 1918; vols. III & IV, 1935.
Industrial Government, with others. New York: Macmillan, 1921.
Labor and Administration. New York: Macmillan, 1913.
Myself: The Autobiography of John R. Commons. New York: Macmillan, 1934.
Principles of Labor Legislation, with John B. Andrews. New York: Harper and Brothers, 1916 (revised editions in 1920, 1927, and 1936).
Trade Unionism and Labor Problems, ed. Boston, MA: Ginn and Company, 1905 (2nd ed., 1921).

References and Further Reading

Brody, David. "Reconciling the Old Labor History and the New." *Pacific Historical Review* 62:1 (1993): 1–18.
Fink, Leon. "Defining the People: The Wisconsin School of Labor History and the Creation of the American Worker." In his *Progressive Intellectuals and the Dilemmas of Democratic Commitment*. Cambridge, MA: Harvard University Press, 1997, pp. 52–79.
Harter, Lafayette G. Jr. *John R. Commons: His Assault on Laissez-Faire*. Corvallis: Oregon State University Press, 1962.

See also **Commission on Industrial Relations (1910s); Historiography of American Labor History; Perlman, Selig; Taft, Philip; Workers' Compensation**

COMMONWEALTH v. HUNT (1842)

The landmark case of *Commonwealth v. Hunt* (1842) was the first instance when a state supreme court ruled that laborers could lawfully organize.

In the first decades of the nineteenth century, tradesmen were largely independent. During the 1830s, early advances in industrialization began to effect changes in ways that goods were produced, increasingly diminishing the control tradesmen held over their labor. In response, some journeymen organized to fight primarily against low wages. The Boston Journeymen Bootmakers' Society formed in 1835 for these aims. It successfully organized strikes in 1835 and 1836 to raise the wages of its members.

The elite denounced labor societies, citing two main objections. First, it claimed that such collectives violated the individual worker's right to contract. Second, it argued that by organizing on issues of pay and work hours, the collectives interfered with the free market. To destroy the associations, the elite solicited state district attorneys to prosecute workers who organized for criminal conspiracy.

American judges and legal scholars debated how the common law conspiracy doctrine should be applied in the states. Most judges held that an otherwise lawful act when committed by an individual (such as a demand for higher wages) became criminal under the conspiracy doctrine when committed in collective (as a restraint on free trade). There were some lawyers, however, who argued that the underlying act had to be criminal or at least unlawful (a civil offense) to substantiate the crime of conspiracy.

In the 1840s, the Massachusetts courts addressed the issue of whether forming a labor collective substantiated a charge of criminal conspiracy. In 1840, a Massachusetts trial court found seven members of the Boston Journeymen Bootmakers' Society guilty of criminal conspiracy for forming a union. The journeymen appealed. Two years later, Chief Justice Shaw of the Massachusetts Supreme Court reversed the convictions. Agreeing that the underlying alleged acts were all lawful, Shaw ruled that these acts, even when committed in combination, could not substantiate a charge of criminal conspiracy.

Shaw's decision did rule that unions were lawful, but it did not allow unions to engage in strikes. Shaw, who was not known as a friend to labor, viewed the collective as a unit created by a contract entered into voluntarily by autonomous individuals. Once formed, the collective operated as a liberal entity within the free market; however, it was also bound by the rules of contract. If the collective entered into an employment contract, its existence would not protect it from prosecution for violating that contract by striking.

Union activists who hoped that *Hunt* was part of a movement to provide laborers with some support were ultimately disappointed. There had been two recent political acts that imposed some limited regulation on industry. In 1840, President Van Buren had issued an executive order establishing a 10-hour day for federal employees, and in March 1842, the Massachusetts legislature made it unlawful to employ children under 12 for more than 10 hours a day in the mills. After the Civil War and through most of the nineteenth century, however, prosecutors continued to charge striking laborers with criminal conspiracy. It would take almost a century before state courts provided any meaningful support for laborers.

GWEN HOERR JORDAN

References and Further Reading

Hattam, Victoria C. *Labor Visions and State Power: The Origins of Business Unionism in the United States*. Princeton, NJ: Princeton University Press, 1993.
Holt, Wythe. "Labour Conspiracy Cases in the United States, 1805–1842: Bias and Legitimation in Common

Law Adjudication." *Osgoode Hall Law Journal* 22 (1984): 591–663.

Juravich, Tom, William F. Hartford, and James R. Green. *Commonwealth of Toil: Chapters in the History of Massachusetts Workers and Their Unions.* Amherst: University of Massachusetts Press, 1996.

Levy, Leonard W. *The Law of the Commonwealth and Chief Justice Shaw: The Evolution of American Law, 1830–1860.* New York: Harper & Row, 1957.

Nelles, Walther. "Commonwealth v. Hunt." *Columbia Law Review* 32, no.7 (1932): 1128–1169.

Tomlins, Christopher L. *The State and the Unions: Labor Relations, Law, and the Organized Labor Movement in America, 1880–1960.* New York: Cambridge University Press, 1985.

Cases Cited

Commonwealth v. Hunt, 4 Metc, 111 (1842).

COMMUNICATIONS/TELEGRAPHY

Ever since 1845, when the company formed by American inventors/entrepreneurs Samuel Morse and Alfred Vail first linked up the East Coast cities of Washington DC, Baltimore, Philadelphia, New York, and Boston in a chain of electrical communication, the telegraph has been seen both as a technological revolution and as a commercial milestone. The wired electromechanical technology of Morse's dot-and-dash "key" would inspire a cascade of similar devices such as stock tickers, alarm systems, rudimentary fax machines, and, of course, telephones. And the organizational innovations that enabled local branch telegraph operators to respond to orders from managers at urban, regional, and national scales would help one firm, Western Union, become the first ever to grow literally coast-to-coast in its rise to what many at the time called "natural monopoly" power (a monopoly allowed to exist by the government because duplicating such expensive technology over such a vast geography seemed absurdly wasteful). However, lurking behind both the "lightning technologies" and the firms that developed and owned them was a vast reserve of human labor that was also crucial to the century-long success of the telegraph.

Certain categories of telegraphic labor remained relatively constant, from the technology's birth in the mid-nineteenth century to its decline in the mid-twentieth: lineworkers and machinists constructed and maintained the physical plant of poles, wires, and repeaters; male and female operators sent and received coded messages using this infrastructure; young messengers ferried those messages in printed form to and from the office; clerks of all sorts interacted with customers and managed complicated work schedules or pricing schemes; and managers at every level attempted to keep the entire process running as if it were one large machine. But at any particular moment, exploring the telegraph industry's division of labor reveals that its simple advertising stereotypes of lonely rural telegraph operators or eager urban messenger boys masked a complicated and polarized set of working conditions, which varied not only by skill and technology but also by geography.

Working in the Telegraph Industry

Of all the workers within the telegraph division of labor, the operators were perhaps the best known. Idealized as a standardized job, the work of sending and receiving telegraphic messages always varied with the type of technology employed and the level of skill demanded in any particular setting. Operators in small railroad offices with light traffic might serve additional functions as managers, lineworkers, ticket agents, or even messengers. They were often employed in subcontracting arrangements and paid in part by rail companies, which received free telegraph time in return. Operators in larger commercial offices would be separated into different grades, from contingent "on-call" daily labor to salaried branch managers. At all levels, their working day waxed and waned with buy/sell orders, press messages, greeting messages, and bulk corporate telegrams all coming in at different times and demanding different levels of skill and speed. Eventually, specialized operator niches for commodity exchanges, news wire services, and the leased lines of private corporations emerged. And gradually, the skill of tapping and listening with Morse code was rendered unnecessary with the development of typewriterlike "Automatic" keyboards. As Thomas Jepsen has shown, female operators were present even during the rise of the telegraph during the Civil War; however, turn-of-the-century urbanization, mechanization, and competition in the telegraph began to favor the employment of young women in the large commercial offices, a transition accelerated even further in the 1920s as the telegraph companies began using the telephone for message collection and even message distribution.

No matter what the context, operators were not simply message encoders and decoders. In the early days of the telegraph, operators were expected to "walk the line" to find the source of a transmission break. Paul Israel has shown that as the industry matured, it was operators with their tacit knowledge of the equipment and its limitations who offered some of the most important technological improvements to management. But the hallmark of the expanding and consolidating telegraph industry was an increasingly detailed division of labor: linework became the province of a skilled electrical trade, and invention moved increasingly out of the machine shop of on-the-job experience and into the laboratory of college-taught electrical theory.

A similar set of polarizations based on geography confronted telegraph clerks and messengers. In small towns and railway offices, a messenger or clerk was likely to be related to the local operator or manager. These settings provided messengers and clerks with the greatest opportunity to use their job as an apprenticeship and "learn the key" to advance into an operator slot. In the larger cities and commercial offices, by contrast, clerical work was highly routinized, and messenger work experienced such high turnover that advancement into operator jobs was rare. Inside the large commercial office, systems of pneumatic tubes might be tended by girls on roller skates transferring printed messages from station to station. Clerks who scheduled messenger routes might demand kickbacks or favors from the boys. Messengers themselves would be kept seated in back rooms with separate entrances, in order to control their behavior (and keep them out of the customer's sight). And managers used a variety of tactics, from assessing fines to mandating uniforms, to attempt to control the messenger's labor in the streets and at the site of the customer.

As Gregory Downey has shown, messengers in particular vexed the telegraph managers with their paradoxical labor role—simultaneously a technological bottleneck and a service and advertising necessity. Managers continually attempted to use technology to either enhance the telegraph messenger (by outfitting him on bicycles and motorcycles) or to replace the telegraph messenger (whether through telephone operators or rudimentary fax machines). Western Union messengers were advertised as hourly labor to customers, in what was arguably the first nationwide "temporary agency." Or they might be used as a nationwide marketing force, distributing free product samples, promotional leaflets, or political advertising to targeted urban and suburban neighborhoods. The telegraph industry went to great lengths to ensure its supply of messengers, even in the face of the tougher child labor and mandatory education laws of the 1910s and 1920s, culminating in an in-house Western Union "continuation school" in New York City that graduated hundreds of boys annually in the 1920s and 1930s.

Organizing the Telegraph Industry

From the very start, the widely varying working conditions and wage relations within the telegraph labor force, coupled with constant management pressures to cut office costs and increase message speed, made telegraphers of all kinds ripe for labor-organizing efforts. But at the same time, as Edwin Gabler has argued, the widely held perception of telegraph work (especially skilled male operator work) as a "middle-class profession" helped structure early telegraph organizations as benevolent societies and "company unions" rather than industrial labor organizations.

The first major labor action against management came with the 1883 strike of the Brotherhood of Telegraphers (affiliated with the Knights of Labor) against Western Union (then under the control of robber baron Jay Gould). The unusual combination of both operators and linemen lent power to the month-long strike, but the lack of participation from press and railroad telegraphers (who soon split off into their own associations) helped doom the effort. Another try began in 1903 with the formation of the Commercial Telegraphers Union (CTU), affiliated this time with the trade unions of the American Federation of Labor. A wildcat strike in 1907 had as its only positive result the initiation of a government investigation of the telegraph industry. Soon after, in 1909, American Telegraph & Telephone (AT&T) purchased a controlling interest in Western Union in an attempt to bring order to the labor and technology of both systems. AT&T relinquished control in 1914, only to see the post office take over both the telegraphs and the telephone industry through World War I. The outcome of both AT&T and government management control was the creation of a company union, the Association of Western Union Employees (AWUE), and the demoralization of the CTU through the 1920s.

Surprisingly perhaps, it was the telegraph messengers, courted by a new industrial union calling itself the American Communications Association (ACA), who helped bring about the legal end of the AWUE company union in the 1930s. Organizing efforts through World War II pitted the more radical ACA against the more conservative CTU; the ACA won victories in New York City (8,000 workers, including hundreds of messengers), but the CTU swept the rest of the nation's telegraph sites (and the remaining 50,000 or so telegraph employees). However, winning the right to representation was in a way an empty victory for the telegraph workers: after its wartime bubble burst, the telegraph industry would enter a slow but steady period of decline. After several attempts at modernization (and decades of labor attrition), Western Union, rechristened New Valley Corporation after selling its brand name, finally went bankrupt in the early 1990s. Yet, as Tom Standage illustrates, studying the "Victorian Internet" that was the telegraph may yet prove useful, especially in revealing (and revaluing) the hidden labor behind information and communcation networks today.

GREGORY J. DOWNEY

References and Further Reading

Downey, Gregory J. *Telegraph Messenger Boys: Labor, Technology, and Geography, 1850–1950*. New York: Routledge, 2002.

Gabler, Edwin. *The American Telegrapher*. New Brunswick, NJ: Rutgers University Press, 1988.

Israel, Paul. *From Machine Shop to Industrial Laboratory: Telegraphy and the Changing Context of American Invention, 1830–1920*. Baltimore: Johns Hopkins University Press, 1992.

Jepsen, Thomas C. *My Sisters Telegraphic: Women in the Telegraph Office, 1846–1950*. Athens: Ohio University Press, 2000.

Standage, Tom. *The Victorian Internet: The Remarkable Story of the Telegraph and the Nineteenth Century's On-Line Pioneers*. New York: Walker and Company, 1998.

COMMUNIST PARTY

The Communist movement in the United States was founded when left-wing radicals split away from the American Socialist Party (SP) in 1919 to create their own organizations. The two Communist parties that first emerged out of the SP differed from moderate socialists over trade union and political tactics, and support for American involvement in World War I, but from the beginning the Communists defined themselves primarily as belonging to an international working-class movement that had originated with the Bolshevik revolution and was centered in Moscow. American Communists pledged to conform to the revolutionary program of the Communist International (Comintern), founded by Lenin in Moscow in March 1919. Although it was composed of representatives from Communist parties from around the world, until its dissolution in 1943, the Comintern was dominated by Russian Communists. Because of its revolutionary prestige and resources, the Comintern exercised great political influence on the American Communist movement. Directives from the Comintern, reinforced by its undercover representatives in the United States, compelled the first two American Communist parties to merge and create a legal political organization, the Workers' Party, in 1921.

A large majority of the early American Communist movement were immigrants, many of whom had belonged to the earlier "language federations" of the Socialist Party, including Finns, Russians, Letts, Ukranians, Poles, and Hungarians. These groups faced intense nativist hostility throughout the 1920s. Immigrant radicals of all persuasions were subject to immediate deportation by the Immigration and Naturalization Service and had been arrested and detained by the hundreds during the Palmer Raids of 1919–1920. In the first decade and a half of its existence, the Communist movement faced intense official repression. Twenty of its leaders were arrested at its 1922 national convention. Justice Department and Bureau of Investigation agents worked with local police to circulate lists of Communists and affiliated radicals to trade unions in order to effect their expulsions.

The early Communists advocated "mass strikes," and some claimed to see revolutionary potential in the unprecedented strike wave of 1919, but at first very few had connections with or practical knowledge of the organized labor movement. A survey by the party in 1922 found that of its membership of 5,000–6000, only about 500 were native-born, and only 5% of the total were actively involved in trade union work. The founding manifestos of the early Communist movement expressed contempt for the American Federation of Labor (AFL), with its official model of craft-union voluntarism. Most Communists were sympathetic to the revolutionary industrial unionism of the Industrial Workers of the World (IWW). The IWW, more committed than the AFL to organizing immigrants, the unskilled, transients, and African-Americans, had generated large strikes and organizing campaigns in the period before World War I, but a large portion of its leadership was arrested and imprisoned during the war itself. William D. "Big Bill" Haywood, the personification of IWW militancy, fled to Moscow in 1921 to avoid a long prison sentence. The IWW was able to maintain only a tenuous or sporadic existence in working-class communities in the 1920s.

It was only after the Comintern's shift to a united front strategy after 1921 that the American party began to actively search for a route to influence within the American Federation of Labor, which had achieved huge increases in membership during World War I. This change in perspective in the early 1920s was consistent with the ideas of several influential syndicalists in the party, including James P. Cannon and Earl Browder, who were conscious of the weaknesses of the IWW and comprehended the militancy and radicalism that persisted within America's craft-conscious union tradition. Larger unions such as the United Mine Workers (UMW), the International Association of Machinists, and the Amalgamated Clothing Workers harbored significant left-socialist minorities that were deeply resentful of the labor-management cooperation plans, or "class collaboration," practiced by much of America's union leadership in the postwar era.

The party recruited William Z. Foster, a radical syndicalist who had helped initiate large AFL organizing campaigns in the meatpacking and steel industries in WWI. Foster attended the first Congress of the Red International of Labor Unions (Profintern) in Moscow in 1921. The head of the Profintern, Solomon Lozovsky, promised Foster and the small group of labor radicals he headed, the Trade Union Educational League (TUEL), financial support. Lozovsky and Foster agreed that Communist activists, while at some unspecified point responsible to the political leadership of the party, should exercise a degree of tactical flexibility and independence in their efforts to exert influence within existing unions. The TUEL, with its cohort of militant but pragmatic and experienced labor organizers dedicated to "boring from within" the AFL, became the focus for Communist activities in the labor movement in the 1920s. The powerful Chicago Federation of Labor worked closely with the TUEL, and Eugene Debs offered his approval of its aims.

The main issue taken up by Communists in the labor movement in the early 1920s was "amalgamation." This referred to ongoing (since before WWI) attempts by labor progressives and radicals to erase craft jurisdictional disputes and overhaul the structures of existing unions in order to make them more "industrial" in nature. By 1923, amalgamation resolutions, usually devoid of overtly Communist "line" or ideology, had been endorsed by hundreds of labor groups across the nation, including 16 state federations and 14 national unions. However, amalgamation was a cause that could only be taken up internally and provoked intense opposition among the officialdom. Anti-Communists also vigorously opposed the existence of Communist cells in the unions as a form of dual-unionism that ultimately undermined solidarity and effectiveness.

The Communists in the TUEL often considered themselves to be operating largely apart from the political apparatus of the party, and more "political" socialists like Charles Ruthenberg, Jay Lovestone, and Benjamin Gitlow openly opposed what they termed "Fosterism," or the TUEL's largely syndicalist emphasis on immediate demands or purely trade-union issues. The TUEL established active dissident cells in a large range of unions, including the railroad federations and shopmen's unions, the International

Association of Machinists, the United Mine Workers, and the main clothing and garment workers' unions.

The divisions between unionists and self-styled "political" Communists within the party were exacerbated as a result of controversy over labor party politics in 1923–1924. The Comintern intervened as well, demanding resolutions and tactics during this period that immensely complicated Communist unionists' ability to maintain alliances with union progressives. The Communists ended up running their own candidates in opposition to the Progressive Party in the presidential election of 1924.

In 1926, Communists helped lead a large and violent strike of textile workers in Passaic and established a strong "Save the Union" movement in the United Mine Workers. However, by the late 1920s, the TUEL as an organization had been largely dissolved. Union officials relentlessly attacked the TUEL, portraying amalgamation (and any other cause promoted by dissidents in their unions) as a power grab by the Communists. Within the party itself, trade union activists were often attacked as "mere" syndicalists, and the "boring-from-within" rationale was criticized for its lack of attention to organizing the unorganized.

With many AFL unions moribund or ineffective by the late 1920s, the Communists, under orders from the Comintern in 1928–1929, organized a new federation of independent unions, the Trade Union Unity League. The TUUL created opportunities for Communist activists to organize in areas that had previously been neglected. The Communist-led National Miners' Union, for instance, created a strong presence in the bituminous coalfields of western Pennsylvania and eastern Ohio during the first years of the Depression, eventually leading a large strike in 1931 that included a large number of blacks who were unemployed or had been denied membership in the UMW. The new Communist unions that were formed in a number of industries beginning in 1929 achieved few tangible organizational or strike successes. However, by 1934, the year the TUUL was formally dissolved, Communist organizers had "colonized" a number of strategic auto, rubber, meatpacking, textile, and steel plants, and had made important progress in establishing a new type of Communist unionism, more suited to the organization of African-Americans, women, and mass-production workers.

The Great Depression offered a tremendous challenge to American Communists. The party achieved an unprecedented level of credibility in American culture, as illustrated, for instance, by the endorsement of the 1932 presidential campaign of William Z. Foster and James Ford by a number of prominent American writers and intellectuals, including Sidney

Hook, Edmund Wilson, John Dos Passos, Theodore Dreiser, and Langston Hughes.

The labor movement, however, remained the most important focus for Communist organizing, and it was the influence that Communists gained in the Congress of Industrial Organizations (CIO) in the 1930s that provided them with their base of power in the political coalitions related to FDR and the New Deal. When John L. Lewis of the UMW broke with the leadership of the AFL in 1935 and created the CIO, he immediately turned to experienced Communist organizers to assist in solidifying and extending the gains of the new industrial union federation. Communists were vital in organizing the steel and automobile industries and were a crucial factor in carrying out what was perhaps the most important strike in American history, the 1937 sit-down in Flint, Michigan, that forced General Motors to recognize the United Auto Workers.

Communist unionists were often capable of flexible adaptation to local circumstances, and with noteworthy exceptions, were inclined to put the immediate demands of workers ahead of doctrinal shifts mandated by the Comintern. During the period of the CIO's formation, the Communist Party's popular front ideology coincided with its support of industrial unionism, antifascism, and alliance with New Deal and other progressive social forces. Communists played crucial roles in the formation of major CIO affiliates such as the United Auto Workers, the United Electrical Workers, the International Longshoremen's and Warehouse Union, and the Packinghouse Workers. They held various important positions of leadership in these unions, as well as in the Food and Tobacco Workers, the Mine, Mill, and Smelter Workers, the Fur and Leather Workers, and the Transport Workers. Although Communist Party members constituted only approximately 1% of the membership of the CIO, by the end of WWII they exercised decisive influence in 14 unions, with an estimated membership of 1.4 million, with another 1.5 million workers belonging to unions divided between pro- and anti-Communist leadership (of approximately 6.2 million total CIO members). Many influential CIO unionists were active leftists who never belonged to the party but sympathized with Communist positions on most issues.

One of the Communist Party's most distinctive characteristics was its strong advocacy of economic and civil rights for African-Americans. The party's position in this respect developed partly out of changes mandated at the Sixth Congress of the Communist International in 1928. There, the policy emerged that American Communists should demand "Negro self-determination in the black belt," or a separate nation in heavily black sections of the American South. Despite its provenance in the Comintern apparatus, the self-determination program opened up possibilities for mobilizing around explicitly racial issues. One effect was helping Communists establish outposts for organizing in the South in the 1930s; Communists were able to employ the self-determination slogan to effectively advance union and unemployed organizing in the Birmingham area, for instance. The party's defense of the Scottsboro boys, arrested in Alabama for a rape they did not commit, added to the status of the party in African-American communities. Communists were also active in dangerous campaigns for sharecroppers' unions. Anti-eviction actions and involvement in unemployment and poor relief campaigns attracted some blacks to the party.

In the labor movement, Communist organizers showed in a number of instances that they were capable of sacrificing principles of racial equality or integration in order to maintain solidarity with white majorities. However, when compared with the records of other CIO unions and organizers, Communists were in general known for their aggressiveness in defending the rights of black workers. This was often true in conflicts where Communists could have made easier advances by compromising with racists. Communist-influenced CIO affiliates such as the Mine, Mill, and Smelters Union and the Food and Tobacco Workers were noteworthy in this regard.

American Communists generally limited the role of women in party and union leadership. There were several noteworthy exceptions in the electrical workers, office workers, and needle-trades unions. In the Food and Tobacco Workers and Electrical Workers unions, with their large proportions of female members, Communists supported job protection and pay equity.

The question of whether the American Communist movement owed its character, accomplishments, and failures primarily to the Comintern and the directives of Soviet politicians, or whether it was a relatively independent political movement that responded primarily to social and economic conditions in the United States, retains its interest to historians of American politics. Much recent research and writing has emphasized the role of American Communists in transmitting strategic intelligence information to the Soviet Union, and maintains that the party was essentially a "Soviet world" dominated by the malign interests and ideology of the Soviet Union.

Although this interpretation tends to focus on only one particular area of Communist activity, it echoes a persistent theme in attacks on the party throughout its history. According to influential critics in the labor movement, Communists were ultimately unable to represent the best interests of organized workers because of the party's strong adherence to Soviet political "line" and ideology. Several salient episodes in the party's history illustrate this argument.

In 1939, as a result of the German-Soviet Nonaggression Pact, the American party suddenly shifted away from its earlier antifascist, pro-Roosevelt perspective and declared its neutrality toward what was now called an "imperialist war" in Europe. From 1939 to 1941, Communists were prominently involved in large strikes in American defense-related industries, allowing employers and their allies to exacerbate fears of "sabotage" of American preparedness efforts. However, these strikes arose out of indisputably local grievances, and during this period many Communist-led unions with defense contracts, including the longshoremen and electrical workers, did not strike.

Following the Nazi invasion of the Soviet Union in 1941, Communist-influenced unions were particularly active in promoting unhindered production for the war effort, vigorously promoting the no-strike pledge and, in some cases, speedups and incentive pay plans. The party attacked the African-American unionist A. Philip Randolph's March on Washington campaign to achieve equal employment in defense industries because of its supposed potential to undermine workplace unity. Under General Secretary Earl Browder's expansive interpretation of the Soviet Union's wartime-alliance posture, the party advocated extension of the no-strike pledge into the postwar period. These positions were not detrimental to the CIO politically or to its tremendous growth in membership during the war. However, in the automobile industry in particular, the Communist pro-production policy would provide one basis for effective attacks on Communist unionists in the first years of the Cold War.

The Communist Party was powerfully affected by the change in U.S.-Soviet relations after World War II. The famous "Duclos letter" originated in Moscow in 1945. It strongly criticized Browder's projections of "class peace" in America in the postwar era and was the principal catalyst for an abrupt change in the party's leadership. Although dismaying to many, Browder's expulsion had little immediate effect on party membership as a whole.

The first years of the Cold War era provided the context for the re-emergence of highly effective anti-Communist forces in the labor movement. The party's tightly disciplined and secretive caucusing methods allowed its opponents to portray it as a devious and essentially undemocratic influence. Many New Deal progressives, including the "center" leadership of the CIO and its president, Philip Murray, were initially hopeful for a generally pro-Soviet political atmosphere after World War II. However, as American foreign policy turned aggressively anti-Soviet, a range of criticisms of the party from church groups, the leadership of the AFL, and prominent unionists like Walter Reuther, elected president of the UAW in 1946, put heavy pressure on Communists and their allies. The Taft-Hartley Act, passed by the new Republican congress in 1947, contained a clause that required union officials to sign anti-Communist affidavits in order to participate in National Labor Relations Board (NLRB) deliberations.

In 1948, the American Communist leadership, responding to signals from Soviet sources, strongly pressured their union cadre to endorse the third-party presidential campaign of Henry Wallace. It is noteworthy that Communist leaders made their individual endorsements of Wallace nonbinding on their memberships. Wallace was a vigorous critic of Truman's foreign policy and developed little rank-and-file support. The anti-Wallace forces in the CIO ranged from principled anti-Stalinists to rank opportunists. The CIO leadership decided it could not tolerate an independent Communist political voice in its councils and unambiguously aligned with Truman and the emerging anti-Communist consensus. Following the 1948 elections, the CIO began a campaign of dismissals, "raiding" of locals, and expulsions of entire unions that permanently crippled the influence of Communists in the labor movement. By 1950, the CIO had expelled 11 unions representing between 17% and 20% of its total membership.

The expulsion of powerful Communist-led unions from the CIO had a dramatic effect on the American labor movement. CIO unions that were Communist-led or had a strong Communist presence before 1949 were in general more democratic in governance, less inclined to cede management prerogatives in their contracts, and more responsive to the racial grievances of their members than were unions without significant Communist influence. Consistent with the earliest syndicalist inclinations of American Communism, the party's organizers exhibited a predisposition to equate workers' "immediate" demands, and mobilization on the shop floor, with their movement's highest political purposes. The persecution of Communists contributed to the acceptance of precisely formalized labor-relations strategies developed by unions and corporate management after World War II. It cemented the CIO's political alliance with the Democratic Party, reducing its effectiveness as an independent political voice.

The Communist Party was further decimated in the 1950s by the wide-scale political repression of the Red Scare and McCarthyism. The revelation of the crimes of Stalin's police state at the Twentieth

Congress of the Soviet Communist Party in 1956 created intense disillusionment within the party and a steady decline in membership. The party's unwillingness to abandon principles of Leninist political organization caused an exodus of reformists, as did the Soviet repression of the Hungarian revolution of 1956. By 1958, the party's membership had fallen to approximately 3,000, from a high point of nearly 66,000 (with thousands of close supporters and sympathizers) in 1939. In later years, following party leader Gus Hall's support of an attempted coup against Mikhail Gorbachev in 1991, the Communist movement split between democratic reformers and hard-liners. At present, the Communist Party has ceased to exist as an influential political force on the American left.

EDWARD P. JOHANNINGSMEIER

References and Further Reading

Barrett, James. *William Z. Foster and the Tragedy of American Radicalism*. Urbana: University of Illinois Press, 1999.
Draper, Theodore. *American Communism and Soviet Russia*. New York: Viking, 1960.
———. *The Roots of American Communism*. New York: Viking, 1956.
Isserman, Maurice. *Which Side Were You On? The American Communist Party during the Second World War*. Middletown, CT: Wesleyan University Press, 1982.
Johanningsmeier, Edward P. *Forging American Communism: The Life of William Z. Foster*. Princeton, NJ: Princeton University Press, 1994.
Klehr, Harvey, John Earl Haynes, Fridrikh I. Firxov. *The Soviet World of American Communism*. New Haven, CT: Yale University Press, 1995.
Ottanelli, Fraser M. *The Communist Party of the United States*. New Brunswick, NJ: Rutgers University Press, 1991.
Rosswurm, Steve. *The CIO's Left-Led Unions*. New Brunswick, NJ: Rutgers University Press, 1992.
Zeitlin, Maurice, and Judith Stepan-Norris. *Left Out: Reds and America's Industrial Unions*. Cambridge: Cambridge University Press, 2003.
Zieger, Robert H. *The CIO: 1935–1955*. Chapel Hill: University of North Carolina Press, 1995.

See also **Browder, Earl; Foster, William Z.; Haywood, William D. "Big Bill"; Industrial Workers of the World; Socialist Party of America**

COMPANY TOWNS

During the nineteenth and twentieth centuries, industrial capitalists and private corporations came into sharp conflict with the labor movement and portions of the general public throughout the United States over the issue of the nature and significance of company towns. Although the term "company town" has sometimes been loosely applied to various settings, the classic company town was one in which the influence of a sole dominant employer, often the founder of the town, was such that it single-handedly determined the economic, political, and social life of the affected geographical area as well as the working and living conditions of its employees. Indeed, the very existence of company towns raised fundamental issues related to workers' rights, monopoly capitalism, civil liberties, and the meaning of citizenship.

The quality of employment, housing, and resources in company towns varied greatly; and not all were successful profit-making enterprises. Nevertheless, the very erection of these towns gave employers an unprecedented degree of control over their employees and their families, a degree of control that did not exist in independent towns or cities where multiple industries and companies co-existed. The dependence of working people on one single source for all the necessities of living, including their jobs, their wages, their working conditions, their housing, their utilities, their store supplies, and their medical care, was absolute. No one doubted where the source of real authority lay. Unions, independent worker organizations, credible business competition, an autonomous media, and critical governmental or public oversight were typically precluded from these environments. Companies were free to pay degrading wages in scrip rather than bona fide currency; to allow foremen to make arbitrary or dangerous demands at work; to require employees to shop only at company stores where they paid elevated prices; to discharge and blacklist workers for virtually any reason; to use private police forces and a spy system to preclude free assembly and free speech; to evict families and cut off store credit when workers engaged in strikes; and to dictate workers' choices at elections. Maintaining a pliant and nonunionized labor force in company towns meant keeping workers isolated from the American labor movement and ensuring that the towns themselves were immune from the broader democratic influences of the outside world.

The history of company towns is inextricably linked to the story of the rise, evolution, and eventual decline of industrial capitalist development in the United States. That history falls roughly into three eras: (1) from the early nineteenth century to the Civil War; (2) from the 1880s to the New Deal and World War II; and (3) from about 1950 to the early twenty-first century.

Company towns were relatively scarce in the early nineteenth century, when large-scale capitalist industry was local or regional. Many of those that did exist were products of the pioneering textile industry in

New England. Samuel Slater's erection of textile factories and the establishment of company towns such as Pawtucket, Rhode Island, in the 1790s set the precedent for the Boston Associates and other textile financial concerns to develop similar enterprises in Lowell, Lawrence, and elsewhere. The number and size of company towns dramatically increased after the Civil War, when industrial development expanded throughout the entire country. Many prominent Gilded Age mining, steel, textile, and railroad corporations established them during the heyday of their productive operations from about the 1880s to the New Deal and World War II. Subsequently, the rising power of the labor movement, the passage of New Deal reforms, and working people's access to greater mobility through the automobile led corporations to re-evaluate their policies and business strategies. Many began to sell off company houses and properties, and by the end of World War II, company towns in the United States were declining, disappearing, or re-emerging in modified forms. The shift to a postindustrial economy in recent decades has left much of the nation's former industrial heartland, including the company towns that lay within the "rust belt," economically devastated.

The primary reason industrial employers established company towns in the United States was to attract and retain a pliant, loyal, and docile work force whose productive labor would ensure substantial profits for the owners and shareholders. The directors of the large, powerful corporations based in New York or Philadelphia that conducted business on an international scale had broad business goals in mind when they drew up comprehensive plans for their towns. Many of those they erected were, of necessity, located in sparsely populated rural areas where labor was scarce. Mining companies, for example, had no choice but to set up their operations near the valuable mineral deposits they sought to extract, and textile companies dependent on abundant water power had to build their factories near rivers. In such instances, the ability to offer potential employees housing, credit, and accessible merchandise gave business enterprises a valuable tool for recruiting the needed labor force.

Also, competition for labor was often fierce during the period of industrial expansion before World War I, and unskilled and semiskilled laboring jobs were plentiful. The Berwind-White Coal Mining Corporation was only one of the many coal companies that used the resources of its company towns as an inducement for southern and eastern European immigrants to come to work for it rather than to go to work in the mines of one of its competitors. Once workers and their families settled in such company towns, the irregular work of the mining industry, the payment of low wages, and compulsory company store credit made it difficult for the indebted workers—or their children, the company's future labor force—to migrate away. The establishment of company stores and company housing thus served the interests of the employers in many ways and suggests that their overall worth cannot be judged solely in narrow economic terms such as how much or how little profit a given store or housing project made.

Corporate Justifications and Workers' Protests

From the outset, the founders of company towns justified their creation of the towns in paternalistic, humanitarian, and altruistic terms while ignoring their own self-interested motivations and other key labor and civil rights issues. The early nineteenth-century textile magnates may have created good housing and been influenced by the reform impulse of the era or by the well-publicized utopian social experiments of Robert Owen and others in Europe and the United States, but the primary reason they created the towns was to make money, run a profitable business, and resolve the "labor problem," as they saw it, in their own terms. In a similar manner, throughout the Gilded Age and Progressive Era, gigantic coal and steel corporations and their supporters attempted to counter growing public criticism by describing their company stores, company houses, and company towns as contributions to the workers' "welfare" and evidence of the capitalists' "philanthropy."

Workers often ridiculed such claims. Throughout U.S. history, they frequently protested arbitrary company-town rule at the workplace and in the community at large. They quit jobs, migrated elsewhere, attempted to organize unions and other independent organizations, engaged in strikes, joined political parties, and lobbied state legislatures for relief. They had occasional successes. For example, hard coal miners who had long protested the existence and policies of company stores, which they called "pluck-me" stores, finally succeeded in 1891 in getting passage of a Pennsylvania state law that prohibited industrial employers from owning them. However, coal, steel, and textile corporations easily skirted the intent of the new law by merely incorporating their stores under a different name. The gap in power relations between the capitalist class interests and the labor movement was too great for workers to end the enormous corporate power inherent in company-town rule. Working people were successful in curbing the worst abuses of company-town rule only after the labor movement mobilized in the 1930s and made substantial change possible by securing passage in 1935 of the Wagner Act, which guaranteed workers the right to organize and bargain collectively. They publicized abuses that led to the abolition of private police systems and gained the enactment, on the state and federal levels, of other New Deal legislation that extended civil liberties to these regions and ensured workers greater economic and political rights.

It is probably not accidental that many of the nation's most important strikes, and many of the most infamous examples of labor violence, took place in such company towns as Homestead, Pullman, Lattimer, Lawrence, Ludlow, Windber, Honea Path, and Flint. Such conflicts undermined the contentions of industrial employers that these were "model" towns that had resolved the "labor problem." Indeed, they revealed that many working people considered their employers autocratic and their company towns "slave" towns. One of the major demands of nonunion miners who joined a national coal strike in 1922 was "to secure the rights of free Americans." Such strikes called public attention to serious issues inherent in company-town rule in a nominally democratic society. Foremost of these was the suppression of basic constitutional rights and civil liberties, a suppression that violated the rights of the working classes, middle classes, and all Americans.

Pullman, Illinois, stands out as the classic example of a company town that exemplified the differing perspectives of industrial capitalists, workers, the public, and the government. George M. Pullman, the wealthy owner of the Pullman Palace Car Company, one of the country's richest and most successful railroad car-building corporations, founded the town in 1880 as a profit-making business enterprise and as a means to solve the problem of growing labor unrest that became apparent after the railroad strikes of 1877. From the outset, the company, as sole property owner, had absolute authority throughout the well-built, attractive town. Pullman himself had instituted an elaborate spying system and prohibited unions, taverns, brothels, independent businesses, and other "outside" influences he deemed harmful.

Initially, the public heralded the "model" town and the founder's paternalism, but there was occasion to rethink such views after May 11, 1894, when Pullman workers went out on strike during the depression and the local work stoppage turned into one of the most important strikes and boycotts in the nation's history. Pullman workers cited their many grievances, including their lack of a voice at work or in town, wage cuts, high rents, company stores, and their inability to form unions or exercise their constitutional rights. As one striker expressed it, "We are born in a Pullman house, fed from the Pullman shop, taught in the Pullman school, catechized in a Pullman church, and when we die we shall be buried in the Pullman cemetery and go to the Pullman hell." By contrast, George Pullman and company officers argued that property rights were sacred and inviolable; that workers had no legitimate rights but were, in effect, commodities subject only to the law of supply and demand; and that neither government nor any other third party had any right to tell a company how to run its business.

Although the Pullman workers and the American Railway Union, the fledgling industrial union that took up their cause, ultimately lost the strike, George Pullman, the notion of paternalism, and the myth of the "model" town lost, too. In 1898, the Illinois Supreme Court ruled that the town of Pullman was a company town and, therefore, incompatible with American democratic institutions. Because the railroad car company exercised a monopoly over both employment and town facilities, the court later ordered the company to sell off the town's properties and businesses.

Other states were not bound by the Illinois court decisions, however, and company towns continued to flourish in the twentieth century. For example, from the 1920s on, textile companies moved south, where they established many such towns. Company towns became an important issue during the New Deal. Eleanor Roosevelt, an ally of the labor movement, decried the dependent conditions of the workers she visited in various mining and other company towns in the 1930s, and it is significant to note that when a New Deal Democrat, Pennsylvania Governor George Earle, denounced company towns as symbols of "economic serfdom" in 1937, there were 1,200 such towns within that state alone.

Company towns were an integral feature of industrial capitalist development in the United States and a prime example of the inordinately unequal power relations that prevailed between business and labor throughout most of the nation's history. Reform of company towns became possible under the New Deal, but those reforms were limited, and the unequal gap that existed in power relations between the capitalist classes and working people in the early twenty-first century was arguably as great as it was before the New Deal. The alliance between business and government, the triumph of global capitalism, and the decline of the labor movement in the post-New Deal era left industrial workers such as those in Flint,

Michigan, or abandoned one-industry towns such as Homestead, Pennsylvania, in deep straits. Although classic company towns have declined in numbers, their legacies, their problems, and their modified versions live on under new circumstances. Meanwhile, none of the major contested issues of workers' rights, civil liberties, the viability of democracy, and the nature of capitalism, issues that lay at the center of the historic conflicts over company towns and subsequent assessments of their role in U.S. history, were resolved.

MILDRED ALLEN BEIK

References and Further Reading

Allen, James B. *The Company Town in the American West.* Norman: University of Oklahoma Press, 1966.

Andrews, Gregg. *City of Dust: A Cement Company Town in the Land of Tom Sawyer.* Columbia: University of Missouri Press, 1996.

———. *Insane Sisters: Or, the Price Paid for Challenging a Company Town.* Columbia: University of Missouri Press, 1999.

Beik, Mildred Allen. *The Miners of Windber: The Struggles of New Immigrants for Unionization, 1890s–1930s.* University Park: The Pennsylvania State University Press, 1996.

Byington, Margaret F. *Homestead: The Households of a Mill Town.* New York: Charities Publications Committee, 1910; reprint, New York: Arno Press, 1969.

Carlson, Linda. *Company Towns of the Pacific Northwest.* Seattle: University of Washington Press, 2003.

"Cites Injustices Alleged by Miners," *New York Times,* June 4, 1923, p. 17.

Corbin, David Alan. *Life, Work, and Rebellion in the Coal Fields: The Southern West Virginia Miners, 1880–1922.* Urbana: University of Illinois Press, 1981.

Crawford, Margaret. *Building the Workingman's Paradise: The Design of American Company Towns.* New York: Verso, 1995.

Dublin, Thomas. *Women at Work: The Transformation of Work and Community in Lowell, Massachusetts, 1826–1860.* New York: Columbia University Press, 1979.

Faust, Bob. "Lead in the Water: Power, Progressivism, and Resource Control in a Missouri Mining Community. *Agricultural History* 76, no. 2 (Spring 2002): 405–418.

Fishback, Price. *Soft Coal, Hard Choices: The Economic Welfare of Bituminous Coal Miners, 1890–1930.* New York: Oxford University Press, 1992.

Garner, John S. *The Model Company Town: Urban Design through Private Enterprise in Nineteenth-Century New England.* Amherst: University of Massachusetts Press, 1985.

Hall, Jacqueline et al. *Like a Family: The Making of a Southern Cotton Mill World.* Chapel Hill: University of North Carolina Press, 1987.

Hirshfield, David, New York City, Committee on Labor Conditions at the Berwind-White Company's Coal Mines in Somerset and Other Counties, Pennsylvania. *Statement of Facts and Summary of Committee Appointed by Honorable John F. Hylan, Mayor of the City of New York to Investigate the Labor Conditions of the Berwind-White Company's Coal Mines in Somerset and Other Counties, Pennsylvania.* New York: M. B. Brown. December 1922.

Illinois Labor History Society. *Palace Cars and Paradise, the Pullman Model Town.* 28 minutes. Videocassette. Chicago: Illinois History Society, 1984.

Johnson, Ole S. *The Industrial Store: Its History, Operations and Economic Significance.* Atlanta: University of Georgia, School of Business Administration, 1952.

Keller, Richard C. *Pennsylvania's Little New Deal.* New York: Garland Publishing, 1982.

Lane, Winthrop. *The Denial of Civil Liberties in the Coal Fields.* New York: George H. Doran Co., 1924.

Lankton, Larry D. "Paternalism and Social Control in the Lake Superior Copper Mines, 1845–1913." *Upper Midwest History* 5 (1985): 1–18.

Lindsey, Almont. *The Pullman Strike: The Story of a Unique Experiment and of a Great Labor Upheaval.* Chicago: University of Chicago Press, 1942.

Marcus, Irwin M., Eileen M. Cooper, and James P. Dougherty. "Confrontation at Rossiter: The Coal Strike of 1927–1928 and Its Aftermath." *Pennsylvania History* 59, no. 4 (October 1992): 310–326.

Miller, Donald L., and Richard E. Sharpless. *The Kingdom of Coal: Work, Enterprise, and Ethnic Communities in the Mine Fields.* Philadelphia: University of Pennsylvania Press, 1985.

Miller, George H. "Plan Your Town as Carefully as You Would Your Plant." *Coal Age* 14 (July 28, 1918): 130–132.

Moore, Michael. *Roger & Me.* Written, produced, and directed by Michael Moore. 91 minutes. Videocassette. Burbank, CA: Warner Home Video, 1990.

Nelson, Daniel. *Managers and Workers: Origins of the New Factory Systems in the United States, 1880–1920.* Madison: University of Wisconsin Press, 1975.

Ricketts, Elizabeth. "The Struggle for Civil Liberties and Unionization in the Coal Fields: The Free Speech Case of Vintondale, Pennsylvania, 1922." *The Pennsylvania Magazine of History and Biography* 122, no. 4 (October 1998): 319–352.

Serrin, William. *Homestead: The Glory and Tragedy of an American Steel Town.* New York: Times Books, 1992.

Shifflett, Crandall A. *Coal Towns: Life, Work, and Culture in Company Towns of Southern Appalachia, 1880–1960.* Knoxville: University of Tennessee Press, 1991.

U.S. Strike Commission. *Report on the Chicago Strike of June–July 1894.* Washington, DC: GPO, 1895.

Walkowitz, Daniel. *Worker City, Company Town: Iron and Cotton-Worker Protest in Troy and Cahoes, New York, 1855–84.* Urbana: University of Illinois Press, 1978.

See also **Anthracite Coal Strike (1902); Brophy, John: Congress of Industrial Organizations; De-industrialization; Gastonia Strike (1929); Hapgood, Powers; Homestead (1892); J. P. Stevens Campaign (1963–1980); LaFollette Civil Liberties Committee; Lawrence Strike (1912); Lowell Turnouts (1834, 1836); Ludlow Massacre (1914); Pullman Strike and Boycott (1894); Pullman, George Morimer; Sit-Down Strikes (1937); Steel and Iron; United Mine Workers of America; United Steelworkers of America; Welfare Capitalism**

COMPUTERS

Although computers became a pervasive part of daily life in the United States toward the end of the twentieth century, little has been written about the history of labor in the computer industry. More common are studies of technological innovation, the contributions of key individuals, and the consumption patterns for computers and related technologies. In most of these analyses, labor—particularly blue-collar labor—is an invisible or marginal factor.

Moreover, writing a labor history of the computer industry raises several difficulties. The sheer ubiquity of computers in the late twentieth and early twenty-first centuries in the United States and the broad scope of the industry make it difficult to categorize and draw general conclusions about the labor being performed. Computing includes work in microelectronics manufacture, telecommunications, software publishing, and many other areas. In a 1986 study, the National Research Council divided the computer industry into categories: engineers, computer specialists (including computer scientists, programmers, and software engineers), technicians, operators, and production workers. However, these categories do not account for the large numbers of nontechnical workers in the computer industry, such as those in sales and administration. Growth in online commerce has further diversified the computer industry and blurred the boundaries of traditional labor classification. Because much of our knowledge of computer history derives from the surviving corporate literature, which depicts events and practices from the perspective of management, certain forms of labor are more prevalent in the literature than others.

Early History

Objections to computerization have often framed computers as the enemy of workers, automating their work and performing with greater speed and efficiency the tasks previously undertaken by humans. However, before 1945, the term "computer" referred to a human being, usually a woman. Human computers performed the tedious calculations that filled mathematical tables used for astronomy, maritime navigation, advanced mathematics, ballistics, and other applications during the eighteenth and nineteenth centuries and the first part of the twentieth century.

In the nineteenth century, the mechanization of information processing paralleled industrialization. In 1821, the British mathematician and inventor Charles Babbage modeled his "difference engine," a machine designed to automate the process of producing mathematical tables, on the division of labor advocated by Adam Smith in the *Wealth of Nations* and the intellectual division of labor found in the human table-making "factories" such as those in Napoleon's France. However, Babbage was also an economist best known by his peers for the book *On the Economy of Machinery and Manufactures* (1832), which surveyed manufacturing processes of the period. Economics, manufacturing, and information processing came together in Babbage's subsequent plans for a more general "analytic engine" (1856). Using the nineteenth-century textile mill as a model, Babbage expanded his design for the difference engine to create a more general machine that shared many characteristics found in modern computers, such as memory, the ability to accept programmed instructions, and a central processing unit that he aptly called a "mill."

Across the Atlantic in the United States, Herman Hollerith, an engineer who had worked as a clerk for the U.S. Census Bureau, created the first tabulating machines to save census workers the daily drudgery of computing data by hand and to reduce the time needed to compile census results. With the introduction of tabulating machinery for the 1890 census, government clerks punched data for each U.S. resident onto a perforated card; Hollerith's machinery then tabulated and sorted the information. Each clerk punched an average of seven hundred cards per day, and more than 80 clerks operated the tabulating and sorting machines, each clerk processing one thousand cards or more per hour. Hollerith's Tabulating Machine Company (TMC), formed in 1896, was the forerunner of the computing giant International Business Machines (IBM).

Hollerith's machines did not replace the use of human computers for more complicated projects, such as those directed by the U.S. military during the first part of the twentieth century. Human computers held a place of importance during World War II. Approximately two hundred women with university degrees in mathematics computed ballistics trajectories at the University of Pennsylvania's Moore School as part of the war effort. When the Moore School finished building the first electronic computer, the ENIAC (electronic numerical integrator and computer), in 1945, many of these female computers became the first computer programmers.

In this period, computers, both human and machine, crunched numbers for scientific purposes. Computing was the exclusive domain of trained mathematicians, scientists, and engineers. This changed in the 1950s, when the computer became a data-processing machine marketed to and adopted by the business community.

J. Presper Eckert and John Mauchly, formerly of the Moore School faculty, formed one of the first computer businesses, Electronic Control Company, to sell the first commercial computer (UNIVAC), but IBM and about 30 other firms soon followed and developed their own machines for business applications. By the mid-1950s, IBM machines dominated the market.

The growth of commercial computing expanded the range of tasks performed by workers in the industry and changed the idea of what it meant to be a computer worker. IBM, for example, built a successful sales force based on sales quotas, commissions, and a strict dress code, which remained in place until the 1990s. All salesmen completed a comprehensive training program and were the cornerstone of IBM's marketing strategy. By the mid-1960s, IBM had nearly 250,000 employees, a figure that climbed to 400,000 by 1985. Not all were computer engineers. With a reputation for job security and a public image as a benevolently paternalistic company, IBM became a coveted place to work for white-collar, middle-class employees during the 1960s, 1970s, and 1980s. However, IBM also depended upon a large infrastructure of technicians, clerical workers, administrative staff, training staff, middle managers, and janitorial workers, among others.

Changes in the computer market paralleled changes in the technology and manufacture of a computer's component parts. The first computers used vacuum tubes. Later models used transistors and, eventually, integrated circuits. The manufacture of a reliable component often required a separate set of techniques, tools, and environmental controls than those that led to the initial laboratory prototype. Bell Laboratories announced the invention of the transistor in 1948, but it was 1951 before the first transistors rolled off its assembly line at a Western Electric plant in Allentown, Pennsylvania.

Because new developments within the industry occurred so rapidly, factories often doubled as laboratories for companies that wanted to be innovative and to manufacture these complex component technologies on a large scale. Western Electric, the manufacturing arm of Bell Laboratories, was a pioneer and employed a team of Bell Labs engineers charged with transforming laboratory inventions into reliable mass-produced goods. In this context, the historian Stuart W. Leslie observes, such "plants should be considered a new kind of laboratory, one devoted to process rather than product." Workers followed strict rules concerning clothing, hair, make-up, and the cleanliness of their workspace. In 1960, workers at the Allentown plant assembled transistors largely by hand, and women outnumbered men on the assembly line by a ratio of 7 to 1.

As a branch of Bell Labs, Western Electric sold transistors for telecommunications systems, not computers. However, its manufacturing practices set the standard for the growing semiconductor industry, which supplied the computer industry. Fairchild Semiconductor was one of several companies that adopted Western Electric's techniques, including clean room practices. Located on the San Francisco Peninsula, the area that would become known as Silicon Valley, Fairchild became a major source of silicon components for computers in the late 1950s, selling to IBM, among others. Fairchild pioneered new methods of manufacture such as photolithography, which improved transistor performance and reliability and later made possible the manufacture of integrated circuits. Like the Western Electric work force, Fairchild's consisted of semiskilled female workers as well as groups of engineers charged with increasing factory production capacities. Fairchild raised the standards for its clean rooms, dust-proofing and air-conditioning all assembly and processing areas and prohibiting employees from smoking on company premises. The firm also required workers to adhere to a strict set of manufacturing procedures outlined in lengthy company manuals.

In the mid-1960s, Fairchild cut its labor costs by moving the testing and assembly of its transistors and integrated circuits to Hong Kong, where unskilled laborers were paid 25 cents an hour instead of the $2.80 per hour that Bay Area factory workers commanded. Other semiconductor firms, including Motorola, Texas Instruments, Pacific Semiconductor, and Hoffman Electronics, soon also sent work to Southeast Asia.

From 1960 to 1970, the semiconductor industry witnessed a period of dramatic growth, fueled in part by rising demand from the computer industry. In 1960, Fairchild had 1,400 employees on its payroll. Ten years later, it and its Bay Area spin-off companies employed about 12,000 people. Growing computer sales helped the semiconductor industry to thrive. One thousand computers were shipped in 1957, compared with sales of 18,700 computers in 1967, and many machines contained more than half a million transistors. In 1968, the year that two Fairchild founders, Robert Noyce and Gordon Moore, left to form Intel, Fairchild commanded 80% of the market for integrated circuits for computers. Its victory was short-lived. Intel's introduction of the microprocessor in the 1970s secured its supremacy into the twenty-first century.

The U.S. computer industry enjoyed continued growth throughout the 1970s and 1980s. In 1970, the U.S. Census Bureau estimated that nearly 1.17 million people worked in the computer industry, a figure that grew to 1.6 million people by 1980. Men dominated the computer work force, particularly in the highest-paid engineering positions. Although many of the first computers were female, women and members of minority groups were, and continued to be, underrepresented in engineering and technical positions, disproportionately occupying many lower-paid clerical and factory jobs. A 1986 report from the National Research Council summed up the situation: "High tech may produce integrated circuits, but it does not necessarily produce an integrated work force or eliminate the female/male earnings differential."

Software and Labor

Despite the eventual disparities in pay and promotion for men and women in the computer industry, early computing machines created new areas and opportunities for female labor. Occupations such as computer programmer lacked a gender precedent, and women could fill such positions without challenging gender stereotypes. Programming was often considered an extension of clerical work, which made such jobs logical for female hires. However, the gender composition of the programming work force saw a significant shift during the 1950s. Men conducted the majority of programming work in the United States from then on. The historians Nathan Ensmenger and William Aspray link this demographic shift to the rise of business computing and the increased demand for programmers in industry, which quickly depleted the available pool of mathematically trained female computers and computer programmers.

According to Ensmenger and Aspray, U.S. companies began expressing fears of a programmer shortage as early as 1954, and this anxiety continued throughout the 1960s. At the same time, programmers experienced a professional identity crisis. Industry trade publications debated the skills, education, and abilities required to become a professional programmer. This was before the advent of most university computer science departments, so college-educated students who learned how to program in the 1960s did so informally, usually in a scientific setting. In most cases, these students wrote programs with little regard for their eventual application or the deadline for their completion, considerations at the heart of industry practice. Early programmers often described software writing as more art than science. This frustrated managers, who hoped to standardize programmers' qualifications and abilities and to structure the process of writing software.

As the 1960s progressed, professional computer societies formed and helped to professionalize those involved in software development. Hierarchies of work emerged within the software industry. University-educated systems analysts became the elite of the profession, with the greatest opportunities for advancing to management. Programmers, or "coders," received fewer opportunities for promotion, and their job descriptions required that they possess a technical degree. Software workers, like other white-collar members of the computer industry, did not organize or join unions.

In the 1970s, management focused on controlling the behavior of programmers rather than increasing their output or efficiency. In his 1977 book *Programmers and Managers*, the sociologist Philip Kraft wrote that management practices such as structured programming, modular programming, and the use of prepackaged software programs allowed companies to cut their labor costs by standardizing the work. By dividing software production into a set of smaller steps connected by a routine set of relationships, managers could make software workers interchangeable. These practices transformed programming into a less-skilled form of work and reduced the level of intellectual control that programmers had over software development. Kraft's Marxist-inspired conclusions are not universally accepted, but his work stands as one of the most thorough studies of the programming profession during the 1970s.

Men continued to hold most of the better-paid jobs in the software industry, including those in engineering and systems analysis. Women gravitated toward less-skilled keypunch and data-entry positions. According to the 1980 U.S. Census, women held 92% of all data-entry jobs, but only 22% of all computer scientists and 31% of all computer programmers were female. The percentage of women enrolled in U.S. university computer science programs declined after the 1980s, a phenomenon that social scientists, educators, and computer professionals cannot fully explain. Moreover, corporate practices of sending programming work to other countries negatively affected the employment prospects for U.S. programmers and contributed to an overall decline in computer science enrollments in the first part of the twenty-first century. In 2005, the U.S. Labor Department predicted the employment of U.S. programmers would continue to grow at around the same average rate as other occupations through the year 2012, with most growth occurring in the area of software publishing. However, in areas such as computer manufacturing, the U.S. Labor Department expects a 23.4% drop in the number of U.S. programmers needed through 2012, the second-largest projected decrease in the sector, behind only electrical and electronic equipment assemblers.

The High-Tech Boom

The late 1970s and early 1980s witnessed a radical change in the computer industry. The personal computer, or PC, brought computers into the house as well as the office and made computer technology accessible to lay users, not just hobbyists or experts. This increased the number of workers in the industry and expanded computer industry work to include sales, tech support, product development, and administrative resources for these new markets.

Advances in electronic manufacturing technology also changed the character of labor in the computer industry during the 1980s. Some sectors, such as circuit board assembly, became automated. Demand for U.S. assemblers dropped dramatically, and companies sent most remaining work involving production and assembly of their circuit boards to foreign countries. Subcontractors handled the remaining circuit board assembly work in the United States and paid minimum wage to semiskilled production workers, many of whom were women, minorities, and illegal immigrants who faced routine exposure to hazardous chemicals and fumes.

The commercialization of the Internet in the mid-1990s connected computers in homes and businesses throughout the world and transformed them into a vast global network. This opened new options for work and commerce and fueled an Internet startup, or dot-com, boom in the late 1990s. According to the social theorist Manuel Castells, the 1990s marked the beginning of an information age defined by flexible labor, the individualization of work, and weaker labor movements. His critics argue that this assertion overemphasizes the impact of technology on labor and ignores labor's role in shaping technological change. However, the rapidity of change required workers to master new skills continuously in an industry also marked by high turnover and a lack of job security. Workers throughout the industry did not organize, and unions reported difficulties building membership because workers regularly change jobs, work is often outsourced, and there is no history of organized labor.

In Silicon Valley, the center of the high-tech boom, the numbers of temporary or subcontracted workers increased dramatically, as did the number of intermediary organizations such as temporary help firms, employment agencies, recruiters, and labor contractors. In California's Santa Clara County, home of

Silicon Valley, temporary workers rose from 1.6% to 3.5% of the area's total work force from 1984 to 1998. The geographer Chris Benner cites more telling statistics in *Work in the New Economy*. He writes that while overall employment in Santa Clara County declined by 2% between 1990 and 1994, employment with temporary agencies grew by 30%. Most workers employed by these agencies lacked union representation, although some temporary workers did secure victories against U.S. computer companies. In 2000, long-term temporary workers, or "permatemps," at Microsoft won a $97 million federal lawsuit because the company excluded them from receiving benefits. A number of guilds emerged in the Silicon Valley area during the 1990s, but most acted as training or professional organizations and exerted little power over company regulations or working conditions.

The high-tech boom boosted employment in the computer and information technology sector, and unemployment rates for Silicon Valley were well below the national average from 1995 to 2000. Average payroll figures for salaried and hourly Silicon Valley workers were 84% higher than the national averages in 2000, which drastically inflated living costs in the Bay Area. However, there is some speculation that reported earnings in the industry were artificially inflated because so many of the lowest-paying jobs no longer existed in the United States. Also, the high salaries were offset by the long hours demanded by an industry in which 80-hour weeks were common and celebrated.

During the boom years, the dominant industry culture changed and promoted an image of young entrepreneurialism, quick wealth, and informality. Dress codes relaxed. Many companies strove to create a fun and flexible atmosphere for their employees that also encouraged them to work longer hours. Internet startups and well-established computer companies offered lucrative salaries to attract and retain highly educated engineers and computer scientists. Newspapers regularly ran stories about young employees in the high-tech sector who accrued millions of dollars in stock options before turning 30. Such stories sustained the mythology of the high-tech boom, but accounts of white-collar employees who held service and lower-level administrative and technical positions spoke of long hours, oppressive management, limited family time, deskilled work, and salaries incommensurate with the cost of living in Silicon Valley and other high-tech areas. When combined with criticism of environmental practices of high-tech processing plants during the 1980s and 1990s, which led to such problems as leaks of hazardous substances from underground storage tanks, the dumping of toxic sewage, and the regular exposure of blue-collar plant workers

COMPUTERS

to dangerous chemicals, the picture was much less than ideal. Although some white-collar professionals made significant sums during the high-tech boom, the distribution of wealth was far from equal, with white and Japanese-American men enjoying the highest salaries. One 1996 study of 33 high-tech firms in Silicon Valley found that whites composed 81% of managers. Only 6% of managers working in these firms were black or Hispanic.

After 2000, the industry experienced a downturn when the "dot-com bubble" burst. Many startup companies went bankrupt, venture capital monies dried up, stocks in high-tech companies lost part (if not all) of their value, and workers paid in stock options saw their net worth plummet. The end of the high-tech boom and increased offshore manufacturing, programming, and engineering exacerbated employment instability for workers in the U.S. computer industry.

EDEN MEDINA

References and Further Reading

Babbage, Charles. *On the Economy of Machinery and Manufactures.* Fairfield, NJ: A. M. Kelley, 1986.
Benner, Chris. *Work in the New Economy: Flexible Labor Markets in Silicon Valley.* Malden, MA: Blackwell, 2002.
Blok, Aad, and Greg Downey, eds. *Uncovering Labour in Information Revolutions, 1750–2000.* New York: Cambridge University Press, 2003.
Campbell-Kelly, Martin, and William Aspray. *Computer: A History of the Information Machine.* Boulder, CO: Westview, 2004.
Castells, Manuel. *The Rise of the Network Society.* Malden, MA: Blackwell, 2000.
Ensmenger, Nathan, and William Aspray. "Software as a Labor Process." In *History of Computing: Software Issues*, edited by Ulf Hashagen, Reinhard Keil-Slawik, and Arthur Norberg. New York: Springer, 2002, pp. 139–166.
Kraft, Philip. *Programmers and Managers: The Routinization of Programming in the United States.* New York: Springer-Verlag, 1977.
Lécuyer, Christophe. *Making Silicon Valley: Innovation and Growth of High Tech, 1930–1970.* Cambridge, MA: MIT Press, 2005.
Leslie, Stuart W. "Blue Collar Science: Bringing the Transistor to Life in the Lehigh Valley." *Historical Studies in the Physical and Biological Sciences* 32, no. 1 (2001): 71–113.
Light, Jennifer. "When Computers Were Women." *Technology and Culture* 40, no. 3 (1999): 455–483.
National Research Council. Committee on Women's Employment and Related Social Issues. *Computer Chips and Paper Clips: Technology and Women's Employment.* Washington, DC: National Academy Press, 1986.
Siegel, Lenny, and John Markoff. *The High Cost of High Tech: The Dark Side of the Chip.* New York: Harper and Row, 1985.
U.S. Department of Labor. Bureau of Labor Statistics. "Career Guide to Industries, 2004–05 Edition, Computer and Electronic Product Manufacturing." 2005–. www.bls.gov/oco/cg/cgs010.htm.

CONFERENCE FOR PROGRESSIVE POLITICAL ACTION

The Conference for Progressive Political Action (CPPA) was intended to form a broad political alliance of socialists, unions, and progressives. It was officially founded at a meeting held in Chicago in February 1922, though the idea of building such an alliance had been originally broached by the National Executive Committee of the Socialist Party in September 1921. This initial conference was called by the Railroad Brotherhoods and was attended by other unions, farmers' organizations, and Progressive political organizations. It worked to promote the election of prolabor candidates to public office. It laid the seeds for the Progressive political party that arose most notably around the candidacy of Robert M. La Follette for president in 1924.

The central problem facing the CPPA was whether to act as a third political party. Many of its constituents envisioned the CPPA as an organization that would support prolabor or progressive candidates from the major parties, while others, especially from the Workers Party of America (a precursor to the Communist Party), pushed the CPPA to form a third party. Between its founding and 1924, the Conference for Progressive Political Action provided the administrative machinery and energy to try and build a prolabor political alliance that would include the AFL unions, socialists, and upper-middle-class progressives, and in doing so it built the skeleton of a third party without actually forming one.

This debate and attempts by the Workers Party to enter the organization led to early internal conflicts. At the CPPA's second convention in Cleveland in December 1922, a number of Workers Party members who attempted to attend the conference were denied the right to do so on the grounds that their organization stood in opposition to the goals and ideas of the CPPA. Soon after, the Workers Party focused its energies on the Farmer Labor Party, and even organized the 1924 convention of the Farmer Labor Party to coincide with that of the CPPA. The Workers Party's attacks on the CPPA as an organization that claimed sympathy for a labor party but did not actually want to build one did not prevent the CPPA from being attacked on the right by politicians who denounced it as a Communist front.

In September 1924, the CPPA met in Cleveland with the intention of endorsing either the Republican or the Democratic nominee for president. However, because the Democratic Party convention was so contentious, no Democratic candidate had yet been nominated. When the Wisconsin Republican Senator Robert M. La Follette offered to run, the Conference for Progressive Political Action endorsed him. La Follette also secured the endorsement of the American Federation of Labor and the Socialist Party. Thus, the Conference represented the beginnings of an electoral alliance between progressives, labor, and socialists under the banner of the Progressive Party, the same banner used by Theodore Roosevelt in 1912.

La Follette attacked monopoly as the biggest problem facing the country. This was meant to appeal to farmers and to urban workers. In this as in all other respects, however, La Follette's platform was essentially a restatement of ideas dating back to the Populist era. La Follette had been a liberal senator and was quite popular in Wisconsin, but in his attempt to build an alliance that would include farmers, urban workers, and the liberal sections of the middle class, La Follette could not clearly express the demands of any group.

He received about one sixth of the votes for president, or 4,826,471 out of about 26 million. The Republicans won the election in a landslide. La Follette won Wisconsin and ran second to the Republicans throughout the Midwest, but fared poorly in the South and East. This movement faced numerous difficulties. First, in 1924, the United States was experiencing rapid economic growth and relative prosperity, despite the persistence of poverty for many. Second, the Conference for Progressive Political Action had very limited resources compared with the major parties. It lacked local organizations in most municipalities, did not run local candidates, and had very limited funds. Finally, the Progressive Party was attacked by conservatives as a radical front to telling effect, while its attempt to express the interests of such a wide range of groups prevented it from consolidating a base among either workers or farmers.

In the aftermath of the 1924 election, the CPPA held a Second National Convention in Chicago in February 1925. This convention was split between labor unionists, who wanted a lobbying group that would not form an independent party or run candidates; socialists, who wanted an independent labor party in the fashion of the British Labour Party that would allow organizations like the Socialist Party to affiliate; and liberals, who wanted a third party with traditional individual memberships modeled after the Democrats and Republicans. Immediately after this convention, the Socialist Party held a convention of its own and voted unanimously to withdraw from the CPPA, and the organization was disbanded. In June 1925, Robert La Follette passed away.

The CPPA was at the same time a foretaste of the coalition that was eventually built during the New Deal and the last gasp of the Progressive Era politics that had produced both the Socialist Party and the

Progressive Party of Theodore Roosevelt. The CPPA was formed in reaction to the conservative attacks on unions and progressive ideas that took place in the aftermath of World War I. This coalition of those under attack could not produce a strong enough consensus to paper over their deep differences. Nonetheless, the CPPA did show the possibility of uniting liberals, labor, and socialists around a program of reform.

SAMUEL MITRANI

References and Further Reading
Draper, Theodore. *The Roots of American Communism.* New York: Viking Press, 1963.
La Follette, Robert M. *La Follette's Autobiography: A Personal Narrative of Political Experiences.* Madison: University of Wisconsin Press, 1969.

See also **American Federation of Labor; Communist Party; Socialist Party of America**

CONGRESS OF INDUSTRIAL ORGANIZATIONS

The Congress of Industrial Organizations (CIO) was born first as the Committee for Industrial Organization in the wake of the 1935 American Federation of Labor (AFL) convention, where proponents of industrial unionism were frustrated in their efforts to secure AFL support for a proposal to charter industrial unions in the mass-production industries. Section 7(a) of the National Industrial Recovery Act (NIRA), passed on June 16, 1933, established workers' right to bargain collectively with their employers through representatives of their own choosing; workers had responded by organizing themselves locally and petitioning for admission to the craft union federation or its constituent unions. In the following year, the AFL signed nearly one million new members. But the AFL had then cherry-picked skilled workers from the industrial units, incorporating them into existing AFL craft unions; for the remaining multitudes of unskilled and semiskilled workers whose occupations fell outside traditional craft jurisdictions, the federation created "federal unions" under direct AFL control. This procedure fragmented the unity of newly organized workers, creating categories of discriminatory "Class B" membership for less-skilled workers and undermining strength in the industrial workplace. Tradition-bound AFL leaders' customary caution also clashed with the militancy of freshly organized workers, and disaffection soon prevailed. By late 1934, continued employer intransigence and the weak response of the AFL had exposed the flaws of

Section 7(a) and the inadequacies of AFL leadership. Discontent erupted in a wave of strikes (1,856 in 1934 alone), which were often violently suppressed. San Francisco longshoremen, Minneapolis truckers, and even the long-oppressed "lintheads" of the southern textile industry conducted legendary strikes, with ambiguous results.

The NIRA also revitalized certain key AFL unions. John L. Lewis's United Mine Workers (UMW) had shrunk through the 1920s from nearly one-half million at the end of World War I to a mere 80,000 in 1932; the NIRA sparked a fire of organizing through the Appalachian coalfields, reigniting the miners' fabled militancy. In the Northeast, the Amalgamated Clothing Workers (ACWA) and the International Ladies' Garment Workers' Union (ILGWU) had been devastated by the Depression; now these traditionally militant, socialist-led unions launched successful fresh campaigns. By 1934, all three unions were alive with activity. Significantly, all three were also structurally industrial unions, and they were uniquely positioned within the AFL to respond favorably to the growing demands for industrial organization sweeping through the nation's workplaces. Their leaders—Lewis of the Mineworkers, Sidney Hillman of the ACWA, and David Dubinsky of the ILGWU—argued that the AFL needed to adapt structurally to mass-production industries that cut across traditional craft lines. Their efforts blocked, Lewis, Hillman, and Dubinsky launched the Committee for Industrial Organizations on November 9, 1935. Ostensibly within the AFL, the Committee in fact functioned virtually autonomously from the beginning.

The fortuitous convergence of pressure from the ranks and receptive, well-placed leaders within the AFL set the stage for the most remarkable wave of organizing in U.S. labor history. The final component was the National Labor Relations Act, authored by Senator Robert Wagner (D-NY), which passed on July 5, 1935, and was reaffirmed by the Supreme Court in 1937. The Wagner Act replaced Section 7(a) of the NIRA, which had been ruled unconstitutional in May 1935. The new law expanded worker protections, outlawed employer anti-union practices, and created a three-member National Labor Relations Board (NLRB) with meaningful enforcement power. Most critically, the Act established mechanisms for conducting representation elections and required employers to bargain with winning unions. This new intrusion by the state was regarded with concern by some labor leaders, and Wagner's impact has since been widely debated by historians; but there is little doubt that the Act became a critical tool for CIO organizing.

In November 1936, President Franklin D. Roosevelt was re-elected with strong working-class support. Roosevelt had long coattails, sweeping pro-New Deal, prolabor Democrats into office at the local and state level. Suddenly, the political climate warmed toward the CIO's agenda. With funding from the UMW, a cadre of zealous organizers (many of whom were communists), and the implicit blessing of the Roosevelt administration, the CIO took aim at the heart of the nonunion core industries, launching an extra-ordinary series of dramatic campaigns from 1936 through 1937. The Committee initiated some innovative techniques like the formation of the Steel Workers Organizing Committee (SWOC) in June 1936. SWOC bypassed the AFL's moribund Amalgamated Association of Iron, Steel, and Tin Workers (AA) to take on the powerful steel, industry. Lewis appointed his associate, Philip Murray, to head the SWOC; Murray gladly enlisted the services of numerous left-wing organizers, who fanned out through steel communities from Pennsylvania to Illinois, urging steelworkers to take over AA locals and company unions and affiliate them with SWOC.

But it was the auto workers' victories in the winter and spring of 1936–1937 that truly energized the movement. The critical event was the six-week sit-down strike by GM workers in Flint, Michigan. GM was the largest and most profitable U.S. corporation, the very epitome of twentieth-century corporate power. From December 29, 1936, until February 11, 1937, GM workers occupied Fisher Body One and several other key GM plants. The sit-down was widely supported and skillfully publicized. Community support was strong and creative. Women workers and strikers' wives organized the famous Emergency Brigade that turned the tide in confrontations with police. The auto workers' stunning victory came to symbolize CIO solidarity and militancy, galvanizing not only auto workers but all labor. Though the Supreme Court outlawed the tactic in *NLRB v. Fansteel Metallurgical Corp* (1939), for the moment the sit-down dramatically shifted the balance of power in labor conflicts, and the tactic proliferated through diverse industries. Following the GM success, the formidable U.S. Steel came to terms with Lewis and SWOC, without a strike, in March 1937. United Auto Workers (UAW) membership rose above 200,000 by the end of 1937; SWOC membership soared as well.

The fall of two great citadels of the open shop fired the imaginations of workers in and far beyond the industrial core, and throughout 1937–1938 they organized in droves. Often the organization of a large local plant would inspire a citywide movement organizing everyone from dry cleaners to newspaper reporters, and the struggles often produced an energetic

CIO culture involving men, women, and children in union-linked activities from strike support to baseball leagues to union glee clubs.

The CIO scurried to meet the clamor for organization. In some industries, like meatpacking, the CIO took the initiative, forming the Packinghouse Workers Organizing Committee (PWOC) on the SWOC model. In others, workers organized themselves and then petitioned for CIO charters. In the northeastern electrical industry, for example, workers in individual plants in the great chains organized themselves, often led by communists, linked together to form the United Electrical Workers (UE), and then affiliated with the CIO. Rubber, chemical, food and tobacco workers, pulp and paper workers, California cannery workers, white-collar workers, public employees, and many, many more elected to organize. Nearly three million joined in 1937 alone.

CIO success in the early years put internal organization at the top of the agenda. The ad hoc structure of 1935 could not accommodate the national scope, industrial diversity, and sheer numbers of recruits that constituted the CIO by 1937. At the suggestion of John Brophy, who coordinated daily operations, leaders designed a more formal structure in the spring of 1937, creating regional, state, and local coordinating bodies modeled after the AFL's central labor councils and state federations. The CIO began to charter new industrial unions, and some revitalized AFL affiliates chose to join forces with the CIO. Finally, the Committee created Local Industrial Unions (LIUs) to accommodate workers in marginal occupations not affiliated with national unions.

Like the AFL's Federal unions, the LIUs were serviced directly by the CIO, but unlike the AFL, the CIO was determined to provide real, effective aid to the LIUs. Consequently, as the LIUs proliferated, so did the CIO's bureaucratic apparatus, creating multiple layers of staffers between the leadership in Washington and the rank and file in the shops. The new procedures mandated by the Wagner Act also had an impact on the growth of bureaucracy, putting a premium on the talents of lawyers and skilled negotiators and tending to suppress grassroots militancy.

The CIO's early successes were very impressive, but the Committee faced serious obstacles as well. GM capitulated, but Ford did not; U.S. Steel came to terms, but the large firms collectively known as "Little Steel" remained staunchly and violently anti-union. On Memorial Day, 1937, police killed 10 protesters outside Republic Steel in Chicago, and violence dampened union fervor elsewhere as well. Other problems arose from within labor's ranks. Factionalism disrupted several affiliates, including the important UAW. The CIO's success had also stung the AFL

into renewed activity, and sparks flew as the two groups competed for influence in numerous sites. By articulating a nearly parallel organizational apparatus, the CIO had signaled growing independence from the AFL. Dubinsky, unhappy about the increasing influence of communists and the CIO-AFL rift, led the ILGWU back into the AFL. Finally, the "Roosevelt Recession" of 1938–1939 severely undermined the fragile recovery of the mid-1930s, and the CIO's numerical strength began to evaporate as unemployment spiked again.

It was thus with some ambivalence that, in response to near-warfare with the AFL, the CIO decided to make official what had long been apparent: the Committee constituted a rival federation. On November 14, 1938, the CIO convened a constitutional convention in Pittsburgh, declared its independence, and changed its name to the Congress of Industrial Organizations, still "CIO." John L. Lewis became the federation's first president, serving until his growing isolationism led to a shocking rupture first with Roosevelt and then with the CIO in 1940. Hillman of the ACWA and Murray of SWOC served as vice presidents; Murray took over as president when Lewis left. The secretary was James B. Carey of the UE, the only representative of the new industrial union affiliates. Membership was said to be over 4 million; in truth, it was probably half of that. Financially, the CIO still depended on the UMW and ACWA; dues collection among the new affiliates was spotty at best, especially given widespread "Roosevelt Recession" unemployment.

War and Postwar

War of a different sort saved the CIO. The outbreak of World War II in 1939 led to frenzied rearmament in the United States, and for the first time in a decade, workers were in great demand. Conditions were soon ripe for the CIO to organize remaining holdouts in the core industries. By 1941, SWOC had broken Little Steel; Ford had fallen to the UAW; and Westinghouse had joined GE on the UE roster. Suddenly, CIO core unions were positioned to make real gains. But when the United States entered the war in December 1941, the CIO and AFL were pressured to endorse a "No Strike Pledge" for the duration, an act that effectively stripped labor of its most potent weapon.

To compensate, Roosevelt created the National War Labor Board (NWLB) in January 1942 as a venue to adjust wartime grievances, and the NWLB sweetened the pill by crafting a union security provision called "maintenance of membership" that required workers in union shops to maintain their union membership for the life of the contract. The provision, coupled with the burgeoning war growth of U.S. industry, led to a dramatic expansion of CIO membership. The UAW alone grew from 165,000 to over one million; SWOC, now the United Steelworkers (USW), and UE mushroomed too. By 1945, the CIO claimed over 4.5 million members.

But WWII changed the CIO's character. Commitment to the No Strike Pledge and the snail-paced deliberations of the NWLB enmeshed CIO leaders in an alliance with government that set them frequently at odds with frustrated rank and filers, many of them new to industry and to unions. CIO bureaucracy grew as what the historian David Brody called the "workplace rule of law" displaced direct action, and the creation of the CIO Political Action Committee (CIO-PAC) in 1943 cemented an alliance with the Democratic Party that effectively foreclosed the option of independent political action via a labor party, a notion popular with the CIO's left wing.

Still, the CIO registered significant achievements during the war. With wages capped for the duration by the NWLB's "Little Steel Formula," negotiators instead made headway elsewhere. The 40-hour week with time and a half for overtime became prevalent. Wide wage differentials between skilled and unskilled workers and regional differentials narrowed. Unions won vacation provisions and other "fringe" benefits.

But perhaps the most significant CIO wartime achievement lay in the realm of race relations and, to a lesser extent, issues of gender. The CIO's rhetoric of democratic inclusion was put to the test as women stepped into men's jobs and African-American workers broke through employment barriers, aided by the Fair Employment Practice Committee (FEPC). Racial tensions escalated in war industries and communities, sparking "hate strikes" and race riots. Historians have hotly debated the CIO's commitment to racial equality, but the wartime crisis produced a strong CIO response. In Detroit, site of much racial violence, UAW president R. J. Thomas moved decisively to quash the 1943 hate strikes, upholding the firing of strikers who violated the union's nondiscrimination clause, and the UAW took critical action to protect black citizens during the Detroit housing riots. In key CIO strongholds like auto, steel, and meatpacking, the wartime defense of minority rights along with the creation of a handful of daringly biracial unions in the Deep South laid the foundation for labor's later alliance with the Civil Rights movement.

Women workers benefited from protections inherent in the new workplace "rule of law," generally making wartime job gains, but these proved largely ephemeral, as the gendered division of labor was swiftly reconstituted after the war. The exception was the left-wing UE, where women made significant progress. UE women broke into leadership ranks at all levels, and "women's issues" were incorporated into the union's agenda; both trends continued into peacetime.

The CIO emerged from World War II numerically strengthened, solidly entrenched in basic industry, but having lost, perhaps inevitably, its prewar élan. The center of gravity had moved from the rank and file in working-class communities to the bureaucracy in Washington, DC. The widened gulf between leaders and ranks became institutionalized. Even the extraordinary 1946 strikes, while venting the rank and file's long-repressed frustrations, were remarkably efficient and well-organized, produced by a disciplined machine rather than a vibrant movement.

Nevertheless, labor's new strength produced a powerful backlash. The 1946 midterm elections returned Republican majorities to both houses of Congress, and within months a plethora of antilabor bills had been distilled to the Taft-Hartley Act, passed over Truman's veto in 1947. Taft-Hartley reversed the polarity of Wagner, enhancing management rights while scaling back those of labor. Most ominously, Title I, Section 9-h required union officials to sign affidavits certifying that they were not members of the Communist Party; noncompliance barred unions from access to NLRB machinery.

With the Cold War heating up, Section 9-h shattered the remnants of the uneasy wartime truce within the CIO's left-center coalition. Anticommunist groups within affiliates gained greater legitimacy. Walter Reuther rode the anticommunism issue to the UAW presidency, and then used the affidavit to purge his communist opponents in the UAW and to launch raids against locals in noncomplying unions. Others followed suit, and an orgy of raiding commenced, absorbing energies that might have gone into new organizing. The UE, largest of the left-led unions, endured over 500 raids between 1947 and 1949, when its leaders finally capitulated and signed. Raids unraveled much of the cutting-edge work of CIO affiliates; in Alabama, for example, an overtly racist USW raid destroyed a key local of the biracial Mine, Mill, and Smelter Workers in 1949.

The 1948 election provided the last straw. Hoping to reverse Taft-Hartley, CIO-PAC endorsed Truman and the Democrats; the communists supported Henry Wallace's Progressive Party. In the aftermath, the CIO elected to purge all communists from the federation's ranks. At the 1949 convention, the CIO voted to expel 11 unions, including the UE, with a combined membership of nearly one million.

The CIO emerged purified but with severely diminished momentum. The unfavorable political climate plus the expulsion of dedicated leftist organizers combined to doom "Operation Dixie," the CIO's highly touted campaign to organize the South. It was the last of the great organizing drives, and the CIO affiliates instead came to focus primarily on collective bargaining in already-organized sectors. Gains there were impressive in the 1950s: wages rose on average by 55%, and the strongest affiliates put together impressive "packages" of benefits, including pensions, vacations, health insurance, and even variants of a guaranteed wage. CIO-PAC developed into a powerful engine of research, publicity, and lobbying as activists worked to defend and extend the gains of the New Deal, even beyond CIO ranks. The goal seemed to be social democracy, through the back door.

The year 1952 provoked a new crisis when Republicans again took the presidency and both houses of Congress. That same year, Presidents Murray of the CIO and William Green of the AFL died, and leadership of the rivals devolved to a new generation lacking the visceral antipathy of their elders. The differences between the CIO and the AFL had largely evaporated: both were large, bureaucratic, and somewhat sclerotic organizations. Though the CIO still maintained a progressive veneer, the gulf had decidedly narrowed, and in 1953, the erstwhile rivals signed a no-raiding pact as a prelude to reunion. Merger negotiations provided that CIO affiliates would have a home in the new Industrial Union Department (IUD), to be headed by Walter Reuther; George Meany of the AFL would be president of the new federation. On December 5, 1955, the AFL-CIO held its first joint convention, and "Big Labor" was born.

Conclusion

The CIO's 1955 reunion with the AFL has generally been viewed as evidence of its decline, and indeed, the industrial federation seemed to have reached an organizational impasse. The energizing fervor of the early days was long gone. By 1955, consolidation, not expansion, was the order of the day; the brash, creative organizers had given way to legions of lawyers and lobbyists, guiding labor's program through thickets of bureaucratic regulation. Still, the CIO achievement was monumental. In its late-1930s heyday, the CIO provided an enduring model of principled, inclusive, militant organization powered by the energies of ordinary working men and women. As an institution in Jim Crow America, the CIO was unique in offering a frequently flawed but sometimes

inspiring vision of interracial cooperation and justice. Finally, the CIO had overcome the historically fierce resistance of powerful corporations and brought dignity, the rule of law, and dramatically improved conditions to millions of working people.

LISA KANNENBERG

References and Further Reading

Bernstein, Irving. *Turbulent Years: A History of the American Worker, 1933–1941.* Boston: Houghton Mifflin, 1970.
Cohen, Lizabeth. *Making a New Deal: Industrial Workers in Chicago, 1919–1939.* New York: Cambridge University Press, 1990.
Derber, Milton, and Edwin Young, eds. *Labor and the New Deal.* Madison: University of Wisconsin Press, 1957.
Faue, Elizabeth. *Community of Suffering and Struggle: Women, Men, and the Labor Movement in Minneapolis, 1915–1945.* Chapel Hill: University of North Carolina Press, 1991.
Fine, Sidney. *Sit-Down: The General Motors Strike of 1936–1937.* Ann Arbor: University of Michigan Press, 1970.
Fraser, Steven. *Labor Will Rule: Sidney Hillman and the Rise of American Labor.* Ithaca, NY: Cornell University Press, 1991.
Halpern, Rick. *Down on the Killing Floor: Black and White Workers in Chicago's Packinghouses, 1904–1954.* Urbana: University of Illinois Press, 1997.
Honey, Michael K. *Southern Labor and Black Civil Rights: Organizing Memphis Workers.* Urbana: University of Illinois Press, 1993.
Lichtenstein, Nelson. *Labor's War at Home: The CIO and World War II.* New York: Cambridge University Press, 1982.
———. *Walter Reuther: The Most Dangerous Man in Detroit.* Urbana: University of Illinois Press, 1995.
Lynd, Staughton, ed. *"We Are All Leaders": The Alternative Unionism of the Early 1930s.* Urbana: University of Illinois Press, 1996.
Meier, August, and Elliot Rudwick. *Black Detroit and the Rise of the UAW.* New York: Oxford University Press, 1979.
Preis, Art. *Labor's Giant Step: Twenty Years of the CIO.* New York: Pioneer Publishers, 1964.
Rosswurm, Steve, ed. *The CIO's Left-Led Unions.* New Brunswick, NJ: Rutgers University Press, 1992.
Zieger, Robert. *The CIO: 1935–1955.* Chapel Hill: University of North Carolina Press, 1995.

See also **American Federation of Labor; Anticommunism; Fair Employment Practice Committee; Lewis, John L.; National Industrial Recovery Act; National War Labor Board (WWII); Reuther, Walter; Taft-Hartley Act; World War II**

CONSTRUCTION TRADES

The construction trades make up one of the United States' oldest and largest industries. Throughout the nation's history, construction workers have helped transform the national landscape by erecting private, commercial, and government buildings and by providing the labor needed to construct bridges, dams, canals, roads, and highways. In addition, since the late nineteenth century, the construction trades' powerful labor unions have played an important role in the development of the American labor movement. Over the course of more than two centuries, the world of construction workers has continually remade itself in response to economic, technological, social, cultural, and political changes.

The Construction Trades and Work Culture

In the twenty-first century, the size and significance of the construction industry are matched by its complexity. Workers of all skill levels from more than 20 different trades make up the work force in the industry's three major segments: general building contractors (which includes residential, commercial, and industrial buildings); heavy construction contractors (which includes sewer systems, roads, highways, bridges, tunnels, and dams); and specialty trades contractors (which includes carpentry, masonry, plumbing, electrical work, painting, and heating and air-conditioning work). Contractors in each segment employ helpers, laborers, and apprentices, who perform tasks that require minimal training in order to assist skilled craftworkers. The latter category is vast in and of itself and consists of three general classifications: structural (including carpenters, operating engineers who operate construction machinery, bricklayers, cement masons, stonemasons, roofers, and iron workers who erect structural steel); finishing workers (including lathers, plasterers, marble setters, terrazzo workers, carpenters, ceiling installers, drywall workers, painters, glaziers, roofers, floor covering installers, and insulation workers); and mechanical workers (including plumbers, sprinkler fitters, pipefitters, electricians, sheet-metal workers, and heating, air-conditioning, and refrigeration technicians). Entrance to these skilled trades requires years of vocational education and apprenticeship training, which typically includes both on-the-job and classroom instruction. Skilled building trades workers often go on to become specialty contractors themselves.

The decentralized, intermittent, and physically arduous nature of construction work has distinguished it from other major American industries and has been instrumental in shaping its history. A building project typically involves architects, developers, financiers, contractors, and construction trades workers—each of whom perform a vital function yet to an extent operate independently of one another. Much of the skilled work performed on construction sites is loosely supervised, providing skilled workers with a sense of workplace autonomy. With this independence comes uncertainty. The itinerant nature of the construction industry also necessitates a casual labor market, in which workers are employed on a per-job basis lasting anywhere from a few months to several years. The boom-and-bust pattern of the building industry adds another layer of uncertainty to the construction worker's livelihood. Moreover, because much of the labor is performed outdoors, construction work is seasonal, and job opportunities diminish with the shorter days and poor weather conditions of winter. Thus, construction workers have to consistently confront the prospect of unemployment and rarely expect to have steady work for the entire year. Finally, work in the construction trades is physically demanding and can be hazardous. Building trades workers operate heavy and dangerous machinery, use heavy materials, brave perilous heights, and expose themselves to miserable weather conditions. Consequently, the construction industry ranks among the national leaders in work-related injuries and illness. This physical aspect of the work places heightened importance on workplace camaraderie and cooperation.

Until recently, these aspects of the construction trades have combined to create a distinct work culture that blended craft pride, masculinity, and whiteness. Because of the decentralized nature of the industry, skilled construction workers have historically identified more closely with their craft and/or union than with any particular contractor or employer. Building trades workers express their craft pride in the tools they carry, the jargon they use, the hard hats that protect their heads, and—until the twentieth century—in the clothes they wear (workers in different trades dressed in certain colors of coveralls). This craft pride has shaped a dual identity among construction workers—one that is both individual- and collective-oriented. Since the eighteenth century, skilled workers in the construction trades have placed a high value on individualism, which has in part been steeped in the prospect of becoming self-employed or, in some cases, an employer. On the other hand, workers in the construction trades have a long history of organization. Several forces have driven the collective impulse in the construction trades, but the most important have been to strengthen their bargaining power vis-à-vis employers, to provide support in the form of social and cultural services, and to exert control over the labor market through apprenticeship programs. More generally, craft organizations help to reinforce the collective identity of construction trades workers. Up until the first decades of the twentieth century, craft associations were also organized along ethnic and racial lines, but over time this dissolved into a broader identity with their trade. According to Mark Erlich, a labor historian and a carpenter, the co-existence of an individual and collective consciousness has produced a form a craft unionism peculiar to the building trades.

The construction trades have also fostered a masculine identity, which has found expression in the common inclusion of the word "Brotherhood" in construction union nomenclature, fraternal rituals common to building craft organizations, the sexualized language workers use at the job site, and the risky behavior they exhibit. Significantly, masculinity in the building trades has been predicated upon, and has perpetuated, the virtual exclusion of women from the industry. As the historian Joshua Freeman has pointed out, masculine representations of construction workers—whether in the form of the respectable manliness of the late nineteenth-century artisan, the strong heroic builder of the 1920s and 1930s, or the macho, crude, and rowdy hardhat caricatured in post-World War II popular culture—have shaped the public's image of the industry.

In addition to its male composition, the skilled-construction work force historically has been disproportionately white. The construction trades have always been notorious for nepotism, as craftsmen have preferred to pass along notices of job openings and apprenticeship opportunities by word of mouth to family, friends, and neighbors. In the North in particular, but also increasingly in the South after the 1890s, the skilled trades have traditionally been the domain of whites. And as craftsmen replenished their ranks through personal networks, they institutionalized racial exclusion by closing off opportunities to nonwhites. Thus, for much of its history, workers in the construction industry have existed in a gendered and racialized social world that linked the job site with the community. Only in the late twentieth and early twenty-first centuries, as a result of union struggles and the social movements and reforms of the 1960s and 1970s, did the racial and gender barriers in the construction trades begin to collapse.

The Construction Trades from the Colonial Era to the Gilded Age

The construction trades experienced significant changes between the colonial era and the Gilded Age. At the beginning of this period, the construction industry consisted of a fraction of the number of trades that it does today. Most building tradesmen

during this period could generally be classified as carpenters, lathers, plasterers, painters, glaziers, bricklayers, masons, or stonecutters. Over time, however, technological developments transformed the industry by introducing new building materials, tools, and methods. In some cases, established trades were able to accommodate changes without much trouble. For example, during the twentieth century, lathers gradually made the transition from using wooden strips to using wire and metal mesh in constructing the framework for plaster walls and ceilings. On the other hand, new materials and building methods could pose a threat to established crafts. For example, throughout the colonial and early national periods, carpenters had performed a number of tasks on building projects, from constructing wooden frames to crafting doors, windows, stairs, trim, and mantels. This work was performed entirely on the job site and by hand. By the 1840s, however, this work was beginning to be done in factories and mills—where woodworking machinery steadily surpassed handwork in output and efficiency. The growth of a woodworking industry independent of the construction site would eventually become a major concern for the carpenters' union in the late nineteenth and early twentieth centuries. Carpenters also had to confront the advent of new materials that replaced wood in building structures. The use of metal instead of wood for trim, sash, and doors in the early twentieth century resulted in intense jurisdictional battles between the carpenters' union and the sheet-metal workers' union (see below) and also compelled carpenters to increasingly learn how to work with materials other than wood.

The relationship between construction tradesmen and contractors also underwent important changes between the colonial period and the Gilded Age. Building tradesmen in colonial America borrowed from the European guild system in structuring their industry. Young apprentices were bound to master craftsmen until they learned the trade and reached adulthood. Upon completion of his term, an apprentice became a journeyman and could hire himself out freely, although many journeymen also found it advantageous to continue working for the same master. Ideally, a journeyman sought to become a master craftsman himself by obtaining enough capital to establish his own enterprise. In the early republic, the prospects for social mobility in the construction trades appeared favorable for the journeyman on the make. The high demand for houses and buildings during this period resulted in high wages and steady work and created opportunities for building tradesmen to profit from speculative building. Craft connections were vital in taking the step from journeyman to an independent master craftsman. Master builders were often willing to assist apprentices and familiar journeymen in establishing their own shop. In addition, the more ambitious master craftsmen who engaged in speculative building could provide journeymen with valuable experience by subcontracting out large building projects.

Up until the third decade of the nineteenth century, the relationship among apprentices, journeymen, and master craftsmen maintained a sense of mutual interest and respect. Workers from all three ranks often worked side by side on building projects and were linked by the prospect, if not expectation, that an apprentice would eventually become a master craftsman. Moreover, all members of the construction trades were equally vulnerable to the boom-and-bust cycle of the industry. By the 1820s, however, a gulf had begun to emerge between master craftsmen—who assumed the mantle of contractors/employers—and journeymen/apprentices—who were increasingly coming to resemble employees. This development was manifest in a wave of strikes launched by construction journeymen in the 1820s and 1830s demanding a 10-hour workday. Boston carpenters went on strike in 1825 and 1832, and between 1833 and 1837 building tradesmen in Boston, New York, and Philadelphia went on strike 34 times. Although these protests were ultimately unsuccessful and were not fierce enough to fully disrupt the bond between apprentices, journeymen, and master craftsmen, they did signal a transformation in construction trades labor relations. Building tradesmen continued to organize throughout the antebellum period and after the Civil War. These protests were not confined to eastern urban centers. For example, carpenters in San Francisco went on strike for higher wages in 1849, 1853, and 1860. And in 1867, they formed The House Carpenters' Eight-Hour League, No.1 to fight for an eight-hour day.

The Rise and Fall of the Closed Shop: The Gilded Age to the Great Depression

By the last two decades of the nineteenth century, the construction industry was in the throes of profound changes. The birth of the modern skyscraper in 1885 punctuated the arrival of iron, steel, and reinforced concrete in the construction process. In addition, the emergence of indoor plumbing, electricity, elevators, and steam heating systems introduced newer trades to the industry. Amid these developments, tradesmen continued to organize on the local level and fight for better working conditions and higher wages. Yet gains won by local craft organizations could quickly

be offset by the influx of itinerant tradesmen from other parts of the country. Thus, building tradesmen sought to unite their crafts on the national level. This occurred first in the more established trades but quickly spread throughout the industry: stonecutters (1853); bricklayers (1867); carpenters (1881); plasterers (1882); painters (1887); sheet metal workers (1888); plumbers and steamfitters (1889); electrical workers (1891); operating engineers (1896); iron workers (1896); lathers (1899); elevator constructors (1901); and laborers and hod carriers (1903).

The building trades unions epitomized the organizing model that characterized the American Federation of Labor (AFL) during this period. Union members owed their allegiance to their particular craft first and foremost, and as a result they have been criticized throughout their history for insulating themselves from the broader working-class movement. In the 1930s, for example, building trades leaders opposed organizing industrial workers and fought off the Congress of Industrial Organizations' attempt to organize construction workers on an industrywide basis. Nevertheless, as craft unions became more organized, they formalized apprenticeship programs, regulated itinerant craftsmen, and employed business agents to oversee job sites. Also known as walking delegates, business agents policed the industry for their respective union and ensured that contractors hired dues-paying union tradesmen.

Construction tradesmen in this period also sought unity among workers in all of the building trades. The logic was simple: if striking workers in one trade could depend on workers in the other building trades to strike in sympathy, then the bargaining power of all construction unions would multiply. Collectively, building trades unions hoped that they could achieve a closed shop on each building job. This strategy promised to be more effective as building projects became more costly and contractors faced a heightened need to avoid delays or a loss of skilled craftsmen that an industrywide strike would entail. New York construction tradesmen launched the first such organization in 1884 when they formed the Board of Walking Delegates. Building trades councils were subsequently established in other cities and had an immediate impact. For example, in the four years after Chicago's building trades council was formed in 1890, the number of successful strikes rose to 85% from less than 50% between 1886 and 1890. San Francisco's building trades council, founded in 1896, extended its newfound strength and influence into the political sphere; the city's building tradesmen took control of the Union Labor Party in 1906, and Building Trades Council President Patrick H. McCarthy served one term as mayor of San Francisco

(1910–1912). Most important, building trades councils were instrumental in instituting the closed shop on construction jobs in cities across the country.

While construction tradesmen were forging tighter bonds of solidarity, other forces created divisions among the different trades that still persist to this day. Most important, the introduction of new building materials and methods created jurisdictional conflicts that local building trades councils were ill-equipped to adjudicate. Technological developments affected old and new trades alike. Carpenters battled sheet-metal workers over the right to install metal doors, window frames, and trim, which had once been made of wood and well within the carpenters' domain. With the introduction of reinforced concrete, bricklayers, plasterers, and cement finishers argued over who had jurisdiction to lay the concrete, while ironworkers, lathers, sheet-metal workers, and laborers disagreed over who should install metal reinforcing rods. Elevator constructors and electricians each claimed jurisdiction over the right to wire electric elevators, while hoisting engineers challenged elevator constructors' right to handle elevators after they were built. Finally, it was not always clear how workers using new tools and materials should be organized. For example, the plumbers' union claimed the right to organize steamfitters even though workers in that trade had organized their own union. Amid these competing jurisdictional claims, it was difficult for architects and contractors to determine which union should be doing which jobs on building sites. Consequently, at the turn of the century, building trades unions in cities such as New York and Chicago crippled local building projects through strikes resulting from inter-union conflict. The threat that jurisdictional disputes posed to both business ventures and solidarity among the construction trades aroused anti-union sentiment and inspired union leaders to craft a solution to the problem.

The first attempt to address these issues on a national level came in 1897, when local and national building trades leaders met in St. Louis and established the National Building Trades Council (NBTC). The organization concentrated on the local level and placed strength with the building trades councils, which alienated strong international unions such as the Bricklayers and Carpenters. In addition, the AFL disapproved of the NBTC because it placed too much power at the local level and was not affiliated with the AFL. Construction trades unions tried again in 1903 with the formation of the Structural Building Trades Alliance (SBTA). The SBTA also lived a contentious existence; it allowed rivalries to fester, proved incapable of enforcing decisions, and kept cool relations with the AFL. Finally, the SBTA was scrapped and

replaced by the Building Trades Department (BTD) in 1908. The BTD was chartered by the AFL and, unlike its predecessors, would pass the test of time (it still exists as the Building and Construction Trades Department). Despite its longevity, the BTD has also struggled with recalcitrant member organizations that have refused to concede jurisdiction when the Department has ruled against them. For example, the carpenters' union has either been expelled from or left the Department on several occasions (for example, in 2001) when it disagreed with the organization's actions. Nevertheless, after a rocky start, the Department has proved to be a valuable lobbying organization for the building trades and has managed to broker a modicum of peace among the industry's numerous unions.

In addition to settling jurisdictional disputes, building trades unions in the early twentieth century also vigilantly guarded against any threats to the closed shop. The formation of building trades councils in the late nineteenth century had been matched by similar associations among local contractors. In most cases, a significant number of contractors had risen from the ranks of tradesmen and had once belonged to unions themselves. As long as the closed shop did not disrupt building projects and interfere with profits, contractors were willing to tolerate a rival labor organization. But when contractor associations felt that building trades councils were abusing their power, as they did in Chicago in 1900, they challenged union power. For the most part, aside from cities like Los Angeles, where the closed shop did not take root, contractor associations and building trades councils were able to co-exist through the First World War.

The war itself brought another challenge to the closed shop in the construction industry. Building tradesmen were not of one mind as far as their opinions on the war itself, but as a whole they gave their labor to support their nation's war effort. And although the Baker-Gompers Agreement did not guarantee the closed shop, building tradesmen warily accepted its provisions for the eight-hour day, equal pay for equal work, and labor's right to organize and bargain collectively with workers if they agreed not to strike; some building tradesmen, most notably Carpenters' president Bill Hutcheson, objected to any agreement that did not ensure the closed shop. Ultimately, the war was a mixed bag for building tradesmen. In some cities, it slowed civilian construction projects and created a building slump. On the other hand, building trades workers obtained work on war-related projects —such as the construction of training camps and airfields. More important, construction unions were able to defend their prewar gains, and over the course

315

of the war, membership in building trades unions steadily increased. By 1920, 17.6% of the nation's unionized work force belonged to the construction trades.

The power that building trades unions had enjoyed in the first two decades of the twentieth century finally met its match in the 1920s. Across the country, the closed shop in construction fell victim to a concerted open-shop drive backed by the Chamber of Commerce, National Association of Manufacturers, National Erectors Association, large industrial employers, and local citizen committees. In advancing the American Plan, open-shop forces aroused public support for their cause by blaming high building costs on corrupt unions and the contractors who submitted to union demands. Construction unions, always hindered by their internal divisions, were unable to mount a successful defense. And even in union strongholds like San Francisco and Chicago, the open shop prevailed.

Another Rise and Fall of Union Strength in Construction: The Great Depression to the Present

The open-shop battles of the 1920s quickly became an afterthought during the 1930s. In the first years of the Great Depression, private construction declined precipitously, and by 1933, seven out of 10 building tradesmen were unemployed. As did workers in other sectors in the economy, construction tradesmen looked to the state to create jobs for skilled craftsmen. As a result, the 1930s marked a turning point in the relationship between the construction trades and the federal government. Much to the disapproval of the general public and workers excluded from organized labor, building trades unions fought to ensure that union tradesmen would be hired on Public Works Administration and Works Progress Administration construction projects and insisted that union conditions would be enforced on those jobs. The BTD stepped up its lobbying efforts in order to persuade the Roosevelt administration to pass legislation that would be favorable to the building trades. The most important piece of legislation, the Davis-Bacon Act, was actually passed toward the end of Herbert Hoover's presidency. Also known as the Prevailing Wage Act, the law protected workers from outside competition by requiring contractors to pay tradesmen no less than local prevailing wage standards.

The construction trades continued to benefit from government spending during World War II and the postwar decades. Throughout the war, the federal government invested heavily in the construction of wartime housing and war industry facilities, and unionized building tradesmen were on hand to perform the work. In the postwar period, construction tradesmen continued to profit from Cold War national defense spending, from the government's investment in national infrastructure in the 1950s, and from the 1960s building boom. With most of this work going to union labor, building trades unions' ability to control the labor market ensured that their members would be well paid.

Despite their dependence on federal spending in the postwar period, building trades unions also worried about increased state intervention in industry affairs. The Taft-Hartley Act's prohibition of the closed shop, secondary boycotts, and jurisdictional strikes was a major blow to union strength in the construction industry. The building trades were also hurt in 1957 by the Senate Select Committee, chaired by Arkansas Senator John McClellan, to investigate corruption in the labor movement. The hearings mainly targeted the Teamsters, but the Operating Engineers and Carpenters were also accused of improprieties such as the misuse of union funds, rigging union elections, and bribery. As a result, building trades unions suffered another setback in the court of public opinion and were subjected to the restrictions imposed by the Landrum-Griffin Act.

In the 1960s, the federal government also took steps to open up the construction trades to minorities and women. Since the World War I Great Migration, African-Americans had protested the exclusionary policies of building trades unions. Throughout the eighteenth and nineteenth centuries, blacks, particularly those in the South, had worked as skilled craftsmen—and had firmly established themselves in the carpentry and bricklaying trades in particular. By the middle of the twentieth century, however, most blacks could find only lower-end work as building laborers and hod carriers. Decades of protests culminated in the modern Civil Rights Movement of the 1960s, which finally spurred the government to action. The Philadelphia Plan, implemented in 1969, required contractors to set targets and timetables for the hiring of minority workers on federally funded projects. In 1971, the Philadelphia Plan was amended to include women, and the government set further hiring goals for women in 1977.

The greatest challenge to union strength in the construction trades since the 1960s came from the combined impact of a large, well-funded, anti-union movement and a slumping building economy. In 1969, union and nonunion contractors joined with some of the nation's largest corporations (U.S. Steel, Monsanto, and the Ford Motor Company, among others) to found the Construction Users Anti-Inflation Roundtable (CUAIR), which reorganized as the Business Roundtable in 1972. The Roundtable blamed organized labor for the inflation and high construction costs of the 1960s, and they sought to strengthen contractors' bargaining power by weakening prolabor legislation (such as the Davis-Bacon Act) and employing nonunion construction workers. At the same time, the postwar construction boom that had kept building trades workers employed at high wages on defense, highway, and housing projects dried up in the 1970s. Just as troublesome for building trades unions was their inability to gain a foothold in private residential construction, which also undermined skill requirements through the growing use of prefabricated materials. As a result, even though the building industry recovered in the late 1980s and 1990s, the percentage of unionized construction workers dropped by approximately 50% since 1970.

The world of construction workers continues to change. Federal laws and the rise of nonunion labor have facilitated the entrance of nonwhites and women into the trades. So too, however, have building trades unions. In order to maintain their place in the industry, unions are making more concerted efforts to organize the unorganized. And as they have for over a century, building trades unions continue to forge solidarity amid contentious jurisdictional disputes.

JOHN J. ROSEN

References and Further Reading

Applebaum, Herbert. *Construction Workers, U.S.A.* Westport, CT: Greenwood Press, 1999.
Christie, Robert A. *Empire in Wood.* Ithaca, NY: Cornell University Press, 1956.
Cohen, Andrew Wender. *The Racketeer's Progress: Chicago and the Struggle for the Modern American Economy, 1900–1940.* New York: Cambridge University Press, 2004.
Erlich, Mark. *With Our Own Hands: The Story of Carpenters in Massachusetts.* Philadelphia: Temple University Press, 1986.
Fenton, Edwin. "Italian Immigrants in the Stoneworkers' Union." *Labor History* 3, no. 2 (Spring 1962): 188–207.
Freeman, Joshua B. *"Hardhats: Construction Workers, Manliness, and the 1970 Pro-War Demonstrations." Journal of Social History* 26, no. 4 (Summer 1993): 725–745.
Kazin, Michael. *Barons of Labor: The San Francisco Building Trades and Union Power in the Progressive Era.* Urbana and Chicago: University of Illinois Press, 1989.
Kruman, Marc W. "Quotas for Blacks: The Public Works Administration and the Black Construction Worker." *Labor History* 16, no. 1 (Winter 1975): 37–51.
Lichtenstein, Nelson. *State of the Union: A Century of American Labor.* Princeton, NJ: Princeton University Press, 2002.
Magnum, Garth. *The Operating Engineers: The Economic History of a Trade Union.* Cambridge, MA: Harvard University Press, 1964.
Palladino, Grace. *Skilled Hands, Strong Spirits: A Century of Building Trades History.* Ithaca and London: Cornell University Press, 2005.
Reimer, Jeffrey W. *Hard Hats: The World of Construction Workers.* Beverly Hills, CA: Sage Publications, 1979.
Rilling, Donna J. *Making Houses, Crafting Capitalism: Builders in Philadelphia, 1790–1850.* Philadelphia: University of Philadelphia Press, 2001.
Schneirov, Richard, and Thomas J. Suhrbur. *Union Brotherhood, Union Town: The History of the Carpenters' Union of Chicago: 1863–1987.* Carbondale and Edwardsville: Southern Illinois University Press, 1988.
Segal, Martin. *The Rise of the United Association: National Unionism in the Pipe Trades, 1884–1924.* Cambridge, MA: Harvard University Press, 1970.
Silver, Marc L. *Under Construction: Work and Alienation in the Building Trades.* Albany: State University of New York Press, 1986.
Sugrue, Thomas J. "Affirmative Action from Below: Civil Rights, the Building Trades, and the Politics of Racial Equality in the Urban North, 1945–1969." *Journal of American History* 91, no. 1 (June 2004): 145–173.

See also **Apprenticeship; Davis-Bacon Act; International Brotherhood of Electrical Workers; International Brotherhood of Teamsters; International Union of Operating Engineers; Laborers' International Union of North America; Landrum-Griffin Act (1959); McClellan Committee Hearings; National War Labor Board (WWI); National War Labor Board (WWII); Philadelphia Plan; United Brotherhood of Carpenters and Joiners of America**

CONVICT LABOR IN THE NEW SOUTH

The convict lease—a system of prison administration whereby a state leased its prisoners to a private individual or company for a number of specified years—was not a postbellum or a southern innovation. But it was during that time and in that place that the practice acquired its notorious reputation. The postbellum South is partly defined by images of felons dressed in striped prison garb, laboring on penal farms (a uniquely southern institution) and in dangerous, hot, and unhealthy conditions, whether in southern turpentine, phosphate, or coal mines. Yet these enduring images obscure the halting process through which the convict lease emerged as the foremost method of southern prison administration. Both parties bore responsibility for the lease; as the historian Edward Ayers notes in *Vengeance and Justice*, Presidential Reconstruction, Congressional Reconstruction, and the era of Democratic counter-revolution all "passed without any obvious watershed in the South's penal system" (Ayers, p. 190).

Convict leasing in the postbellum South took one of two basic forms. Under the contract system, as Mark Carleton notes in his book, *Politics and Punishment,* the states leased the labor of their prison inmates, but not actual convicts. In theory, state officials remained liable for feeding, clothing, and guarding the prisoners. South Carolina, Texas, and Virginia all adopted this system of prison management by the 1880s. The convict lease, by contrast, enabled private companies to work prisoners outside the walls of the penitentiary; in return for this greater latitude, they acquired the responsibility of providing their charges with food and health care. All the other southern states adopted this more privatized system (Carleton, p. 22).

The origins of the convict lease rested in the substantial indebtedness of southern states during the post-Civil War period, along with the destroyed or tenuous condition of state penitentiaries following the war. A Tennessee warden criticized its central penitentiary, as Karin Shapiro recalled in her *A New South Rebellion*, as "old and dilapidated, damp and cheerless" (Shapiro, p. 54). Limited state funds with which to rebuild or upgrade state penitentiaries, coupled with a rapidly growing prison population of mostly black inmates, led the states to seek alternative forms of prison management. During the late 1860s and early 1870s, the resulting convict leases had short time frames and consisted of individuals or companies that hired a group of convicts to work within the prison walls to make such goods as harnesses or saddles. Other lessees sought prisoners to work on their sugar cane and cotton farms or in railroad construction. Few of these early state leases were particularly remunerative to the southern states, but as Carleton showed in his history of Louisiana's penal system, the arrangements relieved state governments of what one official called an "expensive luxury"—the need to manage the prisons and to provide food and shelter (Carleton, pp. 9, 42). During the 1870s, however, convicts became omnipresent along railroad routes, while prison leases became ever more economically significant to states and companies alike. By the 1880s and 1890s, the states with the most convicts—Alabama, Florida, Georgia, and Tennessee—had turned to mining companies to house and work prisoners, and so southern convicts increasingly found themselves engaged in far-flung operations under the sole care of private companies. The former slave states had essentially given up all responsibility for the feeding, housing, clothing, and care of their prison inmates.

The financial benefits of the convict lease system to the southern states proved to be considerable. The states saved annual maintenance and transportation costs, estimated at around $250,000 by Tennessee's governor in 1891. He further predicted that a new penitentiary would cost taxpayers roughly $300,000 and take two years to build. In an economic environment in which governments favored low taxes and fiscal prudence, legislators valued such savings. Over time, convict leases also substantially boosted state revenues. Alabama and Tennessee, the states with the most remunerative prison contracts, each received $100,000 per annum from 1880s onward. Shapiro quotes Tennessee's governor as praising the lease as "successful," "relieving [the state] of all business risk and expense, and paying a surplus into the treasury" (Shapiro, p. 53). According to Mancini's review of convict leasing in the American South, by 1898, Alabama received a whopping 73% of its total revenue of nearly $388,000 from the hire of its convicts (Mancini, p. 112). Other southern states, such as Georgia, Mississippi, Arkansas, North Carolina, and Kentucky, also received significant sums from their lessees, ranging between $25,000 and $50,000 per year. Compared with northern prisons in which the inmates worked within the prison walls, the profits garnered from leasing out southern convicts were noteworthy. According to Ayers's calculations, prisons that did not use the lease system earned 32% of their costs, while those that hired convicts to work outside their walls generated income that exceeded prison-related expenditures by 267% (Ayers, p. 196).

The convict lease simultaneously proved highly satisfactory to southern lessees such as coal companies. Coal producers first began employing convict laborers because, as their corporate managers repeatedly reiterated, the South lacked a sufficient pool of free laborers willing to enter the mines, especially at wages they were prepared to pay. Although many southern laborers still had access to agricultural pursuits in the late 1860s and early 1870s, this option lessened considerably as the decade wore on. But as Alex Lichtenstein has shown, by then the South's leading coal companies—such as the Pratt mines in Birmingham; the Tennessee Coal, Iron and Railroad Company (TCIR) in Tracy City, Tennessee; the Knoxville Iron Company in Coal Creek, Tennessee; and the Dade Coal mines in northwest Georgia—all used convicts to mine coal and smelt coke, and all had many reasons to be satisfied with their labor management decisions (Lichtenstein, p. 22). Roughly 27,000 convicts labored in the postbellum South at any one time. But it was less their absolute numbers that were significant than their placement in the key nascent industries of coal mining and iron production.

Though convict productivity was generally lower than that of free miners, the lease provided a steady supply of laborers to these emerging industries. Moreover, the South's leading coal companies all found that the use of convict laborers initially slashed their wage bills. The fees the companies paid to the state, together with the costs of taking care of the prisoners, ranged from 60 cents to one dollar per prisoner per day—one quarter to one half of the daily earnings of fee laborers. Moreover, the presence of convicts kept the earnings of free miners static in real terms over the two decades from 1870 to 1890. Wages earned by miners in Tennessee, for example, dropped from about four dollars a day to under two dollars a day, paralleling a general decline in nineteenth-century prices. Convict lessees also repeatedly found that the presence of unfree miners constrained the ability of free miners to bargain for higher wages or better working conditions. Indeed, during periods of union organizing or labor agitation, the companies proved able to withstand demands for higher wages or better working conditions by threatening to lay off their free workers. They knew they could use convicts to mine enough coal to keep the coke ovens going. The coal barons viewed convict labor as a "club" they could hold over their free miners, correctly calculating that the miners would be reluctant to strike, since company managers could readily replace them with convict laborers. In addition, when the demand for coal lessened during the hot summer months and other periods of economic weakness, the coal companies invariably laid off their free miners, keeping the cheaper convicts at work.

If coal companies used the option of convict labor as a labor-management tool, coal miners sought to eliminate this threat. Mine workers, profoundly cognizant of the effect of convict laborers on their bargaining positions, initiated 21 strikes between 1871 and 1900 against the entry of convict laborers in the mines. The vast majority of these strikes failed. Partly as a result of the convict lease system, the union movement developed shallow roots in the post-Civil War South.

The convicts who labored in the mines and on the farms and railroads of the South were primarily young and unskilled African-American men. Often convicted of trivial offenses, such as the theft of a fence rail or a chicken, these men generally received sentences of one to six years. The social composition of the postbellum South's prison inmates contrasted starkly with that of the pre-Civil War years. Prior to the war, most prisoners were white, had committed serious felonies, and lived in urban centers. African-American slaves who confronted allegations of infringing plantation rules or state laws usually were punished by their masters, out of the purview of state officials. Subject to state courts following their emancipation, black freedmen soon found themselves falling foul of misdemeanor laws and caught up in the justice system. Once convicted, these young black men often received sentences disproportionate to the ostensible crimes they committed and then found themselves working in convict camps dotted around

the South. Cities and towns continued to account for the majority of prison inmates, but postbellum rural areas sent an ever-greater number of felons to the state prisons.

Although historians of the southern convict lease system have generally concluded that convicts typically arrived in the state's prisons as a result of petty pilfering increasingly punished by the state as criminal theft, one scholar, Mary Ellen Curtin, has argued that many convicted criminals in postbellum Alabama faced punishment because of efforts by African-Americans to push the social, political, and economic limits of their newfound freedom. In her book *Black Prisoners and Their World, Alabama, 1865–1900*, Curtin shows that state officials employed the law to direct black farmers' economic activity to white-owned country stores. Those who frequented "deadfalls"—informal, after-hour markets that furnished supplies to African-American farmers—often faced larceny charges. She additionally suggests that many blacks pursued their own court cases, charging fellow African-Americans with wrongdoing. In so doing, Curtin argued that they viewed the law as yet another vehicle by which they could express their recently acquired citizenship.

Whatever the route into the South's criminal justice system, the majority of its inmates were black men convicted for petty offenses, and they soon found themselves laboring on the South's penal farms and its turpentine, phosphate, and coal mines. White men, who typically fell foul of the law only if they had committed a serious crime, such as murder, generally stayed within the walls of the old penitentiaries along with those men too sick or old for hard labor. Women prisoners, who constituted only about 7% of the inmate population, also remained in central prisons, where they made prison clothes and prepared food.

Circumstances at postbellum southern convict camps varied, depending on the kindness of an individual manager and the financial well-being of his company. Some states even set minimum legal standards, though lessees rarely observed them. Moreover, many lessees subleased convicts to third parties, attenuating the state's control even further. Despite variations, convict laborers almost invariably endured horrific living conditions. Shapiro recounts an 1893 visit by a seven-man Tennessee legislative committee to the convict camp in Coal Creek, who found that the stockade consisted of "three box houses or wings"—too small for the number of men it housed and "unsanitary in the extreme." Two men slept to a bed "made of rough plank in a continuous row." The bedding was "filthy to an extreme degree," covered in "grease, grime, and coal dust." The food was no better, apparently "not up to the standard required by law, either in quantity or quality, variety, or method of preparation" (Shapiro, pp. 65–66). Abysmally high death rates further suggest the harshness of the prisoners' circumstances. Mancini observes that in the 1880s, 10% to 15% of Mississippi inmates died during their incarceration (Mancini, p. 139).

Everywhere in the postbellum South, work became the sine qua non of the convicts' lives. They toiled for long hours in hot, dangerous conditions. Although the era's prison reformers assumed that hard labor offered a road to rehabilitation through the inculcation of habits of "diligence" and "temperance," the convict lessees cared little or nothing about the physical or psychological well-being of the convicts. Relentless, backbreaking labor was good for the company profits. As convict lessees tried to extract the maximum amount of labor from their unfree laborers, however, the inmates invariably resisted whenever possible. In the coal mines, resistance generally involved shooting the coal to bits, loading coal cars with unusable slate, and shirking work, oftentimes by feigning illness. An 1894 article in the mining industry's trade journal, cited by Shapiro, bemoaned that convict-mined coal resulted in "badly laid track, badly set props...coal not mined at all, but simply shot to pieces, and finally, loaded up with all the slate, sulfur and other refuse at hand that would help fill up the requisite number of cars for the task" (Shapiro, p. 69). Although convict "trustees" and prison guards sought to induce proper mining techniques and a substantial output from the convicts, the latter had few incentives to accede to these demands. In the time-honored fashion of compelling labor from people who have little incentive to work hard, the guards resorted to both sticks and carrots—whippings alongside small incentives, such as offering small bonuses for mining more tons than one's individual allotment. Yet, as the prison record books make clear, these methods often had fairly limited results. Many convicts resisted work demands, choosing punishment over exploitation.

Faced with such horrendous living and working conditions, and a fearsome death toll, surviving prisoners could only hope that their situations might improve through escape, reduction of sentences for "good behavior," or a gubernatorial pardon. Each of these events occurred with some regularity, offering prisoners some hope of avoiding death at the mines. Statistics varied considerably from state to state and over the course of the postbellum period. In mid-1870s Georgia, according to Ayers, almost half the inmates escaped during their incarceration; in 1880s Tennessee this proportion reached just 8% (Ayers, p. 201). Substantial numbers of prisoners also received reduced sentences or pardons, a phenomenon that suggests that the southern states used these mechanisms to shorten long sentences for inconsequential crimes.

Boxes and boxes of southern governors' papers are filled with petitions for pardon. These appeals for clemency offer fascinating glimpses into notions of culpability and responsibility in the New South, as well as the social mores of justice in this period. If a convict had been drunk when he committed a crime, injured or killed a person known to be a notorious villain, had perpetrated an offense while defending his own honor or that of a woman he loved, or could plausibly claim to be too young or too ignorant to understand the implications of his actions, a petition for pardon often had a good chance of success. The hardship that befell a family following the arrest of the head of family was also a well-worn theme in these appeals.

Prison petitions additionally suggest a great deal about the nature of social hierarchy and race relations in postbellum southern communities. Petitions were often accompanied by dozens of signatures, not just of family members, but also of local notables, judges, jurors, and previous or current employees. Poor black petitioners did well to secure the assistance of these kinds of people, and local elites readily offered such support. They did so to make sure that the criminal justice system retained a personal character, one that tied poor blacks to their paternalistic largesse. Some members of the elite may have offered their support to elicit a sense of obligation from the African-American community, or to remind themselves of their exalted position in southern society. Yet others probably truly believed that justice and redemption were best served by personalizing it.

Government failure did not end here. The relationships between government officials and convict lessees were subject to abuse and corruption. Accusations of bribery dogged the convict lease system, with corrupt government officials and convict lessees in most states acquiring the appellation of a "penitentiary ring," or in the words of Edward Ayers, a kind of "mutual aid society" (Ayers, p. 195). Beyond corruption and a failed criminal justice system, the convict lease further poisoned relationships between southern blacks and whites. The naked distortions of the criminal justice system, the horrendous conditions in which convicts found themselves, the high mortality rates, and the relentless public images of stripe-clothed prisoners pushed to the breaking point all did much to remind African-Americans of the inequities of racism in the postbellum South and beyond.

KARIN A. SHAPIRO

References and Further Reading

Ayers, Edward L. *Vengeance and Justice: Crime and Punishment in the Nineteenth-Century American South.* New York: Oxford University Press, 1984.

Carleton, Mark T. *Politics and Punishment: The History of the Louisiana State Penal System.* Baton Rouge: Louisiana State University Press, 1971.

Curtin, Mary Ellen. *Black Prisoners and Their World, Alabama, 1865–1900.* Charlottesville: University of Virginia Press, 2000.

Lichtenstein, Alex. *Twice the Work of Free Labor: The Political Economy of Convict Labor in the New South.* New York: Verso Press, 1996.

Mancini, Matthew J. *One Dies, Get Another: Convict Leasing in the American South, 1866–1928.* Columbia: University of South Carolina Press, 1996.

Oshinsky, David M. *Worse than Slavery: Parchman Farm and the Ordeal of Jim Crow Justice.* New York: Free Press, 1996.

Shapiro, Karin A. *A New South Rebellion: The Battle against Convict Labor in the Tennessee Coalfields, 1871–1896.* Chapel Hill: University of North Carolina Press, 1998.

See also **New South**

COOPERATION

With the advance of the market revolution in the early nineteenth-century, American labor reformers confronted the seemingly interminable problems of wage labor and high prices with a new idea. Rather than engage in a permanent battle over wages and working conditions, workers, they argued, should own and operate their own cooperative workshops and factories. Instead of dealing with middlemen who needlessly raised the prices of necessary goods, workers should own their own cooperative stores. This strategy, known as "cooperation," was first endorsed by the labor movement in the 1830s and continued to grow in popularity until interest peaked during the Gilded Age under the aegis of the Knights of Labor. After the decline of the Knights in the 1890s, the interest of organized workers in cooperation waned and only sporadically re-emerged, most notably in the volatile years after World War I.

The idea that workers could end wage labor and their exploitation by middlemen through economic institutions of their own design was a powerful lure for many nineteenth-century trade unionists steeped in the political ideals of republicanism and the producer ethos of the skilled male worker. At the same time, cooperation's appeal to working men and women rested in its often perceived practicality. Labor reformers believed that cooperatives would readily succeed in the marketplace and stabilize community life for workers in an unstable industrializing economy. Cooperation was both utopian in its goal to supplant "competitive" capitalism and create what advocates called a "cooperative republic" and practical in its design to meet the immediate needs of its constituents. Cooperators were practical utopians.

Cooperation before the Civil War

During the 1830s, cooperation appeared as a new departure for the emergent labor movement. In 1836, the National Trades' Union proposed cooperation as a way to end strikes permanently. In 1845, the Working Men's Protective Union in Boston established a network of cooperatively owned stores and consumer buying clubs. Within two years, member wage earners had established 40 Protective Union associations in the states of Vermont, Maine, New Hampshire, and Massachusetts. By the late 1850s, members throughout New England, New York, and Canada purchased a variety of goods in over 800 Union "divisions."

During the 1840s and 1850s, skilled workers established a number of cooperative factories and workshops. Iron molders opened foundries in Ohio, Pennsylvania, and West Virginia. Shoemakers started shops in Lynn, Pittsburgh, and New York City. In Boston, tailors set up a cooperative shop; bakers, shirt sewers, and hat finishers did the same in New York. In this latter city, German tailors and cabinet-makers were inspired to cooperate by the movement in their home country. Much of this activity was also supported and nurtured again by Fourierists. They advanced cooperative workshops as a major step toward their own plan of social reconstruction.

The cooperatives established by unions in the 1830s, the numerous Protective Union stores, and the craftsmen's cooperatives of the 1840s and 1850s could not sustain themselves amidst the economic and political turmoil of the era. The first American labor movement was, in fact, destroyed, along with its experiments in cooperation, by the panic of 1837. The Protective Unions experienced debilitating internal conflicts, intense competition from other retail stores, and disruption from the onset of civil war. The early efforts of cooperative production among skilled men also suffered from an unstable economy and wartime upheaval.

Postwar Re-Emergence

Despite its pre-Civil War decline, cooperation continued to appeal to American workers. As the labor movement re-emerged in the 1860s, cooperation particularly excited the movement's new leadership. In Philadelphia, the center of much union activity during these years, a group of immigrants from England established the Union Cooperative Association No. 1. This relatively insignificant grocery attracted the attention and gained the membership of pre-eminent leaders of the labor movement, such as William Sylvis, the president of the Iron Molders' Union, Jonathan Fincher, the labor reform newspaper editor, and John Samuel, the Wilshire-born union activist, cooperator, and future Knights of Labor executive. The Union Cooperative Association was one of the first Rochdale-inspired cooperatives in the United States, and labor leaders saw it as an ideal model for emulation by American workers everywhere.

The Rochdale method of cooperation was developed by a group of weavers, known as the Rochdale Pioneers, in England in the 1840s. The method proved extra-ordinarily successful, and word of this success spread among American workers. By 1863, Rochdale advocates attained considerable influence within the labor movement. Under the Rochdale system, a cooperative store allowed its stockholders one vote regardless of the number of shares held by any individual. Shareholders received a fixed dividend of no more than 5% on their investment. Stores did not extend credit to their members and sold all goods for cash at market prices, with the profits returned to members in proportion to their purchases. According to John Samuel, approximately 100 cooperative stores, many operating under these principles, opened for business during the decade of the Civil War. During the depression of the 1870s, the Sovereigns of Industry, a labor reform organization advocating the establishment of cooperative stores, adopted the Rochdale system. Its 450 local councils in New England and the Middle and Central states each had a purchasing club or store based on this system. A decade later, the Knights of Labor supplanted the Sovereigns, and the Knights' local assemblies operated an unknown number of consumer cooperatives possibly totaling in the thousands.

The workers who endorsed Rochdale stores in most cases also promoted the establishment of producer cooperatives. They often conceived of the cooperative store as a means to accumulate capital for a factory or workshop. Shoe workers and molders were the two most prominent trades involved in cooperative activity, and their respective unions, the Knights of St. Crispin and the Iron Molders' Union, were strong supporters. Between 1866 and 1876, shoe workers operated at least 40 shoe factories and molders at least 36 foundries. Both trades established numerous cooperative stores. In addition, other workers including miners, carpenters, machinists, cigar makers, printers, bakers, coach makers, collar makers, shipwrights, nailers, ship carpenters and caulkers, glassblowers, hatters, boilermakers, plumbers, and iron rollers organized cooperative workshops. In the quarter-century following the Civil War, at least 500 cooperative factories, workshops, and mines opened for business. A majority of these enterprises commenced business in the mid-1880s.

Despite the support of important leaders in the labor movement, and the emphatic support of the Knights of Labor and its General Master Workman Terrence Powderly, national unions launched very few cooperative enterprises of their own. In fact, the role of the Knights' national organization in cooperation was limited by its general assembly's inability to agree upon an effective program. The Knights' most important centralized efforts at cooperation occurred in 1884, when they purchased a coal mine in Cannelburg, Indiana, and in 1886 when they invested in a wagon factory in Homer, New York. In both cases, the Knights operated their enterprises through their national executive board, which proved distant, difficult, and unwieldy. Both enterprises eventually failed.

In the 1870s and 1880s, cooperators achieved much greater success on a local level, where they formed cooperatives often during or after a strike. The rapid growth of the Knights of Labor inspired in many members a growing confidence that a cooperative future was possible. Consequently, local and district assemblies of the Knights sponsored, and at times collaborated, in the formation of many of these cooperatives. The most noted and successful efforts of this kind occurred in Minneapolis, Minnesota, among barrel makers, who formed an important adjunct industry to the city's large and powerful flour mills. By 1887, 62% of the 593 working barrel makers in the city operated seven barrel cooperatives and dominated the industry. They also opened a cooperative store and inspired the formation of at least 15 other cooperative businesses in Minneapolis, including a laundry owned and operated by women. The labor press heralded this success as a model for workers to learn from and emulate.

Why Cooperate?

Workers established cooperatives in this period for a variety of different reasons, some visionary and others practical. Behind cooperation's most radical tendencies was the view of wage labor as inimical to a democratic republic. Workers could only receive the full value of their labor, they argued, and act as fully independent citizens if they operated their own democratic businesses and did away with work for wages. More practically, skilled workers cooperated often to preserve their craft skills and guarantee trade union standards. Working men might also open a cooperative to preserve their status as family bread-winners and exclude women from the workplace. Most cooperators, however, strove to build autonomous democratic institutions, whether they were producer or consumer cooperatives, in order to create stable community lives.

Failure of the Dream

While a handful of cooperatives lasted for years, most, including those in Minneapolis, failed in a relatively brief period of time. The reasons usually cited by contemporaries for failure included inadequate capital resources and managerial experience, hard economic times, opposition from competing grocers or manufacturers, lack of knowledge, and inadequate legal protection for cooperatives as businesses. While these all rang true, other factors contributed to failure as well. Cooperators established their businesses primarily to stabilize their work, family, and community lives. This made their capital investments less responsive and more vulnerable than their competitors' to changing economic conditions. Internal discord between skilled and less-skilled workers could also cause operational problems. In addition, cooperators often required the support of organized labor to provide markets for their goods and for much needed capital. The principal source of such support during the 1880s was the Knights of Labor. When the Knights rapidly lost membership at the end of the decade, that source evaporated. The decline of the Knights also deflated the widespread enthusiasm for cooperation erstwhile members of the movement possessed.

As the institutional support for cooperation dissipated, labor movement cooperators moved in at least two new directions. Some joined socialist organizations, such as the Brotherhood of the Cooperative Commonwealth and the Social Democracy of America. Others participated along with academics and middle-class reformers in a cooperative movement independent of any labor organization. The labor movement itself did not reject cooperation entirely but assumed a much less active and more ambivalent role than in earlier years.

In the 1890s, the American Federation of Labor replaced the Knights of Labor as the dominant national labor organization in the United States.

It assumed a practical stance toward cooperation, rejecting the emancipatory vision associated with the Knights. The AFL believed that consumer cooperation could be a useful tool for trade unionists, and it maintained this position throughout much of the twentieth century. It only halfheartedly supported producer cooperatives. Yet this did not preclude a moment when cooperation would again inspire a grander vision of social transformation among organized workers.

During and immediately after World War I, the AFL endorsed a resurgent consumer cooperative movement around the country. In Seattle, this renewed enthusiasm took a particularly radical form. Following the general strike of 1919 in the city, Seattle's workers joined *en masse* two chains of consumer cooperatives as well as a few producer enterprises. As workers did during the Gilded Age, they hoped to eliminate middlemen, lower prices, and build economic institutions of their own design. Their ultimate goal, as expressed by their local union leadership, was to create a cooperative commonwealth through a peaceful evolutionary process, eventually crowding out privately owned enterprises entirely. Despite widespread enthusiasm and visionary leadership, the depression of the early 1920s overwhelmed these businesses. By 1922, the cooperatives of Seattle had completely collapsed.

The Meaning of Cooperation: Debate among Historians

Though cooperation played an important role in the labor movements of the nineteenth century, it has rarely received full scrutiny from historians. The first historians of cooperation in the 1880s were the most thorough chroniclers of the movement's early years. They wrote approvingly of cooperation as an important but nonideological aspect of the burgeoning labor movement. Workers, in their view, were simply acting pragmatically to solve their various labor problems through self-help measures. John Commons and the historians influenced by the Wisconsin School of labor history argued differently. To them cooperation expressed the ideological, middle-class, and backward-looking nature of the labor movement of the nineteenth century, soon rejected, appropriately, by the practical trade unionism of the American Federation of Labor.

This interpretation generally held sway until the 1970s when historians reassessed the nature of American working-class history. Central to their re-interpretation was the rediscovery of a class consciousness among American workers in the nineteenth century rooted in a working-class interpretation of republicanism. Cooperation fit in this new view as an expression of republicanism's most radical demand for an economic independence incompatible with American industrial capitalism. However, it has also been argued that cooperation was less defined than this view of a radicalized republicanism might suggest. Cooperators, in fact, held only a vague and ill-formed understanding of the producer's place in a republic. Outside of the Rochdale system, cooperators had no fixed guidelines or rules for building cooperatives; and when they established their stores and factories, they often promoted notions of democracy permeated by traditional hierarchies of gender, skill, and race. Cooperation in this view was both an expression of republican independence and a place where the very meaning of that independence was fought over, reinforced, and transformed. This helps explain the fate of cooperation at the end of the century. When cooperatives in the 1880s failed, they did so, in part, because they were themselves a source of conflict. And that failure to emancipate wage laborers surely disillusioned thousands of working men and women about the emancipatory potential of both cooperation and a labor movement based on the ideals of republican independence.

STEVEN LEIKIN

References and Further Reading

Adams, Herbert, ed. *History of Cooperation in the United States.* Johns Hopkins University Studies in Historical and Political Science, Vol. VI. Baltimore: Johns Hopkins University, 1888.

Fink, Leon. *Workingmen's Democracy: The Knights of Labor and American Politics.* Urbana: University of Illinois Press, 1983.

Frank, Dana. *Purchasing Power: Consumer Organizing, Gender, and the Seattle Labor Movement, 1919–1929.* New York: Cambridge University Press, 1994.

Grob, Gerald N. *Workers and Utopia: A Study of Ideological Conflict in the American Labor Movement, 1865–1900.* Chicago: Quadrangle Books, 1961.

Guarneri, Carl J. *The Utopian Alternative: Fourierism in Nineteenth-Century America.* Ithaca, NY: Cornell University Press, 1991.

Laurie, Bruce. *Artisans into Workers: Labor in Nineteenth-Century America.* New York: The Noonday Press, 1989.

Leikin, Steven. *The Practical Utopians: American Workers and the Cooperative Movement in the Gilded Age.* Detroit: Wayne State University Press, 2004.

Montgomery, David. "William H. Sylvis and the Search for Working-Class Citizenship." In *Labor Leaders in America,* edited by Melvyn Dubofsky and Warren Van Tine. Urbana: University of Illinois Press, 1987, pp. 3–29.

Oestreicher, Richard. "Terence V. Powderly, the Knights of Labor, and Artisanal Republicanism." In *Labor Leaders in America,* edited by Melvyn Dubofsky and Warren Van Tine. Urbana: University of Illinois Press, 1987, pp. 30–61.

Parker, Florence E. *The First 125 Years: A History of Distributive and Service Cooperation in the United States, 1829–1954.* Chicago: Cooperative Publishing Association, 1956.

Rachleff, Peter. *Black Labor in Richmond, 1865–1890.* Urbana: University of Illinois Press, 1989.

Ware, Norman J. *The Labor Movement in the United States, 1860–1895.* New York: Vintage Books, 1929.

Wilentz, Sean. *Chants Democratic: New York City and the Rise of the American Working Class, 1788–1850.* New York: Oxford University Press, 1984.

CORONA, BERT (MAY 29, 1918– FEBRUARY 15, 2001)
Activist for Mexican and Mexican-American Rights

Humberto (Bert) Corona was a tireless labor and community activist who devoted much of his life to the needs of Mexican immigrants. Corona was born in El Paso, Texas, in 1918. His father, Noé, served in Pancho Villa's Division of the North during the Mexican Revolution (1910–1920) and advocated local autonomy for rural folk, whom he believed had the right to arm themselves in defense of their interests, enshrined in the Mexican Constitution of 1857. His mother, Margarita, also supported the democratic ideals of the Revolution. Unlike Noé, she was a Protestant, came from a wealthy family, and had obtained a high-level bilingual education through congregational instructors, at the behest of her mother, Ynes, a practicing medical doctor. Meeting after a battle during which Ynes treated several of Noé's men, the couple later married, and at various times lived on either side of the border. In 1924, while living in Chihuahua, Noé and a group of political activists were assassinated. This left a long-lasting impact on Bert, who believed his father to have been a champion of social justice. After Noé's death, Margarita and Ynes moved the family to El Segundo Barrio of El Paso, which had become a refuge for Mexican revolutionaries. In El Segundo, Bert listened to revolutionary tales stressing struggle, sacrifice, and justice.

In addition to this unorthodox education, Corona attended Protestant educational services in El Paso and then later enrolled in Harwood Boys School in Albuquerque, New Mexico. There, he partook in a student-led strike against corporal punishment and historical lessons concerning the Revolution. During the Great Depression, Corona attended El Paso High School, where he joined a study group that discussed fascism, socialism, the Russian Revolution, and the writings of Thorsten Veblen, Upton Sinclair, and Lincoln Steffens. He then began attending the meetings of the *Sociedad Anarcho-Sindicalista*, a group of Mexican laborers who were followers of the anarcho-syndicalist Ricardo Flores Magon. In 1936, Corona moved to Los Angeles after obtaining a basketball work assistance scholarship at the University of Southern California (USC). At USC, Corona joined the Non-Org Movement, a college organization composed of lower-middle- and working-class youth, who often had participated in the Civilian Conservation Corps. The Non-Org fought for university services such as student housing and expressed political support for Republican Spain, the National Labor Relations Act, and other New Deal programs. Through a series of conferences sponsored by the Young Men's Christian Association, Corona and other Mexican students, social workers, and teachers formed the Mexican-American Movement (MAM), which focused on combating discrimination in education, employment, and recreational services. Although MAM disintegrated during the Second World War, between 1938 and 1940, the organization left a positive impact on many Latinas/os, who remained politically active throughout their lives.

Through a USC work assistantship, Corona secured employment at the Brunswig Drug Company. At Brunswig, the Longshoremen's Association, which would be renamed the International Longshoremen's and Warehousemen's Union (ILWU) after it affiliated with the Congress of Industrial Organizations (CIO) in 1937, recruited Corona to picket the transportation of nonunion-affiliated merchandise within L.A. In the fall of 1937, Corona helped form Local 26 of the ILWU, was elected recording secretary, and began organizing workers. In this role, he was mentored by Lloyd Seeliger, a seasoned labor organizer who had joined the International Workers of the World (IWW) at age 13. Seeliger invited Bert to attend labor and political functions and introduced him to the Communist Party of the United States' *Daily People's World*, which covered labor events, strikes, and debates between unions. Describing himself as a progressive who leaned toward the socialist ideology of Lincoln Steffens, Corona always maintained that he had never joined the Communist Party of the United States (CPUSA). Yet, over the course of his life, Corona developed close friendships with a number of communists and worked with unions associated with the CPUSA. Perhaps as a result of these affiliations or his undisclosed membership, the Federal Bureau of Investigation believed Corona to have been a member of the CPUSA from 1940 to 1945. In any event, during the 1930s Corona helped organize 95% of the workers at Brunswig and in his spare time worked to unionize other industries. In 1939, Corona

dropped out of the USC and devoted himself completely to the CIO. By 1941, Local 26 had over six thousand members, Corona was elected president of the local; after being fired from Brunswig during a botched slowdown action, he was immediately hired as a full-time organizer by Harry Bridges, the president of the ILWU.

As a full-time CIO unionist, Corona organized the waste material industry, which employed many Jewish and Mexican female laborers. By meeting the workers' particular linguistic needs (Yiddish and Spanish), drawing on family networks, and organizing cultural events to generate solidarity, Corona was very successful. Through the CIO, Corona befriended Luisa Moreno, a Guatemalan immigrant who worked for the Packing and Allied Workers of America (UCAPAWA) and was then the only Latina/o officer of the California state CIO. Moreno had just formed the Committee on Spanish-Speaking Workers, which focused on the needs of Latina/os within the CIO but also worked with the National Association for the Advancement of Colored People and the Urban League in a few broader Civil Rights struggles. Corona later worked with *El Congreso Nacional del Pueblo de Habla Espanola* (*El Congreso*), an organization created by Moreno and furthered by activists such as Josefina Fierro and Eduardo Quevedo. *El Congreso* combated discrimination and police brutality and sought to expand the educational and employment opportunities of Spanish-speaking people. While organizations such as the League of United Latin American Citizens drew sharp distinctions between the interests of Mexicans who held U.S. citizenship and Mexican nationals, *El Congreso* sought to defend the interests of all Latin Americans, regardless of citizenship. Consequently, *El Congreso* organized numerous Mexican immigrants into the CIO. While the organization dissolved during WWII, several of its founders were later harassed politically during the Cold War. As a result of the passage of the McCarran-Walter Act in 1952, which sanctioned the deportation of immigrants and naturalized citizens considered "subversive," many Latina/o immigrant activists who had built *El Congreso*, including Moreno and Fierro, went into exile to avoid persecution.

In 1941, Corona married Blanche Taff, a middle-class woman of Polish-Jewish descent. The couple met during a unionizing campaign at North American Aviation, during which Blanche participated as a member of the Democratic Youth Federation, an organization of young, militant Jewish-American students who supported unions and the New Deal. Bert and Blanche married, had three children, and on occasion, worked together in the CIO and antidiscrimination activities. After Pearl Harbor, Corona enlisted in the Army Air Corps, but due to his labor and CPUSA affiliations, he was labeled a possible subversive and was never allowed into combat. After completing his military service, in 1945, Corona moved to the Bay Area in California and became involved in electoral politics. He worked with the Independent Progressive Party, which endorsed former Vice President Henry Wallace for the 1948 presidential election. Corona then joined the Community Service Organization (CSO), a predominantly Mexican-American group that concentrated on voter registration drives in order to expand Latina/o representation in California politics. The CSO spearheaded Edward Roybal's election to the L.A. City Council and later mobilized Mexican-Americans to vote for progressive political candidates such as Byron Rumford and Lionel Wilson, African-Americans who ran for state assembly and municipal judgeship positions. During the 1950s, Corona became the northern California regional director of the *Asociacion Nacional Mexico-Americana* (ANMA). Corona was attracted to ANMA because it was created by the Mexican membership of the Mine, Mill and Smelter Workers; the ILWU; the UCA-PAWA; and the Furniture Workers Union. Furthermore, Corona applauded ANMA's commitment to defend the civil rights and culture of Mexican people. During the 1950s, ANMA provided institutional support to laborers involved in various strikes, such as the Salt of the Earth strike and bracero stoppages.

During the 1960s, Corona worked as a labor organizer for the National Maritime Union and as a political recruiter for the Mexican-American Political Association (MAPA), which mobilized Mexicans to obtain U.S. citizenship and to vote for political candidates such as Lyndon B. Johnson in the 1964 presidential election, for Pat Brown in the 1966 gubernatorial election of California, and for Robert F. Kennedy in the 1968 presidential campaign. While Corona often worked in a variety of causes, including antiwar protests during the Vietnam War, and joined forces with incredibly diverse activists and organizations, such as César Chávez and the United Farm Workers Union, Reis Lopez Tijerina and the *Alianza*, Rodolfo "Corky" Gonzales and the Crusade for Justice, and disparate groups that were part of the Chicano Power Movement, in 1968, Corona moved back to L.A. and decided to devote himself to organizing Latin American undocumented immigrants. In L.A., Corona established a chapter of the *Hermandad Mexicana Nacional* (*Hermandad*), an organization formed in 1951 by Phil and Albert Usquiano, two trade unionists who created the group to protect the legal rights of Mexican immigrants. Through the *Hermandad*, Corona labored to provide all Spanish-speaking immigrants with legal counseling, citizenship and English-language classes, and cultural activities, and formed broad-based community coalitions to lobby officials in Washington in regard to immigration legislation. Organizing Latina/o immigrants along the lines of the family unit, the *Hermandad* grew to over 30,000 members. After participating in numerous labor and political struggles, at the age of 82 in 2001, Bert Corona passed away.

JOHN H. FLORES

References and Further Reading

The Bert Corona Oral History Collection, 1937–1945. The California Ethnic and Multicultural Archives, Special Collections, Donald C. Davidson Library, University of California, Santa Barbara.
Corona, Bert. *Bert Corona Speaks on La Raza Unida Party and the "Illegal Alien" Scare*. New York: Pathfinder Press, 1972.
———. *MAPA and La Raza Unida Party: A Program for Chicano Political Action for the 1970's*. National City, California: La Raza Unida Party, 1971.
Garcia, Mario T. *Memories of Chicano History: The Life and Narrative of Bert Corona*. Berkeley: University of California Press, 1994.

See also **Bridges, Harry Renton; Chávez, César Estrada; Cold War; Communist Party; Industrial Workers of the World; International Longshoremen's Association; McCarran-Walter Act (1952); Mexican and Mexican-American Workers; National Association for the Advancement of Colored People (NAACP); Vietnam War**

COXEY'S ARMY

In 1894, in the midst of a severe economic depression, people across the United States had a vivid lesson in the efforts of labor and financial reformers to increase the amount of federal government intervention in the economy. From March through May, they read and sometimes watched as at least a thousand people tried to take part in the first march on Washington. Led by Jacob Coxey, a business owner and Populist from Ohio, and Carl Browne, a labor activist from California, these protesters sought to attack the rampant unemployment that affected directly many of the marchers and to loosen the money supply. The demand was for the federal government to support road building and other improvements by towns, cities, and counties. Workers on these projects would receive a minimum wage of $1.50 a day, almost 80% above the standard for the period. The projects would be financed by no-interest loans to the local governments; in other words, by the federal government issuing more money. For people with debts or the need to borrow, the result would be lower interest rates. Supporters came from the unemployed, labor activists, Populists, and financial reformers. But the proposals and the method of marching directly to the Capitol did not receive universal support from even these groups and were scarcely considered by Congress or the president.

The mixture of attention and disdain reflected sustained questions about the methods and goals of the labor movement in the 1890s in the United States. Some labor activists questioned whether it made sense to appeal for any help from Washington, when the federal government often took an active role in breaking up strikes and in creating policies that protected business. Indeed, federal troops were authorized to stop a train that some supporters of Coxey's Army had seized in Montana; the ensuing battle resulted in two deaths. Such violence fueled the opposition to this cause among most mainstream politicians. Both Democratic and Republican leaders had many reasons to dislike this proposal. Republicans, closely aligned with the interests of large business owners and some established unions, preferred to use taxes on imports to respond to economic changes. Democrats, with a more economically diverse constituency, feared the growth of the national government as a threat to the powers of the states and individuals. Regardless of party, most politicians of the time believed that the appropriate response to an economic crisis was to cut their spending as their revenues fell. For these reasons, there was barely any sustained debate of the demands of Coxey's Army in Washington.

Nevertheless, Coxey's Army demands and methods were not that different from many reformers, both within and outside the organized labor movement. Their proposal called for jobs, not relief. Though their figure for the minimum daily wage was high, it still fit with similar calls by social welfare reformers and labor activists for a family wage. And like other economic reformers of the time, supporters of Coxey's Army understood that federal policy—especially deficit spending and a looser money supply—could have a fundamental effect on the broader economy of the nation. Finally, in mobilizing the poor to demand changes, Coxey and Browne had many counterparts in the vibrant labor and social reform culture of the late 1880s and 1890s. Though newspaper reporters dubbed them Coxey's Army, their official name was the Commonweal of Christ, reflecting their belief in the connections between Christianity and economic equality.

Their method of demanding change by going directly the nation's capital also had parallels with other labor actions of the time, but was unique and untested. Direct demands on local government were commonplace, and some protests focused on state government. In the 1870s, Browne had been an activist with the Workingmen's Party in San Francisco. The party mobilized workers in the city through sustained protests and an electoral campaign that resulted in their control of the city's government. Bolstered by this success, the party tried to build a national movement. Later, in 1893, Browne watched as unemployed workers in Chicago besieged the City Hall with demands for work. Yet, taking to the streets of a familiar locality was quite different than orchestrating a national march to Washington.

In contrast to these local protests in known spaces, Coxey's Army faced logistical, political, and symbolic unknowns. For the 300 supporters who left Ohio with Coxey and Browne on foot on March 26, the nearly 700 miles of marching was difficult. They camped; they foraged for food; and they were threatened by local authorities. For other supporters, traveling from as far west as California and as far north of Boston, the question was how to reach Washington by May 1, 1894. Some hopped trains; one group that included the author Jack London took leaky barges down Midwestern rivers. Not all of these groups made it to Washington for the May 1 march and protest.

The right of the participants to march in Washington was also highly contested for political and symbolic reasons. City authorities, working in concert with federal officials, initially proposed arresting all marchers as vagrants. When that option was dismissed, they turned to strictly regulating the nature of the march. The city authorities granted permission to march down Pennsylvania Avenue but refused the right of the protestors to go to the Capitol Building itself. The Capitol grounds, mainstream politicians declared, deserved protection from such disruptions. Congress needed peace and quiet to deliberate. Populist representatives and senators objected strenuously; they noted the raucous behavior of both elected politicians and lobbyists in the Capitol, and the arbitrary enforcement of this ban.

Nevertheless, on May 1, Coxey's Army, made up of nearly 1,000 marchers, marched in ranks down Pennsylvania Avenue. Thousands of interested Washingtonians and a huge contingent of police watched with interest; some observers cheered regularly. When Coxey and Browne deliberately broke the prohibition on entering the Capitol grounds, they were arrested. Eventually, they served 20 days in jail on the dubious charge of walking on the grass. Supporters of their efforts continued to camp around the nation's capital over the summer of 1894. But the Pullman Strike drew attention from their efforts, and eventually the Maryland, Virginia, and District of Columbia authorities forced them to depart. Still,

Coxey's and Browne's vision of the right of the people to use the Capitol on behalf of their causes gradually became an accepted political tool for protests of national policy. Labor activists remembered Coxey's Army when they took part in the veteran's Bonus Army of 1932, the Negro March on Washington in 1941, the civil rights marches of the 1950s and 1960s, and the Solidarity protests of the 1980s.

LUCY G. BARBER

References and Further Reading

Barber, Lucy G. *Marching on Washington: The Forging of American Political Tradition.* Berkeley: University of California Press, 2002.

Hoffman, Charles. *The Depression of the Nineties: An Economic History.* Westport, CT: Greenwood, 1970.

McMurry, Donald L. *Coxey's Army: A Study of the Industrial Army Movement of 1894.* Seattle: University of Washington, 1968 [1929].

Schwantes, Carlos A. *Coxey's Army: An American Odyssey.* Lincoln: University of Nebraska Press, 1985.

See also **Kearney, Denis; Living Wage; March on Washington Movement; Poor People's Campaign; Pullman Strike and Boycott (1894); Unemployment**

CRIPPLE CREEK STRIKES

Two strikes of the Western Federation of Miners (WFM) bracketed a decade of union power in Colorado's Cripple Creek District in the late nineteenth and early twentieth centuries. The six-mile-square gold-mining district southwest of Colorado Springs took its name from the largest town and supply center. Nine smaller communities—Anaconda, Elkton, Victor, Lawrence, Goldfield, Independence, Altman, Cameron, and Gillet—clustered around the mines and mills. The labor movement and the local economy revolved around gold mining. Gold was discovered in Cripple Creek in 1890. By 1900, miners dug over $20 million from 475 producing mines that supported a local population of some 32,000.

The first Cripple Creek strike, in 1894, secured the eight-hour day, the $3 minimum daily wage, and the right to union membership for the District's miners. Their victory anchored a labor movement that had, by 1902, organized a majority of all workers. Organized labor's power extended from the mines and workplaces to various aspects of social, cultural, and political life. The unions hosted balls, smokers, picnics, political debates, and the annual Fourth of July and Labor Day celebrations. They provided health care, insurance, and sick benefits, buried dead members, or shipped their bodies out of the District for burial. They promoted working-class education, operated reading rooms, and from 1899 to 1903, published *The Victor and Cripple Creek Daily Press*, the masthead of which proudly announced: "The Only Daily Newspaper Owned by Organized Workingmen." Nine WFM locals grounded this vibrant labor community, in a district where six of 10 men worked in mining, and 80% of the population was working class.

The decade of union power ended with the second Cripple Creek strike, one of a series of conflicts in Colorado coal and hardrock mining known collectively as the "Colorado Labor Wars" of 1903–1904. The two Cripple Creek strikes were linked by competition among mine owners as they integrated the local mining industry and contests between capital and labor to control working conditions in industrial mining. In both strikes, the power of the state proved pivotal.

The 1894 Strike

The first Cripple Creek strike occurred in circumstances far from auspicious for labor. The repeal of the Sherman Silver Purchase Act closed silver mines throughout the Mountain West in 1893, throwing thousands of miners out of work just as an economic depression swelled the ranks of unemployed. Miners and mining capital moved to the new gold camp. Two major ownership groups, one led by J. J. Hagerman and the other led by David Moffat and Eben Smith, were laying tracks to connect the District's mines to its mills in Colorado City and Florence. With a surplus of skilled labor and the railroads not yet completed, it appeared a good time to establish owners' control.

For western hardrock miners, it was time to organize. They met in Butte, Montana, on May 15, 1893, to found the Western Federation of Miners. District miners did not attend but asked Colorado WFM organizer Alexander McIntosh for help. McIntosh organized a WFM local in Altman, and then deputized John Calderwood, who organized locals in Victor, Anaconda, and Cripple Creek. Calderwood stayed to lead the union through the first strike.

The first WFM local, Altman Free Coinage No. 19, was founded August 20, 1893, three days after Hagerman's Isabella mine announced it would lengthen the work day from eight hours to 10. The miners refused to work, and the mine temporarily rescinded the order, but the stage was set for the 1894 strike, which concerned hours and wages. Some mines worked eight hours, some nine or 10. The union sought a uniform eight-hour day and a $3 minimum daily wage. A number of mines that were allied with the Hagerman or Smith-Moffat interests announced that on February 1 they would enforce 10-hour shifts. After offers to compromise failed, on February 7, 1894, the miners struck all mines that worked over eight hours. The strike involved fewer than half of the mines, and less than a fourth of the working miners, about half of whom already worked eight hours for $3.

Divisions among owners influenced the outcome. Some held firm for nine or 10 hours; some quickly settled with the union; some threatened a wage cut to $2.50 for an eight-hour day. Calderwood negotiated a special agreement with W. S. Stratton and James Burns, two of the few working-class men who had struck it rich in the District. Their mines paid $3.25 for a nine-hour day shift, and $3 for an eight-hour night shift, an agreement that held until 1896 when they switched to eight hours.

The progress of railroad construction influenced divisions among employers. Mine owners with substantial railroad interests held to nine or 10 hours, content to close their mines or stockpile ore until the railroads arrived to reduce shipping costs.

Another crucial factor was an exercise of state power atypical in western labor conflicts. The mine owners controlled the county government, but Governor Davis Waite, a Populist, supported the strikers. From March through May 1894, local officials, many of them WFM members, faced off against an army of El Paso County sheriff's deputies, who in turn were checked by the state militia. Twice Waite dispatched troops: briefly in March, after Altman officials detained and disarmed six deputies sent to guard the Victor Mine, and in June, after the strike was settled, to disband an army of sheriff's deputies.

By April, 28 mines worked eight-hour shifts, in addition to Burns's Portland and Stratton's Independence; only seven were idled by the strike. In mid-May, Bowers swore in some 1,200 deputies, paid and armed by mine owners, and sent nearly 200 to occupy mines near Victor as the Florence and Cripple Creek Railroad (F&CC) approached. Fearing attack, the strikers entrenched themselves near Altman on Bull Hill. On May 24, they met the deputies near Victor, surrounded the nonunion Strong Mine and its guard of armed deputies, and allegedly blew up the shaft house. Who was responsible remained a subject of local debate. The next day, a striker and a deputy were killed and two men wounded in a confrontation between miners and deputies. Six strikers were jailed. On May 26, Governor Waite asked the strikers to lay down their arms and demanded that Bowers's deputy sheriffs disperse because they constituted an illegal army, usurping the powers of the governor. The

same day, the F&CC reached Victor and the mines the deputies had occupied.

Both sides moved to settle. The miners appointed Waite their sole arbitrator. On June 4, he negotiated with Hagerman and Moffat, the only significant holdouts. As the tracks reached their mines, both conceded the $3 day and eight hours, and promised not to discriminate against union members.

Bowers then advanced on Bull Hill with his 1,200 deputies. Waite sent the state militia and finally threatened martial law to force the deputies to disband. Sheriff Bowers arrested several hundred men for strike-related offenses. Ultimately, only four strikers were convicted, and the Colorado Supreme Court reversed one conviction. Jackson Rhines served six months in county jail for assault. Robert Lyons and Nicholas Tully were sentenced to six and eight years, respectively, for blowing up the Strong Mine, but A. W. McIntire, a Republican who succeeded Waite as Governor, pardoned both. The miners considered Tully, Lyons, and Rhines heroes convicted by antiunion Colorado Springs juries.

Building from the strike victory, the WFM supported the organizing and demands of other workers, using a combination of consumer boycotts and social pressure. If those tactics failed, a number of brief strikes proved effective in getting employers to negotiate. That decade of success informed union strategy as the second strike began.

The 1903–1904 Strike

Competition among owners again proved significant in the second strike, as did state power. Stratton's moderating influence ended with his death in 1902, and younger anti-union owners, led by Charles Tutt, Spencer Penrose, Charles MacNeill, and A. E. Carlton, expanded their holdings. Tutt, Penrose, and MacNeill's United States Reduction and Refining Company (USR&R) was rivaled by the Portland Gold Mining Company, headed by James Burns. The second strike began in August 1902, with the organization of a WFM local at three Colorado City mills: the Portland, Telluride, and USR&R's Standard.

The WFM was an industrial union, committed to organizing all workers in the mining industry to match owners' integrated control of mines, mills, and railroads. Thus, the miners considered it their issue when USR&R fired 42 men identified by a Pinkerton detective as union members. In February 1903, the union requested their reinstatement, a daily wage increase from $1.80 to $2.25, and the right to union membership. USR&R refused to bargain; the millmen struck, and the strike spread to the Portland and Telluride when they, too, denied union recognition. The companies asked a willing sheriff and governor for protection.

Republican James H. Peabody, who belonged to the anti-union Citizens' Alliance, won the 1902 gubernatorial race by a plurality. During his two-year term, Peabody sent troops to strikes throughout Colorado's mills, hardrock mines, and coalfields. The local issues in each strike differed; each escalated as anti-union owners mobilized state support.

As the adjutant general of the National Guard, Peabody appointed Sherman Bell, the manager of the District's Smith-Moffat interests, and ordered him to guard the mills. The WFM then threatened to strike all mines that shipped to the unfair mills. The Portland and Telluride settled, the Standard refused to budge, and on March 17, the WFM struck all mines that shipped to USR&R.

The strike dragged on for 15 months, punctuated by violence, military occupation, and jockeying for control among owners. The union held back as USR&R promised to re-instate some of the fired mill workers. By July, the Portland and Telluride worked an eight-hour day for a $2.25 minimum wage; the Standard paid $1.80. Hoping to force other owners to pressure the Standard, on August 8, Cripple Creek District Union No. 1 struck all mines that shipped to Colorado City. The Portland settled and remained open as a union shop.

The Standard Mill closed due to lack of ore on September 2. The same day, mine owners asked Peabody for troops. Over the objections of local authorities, Peabody sent one thousand National Guard troops on September 4, the costs covered by the mine owners at 4% interest. Using the vague legal justification of "qualified martial law," troops seized the work force of the pro-union *Victor Record*, charged union leaders with two failed train-wrecking attempts, and refused to surrender them to civil authorities.

On November 21, an explosive device killed two men at the Smith-Moffat Vindicator Mine, located in the middle of the main military camp. Citing the attempted train wrecking and the Vindicator explosion, Peabody asserted that Teller County was in a state of insurrection and rebellion and declared martial law on December 4.

On January 26, 15 miners fell to their deaths when faulty machinery severed the cable hauling them to the surface of a nonunion mine. The coroner's jury blamed negligent management; the union blamed incompetent nonunion labor, and the Mine Owners Association (MOA) charged that the union had tampered with machinery that again lay within the main militia encampment. Peabody announced that peace and good order had been restored and suspended martial law on February 2. Later that month, a jury from outside the District acquitted the men accused of attempted train wrecking, given evidence that MOA detectives had staged the incidents.

The struggle continued in economic arenas. The MOA had successfully pressured some mines to fire union workers, and on March 10 instituted a permit system to blacklist WFM members. Cripple Creek merchants had cut off credit to strikers, so the WFM opened four cooperative stores. Each side claimed it was winning.

The tragic end began at 2:15 a.m. on June 6. An explosion ripped through the platform of the Independence F&CC depot, killing 13 nonunion miners coming off shift from Carlton's Findley Mine. Within hours, mine owners and the local Citizens' Alliance forced elected officials to resign, seized control of the local government, provoked a riot, and ransacked the union halls and cooperative stores. A re-activated militia deported over 200 union leaders to Kansas and New Mexico; hundreds of others fled or were "whitecapped" out as the MOA banned union labor from the District. The militia closed the Portland Mine, and an anti-union faction took over the company. In November, MOA gun thugs intimidated voters by killing two union poll watchers. Although the strike was not officially called off until 1907, the aftermath of the Independence depot explosion crushed the Cripple Creek labor movement.

Two years later, Harry Orchard accused an "inner circle" of the WFM of hiring him to murder former Idaho Governor Frank Steunenberg on December 30, 1905, and of paying him to set the bombs at the Vindicator Mine and Independence Depot. WFM leaders William D. Haywood, Charles Moyer, and George Pettibone were kidnapped to stand trial in Idaho. Although Haywood was acquitted, and charges against Moyer and Pettibone were dismissed, who paid Orchard remained historically contested. The outcome in Cripple Creek influenced the WFM to help found the Industrial Workers of the World in 1905. Both strikes wrote significant chapters in the struggle for control of industrial hardrock mining.

ELIZABETH JAMESON

References and Further Reading

Dubofsky, Melvyn. *We Shall Be All*. New York: Quadrangle/The New York Times Book Co., 1969.

Haywood, William Dudley. *Bill Haywood's Book: The Autobiography of Big Bill Haywood*. New York: International Publishers, 1929; reprint ed., New York: International Publishers, 1974.

Jameson, Elizabeth. *All That Glitters: Class, Conflict, and Community in Cripple Creek*. Urbana and Chicago: University of Illinois Press, 1998.

Jenson, Vernon H. *Heritage of Conflict: Labor Relations in the Nonferrous Metals Industry Up to 1930*. Ithaca, NY: Cornell University Press, 1950.

Langdon, Emma F. *The Cripple Creek Strike: A History of Industrial Wars in Colorado*. Denver: The Great Western Publishing Co., 1904–1905; reprint ed., New York: Arno Press and the New York Times, 1969.

Suggs, George G. Jr. *Colorado's War on Militant Unionism: James H. Peabody and the Western Federation of Miners*. Detroit: Wayne State University Press, 1972.

Waters, Frank. *Midas of the Rockies: The Story of Stratton and Cripple Creek*. Chicago: The Swallow Press, Inc., 1937.

CROATIANS

Between 1880 and World War I, an average of 500,000 immigrants arrived in the United States annually. Most of them came from southern, eastern, and central Europe, drawn to U.S. industry's demand for unskilled labor. Former peasants, farm laborers, and casual workers, predominantly men at first, became miners, steel workers, packinghouse workers, and the like. As they adjusted to life in industrial America, many of them participated in the nascent labor movement of the 1910s–1930s, a labor movement that struggled with the increasing ethnic and racial diversity of the working class, the re-organization of production under the influences of Taylorism and Fordism, the emergence of a mass consumer culture, and the rising power of the corporate and industrial elite. Within the heart of this experience were Croatian immigrants and, as time went on, their children.

Croatians came to the United States as they responded to the social forces that transformed the lives of millions of peasants and oppressed minorities throughout southern, central, and eastern Europe. In the 1870s and 1880s, economic and social changes had begun to shake the centralized authority of the Austro-Hungarian Empire, disrupting everyday life and putting political freedom on the historical agenda from the Dalmatian coast to the mountains of Bosnia and Hercegovina. Some launched new political movements for independence, democracy, and even socialism, while others left in pursuit of economic opportunities abroad. Nearly half a million, mostly young men, emigrated between 1905 and 1914, heading to Canada and Australia, as well as the United States. Seeking unskilled jobs in the rapidly expanding mass industries, they settled in the heavily industrialized cities of Pittsburgh, Cleveland, and Chicago and the smaller industrial towns around these cities; the industrial frontier of Michigan, Wisconsin, Minnesota, and Montana; and the coal towns of Pennsylvania, West Virginia, Ohio, and Colorado.

While most of the immigrants arrived thinking of themselves as people from specific provinces—Licani, Slavonians, Dalmatians, Hercegovinians, among others—they would forge a new "Croatian" identity in the diaspora. Some had been influenced, before leaving, by the romantic nationalism that had developed within some of the Croatian provinces. Some sought broader bases for ethnic fraternal benefit societies. Since most of them had found low-paying, dangerous, unskilled work, they needed to provide for themselves and their families in case of injuries or even death. They quickly realized that the larger the base for a mutual benefit organization the better. By the early twentieth century, predominantly local societies had begun to flow into national organizations, first the National Croatian Society in 1897 and then an expanded Croatian Fraternal Union (CFU) in 1924. These organizations themselves promoted a new "Croatian" identity to attract members; and they produced newspapers, poetry, visual art, drama, music, dance, and political ideologies to reinforce this new self-conception. They also provided connections to ongoing political movements in the home country, which was a matter of considerable concern to many of the immigrants.

This new identity, new consciousness, continued to be transformed in response to international influences (the emergence of an independent Yugoslavia in the aftermath of World War I), national pressures (the disruption of new immigration occasioned by the laws of 1923 and 1924, on the one hand, and the concerted campaign to "Americanize" immigrants and their children, on the other), industrial and class experiences (the re-organization of production under the impact of Taylorism and Fordism), the recomposition of the working class (relations among immigrants and the great wave of African-American migration), and the intervention of activists (promoters of ethnic fraternalism, political organizers for homeland movements, trade union advocates, and socialists and communists). Croatian immigrant workers and their children who followed them into the same industries joined the CFU, contributed to political movements geared toward the homeland, and demonstrated an increased interest in the labor movement in the United States.

This reached a climax in the mid-1930s. The Great Depression put new pressures on Croatian and Croatian-American workers. They faced layoffs, reduced work weeks, wage cuts, speedups, and deteriorating working conditions. The New Deal offered them new hopes, ideas, and connections, as they joined political organizations and campaigns, made new alliances with other ethnic workers and even African-Americans, and experienced a level of involvement and empowerment that was inspiring and encouraging. When new unions, industrial unions, emerged within mass production industries, and their organizers produced literature in Croatian, spoke at CFU lodge meetings, participated in Croatian social and cultural events, and even hired Croatian and Croatian-American organizers, the floodgates opened. Tens of thousands of Croatians and Croatian-Americans joined the Steel Workers Organizing Committee, the United Auto Workers, the Packinghouse Workers Organizing Committee, and other new union formations, mostly affiliated with the CIO, and some were even elected officers of the new local unions.

Like other immigrant and ethnic groups in this period, Croatians and Croatian-Americans remade themselves as American workers, drawing on their own particular cultural and political heritages, their experiences of exploitation and empowerment in the United States, their new relationships with other immigrants and ethnic workers, and their dreams of justice and political freedom for their homeland and a better life for their children and grandchildren in the United States. This mix, different in its particulars yet similar in its contours for each southern, central, and eastern European immigrant group in this period of U.S. history, enriched the labor movement and gave it much of its body. Croatian immigrant workers made an important contribution to the larger story of labor in the United States.

PETER RACHLEFF

References and Further Reading

Barrett, James, Rob Ruck, and Steve Nelson. *Steve Nelson: American Radical*. Pittsburgh: University of Pittsburgh Press, 1981.

Cizmic, Ivan. *History of the Croatian Fraternal Union of America, 1894–1994*. Zagreb: Golden Marketing, 1994.

Cohen, Lizabeth. *Making a New Deal: Industrial Workers in Chicago, 1919–1939*. New York: Cambridge University Press, 1990.

Mihanovich, Clement S. *Americanization of the Croats in St. Louis*. St. Louis: St. Louis University Press, 1936.

Prpic, George. *The Croatian Immigrants in America*. New York: Philosophical Library, 1971.

Rachleff, Peter. "The Croatian-American Left." In *Encyclopedia of the American Left*, edited by Paul Buhle, Mari Jo Buhle, and Dan Georgakas. Urbana: University of Illinois Press, 1991.

———. "The Dynamics of 'Americanization': The Croatian Fraternal Union between the Wars, 1920s–1930s." In *Labor Histories: Class, Politics, and the Working-Class Experience*, edited by Eric Arnesen, Julie Greene, and Bruce Laurie. Urbana: University of Illinois Press, 1998.

Stipanovich, Joseph. "Collective Economic Activity among Serb, Croat, and Slovene Immigrants in the United States." In *Self-Help in Urban America*, edited by Scott Cummings. Port Washington, NY: Kennikat Press, 1980.

CUBANS

The ebbs and flows of Cuban immigrants to the United States during the nineteenth and early twentieth centuries fluctuated in tandem with the international market for tobacco products and the development of the cigar industry in particular. Although Cubans lived in the United States prior to the American Civil War (1861–1865), estimates of their numbers do not exceed one thousand, and they were not centered in distinct communities. By the mid-1870s, Cuban communities developed in New York, New Orleans, and Key West. Large-scale Cuban immigration to the United States in the nineteenth century can be traced to two intertwined factors: political and economic. The political factor revolved around the Civil War and the first Cuban War of Independence or Ten Years' War (1868–1878). The economic factor primarily concerned the tariffs that arose in the United States as a result of the Panic of 1857 and the Civil War.

Cigars were highly prized and enjoyed luxury items for the growing bourgeois populations of Europe and the United States during the early- to mid-nineteenth century. Cuban cigars were considered the world's finest due to the quality of the tobacco and the skill of the workers. Small-scale cigar manufacturing facilities were present in Key West, Florida, by the 1830s, and small Cuban communities developed in tandem. The close proximity of Key West to the commercial center of Havana and the tobacco regions of western Cuba provided an ideal setting for cigar production. The short distance from Florida to Cuba combined with friendly diplomatic relations between the United States and Spain allowed workers relatively easy access to labor markets on both sides of the Florida Straits.

The Panic of 1857 and the American Civil War impeded the cigar trade as tariffs on finished goods rose, while tariffs on raw materials remained unchanged. Cuban immigration to Key West was also impacted negatively by the war. As Havana's cigar industry began to feel the effects of the tariffs, a few manufacturers contemplated developing facilities in Key West and western Florida. Large numbers of unemployed workers emigrated to Key West in search of work. Most professionals emigrated to the northeastern cities of the United States—New York, Philadelphia, and Boston—while the wealthiest patricians settled in Europe.

In 1869, the second year of the war, the Spanish cigar manufacturer Vicente Martinez Ybor established his *El Principe de Gales* factory in Key West. Within a decade, Key West emerged as the major manufacturing cigar production center in the United States. Within a year, defeated working-class insurgents found a new home in southern Florida, and Key West also emerged as a major hotbed of Cuban activism. Adhering to various forms of Proudhonian mutualism in the early 1860s, by the 1880s workers organizations in Cuba adopted a more confrontational stance associated with the collectivism of Russian anarchist Michael Bakunin. What developed in the United States was a unique intersection of anarchist internationalism and Cuban nationalism.

Greatly influenced by—if not being members of—radical Cuban labor organizations in Cuba, Cuban immigrants developed a unique set of workplace institutions unknown in any other industry. Perhaps the most unique was the presence of a lector, or reader, in the cigar factory. Lectors read a variety of material—current events in newspapers, political propaganda, serialized novels—and were chosen and paid by the workers themselves.

By the mid-1880s, work disruptions in Key West's cigar industry became commonplace. Facing regular labor stoppages, several manufacturers sought a new location for their factories. Martínez Ybor purchased a 40-acre tract of land east of Tampa in 1885, and Ybor City was founded the following year. Other manufacturers followed his lead, and Ybor City became the new cigar mecca of the United States. Like other factory owners of the time, Ybor envisioned Ybor City as a paternalist company town. Workers were offered the opportunity to purchase their own homes at interest rates uncommon in Western company towns. Many workers gladly took advantage of the offer. Workers also settled with their families, either bringing wives and children from Cuba or marrying within the two growing south Florida Cuban émigré communities.

In addition to anarchism and workplace activism, Cuban independence also figured prominently in the goals and aspirations of the Cuban émigrés, whether upper class, middle class or working class. Cuban revolutionary leader José Martí made a series of visits to Key West and Tampa in early 1892. By the end of the year, during a visit to Tampa, he announced the creation of the Cuban Revolutionary Party (PRC), dedicated to Cuban independence.

The Cigar Makers International Union (CMIU) leader Samuel Gompers and other American Federation of Labor (AFL) leaders realized the difficulties the CMIU faced from a Spanish-speaking population tempered by militant and radical labor activism. The AFL and CMIU leadership also recognized that any popular movement overthrowing Spanish rule would wipe out the legal restrictions in Cuba against labor organizations. In short, the CMIU supported separatism in the hopes that an American version of craft unionism would develop in Cuba. Gompers met with PRC leadership, including Martí, and the anarchist Ramón Rivero felt significantly threatened to found the *Federacíon Cuba de Obreros* to combat the influence of the CMIU. Gompers would become head of the AFL in 1886.

Key West and Ybor City were not the only cities with sizable populations of Cubans and Cuban workers. New York City was the home to a sizable working-class community as well as an intellectual center and home to Cuba's landowning elite and professional and merchant classes. By July 1894, the *Cigar Makers Official Journal* recorded approximately three thousand cigar factories in New York City. Cigar factories varied in size from the *chinchal* (artisanal workshop) to the *fábrica* (factory) and everything between. The sociologist Lisandro Pérez notes that a key difference between the cigar industry in Ybor City/Key West and New York City is that Cubans dominated the cigar trade in south Florida while in New York they were apparently outnumbered by at least six other nationality groups. Another dissimilarity with Key West and Ybor City was that the vast majority of working-class Cubans were men. Living conditions varied, but most did not have the opportunity to rent, let alone own, the single-family dwellings common among their fellows in southern Florida. Most shared a room with three or four other men.

During the nineteenth and early twentieth centuries, cigar rolling in Cuban émigré communities was largely the domain of white males. White women and Afro-Cubans were incorporated into other aspects of the cigar production process. In New York City, the most expensive cigars were typically rolled by *Peninsulares* (Spaniards), while *Creoles* (Europeans born in Cuba) dominated the profession in Tampa and Key West. Banders, strippers or stemmers (workers who removed the center stems from tobacco leaves), casers, and bunchers were almost exclusively Creole. These jobs were the least paying and least prestigious in the cigar rolling hierarchy. At the bottom of the occupational ladder were women and unskilled Cubans, most of them Afro-Cubans and in some rare cases in Ybor City, local Afro-Americans. These tasks did not involve working directly with tobacco but were menial tasks such as sweeping and hauling.

Within the cigar industry in Cuba and south Florida, jobs were segregated more often by sex than by race. In the mid- to late 1800s, black, white, mulatto, and quadroon men mingled on cigar benches while their wives and daughters worked side by side in the stemming rooms. Photographs of workers in Ybor City factories in the late nineteenth and early twentieth centuries capture the multiracial and multicolored labor force that fueled cigar production and distinguished these manufacturing worksites from others in the New South.

In the mid-nineteenth century, Cuban women worked directly with tobacco as strippers and cigarette makers. White Cuban working-class women often worked inside the home, although in rare cases some rolled cigars or made cigarettes in small workshops or factories. Over time, more Cuban women entered the larger tobacco factories. In addition to coming close to monopolizing tobacco stemming, women banded and tubed the cigars.

A commonality shared by Cuban cigar makers in New York City and south Florida, in addition to being educated and radicalized on the shop floor through the lectors, was that the cigar makers also had ample opportunity for developing bonds of solidarity in their communities. Cultural societies and a large number of workers' cooperatives worked out of these centers. A variety of political, economic, social, and philosophical views were discussed, although ideological divisions were common. Every night of the week, one could find working-class speakers airing their views, with the active participation of the public.

After the labor disputes in the émigré working-class communities in 1885 and 1886, anarchists influenced by the particular version of Spanish anarcho-collectivism that was increasingly in vogue in Cuba began to lead the Cuban cigar makers' unions in New York City, Key West, and Ybor City. Émigré Cuban workers managed to establish trade unions with strong ties to those inside Cuba. Cuban labor organizations had attempted to coordinate the activities of Cuban workers in the United States and sought the cooperation of the Knights of Labor, but the main links maintained by these workers were with the labor movement in Cuba. Also, the fact that leaders of the Knights of Labor sided with the prosecution during the trial of the Haymarket anarchists no doubt alienated Cuban workers from this union.

Cuba's second war of independence (1895–1898) and the Spanish-American War (1898) provided further disruptions to the cigar industry. When war erupted in 1895, Cuban anarchists in the émigré communities and on the island engaged in the armed struggle. In this war, the goal for the cigar makers was greater than independence—it was global social revolution. What differentiated the struggle in 1895 from all the previous wars against Spain was the acknowledgment that inequality was the effect of the Cuban social system, not a by-product of Spanish colonial rule.

U.S. victory in the Spanish-American War meant that the Cuban anarchists' dream of global proletarian revolution was thwarted. It also meant that Cuba's tobacco industry—in particular, the Island's plantations—was soon dominated by U.S. tobacco concerns. In the early 1900s, the American Tobacco Corporation (ATC) consolidated control of the most productive tobacco farms, thereby establishing a global monopoly of tobacco cultivation, production, and distribution. Once ATC had total control of the Cuban tobacco market and outsourced production in the United States, Cuban workers left the island in record numbers. The Library of Congress estimates that between 50,000 and 100,000 Cubans moved between Havana and south Florida each year during the first decades of the twentieth century.

By the 1930s, technical advances and mechanization in the industry had dramatic impacts on the cigar industry and Cuban migration patterns. Machine operators, including women, made the skilled male hand-rollers superfluous. Furthermore, the discovery of mild Virginia tobacco, combined with a shift in consumer tastes—and commercial marketing—toward cigarettes, was the death knell of tobacco farming for countries like Cuba known for producing strong, dark tobacco. The North American cigar labor market was decimated, and the migration of Cuban cigar workers slowed to a trickle.

However, the number of political refugees increased under the regime of dictator Fulgencio Batista (1933–1944; 1952–1959) and again dramatically after the ascendancy of Fidel Castro's revolution in 1959. The early exiles tended to be white elites and professionals, while subsequent emigrants were small entrepreneurs, artists, and workers, including Afro-Cubans. Peter Cattan notes that the actual number of Cuban workers in the United States has been decreasing since 1980 due to slow population growth attributable, in large measure, to the Cuban government's restrictions on immigration. The largest Cuban communities in the United States today are the Miami and New York City metropolitan areas.

EVAN MATTHEW DANIEL

References and Further Reading

Casanovas, Joan. *Bread, or Bullets!: Urban Labor and Spanish Colonialism in Cuba, 1850–1898.* Pittsburgh, PA: University of Pittsburgh Press, 1998.
Cattan, Peter. "The Diversity of Hispanics in the U.S. Work Force." *Monthly Labor Review Online*, 116, no. 8 (August 1993): 3–15. http://www.bls.gov/opub/mlr/1993/08/art1exc.htm.

Cooper, Patricia A. *Once a Cigar Maker: Men, Women, and Work Culture in American Cigar Factories, 1900–1919.* Urbana and Chicago: University of Illinois, 1987.

Hewitt, Nancy A. *Southern Discomfort, Women's Activism in Tampa, Florida: 1880s–1920s.* Chicago: University of Chicago Press, 2001.

"Immigration." Library of Congress. http://memory.loc.gov/learn/features/immig/cuban5.html.

Ingalls, Robert P. *Urban Vigilantes in the New South: Tampa, 1882–1936.* Knoxville: University of Tennessee Press, 1988.

Jacobstein, Meyer. *The Tobacco Industry in the United States.* New York: Columbia University Press, 1907.

Mormino, Gary R., and George E. Pozzetta. *The Immigrant World of Ybor City: Italians and Their Latin Neighbors, 1885–1985.* Chicago: University of Illinois Press, 1990.

Pérez, Lisandro. "The Cuban Community of New York City in the Eighteenth Century." Unpublished paper. Presented at the 1985 meetings of the Latin American Studies Association, April 17–20, 1985.

Pérez, Louis A. Jr. *Essays on Cuban History: Historiography and Research.* Gainesville: University of Florida Press, 1995.

———. *Martí in the United States: The Florida Experience.* Tempe: Center for Latin American Studies, Arizona State University, 1995.

Poyo, Gerald. "The Cuban Experience in the United States, 1865–1940: Migration, Community, and Identity." *Cuban Studies/Estudios Cubanos* 21 (1991): 19–36.

———. *"With All and For the Good of All": The Mergence of Popular Nationalism in the Cuban Communities of the United States, 1848–1898.* Durham, NC and London: Duke University Press, 1989.

Stubbs, Jean. "Labour and Economy in Cuban Tobacco, 1860–1958." *Historical Reflections/Reflexions Historiques* 12, no. 3 (1985): 449–467.

———. 1981. *Tobacco on the Periphery: A Case Study in Cuban Labor History*, 1860–1958. Cambridge: Cambridge University Press, 1985.

Vega, Bernardo, and César Andreu Iglesias, eds. *Memoirs of Bernardo Vega: A Contribution to the History of the Puerto Rican Community in New York.* New York: Monthly Review Press, 1984.

Westfall, L. Glenn. *Don Vicente Martinez Ybor, the Man and His Empire. Development of the Clear Havana Industry in Cuba and Florida in the Nineteenth Century.* New York: Garland Publishing, Inc., 1987.

See also **Cigar Makers International Union**

CULTURE, WORKING-CLASS

Working-class culture is a complex and contested concept, whether viewed from the perspective of historians who have studied it or from the groups to whose "culture" the phrase seems to refer. Among historians of the U.S. working class, analyses foregrounding the "cultural" dimensions of workers' work, home, and/or leisure lives remain controversial (though such analyses are not as "new" as some of their proponents or critics suppose). The study of working-class culture necessarily expands the focus on union organization that the generation of historians who first institutionalized "labor history" placed at the center of their project, and also calls into question the centrality to workers' lives of the material and power struggles centered in the workplace that were the focus of later generations of historians. While practitioners of working-class cultural history argue that this expansion of focus more accurately represents the range of actual concerns of workers and their communities, others question the historical significance of studies not focused on workplace and political conflicts aimed at transforming oppressive class relations.

Even assuming its validity as a focus of working-class history, "working-class culture" is a vast and internally divided topic. In its modern anthropological sense, after all, "culture" covers an immense terrain. As applied to the lives of workers, this terrain potentially encompasses workplace skills and routines, political convictions ranging from revolutionary radicalism to nationalistic patriotism (albeit not always for the workers' current country of residence), domestic arrangements, gender relations, religious belief (and related institutionalized rituals and lay practices), ethnic identities and the cultural practices associated with them (including language, family structure, foodways, music, spoken and written narrative and verse, arts and crafts, religion, along with a variety of transnational affiliations), and engagement with an expanding range of commercial cultural forms (theater, dance halls, radio, recorded music, movies, television, newspapers, books), participation in consumer culture, navigations and understandings of space and region, and constructions of divisions of race, ethnicity, and gender as well as class acquired from a variety of sources, to name only some of the topics that have engaged historians of working-class experience. A tall order for any single study—indeed it is common for scholarship in the field to be faulted for missing some dimension of its subjects' cultural world—this range of potential subject matter also invites scrutiny as to the relevance of its various dimensions to the dynamics of class identity or agency that are usually important to labor and working-class history. More perplexing, still, may be the ways in which the inclusive anthropological notion of culture, though in many ways more amenable to the egalitarian spirit of much labor and working-class history than more hierarchical literary or "high" cultural traditions, poses some knotty conceptual dilemmas of its own for the projects of working-class historians.

A key problem with the anthropological notion of culture is its assumption of unity within "the culture" under study. Though many anthropologists themselves now question this assumption—revising it to make sense of increasingly mobile cultural identities that cross the borders containing the place-bound cultures analyzed within the ethnographic tradition that produced it—its dilemmas remain for the many disciplines informed by anthropology's widely influential concepts. For scholars examining working-class history, distinctions of race, ethnicity, and gender, most prominently, as well as a host of other divisions complicate any efforts to comprehend working-class culture as an actual or potential "whole." In the late twentieth and early twenty-first centuries, race and ethnicity were especially important fault lines within the study of working-class culture, which historians saw as an in which racially indeterminate "new immigrants" of the turn of the twentieth century came to embrace the privileges of "whiteness," and sometimes to bridge or dismantle them.

Whatever the dilemmas posed by anthropological notions of culture, historians interested in the problems, perspectives, and interests of working-class people tend to be decidedly less friendly to concepts of culture that derive from scholarly traditions of literary criticism or intellectual history. Historians studying people whose own organizational and political cultures often emphasized how economic divisions rooted in material life shaped and curtailed their own aspirations look with understandable suspicion on the "cultural" or "linguistic" turn. They associated it with a literary history that highlighted discursively constructed cultural categories beyond which determinations of material life or experience remain obscure. They may also resent insinuations that social-scientific methods of analysis render them obtuse to textual constructions of documents they examine for a bedrock of fact. Even so, the methods of textual scrutiny and "discursive" analysis associated with the "cultural turn" have proved useful to working-class historians interested in the intellectual categories that shaped many of the governmental, social-scientific, legal, and scientific sources on which historians rely to reconstruct working-class lives. Combined with efforts to interpret working-class appropriations and reconfigurations of such categories, such studies yield insights into plebeian participation in cultural traditions that would otherwise remain the preserve of historians of more elite and powerful groups.

Battles between "documentary" social historians and "textual" cultural historians have given way to cross-disciplinary efforts to make sense of the capital, labor, and cultural flows in an era of fast-paced global production. A concurrent turn toward the analysis of empire and colonialism and their significance for constructions of a range of social categories within imperial nations, including class, has set challenging new cultural questions on the agendas of working-class historians, from the global mapping of class identities to the imperial hierarchies implicated in workers' political and popular culture. Recognizing that a short encyclopedia entry can scarcely do justice to the broad field of "working-class culture" either in this scholarship or in the past, the remainder of this essay addresses some key areas of innovation and debate over the decades since "culture" became an indispensable dimension of scholarship on the U.S. working class.

Cultures of Labor, Organization, and Working-Class Experience

Since the 1960s, scholars who focus on workers' "culture" as an object of historical analysis have seen themselves as broadening the terrain of labor and working-class history beyond the organizational and economic focus of earlier generations of labor historians. But many of their most important insights into the cultural dimensions of workers' lives—their beliefs, values, language, stories—have actually focused on the very topics of workplace skills and experience, labor organizations that aim to shape the job from below, and political action that takes such aims into realms of electoral and revolutionary action that absorbed the attention of labor historians from the early twentieth century on. Conceptualized and analyzed as workers' culture, these dimensions of workers' lives as expressions of working-class cultural expression and intellectual life, these shop-floor and organizational dimensions of workers' lives, turn out to have wide significance beyond the domains of factory and union.

Though not the first scholarship on U.S. working populations to do so, Herbert Gutman's classic "Work, Culture, and Society in Industrializing America" articulated with particularly resounding effects the importance of "culture," in the anthropological sense, to studies of work and workers in the United States. In this essay, Gutman pointed to burgeoning nineteenth-century factories as sites of particularly profound cultural conflicts between employers' expectations and the cultural aspirations and practices workers brought from rural backgrounds and artisanal pasts to new forms of industrial employment. Religious convictions, traditional habits of work, nostalgia for outdoor work, among other cultural constructions, all posed challenges to the rigors of industrial labor. A companion piece in the collection named after Gutman's influential article emphasized the importance of class divisions, forged at the workplace and expressed in working-class organization, to the wider culture of Protestant religious practices and values of sobriety and self-control that had been attributed predominantly to middle-class clergy, reformers, and parishioners.

Over the next 20 years, his example inspired and provoked a range of scholarship that looked to emerging factory experiences and the struggles, organizations, and politics they provoked in order to understand the sources of wider shifts in "national" culture, particularly in the nineteenth century. Artisanal journeymen who found their status as craftsmen degraded by the shift to wage labor became the architects of a working-class republicanism that claimed for workers the republican ideals of independence and virtue associated with a more elite revolutionary generation; immigrant heirs to the European class struggles of 1848 transplanted class-inflected concepts of liberty to antislavery organizations; even women workers, often slighted in histories that attended to the cultural constructions emanating from not only predominantly male but also masculinist constructions of working-class values and political culture, defiantly engaged middle-class gendered ideals of domesticity and femininity in their encounters with work, charitable, judicial, and political authorities, male and female. In the late twentieth and early twenty-first centuries, historians of maritime labor in the seventeenth and eighteenth centuries, such as Marcus Rediker, have mined the Atlantic, cross-racial world of sailors to find shipboard languages, narratives, and struggles that contributed strong plebeian voices to the intellectual history of eighteenth-century revolution.

Studies of workers' contributions to broad national and transnational cultural currents have necessarily also broadened the "culture" of workers' organizations themselves beyond the issues of wages and contracts that occupied earlier generations of labor history scholars. From shipyard locals, whose contracts enshrined the ideals of leisure and cultural development associated with shorter hours, to Knights of Labor assemblies that drew on the rituals of secret fraternal societies to instill and maintain a sense of the dignity of craft, even across craft, gender, and racial lines, nineteenth-century workers extended the efforts of their organizations to the realm of culture. Iron and garment workers of the late nineteenth century, as David Montgomery has shown, fashioned out of their workplace lives ideals of mutualism that their unions enunciated and pressed into American reform and political debates. Radical political organizations of the nineteenth and twentieth centuries also expressed values forged on the job, translating individualist traditions of sobriety and independence into a socialist register, providing the communities of discourse in which working-class intellectuals could concoct new theories of mobilization and education, and establishing written and public venues for the performance of the music, poetry, and narrative that emerged from struggles over control at the workplace.

But the nexus of working-class organization and culture was not tied only to the job, as many studies of work and community have demonstrated. Labor historians concerned with workers' culture have also shown the vital importance of neighborhoods and households, saloons and churches, parish priests and local entrepreneurs, immigrant organizations and foreign language newspapers to the values and aspirations realized through union organization in the late nineteenth and early twentieth centuries. In some cases, certain ethnic identities came to infuse multiple dimensions of working-class culture for other ethnic groups, as when Irish-Americans came to dominate many of the labor as well as the parish, drinking, theatrical, and political cultures encountered by Eastern and Southern European newcomers to the United States in the late nineteenth century. Combining some of the complicating themes addressed below, historians like Lizabeth Cohen have also insisted on new media of commercial and consumer culture, such as radio, movies, and chain stores, as venues that both reinforced and bridged the ethnically diverse cultures of unorganized workers in ways that prepared the way for the appeal of mass industrial unions in the 1930s. These unions, in turn, spawned what Michael Denning recognizes in the 1930s and after as a "laboring" of U.S. culture at large, as culture "high" and "popular" became infused with a range of concerns that linked the CIO, the pan-ethnic cultures of many of its members, the internationalist ideals of radical antifascism, and demands for and provisions of the incipient welfare state associated with New Deal programs. Promising in its appeal to the multiple cultural roots of "everybody who's nobody," as Paul Robeson sang it in "Ballad for Americans," this labored culture also fractured over the very boundaries implicit in the organizational and governmental programs on which it thrived.

Race, Ethnicity, and Gender

That splintering had much to do with the fissures of race, ethnicity, and gender that many historians of working-class experience have emphasized as limits to the mutualism expressed by the organizational cultures described above. The very ethnic traditions, organizations, and neighborhoods that served as resources for working-class organizations and their ideals of solidarity also proved to be obstacles to the solidarities some radicals and organizers assumed to be natural expressions of shared class oppressions and struggles. Ethnic solidarity and tradition—as well as religious and nationalistic allegiances that accompanied them—often provided access to the economic security that labor organizations and their historians associate with the shared culture of work, thus demonstrating that the shared values of "working-class culture" had itself to be produced out of a range of competing affiliations.

Some ethnic boundaries were more readily bridged by a shared "working-class culture" than others. An important strain of working-class cultural history examines the ways in which some racialized ethnicities have been systematically subordinated as successive waves of immigrant populations constructed working-class cultural institutions—and more amorphous spaces of working-class cultural affiliation—out of the lineaments of white privilege. In the works of David Roediger and Alexander Saxton, the hoary nineteenth-century ideals of manly independence and republican virtue that wage laborers translated into working-class terms made sense only in tortuous distinction to slave labor and the reviled African-Americans associated with it. Both in popular venues like minstrelsy—one of the first forms of public culture performed for distinctively working-class audiences—and in political and organizational mobilizations, wage workers demonstrated an ambivalent identification with and ridicule of African-Americans that inflected the cultures of working-class identity and organization henceforth. While some critics complain that this rendering of the white racialization of working-class culture in the United States obscures the social and economic sources of racial division in favor of undocumented psychological and symbolic categories, focus on the cultural work of white privilege has produced important insights into the role of working-class culture and institutions as crucibles of racial identity. The identification of race as a key problem not only for elite intellectual theorists of biological difference but also for union locals and socialist parties has also focused attention on these venues as important sites for innovative conceptualizations of racial differences and solidarities. A further theme in working-class cultural studies attuned to issues of race and ethnicity is to reclaim the cultures of solidarity produced by African-American, Asian-American, Latina/o and other racialized workers. This scholarship has emphasized the sources of working-class culture in long and dispersed traditions of anti-racial protest and also emphasized the significance of the "hidden transcripts" of everyday interchanges, jokes, and stories as sources of more substantial challenges to racial and economic injustice.

The gendered identities and experiences of both women and men as workers within the industrial workplaces that have absorbed much of the attention of labor historians and in the broader communities that housed, fed, and entertained them also complicate renditions of a single shared working-class culture. The very conception of working-class dignity associated with such cultures was gendered in ways that excluded women from participating in its rituals of manliness, and focused these rituals on the cultivation of particular versions of masculine identity that had racial and ethnic boundaries of their own. Moreover, the dignity of labor pursued in the cultures of working-class organization was often defined against dependency associated with women's status in nineteenth-century households. Working-class women themselves shouldered a range of labors within and outside the household that sustained working-class cultures without being celebrated within them. When they did venture into wage labor, they were often shunned from the fraternities of working-class solidarities. For all these reasons, the study of women workers, and more broadly of gender within working-class culture, has necessarily reshaped the boundaries of workplace and institutions within which the historical cultures of workers as a class have often been sought: taking that study to tenements, porches, strike kitchens, breadlines, gossip columns, and fashion debates. As the availability of consumer goods at lower prices gradually replaced some of the household production women contributed to working-class households, moreover, their status as "consumers," and their relations to women who often staffed the proliferating sites of consumer culture, challenged the producerist themes prominent in the culture of working-class organization. Often bringing commercially inspired definitions of style onto the picket lines, such women—and not a few men, like the well-dressed pachucos of postwar working-class racial tensions—traced the complex nexus of working-class and popular culture.

Popular Cultural Spaces and Leisure

The commercial origins of workers' popular cultural pursuits have posed special dilemmas for the study of an identifiably working-class culture. While working people have patronized, labored in, shaped, and rendered popular a range of influential forms of commercial forms, the sometimes ephemeral and escapist character of such expressions render them questionable vehicles of "class" identities. An important vein of scholarship on U.S. working-class culture points to the "working-class accents," to borrow Michael Denning's phrase, in commercial cultural fare ranging from dime novels to vaudeville theater to movies to television. As important, they have shown that commercial culture is a terrain on which the fault lines of a presumptively shared "class" culture are probed and negotiated: where "hillbilly" music encounters African-American blues, homosocial worlds of working-class men experiment on dance floors with new relations to women, and so on. The results do not always or even usually make for shared class-specific values bridging such divides, as popular culture is as important a source of divisive self-constructions as it is a venue for expressing and exploring cross-racial or gender-bending class solidarities. More challenging still, perhaps, are the studies of working-class engagement with popular culture that remind us of the role that the enticements to abundance, self-expression, and frivolity associated with commercial and popular culture might play in a cultural tradition often associated with solidarities formulated around scarcity, mutuality, and hard work. Opening on to a wide range of studies of workers at play, such themes stretch definitions of the "will" contained in the mid-nineteenth-century anthem to a working-class mutuality that looked beyond the cultures of work itself: "eight hours for what we will."

KATHRYN J. OBERDECK

D

DANBURY HATTERS CASE: *LOEWE v. LAWLOR* (1908, 1915)

Loewe v. Lawlor, the 1908 U.S. Supreme Court case (with a ratification of the related financial judgment in 1915), is one of the most notorious anti-union judicial decisions in American history. In what became known as the "Danbury Hatters' case," the Supreme Court struck a blow against labor by subjecting individual unionists engaged in a secondary boycott to financial penalties for their violations of antitrust law.

During the late nineteenth and early twentieth centuries, Americans were attempting to come to grips with a variety of novel forms of large organizations, particularly new corporate behemoths that threatened to monopolize fields ranging from tobacco to oil. The foundational piece of national legislation meant to restrain the power of large corporations was the Sherman Anti-Trust Act of 1890. The intent of this law was to prohibit corporate restraint of trade in interstate commerce. As the twentieth century dawned however, employers faced with the increasing power of unions realized that courts might be sympathetic to using the Sherman Act to restrain similar combinations organized by workers.

Local as well as national conditions were critical to the eventual resolution of the case that became *Loewe v. Lawlor*, which dragged on for a decade and a half. In 1902, workers affiliated with the American Federation of Labor's (AFL's) United Hatters of North America struck the shop of Dietrich Loewe, a small manufacturer in the hat capital of Danbury, Connecticut, as part of an industrywide organizing effort.

When Loewe broke off negotiations, the union launched a national boycott of his products.

Supported by the American Anti-Boycott Association, an association of small Connecticut proprietors, Loewe retaliated with a lawsuit that ultimately landed in front of the U.S. Supreme Court in 1907. The following year, the Supreme Court ruled, in a unanimous decision written by Chief Justice Melville Fuller, in favor of Loewe. The court held most generally that unions were indeed subject to antitrust legislation and that they would not be allowed to restrain interstate trade. In particular, the court declared illegal the union's secondary boycott. Such boycotts were meant to pressure companies not involved in an immediate conflict between workers and an employer not to purchase nonunion or "unfair" products. The Taft-Hartley Act of 1947 declared secondary boycotts illegal, although unions have earned certain rights to picket informationally about unfair goods.

Along with their formal ruling, the Supreme Court sent the case back to the federal district court, with the trial beginning in 1909. At issue was whether Loewe could seize as damages the assets not just of the poor and unincorporated union itself, but of all individual union members involved even in the most indirect way in the strike or boycott. The judge and jury found in favor of Loewe, and a second trial in 1912 brought an even larger financial settlement for the hat manufacturer. The U.S. Supreme Court, in a decision written by Justice Oliver Wendell Holmes, subsequently upheld the lower courts in the 1915 ruling of *Lowler v. Loewe*. Nearly 200 members of the United Hatters—most of whom had not worked for Loewe or even had knowledge of the boycott—then had their property attached. The threatened loss of their homes led the AFL to proclaim a 1916 Hatters' Day to raise funds. After many attempts to fight the judgment, the union finally in 1917 paid Loewe $234,192 in damages. Ironically, while the larger battle over who had legal responsibility for union actions played itself out, Loewe apparently remained on good terms with local unionists—even those who suffered under the court's financial judgment. Many apparently recognized that such small proprietors would indeed have suffered irreparable financial harm by following these particular union wages and rules.

The Clayton Act of 1914 promised some relief to unions from antitrust prosecutions, but injunctions continued to cripple many organizing efforts. And in the end, *Loewe v. Lawlor* can hardly be viewed as anything but an almost-crippling blow to the organization of labor. Still, even the arguments made on behalf of Loewe did offer some glimmer of hope that the legal environment of the Progressive Era would provide increasingly legitimacy to workers' organizing, moving unions from illegal conspiracies that business elites wished to stamp out completely to accepted actors in a pluralist political economy oriented around the rights of groups, and not just those of sovereign individuals.

ROBERT D. JOHNSTON

References and Further Reading

Ernst, Daniel R. *Lawyers against Labor: From Individual Rights to Corporate Liberalism.* Urbana: University of Illinois Press, 1995.
Forbath, William E. *Law and the Shaping of the American Labor Movement.* Cambridge, MA: Harvard University Press, 1991.
Orren, Karen. *Belated Feudalism: The Law, Labor, and Liberal Development in the United States.* Cambridge, UK: Cambridge University Press, 1991.

Cases and Statutes Cited

Lawlor v. Loewe, 235 U.S. 522 (1915).
Loewe v. Lawlor, 208 U.S. 274 (1908).

DAVIS, LEON (1906–1992)
Hospital Workers' Union

Leon Julius Davis, longtime leader of Hospital Workers' Union, Local 1199, was a pioneer in hospital worker organizing and also a shrewd survivor within the "lefting" of the American labor movement. Born to a family of religious Jews in Pinsk, a peasant village near Brest-Litovsk in what was then White Russia, on November 21, 1907, Davis migrated to the United States in 1921 and attended the Columbia School of Pharmacy (1927–1929), leaving to become a drugstore clerk and an activist for the Trade Union Unity League, the labor organizing arm of the Communist party. In 1932, he was a founder of the Pharmacists' Union of Greater New York and remained an organizer when the union became Local 1199 of the Retail Clerks International (American Federation of Labor [AFL]) in 1936.

Within a year, however, Davis's organization had disaffiliated with the AFL and participated in the founding of the Retail, Wholesale, and Department Store Union (RWDSU-CIO), with which Local 1199 subsequently affiliated and in which Davis became an international vice-president in 1955. In 1969, Davis was elected president of Local 1199, National Union of Hospital and Health Care Employees, while retaining presidency of Local 1199, the New York Drug and Hospital Union, a post which he had held for the previous two decades.

Davis retired from both positions in 1982, only to see his union suffer a period of prolonged internal turmoil. He died in Queens, New York, following his second heart attack in 1992. A crowded memorial service in Lincoln Center's Avery Fisher Hall featured eulogies from Coretta Scott King and New York City Mayor David Dinkins, as well as many long-time union brothers and sisters.

Under President Davis's leadership (and with the assistance of key colleagues Elliott Godoff, Moe Foner, and Jessie Olson), Local 1199 mixed political idealism with a hard, pragmatic edge. Even as a small drugstore union, Local 1199 displayed a distinctive spirit. For one, interracial and interethnic solidarity proved an essential ingredient of drugstore unionism. Partially as a response to an anti-Semitic quota system affecting medical schools, Jews dominated the pharmacist trade in New York City, even as porters and stockmen were predominantly black. In 1937, the union launched a successful campaign in Harlem, beginning with open-air meetings of the unemployed and ending with strike threats, to secure jobs for black pharmacists and to promote the invisible porters to the position of "soda men." In response, when the union faced a fierce attack from both anti-Communist governmental probes and rival Congress of Industrial Orgaizations (CIO) locals in 1948, black Harlem pharmacists stepped in to protect 1199's jurisdiction. Another important principle was militant, industrial unionism. What began as a pharmacists' organization not only quickly incorporated the less-skilled drugstore employees into its ranks but also developed a creative, participatory approach to organizing.

In 1957, as Local 1199 emerged from a decade of defensive, jurisdictional battles with a small but secure base of 6,000 NYC drugstore members, Davis searched for a new organizing challenge. Connecting with Elliott Godoff, a hospital organizer refugee from the left-wing—and by then defunct—United Public Workers of America, Davis led his union into a new and grand adventure into the giant, nonprofit hospital sector of the city and beyond. Beginning with Montefiore Hospital in 1958 and continuing with a significant breakthrough following the nation's first major hospital strike in 1959, Local 1199 transformed itself from a bit player to a major figure within the city's labor and political firmament.

By the 1960s, Davis and what was now District 1199 began to fan out throughout the country to organize health care workers in all sections of the health care industry, from hospitals and nursing homes to mental health clinics. The growth and organization of the hospital workers' union, however, was more than just a labor union struggle, since Davis and 1199 members used their organized strength to demand social and economic changes for all workers. Adopting the slogan "Union Power-Soul Power," Davis joined forces with the Rev. Martin Luther King Jr.'s Southern Christian Leadership Conference in a new spirit of labor movement building. At the height of civil rights (and later anti-Vietnam War and women's rights) struggles, 1199ers were visibly out front, with Davis regularly leading a black, brown, and white coalition in the streets as well as at ballot boxes on a never-ending host of progressive campaigns. An extended confrontation with nearly 1,000 arrests, for example, accompanied Local 1199-B's ultimately stymied campaign in Charleston, South Carolina, in 1969.

LEON FINK

References and Further Reading

Fink, Leon, and Brian Greenberg. *Upheaval in the Quiet Zone: A History of Hospital Workers' Union, Local 1199.* Urbana: University of Illinois Press, 1989.

See also **New York City Hospital Strike (1959)**

DAVIS, RICHARD L. (DECEMBER 24, 1863–JANUARY 15, 1900)
National Executive Board of the United Mine Workers of America

In 1896, Richard L. Davis became the first African-American to be elected a member of the National Executive Board of the United Mine Workers of America (UMWA), a position he held for two years. Although historians have lavished attention on the scores of letters he wrote during the 1890s to the *United Mine Workers Journal*, they have put little effort into reconstructing Davis's socio-economic background. Through the letters, scholars have assessed the extent to which the UMWA lived up to its constitutional commitment to interracial organizing, as well as the union's treatment of black workers and its willingness and ability to curb the racist actions of rank and file white miners. The result of all this attention has been a sharp debate among labor historians over the possibilities and limits of interracial unionism in the Gilded Age and Jim Crow United States. Writing amid the Civil Rights movement in the late 1960s, Herbert Gutman's examination of Davis's letters led him to argue that even in the Jim Crow era, black and white miners could achieve labor solidarity. Herbert Hill offered a stinging rebuke amid the political polarization of the Reagan years, stressing the limits of interracial fellowship. Hill contended that the UMWA failed to achieve its promise of solidarity and equitable treatment of black and white workers, and that the union failed to monitor and control the racism of white workers, who exhibited little real commitment to organizing across the color line.

Born on December 24, 1863, in Roanoke, Virginia, Davis began his working life at age eight in a tobacco factory, a job he held for nine years. Eventually dismayed by poor wages and working conditions, he sought employment as a coal miner. For a year or so, he drifted through West Virginia's Kanawha and New River regions, arriving in the Hocking River Valley town of Rendville, Ohio, sometime during 1882. Soon thereafter he joined the segregated "colored" Knights of Labor Local 1935, which had just been formed that year. By the mid-1880s, Davis already evinced a strong desire to bring all of Rendville's African-American miners into the union. As Charles Nelson recounts in "A Story of Rendville," Davis soon became active in labor organizing, sending a letter to the Knights of Labor's national leader, Terence Powderly, that proclaimed, "We [L.A. 1935] will never relinquish our work until the bulk of our brethren are brought within the folds of our noble order."

When the Knights began to wane in the late 1880s and early 1890s, Davis lost no time in joining the newly formed UMWA. He attended its founding as a delegate in 1890 and served on the executive board of District 6 until his election to the national executive board six years later. As a roving labor organizer, Davis spent his time organizing new locals, settling disputes between miners and their employers—usually over pay and working conditions— and negotiating arrangements between white and black workers. Racial disputes among miners typically concerned the equitable distributions of work and supervisory positions in the mines. Most of Davis's work was based in Ohio, but special assignments took him to western Pennsylvania, Virginia, West Virginia, and Alabama. His rich and compelling letters written to the *UMWJ*, which he wrote during his travels as an organizer, reveal much about him and his aspirations, as well as about the difficulties he faced in Ohio and elsewhere. Davis evinced a steadfast commitment to working people and their institutions. But he was never starry-eyed about this commitment. He constantly found himself chiding black mineworkers for wanting to organize separately, lambasting white unionists for treating their fellow black workers unfairly, and holding the union to account for failing to live up to its espoused promises. These failings irked Davis and added to the difficulties he faced negotiating decent wages and fair working conditions during the economically tough 1890s.

In addition to the considerable commitments Davis made to the miners of Hocking Valley, he sank familial and political roots in Rendville. In 1887, he married Mary Bailey, and she and Davis had two daughters together. Like her husband, Mary was literate, and both their daughters attended school in Rendville. Long after Davis's premature death in 1900, Mary and the two children continued to call Rendville home, with Mary earning a living by dressmaking and by taking in boarders. Besides raising a family in Rendville, Mary's husband exhibited political commitments to Ohio's Republican party. He lent his support to congressional candidates with a commitment to labor and shared platforms with gubernatorial candidates and state senators to commemorate Labor Day.

We do no know why Davis merely passed through Kanawha and the New River Region of West Virginia, but when he reached Rendville, he found work as a coal miner and almost certainly, a receptive community as well. As a coal miner, he attained the respected position of checkweighman—the person who recorded the weight of the coal the miner's mined. Since coal companies paid miners according to the amount of the coal they dug from the earth, this position determined the miners' wages. He also likely found a community of fellow black citizens who attained considerable prominence in the community, whether as politicians, proprietors, or professionals. At times, these men chose to act as a black community but at other times, aligned with their white neighbors. How they chose to exercise their political and organizational will depended on the particular issue at hand. To secure the election of political candidates favorable to labor issues, blacks and whites lent their voices jointly to campaigns. To prevent a rumored lynching, the black community informed local white police officers that retribution would follow should the authorities permit such an affront to justice.

Following the depression of the 1890s and the re-opening of a mine at which Davis had labored for many years, he found himself blacklisted and unable to secure work. Why Rendville coal operators blacklisted Davis remains unclear, but the effect was to leave him in difficult economic circumstances. Davis pleaded with the UMWA, the organization that he had served so ably, to assist him with work or financial assistance in this time of great need. The union failed him. At the time of his death on January 15, 1900, he was still not working as a miner, though some reports suggest that he may have become a village constable. The cause of Davis's untimely death remains murky, with some accounts suggesting he died of typhoid after catching it from contaminated well water. Other reports suggest he died of pneumonia. Whatever the cause, Rendville and its working people had lost a staunch advocate, and the United States one of its first black industrial labor organizers.

KARIN A. SHAPIRO

References and Further Reading

Gutman, Herbert G. "The Negro and the United Mine Workers of America: The Career and Letters of Richard L. Davis and something of their meaning: 1890–1900." In *The Negro and the Labor Movement*, edited by Julius Jacobson. New York: Anchor Books, 1968.

Hill, Herbert. "Myth-Making as Labor History: Herbert Gutman and the United Mine Workers of America." *International Journal of Politics, Culture, and Society* 2 (1988): 132–200.

———. "Rejoinder to Symposium on Myth Making as Labor History: Herbert Gutman and the United Mine Workers of America." *International Journal of Politics, Culture, and Society* 2 (1989): 587–595.

Letwin, Daniel. *The Challenge of Interracial Unionism: Alabama Coal Miners, 1878–1921.* Chapel Hill: University of North Carolina Press, 1998.

Lewis, Ronald L. *Black Coal Miners in America: Race, Class, and Community Conflict, 1870–1980.* Lexington: University of Kentucky Press, 1987.

Lichtenstein, Alex. "Racial Conflict and Racial Solidarity in the Alabama Coal Strike of 1894: New Evidence in the Gutman-Hill Debate." *Labor History* 36 (Winter 1995): 63–76.

Nelson, Charles H. "The Story of Rendville: An Interracial Quest for Community in the Post Civil War Era." *Buckeye Hill Country: A Journal of Regional History* 1 (Spring 1996): 25–35.

Tribe, Ivan M. *Sprinkled with Coal Dust: Life and Work in the Hocking Coal Region, 1870–1900.* Athens County, Ohio: Historical Society and Museum, 1989.

DAVIS-BACON ACT

When enacted on March 3, 1931, the Davis-Bacon Act, also known as the Prevailing Wage Law, became the nation's first federal law to secure a minimum wage for nongovernment workers. In short, the law requires contractors working on federal or federally assisted building projects to pay workers no less than the local prevailing wage rates for each trade.

Prior to the 1960s, the Davis-Bacon Act inspired little controversy. Amid the economic crisis of the Great Depression, the act was an easy sell for Congressman Robert Bacon (Republican, NY) and Senator James Davis (Republican, PA). The American Federation of Labor's (AFL's) Building Trades Department lobbied hard for the legislation, but they were joined by others outside of the house of labor. Most notably, contractors who had entered into agreements with local building trades unions sought protection from outside contractors who employed cheap, nonunion labor. In general, supporters of the Davis-Bacon Act hoped that it would bring a degree of order to an unpredictable industry at a time when the living conditions of the working class were rapidly deteriorating.

For the remainder of the Depression and throughout World War II, the Davis-Bacon Act determined wages on all federally funded construction projects (including WPA, PWA, and defense projects). Numerous states followed by passing "Little Davis-Bacon Acts" to cover state-funded projects (although several states had already enacted prevailing wage laws prior to 1931). During the postwar period, the Building Trades Department fought to preserve the prevailing wage system and to extend its coverage to include federally assisted projects. These efforts bore fruit, and as a result building trades unions positioned themselves to profit handsomely from postwar government construction. The 1956 interstate highway bill included a prevailing wage provision, and in 1964, Congress amended the Federal Airport Act and the National Housing Act to work in accordance with the Davis-Bacon Act. Also in 1964, Congress amended the act to include fringe benefits, such as health and life insurance, and vacation and holiday pay.

The government's postwar spending in defense and heavy construction, coupled with the 1960s construction boom, fostered union strength and rewarded building trades workers in the form of steady employment and high wages. This prosperity in turn generated a backlash. In 1971, rising wages coupled with a flurry of strike activity in the construction industry prompted President Richard Nixon to suspend the Davis-Bacon Act for one month. More threatening than the Nixon administration's attempts to curb inflation and to stabilize the industry, however, was the formation of a movement to challenge the power of building trades unions.

In 1969, union and nonunion contractors joined with some of the nation's largest corporations (U.S. Steel, Monsanto, and the Ford Motor Company, among others) to found the Construction Users Anti-Inflation Roundtable (CUAIR), which reorganized as the Business Roundtable in 1972, to strengthen contractors' bargaining power. Since members of the Roundtable blamed rising construction costs on union wage rates and benefits, the Davis-Bacon Act was a natural target. The prevailing wage system may have served a purpose during the economic crisis of the 1930s, they argued, but in the 1960s the law handcuffed the economy by inhibiting the growth of the nonunion sector of the construction industry and by causing inflation to spiral out of control. In addition, opponents of the law claimed that in practice it was inefficient, arbitrary, and poorly administered. Since an amendment to the act in 1935, the Department of Labor has been responsible for determining the prevailing wage for a given locality (in the law's original form, that responsibility was assumed by contractors and contracting agencies). Opponents of the law have contended that the Department of Labor lacks the resources to meet the task of conducting accurate wage surveys in thousands of localities for thousands of construction projects each year. Instead, critics have charged that the DOL tends to make union rate the *de facto* prevailing wage (supporters of the act have countered that less than half of wage determinants match union scales).

Throughout the 1970s, the Roundtable, the Associated Builders and Contractors (ABC), and other open-shop organizations attacked the Davis-Bacon Act with a combination of publicity and legislative lobbying. In addition to spending $1.2 million to run its own series in *Reader's Digest* in 1975, the Roundtable financed several academic studies that buttressed its call for the repeal of federal and state prevailing wage laws. Their efforts were buoyed in 1979, when the federal government's General Accounting Office condemned the law in a report decisively titled *The Davis-Bacon Act Should be Repealed*. Ideally, the Roundtable and ABC hoped that they could convince Congress to repeal the act. But alternatively they supported legislation that would restrict its reach by removing certain projects from the Department of Labor's jurisdiction and by attaching provisions to appropriation bills that would limit the act's applicability.

Their efforts notwithstanding, open-shop campaigns to repeal or amend the Davis-Bacon Act have been unsuccessful (although several state prevailing wage laws were repealed in the late 1970s and early

1980s). This is in large part because of the ability of building trades unions, which frequently feud with one another, to unite in defense of the law. Organized labor has considered prevailing wage laws vital to the maintenance of a quality standard of living for construction workers. Union solidarity on the issue was manifest in the activities of the Building Trades Department (BTD). To counter the Roundtable's publicity campaign, the BTD established the Center to Protect Workers' Rights (CPWR) in 1979. One immediate task of the CPWR was to fund scholarly research, free from anti-union bias, on the inflationary impact of the Davis-Bacon Act. Armed with these articles and other research materials prepared by the CPWR, the BTD waged a spirited lobbying campaign of their own. With the support of the Department of Labor, which has generally supported the Davis-Bacon Act, organized labor was able to prevent open-shop forces from gaining the support they needed in Congress.

On the other hand, by 1990, the open-shop movement had begun to retreat from its aggressive stance. For one, the inflationary period of the 1960s had passed. Also construction unions no longer held the upper hand in collective bargaining. Whereas 80% of the industry's workforce was unionized in 1969, only 35% carried union cards in 1990. Nevertheless, the Republican party continues to try to weaken the Davis-Bacon Act. In 2005, in the wake of Hurricane Katrina, President George W. Bush attempted to suspend the act in those parts of Alabama, Florida, Louisiana, and Mississippi devastated by the hurricane. However, he withdrew his suspension after his action met with intense political opposition.

JOHN J. ROSEN

References and Further Reading

Erlich, Mark. *Labor at the Ballot Box: The Massachusetts Prevailing Wage Campaign of 1988*. Philadelphia: Temple University Press, 1990.
Goldfarb, Robert S., and John F. Morall. "The Davis-Bacon Act: An Appraisal of Recent Studies." *Industrial Labor Relations Review* 34, 2 (Jan. 1981): 191–206.
Gujarati, D. N. "The Economics of the Davis-Bacon Act." *Journal of Business*. 40, 3 (July 1967): 303–316.
Palladino, Grace. *Skilled Hands, Strong Spirits: A Century of Building Trades History*. Ithaca, NY, and London: Cornell University Press, 2005.

DAY, DOROTHY (1897–1980)
Catholic Labor Activist

Bohemian, radical activist, journalist, charity worker, and devout Catholic, Dorothy Day founded the *Catholic Worker* newspaper and the movement it inspired.

Raised in a respectable middle-class household in San Francisco and Chicago, Day rebelled against the culture of her upbringing and became involved in a socialist organization at the University of Illinois. After two years in Urbana, she went to New York, where she embraced the world of early twentieth-century Greenwich Village: literary, radical, and religiously agnostic. She wrote first for a socialist daily, the *New York Call*, then for a Marxist magazine, the *Masses*. Her social circle included many prominent writers and editors of the day, including Max Eastman, John Dos Passos, Malcolm Cowley, Allen Tate, Caroline Gordon, Hart Crane, and Eugene O'Neill.

The birth of her daughter in 1926 crystallized a developing religious sense, and Day had the girl baptized in the Catholic church; Day herself became Catholic the following year. She dedicated her life to her daughter and to the working class of New York City.

Conversant with, and sympathetic to, the socialist and Communist strains of thought to which she was exposed, Day nonetheless charted a different course, one more compatible with the Catholic faith to which she was newly wedded. She was confirmed in her tendencies by the preaching of an eccentric French philosopher, Peter Maurin, whom she met in 1932. Maurin, newly arrived in the United States, taught a brand of personalist philosophy that was at once devoutly Catholic and profoundly radical. He advocated abolition of the wage system but envisioned it occurring through a return to agriculture rather than through worker ownership of industry. Day absorbed his thought and sought to put it into practice.

Convinced of the evils of both the state and capitalism, Day applied herself to undermining both. She started a newspaper, the *Catholic Worker*, the first issue of which appeared on May Day, 1933. Sold at a penny a copy, it was intended not to make a profit, but to inspire working people to bring about a society that reflected the principles of cooperation and sharing rather than competition and profit making. It also aimed to bring to workers a friendly face of Catholicism, to attract those who were inclined to dismiss the church as a force for the status quo.

Day was not content to limit her work to the publishing world, where her efforts on behalf of workers might remain at a distance from their plight. She sought also to remedy the ills of society directly through "houses of hospitality." Similar in some ways to the settlement house movement headed by Jane Addams, the Catholic Worker houses that Day and her increasing number of followers organized were

Dorothy Day, half-length portrait, seated at desk, facing right. Library of Congress, Prints & Photographs Division, NYWT & S Collection [LC-USZ62-111099].

open to the indigent, the homeless, or to anyone who needed lodging. Residents were expected to participate in the work of the movement, from housework to printing and distributing the *Catholic Worker*. Inspired by the teaching of Day and Maurin, Catholic Workers also founded communal farms.

In the context of a late 1930s breakdown of initial Catholic consensus in favor of the New Deal, the Catholic Worker movement became more controversial within the church. No one questioned Day's personal morality or standing in the church (she vocally defended the church's moral teachings), but her unorthodox methods attracted some criticism. For one, her mission operated outside the traditional structure of Catholic charity, outside even the purview of Catholic clergy. Increasing Catholic (and broader American) fears of radicalism and communism also called into question an organization that frequently cooperated with such elements.

In the early days of the movement, Day and Maurin had disagreed over the issue of organized labor. Maurin opposed union organization as a capitulation to the modern industrial system, while Day and most Catholic Workers actively supported the labor movement. The Association of Catholic Trade Unionists (ACTU) grew out of a meeting that occurred at the Catholic Worker headquarters in New York.

By the late 1930s, however, Day had become disillusioned with the trajectory of American unions. Her paper began criticizing the ACTU and organized labor for sacrificing the spiritual end of a radical transformation of work in favor of the more materialistic goals of higher pay and better working conditions. The difference led to a break between the New York Catholic Worker, led by Day, and the ACTU, led by former Catholic Worker, John Cort.

Another point of contention was Day's unbending pacifism, which became increasingly notable as the United States prepared for and entered World War II. The issue provoked another break in the movement in 1940, as the Chicago Workers, led by John Cogley, decided that Christian commitment to the working class was compatible with American military action against fascism.

The Catholic Worker movement was then probably at its apex. The paper reached its highest circulation in 1940 at 185,000. It lost 100,000 subscriptions (many of them bulk requests from Catholic pastors) during the war because its pacifist stance contradicted the strongly prowar views of many of its readers. In the more prosperous, less radical 1940s and 1950s, moreover, workers were more likely to identify with mainstream unions than with Day's iconoclastic, communitarian movement.

The *Catholic Worker*, nonetheless, is still published, and Catholic Worker houses operate in many urban centers around the United States. In 1959, she again provoked controversy among Catholics and others with her positive assessment of Fidel Castro's Cuban Revolution. Day's protests against air-raid drills in New York landed her in jail in the 1950s, and she joined anti-Vietnam demonstrations in the 1960s and 1970s. Meanwhile, she continued to manage the New York house of hospitality and traveled the country to frequent speaking engagements. Still a controversial figure within the Catholic church, Day is nonetheless widely revered, and her cause for canonization as a saint has been introduced.

KEVIN E. SCHMIESING

References and Further Reading

Day, Dorothy. *The Long Loneliness*. San Francisco: Harper, 1997.

Fisher, James Terence. *The Catholic Counterculture in America, 1933–1962*. Chapel Hill: University of North Carolina Press, 1989.

Miller, William. *A Harsh and Dreadful Love: Dorothy Day and the Catholic Worker Movement*. New York: Liveright, 1973.

Piehl, Mel. *Breaking Bread: The Catholic Worker and the Origin of Catholic Radicalism in America.* Philadelphia: Temple University Press, 1982.

Roberts, Nancy L. *Dorothy Day and the Catholic Worker.* Albany: State University of New York Press, 1984.

See also **Association of Catholic Trade Unionists**

DEBS, EUGENE V. (1855–1926)
Cofounder, American Railway Union; Leader, Socialist Party of America

Eugene V. Debs, the nation's most prominent socialist by the early twentieth century, was born into a middle-class family in Terre Haute, Indiana, in 1855. Despite the pleas of his parents to remain in school, Debs became a paint scraper for a local railroad. He then tramped around the Midwest looking for a job as a railroad fireman. Returning to Terre Haute in the mid-1870s, Debs attended an organizing meeting of the International Brotherhood of Locomotive Firemen (BLF). He was elected recording secretary of the new local and thus began his trade union career.

Debs firmly believed that a balance between labor and capital could be achieved, each one recognizing the worth of the other. The year 1885 was a dramatic one for Debs, since it began his turn away from a collaborative relation with railroad management to a more adversarial one. To counter the threatening power of the railroad corporations, Debs floated the idea of creating a federated council of the railroad brotherhoods. The federation principle was one that held enormous symbolic value for Debs. It was perceived as a unified response to railroad power. His basic argument was that the federation would ensure fewer strikes because employers would think twice before combating their workers.

Spurring Debs on was a record of defeated railroad strikes. Other than the weight of owner resistance, it was the propensity of the railroad brotherhoods to scab on one another that effectively defeated the strikes. But the established railroad brotherhoods rejected Deb's idea of a federation. Correspondingly in 1893, Debs took the dramatic and fateful step of helping to form the American Railway Union (ARU). The principles differed markedly from the federation idea, however. The organizers wanted to accept all white railroad workers into the ARU. Importantly, African-Americans were not invited to join. Bringing together all white railroad workers under one umbrella would counter the railroads' power. Debs had clearly embraced the ideal of industrial unionism.

Daily, hundreds of railroad workers signed up for the ARU, and Debs was hard-pressed to keep up with the organizing calls and speeches demanded. Within weeks after a successful strike against the Great Northern Railroad, the ARU had grown to 150,000 members, dwarfing the combined membership of the railroad brotherhoods. For Debs, caution was the key. He tried mightily to remind the members that they should avoid unnecessary entanglements that might severely test the youthful ARU. Unfortunately for Debs and the ARU, such advice was ignored during a strike of Pullman car workers.

Just outside of Chicago, George Pullman had created a company town that bore his name. Manufacturing luxury passenger cars, the Pullman Company controlled much of the workers' lives. While the system was grudgingly accepted by the Pullman workers, after the economic downturn of 1893–1894 saw cuts in wages but no accompanying cut in costs, the workers demanded that the pay cuts be rescinded. Pullman refused and fired those who had tried to obtain an audience with him to discuss the cuts. In response, the workers went on strike.

The strikers called on the ARU for support. Debs was comfortable in providing money and giving speeches on their behalf, but just as he feared, the ARU was dragged into a momentous confrontation against the combined weight of the railroad capital. As the boycott spread, those ARU members who refused to operate trains with attached Pullman cars were dismissed. In turn, the workforces struck in protest. Very quickly the boycott was transformed into a strike. Correspondingly, the owners turned to the federal government for help, approaching Richard Olney, the U.S. Attorney General, for support

Olney obliged by obtaining a sweeping federal injunction. Debs and other leaders were specifically enjoined from issuing both instructions and funds to the ARU strikers. In effect, the purpose was to strangle the strike. Debs initially ignored the injunction but soon found himself under arrest. Debs was joined by six other ARU leaders. With the leadership of the ARU neutralized, the strike effectively came to an end. Debs and his associates appealed their conviction but were sentenced to 6 months in prison.

The strike had been a disaster for the ARU. Thousands of ARU members were summarily dismissed and blacklisted from railroad employment. The defeat also confirmed Debs's hostile attitude toward the federal government. Its intimate relationship with railroad owners, and its readiness to apply injunctive law against the ARU, confirmed Debs's belief of the essential corruptness of the established political parties. The strike defeat opened the road for Debs to begin his socialist career. Debs joined others in forming the Socialist Party of America (SPA). Debs's socialism was a unique blend of American radicalism and vulgar Marxist principles. Debs girded himself for the 1908 presidential election. A special train (Red Special) was commissioned to take the 52-year-old Debs on a campaign tour that included over 34 states. Debs gave his all in trying to convince the audiences to vote the socialist ticket. Talking for hours, his impact on the listeners was generally profound. Cynical audience members were won over by his charm and magnetism. Unfortunately, the SPA's 1908 showing was deeply disappointing. Although gaining votes in the southwest, the ticket only increased its vote tally by a mere 18,000 votes to 420,000. Buoying Debs, however, were important socialist gains at the municipal level. Socialists mayors had been elected in Schenectady and Milwaukee, and Victor Berger had been elected to Congress. Just as vital was the increasing membership in the SPA. The 1912 election confirmed the growth of the SPA and that its message was being adopted by increasing numbers of voters. Overall, Debs polled 900,000 votes, 6% of the total vote.

The years 1913–1917 were eventful in turning Debs's attention away from domestic affairs to that of the international arena. As President Woodrow Wilson stepped up his preparedness program for involving the United States in the war, Debs acted in kind. Once President Wilson obtained a declaration of war in April 1917, the SPA convened to respond. The SPA came out forcefully against the war. Within weeks of the declaration of war, the forces of reaction threw their full weight against those judged to be disloyal. Socialist newspapers were closed down, and party offices ransacked. Nurturing this oppressive atmosphere was the passage of two legislative acts, the Espionage and Sedition acts. In sum, these acts acted as breaks on any form of criticism of government action during the war, whether it was of conscription or of general policy.

Debs was horrified by the turn of events during 1917. His lecture tours had been canceled, and the suppression of the socialist press ensured that his voice could not get out. Debs became depressed by his collapsing world. Socialists were literally being hunted down by either government agents or vigilantes, and the socialist press had been destroyed. It was perhaps the scale of the repression that dampened Debs's spirit, as well as his deteriorating health.

In 1918, when Debs was 63, friends and colleagues were in jail, and the socialist vision of eventual success seemed a distant dream. Debs decided to join his comrades in prison. In early June he gave several speeches outlining his opposition to the war but was frustrated by no response by either federal or state authorities. His dream would be realized, however, with his June 16, speech in Canton, Ohio.

Twelve hundred people were packed into the hall, as were government agents and stenographers. Debs attacked the notion that the United States was a democracy: "They tell us that we live in a great free republic; that our institutions are democratic; that we are a free and self-governing people. This is too much; even for a joke." To prove his point, he then spoke out on the persecution of hundreds of socialists and Wobblies wasting away in prison. Then specifically he announced, "The master class has always declared the wars; the subject class has always fought the battles. The master class has had all to gain and nothing to lose, while the subject class has had nothing to gain and all to lose—especially their lives."

The stenographic record was given to the U.S. Attorney's office in Cleveland. Two weeks later, an indictment was handed down that Debs had violated the Espionage Act, and he was arrested on June 30, 1918. The trial was set for September 9, 1918, and Debs and his battery of lawyers were prepared. As the prosecution brought in its witnesses, the defense offered little in the way of cross-examination. The strategy was clear, Debs had no intention of disputing any of the facts of the case; that is, they would not deny that Debs had spoken out against the war and U.S. government policy. The point was that Debs had every right to say what he did; it was purely an issue of freedom of speech. After the prosecution witnesses had finished their testimony, Debs took the stand in his own defense. Using examples of George Washington, Samuel Adams, and Abraham Lincoln, Debs argued that it was an American tradition to oppose unjust government policies that ushered in autocracy. So while admitting he had opposed the government's declaration and running of the war, he merely argued it reflected a common American tradition of resistance to oppression.

Not surprisingly, the jury found Debs guilty of the conspiracy charges. Debs's lawyers immediately appealed the decision to the U.S. Supreme Court. On March 10, 1919, the Court denied the appeal by arguing that Debs had deliberately tried to obstruct wartime recruitment. On April 13, 1919, Debs began his first day in federal prison in Moundville, Ohio. Debs was asked once again to stand for election in 1920 as the Socialist Labor Party (SLP) candidate; he reluctantly agreed. The campaign re-invigorated Debs, but the results were deeply disappointing. Nearly gaining one million votes, the percentage had dropped from 6% to 3%. Still the result was remarkable. The year 1920 saw the height of the Red Scare, with its accompanying ransacking of socialist and Communist offices and arrests of leaders and followers alike.

With the election of Warren Harding, the push for a pardon for Debs began in earnest. Eventually, a halfway measure of amnesty was offered. Debs was not happy with the decision. True, he gained his freedom, as did 23 other political prisoners, but many other left-wing radicals were left in prison. On December 26, 1921, he was released and whisked to Washington, D.C., for a private audience with President Harding.

By 1926, Debs was ill and exhausted. His trademark enthusiasm had deserted him, leaving audience members wondering what had happened to the once-dynamic leader. He increasingly checked himself into sanatoriums, suffering from exhaustion. After a trip to Bermuda in 1926 (his first trip abroad), he caught a cold on the return voyage. Months of rest could not revive Debs's energy, and after a heart attack, he lapsed into a coma. On October 20, 1926, Debs died. There was a huge outpouring of sorrow once the news became public.

Throughout his early life, Debs grappled with questions of trade union principles and socialist ideology. The common thread was his immense compassion for working people. Once committed to the socialist ideal of creating an alternative to the rank injustices of capitalist encroachment, he never wavered. Debs led a particularly long and dramatic life. His legacy included the formation of a vital trade union movement and a socialist party that thundered its way across the American political landscape.

COLIN DAVIS

References and Further Reading

Buhle, Mari Jo. *Women and American Socialism, 1870–1920*. Urbana: University of Illinois Press, 1981.

Ginger, Ray. *The Bending Cross: A Biography of Eugene Victor Debs*. Kirksville, MO: Thomas Jefferson University Press, 1992.

Green, James. *Grass-Roots Socialism: Radical Movements in the Southwest, 1895–1943*. Baton Rouge: Louisiana University Press, 1978.

Laslett, John H. M., and Seymour Martin Lipset. *Failure of a Dream? Essays in the History of American Socialism*. Berkeley: University of California Press, 1984.

Miller, Sally. *Race, Ethnicity, and Gender in Early Twentieth-Century American Socialism*. New York: Garland, 1996.

Salvatore, Nick. *Eugene V. Debs: Citizen and Socialist*. Urbana: University of Illinois Press, 1982.

Shore, Elliot. *Talkin' Socialism: J. A. Wayland and the Role of the Press in American Radicalism, 1890–1912*. Lawrence, KS: University of Kansas Press, 1988.

See also **American Railway Union**

DE-INDUSTRIALIZATION

Originally coined in its modern usage in 1982 by economists Barry Bluestone and Bennett Harrison, de-industrialization denotes the removal or substantial reduction of manufacturing activity in a region or country. In the twenty-first century, the term is used variously to describe: a process that inevitably happens in advanced economies and is a net positive for those economies; a disaster akin to a hurricane for regions and countries when and where it happens; or a result of a mistaken economic policy that (either accidentally or intentionally) reduces wages, working conditions, and living standards in a "race to the bottom." The meaning of de-industrialization has been and is still contested terrain.

What is contested is the general importance of manufacturing to a modern economy and whether, despite the pain experienced by laid-off workers and abandoned communities, de-industrialization is inevitable and necessary to positive economic growth.

A loose "periodization" frames much popular understanding of de-industrialization. In this frame, the United States and other advanced countries have moved from an agrarian to an industrial to a postindustrial service society. As a broad description of the past two or three hundred years, this frame is not inaccurate in pointing to fundamental shifts in the relative importance of three kinds of basic economic activity. But insofar as it suggests that manufacturing is now unimportant, this basic way of defining our society as postindustrial misses many of the contested issues involved with de-industrialization.

Manufacturing *is* relatively less important to our economy and society than it used to be, just as agriculture is. But few economists or other scholars think that means that making and growing things is no longer fundamentally important to our or any other economy. At the end of the twentieth century, total manufacturing output was actually larger in the United States than it was in 1960, when we were uniformly described as an advanced industrial society. As a share of Gross Domestic Product (GDP), however, manufacturing had declined since then from nearly 30% to less than 15%. Even in 1960, services accounted for a majority of GDP (nearly 60%), but by the end of the century it had risen to nearly 80%.

The relative decline in manufacturing employment is even steeper. Though in 2000, there were about 2 million more factory jobs than there had been in 1955, manufacturing's share of total employment had fallen from nearly one-third to less than one-seventh during that time. Thus, even when manufacturing jobs were still increasing into the 1970s, service-sector jobs were growing much faster, moving from a bare majority of total employment in 1960 to more than 80%. (Service-sector jobs cover a wide variety of occupations from teachers, managers, doctors, and lawyers on the higher income end to janitors, child-care workers, waitresses, and hotel maids on the low end, with truck drivers and airline workers mostly in the middle.)

As Rowthorn and Ramaswamy show in their report for the International Monetary Fund (IMF), the relative rise of the service sector versus manufacturing is common among all advanced industrial countries since at least 1960. But this relative decline is not what is usually meant by de-industrialization. As long as manufacturing activity, whether measured by output or jobs, is still growing or at least not declining substantially, there is not yet de-industrialization. A country or region may be moving from an industrial to a postindustrial society without de-industrialization occurring at all.

National De-Industrialization

De-industrialization did not begin for the United States as a whole until 1977, when manufacturing employment peaked at 19.6 million jobs. Though there had been ups and downs before then, particularly during the Great Depression of the 1930s, factory jobs had been increasing fairly steadily through the late nineteenth century, beginning the twentieth century with about 5 million and quadrupling by 1977.

The period from 1977 to 1986, during which the worst economic recession since the 1930s occurred, saw a dramatic period of plant closings in what began to be called the Rust Belt in the Northeast and Great Lakes, as well as through the Great Plains and into California. This is when the term was originally coined, but de-industrialization was largely a regional phenomenon at that time. As the national economy recovered in the late 1980s, manufacturing employment briefly reached 19 million again in 1988 before beginning a longer, steadier decline to just over 17 million by the year 2000. By then, it seemed to many that the period of de-industrialization had ended, as new industries in electronics and pharmaceuticals had begun growing even as such traditional industries as steel, auto, and rubber continued to decline. The relatively mild recession with which the twenty-first century began, however, initiated a new round of manufacturing job losses. By 2003, manufacturing employment had dropped to 14.5 million. Thus, the quarter century from 1977 to 2003 saw the loss of more than one-quarter of U.S. factory jobs. This is de-industrialization at the national

level, and we are still in the middle (or possibly at the beginning) of this process.

The decline in total manufacturing output is not nearly so dramatic as the decline in employment, a real (inflation-adjusted) loss of a little more than 3% from 1977 to 2003, as measured by the dollar value of shipments. This discrepancy between a 25% loss in jobs and a 3% loss in output is the result of very large increases in manufacturing productivity since the 1980s. The reasons for these large gains in productivity are complex, including industry restructurings around investments in new (often computer-controlled) machinery; shifts to such industries as pharmaceuticals and electronics; and old-fashioned "labor speed-up," based on the dramatic loss of union power in manufacturing during this period.

Thus, as with agriculture before it, manufacturing remains an essential economic activity in the United States, producing about as much as it ever has. But after growing, often dramatically, for more than two centuries, output has leveled off, and employment is declining steadily and substantially at the national level.

Regional De-Industrialization

Regional de-industrialization, on the other hand, is a more dramatic and much more traumatic phenomenon, since the period from 1977 to the mid-1980s saw what one steelworker leader described as a "creeping holocaust" through the Northeast and midwestern manufacturing belt. Steel towns like Lackawanna in New York; Bethlehem, Johnstown, Homestead, and McKeesport in Pennsylvania; Cleveland, Youngstown, and Steubenville in Ohio; Chicago in Illinois; and Geneva in Utah lost all or almost all of their mills and the hundreds of thousands of jobs they provided. Auto assembly plants were closed in the same states and in Michigan and California, and auto parts factories—making everything from valves to windshield wipers—shut down after 50 years or more of driving the local economies of dozens of towns and cities in the Rust Belt and elsewhere. Plants making radios and televisions, tires, elevators, textiles and clothing, paper products, farm equipment, and machine tools were shut down. A major part of what had been the heart of the post-World War II U.S. industrial economy disappeared in less than a decade.

The ripple effects of this rapid de-industrialization of the U.S. industrial heartland were devastating to scores of communities. The loss of jobs meant the loss of consumer-spending power for everything from department stores to barber shops, auto dealerships to restaurants and grocery stores. It also meant a declining tax base with which to fund public education, fire and police departments, and other public services, which often deteriorated dramatically. Some of these communities have recovered or semi-recovered in the past 20 years. Many have not. Many had adjusted to lower standards of living, declining populations, and reduced public services and seemed on the upswing during the late 1990s' economic boom, only to see what turned out to be temporary gains washed away in the economic recession and stagnation of the early twenty-first century.

Most of the communities devastated by de-industrialization in the late 1970s and early 1980s suffered it as they would a natural disaster, waiting for it to end and then cleaning up as best they could. But some fought to save specific plants and mobilized across communities and industries to mount pressure for a national effort at re-industrialization. These "fight backs," usually led by union-community coalitions, were mostly unsuccessful. Though many succeeded in retaining specific plants for a while longer (in several cases, for decades longer), the possibility of a concerted industrial policy by the federal government to save and grow manufacturing jobs disappeared during that time. The methodologies developed by the anti-shutdown movement, then, have been further refined since, often with the help of local and state governments, but the rich debate about the possibility of re-industrializing had largely been put aside by the time a second round of de-industrialization began in the early years of this century.

Fighting Back?

The main lesson from the antishutdown movement during the initial period of de-industrialization is that while many plant closings are inevitable due to economic conditions, many plants can be saved by changes in ownership (including partial or full employee ownership), new business strategies, enlisting the participation of workers in managing production, and using local and state government financing authority to obtain private investment in new technology. Saving existing plants and attracting new ones has often also involved concessions in wages and work rules by labor unions and economic development subsidies from local governments, not all of which have been worthwhile in terms of jobs saved or gained. But clearly at the local level, de-industrialization is not completely analogous to an earthquake or tornado. Industrial retention and attraction are now standard

parts of most state and local government economic development activities.

At a national level however, the primary view is that de-industrialization in general and any individual plant closing in particular are likely both inevitable and a long-term positive for the economy as a whole. The closing of factories, it is pointed out, is as old as the industrial revolution itself. Many of the first Pittsburgh-area iron mills in the nineteenth century were shut down as they were replaced with newer, much larger steel mills on the Monongahela and Allegheny rivers. Likewise, the opening of Ford Motor Company's River Rouge complex outside Detroit displaced workers from earlier Ford plants in the Detroit area. Indeed, the rise and fall of entire industrial regions is nothing new to the last quarter of the twentieth century. One of the original iron-making regions of western Pennsylvania, for example, was in the Juniata Valley, an area well east of Pittsburgh that has long been a bucolic landscape with little remaining evidence of its industrial past. Likewise, Titusville, where oil was first discovered, has not produced any oil for more than a century. The dynamism of capitalism's "creative destruction" requires the competitive fury of new plants replacing old ones and new industries rising as old ones decline. Today, this same process goes on, as biogenetic drugs replace more traditional remedies even as the pharmaceutical industry as a whole grows like auto and steel in their heydays.

For government to intervene in this process in efforts to preserve some industries and plants while nurturing others, called industrial policy in the 1980s, would interfere in the natural workings of a free market and would result in less overall economic growth, and thus less economic activity and fewer jobs, not more. Besides, the argument goes, from a national perspective, the Rust Belt's industrial loss was the Sun Belt's gain, as many factories and their jobs migrated South and as new, smaller facilities based on new technology, like steel minimills, were more expeditiously dispersed throughout the country instead of being concentrated in just a few areas.

Opposed to this view is one that sees a large part of de-industrialization as unnecessary and wasteful, allowed, if not caused, by government economic policies that misunderstand the dynamics of a mature industrial economy. The overall effects of de-industrialization, this view holds, are much larger than the long string of devastated factory towns and neighborhoods. They include a quarter-century's decline in real wages for the 80% of the private-sector workforce that is defined as production and nonsupervisory workers, the loss of health insurance and pensions for growing millions of workers, and the steady deterioration of working conditions in offices and stores as well as in factories. Some see this as a conscious policy begun in the 1970s to break the power of union workers, thereby making all workers more manageable. But most see it as a necessary result of conservative economic policies that counsel increasing reliance on the free market unrestrained by government interference. This is exactly the wrong approach, according to this view, to any mature industry, which once it is in place represents an investment not only in capital equipment, but also in worker skills and public infrastructure that should not be discarded lightly. Government supervision of the market process is all the more necessary once relative profit rates decline, as they inevitably do in the mature phase of any industry.

In the late 1970s and early 1980s, various re-industrialization programs were put forward not only by unions and labor-community coalitions like the Tri-State Conference on Steel (in Pennsylvania, Ohio, and West Virginia) and the Oakland (California) Plant Closures Project, but by investment bankers like Felix Rosalyn and even *Business Week* in special issues in June of 1980 and 1981. Though different in the roles they prescribed for various levels of government, all saw strategic public investments as required not necessarily to save particular factories, but to preserve productive equipment, work cultures and skills, and public infrastructure that with a little help could have had a future. By the late 1980s, this was "the road not taken," but it has been sustained in other venues in opposition to so-called free trade agreements and even an early twenty-first century re-industrialization program called the Apollo Alliance for Good Jobs and Clean Energy. Apollo Alliance proposes a $100 billion government investment fund over 10 years to nurture emerging industries in such alternative energy sources as wind, solar, biomass, and geothermal; and in hybrid cars; more efficient appliances; wind turbines; high-performance buildings; high-speed rail and other public transportation. Building on current competitive advantages enjoyed by U.S. manufacturing, the Apollo Alliance envisions a program of public investment that would lead to energy independence, a dramatically cleaner environment, and three million new manufacturing jobs.

It may make sense to describe the United States as a postindustrial society, but de-industrialization is likely to remain contested terrain. Just as government agricultural policy has remained an area of contention in all industrial and postindustrial societies, the issue will continue to be whether passively to accept the impartial workings of the free market or whether as citizens in a democracy to require our government to pursue better outcomes than the unaided market is likely to provide. If de-industrialization is inevitable, then all a democratic society can do is minister to those harmed by the process. If it is not inevitable or not entirely inevitable, then the issue is not simply about what to do for the injured, but what to do to stop, reverse, or retard the de-industrializing.

JACK METZGAR

References and Further Reading

Bensman, David, and Roberta Lynch. *Rusted Dreams: Hard Times in a Steel Community*. New York: McGraw-Hill, 1987.

Bluestone, Barry, and Bennett Harrison. *The De-industrialization of America: Plant Closings, Community Abandonment, and the Dismantling of Basic Industry*. New York: Basic Books, 1982.

Cowie, Jefferson, and Joseph Heathcott. *Beyond the Ruins: The Meanings of De-industrialization*. Ithaca: Cornell, 2003.

Fingleton, Eamonn. *In Praise of Hard Industries: Why Manufacturing, Not the Information Economy, Is the Key to Future Prosperity*. New York: Houghton Mifflin Buttonwood Press, 1999.

Linkon, Sherry Lee, and John Russo. *Steeltown U.S.A.: Work and Memory in Youngstown*. Lawrence: University of Kansas, 2002.

Lynd, Staughton. *The Fight against Shutdowns*. San Pedro, CA: Singlejack Books, 1982.

Rowthorn, Robert, and Ramana Ramaswamy. "De-industrialization: Causes and Implications." *A Working Paper of the International Monetary Fund*, 1997.

DELANO GRAPE STRIKE (1965–1970)

The Delano Grape strike in California ushered in a new era of unionization of farm workers. Poorly paid, living in substandard housing, subjected to intolerable working conditions, with no political or economic base to advocate for their concerns, agricultural workers were among the most exploited segments of the American labor force. Although attempts to organize farm laborers had occurred throughout the twentieth century, these initiatives were characterized by outbreaks of militancy, limited government responses to ameliorate circumstances, ruthless actions to crush organization by corporate agriculture, and the ultimate defeat of union drives. This protest, unlike previous uprisings, drew strength from a vigorous civil rights movement and the use of the philosophy of nonviolence successfully employed by Mahatma Gandhi and Martin Luther King, Jr. Of critical significance was the emergence of local leadership that was able to inspire solaridarity on the part of the multicultural and seasonal workforce. The movement also benefited from the repeal of the *bracero* (guest worker) program, which had undermined past efforts through the availability of plentiful labor from Mexico.

The Delano strike eventually led to the development of the United Farm Workers of America (UFW), the first enduring union to organize agricultural laborers successfully.

Although the Delano strike is generally associated with the emergence of the charismatic César Chávez, it was actually initiated by the American Federation of Labor (AFL)-Congress of Industrial organizations (CIO)-affiliated Agricultural Workers Organizing Committee (AWOC), a predominately Filipino local, led by Larry Itliong and Ben Guines. The strike first erupted in the Coachella Valley in the southern part of the state. In early spring 1965, grape growers offered domestic Filipino workers $1.25 an hour and 10 cents a box for field packing. This amount was below $1.40, the prevailing per hour wage set for *bracero* workers by Secretary of Labor Willard Wirtz. The AWOC went on strike for the higher rate. Refused access to *bracero* labor, the growers quickly capitulated to workers' demands. When the grape harvest moved to central California, growers there offered $1.20 an hour and 15 cents a box, setting the stage for another confrontation. The AWOC leadership approached the National Farm Workers Association (NFWA), headed by César Chávez and Dolores Huerta, whose membership worked along side the Filipinos at many of the same vineyards, for their support.

More than 2,000 NFWA members enthusiastically joined over 1,000 Filipino AWOC strikers. During the early stages of the strike, it became apparent that the NFWA had stronger support and backing, and the two groups merged into the United Farm Workers Organizing Committee (UFWOC) with Chávez as the director, assisted by Itliong. Even with a stable leadership, the union faced the daunting task of challenging the overwhelming power and influence of agribusiness. Although workers eagerly took to the picket lines, it was clear a protracted strike would be insufficient to prevail against the vast resources of corporate agriculture. With the coffers of the union strained, notwithstanding substantial pledges of financial support from United Auto Workers President Walter Reuther, who visited Delano, and AFL-CIO President George Meany, Chávez and his team devised a broader plan to place the struggle before the public nationwide. The union leadership issued direct appeals to students, church groups, civil rights activists, and urban unions to support a boycott. Donations and volunteers poured in.

Initial actions focused on picketing of the San Francisco docks, where members of the International Longshoremen's and Warehousemen's union refused to load grapes. But soon the strategy evolved to the boycott of individual brands and then to the entire grape industry. By the fourth year of the strike, UFWOC boycott offices existed in over 40 major cities, and smaller communities hosted active boycott committees. Student volunteers and striking farm workers and their families staffed the operations in spaces offered by unions, churches, and other sympathetic groups. Such grassroots efforts along with marches, masses, vigils, nonviolent demonstrations, and fasts by Chávez kept the union's cause before the public, aided by favorable accounts in the mainstream, national press. Television news programs along with magazines like *Look, Saturday Evening Post,* the *New Yorker,* and *Business Week* covered the strike and boycotts. *Time* featured Chávez on its cover in 1969. Supportive politicians came to the defense of the union. Early in the strike, Senator Robert F. Kennedy, a member of the Senate Subcommittee on Migratory Labor, brought important publicity to the farm workers' cause when the committee conducted hearings in Delano.

As in the past, agribusiness mobilized their extensive resources to thwart the union's campaign. In the early stages of the dispute, growers resorted to their conventional tactics of evicting strikers from their labor camps. They used intimidation by hiring armed guards, displaying guns, covering pickets with sulphur intended for vines, and assaulting protestors. Repeating a standard practice, owners recruited strikebreakers to replace their lost workforce. Accustomed to the traditional support from local courts, growers won injunctions that limited the number of pickets. Siding with influential agribusiness, local law enforcement detained pickets, engaged in mass arrests, and overlooked grower harassment of picketers. Agribusiness also relied on the policies of the Farm Placement Bureau and the Immigration and Naturalization Service to support its position. Growers invited rival unions to organize their workers in order to forestall unionization by the UFWOC.

Despite this bitter opposition, the union persisted. The first crack in the united front of agribusiness came with Schenley Industries and its 5,000-acre wine-grape vineyard. The large company already had contracts with unions in other sectors of its business. The union focused its boycott on Schenley's other highly visible products, such as Cutty Sark. Fearful of damaging its liquor sales and its positive labor relations image, Schenely agreed to negotiate. The 1966 contract stipulated a $1.75 per hour wage. Perhaps the most telling concession was the replacement of the despised labor contractor system with the union hiring hall. Other wineries followed Schenley's lead. The UFWOC signed contracts with Almaden, Paul Masson, Gallo, Christian Brothers, and others.

However, table-grape growers, such as the DiGiorgio Corporation, held out. After succumbing to pressures to hold secret-ballot elections, the company invited the teamsters to organize its work force in order to derail the union's effort. After the UFWOC won, DiGiorgio undermined the contract through evasion, obstruction, and noncompliance. Denied a successor clause, the UFWOC lost the contract when DiGiorgio sold its holdings in 1968. Encouraged by these developments, the industry refused to bargain. California agribusiness banded together in a coalition to finance a two-million-dollar public relations campaign to protest the union, attacking it as subversive. In the face of this intransigence, the UFWOC abandoned its tactic of focusing on one company at a time in favor of an industrywide approach.

For two more years, the union pressed its case. The final breakthrough came in 1970, when the UFWOC won three-year contracts with growers first in the Coachella Valley and then in the Delano area. With these contracts, the union covered 85% of the table-grape industry. Wages ranged from $1.75–$1.80 per hour and 25 cents per box piece rate, with also a stipulation of annual raises. Strict pesticide regulations protected workers. Growers contributed to the union health plan and to a pension fund for retired and disabled workers. The union hiring hall replaced the labor contractor system, and a formal worker grievance procedure was established. Working conditions improved with such provisions as rest breaks, cool drinking water, and sanitation facilities in the fields. Although the union would face serious challenges from agribusiness in the future, the five-year struggle achieved an historic victory. The UFWOC had established it legitimacy as a union and a political force. It had also succeeded in permanently altering the traditional power relations between farm workers and agribusiness.

MARGARET ROSE

References and Further Reading:

Dunne, John Gregory. *Delano: The Story of the California Grape Strike.* New York: Farrar, Straus & Giroux, 1967.

Jenkins, J. Craig. *The Politics of Insurgency: The Farm Workers Movement in the 1960s.* New York: Columbia University Press, 1985.

Levy, Jacques. *Cesar Chavez: Autobiography of La Causa.* New York: W.W. Norton & Company, Inc, 1975.

Majka, Linda C., and Theo J. Majka. *Farm Workers, Agribusiness, and the State.* Philadelphia, PA: Temple University Press, 1982.

Nelson, Eugene. *Huelga: The First Hundred Days of the Great Delano Grape Strike.* Delano, CA: The Farm Worker Press, 1966.

Rose, Margaret. "'Woman Power Will Stop Those Grapes:' Chicana Organizers and Middle-Class Female Supporters in the Farm Workers' Grape Boycott in Philadelphia, 1969–1970." *Journal of Women's History* 7, 4 (Winter 1995): 6–36.

———. "Dolores Huerta: The United Farm Workers' Union." In *The Human Tradition in American Labor History,* edited by Eric Arnesen. Wilmington, DE: Scholarly Resources Inc, 2004.

See also **Agricultural Labor Relations Act; Chávez, César; Huerta, Dolores; United Farm Workers' Union**

DeLEON, DANIEL (DECEMBER 14, 1852–MAY 11, 1914)
Socialist Labor Party Leader

Daniel DeLeon was a well-known socialist and labor leader active in the United States. He was especially known through his association with the Socialist Labor party (SLP).

DeLeon was born on the Dutch-owned island of Curacao, which is just off the coast of Venezuela. His parents were Salomon and Sarah, who were Dutch Jews. DeLeon received his education in Europe, where he pursued the study of medicine and languages during the 1860s and early 1870s. In 1874, he immigrated to the United States, where he then took up a position as a schoolteacher in New York. He soon began studying law at Columbia University (then Columbia College). After graduating, DeLeon won two prestigious prizes for his essays *Constitutional History and Constitutional Law* and *International Law.* After a short stint practicing law in Texas, he returned to Columbia, serving the school as a lecturer on International law.

In 1882, DeLeon married Sarah Lobo before returning to New York, where he was then practicing law. In 1883, his first son, Solon, was born, with a second son born the following year.

While at Columbia, DeLeon started involving himself in reform movements. He especially took to Edward Bellamy, Henry George, and the Knights of Labor (KOL). Bellamy is best known for his utopian socialist novel, *Looking Backward,* the KOL for its stance on industrial unionism, and George for his "single-tax" platform. DeLeon would eventually join the KOL in 1888.

DeLeon was becoming active in politics as well. In the presidential election of 1884, he openly supported the candidacy of Grover Cleveland, as well as that of the United Labor party, for whom George was the New York mayoral candidate in 1886. It was through his work supporting George that DeLeon became more involved with both socialist and labor reformers. But DeLeon's growing belief in socialism would have a detrimental effect on his position at Columbia. He was denied tenure by Columbia, mostly due to his increasing socialism, and DeLeon would resign from the school.

Sarah DeLeon passed away in 1887 from an infection brought on by a premature birth, shortly followed by the death of their youngest son. In 1892, DeLeon married his second wife, Bertha Canary, whom he met in Kansas while on a speaking tour for the Socialist Labor Party (SLP). Bertha was a former teacher herself and would give birth to five children during the marriage.

In 1890, DeLeon joined the SLP, and began to serve the party as a speaker and a writer. He rose quickly in the party. In 1891, he was appointed the assistant editor of the party's English-language journal *The People*, a paper to which he would become editor in 1892 after the current editor, Lucien Sanial, resigned due to failing eyesight. DeLeon would maintain this position until his death.

DeLeon would also translate works of Karl Marx, and other radical thinkers, into English. When DeLeon first joined the SLP, it was not as cohesive a party as it could have been and was in fact criticized by Marx's partner, Frederick Engels, because of the group's ethnic composition, which was virtually all German immigrants. Through translating radical works, DeLeon helped to shape the SLP into a Marxist party. DeLeon also drew on his experiences in the KOL. It was by blending Marx with his views of the American economic system that enabled DeLeon to shape the SLP. Like many others, DeLeon felt that capitalism had outlived its usefulness. Unlike many radicals, DeLeon favored a peaceful type of revolution through electoral and parliamentary means, and educating the public on economic and political matters.

DeLeon incorporated his views several important lectures that he hoped would enlighten his audiences. The series included *Reform or Revolution* (1896), *What Means This Strike?* (1898), *The Burning Question of Trades Unionism* (1904), and *Socialist Reconstruction of Society* (1905). These lectures would later be published together under the title *Socialist Landmarks*. Other works by DeLeon also analyzed the role of Marxism to history and society. *As to Politics*, *Abolition of Poverty*, *Two Pages from Roman History*, and *Fifteen Questions about Socialism* all discussed ways in which socialism could be used to replace capitalism.

In 1895, DeLeon broke with the KOL and affiliated with a new, radical organization, the Socialist Trades and Labor Alliance (STLA), a group that achieved little by way of concrete organizational success. The STLA, with a heavily German membership, promoted not only the socialist agenda, but hoped to compete against the American Federation of Labor (AFL) in organizing workers.

While DeLeon helped to shape the SLP and spread its message of socialism, he was not without his detractors. Eugene V. Debs, the leader of the Socialist Party of America (SP), thought DeLeon was too dogmatic. In 1905, DeLeon took part in the formation of the Industrial Workers of the World (IWW) in Chicago, along with other radicals, such as Debs and Mother Jones. Three years later, however, the IWW expelled DeLeon over ideological differences.

As a way to reward DeLeon for his translating work, especially the Eugene Sue novel *Mysteries of the People*, the SLP collected just over one thousand dollars for DeLeon, and along with a half-acre of land they acquired, gave these gifts to him. Using some additional borrowed funds, DeLeon built a house and moved in his family. However, during early 1914, DeLeon grew ill and was eventually bedridden. He was admitted to Mount Sinai hospital in New York City, where he had an infection of the heart muscles. Since there were no known cures for his illness at the time, DeLeon became comatose and died on May 11, 1914.

MITCHELL NEWTON-MATZA

References and Further Reading

Kraditor, Aileen. *The Radical Persuasion*. Baton Rouge: Louisiana State University Press, 1981.
Petersen, Arnold. *Daniel DeLeon: Pioneer Socialist Editor*. New York: New York Labor News, 1966.
———. *Daniel DeLeon: From Reform to Revolution*. New York: New York Labor News, 1946.
Raiskii, Leonid. *The Struggle against Opportunism in the American Labor Movement: An Appraisal of Daniel DeLeon*. New York: New York Labor News, 1959.
Reeve, Carl. *The Life and Times of Daniel DeLeon*. New York: AIMS, 1972.
Seretan, Glen L. *Daniel DeLeon: The Odyssey of an American Marxist*. Cambridge, MA: Harvard University Press, 1979.
Stalvey, James Benjamin. *Daniel DeLeon: A Study of Marxian Orthodoxy in the United States*. Urbana: University of Illinois Press, 1946.

See also **Debs, Eugene V.; Industrial Workers of the World**

DELLUMS, C. L. (JANUARY 1900– DECEMBER 8, 1989)
Brotherhood of Sleeping Car Porters

Born in January 1900 in Corsicana, Texas, C. L. Dellums moved to Oakland, California, in 1924 with the hopes of attending law school at the University of California. Shortly after arriving, however, his life took an unexpected turn when he took a job with the Pullman Company. Working as a Pullman porter, Dellums became good friends with Morris "Dad" Moore, a cantankerous retired porter in his late seventies. Moore had become an enthusiastic follower of A. Philip Randolph after three porters invited the publisher of the black monthly magazine the *Messenger* to lead a new porters' union in 1925. Dellums was also impressed with the inchoate union's leader. Although he had been in the Bay Area only a short time, Dellums had plenty of first-hand knowledge of the long hours, low wages, and harsh working conditions that a job with the Pullman Company entailed. Willing to risk company reprisals, he joined Moore in organizing the Oakland local of the Brotherhood of Sleeping Car Porters (BSCP).

Dellums was well-suited for the task. He considered himself the son of a slave (his father was born about two months before Texas ratified the Thirteenth Amendment), had witnessed racial injustice in his native Texas, and was disturbed on discovering the extent of racial discrimination on the West Coast. Having taught school in Texas for four years, Dellums was also an effective orator. And when push came to shove, he did not hesitate to back up his words with his fists and powerful 6-foot frame.

Dellums' dynamic leadership would help make Oakland a BSCP stronghold. But the fight against Pullman, leadership came with a price. After he helped form the Oakland local of the BSCP in 1926, the Pullman Company rewarded his efforts by firing him from his job, a fate that would befall hundreds of other organizers. His short career as a porter having ended, Dellums survived with the help of donations from his fellow porters and was able to work for the union full time. In 1928, he became secretary-treasurer of the Oakland local and became president on Dad Moore's death in 1930. At the first BSCP national convention in 1929, he became one of seven vice-presidents. From his positions of leadership in the national union and the Oakland local, Dellums helped lead the fledgling union in its fight for recognition, which finally came in 1937.

As Dellums battled Pullman, he also became a leading activist in west Oakland, the city's working-class African-American community. In addition to his position within the BSCP, he was an active member of both the Alameda County National Association for the Advancement of Colored People (NAACP) and the Alameda County Central Labor Council. Through these organizations, he linked labor and civil rights organizations as he worked to improve living and working conditions for his neighbors during the

Great Depression and World War II. In the late 1930s, he spearheaded a coalition comprised of the Congress of Industrial Organizations (CIO), Labor's Non Partisan League, and the League of Women Voters in securing federal funds for the construction of low-income public housing in Oakland. At the same time, he led a campaign against the discriminatory hiring practices of the Key System, a transportation network that linked the East Bay and San Francisco. He helped bring the case before the World War II Fair Employment Practices Committee (FEPC), which ruled against the company and its union.

In the years before World War II, Dellums also sought to secure jobs for blacks through his involvement in the National Youth Administration (NYA). Dellums was instrumental in shaping NYA policy in the Bay Area and helped make it the most successful New Deal Agency in terms of supplying jobs for African-Americans in California. Dellums was one of three blacks to serve on the NYA California State Advisory Committee. He viewed this position as an opportunity to improve the state's race relations, and he used his influence to strengthen the agency within the state and to push for increased black employment in the defense industry. In 1941, Dellums joined seven other African-Americans on a newly established black statewide advisory committee, a subcommittee designed to extend the reach of the NYA to provide for more extensive job training and permanent job placement for black—and eventually other minority—youths.

In the decade following World War II, Dellums reached the height of his political influence in the East Bay and California more generally. He remained a BSCP vice-president and became chairman of the NAACP West Coast regional office on its inception in 1944. Moreover, his work with Randolph and the BSCP and his experiences in black Oakland's prewar and wartime struggles left an indelible mark on his postwar activism, which was inspired by his faith that the labor movement, civil rights movement, and Democratic party liberalism could reinforce each other to bring about positive social change. His role in forging a statewide labor-civil rights coalition was instrumental in the revitalization of California's Democratic party in the postwar period (his nephew, Ronald Dellums, would become an influential Democratic congressman).

During the 1950s, Dellums directed most of his political energy toward the creation of a state fair employment practices (FEP) law. Although the wartime federal agency turned out to be something of a paper tiger, Dellums hoped that an effective statewide commission would provide a valuable weapon in the fight against employment discrimination and in creating a stronger, more inclusive labor movement.

The movement for an FEP law was initially limited to NAACP leaders and African-American legislators Gus Hawkins and Byron Rumford. In 1952, however, Dellums and other NAACP leaders enlisted leaders of the state American Federation of Labor (AFL) and Congress of Industrial Organizations (CIO), along with a handful of civil rights organizations, into the cause. Their efforts bore fruit in 1959, when Democratic Governor Edmund "Pat" Brown signed the state FEP law. Dellums was immediately appointed to the new committee, where he would serve for the next 26 years.

All the while, Dellums continued his leadership within the BSCP. Pursuant to a pre-arranged agreement among the union's founding members as to the line of succession, Dellums replaced Randolph as the union's president when the leader left the post in 1968. By that time, Pullman porters were a dying breed, and the union's membership was in sharp decline. Its future in doubt, Dellums tried in vain to sustain the BSCP as an independent union. However, in 1978, economic realities forced the union to merge with the Brotherhood of Railway and Airline Clerks.

Dellums died of a heart attack in his West Oakland home on December 8, 1989.

JOHN J. ROSEN

References and Further Reading

Anderson, Jervis. *A. Philip Randolph: A Biographical Portrait*. Berkeley: University of California Press, 1972.
Broussard, Albert. *Black San Francisco: The Struggle for Racial Equality in the West, 1900–1954*. Kansas: University of Kansas Press, 1993.
Rhomberg, Chris. *No There There: Race, Class, and Political Community in Oakland*. Berkeley: University of California Press, 2004.
Santino, Jack. *Miles of Smiles, Years of Struggle: Stories of Black Pullman Porters*. Urbana and Chicago: University of Illinois Press, 1989 and 1991.
Self, Robert O. *American Babylon: Race and the Struggle for Postwar Oakland*. Princeton, NJ: Princeton University Press, 2003.

See also **Brotherhood of Sleeping Car Porters; Randolph, A. Philip**

DELMARVA POULTRY JUSTICE ALLIANCE

Faced with declining membership, a hostile political climate, and diminished social legitimacy, unions during the last three decades have attempted to fashion more favorable circumstances for organizing and collective bargaining by developing alliances with community groups and religious organizations. The Delmarva Poultry Justice Alliance (DPJA) is an important example of these phenomena. As an innovative labor-community coalition seeking to influence the corporate behavior of the poultry industry, it has won widespread attention for its efforts on behalf of growers who raise chickens, the workers who prepare them for consumption, and the communities where poultry facilities are located.

The Delmarva peninsula encompasses the state of Delaware and the 11 eastern shore counties of Maryland and Virginia, and some of the country's largest and most powerful poultry producers, most notably Perdue Farms and Tyson Foods, have a substantial presence there. The Delmarva poultry industry has been highly resistant to union penetration, with less than 20% of its workers under union contracts. The industry's competitive need to promote cost cutting and efficiency has resulted in low wages and onerous working conditions for most poultry workers, near poverty-level wages for the growers who raise chickens for the large processors, and charges of environmental damage caused by careless disposal of the waste generated in chicken processing.

The DPJA was launched in 1995 by the Reverend Jim Lewis, an Episcopal priest with a background in social activism. Lewis carefully assembled various constituencies affected by the poultry industry—growers, catchers, processors, environmentalists, civil rights activists, church people—and after a two-year dialogue, participants agreed in 1997 to form an organization, the DPJA. The parties agreed that the new organization would be rooted in a specific set of ethical commitments: protecting the environment; producing safe, healthy food; and promoting fair treatment for workers and growers. With these commitments in mind, the DPJA sought to draw attention to the labor and environmental practices of the industry and create a grassroots movement that would press for more responsible corporate behavior.

Already a member of the DPJA, the United Food and Commercial Workers' Union (UFCW) became more deeply involved in the alliance after a wildcat strike at a processing plant following the dismissal of a union member who was an undocumented worker. Prodded by other members of the alliance and realizing that it had not been fully responsive to the needs of its immigrant members, the union began a concerted program to reach out to its mostly Latino membership. This effort led to closer collaboration with DPJA in some significant initiatives that directly challenged the power and authority of the Delmarva poultry industry and gained national attention.

One of the alliance's most notable achievements has been its work assisting the UFCW in organizing chicken catchers, a group of mostly African-American men who capture broilers and load them for transportation to processing plants. Perdue Farms had declared its catchers "independent contractors" in order to avoid paying them benefits and overtime. Along with the UFCW, DPJA pressed the Clinton administration to launch what became known as its "poultry initiative" to investigate wage and hour violations in the industry. Subsequently, the alliance supported a successful lawsuit against Perdue charging violations of the Fair Labor Standards Act (FLSA) and state wage and hour laws. The alliance also provided critical support for the UFCW's successful organizing campaigns among catchers at several Delmarva facilities. These victories in 2000 and 2001 marked the first time in Perdue's history that unions had won National Labor Relations Board (NLRB)-sponsored representation elections. As was the case with the lawsuit against Perdue, DPJA and the UFCW had demonstrated that it was possible for poultry workers to take on the industry successfully through a combination of grassroots mobilization, government intervention, and the glare of media attention.

The future potential of labor-community alliances will hinge on their ability to develop stronger grassroots involvement among their constituents, offer a compelling vision of what constitutes the good of the community, and gain sufficient power to bargain on their agendas. The brief but compelling experience of the DPJA suggests that well-conceived labor-community partnerships offer the union movement a powerful opportunity to reclaim its moral authority as a respected advocate for the public good.

ROBERT BUSSEL

References and Further Reading

Bussel, Robert. "Taking on 'Big Chicken': The Delmarva Poultry Justice Alliance." *Labor Studies Journal* 28, 2 (Summer 2003): 1–24.

Craft, James A. "The Community as a Source of Union Power." *Journal of Labor Research* 11, 2 (Spring 1990): 145–160.

Griffith, David. "Hay Trabajo: Poultry Processing, Rural Industrialization, and the Latinization of Low-Wage Labor." In *Any Way You Cut It: Meat Processing and Small-Town America*, edited by Donald D. Stull, Michael J. Broadway, and David Griffith. Lawrence, KS: University Press of Kansas, 1995.

Horowitz, Roger, and Mark J. Miller. "Immigrants in the Delmarva Poultry Processing Industry: The Changing Face of Georgetown, Delaware and Environs." *JSRI Occasional Paper No. 37.* East Lansing, MI: The Julian Samora Research Institute, Michigan State University, 1999.

Voices and Choices: A Pastoral Message on Justice in the Workplace from the Catholic Bishops of the South. Cincinnati, OH: St. Anthony Messenger Press, 2000.

DEPARTMENT OF LABOR

The establishment of a cabinet-level Department of Labor in 1913 was the culmination of a 50-year effort by organized labor to establish an official working-class presence in the federal government. Public Law 426-62: An Act to create a Department of Labor, states, "The purpose of the Department of Labor shall be to foster, promote, and develop the welfare of the wage earners of the United States, to improve their working conditions, and to advance their opportunities for profitable employment." Over the next 90 years, the department, rather than serving as a working-class presence in the president's cabinet, developed into a bureaucracy regulating the bounds of American labor relations.

As originally established, the Department of Labor consisted of four bureaus: the Bureau of Immigration, the Bureau of Naturalization, the Children's Bureau, and the Bureau of Labor Statistics. President Woodrow Wilson appointed William B. Wilson as the first secretary of the Department of Labor. One portion of the act creating the Department of Labor stated "That the Secretary of Labor shall have power to act as mediator and to appoint commissioners of conciliation in labor disputes whenever in his judgment the interests of industrial peace may require it to be done...." The U.S. entry into World War I on April 6, 1917, coincided with an unprecedented strike wave within the United. States. The mounting pressure of disputes during the war transformed Secretary Wilson's *ad hoc* conciliation efforts into the formal creation of the United States Conciliation Service in 1917.

Other agencies were also created to meet the exigencies of war labor problems. In an attempt to rationalize the government's labor relations machinery, President Woodrow Wilson issued an executive order creating the War Labor Administration (WLA), to be directed by Labor Secretary William Wilson.

The creation of the National War Labor Board (NWLB), which served as a "supreme court" for labor relations during World War I, was a key development within the WLA. The NWLB transformed American labor management relations from a private one to a semiprivate one, setting a powerful historical precedent. For while the board outlawed strikes and lockouts for the duration of the war, at the same time it recognized the right of workers to organize and the principle of the 8-hour day, and promulgated the idea that workers were entitled to a living wage. From 1917–1919, union membership grew from around 3 million members to 5 million members. The NWLB set precedent in other ways, however, in that it established a center of government regulation of collective bargaining outside the Department of Labor.

The elections of 1918, a Republican party landslide, presaged a return to the normalcy of the 1920s. Labor began to lose power as the U.S. demobilized after the armistice ending World War I in November 1918, and during the next few years, the labor machinery set up by the government during World War I was dismantled. By the end of 1919, the NWLB was no longer in existence. Funds for the United States Employment Service (USES), which helped place 5 million workers during World War I, were slashed, and the number of cases handled by the United States Conciliation Service dropped from the 1,780 handled in 1919 to 370 in 1922.

The primary concern of the new secretary of labor, John J. Davis, was immigration control. In 1921 and 1924, the Congress passed, and Presidents Coolidge and Harding signed, laws restricting immigration. More than 800,000 immigrants came to the United States in the fiscal year ending June 30, 1921. The new immigration laws reduced the number of immigrants legally admitted to the United States from areas other than Mexico and British North America to 354,000 under the 1921 law, and to 164,000 under the 1924 law. Seventy-five percent of the Department of Labor's personnel were dedicated to the enforcement of immigration law. Although the Bureau of Labor Statistics, Conciliation Service, and USES continued to operate, Secretary of Labor Davis did not play a major role in the cabinet, as reflected by a letter Davis wrote to President Coolidge in 1924, in which he stated, "Being at the tail end of the Cabinet, after all the others have taken up their questions with you, I somehow feel that I ought not to take up more of your time."

The Great Depression, which began in 1929 and was a phenomenon of unprecedented magnitude, ended Republican dominance of American politics. Twenty-five to thirty-five of the workforce was out of work. By March 1933, payrolls had nosedived to about one-third of what they had been in 1926. In an effort to protect wage levels from collapse, President Hoover's secretary of labor, William N. Doak, and newly elected Pennsylvania Senator and former Labor Secretary James J. Davis worked together to pass the Davis-Bacon Act of 1931, which established the requirement for paying "prevailing wages" on public works projects.

Franklin D. Roosevelt was elected president in 1932, and he appointed Frances Perkins secretary of labor in March 1933. Perkins was trained as a social worker, and she had worked in settlement houses such as Hull-House. She held many important state labor-related jobs under New York Governors Franklin Roosevelt and Al Smith. Secretary Perkins' background greatly effected her administration of the Department of Labor and would set the course for the future development of the department. Against a background of labor strife, Perkins' style of leadership was seen by labor leaders (and some labor historians) as ineffectual. While holding a strong belief in the right of unions to organize, Perkins saw collective bargaining as a way to raise conditions of employment above minimum, government-imposed standards of employment.

Thus, while Secretary Perkins was not a primary mover behind the establishment of the National Labor Relations Board established by the Wagner Act, or the National War Labor Board of World War II, she was a leader in the passage of the Wagner-Peyser Act of 1933, which re-invigorated the USES as an employment agency; the Social Security Act in 1935, which established a pension system for all American workers; and the Fair Labor Standards Act of 1938, which established a federal minimum wage. In addition, the establishment of the Division of Labor Standards in 1934 as a service agency to promote, through voluntary means, improved conditions of work, was reflective of Secretary Perkins' approach to labor problems and reflects to some degree the approach of the department today.

It was World War II that effectively ended the Depression in the early 1940s. Perkins remained secretary of labor until June 30, 1945, resigning after 12 years, the longest period of service for any labor secretary. During World War II, however, the department was eclipsed by other federal wartime labor agencies, such as the War Manpower Commission and the second National War Labor Board. In addition, the Immigration and Naturalization Service, the largest component of the Labor Department, was transferred to the Department of Justice in 1940.

After the death of President Roosevelt, Vice-President Harry S. Truman succeeded to the presidency and appointed former Senator Lewis B. Schwellenbach of Washington State as secretary of labor. Secretary Schwellenbach faced several tough issues on his assumption of office on July 1, 1945. In part due to postwar "strike weariness," Republicans again gained control of the Congress in 1946. In 1947, Congress passed the Taft Hartley Act over President Truman's veto. The act included provisions for cooling-off periods and outlawed the closed shop. Perhaps most important to the Department of Labor, Taft-Hartley removed the U.S. Conciliation Service from the department and made the new Federal Mediation and Conciliation Service an independent agency. Congressional appropriations for the Department of Labor were cut dramatically.

President Truman appointed Maurice Tobin as secretary of labor after Secretary Schwellenbach's death in June 1948. Tobin was made responsible for wartime labor supply after the eruption of the Korean War in 1950 and created the Defense Manpower Administration. As a result of the department's new responsibilities, much of the funding taken away from the Department of Labor was restored. In addition, reflecting continuing U.S. interests in foreign affairs after World War II, Tobin continued the build the department's international responsibilities begun by Schwellenbach, including active participation in the International Labor Organization.

Labor historians often refer to gradual establishment of postwar corporate consensus or corporate liberalism in the late 1940s and early 1950s. Based somewhat on the ideas of economist John Maynard Keynes, corporate liberalism was a system where employers and labor leaders increasingly shared the same goals, building a kind of day-to-day cooperation between company and union, guaranteeing economic stability, and protecting the rights of workers through nondisruptive collective action. Wages and benefits, rather than social reform, became the chief concern, of unions.

President Dwight David Eisenhower, elected president in 1952, appointed Martin P. Durkin, a former steamfitters apprentice and a leader in the plumbers' union, as secretary of labor in January 1953, but a failure to amend the Taft-Hartley Act and Durkin's feeling of isolation within Eisenhower's cabinet led to his resignation in September 1953. Eisenhower then appointed James P. Mitchell as labor secretary in October 1953.

Secretary Mitchell, a former labor relations executive in the retail industry and a manpower expert for the Department of Army during World War II, was the first of three secretaries of labor who would establish the modern department's identity. By establishing Department of Labor hegemony over most Eisenhower administration functions relating to labor, increasing the level of professionalism within the agency, and effectively setting up the administration of the Landrum-Management Reporting and Disclosure Act (LMRDA) of 1959 (better known as the Landrum-Griffin), which subjected the internal affairs of unions to detailed government regulation, Secretary Mitchell firmly established the Department of Labor within the new "corporate consensus." In addition, known as the "social conscious" of the Eisenhower administration, Mitchell brought official attention, if not effective action, to the fight against employment discrimination and the plight of migrant workers.

On December 15, 1960, shortly after he had been elected president, John F. Kennedy nominated Arthur J. Goldberg to be secretary of labor. Goldberg had a long career in organized labor, formerly serving as general counsel for the American Federation of Labor (AFL)–Congress of Industrial Organizations (CIO). Among Goldberg's accomplishments during his brief tenure was convincing President Kennedy to appoint a presidential committee on equal employment opportunity and increasing the number of minority employees to 30% of the department's workforce. A proponent of mediation and conciliation, Goldberg helped settle a major steel strike in 1961, as well as a strike of the Metropolitan Opera Company. Looking back on his tenure just more than 25 years later, Goldberg claimed that more labor legislation was enacted from 1961–1962 than was previously enacted under any other secretary of labor. Among these legislative successes was the enactment of the Manpower Development and Training Act (MDTA) of 1962. From 1962–1972, 2 million individuals were enrolled in MDTA programs.

In August 1962, President Kennedy appointed Secretary Goldberg to the United States Supreme Court and replaced him in September with Willard Wirtz, Goldberg's undersecretary of labor. Wirtz, a former Northwestern University law professor who had served on the World War II Wage Stabilization board and who later had been recognized as a leading labor arbitrator, served both President Kennedy and President Lyndon B. Johnson until January 1969.

Wirtz led the department during a period of unprecedented federal government activism not seen since the 1930s. The Economic Opportunity Act of 1964 (EOA) was the centerpiece of the War on Poverty, which in turn was a major thrust of the Great Society legislative agenda of the Johnson administration. The EOA was passed in August 1964, and established the Office of Economic Opportunity, directed by Sargent Shriver, who served until 1969.

Although the new EOA programs were established outside Department of Labor, Wirtz believed that the department provided "a regiment for the war on poverty." Internally, Wirtz led the Department of Labor as it coordinated the department's burgeoning training and education programs, establishing for instance the Manpower Administration (MA) in February 1963. The MA included not only the Bureau of Employment Security and the Bureau of Apprenticeship and Training, but also the recently established Office of Manpower, Automation, and Training (OMAT). During the Nixon administration, EOA was dismantled, and the MA absorbed the most important of the defunct agency's jobs programs—the Neighborhood Youth Corps and Job Corps. In addition, following passage of the Civil Rights Act of 1964, an Office of Federal Contract Compliance was established to see that contractors were not discriminating against their employees.

In 1968, disagreements with President Johnson over a proposed reorganization of the Department of Labor and with the administration's Vietnam policy nearly led to Wirtz's resignation, but he ultimately served out his term. He was the last of three secretaries of labor who served a total of 16 years, providing the department with a much-needed opportunity to consolidate and strengthen its bureaucratic structure. During the next 16 years, there were to be nine labor secretaries.

After Richard Nixon was elected president, he selected George P. Shultz, dean of the Graduate School of Business at the University of Chicago, as his first secretary of labor in January 1969. An important economic adviser to the president, Schultz helped draft plans for many of the Nixon administration's domestic programs, including federal revenue sharing.

Internally, Secretary Schultz sought to organize a comprehensive manpower system within the department as it absorbed such EOA programs as the Job Corps and the Neighborhood Youth Corps. His tenure as labor secretary is perhaps best known, however, for his support of the Philadelphia plan, an attempt to end job discrimination in the construction industry by establishing goals for black employment on federal construction projects. Developed over many years within the Department of Labor, the plan required Philadelphia construction companies with federal contracts to hire minority workers. The Philadelphia plan was bitterly resented, however, by craft unions within the AFL-CIO. The Philadelphia plan, established in other areas of the country, morphed into Hometown plans, agreements among local contractors, unions, community-based organizations, and contracting agencies to work together to identify minority and female workers, prepare them for employment, and assist in their placement in jobs available in the federal contractor workforce.

Secretary Schultz was appointed as director of the new Office of Management and Budget (OMB) in June 1970, and Under Secretary James D. Hodgson was named by President Nixon as his replacement on July 2, 1970. Hodgson had previously served as vice-president for industrial relations at Lockheed Corporation. Hodgson's proudest accomplishment as secretary was the passage of the Occupational Safety and Health Administration (OSHA) Act of 1970, setting standards of on-the-job safety and health for 60 million workers. An outgrowth of many years of gradually increasing state and federal regulation of workplace safety regulations, the bill greatly expanded the department's regulatory activities. No longer simply a voluntary organization, as was the Department of Labor Standards, OSHA federal inspectors found violations in 80% of the 9,300 workplaces inspected during the first 6 months of operation after the law went into effect.

During Hodgson's tenure, unemployment increased from 4.7% to about 6% in 1972. During this period of recession, the Department of Labor administered the first new public employment program since the 1930s under the Emergency Employment Act of 1971, which provided 170,000 public-service jobs. As a public spokesperson for an administration not popular with a union constituency, however, Hodgson was subject to considerable attack, especially by AFL-CIO President George Meany. Shortly after President Nixon's reelection, Hodgson resigned.

He was replaced by Peter J. Brennan, a lifelong Democrat who began his career as a painter, and eventually became president of the New York State Building and Construction Trades Council. Brennan, brought to Nixon's attention by his support of the president's Vietnam policies, became secretary on January 31, 1973. During his tenure, the Comprehensive Employment and Training Act (CETA) passed in 1973. CETA used "revenue sharing" to transfer funding decision-making authority for vocational-training programs (including stipends for trainees) as well as for public-service employment to local government. Also passed during Brennan's term of office was the Employee Retirement Income Security Act (ERISA) of 1974, which gave the department a major role in the regulation of pension or welfare benefit plans for their employees. In addition to reporting requirements on the fiduciaries, certain employers and plan administrators fund an insurance system to protect some benefits, with premiums paid to the Pension Benefit Guaranty Corporation (PBGC).

Brennan served under President Nixon and later Ford after Nixon's resignation. Brennan resigned in February 1975, and was replaced by John T. Dunlop. An economics professor at Harvard University, Dunlop had worked for the Bureau of Labor Statistics under Frances Parkman and had known each secretary of labor since Parkman. He also served as director of the Cost of Living Council, which administered price and wage controls implemented in 1971.

Secretary Dunlop believed in a strong collective-bargaining system, informal mediation, and cooperative problem solving. He was concerned with the growth of the number of regulatory programs administered by the Labor Department, which had grown from 40 in 1960, to 134 in 1975, and was also concerned about limitations on bringing about social change through legal compulsion.

Developing labor standards under Section 13 of the Urban Mass Transportation Act, Dunlop advocated "negotiated rulemaking," convening labor and management representatives to seek agreement on standards to be issued into the Federal Register for comments and subsequent issuance. Negotiated rulemaking has grown as a form of establishing federal regulations and is extensively used by the Environmental Protection Agency and other federal agencies.

Dunlop resigned from his position as secretary of labor in January 1976 over President Ford's veto of the Common Situs Picketing bill that would have allowed a striking union to picket all contractors at a construction site. Dunlop had worked to pass a bill he believed acceptable, and Ford's veto, Dunlop believed, was a fatal blow to his credibility as secretary of the Department of Labor.

Ford replaced Dunlop with William J. Usery. Jr., in February 1976. Active in the International Association of Machinists, Secretary Usery served as assistant secretary of labor for labor-management relations from 1969–1973, and in February 1973, was named director of the Federal Mediation and Conciliation Service, eventually replacing Dunlop after his resignation. During his short tenure as secretary, Usery helped to bring about resolutions to a long-running rubber industry strike and a potentially crippling truck strike. After his election to the presidency in 1976, Jimmy Carter appointed Ray Marshall as secretary of labor in January 1977. Marshall had taught at the University of Texas for many years and published many books and scholarly articles on race and labor.

Secretary Marshall cited several accomplishments that he was particularly proud of during his term in the White House. During his tenure, the Federal Mine Safety and Health Act was passed in 1977, and Marshall set up the Mine Safety and Health Administration to administer the act. He sought to strengthen OSHA, placing it under the leader ship of Dr. Eula Bingham, who worked to simplify OSHA regulations and concentrate on problems known to exist in the workplace. Under his stewardship, the budget of Comprehensive Employment and Training Administration (CETA) was increased to $8 billion, and the number of public-service jobs increased from 310,000 in 1976, to a peak of 725,000 in 1978.

Primarily due to a lethal combination of "stagflation" and a perceived ineptness in foreign policy exacerbated by the Iranian hostage crisis, President Carter was not re-elected for a second term. Ronald Reagan became president in January 1981, and appointed Raymond J. Donovan, a vice-president in charge of labor relations for the Schiavone Construction Company. Donovan sought to support the Reagan administration's goal of bringing regulatory relief to American business.

Discretionary spending in the Department of Labor was slashed by 60%, and department, employment fell 21%. Within the department, the new OSHA administration adopted a regulatory approach that emphasized voluntary compliance. The CETA funding was cut from $8 billion to $3.7 billion, largely through the elimination of public-service jobs. In 1982, Congress replaced CETA, which was expiring, with the Job Training Partnership Act (JTPA). The new law gave the states more control over how they distributed vocational-training funds and ended federal funding for public-service employment programs. In March 1985, Secretary Donovan, under indictment on charges of grand larceny in connection with the building of a New York City subway project, resigned.

Over the next 20 years, seven individuals, five of whom were women, would serve as secretary of labor. Under those secretaries, major emphasis was placed on managerial efficiency of the Department of Labor's bureaucratic structure, an emphasis on less rigorous enforcement on departmental regulations, and job training.

Secretary Donovan was replaced by William Emerson Brock, who became secretary of labor in April 1985. Brock, a former Tennessee senator, worked to increase the efficiency of the Department of Labor. Under Brock, OSHA explored mediated rule making, instituted a Secretary's Management System to track and assure the meeting of departmental goals, and initiated a Workforce in the Year 2000 project to make plans to meet future skilled labor needs. Secretary Block left office in October 1987, and was replaced by Ann Dore McLaughlin, formerly assistant secretary of the treasury and under secretary of the interior. Serving in the final two years of the Reagan administration, Secretary McLaughlin stressed economic growth as a job-creating mechanism and advocated nongovernmental action to help resolve the dueling demands of family and work life.

In January 1989, President George Bush appointed Elizabeth Hanford Dole to be labor secretary. Secretary Dole had a long career of government service, including a stint as secretary of transportation under President Reagan. Under her leadership, the Department of Labor instituted a Glass Ceiling initiative to reduce barriers for women and minorities in corporations. In addition, the minimum wage was raised but was accompanied by an amendment to the Fair Labor Standards Act (FLSA), which provided for a special subminimum youth-training wage, much opposed by organized labor.

After serving as secretary for not quite 2 years, Dole resigned to become president of the American

Red Cross. President Bush then appointed Lynn Morley Martin to be secretary in February 1991. Secretary Martin, a former high school economics teacher who later served 11 years in the U.S. House of Representatives, continued much of the work begun by Dole, formally establishing a Glass Ceiling Commission and developing programs to improve the delivery of employment programs.

Robert B. Reich was appointed secretary of labor by President Clinton in January 1993. Secretary Reich, formerly a professor at Harvard University, had served with the policy-planning staff of the Federal Trade Commission and as an assistant to the solicitor general in the Ford administration. An enthusiastic advocate for labor in the cabinet, Reich focused on developing skills-building programs to assist American workers. For instance, the School to Work Opportunity Act of 1994 sought to expand apprenticeship programs and employer internships, integrating academic study with work world experiences. He also was instrumental in passing the Family Leave Act, which allowed workers leave from work due to the birth or adoption of a child or to take care of an ill family member.

At the same time, however, Reich oversaw the streamlining of the Department of Labor, during which the Department of Labor staff was reduced by 1,000 employees. The political goal of balancing the budget outweighed Reich's other interests, such as addressing the growing gap between rich and poor. Secretary Reich resigned after President Clinton's re-election and was replaced by Alexis Margaret Herman in April 1997. Secretary Herman served previously as director of the Women's Bureau. Herman continued to administer the skills-building program of Reich, as well as orienting the department to implement the Personal Responsibility and Work Opportunity Reconciliation Act of 1996, which increased the emphasis on the need to move welfare recipients from welfare to work.

After his election in 2000, President George W. Bush appointed Elaine L. Chao as secretary of labor in January 2001. Prior to her appointment, Chao served as director of the Peace Corps and deputy secretary at the U.S. Department of Transportation, as well as a fellow at the Heritage Foundation, a conservative think tank. Under Chao, the department updated the white-collar exemption of the Fair Labors Standard Act, an update that was in general opposed by organized labor, and the 2002 discretionary budget of the department was cut by 9%. Secretary Chao also oversees the Department Center for Faith-Based and Community Initiatives. As of November 2005, Secretary Chao has been the longest serving secretary of labor since Secretary Wirtz left office in January 1969.

The U.S. Department of Labor FY 2003–2008 Strategic Plan September 2003 states, "The Department of Labor promotes the welfare of job seekers, wage earners, and retirees of the United States by improving working conditions, expanding opportunities for training and profitable employment, protecting retirement and health care benefits, helping employers find workers, strengthening free collective bargaining, and tracking changes in employment, prices, and other national economic measurements." The specificity of the department's mission statement reflects the development over 90-plus years of government bureaucratic regulation of American labor. It reflects a department that is perhaps far less representative, and far more regulative, of American labor than the original advocates of a Department of Labor envisioned.

JAMES G. CASSEDY

References and Further Readings

Bernstein, Irving. *The Lean Years: A History of the American Worker, 1920–1933.* Boston: Houghton Mifflin Company, 1960.

Brennan, Peter J. "A Benchmark of Progress: 1973–75." *Monthly Labor Review.* 111, 5 (February 1988): 44–45.

Brock, William E. "Workforce 2000 Agenda Recognizes Lifelong Need to Improve Skills." *Monthly Labor Review.* 111, 5 (February 1988): 54–56.

Dubofsky, Melvin. *The State and Labor in Modern America.* Chapel Hill: The University of North Carolina Press, 1994.

Dunlop, John T. "Some Reflections of a Brief Tenure." *Monthly Labor Review* 111, 5 (February 1988): 46–49.

Fink, Gary M. "F. Ray Marshall: Secretary of Labor and Jimmy Carter's Ambassador to Organized Labor." *Labor History* 37 4 (Fall 1996): 463–479.

Goldberg, Arthur J. "Labor-Management Relations: A High Priority, 1961–1962." *Monthly Labor Review* 111, 5 (February 1988): 38–39.

Grossman, Jonathan. *The Department of Labor.* Washington, DC: Praeger Publishers, 1973.

Guzda, Henry P. "James P. Mitchell: Social Conscience of the Cabinet." *Monthly Labor Review* 114, 8 (August 1991): 23–29.

Hodson, James P. "Enactment of OSHA Required Ingenious Compromises and Strategies." *Monthly Labor Review* 111,. 5 (February 1988): 41–43.

McCartin, Joseph A. *Labors Great War: The Struggle for Industrial Democracy and the Origins of Modern American Labor Relations, 1912–1921.* Chapel Hill: The University of North Carolina Press, 1997.

MacLaury, Judson. "A Brief History: The U.S. Department of Labor." http://dol.gov/asp/programs/history/hs75menu.htm.

Marshall, Ray. "Establishing an Agenda for the Department of Labor." *Monthly Labor Review* 111, 5 (February 1988): 52–54.

Records of the United States Department of Labor (Record Group 174) are to be found at the National Archives and Records Administration (NARA), College Park,

Maryland. Other related records found at NARA include the records of the National Labor Relations Board (Record Group 25), Records of the Women's Bureau (Record Group 86), Records of the Occupational Safety and Health Administration (Record Group 100), Records of the Children's Bureau (Record Group 102), Records of the Federal mediation and Conciliation Service (Record Group 280) and many others.

Reich, Robert B. *Locked in the Cabinet.* New York: Alfred A. Knopf, 1997.

Renshaw, Patrick. *American Labor and Consensus Capitalism, 1935–1990.* Jackson: University Press of Mississippi, 1991.

Rourke, Francis E. "The Department of Labor and Trade Unions." *The Western Political Quarterly* 7, 4 (December 1954): 656–672.

U.S. Department of Labor. History at the Department of Labor. http://dol.gov/asp/programs/history/.

Usery, W. J., Jr. "Government's Role in Promoting Labor-Management Cooperation." *Monthly Labor Review* 111,. 5 (February 1988): 49–51.

Wandersee, Winifred D. "I'd Rather Pass a Law Than Organize a Union: Frances Perkins and the Reformist Approach to Organized Labor." *Labor History* 34, 1 (Winter 1993): 5–32.

Wirtz, Willard. "Humanitarian Initiatives During the 1960s." *Monthly Labor Review* 111, 5 (February 1988): 39–41.

Zieger, Robert H. *The CIO, 1935–1955.* Chapel Hill: The University of North Carolina Press, 1995.

DILLINGHAM COMMISSION

In the 400 years since Europeans began a campaign to colonize North America, the labor of migrant peoples has propelled the phenomenal economic growth of these two continents. For the majority of our history as a nation, immigration to the United States remained almost wholly unrestricted; the first official ban on any immigrant group came in 1882, in the form of the Chinese Exclusion Act. However over the following four decades, Congress repeatedly sought to keep out undesirable groups. Gathering support among many Americans, and the American Federation of Labor (AFL), restrictionism reached its zenith in 1921 and 1924 with the passage of the Quota Act and its follow-up, the Immigration Restriction (or Johnson-Reid) Act. These laws created, and later tightened, a system of quotas based on national origins. The Johnson-Reid Act designed these annual immigration quotas to reduce dramatically the volume of fearsome "new immigrants" (from southern and eastern Europe) in favor of old-stock immigrants whose homelands included Great Britain, Germany, and Scandinavia. Before Congress agreed to recast so dramatically this country's immigration policy, members investigated the immigration problem through the work of the Dillingham Commission.

What happened in the early part of the twentieth century to shift the mood of the country in favor of immigration restriction? By the early 1910s, the American melting pot—revered for its ability to absorb and recast ethnic identity—had received a noticeably different infusion into its native cultural stock. A profound shift in immigration patterns had occurred in the late nineteenth and early twentieth centuries as southern and eastern Europe now provided the majority of immigrants to the United States, where northern and western Europe had previously. Concern over these unmeltable ethnics mounted in an intellectual climate dominated by a rigid biological understanding of race. Additional pressure came from organized labor as skilled workers rallied against the downward force that they felt immigrant low-wage workers were exerting on wages and working standards. The bulging industrial cities of the turn of the last century attracted millions of migrants annually, many of whom relied on informal informational networks and returning migrants to decide where to live and work in the United States. By the early twentieth century, industrial unionism had built a presence in urban factories; as waves of mostly poor peasants from Europe continued to land on U.S. shores. Native-born people in the trade union movement (including pioneer labor historian John R. Commons) worried about the effect that a constant supply of cheap labor would have on the skilled workingman.

At this time, both public pressure and private concern motivated legislators to act purposefully to shape the movement of people to the United States. The first attempt at restriction of European immigration came in 1907, in the form of a mandatory literacy test (the favored provision of Senator Henry Cabot Lodge's Immigration Restriction League), the successful completion of which was necessary for admittance. That year the literacy test failed to pass into law, and President Theodore Roosevelt responded by appointing a commission of legislators, academics, and private citizens to investigate the condition of immigrants and suggest further governmental action. Named in honor of its chairman, Senator William P. Dillingham of Vermont, the Dillingham Commission's mandate charged it to "make full inquiry, examination, and investigation, by subcommittee or otherwise, into the subject of immigration." In the heightened climate of controversy that gave rise to its existence, the commission conducted its work in private and did not hold any public hearings nor publish its data for almost four years.

Despite its public silence, the Dillingham Commission was diligent in its investigation and finally produced a response by 1911: forty-one volumes of reports, statistics, recommendations, and assessments on the subject of immigration and its relationship to American economy and society. Almost three-quarters of the report focused exclusively on the role of immigrants in American industry. Other volumes covered a variety of topics; four books examined immigrant charitable institutions and the employment, intelligence, and physical characteristics of the native-born children of immigrants, as well as the propensity of immigrant women to reproduce. Members of the Dillingham Commission were also interested in the history of federal and state legislation pertaining to immigration. Throughout the report, the various authors compiled a mountain of statistics in order to compare how immigrants lived and worked across generations and in other parts of the world. As documents created in response to a specific socio-economic question, that of the impact of immigrants on U.S. culture and the economy, the prodigious output of the commission is a valuable tool to study immigrant workers at a time when over 20% of the U.S. population was foreign-born.

Many immigration historians have placed the Dillingham Commission at the beginning of the formal legislative road to immigration restriction, which was fully achieved in 1924. According to this interpretation, the Dillingham Commission Report provided a scientific argument for immigration restriction. But while the congressional members of the Dillingham Commission looked at immigration as "primarily an economic problem," the hundreds of field researchers and mostly nameless authors (the notable exceptions being economists Jett Lauck and Jeremiah Jenks, and the father of modern anthropology, Franz Boas) who compiled the report's other 40 volumes offered few opinions. Ultimately, Senator Dillingham's summary (Volume 1, *Abstracts of Reports*) manipulated and largely ignored the findings of the other 40 volumes in order to argue the need for immigration restriction. Viewed in its entirety, the material collected by the Dillingham Commission describes very specifically how immigrants lived and worked across the United States during a decade when over 8.8 million immigrants entered the United States (a volume not surpassed until the 1990s).

Immigration to the United States from Europe decreased dramatically after 1924; whether this was the result of the Johnson-Reid Act or a byproduct of shifting labor markets and migration streams in post-World War I Europe is debatable. Either way, immigration restrictionists declared the quota system a success, and industrial unionism continued to gain clout among Americanized workers. Ironically, the state likely played a minor role in determining migration patterns, since economic forces exerted greater control. Thus, the significance of the Dillingham Commission in labor history rests on the depth and breadth of its monumental study, which helps to document the historically changing role that immigrants and their children played in the twentieth-century workplace.

LAUREN H. BRAUN

References and Further Reading

Commons, John R. *Races and Immigrants in America*. New York: Macmillan, 1920.

Higham, John. *Strangers in the Land: Patterns of American Nativism 1860–1925*. 2nd ed. New Brunswick, NJ: Rutgers Univ. Press, 1988.

Lee, Erika. *At America's Gates: Chinese Immigration during the Exclusion Era, 1882–1943*. Chapel Hill, NC: Univ. North Carolina Press, 2003.

Tichenor, Daniel J. *Dividing Lines: The Politics of Immigration Control in America* Princeton, NJ and Oxford, UK: Princeton Univ. Press, 2002.

Thistlethwaite, Frank. "Migration from Europe Overseas in the Nineteenth and Twentieth Centuries." In *A Century of European Migrations, 1830–1930*, Edited by Rudolph J. Vecoli and Suzanne Sinke. Urbana: Univ. of Illinois Press, 1991. (reprint).

United States Immigration Commission. *Reports of the Immigration Commission*. 41 vols. Washington, DC: U.S. Government Printing Office, 1911. New York: Arno Press, 1970. (reprint).

See also **American Federation of Labor; Commons, John Rogers**

DIRECTORS GUILD OF AMERICA

Directors formed what is now called the Directors Guild of America (DGA) at the beginning of 1935, two years after writers and actors had unionized. Unlike writers and actors, the directors chose not to affiliate with any national labor organization, preferring to keep their independence. From the beginning, they established a tradition of strong member control for the group: None of the elected officers is paid, and the executive director serves at the pleasure of the all-volunteer governing board.

Before applying for recognition to the National Labor Relations Board in 1938, the directors reached out to include assistant directors in their group. Nonetheless, in the early years the DGA was sometimes characterized as a gentleman's club made up of rich men. Such a portrait of directors as a group of highly privileged individuals however was somewhat misleading, for the livelihood of many of them was hardly secure. In 1930, about half were unemployed.

This least unionlike of unions has amassed an enviable record of achievements over the years.

These include such traditional union issues as minimum salaries, improved working conditions, residuals (a form of royalty payments), and health and retirement benefits. The guild's only strike, a very brief one in 1987, was over residuals. Under President Robert Aldrich in the early 1970s, the guild vastly expanded its staff so that it could effectively manage its ambitious programs, collecting residuals from the studios and producers on behalf of its members and administering its health and pension plans with monies from members' dues and studio contributions. By 1996, when membership had reached 10,000, annual residual payments handled by the guild had grown to over $100 million, while pension and health plan assets topped $1 billion.

As successful as the DGA has been in negotiating these bread-and-butter labor issues, however, they have not been the organization's primary concern. Instead, the group has followed a policy of yoking such issues to a visionary creative-rights agenda. The DGA's creative-rights agenda was largely developed by Frank Capra, one of the shaping forces in the guild's formation. Capra continued to assert a powerful influence over the organization's creative rights policy until the 1960s, occupying a variety of positions, both official and unofficial, over the years. Under Capra's leadership, guild members won the right to adequate time for preparation and rehearsal before the actual shooting of a film begins and the right to supervise directors' cuts on the productions they helm. Beginning in 1986, the DGA also spearheaded the drive to halt the colorization of black-and-white movies. Most important to the guild's creative-rights itinerary is Capra's slogan "one man, one film." To this end, the group oversees all directorial credits so that only one director is officially recognized on any given production even when more than one have been involved.

Creative-rights issues have led to bitter acrimony between the DGA and the Writers Guild over the years. The DGA rules stipulate that writers are not permitted on movie sets. The writers have been further enraged by the DGA's tacit endorsement of the so-called "possessory credit" ("a film by — —" or "a — — film"). The writers claim that such a credit belies the group nature of moviemaking and is granted indiscriminately to directors of all stripes. In 2003, the directors attempted to soothe the writers' ire by creating guidelines aimed at limiting the use of such credits, but the issue remains a sensitive one between the two guilds.

The Red Scare during the late 1940s and early 1950s ushered in the DGA's only major crisis. Two of its members, Herbert Biberman and Edward Dmytryk, were part of the Hollywood Ten jailed for refusing to "name names" of fellow Communist sympathizers to the House Un-American Activities Committee. Then in 1950, Guild bigwig Cecil B. DeMille, responding to the pressure the House Committee was putting on Hollywood labor, attempted to oust then-Guild President Joseph L. Mankiewicz because Mankiewicz had refused to force DGA members sign an oath of loyalty to the U.S. government. After a fractious 7-hour special meeting at the Beverly Hills Hotel, the group rallied in support of Mankiewicz. However, the re-instated guild president reversed himself a few days later, sending a letter to all DGA members asking them to sign the disputed loyalty oath. The other talent guilds soon followed suit.

During the 1950s, the guild fell on hard times, and membership languished. However, during this decade, the DGA won jurisdictional rights over television. Its merger with the New York-based Radio and Television Directors Guild in 1960 further strengthened its base. In 1964, the guild established a New York office in addition to its headquarters in Los Angeles. That same year, the DGA began a training program for assistant directors, and in the years that followed, it added numerous other educational and outreach programs designed to benefit its members and promote the cause of directors within the industry and among the public at large. By 2004, DGA membership included directors of movies, television, radio, and commercials, along with unit managers, who had been admitted to the guild in 1964.

Beginning in the 1980s, the DGA became active on issues of diversity, sponsoring mentoring and networking programs for women and minority member as well as mounting legal battles against discrimination at the studios. The guild also began collecting and publicizing data on the employment of female and minority directors in the industry. It was the first of the Hollywood labor groups to become active on these issues. By the turn of the century, however, these programs had produced little in the way of results. The number of female and minority guild members employed as directors continued to be negligible. Moreover, it took until 2002 for the guild itself to elect a female president, Martha Coolidge, and by 2006, the group had yet to elect a president who represented a minority group.

As the DGA moved into the twenty-first century, two new concerns faced it. The studios were refusing to share the significant profits accruing from the burgeoning market in DVDs by increasing residual payments to the unions. In addition, runaway productions were taking advantage of cheap foreign workers in the place of more expensive union labor. Both of these issues represent a growing concern for the actors and writers as well as the directors. As a result, the three groups have mounted cooperative efforts to win gains for their members.

The global, technologically sophisticated marketplace of the twenty-first century has brought other issues to the fore for the DGA as well. Recognizing the reality of modern internationalized movie-making practices, the DGA has sought to form alliances with other directors' groups around the world. However, this effort has at times been hampered by the resentment felt by directors in other nations toward the stranglehold Hollywood frequently has on their home markets. Meanwhile, the guild's commitment to keeping its members up to date on matters of professional interest faces ever-more daunting tests as filmmaking moves into the digital era, in which technological imperatives and industry practices are evolving at an ever-more dizzying pace. But there is little doubt that the guild will prove equal to this challenge as it has to all others. In a time when the strength of most unions is ebbing, mentions of the DGA in the Hollywood trade press are routinely preceded by the word "powerful." That power has served the group well in the past and is likely to continue to do so in the future.

VIRGINIA WRIGHT WEXMAN

References and Further Reading

Geist, Kenneth. *Pictures Will Talk: The Life and Films of Joseph L. Mankiewicz*. New York: Da Capo, 1978.

McBride, Joseph. *Frank Capra: The Catastrophe of Success*. New York: Simon and Schuster, 1992.

———. *Searching for John Ford*. New York: St. Martin's Griffin, 2001.

Robb, David. "Directors Guild Born out of Fear 50 Years Ago." *Daily Variety*, 29 (October 1985,): 21-50.

Spergel, Mark. *Reinventing Reality: The Art and Life of Rouben Mamoulian*. Metuchen, NJ: Scarecrow Press, 1993.

Youngerman, Joseph. *My Seventy Years at Paramount and the Directors Guild of America*. Los Angeles, CA: Directors Guild of America, 1995.

DISFRANCHISEMENT

From 1890–1908, every state of the former Confederacy rewrote or amended its constitution to deprive around two million African-American men of the right to vote, a right they had obtained 30 or so years earlier during Reconstruction. Along with virtually all of the African-American men, hundreds of thousands of poor and illiterate white men also lost their voting rights.

Disfranchisement was a draconian movement unprecedented in the modern history of representative government; it took away the guaranteed right to vote from at least one-fourth of the eligible electorate. The United States was therefore out of step with every other democratizing nation in the modern era when expansion of the suffrage, rather than its contraction, was the overall trend. Not until 1965 and the passage of the Voting Rights Act were these rights restored to blacks, a century after their initial acquisition.

Outcome

This reactionary development, which amounted to nothing less than the final stage in the counter-revolution against Reconstruction, had a decisive impact on the political system of the southern states. It destroyed the Republican party and what was left of the Populist party, and it eliminated from the polity millions of voters who could not meet the new requirements for voting. These qualifications consisted primarily of evidence of continuous residence in one place, ability to read, and payment of an annual poll tax. They were not especially severe, but they proved sufficiently onerous, as their proponents well knew, to prohibit almost all black men and a large segment of white men from qualifying to vote. In effect, landless tenants and sharecroppers in the countryside as well as most working people in the cities were disfranchised. Those blacks who were disfranchised by the new requirements as well as the few who could meet them were then barred from what soon became the real election, the nominating primary of the Democratic party. And this was achieved through either state legislation or party rules that restricted participation to whites only, thereby creating an institution known as the white primary.

The political system that resulted from these changes was called the "solid South." It possessed three general features. First, it was a one-party system with the Democratic party pre-eminent and its dominance undisputed in all but a few of the upper southern states, such as Tennessee and North Carolina, where the mountain regions still generated a competing Republican presence. Second, the electorate was severely restricted. It was limited to whites, and only those among them who could meet the voting requirements, namely, the better off and the middling sorts. Essentially, the electorate was purged of most of the men who were laborers whether they lived and worked in cities or on farms and plantations.

And the third feature of the solid South was the vastly disproportionate influence and power its members wielded in the national Democratic party and in Congress. Because the South was solidly Democratic and because its Congressmen, once elected, were very difficult to unseat, since there was no Republican opposition in the general election, the region's Democrats were able to guarantee victories in the southern states to Democratic presidential candidates, and they were also able to use their incumbency and seniority in the Senate and House of Representatives to control committees and influence legislation. Of most concern to them was legislation likely to upset the region's system of white racial dominance on which disfranchisement and the solid South were based. Worrisome but less threatening than antidiscrimination measures were laws that benefited labor and endangered the South's ability to hold workers under tight control and keep wages low, a comparative advantage the region's political and economic leaders strove vigorously to preserve. Their efforts ran into considerable opposition, however, in the 1940s and 1950s, after the Second New Deal, when the Democratic party became closely aligned with organized labor, now more assertive after the formation of the Congress of Industrialized Organizations (CIO), as well as with the interests of working people in the northern cities.

Origins

The solid South was the direct political consequence of disfranchisement. And the maintenance of white supremacy as well as the control of labor and the exploitation of working people comprised the broader economic and social order it was intended to protect and sustain. But what was the cause of disfranchisement? Who were its initiators, and what were their intentions? Historians always have to beware of the logical fallacy of deriving intention from outcome and thereby overlooking what has, in recent years, been described as unintended consequences. But in this case, intention and outcome were directly correlated. The disfranchisers were remarkably successful. Indeed, the outcome proved to be even more favorable than they had hoped. They obtained everything they wanted, and then some. Dominance over the South's politics and therefore over its recently emancipated black population was the disfranchisers' objective. But once they gained control over the political system, they discovered the enormous leverage this power and unity gave them within the nation at large through the Democratic party and the organizational structure of Congress. Because of this unanticipated bonus, southern Democrats were able to consolidate their regional power further by using their national influence to protect what they believed to be the region's interests against the growing

criticism, even hostility, of the rest of the nation that arose after World War II.

The movement to end black voting emerged in the 1890s, a turbulent decade in American political history when farmers in the South and West were experiencing severe economic distress that neither of the two major parties seemed able to respond to. In the South, a new and more assertive farmers' organization, the Farmers' Alliance, had arisen in the late 1880s, and it mobilized small-to-middling farmers, mainly whites but also blacks to some extent. Soon the alliance entered the political arena and played a large role in forming the People's party, or Populists, who challenged the Democrats, either as a third party or more dangerously, through fusion arrangements with the Republicans. In every state, the Democrats faced serious insurgencies, none more so than in North Carolina and Louisiana, where Populist-Republican fusion produced anti-Democratic electoral majorities, and in North Carolina, where Republican managed to win control of state government from 1894–1898.

The initiative for disfranchisement was spurred by a sense of urgency at the prospect of a resurgent republicanism and of an opposition broadened and invigorated by populism. But the concern behind disfranchisement preceded the crisis of the 1890s. Ever since the end of Reconstruction, when they had succeeded in overthrowing the Republican-controlled governments one by one, Democrats had been frustrated by the large number of blacks who still had the right to vote. Their numbers constituted a direct threat to Democratic ascendancy in black-majority districts, while elsewhere they remained a bloc of voters whom the Democrats could not reach and win. Unwilling to accept the legitimacy of blacks' right to vote and participate in the political process, Democrats used physical violence in order to deter blacks from voting altogether, or they resorted to ballot box fraud by tampering with the ballots cast by black voters so that they ended up in the Democrats' boxes.

In the 1890s, the Democrats arrived at the decision to eliminate the black vote altogether rather than continue to engage in electoral activities that, despite their effectiveness, were nevertheless humiliating, tiresome, and patently illegal. And this change of strategy became more urgent and necessary with the growing turbulence and insurgency in the region's politics. Beginning with Mississippi in 1890, before the Populist party had even formed, the movement got under way as the southern states either called a constitutional convention or ratified constitutional amendments for the purpose of eliminating black voters by introducing new voting requirements that almost all blacks could not meet. Conventions were held in Mississippi (1890), South Carolina (1895), Louisiana

(1898), and Alabama and Virginia (1901), while constitutional amendments were enacted and then ratified in Tennessee (1890), Florida (1889), Arkansas (1892), North Carolina (1900), Texas (1902), and Georgia (1908). The initiators of disfranchisement were all Democrats, for this was fundamentally a partisan maneuver. Even though different interest groups and factions within the party led off the move to disfranchise and even though serious debates arose during the entire process, the conventions were overwhelmingly Democratic in composition, and the entire operation, whether by constitutional convention or amendment, was carried through by the party leadership, and not by the rank and file.

Loophole Clauses

The most problematic aspect of this process was the need to comply with the Fifteenth Amendment to the U.S. Constitution, ratified in 1870 during Reconstruction, which forbade denial of the right to vote "on grounds of race, color, or previous condition of servitude," a clear prohibition against disfranchising blacks alone. The restrictions on voting were therefore based on grounds other than race—residence, literacy, tax payments, and so forth. Naturally enough, these kinds of requirements would eliminate many whites as well. Therefore, each state concocted a loophole clause to enable whites to vote if they took advantage of it. These clauses were criticized vigorously by the Democratic press at the time because they were so obviously fraudulent that they would taint what many considered a cleaning-up of a deeply corrupt electoral system and would also expose the party to ridicule. The grandfather clause allowed people to vote whose immediate ancestors had possessed the right to vote before 1867, which happened to be the very year in which blacks had first obtained the vote. The other device that emerged was the understanding clause, which permitted men to vote who could pass a test given by the registrar that showed they understood a particular clause or section of the state constitution. Both of these exceptions were clearly intended to be discriminatory and fraudulent. And they reveal conclusively that getting rid of the black vote was the overriding objective of disfranchisement

Interestingly, few whites took advantage of this special offer. Exactly why they did not remains speculative. Perhaps they found the need to appear before a registrar and admit one's illiteracy and poverty too humiliating to undergo. Or perhaps they did not care enough about losing the vote to take the trouble to go through the procedure. Whatever the reason, they passed up the opportunity to register and participate. And this was a cause of some surprise to the Democrats, who had gone to great lengths to include these loopholes for the benefit of whites who would not meet the new strictures. Nevertheless, they took no action to get these whites to register, and they expressed little concern that they would lose the vote.

While blacks were undoubtedly the target of disfranchisement, the Democratic leadership evidently considered that disadvantaged whites were expendable as voters. Their loss was a by-product of disfranchisement, but not an entirely unwelcome one. Although indisputably secondary to race, the class dimension seems nonetheless to have been an aspect of the maneuver. The southern Democrats were obsessed about race, but they were also worried about class.

MICHAEL PERMAN

References and Further Reading

Bloom, Jack M. *Class, Race, and the Civil Rights Movement.* Bloomington: Indiana University Press, 1987.
Key, V. O., Jr. *Southern Politics: In State and Nation.* New York: Alfred Knopf, 1949.
Kousser, J. Morgan. *The Shaping of Southern Politics: Suffrage Restriction and the Establishment of the One-Party South, 1880–1910.* New Haven, CT: Yale University Press, 1974.
Perman, Michael. *Struggle for Mastery: Disfranchisement in the South, 1888–1908.* Chapel Hill, NC: University of North Carolina Press, 2001.
Woodward, C. Vann. *The Strange Career of Jim Crow.* 3rd. ed. New York: Oxford University Press, 1974

See also **African Americans; Civil War and Reconstruction; Slave Trade**

DOCK AND COTTON COUNCIL

The Dock and Cotton Council (D&CC) was organized on the waterfront in New Orleans in October 1901. It represented all of the screw men, longshoremen, teamsters, coal wheelers, steamboat hands, cotton scale hands, weighers, and yardmen, black and white alike. While member unions were organized along strictly segregated lines, the council took its strength from a biracial leadership that drew delegates from every member union. The council president always came from the ranks of the strongest labor organization on the waterfront, the white-cotton screw men, and the secretary came from the black longshoremen, one of the oldest and most numerically significant organized groups. The council's vice-president also usually came from the black longshoremen. Because of the mostly unskilled nature of their work, the waterfront workers of all trades and both races recognized that they must join together in order to control the labor supply. They also benefited from the leadership of the elite cotton screw men, who were called the aristocrats of the levee because their particular skills were in such high demand. Hence, the council appeared in a segregated city where all of the American Federation of Labor (AFL) unions were divided by race. Away from the docks, the AFL chartered two separate central labor councils for the two races, but the integrated D&CC represented all of the dockworkers. After the fall of 1902, the council mandated equal work sharing between the races, though the union whites still controlled the best jobs.

As the workers' biracial alliance remained solid over the next several years, labor conflict continued to characterize relations between employer and workers. The first real test of the council came in 1907, when the shippers instituted a brutal speed-up directed primarily against the highly skilled screw men. After several days of protests, the council called for a general strike. When over nine thousand workers from all skill levels responded in perfect racial solidarity, they completely shut down the docks. After 10 days, the shippers asked for arbitration. As was their standard practice, the dockers sent an integrated set of delegates to negotiate a permanent settlement for the council at the conference table.

The poststrike conferences in 1907 and 1908 were enlivened by the resistance of the employer representatives to the integrated delegation of workers. Nonetheless, a five-year contract that specified fair wage rates and decent work rules resulted from the negotiations. As Eric Arnesen notes, "The hatchet was buried" in early May of 1908, and labor peace prevailed along the New Orleans wharves for over a decade. The shippers even came to praise the D&CC as a kind of partner they could count on to deliver a reliable labor force. Likewise, the leaders of the council made job security their over-riding concern in exchange for decent wages and working conditions. During this time, all of the members of the D&CC were finally part of labor's privileged elite. They belonged to the national AFL but remained united across racial lines because they all belonged to the council. It was truly a remarkable alliance, a unique product that was just as much time-based as it was on the strength of craftsmen whose skills were nearing obsoleteness.

In the next 15 years, increasing technology gave more power to the employers. When a high-speed cotton press became widely available after World War I, it made the shippers much less beholden to the cotton screw men. In addition changing demographics weakened the council. As the number of black screw men and longshoremen continued to

increase dramatically, the new demographics rendered equal work sharing inherently discriminatory.

Racial conflict was not the direct cause of the collapse of the council, however, because a more immediate threat came against the screw men, their elite work rules and more literally, their jobs. The D&CC held solid through the labor skirmishes of 1921 and 1922, but in 1923, the entire waterfront union coalition fell apart following a devastating strike.

During contract renewal negotiations in 1923, the screw men threatened to strike because the shippers refused to incorporate the old work rules into the proposed new contracts. Many white longshoremen supported them. The majority of African-Americans, however, were reluctant to go along because they feared a strike might fail. When the issue came to a vote, less than 20% of black longshoremen supported the strike that was being pushed so hard by a minority of the whites. Inexplicably, the strike still won approval that September, and 1300 men walked off the wharves, black and white going out in apparent solidarity.

The shippers and their agents refused to negotiate with the men or recognize the strike. Instead, they revived an old mechanism to hire strikebreakers. Called the shape-up, it was a system that prevailed in most other American ports but was not widely used in New Orleans since at least the 1880s because the organized workers would not allow it. In 1923, when the shippers imported hundreds of strikebreakers to cross the picket lines, the new recruits came together at designated "shaping places" where foremen hired individual men for a single day's work. As a result, the shippers never had to negotiate with the experienced strikers because they quickly trained a whole new labor pool. Meantime, they took their case against the D&CC into federal court, where a judge issued an injunction prohibiting the strikers from interfering with commerce on the docks. Armed with that court order, the shippers forced the pickets to quit the strike without a settlement. There was not only no contract left on the table, but for way too many of the strikers, no job. That was the end of the D&CC, though the New Orleans International Longshoremen's Association (ILA) managed to stay alive—just barely.

EDIE AMBROSE

References and Further Reading

Ameringer, Oscar. *If You Don't Weaken.* Henry Holt: New York, 1940.
Arnesen, Eric. *Waterfront Workers of New Orleans, Race, Class and Politics, 1882–1923.* Oxford, UK: Oxford University Press, 1991.
———. "It Ain't Like They Do in New Orleans": Race Relations, Labor Markets, and Waterfront Labor Movements in the American South, 1880–1923." In

Racism and the Labor Market: Historical Studies, Marcel van der Linden and Jan Lucassen, eds. Bern and New York: Peter Lang, 1995.

Marshall, F. Ray. *Labor In the South.* Cambridge, MA: Harvard University Press, 1967.

Northrup, Herbert R. "The New Orleans Longshoremen." *Political Science Quarterly* 57 (1942): 526–544.

Rosenberg, Daniel. *New Orleans Dockworkers: Race, Labor and Unionism, 1892–1923.* New York: State University of New York Press, 1988.

Wells, Dave, and Stodder, Jim. "A Short History of New Orleans Dockworkers." *Radical America* (1976): 43–64.

See also **American Federation of Labor; Injunctions; International Longshoremen's Association**

DOMESTIC SERVICE

A dichotomy between the domestic realm, considered the provenance of women, and the market, deemed the domain of men, has had powerful labor market effects throughout American history, relegating women to lower paying, undesirable jobs at the margins of the paid workforce and complicating efforts at government reform and shop-floor organizing. Distinctions based on race, class, and caste have strengthened these prescriptions, relegating poor women, immigrant women, and women of color to the lowest rung of the ladder of paid employment, that is, to domestic service. From before the founding of the republic to the 1940s, more American women workers labored in the private homes of other Americans than worked in any other job. The degradation of domestic workers (including their presumed laziness, sexual availability, and inherent servitude) has served metaphorically and in practical terms as a foil for the pristine, white, middle-class American woman.

Female domination of any job category rightly sends up red flags to students of labor history. According to census figures, from 1870–1930, almost 90% of domestic servants were women. (Historians consider this a considerable undercount based on the inclusion of male porters in the domestic servant job category.) Whether servants, maids, cooks, housekeepers, laundresses or nannies, through the ages U.S. domestic workers have managed all aspects of social reproduction for those who could afford to hire them. In turn, the wages paid to domestic workers have provided indispensable economic support to these women, both native-born and immigrant, and their own families. And yet, since it requires no formal education, offers no possibility of promotion, pays notoriously badly, and leaves workers vulnerable to sexual and other kinds of exploitation by employers, domestic labor has always been among the lowest status and least desirable jobs available to women.

Few who have worked as domestics have written about their experiences, but journalistic accounts and oral histories emphasize social isolation as one of the most punishing features of domestic service. Atomization has wrought economic as well as psychological implications: Unions, historically male and manufacturing-oriented, never put sufficient effort into organizing domestics to overcome these barriers. At the same time, domestic workers have been excluded from almost all government labor regulation—whether concerned with safety, wages and hours, retirement, or the right to organize. For these reasons, the case can be made that no other category of free labor has left workers as vulnerable to the wiles of individual employers or the vicissitudes of the economy as domestic labor.

Some historians consider the early republic the "golden age of domestic service" when a fresh democratic ethos blunted social distinctions between mistresses and their domestic servants. In rural communities, young, native-born women aided in the home production of clothes, food, and such necessities as soap. In towns in the North and center of the country, young women, fresh off ships from Scandanavia, Ireland, and Germany, became American in the homes of their employers. On the West Coast, an influx of Chinese men and women dominated the field. But as the home shifted from a site of production to a locus of consumption, the domestic servant found her role shifting from an apprentice to family life to a mere expression of the will of her mistress or master.

During the mid-to-late nineteenth century, race and gender remained the principal axes of social organization and the primary determinants of who worked for whom and in what capacity. By 1855, 25% of the almost one million Irish girls and women in New York City worked as domestics. Driven from their native land by successive waves of famine, by age 14, 60% of Irish females no longer lived with their own families. "Bridget," the derogatory nickname Protestant employers assigned their Irish household help, faced anti-Catholic sentiment as well as general disdain for her character. Immigrant and native-born girls who found live-in work an ill fit with married life and motherhood could shift their dependency, relying on their husbands' wages; poorly paid piecework like hat braiding, which they could take into their homes; or a job in a mill or factory.

Approximately half a million free African-Americans lived in northern cities like Philadelphia, Boston, and New York by 1860. At least half of the women labored as domestics. Because African-American men earned significantly less than their white counterparts, even for the same work, African-American women had no choice but to continue working after marriage and the birth of their own children, making working mothers a fixture of African-American family life. By 1900, in New York City, 31% of African-American women worked for a wage, as compared to 4% of white women.

In the South, by contrast, domination of domestic service by African-American women was unchallenged. Even the poorest white woman turned her nose up at the idea of work in another white person's home. Moreover, prevailing wages for the job were so low that all but the most impoverished white families could afford to employ an African-American woman to cook, do washing, and help mind children. While almost any other kinds of work might have been preferable, free African-Americans found their options severely limited by black codes, local regulations that imposed occupational barriers and curfews on African-Americans, limiting the kinds of paid work available to them. In 1808 and 1836, for example, the city council of the District of Columbia approved such legislation. The prevalence of such racist laws wrought predictable results even in the upper South. By the 1890s, regardless of their abilities and experience, most African-Americans worked in low and unskilled trades.

After Emancipation, African-American women who trekked North shattered the existing mold of domestic service by insisting on day-work rather than live-in situations. By World War II, what had been a predominantly white, live-in occupation had gradually become a day job dominated by African-Americans. Although day workers might lose money on the new arrangement—needing to pay room and board out of the same meager wage they received when they lived-in—they strongly preferred living apart from their employers, being assured at least some time off and their own sliver of private physical space.

Forces of urbanization and industrialization also changed the experience of domestic service. Compulsory education extended new options to girls. Fresh labor market opportunities attracted others. Qualified women leapt at the chance to take clerical or retail work or to become teachers. Relative to other types of paid work, domestic service began to diminish. An Irish woman in her early twenties who had left domestic employment to work in a commercial laundry preferred her new job, finding it "no harder, giving more time after work hours, and being better paid."

Private domestic service remained the single largest job category for women until the 1950 census. Labor and feminist movements made remarkably few inroads in the sector, leaving intact its essentially feudal structure. Suffragist Charlotte Perkins Gilman envisioned cooperative household arrangements that would alleviate the isolation and stigma of housework while freeing women to engage in other pursuits. While this remained a pipedream, Progressive Era reformers did win legislation prohibiting child labor and in some states, establishing protective legislation controlling the hours of women's work. Yet domestic labor itself remained a peripheral concern. Such feminist leaders as Alice Paul of the National Women's party foreshadowed the blind spots of the feminist movement of the 1960s, which would also be dominated by middle-class white women, when she rejected appeals for inclusion by domestic workers, instead concentrating on the status of teachers, clerical workers, saleswomen, and wealthier women financially dependent on their husbands. Paul deflected such appeals by noting that the problems facing domestic service were fundamentally racial—not tied to sex.

Organized labor proved slightly more receptive to overtures by domestic servants. At various times, the Knights of Labor, the Industrial Workers of the World, the Women's Trade Union League, and the Young Women's Christian Association each recognized associations of domestic workers. Household workers locals could be found in Tulsa and Lawton, Oklahoma, in Richmond, Virginia, in Mobile, Alabama, and in Philadelphia, Pennsylvania, and other large towns at various moments throughout the late nineteenth and early twentieth centuries. When 3,000 laundresses, cooks, and maids organized a strike in Atlanta in the 1880s, the city council crushed the strike, imposing a $25 fee on the strikers (the same amount charged to business owners) and jailing some of the movement's organizers. In the face of strong-arm tactics, momentum proved difficult to sustain. A brief resurgence of organizing among domestics during World War I produced 10 locals of the American Federation of Labor (AFL) nationwide by 1920. By 1923, however, none remained. Perhaps even more than other female workers, domestics faced resistance from traditional male unions as well as from the middle-class establishment, male and female. Combined with the abundance of an unskilled labor force, the low status of the workers, their isolation from one another, and the personalized nature of the relationship between the domestic and her employers, the obstacles proved overwhelming.

In the absence of formal contract negotiations, immigrant and native-born domestic workers developed their own strategies for expressing work-related grievances—short of quitting, which meant risking economic destitution for their families. Within the seven-day workweek, such opportunities abounded.

To make their jobs livable, they experimented with tardiness, absenteeism, petty theft, and outright sabotage. Employers tended to dismiss such behaviors as endemic to the employees' race or ethnicity, waxing elegiac about the servant problem.

While it is hard to imagine a category of workers in greater need of an economic safety net, domestic workers were specifically excluded from the regulation and protection extended to workers in other industries during the New Deal. Leaders of sympathetic organizations, such as the YWCA, lent their efforts to worker-led letter-writing campaigns, urging lawmakers to include domestic work in the National Recovery Administration and the Fair Labor Standards Act. Ultimately, they were excluded from both. Lawmakers saw little cause for controversy: The private nature of domestic employment rendered impractical the administration and enforcement of such reforms as overtime pay, a limited workweek, and a guaranteed minimum wage. Practical complications aside, traditional paternalism was the root cause of their resistance. By excluding domestic servants from unemployment insurance, workers' compensation, and old-age insurance, members of Congress intensified employers' control.

For a sense of just how many people made their living at domestic service, a survey conducted by the future Nobel economist Joseph Stigler in 1939 found that as many Americans worked in domestic service as were employed in coal mines, automobile manufacturing, and railroads combined. At the same time, the composition of the domestic workforce was shifting. By 1940, 47% of the women who performed domestic work in private homes were nonwhite, while nonwhite women accounted, on average, for only 14% of other categories of worker. The influx of immigrants and their comparatively unproblematic acceptance by white Americans in other sectors had reduced their proportionate employment in domestic service. Mobilization of the home front during World War II marked the last significant exodus of women from the domestic service sector. However, the postwar expulsion of women from well-paying war jobs was even more severe for blacks, increasing their representation in private household service. By 1944, African-American women did over 60% of such work.

A second burst of organized feminism in the 1960s once again raised popular consciousness about the rights of women but again failed to reckon with the layers of oppression that burdened poor women of color, that is, the women most likely to work as domestics. While this movement dramatically changed the way many working women thought about themselves and their work, the middle- and upper-class white women who led the movement failed to detect that for women trapped in domestic service and other feminized wage labor, employment was the cause of their suffering, not the answer to it. An intense focus on a woman's right to paid work ignored the central concerns of domestic workers and other low-wage workers who already worked for pay.

By the second half of the twentieth century, the nonwhite cleaning lady and nanny had become fixtures of the American labor market. During the 1970s, federal lawmakers extended labor legislation (such as the Fair Labor Standards Act [FLSA]) to such workers. However, the reduction in hours per employer has meant that most domestics now work in more than one household—sometimes more than one per day—and often do so off-the-books. Reliable statistics are difficult to find, but high-profile "nannygate" scandals have exposed the tendency of private employers not to declare their household employees for tax purposes, thus leaving domestic workers outside the formal labor market and ineligible for benefits that under current federal law they might now rightly claim.

As educated American women have blazed into the professions and the business world, they and their families have deepened their dependence on a class of housekeepers and nannies. African-American women are still disproportionately represented, but today's domestic workers are also increasingly nonwhite immigrant women who remit a portion of their wages to their families in their countries of origin—often poor nations with weak economies and heavy debt burdens to the United States and the rest of the West. Moreover, in the atmosphere of homeland security that engulfed the nation after the attacks of September 2001, fear of deportation (for themselves or their loved ones), now mingles with historical fears of exploitation among members of the domestic workforce.

ANASTASIA MANN

References and Further Reading

Jones, Jacqueline. *Labor of Love, Labor of Sorrow: Black Women, Work, and the Family from Slavery to the Present*. New York: Basic Books, 1985.

Katzman, David M. *Seven Days a Week: Women and Domestic Service in Industrializing America*. New York: Oxford University Press, 1978.

Kessler-Harris, Alice. *Out to Work: A History of Wage-Earning Women in the United States*. New York: Oxford University Press, 1982.

Palmer, Phyllis. *Domesticity and Dirt: Housewives and Domestic Servants in the United States, 1920–1945*. Philadelphia, PA: Temple University Press, 1989.

Van Raaphorst, Donna L. *Union Maids Not Wanted: Organizing Domestic Workers, 1870–1940*. New York: Praeger, 1988.

DOMINANCE AND INFLUENCE OF ORGANIZED LABOR: 1940s

If the 1930s were the seedtime for the modern labor movement, then the 1940s constitute the harvest years when organized labor blossomed and bore fruit. During the decade, unions reached their apex of power and influence in American society. For this brief historical moment, they were a significant progressive force shaping politics, society, and the economy. Unions were integral cogs in the wheels of the New Deal state, and in some cases labor leaders themselves became powerbrokers with the ability to make presidents. But at the moment of its apogee, organized labor discovered its grip on American politics fleeting and its authority in the economy and the society rather illusionary. Unions ended the decade far weaker and more vulnerable than they began it.

The Great Depression of the 1930s and President Franklin D. Roosevelt's New Deal had helped to spark the organizational drives that reversed labor unions' precipitous decline during the Republican-dominated 1920s. However, it was the coming of the Second World War that created the conditions for unprecedented growth, scarcely imaginable during the doldrums of the Great Depression. Take the shipbuilding industry as an example. In 1920, the major shipyards built almost 3.5 million deadweight tons of new shipping. In the final year of President Herbert Hoover's administration, that yearly output had plummeted to 355,771, and in 1935, the Great Depression's nadir, only 49,000 tons of new shipping were launched. Late in the New Deal, President Franklin D. Roosevelt tried to foster growth in the shipbuilding industry by requisitioning new ships for the Merchant Marine and the United States Navy. The initial plan to revive this sick industry was to contract 50 ships a year for 10 years. The outbreak of war in Europe in 1939 vastly accelerated and expanded FDR's timetable. By 1940, Roosevelt's government was ordering 200 ships a year, and that number grew substantially. At the war's height in 1944, over 20 million tons were launched in that single year. The beneficiaries of this wartime boom were of course the military brass, the shipyard owners, and the laborers who built the ships. Because closed-shop contracts were so common in shipyards, nearly all shipbuilding workers belonged to a union. Most but not all were affiliated with an international of the American Federation of Labor (AFL). For instance, the International Brotherhood of Boilermakers dominated in many yards. But other smaller AFL unions, such as the blacksmiths, the metal polishers, and the stove workers also did exceedingly well during the early 1940s.

Similar patterns existed elsewhere. For example, the construction industry experienced an unprecedented recovery in the early 1940s. The Great Depression had all but stopped private construction both for homeowners and for businesses. The worst year was 1935, when at no point was the unemployment rate for construction workers under 45%. Such New Deal work programs as the Works Progress Administration helped a little, but jobs were scarce, and wages remained low for the entire 1930s. Some advances were made. In 1939, in Los Angeles, city leaders arranged for new construction loans totaling $33 million in order to restart the city's lagging building industry. That development was Lilliputian compared to the money the federal government spent on construction immediately before and during the Second World War. For example, the Roosevelt administration spent more than $33 million on a single U.S. Marine base in San Diego, where union workers belonging to the AFL built a new training station, a hospital, an air station, an armory, and defense housing. And again it was unions that reaped the benefit from this new war-spurred growth.

In general terms, because of the economy's revitalization, the 1940s saw union penetration in the American economy like never before. In 1930, there were roughly 49 million workers in the labor force. Only about 3.5 million, or 7% belonged to a union. In 1940, the U.S. labor force was comprised of 53 million workers, 17% were in unions. The wartime peak in union numbers came in 1945, when there were almost 15 million unionists working. They amounted to about a quarter to a third of the labor force. In some areas, such as airplane manufacturing, lumbering, and shipbuilding, that percentage was much higher. Significantly, union growth kept pace with the expansion of the labor force after the Second World War. In the decade's last year, the total number of workers was nearly 64 million, and union workers represented about 23%. It was a decline from the war years, but the numbers of workers in unions did not return to the levels of the late 1920s or early 1930s.

The sensational increase in the size and numbers of unions in the 1940s was matched by a similar rise in their political power and social influence. Even by 1939, President Franklin D. Roosevelt was drawing union leaders into the preparations for defense. Simply, FDR needed their technical expertise, their ability to mobilize and train workers, and their cooperation for harmonious labor relations. Unions were the key to a smooth conversion to war production. In shipbuilding for example, a number of sticky problems had arisen after the federal government began to order dozens of new naval vessels in early 1940. There were labor and material shortages as well as strikes as unions sought to bargain for equitable wage and overtime rules. By January 1941, these roadblocks to production were quickly becoming a major impediment to the re-arming of the United States. At this critical juncture, the AFL's Metal Trades Department, led by the fiery John Frey, hammered out a solution. During a general meeting of the department, Frey and other leaders from the boilermakers and other metal unions devised a stabilization agreement. For shipbuilding, the nation was divided into four regional production zones governed by stabilization boards made up of employers, unionists, and federal officials. These boards determined wages and helped ensure efficient production. Unions also pledged not to strike during the defense emergency. Employers promised not to lock their unions out of the shipyards. Disputes were to be handled by federal mediation boards, and not job actions of any kind. For unionists, the trade-off was very beneficial. For the duration, shipyard owners recognized their unions, agreed to bargain collectively, and granted them the closed shop. The agreement was so groundbreaking and useful that nearly all other major wartime industries, such as airplane manufacturing, used this stabilization program first proposed by the AFL's Metal Trades Department.

The agreement fashioned by the Metal Trades department and the shipbuilders was reflective of a new—albeit short-lived—spirit of labor-business-government cooperation. Even before the Japanese attack on Pearl Harbor, labor unions were becoming an important part of the overall management of the defense effort. However, in the deadly raid's aftermath, President Roosevelt made sure that labor was represented in every major war agency. The Office of War Production, for example, had the Congress of Industrialized Organizations' (CIO's) indomitable Sidney Hillman as its cochair. Furthermore, both the AFL and CIO had representation on the National War Labor Board (NWLB), which was FDR's main agency to settle wage, working-conditions, and benefit disputes between unions and employers during the war. Despite being under constant criticism from politicians, employers, and unions, the NWLB was an effective administrative tool for creating labor peace. This reconciliation between feuding parties in the American economy briefly stretched to include the two labor federations. Both the AFL and CIO had been warring since 1935. With the Second World War clearly on the horizon, President Roosevelt had sought to heal the breach between them. Well into the war, peace was within reach, although in the end neither the AFL nor the CIO was ready to

commit to a singular and unified American labor movement.

Regardless, the early 1940s was an exceptional period for American labor unions. They had grown in size and numbers scarcely imaginable just 10 years earlier. Moreover, they were now a staple part of American politics, particularly liberal politics. Both the CIO and the AFL had transformed themselves under the new realities of the New Deal. By the early 1940s, union leaders were making the most of their newly found political power. For instance, in 1943, Hillman and other CIO leaders formed the Political Action Committee (PAC) to support President Franklin Roosevelt's bid for an unprecedented four terms in office. The Congress's PAC indeed had an impact on the election, and it became a model for future interest groups that sought to influence American elections.

Unionists' leverage in politics was not confined to voting. In the 1940s, labor unions developed an agenda to recast economic relationships and national-spending priorities. The greatest fear of all workers, both organized and unorganized, was that after the war, the Great Depression would return. In fact, many senior labor economists, such as the AFL's Boris Shishkin, predicted even higher rates of unemployment in the late 1940s than had been the case in the mid-1930s. To insulate and to inoculate workers from the violent throes of postwar reconversion, the AFL and CIO developed a detailed blueprint to ensure prosperity. It involved three major ideas: full employment, national health care, and civil rights.

Full employment was the buzzword of the mid-1940s. The idea centered on the notion that the federal government with the assistance of corporate and union leaders could foster economic growth through careful planning and the use of pump-priming spending in recession times. The intellectual roots of full employment extended back into the early days of the New Deal when such social and economic planners as Harold Ickes had used Roosevelt's alphabet agencies not only to create economically significant and consequential public-works programs, but also to form federal planning boards to spark further reform. The last such board, the National Resource Planning Board (NRPB), had issued several influential reports during the Second World War, but its *Security, Work, and Relief Policies* (1942) was path-breaking. The NRPB called for comprehensive and thoughtful social programs and economic planning to create permanent affluence in the United States. Full employment was possible, liberals argued, with proper forethought and effective use of the vast resources of the federal government. The leaders of the AFL and CIO latched onto the notion of full employment. To them, the hook was the ways in which planners thought full employment might be achieved. Many economists, such as Alvin H. Hansen, argued that with federal investment in highways and new construction, particularly in housing and urban renewal, full employment would be easily realized. American workers knew that there had been very little new building for private or commercial use since the late 1920s. It was easy for them to see their own interests in full employment.

Similarly, the working class was drawn to another postwar war liberal idea: national health insurance. The idea had received serious thought during the 1930s. In the 1940s, the big labor federations began to push for it. For example, at its 1944 Post-War Forum, the AFL adopted the stance that the federal government ought to foster a national system of health insurance so that all workers would have access to quality medical care when ill as well as wellness checkups when not. Additionally, the AFL backed proposals to lessen the chances of needing medical assistance. For example, the federation leaders agreed with the NRPB that children of the working poor should have access to free lunches. Similarly, they approved of plans to improve the insurance systems that govern industrial accidents, strengthening the carrot-and-stick scheme that encouraged employers to create safe working environments.

These ideas were not based on abstract theory. Rather, workers' calls for better medical and health insurance systems were a reaction to the experiences of the Great Depression and the Second World War. During the 1930s, there was a marked decline in the overall health of the working class. The causes were as obvious then as now. And the young and the elderly bore the brunt of the health-related problems as a result of malnourishment. Although the food crisis of the Great Depression lessened significantly during the 1940s, there were still new challenges. During the Second World War, industrial accidents and injuries rose considerably. In fact, for the first two years of the United State's direct involvement in the war, the shopfloor was more dangerous than the front lines. More Americans died and were maimed in factories than in combat until the end of 1943. On average each year, from 1941–1945, over 2 million wartime workers were killed or seriously injured laboring for the arsenal of democracy. When one considers the vast numbers of military causalities in addition to the industrial ones, the United States experienced an enormous health crisis in the 1940s. Workers and veterans wanted the federal government to help provide health care, assistance, and insurance in order to gain access to the best medicine available.

Finally, unions used their political power in the 1940s to press for the expansion of civil rights for all Americans. One unionist in particular labored mightily and indefatigably to improve the lives of black and other minority workers: A. Philip Randolph, the president of the Brotherhood of Sleeping Car Porters (AFL). At the start of a defense preparedness program in 1940, Randolph began pressuring the federal government to do something to stop the rampant discrimination against African-Americans. The situation had become quite desperate, and it was a national problem. Minority workers were barred from 50% to 90% of all defense-related jobs in every region of the country. Not only was this an affront to U.S. democratic beliefs, but it was also a security, economic, and military liability in the age of total war. Regardless, it took Randolph's pledge of a march on Washington to protest employment bias in the war industries to force President Roosevelt to act. In exchange for Randolph's promise to call off the march, in June 1941, FDR issued Executive Order 8802, which banned job discrimination in the federal government and in defense factories. Although the order and the agency set up to enforce it, the Fair Employment Practice Committee (FEPC), had a limited impact, the precedent was nonetheless set. And after the war, both the AFL and CIO continued to press for a permanent FEPC and the establishment of civil rights in other areas of American life, albeit with varying commitment. The CIO was nearly always stronger on civil rights issues than the AFL.

This far-reaching postwar agenda was organized labor's attempt to make hay from those seeds sown during the early New Deal. Working-class leaders had every reason to be optimistic that their goals would be realized. Both the AFL and CIO were significant forces in American politics. Not only had the federations influenced the 1944 presidential election, but representatives of both groups had also participated and shaped the wartime bureaucracy and government. Organized labor also had the numbers, especially by the mid-1940s, when union membership was at its historic peak. And finally, union leaders believed that they had the general support of Americans, since they had contributed mightily to the "arsenal of democracy," to the Allied victory over fascism. But this sanguine, confident outlook proved misplaced. Organized labor was neither as strong nor as influential as it seemed. By the end of the decade, American workers were on the defensive; thus, power dwindling at the dawn of the Cold War set up a decades-long decline.

Organized labor's efforts to reshape the United States began before the end of the Second World War and centered on voting booths, conference tables, and picket lines. During the 1944 presidential election, unionists had backed Franklin Roosevelt's four freedoms, particularly the notion to eliminate want. Additionally, union leaders met many times at various conferences, including ones with the leaders of business, to hammer out a postwar blueprint to establish full employment, national health insurance, and civil rights. Frustrations both with the politics and with negotiations with employers led to a dramatic increase in the number of strikes from 1944–1946. Although history books tend to emphasize the strike wave of 1946, workers started protesting low wages and insufficient benefits years earlier. In 1943, twice as many workers were involved in strikes as the year before. There were nearly 3,800 strikes in 1943 and almost 5,000 in 1944. In 1945, there were 4,750 work stoppages and in 194, 5,000 involving 4.6 million workers. At its crest, the 1945–1946 strike wave was larger than the famous 1919 strikes. Generally, unionists fought for cost-of-living adjustments; increased benefits, such as health care; and improved working conditions. They also sought to realize their postwar agenda. The most famous example was the United Automobile Workers' (UAW's) strike against General Motors. Union President Walter Reuther not only demanded a wage and benefit hike but also called on GM to "open the books." In other words, the UAW wanted to share in the governance and management of the corporation. In a pattern that played out frequently in 1945 and 1946, the union lost the strike, making only marginal gains. Strikes led by the United Mine Workers and the United Steelworkers met similar fates. The failures of the postwar strikes presaged larger, more devastating defeats for organized labor in the 1940s and beyond.

Several things conspired to sap American workers of their power in politics and society during the latter part of the 1940s. First and foremost were the divisions and diversions in American politics and within the labor movement generally. Beginning as soon as the Second World War ended, a conflict between the United States and the U.S.S.R. ensued. This Cold War in which the two main belligerents never met tête-à-tête transformed world and domestic politics and priorities. In postwar America, arguing for an expansion of the New Deal to provide jobs to the unemployed, to ensure national health care, and civil rights smacked of communism to the political right, many of whom held the reigns of power in Washington, D.C., and in many states and cities. They worked to stop labor's postwar agenda in its tracks. National health insurance legislation failed, as did nearly all civil rights initiatives. In 1946, Congress did pass a full-employment bill, but it was so watered down that it barely had any meaning or impact on American workers. Making matters worse, in 1947, Congress passed—over President Harry S. Truman's veto—the Taft-Hartley Act, a series of amendments to the 1935 Wagner Act designed severely to restrict the political and economic power of labor unions.

These political cleavages that resulted in legislative setbacks were mirrored inside organized labor. Both the AFL and CIO struggled over the issues of anti-communism and support of American foreign policy. In the end both federations purged their memberships of the avowed radical Left. As a result, some of the most dedicated unionists for issues like civil rights were booted out of the labor movement. As a result, organized labor's social agenda and organizing aspirations went unrealized. Moreover, although by the mid-1940s, labor leaders were generally supportive of civil rights reform, not all were. During the famous Operation Dixie when the CIO sought to organize unorganized factory workers the South, union leaders failed to take a strong enough stand on civil rights, a fact that contributed to the operation's demise. The AFL and later the AFL-CIO had its racial problems, too. Clashes at conventions over the issues of fair employment, for example, were frequent and quite telling of the resistance of white unionists to support the struggles of African-American workers. Perhaps nothing demonstrated this more than the infamous 1959 AFL-CIO Convention. After Randolph, still the head of the Brotherhood of Sleeping Car Porters and an AFL-CIO vice-president, introduced a resolution that called for the expulsion of unions that discriminated against blacks, none other than the president of the AFL-CIO, George Meany, shouted Randolph down, cursing at him and viciously exclaiming, "Who the hell appointed you the guardian of all Negroes." During the 1940s, and well into the 1950s, the AFL-CIO offered only a tentative and quite limited program for black workers inside and outside the labor movement. As a result, African-Americans generally did not look to labor unions to provide solutions to their most pressing problems. And they were not alone.

Despite their large numbers, by the end of the 1940s, the labor movement was having trouble gaining new recruits. Part of the problem was that many of the new wartime unionists had not joined freely, but they had to become members of the AFL or CIO because the local had a closed-shop agreement with the employer. These arrangements often created resentments— especially with people who were unaccustomed to the labor movement. In any event, all of these problems—the legislative defeats, the political schisms outside and inside the labor movement, and the problem of recruiting new members—which at the time perhaps did not seem so significant, did set organized labor and the American working class in general down a bleaker path. Just two decades later, many of the wage, benefit, and political gains made during the 1940s were in serious jeopardy. Looking back six decades later, the 1940s appear as a moment of missed opportunities and spoiled chances.

ANDREW E. KERSTEN

References and Further Reading

Brinkley, Alan. *End of Reform: New Deal Liberalism in Recession and War*. New York: Vintage, 1996.

Dubofsky, Melvyn, and Warren Van Tyne. *John L. Lewis*. Urbana: University of Illinois Press, 1986.

Griffith, Barbara. *The Crisis of American Labor: Operation Dixie and the Defeat of the CIO*. Philadephia, PA: Temple University Press, 1988.

Kersten, Andrew E. *Labor's Home Front: The American Federation during World War II*. New York: New York University Press, 2006.

Lichtenstein, Nelson. *Labor's War at Home: The CIO in World War II*. Cambridge, UK: Cambridge Univ. Press, 1982.

Lichtenstein, Nelson. *The Most Dangerous Man in Detroit: Walter Reuther and the Fate of American Labor*. New York: Basic Books, 1995.

Phelan, Craig. *William Green: Biography of a Labor Leader*. Albany: State University of New York Press, 1989.

Taft, Philip. *The AFL from the Death of Gompers to the Merger*. New York: Harper, 1962.

Whitney, Fred. *Wartime Experiences of the National Labor Relations Board, 1941–1945*. Urbana: University of Illinois Press, 1949.

Zieger, Robert H. *The CIO, 1935–1955*. Chapel Hill: University of North Carolina Press, 1995.

DONAHUE, THOMAS (1928–)
President, AFL-CIO

Thomas Reilly Donahue was the third president of the American Federation of Labor (AFL)-Congress of Industrialized Organizations (CIO), from August to October 1995. Donahue became president when dissident members of the AFL-CIO's executive committee pressured Lane Kirkland to resign from the position. Donahue, who had been the secretary-treasurer of the federation since 1979, and a close friend and associate of Kirkland, was selected by the executive committee to fill Kirkland's term of office until elections could be held at the October AFL-CIO convention. At the convention, however, Donahue was defeated during the first contested election in AFL-CIO history by his long-time friend, John Sweeney, the head of the Service Employees' International Union (SEIU).

Donahue was born in 1928 in the Bronx, New York, to a family of Irish Catholics. He served in the U.S. Navy as a seaman from 1945–1946, and after his discharge, he earned a B.A. from Manhattan College in Labor Relations in 1949 and an LL.B from Fordham School of Law in 1956. After leaving college, Donahue began a lifetime association with the labor movement, beginning with a position as an organizer for the Retail Clerks' International Union. In 1949, Donahue joined the staff of the Building Service Employees' International Union (BSEIU), the union in which he would remain until he joined George Meany's staff at the national AFL-CIO in 1973. During his career with BSEIU (and after it changed its name, SEIU), Donahue held a variety of positions, beginning with Education Director for New York's Local 32B and extending all the way through the first vice-presidency, which he held from 1971–1973. Donahue also held a number of important government appointments. In 1957, he was selected to serve as the labor program coordinator for Radio Free Europe, and from 1967–1969, he served as the assistant secretary of labor for Labor-Management Relations under President Lyndon Johnson.

WhenLane Kirkland became AFL-CIO president in 1979 after Meany's retirement, Donahue became the federation's secretary-treasurer, a position he held until his elevation to the presidency in 1995. As secretary-treasurer, Donahue was a strong supporter of Kirkland and his policies, including Kirkland's anti-communism and his desire to free Eastern Europe from Soviet control. This closeness to Kirkland became a detriment when the leaders of many of the federation's largest unions joined together in a New Voices coalition in 1995 with the goal of radically transforming the AFL-CIO. The New Voices coalition, led by SEIU president John Sweeney and United Mine Worker's (UMW) president Rich Trumka, had a number of criticisms of federation policy under Kirkland. Most importantly, Sweeney's allies felt that the federation should take a more active hand in organizing nonunion workers. Whereas Kirkland (and Meany before him) believed that organizing was primarily the responsibility of individual international unions, Sweeney wanted the AFL-CIO to devote 30% of its budget to supporting organizing drives. In addition, the New Voices coalition felt that Kirkland had devoted too much attention to international affairs, particularly his anti-Communist work in Poland. Finally, the dissident faction laid the blame for the Republican landslide of 1994 and the passage of North American Free Trade Agreement (NAFTA) at Kirkland's feet.

While Kirkland and Donahue retained the loyalty of the majority of unions in the federation, Sweeney and the New Voices coalition controlled the AFL-CIO's largest unions, ensuring that they would be able to win any disputed elections at the annual convention. Donahue and Sweeney both engaged in a spirited campaign running up to the convention, including a number of debates between the two candidates. Ironically, the two men were not only close friends, but also in agreement on almost all of the issues that supposedly divided their coalitions. Both supported an increased focus on organizing, and both supported expanding the executive committee of the AFL-CIO to include more women and minorities. Sweeney, however, took consistently more militant positions on these and other issues. When it became apparent that Sweeney controlled the most delegates at the convention, Donahue stepped aside, and Sweeney became the fourth president of the AFL-CIO.

AARON MAX BERKOWITZ

References and Further Reading

Puddington, Arch. *Lane Kirkland: Champion of American Labor*. Hoboken, NJ: Wiley, 2005.

"DON'T BUY WHERE YOU CAN'T WORK" CAMPAIGNS

From the late 1920s to the late 1940s, African-Americans created Don't Buy Where You Can't Work campaigns, employing consumer boycotts and picket lines to force white-owned companies in segregated black neighborhoods to hire black workers. Picketers in the campaigns carried signs reading, "Buy Where You Can Work! No Negroes Employed Here!" or similar messages. The campaigns grew out of African-American consumers' long-standing grievances against the increasing numbers of white-owned chain stores that cropped up in segregated, urban, black neighborhoods. Consumer boycotts appealed to African-Americans with a wide range of political and ideological positions. Black business leaders, for example, relished the opportunity to increase black consumers' buying power and raise the racial consciousness of their buying decisions. Similarly, the New Negroes who emerged from the Harlem Renaissance period saw consumer boycotts as effective means to act on African-Americans' self-dependence. Don't Buy Where You Can't Work campaigns directly opened hundreds of jobs for un- or underemployed black workers, while many stores changed their hiring practices in order to avoid becoming targets of jobs campaigns. By the late 1940s, African-Americans commonly held clerical and sales positions in black neighborhoods.

Boycott movements occurred in at least 35 cities throughout the nation but emerged most often in northern cities where the World War I era African-American migrants gathered and created significant centers of consumer power. In 1929 and 1930, A. C. MacNeal and Joseph D. Bibb, editors of the African-American newspaper, the *Chicago Whip*, publicized the efforts of a small group picketing a local grocery store. Although this was not the first such consumer boycott, it was the first Don't Spend Your Money Where You Can't Work campaign to capture national attention. After winning jobs at the grocery store, the Chicago movement embarked on a more ambitious struggle against Woolworth chain stores, winning approximately 300 jobs for black workers. From 1930–1941, numerous groups created similar efforts in such cities as Toledo and Cleveland, Ohio; Detroit, Michigan; New York, New York; Washington, D.C.; and Baltimore, Maryland. Boycott movements emerged even in a few southern cities, such as Richmond and Newport News, Virginia, although such direct-action techniques were possible only where not precluded by the threat of retaliatory violence.

Large, segregated, urban African-American communities during the Great Depression were fertile ground for Don't Buy Where You Can't Work campaigns. By the beginning of the Depression, African-Americans had been migrating to southern and northern cities in great numbers for almost three decades. Migrants represented a large consumer market. Unlike earlier communities of European immigrants, large, segregated African-American neighborhoods depended on numerous white-owned retail chain stores, which became the jobs campaigns' favorite targets. At the same time, urban African-Americans also forged the civic, media, and political networks that enabled direct-action campaigns. In addition, the Depression created widespread desperation and popular support for militant struggles for economic improvement.

Although Depression Era African-American urban communities created numerous consumer-based jobs campaigns, most Don't Buy where You Can't Work campaigns did not receive mass support. The Chicago campaign of 1929 and 1930, for example, depended on paid picketers and failed to win the backing of the city's most important black newspaper, the *Chicago Defender*. The campaign therefore disintegrated when the *Chicago Whip* folded in bankruptcy and employers secured a court injunction against the picket lines. The most successful movements relied on the backing of popular local black newspapers. The 1934 campaign in Harlem and Cleveland's Future Outlook League—both of which built mass community support—benefited greatly from the publicity provided by the *New York Age* and the Cleveland *Call & Post*. For the most part, however, Don't Buy Where You Can't Work campaigns suffered from the impression that they benefited a relative few workers, generally caused violence, and trampled on employers' rights to make hiring decisions. In addition, unlike the interracial industrial union movement of the 1930s and 1940s or the Civil Rights Movement of the 1950s and 1960s, race-conscious Don't Buy Where You Can't Work campaigns did not generally win a significant number of white supporters.

For many people concerned with the lack of buying power in African-American communities, and frustrated with the obvious shortage of black faces behind the counters of white-owned stores, Don't Buy Where You Can't Work campaigns represented distinctive alternatives to the many other examples of unemployed, labor, and civil rights organizing of the 1930s. Consumer boycotts benefited from the fact that their appeal often crossed customary divisions within black communities. The symbolic importance and potential for upward mobility black clerks in black neighborhoods represented appealed to middle-, working-class, and poor African-Americans. Don't Buy Where You Can't Work campaigns also confronted color prejudice by demanding that stores hire dark-skinned African-Americans. In addition, women and men often marched alongside each other in the same direct-action movements. Middle- and working-class women, in particular, played an especially important role. As the managers of household economies, African-American women created the networks that made consumer boycotts effective.

Contemporaries on the right and left criticized Don't Buy Where You Can't Work campaigns. White business owners, politicians, and media outlets undercut popular support for the campaigns by claiming that picketers used violent intimidation against employers, although it was generally unclear whether the violence resulted from the actions of pickets, employers, the police, or bystanders. Conservative critics also secured court injunctions against picket lines by arguing that the boycott movements violated what they saw as employers' inviolable rights to control hiring decisions. Left-leaning critics dismissed consumer-based campaigns for different reasons. They argued that consumer boycotts were bourgeois movements that would benefit only a few people who secured white-collar positions. In addition, especially before the Popular Front period, Communist leaders argued that race-conscious boycotts would divide white and black workers.

Until 1938, court injunctions against picket lines comprised the most important barriers to Don't Buy Where You Can't Work campaigns. The 1932 Norris-LaGuardia Act sanctioned picketing in legal labor disputes, but lower court and appellate court judges decided that protests against racially discriminatory hiring practices were not legal labor disputes. This changed when Washington, D.C.'s New Negro Alliance faced an injunction against its pickets against the Sanitary Grocery Company's stores; the alliance brought its case to the Supreme Court. In the majority opinion in *New Negro Alliance v. Sanitary Grocery Co.* (1938), Justice Owen J. Roberts expanded the definition of a legal labor dispute to include cases in which the disputes "arise with respect to discrimination in terms and conditions of employment based upon differences of race or color."

In the wake of the New Negro Alliance decision, a renaissance of Don't Buy Where You Can't Work campaigns spread across the country. The New Negro Alliance won jobs for black workers with local department stores and breweries in Washington, D.C. Harlem's Greater New York Coordinating Committee, led by Reverend Adam Clayton Powell, secured an agreement with the local chamber of commerce that all retail stores in the area would increase the proportion of African-American white-collar workers. In Chicago, the Negro Labor Relations League and the Chicago Urban League's Council of Negro Organizations led a successful campaign to secure driver-salesmen jobs for black men with local dairies. The St. Louis Clerks' Circle, in cooperation with the local Urban League branch, won hundreds of white-collar jobs for black workers. Cleveland's Future Outlook League created what was perhaps the most dynamic movement in the wake of the New Negro Alliance decision.

Historians disagree on the question of how Don't Buy Where You Can't Work campaigns fit into the long history of nonviolent direct action in the African-American freedom struggle. Some scholars have looked at the campaigns as part of the long continuous history of nonviolent militancy stretching from resistance to slave owners, boycotts of discriminatory schools and transit systems in the early twentieth century, consumer boycotts in the 1930s, and nonviolent direct action of the 1950s and 1960s. In contrast, historians August Meier and Elliott Rudwick have convincingly argued that the Don't Buy Where You Can't Work campaigns are the best illustrations of discontinuity in the history of African-American nonviolent resistance to racial oppression. There is no easy way to draw a link between Don't Buy Where You Can't Work campaigns and later movements to desegregate public accommodations in predominately white neighborhoods. In addition, despite the fact that both used nonviolent pickets and focused on retail businesses, the 1930s consumer boycott movements had little in common with the civil rights movements of the 1950s and 1960s. The later movements' ability to mobilize mass interracial support, their thoroughly articulated commitment to nonviolent resistance based on Christian morality, and their focus on integration and legal rights distinguish these predecessors from Don't Buy Where You Can't Work campaigns. During the 1960s, Operation Breadbasket, under the leadership of Reverend Jesse Jackson, revived economic boycotts against large-scale retail establishments in Chicago. This incarnation of consumer boycotts, however, occurred after the civil rights' victories of the mid-1960s, when African-American political movements began to shift their focus from legal rights to economic power, and from integration to nationalism.

JEFFREY HELGESON

References and Further Reading

Greenberg, Cheryl. *"Or Does It Explode": Black Harlem in the Great Depression*. New York: Oxford University Press, 1991.
Hunter, Gary Jerome. "'Don't Buy from Where You Can't Work': Black Urban Boycott Movements during the Depression, 1929–1941." PhD. dissertation, University of Michigan, 1977.
Kelley, Robin D. G. *Race Rebels: Culture, Politics, and the Black Working Class*. New York: Free Press, 1994.
Lamon, Lester. *Black Tennesseans, 1900–1930*. Knoxville: University of Tennessee Press, 1977.
McDowell, Winston. "Race and Ethnicity during the Harlem Jobs Campaign, 1932–35." *Journal of Negro History* 69 (Summer-Fall 1984): 134–143.
Meier, August, and Elliott Rudwick, *along the Color Line: Explorations in the Black Experience*. Urbana: University of Illinois Press, 1976. (reprinted. 2002)
Pacifico, Michele F. "'Don't Buy Where You Can't Work': the New Negro Alliance of Washington." *Washington History* 6, 1 (Spring-Summer 1994): 66–88.
Phillips, Kimberly L. *Alabama North: African-American Migrants, Community, and Working-Class Activism in Cleveland, 1915–1945*. Chicago: University of Illinois Press, 1999.
Skotnes, Andor. "'Buy Where You Can Work': Boycotting for Jobs in African-American Baltimore, 1933–34." *Journal of Social History* 27 (Summer 1994): 735–761.
Spear, Allan H. *Black Chicago: The Making of a Negro Ghetto*. Chicago, IL: University of Chicago Press, 1967.
Wye, Christopher G. "Merchants of Tomorrow: The Other Side of the 'Don't Spend Your Money Where You Can't Work' Movement." *Ohio History* 93 (Winter-Spring 1985): 40–67.

Cases Cited

New Negro Alliance v. Sanitary Grocery Co., 303 U.S. 552 (1938).

See also **Future Outlook League of Cleveland; Norris-LaGuardia Federal Anti-Injunction Act**

DORR WAR

The colony of Rhode Island, founded in 1636 by Roger Williams, was an oasis of religious and political freedom in New England. Although nearby settlements coveted the diminutive area, Williams and especially Newport physician John Clarke secured a liberal charter in 1663 from King Charles II, son of the slain monarch executed during the Puritan revolution in England. The document actually encouraged Rhode Island to experiment with religious toleration and representative democracy in the face of neighboring Puritan orthodoxy and the religious fratricide that recently ripped the mother country. The charter empowered the Rhode Island General Assembly to determine voting rights. These early legislators tied the franchise to land ownership, empowering most residents in this agricultural area.

After the American Revolution grafted some of the Ocean State's liberal tradition into the nation's new polity, Rhode Island engineered the country's industrial revolution at Slater's Mill in Pawtucket in 1790. In the ensuing half-century, native-born citizens and immigrants flocked to the expanding textile industry that paid workers, including children, in hard currency. As pioneering factory laborers abandoned farms, they also lost the land that allowed them to reach the $134 threshold to vote. By 1840, almost 60% of adult white males did not own enough property to qualify to cast a ballot.

Nor could they serve on a jury, initiate legal action, or participate in other civic functions. Nonetheless, they still had to pay taxes and perform militia and fire brigade service. The state degenerated into a declining democracy, governed by an ancient English parchment. The King Charles Charter, once a blueprint for enlightened and tolerant government, now accomplished the opposite of its original intent.

Furthermore, Rhode Island's earliest rural towns enjoyed greater representation in the legislature despite dwindling populations and paltry tax payments while the new industrial cities suffered from under representation while paying the lion's share of financial assessments. The tiny municipality of Middletown, for example, with a population of 1300 sent four delegates to the general assembly while the capital city of Providence with 23 thousand inhabitants had the same number of representatives. Adding insult to injury, the eldest sons of eligible voters could cast a ballot under the antique provisions of primogeniture that harked back to medieval Europe and outlasted the American Revolution.

Numerous attempts at constitutional change in the first two generations of the nineteenth century failed despite a powerful alliance between skilled workers and some of Rhode Island's elite, most notably Thomas Wilson Dorr, a Harvard-educated lawyer imbued with the democratic passion of the Founding Fathers not to be taxed without democratic representation. The aristocratic Dorr championed the rights of the handful of pre-famine Irish-Catholic immigrants who became a flashpoint in the Yankee backlash to reform. On a personal level, he also supported voting privileges for African-Americans, a stand that his followers narrowly defeated as too provocative in a constellation of already radical proposals.

In the face of the state's ruling class—a group of about 8,000 freemen in a population of about 100 thousand—Dorr brilliantly orchestrated the passage of a People's Constitution in 1841. In a scrupulously documented three-day election, the forces of change allowed both freemen who could already vote as well as those who would be empowered under Dorr's proposed liberal provisions. In a stunning victory, Dorr and his followers won a clear majority from both sets of voters who endorsed a new constitution that did away with most financial qualifications.

The political leadership of the ruling opposition (the Whigs)—unwilling to recognize the legitimacy of the extralegal election—organized their forces into the Law and Order party and prepared a multifaceted reaction, especially on the judicial and military front. They finally offered some reform measures of their own (although they had fought all such measures prior to the reform election) while at the same time the state Supreme Court accused the Dorr juggernaut of treason against the state. Lines had hardened since the astonishing victory of the People's Constitution. The Law and Order party fanned the flames of class warfare and prejudice against the state's small Irish immigrant population in order to unite its own conservative Yankee base. The local press, stalwarts of the status quo, forcefully attacked the radical nature of the reforms. The state militia prepared to mobilize.

Scheduled elections in the spring of 1842 pitted moderate Democrats against the ruling Whigs, who won handily. However, Dorr's backers scheduled another extralegal vote at the same time and chose Dorr as the state's chief executive along with a slate of delegates. Rhode Island now had two sets of governors and legislators.

Dorr, Rhode Island's inadvertent leader, threw caution to the wind and led his forces in an inconclusive midnight attack on the state arsenal in May 1842. Ironically, some of Dorr's own patrician relatives defended the armory. Another battle followed in the northern part of the state as textile workers and other laborers continued to back Dorr while his more genteel supporters left the fold as events turned

violent. The Law and Order group unleashed the militia and, in a remarkable and creative tactic, attracted the state's African-American population into their ranks by guaranteeing them the right to vote. One local congressman remarked that his constituents would rather see blacks vote than the despised Irish.

In a mopping-up operation, the state militia arrested several hundred "Dorrites," including the working-class leader, Seth Luther, as well as Dorr. Sentenced to life imprisonment in 1844, he was pardoned several years later but died of poor health in 1854. Issues from the relatively bloodless insurrection landed in the United States Supreme Court, initiated a thousand-page indictment of Law and Order rule by Congressional Democrats, and became a part of the 1844 Democratic presidential election that featured the slogan, "Polk, Dallas, and Dorr." Although the forces of Law and Order instituted some of Dorr's reform package, especially for native-born citizens, vestiges of voter restraints lasted late into the twentieth century. An immediate outcome of the conflict enfranchised hundreds of black voters for supporting the conservative forces while Irish-Americans, and later immigrants, remained the most disenfranchised caste outside the southern states.

SCOTT MOLLOY

References and Further Reading

Conley, Patrick T. *Democracy in Decline: Rhode Island's Constitutional Development, 1776–1841*. Providence, RI: Rhode Island Historical Society, 1977.
Gettleman, Marvin E. *The Dorr Rebellion: A Study in American Radicalism, 1833–1849*. New York: Random House, 1973.
Mowry, Arthur May. *The Dorr War*. Providence, RI: Preston and Rounds, 1901.

See also **Luther, Seth**

DRUM, FRUM, ELRUM

In 1968, black autoworkers in Detroit began to organize militant, race-based revolutionary unions that openly proclaimed a black Marxist-Leninist position. *DRUM* (Dodge Revolutionary Union Movement), *FRUM* (Ford Revolutionary Union Movement), and *ELRUM* (Eldon Avenue Revolutionary Union Movement) were the largest and most active of the affiliated unions. Founding members of the revolutionary union movement included John Watson, Ken Cockrel, Mike Hamlin, Luke Tripp, General Baker, Chuck Wooten, and Ernest Allen. Former Student Non-Violent Coordinating Committee (SNCC) and Black Panther party organizer James Forman joined the group later as well. In early 1969, The League of

Revolutionary Black Workers was established to coordinate the policies, strategy, and activities of the various revolutionary unions.

Following the July 1967 uprising, black auto workers began meeting for discussions in caucus-style assemblies at the Dodge Main plant (Hamtramck assembly plant). The *Inner City Voice*, a radical black newspaper, also began to appear in publication in Detroit's ghettos in September of the same year. In May of the following year, the paper's editors united with nine black workers at Dodge Main to form DRUM. DRUM was organized in the immediate aftermath of a spontaneous, interracial wildcat strike by 4,000 workers at Dodge Main on May 2, 1968. Seven workers were fired (five black, two white), while all but two (both black) were eventually rehired. Following the strike and firings, DRUM began publishing a weekly newsletter entitled *drum*. The first issue was devoted to an assessment of the recent strike and argued that it was caused by a production speed-up from 49 to 58 units per hour. In addition, the newsletter highlighted the double standard with which the striking black workers were treated and attacked Chrysler for racist labor practices. Subsequent newsletters expanded on the union's positions and explained why a new structure outside of the United Auto Workers (UAW) union was necessary. DRUM noted that black workers represented 60% of the laborers at Dodge Main, worked in unsafe and unclean conditions, and were the target of racist procedures within both the plant and the union hall. The DRUM consistently argued that UAW leadership failed to address the grievances of black workers sufficiently. It therefore felt that black autoworkers should have a separate contract and be able to conduct direct negotiations with Chrysler. Relations between DRUM and the UAW deteriorated further when the UAW publicly endorsed the Detroit Police Department's annual field day celebration. Most white members and leaders of the UAW regarded DRUM as extremist and worried it would splinter the unionized Dodge workforce.

The DRUM organized a series of rallies and wildcat strikes against Chrysler in the summer and fall of 1968 that succeeded in attracting more members but failed to produce concrete improvements. After a mass rally on October 24, 1968, at Chrysler's Highland Park headquarters drained DRUM's treasury, the group attempted to raise both funds and the revolutionary consciousness of workers through a fund-raising raffle on November 17 in which the prizes were an M-1 rifle, a shotgun, and a bag of groceries.

The DRUM was also known for maintaining a confrontational posture toward those within the black community whose activities were seen as inconsistent with DRUM policies. In its first newsletter, DRUM editors identified particular black workers within Chrysler plants who worked closely with management or refused to strike as "Uncle Toms." Likewise, when the Detroit chapter of the Urban League held a luncheon at the Statler-Hilton Hotel in November 1968 to present equal-opportunity employment awards to Chrysler, Ford, and General Motors, uninvited DRUM workers wearing heavily soiled work clothes created a disruption by parading through the formal luncheon with protest signs.

The DRUM activities during 1968 inspired other black autoworkers in Detroit to establish their own revolutionary unions. The FRUM and ELRUM, both organized in November of 1968, were the most prominent. Others included Mack Stamping (MARUM), Forge (FORUM), Jefferson Ave. (JARUM), Cadillac (CADRUM), Chrysler (CHRYRUM), Mount Road Engine (MERUM), as well as two nonauto affiliates, United Parcel Service (UPRUM) and Detroit News (NEWRUM). The ELRUM was especially problematic for Chrysler because the Eldon Avenue plant was Chrysler's only gear and axle plant, making the company vulnerable to a strategic shut-down. In fact, when ELRUM completely shut down plant production with its first wildcat strike on January 27, 1969, Chrysler responded by firing 26 striking workers. Although most fired workers were eventually rehired, the president of ELRUM, Fred Holsey, was not. The ELRUM strike was significant for two reasons. First, a higher percentage of black workers took part than in previous actions; and second, black workers represented an even larger proportion of the labor force at the Eldon Ave. plant than at the Hamtramck assembly plant. In 1970, ELRUM initiated two more wildcat strikes. In April, ELRUM workers maintained a three-day strike to protest the firing of John Scott, a worker accused of threatening to beat a foreman with a pinion gear in self-defense. As a result of the strike, Scott was rehired, and the foreman was removed from his position. In addition, a wildcat strike against unsafe working conditions at the Eldon Ave. plant occurred in May when jitney operator Gary Thompson was killed in a job-related accident.

The Revolutionary Union Movement (RUM) in Detroit gradually faded out of existence as a result of internal dissention. A major split emerged in 1970 between revolutionary Black Nationalist workers and Marxist-Leninist organizers and intellectuals. In addition, the RUM organizations faced consistent opposition from management, local and international UAW leadership, and law enforcement agencies. Because of the flexible and transitory nature of the RUM organizations, an accurate count of RUM membership is not possible. However, it is clear that thousands of black workers took part in RUM, and it inspired wildcat strikes and other organizing activities. Judging from newsletter distribution, tens of thousands of black workers across the nation were sympathetic to RUM efforts. The RUM model spread beyond Detroit's auto plants throughout the late 1960s and early 1970s. Affiliated revolutionary unions were organized in New Jersey's and Georgia's auto plants; within New York's, San Francisco's, and Chicago's transit systems; among members of the U.S. Steelworkers union and the Building Service Employees International; and even inside the American Federation of Teachers.

JOSEPH LIPARI

References and Further Reading

Georgakas, Dan, and Marvin Surkin. *Detroit: I Do Mind Dying, A Study in Urban Revolution.* New York: St. Martin's Press, 1975.
Geschwender, James. *Class, Race, and Worker Insurgency: The League of Revolutionary Black Workers.* Cambridge, UK: Cambridge University Press, 1977.
Thompson, Heather Ann. *Whose Detroit? Politics, Labor, and Race in a Modern American City.* Ithaca, NY: Cornell University Press, 2001.

See also **The League of Revolutionary Black Workers**

DUAL UNIONISM

Labor-opposition groups faced a chronic paradox. The characteristic form of workers' organization under capitalism, unions, gathered individuals together on the basis of shared interests and grievances, contributing perhaps in the process to a heightened sense of working-class solidarity. Activists who established competing, dual unions were apt to be branded traitors sowing seeds of division. Often, to leave the established union and to start a new organization in competition with it was to cut oneself off from the heart of the working-class community and to abandon what appeared to be the natural base for the creation of a radical movement. Yet labor unions were reformist by nature, designed not to transform society but to win limited concessions from employers. American Federation of Labor (AFL) and other unions were often inhospitable environments dominated by conservative, white, male business unionists inclined to inhibit or repress whatever radical potential workers might display. This tension between the vital role of unions in working-class life and the difficulty many radical activists had in working within them lies at the heart of the history of dual unionism in the United States.

The basis for dual unions might be racial or ethnic as well as political. Anarchists established separate union federations in Chicago, New York, and other cities during the 1880s. A revolutionary principle was involved. In building this movement, anarchists hoped to harness the power of the unions to destroy the capitalist state, undermine private property, and build a libertarian society. But the constituent organizations that formed these new federations were most frequently dual ethnic unions based in German, Czech, and other recent-immigrant communities. Feeling unwelcome in the mainstream unions, the immigrants organized their own, which tended to be far more radical than craft union counterparts. Also in the 1880s, "trade assemblies" of the Knights of Labor, with its expansive labor reform ideology, overlapped and sometimes competed with craft unions in the same industries. Black workers, particularly in the World War I and 1920s era, sometimes chartered new organizations outside of the AFL and the railroad brotherhoods when the existing unions insisted on maintaining the color line.

There was an implicit radical logic in the actions of the anarchists, and later the socialists, in constructing such separate radical movements; the business unionists seemed not only disinterested but often hostile to change. But there is no doubt that their actions frequently led to splits even among the radicals themselves and further alienated them from the mainstream unions. When the Socialist Labor Party (SLP) launched the Socialist Trades and Labor Alliance (STLA) in 1895, the move failed to win not only most unionists, but even some of the party's own members who preferred to remain in the AFL to contest for power in what was already a mass organization. The split caused within the SLP over the issue of dual unionism helps to explain the appearance of the Socialist Party of America (SP) in 1901. Most SP members preferred to join existing unions and work within the AFL. The failure of groups like the STLA and the relative strength of socialist influence in the AFL around the turn of the century suggest the wisdom perhaps of the SP argument.

By far the most famous organization to embrace the principle of dual unionism, the Industrial Workers of the World (IWW) won considerable strength among diverse groups of unorganized workers between its birth in 1905 and its eclipse during the 1920s. Anarchosyndicalists, the Wobblies envisioned a new federation of revolutionary industrial unions, each one organizing all of the workers in its respective industry regardless of skill, race, nationality, sex, or politics. The decision to obliterate the color line was striking in an era of rampant segregation and discrimination in which many AFL and railroad unions specifically barred African-Americans, Chinese, and other workers of color. Wobbly activists provided charismatic leadership for a whole series of mass strikes by immigrant men and women in the textile, steel, auto, and other industries from 1909–1913. Although the AFL employed the term dual unionism often in its attacks on the IWW, some of these IWW unions did not compete directly with existing mainstream unions. In some cases, they organized in industries where no unions of any description existed, as in their efforts to build agricultural unions in the World War I era. In other cases, they were not really competing because they organized among despised immigrant, Asian, and black workers where the AFL unions were making no efforts themselves. Even where they did not compete directly with AFL unions, however, the IWW projected a far more inclusive and militant model of unionism and in this sense threatened the vested business unions. In part because they were facing enormous odds, however, IWW organizations tended to be fleeting. Most were either destroyed in employer and government counterattacks or simply withered away by the early twenties.

Coming directly out of the IWW, William Z. Foster and his Syndicalist League of North America (SLNA) developed an alternative to dual unionism based in part on the French syndicalist model. Foster argued that rather than abandon the mainstream unions, activists must transform them into revolutionary weapons through a process he called "boring from within." A militant minority within each of the unions would agitate for a more aggressive line and for the organization of the unorganized. Although neither the SLNA nor a later organization, the International Trade Union Educational League, ever grew substantially, the group of syndicalists around Foster played important roles in the World War I organizing drives, which seemed to demonstrate the effectiveness of working within existing unions. The concept of boring from within won even greater acclaim when it was embraced by Lenin and his new Red International of Labor Unions in 1921.

Although originally inclined toward dual unions and shrill attacks on the AFL, the new Communist movement abandoned any plan to integrate with the IWW and firmly rejected the dual-union strategy from 1921–1928. In the process, the movement enjoyed some success. Employing Foster's Trade Union Educational League (TUEL) as a base, Communist unionists and their allies organized oppositional groups within several important unions, though the league's members were subject to constant expulsions, particularly in the mining and needle trades industries. These expulsions and a new turn in Communist trade union policy provided the basis for a new dual-union initiative in late 1928—the Trade Union Unity League (TUUL). The new league established revolutionary unions in several industries where they competed directly with existing AFL organizations, notably in mining, metalworking, and the garment and auto industries. The TUUL organizations led a series of spectacular strikes in 1929 and the early 1930s, facing considerable violence from employers' forces, vigilantes, and police.

When it was liquidated with the appearance of the new Popular Front line in 1935, many of the TUUL's activists emerged as organizers in the Congress of Industrial Organizations (CIO). Organizers for this new federation of industrial unions competed in some cases with weak, existing AFL unions in basic industry and in other cases led drives where no unions existed at all. In bitter conflicts between the two federations, AFL organizers often leveled the dual-union charge at the new CIO. The rivalry ended only with the expulsion of the CIO's left-wing unions in 1949, and the merger of the two federations in 1955. In order to undermine the left-wing unions, the CIO chartered a series of dual unions that competed with them, often successfully, in the 1950s.

Given frequent tension between conservative leaderships and rank and file activists, the danger of competing breakaway unions was always present. One of the most spectacular and violent of these conflicts involved the struggle between the United Mine Workers of America (UMWA) and the Progressive Miners of America (PMA), established in 1932 by radicals in Illinois District 12. The breakaway union competed directly with the UMWA for membership, occasioning considerable violence in the Illinois coalfields throughout the 1930s, and it declined only gradually after the UMWA returned to the AFL in 1946.

With newer industrial unions more open to unskilled, women, and minority workers and rank-and-file movements scoring notable successes in the late 1960s and 1970s, breakaway unions were less common in the postwar era. By the end of the twentieth century, with the labor movement under attack and in decline, union mergers were far more typical. The notion of launching new unions in such an inhospitable climate was undoubtedly a daunting prospect.

Dual unions never won most workers to a radical union program. Yet anarchist, IWW, syndicalist, Communist, and other radical organizers played important roles in organizing the unskilled, women, and minority workers excluded by the mainstream unions. In the process, they pioneered new forms of organization and new strategies and kept alive an alternative vision of the labor movement as a vehicle for social change.

JAMES R. BARRETT

References and Further Reading

Barrett, James R. "Boring from Within and Without: William Z. Foster, the Trade Union Educational League, and American Communism in the 1920s." In *Labor Histories: Class, Politics, and the Working-Class Experience*, edited by Eric Arnesen, Julie Greene, and Bruce Laurie. Urbana, IL: University of Illinois Press, 1998.

Cochran, Bert. *Labor and Communism: The Conflict That Shaped America Unions.* Princeton, NJ: Princeton University Press, 1977.

Dubofsky, Melvyn. *We Shall Be All: A History of the Industrial Workers of the World.* Chicago, IL: Quadrangle Books, 1969.

Johanningsmeier, Edward P. "The Trade Unity League: American Communists and the Transition to Industrial Unionism, 1928–1934." *Labor History* 42, 2 (2001): 159–177.

Nelson, Bruce C. *Beyond the Martyrs: A Social History of Chicago's Anarchists, 1870–1900.* New Brunswick, NJ: Rutgers University Press, 1988.

Rosswurm, Steve, ed. *The CIO's Left Led Unions.* New Brunswick, NJ: Rutgers University Press, 1992.

Saposs, David. *Left Wing Unionism: A Study of Radical Policies and Tactics.* New York: International Publishers, 1926.

Zieger, Robert H. *The CIO, 1935–1955.* Chapel Hill, NC: University of North Carolina Press, 1995.

DUBINSKY, DAVID (1892–1982)
President, International Ladies' Garment Workers' Union

An influential American trade union leader and official who served as president of the International Ladies' Garment Workers' Union (ILGWU) from 1932–1966. Dubinsky (originally Dobnievski) was born in Brest-Litovsk in Russian Poland on February 22, 1892, the youngest of six children in an impoverished Jewish family. His father moved the family to Lodz where he operated a bakery and where at age 11 David began his working life. At 14, Dubinsky joined a bakers union affiliated with the German Jewish Workers' Union—or the Bund—an ideological organization consisting mainly of Jews in Eastern Europe and Russia. The union advocated global socialism. Dubinsky was soon arrested and imprisoned by the Russian Czar's police. Though he was to be exiled to Siberia, Dubinsky managed to escape and secured passage to the United States, where he entered New York on New Years' Day, 1911.

Dubinsky apprenticed as a fabric cutter in New York's bustling apparel trade and joined the prestigious Local 10—the cutters' union affiliate —of the ILGWU. At age 29, he was elected head of the local and soon rose to be an officer in the ILGWU, served as union secretary-treasurer, then president from 1932 until his retirement in 1966. At the outset of his term as president, the ILGWU had been decimated by the industrial slowdown precipitated by the Great Depression. The union was also nearly bankrupt from dwindling membership and an internal struggle between Communist and moderate forces. Denouncing Stalinist-led unionists, Dubinsky allied the ILGWU with Franklin Roosevelt's New Deal and advocated the democratic reform of industrial capitalism to ameliorate poverty, human suffering, and fairer treatment of workers. He served as a vice-president of the American Federation of Labor (AFL), the first garment workers' union president to serve on the labor federation's executive council, and he led the union in joining the Committee for Industrial Organizations (CIO). Dubinsky was also influential in securing the American labor movement's affiliation with the International Labor Organization—a dramatic policy shift that replaced American labor's isolationist history with a broader agenda of international worker solidarity. However, when the AFL suspended the CIO unions (1936), Dubinsky resigned from the federation. At the same time, he opposed the establishment of the CIO on a permanent independent basis, and in 1938 he also broke with it, thus making the ILGWU independent until 1940, when it reaffiliated with the AFL. In 1936, he was one of the founders of the American Labor Party in New York. When it fell under Communist influence, he resigned and played a key role in founding the Liberal Party. In 1945, he again became a vice-president and member of the executive council of the AFL, retaining the position after it merged with the CIO in 1955. His efforts at ousting corrupt union leaders culminated in the new ethics standards adopted by the AFL-CIO in 1957.

Along with such influential labor leaders as John L. Lewis, Sidney Hillman, George Meany, and Philip Murray, Dubinsky played a central role in building the American labor movement and advocating on behalf of workers. A firm believer in social unionism and economic justice, Dubinsky and other ILGWU leaders—men and women—successfully negotiated employer contributions to a health and welfare fund, a member pension fund, vacation time, and equitable compensation. From the late 1930s–1950s, Dubinsky led strong organizing campaigns to unionize apparel manufacturers who had begun to locate outside of the metropolitan New York area in search of cheaper, nonunion labor. Dubinsky was among few pioneering labor leaders and unionists who foresaw the threat from the movement of capital ever in search of cheaper labor (a threat that would be global by the end of the twentieth century). Such manufacturers were known as "runaway" factories and usually secured contracts to produce goods for New York-based jobbers. Yet they typically paid workers a fraction of what unionized New York workers earned, ignored minimum-wage and maximum-hour laws, and skirted statutory mandates when it came to workers' compensation, workplace safety, and child labor. Dubinsky saw to the establishment of union locals and affiliates in locales that were increasingly popular in runaway factories, including Scranton and Hazleton, Pennsylvania; and locales in upstate New York and New England.

Dubinsky was also influential in establishing cultural and social institutions that served ILGWU members' needs. These included a New York-based union leadership school; a Labor Stage for worker-based performing arts; the ILGWU's vacation and education resort, Unity House, in the Pocono Mountains of Pennsylvania; a union-owned radio station; and he was influential in establishing union-operated health care centers in key apparel-making hubs, including Manhattan, and Allentown and Wilkes-Barre, Pennsylvania. The ILGWU also constructed housing for member-retirees in New York.

With a membership that approached one-half million by the 1960s, the ILGWU had grown to be one of the most powerful labor institutions in the United States. Dubinsky ensured the union's role in local, state, and national politics by aligning it with influential and progressive Democratic politicians and policymakers. The ILGWU proved to be an influential lobbyist in the U.S. Congress, with various presidential administrations, and in state capitols around the nation but especially in the industrial Northeast. The union was a natural ally of Presidents John F. Kennedy and Lyndon B. Johnson and progressive legislators at the state and national levels.

Retiring as president in 1966, Dubinsky assumed the role of director of the ILGWU's Retiree Services Department where he served union 1981. He continued to provide advice and counsel to the ILGWU, the AFL-CIO, and the labor movement. Dubinsky passed away on September 17, 1982 in New York. He was inducted into Labor's Hall of Fame in January 1994.

KENNETH WOLENSKY

References and Further Reading

Danish, Max. *The World of David Dubinsky*. Cleveland, OH: World Publishing, 1957.
Dubinsky, David. *A Life with Labor*. New York: Simon and Shuster, 1977.
Lorwin, Louis. *The Women's Garment Workers*. New York: Arno, 1969.
Tyler, Gus. *Look for the Union Label*. Armonk, New York: M.E. Sharpe, 1995.
Wolensky, Kenneth C., Nicole H. Wolensky, and Robert P. Wolensky. *Fighting for the Union Label*. University Park: Pennsylvania State University Press, 2002.

See also **International Ladies' Garment Workers' Union**

DU BOIS, W. E. B. (FEBRUARY 23, 1868–AUGUST 27, 1963)
African-American Activist and Author

Probably the most prominent African-American intellectual in American history, W. E. B. Du Bois wrote many works on labor and working-class issues in his voluminous publications. His 95 years took him on an ideological odyssey, from Gilded Age *laissez faire* liberalism, through twentieth-century progressivism and liberalism, ending up as a Communist expatriate.

Du Bois was born in Great Barrington, in western Massachusetts. A precocious student, he was the first black graduate of his integrated high school and attended Fisk University in Tennessee, thence transferring to Harvard. He earned his B.A. and M.A. there and after two years at the University of Berlin, a Ph.D. He began to teach at Wilberforce University and worked as a teacher and writer, along with his political activism, for the rest of his life. His education was both wide and deep, with training in classics, history, and economics. In 1896, he married Nina Gomer. The couple had two children—Burghardt (who died at the age of three) and Yolande.

Du Bois's early views on labor and political economy were quite conventional. Like most of the educated middle class, black and white, Du Bois held classical liberal, or *laissez faire*, opinions. He described himself as favoring free trade and good government along with other Mugwump reformers of the 1880s. He decried the violent labor unrest of the Gilded Age and approved of the Haymarket executions. While in graduate school in Berlin, he outlined a novel in which an African-American entrepreneur's business was destroyed by his white workers at about the same time as the Pullman strike. On the other hand, Du Bois admired Prussian state socialism while studying in Berlin and sketched another novel whose protagonist was a socialist. He found himself in the great battle between classical and historical schools in the university's department of economics and later claimed that he considered himself a socialist while in Berlin. He had lauded Bismarck in his

Dr. W. E. B. Dubois. Library of Congress, Prints & Photographs Division [LC-DIG-ggbain-07435].

Fisk University commencement address and wore the Kaiser's goatee and mustache for his entire life.

His early sociological studies were also consonant with the liberal ethic of individual responsibility, self-control, self-help, and the Victorian moral code. In the *Philadelphia Negro* (1899), a path-breaking depiction of the city's black population, he condemned white prejudice and discrimination but emphasized the need for black responsibility and maintained his faith in free enterprise and economic competition. It sometimes sounded as if Du Bois were, in the phrase of a later generation, "blaming the victim." He also encouraged blacks to show greater interest in business and called for "Negro Businessmen's Leagues," an idea that Booker T. Washington turned into the National Negro Business League.

Though he later made his mark as the main opponent of Booker T. Washington, the two were quite close in the 1890s. Du Bois congratulated Washington on his "Atlanta Compromise" address, in which he urged blacks to defer demands for political and social equality and focus on economic progress, calling it "a word fitly spoken." "Here might be the basis of a real settlement between whites and blacks in the South," he wrote. Du Bois repeatedly considered working under Washington at the Tuskegee Institute. Their different opinions on education—Du Bois stressing liberal training for the elite, Washington industrial

and vocational schooling for the masses—have also been exaggerated. Their estrangement was largely due to Du Bois's independent spirit, which recoiled against the centralized control that Washington exercised trough the "Tuskegee machine."

Du Bois's later radicalism, and his propensity to revise the story of his life in his numerous autobiographies, has obscured his early conservatism. Around the turn of the century, Du Bois was beginning to work with black leaders who would come to break with Washington. One of these organizations was Alexander Crummell's American Negro Academy, an attempt to form a black professional society, as opposed to Tuskegee's focus on practical, vocational, industrial education. Du Bois presented a paper to the academy in 1897 entitled "The Conservation of Races." In it he criticized the individualism and assimilationism dominant among American Negroes and hoped that they would recognize and preserve their distinct cultural gifts. Their "spiritual, psychical" nature would "soften the whiteness of the Teutonic today," Du Bois wrote. "We are that people whose subtle sense of sound has given America its only American music, its only American fairy tales, its only touch of pathos and humor amid its mad money-getting plutocracy." Throughout his life, Du Bois would try to advocate a system in which blacks could retain their distinct identity and yet contribute fully to a white-majority society. Neither separatism nor assimilation but pluralism was his goal.

Thus, both his views on race and labor exhibited the characteristic "double consciousness" that Du Bois described in the *Souls of Black Folk*. In the early twentieth century, as he openly broke with Washington, Du Bois grew closer to white progressives and socialists.

Many of these dissidents came together in the Niagara Movement of 1905. Its "Declaration of Principles" stated, "We hold up for public execration the conduct of two opposite classes of men: The practice among employers of importing ignorant Negro-American laborers in emergencies, and then affording them neither protection nor permanent employment; and the practice of labor unions in proscribing and boycotting and oppressing thousands of their fellow-toilers, simply because they are black."

Like many progressives, Du Bois was profoundly ambivalent about organized labor. His early liberalism still shone through the rising socialism of these decades. His two works that addressed black labor most closely, *the Negro Artisan* (1902) and the *Negro American Artisan* (1912), were extremely critical of organized labor. His 1909 address to the National Negro Committee (a forerunner to the National Association for the Advancement of Colored People) expressed liberal labor principles in showing how white workers sought to eliminate black competition and used government power to do so. He carried this analysis into the *Crisis*, the NAACP monthly that he edited. "So long as union labor fights for humanity, its mission is divine," he wrote. "But when it fights for a clique of Americans, Irish [,] or German monopolists who have cornered or are trying to corner the market in a certain type of service, and are seeking to sell that service at a premium, while other competent workmen starve, they deserve themselves the starvation which they plan for their darker and poorer fellows." Too often he saw the latter as the nature of the American labor movement. Though he supported Woodrow Wilson in 1912 (the year after briefly joining the Socialist party), Du Bois's economic philosophy was socialist by World War I.

But he was unable to accept the socialist explanation for discrimination in organized labor—that employers fomented racial discord in order to frustrate proletarian solidarity. He saw too many cases in which white workers excluded and discriminated against blacks for their own advantage to believe that the race problem would resolve itself once capitalism was abolished. He was also skeptical about programs that emphasized race consciousness too much, such as Marcus Garvey's Back to Africa movement or the Communist party's calls for a separate African-American state in the black belt of the South.

Du Bois surmised that although white workers were more easily exploited under segregation, they enjoyed a "social and psychological wage" due to their superior social status. This insight, adumbrated in the cultural approach of his "Conservation of Races" essay, has been invoked in recent years by cultural studies theorists who describe the "construction of whiteness." His suspicion of left-wing alternatives to the trade-unionist AFL also followed form his belief that race consciousness was not simply a by-product of class struggle. He wrote after the 1917 race riot in East St. Louis, which was largely a reaction to the migration of black workers into that city, that "there is absolutely no hope of justice for an American of Negro descent" under AFL leadership. Ten years later, when the AFL lobbied for legislation to curb the use of injunctions in labor disputes, Du Bois told the NAACP leadership that these generally anti-union devices had often benefited black workers.

By the time that organized labor began to gain political power under the New Deal, Du Bois was moving in a retrograde direction. His response to the severe privation and unemployment of the Great Depression was to emphasize black economic cooperation. Race consciousness had always been a part of Du Bois thinking, and it returned in the 1930s, in a

way similar to that of his great antagonists, Booker T. Washington and Marcus Garvey. Du Bois' argument that blacks could turn segregation to their own advantage—that there could be "segregation without discrimination"—led to his resignation from the NAACP in 1934.

Du Bois returned to full-time teaching and writing at Atlanta University. His Marxian views on American labor can be seen in his monumental 1935 book, *Black Reconstruction in America*. Du Bois had been arguing for a new view of Reconstruction, stressing the role played by African-Americans in it and the positive results that it achieved, for decades. In this book, he described how the slaves helped to win their own freedom by refusing to work, in what he described as the first general strike in American history. He also praised the active role that the Reconstruction governments played in the political economy. Slowly, this black- and labor-centered revisionist view of Reconstruction gained power in the academy and has been the dominant one since the 1960s. Applying the sociological methods that he had pioneered at the turn of the century, Du Bois prepared the ground for a new generation of social historians in the 1960s, who explored American society "from the bottom up."

Du Bois became increasingly alienated from American politics and turned radical in the last third of his life. He returned briefly to the NAACP in 1944 as their director of special research but soon left again as the rift between him and Walter White widened. He turned his attention increasingly to world affairs. He was impressed by the success that the Japanese showed in ousting European colonial powers from Asia, despite their brutal treatment of Chinese, Koreans, Filipinos, Indonesians, and others. His affinity for the Soviet Union grew, especially after his second marriage to Shirley Graham in 1951. In Leninist fashion, he saw the problems of African-Americans as part of a global phenomenon whereby European capital exploited the resources and labor of the colored Third World. He supported Stalin throughout the Cold War. He was unsuccessfully prosecuted for serving as an officer of the Peace Information Center, a Soviet propaganda organization. Finally, in 1961, Du Bois joined the U.S. Communist party and moved to Ghana. Most historians and biographers avert their eyes at these last years in which he supported regimes unarguably more repressive than the Jim Crow South and focus on his earlier and otherwise illustrious career. He died in Ghana in 1963, the day before the March on Washington for Jobs and Freedom was held in Washington, D.C.

Du Bois's long and prolific career thus contains a multitude of significant ideas. Nobody struggled longer to understand the roles that race and class play in American and world civilization. These problems and his work will surely continue to compel the attention of intellectuals of future generations.

PAUL D. MORENO

References and Further Reading

Boston, Thomas D. "W. E. B. Du Bois and the Historical School of Economics." *American Economic Review* 81 (1991).

Lewis, David Levering. *W. E. B. Du Bois: Biography of a Race, 1868–1919*. New York: Holt, 1993.

———. *W. E. B. Du Bois: The Fight for Equality and the American Century, 1919–63*. New York: Holt, 2000.

Lester, Julius, ed. *The Seventh Son: The Thought and Writings of W. E. B. Du Bois*. 2 vols. New York: Random House, 1971.

The Papers of W. E. B. Du Bois. 89 reels of microfilm. Sanford, NC: Microfilming Corporation of America, 1980–19881.

Wolters, Raymond. *Du Bois and His Rivals.* Columbia, MO: University of Missouri Press, 2002.

DUNLOP COMMISSION

The Dunlop Commission was established by the Clinton administration in March 1993, and was formally known as the Commission on the Future of Worker-Management Relations. It was known as the Dunlop Commission because John T. Dunlop, a Harvard University professor and prominent mediator who was labor secretary in the Ford administration, chaired it. The commission was established by the Clinton administration under the auspices of Labor Secretary Robert Reich and Commerce Secretary Ronald Brown. Reich had been a noted labor economist and academic prior to his appointment as labor secretary by President Clinton. The commission was created in response to the 1992 Electromation decision issued by the National Labor Relations Board. The board ruled in that decision that some labor-management cooperation mechanisms violated Section 8(a)(2) of the National Labor Relations Act. The Dunlop Commission was an effort to create a new compromise between labor and management by offering organized labor easier union recognition, while also offering business new methods of promoting labor-management cooperation.

The commission pursued three main objectives. The first was to determine what new methods or institutions should be encouraged or required to enhance workplace productivity through labor management co-operation and employee involvement. The second was to identify what changes should be made in the present legal framework and practices of collective bargaining to enhance cooperative behavior, improve productivity, and reduce conflict and delay. The third was to examine what should be done to increase the extent to which workplace problems are directly resolved by the parties themselves rather than through state and federal courts and regulatory bodies. These seemingly innocuous objectives aroused a range of responses from commentator across the political spectrum.

The commission conducted a number of hearings, with 11 held in Washington and an additional six meetings held around the United States. It heard presentations from 354 witnesses and accumulated 3,858 pages of transcripts. The report that the commission produced reviewed the changing environment of worker-management relations, employee participation, and labor-management cooperation in American workplaces; worker representation and collective bargaining; and employment regulation, litigation, and dispute resolution. The favorable response of the labor movement to the report and the business community's largely negative response were based on the report's recommendations.

The report identified many changes in the American economy, including a decline in long-term productivity, the impact of technology on the workplace, stagnant real hourly compensation, and a growing division between full-time and part-time employment. A decline in collective bargaining and fewer strikes and lockouts were also discussed. The report suggested that the American economy could not continue on the route that it was proceeding and mentioned the growing bifurcation of the workforce as a particularly significant issue.

Several trends in the workplace were identified in the commission's report. Employee participation was identified as a growing, partially diffused development across the United States. It was further suggested that from 40 to 50 million workers would like to participate in decisions on the job if they had the opportunity to do so. Labor and management expressed differing views about the role of employee participation on the workplace. Union representatives argued before the commission that they viewed employee participation as an opportunity to improve both productivity and workplace democracy and viewed independent representation as necessary to achieve these objectives. Management saw employee participation as part of the work process, and felt that effective worker representation could be achieved in both unionized and nonunionized workplaces. While long-term employee participation in the workplace could lead to improved economic performance, the report noted that historical and contemporary evidence indicated the fragility of employee-participation structures. A number of issues were identified as barriers to implementing a viable employee-participation plan.

The report identified several flaws in the labor relations system in the United States. The number of National Labor Relations board elections for union certification had fallen in recent years, and representation elections were identified as conflictual activities for workers, companies, and unions. Workers who exercised their legal rights under the National Labor Relations Act faced the possibility of discharge or unfair discrimination for exercising those rights. Approximately one-third of workplaces that vote for union representation did not conclude a collective agreement, and the report further noted that there was a negative side to American labor relations in which employers facing an organizing drive violated the rights of workers wishing to organize.

The various changes in the economy, the workplace, and in the labor relations system were also linked to a complex legal framework. The report noted that the number of federal laws governing the workplace had grown significantly since the 1960s, with the Department of Labor solely responsible for enforcing these laws. A large increase in litigation related to the workplace had led to a backlog for the Department of Labor agencies responsible for administering the various labor laws. The report identified over reliance on civil courts as a problem with resolving workplace disputes. The use of other methods of dispute resolution in other countries, such as tripartite employment courts, was noted, and the commission suggested the possibility of the United States introducing such methods.

The Dunlop Commission was part of a select number of similar commissions and committees in twentieth-century American history. Four Congressional commissions on labor-management relations had been established in the twentieth-century: The 1898–1901 U.S. Industrial Relations Commission, the 1912–1915 U.S. Commission on Industrial Relations, the 1936–1940 LaFollette Committee, and the 1957–1960 McClellan Committee. Presidential commissions were established in 1919 by President Wilson and in 1945 by President Truman. A further two labor-management committees were established by President Johnson in the mid-1960s and by President Ford in 1975. The Dunlop Commission was thus part of an important sequence of commissions and committees established by Congress and the president for the purpose of examining labor-management relations.

The commission ultimately could not establish a basis for a compromise between labor and business that would balance the need for easier union recognition and better labor-management cooperation. Business was uninterested in accepting measures that would strengthen unions in return for new schemes for labor-management cooperation. The failure of the commission to meet this objective represented broader difficulties with creating a basis for a national consensus on labor-management relations in the late twentieth century. This difficulty with reaching a consensus also occurred as the American workforce experienced the changes described in the commission's report, including economic restructuring, increased job insecurity, and growing demographic change. The creation of the Dunlop Commission did, however, mean that the executive branch of the federal government was prepared to make an effort to address these changes in order to determine how workplace policy in the United States should be shaped in the future

JASON RUSSELL

References and Further Reading

Dunlop, John Thomas. *Industrial Relations Systems*. Boston: Harvard University Press, 1993.

Fact Finding Report: Commission on the Future of Worker-Management Relations, 1994. Washington, DC: United States Department of Labor/United States Department of Commerce.

Reich, Robert. *Locked in the Cabinet*. New York: Vintage, 1998.

E

EDUCATION, LABOR

Labor education programs in the United States have been characterized by three basic assumptions: That workers' interests are best served through alternative, independent working-class educational institutions; that education is key to political development and organizational strength; and that individual worker students bring a formal knowledge of the workplace and of the broader world that create a special pedagogical environment. Despite these common views, the workers' education movement in the United States has been marked by considerable variation in terms of goals, funding, pedagogy, and political commitment. With programs ranging from craft-centered guilds and mechanics' institutes to schools representing the full assortment of labor philosophies from Marxist and progressive politics to religious-based, feminist- and union-sponsored colleges dedicated to everything from organizing, social conservativism, and reform to public speaking and vocational advancement, the goals of labor education represent a spectrum for understanding the ideas that have shaped labor in the United States. Often the sights of important pedagogical experiments, worker-centered schools and their curriculums, impacted broader developments in American education, such as the expansion of adult education programs and evening division courses, especially in the post-1945 period. This dynamic blend of function and innovation makes these educational programs one of the labor movement's greatest contributions to American cultural history.

Early Precedents of Labor Education in the United States

Traditions of labor education were first transplanted to the United States from Europe in the colonial period through the establishment of craft guilds. Overseeing apprenticeships for young male craft workers, guilds served important social needs and welfare functions while also providing a more general education in reading and civics. Similar associations arose to represent artisans in the mechanical arts, and by the 1830s, mechanics' institutes were important features of a new urban culture, providing educational opportunities for a mostly male clientele through establishment of reading rooms and libraries, public lecture programs, and formal schools that offered a range of classes focused primarily in the sciences. The most successful of these schools was Philadelphia's Franklin Institute. Founded in 1824, it maintained a permanent faculty that offered courses in technology and business, while sponsoring annual competitions for aspiring engineers. Mechanics' institutes continued earlier guild traditions stressing social harmony between master craftsmen and younger apprentices, while emphasizing individualistic values that placed hard work and upward mobility as central tenants of a uniquely American character.

With industrial expansion in the early nineteenth century, and the corresponding sharpening of class interests, alternative views of labor education soon emerged. Early labor activists, such as Frances

Wright and Robert Dale Owen, called for the establishment of a nonsectarian, national public education system to foster democratic civic values and social equality. Yet the development of state-sponsored education at the primary and secondary levels focused primarily on socializing workers into accepting the capitalist values of their employers. Additionally most workers had limited access to formal education, with the majority of youth discontinuing school at an early age to enter the industrial workforce. Many workers continued to seek education in informal ways. In response workers and their associations inaugurated new types of worker-controlled schools outside of the mainstream educational system. Increased European immigration, particularly from Germany and Eastern Europe, energized this new development in labor education in the post-Civil War period. Independent schools, usually conducted in the evening or on Sundays, played important roles in an alternative workers' culture, stressing collective, political, and workplace goals. German groups, such as the *Arbeiter-Verin*, provided coherence for immigrant workers and adapted European political commitments to the American environment. Similar schools were prevalent in most immigrant communities, with classes sponsored in the 1890s and early 1900s in New York City by the United Hebrew Trades (UHT) and in Duluth, Minnesota, by the Finnish People's College. Many of these programs also stressed the involvement of women as both teachers and students, marking a break from earlier traditions.

One of the defining characteristics of the labor schools of the late nineteenth and early twentieth centuries was their emphasis on political education. In this effort there was a marked shift away from the mechanical arts toward the humanities, with curriculums focusing on history, political organization, sociology, and the law. Seeing education as key to forging a mass movement, labor schools played prominent roles in radical political strategies. From the 1880s on, socialist parties of all types actively supported independent educational efforts. Foremost among these was New York City's Rand School of Social Science. Founded in 1906, the Rand School, like most labor colleges, catered to a part-time student body, with a peer-centered curriculum that focused on question-and-answer sessions and reading groups rather than lecture methods. One of the most successful labor programs in the twentieth century, the school was in operation for almost 50 years, and its history marked by themes shared by many labor colleges of this era. Although always committed to socialist change, the school's faculty and students often disagreed on strategy, with outside attempts by various leftist groups to direct the curriculum sometimes exacerbating the infighting. The Rand School of Social Science's open embrace of Marxist ideology also brought on government surveillance and repression, resulting in its eventual demise in the 1950s.

Further to the left, the Communist Party of the United States of America (CPUSA) also adopted a rigorous program of labor education. Communist activists in the 1920s and 1930s paid close attention to all independent and union-sponsored workers' schools, infiltrating many programs to steer them toward more revolutionary goals. The CPUSA also initiated a variety of educational efforts aimed not only at adults, but at adolescents and children through such programs as the Young Pioneer's summer youth camps that provided a utopian environment where youths participated in programs that included dance, music, sports, and theater within a cooperative setting. In the 1940s, New York City's Jefferson School of Social Science emerged as the central school for the party's national network of labor schools. Like the Rand School of Social Science, the Jefferson School faced severe government repression through its years of existence and eventually disbanded in 1956.

Labor colleges across the political spectrum adapted innovative pedagogies, a hallmark of the workers' education movement. Many of these developments drew on the ideas of progressive education that emerged in the United States in the early twentieth century. Centered on the theories of John Dewey and other innovators, progressive education sought a more collaborative classroom model, de-emphasizing formal lectures and stressing group discussions and interaction. For the most part, labor school faculty came from the working class, with many courses taught by trade unionists with experience in organizing and strike campaigns, newspaper editing, collective bargaining, and political strategy. Besides these organic intellectuals, labor education efforts were also supported by university-trained teachers in history, sociology, and the legal profession, who advanced the cause of labor by offering their expertise in the classroom.

Women played an important role in implementing new ideas in labor education settings. Jane Addams's early experiments at Hull-House in Chicago was a model for many similar programs, with urban settlements offering classes in nutrition, childcare, consumer habits, and English language instruction. These experiments in urban education helped inform broader experiments in the field of labor education. In 1914, the National Women's Trade Union League formed the Training School for Women Workers in Chicago. This groundbreaking program introduced women to a range of practical skills useful in union work, such as journalism and public speaking. From this additional programs for women appeared, including the Bryn Mawr Summer School for Women Workers in Industry. Formed in the summer of 1921 at Bryn Mawr College outside Philadelphia, this residential program stressed women's role in bringing about social harmony, reflecting a middle-class uplift ideology that distanced it from more radical curriculums. Bryn Mawr's director Hilda W. Smith, a social worker and veteran of the suffragist movement, would emerge as an important leader within labor education for over a generation.

Trade Unions and Workers' Education

Organized labor has played a fundamental role in shaping the history of labor education in the United States. As part of its earliest organizing efforts in the 1870s, the National Labor Union established reading rooms and libraries in chapters across the country, with identical efforts embraced by the Knights of Labor and the American Federation of Labor (AFL). The International Ladies' Garments Workers' Union (ILGWU) pioneered union sponsorship of workers' education, formally establishing an education department to oversee an expanded program in 1914. Modeled after the schools of the United Hebrew Trades, the ILGWU program implemented courses in trade unionism and the humanities while also organizing such cultural activities as museum trips and concerts. In the 1920s, the AFL officially recognized the importance of labor education by advocating resources to adopting education departments in local unions. This move also reflected the AFL's wariness about the radical political agenda that marked many labor schools of the era. Through the 1920s and 1930s, AFL unions adapted educational programs, with noteworthy sections in the National Maritime Union of America and the Amalgamated Meat Cutters and Butcher Workmen. The AFL's union of local government workers, the American Federation of State, County and Municipal Employees (AFSCME) was active in workers' education, sponsoring summer training seminars and a large education and research center that focused on government reform and the promotion of civil service initiatives.

The 1920s saw the emergence of a number of independent labor colleges. Perhaps the most influential of this era was Brookwood Labor College, located in Katonah, New York. Brookwood's early curriculum was influenced by its director, A. J. Muste, a former labor official who turned to education as a way of furthering the cause of labor at a time of organizational decline. Unique as a residential program, Muste implemented a standard two-year course load that combined book learning in a nonhierarchical classroom setting along with a wide range of extracurricular activities, such as debate clubs, music, and theater. The school did have formal links to organized labor, with its staff represented by the American Federation of Teachers, Workers' Education Local 189, which pioneered in promoting the workers' education movement across the United States. Brookwood Labor College provided an educational experience for hundreds of graduates who eventually emerged as leaders of a revived labor movement in the 1930s.

One of the most important developments in labor education in the 1920s was the establishment of two agencies dedicated to the promotion of workers' education on a national scale. Founded in 1921, the Workers' Education Bureau of America served as an informational clearinghouse for labor education, organizing forums around the country and assisting local programs. The American Labor Education Service (ALES), established five years later, had a similar agenda, functioning as a general advisory service and providing information for education directors through the publication and distribution of labor education pamphlets, biographies of leaders, and books on U.S. labor history. The ALES also provided field services for existing labor education programs and encouraged new ones through the organizing of regional and local conferences and the publication of a national registry of workers' education teachers.

Organized labor's membership growth in the New Deal period saw a parallel expansion in workers' education programs. The Workers' Education Bureau of America and ALES, along with AFT Workers' Education Local 189 oversaw the rising popularity of these classes by sponsoring the adoption of a federal project for labor education with the Federal Emergency Relief Administration's Emergency Education Program. Organized by Smith in 1934, the Emergency Education Program trained approximately 1,700 teachers in a series of six-week courses offered at university and college campuses across the United States. The first federally funded teacher program in U.S. history, the initiative shared similar experiences with labor education programs through the twentieth century, with competing labor and political groups contesting the agency's objectives. Like other New Deal cultural initiatives, the Emergency Education Program was criticized for fostering politically leftist views and was eventually abandoned. Official government support of labor education continued however through the Labor Education Service Branch. Under direction of the Department of Labor, this branch was officially nonpartisan, performing as a distributor of information and research services while fostering voluntary programs that stressed union responsibilities in collective-bargaining agreements.

Besides union-supported educational workshops, the New Deal and World War II periods are noteworthy for the development of worker-based education in all regions of the nation. Schools were established in the Far West, including the California Labor School in San Francisco and such southern institutions as the Georgia People's School, the Southern School for Workers in the South, and the residential program at Highlander Folk School at Monteagle, Tennessee. A variety of religious-based labor schools also appeared. Pendle Hill, established by the Religious Society of Friends (Quakers) in 1930 in Wallingford, Pennsylvania, had a regional reputation for its seminars and summer programs based on the Brookwood model. Catholic labor colleges also marked the educational landscape. Stressing a belief in social justice while advocating antiradical political objectives, such schools as the Xavier Labor School in New York and the Comey Institute in Philadelphia emerged as models for similar experiments around the country. Some of these programs, such as the courses run by LaSalle College's Brother Alfred, also introduced arbitration associations that proved important in settling labor disputes well into the postwar period.

Within the house of labor in the 1930s and 1940s, the Congress of Industrial Organizations (CIO) embraced the concept of labor education more fully than the AFL, incorporating education into its major organizing campaigns. More importantly it saw the function of education as a tool in the broader transformation of American institutions. Through its Education and Research Department, the CIO served all of its international unions, providing important information concerning the national economy and the political objectives of the labor movement. In this way, by educating leadership and members, the CIO could promote an economic program that could be advanced by informed advocates in community forums across the country. The United Auto Workers (UAW) was the most active union within the CIO in its embrace of labor education, reflecting the social unionism of its leader Walter Reuther, a graduate of Brookwood Labor College. Throughout his years as UAW head, Reuther advanced the idea of union-sponsored education courses as a key aspect of an engaged trade unionism. Under his direction, the union eventually established the UAW Family Education Center, located in Black Lake, Michigan, as a yearlong education and recreation center.

College- and University-Based Labor Education Programs

The relationship between labor and institutions of higher learning was well-established early in the twentieth century, with successful experiments at Bryn Mawr College and numerous other colleges and universities. These links were strengthened in the post-1945 period. Several reasons account for the turn toward university- and college-based worker education programs in this era. The success of labor programs at universities, especially through the federal programs of the 1930s, showed administrators the financial benefit of providing continued course offerings to nontraditional students. This coupled with the new veterans' education benefits sponsored through the G.I. Bill paved the way for increased interest in labor-oriented adult education in the United States. Changes in labor's relation to the state also shifted its educational prerogatives by the postwar period. New Deal legal reforms created a new federally mandated collective bargaining order in American industry that called for the training of labor experts to facilitate workplace agreements and to oversee labor peace. Both business and labor interests took advantage of new labor management programs that were initiated across the nation. Finally McCarthy period government suppression of politically leftist labor schools shifted the priorities of labor education away from oppositional agendas toward more mainstream political goals.

Although numerous universities had been active in promoting labor education, the University of Wisconsin at Madison developed the most respected program linking higher academics to the cause of progressive labor. Steered by John R. Commons, an economist who had allied with radical causes in his early career, Wisconsin was a center for labor theorists and intellectuals in the years before World War I. The political climate at Madison was fostered by the university's relationship with Governor Robert M. LaFollette, who actively sought faculty input as he crafted reforms that reshaped the state's workplace policies. The program at Wisconsin provided education not just for academics allied to labor's cause, but to average union members through the School for Workers, which remains the oldest running university-based labor education program in North America. Cornell University's School of Industrial and Labor Relations continued this model, often seen as the foremost post-1945 professional labor program in the United States. Established as the New York State School of Industrial and Labor Relations by the New York state legislature in 1945, the school was sponsored to help improve labor relations in the state. The only four-year undergraduate institute in the United States that offers a labor management BA, Cornell's labor relations school has been active in supporting union-friendly programs by placing experienced union activists on its faculty and by offering seminars on such topics as steward training and organizing. Similar programs have been implemented in hundreds of colleges and universities across the United States, often in alliance with union education departments.

The stronger alliance between organized labor and higher education in the post-1945 period reflects a corresponding decline in class-consciousness among American workers. The disappearance of alternative, independent labor schools suggests the parallel decline of a separate working-class culture that marked the rise of labor education in the mid-nineteenth century. Some within the labor movement have sought to revive the earlier traditions of independent educational programs directed by labor for its own interests. The National Labor College in Silver Springs, Maryland, established by the AFL-CIO in 1974, was seen by many as a move in this direction. The school's primary goal has been to develop professional staff for national unions, with expertise in collective bargaining, legal studies, statistics, and economics, although the overall climate at the institute has often fostered a more class-based political consciousness. In the 1990s, the National Labor College received recognition as an independent, accredited institution of higher learning, changing its name to the George Meany Center for Labor Studies. One of the highlights of this center has been the inauguration of an organizing institute meant to energize a new period of membership growth. Although this objective has not been realized in the first decade since its founding, organized labor continues to stress the need for education. In the cyclical patterns of U.S. labor history, labor education has been a source of direction and hope in times of decline, serving as a tool for planning new courses of action. As organized labor seeks new paths in the twenty-first century, labor education continues as a long, viable tradition within American labor culture.

FRANCIS RYAN

References and Further Reading

Adam, Thomas. *The Worker's Road to Learning*. New York: American Association for Adult Education, 1940.

Altenbaugh, Richard J. *Education for Struggle: The American Labor Colleges of the 1920s and 1930s*. Philadelphia, PA: Temple University, 1990.

———. "The Children and Instruments of a Militant Labor Progressivism: Brookwood Labor College and the American Labor Movement of the 1920s and 1930s." *History of Education Quarterly* (Winter 1983): 395–411.

Barbash, Jack. *Universities and Unions in Workers' Education*. New York: Harper, 1955.

Brameld, Theodore. *Worker's Education in the United States*. New York: Harper, 1941.

Catlett, Judith L. "After the Goodbyes: A Long-Term Look at the Southern School for Union Women." *Labor Studies Journal* 10, 3 (1986): 300–311.

Coit, Elanor G., and John D. Conners. "Agencies and Programs in Workers' Education." *Journal of Educational Sociology* 20, 8 (April 1947): 520–528.

Gettleman, Marvin E. "No Varsity Teams: New York's Jefferson School of Social Science, 1943–1956." *Science and Society* 66, 3 (Fall 2002): 336–360.

Kornbluh, Joyce L., and Mary Frederickson. *Sisterhood and Solidarity: Workers' Education for Women, 1914–1984*. Philadelphia, PA: Temple University, 1984.

———. *A New Deal for Workers' Education: The Workers' Service Program, 1933–1942*. Urbana: University of Illinois Press, 1987.

Rosswurm, Steve, "The Catholic Church and the Left-Led Unions: Labor Priests, Labor Schools, and the ACTU." In *The CIO's Left-Led Unions*, edited by Steve Rosswurm, New Brunswick, NJ: Rutgers University Press, 1992.

Schneider, Florence Hemley. *Patterns of Workers' Education: The Story of the Bryn Mawr Summer School*. Washington, DC: American Council on Public Affairs, 1941.

Wertheimer, Barbara M. *Labor Education for Women Workers*. Philadelphia, PA: Temple University, 1981.

Wilentz, Sean. *Chants Democratic: New York City and the Rise of the American Working Class, 1788–1850*. New York: Oxford, 1984.

See also **Brookwood Labor College; GI Bill; Muste, A. J.; Reuther, Walter; Wright, Frances**

ELAINE, ARKANSAS MASSACRE (1919)

In the fall of 1919, an incident outside a church where an African-American union meeting was taking place led to a massacre of over a hundred African-Americans. Viewed in the context of the Red Scare and labor strife, both of which were attracting attention across the country, any activism on the part of African-Americans represented a particularly threatening challenge to the system of peonage in place on southern plantations. In fact African-Americans in the Arkansas delta and elsewhere in the South had endured segregation and disfranchisement long before the post-World War I Red Scare, and while it is true that the war gave returning black servicemen a sense that they should exercise their rights more forcefully, African-Americans had never been totally quiescent and subordinated. Long before the massacre at Elaine, individual sharecroppers and tenants had attempted on occasion to secure their fair share of the crop settlement from their landlords, and sometimes these confrontations led to violence. What was different in 1919 was that blacks had banded together under the banner of the Progressive Household Union of America and hired an attorney to represent them in suits they planned to file. The threat of a united force of African-Americans availing themselves of legal counsel prompted a swift and deadly response from planters who were able to use racism and the rumor of race war to unite whites across class boundaries to quash the black union.

Some time during the spring and summer of 1919, Robert Hill, an African-American farmer, began organizing the Progressive Household Union of America. He organized local chapters and collected dues, preaching the need to band together and file suit against planters in order to secure a fair settlement at the end of the crop year. During the last years of World War I, cotton prices had recovered after decades of disappointing returns, and African-American sharecroppers believed they deserved to share in the bonanza, but their planters thought otherwise and kept them indebted. Planters became aware of the union and grew increasingly alarmed, some of them circulating rumors that the union meant to murder whites and take their lands. In fact Hill had hired a white attorney from Little Rock, U.S. Bratton, to represent the union, and he had sent his son to Phillips County to interview members of the union in order to gather evidence. Young Ocier Bratton was in town on the morning of October 1, 1919, when the massacre got underway and was himself arrested and held in the Phillips County jail.

The evening before Bratton's arrest, a group of black sharecroppers were holding a meeting in a black church at Hoop Spur, a small hamlet near Elaine, when a car carrying two deputies and a black driver stopped just a few yards up the road. What happened next remains a matter of conjecture, but either the black union sentries standing at the door or the deputies opened fire. Both of the deputies were wounded, one of them mortally. The black driver made his way back to Helena, Arkansas, and alerted authorities, although the substance of his exact report remains unknown. The first news stories printed in the next morning's papers suggested that the officers had encountered bootleggers, but within hours rumors of an alleged insurrection of black sharecroppers spread throughout the county. A posse was dispatched, and soon the alarm attracted gangs of whites from other Arkansas counties as well as from across the river in Mississippi and Tennessee. Soon any semblance of order dissolved into chaos as whites rampaged against blacks, most of whom had played no part in the union organizing. Estimates of the total death toll among blacks ranged from 26—the official total—to 856. In fact it is likely that from 100–200 African-Americans lost their lives. Governor Charles Brough authorized the use of federal troops, veterans of the Great War stationed at Camp Pike, to restore order. Arriving on the morning of October 2, 1919, they disarmed blacks and whites, but historians debate the role the federal troops played in adding to the black death toll. Only five whites died, one of them a soldier.

On October 27, the Phillips County Grand Jury began to meet and four days later charged 122 African-Americans with participating in the riot. The only white man to face the threat of prosecution was Ocier Bratton, who was accused of having incited the African-Americans, but he never came to trial. Allegations later surfaced that the black prisoners were tortured into confessing to various crimes, including murder. After brief and cursory trials, some of which lasted no more than a few minutes, 65 were sentenced to prison and 12 to death. A concerted effort to spare the 12 condemned men from the gallows then ensued, with African-Americans in Arkansas participating in raising funds to represent them. The National Association for the Advancement of Colored People (NAACP) sprang into action and hired two Arkansans, one of them black and one white, to appeal the convictions of the Elaine Twelve. Scipio Jones, a noted African-American attorney from Little Rock, was joined by George Murphy, a Confederate veteran, in pursuing the cases. The Arkansas Supreme Court upheld convictions in six of the cases, which came to be known as the "Moore defendants," but required new trials in the other six cases, which came to be known as the "Ware defendants." The Arkansas Supreme Court was convinced by Murphy's argument that the original trial court had failed to designate which degree of murder Ed Ware and five others were guilty of having committed. New trials were ordered, but they were soon convicted once again and on July 23 were again sentenced to death. Later that year however, the Arkansas Supreme Court again overturned the convictions, this time on the basis of the fact that blacks had been excluded from the jury. While the local courts delayed retrying those cases, the NAACP relentlessly pursued further appeals in the other cases—the Moore cases—and the appeals eventually made their way to the United States Supreme Court, which called for new trials. By that time, no one in Arkansas wanted to revisit the cases, and by January 1925, the last of the Elaine Twelve were freed.

JEANNIE M. WHAYNE

References and Further Reading

Butts, J. W., and Dorothy James. "The Underlying Causes of the Elaine Riot of 1919." *Arkansas Historical Quarterly* 20 (Spring 1961): 95–104.

Cortern, Richard C. *A Mob Intent on Death: The NAACP and the Arkansas Riot Cases.* Middletown, CT: Wesleyan University Press, 1998.

McCool, B. Boren. *Union, Reaction, and Riot: A Biography of a Race Riot.* Memphis: Bureau of Social Research, Division of Urban and Regional Studies, Memphis State University, June 1970.

Rogers, O. A., Jr. "The Elaine Race Riots of 1919." *Arkansas Historical Quarterly* 19 (Summer 1960): 142–150.

Stockley, Grif, *Blood in their Eyes: The Elaine Race Massacres of 1919.* Fayetteville: University of Arkansas Press, 2001.

Taylor, Kieran, "We Have Just Begun: Black Organizing and White Response in the Arkansas Delta, 1919." *Arkansas Historical Quarterly* 63 (Autumn 1999): 265–284.

Waskow, Arthur I. *From Race Riot to Sit-In, 1919 and the 1960s: A Study in the Connections between Conflict and Violence.* Garden City, NY: Doubleday & Company, 1966.

Whayne, Jeannie M. "Low Villains and Wickedness in High Places: Race and Class in the Elaine Race Riot." *Arkansas Historical Quarterly* 63 (Autumn 1999): 285–313.

White, Walter. "'Massacring Whites' in Arkansas," *The Nation* (December 6, 1919): 715–716.

Woodruff, Nan Elizabeth. *American Congo: The Africa-American Freedom Struggle in the Delta.* Cambridge, MA: Harvard University Press, 2003.

ELECTROMATION v. *TEAMSTERS LOCAL 1094* (1992)

The case of *Electromation v. Teamsters Local 1094*, decided by the National Labor Relations Board (NLRB) in December 1992, had dramatic implications for the corporate administration of nonunion employee cooperation efforts. Since the return and proliferation of these programs in the 1980s under such names, for example, as quality of work life programs, quality circles, and employee involvement programs, these cooperative efforts have been of intense concern for unions who often felt that their implementation was at best a union-substitution strategy and at worst an outright anti-union instrument designed to prevent the formation of independent unions. Thus many union proponents viewed such vehicles as nothing more than modern-day company unions that were made illegal under Section 8(a)(2) of the 1935 National Labor Relations Act. Specifically Section 8(a)(2) prevents an employer from either controlling or obstructing the establishment or management of any labor organization or from supporting it, financially or otherwise, in any manner. Prior to the Electromation decision, the NLRB interpreted this provision quite narrowly in prohibiting certain types of employee dealings with management. However the board's decision in this case resulted in the NLRB creating tests for deciding the legality of union-management cooperation programs in nonunion settings.

Electromation, a nonunion electrical parts manufacturer, established action committees of employees after Teamsters Local 1094 launched an organizing drive at the company. These committees discussed a variety of personnel issues, including absenteeism, the no-smoking policy, attendance bonuses, communication, and pay increases for the company's top jobs. The Teamsters requested employer recognition after the committees' creation and filed an unfair labor practice charge with the NLRB, arguing that the company had violated Section 8(a)(2) of the NLRA. Specifically the union claimed that the committees were labor organizations that Electromation had dominated and unfairly supported. Ruling that the action committees were controlled by the company, the NLRB ordered Electromation to dissolve the committees.

In the post-Electromation environment, nonunion employers who engaged in employee-participation efforts became concerned that their programs might be illegal with regard to the current interpretation of Section 8(a)(2). Based on NLRB and court rulings after the Electromation decision, employee-participation programs will probably be determined to be legal assuming the following seven conditions are present. First employee representatives are elected by coworkers to serve on the committees with terms of service regularly rotated among employees. Second employees cannot be unhappy with these participation programs, and these cooperative efforts cannot exhibit any type of anti-union bias. Third a union organizing drive cannot be taking place when these programs are created. Fourth employee participation is not coerced but voluntary. Fifth employees are allowed to join a union. Sixth the participation committee has the power to make and implement final and binding decisions, and seventh the topics discussed by these committees can be only ones that are not subjects determined to be bargained in contract negotiations.

While the Electromation decision neither led to increased union-organizing success nor to arresting the continuing decline in U.S. union density in the late twentieth century, it did make nonunion employers more cautious in the implementation of their employee-participation programs. In that sense employees gained some leverage in the workplace and clearly benefited from the decision. It remains to be seen however whether unions can use the Electromation decision to their advantage in developing successful union-organizing strategies in the first decade of the twenty-first century.

VICTOR G. DEVINATZ

References and Further Reading

Gely, Rafael. "Where Are We Now: Life after Electromation." *Hofstra Labor and Employment Law Journal* 45 (Fall 1997): 45–74.

LeRoy, Michael H. "Employer Domination of Labor Organizations and the Electromation Case: An Empirical Public Policy Analysis." *George Washington Law Review* 61 (August 1993): 1812–1852.

Moe, Martin T. "Participatory Workplace Decision Making and the NLRA: Section 8(a)(2), Electromation, and the Specter of the Company Union." *New York University Law Review* 68 (November 1993): 1127–1186.

Stokes, Michael L. "Quality Circles or Company Unions? A Look at Employee Involvement after Electromation and DuPont." *Ohio State Law Journal* 55 (Fall 1994): 897–927.

EMANCIPATION AND RECONSTRUCTION

Emancipation and the reconstruction of the American South during and after the Civil War involved the reorganization of both the antebellum South's labor system and racial order. The abolition of slavery was also an essential element of the transition to more distinctly capitalist social relations in the South.

Slavery and the Old South

On the eve of the Civil War, nearly four million slaves labored on plantations and farms in 15 states from Delaware to Texas. Between one-quarter and one-third of white households throughout the slave states held slaves. Most slaveholdings were relatively small. The large majority of slaveholders held fewer than 20 slaves, with most of these owning one or two, but the majority of slaves lived on plantations with holdings of more than 50 slaves. In addition to raising cotton, the South's most important staple crop, slaves grew tobacco in Virginia, North Carolina, and Kentucky; rice along coastal South Carolina and Georgia; and sugarcane in southeastern Louisiana and eastern Texas. They also worked on the smaller landholdings of yeoman farmers, both within the plantation belt and in the upcountry.

The South before the Civil War was a predominantly rural and agricultural society, but thousands of slaves also labored in the South's small industrial sector, in factories, on railroads, or in building canals. Many slaves also lived and worked in southern cities, mostly as domestic servants or manual laborers. Skilled slaves were often hired out by their owners. They were permitted a considerable degree of independence in their daily lives and allowed to retain some of the income they earned for their masters.

While scholars have debated the question of whether the slave South was a genuinely capitalist society—with some maintaining that it was not, since slaves could not sell their labor (or more accurately, their "labor power") on a free and open market–there is no doubt that slaveholders operated within the capitalist system and were motivated by a desire to maximize profits through the production of staple crops for sale on domestic and international markets. Moreover scholars also debate whether or not slavery impeded southern industrial development and economic progress, but they agree that slavery as a labor system was both efficient and highly profitable.

The Civil War and the Abolition of Slavery

Although President Abraham Lincoln and most northerners originally viewed the Civil War as a war not to abolish slavery but rather one to preserve the Union, the war ultimately resulted in the abolition of slavery. The flight of thousands of slaves from plantations in areas of the South where the Union army gained control compelled Lincoln, the federal government, and the North at large to confront the issue of slavery. Lincoln and most northerners eventually came to see the necessity of abolishing slavery as a means of both winning the war and undertaking the reconstruction of southern society, resulting in Lincoln's Emancipation Proclamation of January 1, 1863.

Both before and after this date, the fugitive slaves who sought refuge behind Union lines forced federal, military, and civilian officials to provide humanitarian assistance as well as to begin to institute programs of free or compensated labor. On farms and plantations in northern Virginia and along the Virginia and North Carolina coast, on the South Carolina Sea Islands south of Charleston, throughout the Mississippi River valley, and in southern Louisiana, former slaves worked for wages or for a share of the crops under federal auspices. They labored on plantations whose owners had remained on the arrival of Union troops as well as on abandoned or confiscated plantations under Union military control. In addition former slaves worked in freedmen's villages, home colonies, or contraband camps established by federal, military, and civilian officials and often administered by northern reformers and missionaries.

The features of wartime free labor varied from state to state and among the different crop regions, and former slaves did not benefit from many of the rights that northern workers enjoyed, such as geographical mobility and the right to negotiate their own terms of employment. Nonetheless wartime free labor instituted the principle of compensated labor while prohibiting corporal punishment, the sale of human property, and other practices of slavery. By the end of the war, as many as a half-million former slaves had some experience with wartime free labor, while another quarter-million black men and women worked in the Union army for pay as military laborers (in addition to some 200 thousand black men who formally served in the Union army and navy).

Presidential Reconstruction and the Problem of Labor

The large majority of slaves did not gain their freedom until the end of the war, and the abolition of slavery was not complete until formal ratification of the Thirteenth Amendment to the U.S. constitution in December 1865. But throughout the former slave states, both in areas that had experienced wartime free labor and those that had not, the central issue was the same: The conflict between former slaveholders and former slaves (or freedmen) over the control of economic resources, especially land and labor. Many if not most former slaveholders remained adamantly opposed to the freeing of their slaves, but even for those who had reconciled themselves to emancipation, the primary goals of all planters were to retain control over labor and to secure a dependable labor force to operate their plantations. They continued to envision themselves as the primary source of authority on their estates, with decision-making power in all aspects of plantation management and in the laborers' working lives, including the issue of compensation. For freedmen by contrast the primary goals were to achieve a measure of independence in their daily working lives and to escape gang labor under white supervision, as had been customary under slavery. Former slaves also demanded a voice in determining such basic matters as the hours, pace, and conditions of labor, as well as the mode and level of compensation. Most freedmen envisioned access to economic resources, in particular the ownership of land and other forms of productive property, as the best means of securing their freedom. For them freedom meant more than simply returning to work on the plantations for meager compensation.

In the immediate postwar period, the former antebellum political leadership, which was largely dominated by planters, returned to power under the policies of Lincoln's successor, Andrew Johnson. A southern Democrat who had remained loyal to the Union, Johnson saw Reconstruction as a matter of restoration rather than as one of fundamentally restructuring southern society. Johnson had little concern for black civil or economic rights and was adamantly opposed to an expansion of federal authority. Under Johnson's policies, southern white leaders enacted a series of laws known as the "black codes" that essentially defined black people as second-class citizens and that were designed to restrict the freedmen's economic opportunities and to bind them to the plantation system. Although the black codes were effectively negated by military authorities and by the 1866 Civil Rights Act, planters continued to use local law enforcement and the courts to reestablish control over labor.

Freedmen were not without resources. Near the end of the Civil War, the Republican majority in Congress had created the Bureau of Refugees, Freedmen, and Abandoned Lands, commonly known as the Freedmen's bureau. A division of the War Department, the bureau was entrusted with authority over all matters concerning freedmen and the transition to freedom. In particular the bureau picked up where military authorities had left off at the end of the war in overseeing creation of a system of free labor for the South. It was also given control over the nearly one million acres of abandoned and confiscated land in the former Confederacy and was authorized to begin the process of dividing this land into 40-acre plots for distribution among freedmen.

As broad as the bureau's mandate was however, it never received adequate resources to fulfill its mission, and it was consciously created as a temporary agency rather than as a permanent or even long-term one. In this respect the bureau reflected divisions among Republicans and many northerners over the federal government's role in addressing the economic status of the former slaves and the reconstruction of southern society. Radical Republicans believed that the federal government had a responsibility to provide substantial and long-term assistance to freedmen in order to address the distinct historical experience of enslavement. Moderate and conservative Republicans by contrast argued that the federal government should guarantee freedmen legal equality and the right to enter into contracts voluntarily within the capitalist marketplace, or what some thought of as "contract freedom," but that freedmen should receive no special treatment or dispensations from the federal government.

An opponent of the bureau, Johnson interfered in its operations and was eventually able to prevent it from carrying out its mission of providing land to freedmen. Instead he saw that almost all of the bureau-controlled land was returned to its former owners, thus delivering a crippling blow to the prospects of the federal government making land available to former slaves. Nonetheless, despite all of the difficulties under which the bureau operated before its closing at the end of 1868, freedmen came to see it as an important ally in the struggle with planters over the new labor system, and they did not hesitate to petition bureau agents for assistance in securing their rights as free workers.

Radical Reconstruction and the Evolution of the South's Labor System

By early 1867, Republicans had broken with Johnson over Reconstruction, and most northerners had likewise rejected Johnson's conservative policies and supported Republicans on the need to guarantee legal equality and contract freedom. With the implementation of radical (or congressional) Reconstruction in 1867 and 1868, black men gained the right to vote, hold office, and otherwise shape the creation and implementation of public policy. Although black office holding and leverage over local and state government varied from state to state until Reconstruction ended in 1877, black political power profoundly influenced the evolution of labor relations throughout the South. Former slaves came to see the issues of legal and political equality and those involving land, labor, and economics as inseparable and indeed as interdependent parts of the same struggle to define freedom. Planters for their part attempted to use both legitimate state power and when necessary, extralegal violence to thwart black political and economic aspirations.

As freedmen gained access to political power during the late 1860s and the 1870s, the South's new labor system slowly took definitive shape, although the manner in which labor was organized and the mode of compensation varied among the different crop regions. In the cotton South, the system that came to be known as sharecropping would eventually predominate, although this term is often used to describe a host of different labor arrangements. In essence sharecropping was a system in which the planter or landlord provided land, work animals, implements, and other forms of working capital, while the laborer, or sharecropper, provided labor and perhaps some working capital of his or her own. The sharecropper

and his or her family rented and worked a specified amount of land, usually purchasing necessities on credit from the landlord or a local merchant. At the end of the crop season, landlord and sharecropper split, or shared, the crop, and the sharecropper's account was settled with the proceeds of his or her share. The laborer's share of the crop depended on the assets he or she originally brought into the bargain. In instances where a sharecropper owned a mule or farm implements, he or she could negotiate a better deal for as much as half the crop; in cases where the sharecropper brought only his or her labor, with the planter providing everything else, the sharecropper received a considerably smaller share. In either case sharecropping was in theory a form of wage labor, since the landlord retained control of the crop and compensated the sharecropper for labor with a share of the crop instead of cash. In some instances freedmen who had accumulated the necessary assets to work their own farms but who lacked only land rented land for a cash payment and were able to retain control of the entire crop. Such arrangements were known as tenancy.

There has been much scholarly debate about the origins and development of sharecropping. Some scholars have maintained that sharecropping emerged out of the natural workings of the free-market system. Others however attribute its origins to the immutable class conflict between former slaveholders and freedmen in the contest over the South's new labor system. Nonetheless most scholars agree that sharecropping evolved in response to the contending desires of planters and freedmen as well as to the particular economic conditions that prevailed in the postwar South. Since it required little cash, sharecropping was attractive in a region that notoriously lacked capital. Since both landlord and laborer had a stake in the crop, sharecropping spread the risk of failure or success between the parties. But most importantly sharecropping gave freedmen a measure of control over their daily working lives, and offered them the possibility of capital accumulation and eventual land ownership even as it ensured planters a stable labor force and overall control over plantation management.

Although various kinds of sharecropping or rental arrangements also prevailed on the upper South's tobacco plantations, sharecropping was not so ideally suited to the South's other crop regions. On southern Louisiana's sugar plantations, which had traditionally been characterized by large concentrations of land, labor, and capital, highly integrated plantation organization survived after slavery, with laborers continuing to work in gangs under white supervision and to live in centralized quarters. In return, sugar workers received monthly or daily cash wages in addition to rations, housing, and the right to keep garden plots. Despite the similarities in plantation routine during and after slavery in the sugar region, workers nonetheless used their skills and knowledge of the complex process of sugar production to gain important leverage in determining the conditions of labor. In the rice kingdom of low-country South Carolina and Georgia by contrast, a wide array of labor arrangements initially replaced slavery, but production never reached antebellum levels, and the story of the postbellum rice industry in the low country was one of irreversible decline and eventual demise. Indeed coastal South Carolina and Georgia were one of the few areas of the postwar South where the antebellum plantation system was replaced by extensive, small-scale black landholding and where the production of staple crops was supplanted by subsistence agriculture and truck farming.

If the low country was exceptional for the demise of its plantation system, it was not so for the presence of black property holders. Throughout the rural South, but especially in the tobacco regions of Virginia and North Carolina, parts of the South Carolina piedmont, the interior of the Yazoo-Mississippi delta, as well as in the low country, former slaves managed to acquire property. Individual black families marshaled together their meager resources or demonstrated an entrepreneurial spirit by putting domestic and household production toward acquisitive ends, so that places like Promiseland, South Carolina, and Mound Bayou, Mississippi, became thriving and self-sufficient communities of black property holders. By 1900, approximately one out of every four southern black farmers owned the land they worked.

Some scholars have debated the question of whether the former slaves in the postbellum southern countryside constituted either a black peasantry or a rural proletariat. Perhaps less important than ascribing such labels is a recognition that a complex array of labor arrangements and methods of compensation coexisted within the southern agricultural sector. Moreover the status that individual blacks occupied was not static; instead individuals moved up and down the economic ladder over time as circumstances and conditions changed. Likewise the various members of black families and households undertook a number of different economic activities simultaneously, all working toward the goal of autonomy and independence.

Urban and Non-Agricultural Labor

One of the most dramatic developments in the postbellum South was the migration of thousands of former slaves from plantations and the countryside to urban areas. Black people were attracted to what they believed were the greater economic opportunities that cities had to offer, as well as to the schools, churches, and benevolent and fraternal societies that tended to cluster in urban areas. Both the overall populations and the black populations of such cities as Washington, D.C., Richmond, Charlotte, Atlanta, Memphis, and New Orleans increased dramatically, while other cities, such as Charleston and Mobile, experienced significant black population growth.

The overwhelming majority of black men and women in cities were engaged in manual labor. Most men were employed as unskilled day laborers, although some obtained skilled employment, and most women worked as domestic servants. Cities were also home to the very small minority of black people who achieved professional or middle-class status, mostly as doctors, lawyers, educators, newspaper editors, and ministers, as well as to those very few African-Americans who became entrepreneurs by starting up, for example, black insurance companies.

Although they suffered severe racial discrimination, black people also found employment in the South's slowly expanding industrial sector. Many black men worked in the coal mines of Appalachia, in the naval stores industry, and in the South's burgeoning timber industry, while others were employed in iron foundries or steel mills, such as those in Birmingham, Alabama. Black men and women also labored as a small proportion of the workforce employed in the textile mills of piedmont South Carolina and North Carolina. Perhaps most tragically many thousands of black people, the large majority men but some women, endured horrific working and living conditions as convict laborers throughout the South, especially in Georgia, Alabama, Louisiana—where a seven-year term was equivalent to a death sentence—and Mississippi, home to the infamous Parchman farm.

Black Labor in the Post-Reconstruction South

Although former slaves and their descendants faced overwhelming obstacles during Reconstruction in achieving economic independence, their prospects for attaining that goal dramatically worsened at its end in 1877. In a process that began in several states before that date but that intensified and became widespread after it, the southern white propertied classes, including many planters and former slaveholders, regained political power and proceeded to use the mechanisms of local and state government to re-establish control over labor. Combining their still-formidable financial power with the force of law, planters and other capitalists restructured legal and economic relations to their own benefit and to the disadvantage of labor. Most black sharecroppers found sharecropping to be a permanent status instead of a stepping stone to independent property ownership, with many reduced to the condition of debt peonage, although historians have debated the extent of this practice. Wage laborers for their part similarly found themselves with few options to that of selling their labor within a capitalist marketplace that was skewed in the interests of capital. Starting in the 1890s moreover, southern state governments moved systematically to impose legal segregation and to strip voting rights from black men, while lynching, race riots, and other forms of racial violence became increasingly commonplace. Black people may not have been legally re-enslaved in the decades following emancipation, but the overwhelming racial and economic oppression that they endured by the turn of the century made a mockery of black freedom, and it has caused scholars ever since to wrestle with the question of how different the new South was from the old South.

JOHN C. RODRIGUE

References and Further Reading

Higgs, Robert. *Competition and Coercion: Blacks in the American Economy, 1865–1914.* Cambridge, UK: Cambridge University Press, 1977.

Holt, Sharon Ann. *Making Freedom Pay: North Carolina Freedpeople Working for Themselves, 1865–1900.* Athens: University of Georgia Press, 2000.

Hunter, Tera W. *To Joy My Freedom: Southern Black Women's Lives and Labors after the Civil War.* Cambridge, MA: Harvard University Press, 1997.

Mandle, Jay R. *The Roots of Black Poverty: The Southern Plantation Economy after the Civil War.* Durham, NC: Duke University Press, 1978.

Montgomery, David. *Beyond Equality: Labor and the Radical Republicans, 1862–1872.* New York: Alfred A. Knopf, 1967.

Morgan, Lynda J. *Emancipation in Virginia's Tobacco Belt, 1850–1870.* Athens: University of Georgia Press, 1992.

Outland, Robert B., III. *Tapping the Pines: The Naval Stores Industry in the South.* Baton Rouge: Louisiana State University Press, 2004.

Penningroth, Dylan C. *The Claims of Kinfolk: African-American Property and Community in the Nineteenth-Century South.* Chapel Hill: University of North Carolina Press, 2003.

Ransom, Roger, and Richard Sutch. *One Kind of Freedom: The Economic Consequences of Emancipation.* Cambridge, UK: Cambridge University Press, 1977.

Reidy, Joseph P. *From Slavery to Agrarian Capitalism in the Cotton Plantation South: Central Georgia, 1800–1880.* Chapel Hill: University of North Carolina Press, 1992.

Rodrigue, John C. *Reconstruction in the Cane Fields: From Slavery to Free Labor in Louisiana's Sugar Parishes, 1862–1880.* Baton Rouge: Louisiana State University Press, 2001.

Saville, Julie. *The Work of Reconstruction: From Slave to Wage Laborer in South Carolina, 1860–1870.* Cambridge, UK: Cambridge University Press, 1994.

Wayne, Michael. *The Reshaping of Plantation Society: The Natchez District, 1860–1880.* Baton Rouge: Louisiana State University Press, 1983.

Willis, John C. *Forgotten Time: The Yazoo-Mississippi Delta after the Civil War.* Charlottesville: University Press of Virginia, 2000.

Woodman, Harold D. *King Cotton and His Retainers: Financing and Marketing the Cotton Crop of the South, 1800–1925.* Lexington: University of Kentucky Press, 1968.

See also **Abolitionism; African Americans; Antebellum Era; Barbers; Brotherhood of Timber Workers; Civil Rights; Civil War and Reconstruction; Colored Farmers' Alliance; Company Towns; Disfranchisement; Du-Bois, W. E. B.; Gender; Gilded Age; Greenback Labor Party; Gutman, Herbert; Historiography of American Labor History; Knights of Labor; Ku Klux Klan (Reconstruction and WWI Era); Louisiana Sugar Strike (1887); National Association for the Advancement of Colored People; New Orleans General Strike (1892); New South; Peonage; Railroads; Sharecropping and Tenancy; Slave Trade, Domestic; Strikebreaking; Tennessee Convict Uprising (1891–1892); Thirteenth Amendment; Union League Movement; Washington, Booker T.**

EMPLOYEE REPRESENTATION PLANS/COMPANY UNIONS

Company unions (also known as work councils or employee-representation plans) date back to the late nineteenth and early twentieth centuries, when the emergence of large-scale and impersonal economic enterprises and a rise in worker militancy and trade unionism began to pose major threats to the efficiency, autonomy, and power of American employers. Shop committees and informal company-specific worker organizations had existed in the nation's factories in the nineteenth century—as early as 1833—but employers became interested in initiating and controlling such bodies in the 1890s and early twentieth century, when early welfare capitalist experiments promoting industrial "betterment," labor-capital mutualism, and company loyalty began to spread through the nation. Some of the earliest examples of such initiatives came in smaller firms that were making adjustments to workforce expansion—and in the service sector. The adoption of company unions however became most pronounced later in larger industrial firms and in the railroad industry.

Perhaps the earliest example of a true company-initiated union can be found in the Filene Cooperative Association (FCA), a company union of female employees established in 1898 and formalized in 1905 at the Filene Boston department store. It was an innovation that came with a variety of other welfare capitalist initiatives: Medical care and insurance, social and athletic programs, company-sponsored cultural activities—all designed to address issues of worker alienation, low morale, and efficiency. The FCA was modeled on the structure of the US government, with the chief executive officer at the top and two representative deliberative bodies—one elected by the workers, the other appointed by the company president—charged with resolving wage disputes and the varied grievances of the department store's workers. Company officers also served as a cabinet of sorts. The FCA also worked closely with Filene's welfare work department, charged with overseeing the general welfare of employees.

Other employers were motivated to adopt employee-representation reforms out of social gospel motives. Such employers as Holbrook FitzJohn Porter, vice-president of the Nernst Lamp Company, were motivated by a religious conviction heavily influenced by social gospel theologians. In addition to the usual panoply of welfare activities undertaken by the firm, Nernst established a factory committee in the winter of 1903–1904 made up of rank-and-file shop and clerical workers and line-level supervisors.

Though Nernst's and Filene's motives in adopting company unionism were not directly related to a union threat, this was not true of other firms. In fact many company unions were specifically created by executives hoping to avoid strikes and trade unions. The Pittsburgh Railroad for example emerged from the Railroad Strike of 1877 determined to avoid such destructive conflagrations with employees in the future; it did so by actively promoting company unions with limited but significant power. The Packard Piano Company of Ft. Wayne, Indiana, hired Industrial Relations Consultant John Leitch of Philadelphia in 1912 to address employee problems that threatened production. Leitch formulated a company union model not dissimilar from that of Filene's, again modeled on a two-house congressional structure. One house, an industrial House of Representatives, was made up of representatives elected by workers, and the other, a Senate, by foremen; the cabinet was entirely composed of corporate executives. Since both houses and the cabinet were required to approve all proposals, and one house and the cabinet was entirely composed of supervisory and administrative

personnel, there was no doubt that real power remained firmly in the hands of management. Because of this, it was not surprising that so many firms looking for mechanisms to address labor problems began to mirror the so-called Leitch plan. Goodyear Tire and the Durham Hosiery Mills of North Carolina were but two of 20 firms that adopted it.

Not surprisingly radicals and trade unionists were extremely critical of company unions in whatever form; the movement toward company unions became a significant one during the 1910s and into the 1920s, and few trade union leaders could ignore it. Common criticisms emphasized the hollowness of corporate-initiated and structured representative schemes and the blatant anti-union motives behind many of them. In spite of such criticisms, the movement continued to grow through the 1910s. Besides the initial stimulation of the movement by Leitch's active proselytizing of his ideas (see, in particular, his classic *Man to Man: The Story of Industrial Democracy*), company unions were most pronouncedly catalyzed by the Colorado Industrial plan (or Rockefeller plan), which emerged in the wake of the Ludlow Massacre of April 1914. The Rockefeller family was the largest stockholder in the Colorado Fuel and Iron Company, the firm against which 9,000 miners affiliated with the United Mine Workers' (UMW) Union struck in the late summer and early fall of 1913. The strike was broken by the use of the Colorado National Guard. The guard attacked a striking miners' camp in Ludlow; gunfire took the lives of 10 men and a child, and a deadly tent fire (the guards had set miner tents on fire) led to the suffocation of another 11 children and two women. Following this, and in response to public outrage against the firm and the Rockefellers, John D. Rockefeller Jr. hired Clarence J. Hicks, who had extensive experience in administering welfare work at International Harvester, and W. L. Mackenzie King, former Canadian minister of labor (and future Canadian prime minister), to reform the labor practices of the firm. One of the results of their collaboration was an employee representation plan (ERP). The plan created local district committees democratically elected by the miners who would attempt to resolve grievances brought forward by workers. If workers could not get satisfaction from foremen or mine superintendents, they could appeal directly to a Joint Committee on Industrial Cooperation and Conciliation or the firm's president (through a presidential industrial representative who periodically visited each mining district). Without a viable alternative—since the UMW had been defeated in the strike—84% of voting workers gave their assent to the plan in 1915.

The Colorado Industrial plan was extended to other Rockefeller firms, such as Standard Oil, and soon—in a variety of forms—it spread throughout the nation, as Midvale Steel Company, Bethlehem Steel, and many other firms adopted it. Perhaps the greatest catalyst for the expansion of the movement however was World War I, when government promotion efforts and labor shortages both came into play as motivating factors. With wartime production and efficiency key considerations, and anxiety over possible strikes and violence in the nation's shipyards and railroads rising, the Wilson administration looked to various forms of employee representation to ward off these threats.

Government wartime agencies, including the War Labor board, the Shipbuilding Labor Adjustment board, the U.S. Railroad Administration, and the U.S. Fuel Administration, established shop committees in various strategic industrial settings. The U.S. Railroad Administration, for example, created a national board with equal representation of labor and capital charged with settling railroad disputes. It in turn fostered the creation of local shop committees to alleviate an impossible burden of dealing with thousands of grievances from around the nation. By 1919, more than a hundred firms had adopted some form of employee representation under government pressure, and many more did it voluntarily (many perhaps in anticipation of government pressure). As many wartime employee-representation initiatives were government- rather than company-initiated, it may be questionable whether to consider wartime shop committees true company unions; nonetheless they borrowed much from prewar corporate experiments, including the Rockefeller plan and the Leitch plan. In the context of World War I idealism, and calls by the Wilson administration to spread democracy around the world, it was a natural leap to apply such ideas to the industrial realm. The language of industrial democracy began to resonate with both labor and progressive employers. Of course it meant different things to these two disparate groups. For the former it meant real independent trade unions; for the latter it meant the Leitch plan or the Rockefeller plan or a half-dozen other variations on the theme.

The wartime experience had a postwar legacy. With growing fears of a spreading Bolshevik revolution, with domestic postwar worker militancy on the rise (the 1919 national steel strike being one important example), with a trade union movement growing dramatically (it grew by 50% from 1916–1920), and with Wilsonian democratic rhetoric pervasive, a significant number of large employers began to recognize the need to implement some form of industrial democracy in harmony with the nation's democratic political traditions. Some believed that employee representation would, like other welfare capitalist initiatives, bring workers closer to management and teach them a respect for the often-unpleasant responsibilities of supervisory personnel and managers. Though the recession of 1920–1921 and escalating worker expectations—reflected in a growing number of labor grievances brought forward for review by worker and company representatives—led employers to slow their adoption of shop committees and other forms of company unions (especially the Leitch plan), the overwhelming tendency in the postwar era was toward an increasing adoption of company unionism.

The number of workers covered by employee representation plans grew through the decade of the 1920s; by 1928, around 1.5 million workers were operating under the umbrella of one or another form of ERP, most of them employed by large firms. There is little unanimity among scholars on the question of to what extent workers accepted or embraced employee-representation initiatives. Some historians emphasize success, others hostility or apathy. Some scholars measure the notion of success from a managerial perspective, others from labor's point of view. A significant recent group of revisionist historians and economists, such as Daniel Nelson, David Fairris, and Bruce E. Kaufman, argue that there was much that was positive about the development of employee-representation plans in the first three decades of the twentieth century, that in fact, many plans improved industrial relations and furthered the interests of both workers and management. Most labor historians however are less sanguine about ERPs.

It is clear the record is varied both within and across firms. In several instances, company unions became quite powerful and effective in extracting wage increases and improvements in working conditions. Employees of Kimberley-Clark, Colorado Fuel and Iron, Standard Oil experienced concrete improvements in wage and working conditions. One detailed analysis of grievances adjudicated by Bethlehem Steel Company's ERP noted that over 1,600 grievances out of 2,300 were settled in favor of the employees. Labor Economist William Leiserson noted in the 1920s—the heyday of the company union movement—that between two-thirds and 70% of grievances brought up for review by ERPs were settled in the employee's favor. In some instances shop committees and councils did help reduce labor turnover and seemed to contribute to worker loyalty to the firm—goals that promoters of company unions had argued to justify their adoption. But it is hard to identify a consistent long-term pattern of significant improvements—either from a labor or managerial perspective. As Leiserson also observed, a pro-employee predisposition was most evident in the initial years of an ERP's operation.

On the other side, more than one scholar has identified a correlation between representation plans and wage cuts, suggesting that companies may have adopted company unions in part in anticipation of wage decreases—as a mechanism to ward off or limit labor unrest. Company unions tended to draw in family men, generally more moderate—even conservative—than younger, single workers. This had important implications on the intensity and level of worker militancy and activism within such unions. Furthermore representatives were not labor or economic professionals and dealt only with local conditions. They rarely developed a more national and global perspective on the economic conditions they were often the victims of—perspectives that international and national trade union officials more often had. These are all arguments made by some business and labor historians, as well as union organizers, against the long-term effectiveness of company unions in promoting the interests of employees. Similarly contemporary businessmen and scholars noted that escalating grievances and heightened expectations in the wake of the creation of employee-representation plans introduced as many labor relations crises as they may have tried to ward off.

Through the 1920s, so long as companies and their company unions delivered some concrete benefits to workers, employee-representation plans were often accepted as the only viable route to settle grievances. Yet with the coming of the Great Depression and the New Deal, the equation that sustained company unionism changed dramatically. Economic downturn meant corporations were less able to satisfy worker expectations, and government's aggressive intrusion into labor-management relations—one hostile to company unions—soon created a major crisis for American corporate managers. From 1928–1932, the years encompassing the early years of the Great Depression, many firms began to abandon company unions, resulting in an 18% decline in employees represented by them. This pattern was temporarily reversed with the passage of the National Industrial Recovery Act of 1933, which recognized—under Section 7(a)—labor's right to collective bargaining and to establish independent trade unions. In defensive reaction, firms throughout the nation began to implement employee-representation plans to head off independent trade unions. The result was an increase in the number of workers covered by such plans from 1.8 million in 1934 to 2.5 million in 1935. A growing and widespread hostility to this blatant attempt to block the growth of true independent labor organizations finally led to a legal prohibition against company unions and all forms of employer-dominated labor organizations, codified by Section 8(a)(2) of the Wagner Act (National Labor Relations Act) of 1935. When the Supreme Court failed to overturn the act in 1937, the government began aggressively to break up company's unions. The 1938 Newport News Shipbuilding and Dry Dock Case (*Newport News Shipbuilding & Dry Dock Co. v. Schauffler*, 303 U.S. 54) was the landmark Supreme Court case that finally terminated the 35-year-old movement.

The hundreds of company unions throughout the nation in the mid-1930s followed various tracks following the government prohibition. Some chose the path of establishing independent, nonaffiliated unions. This was the case with the Gadsden, Alabama Goodyear Tire plant. Workers violently rejected attempts by the American Federation of Labor (AFL) and the Congress of Industrialized Organizations (CIO) to organize plant workers. Instead they chose to establish the Etowah Rubber Workers' Association. A significant percentage of workers enrolled in company unions followed a similar track; from 1935 to the early 1940s, around half of all workers enrolled in company unions and newly established independent unions voted against affiliation with AFL or CIO unions in National Labor Relations Board (NLRB)-supervised elections.

On the other hand, there were also numerous examples of company unions being either rejected when viable alternatives were offered to workers or becoming springboards to trade independence in the 1930s. Trade union organizers captured employee-representative committees at Pittsburgh's steel mills and lobbied effectively for employee support of the CIO. In early 1937, US Steel finally accepted the Steel Workers' Organizing Committee (SWOC), affiliated with the CIO, as the bargaining unit of their employees. A similar transition took place at General Electric—though it took various routes in the firm's diverse plants. There at the firm's West Lynn, Massachusetts, plant, a works' council had been in existence since 1918 (formed in response to government pressure). But led by a militant pattern maker named Al Coulthard, a concerted effort began in the early 1930s to replace the works' council with an independent union. In an election monitored by the New England Regional Labor Council, Coulthard's independent union defeated the council by a margin of 82% to 18%. In the Schenectady Works of General Electric, one of the firm's largest production centers, industrial union organizers—several of them Communists—became active in the firm's works' council, originally established in 1924. Already under pressure to comply with Section 7(a) of the National Recovery Act (NRA) management first attempted to convince government watchdogs that the firm was already in compliance with the law. The firm modified the council in late 1933 though, changed the Schenectady organization's name to the Workers' Council, strengthened grievance procedures, and increased worker input into wage determinations. To assuage workers further, management announced a wage increase of 10% on April 1, 1934, and cited the effective negotiation pressure of the council as a factor in the wage increase. With the power of the council increasing, labor militants began to look to it as a mechanism to accomplish more dramatic changes in the firm. They flocked into its ranks and began to advocate for an open NLRB election to replace the council with an independent industrial union. The final result of that process led to the formation of Local 301 of the United Electrical, Radio and Machine Workers of America (UE) in early 1937.

The later 1930s witnessed an end to company union initiatives. The legacies of these initiatives and the company union movement as a whole were mixed, but in their final years, employee-representation plans and workers' councils formed bridges to independent trade unionism—small, independent, and local, as well as large, affiliated, and national. The ideas and ideals of company unionism, often more than the realities, seemed to keep alive the idea of industrial democracy among workers. And as historian Irving Bernstein has noted, whether sustaining or contradicting those ideas and ideals, company unionism offered workers a language that they could use to fashion a more truly democratic and independent form of unionism, reflected in the rise of the CIO unions in the late 1930s.

Gerald Zahavi

References and Further Reading

Bernstein, Irving. *The Lean Years*. Boston: Houghton Mifflin, 1960.
Brandes, Stuart D. *American Welfare Capitalism, 1880–1940*. Chicago, IL: The University of Chicago Press, 1976.
Fairris, David. "From Exit to Voice in Shopfloor Governance: The Case of Company Unions." *Business History Review* 69 (Winter 1995): 493–529.
Kaufman, B. E. "The Case for the Company Union." *Labor History* 41:3 (2000): 321–351.
Kaufman, Bruce, and Kleiner, Morris, eds. *Employee Representation: Alternatives and Future Directions*. Madison, WS: IRRA, 1993.
Leitch, John. *Man to Man: The Story of Industrial Democracy*. New York: B. C. Forbes Company, 1919.
Nelson, Daniel. "The Company Union Movement, 1900–1937: A Reexamination." *Business History Review* 56 (Autumn 1982): 335–357.
Patmore, Greg. "Employee Representation Plans in North America and Australia, 1915–1935: An Employer Response to Workplace Democracy." Sidney, Australia: Conference paper presented at the 2001 Workplace Democracy Conference, Labour Council of NSW/ Work and Organisational Studies, School of Business, University of Sydney, June 2001. Available on line at: *Worksite: Issues in Workplace Democracy*. www.econ. usyd.edu.au/wos/worksite/employer.html.

EMPLOYEE RETIREMENT INCOME SECURITY ACT (1974)

Most laws relating to private-sector pensions in the United States are contained either in federal tax law or in the Employee Retirement Income Security Act (ERISA), which was first enacted in 1974. Although ERISA also deals with so-called "employee welfare plans," including, for example, health plans, pension provisions take up its bulk.

The ERISA does not require any employer to establish a retirement plan and does not dictate retirement benefits. However it does subject those pension plans that are established to numerous legal requirements, mainly aimed at ensuring that pension plans are actually used for the benefit of covered employees. The ERISA is a very large and extremely complex law, encompassing many disparate goals.

The ERISA regulates both "defined-benefit" and "defined-contribution" retirement plans. (The former term refers to a plan wherein benefits are based on a specifically defined formula, usually based on years of service and salary at or around the time of retirement. The latter refers to a plan wherein benefits are based on the size of an account to which the employee, and sometimes the employer as well, has/have contributed.) However defined-benefit plans are the type that is truly contemplated by the law and thus such plans are far more regulated by ERISA.

The Problem of Retirement

Pensions as we know them did not always exist. Neither for that matter did retirement. Prior to the Civil War, as a general rule most Americans appear to have died relatively young, worked until they died, and worked in an agricultural environment. Retirement was mostly unknown. Following the Civil War however, more people came to work in industry, where older people are commonly thought to be of less use than in agriculture. Further the population of the country generally aged from the Civil War to the 1930s. The concept of the pension slowly began to develop as a way of ensuring an income for people who were considered to be of no further use as workers.

The first American pensions appear to have been exclusive to either disabled or retired Civil War veterans (sources differ). Despite various administrative problems, the program was popular and became an important precedent. Though there is some disagreement, most sources indicate that first American private-sector pension plans were established in 1875 (by the American Express Company) and in 1880 (by the Baltimore-Ohio Railroad Company).

From here pensions grew only in number, size, and importance. Pension plans appear to have become major financial players relatively early in their history.

The Rise of ERISA

Government accommodation and regulation of pensions dates back to the Revenue Acts of 1921 and 1926, which first gave pensions a special tax status. Other laws were enacted throughout the 1940s, 1950s, and 1960s.

Pension reform began in earnest however in the late 1950s, in response to a series of major pension-related scandals; two particularly important ones involved Teamsters union leader James "Jimmy" Hoffa, and another involved the Studebaker car manufacturer. A series of federal laws, dating back to 1958, ultimately discredited Welfare and Pension Plan Disclosure Act of 1958 (WPPDA), and a Presidential Committee on Corporate Pension Funds (put together by President John F. Kennedy in response to the Studebaker scandal) led up to the enactment of ERISA. Following the issuance of the presidential commission's report, New York Senator Jacob K. Javits took the lead on the issue and is usually credited with principal authorship of the bill that eventually became ERISA some years later in 1974 (PL 93-406, also known as the Pension Reform Act). Why ERISA went through exactly when it did is an extremely interesting question to which the answer is rather murky.

Although ERISA has been amended several times since 1974 (most notably by the Revenue Act of 1978 and the Retirement Equity Act of 1984), its essentials appear to have remained very similar since its initial enactment.

The Basics

Many of ERISA's provisions are detailed, technical, and complicated. However the basics of the law are fairly easy to summarize in the broadest terms.

Without requiring employers to establish pension plans or mandating what benefits are payable, ERISA subjects pension plans to various requirements. For example requirements for vesting in a plan (vesting refers to the point after which an employee can draw benefits after reaching normal retirement age for the plan even without long service to the employer) were enacted. These requirements are considered important because they limit the ability of employers to take away employees' pensions entirely by firing them late in their careers and assist employees in changing jobs without losing their pensions entirely. Toward similar ends, requirements for benefit accrual were also established.

Provisions were also made requiring employers to report, regularly and accurately, to members regarding the benefit package and the fiscal health of the plan. Requirements for investment and financial management were also enacted. In general investors for the plan are required to make investments for the exclusive benefit of plan members, are required to invest prudently (considered to be a higher obligation than the "reasonable man standard" that often appears in other areas of law), and mandated to diversify investments unless prudence clearly dictates otherwise. Further an agency called the Pension Benefit Guaranty Corporation (PBGC) was established to pay benefits for plans that failed.

In general ERISA regulates traditional defined-benefit pension plans, wherein benefits are based on a formula that is known from the outset, more so than defined-contribution plans, such as 401(k) plans, where benefits are determined by the size of an account. The latter were not as popular when ERISA was enacted as they are now and in some circles are considered to be less retirement plans per se then deferred-compensation or assisted-savings programs. Defined-contribution plans are regulated by ERISA, only somewhat less so.

Current Issues

Within the last few years prior to the writing of this article, pension-related scandals have once again shined a spotlight on ERISA and led to calls for its amendment. At the time of writing, some proposals have been enacted, but many have not, and the basic provisions of ERISA as previously described remain about the same. To an extent ERISA's reporting requirements have been strengthened, along with other reporting, accounting, and auditing requirements for businesses.

Employer advocates generally argue for ERISA's provisions to be strengthened in light of the various scandals where plans proved to be underfunded and instances where employers and plan managers have either violated ERISA or have sought to subvert its intent while remaining within its letter. On the other hand, some employers have argued for a lessening of ERISA's requirements, arguing that due to certain financial techniques, pension plans can coast for longer periods of time without being actually sound actuarially.

At the time of writing, many companies under financial stress have begun to seek the protection of the courts through the bankruptcy laws, and pension obligations, typically considered particularly expensive for companies, have often been the first targets of discharge or lessening of company debt pursuant to the bankruptcy laws. A study issued by the PBGC late in 2005, for example, showed that 9.4% of pension plans covered by ERISA had frozen benefit accruals; this means that while the plans were still in existence, members' benefit levels were frozen and could not grow any further despite their continuing to work for the firm.

Even before the recent rash of "dumping" of obligations, the PBGC was considered to be on rather shaky financial ground, and the increasing reliance on it to pay the pension obligations of ostensibly bankrupt firms has not helped matters. These factors together with other circumstances have led some commentators to worry that a crisis looms in the nation's private-sector retirement system.

STEVEN D. KOCZAK

References and Further Reading

Henle, Peter, and Raymond Schmitt. "Pension Reform: The Long, Hard Road to Enactment." *Monthly Labor Review* (November 1974): 3–12.

Koczak, Steven D. *Pension and Welfare Benefits Administration. General Information about ERISA* (pamphlet). Washington, DC: United States Department of Labor, 1987.

———. Pension and Welfare Benefits Administration. *Troubleshooter's Guide to Filing the ERISA Annual Report.* Ibid., 2001.

Langbert, Mitchell. "ERISA: Law, Interests, and Consequences." *Journal of Economic Issues* 17 (1994): 277–289.

Pension Benefit Guaranty Corporation. www.pbgc.gov

Sass, Steven A. *The Promise of Private Pensions: The First Hundred Years.* Cambridge, MA: Harvard University Press, 1997.

Seburn, Patrick W. "Evolution of Employer-Provided Defined-Benefit Pensions." *Monthly Labor Review* (December 1991): 16–23.

U.S. Department of Labor, Pension and Welfare Benefits Administration. www.dol.gov/dol/pwba

Woodruff, Alan P. The ERISA Law Answer Book. New York: Aspen Publishers, 1998.

ENGLISH WORKERS

English workers played crucial roles in American labor history. Among all immigrants they made unique contributions to the development of industry and labor organization. This was due to an essential fact: Great Britain—England especially—was the world's first industrial nation and until the late nineteenth century, led the world in industrial technology and manufacturing. It had the world's most advanced and diversified economy and labor force, with the largest share of its population working in modernizing industries. Thus English workers in the United States—from the Revolution through the nineteenth century and beyond—offered valuable skills and experience. They brought a transatlantic industrial revolution from Britain to the United States that profoundly changed the American economy and society.

Another feature that distinguished the English from other immigrants in American labor was the fact that they already shared the same language and basic religious and political culture with most white Americans. England after all was the mother country and had planted a culture that remained essentially English after the Revolution in spite of the arrival of many non-British peoples. English workers in the United States then found a culture and institutions that were more familiar than different. They were "invisible immigrants" in the sense that they were often not seen as true foreigners but as cousins of the same stock. They blended in quickly with the larger American society. Sometimes the English did feel hostility from overly patriotic Americans who questioned their loyalty—especially in the years immediately after the Revolution, during the War of 1812, and other times of tension between the two nations. But generally the English were warmly welcomed and appreciated for their skills, hard work, common values, and quick assimilation to American life. They did not form ethnic communities or establish ethnic presses or other institutions like other immigrant groups did. Thus the English entered American labor quickly, often in leading roles. The great majority were not fleeing poverty but seeking greater opportunities in America. Some however were indeed poor. As early as the 1770s, the English in American cities began establishing St. George societies to assist English newcomers who needed help to get established as workers in the United States.

Industrial Skills

The industrial revolution is closely associated with innovation in textiles, and all of the major breakthroughs occurred in England: James Hargreaves's spinning jenny (1764), Richard Arkwright's water frame (1769), Samuel Crompton's spinning mule, and Edmund Cartwright's power loom (1785). The transfer of these innovations from Britain to the United States occurred quickly through English immigrants like Samuel Slater. He had been an apprentice to one of Arkwright's partners and came to the United States in 1789. Slater was responding to advertisements for skilled mechanics that American state legislatures published in English newspapers—so strong was the American demand for advanced skilled labor and the accurate perception that England was the source. Slater, like other early skilled workers heading for the United States circumvented the English law that forbade the emigration of skilled workers by simply declaring himself an apprentice. In 1790, Slater signed a contract to build a water-powered cotton-spinning mill based on Arkwright's designs, and he set up his own factory in Pawtucket, Rhode Island, in 1793. After his brother joined him from England, he built another mill in a town soon-called Slatersville. He also expanded his operations in Massachusetts. Slater employed other English workers along with local people, and he established a family system of labor, which combined some aspects of Arkwright's management system with new approaches to avoid England's tendency for horrible factory conditions. By the time of his death in 1835, Slater was involved with 13 textile mills. Another important English immigrant, Arthur Scholfield, similarly brought the latest textile technology to Pittsfield, Massachusetts, and his five brothers and their families to help him. Other less spectacular examples of English immigrants building textiles mills in the United States or bringing the latest skills are common and stretch into the mid-nineteenth century and beyond.

What happened in the transfer of textile technology and skills occurred in most industries. The early iron mills of Pennsylvania and Ohio relied heavily on English people who discovered ore bands and exploited them and others who brought experience with modernizing iron production from England. English workers helped build the first U.S. iron-rolling mill in Pittsburgh in 1812, and they brought the boiling method for puddling iron in 1837. The English introduced the method of coal-fired blast furnaces and the technology to build the first coke ovens in the 1830s. They also introduced the production of blister and crucible steel and helped develop the first U.S. rail production. Naturally the English rose quickly in the mills as supervisors and owners. And when steel began to replace iron—after the Bessemer process was brought from England following the Civil War—it was often with the help of English workers who had acquired the necessary skills and experience in their native land. The English also transferred the necessary workers and tools to establish the modern brass-making industry in Connecticut. In the 1830s, potters from Staffordshire established the pottery industry in East Liverpool, Ohio, and in Trenton, New Jersey. For decades English workers dominated and developed the industry in those cities, such that by the post-Civil War Era, the Americans could successfully compete with the English in pottery.

The English were especially important in American mining. Since the Middle Ages, the English had pioneered coal mining, and in the eighteenth and early nineteenth centuries they created the modern coal-mining industry. As their mines plunged more than a thousand feet below the earth's surface and even under the sea bed, they developed new techniques of ventilation, water pumping, and safe methods of tunneling. Mining—whether of coal or ores—was a skilled craft until mechanization took over in the late nineteenth century, and the English (as well as the Welsh and Scots) brought that skill and experience to the United States. They opened the coalmines of Pennsylvania, Ohio, Illinois, and other key states. In the 1850s alone, at least 37,000 British miners (most of whom were English) arrived in the United States, and they rose quickly to become mine bosses and owners. All over Pennsylvania and the Midwest, English workers discovered and developed important coal seams.

In other areas of mining, too, the English were instrumental. The Cornish—though ethnically distinct—were considered English as well, and they opened up the lead mines of the upper Mississippi River valley, especially in southwest Wisconsin, northwest Illinois, and eastern Iowa. The same was true of the iron and copper mines in upper Michigan and other areas in the Midwest. And of course when gold was discovered in California, and silver throughout the American West, the English were quick to exploit the new opportunities. They could apply their mining skills to the more precious ores, and with their common language and ease of participation in American life, they could move throughout the country rapidly to make the most of their situations. Virtually wherever one looks at American mining, one sees the English in prominent numbers and roles.

An overview of the occupational background of English workers in the United States reveals a remarkable diversity and comparatively high level of skill. During the late 1820s and 1830s, the English arriving in the United States were largely farmers and pre-industrial craft workers—especially building trades workers, miners, woodworkers, and so on.

Also prominent were skilled industrial workers in textiles and iron. They were generally not desperately poor or escaping technological displacement but could afford to travel as families in search of richer American opportunities. More poor workers arrived during the famine years of the late "hungry forties," but during the prosperous midcentury, farmers and engineers and skilled machinists (who were generally doing well in England) were entering the United States in significant proportions. In 1851 alone, an estimated 440 engineers and 660 ironworkers came from Britain (mostly England) to the United States. This was just what the young, industrializing nation needed for economic development.

During the 1860s, early 1870s, and 1880s, English immigration to the United States rose. They came increasingly from urban areas and were mostly building trades workers, miners, and unskilled workers. Many professionals, including lawyers, teachers, and clerks, also arrived throughout the century. A surprising number of all of these people from industrial and professional backgrounds took up farming in the United States. The availability of cheap, fertile land had attracted many of the English to the United States in the first place. And though most of them had nonagricultural occupations in England, many had been raised on or near farms. Farming was in their blood, and land ownership was a powerful incentive for their move. Thus when the English came to the United States and took up work in industry, mining, the building trades, and other nonagricultural fields, it was often a means to acquire the necessary capital to purchase land and take up farming.

English women in the United States were most commonly textiles workers, seamstresses, or domestic servants; but many were also active in teaching and medicine. They made essential contributions to family incomes and were also crucial for agriculture. They played more diverse roles in American labor than other immigrant women. Altogether the English contributed valuable industrial skills and experience and accelerated the growth and development of the United States. The 1890 United States census shows that the English were still much more likely than other immigrants to have skills and to be working in textiles, iron and steel, machine making, and other various skilled occupations.

Labor Organization

English workers also contributed to labor organization. For though the Americans were leaders in political democracy, the British were the leaders in industrial democracy. English workers coming to the United States carried their awareness of the need for labor unions and their experience in attempting organization. Some had been Chartists, demanding full democratic rights, but many more simply had a determination to reform the industrial system to benefit the workers. Some American businessmen who recruited skilled English workers were surprised to find that they now had employees who were organizing fellow workers for better pay and conditions, and some avoided hiring the English precisely for that reason. One of the earliest U.S. labor organizations—New York's Workingmen's party—was established in 1829 under the leadership of English immigrants, and in the 1840s, the arrival of English Chartists helped bolster the state's labor movement. In 1850, when Parliament began to devise safety codes and inspection systems in response to the miners' agitation, English miners brought their determination to accomplish the same goals in the United States. They led the formation of the American Miners' Association in 1861.

The importance of the English in American labor organization is also illustrated in the life of Samuel Gompers. Born in London's East End to Dutch Jewish immigrant cigar makers, he came to the United States with his family in 1863, with financial help from his father's trade union. Starting out as a cigar maker in New York, Gompers began meeting with other skilled workers and used the British experience with labor organization to demand higher dues from the workers to allow benefits like sick relief, unemployment compensation, and especially a strike fund. With this British model, Gompers established the Federation of Organized Trades and Labor Unions in 1881, which he transformed into the American Federation of Labor in 1886, serving as its president. Because of the role of Gompers and many other English workers, the American labor movement grew with more speed.

The peak number of English-born people in the United States was recorded in the 1890 census at over 900,000. In the twentieth century, the numbers fell as the English were drawn more to the Commonwealth. But the English were still important for the American labor force. They were more concentrated in the professions, as the "brain drain" from Britain to the United States brought more educated people into the universities, the entertainment industry, medicine, and high technology. Altogether the English made an enormous impact and contribution to American labor.

WILLIAM E. VAN VUGT

References and Further Reading

Berthoff, Rowland Tappan. *British Immigrants in Industrial America, 1790–1950*. 1953. Reprint, New York: Russell & Russell, 1968.

Erickson, Charlotte. *American Industry and the European Immigrant, 1860–1885*. 1957. Reprint, New York: Russell and Russell, 1967.

Erickson, Charlotte J. *Invisible Immigrants: The Adaptation of English and Scottish Immigrants to the United States*. Leicester, UK: Leicester University Press, 1972.

———. *Leaving England: Essays on British Emigration in the Nineteenth Century*. Ithaca, NY: Cornell University Press, 1994.

Jeremy, David J. *Transatlantic Industrial Revolution: The Diffusion of Textile Technologies between Britain and America, 1790–1830s*. Cambridge, MA: MIT Press, 1981.

Van Vugt, William E. *Britain to America: Mid-Nineteenth-Century Immigrants to the United States*. Urbana: University of Illinois Press, 1999.

Yearley, Clifton K. *Britons in American Labor*. Baltimore, MD: Johns Hopkins University Press, 1957.

ENVIRONMENTALISM

American environmentalism, from its Progressive Era antecedents to the first Earth Day in 1970 and beyond, must be understood as one of several social movements that arose in response to the profound changes in American political economy and society that began during the second half of the nineteenth century and continued into the twentieth century. Like trade unionism, progressivism, and New Deal-style industrial unionism, the conservation and environmental movements emerged as a result of the United States' transformation from an agrarian and rural society into a predominantly industrial and urban society. As two distinct responses to this same fundamental development, the environmental movement and the various movements organized by, or on behalf of, the working class have experienced a history of uneasy coexistence. The two reform impulses have complemented one another to the extent that they each have posed challenges to the modern corporate-industrial economy, most often by looking to the federal government to curb the excesses of the corporate-industrial order. Ultimately however different constituencies and different goals have led to many intractable contradictions between environmentalism and working-class movements.

Origins of American Environmentalism, 1890–1945

The roots of modern American environmentalism are found in the Progressive Era conservation movement that emerged at the end of the 1800s. This conservation impulse was a response to three late nineteenth century developments in the American political economy: Industrialization, urbanization, and the symbolic closing of the frontier due to the westward expansion of settlement. Industrialization ensured that the exploitation of the nation's timber and mineral resources occurred at unprecedented levels, while the westward spread of settlement meant that fewer land remained immune to this new level of exploitation. Urbanization placed seemingly unsustainable demands on the nation's forests, rivers, and farmlands and also created new environmental problems in the form of urban air and water pollution. These developments engendered a sense of anxiety among many Americans that the public domain was vanishing and that the U.S. economy was exploiting the nation's natural resources at an unsustainable pace. Perhaps historian Roderick Nash in his seminal *Wilderness and the American Mind* has explained this development most succinctly: Americans' concern for the nation's remaining natural areas became more pronounced as the advance of the urban-industrial economy threatened to destroy those areas.

Progressive era conservation was above all else a federal-level legislative and administrative response to this anxiety over dwindling natural resources. As early as 1864, George Perkins Marsh, considered by most historians to have been an early prophet of American environmentalism, cautioned against the overexploitation of American resources. In his book *Man and Nature*, Marsh warned that the rampant deforestation he observed in his native New England and in neighboring New York threatened environmental catastrophe in the form of soil erosion, flooding, and localized climate change. But for decades his warnings went unheeded. Such legislation as the Homestead Act (1862), the General Mining Law (1872), the Desert Land Act (1877), and the Free Timber Act (1878) reflected preconservation, *laissez faire* attitudes. The framers of such laws sought to promote economic growth simply by giving away to private developers the rights to public land, timber, and mineral resources. The Progressive conservation movement therefore signified an important revolution in the management of the nation's natural resources. In contrast to the long tradition of the *laissez faire* approach to natural resource policy, Progressive Era conservation policies inserted the federal government into the long-term management and regulation of American forests, soils, and rivers. The United States Forest Service (USFS) was created in 1905 and charged with managing federally owned forestlands. The Newlands Act (1902) created the Bureau of Reclamation, an agency charged with managing rivers and irrigation projects in the arid American West. The goal of these two agencies was to shift away from concerns over immediate profitability in order to promote long-term, efficient economic development. On the other hand the American Antiquities Act (1906) authorized the president to designate as national monuments areas of historical or archaeological significance for the expressed purpose of exempting these lands from economic development in perpetuity. Congress created the National Park Service (NPS) in 1916 in order to manage these and other preserved lands. As this list suggests, the new managerial role for the federal government was contradictory from the outset. The Bureau of Reclamation and the USFS clearly intended to use federal power to promote the orderly and efficient use of the nation's natural resources. Such legislation as the Antiquities Act and such agencies as the NPS envisioned the federal government as the guardian of the nation's wild or natural places.

The questions often debated by historians of Progressive Era conservation are who spearheaded these legislative and administrative changes in conservation policy, and who benefited from these changes? Samuel P. Hays, in his classic *Conservation and the Gospel of Efficiency: the Progressive Conservation Movement, 1890–1920*, argued that elite, scientific-minded experts foisted these conservation policies on the public and managed the nation's public lands to the benefit of American industry. Hays' archetypal conservationist was Gifford Pinchot, considered by historians the founder of American forestry. Pinchot espoused a utilitarian view of conservation that called for the "right use" of natural resources to benefit the greatest number of people for the longest amount of time. Natural resources, Pinchot argued, should not be squandered by rapacious American industry, but nor should those natural resources be "locked up" or preserved from all economic development. As chief forester of the USFS, Pinchot developed the policy of sustained-yield forestry, whereby the national forests were managed as a crop with the goal of promoting future economic development. Historian Stephen Fox, on the other hand, argued that the Progressive Era conservation impulse is best understood as a fight between the people and the interests. In *The American Conservation Movement: John Muir and His Legacy*, Fox stressed the degree to which preservationists like John Muir, avid outdoorsman, founder of the Sierra Club, and tireless promoter of the preservation of spectacular natural landscapes, spoke on behalf of the people and against the interests of logging, mining, and ranching elites. The creation of 13 national parks from 1872–1913 at the insistence of preservationists like Muir, Fox argued,

was fundamentally a democratic development and represented the protection of public lands from private industry.

One possible way to reconcile this debate and also to assess the legacy of Progressive Era conservation movement is to acknowledge the degree to which the Progressive Era conservation movement—including Muir's preservationist Sierra Club—was largely an elite affair, as Hays suggested. Indeed conservationists shared many of the anti-immigrant and illiberal attitudes toward the working class with other Progressive Era reformers (the notorious nativist Madison Grant for example, was also a member of the Save the Redwoods League, a founder of the Bronx Zoo, and on the board of trustees at the American Museum of Natural History). But it is equally important to acknowledge that government regulation of the nation's natural resources amounted to a revolutionary break with past *laissez faire* policies, regardless of the business-friendly mentality of Pinchot and other utilitarian conservationists. At the end of the Progressive Era then two competing strands of thought—one utilitarian, the other preservationist—had emerged, each with its own elite constituency.

Indeed the flurry of conservationist and preservationist legislation passed during the Progressive Era is a testament to the fact that the earliest environmental impulse was a movement among elites. It is important to note however that Pinchot and other Progressive Era conservationists, such as Senator George Norris and Senator Francis Newlands, did view conservation as a way to promote social equity through a more even distribution of natural resources. But without a self-organized movement among the working or even the middle classes, promises of social equity made by conservationists inevitably went unfulfilled.

Just as American business leaders during the 1920s were able to co-opt the language and logic of the labor movement by calling for American plans and company unions, so, too, were industrialists able to bend the language and logic of Progressive conservation to their needs. Such industry-dominated groups as the American Forestry Association used Pinchot's language of "multiple" or "right" use, initially intended to ensure a wide distribution of forest resources, to argue successfully for repeated rounds of road building and logging in the national forests that favored larger timber companies. Similarly large agribusiness interests in such states as California secured extensive Bureau of Reclamation irrigation projects, justifying their actions using the egalitarian promise of 160-acre homesteads even as these agribusiness interests circumvented such acreage restrictions. Senator Newlands, the author of the legislation that created the Bureau of Reclamation, had envisioned the 160-acre limit as a way to ensure that the benefits of irrigation would flow in democratic fashion to small-family farmers. But quickly the scope of the bureau's projects made Newlands' idea seem quaint at best, and downright backward as far as agribusiness interests were concerned. The failure to make strides toward a more equal distribution of natural resources continued unabated during the New Deal Era. The Tennessee Valley Authority (TVA) was created in 1933 and charged with building a series of dams in order to promote hydroelectric power, flood control, and economic growth in the Tennessee River valley. The brainchild of Senator Norris, the TVA was supposed to promote social equity by bringing low-cost, publicly generated electricity to one of the more impoverished regions of the South. But to such critics as Benton MacKaye, a forester, regional planner, and creator of the Appalachian Trail idea, the TVA quickly sacrificed socially and ecologically sound regional planning at the altar of economic growth. Similar disappointments followed the construction of the Bonneville Dam on the Columbia River. The absence of a self-organized conservation movement among the middle and working classes, along with the Depression Era need to alleviate unemployment and create economic growth, meant that conservation projects placed the federal government squarely in the role of increasing the productive capacity of the nation's environments. The goal of an equitable distribution of natural resources, always less important to Progressive Era and New Deal Era policymakers than the developmental imperative that lay behind these utilitarian conservation works, was in eclipse by the end of the New Deal.

Modern American Environmentalism, 1945–2005

Modern American environmentalism began when increasing numbers of Americans recognized that the environmental consequences of post-World War II economic growth not only jeopardized the health of distant national forests or national parks but also threatened public health and quality of life at home in their own neighborhoods. Just as Progressive Era conservation and preservation stemmed from the development of the urban-industrial economy during the late nineteenth century, the development of modern environmentalism reflected significant shifts taking place in the American political economy during the middle of the twentieth century. Economic

growth led to an expanding middle class and a new consumer-oriented economy. Suburbanization invaded previously undeveloped lands at the edge of urban areas, and automobiles soon rivaled factories as a source of air pollution. Spurred by wartime innovation, newer industries, such as plastics, pesticides, chemicals, petroleum, and nuclear energy, grew tremendously. Moreover the large-scale public-works projects begun in the 1930s yielded truly Herculean levels of environmental transformation by the end of World War II. By the mid-1940s, for example, the Bureau of Reclamation's numerous hydroelectric dams had so thoroughly harnessed the Columbia and Colorado rivers that the bureau was capable of generating more electricity than any other entity, public or private, in the world. Clearly then economic growth in the postwar United States was predicated on massive changes in the American landscape and came at a high environmental price. Modern American environmentalism thus grew from a paradox at the heart of the new postwar American political economy: Robust economic growth made economic security more widespread than ever before in American history, but many Americans in the expanding middle class found their newfound sense of economic security almost immediately undercut by fears that economic growth jeopardized both environmental stability and public health. Post-World War II environmentalism was therefore more democratic than the earlier eras of expert-led conservation in the sense that during the postwar era, the environmental impulse was more widely shared. But for much of this era, environmentalism was still open to charges of elitism because it was largely a middle-class movement, a characteristic that distinguished environmentalism from the organized labor movement.

The first stage of postwar environmentalism involved the protection of iconic public lands and dramatically expanded the constituency of environmental organizations beyond their historically elite base and into the ranks of the expanding middle class. The familiar debate between preservationists and utilitarian conservationists that had been raging since the 1890s came to a head in the early 1950s when the Bureau of Reclamation announced plans to build a dam at Echo Park inside Colorado's Dinosaur National Monument. This proposal was part of the larger Colorado River Storage Project (CRSP) and reflected the utilitarian spirit of Progressive and New Deal Era conservation. It would have flooded federal lands that were supposedly protected from economic development. Led by David Brower, the Sierra Club's dynamic new executive director, more than a dozen preservationist organizations waged a publicity campaign that forced the Bureau of Reclamation to scrap its plans for Echo Park due to the public outcry. What was remarkable about this episode was that the Echo Park project would have been so very unremarkable during the 1930s or 1940s. But as middle-class Americans flocked to the national parks during the 1950s and 1960s, they could be mobilized to defeat public-works projects that adversely affected these public recreational lands. Dams in the works for Glacier, Big Bend, Kings Canyon, and Grand Canyon national parks were also scrapped as a result of this middle-class hostility toward such proposals. The fight against the CRSP marked the apogee of the preservationist strain of environmentalism that began with Muir. During this era the Sierra Club and other preservationist organizations first enjoyed widespread public support. Such organizations expanded beyond their historically elite base in the decades following the 1950s, as many middle-class Americans decided that at least the nation's publicly owned parklands should be protected from rampant economic development. This first stage of postwar environmentalism questioned the logic of incessant economic growth but only as far as iconic public lands were concerned.

The 1960s and 1970s were important decades during which the environmental movement articulated a more direct challenge to the logic of continuous economic growth. This was the second stage of postwar environmentalism. A series of high-profile environmental problems surfaced during this era. Scientists linked smog clouds over Los Angeles and other cities to automobile exhaust; middle-class Americans in suburbia found their drinking water contaminated by pollutants traced back to phosphates found in household laundry detergents; ecologists declared Lake Erie to be ecologically dead in the mid-1960s due to industrial pollutants; Cleveland's Cuyahoga River became so polluted that it famously caught fire in 1969, and so on. But perhaps the most startling revelation occurred in 1962 with the publication of Rachel Carson's *Silent Spring*. Widely regarded as one of the most influential books in the history of American environmentalism, Carson's book revealed to unsuspecting Americans the degree to which such chemicals as DDT had deleterious—and even fatal—impacts on animal life throughout the food chain and could cause significant health problems in humans. In the wake of *Silent Spring,* many Americans came to consider pollution and toxic chemicals as direct threats to their health, security, and quality of life. As these connections between public health problems and environmental degradation on the one hand and unrestrained economic growth on the other became increasingly obvious, environmentalists began to call for a series of regulations that marked a significant departure from the earlier concern with iconic

parklands. Now the actions of privately owned businesses and the use of privately owned resources that polluted the air, water, and land were to be regulated. The Clean Air Act (1963) and the Clean Water Act (1972), both of which were amended several times in the coming decades, sought to reduce air and water pollution to safe or acceptable levels by requiring industry to restrict its emissions of harmful materials. The National Environmental Policy Act (1970) mandated environmental impact statements (EIS) in order to evaluate the wisdom of proceeding with industrial projects likely to adversely affect the environment. The Environmental Protection Agency (EPA) was created (1970) to oversee the regulation of air and water quality, solid-waste disposal, and to supervise the EIS process. Congress banned the use of DDT (1972), and the Toxic Substances Control Act (1976) called for more stringent monitoring of the use and disposal of industrial chemicals. The Endangered Species Act (1973) mandated the protection of species designated by scientists as threatened or endangered without any consideration of the economic consequences of protection. And the Comprehensive Environmental Response, Compensation, and Liability Act, better known as the Superfund Act, was passed in 1980 and authorized the creation of an environmental rehabilitation fund to be financed by a tax on the chemical industry. It also authorized the EPA to sue corporations for clean-up costs if corporate negligence could be proven. Taken collectively these environmental measures amounted to a frontal assault on corporate U.S. managerial prerogatives to use their privately owned resources as they saw fit.

The environmental reforms achieved during the 1960s and 1970s were far from perfect, and many environmentalists argued that they did not go far enough, but the conservative backlash against environmental regulations since 1980 suggests the degree to which environmental legislation did in fact place significant restrictions on managerial prerogatives. Since 1980, capital and its conservative political allies have argued that environmental regulations hurt the American economy and cost Americans jobs. The "job blackmail" or "jobs versus the environment" debates that have raged since 1980 are examples of this. These arguments had salience in large part due to the wrenching economic changes that the American economy experienced during the late 1970s and early 1980s. Ronald Reagan's famous proclamation that "government is the problem" led him to slash the EPA's budget, for example, and appoint a series of cabinet-level officials hostile to the very idea of federal management of natural resources, ostensibly in the name of increasing the productivity of private enterprise and boosting employment for American workers. In addition to this pragmatic argument that environmental regulations cost jobs and hurt the economy, the conservative backlash against environmentalism has also been bolstered by the larger ideological shift toward private property rights in American political culture that has accompanied the resurgence of the conservative movement. The Wise Use movement, a movement consisting of a coterie of wealthy western miners, ranchers, loggers, and landowners assuming the appearance of a grassroots uprising, has argued that the federal government had no right to regulate any use of privately held lands and demanded an end to government regulation of natural resource use. Similarly the Republican party's 1994 Contract with America included an effort to re-interpret the Fifth Amendment to include a "takings clause." Traditionally under the rules of eminent domain, the government compensated private landowners only if their property was physically occupied. The proposed takings clause called for remuneration if any restrictions whatsoever—including regulations designed to reduce pollution or protective actions mandated by the Endangered Species Act, for example—were placed on private owners' land use options. Such a clause would make most environmental regulations unaffordable. The backlash against environmental regulations was part of the larger ideological movement to free the private sector from as much governmental regulation as possible.

Modern American Environmentalism and the Labor Movement, 1945–2005

In 1990, environmentalists successfully petitioned to have the northern spotted owl listed as threatened under the Endangered Species Act. This triggered actions to protect the owls' habitat, the old growth forests of the Pacific Northwest. The timber industry ominously predicted the loss of over 100,000 jobs if these forests were removed from the market. Environmentalists argued that this was an exaggerated threat and that any jobs lost were the result of a timber industry that was ailing regardless of whether or not remaining old growth forests were cut. Members of Earth First!—a grassroots environmental organization—heightened the tension when they engaged in direct-action protests that included "monkey wrenching," or the sabotaging of logging equipment. Afraid of losing their jobs and resentful of what they perceived as environmentalists' economic and cultural elitism, blue-collar loggers sided with the timber industry. The ensuing fight between environmentalists and workers quickly came to epitomize what is often

assumed to be the inherent disconnect between the environmental and labor movements. As this disagreement between loggers and environmentalists suggests, it is important to acknowledge the deep fissures that exist between the labor and environmental movements. Both movements challenged the prerogatives of industry, but environmentalism and organized labor have historically represented different constituencies that did not always challenge the corporate-industrial order in the same way. Middle-class environmentalists ensconced in professional jobs were free to question the logic and desirability of incessant economic growth, particularly in such extractive industries as logging. Labor unions, constrained by patterns of firm-centered collective bargaining in place since the Wagner Act, were understandably devoted to ensuring the health of their industry and hesitated to endorse any measures that threatened its economic growth. Different constituencies and different core values have meant that labor and environmentalism have often been at odds.

But collaboration between environmentalists and organized labor has not been impossible, and the assumption that there is an irresolvable conflict between organized labor and environmentalism is incorrect. Before the 1970s, there were considerable areas of overlap between the two movements, particularly when workers' health and the health of working-class communities were concerns. Middle-class Americans may have been worried about the negative environmental impacts of industrial processes, but without a doubt working-class Americans and their communities were the most adversely affected by industrial pollutants, and unionized workers often pushed for reforms that in retrospect seem like early instances of what would later be considered environmental demands. The United Steelworkers (USW) began supporting clean air measures as a result of the infamous killer smog incident in 1948, when local weather patterns trapped polluted air over the working-class city of Donora, Pennsylvania, killing 20 people. The steelworkers supported federal clean air measures through the landmark legislation of the 1970s, as did the United Auto Workers (UAW), the International Association of Machinists (IAM), and even the United Mine Workers (UMW) (so long as smokestack "scrubbers," and not alternative sources of energy, provided the basis for the clean air acts). Workers' health was also an issue that led to unions articulating environmental demands. The United Farm Workers (UFW) for example teamed with environmental organizations in order to reduce pesticide use in California agribusiness during that union's organizing campaigns in the late 1960s. A similar concern with toxins in the workplace led the USW,

IAM, UAW, and the Oil, Chemical, and Atomic Workers (OCAW) to lobby for the passage of the Occupational Safety and Health Act (OSHA) in 1970. Although most environmentalists failed to openly support OSHA, several mainstream environmental organizations, including the Sierra Club, Friends of the Earth, the Earth Defense Fund, and the Izaak Walton League, supported OCAW's 1973 strike and boycott against the Shell Oil Company, a strike designed to force Shell to comply with OSHA regulations. In the wake of this strike, formal alliances were sought by labor and environmental leaders. Environmentalists for Full Employment (EFFE) was founded in 1975 in order to provide a way for environmentalists to reach out to the organized labor community. And in 1976, the leaders of over 100 labor and environmental organizations attended the Working for Environmental Justice and Jobs conference held at the UAW's Black Lake center in Michigan. Such alliances were instrumental in getting the Clean Air, Clean Water, Toxic Substance Control, and Superfund acts passed. This list suggests that when the health and safety of workers and their communities were concerns, support for environmental causes has been possible among the ranks of organized labor.

But these labor-environmental alliances fractured during the 1980s and 1990s. This happened for several related reasons. The alliances between labor and environmental groups forged during the 1970s were for the most part created only at the leadership levels. Such alliances failed to address the significant cultural and class differences between the rank-and-file of the two movements. And the resurgence of free-market conservatism created a hostile political climate during the 1980s and 1990s, making these decades a period of retrenchment for both environmentalism and organized labor. Indeed the most significant instance of labor-environmental collaboration during this period highlights the tenuousness of the labor-environmental alliance. From 1984–1989, members of the Oil, Chemical, and Atomic Workers engaged in a bitter dispute with the management of chemical giant BASF at that company's Geismar, Louisiana, facility. Capitalizing on the chemical industry's checkered environmental record, OCAW allied with a collection of citizen's environmental groups and local chapters of national environmental organizations, such as the Sierra Club. The OCAW and the environmentalists publicized BASF's many violations of federal and state environmental laws and argued that only a unionized workforce could force the company to comply with environmental regulations. The resulting public pressure forced BASF to reinstate locked-out union workers in 1989, a rare victory for both organized labor and environmentalists during an era characterized by concessionary bargaining and the permanent replacement of striking workers. But the conditions under which this successful labor-environmental alliance was forged suggested just how unlikely other such alliances had become: The workers at BASF had already lost their jobs and were therefore immune to jobs-versus-the-environment arguments; BASF was committed to expanding its Louisiana facilities and therefore could not credibly threaten to move its operations elsewhere; and local residents were easily persuaded that BASF's operations had a deleterious impact on their health and safety. Indeed most of the labor-environmental relations during the last two decades have gone the other way. In addition to the divisive fight between environmentalists and loggers in the Pacific Northwest, there were other high-profile disputes between organized labor and environmentalists. The UMW broke with environmentalists over the acid rain provisions contained in the Clean Air Act of 1990. More recently, the UAW has resisted calls for strengthening the federal Corporate Average Fuel Economy (CAFE) standards for cars and trucks sold in the United States. In a classic case of jobs-versus-the-environment logic and despite significant improvements in fuel economy technology, U.S. automakers maintain that the implementation of more stringent CAFE standards will result in the loss of union jobs. The UAW, already buffeted by declining union density due to foreign competition and automation, continues to side with the auto industry on this issue.

Conclusion

The history of American environmentalism demonstrates that environmentalism and the labor movement have not simply been driven apart by the machinations of corporate managers and political conservatives hostile to all intrusions into the free market. There are fundamental differences between the two movements that have made cooperation difficult. During the Progressive and New Deal eras, the conservationist and preservationist impulses were primarily confined to elites, did not have a broad popular base, and had little relation to the labor movement of those times. Since 1945, environmentalism has developed a much larger constituency but one that was for the most part confined to the middle class. Cooperation among environmentalists and organized labor was not impossible, particularly where labor issues dovetailed with environmental health and safety concerns. But tensions between middle-class environmentalists and organized labor's working-class membership were exposed when declining union density, structural changes in the American economy, and a hostile political environment severed the fragile links between the two movements. The fundamental class differences between the two movements must be acknowledged.

It may be too simple to argue that workers and environmentalists have been driven apart by their enemies then, but the current excesses of global corporations and the ideology of free trade may yet drive these two movements together. It is not surprising that an era in which private property rights are celebrated and the public sphere is disdained has also been an era that produced a corporate order committed to rolling back labor and environmental regulations even though these regulations were the result of laws passed by democratically elected Congresses. As free trade makes it easier for corporations to circumvent such labor and environmental standards, members of the two movements have come to see each other as potential allies. The 1999 protests against the World Trade Organization at its meeting in Seattle, when tens of thousands of laborites and environmentalists marched together as part of a new coalition called the Alliance for Sustainable Jobs and the Environment, could thus come to symbolize the beginning of a new era of labor-environmental cooperation.

KEVIN NOBLE POWERS

References and Suggested Reading

Cronon, William, ed. *Uncommon Ground: Rethinking the Human Place in Nature*. New York: W. W. Norton & Co., 1996.

Fox, Stephen R. *The American Conservation Movement: John Muir and His Legacy*. Madison: University of Wisconsin Press, 1981.

Gottlieb, Robert. *Forcing the Spring: The Transformation of the American Environmental Movement*. Washington, DC: Island Press, 2005.

Hays, Samuel P. *Beauty, Health, and Permanence: Environmental Politics in the United States, 1955–1985*. New York: Cambridge University Press, 1987.

———. *Conservation and the Gospel of Efficiency: The Progressive Conservation Movement, 1890–1920*. Cambridge, MA: Harvard University Press, 1959.

———. *A History of Environmental Politics since 1945*. Pittsburgh, PA: University of Pittsburgh Press, 2000.

Kline, Benjamin. *First along the River: A Brief History of the U.S. Environmental Movement*. San Francisco, CA: Acadia Books, 1997.

Koppes, Clayton R. "Efficiency, Equity, and Esthetics: Shifting Themes in American Conservation." In *The Ends of the Earth: Perspectives on Modern Environmental History*, ed. Donald Worster,. New York: Cambridge University Press, 1988.

Merchant, Carolyn. *The Columbia Guide to American Environmental History*. New York: Columbia University Press, 2002.

Minchin, Timothy. *Forging a Common Bond: Labor and Environmental Activism during the BASF Lockout*. Gainsville: University Press of Florida, 2003.

Nash, Roderick. *Wilderness and the American Mind*. New Haven, CT: Yale University Press, 1967.

Obach, Brian K. *Labor and the Environmental Movement: The Quest for Common Ground*. Cambridge: Massachusetts Institute of Technology Press, 2004.

Rome, Adam. *The Bulldozer in the Countryside: Suburban Sprawl and the Rise of American Environmentalism*. New York: Cambridge University Press, 2001.

Rose, Fred. *Coalitions across the Class Divide: Lessons from the Labor, Peace, and Environmental Movements*. Ithaca, NY: Cornell University Press, 2000.

Rothman, Hal. *Saving the Planet: The American Response to the Environment in the Twentieth Century*. Chicago, IL: Ivan R. Dee, 2000.

Runte, Alfred. *National Parks: The American Experience*. Lincoln: University of Nebraska Press, 1979.

Sale, Kirkpatrick. *The Green Revolution: The American Environmental Movement, 1962–1992*. New York: Hill & Wang, 1993.

Steinberg, Theodore. *Down to Earth: Nature's Role in American History*. New York: Oxford University Press, 2002.

Sutter, Paul S. *Driven Wild: How the Fight against Automobiles Launched the Modern Wilderness Movement*. Seattle: University of Washington Press, 2002.

Worster, Donald. *Dust Bowl: The Southern Plains in the 1930s*. New York: Oxford University Press, 1979.

———. *Rivers of Empire: Water, Aridity, and the Growth of the American West*. New York: Pantheon Press, 1985.

EQUAL EMPLOYMENT OPPORTUNITY COMMISSION

Title VII of the Civil Rights Act of 1964, which prohibited employment discrimination on the basis of race, color, national origin, religion, or sex, established the Equal Employment Opportunity Commission (EEOC). Initially EEOC sought compliance from employers, labor organizations, and employment programs but could not directly enforce Title VII. Subsequent legislation expanded EEOC's powers and jurisdiction, which came to include disability, age, and pregnancy discrimination and sexual harassment. Yet EEOC's growing authority as the lead enforcement agency in workplace discrimination did not bring parallel increases in resources and funding.

The EEOC operates under five bipartisan commissioners and a general counsel, appointed by the president and confirmed by the Senate. Commissioners serve staggered five-year terms, and the general counsel a four-year term. The president designates a chair, who is chief executive officer of EEOC. Franklin D. Roosevelt, Jr., served as first chair (1965–1966).

Following him were Stephen N. Shulman (1966–1967), Clifford L. Alexander, Jr. (1967–1969), William H. Brown, III (1969–1973), John H. Powell (1973–1975), Lowell W. Perry (1975–1976), Eleanor Holmes Norton (1977–1981), Clarence Thomas (1982–1990), Evan J. Kemp, Jr. (1990–1993), Gilbert Casellas (1994–1997), Ida L. Castro (1998–2001), and Cari M. Dominguez (2001–2006).

The Early EEOC

The EEOC's initial lack of enforcement powers was a key concession to Republicans and conservative southern Democrats in congressional debate over the Civil Rights Act. What helped the act pass in mid-1964 was elimination of proposed EEOC power to issue cease-and-desist orders or initiate litigation. Congress authorized EEOC only to interpret Title VII and to investigate and "conciliate" charges of discrimination filed by workers.

Per Title VII, EEOC was to issue employment guidelines and with individual complaints, determine whether there was reasonable cause to believe that illegal discrimination had occurred. When EEOC found reasonable cause, it was to seek compliance with Title VII "by informal methods of conference, conciliation, and persuasion." If conciliation failed, EEOC could recommend legal action to the U.S. Attorney General, who was empowered to sue where "patterns or practices" of systematic discrimination were found (in the first year, only 11 cases were so referred). Or far more likely, EEOC advised the complainant of her or his right to file a civil action within 30 days.

What limited power the early EEOC had it applied unevenly, critics charged. Leaders of the new commission made clear that they considered sex discrimination less important than racial discrimination, a belief encouraged by the last-minute inclusion of sex in Title VII, a bill otherwise devoted to African-American rights. Working women certainly took the new law seriously—a full third of the complaints filed in 1966 concerned sex discrimination (53% concerned race). Feminists outside and within EEOC, including founding Commissioners Aileen Hernandez and Richard Graham and lawyer Sonia Pressman Fuentes, pressed for more action on women workers' behalf. Veterans of the African-American freedom struggle wondered why the new commission—a product of civil rights activism—was dominated by political insiders and bureaucrats with business ties but little relevant experience.

Making Title VII Meaningful

The early EEOC accomplished much simply in interpreting what Title VII meant and required. Congress had been vague in many areas, so it fell to EEOC to specify the parameters of employment discrimination—and it did so expansively. Particularly important was the commission's insistence that illegal discrimination did not require intentional acts that overtly targeted individuals (known as "disparate treatment"). Discrimination also occurred, EEOC argued, when an employment policy adversely and disproportionately affected a protected group, regardless of appearance or intent (known as "disparate impact"). If an employer did not prove the business necessity of such a policy, EEOC considered it illegal. Similarly EEOC narrowly interpreted the bona fide occupational qualification, or BFOQ, exception to Title VII. The BFOQ clause of Title VII allowed employers to discriminate on the basis of sex, national origin, or religion (but not race) if they showed that doing so was "reasonably necessary" to "normal" business operations. The EEOC decided this applied only rarely, such as in acting or in the hiring of a minister, priest, or rabbi. Finally believing employers were obliged not merely to stop discriminating but also to address ongoing effects of past bias, EEOC promoted affirmative action programs.

As the commission's interpretations and *amicus* briefs proved increasingly persuasive to the courts by the 1970s, workers and EEOC together gave Title VII force and meaning. Successful targets included the blatant sex typing of occupations as well as seemingly neutral educational requirements and tests whose effect was not to ensure skill levels, but to bar minorities from jobs and promotions. Workers' own organizations came under fire, too. The EEOC investigated unions for colluding in employer discrimination and even enforcing inequality through seniority systems. In some occupations and industries, EEOC-supported worker activism brought dramatic change: Airline flight attendants no longer had to be single, under 35, and female, while in the heavily southern textile industry African-Americans went from holding a mere 3% of jobs in 1960 to over 18% by 1978.

Growing Power and Responsibilities

In 1972, EEOC gained enforcement power. Congress decided it had underestimated the extent of discrimination and overestimated the potential of voluntary compliance with Title VII. With the Equal Employment

Opportunity Act of 1972, Congress amended Title VII to give EEOC right-to-sue powers, including "pattern and practices" suits previously under the U.S. Attorney General's purview. The act also expanded Title VII coverage to civil service at federal, state, and local levels and to educational institutions, and lowered its minimum threshold from 25 to 15 employees.

Within three years, EEOC had filed more than 450 lawsuits on individual charges. It also began systematic attacks on racial and gender discrimination at some of the nation's largest employers, including AT&T, Ford, and Sears Roebuck. Such efforts resulted in several high-profile agreements: with AT&T in 1973, then the nation's largest private employer; the nine largest steelmakers in the U.S. and the United Steelworkers in 1974; General Electric in 1978; the Associated Press in 1983; and General Motors and the United Auto Workers in 1984. These agreements brought workers millions in back pay and featured affirmative action plans to move more women and minorities onto and up the employment ladder, out of blue- and pink-collar ghettoes. Hardly all investigations resulted in such successes, however.

In the late 1970s, EEOC's increased powers expanded to new areas of discrimination. The Carter administration gave EEOC responsibility for enforcing the Equal Pay Act of 1963 and the Age Discrimination in Employment Act of 1967, previously the Department of Labor's duty. By the 1980s, age discrimination was the fastest growing area of workers' complaints. In 1978, Congress passed the Pregnancy Discrimination Act, amending Title VII to prohibit bias against pregnant workingwomen. When EEOC issued its first guidelines on sexual harassment in 1980, it brought yet another area of discrimination under sustained scrutiny. (Ironically charges of sexual harassment against former EEOC Chair Clarence Thomas while he was vetted for the U.S. Supreme Court in 1991 dramatically raised public awareness of this newer area of sex discrimination.)

The early 1990s brought a final wave of expansion in EEOC's jurisdiction and authority. Congress charged the commission with enforcing Title I of the Americans with Disabilities Act of 1990, banning discrimination in employment based on disabilities. Congress also responded to the growing conservatism of the courts with another Civil Rights Act in 1991. It revised Title VII to reflect EEOC standards for defining and proving discrimination; enabled workers to seek damages, along with back pay and reinstatement; and extended Title VII coverage to Americans working overseas.

Underfunded and Always Behind

Whatever the political climate, EEOC never enjoyed adequate resources to investigate, let alone conciliate or litigate, the flood of workers' complaints it received. The original EEOC, with fewer than 100 employees and a budget of $2.25 million, expected 2,000 complaints in its first year. It received nearly 9,000. Though it quickly expanded, the commission would only fall further behind as its caseload swelled and Congress provided budgets of far less than requested. Pursuit of voluntary employer compliance brought limited results at best. Successful conciliations ran in the low hundreds annually for the first several years, while new charges were in the several thousands. With new power and expanded jurisdiction came even more complaints. After a decade the backlog of unprocessed cases topped 100,000 and the average complaint took more than two years to resolve (Title VII's original timeframe was 60 days). Other problems became clear by the mid-1970s: Efforts to monitor employer compliance with settlements were lax or nonexistent, and high turnover at the top had created instability.

By the mid-1970s, many believed EEOC desperately needed reform. Carter-appointed Chair Eleanor Holmes Norton instituted speed-up processing of new charges and backlog-reducing measures. Norton's reforms did slash the backlog, but critics saw a new policy of indiscriminate settlement, regardless of a case's merit. Under Reagan-appointed Clarence Thomas, EEOC recommitted itself to full investigations of individual complaints and pulled back from higher impact systematic approaches. The change in focus, combined with staff reductions due to funding cuts and increased responsibilities, saw the number of unprocessed charges skyrocket again in the 1980s. Under President Clinton's appointees, new systems of prioritizing investigations and voluntary mediation reduced the backlog again, with less controversy.

Throughout its history, EEOC has struggled to provide individuals with relief while attacking discrimination broadly and to fulfill its educational and conciliation mandates (or claims adjuster role according to critics) while wielding regulatory and litigation powers. Perpetual underfunding, despite increasing responsibilities, has necessarily limited the commission's agenda and impact. Whatever the enforcement philosophies and achievements of successive EEOC regimes, many thousands of workers have had their charges of discrimination lost in the political and bureaucratic shuffle. But those who did succeed in pressing complaints have helped, and been helped by, EEOC in banishing more egregious forms of discrimination from many American workplaces.

KATHLEEN M. BARRY

References and Further Reading

Graham, Hugh Davis. *The Civil Rights Era: Origins and Development of National Policy, 1960–1972.* New York: Oxford University Press, 1990.

Hamilton, Konrad Mark. "From Equal Opportunity to Affirmative Action: A History of the Equal Employment Opportunity Commission, 1965–1980." Ph.D. dissertation, Stanford University, 1998.

Kessler-Harris, Alice. *In Pursuit of Equity: Women, Men, and the Quest for Economic Citizenship in Twentieth-Century America.* New York: Oxford University Press, 2001.

MacLean, Nancy. *Freedom Is Not Enough: The Opening of the American Workplace.* Cambridge, MA: Harvard University Press, 2006.

Maschke, Karen J. *Litigation, Courts, and Women Workers.* New York: Praeger, 1989.

Minchin, Timothy J. *Hiring the Black Worker: The Racial Integration of the Southern Textile Industry, 1960–1980.* Chapel Hill: University of North Carolina Press, 1999.

U.S. Equal Employment Opportunity Commission. "EEOC History: 35th Anniversary: 1965–2000." www.eeoc.gov/abouteeoc/35th/index.html (2000-).

Cases and Statutes Cited

Age Discrimination in Employment Act of 1967, Act of Dec. 15, 1967, 81 Stat. 602.

Americans with Disabilities Act of 1990, Act of July 26, 1990, 104 Stat. 327.

Civil Rights Act of 1964, Act of July 2, 1964, 78 Stat. 241.

Civil Rights Act of 1991, Act of Nov. 21, 1991, 105 Stat. 1071.

Equal Employment Opportunity Act of 1972, Act of Mar. 24, 1972, 86 Stat. 103.

Equal Pay Act of 1963, Act of June 10, 1963, 77 Stat. 56.

Pregnancy Discrimination Act, Act of Oct. 31, 1978, 92 Stat. 2076.

See also **Civil Rights Act of 1964/Title VII**

EQUAL PAY ACT OF 1963

Support for a federal equal pay law for women dates back to the nineteenth century. Male unionists had long supported equal pay, especially in industries where the replacement of men with women loomed large. It took concrete form as a legislative campaign however only when large numbers of women entering the World War II production workforce demanded that they be paid on a par with men. In general women were not, but they did take up jobs previously designated as men's jobs and destabilized the notion that women were unfit to perform certain kinds of work. Women came to expect more money and greater status in the workplace and union with this new responsibility. At the very least, they wanted to be paid what men working alongside them were paid.

As reasonable as equal pay legislation seemed in the 1940s, it would take nearly 20 years for Congress to pass an equal pay law. The reasons for the delay in passage were many: Legislators waffled on the wording of the proposed law; union leaders failed to invest the necessary resources to promote the measure; and officials in the executive branch during the presidency of Republican Dwight Eisenhower in the 1950s did not pursue such social legislation as equal pay.

The real force behind moving equal pay legislation through Congress came from a loosely formed coalition that was sponsored by the U.S. Women's Bureau. The so-called Women's Bureau coalition had as its members unionists and those representing liberal interest groups, some of whom had their roots in the progressive movement. The new administration of Democrat John Kennedy, elected in 1960, was not only more open to social legislation than the Republicans but included several unionists receptive to women's issues. Esther Peterson, a longtime union staff member, revitalized interest in equal pay legislation from her post as Women's Bureau head and assistant secretary of labor for President Kennedy. The legislation, along with President Kennedy's Commission on the Status of Women, expansion of the Fair Employment Standards Act to include low-paid and marginalized workers, and the enactment of a federal law providing daycare support, marked a period of transition to support for gender equality.

Conservative legislators and the business community weakened the measure considerably. The act, modeled on the Fair Employment Standards Act coverage, exempted employers with fewer than 25 employees and permitted a gradual elimination of wage differentials between men and women workers. Unionists helped defeat an attempt by conservatives to include a provision in the bill postponing the effective date of the Equal Pay Act in the case of employees covered by current labor-management contracts until two years after enactment or until contracts expired. They worried that such an allowance would set a dangerous precedent when they called for examining the minimum-wage or maximum-hours provisions of the Fair Labor Standards Act.

In its first decade of enforcement, court decisions interpreted the meaning of equal pay broadly by refusing to limit the measure to identical jobs. As a result the government awarded 171,000 employees $84 million in back pay. The law was one of several signs in the early 1960s that support for gender equality in the workplace was on the rise. The new law underscored a shift in working women's sentiment that would manifest itself over the course of the next decade in feminist activism.

DENNIS A. DESLIPPE

References and Further Reading

Cobble, Dorothy Sue. *The Other Women's Movement: Workplace Justice and Social Rights in Modern America.* Princeton, NJ: Princeton University Press, 2004.

Deslippe, Dennis A. *"Rights, Not Roses": Unions and the Rise of Working-Class Feminism, 1945–1980.* Urbana: University of Illinois Press, 2000.

Gabin, Nancy F. *Feminism in the Labor Movement: Women and the United Auto Workers, 1935–1975.* Ithaca, NY: Cornell University Press, 1990.

Harrison, Cynthia. *On Account of Sex: The Politics of Women's Issues, 1945–1968.* Berkeley: University of California Press, 1988.

Kessler-Harris, Alice. *In Pursuit of Equity: Women, Men, and the Quest for Economic Citizenship in Twentieth-Century America.* New York: Oxford University Press, 2001.

Laughlin, Kathleen A. *Women's Work and Public Policy: A History of the Women's Bureau, U.S. Department of Labor, 1945–1970.* Boston, MA: Northeastern University Press, 2000.

See also **Fair Labor Standards Act; Peterson, Esther; Women's Bureau**

ERDMAN ACT

The Erdman Act bears witness to the critical position railways and railway unions played in the evolution of twentieth-century labor law and practice. The act extended the *de facto* protection of the federal government to the four railway-operating brotherhoods (engineers, firemen, conductors and trainmen) while simultaneously making industrywide strikes difficult if not impossible to sustain. Representing the first substantive effort by the federal government to move beyond simply assisting in the suppression of strikes, the act emerged from 20 years of widespread agitation by railway employees for a determinative voice in the circumstances, wages, and administration of their work.

Though its genesis lay in suggestions found in the report of the United States Strike Commission's investigation of the 1894 Pullman strike, the bill reflected the concerns of its primary author, President Grover Cleveland's attorney general, Richard Olney. He sought to find a path to labor peace that recognized the legal existence of the operating brotherhoods but which also prevented railway employees from substantially interfering with interstate commerce through strikes and boycotts. Drafted in 1895, the bill saw debate in several sessions of Congress before President William McKinley signed it into law on June 1, 1898.

The act called on the chairman of the Interstate Commerce Commission and the commissioner of labor to mediate disputes between railways and their operating employees at the request of either party. If mediation failed, the act provided for the creation of a three-member panel of arbitration, composed of a neutral party and one delegate each from the disputants. Unlike the provisions of the Arbitration Act of 1888, the decision of the arbitration panel would be enforceable by law in federal courts and stand for one year. The act required parties in arbitration to maintain the *status quo antebellum* for up to six months. Furthermore the bill proscribed a series of anti-union practices that the railway brotherhoods found particularly noxious, including yellow-dog contracts, discrimination against union members, blacklists, compulsory participation in company-sponsored insurance and relief associations, and finally mandated specific fines for violations of those prohibitions.

In practice the act fell far short of its promise. After an initial attempt to use its arbitration procedures failed because the railroads in question refused to participate, the law fell into disuse. However from 1906–1913, when it was superseded by the Newlands Act, railways and unions brought a total of 61 requests for action of which more than half were eventually settled by mediation, arbitration, or a combination of both.

Traditionally scholars of American labor have interpreted the Erdman Act as a tentative first step toward extending the protection of the state to unions and workers but one that was quickly stymied by a conservative Supreme Court in the *Adair v. United States* decision of 1908. However in recent years a number of legal and political scholars have argued that this interpretation ignores a long-standing congressional penchant for deferring difficult or unpopular questions to the federal courts. Debates on this issue continue.

SCOTT E. RANDOLPH

References and Further Reading

Eggert, Gerald G. *Railroad Labor Disputes: The Beginnings of Federal Strike Policy.* Ann Arbor: University of Michigan Press, 1967.

Lecht, Leonard A. *Experience under Railway Labor Legislation.* New York: Columbia University Press, 1955.

Lovell, George I. *Legislative Deferrals: Statutory Ambiguity, Judicial Power, and American Democracy.* Cambridge, UK: Cambridge University Press, 2003.

Stromquist, Shelton. *A Generation of Boomers: The Pattern of Railroad Labor Conflict in Nineteenth-Century America.* Urbana: University of Illinois Press, 1987.

Cases and Statutes Cited

Adair v. United States, 208 U.S. 161 (1908)
Newlands Act, 38 Stat. 103 (1913)

EVANS, GEORGE HENRY (1805–1856)
Jacksonian Era Labor Activist

Born in 1805, George Henry Evans was a printer, writer, political activist, and land reform advocate who participated in many of the reform activities of the Jacksonian era labor movement, including the Working Men's party, the bank crusade, the National Trades' Union, and the National Reform Association. Born in Bromyard, Herefordshire, England, Evans emigrated to the United States at the age of 15 with his father and brother and was apprenticed to an Ithaca printer soon thereafter. Under the influence of several mentors, he immersed himself in the works of eighteenth-century radicals Thomas Paine and Thomas Jefferson. Emulating his hero, Paine, Evans became an atheist and an anticlerical. From 1824 to 1827, Evans edited the Ithaca *Museum and Independent Corrector,* through which he made use of his Jeffersonian-Paineite education by attacking political chicanery, social inequality, and the religious revival known as the Second Great Awakening, which was then sweeping western New York.

Apparently ambitious by nature, Evans moved to New York City in 1827, and in 1829 began publishing the *Working Man's Advocate,* which started as the semi-official organ of the New York Working Men's party and which under differing names and a few pauses, Evans published for 20 years. Though Evans was neither a labor union member nor a union leader, he was nevertheless a consistent and committed voice for the constellation of reforms, including hard money, free public land, opposition to chartered monopoly, shorter working hours, universal education, secularism, and poll tax abolition, that characterized labor-oriented reform in the Age of Jackson. In short he was sympathetic to the constituency and aims of the labor movement, whose leaders were frequently his closest ideological and political allies. Most importantly Evans was always true to the spirit and ideals of Jeffersonian and Paineite republicanism, from its emphasis on the ownership of land by nearly everyone as a great bulwark to the Republic to its strict insistence that all men are created equal; from its Enlightenment optimism to its skeptical stance toward organized religion. The *Declaration of Independence,* the *Rights of Man,* and the *Age of Reason* constituted the holiest books of his radical Bible. After the demise of his last reform journal, *Young America,* Evans retired to his New Jersey farm, where he died in 1856.

Evans first got involved in labor politics in October 1829, when he began publishing the *Working Man's Advocate.* A young man of 24, Evans was never a leader of the Working Men's party, though as editor of the *Advocate* he was drawn into the internecine, three-way factional struggles that characterized the party in 1829 and 1830. Thomas Skidmore, an autodidact machinist whose polemical book, the *Right of Man to Property,* advocated the redistribution of wealth and abolition of inheritance, was the leader of the party in its early days, when it won several local races and seemed poised for even greater successes. Shortly after the November 1829 elections however, an alliance between Robert Dale Owen and Fanny Wright, who urged universal free education as a panacea, and Henry Guyon and Noah Cook, who were politicos attempting to use the party as a weapon against the regular Tammany Hall Democrats, forced Skidmore out of the party. Within months Guyon and Cook had managed to expel Owen and Wright as well. Though initially attempting to mediate these disputes, Evans eventually turned against the radicalism of Skidmore and embraced Owen's State Guardianship plan for universal public boarding schools. Divided into three separate parties however, the Working Men's movement achieved little further success and was dead by 1831.

For the two years following the demise of the Working Men's party, Evans continued to publish his newspaper and attempted to keep the spirit of reform alive with proposals for public bathhouses (to improve the public health), abolition of the military academy at West Point, hard-money opposition to chartered banks, and antisabbatarianism. The latter of course reflected the anticlerical influence of Paine, as Evans argued that laws prohibiting activities on Sunday amounted to an imposition of the Christian religion on the populace in violation of the Constitution.

The bank issue, which Evans raised as early as 1831, became a political issue of national importance in 1832, when Congress, at the urging of Nicholas Biddle, president of the Bank of the United States, renewed the bank's charter four years early, and President Andrew Jackson vetoed the legislation. The banking issue resonated deeply in the urban working class. Small-scale artisans and others in the laboring classes had long argued that the banking system was rigged to hold down the honest mechanic by limiting access to capital to those with wealth or political connections. Further employers paid wage laborers not in hard specie, but in bank notes that often proved to be fraudulent or worthless. Thus the bank issue was, unbeknownst to the inept Biddle and the bourgeois Whig party, a labor issue, which Henry Clay handed to Andrew Jackson, who turned a simple veto into a powerful statement of the populist sympathies of the Democratic party that still resonates today. Evans, who however was always more of a Jeffersonian than a Jacksonian, entered the fray only in 1833, and added nothing new to the debate, preferring to reprint the contributions of others, such as *New York Post* editor William Leggett. Early in 1835, in response to the New York Assembly's grant of several new state bank charters, Evans helped organize and became vice-president of an organization called "The Working Men Opposed to Paper Money," which helped organize antibank sentiment into an electoral force, which contributed to Democratic political victories.

Evans's first direct participation in labor union activity was short-lived. In 1834, Evans gave needed editorial support to the new National Trades' Union, (NTU) which proposed to unite the various local trades' confederations into a national organization. The NTU specifically recommended that its members read the *Advocate*, along with several other reform journals. At the NTU's inaugural convention however, Evans was greatly disappointed by the decision to abjure politics and focus on the hours of labor and wages. By mid-1835, Evans was in serious financial difficulty and relocated to his New Jersey farm, giving up his journalism for about five years.

In 1840, Evans emerged from his self-imposed political exile advocating the panacea of free public land. The idea that the federal government should give away public lands to those willing and able to till its soil was not new: The NTU had urged free public land in 1834, and many others before and after as well. Most importantly to Evans, his old hero Thomas Paine had urged, in *Agrarian Justice*, that uncultivated land was the "common property of the human race," though he had made no specific proposal for its distribution. Drawing on the ideas of Paine, Thomas Skidmore, English radical political economist Thomas Spence, and French Associationist

Charles Fourier, Evans argued that because property is the produce of labor, and land is not the produce of labor, land cannot be property. Thus Evans concluded, land should not—indeed could not—be bought or sold. He proposed that the federal government should give away public land in the form of 160-acre, nonalienable homesteads to anyone willing and able to use that land productively. On death the homesteads would be distributed to others: An arrangement not unlike the life tenancy that had once characterized the holdings of many English yeomen. He further urged the abolition of all laws for the collection of debts, imprisonment for debt, long hours of labor, chattel slavery, and wage slavery.

In 1844, along with the Irish Chartist Thomas Devyr, Evans was instrumental in the founding of the National Reform Association (NRA), whose stated purpose was to pursue land reform along the lines Evans was advocating. Evans published and edited the NRA's triweekly journal, the *People's Rights,* while reviving the *Advocate* as well. The availability of so much land in the West, particularly in light of the controversies over the annexation of Texas and the Oregon boundary, made land reform a fairly salient issue in the politics of the 1840s, and Evans's talents as a writer ensured that land reform became a well-known cause. Nevertheless Evans's proposal, especially the requirement that land be neither bought nor sold, was still too radical for most Americans or for passage by Congress. Urban workers and their unions, too, failed to flock to the plan, since they were more concerned with economic issues related to the work place. By 1848, the NRA and radical land reform were dead issues, though both continued in one form or another for several years. When Congress did finally pass land reform, the legislation provided only for cheap, but not free and not inalienable, homesteads. Disillusioned by the failure of radical land reform, Evans retired from politics in 1849 and returned to his farm for the last time.

Though Evans met limited success in his career as a reformer, his contribution to the American labor movement goes well beyond a tally of wins and losses. Evans was the prototypical radical printer turned reform journalist, an originator of a tradition that would include John Swinton, J. A. Wayland, and George E. McNeill. His participation in left wing politics was almost always a consequence of his work as a newspaper or book publisher, and though he barely transcended his Paineite and Jeffersonian roots, he always lived up to them.

MATTHEW S. R. BEWIG

References and Further Reading

Earle, Jonathan H. *Jacksonian Antislavery and the Politics of Free Soil, 1824–1854*. Chapel Hill: University of North Carolina Press, 2004.

Evans, George Henry. *History of the Origin and Progress of the Working Men's Party of New York*. New York: 1842.

———, ed. *The Complete Works of Thomas Paine*. 8 vols. Granville, NJ: 1839.

Hugins, Walter. *Jacksonian Democracy and the Working Class*. Stanford, CA: Stanford University Press, 1960.

McFarland, C. K., and Robert L. Thistlethwaite, Twenty Years of a Successful Labor Paper: The *Working Man's Advocate*, 1829–1849," *Journalism Quarterly* 60, 1 (Spring 1983): 35–40.

Pessen, Edward. *Most Uncommon Jacksonians*. Albany: State University of New York Press, 1967.

Pilz, Jeffrey J. *The Life, Work, and Times of George Henry Evans, Newspaperman, Activist, and Reformer*. Lewiston: The Edwin Mellen Press, 2001.

Schlesinger, Arthur M., Jr. *The Age of Jackson*. Boston, MA: Little, Brown and Company, 1945.

Wilentz, Sean. *Chants Democratic*. New York: Oxford University Press, 1984.

See also **American Exceptionalism; Great Migration**

F

FAIR EMPLOYMENT PRACTICE COMMITTEE

In its day, President Franklin D. Roosevelt's Fair Employment Practice Committee (FEPC) was the most controversial federal government agency ever created. The FEPC's mission was to receive, address, and resolve any instances of employment discrimination by employers with defense contracts. If today the elimination of job bias remains a radical, "hot button" political issue, in the 1940s any notion of altering American race relations bordered on the revolutionary. President Roosevelt himself wanted little to do with fighting job discrimination while he was preparing the United States to potentially fight fascism in Europe and in Asia. He was forced, however, by a group of African-American civil rights leaders, most notably A. Philip Randolph, to deal with unfair employment practices. Although Roosevelt's FEPC did yeoman work, it ultimately failed to redress the fundamental racial and ethnic injustices in the American economic system. Still, the Committee's work and the efforts of the civil rights groups that supported it provided the necessary impetus and substance to transform the struggle for equality in the twentieth and twenty-first centuries.

The origins of the Fair Employment Practice Committee lay in the rapid mobilization of the United States for military conflict beginning in late 1939. When Hitler unleashed his Nazi forces upon Europe, President Roosevelt started to prepare the United States for the inevitable. The federal government poured billions of dollars in the economy to equip and train millions of soldiers. And despite the approach of war clouds, there was one practical benefit from this massive spending. As Americans began to pound ploughshares into swords for the second time in 20 years, the Great Depression in the United States dissipated and eventually disappeared. One group of Americans, however, was left out of the new emergency-spurred prosperity: African-Americans.

This was nothing new to black workers. Historically, they were the most-downtrodden of the working class. Emerging from centuries of chattel slavery, African-American workers had only known a few years of opportunity and hope during the later years of the Civil War and the first few years of Radical Reconstruction. By the 1880s, the old patterns had returned. In no way were black workers on equal footing with that of whites. The Great Depression had made matters worse, as they were pushed to lower rungs of the economic ladder as white workers took jobs that they previously had refused such as domestic servants, hod carriers, and common laborers. The New Deal had provided some relief, but not all of Roosevelt's alphabet agencies treated blacks the same. The National Youth Administration and especially the Works Projects Administration were sympathetic and helpful to African-American workers. Other agencies, such as the Civilian Conservation Corps, reflected the norm of American race relations. The CCC discriminated and segregated, treating needy blacks as second-class citizens.

As the New Deal gave way to defense mobilization, conditions for blacks remained all too similar. For example, six months after the Japanese attack on Pearl Harbor, African-American workers were barred from about half of all available work in defense factories. The situation was bad in the South but worse in other sections of the nation. In 1942, one out of every two war jobs in Texas were for whites only. In Michigan, the figure was eight out of every 10 jobs. And in Indiana, 94% of all available war work was for whites only. Black leaders of the National Association for the Advancement of Colored People (NAACP), the National Urban League, and other groups shared the frustrations of black workers as their complaints to local employers and local government officials fell on deaf ears. NAACP head Walter White described the situation succinctly when he said that blacks had been "left out in the cold."

If the economic reality for black Americans in 1940 and 1941 was not unusual, their reaction was. In stark contrast to the general support African-Americans gave the Wilson administration during World War I, blacks across the political spectrum and across class lines voiced disgust with the mobilization effort. The vanguard of this discontent was a newly established civil rights organization, the March on Washington Movement. In spring 1941, A. Philip Randolph, the head of the Brotherhood of Sleeping Car Porters (AFL), called on 100,000 African-Americans to march on Washington, DC, to protest discrimination in defense employment and the military. But FDR's actions were woefully inadequate to deal with the enormity of the problem. A Socialist and a strident advocate for civil rights and black labor rights who had actually opposed American intervention in World War I, Randolph hoped to push President Roosevelt into more dramatic and effectual action. And he knew that he had the president cornered. FDR did not want a march on Washington to protest racial discrimination. Not only would such an event embarrass the "arsenal of democracy," but it could also provoke a race riot in the nation's capital. In late June 1941, Roosevelt called both Randolph and the NAACP's Walter White to the White House. There Randolph repeated his pledge to march unless FDR did something to rectify the issue. At that point, Roosevelt turned to White, the more conservative of the two, and asked how many would march. Although he did not know for sure, White told the president that Randolph would bring 100,000 African-Americans down Pennsylvania Avenue. In return for calling off the march, Roosevelt then told the civil rights leaders that he would issue an executive order banning discrimination in defense factories. Although Randolph did not get everything he wanted—no mention was made of discrimination in the military—he agreed

and called off his march. On June 25, 1941, FDR signed Executive Order 8802, which established the policy of the United States that "there shall be no discrimination in the employment of workers in defense industries or Government because of race, creed, color, or national origin." Executive Order 8802 also created the Fair Employment Practice Committee to enforce the ban.

The creation of the FEPC was tremendously significant. For the first time since Reconstruction, the federal government had set up an agency specifically designed to deal with the problems of minority workers. Additionally, it was a major advance in the struggle to solve what Swedish sociologist Gunnar Myrdal called the "American dilemma," that is, the problem of a nation that had not fulfilled the promise of its founding, which had been based upon ideas of liberty and civic virtue. Yet, there were limits to what the FEPC could do. First, the Committee was a part of administrative law. As such, it had no access to the federal courts to subpoena, fine, or jail offenders of Executive Order 8802. The Committee's members would have to use moral suasion and forceful persuasion to convince recalcitrant employers to stop their unfair employment practices. Second, the Committee was limited by a meager budget and a small staff, which at no time numbered over 130. Finally, the FEPC could work only with employers with federal contracts or with federal agencies. Employers outside the contracting systems or attached with a state or local government were beyond its purview.

Despite these shortcomings and handicaps, the Fair Employment Practice Committee accomplished much during its short five-year life. From June 1941 to June 1946, the FEPC processed over 12,000 complaints of job discrimination and settled nearly 5,000 to its satisfaction (42%). From August 1944 to August 1945, it held 15 public hearings, docketed 3,500 cases, and resolved over 1,100 of them. Two examples will have to stand for thousands. In January 1942, six ranking members of the FEPC held a public hearing in Chicago, Illinois, to resolve several dozen complaints against employers in the Windy City and in Milwaukee, Wisconsin. Among the companies appearing that day was A. O. Smith, a manufacturer of various military supplies. At that time, A. O. Smith's managers had hired not a single black worker. After several days of public castigation and behind-the-scenes negotiations, A. O. Smith relented. By the war's height in 1944, it employed over 800 African-Americans, who made up over 5% of its workforce. These instances of success were, of course, tempered by failures. In 1943, Willie Webb, a black woman from Cincinnati filed a complaint with the FEPC. Although she had amassed over 500 hours of training as a welder, officials at the Crosley Radio Corporation, maker of naval signaling equipment, had denied her a position. In March 1945, the FEPC held a public hearing in Cincinnati to redress Webb's grievance and those of nearly 50 other black women and 20 black men. Although there were some breakthroughs at these hearings, most Cincinnati employers continued to ignore Roosevelt's fair employment policy. The Cincinnati hearings, which were among the FEPC's last, illustrated the pattern of discrimination that the Committee's members discovered. In northern areas with tight labor markets, change was quite possible. In border areas and in the South, regardless of labor conditions, the FEPC had an extraordinarily hard time easing the color line in employment. It is important to emphasize that tight labor markets alone did not create equal employment opportunities, as the 1942 Chicago hearings well illustrated.

Despite the FEPC's accomplishments and activities, or perhaps because of them, its days were numbered. Congressional conservatives in both the Republican Party and the Democratic Party had vehemently opposed the Committee since its creation in 1941. However, after 1943, when the FEPC was reorganized and strengthened, congressional leaders sought to destroy it. Since the late 1930s, a coalition of conservatives had presented numerous problems for the Roosevelt administration. The advent of World War II had quelled much of the rancorous politics of the late New Deal. But by 1944, FDR and his alphabet agencies were once again the target. Of particular concern was the FEPC, which according to Democratic Representative John Rankin (Miss.) was in essence a Communist plot to subvert the American way and Christianity. With the cooperation of key Republicans such as Senator Robert A. Taft (Ohio), Congress successfully cut all funding for the FEPC, thus killing it at the source. The Committee also suffered a severe political blow when President Roosevelt died in April 1945. President Harry S. Truman was initially unsupportive and did nothing as the Committee disappeared.

Although it was a short-lived and small New Deal agency, the Fair Employment Practice Committee had an enormous influence. Some of the Committee's members went on to significant careers in politics and the federal government. One such person was Elmer Henderson, who as an FEPC official began legal proceedings against the Southern Railway Company, which had discriminated against him. The lawsuit eventually went to the U.S. Supreme Court. In 1950, the Court sided with Henderson and in so doing overturned its previous decision in *Plessey* v. *Ferguson*. From the 1950s through the 1980s, Henderson worked on Capitol Hill as a political liaison between the Congress and various presidents.

The FEPC was also important because after World War II, it became *the* model for civil rights reform for more than 30 years. From 1946 to 1964, 35 states and over 200 cities passed fair employment laws and ordinances. One of the central organizations pushing for these kinds of reforms was A. Philip Randolph's postwar civil rights group, the National Committee for a Permanent FEPC (NCPFEPC). The NCPFEPC's central goal was a new federal FEPC, but it did work with state and local groups like the Committee for a Pennsylvania FEPC and the Ohio Commission for Fair Employment Practice Legislation. Although by the 1960s more than half of the states had fair employment laws and agencies, most of them were weak and ineffectual. The powerful and well-funded New York State Committee Against Discrimination was the exception. Wisconsin's FEPC, for example, was run by a single woman, Virginia Huebner, who had neither the legal power, staff, or time to adequately address the serious problems of discrimination in the Badger State.

The failures and frustrations of state FEPCs added momentum to the movement to re-create the federal FEPC, which culminated in the passage of the 1964 Civil Rights Act and the creation of the Equal Employment Opportunity Commission (EEOC). Although similar, the EEOC and the FEPC differ in several ways. Because it was established by a statute, the EEOC has had access to federal courts. Moreover, it has an expanded mission. The EEOC is charged with eliminating job bias against workers because of race, color, religion, national origin, *and* sex. In the early 1970s, the EEOC was re-organized and given more powers. And yet, like the FEPC, the EEOC has found that fighting job bias is no easy task. Like the original FEPC, the modern version has had to fight racially insensitive employers and unions as well as constantly battle with conservative politicians who wish to eliminate it.

ANDREW E. KERSTEN

References and Further Reading

Arnesen, Eric. *Brotherhoods of Color: Black Railroad Workers and the Struggle for Equality.* Cambridge, MA: Harvard University Press, 2001.

Daniel, Cletus E. *Chicano Workers and the Politics of Fairness: The FEPC in the Southwest, 1941–1946.* Austin: University of Texas Press, 1990.

Kersten, Andrew E. *Race, Jobs, and the War: The FEPC in the Midwest, 1941–46.* Urbana: University of Illinois Press, 2000.

Reed, Merl E. *Seedtime for the Modern Civil Rights Movement: The President's Committee on Fair Employment*

Practice, 1941–1946. Baton Rouge: Louisiana State University Press, 1991.

Ruchames, Louis. *Race, Jobs, and Politics: The Story of the FEPC*. New York: Columbia University Press, 1953.

FAIR LABOR STANDARDS ACT

The passage of the Fair Labor Standards Act (FLSA) by Congress in June 1938 marked a historic turning point for labor in the United States. For the first time, the federal government mandated wages and hours standards for the majority of the nation's workers, a goal that reformers had sought since the Progressive Era.

The Minimum Wage Movement Begins in the United States

While nations such as Great Britain and Australia possessed national minimum wage laws by 1910, the first minimum wage law in the United States did not exist until two years later, when Massachusetts established a minimum wage commission. Efforts to expand this precedent proceeded fitfully for the next two decades. While the Supreme Court upheld minimum wage legislation for male workers in *Stettler v. O'Hara* (1917), six years later it rejected a similar law for women workers (*Adkins v. Children's Hospital*). The minimum wage movement lost its momentum after 1923, and although reformers in several states, most notably New York, continued the fight, the *Adkins* precedent seemed to foreclose any national effort.

The Great Depression Provides Further Impetus

The Great Depression did not start immediately after the stock market collapses of late October 1929, but by late 1932, the dire salary situation facing labor became painfully evident. From 1929 through 1933, the weekly wages of manufacturing workers in the United States decreased from approximately $25 to less than $17, a decline of 33%. With an accompanying decline in retail sales from $48 billion to $24 billion in the same four years, the need to stabilize workers' salaries so as to increase consumption, and thus revitalize the nation's economy, became a primary objective of President Franklin D. Roosevelt when he assumed office in March 1933. The passage by Congress of the National Industrial Recovery Act (NIRA) in May 1933 reflected this concern.

The NIRA Sets a Precedent for Federal Hours and Wages Legislation

The NIRA lasted only two years, but it proved the first significant step toward federal hours and wages legislation. Not only did the NIRA establish the National Recovery Administration (NRA), but Section 7(a)(3) of the statute required that "employers shall comply with the maximum hours of labor, minimum rates of pay, and other conditions of employment approved or proscribed by the President." As the NRA's committees worked with both management and labor to establish industrial hours and wages standards, President Roosevelt advanced the idea of voluntary agreements with employers, known as the President's Reemployment Agreement (PRA). By 1935, over two million agreements came into effect, covering over 16 million employees throughout the nation.

Although the Supreme Court declared the NIRA unconstitutional in May 1935, U.S. Secretary of Labor Frances Perkins continued the momentum for federal labor standards with the Walsh-Healey Public Contracts Act, passed by Congress in 1936. The Act required federal contractors to meet minimum wage standards. Perkins also held seven national minimum wage conferences during the first Roosevelt administration.

The Introduction of the FLSA

By early 1937, several key forces united behind a federal labor standards law. The American Federation of Labor (AFL) traditionally opposed federal legislation, fearing interference with both trade unionism and labor negotiations. But the AFL changed its viewpoint after experiencing positive results with the NIRA. The new Congress of Industrial Organizations (CIO), which represented millions of unskilled workers throughout the United States, also supported federal legislation, particularly through its influential vice president, Sidney Hillman. Buoyed by his unprecedented re-election mandate in 1936, moreover, President Roosevelt decided to prepare a presidential message to Congress on the subject.

On May 24, 1937, as Roosevelt sent his message to Congress, selected congressmen introduced the administration's measures in both houses of Congress. Known as Senate Resolution (S.R.) 2475 and House Resolution (H.R.) 7200, the original bills provided, among other features, for a five-member Fair Labor Standards Board; a minimum wage of not more than 80 cents per hour, or $1,200 a year; the mandating of a 40-cent-per-hour, 40-hour workweek except in unusual circumstances; and the prohibition of interstate shipment of goods produced with "oppressive child labor."

The FLSA Is Passed

As is usual with major legislation, the final law proved far different from the original statute. In addition, new political factors complicated the passage of the FLSA. The failure of Roosevelt's attempt to reform the U.S. Supreme Court by mid-1937 damaged his credibility and solidified the growing congressional coalition of conservative Republicans and southern Democrats. Business interests feared government interference with their affairs, while southerners opposed a federal labor law that favored the North's higher wages.

Thus, while the Senate quickly reported out an amended version of S.R. 2475 in July 1937, the House Rules Committee delayed consideration of H.R. 7200 on the legislative floor. AFL leaders also objected to the Senate proposal because their recommendations failed to make the final version. Although the entire House of Representatives voted to discharge H.R. 7200 from the Rules Committee in December 1937, the bill eventually returned to the House Labor Committee. A final, compromise measure passed both houses of Congress in June 1938, and Roosevelt quickly signed the bill.

The new statute created a Wage and Hour Division in the U.S. Department of Labor; mandated a 40-cent-per-hour minimum wage by 1945; required a maximum workweek of 44 hours, with a reduction to 40 hours by 1940; established an overtime wage rate at one and a half times the regular rate of pay; and prohibited "oppressive" child labor. While no regional wage differentials were recognized, southern concerns were implicitly accepted by the exclusion of agricultural employees, among other workers, from the law's provisions.

"That's that," President Roosevelt exclaimed as he signed the FLSA on June 25, 1938. Ironically, Roosevelt's expression signified more than just a sigh of approval; the new measure represented the last significant legislative achievement of the New Deal. Conservative gains in the 1938 congressional

elections, and the burgeoning war in Europe, ended any further domestic reform until after World War II.

The FLSA Passes Constitutional Muster

Business interests challenged the new federal law in two cases, *United States v. Darby* and *Opps Cotton Mills, Inc., et al. v. Administrator of the Wage and Hour Division of the United States Department of Labor*. The cases quickly reached the U.S. Supreme Court, which announced its decisions in February 1941. By this time, the nation's highest court had sanctioned minimum wage legislation in *West Coast Hotel Co. v. Parrish* (1937), and President Roosevelt's several Court appointments from 1937 through 1940 had replaced conservatives with justices sympathetic to the New Deal.

Not surprisingly, the Court upheld the FLSA in both cases, rejecting the claim that the statute regulated only the manufacture of goods, and thus failed to involve Congress's power to regulate interstate commerce under the U.S. Constitution. The Court held that the power to regulate interstate commerce encompassed the production, as well as the transportation, of goods and that the FLSA could thus prohibit the shipment of goods in interstate commerce produced under its "forbidden substandard labor conditions." The justices also rejected the claim that the FLSA's minimum wage requirements violated employers' rights, citing *West Coast Hotel Co. v. Parrish*.

The Continuing Effect of the FLSA

The FLSA's original hours and wages requirements came into effect well before the prescribed deadlines, as industrial committees appointed by the Department of Labor quickly enacted the mandated standards. The first FLSA amendments, passed as part of President Harry S. Truman's "Fair Deal" program in 1949, increased the minimum wage to 75 cents per hour and also expanded coverage to airline and cannery employees. Except for an increase of the minimum wage to $1 an hour in 1955, no major changes then occurred until the first year of John F. Kennedy's administration. The hourly minimum wage became $1.25, and retail and service employees now received coverage. Congress's 1966 amendments proved the most significant changes to the FLSA since its original passage, as over nine million workers now became eligible for a floor wage.

By the beginning of the twenty-first century, continuing FLSA amendments brought the minimum wage to $5.15 an hour. Many labor advocates argued, however, that the minimum wage failed to provide workers with adequate incomes for their families. Business interests and their conservative supporters in Congress claimed, in turn, that a large increase in the floor wage would mean higher labor costs, forcing layoffs. The federal government under President George W. Bush also passed regulations restricting the use of overtime pay for certain classes of so-called white-collar employees. These controversies demonstrated that the FLSA not only stood as one of the most significant labor laws of the 1930s, but also remained viable in a new century.

JOHN THOMAS MCGUIRE

References and Further Reading

Ehrenreich, Barbara. *Nickel and Dimed: On (Not) Getting By in America*. New York: Henry Holt, 2001.

Kennedy, David M. *Freedom from Fear: The American People in Depression and War, 1929–1945*. New York: Oxford University Press, 1999.

Levin-Waldman, Oren M. *The Case of the Minimum Wage: Competing Policy Models*. Albany: State University of New York Press, 2001.

Nordlund, Willis J. *The Quest for a Living Wage: The History of the Federal Minimum Wage Program*. Westport, CT: Greenwood Press, 1997.

Cases and Statutes Cited

Adkins v. Children's Hospital, 261 U.S. 525 (1923)

Opps Cotton Mills, Inc., et al. v. Administrator of the Wage and Hour Division of the United States Department of Labor, 312 U.S. 126 (1941)

Stettler v. O'Hara, 243 U.S. 629 (1917)

United States v. Darby, 312 U.S. 100 (1941)

West Coast Co. v. Parrish, 300 U.S. 379 (1937)

Fair Labor Standards Act of June 14, 1938, S. 2475

National Industrial Recovery Act, Public Law No. 67, 73rd Congress

FAMILY AND MEDICAL LEAVE ACT

The Family and Medical Leave Act of 1993 (the official citation is Public Law 103-3) guarantees unpaid but job-protected leave to many, but not all, working Americans.

Covered employees are guaranteed up to 12 weeks of such leave during any 12-month period, for personal or family medical conditions (work-related or otherwise), the addition of a child into the family (by birth, adoption, or foster care), or like matters.

The impact of the Act is commonly regarded as positive upon employees and negligible or minimal upon employers, despite complaints by employers at the time of enactment (and continuing to this day).

History

Like many laws, the Family and Medical Leave Act (FMLA) as an idea was around for some time prior to its eventual enactment. As working Americans increasingly complained of difficulties managing work/life issues, and as an apparently decreasing willingness of employers to accommodate their concerns spread, they turned to public policy makers. In turn, policy makers looked outside the United States for inspiration. While family and medical leave, usually paid as opposed to unpaid, seemed to be common (and indeed typical) across Europe, in the United States guaranteed leave for non-work-related disability was rare, and for such leave to be paid was even rarer. For example, in the early twenty-first century, only six states had a form of off-the-job disability insurance, and even then it was typical for the covered individual's job to not be guaranteed upon recovery or upon this paid leave running out.

The idea saw bill form during the administration of President George H. W. Bush (1989–1993, referred to as the "First President Bush" to differentiate him from his son, who also served). President Bush, however, based upon the objections of business, vetoed the bill twice, once in 1990 and once in 1992.

Democratic presidential candidate William J. "Bill" Clinton, during the election of 1992, announced that he would sign the bill if he were elected, and Congress passed it again. After he assumed office in 1993, Congress did just that, and President Clinton signed it as Public Law 103-3. For most employers, the act was effective August 5, 1993.

Main Provisions

The FMLA guarantees covered employees up to 12 weeks of unpaid, but job-secure (in other words, an employer cannot legally fire an employee for taking FMLA leave) family and medical leave, during a 12-month period. The employer is allowed to define the start date of the 12-month period. It could be the calendar year or any 12-month period following the enactment of the FMLA.

Quoting directly from a U.S. Department of Labor document, covered employers include government entities (including state, local, and federal employers)

and private businesses that employ 50 or more employees in 20 or more workweeks.

To be eligible for FMLA benefits, an employee must:

- Work for a covered employer (see above)
- Have worked for that employer for a total of 12 months
- Have worked at least 1,250 hours over the previous 12 months
- Work at a location inside the United States, or in any territory or possession of the United States

Covered forms of family and medical leave include time off for the birth, adoption, or foster care of a child (this child-care leave must be concluded within 12 months of such birth, or adoption, or start of foster care); to care for an immediate family member with a serious health condition; or for employees unable to work because of a serious medical condition (including both job-related and non-job-related conditions) to recover or take care of themselves. This guaranteed leave is unpaid.

The Act appears to be considered a "floor" rather than a "ceiling," and provisions of collective bargaining agreements or employer policies can supplement it.

Employees have been allowed to switch back and forth between FMLA leave and other forms of leave offered by their employers, sometimes during the same working day. For example, an employee could be considered to be on FMLA leave for, say, four hours in a given day, and then take four hours of "personal time" as granted by the employer.

While sometimes employers complain that the administrative tasks associated with these practices are onerous, and that some employees take advantage of the system, there appears to be very little, if any, evidence that it actually is all that much of a burden. Further, employers are often granted the right to determine if a given use of leave is FMLA leave or some other kind of leave.

Significance and Current Issues

At the beginning of the twenty-first century, the FMLA seemed to be relatively stable. Some "noise" from the administration of President George H. W. Bush (the son of the earlier President Bush, who vetoed the first version of the FMLA) was made about modifying the Act so as to limit the ability of employees to mix and match FMLA leave and other

forms of leave. These measures did not appear to be a high priority for the administration, however.

Also, the second Bush administration rolled back regulations propagated under President Clinton allowing states to compensate employees on FMLA leave for birth or adoption of children using Unemployment Insurance (UI).

There were some important, but technical, issues involving the interaction of FMLA leave and state workers' compensation programs that had yet to be worked out. The FMLA could apply to work-related injuries or illnesses, which were also, by definition and intent, the domain of state workers' compensation programs. It was often not clear, for example, if employees on workers' compensation had to be required to draw upon their FMLA leave.

The broader significance of the FMLA for working-class life is a matter for debate. It certainly, by definition, provides protections that did not exist prior to its enactment. However, the fact that the leave is unpaid has, in the arguments of some commentators, effectively granted rights that members of the working class literally cannot afford to exercise. The Act has, however, clearly been an extremely important right to specific members of the working class in certain specific circumstances.

At the beginning of the twenty-first century, the Act covered roughly 60% of the American workforce. Some working-class advocates wanted to see that figure increased, but this, too, seemed rather unlikely.

STEVEN D. KOCZAK

References and Further Reading

Leonard, Bill. "Senate Beats Back Bid to Expand FMLA." *HR Magazine* (August 2004).
Minton-Eversole, Theresa. "DOL Reviewing 'Baby UI' Comments." *HR Magazine* (March 2003).
Shaller, Elliot H., and Mary K. Qualiana. "The Family and Medical Leave Act." *Employee Relations Law Journal* (Summer 1993).
United States Department of Labor. Employment Standards Administration. *Fact Sheet #28: The Family and Medical Leave Act of 1993.*
Waldfogel, Jane. "Family and Medical Leave: Evidence from the 2000 Surveys." *Monthly Labor Review* (September 2001).
Waldfogel, Jane, Yoshio Higuchi, and Masahiro Abe. "Family Leave Policies and Women's Retention after Childbirth: Evidence from the United States, Britain, and Japan." *Journal of Population Economics* 12 (1999): 523–545.
Winters, Jeffrey. "The Daddy Track: Men Who Take Family Leave May Get Frowned Upon at the Office." *Psychology Today* (September–October 2001).

FAMILY WAGE

The term "family wage" is a key word in academic discourse about the history of the sexual division of labor and is also central to public policy and religious debates about the historical relationship among wage labor, morality, and family life. In contrast with the term "living wage," with which it is often paired, working-class Americans have rarely used the term "family wage." Among the social workers and policy makers who popularized the term in the post-World War I years, and the political commentators and academics who re-introduced it in the late twentieth century, the phrase came to stand in for two somewhat contradictory notions, both with authentic roots in American labor history: the ideal of a male breadwinner who could support his family on his wages, on the one hand, and the reality of the "family wage economy," in which all family members contributed their wages as a cooperative survival strategy, on the other. Many commentators assume that over the course of the twentieth century, America has moved from the former to the latter, that is, from a country in which male breadwinners predominated to one of multiple wage earners. In fact, throughout American history, most families have needed more than one breadwinner to support themselves, and it was only for a brief period in the United States—beginning in the 1920s—that a majority of American families consisted of a breadwinner husband, a homemaker wife, and children at school rather than the workplace. The stresses of the Depression and the increasing number of married women in the workplace during World War II and in the postwar years made this supposed "norm" surprisingly short-lived. What is often taken as the rule, in other words, is really the exception. While it is true that two-earner families have become increasingly common since World War II, the reality is that two meanings of the family wage—the ideal of the male breadwinner and the family wage economy—have been paired in tension from the very beginning of the development of a wage labor economy in the early nineteenth century.

The family wage—understood as a male breadwinner capable of supporting a family on his wages—was a long-standing ideal for working-class families, dating back to the early nineteenth century.

As wage labor became increasingly common in the early nineteenth century, and as the republican ideal of independent proprietorship became correspondingly rarer, many male workers, and their families, demanded a subsistence wage that would enable them to support their families and even to have savings for retirement. This version of the family wage, based on socially defined needs of workers as citizens and family supporters, provided workers with an alternative to the "natural laws" of supply and demand, which employers used to justify low wages. With this notion of the family wage, workers for the first time adopted the idea of wage labor, which they had previously rejected, as acceptable. These moral economic claims also promoted a sexual division of labor—male breadwinners, female homemakers—consistent with the Victorian ideal, if not the reality, of "separate spheres" for men and women. "We must strive to obtain sufficient remuneration for our labor to keep the wives and daughters and sisters of our people at home," a Philadelphia trade union declared in the 1830s (Carlson, 2001). As the American labor publication, the *Ten Hour Advocate*, editorialized in 1846: "We hope the day is not distant when the husband will be able to provide for his wife and family, without sending the [wife] to endure the drudgery of a cotton mill" (May, 1982, p. 401). Despite these clarion calls for a single male breadwinner, even in the nineteenth century, the reality was that working-class families typically relied on a family economy consisting of husbands, wives, and children, all earning wages and helping, in varying degrees, with household labor. The Victorian ideal of "separate spheres" was far more descriptive of middle-class families than it was of laboring families. In the early twentieth century, as an increasing number of wives entered the paid labor force, the reality was often even further from this family wage ideal. And it is widely acknowledged that by the late twentieth century, this ideal bore little relation to reality for most American families, which consisted largely of dual wage earners and of single-parent breadwinners.

Throughout the late nineteenth century and into the twentieth century, American workers and their organizations demanded "living wages" that would enable them to support their families, participate in public life, and maintain an "American Standard of Living." While initially these demands for what later became known as "family wages" were derided as "communistic," many distinctly non-Socialist reformers, religious leaders, politicians, and businessmen came, for a variety of reasons, to support the idea of a family wage. In 1914, the pioneering automaker Henry Ford, for example, began offering his male workers five dollars per day (at a time when the typical wage for a worker was about half that much) as a means of promoting mass consumption, minimizing class conflict, and solidifying traditional gender relations in working-class families. According to Ford, "The man does the work in the shop, but his wife does the work in the home. The shop must pay them both…. Otherwise we have the hideous prospect of little children and their mothers being forced out to work" (May, 1982, p. 415).

Ford and other employers, such as Edward Filene, the Progressive department store owner, were echoed by proponents of Social Gospel Protestantism, who embraced the idea that working people should earn enough to provide the essentials of food, clothing, and shelter for a family as well as the creature comforts and respectable consumer satisfactions of life in an industrializing America. Many reformers, alongside many workers, who held the ideal of the male breadwinner as a goal, used the phrase "family wage" as shorthand for the effort to promote a wage that would support a single breadwinner for a family. As the Progressive economist Robert W. Bruere noted, "Too many employees are in the habit of interpreting the family wage as meaning the total earnings of all members of the family, rather than the wage paid to the head of family alone." In 1919, Bruere called for a "minimum guaranteed family wage," and in so doing became one of the first to use the phrase "family wage" (Bruere, pp. 95–100).

The Roman Catholic Church has, since the late nineteenth century, also strongly supported the effort to secure a single breadwinner "family wage." Pope Leo XIII's 1893 encyclical, *Rerum Novarum* ("The Condition of Labor"), pointed to the familial nature of the just wage. Forty years later, Pope Pius XI called explicitly for a family wage for every male adult, as a matter of social justice. In books such as *A Living Wage* (1906) and *Distributive Justice* (1916), Father John A. Ryan, the leading American advocate, called the family wage the linchpin of a moral economic system. Ryan declared that "the laborer has a right to a family living wage because this is the only way in which he can exercise his right to the means of maintaining a family." The welfare of society made it "imperative that the wife and mother should not engage in any labor except that of the household." Ryan insisted that "the State has both the right and the duty to compel all employers to pay a Living Wage." In 1981, Pope John Paul II's encyclical, *Laborem Exercens* ("On Human Work") continued the Church's call for family wages: "Just remuneration for the work of an adult who is responsible for a family means remuneration which will suffice for establishing and properly maintaining a family and for providing security for its future." John Paul II noted his preference for this remuneration to be given "through what is called a family wage—that is, a single salary given to the head of the family for his work, sufficient for the needs of the family without the other spouse having to take up gainful employment outside the home" (http://www.vatican.va/holy_father/ john_paul_ii/encyclicals/documents/hf_jp-ii_enc_ 14091981_laborem-exercens_en.html).

If a consensus in favor of the family wage formed in the first half of the twentieth century, it is important to note that the concept was never without its critics. These critics came from opposite ends of the political spectrum. Many business leaders and politicians believed that the family wage interfered with the free market for wages and freedom of contract. The family wage concept was also criticized by some feminists both in and out of the labor movement who believed that it undermined the idea of equal pay for equal work. They argued that the family wage ideal sanctioned gender discrimination and a sexual division of labor, in which women earned lower wages. Historians generally concede that the family wage ideal served a masculinist ideal of male breadwinners, which contributed to the difficulties of female breadwinners to breach the sexual division of labor that rewarded "male" jobs more highly than "female" jobs.

Whatever the historical costs or benefits of the family wage ideal, by the late twentieth century, there was a widespread consensus that this ideal was in crisis. And in recent decades, a call for a revived family wage has been made by a diverse coalition of conservative Christian promoters of "family values" as well as laborite supporters of living wages. The former believe that a family wage will provide incentives for the return of the "traditional" family of stay-at-home moms and working dads. The latter believe that it is necessary to recognize that workers, including many single mothers, support families. The slow increase in the legal minimum wage, making it worth less in real dollars in the 1990s and 2000s than it was in the 1960s and 1970s, suggests that these pleas have not been widely heeded in policy. Moreover, despite the diverse coalition of support for the family wage, critics remain. As one critic recently suggested, "returning to a system of male breadwinning is an unworkable and for many families, an undesirable solution." Feminist advocates of the living wage argue that the solution to the family wage problem is not to pay men more but to compensate women for their labor. "The breadwinner-homemaker household is a short-lived arrangement that, even at its height in the 1950s, never met the needs of countless women, men and children" (Letter from Kathleen Gerson, "Homemaker Nostalgia," *New York Times*, September 12, 1995). So the consensus that the family wage ideal collapsed in the last third of the twentieth century has not led to a clear solution to this problem, since for many critics, it was the family wage ideal itself that was the problem. With increasing globalization and economic insecurity, debates about the family wage will doubtless continue well into the twenty-first century.

LAWRENCE GLICKMAN

References and Further Reading

Bruere, Robert. "Can We Eliminate Labor Unrest?" *Annals of the American Academy of Political and Social Science* 81 (Jan. 1919): 95–100.

Carlson, Allan C. "The Changing Face of the American Family." The Family in America 15:1 (Jan. 2001). http://www.profam.org/pub/fia/fia_1501.htm.

———. "What Happened to the 'Family Wage'?" *Public Interest* 83 (Spring 1986): 3–17.

Christensen, Bryce J. et al. *The Family Wage: Worker, Gender, and Children in the Modern Economy*. Rockford, IL: Rockford Institute, 1988.

Coble, Dorothy Sue. *The Other Women's Movement: Workplace Justice and Social Rights in Modern America*. Princeton, NJ: Princeton University Press, 2003.

Glickman, Lawrence B. *A Living Wage: American Workers and the Making of Consumer Society*. Ithaca, NY: Cornell University Press, 1997.

May, Martha. "Bread before Roses: American Workingmen, Labor Unions, and the Family Wage." In *Women, Work and Protest: A Century of Women's Labor History*, edited by Ruth Milkman. Boston: Routledge and Kegan Paul, 1985, pp. 1–21.

———. "The Historical Problem of the Family Wage: The Ford Motor Company and the Five-Dollar Day." *Feminist Studies* 8 (Summer 1982): 399–424.

Maclean, Nancy. "Postwar Women's History: The 'Second Wave' or the End of the Family Wage?" In *A Companion to Post-1945 America*, edited by Jean-Christophe Agnew and Roy Rosenzweig. Oxford: Blackwell, 2002, pp. 235–259.

Milkman, Ruth. *Gender at Work: The Dynamics of Job Segregation by Sex during World War II*. Urbana: University of Illinois Press, 1987.

Tucker, William. "A Return to the 'Family Wage.'" *Weekly Standard* (May 13, 1996): 27–31.

FANSTEEL v. UNITED STATES (1939)

Nineteenth-century striking workers effectively prevented continued production by removing their tools and knowledge from the workplace. Twentieth-century employers could continue mass production during strikes by bringing in new workers to run the massive machinery and assembly lines. Workers could be sure of stopping production only by sitting down at their machines. The first such strike occurred at a General Electric plant in Schenectady, New York, in 1906. It was revived by tire and rubber workers from 1934 to 1936 in Akron, Ohio, most often over use of non-union workers, speedups, and work rule changes, and most often as spontaneous rank-and-file beginnings. Most of these strikes started among younger workers on the night shift. In 1936–1938, a wave of more than 62 sit-down strikes spread to other industries attempting to force employers to bargain with unions, the most famous being the autoworkers strike in Flint, Michigan. In the vast majority of sit-downs, little damage was done to plants and machinery, and then mostly during eviction attempts.

The U.S. Supreme Court decided the legality of the sit-down tactic under the National Labor Relations Act (NLRA), *NLRB v. Fansteel Metallurgical Corp.*, 306 U.S. 240 (1939). Fansteel processed rare metals in Waukeegan, Illinois. The Amalgamated Association of Iron, Steel, and Tin Workers of North America, Lodge 66, affiliated with the CIO, first attempted to represent Fansteel employees during September 1936. The plant superintendent, A. J. Anselm, replied that the company would not deal with an outside union. The company hired the operative Alfred Johnstone, National Metal Trades Association, to infiltrate and spy on union activities, isolated the union president, John Kondrath, next to the superintendent's office, and enlisted employees in a company union. On February 17, 1937, Lodge 66, representing 155 of 229 employees, again demanded collective bargaining and was refused. At 2:00 p.m. that day, the union determined to strike by sitting down. By 2:30, approximately 95 employees seized key buildings 3 and 5.

At 6:00 p.m., Anselm, company counsel, and two policemen approached the seized buildings, announcing in a loud voice that the men were illegally trespassing and were all fired. The next day, the company sought an injunction against continued possession of the buildings. On February 19, the sheriff passed copies of the writ through an open window to Swanson and Warner, the respective leaders in the two buildings. Later that day, the sheriff, with approximately one hundred deputies, tried to forcibly evict the men with tear gas bombs, a battering ram, and baseball bats. They were met by a fire hose and a hail of nuts, bolts, small tools, parts, and sulphuric acid until the sheriff withdrew after two hours.

At dawn, February 26, the sheriff, with a slightly larger force, wheeled a truck with a 30-foot armored scaffold to the buildings. From the higher vantage, they fired tear and emetic gas into the windows. After an hour of pitched battle, the occupying men scattered and fled.

The company suffered $75,000 in broken windows, small tools, and parts thrown from the building, all of which occurred during the two stormings of the buildings, but no major damage to the heavy machinery. During and after the strike, the company solicited individual employees and strikers to return to work, rehiring 35 of the sit-downers. After the strike, the company encouraged membership in a new union, the

Rare Metal Workers Union No. 1, providing it with a place to work and meet, and supplies.

Thirty-nine of the sit-downers were prosecuted for contempt in state court. They were fined between $100 and $1000 and jailed for 10 to 240 days.

The National Labor Relations Board, 5 NLRB 124 (1938), found violations of the NLRA, sections 8(1) interfering with the right to self-organize, 8(2) supporting a company union, 8(3) discriminating against union activity, and 8(5) refusing to bargain and attempting to bargain with individuals. The Board ordered reinstatement of all the strikers and bargaining with the union under its remedial power to effectuate the purposes of the NLRA. It argued that allowing the seizure to disqualify the workers from relief would reward the company for its unfair labor practices.

The Seventh Circuit Court of Appeals refused to enforce the order 2-1, and the Supreme Court affirmed 7-2. Recognizing the existence of the unfair labor practices, Chief Justice Hughes nonetheless stated, "We are unable to conclude that Congress intended to compel employers to retain persons in their employ regardless of their unlawful conduct— to invest those who go on strike with an immunity from discharge for acts of trespass or violence against the employer's property." The only concession to the Board suggested a Board-supervised election to determine the majority's representation choice. The dissent by Justices Reed and Black would have returned the parties to the same position they were in before the unfair labor practices and the strike, enforcing the Board's order, arguing it is too easy for employers to get away with unfair labor practices as long as the employer has a nonrelated reason to fire the strikers.

The loss of the sit-down had legal, economic, and organizational consequences. First, sit-downs largely worked for meeting workers' demands. Second, aside from removing a key tactic in the successful organization drives of the CIO in the late 1930s, the majority's rationale weakened the Act's reach by elevating the property rights of employers over the organizing abilities of workers. This was a judicially imposed choice not mandated by the NLRA. Third, another loss to labor was the increased solidarity among the rank and file who had time to talk about their work and get better acquainted during the strikes. This held over in the form of increased demands from workers in those plants experiencing sit-downs. Finally, usually short sit-down tactics were perceived by workers as spontaneous rank-and-file actions, the removal of which encouraged centralization of bargaining and grievance machinery.

KENNETH M. CASEBEER

References and Further Reading

Brecher, Jeremy. *Strike!* Boston: South End Press, 1972.
Fine, Sidney. *Sit-Down: The General Motors Strike of 1936–1937*. Ann Arbor: University of Michigan Press, 1969.
Hansen, Drew D. "The Sit-Down Strikes and the Switch in Time." *Wayne Law Review* 46 (Spring 2000): 49–133.
Klare, Karl E. "Judicial Deradicalization of the Wagner Act and the Origins of Modern Legal Consciousness, 1937–1941." *Minnesota Law Review* 62 (1978): 265–339.
Nelson, Daniel. "Origins of the Sit-Down Era: Worker Militancy and Innovation in the Rubber Industry, 1934–38." *Labor History* 23 (1982): 198–225.
Pope, James Gray. "Worker Lawmaking, Sit-Down Strikes, and the Shaping of American Industrial Relations, 1935–1958." *Law and History Review* 24, no. 1 (2006).

Cases and Statutes Cited

Fansteel Metallurgical Corp. v. Lodge 66, 1 Labor Cases 506 (Il. 1938)
Fansteel Metallurgical Corp. v. NLRB, 98 F. 2d 375 (1938)
In Re Fansteel Metallurgical Corporation and Amalgamated Association of Iron, Steel, and Tin Workers of North America, Lodge 66, 5 NLRB 124 (1938)
NLRB v. Fansteel Metallurgical Corp., 306 U.S. 240 (1939)

See also **Amalgamated Association of Iron and Steel Workers; Sit-Down Strikes (1937)**

FARM EQUIPMENT AND METAL WORKERS UNION

The Farm Equipment and Metal Workers Union (FE), a relatively small union that was influenced by the U.S. Communist Party (CPUSA), had a jurisdiction that overlapped with the much larger United Auto Workers union (UAW). Beginning as the Farm Equipment Division of the Steel Workers Organizing Committee in July 1938, the Congress of Industrial Organizations (CIO) chartered the FE as the international union whose jurisdiction encompassed the farm implement industry. At its peak, the FE had 70,000 members, with its major base of strength located in the plants of the International Harvester Corporation, where the union represented 40,000 workers. During the 17 years (1938–1955) of the union's existence, the FE pioneered an independent shop floor unionism and was a vigorous proponent of racial egalitarianism and civil rights for its African-American members.

Believing that the workers were involved in a constant struggle with capital, the FE at both the national and local levels encouraged a shop floor unionism based on direct action at the point of production in defending workers' rights. This militancy was expressed in the union's continuous use of work stoppages—both authorized and unauthorized—throughout most of the union's life. For example, at Harvester during the years between 1945 and 1951, the FE engaged in 849 strikes, while UAW members participated in 171 walkouts.

With regard to the union's commitment to racial egalitarianism within the workplace and the union, the FE was successful in its fight to upgrade African-American workers to better jobs. For example, at the McCormick Works (Chicago), where 80% of the employees were white, although the majority of blacks still labored in the foundries, FE Local 108 won the right for African-Americans to hold jobs as assemblers, inspectors, welders, and polishers by 1949. Furthermore, blacks were amply represented in the local's leadership positions, ranging from shop steward to the executive board. And in the 1949 elections, four of the 11 executive board members and three of the seven grievancemen voted in were African-American. FE Local 236's (Louisville) record on fighting for racial equality was as good if not better than that of Local 108. It had obtained a nondiscrimination clause in its 1946 contract with Harvester and aggressively fought to desegregate Louisville's white-only parks and hotels.

The FE's Relationship with the UAW, 1945–1949

Until 1945, the rivalry between the UAW and the FE was handled by the two unions splitting up the jurisdiction over the relevant industrial units, with the FE organizing the agricultural implement factories and the auto union maintaining control over the truck plants. However, after World War II, this arrangement abruptly ended, with the two unions competing to organize new plants. In addition, the UAW attempted to raid, that is, to replace one union with that of another as the collective bargaining agent, the FE plants for the first time.

In 1947, the UAW membership rejected a proposed merger of the FE into the auto union when Walter Reuther, the UAW president, and his faction (the Reuther Caucus) actively opposed the combination on the grounds that FE's addition to the UAW would tip the balance of power within the union in the direction of the CPUSA-supported Thomas-Addes forces. That same year, the passage of the Taft-Hartley Act, with its requirement that all union officials sign noncommunist affidavits in order to retain National Labor Relations Board (NLRB) protection, had severe consequences for the FE when the union's officers refused to comply.

FE Local 105, which represented 16,000 production workers at the Caterpillar Tractor Company's Peoria plant, struck Caterpillar in early April 1948 when its contract expired. Arguing that since the union had not fulfilled the Taft-Hartley Act requirements, Caterpillar ceased bargaining with Local 105 in March, stating that it did not want to spend time negotiating with a union that might be replaced by a legitimate labor organization certified by the NLRB at a later date. Shortly thereafter, four unions initiated organizing drives in order to lure the Caterpillar employees away from Local 105. With the FE ineligible to be on the ballot, the runoff election between the UAW-CIO and the UAW-American Federation of Labor (AFL) resulted in the former obtaining bargaining rights for the Caterpillar workers and depriving the FE of nearly 25% of its membership.

Shortly after the Caterpillar debacle, the FE officers complied with the Taft-Hartley Act affidavits, which made other UAW raids on FE plants later in the spring of 1949 unsuccessful. The FE soundly defeated the auto union at the John Deere Plow Works in Moline (Illinois) and the Oliver plant in Iowa.

The UAW's Raids on the FE, 1949–1954

When the CIO expelled the FE in the fall of 1949, along with 10 other Communist-led unions, the federation sanctioned raids by the UAW against the FE. In an attempt to protect itself from these attacks, the FE merged with another CIO union that had also been expelled for its ties with the CPUSA, the United Electrical, Radio and Machine Workers of America (UE), also becoming known at this time as the FE-UE.

The UAW-FE rivalry, which accelerated after the union's expulsion from the CIO, reached a crescendo in 1952 when the union struck Harvester and the UAW provided no support to the beleaguered FE. In June 1952, two months before the strike, the UAW launched an unsuccessful raid against FE Local 108. With the hostility between the two unions having reached a feverish pitch, Harvester had steeled itself to engage the FE in an all-out struggle.

The FE strike, which commenced on August 21, 1952, involved approximately 30,000 workers in eight Harvester plants throughout the United States. In an attempt to break the work stoppage, the company kept its plants open and conducted a vigorous campaign, encouraging the strikers to return to work. With McCarthyism nearing its peak in 1952, Harvester took advantage of the anti-Communist fervor sweeping the country to sway public opinion against the FE. The corporation took out advertisements in the Chicago newspapers emphasizing the intimate connection between the FE leaders and the CPUSA. Another devastating blow to the union occurred when the House Un-American Activities Committee arrived in Chicago a mere two weeks into the strike in order to examine the influence of Communism in Chicago unions.

Despite the walkout's violent nature, employees *were* returning to work. By the end of the first week in November, a considerable percentage of workers had crossed the picket lines in all eight plants. With the strike disintegrating at an astonishingly rapid rate, Geralde Fielde, the FE Secretary-Treasurer, ended the work stoppage on November 15 by signing a contract that totally capitulated to Harvester on all of the union's original demands.

The conclusion of this disastrous strike against Harvester only emboldened the UAW in its raids of the weakened FE. At this time, the auto union consciously selected plants where the "back-to-work movement" had been the strongest in order to petition the NLRB for new representation elections. However, the UAW was unsuccessful in ousting the FE at these factories. The Richmond (Indiana) plant workers voted for the FE over the auto union by a 2-to-1 margin. At the West Pullman plant in Chicago, the level of victory was even greater, with the FE beating the UAW 3-to-1. Realizing that it had no chance to defeat the FE at the Farmall (Rock Island, Illinois) plant, the auto union dropped out just two days before the NLRB election.

In spite of the union's ability to successfully retain its membership in these poststrike raids, problems within the FE first surfaced in two Harvester plants in the Quad Cities of western Illinois in the middle of August 1953. At the East Moline and Rock Island facilities, the workers conducted membership referendums and voted to disaffiliate their two locals from the FE. The East Moline NLRB representation election, held on May 26, 1954, led to the first irreparable crack in the FE Harvester chain when the workers voted to affiliate with the UAW rather than to remain in the FE.

However, raids were not the FE's only worries at this time. With McCarthyism still in full force throughout the nation, the FE was confronted with the Communist Control Act of 1954. The Act granted the attorney general the authority to use the Subversive Activities Control Board to decree that a union was controlled by Communists, thus depriving it of any protection under the National Labor Relations Act (NLRA). In addition, if a mere 20% of a

Communist-controlled union's members demanded a representation election, the union could re-organize under new non-Communist leadership and still be able to retain its contract and have access to both the NLRA and the NLRB.

After the defection of the East Moline plant, the next plant to leave the union for the UAW was Farmall. After these two losses in the Quad Cities, the movement expanded to include the Chicago Harvester plants, the stronghold of the FE membership, and finally to all of the union's plants.

The FE's Affiliation with the UAW, 1955

At the end of January 1955, a committee of five top-level FE officers met with a comparable committee of UAW representatives. This meeting, called under the guise of achieving unity between the two unions during the upcoming negotiations at Harvester, however, was little more than a way for the FE leaders to see what they could get from the UAW for bringing their members, as a group, into the auto union.

In the middle of March 1955, the FE Harvester Conference Board voted for disaffiliation from the United Electrical Workers Union and decided to join the UAW as a group. Under the arrangement, the auto union agreed to retain the former FE staff representatives (except for the president, Grant Oakes, and the secretary-treasurer, Gerald Fielde) for the FE bringing their locals into the UAW. In the subsequent NLRB representation elections held in the former FE Harvester plants in May and June 1955, the UAW won all elections over the rival AFL unions and the "no union" choice by decisive margins. The end of the FE, and its rivalry with the UAW, came with a whimper, not a bang.

VICTOR G. DEVINATZ

References and Further Reading

Devinatz, Victor G. "An Alternative Strategy: Lessons from the UAW Local 6 and the FE, 1946–1952." In *Beyond Survival: Wage Labor in the Late Twentieth Century*, edited by Cyrus Bina, Laurie Clements, and Chuck. Davis., Armonk NY: M. E. Sharpe, 1996, pp. 145–160.
Gilpin, Toni. "Labor's Last Stand." *Chicago History* 18, no. 1 (Spring 1989): 42–59.
———. "Left by Themselves: A History of the United Farm Equipment and Metal Workers Union, 1938–1955." Ph.D. diss., Yale University, 1992.
Rosswurm, Steven, and Toni Gilpin. "The FBI and the Farm Equipment Workers: FBI Surveillance Records as a Source for CIO Union History." *Labor History* 27, no. 4 (Fall 1986): 485–505.

FARMER-LABOR PARTY

The Farmer-Labor Party (FLP) was an attempt in the post-World War I years to establish a viable third-party political party uniting workers from all aspects of society.

The impetus for a labor party after WWI came from many sources. Another influence came from the success of the British Labour Party. Many believed that similar successes could come from a similar American organization.

At the time of the formation of the FLP, many labor organizations across the country were starting to organize their own political parties. While it is uncertain where the first true labor party was formed, there was considerable action in several states. In Chicago, under the call of the Chicago Federation of Labor (CFL), unsuccessful attempts came in 1905, 1908, and 1910. According to some scholarship, the first vital party was formed in 1918 in Bridgeport, Connecticut. In Minnesota, a Farmer-Labor Party was begun in the same year as in Connecticut. The Minnesota party had some success with the election of three governors and four U.S. senators. The party called for protecting both farmers and labor unions, and government control of some industries. But it was especially in the Chicago arena that the ideas came together.

John Fitzpatrick, the longtime CFL president, pushed for independent political action, an act which he knew would meet with opposition by the American Federation of Labor (AFL) president, Samuel Gompers. While not opposed to political action itself, Gompers believed in nonpartisan political action by supporting those who would promote labor concerns. Radical groups such as the Socialists were also opposed to the idea of a labor party for two reasons. First, they argued it would divide the working-class vote at the polls, and two, it would take away from their own publicity and membership.

The CFL started developing the drive for the national party in 1918, when it first formed a local party for Cook County (the county in which Chicago is located), and then a state party afterward. Neither party met with much, if any, success. During August 1919, along with 30 representatives from across the country, the CFL called for the formation of a national party. Each city's central labor body was permitted to send one delegate each, and local parties and unions could send one delegate for every 500 members. The convention met three months later in Chicago. With over 1,200 delegates in attendance, party officers were chosen, and a party platform developed, mostly taken from that of the Illinois party. Also in attendance were the single taxers, farmers,

and the progressive "Committee of 48." Since the national elections were not until the following year, that first convention did not feel any need to make major decisions, including a candidate for the presidency.

The next national convention met in Chicago during July 1920. At this time, the party blended many groups into one, and a new name was chosen—the Farmer-Labor Party. Delegates from the Non-Partisan League, the World War I Veterans, the Single Tax League, the Farmers' League, and the Committee of 48 attended. To promote their activities, the FLP especially used the CFL newspaper *The New Majority*, which was initially founded to promote the CFL's local political activities.

The platform, once again, was based upon that developed in Chicago. The 48ers objected to many of its provisions, such as the "democratic control of industry," which they believed to be too socialistic. The 48ers had no objections to antimonopoly provisions, but they were dead set against any sort of nationalization of any industry. The platform also called for recognizing the Soviet Union, civil rights for African-Americans, and nationalization of the mines, among other provisions.

The 48ers would also become disappointed with the FLP's choice for a presidential candidate. Instead of choosing LaFollette, the convention nominated Parley Parker Christensen, of Salt Lake City, and Max S. Hayes, a former Socialist candidate, for vice president. Furthermore, LaFollette expressed no interest in being a candidate. To many, the 48ers were latecomers to the movement and wanted to take over the FLP merely to promote their own agenda. Since the 48ers had no sort of a majority, their ideas were overridden.

The election in November 1920 was an utter disaster for the FLP. Warren G. Harding won by a landslide, easily defeating James Cox, the Democratic Party candidate. Christensen received less than a quarter of a million votes, not even 1% of the total. The Socialist labor leader Eugene V. Debs, currently serving time in prison for having violated the WWI Espionage and Sedition Acts, received just over 900,000 votes. Furthermore, the local parties created by the CFL suffered mostly devastating defeats as well. Any successes were in winning seats on the local level in places such as Illinois, New York, Washington, and Minnesota.

The CFL called for constant organization, believing that any hope for success in future elections depended upon not waiting for another election, but rather keeping their platform before the public. But the defeat in 1920 took its toll on the party. The next congressional elections would be in 1922, and calls were made to prepare. Popular sentiment toward the party was fading, and fast. Despite trying to portray itself as a party for all Americans, the FLP could not interest the general public, including labor's own rank and file. The Socialists proposed a meeting with the National Executive Committee to discuss possible options, but was turned down.

The CFL also began a "member contest," a last-ditch effort to keep the party moving by heavy recruitment of new members. The winners would be given dues for 12 months, a 12-month subscription to the *New Majority*, and an invitation to the next party dinner. The *New Majority* never reported the results.

At the 1923 convention, policy would be dictated by the Communists, led by Fitzpatrick's former organizing partner, William Z. Foster. With the FLP in a weakened state, the Communists were able to impose their will on the convention. Many of the less radical FLP members withdrew from the party, with Fitzpatrick himself furious at the move. To ally themselves with the Communists was political suicide, especially during the early 1920s when the first Red Scare took aim at any radicals, real or perceived. With the Communists in control, the FLP name was changed to the Federated Farmer-Labor Party.

In May 1924, Fitzpatrick and the CFL abandoned the idea of independent political action. The repeated failures, and the party takeover by the Communists, sent the CFL straight back into the AFL fold of nonpartisan political action. In a speech, Fitzpatrick lamented the turn of events while praising the AFL tactics. To further separate themselves from the now-defunct FLP, the CFL changed the name of its paper from the *New Majority* to *Federation News*, a name that remains into the present day. *Federation News* also declared its allegiance to AFL policies. While the party was dead on the national scene, the FLP continued to exist in Minnesota. In 1944, the Minnesota Democratic Party, led by the verbose Hubert H. Humphrey, merged with the FLP, then becoming known as the Minnesota Democratic-Farmer-Labor Party.

The FLP's failure stemmed from its lack of popular support, organization, funds, and coverage from the mainstream press, as well as staunch opposition from the leadership of the AFL.

MITCHELL NEWTON-MATZA

References and Further Reading

Federation News.

Fine, Nathan. *Farmer and Labor Parties in the United States, 1828–1928*. New York: Russell and Russell, 1961.

Greene, Julia. "The Strike at the Ballot Box: The American Federation of Labor's Entrance into Election Politics, 1906–1909." *Labor History* 32 (Spring 1991): 165–192.

Horowitz, Roger. *The Failure of Independent Political Action*. Bachelor's essay, 1982.

Keiser, John Howard. *John Fitzpatrick and Progressive Unionism*. Ph.D. diss., Northwestern University, 1965.

New Majority.

Newton-Matza, Mitchell. *Intelligent and Honest Radicals: The Chicago Federation of Labor and the Illinois Legal and Political System, 1919–1933*. Lanham, MD: University Press of America (forthcoming).

Shapiro, Stanley. "Hand and Brain: The Farmer-Labor Party of 1920." *Labor History* 26 (Summer 1985): 405–422.

Staley, Eugene. *A History of the Illinois State Federation of Labor*. Chicago: University of Chicago Press, 1930.

Stedman, Murray, and Susan Stedman. *Discontent at the Polls: A Study of Farmer and Labor Parties*. New York: Russell and Russell, 1967.

FARM LABOR ORGANIZING COMMITTEE

The Farm Labor Organizing Committee (FLOC) represents the most successful and long-lasting unionization effort among Midwestern farmworkers in the twentieth century. Created in 1967 to address the needs of migrant farmworkers who toiled on tomato farms in Ohio, FLOC has since expanded to include farmworkers in the South as well.

FLOC is very much associated with its founder, Baldemar Velasquez. Born in Texas in 1947, Velasquez worked as a migrant laborer with his family, regularly traveling between the Southwest and the Midwest. In 1954, the Velasquez family settled in Putnam County, Ohio, where they continued to work together in the fields. However, Velasquez also attended school, and after graduating from high school, he enrolled in college at Bluffton College in Ohio, where he took part in the emerging civil rights and free speech movements.

In 1967, based on his own experience in the fields as well as the supportive influence of Jesse Salas, who was already organizing pickle fieldworkers in Wisconsin, Velasquez decided to organize FLOC. He envisioned FLOC as a way to address the kinds of hardships he and thousands of Mexican and Mexican-American migrant farmworkers faced in Ohio— low pay, substandard housing, isolation, and limited educational opportunities. Since almost all the farmers who grew tomatoes owned relatively modest family farms, the FLOC organizers' first strategy revolved around trying to pressure individual growers to work voluntarily with them to improve living and working conditions as well as wage rates. Velasquez and his fellow organizers soon realized, however, that even gaining access to farmworkers would present a formidable challenge. Many farmers refused to allow FLOC organizers to visit with or speak to the migrant farmworkers. As such, FLOC organizers challenged their exclusion in court, and thereby successfully gained access to migrant workers, though they were not allowed to photograph the workers' living conditions inside migrant camps. FLOC also attempted to reach as many farmworkers as possible by sending organizers to Texas each winter to meet with migrant workers who would be traveling in the spring to work in Ohio. Equally important, FLOC began a well-organized publicity campaign to highlight the plight of migrant workers in the Midwest. This publicity campaign included a traveling theater, a bilingual union paper (*La Voz del Campensino*), and a radio program.

After failing to convince the farmers to address the working and living conditions of migrant workers, in September 1968, FLOC organized a strike against 10 Ohio farmers, including grower James Ackerman. FLOC demanded wage increases, life insurance, day care, paid hospitalization, and various wage guarantees to protect workers in case of inclement weather and delayed growing seasons. Though most growers refused to negotiate with FLOC, five growers agreed to sign a contract establishing FLOC as the sole bargaining agent and labor recruiter. The growers also agreed not to discriminate against union activists as well as to provide a minimum wage and limited insurance during the growing season. In return, FLOC members agreed to remain in the fields until the end of the growing season. Within a couple of weeks, a total of 21 farmers signed contracts with FLOC as well.

By 1969, FLOC's membership had grown to three thousand workers, and organizers looked forward to even more victories. However, FLOC soon faced an increasingly organized and militant opposition as various growers, associations, including the Farm Bureau, went on the offensive. Of the 21 growers who had signed the FLOC contract in 1968, 12 simply stopped growing tomatoes, while others tried to undermine FLOC by offering workers minimum wage increases on their own. Although FLOC officials were successful in using the court to force the growers to abide by the 1968 agreement, and even successfully negotiated two-year contracts with 11 growers, the prospect of trying to convince dozens of individual growers to sign contracts each year forced FLOC organizers to rethink their organizing strategy. Velasquez feared that negotiating contracts with individual growers would not deliver the kinds of long-term benefits that he and his associates hoped to achieve. Moreover, even the recently hard-won victories provided plenty of evidence that the strategy of negotiating one-on-one with Ohio's farmers left FLOC in a particularly vulnerable position.

In the post-1969 period, FLOC directed its energies toward challenging the processors with whom the farmers contracted to grow tomatoes—most importantly, the Campbell Soup Company—rather than just the farmers. The idea was that if organizers could convince the processors to sign multiparty contracts, this would force growers and farmworkers to recognize their common interests as well as ensure uniform wage rates and better living conditions for the thousands of farmworkers dispersed throughout the Ohio countryside. To achieve these multiparty three-way contracts, however, FLOC had to get the processors to come to the bargaining table.

The battle to convince Campbell Soup to engage in three-way collective bargaining and to sign multiparty contracts lasted for seven years. During that time, FLOC expanded its public relations campaign by calling for a national consumer boycott of all Campbell's products. In 1983, FLOC also engaged in a well-publicized protest walk from Ohio to Campbell's headquarters in Camden, New Jersey. By 1986, these efforts to reach out to the broader public paid off when Campbell Soup finally agreed to engage in three-way collective bargaining. Soon thereafter, other processor companies also agreed to three-way contracts, including Heinz, Vlasic, Aunty Jane, Dean Foods, and Green Bay Foods.

While FLOC organizers continued to organize farmworkers in the Midwest in the 1980s and 1990s, they also recognized the fact that since the market for tomatoes was becoming more national and international, they, too, needed to begin to organize workers outside the Midwest. Therefore, in 1997, FLOC expanded its organizational strategy by looking to organize farmworkers in North Carolina. Doing so posed new challenges. In contrast to the relatively homogenous farm labor force in Ohio, the nearly 40,000 migrant farmworkers in North Carolina included significant numbers of single men from diverse backgrounds, including the United States, Mexico, Central America, and the Caribbean. The prospect of successfully organizing this diverse workforce was further hampered by the very antiunion environment of this conservative southern state.

FLOC began its 1997 organizing campaign in North Carolina by directing its attention to the Mt. Olive Pickle Company. Though FLOC hoped that Mt. Olive would cooperate and help pressure local farmers to engage in three-way bargaining, Mt. Olive proved to be a formidable opponent. Mt. Olive executives insisted that since they hired neither the farmers nor the farmworkers, they had no authority to engage in any kind of bargaining. To counter Mt. Olives' intransigence, FLOC began another public relations campaign, including a well-publicized boycott, which received support from over two hundred labor, community, and religious groups. Mt. Olive responded with its own campaign, which received support from many antiunion conservatives. However, after a seven-year battle and a five-year boycott, in 2004, the Mt. Olive Pickle Company and the North Carolina Growers' Association capitulated to FLOC's call for three-way multiparty bargaining. In addition to agreeing to negotiate living and working conditions, Mt. Olive also pledged to increase the growers' pay by 10% over a three-year period to encourage them to increase the workers' pay as well. The 2004 victory provided FLOC with renewed optimism about organizing migrant farmworkers in the twenty-first century.

KATHLEEN MAPES

References and Further Reading

Morrissey, Marietta. "The Political Economy of Northwest Ohio Agriculture and Options for Labor Organization." *Migrant World Magazine* 27, no. 3 (1997): 18–23.

Rosenbaum, Rene Perez. "Unionization of Tomato Field Workers in Northwest Ohio." Labor History 35, no.3 (1994): 329–344.

Valdes, Dennis Nodin. "From Following the Crops to Chasing the Corporation: The Farm Labor Organizing Committee, 1967–1973." In *The Chicano Struggle: Analyses of Past and Present Efforts*, edited by T. Cordova, et al. Binghamton, NY, 1984.

FEDERAL BUREAU OF INVESTIGATION

The U.S. Department of Justice initially relied on other federal agencies to conduct investigations. A 1908 bill to create a Bureau of Investigation failed due to congressional opposition to a central spy agency. President Theodore Roosevelt insisted that the Department needed detectives and instructed his attorney general to create the Bureau after Congress adjourned. In 1935, it was renamed the Federal Bureau of Investigation (FBI).

Starting as a small agency with narrow jurisdiction, the FBI grew rapidly under J. Edgar Hoover, director from 1924 until his death in 1972. Hoover had joined the Justice Department in 1917 and headed the Radical Division, quickly renamed the General Intelligence Division, from 1920. Hoover amassed huge files, which he used to create a political role for the FBI that, for most of the twentieth century, exceeded its statutory responsibility. He maintained

dossiers on every member of Congress, the Supreme Court, Cabinet, and the eight presidents under whom he served. He shaped the Bureau's internal labor policies and its approach to labor organizations. Determined to control personnel, Hoover refused to cooperate with the Civil Service, and he barred African-American men as agents.

Bureau agents participated in the 1917 Espionage Act raids against immigrant working-class radicals, Socialists, the Industrial Workers of the World, and critics of the war. Despite lack of authorization, the Bureau assisted the Immigration Department in 1919 to arrest 750 immigrants, of whom over 200 were deported. Hoover helped organize the 1920 Palmer Raids, mass arrests of four thousand radicals in 33 cities, made possible by undercover agents in positions of sufficient leadership in the radical movement to organize the simultaneous meetings.

Federal officials claimed lack of jurisdiction, however, to investigate the 47 murders during the 1917 East St. Louis race riot, an antiblack rampage ignited by white craft workers. The FBI did investigate the East St. Louis black community for any influences which might foster attacks on whites, and it worked with employers to portray the riot as proving the dangers of unions. The FBI did not investigate any lynchings, averaging 65 per year during and after World War I, often the result of white hostility to black men in uniform. Nor did the FBI evince interest in labor racketeering. According to James B. Jacobs, the FBI devoted few resources to organized crime while Hoover was alive. Popular impressions to the contrary stem from confusion with other agencies (Al Capone was stopped by Treasury agents) and from Hoover's extraordinary promotional skills. The FBI joined with the Military Intelligence Division of the Army and the Office of Naval Intelligence to investigate the 1919 Steel Strike. FBI agents infiltrated the 1922 Railroad Shopmen's strike. Unable to develop evidence of radicalism, agents nonetheless helped make the case for federal troops. Although the General Intelligence Division was abolished in 1924, the FBI maintained its files on labor organizers and worked with plant security forces to develop fingerprint collections with which labor activists were tagged for blacklisting.

In 1932, the FBI infiltrated the Bonus March, a nonviolent demonstration by veterans, in an unsuccessful search for evidence to support President Herbert Hoover's claim that the marchers were Communists or criminals. The FBI used wiretapping extensively in violation of the 1934 Communications Act and helped train other police forces in its use. Wiretapping and related practices such as break-ins and mail intercepts were illegal, and illegally obtained evidence was inadmissible in court. However, the FBI found them effective in antiunion operations where the objective was disruption and provocation rather than prosecution. The FBI also shared wiretap information with employers.

The 1942 FBI break-in at the Los Angeles Communist Party headquarters provided the membership lists underpinning the Hollywood movie studios' blacklist. From 1934 to 1945, the FBI participated in an unsuccessful campaign to deport Harry Bridges, the president of the International Longshoremen's and Warehousemen's Union. Other labor targets in the 1940s included the Congress of Industrial Organizations (CIO), including CIO leader and key Roosevelt ally Sidney Hillman, the National Maritime Union, the United Mine Workers, and the New York City Teachers' Union. In 1946, Hoover proposed to President Harry Truman an emergency detention list including labor and civil rights leaders, which Attorney General Tom Clark authorized two years later. The FBI launched an anti-Communist and antiunion educational campaign in 1946, using cooperative columnists to disguise the FBI initiative.

President Truman's 1947 Federal Employee Loyalty Program increased both the FBI's surveillance mandate and its de facto unaccountability to constitutional standards. FBI files, inadmissible in court, proved decisive in loyalty dismissal proceedings. After the accused lost their positions, continued FBI surveillance and visits to prospective employers enforced blacklisting. FBI files on homosexuals, compiled without authorization since 1937, led to dismissals of thousands of federal employees.

The FBI provided information for congressional investigations of union activists, particularly leftists in the CIO, and shared information with plant security. In the 1953 House Committee on Un-American Activities hearing in Pittsburgh, the FBI supplied information about the United Electrical, Radio and Machine Workers of America that it had received from the manufacturers' labor spies and an FBI informer on the union's staff.

The FBI also gave information about union leftists to selected union leaders. James Carey, president of the International Union of Electrical Workers, started exchanging information with the FBI in 1943. In the March 1952 Detroit hearing against United Auto Workers (UAW) Local 600, the FBI provided CIO Vice President Walter Reuther with information from an informer in the local. The FBI spied on A. Philip Randolph, especially regarding the World War II-era March on Washington Movement for fair employment, and also reported to Randolph about possible Communist influence within the march.

The FBI engaged in disruption of black organizations. When the Memphis sanitation workers struck in 1968 and organized in the American Federation of State, County, and Municipal Employees, the FBI filed reports on the strikers (and shared information with the antiunion mayor) from the strike's inception. After Dr. Martin Luther King's assassination, the FBI continued to monitor the Poor Peoples' Campaign, sharing information with the Military Intelligence Division and Central Intelligence Agency, as well as leaking derogatory gossip to reporters. A paid FBI informant provided the diagram of the apartment in which Fred Hampton, a charismatic young Black Panther Party leader, was shot while asleep by the Chicago police in 1969. FBI testimony, disputed by historians and Amnesty International, led to the sentence of life imprisonment for the American Indian Movement member Leonard Peltier following a shoot-out at the Pine Ridge Reservation in 1975.

After Hoover's death, the FBI began to focus more on organized crime. The passage of the Organized Crime Control Act of 1970 (including the Racketeer Influenced and Corrupt Organizations [RICO] Statute and the Witness Security Program) provided the FBI with tools to combat labor racketeering; it focused especially on corrupt locals within the International Brotherhood of Teamsters. There has been debate within the union movement whether the FBI can be effective against labor racketeering, as it remains closely attuned to the demands of the presidency and largely immune to working people's priorities for law enforcement and union democracy.

GERDA W. RAY

References and Further Reading

Jacobs, James B. *Mobsters, Unions, and Feds: The Mafia and the American Labor Movement.* New York: New York University Press, 2006.
Kornweibel, Theodore Jr. *"Investigate Everything": Federal Efforts to Compel Black Loyalty during World War I.* Bloomington: Indiana University Press, 2002.
Lowenthal, Max. *The Federal Bureau of Investigation.* New York: William Sloane Associates, Inc., 1950.
O'Reilly, Kenneth. *Hoover and the Un-Americans: The FBI, HUAC, and the Red Menace.* Philadelphia: Temple University Press, 1983.
Schultz, Bud, and Ruth Schultz. *The Price of Dissent: Testimonies to Political Repression in America.* Berkeley: University of California Press, 2001.
Theoharis, Athan G. *The FBI & American Democracy: A Brief Critical History.* Lawrence: University Press of Kansas, 2004.

See also **Bridges, Harry Renton; Communist Party; Hillman, Sidney; Hoffa, James R.; House Un-American Activities Committee/Dies Committee; Industrial Workers of the World; International Brotherhood of**

FEDERAL COAL MINE HEALTH AND SAFETY ACT

In 1969, President Nixon reluctantly signed the Federal Coal Mine Health and Safety Act (FCMHSA) in the face of a rank-and-file movement of U.S. coal miners. It heralded a paradigm shift by comprehensively committing the federal government to creating and enforcing safety standards, and compensation for disease, in America's most hazardous industry. The prior reliance on states' initiatives had resulted in a dismal record on coal-mine safety in the United States, with over 90,000 officially reported fatal accidents from 1906 to 1970 (in bituminous mines alone), over 1.5 million injuries from 1930 to 1969, and likely even higher numbers killed and disabled more slowly by black lung disease.

Among other measures, the 1969 Act mandated federal inspections of each underground mine; fines for violations, with criminal penalties for willful violations; and the right of miners to request federal inspections. Soon, the groundbreaking 2 mg. of respirable dust per cubic meter of air rule was adopted, and coal miners were given periodic X-ray exams, with the right to demand less dusty work when black lung (Coal Workers' Pneumoconiosis, or CWP) was detected. The 1978 amendments created the Mine Health and Safety Administration (MSHA) within the Department of Labor (DOL) to take charge of mine safety matters, replacing the historically passive Department of the Interior. Proposals in 1978 for safety representatives, chosen by the miners, who would carry out the sampling of respirable dust, were rejected as a radical infringement on property rights.

Title IV of the FCMHSA (amended expansively in 1972 and 1978 and restrictively in 1981) created a federally administered black lung benefits program. The industry promptly challenged its constitutionality and lost in the Supreme Court. Title IV was originally a temporary federal commitment, under which:

(1) benefits would be paid from government revenues to those older disabled miners and widows still surviving the pre-1970 cover-up and abuse;
(2) a model adversarial workers' compensation program would then be created, followed by,
(3) adoption of similar programs by the states.

In practice, the backlog of older miners was too great, and the bureaucracy too unwieldy, to dispose of both rapidly and fairly. Furthermore, epidemiological evidence showed that the disease was more widespread than had been thought, because many miners whose X-rays were negative for the "textbook" picture of CWP nonetheless had coal dust-induced disease—both "classical CWP lesions" and Chronic Obstructive Pulmonary Disease (COPD), which was shown to result from coal dust exposure as well as from smoking.

The states could not rise to the challenge. In 1978, the federal program was made permanent, and the legal definition of pneumoconiosis was amended to include all respiratory disease arising out of coal-mine dust. An industry-financed Trust Fund was established for the older miners, whose last coal-mine work was prior to 1970. Those miners were freed from the opposition of the individual employers to their claims.

Then the 1981 amendments, supported by the coal industry and President Reagan, abolished several of the lenient eligibility provisions that had been won by the continuing vigilance of black lung activists. The approval rate plummeted from a high of 37% to a low of 5%. The decline also resulted from the shrinking number of "Trust Fund" cases and, concomitantly, the growing involvement of individual coal-mine operators. Their armies of well-paid lawyers and medical consultants vastly "outgunned" claimants on fixed incomes, and their appeals against the few claims awarded dragged on for years. In 2000, miners and their advocates won passage by the Clinton Administration of long-sought changes in the DOL's implementing regulations. These rules sought to level the field by limiting the quantity of evidence that could be submitted by employers, and they explicitly recognized the link between COPD and coal dust. The industry filed suit against the regulations and lost, but continued challenging the rules case by case.

One generation into the FCMHSA, mine fatalities have been greatly reduced (only in part because there are far fewer underground miners). Over 600,000 miners and widows have been awarded billions of dollars in benefits, and a network of clinics for diagnosis and treatment has been created. On the other hand, fatal accidents have still not been eliminated, especially at cost-cutting, often nonunion mines. It was revealed, in the late 1990s, that leaving the operators in charge of collecting and submitting dust samples for analysis had resulted in widespread fraud, condemning many miners unnecessarily to future disabling black lung. The problems with dust control added a certain irony regarding the resources—public and private—expended on adversarial battles over black lung claims, a situation which the 2000 regulations may partly alleviate.

The compensation aspect of the Act, "paying the piper" for years of accumulated neglect, has probably generated the most sustained adversarial conflict. Efforts to use black lung benefits as a model for federally administered compensation of all chronic occupational disease have thus far failed, despite government findings (1978) that 20% of Social Security Disability beneficiaries were disabled because of their jobs, and that only 5% of those with work-related illnesses were receiving state compensation. On the prevention side, the FCMHSA helped break ground for the Occupational Health and Safety Act one year later. Thus, the impact of the Act on coal miners and, to a degree, on workers in general has been substantial.

PAUL SIEGEL

References and Further Reading

Barth, Peter S. *The Tragedy of Black Lung: Federal Compensation for Occupational Disease.* Kalamazoo, MI: W. E. Upjohn Institute for Employment Research, 1987.

Derickson, Alan. *Black Lung: Anatomy of a Public Health Disaster.* Ithaca, NY: Cornell University Press, 1998.

———. "The Role of the United Mine Workers in the Prevention of Work-Related Respiratory Disease, 1890–1968." In *The United Mine Workers of America: A Model of Industrial Solidarity?* edited by John H. M. Laslett. University Park: University of Pennsylvania Press, 1996, pp. 224–238.

Harris, Gardner, and Ralph Dunlop. "Dust, Deception and Death." Series in *The Courier Journal.* April 19–April 26, 1998. Louisville, KY.

Hume, Brit. *Death and the Mines: Rebellion and Murder in the United Mine Workers.* New York: Grossman Publishers, 1971.

Judkins, Bennett M. *We Offer Ourselves as Evidence: Toward Workers' Control of Occupational Health.* New York: Greenwood Press, 1986.

Smith, Barbara Ellen. *Digging Our Own Graves: Coal Mines and the Struggle over Black Lung Disease.* Philadelphia: Temple University Press, 1987.

Statutes and Cases Cited

National Mining Assn v. Chao, 292 F.3d 849 (DC Cir. 2002)
Usury v. Turner Elkhorn, 428 US 1, 18 (1976)
Black Lung Benefits Act of 1972, PL 92-303
Black Lung Benefits Amendments of 1981, PL 97-119
Black Lung Benefits Reform Act of 1977, PL 95-239
Federal Coal Mine Health and Safety Act of 1969, PL 91-173
Federal Mine Safety and Health Act of 1977, PL 95-164

Federal Regulations

Department of Labor/Employment Standards Administration, 20 CFR Part 718 et al., *Federal Register,* December 20, 2000.

See also **Black Lung Associations; Boyle, W. A. Tony; Federal Coal Mine Health and Safety Act; Miller, Arnold; Miners for Democracy; United Mine Workers of America**

FEDERAL EMERGENCY RELIEF ADMINISTRATION

In 1933, the Roosevelt administration unveiled the Federal Emergency Relief Administration (FERA) as part of its New Deal economic reform program. Congress allocated $500 million to fund the program that provided large-scale direct relief to the many unemployed of the Great Depression. The program operated by providing block grants to states, which provided matching funds, allowing states to stretch their limited relief funds greatly. This represented a sharp break with prior policy, as the federal government had previously tended to leave poverty relief to states and had traditionally been extraordinarily hesitant to provide any direct relief whatsoever.

Franklin D. Roosevelt appointed Harry Hopkins to head FERA. Hopkins was an enthusiastic supporter of the agency, eager to spend money to alleviate the suffering of those in need, and eventually Hopkins proved to be one of the most popular and influential advisors to Roosevelt. Hopkins sought not only to disburse FERA funds directly to the needy, but also to use FERA as a laboratory to experiment with novel forms of poverty relief.

The agency did not disburse cash in most cases; rather, recipients received coupons to buy necessities like food, fuel, and clothing. Still, from the outset, the idea of giving unearned money to the needy troubled everyone involved in the program, including Hopkins and Roosevelt. Most government officials and local reformers favored a system of earned stipends. Thus, FERA chartered the first of the work relief programs of the New Deal, the Civil Works Administration (or CWA). The CWA put the nation's unemployed to work building schools, roads, parks, and other public improvements. The CWA eventually employed over 4 million workers. While the CWA was not part of the original legislative intent in creating FERA, it quickly became the most popular part of the program, both for the program's participants and for those who disapproved of direct government assistance to the poor. There were critics, however. Conservatives saw the CWA as a mass program of busy work. The American Federation of Labor (AFL) feared the CWA's real potential to undercut union wages, as CWA workers received a bare living stipend. Thus, the union movement would push to make CWA workers paid a prevailing local wage. Overall, union leaders remained wary of the program, as government work relief had the potential to replace high-paying private sector jobs with low-paying government work relief.

FERA was an enormously popular measure of the Roosevelt administration's New Deal. It greatly expanded the ability of government to provide relief to those most in need, and served as a model for later programs like Aid to Families with Dependent Children (AFDC) that provided a more thorough social welfare system. Congress perceived the popularity of the most popular program of FERA, the CWA, and extended it. But Roosevelt and Hopkins both saw government relief as a temporary expedient for relieving poverty. They ended the CWA in the spring of 1934. The program served as the inspiration, however, for later, larger New Deal work relief programs such as the Works Progress Administration and the Public Works Administration.

STEVEN DIKE-WILHELM

References and Further Reading

Leuchtenburg, William E. *Franklin D. Roosevelt and the New Deal, 1932–1940*. New York: Harper and Row, 1963.
Rauch, Basil. *The History of the New Deal, 1933–1938*. New York: Creative Age Press, Inc., 1944.
Watkins, T. H. *The Great Depression: America in the 1930s*. Boston: Little, Brown, and Company, 1993.

FEDERAL MEDIATION AND CONCILIATION SERVICE

The U.S. Congress established the Federal Mediation and Conciliation Service (FMCS) with Sections 202–205 of the Taft-Hartley Act of 1947. Taft-Hartley charged the FMCS with preventing strikes, lockouts, and other work stoppages by working to settle labor disputes with mediation and conciliation. Taft-Hartley created the FMCS as an independent organization, separate from the U.S. Department of Labor. Further, the mediation services that the U.S. Department of Labor had provided were transferred to the FMCS.

The FMCS is divided into an Eastern and Western region, which are subdivided into 10 districts and 70 field offices. The national office is in Washington DC. Contact information for the national, regional, and district offices is available on the FMCS Web site (www.fmcs.gov).

The Federal Mediation and Conciliation Service offers mediation services during collective bargaining negotiations. Any party to a collective bargaining dispute can request that the FMCS provide a free mediator during a contract negotiation. Mediators will attempt to help both sides come to an agreement.

They may make suggestions, but all of their recommendations are nonbinding. In addition to providing mediation during a contract negotiation, the FMCS can also provide grievance mediation. While the FMCS does not mediate routine grievances, it will attempt to mediate chronic problems between employers and employees, with the goal of improving overall workplace relations. The FMCS has turned increasingly toward preventative measures such as grievance mediation to stop labor disputes before they begin.

Federal law requires both employers and unions to notify the FMCS 60 days before they intend to terminate or renegotiate a contract. The FMCS Web site provides an F-7 form to notify the agency about a potential labor dispute. Once the FMCS receives an F-7 form, it will assign a mediator from the nearest regional office. Depending on the circumstances of the negotiations, the mediator could become very involved or relatively uninvolved.

The FMCS also serves as a reference for parties that wish to pursue arbitration. If the parties to a labor dispute choose to submit to arbitration, the FMCS will provide a list of "qualified neutrals" who will hear a case and produce a solution. The FMCS will also produce a panel of seven prospective arbitrators. The two parties to the dispute can then either mutually agree on an arbitrator, or each side can rank the panel by preference. The FMCS will then review the two lists and appoint an arbitrator from the panel. Whereas FMCS mediators make suggestions that either party can choose to adhere to or ignore, a decision produced by an arbitrator is legally binding.

The creation of the FMCS in the Taft-Hartley Act was a part of the broader trend to limit the militancy of labor. The FMCS was also emblematic of the move toward cooperative rather than antagonistic labor relations—which some have praised, and some have seen as hostile toward labor.

STEVEN DIKE-WILHELM

References and Further Reading

Koretz, Robert, ed. *Statutory History of the United States: Labor Organization*. New York: Chelsea House, 1970. www.fmcs.gov.

See also **Taft-Hartley Act**

FERRELL, FRANK
Knights of Labor

In the mid-1880s, at the height of the Knights of Labor's strength, Frank Ferrell was the best-known

African-American labor activist in the United States. A native of Brooklyn, New York, and a member of the "Home Club" organization within District Assembly 49 (DA 49), Ferrell burst onto the national scene during the Knights' October 1886 "General Assembly" in Richmond, Virginia. This national convention, only months after a nationwide strike for the eight-hour day and the dramatic Haymarket events in Chicago, attracted press coverage across the country. Reporters, who expected the assemblage of nearly 1,000 delegates to pass historic resolutions on the eight-hour day, strikes, relations between the Knights and trade unions, violence, legal repression, and a call for amnesty for the Haymarket martyrs, instead found issues of race relations (popularly known as "social equality") dominating the gathering's two weeks. And at the center of these issues was Frank Ferrell.

Ferrell traveled to Richmond as the only African-American among DA 49's 60 delegates. In a letter to the *New York Sun* posted just before it left via steamship for Richmond, the delegation pledged to challenge the system of racial segregation that had emerged in the former capital of the Confederacy and many other southern cities. When they arrived in Richmond, they attempted to register in a white-only hotel, where they had made reservations beforehand. When the desk clerk refused Ferrell admission, all 60 delegates walked out and secured lodging in a variety of African-American establishments. This action scandalized the local press, which regaled its readers with daily front-page stories of black and white delegates sharing rooms ("sleeping together") and assertions that such behavior revealed that the Knights stood for "social equality." Some articles even quoted wealthy whites' complaints about a new "impudence" evinced by local African-American servants. The national media echoed such concerns. "Genuine social equality can be witnessed" at one black hotel, reported the *New York Tribune*.

Ferrell and his New York compatriots launched additional challenges to local racial mores. On the steamship that carried them to Richmond, they had met a touring Shakespearean drama troupe on its way to perform *Hamlet* at the nationally recognized Richmond Academy of Music. The thespians gave the labor delegates free tickets to the opening night of the show. All of the tickets were in the traditionally whites-only orchestra section, and Ferrell's insistence, with the support of his allies, that he not be banished to the "colored gallery" occasioned uproar and a near riot. Once again, Ferrell and his colleagues made front-page news, locally and nationally, as purveyors of "social equality."

This perception was given added significance by the decision of Knights' General Master Workman Terence Powderly to invite Ferrell to introduce him to the assemblage at the opening session of the convention. DA 49's leaders had actually asked for more, urging that Ferrell introduce Virginia's governor, Fitzhugh Lee, the nephew of Robert E. Lee and a well-known white supremacist. Unwilling to go quite that far, Powderly did place Ferrell on the stage with Lee and himself, which offered a striking visual image of the labor organization's commitment to racial equality. Ferrell told the audience, "One of the objects of our Order is the abolition of those distinctions which are maintained by creed or color." Powderly's remarks affirmed Ferrell's: "When one that happened to be of a dark skin, of a delegation of some sixty men, could not gain admission to the hotel where accommodations for the delegation had been arranged, rather than separate from that brother, they stood by the principles of our organization which recognizes no color or creed in the division of men." He then explained his selection of Ferrell to introduce him to the General Assembly as evidence that "we practice what we preach."

These actions provoked responses not only in the media, but also in the ranks of the Knights. Some delegates praised Powderly, Ferrell, and DA 49, while others, particularly white southerners, condemned them. The African-American community, including not only members of locals affiliated with Black District Assembly 92 but also political activists, businessmen, and professionals, embraced Ferrell, DA 49, and the Knights. Midway through the convention, a parade saw black participants far outnumber white ones. The thousands of black spectators who lined the parade route led one correspondent to speculate that "the entire colored population of Richmond" was in attendance. A week later, when the General Assembly came to a close, local black activists organized a banquet to honor DA 49 and Frank Ferrell. They packed the hall above a prominent funeral parlor, listened to speeches from local African-American activists, and gave toasts in honor of their guests from New York.

Over the next four years, the Knights of Labor slid down a slope toward overall decline, losing numbers, strength, and power. Interestingly, though, their popularity among African-Americans, especially in the South, even the rural South, actually grew. Frank Ferrell had fired their imaginations, while Terence Powderly and the Knights of Labor had reached out publicly to him in a way that suggested that they did, indeed, practice what they preached.

PETER RACHLEFF

References and Further Reading

Fink, Leon. *Workingmen's Democracy: The Knights of Labor and American Politics.* Urbana: University of Illinois Press, 1983.

Foner, Philip S. *Organized Labor and the Black Worker.* New York: International, 1981 [1974].

Foner, Philip S., and Ronald L. Lewis, eds. *The Black Worker during the Era of the National Labor Union.* Philadelphia: Temple University Press, 1978.

Gutman, Herbert. "The Negro and the United Mine Workers of America: The Career and Letters of Richard L. Davis and Something of Their Meaning, 1890–1900." In *Work, Culture, and Society in Industrializing America.* New York: Vintage, 1977 [1966].

Kessler, Sidney. "The Organization of Negroes in the Knights of Labor." *Journal of Negro History* 37, no. 1 (1952): 248–276.

McNeill, George E., ed. *The Labor Movement: The Problem of To-Day.* New York: Augustus M. Kelley, 1971 [1887].

Phelan, Craig. *Grand Master Workman: Terence Powderly and the Knights of Labor.* Westport, CT: Greenwood Press, 2000.

Powderly, Terence V. *Thirty Years of Labor, 1859–1889.* New York: Augustus M. Kelley, 1967 [1890].

Rachleff, Peter. *Black Labor in Richmond, 1865–1890.* Urbana: University of Illinois Press, 1989 [1984].

Weir, Robert E. *Beyond Labor's Veil: The Culture of the Knights of Labor.* University Park: Pennsylvania State University Press, 1996.

———. *Knights Unhorsed: Internal Conflict in a Gilded Age Social Movement.* Detroit: Wayne State University Press, 2000.

See also **Haymarket Affair (1886); Home Club; Knights of Labor**

FILM

At the start of the twentieth century, leisure in the United States was stratified by class and marked by a distinct gulf between high-brow and low-brow entertainments. Movies emerged in the early twentieth century as a primarily working-class pleasure, and working people were simultaneously the primary consumers, producers, and subjects of the early silent films. As nickelodeons and storefront theaters proliferated in American cities, movies quickly surpassed dance halls, vaudeville theaters, amusement parks, and other cheap amusements to become the mainstay of working-class leisure.

During this period, too, the experience of moviegoing was quite different from that of more respectable, high-brow entertainments. Working-class movie audiences were not passive cultural consumers; rather, they actively engaged with the movies and each other. As audiences cheered their heroes and hissed the villains, sang along with the musical accompaniment or talked amongst themselves, a trip to the movie theater became a distinctly communal and participatory experience and one that contrasted sharply with the regimentation of the workplace. Moviegoing was also critically important in reshaping women's leisure and use of public space. Theaters encouraged women to bring children to the show, and movie houses were a key site for family-centered leisure. Single women, too, were ardent filmgoers, and "movie-struck girls" relied on film images in negotiating new freedoms and gender conventions. For young women and men, movie theaters also offered an ideal space for sociability and new opportunities for romance both on- and off-screen. The appeal of movies crossed racial as well as ethnic and gender lines. Though many theaters remained racially segregated, African-Americans were avid consumers, not only of mainstream movies, but also of "race films," produced by African-American filmmakers specifically for black audiences. Thus, both the content and experience of these early silent films helped to bridge ethnic, religious, gender, and sometimes racial divisions within the laboring population.

In the years before World War I, when relatively little capital was required to produce the one- and two-reel silent shorts, film production was remarkably fluid. Small-scale entrepreneurs, often immigrants, and women (who worked in the film industry in greater numbers and more diverse positions during this period than ever again) vied with established companies like Biograph and Edison to meet the seemingly insatiable demand for movies. Lary May estimates that in 1912, nearly 100 small companies scattered throughout the East and Midwest were involved in film production. The entrepreneurial nature of early film production translated into a complex amalgam of film styles and subjects, ranging from documentaries to melodramas and comedy to romance.

Though film historians continue to debate the significance and extent of class representations in early silent films, many have argued persuasively that these movies exhibited a distinct working-class sensibility. The silent era's slapstick comedies were as popular as they were potentially subversive. Mack Sennett's bumbling Keystone Kops lampooned law and order and police authority, while Charlie Chaplin's Little Tramp mocked everything from middle-class pretensions to gender roles to the mechanization of labor. The social realism of Progressive Era art and literature also influenced silent films. As in the paintings of the Ashcan School or the photography of Lewis Hine, images of the modern city, the bustle of street life, and the diversity of working people, predominated in silent film. The hardships as well as the dignity of working-class life were dramatized in a wide range of movies, from "social problem" films to less politically explicit melodramas and romances. A number of prominent filmmakers shared the Progressive Era's reform impulse. Lois Weber, for example, used film to explore issues of birth control, divorce, child labor, and capital punishment, while D. W. Griffith—though perhaps better known for his epic defense of white supremacy in *The Birth of a Nation* (1915)—also sympathetically contrasted the exploitation of workers with the decadence of capitalists in *A Corner on Wheat* (1909). Movies like *The Jungle* (1914), an adaptation of Upton Sinclair's muckraking novel, and *The Blacklist* (1916), which dramatized the Ludlow Massacre of striking mine workers, not only depicted struggles for justice against corrupt bosses and politicians, but also encouraged working-class solidarity.

Steven J. Ross has also identified a thriving pre-World War I worker film movement composed of radical filmmakers, often affiliated with labor organizations or socialist movements. Drawing inspiration and material from the labor struggles of the period, from the 1909 Uprising of the Twenty Thousand to the free speech fights of the Industrial Workers of the World, the movies of the worker film movement emphasized collective action and the power of an organized working class to reform the public sphere. These radical films competed with films produced by conservative business interests, making movies an ideological battleground over representations of labor militancy. Where the worker film movement depicted unionists engaged in rational and peaceful negotiations or social action, the conservative labor films depicted passive workers becoming unruly mobs under the influence of wild-eyed anarchists. Whatever their political perspective, the confrontational class politics in these labor-capital films worked to raise political consciousness and shape audience response to the world of work.

From the beginning, then, movies were broadly understood not simply as entertainment but as a powerful vehicle for shaping public consciousness and behavior. As such, movies quickly became a site of contention for middle-class reformers. While some applauded the democratizing and Americanizing potential of movies, others argued that movies encouraged crime, juvenile delinquency, and sexual promiscuity. Closely linked to the Progressive Era antivice crusades, the campaign against the movies called for the voluntary regulation not only of film content but also of theaters themselves, which were seen as sites of urban disorder and immorality.

The Rise of the Studio System

During the 1920s, the film industry and the movies themselves changed dramatically, as the entrepreneurial mode of production gave way to the studio system. As filmmakers and small production companies struggled to meet the growing demands for longer and more sophisticated films, the pressure to centralize and standardize the production process became overwhelming. Between 1915 and 1930, nearly every aspect of filmmaking was standardized, economized, and regimented, and film production was centralized in the business-friendly frontier town of Hollywood, though the marketing and administrative functions remained in the corporate offices in New York. By 1930, eight vertically integrated companies dominated the film industry, together producing up to 600 full-length features a year.

The consolidation of film production under the Hollywood studio system affected movies and audiences in myriad ways. During the 1920s, studios sought to expand their audience, investing in opulent theaters in more affluent neighborhoods to attract middle-class patrons. These movie palaces helped to make moviegoing respectable and, in the process, significantly changed the ways movies were watched and experienced by audiences of all classes. Ticket prices rose to match the rising costs of film production. The star system spurred higher salaries for actors as well as a full-blown publicity machine to nurture the emerging fan culture around major movie personalities like Clara Bow, the "It" Girl, and "Hollywood's Sweethearts," Mary Pickford and Douglas Fairbanks. The introduction of talkies in the late 1920s had a significant impact on the film industry as well, requiring the studios not only to retool theaters to accommodate the new technology, but also to recruit and maintain a stable of more sophisticated writers. As the studios' financial investment in film production soared and each studio produced fewer, more expensive movies each year, box office returns took on an inordinate importance. In sharp contrast to the pre-World War I era, the new studio moguls were less willing to take a chance on controversial subjects or specialized films that seemed unlikely to appeal to a broad audience. Despite—or perhaps because of—their own immigrant and working-class backgrounds, the Hollywood moguls were deeply conservative and antagonistic to the use of movies to raise public consciousness or dramatize social issues. Insisting that movies were simply "entertainment," Harry Cohn once famously growled, "If you want to send a message, use Western Union." As movies became the epitome of mass culture in the 1920s, the worker film movement and the culture of the masses of the pre-World War I era dissipated. Though working people continued to be represented on film, themes of working-class solidarity and collective action gave way to stories of cross-class romance and upward mobility.

This trend held to a great extent through the 1930s, despite the widespread economic dislocation of the Depression and the resurgence of the labor movement under the New Deal. Hollywood's initial response to the Depression was mixed. Hoping to attract the dwindling audience to theaters, the studios offered wildly extravagant entertainments like *Gold Diggers of 1933*, which infused a conventional rags-to-riches romance and glitzy musical numbers (most notably "We're In the Money") with both escapist glamour and a working-class élan. In contrast to the frivolity of much of the film, *Gold Diggers* closes with "Remember My Forgotten Man," which invoked breadlines, homelessness, and the Bonus Marchers. The early 1930s were also the heyday of the fallen woman film and the gangster film, both of which suggested that economic hardship had led to the moral downfall of these protagonists. The backlash against the perceived violence and immorality of these films, however, also spurred the creation of the Production Code Administration (PCA) in 1934 to forestall government regulation and assuage conservative organizations like the Legion of Decency. In its zeal to banish offensiveness from movies, the Code sharply defined the representational parameters of Hollywood films during this period, imposing sharp restrictions on a wide range of issues, primarily sexuality, but also class, race, labor relations, and particularly any negative representation of capital and business.

Thus, the films of the 1930s reflect both the conservatism and self-censorship of the Hollywood studios and the revitalized class consciousness and populist ethos of the New Deal era. On the one hand, movies such as *Black Fury* (1935) and *Black Legion* (1936) depicted labor unions as corrupt institutions that led passive workers astray, while on the other hand, movies like *The Grapes of Wrath* (1940) sympathetically dramatized the struggles of working people while gritty films such as *I Am a Fugitive from a Chain Gang* (1932) and *Dead End* (1937) suggested the social realist tradition was alive and well. Certainly, class remained a central pre-occupation across film genres, though the overwhelming emphasis in films of the 1930s is on upward mobility, individual success, and personal solutions to political problems. Nonetheless, the cross-class romance theme in screwball comedies like *Easy Living* (1934) or *My Man Godfrey* (1936) offered numerous opportunities to poke fun at the pretensions of the rich and to applaud the "regular Joe." Both comedies and melodramas of the 1930s also featured the "city boy," epitomized by James Cagney, Humphrey Bogart, and John Garfield, and the "wise-cracking dame," epitomized by Rosalind Russell, Myrna Loy, and Barbara Stanwyck, new models of masculinity and femininity that were deeply inflected with a working-class sensibility even when the films in which they appeared elided working-class politics.

A more direct result of the New Deal-era resurgence of labor came in the intense and convoluted struggles to unionize key sectors of the film industry itself. The screenwriters, always the most politicized of the talent workers, led the way, founding the Screen Writers Guild (SWG) in April 1933; the Screen Actors Guild (SAG) followed suit three months later, while the Directors Guild was founded in 1936. The studio moguls fought unionization with belligerence and divisiveness. Though the 1935 National Labor Relations Act authorized collective bargaining, it was ignored by the studios. The threat of an actors' strike two years later finally forced the studios to recognize SAG in 1937. Despite recognition of SWG by the National Labor Relations Board in 1938, the screenwriters battled the studios and the company union, the Screen Playwrights, before a contract agreement was reached in 1941. This bitter and protracted unionization battle between the talent guilds and the studios reinforced the participants' sense of themselves as cultural *workers* and gave birth to a highly politicized left-liberal cadre in Hollywood.

These progressive filmmakers were key players in the New Deal-era "laboring of American culture" described by Michael Denning. Despite the creative and political constraints imposed by the studio heads and the PCA censors, Hollywood progressives consistently attempted to address issues of class and labor, with varied success. Ironically, perhaps, film radicals gained a new legitimacy during World War II, as the studios drew upon their political expertise to produce hundreds of films depicting the threat of fascism and explaining "why we fight" to American moviegoers. Nonetheless, with the oversight of the Office of War Information, which declared a moratorium on social problem filmmaking for the duration, Hollywood representations of class and labor were largely refracted through the lens of patriotic Americanism. Films depicting the home front emphasized the contributions of laboring men and women to the war effort, while war films depicted military units as cross-class microcosms of the American melting pot fighting to preserve the American way of life.

The immediate postwar period in Hollywood witnessed a volatile jurisdictional struggle between Hollywood craft unions, as the left-liberal Conference of Studio Unions (CSU) battled unsuccessfully against the mob-controlled International Alliance of Theatrical Stage Employees. Two protracted CSU strikes between 1945 and 1947, marked by red-baiting and violent clashes between strikers and studio police, augured both the burgeoning anti-Communist climate and the breakdown of the left-liberal coalition of the Popular Front period. As Lary Ceplair and Ken Englund suggest, the conservatism of the studios' postwar agenda was signaled as early as 1945, when Eric Johnston, the new head of the Motion Picture Producers Association, announced to a meeting of the Screen Writers Guild, "We'll have no more *Grapes of Wrath*, we'll have no more *Tobacco Roads*, we'll have no more films that deal with the seamy side of American life. We'll have no more films that treat the banker as a villain." Nonetheless, Hollywood progressives greeted the postwar period with enthusiasm, eager to tackle the domestic social problems that had been discouraged by the Office of War Information during the patriotic frenzy of the war years. Postwar films like *Crossfire* (1947) and *Gentleman's Agreement* (1947) indicted American anti-Semitism while *Pinky* (1949), *Home of the Brave* (1949), and others explored the problem of racism. This flurry of progressive filmmaking was cut dramatically short, however, by the postwar investigations into subversion in the film industry by the House Un-American Activities Committee (HUAC), which resulted in the blacklisting of the Hollywood 10 in 1947 and hundreds more Hollywood leftists during a second round of hearings in the early 1950s.

The Postblacklist Period

With Hollywood's postwar attack on domestic social problems derailed by the HUAC investigations, dissent—particularly around issues of class—in 1950s films merely seeped through the cracks of the Cold War consensus, confined largely to *film noir*, with its sordid settings, paranoid protagonists, and existential despair, and to juvenile delinquency films like *The Blackboard Jungle* and *The Wild Ones* (as well as a whole slew of B films), featuring alienated, angry youths rebelling against a conformist adult world. During this period, blacklisted producer Adrian Scott identified several troubling trends in Hollywood filmmaking: a postwar cycle of anti-Communist films (which bombed at the box office), films glorifying the American businessman and the capitalist order, and films glorifying the military might of the United States. Most disturbing to him, however, was that, in the vacuum created by the blacklisting of radical

cultural workers, liberal filmmakers abandoned social and economic causality and wholeheartedly embraced the individualistic, psychological solutions of the postwar therapeutic culture.

The widespread affluence and decline of labor militancy in the Eisenhower years also re-inforced the notion that the problem of class in America had finally been solved. In this context, sympathetic or overtly political images of the labor movement and working-class people were few and far between. Nonetheless, Judith E. Smith points to the persistence of an ethnic or working-class sensibility in a handful of films she describes as "everyman's love stories": *Born Yesterday* (1950), *Marty* (1955), *The Marrying Kind* (1952), and *A Raisin in the Sun* (*1961*). In contrast, *On the Waterfront* (1954) resurrected earlier images of corrupt unions and powerless workers, and in the wake of director Elia Kazan's decision to name names to HUAC, raised troubling questions about labor solidarity and the politics of informing. One striking exception to this trend was *Salt of the Earth* (1953). Produced outside the studio system on a shoestring budget by a handful of blacklistees, the film dramatized a strike by Latino mine workers in New Mexico. Though distribution of the film was blocked in the 1950s by the major studios and the anti-Communist network, *Salt of the Earth* was rediscovered in the 1970s and praised for its progressive treatment of gender and race as well as its powerful evocation of labor solidarity.

Despite the collapse of the studio system and the resurgence of progressive political movements in the 1960s and 1970s, the New Hollywood, built by independent production companies, powerful agents, and multi-industry conglomerates, did little for the representation of the labor movement and the working class. Though certainly a number of Hollywood films from this period, such as *Norma Rae* (1979), *Bound for Glory* (1976), and *Silkwood* (1983), offered sympathetic portrayals of working-class consciousness and the possibilities of collective action, for the most part, Hollywood continued to depict unions as cynical and corrupt in such films as *F.I.S.T.* (1978), *Blue Collar* (1978), and *Hoffa* (1990). Since the 1980s, a number of independent filmmakers have offered exceptionally progressive labor films, including John Sayles' *Matewan* (1987), a dramatization of cross-race solidarity in a 1920s West Virginia coal strike, as well as Ken Loach's *Bread and Roses* (2000), which depicts the struggles of two Latina immigrant sisters to win justice for janitors. Perhaps the most significant film representations of working-class life and labor since the 1970s have come from documentary filmmakers, from Barbara Koppel's *Harlan County, USA* (1976) and *American Dream* (1991) to Michael Moore's

Roger and Me (1989) and The Big One (1997). Though the New Hollywood offers increasing opportunities for independent filmmakers, the future of labor and film remains to be seen.

JENNIFER LANGDON-TECLAW

References and Further Reading

Ceplair, Lary, and Ken Englund. *The Inquisition in Hollywood: Politics in the Film Community, 1930–1960.* Berkeley: University of California Press, 1979.

Denning, Michael. *The Cultural Front: The Laboring of American Culture in the Twentieth Century.* London and New York: Verso, 1996.

DiBattista, Maria. *Fast-Talking Dames.* New Haven, CT: Yale University Press, 2003.

Doherty, Thomas. *Pre-Code Hollywood: Sex, Immorality, and Insurrection in American Cinema, 1930–1934.* New York: Columbia University Press, 1999.

May, Lary. *The Big Tomorrow: Hollywood and the Politics of the American Way.* Chicago: University of Chicago Press, 2000.

———. *Screening Out the Past: The Birth of Mass Culture and the Motion Picture Industry.* Chicago: University of Chicago Press, 1980.

Rabinovitz, Lauren. *For the Love of Pleasure: Women, Movies, and Culture in Turn-of-the Century Chicago.* New Brunswick, NJ: Rutgers University Press, 1998.

Ross, Steven J. *Working-Class Hollywood: Silent Film and the Shaping of Class in America.* Princeton, NJ: Princeton University Press, 1998.

Schatz, Tom. *The Genius of the System: Hollywood Filmmaking in the Studio Era.* New York: Pantheon Books, 1988.

Sklar, Robert. *City Boys: Cagney, Bogart, Garfield.* Princeton, NJ: Princeton University Press, 1992.

Smith, Judith E. *Visions of Belonging: Family Stories, Popular Democracy, and Postwar Democracy, 1940–1960.* New York: Columbia University Press, 2004.

Stewart, Jacqueline Najuma. *Migrating to the Movies: Cinema and Black Urban Modernity.* Berkeley: University of California Press, 2005.

Zaniello, Tom. *Working Stiffs, Union Maids, Reds, and Riffraff: An Organized Guide to Films about Labor.* Ithaca, NY: ILR Press/Cornell University Press, 1996.

FINNS

The Finnish presence in North America dates to the 1600s, when Swedish colonizers relied on Finns for their skills as woodsmen. Though Finns were few in number, historians have argued that they set the pattern of colonial backwoods homesteading. After this initial foray, the Finnish migrant stream dried to a trickle until the high tide of Finnish immigration came on suddenly at the turn of the twentieth century, when hundreds of thousands joined the millions of New Immigrants then filling the ranks of the industrial workforce of the United States. Immigrant Finns confronted racism, nativism, grinding work, and horrible conditions, but they organized and confronted these obstacles with a unique brand of ethnic radicalism that persisted through the conservative 1920s into the post-World War II era.

"America Fever" began in the extreme northern part of Finland in the 1860s. Michigan's Upper Peninsula drew large numbers of Finns after a copper company recruited a number of them to work its mines. These miners sent word home, and the urge to move west spread to more populous industrialized regions of Finland, themselves undergoing economic and industrial transformations that displaced thousands of farmers and workers. In all, some 350,000 Finns, one ninth of the total population of Finland in 1900, left for the United States, the vast majority arriving between 1900 and 1914. From the Upper Peninsula of Michigan, Finns spread out to settle in the Northeast, the Upper Midwest, the Mountain West, and the Pacific Northwest, drawn to jobs through transatlantic networks of kin, community, and friendship. With the development of Minnesota's Mesabi and Cuyuna Iron Ranges in the late 1890s, large numbers of Finns moved there, and within a short time most Iron Range communities possessed their own "Finntowns," pejoratively dismissed as "Pig Towns" or "Finn Hells" by some of their neighbors. By 1920, almost 150,000 Finns lived in northern Minnesota alone, but Finnish enclaves could be found in mining communities across the American West.

Finnish miners faced harsh lives in the raw, undeveloped mining towns of the Midwest and West. A few miners lived in company towns—model villages of trim cottages and clean streets—but in Minnesota, most lived in "locations," temporary towns built in close proximity to mines that could be easily moved should the mining companies wish to extract the underlying ore. Though some of these locations were relatively clean, most were ramshackle and squalid affairs thrown up by residents with little or no assistance from the companies. In addition to their refusal to concern themselves with the living conditions of employees, mining companies in Michigan, Minnesota, and western states like Montana and Arizona kept costs low by refusing to pay for safety devices in the mines, employing industrial spies to discourage unions, ethnically and racially segmenting their workforces to keep wages down, and using brutal strikebreaking tactics when necessary. Finns also faced virulent racism and nativism encouraged by companies, which in one instance in Minnesota tried to have some Finn union organizers deported as "Mongolians."

While many Finns arrived in the United States already radicalized by events in Europe, especially those who arrived from the urban areas of Finland after the abortive 1905 Revolution in Russia, most joined unions as a result of the conditions they encountered in the mines; Finnish miners embraced labor radicalism in this hostile environment. Though not all Finns joined radical labor unions—there were strong divisions between Church Finns (deeply religious men and women also known as "white" Finns or Temperance Finns) and the radials ("Red" Finns)—they nevertheless gained a reputation for a propensity toward radicalism wherever they worked. Finns spearheaded organizing efforts with the Western Federation of Miners and the Industrial Workers of the World (IWW) in the mining regions of Michigan, Minnesota, Montana, and Arizona, though the locus of their activity remained in the Upper Midwest.

Finnish immigrant miners first distinguished themselves in the 1907 strike against Minnesota iron-mining companies, an industry dominated by a U.S. Steel subsidiary, the Oliver Mining Company. Iron miners suffered from lower pay than their native-born coworkers. They had to pay the cost of materials like tools and explosives. The work season forced them to shift for themselves over the long winter months, when Lake Superior shipping routes were icebound. Most important, miners complained of a dismal record of safety in the underground mines. When the Western Federation of Miners began to organize on the Range, Finns proved to be eager and enthusiastic members, and when a wildcat strike broke out at a Range sawmill in the summer of 1907, Finns quickly turned it into a general strike against the mine companies. The companies fought back and imported Eastern European strikebreakers, blacklisted hundreds of Finnish miners, and induced local merchants to cut off the credit of striking miners. By the end of the summer, the strike had been defeated. Finnish miners responded in a number of ways: some left the Range for other mining regions—notably in the Mountain West—while those who remained formed cooperative stores (many of which survived into the 1950s) and flocked to the Industrial Workers of the World.

This pattern repeated itself again in a 1913 strike against Michigan's copper mines that involved almost 15,000 copper miners, most of them Finns, who struck for 265 days before giving in to company pressure. As in Minnesota, companies turned to strikebreakers, threats of violence, and blacklists. In the 1916 Mesabi Iron Range strike, Finns again took leadership roles and turned their extensive network of Finn Halls into headquarters for IWW organizing efforts. One-time strikebreakers from Italy, Russia, Croatia, Serbia, and Montenegro joined the Finns to demand equal pay, better and safer conditions, and more benefits. The Oliver Mining Company recruited over a thousand armed guards and engaged in a systematic campaign of threats and violence to suppress this strike of some 20,000 miners, ultimately instituting one of the most extensive industrial spy networks in the country, which effectively forestalled future strikes.

The decline of iron and copper mining and the consequences of immigration restriction in the 1920s took their toll on the once-flourishing Finnish enclaves. Finns still constitute a visible ethnic presence where they settled the most thickly, however. Snatches of Finnish polkas can yet be heard in the backyards of western mining towns like Butte, Montana, and distinctive blue-and-white bumper stickers bearing slogans like "*Suomi* (Finland) Power" and "*Sisu*" (Strength) can be seen across Michigan's Upper Peninsula and in northern Minnesota, proclaiming the tenacious ethnic pride of local residents.

GERALD RONNING

References and Further Reading

Chrislock, Carl H. *The Progressive Era in Minnesota: 1899–1918*. St. Paul: Minnesota Historical Society, 1971.

Gudmundson, Wayne. *Testaments in Wood: Finnish Log Structures at Embarrass, Minnesota*. St. Paul: Minnesota Historical Society, 1991.

Hoerder, Dick, ed. *American Labor and Immigration History, 1877–1920s: Recent European Research*. Urbana: University of Illinois Press, 1983.

Hoglund, Arthur W. *Finnish Immigrants in America, 1880–1920*. Madison: University of Wisconsin Press, 1960.

Holmio, Armas K. E. *History of the Finns in Michigan*. Detroit: Wayne State University Press, 2001.

Hummasti, Paul G. *Finnish Radicals in Astoria, Oregon, 1904–1940: A Study in Immigrant Socialism*. New York: Arno Press, 1979.

Jordan, Terry G., and Matti Kaups. *The American Backwoods Frontier: An Ethnic and Ecological Interpretation*. Baltimore: Johns Hopkins University Press, 1989.

Kivisto, Peter. *Immigrant Socialists in the United States: The Case of the Finns and the Left*. Rutherford, NJ: Fairleigh Dickinson University Press, 1984.

Ronning, Gerald. "Jackpine Savages: Discourses of Conquest in the 1916 Mesabi Iron Range Strike." *Labor History* 44, no. 3 (August 2003): 359–382.

Ross, Carl. *The Finn Factor in American Labor, Culture, and Society*. New York Mills, MN: Parta Printers, 1977.

Salerno, Salvatore. *Red November, Black November: Culture and Community in the Industrial Workers of the World*. Albany: State University of New York Press, 1989.

FITZPATRICK, JOHN (1871–1946)
President, Chicago Federation of Labor

John Fitzpatrick was one of the most important Chicago labor leaders in the first half of the twentieth century, and was also a national leader of what historian John Keiser labeled "progressive unionism" between 1915 and 1925.

Born in Ireland, Fitzpatrick came to America in 1882 following the death of both of his parents. He found work in Chicago's stockyards, and in the wake of the labor unrest in 1886 in favor of the eight-hour day, Fitzpatrick joined the International Union of Journeymen Horseshoers of the United States and Canada and the Blacksmiths, Drop Forgers and Helpers Union. He held a number of positions within these unions, including business agent, treasurer, and president. The office for which he is best known, however, was the presidency of the Chicago Federation of Labor (CFL), which he held from 1904 until his death, from a heart attack, in 1946, with one short interruption.

Fitzpatrick won the CFL presidency through the efforts of local progressives and municipal reformers, including the recently formed Chicago Teachers Federation. In fact, Fitzpatrick represented one of the best efforts at combining progressive reform and labor activism. Nevertheless, Fitzpatrick's program was ultimately a failure, and by 1925, he was forced to repudiate many of the reforms he had fought for. To a large extent, this failure was a result of the structural difficulties inherent in progressive unionism, particularly the need to steer between the extremes of Gompers-style trade unionism on the right and revolutionary socialism on the left. When the strength of the left began to decline in the 1920s, Fitzpatrick was easily tarred by his "conservative" opponents within the American Federation of Labor (AFL) for his closeness to socialists and Communists like William Z. Foster.

Fitzpatrick was instrumental in two major organizing campaigns, the drive to unionize the Chicago stockyards in 1917 and the national steel strike in 1919. In both campaigns Fitzpatrick, along with Foster, his friend and ally, pioneered the notion of "federated" unionism, a position halfway between the trade unionism advocated by the AFL and the more radical industrial unionism called for by groups like the Industrial Workers of the World (IWW). Drawing on the example of the railroad brotherhoods, under federated unionism an umbrella organization was created that contained delegates from all of the trades present in a given industry. This organization would then coordinate organizing activities for the industrywide organizing campaign, while the international unions would retain their authority over collective bargaining.

Federated unionism was initially successful in both campaigns. The Stockyards Labor Council and the National Committee for Organizing Iron and Steel Workers (both of which were chaired by Fitzpatrick), the umbrella organizations in the stockyards and steel campaigns, respectively, managed to temporarily head off jurisdictional disputes between the various trade unions involved in the campaigns, and considerable numbers of workers were organized. Both campaigns, however, were ultimately defeats for the labor movement. While much of the blame has been placed on the growing business intransigence toward unions after the war and the conservative, antilabor consensus that began to dominate in the 1920s, the inability of the various trade unions to cooperate long-term also played a major role in the campaigns' defeats. In the stockyards, for instance, the Amalgamated Meat Cutters withdrew from the Stockyards Labor Council and attempted to claim the newly organized packinghouse workers for itself, precipitating the defeat of the federated unionism attempt. Nevertheless, Fitzpatrick and Foster's attempts at federated unionism served as one of the important precursors to the wave of industrial unionism under the Congress of Industrial Organizations (CIO) that occurred in the 1930s.

Fitzpatrick was also closely involved with the American Labor Party movement, which arose in the aftermath of World War I. The Chicago Federation of Labor created one of the earliest of these labor parties in 1918, and Fitzpatrick and the CFL were instrumental in creating the Illinois State Labor Party as well as the national Farmer-Labor Party in 1920. Fitzpatrick himself ran for office twice on the Labor Party ticket, first for the Chicago mayoralty in 1919 and then for United States senator in 1920. The various labor parties, however, largely failed to appeal to workers, and the Labor Party's share of the vote steadily declined after its founding. In an attempt to broaden its appeal, Fitzpatrick advocated amalgamating the Labor Party with other independent political movements, including the National Non-Partisan League, an organization of small farmers. This union led to the creation of the Farmer-Labor Party in 1920.

Unfortunately for the Labor Party movement, Fitzpatrick decided to extend his attempts at amalgamation to include a number of small left-wing and socialist parties. Among these was the Workers Party, which was, at the time, the secret, aboveground arm of the American Communist Party. In 1923, William Z. Foster, who had by then become a member of the Communist Party, betrayed his former ally, Fitzpatrick, and helped pack the July Farmer-Labor Party convention with Communists. Foster succeeded, and a new party, the Federated Farmer-Labor Party, controlled by the Communists, was created. This split created a great deal of confusion and led to the decline of the Farmer-Labor movement outside of Minnesota.

Fitzpatrick and his progressive unionism had long been a thorn in the side of Samuel Gompers, and the head of the AFL took the Farmer-Labor debacle as an opportunity to re-assert his control over Fitzpatrick and the CFL. During the 1923 AFL convention, a resolution favoring independent political action on the part of labor was soundly defeated. This turn of events, along with consistent pressure from Gompers, left Fitzpatrick to choose between abandoning his advocacy for the Labor Party and other progressive causes or leaving the AFL. Lacking an independent base of support outside of his position in the CFL, Fitzpatrick chose to remain within the AFL and moderate his positions. He remained a major labor leader on the Chicago scene for the next 20 years, although his role as a national labor leader waned with the defeat of progressive unionism.

AARON MAX BERKOWITZ

References and Further Reading

Barret, James. *William Z. Foster and the Tragedy of American Radicalism.* Urbana: University of Illinois Press, 1999.
Keiser, John. "John Fitzpatrick and Progressive Unionism, 1915–1925." Ph.D. diss., Northwestern University, 1965.
McKillen, Elizabeth. *Chicago Labor and the Quest for a Democratic Diplomacy, 1914–1924.* Ithaca, NY: Cornell University Press, 1995.

See also **Chicago Federation of Labor**

FITZSIMMONS, FRANK E. (1906–1981)
President, Teamsters Union

Succeeding James R. Hoffa as the leader of the largest union in the United States, Frank E. Fitzsimmons had originally been appointed as a caretaker, who would hold his predecessor's place during his jail term. But the unassuming Fitzsimmons made this position his own and led the Teamsters through a period of continued growth and controversy from 1967 to 1981.

Fitzsimmons was born in Jeannette, Pennsylvania, a small town outside of Pittsburgh. The family later moved to Detroit, and at age 16, with his father ailing, Fitzsimmons left school to begin working in a local factory. He eventually became a long-haul truck driver and through that job joined the Teamsters Union in 1934. His fellow drivers elected him to the post of shop steward, and through that position he met Hoffa, then an ambitious business agent for a Teamsters local in Detroit. With Hoffa's support, Fitzsimmons steadily progressed up the union's ranks, becoming a business agent in Hoffa's Local 299 in 1937, and then vice president of the local in 1940. By 1961, Fitzsimmons was elected thirteenth vice president of the national Teamsters union, making him a member of its ruling General Executive Board. As a trusted Hoffa loyalist, but also one whose ambitions and abilities seemed limited, Fitzsimmons became Hoffa's choice to lead the union in his place when he faced the certainty of a prison sentence. In 1966, Hoffa convinced the union's convention to create a new position, general vice president, who would be empowered to lead the union in the general president's stead. Hoffa then supported Fitzsimmons's election to that new post. The next year, in 1967, when Hoffa began serving a 13-year jail sentence, Fitzsimmons assumed the role that Hoffa had created for him.

But Fitzsimmons soon proved himself to be more than a mere placeholder for Hoffa. As general vice president, he ran the union in his own way, telling other members of the General Executive Board that he would let local and regional Teamster leaders operate with more autonomy, thus reversing Hoffa's policy of centralization within the union. That policy, as well as the solid gains Fitzsimmons won in national trucking industry contract negotiations in 1967 and 1970, helped him build up a core of his own supporters. When Hoffa, in an effort to win parole, resigned all of his union offices in 1971, Fitzsimmons was unanimously elected general president by the Teamsters convention in 1971.

In some ways, the union prospered during his leadership. Membership grew from 1.6 million in 1967 to 2.1 million by 1975, and wages and benefits increased steadily. But the union remained notorious for its corruption and its alleged connections to organized crime. That notoriety was only further heightened by the disappearance in 1975 of Hoffa, widely believed to have been killed by the Mafia. Like his predecessors, Fitzsimmons took no real constructive action to deal with the problem of corruption, limiting himself to indignant attacks on the union's critics. He died in office in 1981, a victim of lung cancer.

DAVID WITWER

References and Further Reading

Brill, Steven. *The Teamsters.* New York: Simon and Schuster, 1978.

See also **Hoffa, James R.; International Brotherhood of Teamsters**

FIVE-DOLLAR DAY

In a decisive series of industrial and technical innovations, Ford factory managers, engineers, and others developed sequential methods of mass production in the Highland Park Plant between 1910 and 1914. Then, in January 1914, Henry Ford astounded the nation when he announced that the Ford Motor Company would pay its workers the then unheard-of sum of $5.00 a day, about double the existing rate for factory work. *The Wall Street Journal* proclaimed that Ford was a "traitor to the capitalist class," since his announcement would destroy prevailing wage rates. The Socialist *Milwaukee Leader* praised Ford for the "large melon" that he offered to American workers. Workers from around the nation swarmed into Detroit in an effort to obtain the Ford jobs with the big wages. On a freezing January day, Ford officials turned fire hoses on workers who massed at the factory gates and who sought the Ford jobs that paid the big money.

The famous Five-Dollar Day was much more complicated than simply a generous increase in the wages of Ford automobile workers. It was a grand experiment in welfare capitalism rooted in the transformation of production and intended to fashion the new worker for progressive or line production in the mechanized Ford plant. It arose from Henry Ford's desire to produce the extremely popular "motorcar for the great multitude," from the modern production methods to satisfy the huge demand for the Model T Ford, and from the need to instill the necessary work and industrial discipline in the habits and culture of a largely unskilled immigrant workforce.

In the recently mechanized Ford plant, mass production truly revolutionized the nature of factory work and the social composition of the workforce. The most salient feature of the Fordist work regime was the drastic removal of skill in factory work. At their machines and on the assembly lines, work became simplified, routinized, and monotonous. Far fewer skilled and semiskilled workers were required for the actual production of automobiles. Large numbers of unskilled Southern and Eastern immigrants replaced the more skilled Northern European and American-born workers. But this new immigrant workforce, a majority from pre-industrial parts of Europe, did not have the industrial skills and work discipline for modern factory work.

As mass production unfolded, absenteeism and labor turnover soared in the newly constructed Highland Park Plant. By 1913, absenteeism averaged 10% of the workforce through the week; turnover reached an astonishing 360%. In other words, an average of 1,500 extra workers needed to be hired each day to work at machines and to maintain production. Or each year, Ford personnel managers needed to hire around 54,000 workers to ensure a workforce of 15,000. In many ways, Ford workers expressed their widespread dissatisfaction with tedious and repetitive jobs at machines and on assembly lines. In addition to high rates of absenteeism and turnover, they soldiered and malingered, restricted output, and began expressing an interest in various forms of unionism. Ford officials sorely needed some mechanism to stabilize, regularize, and reward its largely immigrant labor force.

Consequently, Ford and his factory managers instituted the now famous Five-Dollar Day. This was not a wage increase but rather a sophisticated profit-sharing scheme to reshape the habits and culture of a largely immigrant workforce. Under this unique scheme, a worker's daily compensation was divided into two parts—wages (approximately $2.40 for an unskilled worker) and profits (about $2.60). All workers received their wages for the tasks that they performed in the mechanically and organizationally controlled work environment of the Highland Park Plant. In order to receive their profits, they needed to prove their "worthiness" and demonstrate what Ford officials labeled "right living." Developed in the Progressive Era, when social reformers believed that a good environment produced good people, Ford and his associates felt that a good home created good habits, which in turn generated good workers.

To implement this innovative program, Ford officials created the Sociological Department (later called the Educational Department) to ensure that Ford workers were worthy and lived according to the appropriate Ford standards. Almost immediately after the Five-Dollar Day's announcement, Ford officials established a staff of more than 100 investigators to examine a Ford worker's production figures, to investigate a worker's home conditions and habits, and to assess whether or not the worker merited Ford profits. Embedded in the Sociological Department standards were distinct American and lower-middle-class values. The Ford investigators approved profits for hard workers who lived with their families in neat and clean homes and who neither stayed out late, drank alcohol, nor smoked. If a worker did not meet these criteria, the investigator typically allowed six months for the reform of living conditions and work habits or recommended dismissal. For approved workers, the investigators conducted follow-up visits to ensure that they did not become backsliders.

As part of the acculturation to modern factory work, Ford officials also established the Ford English School for non-English-speaking workers. Meeting after work hours, foremen instructed laborers in the rudiments of the English language, the proper industrial habits and work discipline, and the skills needed in a modern industrial society. In addition to procuring the advice of investigators and establishing English School instructors, Ford labor managers produced lavishly illustrated pamphlets and brochures that provided detailed information on how best to satisfy the Ford requirements and to receive the Five-Dollar Day.

Over the short term, the Five-Dollar Day was enormously successful. Workers simply accepted the trade-off of high wages for boring and degraded work. The technical advantage of progressive production allowed Ford to pay the high level of compensation. Absenteeism and labor turnover fell to more reasonable and manageable levels. Those workers who resented the encroachment into their personal lives moved on to other less-intrusive firms. With the high "wage," Ford was able to select and to skim off the cream of the Detroit workforce to work in the Highland Park Plant.

But over the long term, other Detroit automobile firms soon adopted the Ford technical innovations and also increased their workers' pay. In the same time, wartime inflation eroded the incentive to change worker attitudes and values. At the end of the First World War, a Ten-Dollar Day would be needed to provide the same financial incentive. Moreover, against the background of postwar labor activism, Ford labor policies became more brutal in the wake of the antiunion offensive known as the American Plan. By the 1920s, the Sociological or Educational Department transmuted into Harry Bennett's notorious Service Department, which took the lead in Ford labor relations and which created a harsh regime of factory spies and shop-floor thugs to monitor and discipline underperforming and dissident Ford workers.

STEVEN MEYER

References and Further Reading

May, Martha. "The Historical Problem of the Family Wage: The Ford Motor Company and the Five Dollar Day." *Feminist Studies* 8 (1982): 399–424.

Meyer, Stephen. *The Five Dollar Day: Labor Management and Social Control in the Ford Motor Company, 1908–1921.* Albany, NY: SUNY Press, 1981.

FLETCHER, BENJAMIN HARRISON (1890–1949)
Industrial Workers of the World

Benjamin Harrison Fletcher was an important African-American labor activist in the most influential radical union of the early twentieth century, when few blacks were permitted in unions and fewer still belonged to left-wing organizations. Fletcher helped lead the largest, most powerful, and longest-lasting interracial union of the era, Local 8, which was Philadelphia's longshore union belonging to the Industrial Workers of the World (IWW), nicknamed the Wobblies.

Fletcher began his career in the IWW as a young man. Born in Philadelphia in 1890, Fletcher seemed a typical young black man, working as a day laborer and longshoreman. One of the better jobs a black man could find in early twentieth-century Philadelphia was longshoring, which involved the loading and unloading of ships. Around 1912, he joined the IWW and the Socialist Party. It is not known how he became radicalized; presumably, he heard Wobbly soapbox speakers address working-class audiences in his riverside neighborhood. Fletcher became a local activist, beginning a long career in public speaking that won him many accolades for his fine voice and incisive arguments for overthrowing capitalism, the goal of both Wobblies and Socialists.

Fletcher was the most prominent member of Local 8. In May 1913, thousands of longshoremen struck for better wages and union recognition: their new union, the IWW; their best-known leader, Fletcher. Local 8 and Fletcher seemed to prove one of the Wobblies' central tenets: race was used to divide workers who shared a more important identity, that of class. While this notion is hotly debated, Local 8 undeniably proved that interracial unionism was possible, and arguably essential, to working-class might.

However, that power did not last, and Fletcher, again, proved central. As America formally entered World War I, Philadelphia became one of the nation's most important ports. Though they engaged in but a single work stoppage (Local 8's birth was celebrated annually with a one-day strike), the government targeted Local 8's leaders in its national raids on the IWW. Fletcher was the only African-American among the hundred Wobblies tried for treason in 1918. Though no evidence ever was provided against Fletcher, Local 8, or even the IWW (most "evidence" was statements of the IWW's anticapitalist beliefs, not any planned actions to interrupt the war effort), all of the defendants were found guilty. Fletcher's punishment was 10 years in the federal penitentiary in Leavenworth, Kansas, and an astronomical $30,000 fine. As the sentences were announced, the Wobbly leader William D. "Big Bill" Haywood reported, "Ben Fletcher sidled over to me and said: 'The Judge has been using very ungrammatical language.' I looked at his smiling black face and asked: 'How's that, Ben?' He said: 'His sentences are much too long.'" Fletcher's release became a celebrated cause among black radicals, championed by *The Messenger*, a monthly coedited by A. Philip Randolph. Fletcher served around three years, pardoned along with most other Wobblies in 1922.

After his release, Fletcher remained committed to IWW precepts, though he never played as active a role, especially after Local 8 collapsed amid a brutal lockout in late 1922. Fletcher briefly organized the Philadelphia Longshoremen's Union but rejoined the IWW by 1925, though Local 8 never resumed its former influence. He occasionally gave speeches, on tours and street corners, into the 1930s. Fletcher's health failed while he was still young, typical for longshoremen, and he suffered a stroke in his 40s. In the 1930s, he rolled cigars, moved to New York with his wife, and managed a small apartment building owned by a fellow old-time Wobbly, before dying in 1949.

Fletcher was unique as a black leader in the IWW. The union that he helped lead for a decade, Local 8, stands at the pinnacle of interracial equality in the Progressive Era. Widely acclaimed while alive, he is now largely forgotten, although his legacy of working-class power and racial equality lives on.

PETER COLE

References and Further Reading

Cole, Peter. *Black Wobbly: The Life and Writings of Ben Fletcher*. Chicago: Charles H. Kerr, forthcoming.
———. *Wobblies on the Waterfront: Interracial Unionism and the IWW in Progressive Era Philadelphia*. Urbana: University of Illinois Press, forthcoming.
Kimeldorf, Howard. *Battling for American Labor: Wobblies, Craft Workers, and the Making of the Union Movement*. Berkeley: University of California Press, 1999.
Seraile, William. "Ben Fletcher, I.W.W. Organizer." *Pennsylvania History* 46 (1979): 213–232.

See also **Haywood, William D. "Big Bill"; Industrial Workers of the World**

FLYNN, ELIZABETH GURLEY (1890–1964)
Industrial Workers of the World, Communist Party of the United States

Elizabeth Gurley Flynn, nicknamed the "Rebel Girl," remains one of the premier female radicals in U.S. history. An activist while still a teenager (hence her nom de plume), Flynn remained committed to the Left for 60 years. As a leader of both the Industrial Workers of the World (IWW) and the Communist Party of the United States of America (CPUSA), Flynn deserves the attention she has received.

Born into an Irish-American family, Flynn learned her politics and activism from her parents, both of whom were socialists. Flynn's father also was involved in the struggle for Irish independence, and thus steeped his daughter in a transatlantic world of resistance. Not surprisingly, Flynn became a socialist. Famously, Flynn gave her first public speech, titled "Women under Socialism," at 15.

Shortly thereafter, Flynn joined and became a leader of the soon-legendary IWW, often called the Wobblies. Like many of her time, she felt that the Wobblies were the leading organization in an era of revolutionary change that soon would occur. She became a much-sought-after public speaker, traveling nationwide to spread the IWW gospel of industrial unionism, direct action tactics, and socialism. She spoke in countless towns to untold numbers of workers, often the only woman present. Flynn took part in many a strike but none more famous than the 1912 Lawrence, Massachusetts, "Bread and Roses" affair. After the first Wobbly leaders were arrested on false murder charges, Flynn and "Big Bill" Haywood took the reins, leading 25,000 textile workers, mostly immigrant women, to a stunning victory. Flynn helped a young Margaret Sanger to organize the much-publicized "Children's Crusade," which sent children of strikers to sympathetic families across the Northeast. After she visited with him in his Utah jail cell, where he sat on a still-controversial murder conviction, Joe Hill, the famous bard of the IWW, wrote a song about Flynn called "The Rebel Girl."

Flynn was the author of the controversial pamphlet "Sabotage," written in 1913 during a Paterson, New Jersey, silk strike. The use of the term "sabotage" typically is presumed to suggest violence, but Wobblies took it to mean slowing down on the job, in order to pressure employers to concede demands by hitting them in the pocketbook. In that pamphlet's preamble, Flynn wrote, "Sabotage is to this class struggle what the guerrilla warfare is to the battle. The strike is the open battle of the class struggle, sabotage is the guerrilla warfare, the day-by-day warfare between two opposing classes."

When World War I erupted, most Wobblies took an antiwar stand, though the organization as a whole did not; yet despite this official nonposition, the IWW—Flynn included—came under government attack. When 166 leaders of the IWW were arrested nationwide, Flynn was the only female in the bunch. Due to her prominence, Flynn had more options (read: wealthy supporters) than most of the accused. She split with the other defendants, believing that the only way to get a fair trial was to have individual

Elizabeth Gurley Flynn, Dr. Mary Engi(?), R. Marsh(?), and Helen Schuster walking side by side on sidewalk. Library of Congress, Prints & Photographs Division [LC-USZ62-55896].

ones; by contrast, most stood together *en masse* in a single trial of 100 defendants. Flynn was found innocent, while the entire large group was found guilty. In the process, Flynn incurred the wrath of many fellow Wobblies.

Just as she was active in IWW free speech fights in the 1910s, Flynn was at the forefront of the international cause célèbre of the 1920s, the fight to save Sacco and Venzetti, two Italian-born anarchists sentenced to die by the state of Massachusetts. Along with many other leftists, anarchists, and civil libertarians, Flynn championed their case until they were executed in 1927.

In 1937, Flynn joined the CPUSA, which was at the height of its influence in U.S. history. She quickly took charge of the Women's Commission for the next decade. She ran for U.S. Congress, as a Communist, in 1942, and won 50,000 votes, championing the most oppressed Americans, whom she identified at that time to be African-American women. Flynn was one of the leaders of the CPUSA and recognized as the premier woman in it.

During the high point of domestic anticommunism during the early years of the Cold War, many Communists were imprisoned, and Flynn led the fight for their release. Flynn herself was arrested under the Smith Act in 1951, and then ran for Congress again, this time from a jail cell. Her campaign slogan was, "Vote No! to McCarthyism. For Peace and Jobs! Amnesty for all." Flynn served three years in the Alderson Women's Federal Prison in West Virginia.

Later in life, at the age of 65, Flynn wrote her autobiography, *I Speak My Own Piece*, now seen as a masterpiece among those interested in women of the Left.

She continued to suffer from persecution because of her political affiliations. In 1961, she was elected chairperson of the CPUSA. In January 1962, the State Department revoked Flynn's passport, as well as several other Communists'. Flynn protested that denying citizens the ability to leave the country freely because of their political beliefs was unconstitutional. The Supreme Court ruled in Flynn's favor in 1964. Subsequently, Flynn returned to the Soviet Union, where she died. The Soviet Union held an official state funeral for her. Communists from across the world mourned her passing.

Though she became gray-haired and a Communist, many considered her the "rebel girl" of Joe Hill's song and a Wobbly. As the *New York Times* reported in its front-page obituary, Flynn remained true to her beliefs to the end: still dreaming of a socialist America and world. For more than 50 years, Flynn worked with most of the leading, radical lights of the American labor movement: "Big Bill" Haywood, Gene Debs, Mother Jones, Joe Hill, Frank Little, Earl Browder, and many more. As with the remains of the Haymarket martyrs and her fellow Wobbly-turned-Communist Haywood, Flynn's remains are buried at Chicago's famous Waldheim Cemetery.

PETER COLE

References and Further Reading

Camp, Helen C. *Iron in Her Soul: Elizabeth Gurley Flynn and the American Left*. Pullman: Washington State University Press, 1995.

Dubofsky, Melvyn. *We Shall Be All: A History of the Industrial Workers of the World*. 2nd ed. Urbana: University of Illinois Press, 1988.

Flynn, Elizabeth Gurley. *The Rebel Girl: An Autobiography, My First Life (1906–1926)*. New York: International Publishers, 1973. http://www.pbs.org/joehill/faces/Flynn.html.

FONER, MOE (AUGUST 3, 1915– JANUARY 10, 2002)
1199/SEIU, New York's Health and Human Service Union

Moe Foner was 1199/Service Employees International Union (SEIU), New York's Health and Human Service Union's longtime executive secretary and campaign strategist, whose public relations efforts helped establish 1199 as the nation's first union for employees in private, nonprofit hospitals.

Born in Williamsburg, Brooklyn, the son of Russian and Polish immigrants, Foner was the third of four boys. His older brothers, the twins Jack and Phil, became well known as college teachers and as authors of numerous publications on American labor and black history. His younger sibling, Henry, was president of the Fur and Leather Workers Union in New York.

Joining and then also managing his brothers' band in his teen years, Foner discovered both radical politics and an ability to orchestrate diverse talents. Moe attended Brooklyn College, where, in 1934, he joined the Young Communist League. After graduating, he worked in the registrar's office at City College of New York (CCNY). In 1941, Moe and Phil, along with some 50 other CCNY employees, were fired as a result of investigations by the Rapp-Courdert committee, which had been created by the New York State legislature to purge alleged Communists from the government.

Foner married Anne Berman in 1941. He was drafted into the army during World War II and served as a commissary clerk on Governor's Island, New York. After the war, as the education director for Department Store Local 1250, Foner staged *Thursdays 'Til Nine*, a musical review based on the job experiences of store workers, some of whom also performed in the show. For Foner, union-produced cultural programs were neither "fluff" nor a diversion from labor's bread-and-butter concerns. Such events served as a vital link, beyond dues paying and contract gains, between the union and its members.

In 1950, Local 1250 was absorbed into District 65, Wholesale and Warehouse Workers Union. An intense internal struggle developed within 65 over the Taft-Hartley Act's requirement that labor officers sign non-Communist affidavits. Foner, caught in the middle of the dispute, left in 1952 to join the staff of Local 1199, Retail Drug Employees Union, as activities director and editor of *1199 News*. In the late 1950s, Leon Davis, president of 1199, recruited Elliot Godoff, a pharmacist and skilled organizer, to launch a union campaign among workers in New York City's voluntary, not-for-profit hospitals. Foner's effective marshaling of support from prominent public figures like Eleanor Roosevelt and his ability to enlist hardbitten news reporters to cover the strike were critical to the success of the union's first major effort, at Montefiore Hospital in the Bronx, New York. For his efforts as a labor publicist in this campaign, Foner received the Silver Anvil Award from the American Public Relations Association.

Firmly entrenched in New York City, 1199 secured a breakthrough contract in 1968 establishing a $100-per-week minimum salary for its members. The following year, attempting to build on its success in the New York metropolitan area, the union launched a "union power, soul power" national campaign in Charleston, South Carolina. Four years later, after successful efforts in Philadelphia and defeats in some other cities, 1199 established itself as the National Union of Hospital and Health Care Employees. In each of these union drives, Foner orchestrated public support of 1199 from civil rights leaders such as Dr. Martin Luther King (who described 1199 as "my favorite union"), Bayard Rustin, and A. Philip Randolph, and from labor movement leaders such as Harry Van Arsdale, president of the Central Labor Council, and Walter Reuther, president of the United Auto Workers.

With Davis's health deteriorating, issues of succession and merger dominated 1199 in the 1980s, leading to an internal rift in 1982 between the New York metropolitan area local and the national union. Under the leadership of Dennis Rivera, who became president of the New York union in 1989, 1199 was reunited. Then, in 1998, the long-sought merger of health care unions was accomplished as 1199: National Union of Health and Human Service Employees Union, SEIU, AFL-CIO.

Foner retired as 1199's executive secretary in November 1982 during the civil war that rent the union. Nevertheless, working under the banner of "Bread and Roses," he continued to produce theater projects, art and photography exhibits, concerts, lectures, and other cultural programs for 1199. One of his last projects before his death, "Unseen America," distributed cameras to working people and to the homeless and then enabled them to exhibit their photographs in 1199's gallery. In Bread and Roses, as in his lifelong commitment to the labor movement, Foner held to a vision of creating a fairer, more humane world. Foner passed away at age 86 on January 10, 2002.

BRIAN GREENBERG

References and Further Reading

Fink, Leon, and Brian Greenberg. *Upheaval in the Quiet Zone: A History of Hospital Workers' Union, Local 1199.* Urbana: University of Illinois Press, 1989.

Foner, Moe, Dan North, and Ossie Davis. *Not for Bread Alone: A Memoir.* Ithaca, NY: Cornell University Press, 2002.

FOOD, TOBACCO, AGRICULTURAL, AND ALLIED WORKERS OF AMERICA
See **United Cannery, Agricultural, Packing, and Allied Workers of America**

FOOD PROCESSING

Of all industrial products, processed food is unusually ubiquitous. American consumers encounter it repeatedly each day. In fact, few commercially available foods are truly unprocessed. Even the freshest produce is extensively manipulated before it finds its way onto supermarket shelves. But unlike most industrial products, food also makes up and becomes part of what we are. On the one hand, its prevalence makes processed food easy to take for granted. On the other hand, our close relationship with it makes understanding the history of processing and the workers who manufacture the food we eat especially important.

Like the varieties of food available, the industry's activities are diverse, ranging from fresh produce packing to engineering food-related chemicals, with much in between. Each of these sectors has its own labor history, and as a result, overarching generalizations about food-processing work must be qualified. However, several trends have helped shape the experience of food workers in the United States since colonial times. First, processing has transformed from a geographically distributed sector composed primarily of small- to medium-scale firms into one that is both geographically and industrially concentrated. Second, a sector that was once very skilled has become predominantly unskilled. Deskilling throughout the

industry—through the combined effects of mechanization and increasingly minute divisions of labor—has led to a mounting lack of political leverage for food workers. But while some aspects of processing have become almost completely automated, others have proven nearly impossible to mechanize entirely, resulting in a continuous need for unskilled workers. Third, the industry has historically fulfilled its labor needs by hiring new immigrants from Europe, Asia, and Latin America, African-Americans, and female workers. Fourth, the industrialization of processing work has often been facilitated by the support of the state.

From Colonial America to the Civil War

Processing played an important role in the colonial and early American economies. Preserved cod—split, salted, and packed in barrels—was one of the most prolific and profitable colonial exports. Baking, brewing, and cheese making were small-scale, geographically dispersed, skilled operations. Although processed, these foods were highly perishable, forcing processors to locate near raw materials and markets. For these same reasons, slaughterhouses were built close to centers of consumption. Live animals were herded to slaughterhouses, where skilled groups of workers killed and prepared carcasses for shipment. Retail butchers then carved these into cuts of meat.

Food processors began to mechanize operations at an early date. In the 1780s, Oliver Evans patented a partially automated flour mill, which used a water wheel to power conveyors, a grindstone, and a mechanical sifter that separated kernels from flour. Evans marketed his design by emphasizing that it produced more, higher-quality flour than traditional mills, yet it required only half the workers. Reducing labor led to significant cost savings for mill owners, and it decreased their vulnerability to worker control.

A growing network of navigable waterways aided the food industry's westward expansion. Grain and livestock, especially, were produced in increasing quantities in the West and shipped to eastern markets. One of the first western meat centers, Cincinnati, shipped livestock and preserved pork to eastern packinghouses and butchers via the Ohio and Mississippi rivers and New Orleans. These meatpackers began applying assembly line-style divisions of labor to the disassembly of animals during the 1830s, significantly changing the experience of packinghouse work. Workers led livestock up ramps to the top floor of multistoried packinghouses, where animals were slaughtered. Carcasses were then attached to hooks hanging from overhead rails, and gravity moved them from floor to floor, where other workers performed specific cuts on the passing carcasses. In this fashion, by the 1840s, 20 workmen could incrementally disassemble 77 hogs an hour.

Civil War and Nineteenth-Century Expansion

While the Civil War devastated the southern economy, northeastern and western food processors thrived. The army purchased vast amounts of food: Union soldiers consumed some 500 million pounds of meat and ate enormous amounts of canned food, such as condensed milk and pork and beans. Wartime demand, in fact, was instrumental in establishing canning as a major food industry, the output of which doubled each decade between 1890 and 1960 (with the exception of the 1930s). Early canneries were for the most part coastal, labor-intensive, small- to medium-scale operations. Some steps in the canning processes, particularly hand-soldering tins and cooking, required significant skill. At the same time, many jobs, such as sorting and slicing produce or scaling salmon, required only minimal training. Cannery owners staffed these jobs with unskilled, seasonal workers who could be hired and fired as business waxed and waned.

The division of skilled and unskilled cannery work was racialized and gendered. In the mid-1800s, white, male workers occupied most skilled positions, while immigrant workers performed unskilled tasks. In California and along the West Coast, Chinese barred from gold prospecting did the bulk of the unskilled work; however, with the Chinese exclusion legislation beginning in the 1880s, the Chinese population began to decline. From 60% of the cannery workforce in 1870, Chinese workers accounted for only 4% by the end of the first decade of the twentieth century. Cannery owners replaced Chinese workers with female workers, who they assumed would accept low wages and seasonal employment, and would be unlikely to organize. By 1900, there were approximately 16,000 female cannery workers in California, nearly all of whom were paid less than their male coworkers and were assigned to unskilled jobs. Even so, many saw cannery work as a step up from domestic employment.

The potential for worker control in nineteenth-century canneries was high, and skilled workers in particular exercised significant autonomy over their daily lives. In part as an effort to gain more control over the manufacturing process, owners installed mechanical processing machines. The machines eliminated both skilled and unskilled jobs, smoothed seasonal labor cycles, and increased production speeds.

In addition, machines could also help achieve racial goals. The inventors of a machine called the "Iron Chink," which could eviscerate 43 salmon a minute, boasted that each one could replace more than 10 skilled Chinese workers. Realizing the effects of mechanization, workers strenuously, sometimes violently, resisted. In one cannery, a guard brandished a gun while a machine was installed.

Produce canneries were supplied by growers who themselves sometimes seemed more like manufacturers than farmers. In the late 1800s, Atlantic Coast market gardeners used hothouses, sophisticated botanical knowledge, and efficient transportation systems to distribute their perishable products. California growers of fruits and vegetables soon joined these eastern growers. In 1887, the first ice-cool railcar filled with oranges departed from California toward eastern markets, and before the year was out, one million boxes had followed. By the turn of the century, southern California produced 77% of the United States' oranges and 90% of its lemons. Heavily capitalized, these growers employed migrant Asian-American and later Mexican-American workers, relied heavily on transportation, and utilized sophisticated production technologies and marketing techniques.

Civil War demands and an increasingly extensive rail network pushed Chicago to the forefront of meatpacking, and by 1900, fewer than half a dozen Chicago meatpackers controlled 90% of the American red meat market. Prior to the 1850s, Chicago meatpackers (like their Cincinnati competitors) mostly shipped live animals and whole carcasses to eastern slaughterhouses. However, with the development of ice-cooled storage and railcars in the 1860s, Chicago packers began to ship "dressed" cuts of meat. In the years between their opening in 1865 and the turn of the century, the yards processed 400 million cows, pigs, and sheep. By 1900, the yards had a daily processing capacity of 455,000 animals. Meatpackers became the city's largest employer, with approximately 25,300 laborers in 1899.

Chicago meatpackers deployed the assembly line on an unprecedented scale. Steam power carried carcasses suspended from overhead rails throughout the packinghouse, and networks of pipes transported animal bits from one part of the factory to another. But meat processing proved difficult to mechanize completely, prompting managers to rely on a minute division of labor. The result was a mechanized yet labor-intensive manufacturing process, in which a single animal would pass in front of more than 150 workers before exiting the factory. The division of labor shifted the composition of the workforce toward unskilled workers, a change that increased line speeds and reduced worker autonomy.

Workers in the Chicago packinghouses in the late 1800s were a mix of European immigrants. Established Germans and Irish held the more skilled jobs, while more recent Central and Northern Europeans held unskilled positions. As the century drew to a close, female workers, mostly in their 20s, worked in increasing numbers in packinghouses. For the most part, they were confined to the least-desirable and lowest-paying jobs in packinghouse canneries and by-product processing. Wages were low: in 1900, average wages were 15 cents an hour, and by World War I, they had increased only a cent and a half.

Packinghouse workers labored and lived in what can only be described as shocking conditions, and attempts to organize in response began in the 1880s. Early strikes in the 1890s, however, were unsuccessful and sometimes violently put down. In 1904, the Amalgamated Meat Cutters and Butcher Workmen (Amalgamated) called its first strike, with demands for improved wages. In response, managers hired African-American strikebreakers. In 1906, Upton Sinclair published his famous muckraking novel, *The Jungle*, based on his experiences living with Union Stockyard workers. A call for organization, Sinclair's book described a world that was smelly, loud, backbreaking, and unsanitary.

Wars and Depressions

Fueled by military food purchases, the processing industry grew during World War I. Working conditions and wages began to improve, while the war also provided opportunities for unions. By 1918, the Amalgamated increased its roster from a low of only 2,000 in 1904 to 28,000. During the 1920s, the food industry concentrated significantly. Large companies dominated nearly all sectors of the industry, from meat to canned and frozen produce, from dairy to baking.

Building on methods for producing and marketing frozen and refrigerated food that had existed since the late nineteenth century, Clarence Birdseye and General Foods began developing an improved method for industrial freezing in the 1920s. Contrary to advertisements that portrayed frozen food as a revolutionary product, links to existing truck farms, canneries, and meatpackers were strong. Early production of frozen food concentrated in the Mid-Atlantic states, most notably in New Jersey, a state that had established itself as a source of fresh and canned produce. Frozen food manufacturing maintained many of the labor relations familiar to the canning and packing activities it supplemented. Introduced at the onset of the

Great Depression, frozen food was slow to take off. In fact, one of the first commercially successful frozen products was concentrated orange juice, invented in 1945. Designed by government researchers as a way to supply troops with vitamin C, frozen concentrated orange juice became an incredibly popular consumer item. For orange growers in Florida and California, concentrated juice provided a way to process surplus harvests into a profitable product.

Canning remained a hazardous, monotonous, and often unsanitary occupation during and after World War I. Gendered and racial divisions of labor persisted, an arrangement that management believed would reduce worker solidarity. Male workers continued to hold permanent, skilled positions, while female workers held seasonal, unskilled ones. In California—which between 1939 and 1950 produced more canned fruits and vegetables than any other state—the number of female cannery workers steadily increased, as did their percentage in the workforce. From 16,000 in 1900, by 1939 there were 75,000; by 1945, 75% of the California cannery workforce were female. The ethnic composition of cannery workers began to change dramatically as well. In 1928, Los Angeles County boasted the highest percentage of Mexican-American cannery workers, at 23.5% of the workforce. By 1975, the California canning industry tallied that upwards of 70% of its workers had Spanish surnames.

During the Great Depression, both the production of processed food and wages for food workers declined. From the perspective of these workers, the government's response was decidedly mixed. While the National Industrial Recovery Act guaranteed collective bargaining rights for most manufacturing workers, it only covered some food-processing workers. At issue was whether these workers were manufacturing or farm laborers (the latter were not covered by the Act). The government adopted a geographic solution to this problem. Processing on the farm was considered agriculture; processing in another place was manufacturing. In practice, this meant that two workers who did the same kind of work might have different labor rights, depending on *where* they worked. The Wagner Act, on the other hand, adopted a definition based on practice. All workers who manufactured food (as opposed to grew and harvested it) could organize. The Wagner Act was a boost for food unions. By the time the United States entered World War II, the Packinghouse Workers Organizing Committed (later the United Packinghouse Workers of America, UPWA) claimed 80,000 members, and Amalgamated 100,000. Similarly, the United Cannery, Agricultural, Packing, and Allied Workers of America made significant gains in organizing women and Mexican-American cannery workers.

As in previous wars, processed food was essential to the defense effort, and World War II pulled the industry from depression. Through the Lend-Lease program, the government purchased vast amounts of processed food to send to Europe. The deployment of American soldiers only compounded demand for specially produced rations, canned food, and meat. Conditions for food workers improved through the course of the war for two main reasons. First, processing was regulated by the National War Labor Board, which enforced a set of minimum labor standards. Second, the war precipitated an industrywide labor shortage. Many male workers were conscripted, while other workers were drawn into different industries. For those who remained, processing wages rose (although they remained lower than other war industries). Doors opened for female workers, who for the first time moved into the skilled and managerial posts previously unavailable to them. At the same time, labor shortages encouraged processors to further mechanize their operations, leading to an overall decrease in their reliance on labor.

Even so, the decades immediately following World War II were a rare period of success for processing unions. Meatpacking workers enjoyed wage parity with other industrial workers for the first time. Even as intense competition raged between rival unions—sometimes prompting red-baiting and illegal agreements between organizers and processors—membership increased dramatically. Unions themselves began embracing African-American and female workers, who historically had been treated as a threat to white, male employment.

Food Technology and Factory Labor

The prevalence of deskilling in food manufacturing was in many ways made possible by the industry's increasing reliance on highly skilled engineers who called themselves "food technologists." Since the turn of the century, these researchers played a central role in developing new sorts of food products and the technologies of industrial food manufacturing. Their role in the industry only grew in the decades following World War I. In university departments of food technology and processors' own industrial laboratories, researchers invented machines, engineered the texture of food, and developed chemical preservatives and flavors.

In many cases, this work was supported by the state through land grant universities, extension stations,

and military funding. In 1972, Jim Hightower and the Agribusiness Accountability Project published *Hard Tomatoes, Hard Times*, a report that criticized public institutions for conducting research and development for the food industry. His report contended that tax-funded research was benefiting large processors to the detriment of workers, consumers, and small businesses. Hightower went so far as to claim that improving food was not the driving motivation behind technological development in the industry. Rather, "The major impetus for food engineering has come from the desire to eliminate labor by mechanizing the harvesting and processing phases of agriculture."

The title of Hightower's report referred to mechanical tomato harvesters and a specially bred thick-skinned tomato that could withstand automated packing and long-distance shipping. The two interrelated technologies were developed in tandem by the University of California and became the subject of a contentious lawsuit over the proper relationship between the state and the agriculture and food industries. Indeed, the debut of this expensive system in the 1960s had striking results. Many small tomato producers could not afford the new technology, and within a few years, 85% were driven out of business, while thousands of migrant fieldworkers saw their jobs eliminated at the same time. Large producers who could afford to purchase the system grew larger.

This case was hardly an isolated one. In dairy processing and cheese making, new machines, processes, and chemicals led to nearly complete automation. For those businesses that could not obtain the credit necessary to finance new technology, the outlook was not good. By 1974, 85% of the dairy processors in business 24 years earlier had closed. A similar situation faced canneries, one quarter of which shut their doors between 1947 and 1954. Other production processes like dehydrating and baking were also extensively automated, while the transfer of more and more processing—for instance, skilled butchering—out of retail markets and into factories affected the daily experience of retail workers.

Hightower's report emphasized the fact that the interrelated processes of mechanization and deskilling were not inevitable or automatic. Widening profit margins and reducing labor requirements in factories required expensive and highly skilled work in the laboratory. While lowering their dependence on one kind of labor, processors were becoming dependent on another. Most important, the financial support provided by the state often masked the true expense of food technologists' work. But the impact on food manufacturing workers seemed clear: many lost their jobs, while those who remained became less and less skilled.

The Work of Food Preparation

The prevalence of processed food in the twentieth century affected the consumer as well. Because processed food could be stored for long periods and transported over large distances, seasonal and geographic variations in food consumption began to decline. Even as class-based differences in diet began to decline, this new diet was more expensive than the old. As Harvey Levenstein notes, even as the income of the average household rose in the 1940s and 1950s, so too did the percentage of its income spent on food—from 22% in 1941 to 26% in 1953. The rising cost of the American diet in the decades following World War II was attributable to increasing consumption of processed foods. In 1953 alone, Americans consumed 16 billion pounds of canned goods. Purchases of frozen foods totaled $2.7 billion in 1959, representing a 2,700% increase over 1949. Consumers were paying not only for the food itself, but also the technology that supported its production. Food processing altered the work of domestic food preparation. Processors claimed that their products dramatically reduced household labor. In a 1957 article titled "Kitchen Revolution," one advocate claimed that processed foods came with "built-in maid service." According to this vision, the tedium of preparation would be transferred from the home to the processing plant. No longer would housewives spend hours preparing dinner. Instead, frozen, precut, and precooked ingredients needed only to be heated and served. The reality, however, was not so simple. If processed food made any one job faster or simpler, it also contributed to rising expectations of what constituted a complete and proper meal. Encouraging this trend, processors published cookbooks—perhaps the most famous of which were authored by the fictional Betty Crocker—with instructions on incorporating new food products into ever more complicated and labor-intensive menus.

Processed food also had a major impact on work in commercial food preparation. Its influences are perhaps most clearly seen in the fast-food industry. Fast food as we recognize it today began in the 1940s in southern California, where companies like McDonald's began as small, family-owned restaurants. These self-service restaurants relied on high volumes of sales from simple menus, a strategy that kept the costs of ingredients low. Fast food caught on, and it quickly became a national business, and then an international business. In 1970, Americans spent $6 billion dollars on it. In 2001, McDonald's was the largest purchaser of beef and potatoes in the United States (and the second largest customer for chicken), and Americans spent $110 billion on fast food.

From its infancy, the fast-food industry has been an avid customer and developer of food technologies like those discussed in the previous section. In 1948, for example, the founders of McDonald's developed the "Speedee Service System." Its purpose was not simply to offer quick service for customers, but also to reduce labor costs for the owner. The system divided the process of preparation into a set of discrete, assembly line-like steps, each of which was performed repeatedly by unskilled workers. The concepts underpinning the system are now commonplace in the fast-food industry. Technologies like computerized ovens with conveyor belts automate preparation. In addition, fast-food companies rely heavily on processing companies for pre-prepared foods, such as precut French fries, seasoned and breaded chicken, shredded lettuce, and shaped burgers. Rarely are these items prepared from scratch within a restaurant itself, further reducing the necessary skill level of workers.

In a highly capitalized industry like fast food, the cost of labor is one of the few variables over which restaurant franchisees have control. While there are certainly exceptions, the industry often keeps labor costs low by hiring young people on a part-time basis. For many of these young people, fast-food work is not a final goal, and many leave after a short time, resulting in a high industrywide turnover rate. For others, however, fast food is one of but a few options. For recent or undocumented immigrants, fast-food work can be relatively easy to obtain. For all workers, long hours are common. Compensation for this repetitive work is low, and in 1990, the 3.5 million fast-food workers represented America's largest minimum wage workers group.

Many obstacles to organization exist. Unionization is often not a priority for young workers, who view the job as temporary. At the same time, the fast-food industry takes advantage of high employee turnover rates. In some cases, fast-food companies have delayed union votes for so long that the organizing workers have simply left to find other work. Moreover, the industry's low skill requirements make organizing workers easy to replace.

The "IBP Revolution"

The decade and a half of union success in the meatpacking industry following World War II began to wane in 1960, when a new company opened its first packinghouse in Iowa. With a plan to take full advantage of nonunionized and highly mechanized production, IBP avoided urban union strongholds by opening its plants in rural areas with lower prevailing wages. Occasionally, it would shut down a unionized plant and re-open it with an unorganized workforce. The depressed economy of the 1980s facilitated IBP's successful transformation of the meatpacking sector. By 1989, IBP was the largest meatpacker in the world with approximately $6.8 billion in sales. Nine of its plants were nonunion, while only three were organized. By the late 1990s, the labor representation that remained was done by the United Food and Commercial Workers, which, while boasting a membership of one million in various food and retail sectors, had been forced to make regular concessions to IBP.

Working conditions in the post-"IBP revolution" period were harsh. Conveyors dictated the work pace more than ever before. Line speeds were high, and repetitive stress traumas, lacerations, and other injuries were all too commonplace. In 1985 alone, meatpacking had the highest worker-injury rate of any industry, with 30.4 injuries per 100 full-time workers—and this was an improvement. Wages fell below other manufacturing industries and to a fraction of what they were in unionized plants. Even though they composed a growing segment of the workforce, female, Mexican-American, African-American, and Asian-American workers were assigned to the worst jobs and were paid less than their white, male coworkers. Job security was nearly nonexistent, since unskilled workers in rural areas with high unemployment were easy to replace.

Poultry processing followed a similar path. Between the 1930s and 1960s, chicken processors began to vertically integrate feed production, chicken rearing, slaughtering, and processing. Consumption of chicken soared during World War II, since it was not rationed like other meats. Originally concentrated near eastern markets in the Delaware-Maryland-Virginia region, the postwar expansion of poultry processing was focused in the South, where lower prevailing wages made factories especially profitable. Attempts by the Amalgamated, UPWA, and the Teamsters to unionize poultry workers met with mixed success, but antiunion campaigns followed in the 1980s and 1990s. Today, a single plant can process 40,000 pounds of chicken a day, and a line worker might conduct the same operation on more than 40 chickens a minute.

Work in poultry factories has been highly gendered and racialized. While the sector historically employed more female workers than red meatpacking, women were in the minority. In the 1990s, approximately two thirds of poultry employees were male. Female workers were generally assigned to lower-paying disassembly line jobs, ostensibly because they were unsuited for jobs that require mechanical skills or heavy lifting. These line jobs have been among the most monotonous and prone to injuries. In 1997 alone, the Occupational Safety and Health Administration (OSHA) reported over three hundred instances of repetitive trauma at a single chicken processor. In 1999, Tyson was fined for violating child labor laws for employing two underage workers, both of whom were casualties of industrial accidents. What has changed significantly, however, is the ethnic composition of the workforce. As white workers left the South in increasing numbers during the last decades of the twentieth century, the poultry industry began employing Mexican and Latin American immigrants, many of whom were undocumented. Processors have been known to use the threat of deportation to force worker concessions.

Alternatives

In the 1970s, activists proposed an alternative to processed food. They conceived of organic food as a rethinking of production, processing, and consumption. By refraining from chemicals and processing and relying instead on small-scale, local production, organic was envisioned as being friendlier to the environment, workers, and consumers. Thirty-five years later, however, organic food has fallen short of its original goals. Nearly all of the large processing companies, using familiar labor strategies, have entered the organic market. The USDA definition of organic permits chemical flavorings and preservatives, making possible mechanically produced and highly processed, yet certified-organic, food.

A history of industrial concentration, worker disempowerment through intense deskilling, gendered and racialized divisions of labor, and state support for businesses over workers has helped to define the work experience in the industry over the past centuries. As attempts to create alternative foodways suggest, industrial food processing, and the labor relations and business organization it relies on, seem to have considerable momentum.

NICHOLAS BUCHANAN

References and Further Reading

Barrett, James R. *Work and Community in the Jungle: Chicago's Packinghouse Workers, 1894–1922.* Urbana: University of Illinois Press, 1987.
Cowan, Ruth Schwartz. *More Work for Mother: The Ironies of Household Technology from the Open Hearth to the Microwave.* New York: Basic Books, 1983.

DuPuis, E. Melanie. *Nature's Perfect Food: How Milk Became America's Drink*. New York: New York University Press, 2002.

Fink, Deborah. *Cutting into the Meatpacking Line: Workers and Change in the Rural Midwest*. Chapel Hill: University of North Carolina Press, 1998.

Friedland, William H., and Amy Barton. "Tomato Technology." *Society* 13, no. 6 (September/October 1975): 34–42.

Hahamovitch, Cindy. *The Fruits of Their Labor: Atlantic Coast Farmworkers and the Making of Migrant Poverty, 1870–1945*. Chapel Hill: University of North Carolina Press, 1997.

Hightower, Jim. *Hard Tomatoes, Hard Times: A Report of the Agribusiness Accountability Project on the Failure of America's Land Grant College Complex*. Cambridge, MA: Schenkman Publishing Co., 1973.

Levenstein, Harvey A. *Paradox of Plenty: A Social History of Eating in Modern America*. New York: Oxford University Press, 1993.

Perry, Charles R., and Delwyn H. Kegely. *Disintegration and Change: Labor Relations in the Meat Packing Industry*. Philadelphia: The Wharton School Industrial Research Unit, University of Pennsylvania, 1989.

Pollan, Michael. "Naturally." *New York Times Magazine*, 31 May 2001: 30–37, 57–58, 63–64.

Ruíz, Vicki. *Cannery Women, Cannery Lives: Mexican Women, Unionization, and the California Food-Processing Industry, 1930–1950*. Albuquerque: University of New Mexico Press, 1987.

Schlosser, Eric. *Fast Food Nation: The Dark Side of the All-American Meal*. Boston: Houghton Mifflin, 2001.

Sinclair, Upton. *The Jungle*. New York: Modern Library, 2002 [1906].

Striffler, Steve. *Chicken: The Dangerous Transformation of America's Favorite Food*. New Haven, CT: Yale University Press, 2005.

Wilde, Mark William. *Industrialization of Food-Processing in the United States, 1860–1960*. Ph.D. diss., University of Delaware, 1988.

See also **Amalgamated Meat Cutters and Butchers Workmen; Bakery and Confectionery Workers Union; Cannery and Agricultural Workers Industrial Union; Domestic Service; International Fishermen and Allied Workers of America; United Brewery Workers; United Cannery, Agricultural, Packing, and Allied Workers of America; United Food and Commercial Workers Union; United Packinghouse Workers of America/Packinghouse Workers Organizing Committee; Waitressing and Waiting/Food Service**

FOOD SERVICE
See **Waitressing and Waiting/Food Service**

FORD, HENRY
See **Assembly-Line Production; Five-Dollar Day**

FOREIGN MINERS TAX

In 1850, the California State Legislature passed the Foreign Miners Tax that would purge thousands of Latino and Chinese miners from the gold diggings. Under the legal doctrine of foreign trespass, all miners who were not citizens of the United States or who had not become citizens under the Treaty of Guadalupe Hidalgo would have to buy a miner's license for a monthly fee of $20 (about $400 in today's currency); the tax collector would receive $3, and the remaining money was split between the county and the state. While the law's professed goal was to raise $200,000 a month from Mexican and South American miners, the tax became a tactic in ethnic cleansing.

On Sunday, May 19, 1850, four thousand armed French, Mexican, and Peruvian miners seized control of the plaza in the California foothill town of Sonora and declared that they would never pay the tax (Holliday, p.173; Lang, pp.30–34). Facing them was a vigilante army of five hundred Anglo tax collectors and miners. When the mob fired on the Latinos, the Chilean and Mexican miners retreated from the diggings, on burro and on foot (Holliday, p. 172; Lang, pp. 30–34). In early June, another vigilante army of three hundred men marched into the Latino diggings in the mining town of Columbia to collect the first tax. But facing protests from Irish, English, Canadian, and German miners, the law was rewritten to exempt any "free white person" or any miner who could become an American citizen.

The tax launched a reign of terror, spurred on by "The Great Greaser Extermination Meeting" in Sonora that demanded that all Latino miners leave the goldfields in 48 hours. Assaults and lynchings followed. Ten thousand Mexican miners returned home. By 1860, four fifths of the Latino population had been driven out of the California mines.

Missing their customers, white merchants from across the Sierras petitioned Governor Peter Burnett to repeal the Foreign Miners Tax (Holliday, 173; Lang, 34, 44–45). While Burnett could dismiss protests by Mexican miners, he listened to the Tuolumne County real estate owners and merchants and had the tax repealed, just 11 months after its passage (Lang, p. 34, 44–45; see also Steven Lavoie, "Miss LIBERTY," in Holliday, p. 172). Years later, white miners still recalled "the long train of fugitives" leaving the gold diggings and returning home: "Some were going North; some South; the great body was probably bound for home; some by way of the sea; others by Los Angeles and the Great Desert" (Johnson, p. 215).

The Chinese were to follow. In 1852, the Chinese formed one tenth of the state's population and nearly one third of the mining population. By 1855, 175,000 miners from all over the world—tense, poor, and disappointed—were crowded along California's rivers, deltas, and beaches. That year the Foreign Miners Tax was reborn, with the express purpose of expelling the Chinese from California. The new tax forced each foreign miner to pay a fee of $3.00 per month for the right to mine; in 1853, it was raised to $4.00, and in 1855, to $6.00, with the provision that each successive year there would be a further $2.00 increase. No Chinese man was allowed to mine for gold until he paid the tax, one half of which went to the county treasury, and the rest to the State of California, with a fixed fee for the tax collector. In practice, the tax was limitless. Between 1852 and 1870, years in which *one billion* dollars worth of *untaxed* gold was mined in California, Chinese miners paid a staggering $58 million to the state, ranging from one fourth to one half of California's revenue.

The tax launched a fierce wave of Chinese expulsions. Although the law stated that private parties had no authority to eject "aliens" who failed to pay the tax, it allowed collectors to seize and sell a Chinese miner's claim and tools. Fraudulent collectors sprang up all over the mountains; real and scam collectors repeatedly visited the same Chinese camps and threatened violence or deportation if the Chinese miner did not pay up. The Chinese miners did their best to avoid the tax. Some bribed the tax collectors; others paid a small amount directly to the collector and agreed not to ask for a receipt. Some simply refused to pay. Others hid in the woods, or in winter, moved into town. Many escaped the tax by going to work for absentee owners or mining corporations, which, as early as 1853, began investing in the costly technology of tunneling and quartz mining. In 1855, groups of Chinese men in Tuolumne and Mariposa counties were killed as they attacked the tax collectors.

Not all Californians agreed that the tax was a good idea. Some worried that it was a form of "taxation without representation" that could lead to Chinese demands for citizenship (Letter from an Old Miner). During the era of abolition, others predicted that it would create a population of paupers who could easily become a desperate class of slaves or burden the state into bankruptcy. And then there was the revenue. The Shasta Miners Convention reminded the legislature that in 1854 alone, the counties and the young state gained $300,000 from the Chinese miners' tax, which would have been lost if it had forced the Chinese out.

On May 8, 1852, the Second Columbia Miners Convention declared that "no Asiatic or South Sea Islander shall be permitted to mine in this district

either for himself *or for others*" and formed a Committee of Vigilance to ensure that none of the "degraded inhabitants of China and Islands of the Pacific" either purchased their own claim or worked for an absentee company (*Alta California*, May 15, 1852). The anti-Chinese movement threatened commercial interests (Johnson, p. 248).

The Foreign Miners Tax cut the Chinese population by the thousands for several years. But new arrivals soon equaled and quickly doubled the number of those who departed the Sonora foothills. Many refugees who returned to China stayed only temporarily (Chiu, p. 142; Coolidge, p. 498).

By 1870, the tax was nullified. At least two legal challenges in California prevailed. In 1870, Congress targeted state laws such as the Foreign Miners Tax when it modified the Civil Rights Act of 1866, and banned any tax imposed on "any person immigrating…from a foreign country which is not equally enforced…upon every person immigrating to such a State from any other foreign country" (Civil Rights Act of 1870, ch. 114, 16 Stat. 140). In 1870, in *U.S. v. Jackson* (26F.Cas 563 [1870 or 1874], a collector of the miners tax), the Supreme Court upheld the constitutionality of the revised Civil Rights Act, and the Foreign Miners Tax became null and void—long after its most egregious effects had passed (McClain, pp. 28–29). Nonetheless, during the two decades of its enforcement, 98% of $4,919,536.40 collected came from Chinese miners.

JEAN PFAELZER

References and Further Reading

Brands, H. W. *The Age of Gold*. New York: Doubleday, 2002.

Chiu, Ping. *Chinese Labor in California: An Economic Study*. Madison: The State Historical Society of Wisconsin, 1963.

Coolidge, Mary. *Chinese Immigration*. New York: Henry Holt, 1909.

Holliday, J. S. *Rush for Riches: Gold Fever and the Making of California*. Berkeley: University of California Press, 1999.

Kim, Hyung-chan. *A Legal History of Asian Americans, 1790–1990*. Westport, CT: Greenwood Press, 1994.

———. "Overview." In *Asian Americans and the Supreme Court: A Documentary History*, edited by Hyung-chan Kim. New York: Greenwood Press, 1992.

Johnson, Susan Lee. *Roaring Camp: The Social World of the California Gold Rush*. New York: Norton, 2000.

Letter from an Old Miner. Mariposa, January 22, 1856. Beineke Library, Yale University, OL2 S 779.

McClain, Charles J. *In Search of Equality: The Chinese Struggle against Discrimination in Nineteenth-Century America*. Berkeley: University of California Press, 1994.

Rawls, James, and Walton Bean. *California: An Interpretative History*. New York: McGraw-Hill, 1988.

Cases and Statutes Cited

U.S. v. Jackson (26F.Cas 563 [1870 or 1874]
Civil Rights Act of 1870, ch. 114, 16 Stat. 140

FOREIGN POLICY

Efforts by American workers to influence foreign relations date back to at least the American Revolution. The historian Dana Frank has noted the key role of sailors and artisans in acts of revolutionary defiance like the Boston Tea Party and the critical participation of workers in economic and military campaigns against the British. The political mobilization of ordinary people during the revolution in turn undermined patterns of social deference and gave birth to an ideology of labor republicanism that stressed equal rights for white male workers and helped lead to broad suffrage for this group by the Civil War. White male workers in the United States thus possessed more political power to influence foreign policy in the late eighteenth and early nineteenth centuries than their counterparts in many other industrializing countries.

Yet the role of the emerging U.S. working class and labor movement in shaping foreign policy before the Civil War remains unclear. As the industrial revolution transformed the Northeast, replacing household manufactures with products from newly created mills and factories, fledgling trade unions emerged to protect the rights of industrial workers. Yet although such unions used local publications to voice occasional opinions on foreign policy issues, they lacked sufficient power to influence national debates over American diplomacy. The dearth of independent labor voices in national debates may have made enfranchised white male workers susceptible to cross-class appeals that urged them to support the quest for continental empire at the expense of people of color, including Native Americans, African-Americans, and the Creole and Mexican populations in the Southwest.

Early Labor Critiques of the International Division of Labor and American Quest for Empire

In the post-Civil War era, elites expanded their appeals to white workers, emphasizing that the country now needed not just a continental but also an overseas empire to ensure a healthy economy. Advocates of an aggressive and militaristic foreign policy, as the historian Kristin Hoganson has argued, also emphasized overseas empire as a way to revitalize American manhood and forge a bond between white brothers of all classes. But several national trade union movements afforded labor activists a forum to promote alternative labor perspectives on foreign policy and empire. No consensus emerged among the nation's trade unions about what role labor should play in shaping the nation's foreign policy between the Civil War and World War I, but healthy debates about the international division of labor and about potential divergences between class interests and so-called national interests helped to clarify what was at stake for workers—both at home and abroad—in supporting U.S. foreign policies.

The short-lived National Labor Union, created in 1866 and led by the dynamic William Sylvis, brought attention to foreign policy issues and questions of international labor solidarity by announcing its intention to affiliate with the initially European-based International Working Men's Association or First International. Leaders of the First International such as Karl Marx emphasized that imperialistic foreign policies grew naturally from capitalism and its never-ending quest for new markets, investments, and natural resources. By encouraging their governments to acquire or dominate new territories and populations, businessmen could enlarge their profits and avoid the contradictions of overproduction and underconsumption even while continuing to exploit workers in their home countries. Marx urged workers to counteract the imperialist designs of government and business through a two-pronged approach that involved supporting the collective actions of international labor organizations and using political channels available within their respective countries.

Sylvis and his supporters within the National Labor Union agreed with Marx about the desirability of limiting the mobility of capital and labor and gaining increased international influence for workers. Although the National Labor Union unraveled before its alliance with the First International was fully consummated, activists within the union helped to publicize the class-based critique of international affairs developed by Marx and other European radicals. American socialists as well as European immigrants to the United States also spread the doctrines of the First International, and by the end of 1871 it boasted 27 sectional chapters and several hundred members in the United States. Perhaps propelled by its popularity in the United States, the First International relocated its headquarters to New York in 1872. But the organization proved faction-ridden and was dissolved at a meeting in Philadelphia in 1876.

The Knights of Labor also helped in unique ways to promote a class analysis of international affairs and U.S. foreign policy. Founded in 1869, this inclusive organization's membership peaked in the mid-1880s at about 750,000 workers. Although some Knights of Labor leaders developed a hostile attitude toward the socialists who dominated the First International, immigrants within the Knights often stressed the linkages between the American class struggle, class struggles in their former homelands, and imperialist domination. Irish-Americans proved an especially important force within the Knights. Weaned on Irish land reform and anticolonial ideologies, Irish-American labor activists naturally conceptualized their trade union battles in the United States as part of a worldwide struggle between the owning and producing classes and used local Knights meetings to raise support for the Irish nationalist cause. Given the internationalist currents flowing through the grassroots intellectual life of the Knights of Labor, it is hardly surprising that Knights chapters spread throughout Canada, and to Ireland, Scotland, and Britain. Although the Knights spent little time lobbying the U.S. government on foreign policy issues, they helped both to advance the cause of international labor solidarity and to lay the intellectual groundwork for an anticolonial critique of U.S. and British foreign policy upon which future immigrant labor activists would build. The Knights of Labor itself, however, would soon be overshadowed by the American Federation of Labor (AFL).

Early International Activities and Foreign Policy of the American Federation of Labor

Founded in 1886, the American Federation of Labor was composed predominantly of craft unions—some of whom had previously belonged to the Knights of Labor—that emphasized improving wages and working conditions for skilled and semiskilled workers rather than eliminating or fundamentally transforming capitalism. Despite its pragmatic focus and narrow membership base, the AFL developed an early interest in the activities of international labor organizations and in giving labor an independent voice in international affairs. In 1889, the AFL worked with the Second International that convened in Paris in 1889 to coordinate the first celebrations of May Day in Europe and the United States. The AFL's relationship with the Second International subsequently cooled, but during the early twentieth century, many individual AFL unions became active in international trade secretariats. These organizations were composed of trade unions from the same industry but different countries that came together to promote their international interests. Among the AFL unions that joined international secretariats in the early twentieth century were the miners, molders, painters, and shoemakers. AFL President Samuel Gompers followed the lead of constituent unions and made the AFL an active member of the International Secretariat of Trade Union Centers, which subsequently became the International Federation of Trade Unions. This organization concerned itself not only with international labor standards but with pacifist endeavors designed to encourage labor mediation of international disputes between nation-states—a cause in which Gompers himself was keenly interested during his early career.

The AFL also demonstrated an early interest in directly influencing U.S. foreign policy, and became particularly active in the debates surrounding the Spanish-American-Cuban-Filipino War and the acquisition of an overseas empire in the 1890s. When Cuba first rebelled against Spain, a majority of delegates to the AFL convention called on the AFL to demand that Congress recognize Cuban belligerency. Supporters of the Cuban rebellion argued that trade unionists in the United States had a responsibility to help fellow Cuban workingmen win their liberty. Yet a vocal minority opposed committing the AFL to support the revolution because it might encourage war with Spain. And war, they argued, always disproportionately hurt workingmen because they were the ones who inevitably did most of the fighting. Interestingly, some also wondered whether labor might be playing into the hands of business leaders in supporting Cuban belligerency, since the United States would no doubt seek to dominate the island nation if Spanish forces were defeated there. As Andrew Furuseth of the Seamen's Union explained at the AFL convention in 1897, the question was really one of "whether the New York speculator or the Spanish capitalist should skin the Cuban workingman." The debate demonstrated that there was no consensus within the ranks of the AFL about supporting nationalist rebellions or about the virtues of an American overseas empire.

For his part, AFL President Samuel Gompers initially supported proposals to recognize Cuban belligerency but opposed President William McKinley's decision to declare war against Spain and to annex former Spanish territories such as the Philippines and Puerto Rico at war's end. Gompers, however, subsequently came to what the historian Delber Lee McKee called a "tacit compromise" with the State Department. The AFL president toned down his opposition to U.S. annexation and imperial control of the Philippines and other acquired islands in return for government and business acquiescence in AFL campaigns to build labor unions in these areas. In contrast to Marx and other socialist theorists, Gompers and his closest colleagues on the AFL Executive Council reasoned that if they could raise labor standards in the island protectorates, then U.S. imperial control might actually benefit U.S. as well as island workers. Goods from these areas would not undersell their American counterparts, and businesses would not be tempted to establish low-wage factories there. Island workers, for their part, might use increased wages to buy American products. Gompers thus proved susceptible to cross-class appeals that emphasized the benefits of U.S. economic expansion and empire for workers both in the United States and abroad. Doubtless cultural messages that proliferated in the American media and in government circles about the need for white men of all classes to participate in the paternalistic oversight of nonwhite races also influenced Gompers. As Delber McKee has documented, Gompers referred to the people in newly acquired territories as "semibarbaric." Initially, Gompers feared that such barbarians might immigrate to the United States and undermine labor standards. But over time Gompers came to believe that such problems could be prevented if island workers were tutored in principles of trade unionism by their more experienced Anglo-Saxon brothers.

World War I

Gompers's interest in cooperating with business and government elites to promote economic expansion and overseas empire led to a full-fledged commitment to corporatist forms of power sharing during World War I. Social scientists use the term "corporatism" to refer to cooperative relationships that develop among business, labor, and the state in modern industrial capitalist societies in order to encourage industrial harmony and efficiency as well as to promote national economic expansion into foreign markets. President Woodrow Wilson (1912–1920) was committed to promoting such a cooperative relationship in the United States, as became clear when he created the Department of Labor and the Commission on Industrial Relations to oversee industrial arbitration and to make recommendations on increasing industrial productivity.

Significantly, when Wilson began to promote military preparedness after the outbreak of war in Europe, he also created a Council of National Defense to develop plans for the conversion from peacetime to military production. AFL President Samuel Gompers eagerly accepted a position on the council and created a labor subcommittee within the council composed of business, government, and labor representatives to study questions of industrial coordination and to draw up guidelines on wages, hours, and mediation in war-related industries. Gompers's writings reveal that he clearly believed he was laying the groundwork for a permanent system of industrial arbitration. When a U.S. declaration of war against Germany seemed likely in March 1917, Gompers called a special labor assembly of the representatives of the AFL's constituent national and international unions and secured a pledge of support for any future U.S. war effort from the meeting. Significantly, AFL-affiliated city labor councils were excluded from the meeting on the grounds that they were centers of pacifism. Local activists in turn charged that the meeting was not democratically constituted and argued that the AFL should instead demand that the government have a referendum vote of the entire population on the question of the war. Gompers, however, ignored such pleas and used the AFL's patriotic pledge as leverage to gain more positions for AFL leaders within emerging war boards. AFL representatives were also asked to serve on the Root Commission to Russia, and the AFL sent two missions to Europe during the war to win support for Wilsonian war aims.

The AFL's support for the war thus won it unprecedented diplomatic and domestic political influence within the Wilson administration. Yet its collaboration with the government also spurred intense criticism from socialists, some Industrial Workers of the World (IWW) members, and many local AFL activists. As the historian James Weinstein has documented, a majority within the Socialist Party of America continued to vigorously oppose U.S. participation in World War I after President Wilson's war declaration and lambasted the AFL for becoming "a fifth wheel on the capitalist war chariot." The syndicalist IWW viewed U.S. involvement in the war as an unfortunate distraction from its efforts to promote one big union and to encourage militant strike activity in the United States. Although some IWW activists cooperated with the government in its efforts to encourage workers to register for the draft, others carried on what the historian Fran Shor has called a "discursive campaign" against both U.S. involvement in World War I and the AFL's collaboration with the government. Both the Socialist Party of America and the IWW faced severe government persecution for their questioning of government policy, and in contrast to the AFL, emerged from the war greatly weakened and faction-ridden.

Some militant AFL-affiliated city labor councils such as the Chicago Federation of Labor (CFL) and Seattle Central Labor Council also renewed their criticism of the AFL by war's end. Such councils, as Gompers and his colleagues correctly assumed, were often more organically connected to immigrant working-class subcultures in the cities they served than to the AFL and became hotbeds of pacifist activity before the United States entered the war. As the historian Elizabeth McKillen has shown, the Chicago Federation of Labor and Seattle Central Labor Council criticized but reluctantly supported the AFL's wartime loyalty pledge after the United States entered the war in1917 because they believed that to oppose the AFL's foreign policy during wartime would be comparable, in the words of one activist, to being a "scab" during a strike. However, both councils doubted the benefits of wartime collaboration for labor and following the armistice created local labor parties in defiance of the AFL's political policies. The parties raised critical questions about the AFL's corporatist approach, arguing that the AFL should not merely seek equal representation with labor in government councils, but should demand representation for labor "in proportion to its voting strength." In contrast to AFL leaders, who hoped for one labor representative on the peace commission that would travel to Paris at the end of the war, CFL activists asked for representation for workers at the peace conference and in future international organizations "in proportion to their numbers in the armies, navies and workshops of the world." Similar labor parties erupted in some 45 other cities in the immediate postwar era and drove the movement to create the national Farmer-Labor party of 1920, a group with a strongly anti-Wilsonian and anti-imperialist agenda.

Gompers and other AFL leaders, by contrast, remained strongly committed to Wilson and a corporatist approach in the postwar era and sought to convert the war boards into permanent arbitration councils. Gompers also joined Wilson at the Peace Conference in Paris and, at Wilson's request, chaired the International Labor Legislation Commission that created the International Labor Organization (ILO). An advisory body to the League of Nations, the ILO was designed to make recommendations regarding questions of international labor standards and other international issues relevant to labor that could be either accepted or rejected by the League and by individual countries. The organization clearly bore the imprint of Gompers's corporatist thinking: it was designed to include not just trade union representatives but national delegations composed of two government, one business, and one labor representative. Critics like Andrew Furuseth of the Seamen's Union complained at the AFL convention in 1919 that to trust business and government leaders in the ILO to deal fairly with international labor standards, one would have to assume that "men all of a sudden have become saints."

European labor leaders initially boycotted the Peace Conference because it refused to allow leaders from the defeated countries on French soil and complained that Gompers and the International Labor Legislation Committee had acted without consulting European labor. Ironically, European trade unionists came to dominate the ILO after the U.S. Congress rejected the Paris Peace Treaty, thereby preventing U.S. representatives from participating in the League of Nations or its advisory bodies. The AFL also distanced itself from the International Federation of Trade Unions and Red International after quarreling with these organizations over their support for international strike and boycott activities.

Interwar Years

Isolated from European labor, the AFL devoted its international energies to improving its relations with Latin American labor movements in the 1920s. During 1918, with the help of secret financial aid from the Wilson administration, the AFL had joined with representatives from several Latin American labor movements to create the Pan American Federation of Labor (PAFL). The official goals of the organization were to raise labor standards in Latin America, curb abuses of labor by international capitalists, and promote the growth of unions in the Americas. AFL leaders also hoped to use the organization to resolve immigration problems between the United States and Mexico and to promote AFL trade union principles in Latin America while undermining those of the Industrial Workers of the World and other radical organizations. The Pan American Federation of Labor, however, declined rapidly in the late 1920s as more left-leaning organizations gained influence in Mexico and Latin America and criticized PAFL as an instrument of U.S. imperialism.

Largely isolated from European and Latin American trade union movements, the AFL at first advocated a nationalist approach to the Great Depression. It resisted Franklin Roosevelt's efforts to promote expanded trade through reciprocal agreements with other countries and instead promoted "Buy American" campaigns and higher tariffs as a way to stimulate the American economy. Yet oppositional subcultures within the AFL helped prevent it from retreating into full-scale isolationism. In particular, the historian Bruce Nelson has documented how maritime workers, whose "legendary rootlessness and transiency" isolated them "from the main integrative institutions of American society," were also natural internationalists who alerted fellow workers to the dangers of fascism. One typical example occurred in July 1933 when workers from American and Danish merchant ships joined together to pull a swastika from a German ship trying to enter Olympia harbor. Concerns about the growth of fascism in Europe helped to provoke AFL boycotts of German and Italian goods and doubtless played some role in the AFL's decision to re-affiliate with the International Federation of Trade Unions in 1937.

The AFL's renewed interest in international labor politics was also likely inspired by the emergence of the Congress of Industrial Organizations (CIO). The CIO is primarily known for organizing mass industrial unions that incorporated most grades of workers in critical industries like steel and rubber. But the CIO also won much sympathy from trade unionists in other countries by initially pursuing a foreign policy that was more accommodating to Latin American nationalism and by seeking to co-operate with trade unions from the Soviet Union during World War II and the early Cold War.

World War II and the Cold War

Because most allied labor movements were hostile to fascism, they were willing to work closely with their governments during World War II on wartime planning issues. But Victor Silverman suggests that the war also encouraged an increased spirit of labor internationalism that pervaded working-class life in the major democracies after 1941. In the United States, increasing numbers of workers no longer felt they could remain isolated from world affairs. Meanwhile, in Britain the war stimulated sympathy for the Soviet Union among workers and resulted in the creation of an Anglo-Soviet Trade Union Committee. The success of this committee in turn led British labor leaders to propose that a new labor organization be created at war's end that incorporated the Soviets. The AFL refused to attend a conference designed to organize the new labor international, but the CIO eagerly sent delegates and played an important part

in the creation of the new World Federation of Trade Unions (WFTU) in October 1945. The CIO distinguished itself within the organization by championing the demands of trade unions from colonial areas for representation independent of their mother countries.

But the new organization soon fell victim to Cold War politics. From the beginning, the AFL's Free Trade Union Committee collaborated with the State Department to weaken the WFTU by sowing discord between the communist and noncommunist European trade union movements. The AFL also successfully worked to prevent international trade secretariats from affiliating with it. The CIO, desperate to appear loyal in the face of mounting anticommunist hysteria at home, asked the WFTU to officially endorse the Marshall Plan. As Peter Weiler has written, the "introduction of the Marshall Plan into the WFTU brought the Cold War directly into the international trade union movement." When the Soviets refused to endorse the Marshall plan, the CIO and many European movements withdrew from the WFTU and joined the AFL in creating the International Confederation of Free Trade Unions (ICFTU). The AFL, CIO, and ICFTU subsequently helped to implement the Marshall Plan in Europe but also played divisive roles within European trade unions movements by encouraging discord between communists and non-communists.

The AFL and CIO's early Cold War foreign policies also produced mixed results in occupied Japan and in Latin America. In Japan, AFL and CIO leaders became part of the Labor Division of the Occupation bureaucracy and helped to establish the legal framework for Japanese workers to organize unions, bargain collectively, and strike. Yet when the Japanese labor movement started to drift to the left, American labor leaders encouraged the creation of anticommunist cells within the movement and eventually called for the development of an anticommunist labor federation in Japan called Sohyo. In Latin America, AFL leaders co-operated with the Central Intelligence Agency and United Fruit Company in undermining the left-leaning government of Arbenz Guzman in Guatemala. After a coup in Guatemala that was partly financed and directed by the CIA, Carlos Castillas Armas took power and proved quite hostile to the Guatemalan labor movement, dissolving thousands of unions. Anticommunism thus re-inforced a longstanding corporatist animus within the American labor movement that placed greater priority on co-operating with American business and state leaders in promoting national foreign policy goals than on encouraging international labor solidarity.

Debate and Changes in the AFL-CIO's Foreign Policy

After the AFL and CIO merged in 1955, the new labor federation struggled to overcome the increasingly negative international image of the American labor movement. During the 1960s, the AFL-CIO created three new labor centers: the American Institute for Free Labor Development (Latin America), the African-American Labor Center, and the Asian-American Free Labor Institute to provide assistance, education, and training for trade unionists from these areas. Yet some charged that paternalistic assumptions about the need for American trade unionists to uplift their less-developed brethren permeated the centers' educational programs. More troubling than charges of paternalism were claims that the institutes worked with the CIA to undermine democratically elected governments in these areas. The American Institute for Free Labor Development, for example, was implicated in U.S. efforts to undermine the governments of Joao Goulart in Brazil in 1964 and Salvador Allende in Chile during 1973. Such disclosures led labor dissidents to conclude that the institutes had been an exercise in trade union colonialism. Grassroots labor groups emerged by the 1980s to oppose the AFL-CIO's foreign policies in Latin America.

The Vietnam War further undermined consensus within the AFL-CIO over foreign policy goals. AFL-CIO President George Meany unwaveringly supported the Lyndon Johnson administration's Vietnam policies, as did the yearly AFL-CIO convention. Newscasts, meanwhile, highlighted hard-hatted unionists attacking antiwar demonstrators. But opposition to the war had always existed within militant subcultures in the labor movement, and after 1967, these groups coalesced in the National Labor Leadership Assembly for Peace. Labor opponents of the war like Walter Reuther grew especially vocal when President Richard Nixon widened the war by bombing the neutral country of Cambodia.

Antiwar labor activists helped to revive debate within the labor movement not only about Vietnam but also about the AFL-CIO's broader foreign policy goals during the Cold War. They questioned not only the morality of AFL-CIO Cold War foreign policies aimed at combating or overthrowing left-leaning governments abroad, but also whether such policies served the economic interests of U.S. workers. By using trade union funds to intervene in the internal political struggles of other countries, they argued, the AFL-CIO had sometimes helped to bring to power right-wing dictators who suppressed workers' rights and who created low-wage economies that encouraged U.S. capital flight and investment overseas. Meanwhile, products from such countries often undersold their American counterparts and caused economic stagnation in the United States. Protests particularly erupted over the role of cheap imports in undermining the sales of American-made products like automobiles.

The end of the Cold War in 1989 helped ensure the birth of a new labor foreign policy. When the reformer John Sweeney was elected AFL-CIO president in 1995, he shut down many of its existing overseas operations, including the CIA-linked American Institute for Free Labor Development, and created in their place the American Center for International Labor Solidarity. The new organization, as the name implied, was designed to encourage transnational labor strategies for counteracting the global machinations of corporations rather than to aid U.S. government interventionism in other countries. Many individual unions within the AFL-CIO have, for their part, also forged ties with foreign union movements in order to develop effective tactics for coping with multinational corporations and the global economy. Meanwhile, the AFL-CIO's continuing opposition to the North American Free Trade Agreement suggests that its leaders have become more critical of the corporatist and Cold War assumptions that freer markets always bring economic expansion and create freer and more prosperous workers. Since bipartisan consensus has often reigned on NAFTA, some activists have rallied behind a new labor party movement as a way to gain an independent voice on foreign policy issues. A new generation of labor leaders also seems dedicated to developing increased international influence by continuing the task of building a strong international labor movement that was begun in the nineteenth century.

ELIZABETH MCKILLEN

References and Further Reading

American Federation of Labor. *Report of the Proceedings of the Annual Conventions of the American Federation of Labor*, 1897–1955.

Andrews, Gregg. *Shoulder to Shoulder? The American Federation of Labor, the United States, and the Mexican Revolution, 1910–1924*. Berkeley: University of California Press, 1991.

Frank, Dana. *Buy American: The Untold Story of Economic Nationalism*. Boston: Beacon Press, 1999.

———. "Where Is the History of U.S. Labor and International Solidarity: Part 1: A Moveable Feast." *Labor: Studies in Working-Class History of the Americas* 1 (Spring 2004): 95–119.

Filippelli, Ronald L. *American Labor and Postwar Italy, 1945–1953: A Study of Cold War Politics*. Stanford, CA: Stanford University Press, 1989.

Greene, Julie. "The Labor of Empire: Recent Scholarship on U.S. History and Imperialism." *Labor: Studies in*

Working-Class History of the Americas 1 (Summer 2004): 113–129.

Hoganson, Kristin. *Fighting for American Manhood: How Gender Politics Provoked the Spanish-American and Philippine-American Wars*. New Haven, CT: Yale University Press, 1998.

Lorwin, Lewis. *Labor and Internationalism*. New York: McMillan, 1929.

McKee, Delber Lee. "The American Federation of Labor and American Foreign Policy, 1886–1912." Ph.D. diss. Stanford University. Stanford, CA, 1952.

McKillen, Elizabeth. *Chicago Labor and the Quest for a Democratic Diplomacy, 1914–1924*. Ithaca, NY: Cornell University Press, 1995.

Nelson, Bruce. *Workers on the Waterfront: Seamen, Longshoremen, and Unionism in the 1930s*. Urbana: University of Illinois Press, 1988.

Schonberger, Howard B. *Aftermath of War: Americans and the Remaking of Japan, 1945–1952*. Kent, OH: Kent State University Press, 1989.

Shor, Francis. "The IWW and Oppositional Politics in World War I: Pushing the System beyond Its Limits." *Radical History Review* 64 (Winter 1996): 74–94.

Silverman, Victor. *Imagining Internationalism in American and British Labor, 1939–1949*. Urbana: University of Illinois Press, 2000.

Snow, Sinclair. *The Pan American Federation of Labor*. Durham: University of North Carolina Press, 1964.

Weiler, Peter. "The United States, International Labor, and the Cold War: The Breakup of the World Federation of Trade Unions." *Diplomatic History* 5 (winter 1981): 1–22.

Weinrub, Al, and William Bollinger. *The AFL-CIO in Central America*. Oakland, CA: Labor Network on Central America, 1987.

Weinstein, James. *The Decline of Socialism in America, 1912–1925*. New York: Monthly Review Press, 1967.

See also **American Alliance for Labor and Democracy; Anticommunism; Cold War**

FOSTER, FRANK K. (D. 1909)
Labor Activist

The 1880s were a tumultuous decade for the labor movement in the United States. Not only did hundreds of thousands of workers join labor organizations, participate in strikes, and struggle for the eight-hour day, but they also engaged in arguments about the form, scope, ideology, strategies, and tactics appropriate for the new labor movement. Frank K. Foster was one of the most important voices in these debates.

Like many of the key labor activists of this era, Foster straddled social classes in his own work and social life. He learned the printer's trade, participated as a leader in the International Typographical Union

(ITU) at the local and national levels, and became editor of several newspapers that not only provided news coverage and editorial statements but also promoted poetry and fiction. Foster himself wrote some of this material and, later in life, published a novel and a collection of poetry.

In the early 1880s, Foster, like many of his peers, sought to maintain membership in both the trade union movement (not only the International Typographical Union, but also the Boston Central Trades and Labor Union, and the Federation of Organized Trades and Labor Unions, the precursor to the American Federation of Labor) and the Knights of Labor (KOL). He was a visible and prominent advocate of both organizations at the national as well as the local levels. At the same time, he was president of the Cambridge local of the ITU, secretary of the Boston Central Trades and Labor Union, and editor of the Haverhill *Daily and Weekly Laborer*, the official Massachusetts newspaper of the Knights of Labor. In 1886, he even sought the Democratic Party nomination for lieutenant governor of Massachusetts.

But by 1886, internal tensions were rippling through the Knights of Labor, revolving around the Order's relationship to the growing trade union movement, the struggle for the eight-hour day, the fallout from the Haymarket violence, arrests, trials, and executions in Chicago, the emergence of socialism and labor politics, and the issues of racial justice raised by the Richmond, Virginia, KOL General Assembly in October 1886. Of course, these conflicts were also overlaid by personality conflicts among key figures in all the movements, from Terence Powderly in the KOL to Adolph Strasser and Samuel Gompers in the American Federation of Labor (AFL), and the likes of Albert Parsons, Daniel De Leon, Eugene Debs, and others, at first on the margins, but increasingly building followings. Activists like Frank K. Foster were caught in the middle, the ground beneath their feet pulling apart into a chasm.

By 1887, Foster—and many of the other men from similar craft and experiential backgrounds—were moving into the trade union camp. They were uncomfortable with the increased criticism of craft unionism, collective bargaining, and the protection of union work rules emanating from within the KOL, as well as the Order's apparent move toward cooperatives, independent labor politics, and ideological radicalism. Foster expressed many of his concerns in a chapter on the history of shoemakers' unionism, which he contributed to George McNeill's seminal volume, *The Labor Movement: The Problem of Today*, in 1887.

In this essay, Foster criticized the pressures being exerted by the Knights of Labor to integrate shoe-makers into "mixed locals" rather than allowing them to maintain their specific, separate trade organizations. At the same time, Foster praised the KOL's commitment to solidarity, their ability to organize community support for striking shoemakers in a number of struggles, and their efforts to promote labor activism.

Indeed, although Foster ultimately moved solidly into the AFL camp, becoming the editor of the *Labor Leader*, the voice of the Massachusetts American Federation of Labor, he never became an advocate of mere "pure and simple trade unionism." While he advocated craft organization, apprenticeship regulations, control over the labor market, and the values of skilled labor, he also upheld principles of solidarity, class organization, and the importance of a broad labor movement. Interestingly, he even became a more outspoken voice for the inclusion of cultural material and perspectives within the movement, encouraging the writing and publication of poetry and fiction. Foster—and many of his peers—continued to see the United States in class terms and to understand workers as producers of a class-based culture that revolved around values of equality, independence, justice, and solidarity. They may have rejected socialist ideologies, the organization of cooperatives, and the practice of independent labor politics, but they remained committed to a vision of broad social transformation.

PETER RACHLEFF

References and Further Reading

Commons, John R., and Associates, eds. *History of Labor in the United States, Volume II.* New York: Augustus M. Kelley, 1966 [1918].

DePlasco, Joseph. "The University of Labor vs. the University of Letters in 1904: Frank K. Foster Confronts Harvard University President Charles W. Eliot." *Labor's Heritage* 1, no.2 (April 1989): 52–65.

Grob, Gerald. *Workers and Utopia: A Study of Ideological Conflict in the American Labor Movement, 1865–1900.* Chicago: Quadrangle, 1961.

Lorwin, Lewis. *The American Federation of Labor: History, Politics, and Prospects.* New York: Augustus M. Kelley, 1966 [1933].

McNeill, George E., ed. *The Labor Movement: The Problem of Today.* New York: Augustus M. Kelley, 1971 [1887].

Weir, Robert. *Beyond Labor's Veil: The Culture of the Knights of Labor.* University Park: Pennsylvania State University Press, 1996.

———. *Knights Unhorsed: Internal Conflict in a Guilded Age Social Movement.* Detroit: Wayne State University Press, 2000.

FOSTER, WILLIAM Z. (1881–1961)
Communist Party Activist

William Zebulon Foster was an American socialist, syndicalist, and communist leader who participated in some of the most dramatic conflicts of twentieth-century American labor and radical history. Coming of age and reaching maturity in the late nineteenth and early twentieth centuries, he was stirred and influenced by militant U.S. trade union struggles raging throughout the nation and by international revolutionary developments in Russia and Europe. His career within the Communist Party (CP), beginning in 1921, encompassed the decades of the Party's most spectacular rise and decline. Foster's ideological loyalties and personal dilemmas reflected the continuing contradictions and tensions inherent in the intersections of national and international radical movements on American soil.

Born in 1881 in Taunton, Massachusetts, to an Irish-Catholic immigrant family, Foster spent most of his youth and young adulthood not in Massachusetts, but in Philadelphia's working-class West End, to which his parents had moved soon after his birth. There, he came into contact with a boisterous, urban political and trade union culture, characterized by militant strikes and numerous competing strains of socialism and syndicalism. Surrounded by constant local and national evidence of the class struggle— the Homestead steel strike of 1892, the Pullman strike of 1894, and the Philadelphia street railway strike of 1895—Foster drank deeply of the culture of working-class radicalism. His early experience with strikes taught him about the "class struggle" and formed the foundations of his lifelong dedication to revolutionary action.

The disintegration of his family following the untimely death of his parents led Foster into an itinerant lifestyle. He traveled widely, developed extensive contacts with a multiplicity of workers, and took up various jobs: newspaper hawker, laborer, steamfitter, fireman, engineer, seaman, railroad worker, and miner. He worked in the streets of West Philadelphia, the packinghouses of Chicago, and the steel towns on the south shore of Lake Michigan, learning from each encounter with skilled and unskilled labor, and with inflexible and exploitative employers.

Drawn into the world of De Leon socialism and into an increasingly international radical community, Foster soon became associated with left-wing socialists who eschewed electoral politics and instead emphasized industrial unionism and worker initiatives.

Though he had joined the Socialist Party in 1901, he was expelled in 1909 during a factional battle between left- and right-wing Socialists in Washington state. Hardly one to stay unaffiliated, Foster soon joined the recently established Industrial Workers of the World (IWW), an organization more consistent with his syndicalist beliefs. He forged broad and disparate contacts with radicals around the country—in Seattle, the Midwest, and especially Chicago, California, New York, Montana, the South, and Canada.

His travels soon widened; he went abroad in 1910 as an IWW representative and attended the International Union Conference in Budapest the following year. He began to expand his familiarity with French, English, and German syndicalism and increasingly identified himself with a worldwide worker movement. Upon his return from Europe, Foster used his own organizational experiences and examples from abroad to develop institutional forms that he hoped would foster industrial and syndicalist unionism in the United States. The British syndicalist Tom Mann's British Industrial Syndicalist Educational League (ISEL), for example, provided Foster with a model for the Syndicalist League of North America (SLNA), founded in 1912, the International Trade Union Educational League (ITUEL), founded in 1915, and later the Trade Union Educational League (TUEL), established in 1920. Through his immersion in the first two decades of the twentieth century in international labor and radical organizations, Foster soon became a global, and globally known, labor activist.

Throughout his career, Foster continually pointed out and sought to remedy the weaknesses inherent in America's undisciplined, parochial, and craft-dominated trade union movement. His early pre-CP activism was heavily focused on nurturing militant strike movements and building an internal left opposition group to challenge Samuel Gompers's leadership in the American Federation of Labor (AFL). All of this was consistent with his early syndicalist ideals. World War I and the growing militancy of workers that came in its wake provided Foster with several opportunities to demonstrate the potential of industrial unionism. In 1917, while a railway car inspector in Chicago and a member of the AFL Railway Carmen's Union, Foster joined with the progressive labor leader John Fitzgerald, president of the Chicago Federation of Labor, in a successful effort to organize wartime packinghouse workers in the city. Over 200,000 workers joined the newly established organization. Then, with his now established and well-earned status as a shrewd and successful organizer, Foster took on his most significant challenge.

It came in the post–World War I era, when he led a coalition of 24 steel industry craft unions in a unified attempt to re-organize the steel industry (an older union, the Amalgamated Association of Iron, Steel and Tin workers had been reduced to impotency by Andrew Carnegie, J. P. Morgan, and a coterie of virulently anti-union steel industry managers). The steel organizing drive of 1918–1919 began brightly, with the rapid recruitment of over 100,000 workers. The steel organizing committee hoped to avoid a strike and sought immediate collective bargaining. Its initial demands included an eight-hour day (it was 12 hours then) and an increase in wages. But Elbert H. Gary, chairman of the board of the United States Steel Corporation, declined to "discuss business" with any trade union representatives. The call went out for a strike, and the Great Steel Strike of 1919 began in late September of that year. Within a week, 350,000 workers in nine states had put their tools down and ceased work. The 1919 Steel Strike anticipated the more general industrywide strikes of the 1930s CIO era in its scope and goals. Foster and his allies were attempting to demonstrate to AFL leaders the potential of industrywide organizing and bargaining. Yet, despite Foster's outstanding organizational and leadership skills, the strike failed, and so did postwar efforts to build an industrial labor movement in the United States.

Though there is disagreement over which factors—domestic or foreign—most heavily shaped the trajectory of Foster's life in the post–World War I period (reflected in the contrasting views of Foster's two major biographers, James Barrett and Edward P. Johanningsmeier), it is certainly obvious that Foster's immersion in international politics had an important influence on his ideological development. His encounter with the Russian Communist Party in 1921 and his growing familiarity with the course of the Russian Revolution led Foster to a belief in the potential power and need for a disciplined, centralized, and militant revolutionary cadre. It also led him into the American Communist Party in late 1921, where he quickly rose to the front ranks of the organization. Three times he ran as the Party's candidate for the U.S. presidency, in 1924, 1928, and again in 1932.

Throughout the 1920s and early 1930s, as Foster navigated between shifting Communist Party lines and existing trade union realities, he was continually forced to compromise his own beliefs on how best to engineer the transition from American business unionism to a revolutionary working-class trade and political movement. Foster's varied work experiences amongst skilled and unskilled laborers, his political and organizational experiences in Seattle and Chicago, and during the steel strike, led him again and again to a recognition of the need to work within existing trade union institutions and transform and radicalize them. But the debates within the CP on organizing autonomous revolutionary unions or "boring from within," supporting or undermining third-party initiatives, and cultivating progressive allies or keeping them at arm's length were not always resolved in harmony with Foster's better judgment. His own experiences taught Foster that working with existing organizations and steering them leftward was the most sensible way to operate within American institutional and ideological realities. That belief was reflected in the Trade Union Education League (TUEL), which he helped found in 1920 and which he brought into the Russian *Profintern* (the Red International of Labor Unions, the RILU) in 1923. The goal of the TUEL was to steer conservative AFL and independent unions to the left by helping to foster insurgent and militant worker movements *within* existing craft-dominated organizations. Nonetheless, Foster was forced to adapt to Party dictates when, during the Stalinist "Third Period" from 1928 until 1934–1935, he yielded to a dual-union emphasis and concentrated his efforts on building competitive and more militant alternatives to existing AFL organizations. The TUEL gave way to the TUUL, the Trade Union Unity League, in 1929, and began immediately to establish new unions. Around a dozen industrial unions were founded in the following six years, in a variety of economic sectors: textiles, marine labor, mining, shoe and leather manufacturing, agricultural labor, and more. More than 50,000 workers were soon organized by TUUL affiliates.

With the rise of the Congress of Industrial Organizations (CIO) and the abandonment of Third Period Communism in 1935, Foster was able to return to a personally more appealing "boring from within" strategy. He and the Party helped funnel hundreds of effective and disciplined Communist organizers into John L. Lewis's newly established industrial union organization, assisting in the transformation of the American labor movement in the 1930s and 1940s.

Following the uncomfortable and potentially disastrous two years of the Hitler-Stalin Pact, Soviet and U.S. unity during World War II helped revive and sustain the Party's effective trade union work. But the political and economic de-radicalization of the Party during World War II by Party head Earl Browder (he transformed the CPUSA into an "association") alienated Foster from Browder and led the former to spearhead efforts to oust Browder in 1946. Adapting to American realities and encouraging wartime unity was one thing; but forsaking basic socialist principles was another. When Browder moved further and further to the right and became almost indistinguishable from Franklin Roosevelt, Foster had enough. The publication of the famous critical letter by French Party leader Jacques Duclos in the late spring of 1945 gave Foster and his allies all the ammunition they needed to purge the now-discredited Browder. Foster succeeded Browder in 1946 and for the remaining 15 years of his life led the Party during its most sectarian and self-destructive period. Unwilling to tolerate deviations from Party discipline, Foster stifled various attempts to reform and democratize the U.S. party during the Cold War years and was unwilling to challenge Moscow's violent put-down of the Hungarian Revolution. Even after Khrushchev's revelation and condemnation of Stalin's excesses in 1956, Foster remained steadfast in holding on to Communist orthodoxy. He became rigid in his dealings with internal dissent and unwilling to tolerate the many calls for reform that spread through the Party's rank and file in the wake of Khrushchev's disclosure of Stalin's many moral and ideological transgressions.

In the final years of his life, in the late 1950s, as he wrestled with illness and remained unbending in his ideological course, Foster watched and—according to many scholars—contributed to his Party's self-destruction. Over 80% of the CP's membership abandoned the organization in the remaining years of the decade. Finally, succumbing to a heart disease that plagued him since the early 1930s, on September 1, 1961, in a sanatorium just outside of Moscow, Foster died.

GERALD ZAHAVI

References and Further Reading

Barrett, James R. *William Z. Foster and the Tragedy of American Radicalism*. Urbana and Chicago: University of Illinois Press, 1999.
Foster, William Z. *Pages from a Worker's Life*. New York: International, 1939.
Johanningsmeier, Edward P. *Forging American Communism: The Life of William Z. Foster*. Princeton, NJ: Princeton University Press, 1994.

See also **Communist Party**

FOURIERISM

Fourierism—also called Associationism by Americans—was a nineteenth-century communitarian movement with wide appeal in the United States. Between 1841 and 1846, idealists and reformers, working under the tutelage of boosters like Albert Brisbane and Horace Greeley, inaugurated 25 communities—including the famous Brook Farm—that housed between 7,000 and 8,000 people. The founding of a few other colonies followed in the 1850s, and the last Fourierite colony lasted until 1892.

The historian Carl Guarneri has estimated that when interested hangers-on are counted among the Associationists, their numbers reached perhaps 100,000. Although none of the Fourierite communities lasted long, while they did last they featured innovative experiments in the management of labor and in progressive education, and were hotbeds of reformist energy.

Charles Fourier, a French cloth merchant and obscure social theorist who lived from 1772 to 1837, was never taken seriously in his own country, where only one Fourierite community was ever constructed. Fourier's ideas were translated to the American context by Albert Brisbane, a native of New York who experienced a forceful ideological conversion while in Europe, and subsequently made popularizing the ideas his life's work. Through the pages of the *New York Tribune* and several books, Brisbane transformed Fourier for an American context, leaving out some of Fourier's more controversial notions.

What was left was "attractive industry," the idea that humans had a limited variety of personality types and that each personality was uniquely suited to a type of industry. Through an emulative vocational education that began as soon as a child could walk and talk, people might be ideally matched with the type of light industry or agricultural work that would uniquely suit them. Accompanied by bands of music and wearing colorful uniforms, they would march to the fields or workshops. There, they would have interesting workdays, full of variety, spurred on to great heights of productivity by friendly competition among "groups" and "series" of workers and by the presence of attractive workmates of the opposite sex. In Fourier's notion, there was someone in a community who was perfect for every job—young boys, who love to play in mud, would naturally serve as garbage collectors for a community, for example.

Fourier had envisioned his communitarians living in phalansteries, symmetrical communities of 2,000 individuals whose geographic planning resembled college campuses. The phalanstery, to be created by members taking out shares in a joint-stock company, was the optimal mix of country and city: a little castle in the midst of the rural idyll. In reality, no Associationist community in the United States was able to attract 2,000 residents—the longest-lived community, the North American Phalanx, had about a hundred. Nor were the Associationists able to construct phalansteries on the scale that Fourier had detailed in his drawings—some, like the community in Ceresco, Wisconsin, had plenty of land but not the capital for grand public buildings; others were swamped with residents and forced to build quickly. Forced to compromise on these key issues, Associationists used available buildings or constructed group housing that resembled the local vernacular architecture.

While Fourier had emphasized agriculture, especially the growing of fruit, as the prime industry for his communities, American Fourierite communities practiced a wide variety of industries, including shoemaking, milling, and tailoring. Like many so-called utopian socialists, Fourier had boasted of the advantages to women of housework being done communally, but some women who joined the communities complained that equality in tasks and pay existed more in theory than in practice. This was a characteristic of the Fourierite communities: even the groups, series, and task rotations so integral to Fourier's plan were impossible to achieve with tens or hundreds rather than thousands of members.

Fourierite communities were notable for their progressive ideas about the education and role of children. In 1844, under the supervision of member George Ripley, the Brook Farm commune became a Fourierite experiment—one that would later be chronicled by Nathaniel Hawthorne in *The Blithedale Romance*. Brook Farm would become best known for its school—a school that attracted children from many of the area's best families. Children in Fourierite communities earned wages for their work and could become self-supporting by the time they were in their teens—a fact that conflicted with traditional family arrangements in some of the communities.

While they lasted, Fourierite communities promised people an altered lifestyle that they hoped would serve as a model for broader societal change. For their residents, they provided an active social life, with musical evenings, lecture series, charades, sledding, and festivals that they created themselves. Fourierite communities were also hotbeds of reform in antebellum America. Reforms embraced by individuals and groups included temperance, vegetarianism, the abolition of slavery, and land reform. Fourierites viewed all of these as inferior to the one great reform: when society was organized around communitarian lines, all of the other issues could easily be mastered.

What explains the popularity of Fourierism? At a time of commercial transformation in America, during which the structure of the workplace was changing and the waged workplace increasingly separate from the home, Americans were attracted to many kinds of alternative living arrangements or "patent office" models for the improvement and reconfiguration of society, including Shakerism, Mormonism, and the Oneida Community. The Fourierites differed from the others by their willingness to embrace new technologies, both in their daily lives and to propagate their propaganda. In addition to Brisbane's column in the *New York Tribune*, Fourierites had their own wide-circulation newspapers, the *Phalanx* and later the *Harbinger*, which helped to spread news of the far-flung communities and to unite physical participants in the program with a network of interested reformers and followers. John Allan and John Orvis, the movement's itinerant lecturers, traveled through upstate New York and Massachusetts and as far west as Wisconsin, taking advantage of the mania for lyceums and self-improvement. Capitalizing on the desire for voluntary association among new urban dwellers, the Fourierites formed clubs of followers in major cities. The response was strongest among the middle classes and skilled artisans.

Despite the strong appeal of both the ideology and its propagation machine, the longest-lived antebellum experiment lasted only 12 years. Individuals chafed under the restraints imposed by a minutely planned vision of society. Strained finances could not cope with fires that claimed major buildings. Perhaps most important, the Fourierites, unlike later Socialists, never rejected the individualist, familial, and private-property-owning aspects of American society, making it easy for members of the communities to drift away and seek their fortunes in the world once the American economic situation improved in the 1850s.

JAMIE L. BRONSTEIN

References and Further Reading

Bronstein, Jamie. *Land Reform and Working-Class Experience in Britain and the United States, 1800–1862*. Stanford, CA: Stanford University Press, 1999.

Delano, Sterling F. *Brook Farm: The Dark Side of Utopia*. Cambridge: Belknap, 2004.

Fellman, Michael. *The Unbounded Frame: Freedom and Community in Nineteenth-Century American Utopianism*. Westport, CT: Greenwood Press, 1973.

Guarneri, Carl. "Reconstructing the Antebellum Communitarian Movement: Oneida and Fourierism." *Journal of the Early Republic* 16, no. 3 (1996): 463–488.

———. *The Utopian Alternative: Fourierism in Nineteenth-Century America*. Ithaca, NY: Cornell University, 1991.

Tomasek, Kathryn Manson. "Children and Family in Fourierist Communities." *Connecticut History* 37, no. 2 (1996–1997): 159–173.

See also **Brisbane, Albert**

FRATERNAL ORDER OF POLICE

To portray the Fraternal Order of Police (FOP) as a genuine labor union is historically inaccurate. During most of its existence, the FOP maintained that the unionization of any police force was dangerous and vigorously resisted any attempt to be labeled a police union by city officials or other labor organizations. Although it has long been organized in a manner similar to labor unions, with local lodges subordinate to state lodges, which are affiliated with the national Grand Lodge, it is only recently that the FOP has adopted the purpose and tactics of traditional labor unions.

Founding

The Fraternal Order of Police was founded in 1915 by two Philadelphia police officers, Martin Toole and Delbert Nagle. The two officers possessed a distinct view of the United States in general, and American police in particular, that stressed the exceptional nature of American civilization and the role of the police as its guardians. They looked to an idealized Roman Empire as their civilizational model and adopted the Roman motto "*Jus, Fidus, Libertatum*" ("Law is the safeguard of liberty") as their own. Ironically, this Roman motto was the source of some confusion within the FOP. Since its founding in 1915, the organization had translated the Latin phrase as "Fairness, Justice, Equality." However, in the early 1920s, a member of the Ladies Auxiliary of the FOP pointed out that the word *fairness* could not be translated from the Roman phrase *Jus, Fidus, Libertatum*. Hence, the translation was adjusted to "Justice, Friendship, Equality." The correct translation (Law is the safeguard of liberty) was not recognized and adopted until 1968, by which time changing the Latin motto on all FOP publications would have been too costly.

The political context during the founding of the FOP accounts for its traditional anti-union stance. Europe was engaged in World War I when the order was founded in 1915. After the sinking of the *Lusitania*, Delbert Nagle, the first grand president of the FOP, assured the public that his organization would be the first to rally around the flag during any national crisis. When the United States entered the war, the FOP passed a resolution pre-emptively endorsing every act of the president. After the war, as anti-German and anti-immigrant sentiments transformed into antiradical hysteria, all forms of workforce organization became suspect in the view of industry and government. Since local police forces were so often used against striking workers, a police union seemed particularly troublesome, if not contradictory.

It was this same tension between the police officers' obligation to break up strikes and their own desire to fight for better pay and working conditions that shaped the stridently conservative identity of the Fraternal Order of Police. From the very beginning, the Order's founders insisted that they had no desire to form a police union. The Order's first constitution reflected this concern; union affiliation and police strikes were strictly prohibited. In fact, when representatives from the American Federation of Labor (AFL) contacted the FOP leadership about building a working relationship, the Order's grand president staunchly refused on the basis that police siding with striking workers could result in social upheaval.

Expansion

The FOP's overt opposition to police unionism during the post-WWI Red Scare stimulated a substantial increase in FOP membership. Ironically, it was the actions of a non-FOP affiliated police force that facilitated the swelling of the FOP's ranks. The widespread labor radicalism of the era produced the first police strike in American history. Boston police officers went on strike in 1919 when the city refused to recognize their affiliation with the AFL. Governor Calvin Coolidge had to call in the National Guard to quell the violence and looting that took place in the wake of the police strike. The corresponding backlash by city officials and the national media produced a nationwide assault on all efforts by police to organize. Although the FOP was not exempt from these attacks (it was repeatedly condemned as radical, anarchist, Bolshevik, and Communist), the Order's forceful denunciation of all things radical and its continued opposition to police unionism and strikes convinced most of its critics that it was sufficiently antiradical. Since most states passed laws banning organized bargaining rights for police officers in the wake of the Boston strike of 1919, the FOP remained as the only viable, nonunion alternative for police officers. From that moment until the 1960s, the FOP lobbied legislative committees and employed publicity campaigns to improve the working conditions of its members.

Membership in the FOP also increased when it proved its ability to delivery better pay and working conditions to prospective members. Originally conceived as a national organization, each gain made by the FOP in its mission to improve the lives of police officers has served as a major selling point in its effort to garner new members. The Order made its first attempt to expand shortly after its inception during WWI. Its first major victory came in 1916 when the Pittsburgh lodge successfully lobbied the city council to give police officers two days off a month with pay. The following year, the original founders mandated the publication of an official FOP journal as a means to communicate with its rank-and-file members and to raise funds through advertising. The use of revenues from the publication soon became a contentious issue within the FOP when Nagle and Toole made the

journal their private enterprise. They were soon purged from the FOP and accused of fraud, misappropriation of funds, and theft (though criminal charges were never brought against them). Despite such an inauspicious end for the Order's founders, the organization grew steadily during the 1920s as antiradical sentiments fueled heightened concern for law and order. The FOP grew so rapidly in the 1930s that a general instability descended upon the Order as huge numbers of new members created new coalitions and factions within the original organization. The ensuing power struggle pitted founding members from the Pittsburgh lodge against new members from Ohio, Indiana, and West Virginia. Fistfights during the Order's annual conventions were not an uncommon occurrence throughout this period. Stronger state lodges emerged from the infighting, and membership tripled from 5,000 in 1930 to 15,000 in 1940. Though concentrated in the Midwest, the FOP was now the largest police organization in the nation, stretching from Pennsylvania to Arizona. During WWII, dissention within the ranks decreased as new membership growth slowed. In 1952, the FOP began publishing its Annual Survey of Salaries and Working Conditions of the Police Departments in the U.S. This allowed all officers, departments, and city officials to have access to comparative statistics on salaries and working conditions from police departments throughout the country. The Annual Survey proved to be the single most important tool in the FOP's lobbying effort on behalf of its members. By 1960, with 500 local lodges and FOP membership at 40,000, the Order had become a powerful national organization able to fight for and defend the interests of police anywhere in United States.

Challenges

The 1960s were the most critical years for the Fraternal Order of Police. A growing emphasis by civil rights organizations on police misconduct led to calls for civilian review boards that would have the power to discipline abusive police officers and overly aggressive tactical units. The Order's uncompromising defense of any officer charged with police brutality brought thousands of officers into the ranks of the FOP. In just five years, the FOP grew by 20,000 members to a total of 60,000 in 1965. Since civilian review boards represented a threat to both local police forces and the local governments that employed them, a close working relationship developed between city governments and local FOP lodges. The Order organized legal defense funds and alarmist publicity campaigns to resist challenges brought by the American Civil Liberties Union (ACLU), Congress of Racial Equality (CORE), Student Nonviolent Coordinating Committee (SNCC), Southern Christian Leadership Conference (SCLC), and even Robert Kennedy's Justice Department. As quoted in Justin Walsh's history of the FOP, "The public should be scared into supporting us," suggested Grand Lodge President John Harrington. The tactic worked; few civilian review boards were ever established.

This period was also marked by a growing police unionization movement across the country. Existing unions such as the International Brotherhood of Teamsters and the American Federation of State, County, and Municipal Employees, as well as new unions such as the National Union of Police Officers, the International Brotherhood of Police Officers, and the International Conference of Police Associations, attracted growing numbers of police officers because of their willingness to engage in collective bargaining and even strikes to fight for the interests of its members, tactics that the FOP leadership had resisted for 50 years. The more militant posture of these unions forced the FOP to adopt a similar stance. A change in FOP attitude toward union activity and strikes became clearly evident by 1967 when FOP members refused to reaffirm the Order's ban on such actions. FOP members engaged in their first strike in Youngstown, Ohio, on September 6, 1967, and received a $100 a month pay raise. The FOP has functioned as a genuine labor union for police officers ever since. By 1975, FOP membership had risen to 120,000.

Political Efforts

Broader issues for which the FOP has lobbied for in the past include effective gun control laws and forced sterilization of repeat offenders. In addition, the FOP has organized against affirmative action hiring of women and minorities and is on record as opposing the hiring of homosexuals. The FOP leadership, in accordance with the more activist posture of the 1960s, endorsed the segregationist George Wallace for president in 1968 and Richard Nixon for re-election in 1972. By 1976, the FOP had begun to routinely endorse and campaign for pro "law and order" politicians.

JOSEPH LIPARI

References and Further Reading

Walsh, Justin E. *The Fraternal Order of the Police, 1915–1976*. Indianapolis, IN: Joseph Munson Co. Inc., 1977.

FREE-SOILISM

"Free-Soilism" refers to the popular mid-nineteenth-century plan to provide cheap federal land in the West to poor settlers while excluding slavery from that same land—in essence, free land and land free of slavery.

Calls for equitable distribution of public land dated back to eighteenth-century Enlightenment radicals. Building on this tradition, Jacksonian-era labor reformers developed the concept of free soil as a cure for low wages and unemployment suffered by urban workers. Free productive land parceled out in small plots would support underemployed workers, end land speculation, and, by drawing labor out of the cities, improve conditions for those remaining behind. Opposition to slavery fed into land reform because slaveholders constituted a powerful interest that threatened to engross public lands at the expense of ordinary Americans. The free-soil critique of slavery owed more to labor reform arguments that banks and corporate monopolies undermined the equality of white citizens than it did to the abolitionist argument that slavery and the racial hierarchy that supported it were morally wrong.

George Henry Evans, an immigrant British printer and editor, led the fight for free soil. He developed his ideas while involved with the utopian Robert Dale Owen and the Workingman's Party in the late 1820s. The agrarian Thomas Skidmore and the anti-slavery Democrat William Leggett also influenced Free-Soilism's development. In the mid-1830s, advocates of free land distribution included the National Trades Union, the antimonopoly Locofoco faction of the Democratic Party, and, for a time, New York City politico Mike Walsh. In 1844, Evans and two other printers organized the National Reform Association, headquartered in New York City. National Reformers promoted free soil by urging workers to "vote yourself a farm."

Evans opposed slavery and was one of the few whites to praise Nat Turner's rebellion. However, Evans also criticized abolitionists for paying more attention to slaves than to white wage earners. That narrowed vision of free labor's concerns enabled Free-Soilers to win support from racist whites who nonetheless worried about the growing power of slaveholders, but it undermined political antislavery's commitment to racial equality. The racism of Free-Soilers led abolitionist followers of William Lloyd Garrison to keep the movement at arm's length.

Nonetheless, as foes of slavery, Free-Soilers attracted some abolitionists who had supported the Liberty Party in 1840 and 1844. Free soil also appealed to tenant farmers in Upstate New York who fought against high rents. Followers of the communitarian theorist Charles Fourier, including Albert Brisbane and, through Brisbane's influence, editor Horace Greeley, also took up the cause of free soil. Along with these constituencies, free soil won adherents in the major parties who worried about the growing power of slaveholders. Northern Democrats witnessed this power in 1844, when southerners blocked New Yorker Martin Van Buren's nomination for president because they doubted his support for slavery's expansion. Similarly, antislavery Conscience Whigs, such as Massachusetts' Charles Sumner, grew restive at the collusion between "the lords of the loom and the lords of the lash"—northern industrialists and southern.

The annexation of Texas in 1845 and the ensuing war with Mexico brought southwestern territories under U.S. control and heightened northern concern that slaveholders would dominate settlement of public lands. In 1846, David Wilmot, a Democratic congressman from north-central Pennsylvania, proposed a ban on slavery in land conquered from Mexico. The so-called Wilmot Proviso was narrowly defeated, but it sparked a new political movement. In 1846, the first Free Soil Party appeared in New York. In New Hampshire, a coalition of free-soil Whigs and Democrats led by John Parker Hale won control of the legislature.

In 1848, the Free Soil Party nominated Van Buren for president. Van Buren campaigned on free soil, but he advocated other labor reform issues such as public works, cheap postage, and the elimination of unnecessary public offices. In the industrial state of Massachusetts, Free-Soilers pushed for the 10-hour day and enjoyed strong support in manufacturing centers like Lynn. Although the Free Soil Party refused to endorse racial equality or immediate emancipation, free black abolitionists like Frederick Douglass and Charles Remond supported it as a necessary step in converting white northerners to antislavery. In the election, Van Buren polled 291,804 votes, 10% of the national total and 14% of all northern ballots. The Free Soil Party did best in rural areas where small farmers had little access to prosperity-generating canals and railroads.

The federal Compromise of 1850, which brought California into the union as a free state, temporarily quieted conflict over western land, but the opening of Kansas and Nebraska to slavery in 1854 re-ignited free-soil protests in the North and spawned the Republican Party. The Kansas-Nebraska Act rescinded an 1820 ban on slavery in these lands by allowing voters in Kansas and Nebraska to decide slavery's status for themselves. Across the North, workers and farmers worried that wealthy slaveholders would buy up the best land, wring profits from it with unpaid slave labor, and drive out ordinary farm families. Exploiting these fears, the new Republican Party promised to provide white families with free homesteads in the West and stop slavery's expansion.

Over the next six years, Republicans challenged the increasingly proslavery and prosouthern Democratic Party for control of the federal government. Like other Free-Soilers, Republicans emphasized slavery's harm to whites and downplayed universal emancipation and racial equality. That argument had mass appeal in the North where anger at the Slave Power had to counterbalance white racism that had in earlier times helped slaveholders win support in the free states.

The Republican Abraham Lincoln's victory in the 1860 presidential election sparked the secession of 11 slave states, and civil war ensued. During the Civil War, Lincoln's administration made good on free-soil promises by passing the Homestead Act of 1862, which gave 160-acre lots to farmers who paid a $10 fee and settled the land for five years. In 1863, Lincoln announced the Emancipation Proclamation, which freed slaves in rebel-held territory, and, in 1865, the Thirteenth Amendment to the Constitution banned slavery throughout the United States.

Frank Towers

References and Further Reading

Blue, Frederick J. *The Free Soilers: Third Party Politics, 1848–1854*. Urbana: University of Illinois Press, 1973.

Earle, Jonathan H. *Jacksonian Antislavery and the Politics of Free Soil, 1824–1854*. Chapel Hill: The University of North Carolina Press, 2004.

Foner, Eric. *Free Soil, Free Labor, Free Men: The Ideology of the Republican Party before the Civil War*. 1970. Reprint. New York: Oxford University Press, 1995.

Lause, Mark A. *Young America: Land, Labor, and the Republican Community*. Urbana: University of Illinois Press, 2005.

See also **Brisbane, Albert; Civil War and Reconstruction; Emancipation and Reconstruction; Fourierism; Evans, George Henry; Leggett, William; Locofoco Democrats; Lynn Shoe Strike (1860); Owen, Robert Dale; Skidmore, Thomas; Walsh, Mike**

FRENCH-CANADIANS

Since the establishment of New France in 1608 and its subsequent conquest by the British following the Seven-Year War, French-Canadian settlers were largely concentrated along the Saint Lawrence Valley, with a significant minority scattered throughout its vast hinterlands. One of the major activities they were engaged in—the fur trade—had taken many of them to the most remote corners of the continent, and even after the Conquest, many remained in the employ of fur companies as voyageurs, *engages*, and artisans. When in 1867 British North America was re-organized into the Canadian Confederation, French-Canadians made up the majority of the population of the newly created province of Quebec.

Throughout much of the nineteenth century, French Canada remained essentially an agrarian society despite the growing importance of proto-industrial activities and a few commercial centers such as Quebec City, Three Rivers, and Montreal—soon to emerge as the province's leading manufacturing and metropolitan area. The co-existence of commercial and subsistence agriculture proved unable to sustain the natural growth of this rural population, whose birthrate was one of the highest in the western world. Moreover, in the absence of adequate public policies to encourage the settlement of largely forested hinterland regions, rural French-Canadians began to overflow from the old parishes toward commercial centers and increasingly across the border and into the United States. Public concern about the loss of population to the United States was voiced as early as the 1830s. By mid-century, the southward population movement seemed to have become irreversible, as ascertained by an 1857 Quebec public inquiry. While the majority crossed into rural districts of neighbouring states, and a few joined the expanding agricultural frontier in the American Midwest, a growing number migrated seasonally to work in canal and railroad construction and logging—thus providing a significant labour input to the initial phase of industrialization associated with antebellum America.

Cross-border migration accelerated dramatically following the Civil War and reached its all-time peak in the 1880s, when the net population loss to the United States for that decade rose to 150,000. Despite the ensuing declining trend, French-Canadians continued to migrate south in large numbers up until the onset of the Great Depression. Estimates covering the 1840–1940 period have placed their net migration to the United States at 900,000.

Despite the multidirectional nature of these cross-border flows, two sections in the United States acted as major poles of attraction: the Great Lakes region, owing—at least initially—to the previous existence of French-Canadian enclaves that had survived the decline of the fur trade; and New England, on account of the geographical proximity of its expanding labour markets.

French-Canadians in the Midwest

On the eve of the Civil War, the states of Michigan, Illinois, and Wisconsin had become the destination for nearly one half of all French-Canadians residing in the United States. Of these, Michigan soon rose as by far the leading pole of French-Canadian settlement. One key factor was the pull exerted by the forestry industry, whose rapid development by the 1860s had made Michigan the major producer state in the union. Many French-Canadian lumberjacks had followed the forestry industry in its continental move from the East to the West; others, encouraged by improvements in fluvial and rail transportation, joined it in Michigan as enclaves and communities started to multiply, particularly in the Saginaw Valley, where much of the forestry production was concentrated. By 1885, French-Canadians made up 13% of the valley's population, with more that half of their labour force employed in logging operations and sawmills—thus making them the largest immigrant group within the valley's forestry industry. So intimately bound was their economic future to that resource industry that when a major strike broke out in 1885 around the issue of a shorter working day—one that proved to be the major labour/capital confrontation in the valley during that era—French-Canadians joined their fellow immigrant and American workers, and offered their community center for rallies and other organizing purposes. Outside the forestry sector, a significant minority of French-Canadians residing in the valley were engaged in skilled trades, either as employees or as independent craftsmen. Others became well established in the service sector (hotels, saloons), often as owners.

In the northern section of Michigan—known also as the Keweenaw Peninsula—French-Canadians began to arrive in the 1850s. To a large extent, their early arrival and subsequent influx were related to the rapid growth of copper mining and its central role in the region's economy. So acute was the labour shortage in this sector that on many occasions employers had to send recruiting agents across the border and entice Canadians with the promise of higher wages. By the end of the century, French-Canadians made up 12% of the peninsula's population and had created a stable institutional network, particularly in the towns of Lake Linden and Calumet.

Not surprisingly, mining-related work became the leading single sector of occupation among French-Canadians, followed by logging and a variety of service-related occupations.

Among the manufacturing centers of the Midwest, it was the city of Detroit that exerted by far the most important pull for French-Canadians. By 1900, they had become the leading immigrant group after the British, the Anglo-Canadians, and the Polish, and were engaged primarily in unskilled and semiskilled occupations.

Migrating to New England

However significant the influx of French-Canadians into the Great Lakes region, its importance within the overall migration movement decreased substantially as the industrial landscape of the nation changed. By the turn of the century, in fact, for every French-Canadian headed to the Great Lakes states, four more were choosing the New England states as their destinations.

During the first half of the nineteenth century, much of the French-Canadian population overflow into New England border counties—from Vermont to Maine—had been essentially an agrarian phenomenon. But with the unprecedented industrial growth marking the "Gilded Age," New England consolidated its role as a major pole of attraction for immigrant labour in the nation.

Of all manufacturing sectors, it was textile production—mostly concentrated in central and southern New England—that drew the largest proportion of French-Canadians. In ever-growing numbers, they discovered the possibilities that the textile mills to the south offered them, and inversely, textile employers discovered the Quebec countryside as a source of labour willing to submit to the particularly harsh working conditions prevailing in that manufacturing sector.

Geographic proximity, of course, played a leading role, particularly now that Quebec had become integrated within the New England rail network. Unlike European immigrants, who were separated from New England labour markets by an often strenuous Atlantic crossing, most French-Canadians only had to reach a nearby rail junction in order to find themselves, in less than a day trip, in any of the labour-hungry industrial centers of New England. Often they were encouraged to migrate by recruiting agents sent by mill owners. Studies of Lewiston, Maine; Lowell, Massachusetts; Manchester, New Hampshire; and Woonsocket, Rhode Island—among others—have traced the early entry of French-Canadians in the textile industry to the 1860s. In many such cases, their arrival and subsequent influx into textile production took on the proportion of a historic immigrant turnover in an industry that had previously relied largely on Irish labour, and before it, on a local Yankee workforce. By 1900, in fact, French-Canadians represented the majority of the population in some large textile centers such as Woonsocket, Rhode Island, as well as in a myriad of smaller mill towns throughout the Blackstone Valley. Moreover, they made up nearly one half of the entire labour force employed in textile manufacturing in Maine and New Hampshire, and in Massachusetts and Rhode Island they accounted for nearly one third of the textile workforce.

But what best explains the historic encounter of rural French-Canadians with the New England textile industry was the particular type of labour market engendered by a production process that was the first one to be mechanized on a large scale and made to depend significantly on the labour of women and children. As a result, hard-pressed small holders, as well as subsistence and tenant farmers in Quebec, saw in textile work a rare possibility to turn several of the family members into wage earners. Not surprisingly, family migration became the main pattern of this movement, resulting in extended kin-based chain migration; and the reliance on the work of children was a key consideration for those envisaging a move south of the border. By 1880, for instance, about 30% of the French-Canadian immigrant population in the state of Rhode Island were children aged 14 and younger—a striking contrast with most European immigrant populations. Perhaps even more significantly, 81% of that population was made up of nuclear families. The same survey revealed that 80.4% of all French-Canadian children aged 11 to 15 were reported at work as against only 8.5% reported at school—thus making this cross-border movement not only a chapter in immigrant working-class history but also a chapter in "children's history." Even when, during the Progressive Era, child labour laws kept a large number of them out of the labour market, French-Canadian older children kept contributing significantly to the family wage. As shown by a New England-wide survey of French-Canadians in the cotton industry produced by the U. S. Senate's Immigration Commission (1908–1911), the earnings of children aged 14 and 15 accounted, on average, for 33% of the total family income, with the earnings of fathers accounting for 52%. Throughout these years, only a small minority of male heads of families gained access to textile manufacturing. The majority of them tended to find work as unskilled day labourers or semiskilled production workers in boot and shoe factories and in brick manufacturing.

French-Canadians and Labour Activism

The stereotype circulated in the 1880s by Massachusetts labour reformers depicting French-Canadians as "the

Chinese of the East" for their ethnic gregariousness, their submission to employers' whims, and their lack of interest in American institutions has long served to explain their low proclivity for labour militancy. In effect, despite the growing instances of French-Canadian workers' resistance unearthed by historians, their participation in the waves of industrial strife marking the Gilded Age and Progressive America bears little proportion to their weight within the New England workforce.

A more historically sound explanation may be found in the previously mentioned demographic and labour-market realities marking their industrial experience, as well as in the organizational priorities of the craft unions prevailing in textile throughout that era, which kept the overwhelming majority of low-skilled, French-Canadian mill workers out of their concerns. Geographic and cultural factors also played their role. Proximity to Quebec, in fact, and the existence—throughout the New England region—of family and kin networks encouraged what one may call "a mobility of abstention." In periods of protracted labour strife, French-Canadians tended to leave their strike-ridden mill towns and head back temporarily to Quebec or join family or relatives in other textile centers. Yet, in some cases, these choices were prompted by a refusal to act as scabs.

But perhaps a more important deterring factor was the significant degree of social control exerted on the community by the church and the local ethnic elite.

It is important to stress that church authorities in Quebec had long condemned out-migration to the United States for the spiritual dangers it posed to those who subjected themselves to the evil influences of urban/industrial life; along with a Quebec nationalist elite, they had also condemned out-migrants for abandoning their fatherland, thus weakening French Canada's political weight within the Canadian Confederation. In the hope of stemming the exodus, they had resorted to repatriation programs as a way to re-channel the southward exodus toward colonisation of Quebec's hinterlands—though with little success. But in the face of the movement's resiliency, the church redefined its mission by joining immigrants in the land of exile in order to ensure that they preserve their French-Canadian traditions (religion, language, family)—thus sheltering them from the evil influences surrounding them.

This posture soon took the force of an ideology known as "*La survivance*" (the survival), which in many areas of settlement pervaded the elaborate institutional network French-Canadians created and which encompassed national parishes, hospitals, French-language schools, mutual-aid societies, recreational activities, and the press.

Just as in Quebec the nascent French-Canadian labour movement was effectively dominated by church officials, who ensured that workers' demands, when economically justified, occur within the framework of enlightened paternalism, so in New England local *curés* exerted intense pressures on their parishioners, viewing, as they did, American labour unions as the embodiment of modernism and socialism, and strikes as a form of disobedience to established authority. But not all French-Canadians yielded to those pressures.

One should not lose sight of the fact that most immigrant communities, regardless of their ethnic backgrounds, experienced the tension of trying to maintain cultural traditions and ethnic associations while at the same time undergoing the Americanisation pressures brought about, most acutely, by the World War I patriotic drives and the ensuing nativist ethos prevailing in much of the country. This tension appears to have been much more pronounced among French-Canadians on account of the growing confrontation in most communities of rival elites: those seeking to enforce *survivance*, and those encouraging naturalisation and participation in the wider civil society. The proximity to Quebec ecclesiastical influences and to the growing Quebec ethno-nationalist movement translated—at least initially—in added ideological ammunition for the former group. Still, this traditionalist-modernist mix defies generalisation, as it varied significantly according to local circumstances and community leadership. But it runs as a common thread in the history of much of New England's "Franco-America," inevitably impacting the types of relations workers had with the local labour organizations and industrial strife.

As resilient as the *survivance* ideology may have been, it did not prevent a new generation of French-Canadian workers—some born in Quebec, but increasingly U.S.-born—from heeding the labour call and joining strikers as the New England textile industry underwent the convulsions associated with the growing competition from southern production, or resulting from the industrial mobilisation of the war period and from the nationwide, historic capital-labour confrontation of the postwar years. A number of skilled workers among them took up labour responsibilities in the United Textile Workers or in other local textile unions such as the Woonsocket-based Independent Textile Union, playing key roles in reaching the mass of French-Canadian unskilled and semiskilled workers. In one of the major textile strikes of the 1920s, fought against the giant Amoskeag corporation, in Manchester, New Hampshire, French-Canadian workers were among the labour activists who spearheaded the nine-month-long confrontation (1922)—thus challenging both the company's entrenched paternalism and their ethnic leaders' call for submission.

While ending in defeat, the Amoskeag strike reflects the transformations occurring in the demographic and political composition of French-Canadian textile workers, and in many ways stands as a rehearsal for the massive, and more successful, organizing drives of the turbulent 1930s, when class interest and solidarity took precedence over ethnic loyalties.

During much of the 1920s, in fact, French-Canadian immigration declined sharply, coming to a virtual end with the onset of the Great Depression. By 1930, nearly two out of three individuals of French-Canadian stock were born in the United States and inevitably subject to the Americanisation influences of the interwar years. To many of them, the labour militancy that swept through the nation, and the ensuing U.S. involvement in the "good war," gave the opportunity to partake in the building of a new, more democratic industrial order, while at the same time adjusting their culture and traditions to a more mainstream vision of Americanism.

BRUNO RAMIREZ

References and Further Reading

Blewett, Mary H. *Constant Turmoil: The Politics of Industrial Life in Nineteenth-Century New England.* Amherst: University of Massachusetts Press, 2000.

Doty, C. Stewart. *The First Franco-Americans: New England Life Histories from the Federal Writers Project, 1938–1939.* Orono: University of Maine at Orono Press, 1985.

Early, Frances H. "The French-Canadian Family Economy and Standard-of-Living in Lowell, Massachusetts, 1870." *Journal of Family History* 7 (June 1982): 180–200.

Frenette, Ives. "Understanding the French Canadians of Lewiston, Maine, 1860–1900." *Maine Historical Society Quarterly* 25, no. 4 (Spring 1986): 198–229.

Gerstle, Gary. *Working-Class Americanism: The Politics of Labor in a Textile City, 1914–1960.* Cambridge, MA: Cambridge University Press, 1989.

Hareven, Tamara K. *Family Time and Industrial Time.* Cambridge, MA: Cambridge University Press, 1982.

Hareven, Tamara K., and Randolph Langenbach. *Amoskeag: Life and Work in an American Factory-City.* New York: Pantheon, 1978.

Lamarre, Jean. *The French Canadians of Michigan.* Detroit: Wayne State University Press, 2003.

———. *On The Move: French-Canadian and Italian Migrants in the North Atlantic Economy, 1860–1916.* Toronto: University of Toronto Press, 1991.

Ramirez, Bruno. "French Canadian Immigrants in the New England Cotton Industry." *Labour/Le Travail* 11 (Spring 1983): 125–142.

Roby, Yves. *The Franco-Americans of New England: Dreams and Realities.* Sillery, Quebec: Septentrion, 2004.

Walkowitz, Daniel J. *Worker City, Company Town: Iron and Cotton Worker Protest in Troy and Cohoes, New York, 1855–84.* Urbana: University of Illinois Press, 1978.

FREY, JOHN
American Federation of Labor

John Frey was a conservative stalwart of the American Federation of Labor (AFL) in the early to mid-twentieth century. In the internal union struggles of the 1930s, Frey argued for the maintenance of the AFL's craft unionist tradition. Frey cut his teeth in the metals unions, serving as vice president of the Iron Molders from 1900 to 1950. Frey also served with the national AFL, as secretary and director of the Metal Trades Department. As head of the Metal Trades Department, Frey sought to defend the old jurisdictions of the craft unions against the emergence of new industrial unions.

Frey's political outlook was generally antistatist. He resisted government involvement in labor, and in the economy generally. In the early 1920s, he opposed the creation of Unemployment Insurance, and in the 1930s, he opposed the creation of the Social Security system. Frey feared that government involvement in the welfare of workers was bound to sap labor's independence. Frey initially supported the Wagner Act of 1935 and the creation of the National Labor Relations Board (NLRB). But the actions of the Board soon seemed to threaten the skilled workers that Frey represented. Because the NLRB tended to favor the creation of large bargaining units, skilled workers were often included with unskilled workers. The ensuing union certification votes tended to favor industrial organization over craft organization. Frey lobbied for changes to the Board's policies of bargaining unit creation, but was largely unsuccessful.

Frey's period of greatest prominence and influence came during disputes between the Congress of Industrial Organizations (CIO) and the AFL. Frey opposed the CIO from the beginning, even when it was created within the AFL as the Committee for Industrial Organization. His opposition to the CIO became still more strident as it split from the AFL and became the independent Congress of Industrial Organizations. In 1936, Frey led the charge from the AFL Executive Council to suspend the 12 major unions of the CIO. Frey charged the Committee for Industrial Organization with "fomenting insurrection." Frey also charged leaders like John L. Lewis and David Dubinsky with encouraging "dual unionism." Frey held that the charters granted by the AFL to affiliates were exclusive, and that the Committee for Industrial Organization was infringing on the rights of craft unions. By encouraging workers to organize into CIO unions in industries where the AFL had granted charters to craft unions, Frey claimed, the CIO was violating the AFL constitution, and should be suspended. Frey prepared a case for the AFL Executive Council against the 12 major unions in the Committee for Industrial Organization, and then presented evidence against them. The ensuing "trial" culminated in the suspension of the 12 unions from the AFL and the eventual schism of the American union movement into the AFL and CIO. In late 1937, as some sort of reconciliation seemed possible, Frey opposed any reunification between the AFL and CIO. He claimed that Lewis's position of leadership in the CIO was weak, that the CIO was suffering financial troubles, and that the intervening year had proved the AFL's old policies of craft unionism were still superior.

Frey continued to hound the CIO even after the split, accusing the CIO of Communist subversion. In 1938, Frey allied himself with Martin Dies, chair of the House Committee on Un-American Activities. He became one of Dies's star witnesses, presenting sensational charges of Communist domination of industrial unions.

Almost every historian of the labor movement in the 1930s demonizes John Frey. Frey operated through underhanded tactics. He was an unapologetic elitist, and his actions sowed division amongst his fellow unionists. These criticisms are accurate and fair. Frey's legacy is basically that of a hit man for the old guard of the AFL. He was resistant to change, unwilling to organize unskilled workers, and vehemently opposed the presence of radicals of any stripe in the union movement. Yet Frey represented a group of workers that were numerous and dedicated to their beliefs. In the world of 1930s unionism, the craft tradition that Frey defended was still surviving, and in some cases thriving.

STEVEN DIKE-WILHELM

References and Further Reading

Bernstein, Irving. *Turbulent Years: A History of the American Worker, 1933–1941*. Boston: 1970.
Morris, James O. *Conflict within the AFL: A Study of Craft vs. Industrial Unionism, 1901–1938*. Ithaca, NY: Cornell University, 1958.
Phelan, Craig. *William Green: Biography of a Labor Leader*. Albany: State University of New York Press, 1989.
Taft, Philip. *The A. F. of L. from the Death of Gompers to the Merger*. New York: Harper and Brothers, 1959.

FUGITIVE SLAVE ACTS

The Fugitive Slave Acts refer to laws passed by Congress in 1793 and 1850 providing for the capture and return of escaped African-American slaves to their owners. Although the Supreme Court upheld the constitutionality of the Fugitive Slave Act in *Ableman v. Booth* in 1859, the acts were eventually repealed in 1864.

Early History

The origins of the Fugitive Slave Acts date back to the colonial period. The earliest act is found in the Articles of Confederation of the New England Confederation of 1643, which contained a clause requiring the return of all fugitive slaves. In 1787, delegates from 12 states met in Philadelphia for what became known as the Constitutional Convention, and wrestled with key issues of slavery, mainly among the northern-southern divide. At this same time, Congress met under the existing Articles of Confederation and passed the Northwest Ordinance (also known as the Ordinance of 1787), which banned slavery in the Northwest Territory and included a clause requiring the return of slaves who escaped to the Northwest Territories. The new U.S. Constitution included a similar fugitive slave clause in Article IV, Section II. It is important to note that the passing of both fugitive slave clauses was a part of major negotiations and compromises between northern and southern states.

Fugitive Slave Act of 1793

Despite the inclusion of a fugitive slave clause in the new U.S. Constitution, states did not always cooperate over the handling of escaped slaves due to major philosophical and legal differences. A conflict that erupted between Pennsylvania and Virginia over an escaped slave named John Davis led to the passing of the 1793 Fugitive Slave Act. This conflict, which lasted over three years, is instructive for understanding the many differences that existed between states over the issue of slavery. Pennsylvania Governor Thomas Mifflin called for the extradition of three men from Virginia accused of kidnapping Davis and returning him to their home state. Virginia Governor Beverly Randolph refused Mifflin's request, claiming that Davis was a fugitive slave who was subject to rendition. Mifflin argued that Davis was actually a free man and thereby protected by law. The Fugitive Slave Act of 1793 was written in response to the

Davis case and was approved by Congress by a strong majority. President George Washington signed it into law in February 1793.

The impact on slaves and even on free African-Americans was tremendous. The act guaranteed the rights of slave owners to reclaim escaped slaves and established the legal processes through which escaped slaves could be apprehended and returned to their masters. All escaped slaves were seen as permanent fugitives. The act made it a federal crime to assist an escaped slave in any way, including giving an escaped slave refuge. Escaped slaves were denied jury trials. Notably, this law denied constitutional rights even to freed slaves. The capturing of slaves became a cottage industry, and even free African-Americans were sometimes kidnapped, seized, and sold back into slavery. The Underground Railroad eventually developed in response to the incredible impact of the Fugitive Slave Act of 1793.

Personal Liberty Laws

Many in the North opposed the 1793 act, and Indiana, Connecticut, New York, Vermont, and Pennsylvania reacted by passing versions of what came to be known as personal liberty laws. These laws were designed to curtail the capture of escaped slaves and to protect free African-Americans. They did so by raising the legal standards in these cases: slave hunters were required to prove that a captive was in fact a fugitive slave, and those captured were often given the right to a trial by jury. However, in 1842, the Supreme Court ruled in *Prigg v. Pennsylvania* that Pennsylvania's personal liberty laws, as well as all related state fugitive slave laws that countered the 1793 Fugitive Slave Act, were unconstitutional—while states were not obligated to enforce the federal law, they could not override it with state-level laws. Massachusetts, Vermont, Rhode Island, and Pennsylvania responded with legislation that forbade state officials from aiding in enforcing runaway slave laws and using state jails to incarcerate fugitive slaves. Slave catchers were left to kidnap fugitive slaves and return them to their owners or hope to appear before federal judges who were not bound by state laws.

Fugitive Slave Act of 1850

Leaders of southern states were angered by northern states' lack of cooperation in capturing escaped slaves and by the growth of the Underground Railroad. Southern leaders' demand for more assistance resulted in the Fugitive Slave Act of 1850. This legislation was part of the Compromise of 1850. The act made federal marshals who refused to enforce the law subject to heavy fines. Any person caught assisting escaped slaves was subject to imprisonment and stiff fines. All law enforcement officials were obligated to arrest anyone even suspected of being a runaway slave, often on very little evidence. Accused fugitive slaves could not testify on their own behalf and were denied the right to a trial by jury. Resistance to the new law continued, however, as abolitionists became more active, Underground Railroad activity increased, and many northern states passed new rounds of personal liberty laws.

Demise of the Fugitive Slave Act

In 1859, the Wisconsin Supreme Court ruled in favor of an abolitionist convicted of violating the Fugitive Slave Act. The Supreme Court, in *Ableman v. Booth*, denied the right of state courts to interfere in federal cases and upheld the Fugitive Slave Act. However, the Fugitive Slave Act was soon to come to an end. In March 1862, the federal government prohibited Union army officers from returning fugitive slaves, effectively annulling the act. On January 1, 1863, the Emancipation Proclamation was signed into effect by President Abraham Lincoln. In 1864, Lincoln signed a repeal of the Fugitive Slave Act. And in January 1865, Congress ratified the Thirteenth Amendment of the United States Constitution, thereby abolishing the institution of slavery.

DAVID PURCELL

References and Further Reading

Bordewich, Fergus M. *Bound for Canaan: The Underground Railroad and the War for the Soul of America*. New York: Amistad, 2005.
Finkelman, Paul. *Slavery and the Founders: Race and Liberty in the Age of Jefferson*. Armonk, NY: M. E. Sharpe, 2001.
Larson, Kate Clifford. *Bound for the Promised Land: Harriet Tubman, Portrait of an American Hero*. New York: Ballantine, 2004.
Paulson, Timothy J. Days of Sorrow, Years of Glory: 1813–1850: From the Nat Turner Revolt to the Fugitive Slave Law. *Milestones in Black American History* series. New York: Chelsea House, 1994.
Pease, Jane H. *The Fugitive Slave Law and Anthony Burns: A Problem in Law Enforcement*. Philadelphia: Lippincott, 1975.

Cases and Statutes Cited

Ableman v. Booth, 62 U.S. 506 (1859)
Prigg v. Pennsylvania, 41 U.S. 539 (1842)

See also **Abolitionism; African-Americans; Civil War and Reconstruction; Emancipation and Reconstruction; Slave Trade; South; Thirteenth Amendment**

FURUSETH, ANDREW (1854–1938)
International Seamen's Union of America

An Oslo-born sailor and fisherman, who jumped ship in 1880 to make his home in San Francisco, Andrew Furuseth was a self-taught exponent of sailor union federation, craft unionism, and ultimately, political regulation of the waterfront. A close friend of the American Federation of Labor (AFL) president Samuel Gompers, Furuseth moved through several union consolidations, from the Coast Seamen's Union (1885) to the Sailors' Union of the Pacific (1891) to the National Seamen's Union (1892) to the presidency of the International Seamen's Union (ISU) of America (1899). Together with James G. Maguire, the San Francisco Democratic congressman and former judge, he had begun crafting seamen's reform bills as early as 1894, and particularly so after 1900, when he practically turned his leadership of the Seamen's Union into a full-time lobbying position in Washington DC. The power and pathos of his argument, together with his sheer persistence of effort, won this ascetic, lifelong bachelor (with a face that some compared to the "prow of a Viking ship") a growing circle of influential friends and admirers.

Undoubtedly, Furuseth's supreme achievement was passage of the Seamen's (aka La Follette) Act of 1915, a complex piece of legislation that, most famously, eliminated the vestiges of coerced labor (that is, heretofore quitting a ship could land a sailor in prison for desertion) for American ships on the high seas. Furuseth's biographer has aptly noted that his subject spent 20 years trying to pass the seamen's bill and another 20 years trying to defend it before unsympathetic administrative and legal authorities. His famous (but perhaps apocryphal) words on the subject of sailor incarceration have been oft-repeated: "You can put me in jail, but you cannot give me narrower quarters than as a seaman I have always had. You cannot give me coarser food than I have always eaten. You cannot make me lonelier than I have always been."

A common defense of the long-standing desertion law had likened a sailor's contract to his duty in a marriage contract. Before the Senate Commerce Committee in 1912, Furuseth quickly dismissed such analogies in favor of a graphic focus on the sailor's world:

When we talk about a ship we always say: "Thank God, I am not married to her."... [The bill] is not worth discussion from that point of view.... I have seen men go ashore and commit misdemeanors to get clear of a vessel. I have seen men eat soap to get clear of a vessel. I have seen men go and put their feet through plate-glass windows to get clear of a vessel.... I have run from a vessel and left L50 due me and was glad I had a chance to run away.

Given the emotional wedge of the desertion issue, it was perhaps not surprising that when, at a key moment in the seamen's bill deliberations in 1915, Furuseth, the crusty old Norwegian leader of the ISU, "personally begged" President Woodrow Wilson "to make him a free man," it moved the president, according to the bill's sponsor, Senator Robert M. La Follette, as "[I] had never seen him moved on any other occasion" (Auerbach, p. 359).

Yet, it was no altruistic game that Furuseth and other advocates were playing. For them, the intended international jurisdiction of the Seamen's Act was more than a desirable extension of the bill's logic: it was the very core of that logic. The reformers' logic began with an appreciation for the American sailor's (and by inference the American shipper's) weak bargaining positions on the world's seas. It assumed a single world market for seagoing labor in the foreign trade. If "sea labor," like any other commodity, were allowed to float at market price, then all would-be employers would have to pay that price. The draconian penalties against desertion, however, prevented the operation of a "free market" in labor, segmenting sailors according to national wage norms, while also preventing lesser-paid sailors from taking advantage of opportunities at higher-wage ports of call. "If conditions can be brought about whereby the wage cost of operation will be equalized," argued Furuseth and the ISU, "the development of our merchant marine and our sea power will be unhampered....The remedy is to set free the economic laws governing wages."

Though an effective advocate of the expansive use of the power of government in the case of the Seamen's Act, Furuseth otherwise generally fit in the most "old school," conservative side of AFL-type craft unionism. A vociferous, openly racist opponent of Chinese (or other Asian) access to maritime work, he also consistently opposed alliances between sailors and longshoremen and fought socialist and "Wobbly" (Industrial Workers of the World, IWW) competitors for sailor loyalty on many occasions. He was also loath to surrender national standard-setting instruments on the high seas for forms of international regulation; he thus opposed both the post-*Titanic* London Conference on Safety of Life at Sea in November 1913 and the formation of the International Labor Organization in 1919, a position which alienated the seamen's leader even from the more pragmatic Samuel Gompers. Altogether, the post-WWI years proved frustrating for Furuseth. Following big gains in membership and wages from 1916 to 1921 (more likely stimulated by wartime demands than the effects of the Seamen's Act), a crackdown by shipowners precipitated a disastrous seamen's strike in 1921. Maritime unionization was effectively curtailed for the next 15 years. When mobilization revived beginning with the San Francisco general strike of 1934, an irascible as well as terminally ill Furuseth found himself unable to stem the tide of left-led militancy. When he died on January 22, 1938, his coffin was placed on display in the auditorium of the Department of Labor Building, the first labor leader to be so honored.

LEON FINK

References and Further Reading

Green, Archie. *"Furuseth's Credo," Calf's Head, and Union Tale: Labor Yarns at Work and Play*. Urbana: University of Illinois Press, 1996.
Hohman, Paul Elmo. *History of American Merchant Seamen*. Hamden, CT: Shoe String Press, 1956.
Lorenz, Edward C. *Defining Global Justice: The History of U.S. International Labor Standards Policy*. Notre Dame, IN: University of Notre Dame Press, 2001.
Nelson, Bruce. *Workers on the Waterfront: Seamen, Longshoremen, and Unionism in the 1930s*. Urbana: University of Illinois Press, 1988.
Weintraub, Hyman. *Andrew Furuseth: Emancipator of the Seamen*. Berkeley: University of California Press, 1959.

FUTURE OUTLOOK LEAGUE OF CLEVELAND

In February 1935, a group of southern-educated, middle-class African-Americans gathered at the home of a local political activist, John O. Holly, in Cleveland, Ohio, to found the Future Outlook League (FOL). Holly, a clerk at the Federal Sanitation Company and president of his electoral precinct's Democratic Club, joined a number of local black professionals and white-collar workers to form the FOL's leadership circle. FOL leaders and allies touted the group as a younger and more militant alternative to the National Association for the Advancement of Colored People (NAACP) and the National Urban League (NUL). The FOL directly challenged both organizations; the League's job campaigns tested the NUL's traditional job-placement role, while its direct action took attention and money from the NAACP's legal actions.

The League was one of a number of organizations—including the Congress of Industrial Organizations (CIO), the National Negro Congress, and the Brotherhood of Sleeping Car Porters—that forged new labor-minded civil rights coalitions to fight racial discrimination in northern cities. The FOL won jobs for many blacks in Cleveland by connecting "Don't Buy Where You Can't Work" campaigns with direct-action techniques such as picketing and letter-writing campaigns. Beginning in July 1938, the FOL also fought for rent decreases and against arbitrary evictions. The League's membership varied a great deal over time. FOL leaders claimed membership of 10,000 in 1936, 18,000 in 1939, and 20,000 in 1943. Historians agree that these numbers were exaggerated; dues-paying members numbered in the hundreds, not the thousands. However, the FOL won power in Cleveland in fights for jobs and tenants' rights. Its influence spread through the FOL's own journal, *The Voice*, and the essential publicity provided by William O. Walker, the editor of Cleveland's black newspaper, the *Call & Post*.

The FOL's programs were remarkably innovative. In 1936, for example, the FOL organized 75 previously independent African-American-owned beauty parlors into the unprecedented Future Outlook League Beauticians Association. More generally, the FOL grounded its direct action on unconventional community organizing techniques. African-American women, who generally controlled household economies, were key organizers of consumer boycotts and acted as "shock troops" on picket lines with black men. The FOL was also exceptionally conscious of not perpetuating the color bias among African-Americans; when employers asked for the lightest-skinned applicants possible, the FOL repeatedly sent prospects with dark skin. Finally, the League created a unique Employees' Association, consisting of dues-paying League members who found jobs through FOL programs. The Association worked to enforce agreements with employers and to improve working conditions. In 1940, the Association became a federally certified labor union, the Future Outlook League Employees Union Local One (EU).

The League's greatest successes came in sometimes-violent struggles to gain jobs for blacks in Cleveland's Central Area, the city's virtually all-black section. A flurry of activity in 1935 won dozens of jobs in retail stores and theaters where the clientele was predominantly black but the workforce was all white. From 1936 to 1940, the FOL continued its campaign to integrate Central Area merchants, while also pressuring the Cleveland Railway Company to hire black motormen and conductors. In 1941, the FOL pressured Ohio Bell Telephone to hire black women. This campaign marked the first time the League fought for jobs outside the Central Area. In addition, many black churches, professionals, and local chapters of the NAACP and the NUL that previously criticized the League's militancy joined in the action. Significantly, African-American women pushed Holly and the leadership circle to pursue direct action against Ohio Bell, as they would in later fights to integrate defense industries.

In 1942, the FOL joined widespread efforts to compel the federal government to enforce integration of defense industries. For the first time, the FOL pursued its agenda through the courts. In two cases—*Effie M. Turner v. Warner and Casey Co.* and *Claretta J. Johnson v. Thompson Products*—the FOL sought to force war industries to employ black women or give up their federal contracts. The case gained national attention but did not directly win any jobs for black women in Cleveland. The local court decided in favor of employers' contract rights. Moreover, by the time the case reached the Ohio Supreme Court, Cleveland's war industries had already succumbed to unprecedented labor shortages and the necessity of hiring black women.

The FOL battled legal obstacles, intransigent employers, uncooperative unions, and unfavorable public opinion. During the League's first three years, employers were able to win injunctions from business-friendly judges who ruled that antiracial discrimination pickets were not legal labor disputes protected under the 1932 Norris-LaGuardia Act. This changed in 1938 when the U.S. Supreme Court expanded the definition of a labor dispute to include protests against racial discrimination. Nonetheless, FOL pickets, which often ended in violence, remained controversial in public opinion. Although it was generally unclear who sparked the clashes—shop owners, League members, or passersby caught up in the excitement—the specter of violence hung over the FOL's activities. Trade unions affiliated with the American Federation of Labor (AFL) presented yet another obstacle to the FOL. In struggles to integrate streetcar conductor and motormen positions, the FOL ran into opposition from the Streetcar Trainmen's Union; and the Bakery Drivers' Union, Local 52, obstructed a 1940 drive to convince local companies to hire black drivers in the Central Area. Finally, money was a constant concern for the FOL; its fluid membership of unemployed and recently employed workers was often unable or unwilling to contribute much-needed sums.

In late 1940s and 1950s, the League's power gradually faded. The FOL won less publicity as it became more of a clearinghouse for social needs. In addition, a grand vision for a $100,000 capital campaign to build a new community center largely failed, and the League came under suspicion for how it allocated the funds it did raise. The political environment of the 1950s destroyed popular support for militant direct action, and the League's original leadership core began to diverge. John O. Holly himself concentrated on a career in local and state politics, without much success. Finally, the FOL's working-class base was generally not as desperate as during the Depression, while other movements captured public imagination. An effort to revive the FOL in the 1960s never gained momentum. The League's decline does not diminish the power and concrete gains it achieved at a key moment for urban black workers. Especially important was the FOL's ability to tap the collective power of jobless African-Americans during the Depression and to respond to demands for direct action from black women and men in Cleveland.

JEFFREY HELGESON

References and Further Reading

Loeb, Charles H. *The Future Is Yours: The History of the Future Outlook League, 1935–1946*. Cleveland: The Future Outlook League, Inc., 1947.

Meier, August, and Elliott Rudwick. "The Origins of Nonviolent Direct Action in Afro-American Protest: A Note on Historical Discontinuities." In *Along the Color Line: Explorations in the Black Experience*. Urbana: University of Illinois Press, 1976, pp. 307–404.

Phillips, Kimberly L. *AlabamaNorth: African-American Migrants, Community, and Working-Class Activism in Cleveland, 1915–1945*. Chicago: University of Illinois Press, 1999.

Zinz, Kenneth M. "The Future Outlook League of Cleveland: A Negro Protest Organization." Master's thesis. Kent State University, 1973.

Cases Cited

Claretta J. Johnson v. Thompson Products
Effie M. Turner v. Warner and Casey Co.
New Negro Alliance v. Sanitary Grocery Co., 303 U.S. 552 (1938)

See also **American Federation of Labor; Brotherhood of Sleeping Car Porters; Congress of Industrial Organizations; "Don't Buy Where You Can't Work" Campaigns; Fair Employment Practice Committee; Injunctions; National Association for the Advancement of Colored People (NAACP); National Negro Congress; National Urban League; Norris-LaGuardia Federal Anti-Injunction Act**

INDEX

Hampton, Fred, 161
Hanley, Edward T., 617
Hansen, Alvin H., 519
Hapgood, Powers (1899–1949), 568–569
  Brophy and, 568
  CIO and, 568
  Cold War and, 568
  CP and, 568
  Pesotta and, 1077
  in Progressive Era, 568
  SP and, 568
  UMWA and, 568, 804
Happy Hooker, The (Hollander), 1139
Harburg, Yip, 927
Hard Tomatoes, Hard Times (Hightower/Agribusiness
    Accountability Project), 465
Harding, Warren G., 440, 1178
  Mingo County War and, 1500
  on prices/social order, 1522
  railroad shopmen's strike and, 1170–1171, 1178
Hardman, J. B. S., 58
Hardy, Charles, 1228
  of BSEIU, 1228
  of SEIU, 1229
Harlan Miners Speak, 973
Harlem Renaissance, Garvey and, 500
Harmon, Dick, of IAF, 50–51
Harper, James, 749
Harrington, Michael (1928–1989), 550, 552, **569–570**, 1250
  Day, Dorothy, and, 569
  DSA and, 570
  DSCO and, 570
  of LID, 796
  Reuther and, 569
  SP and, 569, 1283
  WDL and, 569
  Wechsler on, 796
  YPSL and, 569
  YSL and, 569
Harris, Abram, on African-American labor history, 597
Harris, Alice Kessler, on gender in labor history, 599
Harris v. Forklift Systems, 246, 1232
Hart, John F., of AMC, 62
Hart, Schaffner, and Marx (HSM) Shop, 498, 499
  Anderson, Mary, and, 105
  collective bargaining influenced by, 57–58
  Darrow representation of, 57
  Hillman, Bessie, employment with, 591
  Hillman, Sidney, as employee of, 592
  strike of, 57–58, 591–592, 1201
  UGW and, 57
Hart-Celler Act. *See* Immigration and Nationality Act of 1965
Hartley, Fred A.
  of NRWC, 978
  Taft-Hartley Act by, 978
Hart-Scott-Rodino Antitrust Improvements Act of 1976, 1242
Hartz, Louis, 68, 836
Harvard Trade Union Program, of Slichter, 1277
Harvard Union of Clerical and Technical Workers (HUCTW), 570–572
  AFSCME and, 571
  Dunlop and, 572
  family-oriented benefits of, 572
  feminine model of unionism of, 570
  on jointness, 572–574

on labor-management conflict, 572
NLRB and, 570
organization of, 570–571
Rondeau and, 570, 571
UAW and, 571
"women's way of organizing" unions at, 571–572
Harvest of Shame (Murrow), 894, 1070
Harvey House chain, 1481
Hatch Act, 73, 959
  UPWA/UFWA and, 1445
Hatfield, Sid, 1500
Hathaway, Clarence, 1501–1502
Hattam, Victoria, 70
Hatters, Cap, and Millinery Workers' International Union, 61
Haupt, Georges, on labor history, 596
Hawaii, 573–576
  anticommunism in, 575
  Chinese/Japanese contract laborers in, 574
  HERE in, 576
  HLA in, 574
  ILWU in, 575
  labor challenges in, 575–576
  NLRB and, 575
  plantation economy of, 573
  Polynesian migration to, 573
  resistance/organization in, 574–575
  strikes in, 575
  sugar plantations of, 574
  tourism in, 575–576
Hawaii Laborers' Association (HLA), 574, **576–577**
  Filippinos in, 576
  HSPA and, 577
  Japanese Federation of Labor and, 576
  strike of, 576–577
Hawaii Sugar Planters' Association (HSPA), 576, 1299
  Higher Wages Association demands for, 715
  Japanese Strike in Hawaii and, 714–715
Hayden, Tom, 796
Hayes, Alfred, 590
Hayes, Charles
  on CBTU, 267
  of Congressional Black Caucus, 268
Hayes, Frank, 182
Hayes, John, 146
Hayes, Max S., 440
Hayes, Rutherford B., 259, 786, 1174
  on Burlingame Treaty, 240–241
Haymarket Affair (1886), 103, 115, 153, 219, 448, 516, 524, 532, 556, **577–580**, 744, 746, 761, 814, 887, 1154, 1157. *See also* Parsons, Albert (1848–1887); Parsons, Lucy (1853–1942)
  anarchists' death sentence in, 579, 858–859
  anticommunism and, 115
  Du Bois on, 388
  Gompers on, 579
  in Great Upheaval, 554, 555
  IWPA and, 577
  Jones on, 726
  KOL after, 250
  Labadie and, 759–760
  Morgan, Thomas, and, 924
  Powderly and, 1117
  Red Scare and, 578
  Rodgers and, 1205
  Spies, August, and, 577, 857, 858, 1312
  violence in, 577–578, 858

S

S & S Division. *See* Stewards and Stewardesses Division
"Sabotage" (Flynn), 459
Sacco and Vanzetti, 1211–1214
  appeals of, 1213
  Defense Committee for, 1213
  Flynn and, 1213
  Galleani and, 1211
  Italian immigrant contempt and, 1211
  legacy of, 1214
  Parsons, Lucy for, 1063
  Pesotta and, 1077
  Red Scare and, 1211–1212
  trial of, 1212–1213
Sacco, Nicola, 678, 704, 1525
Sacco-Vanzetti Defense Committee, Lowell of, 1213
Sadlowski, Ed (1938–), 1214–1217
  ENA and, 1215
  Galbraith on, 1214
  of USWA, 1214–1215, 1455
Sadlowski v. United Steelworkers, 1214
SAG. *See* Screen Actors Guild
Sailors' Union of the Pacific (SUP), 177, 1217–1218
  CSU and, 1217
  Furuseth and, 848, 1217
  strike of, 1218
Saint-Simon, Comte de, 1551
Salinas, Carlos, 1012
Salt of the Earth, 910, 1307, 1507
Samuel, John
  on cooperative stores, 322
  of KOL, 322
San Francisco Trades Union, 201
San Francisco Typographical Society, 201
San Joaquin Valley Cotton Strike (1933), 1218–1219
  AAA and, 1219
  CAWIU and, 1218–1219
  Creel and, 206–207
  Mexican-American in, 1218
  migrant farmworkers in, 1219
  NRA and, 1219
  violence in, 206–207, 1219
Sandinista National Liberation Front, Central Americans and, 215, 216
Sanger, Margaret, 459
  SP and, 1283
Sanger, William, 1135
SAPs. *See* Structural adjustment programs
Save your Job, Save Our Country: Why NAFTA Must Be Stopped Now (Perot), 1013
Sayen, Clarence N., ALPA president, 42
SBTA. *See* Structural Building Trades Alliance
Scalise, George, 714, 1228
  of BSEIU, 1228
  indictment of, 1228
Schechter Poultry, 789
Schechter v. U.S., 1485
  NIRA and, 965, 968
Schlesinger, Arthur, Jr., on labor history, 597
Schlesinger, Benjamin, 681
Schneiderman, Rose (1882–1972), 1220–1222, 1514, 1516
  FDR and, 1220
  ILGWU and, 271
  Labor Party and, 1221

New Deal legislation and, 1220
  Newman and, 1007
  NRA and, 1222
  NRA Labor Advisory Board and, 1220
  NWTUL/NYWTUL and, 1220, 1221
  O'Reilly and, 1045
  Roosevelt, Eleanor as friend of, 1221
  women's rights and, 1221, 1222
Schneirov, Richard, 205
Schnitzler, William, 143
Scholfield, Arthur
  as English immigrant, 411
  textiles and, 411
School to Work Opportunity Act, Reich and, 364
Schuberts producing manager, 13
Schultz, George P., 362
Schwarzenegger, Arnold, 204
Schwellenbach, Lewis B. and, 360
Science of Political Economy (George), 514
Scientific management
  AFL on, 1523
  Taylor, Frederick W., on, 1520, 1542
SCLC. *See* Southern Christian Leadership Conference
SCMWA. *See* State, County, and Municipal Workers of America
Scott, Dred, 1267
Scottsboro Case, 1222–1224
  on African-American rape accusation, 1222
  CP and, 1223
  Defense Committee of, 1224
  ILD and, 678, 1223
  NAACP and, 940, 1223
Screen Actors Guild (SAG), 11, 12, 451
Screen Writers Guild (SWG), 451
  HUAC and, 617–618
  NLRB and, 451
SCU. *See* Share Croppers' Union
SDP. *See* Social Democratic Workingmen's Party
SDS. *See* Students for a Democratic Society
Seafarers' International Union (SIU), 849
  ISU and, 1217
  in Maritime Federation of the Pacific Coast, 1218
  in maritime labor, 849
  McGuire Act and, 1217
  strikes of, 1217–1218
  WWI opposition by, 1217
  in WWII, 1218
Seale, Bobby, 159, 161
Seaman's International Union (SIU-AFL), 675
Seamen's Act. *See* LaFollette Seamen's Act (1915)
Seamen's Protective Association, 848
Seattle General Strike, 1336, 1522, 1545
  in strike wave (1919), 1335–1336
Second Confiscation Act, abolition and, 256
Second Great Awakening
  abolition and, 5
  Evans and, 424
Secondary boycott, 34, 172
  ALRA on, 34
  Butchers'/Retail Clerks' unions on, 33
  Danbury Hatters' case and, 341
  Duplex Printing Press v. Deering on, 658
  Hoffa, James R., on, 606
  of IBT, 669
  National Association of Manufacturer on, 776

against NAFTA, 1015
New Voices coalition and, 379, 1343, 1344, 1478
of SEIU, 225, 379, 714, 864, 1229–1230, 1344, 1345, 1406
Union Summer internship program and, 1408
Sweet, James, 1266
SWG. *See* Screen Writers Guild
Swinton, John (1830–1901), 1345–1347
as labor journalist, 1345
Marx and, 1346–1347
Switchmen's Mutual Aid Association, Switchmen's Union of North America and, 1166
Switchmen's Union of North America, Switchmen's Mutual Aid Association and, 1166
SWIU. *See* Service Workers' International Union
SWOC. *See* Steel Workers Organizing Committee
SWP. *See* Socialist Workers' Party
Sylvis, William (1828–1869), 259, 470, 969–970, **1347–1348**
African-American support by, 1347
of IMIU/NLU, 1347
of Iron Molders' Union, 322, 965, 969
of NLU, 205, 965
on women's rights, 971
Syndicalism, 704, **1348–1350**, 1542
of French, 1348
of Italians, 704
IWW and, 1348–1349, 1350
Lawrence Strike and, 1349
union members of, 1350
WWI and, 1349–1350
Syndicalist League of North America (SLNA), 386, 535, 1349
Foster, William Z., and, 386, 478

T

TAA. *See* Teaching Assistants' Association
Tabulating Machine Company (TMC)
Hollerith and, 302
IBM and, 302
Taft, Philip (1902–1976), 598, **1351–1352**
on labor history, 595, 1351
Perlman and, 1352
Taft, William Howard, 261, 722, 788, 985
CIR and, 288
NCF and, 772
on trust-busting, 1241
welfare capitalism and, 1493
Taft-Hartley Act, 60, 64, 77, 80, 360, 361, 378, 438, 461, 527, 601, 628, 645, 659, 664, 677, 684, 691, 741, 754, 805, 871–872, 910, 1066, 1090, 1121, 1245, 1249, 1278, 1279, **1352–1355**, 1416, 1419, 1550
on agricultural labor, 33
ANA and, 1028
anticommunism and, 204, 1354
on blacklists, 164
Chávez and, 33
on closed shops, 1353
on collective bargaining, 969
communism and, 297
consequences of, 1354
DWU and, 1186
FMCS of, 447
Gold, Ben, and, 677
by Hartley, 978
in law labor, 790

NAACP against, 941
NAPE and, 938
NCF and, 722
New Deal and, 1352
NLRB and, 278–279, 967
NNC and, 976
non-communist affidavits of, 1506
Norris-LaGuardia Act and, 1010, 1011
Operation Dixie and, 1041
origins of, 1352–1353
provisions of, 1353–1354
repeal of, 1253–1254
on secondary boycotts, 33, 341, 661, 776, 1353
SNYC and, 976
Steel Strike injunctions of, 1322, 1323
Steel Strike of 1959 and, 1322, 1323
strikebreaking and, 1342
Truman and, 173, 1353
TWUA and, 1042
on union strength, 316
UOPWA and, 1436
Wagner Act and, 310, 1557
"Take This Job and Shove It" (Travis), 928
Talbot, Marion, 610
Talbot, Thomas Wilson, 660
Talking Union, 928
Tammany Hall, 1484
TANF. *See* Temporary Aid to Needy Families
Tappes, Shelton (1911–1991), 1240, **1354–1355**
FEPD and, 1355
TULC and, 1355
of UAW, 1354
TAs. *See* Graduate Teaching Assistants
Task Force on Organized Crime, on racketeering/RICO, 1163
Tate & Lyle
purchase of A. E. Staley, 1
sugar conglomerate of, 1
Taxi and Limousine Commission (TLC), 1299
Taylor, Alva, 1501
Taylor, Frederick W., 130, 263, 1074
against collective bargaining, 277
on scientific management, 1520, 1542
on unemployment, 1464
Taylor, George, 766
Taylor v. Georgia, 1069
TBU. *See* Teamsters' National Union
TCIR. *See* Tennessee Coal, Iron, and Railroad Company
TDC. *See* Teamsters for a Decent Contract
TDIU. *See* Team Drivers' International Union
TDU. *See* Teamsters for a Democratic Union
Teachers' Guild, 1233
Teaching, 1355–1361
AFT in, 1359
centralization of, 1358–1359
in early American, 1355
in Great Depression, 954
Haley on, 953
male teacher recruitment, 1360
marriage bars for, 1359
mid-twentieth century transformation in, 1359–1360
in modern America, 1358–1359
NEA and, 1357, 1359
normals/teacher-training school for, 1357
as profession, 1359, 1360–1361
Progressive Era influence on, 1358